ISBN 978-0-282-36227-0
PIBN 10848990

For support please visit www.forgottenbooks.com

1 MONTH OF
FREE
READING

at

www.ForgottenBooks.com

By purchasing this book you are eligible for one month membership to ForgottenBooks.com, giving you unlimited access to our entire collection of over 1,000,000 titles via our web site and mobile apps.

To claim your free month visit: www.forgottenbooks.com/free848990

English
Français
Deutsche
Italiano
Español
Português

www.forgottenbooks.com

Mythology Photography **Fiction**
Fishing Christianity **Art** Cooking
Essays Buddhism Freemasonry
Medicine **Biology** Music **Ancient**
Egypt Evolution Carpentry Physics
Dance Geology **Mathematics** Fitness
Shakespeare **Folklore** Yoga Marketing
Confidence Immortality Biographies
Poetry **Psychology** Witchcraft
Electronics Chemistry History **Law**
Accounting **Philosophy** Anthropology
Alchemy Drama Quantum Mechanics
Atheism Sexual Health **Ancient History**
Entrepreneurship Languages Sport
Paleontology Needlework Islam
Metaphysics Investment Archaeology
Parenting Statistics Criminology
Motivational

HISTORY

OF THE

Ancient Ryedales

AND THEIR DESCENDANTS IN

NORMANDY, GREAT BRITAIN, IRELAND, AND AMERICA,

FROM 860 TO 1884.

COMPRISING THE GENEALOGY AND BIOGRAPHY, FOR ABOUT
ONE THOUSAND YEARS, OF THE FAMILIES OF

RIDDELL, RIDDLE, RIDLON, RIDLEY, ETC.

*FULLY ILLUSTRATED WITH ENGRAVINGS OF PORTRAITS, RESI-
DENCES, MONUMENTS, COATS-OF-ARMS, AND AUTO-
GRAPHS, ON STEEL, STONE, AND WOOD.*

BY G. T. RIDLON,

AUTHOR OF "EARLY SETTLERS OF HARRISON, ME.," "BURBANK GENEALOGY,"
"HAMBLINS OF BEECH HILL," AND OTHER BIOGRAPHICAL
AND GENEALOGICAL WORKS.

"That the generation to come might know them, even the children which should be born; who should
arise and declare them to their children."— *Psalms 78 : 6.*

MANCHESTER, N. H.:
PUBLISHED BY THE AUTHOR.
1884.

VOX POPULI PRESS:

HUSE, GOODWIN & CO.,

LOWELL, MASS.

READERS' DIRECTORY.

GENEALOGIES and pedigrees are published in nearly as many forms and with as great a variety of classifications as they have authors and compilers. Each writer has his own ideal, and composes accordingly. I have consulted nearly all family histories now in our New England public libraries, and have found many very comprehensive arrangements of family names, but have not adopted any of them as a whole. In reading this book the table of contents should be consulted; here will be found the names by which I have denominated the numerous branches and sub-branches of the family; in most instances each will be distinguished by the name of the town, village, or district, where the ancestors settled, or where a majority of the families have lived. Under these captions each family will be classified by generation, beginning with the name of the person heading the list and running down to youngest children. Each person's name will be attended by a small figure standing above the type line, called a "superior," which denotes the generation to which that individual belongs. All of the second, third, fourth, fifth, and sixth generations will follow in rotation, beginning in each instance with the children of the eldest brother. When passing from a higher to a lower generation the words "second generation," or "fourth generation," as the case may be, will be found between the paragraphs. By this arrangement it will be observed that *own cousins*, being of the same generation, will stand in one category, but their names separated by a light double dash.

There will also be a heavy-faced figure in a parenthesis (4) following each person's name, at the heads of paragraphs, which denotes the number of persons in that branch family of the same *Christian name*, and in every instance will have reference to the *first name* of the individual. Thus, Nathaniel[6] (6), son of Nathaniel[5] (5), will show that in that particular branch of the family there had appeared five Nathaniels before the one first mentioned, and that three generations had been previously recorded. By this simple arrangement no two person's of the same Christian name need be confounded, as they will in no instance stand connected with the same figures. In case a person's name stands in its proper place in some earlier branch of a family, as Thomas[2] (4), and that same person becomes the head of a sub-branch, his name will appear as Thomas[1] (1), with the reference, "See Riddells of Granton," or "See Riddells of Glen-Riddell," as the case may require; so that each may be traced readily, although their names may not be attended with the same figures. In tracing the early families, where the pedigree will embrace from twelve to twenty-eight generations, the reader must observe this distinction.

There will be an Index of Surnames of those intermarried with the Riddell, Ridlon, and Ridley families. In tracing any particular person, if the reader remembers the name of the wife or husband, he may facilitate his search by running down the alphabetical Index of Surnames till he comes to the one desired; then by reference to the page in the Index, that person's birth, marriage, and biographical sketch may be found in the genealogical department of the book.

In nearly all genealogical books there are many repetitions, and the reader must turn from page to page to find all that is published respecting an individual; the trouble occasioned by these complicated arrangements is obviated by the simple plan carried out herein, and what is said of one person will be found in one place, unless alluded to incidentally in some preliminary or descriptive chapter.

There are a short "Appendix" and a supplementary article entitled "Gleanings and Notes," in the last part of this book, wherein may be found many interesting incidents and items respecting families and individuals that could not be properly classified in the body of the work, or were received too late for insertion in their proper place.

NOTE.—This work has been edited in the midst of most pressing professional duties, and could not, therefore, receive that careful attention while going through the press that is necessary in order to produce a book free from typographical errors. Nearly all the materials were furnished in manuscript, and frequently so poorly written that it was impossible to ascertain with certainty the proper spelling of names.—*Author.*

LIST OF ILLUSTRATIONS.

PORTRAITS.

PLATES AND VIEWS.

TABLE OF CONTENTS.

INTRODUCTION AND COMPENDIUM.

HISTORY OF THIS BOOK.

MY early years were spent in the home of my paternal grandparents, — a place where many members of our family connection resorted to discuss the history of the past, — and from listening attentively to the conversation that passed between those godly ancestors as they gathered around the ample hearthstone, I became, at an early age, deeply interested in everything pertaining to the history of my forefathers and their times. This interest increased with my years, and I determined that at some future day I would fully acquaint myself with the history of our family and its origin.

My grandfather was truly a patriarch, for he lived contemporary with *eight generations* of his family. From his standpoint he could look *backward* and remember *three* generations of his predecessors; looking *downward* he could see *four* generations of his descendants, and at the same time he himself was the connecting link of this chain between the first *three* and last *four* generations, making *eight* generations in all. This remarkable acquaintance with so many of his family, supplemented by the possession of a wonderfully retentive memory, which remained unimpaired till he was more than ninety years of age, qualified this venerable man in a peculiar manner to impart information respecting the history and genealogy of his family connections. The elder members of our family seemed pleased to advert to all the traditions known to their ancestors, and delighted to transmit them from father to son, always careful that nothing should be lost. When these discussions were going on I used to draw near my grandfather's knee and listen with the keenest relish to every word spoken, frequently asking questions about the relationship between the various cadets of our family mentioned in the conversation.

During those early years I noticed that frequent allusion was made to "Old Uncle John" and "Old Uncle Abram" in a very emphatic way, — great stress always being laid upon the word "*old.*" This served to excite my curiosity and rekindle the fires of interest, until, as a result of my inquisitiveness, I possessed a very good traditionary outline of the history of my own branch of the family. If I saw one of our surnames in a book or newspaper, it always awakened a new interest and inspired a zeal to investigate more fully the genealogy of all branches of our tribe.

While spending a few days at my grandfather's home in 1868, and discovering the remarkable vividness of his memory, I availed myself of the opportunity to make copious notes respecting the branches and sub-branches of our own line of the family. I was especially careful to learn where all who had removed to distant States, had settled as well as to gain a knowledge of the personal appearance and habits of the heads of the early families. On returning to my own home I arranged and classified my notes, — the first written basis of this book, — and instituted an extensive correspondence at once, directing my attention especially to the acquisition of genealogical information of the descendants of my own ancestor direct, having no object beyond an attempt to make out a tabular pedigree, to be framed and kept in my house. Failing to trace by correspondence several branches broken from the parent stock, I found it necessary to advertise freely in the newspapers in several States, hoping thereby to find the "lost Joseph." In answer to these published inquiries I received many communications from persons bearing our surname, whose families I could not then connect with my own. Letters of this class continued to accumulate as I extended the circle of my investigations, and I was soon aware that our clan had become so numerous that my original plan would be impracticable; hence, knowing by this time that there were in the United States several branches bearing our surname, that were descended from as many distinct ancestors, I abandoned my first plan and adopted one of a broader scope, namely, that of compiling a genealogy of *all* the American families, the orthography of whose names seemed to point to a common derivation. Having fully matured my new plan, I multiplied my queries by correspondence, circulars, and advertisements in historical magazines and newspapers. My mind was now fully enlisted in the work of research, and I decided to "leave no stone unturned" under which there was the least hope of finding a link of our family chain that would add to the interest of my proposed "book of chronicles."

Some families had early removed to the far west, others to Vermont and Massachusetts, and a few to the eastern section of Maine. More than *seventy years* had elapsed since any communication had passed between the New England and western families, and their address, in consequence of change of names in new States, and removals, had been lost, and a long time passed before any information concerning our western friends could be obtained. At length, however, my advertisement reached them, and with the most inexpressible gladness they reported themselves. I shall always remember with emotions of pleasure the satisfaction I experienced when I read the first letter from a representative of the family in Ohio, whither they had emigrated in the year 1800. I made haste to acquaint my aged grandfather with the fact that several of his own cousins, with whom he spent many pleasant days in his childhood, were still living, and that they remembered him well. On hearing the intelligence the dear old man was overcome with emotion and wept for joy. The communications that followed were filled with touching reminiscences of the days when the several families were living neighbors in New England.

During the years I was collecting the records of my own family connection, great confusion was occasioned in consequence of the local mingling of the families that were offshoots of different original stocks. Many descendants of my ancestor had moved to the eastern part of Maine, and were soon living alongside of families named *Ridley*, who had come from Cape Cod, Massachusetts, a few years previously; and having assumed that all were originally from one ancestry, the *Ridlon* family soon changed their name to *Ridley;* this mutation of the surname, supplemented by the frequent correspondence of ages and Christian names between members of the two families, made it very difficult to properly classify their records. The same embarrassment attended my researches in the western and southern States. Many of my advertisements were copied from western to southern newspapers, and I soon found myself in possession of numerous pedigrees from a prolific family in Virginia, Tennessee, and Georgia, of whom I previously had no knowledge; these used the same surname as many of my own kindred, but were evidently descended from another stock. These southern families were wealthy, highly respectable, and well allied by marriage with many of the most eminent families in the southern States; they were deeply interested in my undertaking, and were as anxious to have their genealogy incorporated into my book as I was to publish my own; hence, to give general satisfaction, I again enlarged my plan, and encompassed within the circle of my inquiries the history and genealogy of every family in America known by our surname, not only in the United States, but in all the British North American Provinces.

Thus my undertaking assumed broader proportions from time to time, as I prosecuted my work of gathering records from the several American branches of the connection, until I had canvassed the ground quite thoroughly. In comparing my records in order to arrange them for composition, I was not willing to put the work to press without making a reasonable effort to learn how these numerous families, descended from ancestors widely removed from each other in their settlements in America, were related to each other in the old country; to learn, if possible, whether or not they all sprung from one common stock, and where their progenitors lived. But the work appeared of too great a magnitude, and as turned my mental vision toward foreign lands, with an intense desire to trace the family line across the seas, insurmountable obstacles seemed to arise before me; but while contemplating the subject there was another favorable turn by the wheel of fortune, — a book fell into my hands, in which I found the name and address of one of the family in England. I immediately forwarded a letter to that gentleman, which resulted in the establishment of a correspondence with several representative heads of families in England and Scotland, which has been uninterruptedly continued ever since, hardly a week having passed for eight years, in which letters were not crossing the ocean, to and from this country.

As data of a very interesting character reached me from Great Britain, I continued to amplify my plans and extend the limits of my search. My interest grew with every new accession to my historical materials. I saw that my work, if published as it then was, must present a fragmentary and disconnected appearance; there would be confusion, uncertainty, and dissatisfaction in the mind of every reader of such a book; and after much consideration and weighing of the probabilities of success, I set my mind toward the consummation of a work so great, that, had I known its magnitude at the time, it would never have been undertaken by one of so limited means as I have been confined to during all the years of my investigation. But there was no limit to the range of my examination commenced at that time, short of a history of the family reaching back to the earliest ancestor of whom any account could be found, and covering the centuries during a period of a thousand years. I also enlarged the *character* of my inquiries, seeking to procure not only genealogical but biographical materials for my work. My correspondence had made me aware that the family, from its earliest history, had been ornamented by many distinguished men; that representatives of the old sept had filled important civil and military stations, and hence it was desirable to preserve in a family memorial a comprehensive account of their lives and services.

Anticipating discouragement from those who could not quite appreciate my ambition and family pride, and wishing to evade the taunts and appellations that are usually pronounced upon an enthusiastic antiquary, I kept my new project to myself for a considerable time; but so many calls were made by members of our family in America, for the results of my *original* venture, that a confession of my latest plans was my only apology for what seemed to others an unnecessary delay on my part. "At my first answer no man stood with me." To my relatives and acquaintances my undertaking was "a castle in the air," my "head was turned," and my "whole time was being wasted." To a less determined mind the work would have seemed too much for one to accomplish, but being confident from my previous success that I should not fail, I asked my friends and correspondents to have patience, and, life being spared, I would produce what had been promised. But, as I had anticipated, many were unwilling to be identified with what appeared to be a "wild goose chase," and at my solicitations for aid would ask, "What will all your labor amount to?" "What will your book be good for if completed?" "How many years will it take to finish the work?" etc., etc. Having become better acquainted with the value of such a book than I was when my relatives "made light of it" and manifested so much indifference and stupidity, I· shall now set forth some of the valuable qualities found in a book of this class.

To me the fact that no attempt had ever been made to preserve in permanent form our family history, seemed a sufficient inducement to justify me in making very reasonable effort to procure the materials necessary for such a book as would be of interest to the rising generation. Like all historians, I soon learned that traditionary information, when transmitted by aged people from generation to generation, becomes exaggerated and modified, and that if those who may bear our family name in years to come would possess anything like a correct knowledge of their progenitors, it must be handed down to them by some accurate and enduring medium. The advanced state of civilization seems to demand that every one, as he goes forth to mingle with his fellow-men and assume the responsibilities of his generation, shall become possessed of a fund of information sufficient to qualify him to converse intelligently and instructively with those into whose society he must be constantly thrown; he should be acquainted with the constitution and history of his country, and the principles of government. If, then, the history of the origin, growth, and prosperity of nations be considered a subject worthy of study, why should it be thought unimportant to know something of the inner circle, of the parts and constituent elements that compose the nations and governments of the world? Certainly it is a worthy motive to wish to know the history of those family predecessors in whose veins flowed the same blood that now animates our own frames; those ancestors who have cut away the forests to hew out homes for themselves and their children; the fathers and mothers to whom we are indebted for the names we bear. But, strange as it may appear, there are hundreds of New England families that have no traditionary knowledge of their ancestors; they do not know whether they were derived from the Celts or Scandinavians; they cannot tell the names of their grandparents. There is no excuse for such ignorance and stupidity, nor is it to be commended as having any claims to respect. Such a state of indifference respecting family history may have been "winked at" in colonial times, when the advantages of education were so meagre that few learned to write, but it is now unnecessary and inexcusable.

A well-arranged book of this class has value from several considerations, among them the following which must commend themselves to all intelligent readers : *First*, from the interest we are supposed to possess in the names we bear. Whose interest is not involved in the family name by which they are identified? If a member of the family whose name we bear is honored, our own respect is gratified, and we instinctively feel our family pride rising within us; and, on the other hand, when one of our kindred becomes the subject of disgrace, we afterwards feel chagrined, and acknowledge our relationship with embarrassing feelings. That sentiment of pride in a family name by which a distinguished and worthy ancestry was known, is both natural and commendable, and should be cherished as sacred. In a good family history the virtues of our ancestors and kinspeople are recorded, and in reading of these we are inspired to noble ambition in the emulation of their examples, and in trying to perpetuate in our families the characteristics for which our fathers were deservedly esteemed while living, and lamented when gone; indeed, all thoughtful persons feel inseparably identified with those who bear their names, and have an honest desire to preserve the prestige of those families as a patrimony for the rising generation.

Such a history has value, *secondly*, because of the respect we have for our departed friends. Universal custom has caused all respectable families to feel it a moral obligation to erect some monument to mark the places where their dead are buried; it is a filial and sacred duty to thus preserve the names of our parents, to record their ages and the times in which they lived, in such enduring form. Such monuments have a beneficial influence on the living, and are protected by the most stringent laws; but a comprehensive family history is a monument more enduring than the sculptured marble, which is worn away by the "tooth of time"; a monument of little cost, upon which may be inscribed the names, ages, marriages, and deaths of our entire family connection. Another valuable feature of such a work is the collection of portraits embraced within its pages, and handed down to gratify the desire of the rising generation to mark the resemblance between the several branches of our tribe. In consequence of removals from State to State, local monuments erected by loving hands, are often far away from the friends who would gladly visit them to read again the epitaphs recorded there; but a family memorial in book form may be carried with us and kept always ready for reference; this may be entailed in our families from generation to generation, until so long as there remains one to bear our name they may possess an authentic and chronological history, from the most remote period to the present time.

A book of this character has value, *thirdly*, because it serves as a medium to satisfy the natural desire to be remembered when our work of life is finished. Few persons whose lives have been useful in this world are willing to be forgotten; and yet those in the more humble and obscure walks of life must resign themselves to the probability that in a few years at most, unless their names are recorded on the page of history, they will be lost to memory. There exists in every heart a fond desire to be remembered by kindred and friends, and when separated from them for a short time there is great pleasure experienced in hearing from them by letters, and in knowing—

> "They look for us their homes to share,
> And joyful greetings "wait us there."

A good family memorial has value, *fourthly*, from its relation to local and general history, for which it preserves many valuable data of a character that would otherwise be irrecoverably lost. A work of this class contains descriptions of the lands and homes where our forefathers once lived, and toiled, and died; extracts of wills, deeds, inventories, and journals are here preserved, thus handing forward to other generations a knowledge of original owners of lands, the

comparative value of real estate from time to time since the settlement of
our country, the means used to procure a subsistence, the growth of the popular institutions, and the advance of civilization. Such a history enables us to
know of the difficulties encountered and the struggles passed through by the
pioneers in securing permanent settlements and titles to their lands, since made
productive, beautiful, and valuable by their persevering toils, and thus fostering
a love for the unimpaired preservation and possession of the homesteads of our
departed sires, as a patrimony worthy of our attachment and respect.

In recording the history and genealogy of our own immediate families, we
necessarily incorporate into the fabric, in marriage records, names from other
families, thus conserving the links belonging to other numerous genealogical
chains, which would have been lost in the visionary traditions of fleeting generations; by such means we form a repository to be consulted by antiquaries and
historians who may follow us. We also preserve the original spelling of names
of places and individuals, giving their derivation and marking the mutations that
have occurred from generation to generation. *Fac-similes* of autographs engraved for such a book show the comparative improvement in chirography; dates
of removals indicate the westward movement of the tide of civilization; biographical notices illustrate the advancement in science and art, improvement in
business facilities and educational advantages; and the whole work embodies
almost every element of history from a very remote date to the present, — valuable for preservation and interesting to the general reader.

Having given my reasons for undertaking the compilation of this work, the
circumstances that served to enlarge its scope, and explained its value, I shall
now comprehensively describe some of the *means* employed for gaining information and collecting the data now embodied in it; but in doing this, for want
of space, I must pass unmentioned hundreds of measures, — legitimate enough,
but original with me, — resorted to by me during my investigations.

To many of my correspondents it will be unnecessary to say that I have
been a very inquisitive man, — indeed every successful antiquary must possess
this faculty of asking questions, which is acquired by great application and
experience in historical research. One must not only be able to ask for
what he wants in a concise way, but he must present his interrogations in a
form that causes the one questioned to feel under an obligation to respond. To
awaken an interest in my undertaking with those who were at first indifferent,
and to stimulate them to action in the premises, has demanded tact and ingenuity, and there are many so obstinate, and some so extremely discreet, that all
the skill of correspondence has failed to draw them out. Experience soon
taught me that I must not ask too much in my first communication; a long
list of questions, involving genealogical data relating to several generations,
seemed too much to be undertaken, and the letter would be put aside; then
the success of the effort to procure the records would depend upon the way in
which the second letter of request was composed. In my initiatory inquiry I
would usually state, — truthfully, of course, — that I had in my possession an
account of some branches of this family, and that I could not properly arrange
the records for composition without a statement respecting other families; then
I would ask for the names of grandparents, parents, uncles, or as the case
might be. Supposing this was all I wanted, my requests were, in most instances, granted. To save expense, — believing that every family ought to help
bear the burden of my undertaking, — I did not enclose return postage in my
first communication; but, if I did not receive an immediate reply, I reminded
the person previously addressed, of my wishes, enclosing a stamp, which almost

always brought to me the desired information. In case my first two letters were laid aside without reply, I have written my third with a tone of disappointment, expressed in language a little pointed. I would state that other families had rendered assistance most cheerfully and promptly, that nearly every one felt a deep interest in my work, and would sometimes close by saying "If these questions are not attended to for want of references I can furnish them at any moment." This succeeded, with few exceptions, and letters from those solicited were usually prefaced with an apology for not attending to my wishes sooner, followed by the statement of their willingness to do all in their power to aid me in my researches. Having opened the way, I must then press my claims; after waiting a few days another communication would be forwarded, in which attention was called to some omission in my first, and after thanking my "valuable correspondent" for the interesting information contained in his letter, I would express the hope that the wanting records would be furnished without delay; this was, with few exceptions, successful. Being now possessed of the material relating to the early generations of this family, I would write out my caption and commence the composition and classification of the matter; meanwhile, those families with whom I had corresponded, having acquired new facts concerning their ancestry, which inspired a growing interest in my work, in spite of their first indifference, their family pride would cause them to discuss the traditions handed down to them, which excited their curiosity to know how the family history was progressing. Taking advantage of their interest I was careful to mention incidentally, in my subsequent letter, some historical fact that was new to them, which always served to rekindle their interest and sharpen their desire for a more complete knowledge of their ancestral history. I would now write that I had commenced the composition of their department of my book, and had found that I could proceed no further without certain records of births, marriages, and deaths of the younger generation, — perhaps I omitted the maiden names of wives, — and would suggest that they could never feel any satisfaction in the history of that branch of the family if it appeared in a "disconnected and fragmentary condition," when other sections of my book would be so complete and interesting; that, as there were now so few deficiencies to be filled, I hoped they would do me the favor to provide the names and dates "by return mail."

During the many years employed on my work, I have learned the expediency of adapting my style of correspondence to the characters and circumstances of those families from whom I desired assistance; indeed, it would have been absolutely impossible for me to bring together from thousands of individuals the large collection of records and historical materials found in this book without playing somewhat upon family pride and ambition; by these means the otherwise inaccessible have freely imparted from their stores of genealogical information valuable contributions to my work. Begging pardon for any seeming discourtesy in my methods of investigation, I will state that to me, in my enthusiasm, the end justified the means, and the results now given to the families who have endured my importunity, are of such a valuable character as to modify their impatience and cause them to regard the author's work with feelings of appreciation.

If I was aware that families from whom I wished to obtain information were in affluent circumstances, — if they were pressed with business cares and the entertainment of friends, — I have called their attention to my undertaking in a circuitous way, never failing to mention the many very respectable families of our name in Great Britain. I have shown that representatives of the family had been magnates in every generation; that their original coat-of-arms was granted them for their distinguished prowess and achievements in battle among the Normans; that the "three piles in point" in their escutcheon represent the three nails of our Saviour's cross, and proved in the language of heraldry that early cadets of the family from Normandy had been engaged in the Crusade wars in the Holy Land.

In my communications to individuals supposed to be possessed of something like political aspiration, I have called their attention to the fact that many members of our clan had won distinction in the halls of the English parliament and of the American congress; also, that by two or more alliances with the royal family of England, the blood of our ancestors was fused with that of every monarch that had sat upon the throne since King John. This intelligence was enough to start the "blue blood" in almost any man's veins, and has opened the way for my success in correspondence when, with some families, everything else would have been unavailing.

Families known to be of religious tendencies and identified with church-work, have been advised of the fact that for eminence in piety the ancestors of our tribe were well known; that in their loyalty to the cause of their Lord they had endured every indignity, even to banishment, imprisonment, and martyrdom; and that besides three bishops in the family, there have been about one hundred ministers who bore our surname.

When the person addressed had seen service in the army, and was possessed of a military and chivalrous spirit, I have informed him of the valor of our ancestors, — who had received the honor of knighthood at the hands of their sovereigns, and were made the recipients of many medals for services performed upon the field of battle; how, from the earliest history of our family, it had been represented by its members in every war in which their countrymen had been engaged, and in every case had won distinction and the commendations of their superiors.

If the methods of procedure mentioned in the foregoing pages have failed to awaken sufficient interest in those to whom I applied for data to enlist their attention, I have forwarded advance-sheets, copies of portraits, views of ancient family residences, and photographs. The possession of such mementoes has usually caused those to whom they were presented to feel under some obligation, and many have afterwards proved my most valuable helpers. But the mediums employed which I have already noticed do not involve all the embarrassments with which this work has been attended; indeed, I have considered it good fortune when these simple expedients have been successful. In many instances I have encountered such indifference and stolidity that for a time I was disheartened, and waited for victory in other directions to rekindle my hope. Some have absolutely refused to render aid, and would not allow the records of their families to be published in this book, and this statement must be my only apology for the disconnected appearance of many pedigrees, and the meagre accounts of some branches of the family as found in this genealogy.

In many instances I have employed clergymen, postmasters, town-clerks, and lawyers to copy tombstones, family records, church registers, town books, probate records, etc., and in a few cases these gentlemen have interviewed the families in person, to elicit facts respecting their history. These services have frequently proved expensive, and have only been called into requisition when all other means have failed.

I have depended largely upon church and town records for the births, marriages, and deaths of the early generations, especially in tracing the American branches of the family. For names and places of residence I have consulted the probate records and registers of deeds found in our county houses. Such records have been examined by me personally in several States, and the expense of traveling, to say nothing of my time, has been considerable, having made two tours through the middle, western, and southern States, besides canvassing New England very carefully. I have spent days upon my knees, in the heat of summer and cold of winter, cutting away the moss from old tombstones, that I might copy the inscriptions which, had become nearly obliterated by the wear of time. Months have been spent in the dusky archives of our public libraries in many New England cities, and I have caused to be examined the records at Washington covering the whole period of American history. Nearly every county in the southern States has been canvassed by letters and printed circulars.

Another prolific medium through which much information has reached me, was advertising in local newspapers and historical magazines, both in this country and Europe. Some of these "queries" have been duplicated through the papers in several counties, and have, in many instances, brought me into communication with valuable correspondents and sources of historical data, that otherwise could not have been reached by me; indeed, by this means many branch families have been found, and ancient portraits, views of residences, and coats-of-arms brought to light and placed in my hands. In many papers and magazines, I have published articles of considerable length on our family history, which have reached distant kinspeople, awakening in their minds sufficient interest to prompt them to assist me in my investigations. In addition to these printed communications, I have circulated among the members of the family about three thousand blanks with printed headings, three thousand descriptive circulars, and two thousand copies of a prospectus issued in 1876. Many of these were filled out with records and returned to me, but several hundred were never heard from. Besides the expense of printing, advertising, and postage, considerable money has been expended for copies of engraved portraits, and views of foreign family seats, which have been forwarded to inspire an interest where all other expedients have proved a failure.

To acquaint myself with the customs of those nations among whom our families have figured during the centuries of their existence, it has been necessary for me to read extensively. An American author writes at great disadvantage in consequence of his being so far removed from sources of information that are in other countries, and in being unfamiliar with the systems of government, habits of the people, and the terms used in their literature, especially when his work reaches back to so remote a date as does this book. Having commenced with the best histories of the Scandinavian races, I traced the customs and character of those people downward through their migrations, conquests, settlements in other European countries, and establishment in Normandy in France, where we find the first mention of our family under a distinctive surname. Thence my reading traced them through their wanderings into Germany, Italy, Russia, Iceland, Scotland, England, and the islands of the seas. It was necessary to learn of the arts of war employed in mediæval and feudal times, to acquaint myself with the ancient system of heraldry, names and grades of rank in civil and military official stations, the holding and entail of landed estates, and to acquire a correct knowledge of the technical language used in the literature contemporary with those generations whose history I wished to record. Having been so long resident in Scotland, multiplying and forming distinct branches, settled in widely separated localities, always advancing with the enlightenment and progress of the nation, changing with the changes in government, education, and modes of living, acquiring extensive landed possessions, making improvements in agriculture with the increased facilities introduced, modernizing their family residences to keep pace with the beauties of architecture of every decade, these many generations have figured more or less in the history of the country, from the time when they first sat down there till the present. Hence, the American author who would make any claim to accuracy in statement, is compelled to wade through hundreds of volumes of ancient and modern local history, in order to qualify himself for his work. These books are rare in this country, and as many of them cannot be found in our public libraries, I have found it necessary to purchase expensive genealogical and historical volumes in Europe; others that were out of print have been consulted, and extracts relating to our family copied for my use. To be correct in my descriptions of places where the family have been seated in Scotland and England, I have consulted gazetteers and descriptive maps, many of which have been forwarded to me by friends in those countries. My acknowledgments are due to many of my correspondents in Great Britain for the disinterestedness manifested by them in their researches in my behalf, being in no way connected with the family. These have seen my notices and queries in the papers and magazines, and being near the sources of information, they have kindly examined many ancient books, records, and other documents, from which some have forwarded copious notes appropriate for this book. Gentlemen in official positions which impose many pressing duties, have found the time to render assistance that could not have been available otherwise. The laws of England and Scotland were early applied to the preservation of the records of the old families, and hence the sources there are much more prolific than in this country. Records have been well kept in parishes, and where now extant are almost always within the reach of searchers. Those great repositories of antiquated documents and records of families, the College of Arms and the British Museum in London, and the Register Office and Lyon Office in Edinburgh, have been thoroughly searched for me, and every item coming within the scope of my book culled out and copied. But when the services of solicitors and officials are called into requisition, the expense attending the work of examination and writing of extracts is too heavy for a poor man.

My correspondence has extended to many gentlemen of high rank, members of parliament, ministers in foreign ports, congressmen, eminent judges, authors, bishops, clergymen, presidents of colleges, earls, lords, barons, mayors of cities, governors, State secretaries; indeed all classes, from the peasant in poverty to the millionaire, have been identified with this book by furnishing me such materials as were accessible to them. The record offices and historical libraries have been examined in London, Liverpool, Bristol, Manchester, and Newcastle, in England; Edinburgh, Glasgow, Aberdeen, Galashiels, Hawick, Kelso, Selkirk, and Paisley, in Scotland; Cork, Dublin, Limerick, Belfast, Coleraine, Londonderry, and many small towns, in Ireland. I have also caused the records in Australia, St. Christopher, Barbadoes, Bermuda, Cuba, Isle of Wight, Shetland, Orkney, and Man, to be searched for my work. A correspondence was also carried on for some time with gentlemen in various provinces in France and Germany, but the labor of translating was so great it was discontinued. Parish registers by the hundred have been consulted in Great Britain, and some of them covering a period of more than three hundred years, being without an index and written on vellum, were carefully turned leaf by leaf for me. Scores of ancient church-yards in England and Scotland have been visited in my behalf, and many very interesting epitaphs copied. This class of work was usually undertaken for me by rectors of the churches or the parish clerks. To some I have paid a stipulated fee; others have kindly forwarded the results of their search gratuitously. In several instances, church historians, being acquainted with the records, have drawn elaborate tabular pedigrees in "broadside" for me, filling in names and dates, with chronological classification.

From members of the English and Scottish branches of the family I learned that many of their kindred had settled in the British American Provinces, and I pushed my inquiries into every considerable city and town in those dominions, but for some reason unknown, some Canadian families have not responded to my wishes, and consequently the genealogy of those branches will be found very incomplete.

As the records of different families were received, the envelopes containing them were all numbered, and an epitome of their contents written on the outside; then these were all classified, tied in bundles, and packed away. In 1873, the work of composition was commenced, and for sixty days, during which I attended to all my professional duties (being a settled pastor), I employed all my spare time in writing, frequently at my work till past midnight, and perhaps the most discouraging feature of that task was the fact that more than one-half of the manuscripts was re-written, in consequence of my dissatisfaction with the arrangement of names and the classification; this change necessitated the loss of more than one thousand pages of carefully written foolscap copy, besides hundreds of pages that have since been cut out to make room for *addenda*, and re-composed. No more confusing piece of classification and composition was ever undertaken than that of compiling from thousands of letters, copies of wills, deeds, commissions, account-books, ancient Latin inscriptions, copies of grave-stones, family Bibles, old framed tablets, marriage and baptism certificates, petitions, business charters, bills of sale, notes, receipts, memorandums, diaries, muster rolls, subscription papers, and other papers too numerous to mention here. This will be better appreciated when it is known that the matter comprising some pages in this book has been taken from twenty different sources. These circumstances expose a work of this class to many liabilities to errors in dates and the spelling of proper names; these will, no doubt, be discovered after the book is in print and when too late to correct them. Of course, many of the original letters and old documents were nearly illegible and difficult to read; these have been transcribed as carefully as possible, and when discrepancies appeared I have adopted that rendering which seemed most reliable; where documentary evidence was wanting, statements have been made as *probabilities* and *approximates.* Traditions have been given as historically true only when well authenticated by according testimony. Errors caused by the carelessness of those who furnished me records, I am in no way responsible for; some are, no doubt, the result of oversight upon my own part.

It has been my purpose to incorporate a generous biographical element into this book, but it has been impossible to obtain sufficient interesting materials of that class to give the composition anything like uniformity in appearance. The biographical sketches of members of the Scottish and English families were largely taken from local papers and popular magazines, but some of them have passed through the hands of the family and received their approval; many of the sketches in the American families have been written or revised by the relatives, and were endorsed as substantially correct.

The author does not claim to have compiled a full history or complete genealogy of all branches or sub-branches of those families whose names are found in this book; such a work was never accomplished by the most enthusiastic and successful genealogist, and can never be expected. I have sought diligently and continuously for fourteen years for everything that could in any way add to the interest and value of this book, and do not know how I could have done more under existing circumstances. As before mentioned, I have respectfully applied to many representatives of the several branch families whose records, in part, stand on the pages of this work, and they have obstinately declined to render the least assistance when it was in their power, by devoting only a few hours to correspondence, to have placed in my hands data that would have largely enhanced the value of the book both in historical matter and literary appearance. These families will undoubtedly regret, when they shall see the book, that they did not appreciate my scheme enough to furnish their quota of records; but the opportunity has passed, the links of the chain are missing, and will never be placed historically where they belong. A hundred discouragements not proper to particularize here have been thrown in the author's way while engaged on this work, and one less determined would have forsaken the enterprise years ago. In humble circumstances at the beginning, with a family to support, he has many times applied himself so assiduously to this favorite employment that an overworked brain was warned him of the necessity of rest, and finally, to add the most painful embarrassment that could have been inflicted, he had a slight paralytic shock, which has so impaired the use of the right hand as to incapacitate him from all study and literary work for many months, and from which there is no hope of full recovery.

The cash expense devoted to this undertaking during the past twelve years has been heavy, and was principally sustained by money earned by professional duties, writing for the press, and the sale of small publications that have been prepared within the same time. Many times I have spent my last dollar for stationery and postage stamps, and sometimes could not continue my correspondence for want of means. Two or three gentlemen who have possessed an interest in what I was seeking to accomplish, have generously forwarded money to assist me, and these have my grateful acknowledgments.

At the family meeting held in Philadelphia in 1876, a plan was adopted to raise twelve hundred dollars toward the expense of completing my work, and five hundred dollars were pledged by responsible men, but the arrangement was not fully consummated and proved abortive. This was a very unfavorable result, as engravings had been ordered on the strength of pledges made, and when the money was needed the men were not willing to contribute their proportion unless the whole amount could be raised.

But my work is done, and imperfect as it is, must show for itself the result of my toil. I feel that my object has been a commendable one, and that I have faithfully used the materials placed in my hands. Those who know the least about such a work will have the least forbearance when they discover any mistake in the book, while others will appreciate the attempt made to preserve in permanent form so many records and incidents belonging to our widely scattered kindred. Acknowledging my indebtedness to hundreds who have so kindly and promptly assisted me in various ways, and hoping every book placed in the hands of the family may be preserved with sacred care for the rising generations, I commit the work to the custody of those whose names are embalmed within its pages.

G. T. RIDLON.

MANCHESTER, N. H., March 12, 1884.

HISTORY OF ILLUSTRATIONS.

THE embellishment of this book has been very expensive. Works of a gene-alogical and biographical character are seldom illustrated, except by portraits and autographs, but I have deemed it advisable to insert views of the ancient residences of the principal families in England and Scotland, as well as some of the homestead houses in the United States. Original copies have been hard to obtain, especially in Great Britain, and those now having a place in this book were procured after the author had nearly exhausted his patience in unsuccessful efforts to secure them. Many of these ancient houses had never been photo-graphed, and being far from an artist, original views could only be had by paying considerable sums of money to induce photographers to go from their rooms to make negatives. In some instances proprietors kindly forwarded views made especially for my use, at their own expense. Several of them furnished views taken from different standpoints, that I might make a choice. The views of residences, mills, and monuments were all lithographed from original photographs, with the exception of three, viz., " Friar's Carse," which was copied from a plate in a book, " Glen-Riddle Mills," made from a wood-engraving used for bill-heads by the owner, and " Hillside Farm," which was from a crayon-drawing by the author, consequently known to be correct representations of the places. A few individ-uals having an interest in my undertaking have paid for the views of their resi-dences, the others were printed for me at an expense of five hundred dollars, and paid for from my own pocket. These are all full-page plates in lithography and pen-drawing, printed in three tints, and in the judgment of many who possess artistic taste and culture are pronounced the most beautiful illustrations for a book of this class they have ever seen. I have photographic views of many more old residences of families whose records are in this book, but could not have them printed.

The coats-of-arms, of which there are eight pages, representing twenty different shields, were engraved on box-wood from photographic copies, pen-drawings forwarded from England and Scotland, or from heraldic descriptions found in books, and are printed from color-blocks in gold and tints, at an expense of two hundred and eighty dollars, paid by the author. That with the motto, — " *Jamais Arriere*," — is copied from a photograph taken from a very fine framed drawing made many years ago for Thomas Ridlon of Boston, but I do not know whence he procured it. That with the two greyhounds for supporters was made from a drawing furnished me by Sir Walter-Buchanan Riddell, Bart., of Hep-ple, England, but the colors were assigned by the engraver. The arms of

. Riddell-Carre, combining the quarterings of the two families, was engraved from a wax seal forwarded by Mr. Riddell Carre from Scotland.

The portraits in this history were mostly engraved on steel by Messrs. F. T. Stewart and J. A. J. Wilcox, of Boston, Mass., and are fine specimens of art as well as excellent likenesses of the individuals. These have cost, — the large-sized heads, — from seventy-five to one hundred dollars each, and were paid for by the originals or their families. The group of seven heads of European members of the family, was engraved at my own expense, and cost, with prints, one hundred and eighty-seven dollars. The group engraved on steel, of seven American members of the Riddell and Riddle family, was subscribed for by the men themselves or their relatives, but as two died before the plate was finished, I have been obliged to pay nearly one hundred dollars on the same. The Ridlon group, comprising seven heads, was paid for by individuals. Four of the lithographic portraits were printed at my expense, and cost one hundred and twenty dollars. The portraits of Bishop Ridley, the martyr, — one on steel by John Sartain, and one by the heliotype process, — were made to my order, at a cost of one hundred dollars. That of Mark Ridley, M. D., was lithographed from a copper-plate print found in London, Eng.; and with the one of GlosterRidley, D. D., which was also made from a copper-plate found on the title-page of a book of his poems, were made to my order at an expense of fifty dollars.

The portraits now engraved, with those ordered for this book, including prints, will cost rising two thousand dollars.

Origin and Changes of Surnames.

THE use of established surnames cannot be traced much earlier than the middle of the tenth century. They first came into use in Normandy, in France, and at the coming of William the Conqueror were quite generally introduced into England. Many of the Norman adventurers who assisted in the Conquest, had taken the names of their residences, or of villages near their ancestral chateaux, names that were used with the French preposition *de* before them. Nearly all of the soldiers of William's army went back to their homes in Normandy, and bestowed the lands awarded them in England upon their younger sons, who came over and settled upon them, giving to these new estates their own names. When the Norman-French disappeared from England, the prefix *de* was completely discarded, unless retained for euphony, and the word "of" used as a substitute. The Scotch have a more expressive designation which they apply to families who have a territorial name; they say, "of that ilk." In Scotland, surnames were seldom used till the twelfth century, and were for a long time variable. The assumption of surnames by the common people is everywhere of later date than that by the gentle families. In England, the number of surnames is about forty thousand, or one to every five hundred individuals; in Scotland, far fewer surnames in proportion to the population. Surnames may be divided into several classes, as territorial, characteristic, mechanical, and personal. The names, Fairbanks, Burbank, Burnham, Washburn, Woodbridge, Woodbury, Bradbury, Mansfield, Kilburn, Swinburn, and Riddell, are all territorial in origin. The names, Carpenter, Turner, Weaver, Brewer, Boulter, Chaplin, Goldsmith, Wheelwright, Gardner, Baxter, and Usher, are all derived from the occupation of ancestors of those families. Among the surnames taken from some characteristic of the individual who first used them, are Walker, Sleeper, Springer, Armstrong, Longstaff, Goodman, Lockheart, Douglass, Broadhead, and Longfellow.

The reasons for the use of surnames are obvious. In localities where there were individuals of the same Christian name, they were distinguished by such names as "John the Cartwright" and "John the Carpenter"; and in a short time these became fixed family surnames. This would be true of two persons of one Christian name, dwelling in the same community, the one at *Fairbanks*, and the other at *Mansfield ;* one would be known as "William of Fairbanks," the other as "William of Mansfield," hence these names, so common in England and America.

The original surname from which the various forms of orthography now used by the numerous branches of the family whose genealogy is found in this book are supposed to have been derived, was local or territorial. Much discussion has been had respecting the origin and changes of the surnames Rydale and Ridel, and men of equal scholarship and research do not agree in their conclusions. How, then, can it be expected, that an author writing from an American standpoint, will be able to lift this veil that has for so many generations held the subject in comparative obscurity? I shall only follow those whose advantages have qualified them to write with the claims of accuracy. The Sieur de Ridel, or Monsieur Ridel, whose name appears on the roll of Battle Abbey, the earliest record of the Normans who came with William the Conqueror, was said to be the ancestor of all branches of the Riddell and Riddle family subsequently settled in England and Scotland, and that he was such, some very able antiquaries have maintained during the present century. The surname appears on the pages of the Domesday Book, and in a variety of forms, such as "Ridle," "Ridel," and "Ridell." We must look to Norway or Normandy for the origin of the name. An English authority says, "The name is a local one, from a place in Scandinavia called Rugdal, that is Ryedale, the valley of rye." This has been the opinion held by nearly all writers, and certainly has the best of grounds in history. Members of this Norman family settled in Yorkshire, and named their landed possessions "Ryedale"; thence they settled in Scotland and called their lands there by their own surname.

John Riddell, one of the greatest antiquaries ever known in Scotland, possessed the deepest interest in this subject, and traced the name back to Norman records to procure every item of proof bearing upon its derivation and original orthography, and in his publications he claims for the "Riddells of Riddell," Roxburghshire, Scotland, the "Riddells of Cranstown-Riddell," the "Riddells of Ardnamurchan," and families of the name in England, a common origin. This gentleman, in one of his literary discussions with Mr. Cosmo Innes, who was considered by some equally eminent in the same line of research, took that gentleman to task for asserting in his preface to the "Chartulary of Melrose," that the Riddells only *acquired* their surname from their lands in Roxburghshire, instead of *giving* it to their estate. In a work published by John Riddell, Esq., in 1843, called "*Stewartiana*," he has treated the subject of his family name with great fulness of illustration and instances the Gervase Ridel, who witnessed an inquisition of David, when Prince of Cumbria, A. D. 1116, as of the same family as Walter de Rydale, and mentions Chalmers' "Caledonia" as authority that the Riddells of Roxburgh spread into Mid-Lothian, and gave the name of "Cranstown-Riddell" to their lands there. More recent genealogists, with some claims to consideration, have taken exception to John Riddell's view of the case, and endeavor to prove that the Ridels and Rydales were originally distinct families. An examination of ancient papers has proved that the Riddells of Roxburgh, denominated "of that ilk" in deeds and monastic records, for several centuries from their first appearance in Scotland, are invariably * styled "de Ridale," and the other stock, now represented by the Riddells of Sunart, in Argyleshire, always had their surname spelled "Ridel" without the prefix *de*. Several authors claim "de Ridale" to be a local surname and "Ridel" as strictly personal in its origin and significance. The same writers identify the Ridels of Cranstown with the Ridels of England; these families having sided with the English in the Wars of the Succession,

---

* There was one exception. "Walter Ridel" witnessed a charter by William the Lyon, say A. D. 1165-1174.

lost their estate in Scotland. The de Ridales, who do not appear prominently of that era, though they were near the Border, retained their lands until they sold them at a comparatively recent date. The name of Sir Hugh Ridel stands on the "Ragman's Roll," but none of the other families appear there.

The Ridels of England were chiefly connected with Northamptonshire and Essex. In the "Pipe Roll" (1184) Hugh Ridel is found in possession of the land of Wittering, in the former county, and in the year 1192 Richard Ridel owned the same estate. A century later (1315) a Hugh Ridel petitions Edward II that the lands of Wittering, which had been taken from him by Edward I (because at the request of Simon Frizel, he stayed in Scotland with John de Balliol), and had been given to the petitioner's son, Geoffry Ridel, during the king's pleasure, might be restored to him. Thirty years afterwards (1348) another Hugh Ridell, son and heir of "Mons. Geffrei Ridell," petitions Edward III, for restoration of his lands of "Craneston in Loudion" (Cranstown-Riddell, Mid-Lothian, Scotland), out of which his father had been expelled by the Scots for his allegiance to the English crown, styling this property the "heritage of his ancestors." According to Bridges, they held Wittering till the reign of Edward IV, when the family ended in an heiress.

At the same time the *Ridels* of Wittering and Cranstown appear in the "Pipe Rolls" of Henry II, and Richard I, the *de Ridales* of Roxburghshire, Scotland, are conspicuous in the "Chartulary of Melrose." One deed in that record gives remarkable evidence of four generations of this family co-existent in the twelfth century. Patrick de Ridale; Walter, his son and heir; William, the son and heir of Walter; and William, son of William and grandson of Walter, all appear in this grant to Melrose. The deed that follows the one before mentioned is a confirmation by Eustace de Vesci, their overlord, of the de Ridales grant. Singularly enough, one of the witnesses to this document was Gaufridus *Ridel*, who is not styled *consanguineus*, as he would have been had he been a relative. Hugh Ridel (before mentioned) also attests a confirmation by William the Lyon, of a grant by Patrick de Ridale to Melrose. At the same period the "Pipe Rolls" show that a Patrick and Roger de Ridale flourished in the County of York. Chalmers claims that the first of the Scotch de Ridales came from Yorkshire, and the Christian name Patrick favors that origin. Jordan Ridell of Tilmouth, in Northumberland, in 1230, had in his arms "three bars wavy" the same as the Ridels of Wittering, while the de Ridales had the "chevron between three ears of rye." Another authority claims the surname of the family of Riddell of Sunart, in its original orthography to have been personal and not territorial; that its true form appears to be Rudellus or Rudel, though frequently spelled Ridel at an early date, but in no instance as de Ridel. He believes in three original branches, or distinct families, of the name, but his quotations do not sustain the arguments of others as to the identity between the English Riddells, and those of Argyleshire and Cranstown in Scotland.

In Berwick-on-Tweed and Newcastle-on-Tyne the name has a continuous history. In "Historical Documents, Scotland, 1286–1306," under date Dec. 10, A. D. 1293, letters of safe conduct for "*Phillipus de Ridall, burginsis et mercator de Berewyk*," trading within the kingdom of England, were granted. In the "Wills and Inventories," edited by the Surtees Society, there is the name of a de Ridell continuing the tradition of Philip de Rydale as a burgess of Berwick-on-Tweed. Thomas de Ridell, who was a burgess of Berwick, in his will, 1615, names among his legatees, his nephew, Alexander de Ridell, together with William, a son, and Agnes, daughter of Alexander; and it may be worth

2

mention as a probable indication of consanguinity with the Ridales of that ilk, that among his bequests occurs "five pounds to the building of the stone bridge of Tweed, at Rokisburgh," together with "lxxx bordar" and "c bordar" to the chapel of the B. V. M. at Rokisburgh, besides a "donation to the Abbot and Convent of Kelkow." (Kelso.)

In the "Correspondence, Inventories, etc.," of the Priory of Coldingham, the rental shows (1298) "Johannas Rydell" holding two curucates "in domonico" in Flemington. William de Hylton, the nuns of Berwick, and Matthew de Red-man are severally recorded as holding lands of the said J. Rydell. Under Lamberton, in the same rental, "*Alicia quæ fuit uxor Johannis Rydell*," is mentioned as having her dower of the third part of Flemington forfeited, "*ut dicitur.*" Among the witnesses to the solemn excommunication pronounced at Norham, after the gospel at high mass of the feast of the translation of St. Cuthbert, 1467, against Patrick Home, Protonotary of our Lord, the Pope, and John Home, "*assertus cánonicus*" in the collegiate church of Durham, *Johannis Ridell* is named among the "well-known friends and kinsmen" of the said Patrick and John, who were present on the occasion. In another of the same series of documents may be found evidence that seems to point to the descent of the Ridells of Flemington. It is taken "*Ex Institutus, Thomæ Prioris Dunelmensis,* A. D. MCCXXXV," and mentions among those who owed service to the Priory of Durham, from Coldinghamshire, "*hæredes Galfrid Ridel, et orum hæredes de Flemington.*" It is in evidence that Galfridus Ridel was the name of the contemporary Lord of Blaye, in Aquitaine, whose letters to Henry III, are in "Royal Letters, Roll Series," under date 1247. The form of the name then given, and which is the prevailing form in "Gascon Rolls," Galfridus Rudelli" is suggestive of an eponymous hero, Ruddellus, or Rudel, and not of a territory the name of which had been taken by its owners. Nigellus Ridulli was one of the barons of Gascony, perverted to the king of France by the court of La Marche. Helias Ridell was one of Henry III's faithful barons and men, of whom Geoffrey Neville, Seneschal of Poitou and Gascony, makes supplication in April, 1219. "Galfridus Rydel," "Galfridus Ridelli," and "Gaufridus Rudelli," such are the forms under which appear the Lords of Blaye (in France), senior and junior, who bore that Christian name during the reign of Henry III and Edward II, whose names are found in many public documents in England and Gascony.

At what date the Roxburghshire family gave their name to their lands is not precisely known. Walter de Ridale got his lands from David I, between 1124 and 1153, by charter, and these were subsequently denominated the "Baronies of Riddell and Whitton." Quintin Ridale is the first of this house styled "of that ilk"; he died in 1471. It will be seen that the family at Berwick-on-Tweed and others at Flemington, evidently derived from the family of Blaye, used the prefix "de" with their surname, proving that their possessions in Scotland and England were called Ridell or Rydale. The several branches of the family seem to have followed out their early custom of bestowing their own names upon their lands whenever and wherever acquired, and we have "Cranstown-Riddell," "Glen-Riddell," "Mount-Riddell," "Minto-Riddell," in Scotland; and "Glen-Riddle," "Riddle's Banks," "Riddle's Station," "Riddleton," and "Riddle's Cross-roads," in the United States.

The Norman ancestors held their earldoms for several generations as a distinct family, before a surname was assumed by them, each successor being known by his Christian name; but there are abundant evidences to prove that the surname used by the Roxburghshire and Northumberland families was originally derived from a place known as Ryedale, and the ears of rye and sheaves of grain, almost universally found in their coats-of-arms from their earliest history, should be a sufficient proof, supplemented by the orthography of the name, without looking any further. In early times there was no established form of spelling surnames, and those of the same individual are frequently found in old records in a variety of forms, written undoubtedly according to the fancy of the recorder, and not by authority of the one who bore the name.

Nearly all branches of the Scottish families have spelt the name "Riddell," but there are many old documents on which it is spelled "Riddle" in the Scotch and English houses; and there have been, and are now, many small branches in Scotland and England, claiming descent from the Ryedales, who spell their own names "Riddle"; among them the "Riddles of Troughend," of which the late Edward Riddle, Master of the Greenwich Naval School, was one.

Many branches settled in the north of Ireland; some from the Roxburgh family, some from the Glen-Riddell branch of the same tree; and others evidently descended from the Riddells of Argyleshire, and many of them spell the name Riddle, Riddel, Riddall, and Ruddell.

An early offshoot of the Norman Ridels settled in Germany; and their numerous descendants, now scattered over the wide world, spell their names Ridel, Riedel, Reidel, and Riedell.

One family in the Southern States are descended from emigrants from France, and in the first generations spelt their names Riddelle. Many of the Scotch-Irish families came to the United States, and a majority of them now spell their names Riddle; some Riddile.

A family early settled in Kentucky spelled their surname Ruddle. And descendants of one Virginian branch still spell the name Ruddell, nearly identical with the Latin forms.

The early New Jersey families were Scottish, and uniformly used the orthography Riddell for several generations. But their names on the Colonial records are frequently spelt Riddle, a name now used by their descendants.

The surname *Ridley*, or *de Ridleigh*, like others in this book, has been under much discussion, and authors of great antiquarian information disagree as to its derivation. Some look to their ancient coat-of-arms as proof for their claims that Ridleigh, as the name was spelt in early times, was derived from a place in Cheshire owned by the ancestors of the family, where *reeds* grew. The shield in a coat-of-arms is sometimes called a "field," and as this had an ox passing through reeds in the arms of Ridleigh, it is said the original form was *Reedfield*, "leigh" in the old language meaning a field or meadow. This would seem reasonable enough if we could find the name spelled Reedfield, or Reedleigh, in any old document. Does any such proof appear? Another writer gives the same derivation for the terminal part of the surname, but ascribes another meaning to the prefix "Rid," which, being sometimes spelled "Red" in old English, signifies to clear away or make clean; hence, combined with "leigh," would represent a clean field or cleared land. Nearly all writers have assigned a territorial origin to the surname, but trace it to a source far removed from Ridley Hall in Cheshire, England. In a biographical notice of Bishop Nicholas Ridley, in the Parker edition of his writings, it is stated, "the origin of the name Ridley may be traced more satisfactorily than that of many others now equally illustrious. It appears to have been Scottish, and originally Ridel or Ryedale, of which Riddle is a corruption; and the Riddells of Glen-Riddell might have traced their descent to a common stock with the Ridleys of Willimoteswick." John Ridley, a brother-in-law of Bishop Ridley, was buried in the Haltwhistle Church, Northumberland, England; and his name in the inscription on his tomb is spelled "Redle" or "Ridle," exactly the same as the name of one of the Norman ancestors of the Riddells, as found in the Domesday Book. One ancient author calls Ridley a "gentile name," and another, writing in 1649, mentions Ridley among thirty-seven families of Northumberland "dating back to the Conquest." I have not found any mention of the name dating prior to the settlement of the Norman Ridels and de Ridales in England and Scotland, but the appearance of the surname de Ridleigh or Ridley, in the north, is contemporary with that of Ridale on the border, across the Tyne. In ancient documents, now extant, in the College of Arms, London, and in the British Museum, the surname is spelled Riddley and Ridlea.

The *Ridlers* of England and America descended from a family in Gloucestershire, are an offshoot of the Ridleys of Willimoteswick, and assumed the same arms and crest.

The *Ridlands* and *Ridlons* are descended from an ancient Norman, Robert de Rhuddlan, or de Ryddland, who settled in Wales, and was resident at Rhuddlan Castle on the river Clwyd, in the County of Flint. (See "Rhuddlans and Ridlands," in this book.) The Ridlands descended from one Adam Ridland from the Orkney Islands, were early settled in Shetland, and seem to have spelt their surname uniformly.

Magnus Ridland, or Readlan, came from Shetland to New England in 1718, and after changing his name from Ridland to Readlan and Redlan, finally adopted the form Redlon, and continued it through life. His seven sons spelt their own names Redlon, and so did nearly all of the third generation, although town-clerks and Justices of the Peace frequently wrote their names Ridlon, Redlone, and Ridley. The Buxton branch and the Damariscotta branch of Maine, have always retained their ancestors name of Redlon. The Hollis branch changed to Ridlon first, but the families at Saco, and in other towns, soon adopted the same form. Families in the west, originally from Maine, spell the surname Ridlen, Ridlin, and Redley. Some of the fathers changed the spelling at the request of an old Scotch school-master, under whose instruction they were early placed.

The descendants of Matthias Redlon, who went to Kennebec County, from Saco, Me., nearly all changed their names to *Ridley*, a very unwise action, that has resulted in great confusion and embarrassment ever since. There were families named Ridley, descended from the Cape Cod branch, early settled in eastern Maine, and almost every one addressed the Redlons by that name; they became weary of correcting the mistake, and supposing these Ridleys to be a branch of the same family, adopted their name. Samuel Ridlon and his descendants of Hollis, Me., however, and John his brother, who settled in Vermont, continued to spell their surname Ridlon, while their brothers in the east changed to Ridley.

It is a matter of surprise to many who are unacquainted with family history, that any surname should be changed; but the causes are numerous and traceable. It is well known by all antiquarians, that in early times there was no established rule for spelling in the Old World, and surnames are found in a variety of forms on ancient documents and monumental inscriptions. Few surnames of families whose ancestors were early settled in New England, are now spelled as they were when introduced into the colonies; and if such families could trace their names to an early period in English history, they would undoubtedly find that their ancestors were known by names quite unlike those borne by the early American generations. In the "old English" all surnames now spelt with the letter *i* were originally written with a *y*, as in Chamberlayne and Rydleigh or Rydley.

In the early New England Colonies representatives of several nationalities, English, Scotch, Irish. French, and Scandinavians, were constantly associated, and each, having a pronunciation peculiar to himself, found it necessary to accommodate his language to the understanding of others; in consequence of this modification, constantly carried on, names of men and things in a short time were pronounced quite differently from what they were originally written. As the early settlers had few advantages for acquiring even a primary education, and but few occasions to write their names, justices, clerks, and clergy, who used the pen, wrote surnames as they heard them spoken, following each pronunciation in their spelling as closely as they could: The rising generations, who had a better education, by consulting the records of towns and churches, learned to spell their names as they found those of their ancestors written, and in a few years families were known by surnames very dissimilar to those borne by their progenitors.

With all the mutations through which the surnames used by the various branches of our clan have passed, it is interesting to observe that a marked resemblance has been preserved in the orthography and the significance of them all. The original form seems to have been derived from a dale or dell where rye was cultivated, and properly written would be Ryedale or Ryedell. Dale and dell are synonamous names, as —

"In *dales* and *dells* concealed from mortal sight."

The change from Ryedale and Riddell to Riddle, — as the name is always pronounced by Scotchmen, — has not caused a loss of the full meaning of the original, as a riddle was an instrument by which rye and other grains were winnowed and cleansed; and the change to Ridler and Riddler, makes that form denote one who winnows grain with a riddle or seive. The old English word *Red* or *Rid*, signifies to cleanse or drive out, as, "I will *rid* my fields of evil beasts." The ancient word, *leigh* and *ley*, represented a field or meadow, a low piece of ground, and connected with *rid* would, in its proper spelling, be *Cleared field* or *Cleanland*. If the surname Ridleigh or Ridley was derived from this source, the meaning resembles that of the original Norman name of Ryedale. But if what has been called *reeds* in the ancient arms of the Ridleys of Willimoteswick, should prove to be *rye* instead, — which seems quite probable, — then the full name Ridleigh would be Ryefield or Ryeland, which is the exact equivalent of Ryedale or Ryedell. The same is true of the surname Ridland, as now used by the branch of the family in Sandsting, Shetland Isles. The territorial or local and agricultural significance of the surname has never been lost by the many changes in spelling during thirty generations of the family.

In one ancient coat-of-arms borne by a branch of the Ryedale family from Normandy, there was a plough, and some heralds represent the ox in the ancient arms of Ridley, as drawing a plough through reeds in a field; this fact strengthens the claim to relationship between the two families.

I give below a catalogue comprising the forms of spelling found in books and records, —sixty in all.

RADLEY.	REDLONE.	RIDDLE.	RIDLE.	RIDLING.	RUDDELL.
RADLY.	REDLY.	RIDDLEA.	RIDLEA.	RIDLION.	RUDDLE.
READLAN.	REEDLEIGH.	RIDDLEON.	RIDLEGH.	RIDLON.	RUDDELUS.
READLAND.	REIDELL.	RIDDLER.	RIDLEIGH.	RIDLY.	RUDEL.
REDDEL.	REIDEL.	RIDDLEY.	RIDLEN.	RIEDEL.	RYDALE.
REDDLE.	RIDALE.	RIDEL.	RIDLEON.	RIEDELL.	RYDALL.
REDEL.	RIDDAL.	RIDELL.	RIDLER.	RODLEIGH.	RYDELL.
REDLA.	RIDDALL.	RIDELUS.	RIDLEY.	RUDDALL.	RYEDALE.
REDLAN.	RIDDEL.	RIDLA.	RIDLIEGH.	RUDDEL.	RYEDEL.
REDLON.	RIDDILE.	RIDLAND.	RIDLIN.	RUDDELI.	RYEDELL.

FAMILY CHRISTIAN NAMES.

NAMES distinguishing one individual from another have been in use from the earliest ages of human society. Among the Jews, the name given to a child originated in some circumstance of birth, or was an expression of religious sentiment. Old Testament names are almost all original, given in the first instance to the person bearing them.

The Greeks bore only one name, given the tenth day after birth, which was the right of the father to choose and alter if he pleased. The early Greek names are expressive of some quality held in great estimation, as valor, skill, wisdom, or gracefulness. (Callimachus, excellent fighter; Pherecrates, strength bringer; Sophron, wise; Melanthus, black flower).

The Romans at a very early period bore two names, and subsequently every Roman citizen had three. The names Caius, Marcus, Cneius, like our Christian names, were personal to the individual. These names were given to Roman children at the attainment of puberty in early times, and afterwards on the ninth day after birth. The Roman names were originally less dignified than the Greeks; some were derived from ordinary employments, as Porcius (swine-herd), Cicero (vetch grower); some from personal peculiarities, as Crassus (fat), Naso (long-nosed), and a few from numerals, Sextus, Septimus.

Celtic and Teutonic names, like the Jewish and Greek, were originally very significant, and to check their exuberance the people contented themselves by passing them down from father to son. Many names in Europe, in consequence of the changed speech of the people, belong to an obsolete tongue, and their signification has become unintelligible. Some were derived from God, as Gott-fried, Godfrey, Godwin; some from inferior gods, as Anselm, Oscar, Esmond; others from elves or genii, as Alfred, Alboin, Elfric (Elfking). Bertha is the name of a favorite female goddess and source of light; the same name compounded is Albrecht, Bertram. Many names indicating personal prowess, wisdom, and nobility of birth, belong to the following class: Hildebrand (war brand), Konrad (bold in counsel), Hlodwig (glorious warrior), now called Clovis, and the original of Ludwig and Louis. The wolf, bear, eagle, boar, and lion entered into the composition of the names of men, as Adolf (noble wolf), Arnold (valiant eagle), Osborn (God bear).

The Puritans, acting under strong religious interests would admit of but two classes of names for their children, — those expressive of religious sentiment, such as Praise-God, Live-well, Wait-still, and names which occur in Scripture; hence in the early generations of the New England families the Christian names, Patience, Charity, Mercy, Hope, Grace, and Lovie are of frequent occurrence. The use of two or more Christian names is a comparatively modern practice, as also the use of surnames in place of Christian names

There are a few Christian names in this book worthy of notice in this article. In the Norman house of Ryedale, or Ridel, *Walgrinus* stands at the head of the pedigree, and does not occur again in any branch of the clan. *Galfridus, Gaufridus*, and *Gaufrid* (different forms of the same name) are transmitted from father to son, and from successor to successor, until borne by thirteen or more members of the family.

Geoffrey and *Geofery* are names used during the early generations of the Norman Ridels. *Gervase*, or *Gervasius*, was one of the first of the Anglo-Norman representatives of the race who settled in Scotland, and it is a little singular that this ancestral name was not continued in that branch of the Riddell family; of late, however, after being laid away more than seven hundred years, it has been resuscitated by a descendant of the original Gervasius, and is now used both in Scottish and American branches of the family. The female Christian names, *Geva* and *Grizel*, early introduced into the Ryedale family, have also been revived and bestowed upon children of the Riddell and Ridlon name in Scotland and the United States. Amongst the singular names found in the Scottish house of Ridale, are *Auskittel* and *Quintin*. The former was derived from the family of Aukittell, or Anskitell, now of "Mount Aukitell," and "Aukitill Grove," County Monaghan, Ireland, connected with the "Riddells of Glasslough," by marriage in 1768; the name Quintin appears but once in the Riddell family, and whence derived is not known, but is the name of a saint in the Roman Calendar, and of a distinguished painter, born at Antwerp in 1460.

The name *Hans* in a branch of the family of Roxburghshire, Scotland, early settled in Ireland, as well as the name *Gavin* or *Gawin*, peculiar to a Scotch-Irish branch of the Riddell family, early settled in New Hampshire, were derived from the Hamilton and Douglas families, in which the latter is found as far back as 1520.

The Ridleys of Willimoteswick have perpetuated several ancient Christian names peculiar to the early generations, such as *Nicholas, Christopher, Cuthbert, Launcelot*, and *Mark*. Nicholas Ridley, the Martyr Bishop, was probably named for his uncle, or Sir Nicholas Ridley the "Broad Knight," and having cast a halo over the family name by his religious zeal and great learning, every generation since has had one or more representatives named Nicholas. The father of the Martyr was Christopher Ridley of Unthank, and many have since borne his Christian name, especially descendants from the "Ridleys of Battersea."

Cuthbert Ridley was sometime (say 1625) rector of Simonburn Church, in Northumberland, England; his Christian name has been kept in the Ridley family of Mickley, from father to son for six successive generations, and is now used by descendants in New York.

Mark, as a Ridley name, goes back to 1628, when Dr. Mark Ridley was a surgeon in London. Since that date the name has occurred in the English and American families, and is still used by the descendants of Mark Ridley, who settled in Barnstable County, Mass., as early as 1660.

The Ridley family, now so numerous in the Southern States, have continued the use of the Christian name, *Robert*, borne by their common ancestor, who came from England in 1635. *Bromfield*, a surname used as a Christian name in this family, is still handed down by members in the legal profession.

The name *Magnus* is peculiar to the Redlon and Ridlon families in New England, descended from Magnus Readlan, or Ridland, who came from the Shetland Islands in 1718. The name signifies strength, or attraction, and is from the same root as the ancient names Magi and Magician, applied to those who were supposed to possess some remarkable and mysterious power. From the same Latin root we have magnes, magnet, and magnate. The loadstone, having a hidden power of attraction, has been called in literature, "The mighty magnes stone." Magnus was assumed by many of the ancients as a surname, among them by Pompey, from the greatness of his exploits. The name is common in Norway and Shetland, being directly derived from the kings of the former country and Sweden, of which there were six who bore that name. King Magnus II reigned twenty-eight years previous to 1070 A. D., and his son and successor, Magnus III, fifty-two years, to 1180. In Kirkwall, the principal town of the Orkney Islands, is St. Magnus' Cathedral, founded in 1136 A. D. St. Magnus' Bay, on the west coast of the mainland of Shetland, affords an excellent anchorage for large vessels. Magnus was also the name of a king of the Isle of Man, 1264 A. D.

The name has been handed down from generation to generation, in the Redlon and Ridlon families, but when the author commenced this book, there were but *two* persons in the connection bearing it, and one of them only as a middle name. Since this family history was undertaken, the author has had the honor of bestowing this grand old kingly and ancestral family name upon several little fellows who bear the Ridlon surname, and it is hoped the Christian name *Magnus* will never be allowed to drop out of the old sept.

Matthias is a name much used in the early generations of the Redlon and Ridlon family, and came from the family of Young, in Kittery, Me., of whom the first wife of Magnus Redlon, our common progenitor, was a member. This old scriptural name represents our ancestors on the maternal side, and should be perpetuated by the Ridlons as long as there is one of the name.

The name *Abraham*, in the Ridlon family, was derived from the Townsends, of Saco. Massie, daughter of Abraham Townsend, sometime of Lynn, Mass., was the second wife of Magnus Redlon, and named her eldest son for her father; that son died unmarried, and although the name has been perpetuated in other branches of the Ridlon family, there are now no male descendants of Massie Townsend who bear our surname.

Robert is a name introduced into the Redlon family by the marriage of John Redlon, of Buxton, Me., with a daughter of Robert Brooks. The eldest son was named Robert for his maternal grandfather, and became the head of the Damariscotta Redlons. Another daughter of Robert Brooks was the wife of David Martin, and named a son Robert for her father, from whom by intermarriage subsequently, between the Ridlons and Martins, the name Robert came into the family again, but from the same original source. I incline to the belief that Robert Ridlon, of Hollis, Me. (deceased), was named for a Robert Cousens of his mother's family.

The name *Ebenezer*, of the Buxton family of Ridlons, came from the Youngs of Kittery, by the marriage of Magnus Redlon with Susanna, daughter of Matthew Young, a Scotchman.

Nathaniel came to the Ridlons from the Townsend family; *Thomas*, from the Edgcombs.

HERALDRY.

ALL the ancient nations mentioned in history, wore some kind of defensive armor when in battle; sometimes of leather, of brass, of iron, and of steel. Some of the more luxurious had their coats of mail and helmets richly ornamented with gold and silver. In Bible times the sacred writers were acquainted with shields, breastplates, and helmets. When coats of armor were of thick leather, they were padded with some elastic material that would deaden a blow of sword or spear. Scale armor was composed of plates of brass, iron, or steel, so formed and joined together, as to adapt itself to the necessary movements of the wearer's body. Armor originally only covered the head and the shoulders, but in the days of William the Conqueror, men of war were clothed from crown to toe in armor made of plate, or steel rings. In process of time the old knights and chiefs had devices on their shields which represented their prowess and were sometimes significant of their family name or place of residence; then a crest was worn on the helmet, well known to the followers of the chief, that could be seen in battle, and served as an ensign. These symbols and devices painted on the shields were of endless variety, "from the highest things celestial, to the lowest things terrestrial." Sometimes surcoats made of leather were worn over the armor of polished brass or steel, to protect the wearer from the heat of the sun, and the devices that had been painted on the shield, were also embroidered on these evergarments; thus the arms became visible to every beholder in battle, without the aid of a standard; from this method of displaying emblems and armorial bearings, arose the term, *cote armure*, or coat-of-arms. Many of the ancient monumental effigies in England, represent men dressed in armor, covered with a surcoat on which are their armorial bearings, exactly corresponding with those on their battle shields. In the middle ages, armorial devices had become so systematized that they formed a language which the most ignorant could understand. The learned and the unlearned could read the symbolic picture, which was presented to the eye in a thousand ways, till the system was interwoven with the character and teaching of the people. Nearly every mansion was decorated with armorial insignia; the ancestry of a family was known by the shields in the upper parts of the windows.

The church favored armorial bearings. Knights took their banners to be blessed by the priests before going to engage in the Crusade wars, and on their return, these trophies, covered with honorable decorative charges, were suspended in the churches, and being of a perishable nature, the distinctions were in time permanently displayed in the glass of the windows, the frescoes of the walls, or carved in stone in the building itself.

In the infancy of heraldry, every knight assumed what armorial distinctions he pleased, without consulting his sovereign. Animals, plants, imaginary monsters, things artificial, and objects familiar to pilgrims were adopted; and whenever possible, the object chosen was one the name of which bore some resemblance in sound to suggest the name of the bearer. The Appletons have three apples in their shield; the Bells, three bells; the Masons, three trowels; the Swans, three birds of that name; and the Ryedales, three ears of rye. As coats-of-arms became more numerous, confusion often arose from the use, by different knights, of the same symbols; and this confusion was augmented by the practice of feudal chiefs in allowing their followers to bear their arms in battle as a mark of honor. In this way different coats-of-arms so closely resembled each other, that it was imperative, for distinction's sake, that some restrictions and regulations should be laid down respecting the character, number, and position of the figures represented on the shields. This necessity led, in the course of time, to the development of a regular system of heraldry, and the ancient rolls show that the process was going on in the thirteenth and fourteenth centuries. In England, the assumption of arms by private persons was first restrained by a proclamation from Henry V, which prohibited every one who had not borne arms at Agincourt to assume them, except in virtue of inheritance or a grant from the crown. To enforce this rule, heralds' visitations through the counties were instituted, and continued from time to time, for centuries. So strict were the laws regarding coats-of-arms at this time, that a man who had assumed certain armorial bearings without proper authority, lost one of his ears as a penalty. When herald visitations were instituted, all persons claiming the right to bear arms were warned to assemble at some stated place in the district, and to bring with them all arms, crests, and pedigrees, for examination by the herald's deputy, and present evidence of their genuineness.

In the united kingdom of Great Britain, no one is entitled to bear arms without a hereditary claim by descent, or a grant from the competent authority, this jurisdiction being executed by the Herald's College in England, the Lyon Court in Scotland, and the College of Arms in Ireland. It is illegal to use without authority, not only a coat-of-arms, but even a crest. The passion for outward distinction is so deeply implanted in human nature, that in this country, where all differences of rank are repudiated, men are found assuming heraldic devices, and the interest in this practice has so increased that hundreds of families have framed coats-of-arms hanging on the walls of their houses, engraved on their jewelry, displayed on their stationery, and even painted on the doors of their carriages, in imitation of the aristocracy of Great Britain. Some of these coats-of-arms were authoritatively borne by their ancestors in the old country, and others are fictitious, having been originally drawn or painted by men who early canvassed New England with books containing cuts of shields and appendages, purporting to have been granted to families in England and Scotland, which they claimed our American ancestors had a right to bear, by virtue of relationship.

As many who will read this book do not understand the "language of heraldry," the characters and abbreviations used in describing the coats-of-arms that have been borne by the various branches of the Riddell and Ridley families, will be unintelligible, unless a comprehensive explanation is given, to which reference may be had for directions. Such a chapter will be both interesting and instructive to all who possess any family pride, as well as to the general reader. The following articles, with tables, will be all that is necessary for this purpose: —

Coat of Arms for Riddells
of Roxburgshire, Scotland
✻ see p. 32 for
info/desription

ATTITUDES AND POSITIONS OF ANIMALS IN COATS-OF-ARMS.

When a lion, or other beast of prey, stands upright, with only one eye and ear seen, he is termed *rampant;* when walking forward with one eye and ear seen, *passant;* when sitting with one eye and ear seen, *sejant;* when lying down with one eye and ear seen, *couchant.* If in any of these positions the animal turns his face fully to the front, so that both eyes and ears are seen, the word *guardant* is annexed to those of rampant, passant, sejant, as the case may be. If the animal look backward with only one eye and ear seen in any of the positions above named, the word *regardant* is annexed to those of rampant, passant, sejant, as the case may be. An animal in a coat-of-arms is said to be *saliant* when leaping forward. Animals of the deer kind, when looking full-faced, are said to be *at gaze;* when standing, *statant;* when walking, *trippant;* when looking forward, *springing;* when running, *courant;* and when at rest on the ground, *lodged.* A horse when running, is said to be *courant,* or *full-speed;* when leaping, *saliant;* when standing, *forcene.* Birds when standing with wings down, are said to be *close;* when preparing to fly, *rising;* when flying, *volent;* when stretched out and their breast seen, *displayed;* when wings are open and against each other, they are said to be *endorsed;* only one wing is called *demivol.* Fishes, when placed horizontally, are called *naiant;* when perpendicular, *haurient;* when in an arched form, they are *embowed.*

APPENDAGES TO THE SHIELD.

The helmet, helme, casque, or morion, as it is variously designated, has varied in shape in different ages and countries. The most ancient form is the simplest, — composed of iron, of a shape fitted to the head, and flat upon the top, with an aperture for the light. This is styled the "Norman helmet," and appears on very ancient seals, attached to the gorget, a separate piece of armor which covered the neck. In the twelfth century a change was made, to mark the rank of the individual bearer.

The helmet assigned to kings and princes of royal blood is placed upon the shield in arms with the face full to the front, and composed of gold, with the *beauvoir,* or visor, divided by six projecting bars and lined with crimson.

The helmet of the nobility is of steel, with the five bars of gold, and is placed on the shield in coats-of-arms, inclining to profile.

The helmet of knights and baronets is of steel, full-faced, with the visor thrown back, and without bars.

The helmet of esquires always depicted in profile, is of steel, with the visor closed.

Each of the helmets is placed immediately above the shield, or escutcheon, and supports the wreath, which is under the crest. The lambrequin, a kind of mantle or hood, is placed on the head between the helmet and crest, and depicted, in heralds' language, *flattant* behind the wearer. The shape of the lambrequin was most capricious, for, as it was probably cut through with the sword in battle, it afforded certain evidence of prowess.

The wreath, upon which the crest is usually borne, is composed of two cords of silk twisted together; the one tinctured with the principal metal, and the other with the principal colors in the arms. The wreath, in ancient times, was used to fasten the crest to the helmet. It is made circular, but when seen in coats-of-arms, is seen with the side view.

The crest, or cognizance (derived from the Latin word, *crista,* a comb, or tuft), originated in the thirteenth century; and, towering above other objects, served to distinguish the combatants when engaged in conflict. No crest is ever found on the arms borne by females. Unless otherwise stated, it is always on the wreath; which need not, therefore, be named on the blazon.

Supporters are figures placed on each side of the shield in coats-of-arms; and, as the name indicates, seem to hold it up. In England, the right to bear supporters is confined to Peers of the Realm, Knights of the Garter and Bath, and to those who may have obtained them by royal grant. The Garter-King-at-arms has no right to grant them to any person of lower rank than a Knight of the Bath, unless acting under special directions from the Sovereign; but in Scotland, Lord Lyon may, by virtue of his office, do so without any royal warrant. In Scotland, the right to bear supporters is universally conceded to the chiefs of the various clans.

DIVISIONS OF THE SHIELD.

• The surface of the escutcheon, or shield, is called the field, and is divided into the following parts, A, B, C: the chief, sub-divided into A, the *dexter*, or right-hand chief point; B, the middle chief point; C, the *sinister*, or left-hand chief point; · D, the collar, or honor-point; E, the heart, or fess-point; F, the *nombriel*, or naval-point; and G, H, I, the base, sub-divided into G, the *dexter* base-point; H, the middle base-point; and I, the *sinister* base-point.

TINCTURES USED IN ARMS.

The shield, or escutcheon, in arms is distinguished by certain armorial colors, called tinctures, which are separated by division lines which run across the shield, and are ornamented with animals, instruments, and other objects called charges. The tinctures used in heraldry are metals, colors, and furs; and by the ancient heralds precious stones were used. (See heraldic tables.)

OR — gold, is known in uncolored drawings and engravings by small dots or points on the white surface.

ARGENT — silver, is expressed by a plain, white surface in the shield, in uncolored views.

AZURE — blue, is depicted by horizontal lines, finely drawn across the surface of the shield.

GULES — red, is depicted by perpendicular lines, finely drawn from the top to the base of the shield.

VERT — green, is depicted by lines running from the dexter chief- to the sinister base-points on the shield.

SABLE — black, is depicted by cross-lines running horizontally and perpendicularly across the shield.

PURPURE — purple, is depicted by lines running from the sinister chief- to the dexter base-points on the shield.

ERMINE — a white shield with black spots, representing ermine fur worn by members of the royal household.

ERMINES — a black shield with white spots, — an exact contrast to the former.

ERMINOIS — a gold surface to the shield, with black spots.

PEARL — a shield with black surface, filled with gold spots.

VAIR — composed originally of pieces of fur, but now of silver and blue colors, cut to resemble the flower of the *campanula*, and opposed to each other in rows. When depicted in colors, they are specified *vairé*.

COUNTER-VAIR — differs from *vair* by having the bells, or cups, arranged base against base and point against point, just the reverse of *vair*.

POTENT-COUNTER-POTENT — is composed of figures, resembling crutch-heads, placed in rows upon the white shield.

Old heralds used more minute distinctions. The arms of gentlemen, esquires, knights, and baronets, they blazoned by tinctures; those of the nobility, by precious stones; and those of emperors, kings, and other sovereign princes, by planets.

HERALDIC TABLE.

Colors and Metals.	*Tinctures.*	*Precious Stones.*	*Planets.*	*Names Abbreviated.*
YELLOW, or GOLD.	OR.	TOPAZ.	SOL. ⊙	O., OR.
WHITE, or SILVER.	ARGENT.	PEARL.	LUNA. ☾	A., AR.
BLACK.	SABLE.	DIAMOND.	SATURN. ♄	S., SA.
RED.	GULES.	RUBY.	MARS. ♂	G., GU.
BLUE.	AZURE.	SAPPHIRE.	JUPITER. ♃	B., AZ.
GREEN.	VERT.	EMERALD.	VENUS. ♀	V., VERT.
PURPLE.	PURPURE.	AMETHYST.	MERCURY. ☿	P., PURP.
TAWNY.	TENNE.	JACYNTH.	DRAGON'S HEAD.	T., TEN.
MURREY.	SANGUINE.	SARDONYX.	DRAGON'S TAIL.	SO., SANG.

PARTITION LINES.

The partition lines in heraldry are those that divide the shield, or charge, and are always right lines unless otherwise described by the following names, viz., engrailed, invected, wavy, *nebulé*, embattled, indented, and *dancetté*. Added to these are sometimes ragnly and dove-tails. The following will explain the divisions of the shield in coats-of-arms: —

PER-PALE. The shield divided into two equal parts, by a perpendicular line.

QUARTERLY. The shield divided into four equal parts, by a horizontal and perpendicular lines, crossing at right angles in the center.

PARTY-PER-FESS. The shield divided by a horizontal line into four equal parts, chief and base.

PARTY-PER-BEND. The shield divided into equal parts by a line running from the dexter chief to the sinister base.

PARTY-PER-CHEVRON. The shield divided by lines running from the sinster and dexter naval-points to the centre of the field, in the form of rafters.

PARTY-PER-SALTIRE. The shield divided by two lines running from sinister and dexter naval-points, and crossing each other in heart or fesse-point of the escutcheon.

GYRONNY-OF-EIGHT. The shield divided into eight parts by two lines running horizontally and perpendicularly, crossing in the fesse-point; and two lines running from the dexter and sinister naval-points to the dexter and sinister chief-points.

THE CHIEF. The shield divided by a horizontal line one-third below the top of the escutcheon.

THE PALE. The shield divided, by two perpendicular lines, which leave the field in three equal parts.

THE BEND. The shield divided by two lines that run from the dexter-chief to the sinister-base.

BEND SINISTER. The shield divided by lines running at right angles, and forming a cross with perpendicular and horizontal bars.

THE FESSE. The shield divided by two lines running horizontally across the field at the honor- and fesse-points.

THE SALTIRE. The shield divided by lines running from the sinister and dexter base- to the sinister and dexter chief-points, forming a cross.

THE CHEVRON. The shield divided by rafters, which rest at the dexter and sinister naval-points, and unite at the middle chief-point.

THE BORDER. The shield divided by a line running inside of the border lines of the field, representing a smaller escutcheon of the same form.

THE ORLE. Lines that describe the form of a bow in the center of the field with cross-top.

THE PRETENCE. A small shield in the center of the large one, on which the wife's arms are emblazoned.

THE QUARTER. Lines running from the top and side of the shield, and meeting in the center so as to cut one quarter from the dexter chief.

THE CANTON. Lines that cut out the dexter corner of the shield, upon which is sometimes an open hand.

CHECQUE. Lines running across the shield at right angles, dividing the field into checques.

BILLETS. Three oblong figures, two in the chief and one in the middle, base-point like billets of wood.

THE PAILE. Lines running from the middle base-point to the dexter and sinister chief-points, forming the letter Y.

THE PILE. Lines running from the sinister and dexter chief-points to the middle base-point, in the form of the letter V, — said to represent the three nails of the Saviour's cross, when there are three.

THE FLAUNCE. Lines running from the sides of the shield in the form of half-circles.

LOSENGE. Three small diamond-formed figures, sometimes one within the other, making a border to each.

THE FRET. A large diamond, whose points nearly reach the sides of the shield, crossed by two lines running from sinister and dexter chief-points to sinister and dexter base-points.

LOZENGY. Caused by lines crossing each other in diamond-form.

ARMS OF RIDDELLS, IN SCOTLAND.
[FROM THE LYON OFFICE, EDINBURGH.]

GEORGE RIDDELL, Esq., doctor of medicine, heir male, and representative of the family of Kinglass, who was descended of Riddell of that ilk: Bears quarterly, first and fourth argent on a chevron gules, betwixt three ears of rye, slipped and bladed vert, a mollet of the field of Riddell. Second and third argent, a fess between three bay leaves vert for Foulis, as being descended from Foulis of Ravelston by his great-grandmother, who was aunt to Sir John-Foulis Primrose of Ravelston and Dunipace, Bart.; Crest, a demi-greyhound argent. Motto, "Right to Share." Matriculated 7th August, 1765.

JAMES RIDDELL, Esq., of Riddell-Lodge, in the County of Berwick, and of Belton, in the County of Suffolk (descended of the family of Riddell of Kinglass, by Elizabeth Foulis, aunt to Sir John-Foulis Primrose of Ravelston and Dunipace, Bart.; who was descended of Riddell of that ilk), and who married Mary, eldest daughter of Thomas Milles, Esq., of Billockby-hall, in the County of Norfolk: Bears quarterly, first and fourth argent, on a Chevron invected gules, betwixt three ears of Rye slipped and bladed vert: a cross moline of the field for Riddell; second and third or, a lion passant between three billets sable by the name of Milles. Crest, a demi-greyhound argent. Motto, "Right to Share." Matriculated 7th August, 1765.

JAMES RIDDELL, of Ardnamurchan and Sunart, in the County of Argyle; of Mains, in the Stewartry of Kirkcudbright; of Riddell-Lodge, in the County of

Berwick; of Castlelaw, in the County of Mid-Lothian; of Belton, in the County of Suffolk; and of Caister, in the County of Norfolk, esquire. One of His Majesty's Justices of the Peace for the Counties of Argyle and Suffolk, LL. D., and member of the Society for Encouragement of Arts, Manufactures, and Commerce, whose lady was Mary, daughter and heiress of Thomas Milles, of Billockby-hall, esquire, in the County of Norfolk, and who was third son of Capt. George Riddell, representative of the family of Kinglass, and Christian daughter of Andrew Patterson, of Kirktown, esquire, which George was eldest son of George Riddell, of Kinglass, esquire, and Jean, eldest daughter of Capt. John Taillyeour, which last George, who succeeded his elder brother James Riddell, of Kinglass, who died without issue, was second son of James Riddell, of Kinglass, Commissary General to the Parliament's army in the north in the reign of King Charles I, and Elizabeth, daughter of George Foulis, of Ravelston, esquire, which last James was only son of James Riddell, the only son of Robert Riddell, second son of Walter Riddell, of Riddell, esquire, chief of that name in this kingdom, the thirteenth in descent from Geoffrey Riddell, who obtained from King David I, these lands in the County of Roxburgh, erected on his account into the Barony of Riddell, which Geoffrey was grandson of the Sieur Riddell, who was descended from the House of Anjou, who was one of the noblemen that came from Normandy with William the Conqueror, and had a command in his army at the Battle of Hastings, in the year 1066: Bears quarterly, first and fourth argent, on a chevron invecked gules between three ears of rye slipped and bladed proper, a cross Moline of the field for Riddell; second and third or, a lion passant between three billets sable for Milles. Crest, a demi-greyhound argent. Motto: "Right to Share," and below the shield, *Utile et Dulce.* Supporters: On the dexter, a lady, the emblem of agriculture, holding in her right hand the Zodiac, together with three stalks of corn, and in her left, an imperial crown proper; her upper garment vert, and the under one or. On the sinister, the emblem of Honour, wreathed about the head with laurel, crested with broom, holding a spear in his dexter hand, and a shield in his sinister, whereon are represented two temples proper, vested above a white garment with a robe azure, with a chain around his neck, and bracelets round his wrists or. Matriculated 7th February, 1775.

SIR JAMES-MILLES RIDDELL, of Ardnamurchan and Sunart, in the County of Argyle, Bart., eldest son and heir of Thomas-Milles Riddell, Esq., and Mrs. Margaret Campbell his spouse, which Thomas-Milles was only son of the late Sir James Riddell, also of Ardnamurchan, etc., Bart., by his spouse Mary, only daughter and heiress of Thomas Milles, of Billockby-hall in the County of Norfolk, esquire: Bears quarterly, first on three piles in point gules, surmounted by a bend azure; second quarter counter-quartered, first lozengy or. and gules; second gules. three lions rampant or; third gules. two pales vair a chief or; fourth barry of six or, and sable in chief. a label of six points of the last. Third grand quarter counter-quartered. first azure, a wolf's head erazed argent; second and third argent. three barry gules; fourth barry wavy of six, or. and gules. Fourth grand quarter or. a lion passant. between three billets sable, the badge of a British baronet being placed in the heart-point. Above the shield is placed a helmet befitting his degree with a mantling, gules doubled argent, and on a wreath of his liveries is set for crest a hand issuing out a coronet of an earl of France, holding baton all proper, over which upon an exvol is the motto "*de Apulia,*" and beneath the shield upon a compartment whereon is inscribed *utile dulce*, are placed for supporters, on the dexter a female representing agriculture, habited as the ancient Ceres, holding a plough with her right hand and in her left a poppy-seed vessel with ears of wheat and rye; and on the sinister an armed knight of the eleventh century representing Honour holding a pennon with the red cross of England upon a white field.

These arms are destined by letters-patent from the Lord Lyon, bearing even date with the Matriculation the twenty-second day of April, 1829, to the said Sir James-Milles Riddell, Bart., and his heirs, with due and proper differences according to the law of Arms, the exterior decoration of supporters and the baronet's badge being the distinct ensigns of the said Sir James-Milles Riddell and his male representatives.

ARMS OF VARIOUS HOUSES OF RIDDELL.

1. RIDDELL, of Ardnamurchan and Sunart, Scotland. Or, three piles in point gu., surmounted by a bend az. Crest, a hand issuing from an earl's coronet of France, holding a baton, all ppr. Supporters, dexter, a female, in her exterior hand three ears of rye; sinister, a knight in complete armor. Motto, " *Utile et dulce* " (useful and agreeable). This coat was created in 1778, and has now many quarterings.

2. RIDDELL, of Roxburghshire, Scotland. Ar. a chev. gu. betw. three ears of rye ppr., slipped vert. Crest, a demi-greyhound ar. Supporters, two greyhounds ar. Motto, " I hope to share."

3. RIDDELL, of Minto, Scotland. Ar. a chev. gu. betw. three ears of rye, stalked and slipped vert. Crest, a dexter hand ppr., holding a blade of rye, slipped, or.

4. RIDDELL, Durham and Newcastle, Northumberland. Ar. a fesse betw. three garbs., az. Crest, a demi-lion rampt. erminois, holding betw paws a garb or. Another az.

5. RIDDELL, Norfolk. Sa. three martletts within a bordure engrailed, ar. Crest, a martlett ar.

6. RIDDELL, Bedfordshire. Paley of six ar. and gu., a bend sa.

7. RIDDELL, Middlesex. Gu. a lion rampt or within a bordure. indented. ar.

8. RIDDELL, Oxfordshire and Gloucestershire. Paley of six, or. and gu. on a chief az. three lions. rampt. or. Crest, a talbot's head couped az. garnished and ringed or.

9. RIDDELL, Felton Park and Swinburn Castle. Arg. a fesse. betw three rye sheaves. az. Crest, a demi-lion. couped. or. holding a rye sheaf. az. Motto, " *Deus solus augot arestas.* " *

10. RIDDELL, Glen-Riddell, Dumfrieshire, Scotland. Ar. a chev. gu. betw. three ears of rye ppr. slipped vert. Crest, a sheaf of rye standing upright ppr.†

UNDESIGNATED ARMS OF RIDDELLS.

11. RIDDELL. Or. on a bend. az. three Catharine wheels ar.

---

* According to the appendix of the Carr MS., Thomas Riddell, sheriff of Newcastle-on-Tyne, 1500 A. D., William Riddell, mayor of that city, 1510 and 1526 A. D., William Riddell, sheriff, 1575 A. D., and Peter Riddell, sheriff, all bore arms as follows: " Gu. a lion rampant within a bordure indented arg." Peter, however, bore "a crescent sa. in dexter chief, for difference." It will be seen that these differ from the arms of the Riddells of Fenham, and the Scottish families. Jordan Ridel, of Tilmouth, England, 1230 A. D., " bore five bars wavy" in his shield. Ridall, or Ridhull (Herts), "Or, on a bend az."

† For arms of Riddells of Wittering, see pedigree of that family in body of this book.

12. RIDDELL. Sa. on a fesse betw. three owls ar. five crosses formee of the first.

13. RIDDELL. Ar. three piles gu. a quarter sa.

14. RIDDELL. Or three piles gu. a bendlet. az.

15. RIDDELL. Sa. on a fesse. betw. three owls. or. as many cross-crosslets of the field.

16. RIDDELL. Arg. a chev. gu. engr. betw three ears of rye slipped ppr. in chief an open hand. Motto, "*Utile et dulce.*"

ARMS OF RIDLEYS IN ENGLAND.

1. RIDLEY, Heaton Hall, County Northumberland, Bart. Quarterly first and fourth. gu. on a chev. betw. three falcons ar. as many pellets. for Ridley; second and third ar. three cocks' heads erased, Sa. for White. Crest, a full pass. the tail extended over the back, gu. Motto, "*Constans fideo.*"

2. RIDLEY, Ridley Hall, Chester, and Willimoteswick and Walltown, Northumberland. Gu. a chev. betw. three goshawks, ar. for Wale, Elias Ridley; quarterings ar. an ox pas. gu. through reeds ppr. being the ancient coat of Ridley. Crest, a greyhound courant, ar.

3. RIDLEY, Atkinton and Linley, County Sallop. Ar. on a mount vert, a bull standing, gu. armed or.

4. RIDLEY, Parkend, Northumberland. Gu. on a chev. betw. three falcons ar. as many pellets. Crest, a bull pass. gu.

5. RIDLEY, Shropshire. Gu. a chev. ar. collared gu.

6. RIDLEY, Ticket and Westwood, Northumberland and Yorkshire. Ar. a bull pass. gu. on a mount vert.

7. RIDLEY (as borne by Nicholas Ridley, Bishop of London). Gu. on a chev. betw. three falcons close, ar. as many pellets. Crest, a bull pass. gu.

8. RIDLEY, County Surrey. Gu. a chev. betw. three birds, ar.

UNDESIGNATED ARMS OF RIDLEYS.

9. RIDLEY. Ar. a chev. sa. betw. three cocks' heads. erased. gu. Crest, on a chapeau a salamander in flames ppr.

10. RIDLEY, or REDLEIGH. Gu. a chev. betw. three birds, ar.

11. RIDLEY. Gu. a chev. betw. three birds, ar. Crest, a greyhound courant; ar. collared, or.

12. RIDLEY. Ar. on a mount vert. a bull sa. armed gu.

13. RIDLEY. Az. a chev. betw. three falcons ar. armed and jessed or.

14. RIDLEY. Gu. on a chev. ar. betw. three falcons close, or as many pellets. Crest, a bull pass. gu.

15. REDLEY. Gu. a chev. or.

16. RIDLER. Same as Ridley of Ticket, Northumberland.

17. RIDLEY. Or. surmounted by bend az. with three stars. dexter an open hand gu. Crest, a leopard, collared, chained, garnished, ramp. gd. Supporters, sinister, a unicorn chained and collared; dexter, a tiger ramp. chained. Motto, "*Jamais Arriere*" (never behind).

3

THE ANCIENT NORTHMEN, RIDDELL ANCESTRY.

THE greatest genealogists of England and Scotland have said, "Few families have claims to higher antiquity, than that of Ridel, or Riddell, and fewer still have such grounds upon which to establish their pretensions; indeed, the authorities supporting their history, are such as are rarely found in tracing the genealogy of our old families, especially at a period so remote as that at which theirs commences." As the ancestors of this distinguished family made so conspicuous a figure amongst their countrymen in the early wars, and were identified with all the fluctuations and migrations of their race, it seems proper to present a comprehensive sketch of the history of the ancient nation from which they are descended.

The several tribes of Scandinavians dwelling in Denmark, Sweden, and Norway, originated on the shores of the German Ocean, and during their southern incursions, were called Norsemen, or Northmen, in consequence of their coming from the north of Europe. This was a proper name to apply to this race while they were united as one kingdom, but after their dissolution, the name Norman had reference only to the inhabitants of Norway; they are now designated by the several countries in which they live, namely, Danes, Swedes, and Norwegians. These ancient sea-kings, or vikings, followers of Odin, have a noble history, and their influence upon the civilization of Europe has been remarkable. Belonging to the German race, they shared the love of liberty, the spirit of activity, and the disposition to wander from their native land. They were divided into numerous tribes, early acquainted themselves with the art of navigation, and were addicted to piracy. From the beginning of the eighth century, they commenced to ravage the coasts of various parts of Europe, and planted their feet upon the soil of every country within their reach. Kings everywhere trembled at the name of the Northmen, and nations were almost paralyzed at their approach. To mark the resemblance between the ancient national characteristics of the Northmen and their descendants, representing the ancestry of the Riddell family, we will briefly consider their early appearance and habits. They were broad-shouldered, deep-chested, long-limbed, with slender waists, and small hands and feet; their build told of strength, which was so prized by them that their puny infants were exposed and left to die. Their complexion was almost always fair, and the fair alone were considered beautiful or well-born. One early writer says of the Northman, "His face was large; his forehead broad, with mickle eyebrows; his nose not long, but excessively thick; his upper lip wide and long, while his chin and jaw-bones were enormously broad.

He was thick-necked, and his shoulders of superhuman breadth. In shape well built, and taller than the most of men."

The ordinary dress of the sexes was nearly the same,—a shirt, loose drawers, long hose, high shoes held by thongs twisted about the ankles. They wore a short kilt or skirt at the waist, an armless cloak, with low-crowned broad-brimmed hat, which completed the costume of the men. The underclothing of both sexes was of linen; the outside garments of woolen homespun, most prized when dyed blue or red. In time of war their chieftains put on a coat of mail, woven of small rings of iron or steel, which formed a complete network, and was so flexible—though heavy—as to adapt itself to every necessary motion of the body. In addition to the coat of mail, the ancient Northmen wore a cowl or *corpunchon* of the same material, thrown over the head and shoulders; over this they placed a conical helmet, made of burnished steel and having a neck-piece or visor, which, when closed, completely protected the head and face. At the waist they wore a tunic, called by them the "hauberk," made of rings of steel, which with the "chaussés" or leg pieces made of the same material, constituted the complete equipment of the Northman soldier. The Northman's shield was long and kite-shaped, having two bands for the arm and one for the neck in case they wished to use both hands in battle; these were covered with hard leather, with steel rim and boss, white in time of peace and red in time of war; they were usually ornamented with some fanciful device, but not of an heraldic character. Their arms were heavy lances, steel-pointed with an ashen shaft; battle-axes; and, above all, a broadsword, the darling of the Northmen. Their lances were decorated with long ribbon streamers, called by them "gonfalons."

Norman ships were long, half-decked galleys, propelled both by sails and oars. The bow and stern were high, and were ornamented, the former with a dragon's head, the latter with the tail, and thus a fleet of these ships looked like huge sea-monsters, whose open jaws were ready to crush the foe. The sails were gay, with stripes of blue, green, and red. In the prow stood the warriors, in the stern their chief, and behind him the helmsman. The rowers were protected during action by planks set up along the bulwarks, and on the sides of the vessel was a gangway from which to board an enemy's ship.

The character of these hardy Northmen fitted them for the adventuresome and warlike destinies of the race. Possessed of an independent, haughty, and unyielding disposition, and taught contempt of danger in their struggles for existence in a rugged and barren country, they proved themselves unconquerable. They were cold-blooded and unmerciful toward their enemies, and, as one has said, "hard-featured when angry." All these qualities were common to ancient conquerors, but were developed in a peculiar degree by the Northmen in every generation until their distinctive habits were lost or modified by the blood of other nations.

As we follow the Northmen in their migrations and settlements, another feature of character is conspicuous, namely, their versatility and power of adapting themselves to the various and peculiar conditions of society whither they went. They introduced but few new principles, but readily assumed the language, religion, and ideas of their adopted country, and became absorbed in the society around them; this rule holds good with the exception of Iceland, where they largely predominated over the inhabitants who preceded them. But not so in respect to their influence upon the nations amongst whom they settled, for invariably they became the master-spirits of the age, and deeply affected those with whom they came in contact; they inspired an increased activity, and rapidly developed institutions of literature and art; they invented nothing, but perfected and organized everything; all nations where the spirit of the Northmen has been introduced, have reached the highest degrees of prosperity under their moulding power.

As early as the end of the eighth century the Northmen had discovered and settled the Shetland and Orkney Islands, on the north coast of Scotland. These were subject to the kings of Norway and Denmark, but under the independent government of earls, till the year 1468. While a part of the Northmen were taking possession of the Western Islands, others were moving south and ravaging the coast of France.

Rollo, or Rolf, one of the most famous chieftains of the Northmen, formerly an Earl of Shetland and Orkney, followed by a large number of his countrymen, made an incursion into France, and in the year 885 marched against Rouen, and subjugated everything in his way. Rollo was a great warrior and statesman. He was surnamed the Ganger, or Walker, because he was too tall and heavy for any horse to bear. He followed the calling of a viking for forty years before his conquests in France and settlement at Rouen. He continued his devastating movements until he was granted by treaty in the year 911 the whole province on the west coast of France, which he called Normandy, or "the land of the Northmen," otherwise the Duchy of Normandy, of which Rollo was the first duke. He also married *Gisela*, the daughter of the king of France, embraced Christianity, was baptised, and settled down at Rouen, the capital of Normandy. The province was now divided into counties, and subdivided into earldoms, and the lands bestowed upon the countrymen who had served Rollo, the duke, in his wars. Rollo continued to enlarge his hold in France by the frequent accession of new territory until the time of his death in 932, when his body was entombed in the chapel of St. Romanus at Rouen. He was about eighty years of age.

During all the years through which we have traced the Northmen, representatives of the Ridel, or Riddell, family were acting with them, and accompanied them in all their migrations; indeed, their names appear contemporary with the earliest date of the Norman settlement in France, and always associated with some important movement.

According to the writings of Playfair, Gaulter de Ridel followed Canute, or Cnut, the Danish king of England, on his pilgrimage to Rome, in the year 1025. He took with him two sons, — Oscital and Gaufrid, and the latter having entered into the service of Rollo,* Duke of Normandy, founded a family at Rouen; the descendants of which continued there in affluence till the Revolution of France. Oscital, or Anskitel, as the name was sometimes spelt, returned to Scotland, and became the head of the Ridel, or Ridale, family there.

In the conquest of Sicily, about 1060, by the Normans, two brothers Ridel accompanied their fellow-countrymen, and were afterwards found in distinguished positions. Goffridus Ridel figured there as Duke of Gaeta, as early as the year 1072; and his brother Rignaldus, as Count de Ponté Carvo, in 1098. John Riddell, Esq., the learned and distinguished antiquary of Scotland, found in Norman records proof of the existence of Gulfridus

---

* According to the date given above, there must have been *two* Norman Dukes named *Rollo*, as the first died in 932 A. D.

and Roger Ridel, in possession of estates in Normandy, in the thirteenth century; and also two great branches in France, classed among its magnates there, and allied by marriage with many distinguished families, denominated " Riddells of Baijerae," which terminated in heirs female.

In the absence of records, many of which were destroyed during the Norman wars, it is impossible to discover the dates when lands were bestowed upon the Ridels in the various provinces in France ; but we know they held the earldoms of Angoulesme, Piragord, and Agen, as early as 885; the latter, as will hereafter appear, having been acquired by the marriage of Walgrinus Ridel with Rosalinda. The son and successor of Walgrinus rebuilt the walls of the city of Angoulesme as a defence against the Normans. A family of Ridels also inherited the baronies of Montausier and Blaye, in the province of Guinne ; another family were barons of Bergerac in Piragord; another branch held the barony of Killey in Touraine ; another became possessed of lands in Nogent and Aurillac, in Champagne in France. At what time the Ridels of France acquired the lands called Ryedale, I cannot tell; but it was evidently about the date of the conquest of Apulia, say 1050, for Galfridus Ridel had assisted the Normans in the reduction of this province, and was endowed with valuable lands there as a reward for his valor, and also granted the coat-of-arms which has the motto, "de Apulia," and in the hand of the woman supporting the shield are three ears of rye, hence, I suppose Ryedale was the seat of Galfridus and his successors as long as they held this property ; and as this same cadet of the family assisted his countrymen as followers of William the Conqueror, in the conquest of England, and was well rewarded with valuable grants of land in that country when William was crowned king, it may be presumed, with plausibility, that Ryedale in Yorkshire constituted a part of those lands bestowed by the Conqueror, and were named for the seat of this branch of the family in France. The records in the Lyon Office of Scotland, however, state that the Galfridus who came with the Conqueror, had a command in the Norman army, and that he belonged to the family styled "Riddels of Anjou." His name on the roll of Battle Abbey is Sieur Ridel.

The history of the Norman Ridels in England is of a meagre and somewhat obscure character. From what proof we have at hand, they seem to have held high and prosperous positions under the Norman kings, and were in unbroken communication with their kinspeople in France; indeed, it seems evident that Monsieur de Ridel, who followed the Conqueror to England, returned soon after to look after his property in Normandy, and sent over his sons to settle on the lands granted him in England. One of this family formed an alliance with the noble house of Bassett by marriage ; and another wedded Geva, the beautiful and accomplished daughter of the Earl of Chester, one of whose descendants, Maud, or Matilda, was the wife of David, Earl of Huntingdon, and became the maternal ancestrix of Robert Bruce, King of Scotland. It is not known how many generations of the Ridels continued the residence in England; but the same family held landed estates in Normandy, England, and Scotland at the same time, as will be seen hereafter in the genealogy. Those were times of constant fluctuation, and lands were sometimes quickly gained and as soon lost, by the changes resulting from the Norman wars.

Branches of the Norman stock of Ridel settled early in Italy and Germany, where their descendants have continued ever since, evidently multiplying with every generation, while several of the branch families of

France ended in the male line and lost the name. Nearly all genealogical writers have commenced the history of the Scottish branch of the Norman family of Ridel with the early ancestors of the Roxburghshire Ridales, but cadets of the family held lands in Scotland at an earlier date, as will be seen in the genealogical departments of this book. Cranstown, subsequently known as "Cranstown-Riddell," was in the possession of the Norman Riddells with little intermission for about two centuries, and was probably granted about A. D. 1100. One authority says Oscital Ridel, having finished his pilgrimage to Rome, returned to his native land by consent of King Malcolm Canmore, and gave his lands of Cranstown, Preston, and others, to his son Hugo, who in the year 1110 bestowed the church of Cranstown and certain lands in the barony upon the monastery of Selkirk, which was founded by King David.

Sir Walter Scott, in a very complimentary note in his poem on Doleraine, has made an attempt to prove that the Roxburgh Ridales were established in Scotland at a period far more remote than those of Cranstown, but his conjectures cannot be sustained by any good authority, and are ignored by the best-informed of the family in Scotland. He mentions two stone coffins found in an ancient vault of the old church in the parish of Lilliesleaf, which contained the remains of men of gigantic size, and bearing date as early as A. D. 727 and A. D. 936. Scott also mentions the date 1110 as found in the aisle of the ancient church of the Ridales of Roxburgh, but the late Walter Riddell-Carre says in a communication to the author, "There are memorials cut in the south wall, but they are not of a sufficiently antiquated character, to represent a period so far back, though they may have been recut in modern times, a not unfrequent process employed to preserve dates nearly defaced by time."

When David I, Prince of Cumberland, who was a great colonizer, went into Scotland he was followed by several cadets of the family of England, one of whom, Gervase, or Geoffery Ridale, was a great favorite of King David, being the first High Sheriff of the county and a constant attendant on royalty, as proven by many crown-charters to which he was a witness; one of the most ancient charters witnessed by this man was the celebrated "*Inquisito Principis Davidis*," which was dated A. D. 1116. Walter Ridale, a brother of the preceding, was also a witness to crown and other charters; but that to himself granted by King David, eclipsed them all, being the most ancient charter known from a king to a layman. This document, dated A. D. 1125, granted an estate including lands called Whittun, near the Cheviot Hills, to be held of the crown. These lands were subsequently denominated the "Barony of Riddell and Whittun." This charter styles Walter Ridale "sheriff" and confirms to him all the lands of which his brother Gervase died possessed.

Besides the charter before mentioned, the early ancestors of the Roxburgh family had two bulls; one from Pope Adrian IV, dated A. D. 1155, and another from Pope Alexander III, dated A. D. 1160, which Mr. Nisbit, the well-known Scottish herald and antiquary saw, confirming to the Ridales the lands received by charter from King David I, and other estates not mentioned in that document. It is somewhat remarkable that these lands were held in unbroken succession by the family for nearly *seven hundred years* without an entail; quite long enough to warrant Sir Walter Scott in using the name of "ancient Riddell's fair domain." In a statement from Walter Riddell-Carre, he says, "There are two things that present themselves in a survey of the history of this family which seem remark-

able; on the one hand, the singular good fortune attending them in maintaining the possession of their estates in direct succession for upwards of
six centuries; on the other hand, that having never fallen lower, they
did not rise higher in the scale. Many names once famous have passed
away, and their lands, once called by their names, have gone into other
families, but Riddell after Riddell, of that ilk, followed each other, and
there was never wanting one to transmit the name and honors of the race.
Why, it may be asked, did they not, during that long time, climb to higher
positions, continuing only barons, knights, and gentlemen, while many
less pretentious of antiquity, secured patents of nobility? One explanation may suffice; they held their lands by being contented with an honorable and safe level.

"Medio tutissiman ibis.

"Ambition has not unfrequently hurled headlong those who were determined to ascend higher than a wise Providence intended; while during
the stormy mediæval times many of the Scottish nobles and families of station tarnished their names by acts of violence and treason, no such stain
attaches to the Riddells; they enjoyed the favor and regard of their sovereigns under whom they lived, receiving knighthood at their hands, and
were granted valuable lands as a reward for services faithfully performed.
But they had higher distinctions than mere worldly ones. In those days,
when to give lands to the church for the service of God was thought to
be a pious work, the Riddells were no niggards of their property, and in
after times when their religious faith caused them to suffer for 'conscience'
sake' they were ready for prison or banishment."

This prestige has clung to the family from generation to generation,
passing unimpaired and unsullied from father to son, from their earliest
history. The Roxburgh Riddells seem to have built a castle on their lands,
and also a church, the former a place of great strength, but long since in
ruins, and now only the earthworks can be seen. A stone was found some
years ago near the present mansion, on which were cut the Riddell arms,
connected with those of the Kerrs, proving a very early alliance with that
historical family, — say four hundred years ago. The chapel built by this
family was a pre-reformation one, but the date of its erection cannot now
be certainly known. Scott mentions the demolition of an ancient church
at the time when the stone coffins, before mentioned, were found; but
clear documentary proofs are wanting. It is evident that the early generations of the family were buried there, as bones have frequently been
dug up on the ground where the chapel stood.

The Norman Ridels inherited the national roaming disposition and love
of adventure, and consequently we find them engaged with their countrymen in all their wars and conquests; which may account for the fact that
representatives of the family are found in every country newly acquired
by Norman arms, and always as possessed of landed property. Other
members of the Norman stock were early in Scotland, being well allied
by marriage, and owning extensive lands; some of these lost their holdings and removed to other parts, while some established and distinct families are still represented in the west of Scotland, denominated "Riddells
of Ardnamurchan and Sunart."

The Riddells of Ireland, whose history I will now follow, are nearly all
of Scottish origin, offshoots of the ancient families so long known in the
latter country. There were some, however, who evidently went to Ireland

contemporary with their earliest settlements in England and Scotland, but whether from those branch-families or cadets of some of the houses of France, cannot be determined now with certainty. The first mention of the Riddell name found in Ireland is in a pamphlet published at Downpatrick in 1842, which is entitled, "Notices of the Most Important Events Connected with the County of Down." In this book there is an account of the first settlement of the English in Ulster under Sir John de Courcy, dated A. D. 1177, and among the names of families that were settled in the province at that time were Savages, Whites, Bensons, and Riddells. It cannot be known whether this family continued as residents of Ireland, but it may be presumed that they were only nominal possessors, as none of the more recent families in that country can be traced to so remote a period in settlement. There is abundant evidence to prove that members of the family from England and Scotland held commissions in Ireland at a date long anterior to the colonization of Ulster by the Scottish Presbyterians, but no evidence to show that these men were permanently domiciled there.

In the year 1608 King James commenced the undertaking of settling six counties in the Province of Ulster, in the north of Ireland, with Scottish subjects. James had been successful in crushing the Irish rebellion, and having confiscated two million acres of land, conceived the idea of sending his own countrymen to settle and occupy the newly acquired possession. It was some time, however, before he could successfully execute the plan, as the Scotch people did not view the project with favor and were unwilling to move their families into Ireland. But inducements of such a character were eventually held out by the government that a small colony emigrated from the northwest coast of Scotland in 1612 and planted themselves in Ulster; these were Presbyterian families from the County of Argyle, and it is very probable that families of Riddells accompanied their countrymen to the new settlement. During the following twenty years many ministers with their congregations crossed the Channel and established themselves in the Province of Ulster; from these new tributaries from Scotland the colony began to flourish, and the ratio of migration was augmented to such an extent that in a few years many hundred families were scattered through the north of Ireland.

This intrusion of Scottish subjects upon their confiscated lands excited intense hatred in the Catholic Irish; and those who had been ruined in their estates in the wars of King James only waited a favorable time to make an attempt to recover what they had lost, and rid their country of their Presbyterian neighbors. The Irish not only hated the king, but all his subjects from Scotland, especially those who were known to have taken part in the wars. As was customary in those days, James rewarded his soldiers with grants of land in Ulster, and among that number were three brothers, namely, Hugh, James, and Robert Riddell, presumably descended from the Roxburghshire family, or some of its numerous branches in Scotland, but possibly of the "Riddells of Kinglass," a distinct family. Of these brothers, James was an officer of rank in the army of King James, and all three had fought from *principle* as Presbyterians through the wars. James Riddell had a grant of land (three townlands) in the County of Armagh, in the Province of Ulster; Hugh Riddell received a grant bordering on the Counties of Tyrone and Donegal, not far from that of his brother before mentioned; while Robert Riddell, the third brother, settled on land further south near the city of Dublin. From these three brothers it seems probable that nearly all of the Scotch-Irish Riddells have sprung. Political troubles drove other families of the Scottish Riddells into Ireland at different times, and it is now a well-established fact that some of these were from the branch of the Roxburghshire house denominated "Riddells of Glen-Riddell," in Dumfrieshire, and their descendants are still in the city of Belfast.

In many respects the settlement of these devoted Presbyterians in Ireland was a misfortune; there could be no peace between them and the Catholic Irish. A conspiracy was raised in 1641, which aimed at the complete extermination of the Protestant population of Ireland; and it so far succeeded that *forty thousand* were suddenly massacred in different parts of the island. A contemporary writer states as follows: "No condition, no age, no sex, was spared. But death was the slightest punishment inflicted by the rebels; all the tortures which wanton cruelty could devise, all the lingering pains of body, the anguish of mind, and the agonies of despair, could not satiate the revenge of the Irish." This rebellion continued until 1649, when Cromwell avenged the blood of the slaughtered saints and crushed the insurrection.

After the Restoration in the year 1660, James, a brother of King Charles, was appointed Viceroy of Scotland, and being a bigoted Roman Catholic, the Scottish Presbyterians were the objects of his hatred and persecution. An old writer says, "He let loose upon the Protestants the dogs of war and drove hundreds of them into exile; large numbers escaped to Ireland and joined the remnant of their brethren who had preceded them." Still, there was no peace, liberty, or safety, for these Presbyterians so long as the laws and inhabitants around them were hostile to the principles which they loved dearer than life itself.

Such constancy, steadfastness, and perseverance, as was exhibited by these Scotch people in endeavoring to maintain a footing upon the soil of their adopted country, has seldom if ever been witnessed, but their sufferings availed but little. They held the troops of James in check, while they defended the last stronghold of King William in Ireland; at Londonderry and at Boyne-water they poured out their blood most freely; they suffered every hardship and endured the most severe deprivations for the sake of their religious faith and the protection of their homes, but they were doomed to disappointment under the bloody policy of their enemies. The Rev. David H. Riddle has said of these Protestants, "My forefathers were Scotch Presbyterians, and fought side by side in the 'Logan forces,' and suffered together at Derry, and Enniskillen, and in the revolutionary struggles, and their cherished memories go back to Ulster and Boyne-water, Donegal and Coleraine." From a communication received from Scotland I make the following extract, which was copied from some old book: "Among the families from Scotland who suffered at the siege of Londonderry, were Hamiltons, Morrisons, Pattersons, Grahames, Watsons, Murrays, and Riddels." From another letter written from Ireland in the year 1727, we learn that "Londonderry * was besieged nearly half a

* Londonderry was founded on the site of ancient Derry, which was burned in 1608, on account of its resistance to the authority of King James I. The site was made over to the corporation of London, and the new city of Londonderry became the stronghold of Protestantism. In December, 1688, its gates were closed against King James II, who laid siege to it April 18, 1689. The siege kept up one hundred and five days, when a man-of-war and two ships loaded with provisions ran past the batteries and relieved the starving inhabitants.

year (1689) by the army of King James, when he had all Ireland subdued but Derry and a little place hard by. The besieged defended
themselves, being Presbyterians, till they were so pinched with hunger
that a dog's head was sold cheap enough at half a crown; and yet
God sustained them until King William sent them relief by two ships,
with men and provisions from England, at which sight, before the ships
got up to the city and landed their men, the besiegers moved their camp
and fled to the west of Ireland, where afterwards two bloody battles were
fought and the papists subdued." When every hope of enjoying the liberty of worship and the unmolested possession of their lands had perished, these devoted Christians turned their faces toward the American
Colonies, that they might find an asylum where they could enjoy the peaceful service of God undisturbed; they left the homes granted their fathers
for service in the army, and the graves of their sires, to brave the dangers
of the ocean and the wilderness of a foreign land, in search of a spot
where they could act according to the dictates of conscience and secure
a living for their families.

From the year 1680 the Scotch-Irish Presbyterians commenced to sell
their lands or forsake them, and take ship for America; as their oppres-
sions became more intolerable the ratio of emigration increased, until
thousands of families were scattered through the Carolinas, Virginia,
Maryland, and Pennsylvania; and early in the eighteenth century several
ship-loads came to New England. As soon as the first families had
settled their lands in this country they forwarded letters to their kindred in Ireland, describing the fertility of the soil and the beauties of
the American forests, lakes, and streams in such glowing colors that in a
few years many townships were taken up and settled by Scotch-Irish.
Among these came many of the Riddell family, which had been very
prolific in Ireland. These early settled in the South, in the middle
States, and some in New England. I find the name in New York, New
Jersey, and Virginia, as early as 1650; but by far the greatest number
came over between 1780 and 1800, influenced by the Irish Rebellion.
There were also families of Riddells from Scotland and England, who
settled in the southern States quite early; some of these came in their
own vessels, bringing with them their cattle, implements of husbandry,
furniture, and silver-plate, being families of abundant means. There
were one or more families that came direct to Virginia from France,
and spelled the name for two generations Riddelle. Others came from
Germany and settled in Maryland and New York.

Numbered among the Scotch-Irish who first came to New England,
were three clergymen of the Presbyterian faith, Rev. James Macgreggor,
Rev. William Boyd, and Rev. William Cornwall, who with their congregations left the north of Ireland in 1718. These embarked in five ships,
and about one hundred families arrived in Boston harbor, while twenty
families with their pastor, Mr. Cornwall, landed at Portland, where they
remained through the winter and suffered extremely from cold and for
food. Some unknown poet has commemorated their arrival in the following lines : —

> " In the summer, one thousand seven hundred eighteen,
> Our pious ancestors embarked on the ocean;
> Oppressed by the minions and dupes of their king,
> They quitted sweet Erin with painful emotion.
> On the wide swelling wave,
> All danger they brave,

> While fleeing from shackles prepar'd for the slave,
> In quest of a region where genius might roam,
> And yield an asylum as dear as their home.
>
> Undaunted they press'd to their prime destination,
> Allured by the prospects that Freedom display'd,
> And such was the warmth of their fond expectation.
> That dangers unnumbered ne'er made them afraid.
> How serene was that day,
> And how cheerful and gay
> Were those pilgrims when anchored in old Casco Bay;
> Their prayers then like incense ascended on high,
> And fond acclamations then burst to the sky."

In the spring of 1719 these families sailed to Portsmouth, solicited grants of land, and had leave from the Massachusetts Assembly to look out a tract six miles square in any of the unoccupied territory along the coast, between the Piscataqua River and Casco Bay. They did not all settle in one township, as might have been desired, — probably in consequence of finding the land taken up by others, — but scattered along the sea-shore, in what is now the towns of Kittery, Wells, York, Saco, Scarborough, and Falmouth; sixteen families not finding a place for settlement to please them, went to Nutfield, in New Hampshire, and sat down there. Belknap says, "These were men principally in middle life, robust, persevering, and adventuresome; such as were well suited to encounter the toils and endure the hardships and self-denials of commencing a new settlement. Being industrious and frugal in their habits of life, and being highly favored with the Gospel, they soon became a thriving, wealthy, and respectable settlement." They had sufficient property to enable them to build comfortable houses and profitably cultivate the soil. They introduced the manufacture of linen into the New England Colonies, having taken their "little wheels" with them from Ireland. These were the celebrated Scotch-Irish, — not semi-Irish, or mixed Scotch people, but real, clean-blooded Caledonians; who themselves, or their immediate ancestors, had first come from the "bonnie braes" or the "heather hills" of Scotland, to dwell in the north of Ireland, but who had now removed to America. Nothing was more offensive to these emigrants than to be called *Irish*. Macgregor writes in 1820, "We are surprised to hear ourselves called Irish people, when we so frequently ventured our all for the British Crown and liberties against the Irish papists, and gave all tests of our loyalty which the government of England required, and are always ready to do the same when demanded." The Rev. David H. Riddle once said in an address, "We glory in our Scotch-Irish descent. Why? I can point you to the very spot on the map of old Ireland, — parish of Ray, Donegal County, — whence my grandfather emigrated to the ancient County of York, Pa., and just alongside where the grandfathers and mothers of some now separated, lived and worshipped, wept and prayed together!" These words represent the universal spirit of the Scotch-Irish in every part of the world, — they were never ashamed to own their origin or their religious principles.

Inheriting the characteristics of their ancient Norman ancestors, the Scottish and Scotch-Irish people have laid the foundation for civil and religious prosperity everywhere they have settled. Bold, adventuresome, and persevering; of tenacious, unyielding disposition; blunt, direct, and outspoken; active-spirited, sound in judgment, and far-seeing in their plans; they have been successful in every avocation of life. They have impressed the influence of their characters upon every institution with which they have been identified, developing and applying everything that was for the public weal. Descendants of these early families from Ireland have filled the most prominent professional and civil positions. They have been in congress, — four of the Riddells or Riddles have been congressmen; and on the judges' bench, — four of the Riddle family in the United States have been judges; they have been college presidents and professors, lawyers, physicians, and distinguished clergymen. They have been leading spirits in every public enterprise, stimulating to activity those around them, and shaping the principles and destinies of men and parties. Naturally conservative, and somewhat cold and stern in appearance, yet kind of heart and very generous when others were in need of their assistance.

In personal appearance the Riddells and Riddles have perpetuated the characteristics of their progenitors in Normandy; generally speaking they have been of "sandy complexion," with blue or gray eyes, and long, outstanding brows; foreheads broad and receding; cheek-bones high and prominent; nose large; mouth and chin wide, and face ruddy. Many of the first two or three generations were very large-framed, brawny men, and their strength almost herculean. They generally have broad shoulders, full chests, and long arms; are compactly built, erect, and graceful of carriage. In the military capacity they have been conspicuous, and in the active service cool and brave. True soldierly qualities seem to have been handed down through all generations in every branch of the family, from their Norman ancestors to the present time. From the first mention of the family under the distinctive surname, beginning with the warfare waged by the Northmen, cadets of this stock have cut a prominent figure in all the European and American wars; they were knighted in early mediæval times for valorous service in France and Italy, as well as in later days in England and Scotland; they have received their medals for faithfulness in engagements while holding commissions in the British army, and their names stand upon the rolls at Washington among the most chivalrous and brave of our American officers.

Having presented a comprehensive and succinct history of the family from the earliest time down to the present; having traced them in their movements and settlements in the various countries where they have been domiciled, and having briefly touched upon the prevailing traits of character developed by the race from its origin down to its representatives of the present, I must now invite the reader to an examination of the biographical and genealogical departments of this book for details and individual characters.

GENEALOGY AND BIOGRAPHY.

Earliest in book ✴

RIDDELLS OF NORMANDY AND ARDNAMURCHAN.

Walgrinus Ridel[1] (1), ancestors unknown, styled Prapinquas, or relative of Charles the Bald,* King of France and Emperor of Germany, in the year 886 was created by that prince, Earl of Angoulesme and Piragord. He married Rosalinda, daughter of Bernard, the famous Duke of Aquitaine, who died in 806, and was afterwards canonized, and grandson of Earl Theodoric, one of the chief captains under Charlemagne. In right of Rosalinda, Walgrinus acquired the earldom of Agen. He had issue *two* sons, of whom hereafter. He died in 886, and was succeeded by his eldest son.

SECOND GENERATION.

Alduin Ridel[2] (1), eldest son of Walgrinus[1] (1) was born at Angoulesme, France, and was named for his paternal uncle, Alduin, the famous abbot of St. Denis, and chief minister of France under Louis le Debonnaire. He succeeded to the earldom of Angoulesme, and rebuilt the walls of this chief city of his principality in order to defend it against the incursions of the Normans, who at that time grievously infested the country. He was succeeded by his son, of whom more hereafter.

William Ridel[2] (1), second son of Walgrinus[1] (1), was born at Angoulesme, France, and had for his inheritance the earldoms of Piragord and Agen, and became ancestor of the Earls of Piragord, which branch of the family was afterwards united to this line, as will soon appear.

THIRD GENERATION.

William Ridel[3] (2), son of Alduin[2] (1), was born at Angoulesme, France, and succeeded to the earldom of Angoulesme. He was surnamed " Lector-ferri," or " Taillefer," that is, " Iron-cutter," which name was acquired from his having, in an engagement with the Normans, cloven through with one stroke of his sword the body of Storis, their king, though clad in iron armor, a feat of strength considered worthy of commemoration in that chivalrous age. He was succeeded by his son in 963.

FOURTH GENERATION.

Arnold Ridel[4] (1), son of William[3] (2), was born at Angoulesme, and

* Charles the Bald was son of Louis the Debonnaire (the gentle), and grandson of Charlemagne. The brothers of Charles were Lothaire, Pepin, and Louis.

succeeded to that earldom, but becoming a monk, relinquished that inheritance to his son in 998.

FIFTH GENERATION.

William Ridel (3), son of Arnold⁴ (1), succeeded to the earldom of Angoulesme in 998 A. D.; married Gerberga, daughter of Galfridus I, Earl of Anjou, and sister of Folco III, grandfather of Folco IV, great-grandfather of Henry II, King of England. This representative of the family was a nobleman equally celebrated for his munificence, his valor, and his prudence. He made a pilgrimage to the Holy Land, and died shortly after his return, the eighteenth of the Ides* of April, 1028, leaving *two* sons, who successively became heirs of the earldom, as will afterwards appear.

SIXTH GENERATION.

Alduin Ridel (2), eldest son of William⁵ (3), was born at Angoulesme, France, and succeeded to that earldom. He died in 1034 A. D., and was succeeded by his brother.

Galfridus Ridel (1), second son of William⁵ (3), was born at Angoulesme, France, and succeeded his brother before mentioned in 1034 A. D. He married Petronilla, daughter and heiress of Manard, surnamed "The Rich," Baron of Archiac and Botaville, by whom he had issue *five* sons. He died in 1048.

SEVENTH GENERATION.

Folco Ridel (1), eldest son of Galfridus⁶ (1), was born at Angoulesme, France, and succeeding to that earldom became the ancestor of the earls of that line. This branch ended in Isabella, wife of King John† of England; and from her every sovereign who has since sat on the throne of England was descended.

Galfridus Ridel (2), second son of Galfridus⁶ (1), was born at Angoulesme, France, and became ancestor of this line, as the eighth in succession. He is sometimes called Geoffery, and is particularly mentioned by the author of the lives of the Earls of Angoulesme, as having assumed the surname, and is described in his account of the issue of Galfridus, his father. He had for his inheritance the baronies of Montausier and Blaye, in Guinne; the former he seems to have given up to his younger brother, afterwards mentioned, who was, in consequence, called Arnold de Montausier; the latter possession he held in the same manner as his father had done, when his elder brother, Earl Alduin, was alive. He married Agnes, daughter and heiress of Albert II, Earl of Piragord, who descended, as himself, in the seventh degree, from Walgrinus, the first

---

* The Romans made a threefold division of the month into *Calends, Nones,* and *Ides.* In March, May, July, and October, the Ides fell on the 15th, and in the remaining months on the 13th.

† King John (surnamed "Lackland"), born 24th December, 1166, was crowned 27th May, 1199. He was espoused to Alice, eldest daughter and co-heir of Humbert, Count of Maurien, now Savoy; she died before nuptials, and John married first, Isabella, daughter and heiress of William, Earl of Gloucester, from whom he was divorced; secondly, to Isabella, daughter and heiress of Aymer Taillefer (or Ridel), Count of Angoulesme, by whom (who married secondly, Hugh, Lord of Lusignan and Valence, in Poictou, and dying in 1246, was buried at Fonterand) he left at his decease at Newark Castle, 19th October, 1216, 1, Henry, his successor; 2, Richard, born 1209; 3, Joan, married 1221 to Alexander, King of Scotland; 4, Eleanor; 5, Isabella, married Frederick II, Emperor of Germany. From this we see how the royal family of Europe were connected with the Riddells.

Earl of Angoulesme, who stands at the head of his family. His wife had been married to William, Duke of Gascony, but was separated from him on account of relationship. He had *two* sons,'and dying in 1075 A. D., was succeeded by the eldest.

Arnold Ridel[7] (2), third son of Galfridus[6] (1), was born at Angoulesme, France, and received from his elder brother the barony of Montausier, in consequence of which he was called Arnold de Montausier.

William Ridel[7] (4), fourth son of Galfridus[6] (1), was born at Angoulesm, France, and became bishop of that earldom. He died young and was succeeded by his brother, of whom hereafter.

Aymar Ridel[7] (1), fifth son of Galfridus[6] (1), was born at Angoulesme, France, and succeeded his brother, before mentioned, as bishop of that earldom.

EIGHTH GENERATION.

Helias Ridel[8] (1), eldest son of Galfridus[7] (2), was born at Angoulesme, and succeeded to the earldom of Piragord ; he also became ancestor of the earls named Helias Ridel III, IV, and V, Bosco Ridel II, and of Jordana Ridel, Countess of Piragord, married to Archibald V, Viscount of Comborne, who became the stock of the succeeding earls. Helias was of the Ridels, barons of Bergerac, in Piragord, who all bore, for several generations, the Christian name and surname of Helias Ridel. This branch ended in Margaret Ridel, who was married to Rignald de Pons, ancestor of the once celebrated house of De Pons, in France.

Galfridus Ridel[8] (3), second son of Galfridus[7] (2), succeeded to his father's paternal inheritance of Blaye, in Guinne, and became renowned for his warlike exploits. He assisted the Normans in the reduction of Apulia* (see coat-of-arms), and William the Conqueror in his expedition against England, when he was rewarded (after William was crowned), with large landed estates by that prince. His name appears on the roll of Battle Abbey as "Monsieur Ridel." He married the sister of Roger Biggot, Earl of Norfolk, and died in 1098, leaving *four* sons, of whom more hereafter.

NINTH GENERATION.

Galfridus Ridel[9] (4), eldest son of Galfridus[8] (3), succeeded his father as Earl of Blaye, in Guinne, and became Lord Justiciary of all England, the highest office under the crown, in the time of Henry I. He married Geva, the daughter of Hugh Lumpus, Earl of Chester (and Geva his first wife, daughter of Robert de Buci), nephew to William the Conqueror, by whom he had *one* daughter, his heir. The authority on which he was called chief justiciary of England, is that of Huntingdon, in his *Epistlæ de Mundi Contemptu*, one copy of which, however, omits his name. Dugdale mentions him as united with Ralph Basset and others, in a commission to hear and determine a case relating to the privilege of sanctuary in the church of Ripon, and then adds that he succeeded Ralph Basset as Justice of England. He came to his death Nov. 25, 1120, with prince William, when on his return from Normandy in the "Blanche-Nef," from the carelessness of a drunken crew. The sons of King Henry I, William

---

* Apulia, in the southeastern part of Italy, was taken possession of by the Normans, 1043 A. D. Now named Puglia. Once a province of importance. Now the towns are depopulated, industry has disappeared, and commerce, once so flourishing, has passed away. Agriculture is in a low condition, and the roads are infested with banditti. The people are ignorant and superstitious, but hospitable.

and Richard, and their sister Matilda, with many other persons of distinction, were swallowed up in the sea with the crew, soon after leaving the port of Harfluer.

Hugh Ridel[9] **(1)**, second son of Galfridus[8] **(3)**, was endowed with the patrimony of the lands of Farringdon, in Northamptonshire, besides which he held the barony of Rilly, in Touraine, in France, and the manor of Cranstown, in Scotland. He was ancestor of the "Riddells* of Cranstown-Riddell" in Mid-Lothian, Scotland. Another authority *supposes* him to have been a son of Gervacius Rydale, who stands at the head of the "Riddells of Riddell," in Roxburghshire, Scotland. The Cranstown Riddells were a distinguished, knightly, and baronial family, and gave their name to their lands at a far earlier date than the Roxburgh branch. The barony of Cranstown† was held of the crown by the descendants of Hugh. In a little more than two centuries they became extinct in the male line, and the heir of the last proprietor, dead in 1357, was the wife of John Murray. One writer says, "Oscital Ridal having returned to his native land by consent of King Malcolm Canmore, gave his lands of Cranstown, Preston, and others, to his son Hugo, who in the year 1110 bestowed the church of Cranstown, and certain lands in the barony, to the monastery of Selkirk, which was founded by Prince David." I shall not separate the "Riddells of Cranstown-Riddell" from the family now under notice.

Philip Ridel[9] **(1)**, third son of Galfridus[8] **(3)**, had one son who became head of the family of "Riddells of Riddell," in Roxburghshire, Scotland (which see), one who entered the church and was canonized, and another who became Baron of Varcillac, in Guinne, who also entered the church.

Matthias Ridel[9] **(1)**, fourth son of Galfridus[8] **(3)**, was made abbot of Peterborough monastery, A. D. 1102 (or, as one writer says, in 1105 A. D.), by King Henry I. Matthias appears to have made a conveyance of the manor of Pithesle to his brother, the Justiciary of England, before mentioned. He held the abbacy but a year, dying on the twelfth of the calends of November, the very day twelve months from his entrance. After his death the king again seized upon the monastery, and held it three years.

---

* Riddell, a baronial (Norman) name derived from a Gothic race in Aquitaine, France. Gerard, Baron of Blaye, 1030, granted lands to the Abbey of Fons Dulcis, near Bordeaux, which grant was confirmed by his brother Gerald de Blaye, and his sons Geoffry Rudelli (Ridel), and William Frebelandus (or Ridel); the last named, who was living 1079–1099, married a sister of William de Albini Brito of England, and had sons, Warin, Oliver, and Geoffry; the latter went to Scotland with King David, received grants of land there, and became ancestor of the Riddells of Ridell in Roxburghshire.

Another Geoffry Ridel, of the preceding generation, came to England from Apulia with William Bigod (or Bigot), to assist William the Conqueror, and is mentioned in Domesday Book, 1086. He was Crown commissioner with Ralph Basset, 1106, and succeeded that justiciary, 1120. A collateral branch of this family possessed lands in Normandy, 1165; Geoffrey Ridel occurs in Normandy, 1180; Roger, 1195; Geoffrey, 1198. This note was taken from a book entitled "The Norman People."

† Cranstown-Riddell was acquired by the family of Macgills, in 1561. Sir James Macgill, of Cranstown-Riddell, was created a baronet in 1619, and in 1651, a peer by the title of Viscount Oxenford. The title became extinct at the death of Robert, second Viscount, and the land descended by marriage to Sir John Dalrymple of Cousland, and Fala, whose family succeeded to the earldom of Stair in 1841, and Cranstown-Riddell is still the property of that family. John Dodds is the present factor at Cranstown-Riddell. There is no mansion on the estate now, only a factor's house.

* Go to p. 63/64 – See Sir Auskittel de Ridale

TENTH GENERATION.

Matilda Ridel[10] (1), only child of Galfridus[9] (4), married to Richard Basset, Lord Justiciary of England to King Henry I. He was of an ancient and noble family, being the son of Ralph Basset, Lord Justiciary of England, grandson of Thurstine, who came over with William the Conqueror, great-grandson of Hugh Basset, who lived in the end of the tenth century. Matilda and her husband founded the Abbey of Laud, in Leicestershire. The issue of this marriage was *four* sons, the eldest of whom, in honor of his mother, assumed the name of Ridel, and carried on that family. Ralph, the second son, became ancestor of the Bassets of Drayton, peers of the realm; this branch ended in heirs female, married into the family of Beauchamp, Earls of Warwick, the Earls of Stafford, and the Chaworths. The third son, William, became ancestor of the Bassets of Sapcote, peers of the realm, which branch ended in heirs female about the time of that of Drayton, — the end of the fourteenth century. An account of the fourth son hereafter. Matilda succeeded in 1139 A. D.

Rignald Ridel[10] (1), a son of Hugh[9] (1) succeeded to his father's estates, and left *one* son, his heir, of whom hereafter.

ELEVENTH GENERATION.

Galfridus Ridel[11] (5), eldest son of Matilda[10] (1), born at Blaye, France, in 1129, assumed the surname of Ridel and became the representative of that family, being the twelfth in order of succession. He was Baron of Blaye, in France, and held fifteen knights' fees in England of the king, *in capite,* being lands in Normandy and others in England, as a feudatory. He was one of the chaplains of King Henry II, and was so much in the royal favor, that after Thomas à-Becket was elevated to the primacy of Canterbury, he was appointed his successor as archdeacon of Canterbury, 1162. He was induced to take holy orders by the king's entreaties, as his support against the machinations of Becket, who used to declare that his greatest enemy on earth was Galfridus Ridel, and also to give him on that account, the name of " Archdevil of Canterbury." He was employed still at court, for his name stands second of the *"Assidentes Justiciæ Regis,"* before whom, in 1165, a charter between the abbots of St. Albans and Westminster was executed in the Exchequer. He was sent with John of Oxford, in 1164, to the pope, to obtain his confirmation of the ancient customs and dignities of the realm; and again, in 1169, he was one of the ambassadors to the court of France, with the king's request that Becket, who had withdrawn there, might not be permitted to remain. Both embassies were unsuccessful, but his activity in the king's behalf was not allowed to pass unnoticed. The irritated primate included him in the excommunication which he pronounced in 1169, against several of the bishops and chief men of the kingdom, and in announcing the sentence to the bishop of Hereford, he designated Galfridus an " archdevil." On Henry's remonstrance, however, the pope's nuncios found it necessary to absolve him before the end of the year, he being one of those who personally attended the king. Galfridus' favor increased at court with Becket's oppression, and accordingly, in the same year of the death of the bishop, the See of Ely was placed in his hands and so remained about four years. In 1173 the bishopric was given him, but he was not admitted to it until he had given his solemn protestation in the

4

Chapel of St. Catherine, in Westminster, that he had in no way, knowingly, been accessory to the murder of the archbishop, an accusation not unnaturally made against him, from the active part he was known to have taken in the king's proceedings. He was then solemnly enthroned, but his consecration did not take place, the See of Canterbury being vacant, until October, 1174.

On the retirement of Richard de Luci, in 1179, Bishop Galfridus was appointed, with the Bishops of Winchester and Norwich, to fill the office of Chief Justiciary, and on the division of the kingdom by the Council of Windsor into four judicial circuits, these prelates were respectively placed at the head of three of them. They were superseded the following year, but Galfridus appears to have acted subsequently in court, as he was one of the justices before whom a fine was levied in 1182. In the roll of Richard I, his pleas are recorded as a justice itinerant in no less than five counties. As, however, he died Aug. 21, 1189, in the interval between the death of King Henry and the coronation of King Richard, which took place within thirteen days of Galfridus' death, that monarch, finding that he had died intestate, appropriated to the expense of the ceremony the treasures he found in his coffers, amounting to three thousand and sixty silver marks, and two hundred and five golden ones, no very vast accumulation after ruling so rich a diocese for nearly fifteen years. He had, however, devoted a large sum during his life to the improvement of his cathedral and the erection of the two towers from the foundation. The cognomen, *superbus*, which he acquired, is stated to have been given from the arrogance of his disposition and his want of affability. The history of Ely relates that his tomb was violated, and that his successor, William de Longchamp, on the day of his enthronization, ascended the pulpit, and with the other bishops present, excommunicated all those who had committed the sacrilege, or consented thereto. During his term of office he repaired St. Etheldreda's shrine, and added different vestments and ornaments to those in use ; he gave to the church five rich copes of red silk, bound with gold lace and adorned with golden flowers, one of the copes having a circle of precious stones set in silver, an abbe starred with gold, a mitre, and a noble altar cloth. He also redeemed many ornaments which had been forfeited by his predecessor, and granted and confirmed by charter the sum of one hundred marks to be annually paid to the Sacrist from the treasury, to provide a wax taper to be kept burning constantly before the high altar in the church forever; and two marks arising from lands in Somersham and Stokings, toward finding provision for the convent, and for an allowance of rye and good beer to be made on two days in the year. He had been nominated one of the executors of King Henry's will, which bears date at Waltham, A. D. 1182. The king dying abroad, in July, 1189, he went down (with many other bishops) to Winchester in great state, to await the arrival of the new king, and while there he was taken ill and died a few days after. His body was conveyed thence to Ely* and interred in the cathedral church. Whether he was

---

* The monastery of Ely was founded by Etheldreda, daughter of Anna, King of the East Angles. Her first design was to build the cathedral at Craterdune, about a mile distant from the present city, where Ethelbert, King of the East Angles, is said to have founded a monastery, which was destroyed by the army of Penda, King of Mercia. From the Saxon Chronicles I learn that Etheldreda began her building at Ely in the year 673, and the year following was consecrated abbess of her own foundation. She was born about the year 630, at Ixning, in the western part of

married has been a matter of question by sacred historians. I have found good proof that he was twice married, but the name of his first wife does not appear. He had, however, *two* sons by this wife, of whom hereafter. He married secondly, Sibilla, sister of William Maudit, Lord of Hanslap, and ancestor of the Earls of Warwick, by whom he left *two sons* and *a daughter*, of whom more hereafter. He was inquired after by the pope, and the answer was, "He has a gospel excuse for his absence." When the pope asked what that was, he was answered, "He has married a wife and therefore cannot come." From the foregoing, supplemented by the statement made at his confirmation, namely, that he had not since his admission to holy orders been married or cohabited with any woman, says a sacred writer, "seems to imply that he had been formerly married."

Jordan Ridel[11] (**1**), fourth son of Matilda[10] (**1**) and Richard Basset, assumed the surname of Ridel, and became possessed of lands of Nogent and Aurillac, in Champagne, in France. This is the first time the name *Jordan* occurs in the family.

Hugh Ridel[11] (**2**), only son of Rignald[10] (**1**), was his father's successor, and having no male issue his daughter became heir to his own estate and that of Wittering.

TWELFTH GENERATION.

Margaret Ridel[12] (**1**), a daughter of Hugh[11] (**2**), inherited the estates of her father, and became the wife of Hugh Ridel, of whom hereafter.

Galfridus Ridel[12] (**6**), eldest son of Galfridus[11] (**5**), obtained the principality of Blaye, upon his father's entering the church, and was one of the most celebrated of the troubadour poets. His history illustrates in a most striking manner the age of chivalry in which he lived. He was the favorite minstrel of Geoffrey de Plantagenet Bretagne, and during his residence at the court of England, where he lived in great honor and splendor, caressed for his talents and loved for the gentleness of his disposition, he heard continually the praises of the Countess of Tripoli, — whose fame, in consequence of her munificent hospitality to the Crusaders, who, when returning from the plains of Asia, wayworn, sick, and disabled, were relieved and entertained by her, had spread throughout Christendom, — which praise of her beauty and benevolence, constantly repeated by the returned Crusaders, in their enthusiasm of gratitude, fired the heart of Ridel (sometimes spelled "Rudel") the poet to such an extent that, without having seen her, and unable to bear the torments of absence longer, he undertook a pilgrimage to visit the unknown lady. He quitted the English court against the entreaties and expostulations of his prince, and sailed for the Levant. He became seriously ill on the voyage, and lived but a few hours after the vessel reached the harbor of Tripoli. When the countess

Suffolk; her mother's name was Henswitha. She was first married to Toubert, a nobleman of the East Angles, and afterwards to Egfrid, King of Northumberland, and, persevering with both husbands to live in a state of virginity, she was assisted in building the monastery by her brother Adolphus, at that time King of the East Angles. She died June 23, 679, and was buried in a wooden coffin, in the common cemetery with the nuns, by her orders. The See of Ely was created by King Henry I, in 1109 A. D. The bishops of Ely were Counts Palatine, but their rights as such were nearly all destroyed by Act of Parliament, in the reign of Henry VIII. The arms of Ely are, "Gules, three open crowns, two and one; or, bishop's mitre on top of the shield."

heard that a celebrated poet was on board, who was dying for her love,
she immediately hastened to his side, and taking his hand entreated him
to live for her sake.   Ridel, already speechless and almost in the agonies
of death, revived for a moment at such unexpected tenderness and favor,
and expressing the excess of his gratitude and love, died in her arms.
The countess wept most bitterly and vowed herself a life of penance for
the loss she had caused the world. She commanded that the last song
Ridel had composed in her honor, should be transcribed in letters of gold,
and carried it always in her bosom.   His body was enclosed in a magnificent mausoleum of porphyry, with an Arabic inscription, commemorating his
genius and his love for her.   The song which the minstrel composed when
on this romantic expedition, while his strength was failing, and which was
worn by the countess * within her vest to the end of life, is still extant,
and has been translated into nearly every language in Europe; of these
translations the following by Sismondi best preserves the original curious
arrangement of the rhymes, as well as the piety and tenderness of the sentiment:—

> "Irrité, dolent partirai,
>   Si ne vois cet amour de loin,
> Et ne sais quand je le verrai
>   Car sont par trop nos terres loin.
> Dieu, qui toutes choses as fait,
>   Et formas cet amour si loin,
> Donne force à mon cœur, car ai
>   L'espoir devoir m'amour an loin.
> Ah, Seigneur, tenez pour bien vrai
>   L'amour qu'ai pour elle de loin,
> Car pour un bien que j'en anrai,
>   J'ai mille maux, tant je suis loin.
> J'a d'autre amour ne jowirai,
>   Si non de cet amour de loin, —
> Qu'une plus belle jen'en scais
>   En lien qui soit ni pres in loin!"

The following is as faithful a version anglicized, as the different idioms
of the language will admit of : —

> "Grieved and troubled shall I die,
>   If I meet not my love afar;
> Alas! I know not that I e'er
>   Shall see her, — for she dwells afar.
> O God! that didst all things create,
>   And formed my sweet love now afar;
> Strengthen my heart that I may hope
>   To behold her face who is afar.
> Oh, Lord! I believe how very true
>   Is my love for her, who is afar;
> Tho' for each joy a thousand pains
>   I bear, because I am so far." †

Richard Ridel[12] (1), second son of Galfridus[11] (5), succeeded his
brother, before mentioned, and became possessed of nearly all the family
estates in England. He resumed the surname of Bassett, and his family
became extinct in the male line; consequently the inheritance devolved
upon his brother, of whom hereafter.

---

* Princess Melinsend, daughter of Raimond, Count of Tripoli, the affianced bride
of Manuel, Emperor of Constantinople.
† This poem must have been composed as early as A. D. 1150.

Hugh Ridel[12] (3), third son of Galfridus[11] (5), and eldest by his second wife, Sibilla Maudit, became on the death of his half-brother, who died without male issue, direct ancestor and representative of his family, and was the thirteenth in the order of succession. He possessed the principality of Blaye. His descendants became the representatives of the families of Ridel and Bassett. He married Margaret, daughter of another Hugh Ridel, before mentioned, and in her right acquired the lordship of Wittering, in Northamptonshire, the manor of Cranstown, in Scotland, the barony of Rilley, in Touraine, France, and considerable property in England, as she was heiress of her father, as before mentioned. By this means he became a powerful baron, and his name is truly distinguished in the annals of both England and Scotland. In 1174, he was one of the noblemen who were hostages to King Henry II, for William the Lion, King of Scotland, when taken prisoner at the battle of Alnwick. Through that prince he was allied to the Ajou, Chester, and St. Liz families. He had issue, *three* sons, of whom more hereafter.

William Ridel[12] (5), fourth son of Galfridus[11] (5), by his second wife, Sibilla Maudit, was lord of the manor of Farringdon, in Northamptonshire, and of Primside and Glengarnoch, in Scotland, of which kingdom he was High Chancellor, under William the Lion. He died in the year 1214, leaving an only son, of whom hereafter.

Stephen Ridel[12] (1), a nephew of Bishop Ridel, is said by Dr. Millis to have been archdeacon of Ely in 1210, and resigned this office in 1214. He was chancellor to John Earl Moriton, afterwards King John; and was possessed of several ecclesiastical benefices in this diocese, of which he was deprived by Bishop Longchamp, but probably restored to them again, as he afterwards occurs witness with Richard Barre, archdeacon of Ely, in several charters of Bishop Eustace. The name of this member of the Norman house of Ridel does not stand in the regular pedigree of the main line of the family, and there were, probably, many other junior branches omitted.

THIRTEENTH GENERATION.

Galfridus Ridel[13] (7), eldest son of Hugh[12] (3) and his wife Margaret, succeeded his father as Lord of Blaye, and was nephew of the barons who conspired against King John, in the year 1212. By the death of his nephew Hugh he again reunited to the family the estates of Wittering and Cranstown, but some of the lands possessed by Hugh had been made over by him to Ralph, Lord Basset, his kinsman of Weldon. He married Hawissa, daughter and co-heiress of William Peverel, in whose right he acquired Chiche Notley, and other lands in Essex, amounting to five knights' fees, by whom he had *two* sons, of whom hereafter. Galfridus died in 1249, and was succeeded by his son and namesake.

Hugh Ridel[13] (4), second son of Hugh[12] (3), and Margaret, his wife, died before his father, — previous to 1200 A. D.

Richard Ridel[13] (2), third son of Hugh[12] (3), succeeded to his mother's inheritance, and left *one* son, his heir.

Ralph Ridel[13] (1), only son of William[12] (5), acquired the estate of Strixton, in Northamptonshire, by gift of his kinsman, William Maudit, Earl of Warwick, in 1232, and also the manor of Risby, in Lincolnshire, in right of his wife, Isabella, daughter of Falco D'Oyrie, by whom he had *two* sons, of whom hereafter.

FOURTEENTH GENERATION.

Galfridus Ridel[14] (8), eldest son of Galfridus[13] (7), became ancestor of the main line of the Ridel family, and succeeded his father as the fifteenth in succession in the lordships of Wittering and Cranstown, and in the barony of Blaye. In the king's writs, summoning him and his father to attend the army, and bring fifteen men at least with them into the field, this Galfridus is styled "Galfridus Ridel, junior." He was more than once entrusted with the important charge of forming and settling the articles of peace between the two monarchs of England and France, being chosen on the part of the former. He married the heiress of a large estate in the island of Oleron (her name does not appear), of which King Henry III ordered his Seneschal of Gascony to deliver seisin to her in the year 1234; by her he had *two* sons, of whom hereafter. He died in 1261, a nobleman justly celebrated for his loyalty and the enjoyment of the favor of royalty.

Roger Ridel[14] (1), second son of Galfridus[13] (7), succeeded to his mother's inheritance and enjoyed it in the lifetime of his father, on which account he was always designated "Roger Ridel, the son of Galfridus." He also possessed his father's lands in Normandy, where his posterity seems to have settled, and to have become a distinct and celebrated branch of the Ridel family. One of them, Martin Ridel, was Baron of More and Plainsevett, grand treasurer in France under Louis XIV. Some of the descendants of this man settled in the United States, and spelled their name *Riddelle*.

Hugh Ridel[14] (5), only son of Richard[13] (2), inherited the estates of Wittering and Cranstown; but dying without issue, these estates devolved upon his uncle Galfridus[13] (7), before mentioned.

Robert Ridel[14] (1), eldest son of Ralph[13] (1), having no male issue, gave his lands of Strixton, which he inherited from his father, to the church, in 1282; but his estates in Scotland came to his daughter, of whom hereafter.

Ralph Ridel[14] (2), second son of Ralph[13] (1), had Risby for his inheritance. He married Agnes, heiress of Wildon, in Bedfordshire, by whom he had *two* sons, of whom more hereafter.

FIFTEENTH GENERATION.

Galfridus Ridel[15] (9), eldest son of Galfridus[14] (8), succeeded to his father's estate in 1261. In France we find him several times summoned to meet the king well provided with horses and arms; and in England and Scotland, as a great benefactor to religious houses. He had issue *three* sons, of whom hereafter.

Margaret Ridel[15] (2), daughter of Robert[14] (1), married a daughter of Henry de Cunningham, and became ancestress of the Cunninghams of Glencairn, earls. She was her father's heiress and inherited his estates in Scotland, and her descendants have represented some of the most worthy families in the realm.

Sir John Ridel[15] (1), eldest son of Ralph[14] (2), was a knight and lord of the manor of Wildon in Bedfordshire, in right of his mother, an heiress.

Ralph Ridel[15] (3), second son of Ralph[14] (2), inherited Risby, and had an only daughter, of whom nothing appears except that she was her father's heiress and was married to Sir William Marmion, Knight.

SIXTEENTH GENERATION.

Galfridus Ridel[16] **(10)**, eldest son of Galfridus[15] (9), succeeded his father in 1288, in the barony of Blaye. He was in great favor with Kings Edward I and II; the latter in 1308 wrote a letter in his behalf to the King of France, a copy of which is still preserved. He had *one* daughter, of whom hereafter. Died in 1319 A. D.

Sir Hugh Ridel[16] **(6)**, second son of Galfridus[15] (9), succeeded to the manor of Wittering and Cranstown, and to the barony of Montclare and Piragord, and in consequence of his brother's dying without male issue became eventually head of this family. He served King Edward II in his war against Scotland, and swore fealty to him in 1296. As he held his lands in Scotland of King Edward, as lord paramount in that country; for tarrying too long in Scotland, King Edward took from him his manor of Wittering, and gave it to his son Galfridus. Thus deprived of his rights, Hugh went to his kinsman, Sir William Ridell of Northumberland, who generously settled upon him a part of his revenue.

Sir Nicholas Ridel[16] **(1)**, third son of Galfridus[15] (9), acquired the barony of Sotus, in Agenois in Guinne, and the manor of Sallows, in Norfolk. His posterity became the representatives of this family, as will afterwards appear.

SEVENTEENTH GENERATION.

Alicia Ridel[17] **(1)**, only daughter of Galfridus[16] (10), was married to William Furt, a Baron of Gascony. Her pretensions to the barony of Blaye, were doubtful, as it seems to have been confirmed, like many others, to male heirs only; in which case, it should have devolved upon her uncle Hugh, before mentioned. Alicia, however, having got possession of it, sold her rights and pretensions with regard to it to Edward II, King of England, who had power enough to secure his bargain against any impeachment that could be made against it by a subject, and particularly as Hugh was out of favor at court. A clause, however, was inserted in the deed of conveyance, that, should Alicia's rights be rendered invalid, she should lose the greater part of the purchase-money.

Sir Galfridus Ridel[17] **(11)**, son of Hugh[16] (6), Baron of Montclare and lord of the manors of Wittering and Cranstown; but this last possession he lost during the Scotch wars, in which he took an active part against King Robert Bruce's party. He died in 1346, and was succeeded by his son, of whom hereafter.

William Ridel[17] **(6)**, son of Nicholas[16] (1), succeeded to his father's estate as Lord of Sallows and of the manor of Sallows; he was returned to hold that lordship in 1316; his name is to be found in many benefactories. He had issue *two* sons, of whom hereafter.

EIGHTEENTH GENERATION.

Sir Hugh Ridel[18] **(7)**, son of Galfridus[17] (11), succeeded his father in 1346, as Baron of Montclare and lord of the manor of Wittering. He petitioned King Edward III to procure him the restitution of Cranstown, which his ancestors had held time immemorial of the kings of England. His petition was not successful. He died in 1363 A. D., with-

out issue, whereupon the manor of Wittering, as well as the representation of the family, devolved upon the grandson of Sir Nicholas Ridel,
before mentioned, who entering the church in the year 1300, settled his
manor and lands upon his son.

Sir Nicholas Ridel[18] (2), eldest son and heir of William[17] (6), was
Lord of Sotus and of the manor of Sallows. He afterwards succeeded
to the manor of Wittering, in Northamptonshire, and to Montclare, in
Piragord, upon the death of his kinsman, Hugh Ridel, before mentioned ;
and at the same time assumed the representation of the family under
notice. He died shortly after, in 1363 A. D., leaving two sons, of
whom hereafter.

John Ridel[18] (2), second son of William[17] (6), entered into the church
and became rector of Chigwell, in Essex.

NINETEENTH GENERATION.

Sir John Ridel[19] (3), eldest son of Nicholas[18] (2), succeeded his
father as representative of this family, and inherited the family estates in
England and France; and also procured a charter from King David
II, of Scotland, granting him the manor of Cranstown, which had been
lost by his predecessors ; this property he either sold, or was forced to
relinquish, as we find it possessed by William Watson soon after. Thus
the family, by losing their possessions in Scotland, for many years had
no intercourse with that kingdom, till they acquired other property
there, as will presently appear. Sir John made a conspicuous figure in
the wars between England and France. He was succeeded by his son, of
whom more hereafter.

William Ridel[19] (7), second son of Nicholas[18] (2), acquired the manor
of Walcot, and other lands in Northamptonshire. He made a conspicuous
figure with his brother, before mentioned, in the wars between France and
England ; and dying without issue male his property was divided between his *two* daughters, one of whom was the wife of Sir Richard Griffin, the other of Sir Richard Sutton ; their names do not appear.

Nicholas Ridel[19] (3), third son of Nicholas[18] (2), was proprietor of
the manors of Wittering and Sallows, and Baron of Montclare and Sotus,
in France. He died in 1405, leaving *two* sons, of whom hereafter. Nicholas became head of this family.

TWENTIETH GENERATION.

Hugh Ridel[20] (8), eldest son of Nicholas[19] (3), succeeded to his father's
estates of Montclare, Wittering, and others. He married Elizabeth Cowal,
heiress of Thornby, in Northamptonshire, by whom he had *three* sons, of
whom hereafter. He died in 1422 A. D., and was succeeded by his son.

Thomas Ridel[20] (1), second son of Nicholas[19] (3), appears in the pedigree without mention of his capacity.

TWENTY-FIRST GENERATION.

Nicholas Ridel[21] (4), eldest son of Hugh[20] (8), was lord of the manor
of Wittering. He was strongly attached to the house of Lancaster; and
in honor of King Henry VI he named his son and heir. The whole of
the family estates on the Continent were in his time lost, in consequence
of the province of Guinne being wrested from the English Crown in
1445 A. D. He was succeeded by his son, of whom hereafter.

Sir William Ridel[21] (8), second son of Hugh[20] (8), obtained for his inheritance the manor of Sallows and the barony of Sotus in Guinne, where he distinguished himself in several engagements in which he fought. Having no children, his third brother, of whom hereafter, succeeded to his property; and the son of his brother eventually became head of this family, as will appear.

Thomas Ridel[21] (2), third son of Hugh[20] (8), succeeded to his brother William, before mentioned, as lord of the manor of Wittering and the barony of Sotus in Guinne. In 1422 he entered the service of France when leagued with England, and served as an English Esquire, under his brother Sir William, who was then proprietor of Sallows. He died in 1428, and was succeeded by his son, of whom more hereafter.

TWENTY-SECOND GENERATION.

Henry Ridel[22] (1), son of Nicholas[21] (4), was his father's heir to Wittering and other lands in Northamptonshire. He distinguished himself by his attachment to the house of Lancaster during the civil wars. He was named in honor of King Henry VI. He married Egidia, who survived him some years (he deceased in 1471), and by her had issue, an only daughter and heir, who became the wife of Robert Halley, Esq., who, in her right, enjoyed the lands which belonged to the Ridel family. Thus the manor of Wittering passed out of the family after remaining in their possession above *three hundred years*. Some monuments still remain in the old church at Wittering, especially their coat-of-arms (see their arms in this book), which is on stained glass, in the upper pane of the chancel. The family vault may also be seen. Upon the death of Henry, the representation of the family devolved upon his cousin, of whom hereafter.

Sir John Riddell[22] (4), son of Thomas[21] (2), was lord of the manor of Sallows and Baron of Sotus in Guinne, where he fought in defense of his property, but lost it irrecoverably when that province fell into the hands of the French. He bore his own standard, being a knight banneret, and was served by thirteen esquires. He is the first of this family who is known to have spelled the surname with the double letters. He was returned to hold the manor of "Riddell," in Sallows, in A. D. 1458, and died in A. D. 1474, leaving issue *two* sons, of whom hereafter.

TWENTY-THIRD GENERATION.

Thomas Riddell[23] (3), eldest son of John[22] (4), was styled " of Sallows, Esquire." In his time the family had lost much of its grandeur and influence. The manor of Wittering, and other lands in Northamptonshire, were now lost, and the estates in Guinne, estates which caused the Ridels to have a continued connection with France for *five hundred years*, that is from their existence as a distinct family, now also remained to them no longer. Thomas died in 1505 A. D., and was succeeded by his son.

Robert Riddell[23] (2), second son of John[22] (4), served in the army of France, in the year 1480, and was styled an " English Esquire."

TWENTY-FOURTH GENERATION.

Thomas Riddell[24] (4), a son of Thomas[23] (3), was styled " of Sallows, Esquire." He married Constantina, daughter of John Calle, of Melton, in the County of Norfolk. By an inquisition at the castle of Norwich, it appears that he died Sept. 20, 1545, leaving an only son, then only nine years old, who was his successor.

TWENTY-FIFTH GENERATION.

John Riddell²⁵ (5), only son of Thomas²⁴ (4), succeeded his father when a child.   In the year 1550 he sold his manor of Sallows, and other possessions in Norfolk, to one Nicholas Southerton, being then fourteen years old.   He then went to and dwelt in Scotland, where he was well received by King James I.   He married a daughter of Thomas Urquahart, of Cromerty, by Helen, daughter of Lord Abernethy, of Salton, by whom he had *two* sons.   He died in 1584 A. D.

TWENTY-SIXTH GENERATION.

James Riddell²⁶ (1), eldest son of John²⁵ (5), succeeded to his father's estates.*   He remained in Scotland where his father had settled, and acquired considerable property in the County of Edinburgh ; to this a remarkable addition was made by his marriage with Elizabeth, daughter of Adam Alleyn, Esq., a connection which formed a sufficient induce- ment for him to fix his residence in Scotland.   He died in the year 1620, leaving an only son, his successor.

TWENTY-SEVENTH GENERATION.

James Riddell²⁷ (2), only son of James²⁶ (1),† was styled, "of King- lass, in Linlithgowshire, Esquire."   The estate of Kinglass he purchased soon after his father's death.   He was a man of great talents, and of the most exemplary virtues, both public and private.   To his patriotic endeav- ors Scotland is indebted for the introduction of some of its most valuable manufactures.   To these endeavors his great influence, both in England and Scotland, gave success, as it secured the concurrence and assistance of some of the most eminent men of that time, and particularly that worthy noble- man, the Earl of Crawford and Lindsey, who in one manufactory joined with him in partnership.   Being a man of the most liberal spirit, he was equally respected during the time of the commonwealth, and afterwards under the newly established monarchial government. ‡   Many friendly letters which

---

* About 1595, this James Riddell was made a free denizen of the royal city of Kasimier, and in 1602, he had from Alexander, then King of Poland, all the priv- ileges of a free citizen confirmed to him.   On his return to Scotland he became a burgess and guild-brother of Edinburgh.   He died in 1620.

† The following acrostic in praise of James Riddell and the antiquity of his fam- ily, which was taken from the family papers, is a curiosity worthy a place here.

   " J   I cannot chuse but preyse thy noble name,
      A   As one descended from an ancient stoke ;
      M   Mars into belyck hes renoined thee feme,
      E   Excelling all the base and vulgar sort.
      S   So hold thyself of a brave, loftee mind,
      R   Resembles rycht thee art comyt of that kynd,
      I   Join all the art wyse and judicious ;
      D   Descreet in lyfe and conversatione,
      D   Distroying all evil leafes virtious,
      E   Esteemed, beloved, and of gentill fashoun ;
      L   Loftee and gallant, a youth of pregnant spirits,
      L   Likely by fortune to be raiset by merit."

It is not *known* which James Riddell this was written to, but *believed* to repre- sent the above James, hence placed in this connection.

‡ During the civil wars this James Riddell was much in the confidence of Oliver Cromwell and General Monk ; the former once lodged with him in his house at Leith, and afterwards corresponded with him.   He was appointed by the Scots Es- tates, Commissary General to their forces, in their expedition to the north, and he is so designated in his burgess ticket from the town of Brechin, in 1645.   At Mr.

passed between him and General Monk, together with a passport written, signed, and sealed by the General himself, in November, 1659, are still preserved. Probably the General's affection for Mr. Riddell was stronger on account of his being descended from Beauchamp, Earl of Warwick, and from Galfridus, Lord Ridel. He married Sept. 19, 1639, Elizabeth, eldest daughter of George Foulis, Esq., of Ravelstone, Master of the King's Mint, niece of Sir James Foulis, of Ingleby, in Yorkshire, Baronet, ancestor of Sir Archibald Primrose, by whom he had *nine* sons, the two eldest of whom successively became his heirs, and *eight* daughters, one of whom was the wife of Walter Riddell, of Minto. This marriage is the first alliance between the main line now under consideration, and the Roxburghshire branch, after it was broken off and established as a distinct family. This James died in 1674, aged 66 years.

TWENTY-EIGHTH GENERATION.

James Riddell[28] (3), eldest son of James[27] (2), succeeded his father in the estate of Kinglass, Scotland, and was a captain in the service of the States of Holland. He greatly encumbered his paternal estate, and dying unmarried in 1688, he was succeeded by his brother, as hereafter stated.

George Riddell[28] (1), second son of James[27] (2), was styled "of Kinglass, Esquire," having succeeded his brother James, before mentioned. He married Jane, eldest daughter of Capt. John Tailzeour, by his first wife, who was daughter of Dr. John Evans, rector of Lewisham, in Kent, descended from an ancient family in Wales; by her he had issue *six* sons and *eight* daughters. He was a wine merchant at Leeds, Scotland. He was succeeded in 1706 by his son; the only one known to be then living.

TWENTY-NINTH GENERATION.

Capt. George Riddell[29] (2), eldest son of George[28] (1), in whose time the estate of Kinglass passed out of the family. He married Christiana, daughter of Andrew Patterson, Esq., of Kirkton, by Barbara his third wife, daughter of Colonel MacDougall, a younger son of the family of Treugh, now represented by the Earl of Dumfries, and sister of James Patterson, Esq., of Kirkton, who married the Honorable Catherine, daughter of Lord John Gray, and had issue *nine* sons and *six* daughters. Captain Riddell was a distinguished man.

THIRTIETH GENERATION.

Dr. George Riddell[30] (3), eldest son of George[29] (2), became an eminent physician in Yorkshire, Va., and is supposed to have died before his father, as the succession of the estate devolved upon a younger brother, who was settled at Belton. I have not been able to learn whether this man had a family.

Andrew Riddell[30] (2), second son of George[29] (2), was styled "of Enfield," and is presumably the first of that family, which see for account of descendants. He was an officer in the army.

Riddell's request a church at Leith was restored to the parishioners by General Monk, — it had been used for a stable, — and the citizens conferred upon him a large space in the body of the church for a seat for his family. His passport from General Monk allowed him to pass and repass, free from molestation, with his servants, horses, and arms, about his private affairs. After the Restoration he obtained from Charles II an order for erecting a new manufactory of woolen and tow cards, the first of the kind in Scotland, for which he obtained an act of Scottish Parliament, in 1663.

Sir James Riddell[20] (4), third son of George[29] (2), was styled " of Ardnamurchan and Sunart." He had the honor to be created a baronet by the King's Most Excellent Majesty, Sept. 2, 1778. He was a Doctor of Law, Justice of the Peace for the Counties of Argyle and Suffolk, and member of the Society for Encouragement of Arts, Manufactures, and Commerce. He married first, Mary, daughter of Thomas B. Milles, of Billockby Hall, in the County of Norfolk, by Helen his third wife, daughter of Major Ferrier of Hemsby, and Member of Parliament for Yarmouth, in the same county. By her he had *four* sons and *one* daughter, who, with the second and fourth sons, died young. He married secondly, in 1775, Sarah, daughter of Thomas Burden, Esq., in the county of Durham and York, as heir to her father and grandfather, Henry Foster, Esq.

John Riddell[30] (6), fourth son of George[29] (2), acquired wealth by commerce in Virginia, and is supposed to have taken up his residence in that State, but no account of a family appears in the Scottish pedigree.

Robert Riddell[30] (3), fifth son of George[29] (2), was styled "of Garzield, Dumfrieshire." He married Susanna-Andry Kenneys, and became an officer in the royal regiment of Horse Guards. He died at Musselburgh, in 1802, and his widow at Garzield, in 1806 (?). In the account of his death found in the *Gentleman's Magazine*, Mr. Riddell is styled " of Kennys Hall," in Dumfrieshire, Scotland; no account of a family.

THIRTY-FIRST GENERATION.

Sir Thomas-Milles Riddell[31] (5), eldest son of James[30] (4), was styled "of Mount Riddell," in the County of Stirling. He succeeded his father as second baronet; married, in 1784, Margaret, daughter of Col. Dugald Campbell, by Christiana, daughter of the late Alexander Drummond, Esq., Consul at Aleppo, son of John Drummond of Newton, and sister of Gen. Duncan Campbell of Lochness, in the County of Argyle, by whom he had issue *two* sons and *five* daughters. He died July 19, 1796; his wife died Oct. 31, 1836. Succeeded by his eldest son.

Lieut. George-James Riddell[31] (4), third son of James[30] (4), was styled "of London Stubbs," in the County of Norfolk. He was a most accomplished youth, and an officer of great promise in the second troop of Horse Grenadier Guards. He fell in a duel, April 23, 1783 ; the circumstances, copied from the *Gentleman's Magazine*, are as follows : " A duel was fought between Mr. George Riddell of the Horse Grenadiers, and Mr. Cunningham of the Scots Greys. Both of these gentlemen belonged formerly to the Scots Greys, and had differed at play. Mr. Riddell had challenged Mr. Cunningham, which challenge was declined ; but many of the gentlemen reviving at intervals that circumstance, Mr. Cunningham found it necessary for the full restoration of his honor, that he should call upon Mr. Riddell. This appeal Mr. Riddell considering out of season, declined attending to, till he had consulted his fellow-officers, who agreed there was no obligation on him to answer Mr. Cunningham. This being their determination, Mr. Cunningham resolved upon forcing him to the point, and meeting him accidentally at Mr. Christie's, their agent, spit in his face. Mr. Riddell, observing that this was a fresh insult, he should take notice of it, and took his departure. He then immediately proceeded to make a few arrangements in his affairs ; but before he had completed them, he received a billet from Mr. Cunningham, reminding him of the affront he had passed upon him, and declaring his readiness to give him satisfaction. This note coming while the wafer was yet wet to the hands of Sir James

Jo.^s Milles Riddell

Riddell, who was under some apprehenson of his son's situation, opened it, and having read it, closed it without taking any notice of its contents more than providing in consequence of it, the assistance of several surgeons of the first ability. The meeting was fixed, they were both punctual, Mr. Riddell attended by Captain Topham, of the Horse Grenadiers, and Mr. Cunningham by Captain Cunningham, of the Sixty-ninth Regiment of Foot. Eight paces were first measured by the seconds, and then the contending parties took their ground. They tossed up for the first fire, and Mr. Riddell won. He then fired, and shot Mr. Cunningham under the right breast, the ball passing as is supposed through the ribs, and lodging on the left side near the back. The moment Cunningham received the shot, he reeled, but did not fall; he opened his waistcoat and declared he was mortally wounded. Mr. Riddell still remained on his ground, when Mr. Cunningham, after a pause of two minutes, declared he would not be taken off the field, till he had fired at his adversary; he then presented his pistol, and shot Mr. Riddell in the groin, when he immediately fell and was carried in a coach to Mr. Topham's, where he lingered until seven o'clock on Thursday morning, and then expired." After four hours' sitting, the coroner's jury brought in a verdict of manslaughter.

THIRTY-SECOND GENERATION.

Sir James-Milles Riddell[82] (5), eldest son of Thomas[81] (5), succeeded his grandfather. He was Justice of the Peace, and Doctor of Law for the County of Argyle. He married Mary, daughter of Sir Richard Brooke, Bart., of Newton Priory, County of Chester, and had issue, of whom hereafter. Sir James died at Strontian,* in 1861, and was succeeded by his son, of whom more hereafter.

Campbell-Drummond Riddell[82] (1), second son of Thomas[81] (5), was born Jan. 9, 1796; married in Ceylon, in April, 1830, Caroline-Stuart, daughter of the Hon. John-Rodney Stuart, by his wife, Lady Louisa Stafford, and had issue, of whom hereafter. He was Colonial Secretary of New South Wales. Died in Feb. 1859, aged 62 years.

Christiana-Drummond Riddell[82] (1), eldest daughter of Thomas[81] (5), of whom no particulars.

Mary-Milles-Geva Riddell[82] (1), second daughter of Thomas[81] (5), of whom no particulars.

Sarah-Burden Riddell[82] (1), third daughter of Thomas[81] (5), was married in 1835, to Maj. J. C. Young, of the Seventy-ninth Regiment.

---

* STRONTIAN. — The residence of Sir James-Milles Riddell, Baronet of Ardnamurchan, is surrounded by dressed and planted groves. The neat slated cottages of the village, substantialy built of granite, and sometimes adorned with parasitic plants, contrast strongly with some turf huts, with which they are intermingled, and indicate the neighborhood of a resident proprietor. These cottages were erected for the use of the miners employed in the celebrated Strontian Mines, and the huts previously in existence were purged from their offensiveness, and dressed into comparative beauty; a complete moral change was introduced into the village by Sir James Riddell and his lady; they insisted on cleanliness in and out of doors, and as the hand readily obeys the will, the girls soon caught the spirit of the lesson, and were not only neat and tidy themselves, but carried the same principle into their fathers' homes. About the date of the Revolution, the manufacture of straw plait was introduced by the proprietor, as means of useful employment for the females, and the improvement of the condition of the whole population. There are considerable lead mines on the estate, but I believe they are not worked at present. Strontian is 25 miles in length, by 10 miles in width, and comprises 40,099 acres, inhabited mostly by shepherds, miners, crofters, and farm hands.

Eleanor-Frazer Riddell[22] (1), fourth daughter of Thomas[21] (5), of whom no particulars.

Margaret Riddell[22] (1), fifth daughter of Thomas[21] (5), of whom no particulars.

THIRTY-THIRD GENERATION.

Sir Thomas-Milles Riddell[23] (6), eldest son of James[22] (5), was born Dec. 25, 1822; succeeded his father as third Baronet, in 1861, and is Justice of the Peace, Magistrate, and Doctor of Law for the Counties of Argyle and Inverness; was formerly lieutenant of King's Dragon Guards, and captain of the Perth Militia. He married in 1851, Mary-Anna, daughter of John Hodgson, Esq., of St. Petersburgh. No issue. He has been in Parliament. His heir presumptive, his cousin, of whom hereafter. He is a gentleman of fine personal appearance. See portrait in this book. Residence, Strontian, Argyleshire, Scotland. He died in 1883.

Richard-Brooke Riddell[23] (3), second son of James[22] (5), was born in 1825, and died in 1832.

Mary-Brooke-Geva Riddell[23] (2), daughter of James[22] (5), died in the year 1823.

Mary-Augusta Riddell[23] (3), a daughter of James[22] (5), was married in 1852, to the Rev. H. Cunliffe, Vicar of Shifnal.

Lieut. Rodney-Stuart Riddell[23] (1), a son of Campbell[22] (1), was born in 1838, and is an officer in the Seventieth Foot Regiment. He is heir presumptive of Sir Thomas, his cousin.

Thomas-Milles-Stratford Riddell[23] (7), a son of Campbell[22] (1), was born Jan. 22, 1832.

RIDDELLS OF ENFIELD, ENGLAND.

[KINGLASS BRANCH.]

Col. Andrew Riddell[1] (1), was second son of George (2)*, of the family denominated Riddells of Kinglass, Scotland; he was appointed lieutenant of the Sixty-sixth Regiment of Foot, April 19, 1789; captain, Dec. 4, 1802; captain Fiftieth Foot, May 25, 1803; major by brevet, Dec. 10, 1807, and lieutenant-colonel, June 4, 1814. He was many years on the staff in different parts of England, as an Assistant Quartermaster General. He died at his seat at Enfield, Nov. 16, 1825, leaving issue.

SECOND GENERATION.

John-Rignald Riddell[2] (1), a son of Andrew[1] (1), was of Byculla House, Enfield, and Speacomb Place, Devon. He wrote the author of this book, just as he was to sail for the continent, and promised that, on his return home, where he could have access to his family papers, he would provide full records of his family, but for some unknown reason has made no reply to subsequent letters of inquiry.

---

* Andrew Riddell, the first of Enfield, was the second son of Capt. George Riddell, of Kinglass, and his wife Christiana, daughter of Andrew Patterson, and brother of James, the first of Ardnamurchan.

Jane Riddell[2] (1), only daughter of Andrew[1] (1), of Enfield, was married Jan. 14, 1773, to Robert-Sadlier Moody, Esq., of Asply Guise. She died Oct. 10, 1825, and was buried at St. Mary-le-Bone. Mr. Moody was a commissioner of Her Majesty's Victualling-board; he was born March 21, 1744, died Nov. 9, 1825, and was buried at St. Mary-le-Bone. Rev. Henry-Riddell Moody was a son of Robert.

THIRD GENERATION.

Rignald-Charles Riddell[3] (1), second son of John[2] (1), was married Sept. 8, 1862, to Maria-Isabella, eldest daughter of Augustus-Charles Skymer, Esq., late major of the Sixteenth Lancers. The marriage was at Priestbury.

Walter-Kenneys Riddell[3] (1), third son of John[2] (1), of Enfield, Middlesex, died at Brussels, in 1849.

RIDDELLS OF ROXBURGHSHIRE, SCOTLAND.

[CREATED BARONETS MAY 12, 1628.]

(see p. 45 for start of lineage; p. 48 for Philip, father of this line)

Gervasius de Rydale[1] (1), a son of Philip[9] (1), of that family whose genealogy will be found in this work under the designation of "Riddells of Ardnamurchan, Scotland" (which see), accompanied David, Prince of Cumberland, into Scotland* early in the twelfth century, and became so great a favorite that he was appointed the first High Sheriff of Roxburghshire, and received grants of lands there as a reward for services faithfully performed. He must have been a very influential man, for he was a constant attendant on royalty, as shown by crown charters to which he was a witness, and especially that celebrated document, the "*Inquisito Principis Davidi*," one of the most ancient records in Scotland, being dated as early as A. D. 1116. Gervasius married Christiana de Soulis, and by her had issue, of whom hereafter. His wife was a liberal donor to Jedburgh monastery, and Gervasius, when he was advanced in life, assumed the ecclesiastical garb, and died at Jedburgh in the odor of sanctity. This was a prevailing custom and considered a great privilege, namely, that those who had led a secular and a sinful life sought to atone for the past by dying in a monastery; this practice was also followed by many whose lives had been peaceful and blameless, a manifest reverence in religion, although a religion of error.

Walter de Ridale[1] (1), a son of Philip[9] (1), who was son of Galfridus Ridel of France, and brother of Gervasius, before mentioned, accompanied Prince David to Scotland, and like his brothers, enjoyed the friendship and patronage of royalty. He was a witness to crown and other charters of importance, but that to himself, from King David I, of the

---

* Sir Walter Scott says tradition carries the history of this family to a point extremely remote, and is sanctioned by the discovery of two stone coffins, one containing a pot with ashes and arms, dated A. D. 727; the other dated A. D. 936, and filled with the bones of a man of gigantic size.

One writer says Gervaise Ridale received from Earl Henry, son of David, King of Scotland, a grant of lands called Prenwentsete, now Primside, near Yetholm, about three miles from the English border. *(early history begins p. 34)*

Followed by Riddells of Somerset, New Jersey pp. 297 - Riddles of Hamilton County, OH p. 309

lands of Wester Lilliesleaf, in Roxburghshire, eclipsed them all, being the most ancient charter known from a king to a layman. This charter was granted between 1120 and 1153; it included lands called Whittun, near the Cheviot Hills, the lands to be held of the crown, "*per servitium unius militis sicut unus baronum meorum vicinorum suorum.*" Another authority gives the date of the charter as 1112, confirming possessions to "*Walterus de Ridal de terris de Lilliesleaf et dimidum de Estetho* (or Chetto), *et Whittunes tenen de Rege per servitium unius militis, sicut unus Baronum nostrovum, coram Andræ Episcopo de Catanis, Waltero Filio Allansi et Ricardo de Moravillo.*" This ancient document became so frail by lapse of time that it was legally copied during a court held at Jedburgh, by order of Lord Gray, Justice General of Scotland, in 1556. Nisbit, the antiquary and herald, who flourished in the early part of the last century drew the copy. These lands were subsequently denominated the Baronies of Riddell and Whittun, in part from the possession, and the latter, "*Domini de Riddell and Whittunus.*" The charter styles Walter a sheriff, and confirms to him all the lands of which his brother Gervasius died possessed. This Walter married Ethrida de Percy, sister to the Lord of Oxenham, and having no issue was succeeded by his brother, of whom hereafter. Walter died about the year 1150.

    Sir Auskittel de Ridale[1] (1), son of Philip[2] (1), of the house of Ridel, or Rydale, denominated "of Ardnamurchan" in this work, succeeded his brother Walter, before mentioned. His name is spelled in ancient documents, Anschittal, Auskittil, Anschittil, and Oscittal. The lands of his brother Walter were derived by will, and confirmed by a bull from Pope Adrian IV, dated 8th April, 1155. The bull runs thus: —
"*Adrianus Episcopus, servus servorum Dei, Auskittel Riddell militi, solotem et Apostolicum Benedictionem, sub Beati Petri et nostri protectione suscepimus specialiter ac quæ Walterus de Riddell testamentum suum ante obitum suum faciens tibi nosciter reliquisse, viz., villas de Whittunus, Lilliesclive, Braeheba, etcetera bona a quibuscunque tibi juste colate, nos authoritate sedis Apostolicæ integre confirmamus. Datum Beneventi Septimo ides Aprilis.*" There is another bull from Pope Alexander III, dated 7th of June, 1160, confirming the will of the said Walter de Ridale, bequeathing to his brother Auskittel the lands of Lilliesclives and Whittuns, and ratifying the bargain between Auskittel and Huctrudes ⁄concerning the church at Lilliesclives, in consequence of the mediation of Malcolm II, and confirmed by a charter from that monarch. One authority says, "Oscitel Ridal having returned to his native land with consent of King Malcom Canmore, gave his lands of Cranstown, Preston, and others to his son Hugo (Hugh), who in the year 1110 bestowed the church of Cranstown and certain lands in the barony, to the monastery of Selkirk, which was founded by Prince David during the reign of his brother, Alexander I. This monastery was afterwards transferred to Kelso when David succeeded to the throne." This writer says, "Ocitel married Elena, daughter to Robert de Morville, lord of Riddesdale, in Northumberland, and by her had several sons." His wife seems to have been a sister to Jordanus le Fleming. Auskittel died in 1180, and was succeeded by his eldest son, of whom hereafter. Sir Auskittel was a witness to a charter of confirmation granted to the monks of Kelso in 1159, by Malcolm IV, the grandson of David I. His title represented knighthood.

    Ralph de Ridale[1] (1), a son of Philip (1), and brother of Gervasius and Auskittel, was a donor to Jedburgh Abbey.

SECOND GENERATION.

Walter de Ridale[2] (2), eldest son and heir of Auskittel[1] (1), succeeded his father in the year 1180. He married Guynolda, daughter of Earl Gospatrick, and had issue *two* sons, of whom hereafter.

Hugh de Ridale[2] (1), second son of Auskittel[1] (1), was ancestor of the family denominated "Riddells of Cranstown-Riddell," a distinguished baronial family that flourished about two centuries and ended in heirs female in 1357, the daughter of the last proprietor, Isabella Rydell, having been the wife of John Murray. This family were created baronets, *long* previous to the "Riddells of Riddell" Roxburghshire, and gave their name to their lands which were held of the crown. This Hugh was one of the hostages for the ransom of King William after his capture at the battle of Alnwick, A. D. 1174. See "Riddells of Cranstown."

Jordanus de Ridale[2] (1), third son of Auskittel[1] (1), and brother of the preceding, became ancestor of the family in Northumberland, now denominated "of Felton and Swinburn." See history of this family. Jordanus was named for his uncle Jordanus le Fleming, and was witness to a charter from King William to the Abbey of Dunfermline, together with David, the king's brother, Nicholas the Chancellor, and Robert de Quincey.

THIRD GENERATION.

Sir Patrick de Riddell[3] (1), eldest son of Walter[2] (2), married Christiana, daughter to Eustace de Vescie, by Margaret, illegitimate daughter to King William the Lion, by whom he acquired the lands of Sprouston, for William de Riddell, son of Sir Patrick, is witness to a charter granted by John de Vescie to William de Vescie, "*Dominus de Sprouston de Nova Tirva de Moli,*" and is there described as son to Christian, daughter of Margaret. After succeeding to his estates he made donations to the Abbey of Melrose, and to the monks serving God there; his wife, or widow, confirmed her husband's donations. Christian, his wife, was a member of that border family of de Vescie, of whom one was a feudal lord, appointed to enforce the observance of Magna Charta; her grandfather, "William the Lion," king of Scotland, brother of Malcolm IV, so surnamed from having introduced the lion as the armorial bearing of Scotland; and from this emblem the head of the Herald's Office in Edinburgh is called "Lion-King-at-arms." Sir Patrick had issue *three* sons, of whom hereafter. Sir Patrick was knighted.

FOURTH GENERATION.

Walter de Riddell[4] (2), eldest son of Patrick[3] (1), succeeded as his father's heir, and married a daughter of Hugh de Giffard, "*Dominus de Yester,*" and had issue *two* sons, of whom hereafter. He seems to have been a pious churchman, for he not only confirmed his father's donations to the convent of Melrose, but gave many benefactions himself, not only to the monks of Melrose, but to those of Kelso.

William de Riddell[4] (1), second son of Patrick[3] (1), married Matilda Corbett, and received from his father at the time of his alliance with that lady, a part of his lands at Whittun; but he died without children, and the lands returned to the head of the family.

Gaufred de Riddell[4] (1), third son of Patrick[3] (1), obtained a part of his father's lands, from which he gave many donations to the monks of Kelso, in the reign of Alexander II. No account of a wife or children.

5

FIFTH GENERATION.

Sir William de Riddell[5] (2), eldest son of Walter[4] (2) and his wife Giffard, was knighted at a very early age by Alexander II. He succeeded to his father's property, and married Isabella, who, with himself, granted a considerable estate to the monks of Melrose about the year 1255, by a charter witnessed by their son William, which charter proves the succession as follows: " *Uxor Wilhelmi de Riddell de alia bovata terræ in territorio de Whittun quam pater meus Wilhelmus, parsona de Hunam, emit a Ganfredo Coco,*"—the deed being made "*Pro salute animæ Domini Patricii de Riddell, and Walter, filii ejus, et Wilhelmi, sponci mei.*" It was witnessed by five members of the family which proves four successive descents. The charter translated reads as follows: "Isabella, wife of William of Riddell, gives this out of pasture land in the territory of Whittun, which my father, William, parson of Hunam, bought from Ganfred Coke, for the salvation of the soul of Sir Patrick de Riddell and Walter, his son, and William my spouse."

Patrick de Riddell[5] (2), second son of Walter[4] (2), has left no record of marriage or inheritance.

SIXTH GENERATION.

William de Riddell[6] (3), eldest son of William[5] (2), succeeded his father in the family estates. He was compelled to swear fealty to King Edward I, when he overran Scotland, and is particularly mentioned in the year 1296; but this laird died without issue, and was succeeded by his brother, of whom hereafter.

Galfridus de Riddell[6] (1), second son of William[5] (2), succeeded his brother William, before mentioned, and made many donations to the religious houses of Kelso and Melrose, during the reign of Alexander III. He died about the year 1325, and was succeeded by his son, of whom hereafter. This ancient family name seems to be handed down as proof that this branch of the family was directly connected with that of Angoulesme and Piragord, in France.

SEVENTH GENERATION.

Sir William de Riddell[7] (4), son of Galfridus[6] (1), succeeded his father in the family estates, and received the honor of knighthood at the hand of his king, David Bruce, in whose reign he is mentioned in many of the chartularies and chronicles. He died in the reign of Robert II, and was succeeded by his son, of whom hereafter.

Sir Robert de Riddell[7] (1), probably a brother of the preceding, was a witness to a charter to Kelso Abbey, of land in Mow; and was cautioner for Mow of Mains, who was a hostage in England on account of border disturbances.

Richard de Riddell[7] (1), probably a brother of the preceding, was a witness to two charters to John Kerr, of Auldtownburn; dated respectively in 1357 and 1358. There is no record to prove that these last two Riddells had wives or children; nor that they ever held family property. Their names were found, as above associated, on documents in the charter chest at Fleurs.

EIGHTH GENERATION.

Quintin de Riddell[8] (1), a son of William[7] (4), succeeded his father. He was certainly in possession in 1420, when a Court of Inquisition was held, and the Lilliesleaf lands were then called Riddell, though after that date the old favorite name sometimes crops up. The family surname, however, had been regularly and officially given to the Lilliesleaf property (Whittun continuing as originally), deriving the baronial character from the tenure of the first charter by David I to Walter; and hence the origin of the local name of Riddell, as denoting an estate that previously was not Scotch or known in Scotland. Quintin had a son who seems to have married and had issue, but died before his father; hence the succession fell to a grandson, of whom hereafter. There was a daughter, however, who married to John Scott, of Harden. Quintin was a new name in the family, and from whence derived does not appear, though the name of a saint in the Roman calendar.

TENTH GENERATION.

James Riddell[10] (1), a grandson of Quintin[8] (1), succeeded to the family lands as Laird of Riddell and Whittun, as early as 1498. He had a brother, and son, his successor, of whom hereafter. It appears, from documents found in Edinburgh, that this James was served heir to his grandfather, Quintin, at Jedburgh, the 4th of May, 1471. He married Margaret, daughter of Sir James Lindsay, and besides his successor, before mentioned, he had *two* daughters.

Thomas Riddell[10] (1), was a grandson of Quintin[8] (1), and brother of James, previously mentioned. I find no record of a family or inheritance for this man.

ELEVENTH GENERATION.

John Riddell[11] (1), son of James[10] (1) and Margaret Lindsay, his wife, succeeded his father, and was infeft in the barony of Riddell in 1510. He granted a precept infefting Patrick, Earl Bothwell, in a part of some lands in Lilliesleaf in 1534, which he held of the Laird of Riddell. John died in 1542, and was succeeded by his grandson.

Margaret Riddell[11](1), eldest daughter of James[10] (1), married to Walter Scott of Harden.

Christian Riddell[11] (1), second daughter of James[10] (1), married to Walter Scott of Harden, nephew to the last named.

TWELFTH GENERATION.

Walter Riddell[12] (4), eldest son of John[11] (1), and his apparent heir married Jane ——, and died before his father, leaving issue a son, who succeeded his grandfather.

George Riddell[12] (1), a son of John[11] (1), is particularly mentioned in a legal transaction upon record affecting him.

John Riddell[12] (2), a son of John[11] (1), was denominated "of Robine." I find no other account of this man.

William Riddell[12] (5), youngest son of John[11] (1), probably died when young, as I find no other mention of his name.

THIRTEENTH GENERATION.

Walter Riddell[12] (5), eldest son of Walter[12] (4), succeeded his grandfather, as previously mentioned, and was styled "of that ilk," or "de odem." He married Mariotta, daughter of Sir James Pringle, of Galashiels, A. D. 1543. He died in the beginning of the reign of James VI, and left issue *three* sons, of whom hereafter.

FOURTEENTH GENERATION.

Walter Riddell[14] (6), eldest son and heir of Walter[13] (5), was served to his inheritance in the year 1588. He married a daughter of Sir George

Ramsey of Dalhousie, by whom he had a son and successor, of whom hereafter.

Robert Riddell[14] (2), second son of Walter[12] (5), received a considerable portion of his father's lands at Minto, and became ancestor of the " Riddells of Minto-Riddell."

William Riddell[14] (6), youngest son of Walter[12] (5), received a portion of his father's landed-estates ; no other mention.

FIFTEENTH GENERATION.

Andrew Riddell[15] (2), son of Walter[14] (6), was served heir to his father in 1592, obtaining a charter March 24, 1595. He married first Miss Pringle, daughter of James Pringle, of Galashiels and Smailholm, his cousin, and after her death he espoused Violette, daughter of William Douglas, Esq., of Pumpherston, West-Lothian. He had issue by both wives, of whom hereafter. Andrew was a man of much importance, and having acquired Haining (signifying an enclosed grass-field) from the Scotts, the first possessors of that beautiful estate, held large territorial possessions, and was called the "Baron of Riddell." Though lordly in his possessions, he must have been a man of remarkable humility, for he was offered a baronetcy, which he declined. Andrew died in 1632, and was buried in the ancient "Riddell aisle," in the old Lilliesleaf church-yard, where his monuments may still be seen bearing the following inscription in Latin : "Here lies Andrew Riddell (de odem), who died at the age of 82, on the 4th of March, A. D. 1632. Long live the memory of the dead. The hours fly." On the same stone is the following : "His sorrowing wife, Violette Douglas, has erected this monument to the memory of her most beloved husband, Andrew Riddell, Baron of Riddell, who died in the hope of the resurrection of the just." There are coats-of-arms on the monument. The will of the laird in 1552 proves the old burial place of the family, called the "Riddell aisle," to have been in the choir of the church. There is another stone, no doubt belonging to the family, with no inscription save the words "Pray for the soul." .The present church, a plain structure, stands outside the church-yard wall; it was erected in 1771.

SIXTEENTH GENERATION.

Sir John Riddell[16] (3), eldest son of Andrew[15] (2), by his wife Pringle, was a man of considerable talent, and obtained the honor of a baronetcy, which was refused by his father ; this was conferred on the 14th of May, 1628, about three years after the institution of the order in Scotland. This John was also knighted at an early age. He married first, Agnes, daughter of Sir John Murray, of Blackbarrony, by Margaret, daughter of Sir Alexander Hamilton, of Innerwick, the oldest branch of the Hamiltons. This alliance connected the house of Riddell with many of the most illustrious families in Scotland, for Margaret had a sister married to Sir Robert Kerr, the first Earl of Ancrum, another sister to Sir Robert Halhet, of Pitferran, a third to Patrick Murray, of Phillipshaugh, a fourth to Sir Patrick Scott, of Thirlstane, besides two others married to Sir James Douglas, of Colphople, and to Veitch of Dawick. Sir John married secondly, Jane, daughter of Sir James Anstruther, of Anstruther, relict of James Douglas, commendator of Melrose, who was second son of the Earl of Morton. By the second marriage Sir John had a daughter whose name does not appear, married to David Barclay, Esq., of Colernie, in the County of Fife. At his creation in 1628, Sir John received a part of a

"THE HAINING,"

FROM THE SOUTH-WEST.

territory in Nova Scotia,* under the name of the "Barony of New Riddell." I have not learned what disposition the family made of this land. Sir John had issue *six* children, of whom hereafter.

William Riddell[16] (7), second son of Andrew[16] (2), inherited the landed estate known as "Newhouse," and became ancestor of the "Riddells of Newhouse," about whom there has been so many opinions expressed by genealogists. See article in this book under above designation. He also got a charter of Muselee in 1618, and became ancestor of that branch of the family.

James Riddell[16] (2), third son of Andrew[16] (2), was denominated "of Maybole." I have no other account of this man, but may presume that he became ancestor of some of the junior branches of the Roxburghshire Riddells — possibly was ancestor of the late Robert Riddell, father of Henry-Scott Riddell, the Shepherd Poet of Tiviothead. I have not found the "missing link," but the families always claimed relationship.

Walter Riddell[16] (7), fourth son of Andrew[16] (2), received from his father the lands of Hartride. I have no other mention.

Andrew Riddell[16] (3), was a "favorite son" of Andrew[16] (2), by Violette Douglas, his second wife, and received from his father the beautiful estate called "Haining" in Selkirkshire. This property continued in this branch of the family till the beginning of the seventeenth century, when it was sold to the second son of Pringle of Clifton. Andrew's monument is in the "Riddell aisle," bearing the inscription, "whose life was short and good." His wife was a Stewart of Traquair, and her husband having died young she married secondly Sir William Douglas, ancestor of the Marquis of Queensbury. Andrew left one son, his successor. See "Riddells of Haining."

Margaret Riddell[16] (2), eldest daughter of Andrew[16] (2), married, Robert Rutherford, Esq., of Edgerston.

Isabel Riddell[16] (1), third daughter of Andrew[16] (2), married to Robert Kerr, a brother of Sir Thomas, of Cavers. Two of her sisters married respectively, John Bailie, ancestor of the Baillies of Wellerstain, and Sir John Scott, of Goldielands, while the last and fifth sister lived and died unmarried.

Jean Riddell[16] (1), a daughter of Andrew[16] (2), was born in 1600, and died a maiden lady in 1660. She was buried in the Abbey burying-ground at Jedburgh,† where her monument stands, bearing the following inscription: "Here lies a religious and virtuous gentlewoman, Jean Riddell, daughter of Sir Andrew Riddell of that ilk, who died in the year of God, MDCLX, and of her age 60."

---

* John Riddell, of New Riddell, received a grant of 16,000 acres of land in the Island of Anticostl, in the Gulf of St. Lawrence, dated May 14, 1628, and unlike many other baronets took seizen of his grant — i. e., took it up, but does not appear to have made any use of it. Presumed to have been forfeited by the effluxions of time. — *Nova Scotia Records.*

Baronets of Scotland charge their coat armour with the arms of Nova Scotia, the order having been founded to promote the plantation of that province.

† JEDBURGH ABBEY was founded by King David I, about 1180 A. D. Of this once magnificent structure, the church, — two hundred and thirty feet long, — alone remains. The abbey was rifled and burned in 1523 by the Earl of Surrey, and again by the Earl of Hertford, in 1544. To preserve the beautiful abbey from complete ruin, it was repaired with judicious regard to its ancient architectural designs, a few years ago. This spot is every year visited by hundreds of travelers. I think the stone to the memory of Jean Riddell was discovered by Walter Riddell-Carre, Esq., late of Cavers Carre.

"She lived a holy life,
To Christ resigned her breath.
Her soul is now with God,
Triumphing over death!"

SEVENTEENTH GENERATION.

Sir Walter Riddell[17] (8), eldest son of Sir John[16] (3), was knighted by King Charles, during his father's lifetime. He succeeded to the baronial estates, and married a very p ous woman, Janet Rigg, the daughter of a worthy and godly man, William Rigg, of Aithernie, Fifeshire, by whom he had *five* sons and *two* daughters. Janet Rigg, Lady Riddell, was not only pious, but accomplished, and her father was a man of high principle and character, and moreover extremely wealthy. Mr. Rigg was fined £50,000 Scots, for opposing the introduction of the Five Articles at Perth, by James IV, and also suffered imprisonment in Blackness Castle. His sister, the aunt of Lady Riddell, Miss Catherine Rigg, who married Douglas, of Cavers, was the celebrated Covenanter, and the ladies were descendants of Dr. John Row, of Perth, John Knox's coadjutor. Walter was succeeded by his son.

Sir William Riddell[17] (8), second son of Sir John[16] (3), was made a knight at an early age, and became governor of Desborough, in Holland. He married Windelina Van Bucham, by whom he had a daughter, married to Nicholas Bowyer, Esq.; her name was Anna-Catherine; also other issue.

Capt. John Riddell[17] (4), third son of Sir John[16] (3), was an officer in the service of Holland.

Capt. Thomas Riddell[17] (2), fourth son of Sir John[16] (3); was also an officer in the service of Holland.

EIGHTEENTH GENERATION.

Sir John Riddell[18] (5), eldest son and successor of Sir Walter[17] (8), was third Baronet of Riddell. He was called in the family Sir John Bluebeard, because he had four wives, not at once of course, like Brigham Young. He married Dec. 9, 1659, to Agnes, daughter of Gideon Scott, of Harden, who dying without issue, he married secondly in November, 1661, to Helen, daughter of Sir Alexander Morrison, of Preston Grange, by Jean his wife, daughter of Robert, Lord Boyd. By this union there were a son and daughter, of whom hereafter. He married thirdly, in October, 1669, Margaret Swinton, of Swinton, by whom he had a son and a daughter. He married fourthly, Mrs. Watt, of Rosehill, whose maiden name had been Hepburn. Sir John inherited his mother's religious zeal, and became a zealous Covenanter, and suffered imprisonment for his defence of civil and religious liberty and his non-conformity. He was at this time a member of parliament for Roxburghshire, and was prosecuted for defending his brother, who was a distinguished preacher. He got a remission in 1687, from the king, and died in 1700, a very short time after his fourth marriage, and was succeeded by his son, of whom hereafter.

William Riddell[18] (9), second son of Walter[17] (8), had bestowed upon him the lands of Friarshaw, in Dumfrieshire, and became ancestor of the "Riddells of Glen-Riddell," in that county. He married Elizabeth, daughter of Capt. Francis Wauchope, of the Middey family. See "Glen-Riddell."

Rev. Archibald Riddell[18] (1), third son of Walter[17] (8), the second Baronet, was educated for the church, and became ancestor of the "Riddells of Granton," whom see.

Believed also to be a Walter Riddell, brother in this generation. He appears with Rev. Archibald in New Jersey records on p. 298 / Family genealogy research shows a Walter, but not this page/book here. This book does assume he is a brother though.

RIDDELLS OF ROXBURGHSHIRE, SCOTLAND,　71

Thomas Riddell[18] (3), fourth son of Walter[17] (8), married to Agnes Scott. No other mention.

Andrew Riddell[18] (4), fifth son of Walter[17] (8), married, and had issue *one* daughter, of whom hereafter.

Margaret Riddell[18] (3), a daughter of Walter[17] (8), married to the Rev. Geo. Semple, of Jedburgh; another authority says, "C. Semple, Esq."

Allison Riddell[18] (1), a daughter of Walter[17] (8), married to George Home, Esq., of Barrendean; another authority says, "a brother of Sir William Scott, of Mourton." Possibly both.

Richard Riddell[18] (2), a son of Sir William[17] (8), of Holland.

Anna-Catherine Riddell[18] (1), a daughter of William[17] (8), married to Nicholas Bowyer, Esq.

NINETEENTH GENERATION.

Sir Walter Riddell[19] (9), eldest son of Sir John[18] (8), became the fourth baronet, and inherited the family estates. He married Margaret, daughter of John Watt, of Rosehill, who was also a daughter of his step-mother, and had issue *five* sons and *three* daughters. Sir Walter was a very godly man, and seems to have fully imbibed the piety of his father and grandmother, whose spirit and habits were characteristic of him. He was a great lover of the Scriptures, and was very zealous of their inter-pretation. He was once attending the preaching of his own son Robert, who was minister of Lilliesleaf, when thinking he was not presenting the claims and terms of the gospel correctly, he stopped him with the words, "Robert, that won't do." He was recommended to stop so many people coming upon his property, but his answer was, "The earth is the Lord's." In his days the public road passed close to the back of Riddell House, and its nearness to the kind-hearted baronet's mansion, must have induced a good many "seekers," as beggars were then called, to intrude upon his premises. He died in 1747, and was succeeded by his second son.

Christian Riddell[19] (2), eldest daughter of John[18] (8), married Henry, eldest son of Sir Patrick Nisbet of Dean.

William Riddell[19] (10), youngest son of Sir John[18] (8), died in 1700, *sine prole.* His mother was Margaret Swinton, the third wife of Sir John Riddell.

Margaret Riddell[19] (4), youngest daughter of Sir John[18] (8), was by his third wife, Margaret Swinton.

TWENTIETH GENERATION.

John Riddell[20] (9), eldest son of Walter[19] (9), was remarkable for his talents and accomplishments as an advocate, but predeceased his father at an early age, unmarried.

Sir Walter Riddell[20] (10), second son of Walter[19] (9), succeeded as fifth baronet, in consequence of his elder brother's predeceasing his father. He was in early life a merchant at Eyemouth, probably a dealer in fish and spirits, brandy being largely imported there. He married Jane, daughter of J. Turnbull, Esq., of Houndwood, near Eyemouth; it was a runaway marriage, but the lady had neither money nor rank; the rank was on Walter's side, but as he was at the time only a merchant, the Turn-bulls may have looked down upon him. He died in the year 1765, having had issue *five* sons and *one* daughter, of whom hereafter. He was suc-ceeded by his second son.

Thomas Riddell[20] (4), third son of Walter[19] (9), became ancestor of the "Riddells of Camieston," whose history consult.

William Riddell[20] (11), fourth son of Walter[19] (9), went to Bermuda, in the West Indies, and became ancestor of a small branch family, which soon became extinct in the male line. One of this family seems to have been an eminent physician, and wrote a medical thesis which showed a desire to do good.

Rev. Robert Riddell[20] (3), fifth son of Walter[19] (9), married Esther, daughter of Dr. John Riddell, of Edinburgh, his kinswoman, but had no issue. He was minister of Lilliesleaf, and was sometimes interrupted during his discourses by his father, the baronet, who was a very exact critic.

Elenor Riddell[20] (1), eldest daughter of Walter[19] (9), married to Robert Carre, Esq., of Cavers Carre.

Sarah Riddell[20] (1), second daughter of Walter[19] (9), married to John Forest.

Christian Riddell[20] (3), third daughter of Walter[19] (9), died young, and unmarried.

TWENTY-FIRST GENERATION.

Walter Riddell[21] (11), eldest son of Walter[20] (10), was a captain in the service of the States of Holland; died unmarried before his father, hence did not succeed.

Sir John Riddell[21] (10), second son of Walter[20] (10), succeeded as sixth baronet. Being second son, he was shipped off to Curaçoa, where he was a merchant, but coming home before his father's death, married Jane, daughter of James Buchanan, Esq., of Sunden, in the County of Bedford, to whose estates she succeeded on the death of her brother, Archibald Buchanan, Esq., in the year 1772. He died about three years after he succeeded to the title and estates, at Hamstead, in Middlesex, the 16th of April, 1768, leaving issue *three* sons, the youngest of whom was posthumous

Col. James Riddell[21] (2), third son of Walter[20] (10), was commissioned a lieutenant-colonel in the Dutch service. He was represented as " a fine-looking man." He died advanced in life, but unmarried, in 1804.

Andrew Riddell[21] (5), fourth son of Walter[20] (10), died unmarried.

Capt. Thomas Riddell[21] (5), fifth son of Walter[20] (10), became ancestor of the "Riddells of Beesborough," for an account of whom, see department in this book under that head.

Jane Riddell[21] (1), only daughter of Walter[20] (10), married to John Carre, Esq., of Cavers Carre, Roxburghshire.

TWENTY-SECOND GENERATION.

Sir Walter Riddell[22] (12), eldest son of Sir John[21] (10), succeeded his father in 1768, and died in the seventeenth year of his age, Feb. 7, 1784. He was succeeded by his brother.

Sir James-Buchanan Riddell[22] (3), second son of John[21] (10), was an officer in the First Regiment of Foot Guards, and was drowned at Brunswick while bathing in the river, Sept. 4th, 1784, only a few months after succeeding to the title and estates of the family. Succeeded by his brother.

Sir John-Buchanan Riddell[22] (3), third son of John[21] (10), succeeded his brother as ninth baronet in 1784. He married August 17, 1805, Frances, eldest daughter of Charles, Earl of Romney, and granddaughter, maternally, of the Earl of Egremont. He was a member of parliament

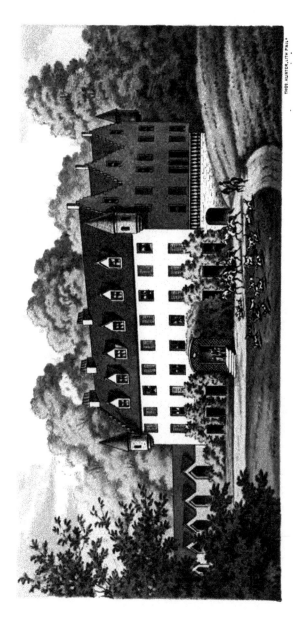

"RIDDELL HOUSE."

Roxburghshire, Scotland.

THOS. HUNTER, LITH. PHILA.

for the burghs of Selkirk and Lanark, and died in the prime of life, and in the midst of incomplete plans, April, 1819, aged 51 years, leaving issue *four* sons and *five* daughters, of whom hereafter. He was succeeded by his eldest son the present baronet, the tenth in succession. Sir John was one of the most devoted agriculturalists the country ever knew; but in carrying forward his improvements on an extensive scale, he seems to have been lavish in his outlay, and became so involved, that after his death the estate of " Riddell-Whittun," which had so long been in the possession of the old family, was sold. Many of the beautiful trees on the lawn and about the grounds were planted by Sir John, and many changes and improvements remain to prove his interest in, and passionate love for, agricultural pursuits.

He was a man of commanding person, and elegant though stiff manners, and as the representative of an old and long line of ancestry, he was doubly respected. His business habits were good, but his affairs became confused, and the property upon which he bestowed so much money was lost to his descendants. High farming and extensive improvements contributed to his troubles; but in pushing his gigantic schemes, he was a great benefactor of the working classes, to whom he gave extensive employment, and the present proprietor is reaping the rich benefits of Sir John's immense expenditure. As this article will close our immediate connection with the old estate so long held, it will be proper to give some description of Lilliesleaf at the time it passed out of the hands of the Riddell family. Lilliesleaf is a parish in the northwest division of Roxburgh-shire, bounded on the northwest by a part of Selkirkshire parish; on the north by Bowden; on the east by Ancrum; on the south by Minto, and a detached part of Selkirkshire; and on the west by Ashkirk. Its extreme length from east to west is five miles; its mean breadth is about two miles and a furlong; and its area is upwards of seven thousand acres. A small stream called Alewater, remarkable for the fine quality of its trout, forms for half a mile the southern boundary; flows three miles northeasterly through the interior, runs three miles debouchingly along the northern and eastern boundaries, and passes away eastward into Ancrum creek. Several broad, low ridges, and waving alternations of slope and valley, diversify the surface of the parish; and though all is capable of cultivation, and at one time subject to the plough, it is now distributed into nearly equal proportions of arable lands and pasture. About six hundred acres are planted, and about fifty are mossy and waste. The soil is partly light sand, partly clay, and partly a rich loam. Two marl-pits have given up much treasure to the arable land. At the death of Sir John Riddell, in 1819, his extensive lands, which had been nearly all disposed in arable farms, were laid out in grass. This is the place commemorated by Sir Walter Scott; in the lines: —

> " Ancient Riddells' fair domain,
> Where Ale, from mountains freed,
> Down from the lakes did raving come;
> Each wave was crested with tawny foam,
> Like the mane of a chestnut steed."

Although the family possessed the estate long enough to entitle the great poet to call it "ancient Riddell," their title did not sustain the highly complimentary note connection with the first line of the above verse. The Riddell family held possession from about 1120 to 1823, in all six hundred and seventy years. Scott endeavors to establish the family as domiciled at Riddell, long previous to the time they acquired it, and mentions the date on the aisle of the old churchyard as being 1110. There are memorials cut in the south wall, but they do not possess a sufficiently antiquated character to represent a period so far back, though these figures may have been re-cut in after times.   There was an ancient church or chapel on the Wester Lilliesleaf or Riddell estate, said to have stood near an old ash-tree not far from the last gate leading from the Eastern Lodge to the mansion-house, not far south from the old castle which stood in the wood a little above where the old Lilliesleaf road to Selkirk passed. At what period the ancient castle, which was probably a place of great strength and security, was built, it would be impossible to say; but it seems probable that the family erected it very soon after acquiring the property in the twelfth century.   It is also difficult to prove when the present "Riddell House" superseded the old castle as a residence, though it gives evidence of great antiquity.   When the present proprietor was preparing to enlarge the ancient house, he erected in the western side of the old mansion, an antiquated stone with the Riddell arms on one side of the shield, and what was supposed to be the arms of the Kerrs on the other side, though the stars are not on a chevron according to the regular cognizance.   This stone is evidently about four hundred years old, and represents an alliance between members of the families of Riddell and Kerr, which actually occurred about that date.   An arch was discovered at the same time, that gave evidence of great antiquity, especially the walls from their hardness, probably caused by using hot lime, as was common in olden times.   The aisle in the old church-yard, which was not reserved when the property was sold, but which was generously restored by the purchaser, was used as a burial-place for the family very early, but *how* early there is no authority to prove.   No doubt they were buried somewhere on the estate from their first settlement, probably at the first chapel, as bones have been dug up there in years past; but in process of time the aisle came to be used, in fact when it was part of the old church, which stood till 1771, the year of the erection of the present one.   The choir of the old church was just where the aisle of the present one now stands.   Whether this ancient church was the original one, cannot be known; but it was evidently a pre-reformation one, and it was thatched with broom, as was the custom in olden times.   "It is to be lamented," says one of the family in Scotland, "that at the sale of the fine old place, the name of Riddell, which was given to it by the family after themselves—a very unusual thing in the history of proprietors—had not been changed, and a new name awarded, or the old one of Wester Lilliesleaf restored.   I have no doubt that the several distinguished branches of the old family, whose ancestors for several centuries enjoyed an unmolested and unbroken possession of the dear old place, find its name now a source of melancholy and unpleasant reflection."

The widow of Sir John Riddell, the last family proprietor of Riddell, who was born Oct. 25, 1778, died July 1, 1868, at the great age of *ninety years*.   She was a woman of great character, and highly respected for her quiet manners and amiable deportment.   She was descended from Sir John Maisham, who had been called "the great Maisham of England."

TWENTY-THIRD GENERATION.

Sir Walter-Buchanan Riddell[22] (**13**), eldest son of John[22] (**11**), succeeded to the baronetcy at the death of his father in 1819. He was born at " Riddell House," Roxburghshire, in 1810 ; married in 1859, Alicia, youngest daughter of the late William Ripley, Esq., formerly of the Fifty-second Regiment. He was educated at Eton and Oxford ; took his degree of B. A. in 1831, that of M. A. in 1834. He was called to the bar at Lincoln's Inn in 1834 ; is now a magistrate for Kent, Northumberland ; judge of the Metropolitan County Courts, and late recorder of Maidstone. He has been a member of parliament. Sir Walter's seat is at Hepple, Northumberland, a property that came to the family from the Buchanans, said to be a beautiful place. He spends much of his time in London. As he has no issue, his heir presumptive is John-Walter, eldest son of Rev. John B. Riddell, who will probably eventually succeed. Sir Walter has manifested a deep interest in this book, and has very kindly assisted the author in many ways. In reply to an invitation to attend the family meeting held in Philadelphia in 1876, he says : " It would have much gratified and interested me, had it been in my power to have visited this proposed family gathering, and also to have witnessed the great exhibition now in progress at Philadelphia, to which Lady Riddell and I have received most kind and pressing invitations from old friends resident in that city. But I am sorry to say that my judicial duties in London prevent my leaving England, besides that I am rather old to begin with the ' New World,' as your mighty continent used to be called before the new career of the United States commenced one hundred years ago. I hope that your genealogical work, with reference to which I have had much interesting correspondence with you, is progressing satisfactorily, and that the proposed family gathering will secure the publication of a family history, in which, if I may presume to consider myself the head of the family, I may deem myself specially concerned and interested. I beg you to present my compliments and the expressions of my hearty good will to the president and gentlemen of the committee arranging the meeting, as well as to the members of the old family and its branches who may attend it, and also to express my great regrets that I am unable to join the assembly."

Rev. John-Charles-B. Riddell[23] (12), second son of John[22] (11), was born in 1814 ; married April 16, 1846, Frances-Sophia, daughter of the late George-James Chalmondly, Esq., and his wife, the Countess Dowager of Romney. He was educated at Eton ; M. A. of Christ Church, Oxford, and late Fellow of All Souls' College. He was rector of Harrietsham, Kent, and Hon. Canon of Canterbury. Mr. Riddell was his brother Walter's heir presumptive to the baronetcy ; he had issue *eight* children, of whom hereafter. Deceased.

Gen. Charles-James Riddell[23] (1), third son of John[22] (11), was born in 1816 ; married in 1847 (Feb. 11th), Mary, second daughter of Lieut.-Gen. Sir Hugh-Dalrymple Ross, K. C. B., and has issue a daughter. He bears the title R. A., C. B.

Gen. Henry-Philip-A. Riddell[23] (1), fourth son of John[22] (11), was born in 1819. I have no record of his marriage. He was educated at Eton and Haileybury college ; was formerly in the Bengal service, and a member of the Legislative Council of India ; is a magistrate for Northumberland. His services under the government have been recognized by the presentation of the medal styled the " Star of India,"[*]

---

[*] **DESCRIPTION OF THE "STAR OF INDIA "** — *The Star.* — Rays of gold issuing from a centre, having thereon a star in diamonds, resting upon a light blue enameled

the highest bestowed for civil services under the crown. He got a companionship and the designation of C. S. I. Mr. Riddell was in the "Old East India Company," and was at one time Postmaster-General of India. He has been a most useful public servant, a man of remarkable ability and energy of character. See his portrait in the group with his brother, Sir Walter, in this book. His seat is Whitefield House, Rothbury, Northumberland, in England, a place he rents of his brother, the baronet.

Frances-Jane Riddell[23] (1), eldest daughter of John[22] (11), was born Aug. 6, 1806, in Edinburgh, Scotland; died in 1869.

Harriet Riddell[23] (1), second daughter of John[22] (11), was born at Riddell House, Roxburghshire, Aug. 29, 1808.

Emily Riddell[23] (1), third daughter of John[22] (11), was born Nov. 19, 1808; married Dec. 21, 1843, to John Adams, Esq., a barrister-at-law (deceased), son of Mr. Sergeant Adams.

Jane Riddell[23] (2), fourth daughter of John[22] (11), was born subsequent to 1810, and before 1819. No other mention.

Charlotte-Mary Riddell[23] (1), youngest daughter of John[22] (11), was born subsequent to 1810, died in 1869.

TWENTY-FOURTH GENERATION.

John-Walter Riddell[24] (13), eldest son of John[23] (12), and his wife Frances-Sophia, was born March 14, 1849; married in August, 1874, Sarah-Isabel, youngest daughter of the late Robert Wharton, Esq., and has issue, of whom hereafter. He was educated at Eton, and Christ's Church, Oxford. He will eventually (should he outlive his uncle) succeed as eleventh baronet. He is in London with his uncle Walter.

Robert-George Riddell[24] (4), second son of John[23] (12), and his wife, Frances-Sophia, was born Sept. 15, 1854; lieutenant Sixtieth Rifles.

Charles-Sidney Riddell[24] (2), third son of John[23] (12), was born Aug. 30, 1858.

Henry-Edward Riddell[24] (2), fourth son of John[23] (12), was born Jan. 25, 1860; officer Royal Camanian Militia.

Frances-Mary Riddell[24] (2), eldest daughter of John[23] (12).

Mary-Amelia Riddell[24] (1), second daughter of John[23] (12).

Sophia-Anna Riddell[24] (1), third daughter of John[23] (12).

Margaret-Charlotte Riddell[24] (4), fourth daughter of John[23] (12).

Mary-Frances Riddell[24] (2), only daughter of Charles[23] (1).

TWENTY-FIFTH GENERATION.

Katherine Riddell[25] (1), eldest daughter of John[24] (13), born Nov. 25, 1875.

circular ribbon, tied at the ends, inscribed with the motto of the order, viz:— "Heaven's Light our Guide," also in diamonds. *The Collar*—Composed of the Lotus of India, of palm-branches, tied together in saltier. and of the united red and white rose. In the centre is an imperial crown; all richly enameled in gold, in their proper colors. *The Badge.*—An onyx cameo of Her Majesty's effigy, set in a perforated and ornamented oval, containing the motto of the order, "Heaven's Light our Guide," surmounted by a star, all in diamonds. The ribbon of the order is sky blue, having a narrow white band toward either side, and is worn from the right shoulder to the left side. *The Mantle.*—Light blue satin, lined with white, and fastened with a cordon of white silk, with blue and silver tassels, on the left side a representation of the Star of the order. This decoration is conferred upon persons who have, by service and conduct in the Indian Empire, merited the royal favor.

Olive-Frances Riddell[26] (1), second daughter of John[24] (13), born May 29, 1877.

Walter-Robert Riddell[25] (14), son of John[24] (13), born April 21, 1879 (as per books), "1883" as per his father's letter.

--------•◦•--------

RIDDELLS OF MUSELEE, SCOTLAND.

William Riddell[1] (1), a son of Andrew[15] (2), the powerful old baron and father of the first Baronet of Riddell, became ancestor of the "Riddells of Newhouse," and of the "Riddells of Muselee." The first property was bestowed by his father; that of Muselee was chartered to him in 1618, and a descendant acquired Bewlie, and both properties continued as a family possession. William married Bessie Ainsley and had issue, of whom hereafter.

SECOND GENERATION.

John Riddell[2] (1), a son of William[1] (1), succeeded to the property of Muselee and Bewlie and became representative of this branch family. He married first, Elizabeth Haliburton, and secondly, Grizel, daughter of Rev. P. Schew; by the latter he had *two* sons and *three* daughters.

THIRD GENERATION.

William Riddell[3] (2), eldest son of John[2] (1) and Grizel, his wife, predeceased his father when young.

Patrick Riddell[3] (1), second son of John[2] (1) and Grizel, his wife, succeeded as representative of this family to Muselee and Bewlie. He married Maria, daughter of Thomas Elliott, ancestor of the Elliotts of Beechwood, and by her had issue *two* sons and *three* daughters.

FOURTH GENERATION.

John Riddell[4] (2), eldest son of Patrick[3] (1) and his wife Maria, succeeded to the property and headship of this family. He married in 1706 Margaret, daughter of Walter Riddell, Esq., of Lilliesleaf, by whom he had *eight* sons and *three* daughters, of whom hereafter.

FIFTH GENERATION.

Patrick Riddell[5] (2), eldest son of John[4] (2), succeeded to the property and representation of this family, and married in 1752 Margaret, daughter of Charles Balfour, Esq., of Broadmeadows, and had issue *six* sons and a daughter.

Walter Riddell[5] (1), second son of John[4] (2).

Andrew Riddell[5] (1), third son of John[4] (2).

William Riddell[5] (3), fourth son of John[4] (2), settled at Berwick-on-Tweed. See "Riddells of Berwick."

Barbara Riddell[5] (1), eldest daughter of John[4] (2).

John Riddell[5] (3), fifth son of John[4] (2).

Alexander Riddell[5] (1), sixth son of John[4] (2).

James Riddell[5] (1), seventh son of John[4] (2).

Mary Riddell[5] (2), second daughter of John[4] (2).

Thomas Riddell[5] (1), eighth son of John[4] (2), settled at Berwick-on-Tweed. See "Riddells of Berwick."

SIXTH GENERATION.

Maj. Charles Riddell[6] (1), eldest son of Patrick[5] (2), succeeded to the estates and representation of this family, and was a major of militia. He was for many years chamberlain to the Duke of Buccleuch, at Branxholm; he died unmarried Dec. 11, 1849, aged 95 years, and was succeeded by his brother, of whom hereafter.

Walter Riddell[6] (2), second son of Patrick[5] (2), succeeded as representative of this family in 1849, at the death of his brother before mentioned. He married a Miss Summerville, and had issue *two* children, of whom hereafter. He was employed as a writer at Jedburgh; now dead.

SEVENTH GENERATION.

Mary Riddell[7] (1), a daughter of Walter[6] (1), was heiress and became representative of the family. She married George Hutton, Esq., son of George-William Hutton, Esq., of Carlton-on-Trent, by Frances, daughter of Bertram Mitford, Esq., of Mitford, in 1855. Mr. Hutton was born in 1807, succeeded in 1835, and assuming the additional name of Riddell became the representative of the family. His wife Mary died, and he married secondly, Hannah-Elizabeth, widow of J. O. Lambert, Esq., and after her death he married thirdly, in 1862, Janetta-Gonville Bromhead, Baroness, and has by the former, with other issue, a son, his successor. Mr. Hutton-Riddell is a magistrate for Notts, Carlton-on-Trent. His address was Newark Notts, Windham Club.

EIGHTH GENERATION.

Capt. George-William Hutton-Riddell[8] (1), eldest son of the late George-William Hutton, Esq., who assumed the additional name of Riddell when he married Mary Riddell, the heiress of Muselee, who died in 1871. He was born in 1836; succeeded his mother and assumed the name of Riddell in 1852; married in 1877 Lady Evelyn-Mary, second daughter of William, second Earl of Craven. Mr. Riddell was educated at Rugby; was late captain of the Sixteenth Lancers. Address, Muselee, Hawick, N. B., Newport Lodge, Melton Mowbray.

Edward-Mitford Hutton-Riddell[8] (1), second son of the late George Hutton, Esq., and Mary, his wife, who was the daughter of Walter Riddell, Esq., of Jedburgh, was born in 1845; married in 1872 Annie-Sophia, youngest daughter of Godfrey Tallents, Esq., of Newark Notts, and has issue a daughter. Mr. Riddell is a magistrate for Notts; his address, Carlton-on-Trent, Newark Notts, Windham Club, S. W.

RIDDELLS OF BERWICK-ON-TWEED.

William Riddell[1] (1), was the fourth son of John[4] (2) (see "Riddells of Muselee") and his wife Mary, daughter of Walter Riddell, Esq., of Lilliesleaf. He married Mary, daughter of Mark ——, and had issue, *three* sons, of whom hereafter. Mr. Riddell was a successful merchant at Berwick-on-Tweed.

Thomas Riddell[1] (1), was the eighth son of John[4] (2), and his wife, Mary Riddell (brother of the preceding). He married in February, 1766, Mary, daughter of Joseph Crosby, Esq., and had issue *six* children, of whom hereafter. Mr. Riddell was a prominent and wealthy merchant at Berwick-on-Tweed. He died on Nov. 10, 1803.

SECOND GENERATION.

John Riddell[2] (1), eldest son of William[1] (1), died young.
Mark Riddell[4] (1), second son of William[1] (1), died unmarried.
William Riddell[2] (2), third son of William[1] (1), married Anne Mark, but died without issue.

Katherine Riddell[2] (1), eldest daughter of Thomas[1] (1), married in February, 1803, to John Lowther, Esq., but died issueless.
Margaret Riddell[2] (1), second daughter of Thomas[1] (1), died when young, unmarried.
John Riddell[2] (2), eldest son of Thomas[1] (1), died unmarried.
Capt. Joseph-Crosby Riddell[2] (1), second son of Thomas[1] (1), was an officer in the army; died in 1833, unmarried.
George Riddell[2] (1), third son of Thomas[1] (1), died an infant.
Capt. George Riddell[2] (2), fourth son of Thomas[1] (1), married, Jan. 22, 1801, Elizabeth-Frances, daughter of Robert Edmerston, and had issue *eight* children, of whom hereafter. He was an officer in the army; died in October, 1823.

THIRD GENERATION.

Rev. Thomas Riddell[3] (2), eldest son of George[2] (2), was Fellow of Trinity College, Cambridge, England, and Vicar of Masham. He died Sept. 30, 1855, unmarried.
Mary Riddell[3] (2), eldest daughter of George[2] (2), died unmarried.
Robert-Edmerston Riddell[3] (1), second son of George[2] (2), died young.
John-Alexander Riddell[3] (3), third son of George[2] (2), was a lieutenant in the Royal Navy; died unmarried.
Elenor-Grace Riddell[3] (1), second daughter of George[2] (2), died unmarried.
Margaret-Crosby Riddell[3] (2), third daughter of George[2] (2), married in 1855 to the Rev. J. A. Carter-Squire, and had *one* son; she died Dec. 6, 1864.
William-Edmerston Riddell[3] (3), fourth son of George[2] (2), married Sept. 17, 1872, Mary, youngest daughter of James Forster, Esq., of Berwick, and had issue *two* sons; died May 29, 1876.
Elizabeth-Frances Riddell[3] (1), youngest daughter of George[2] (2), was a maiden lady, resident at Berwick-on-Tweed; died Oct. 8, 1878.

FOURTH GENERATION.

Walter-James Riddell[4] (2), eldest son of William[3] (3), was born July 25, 1873.
William-Edmerston Riddell[4] (4), second son of William[3] (3), was born Dec. 20, 1874.

---

* In 1293 there was a Phillipus de Rydall, merchant of Berwick, who was trading within the kingdom of England. Another de Ridell was a burgess at Berwick-on-Tweed, in the middle of the fourteenth century. Thomas de Ridell was at Berwick in 1615; he was senior burgess ... "*die Sabb 12° mens Jan. A. D. mill° trescent° quinquag° Oct.°.*" The testator names among his legatees his "*nepos,*" Alexander de Ridell, together with William, son, and Agnes, daughter, of the said Alexander. Among his bequests he gives "five pounds to the building of the stone bridge of Tweed, at Rokisburgh," and "a donation to the abbott and convent of Kelkow" (Kelso).

RIDDELLS OF GLEN-RIDDELL, SCOTLAND.

Walter Riddell[1] (1), first of Glen-Riddell, was son of William[18] (9), styled "of Friarshaw," and grandson of Sir Walter, second Baronet of Riddell, and his wife, Jane Rigg. He married Catherine, daughter of Sir Robert Laurie, Bart., and having purchased Gilmerston, otherwise Snade, he named it Glen-Riddell,* and made it his residence. His marriage was in the year 1694; he had issue *two* (perhaps more) sons, of whom hereafter

SECOND GENERATION.

Robert Riddell[2] (1), eldest son of Walter[1] (1), was his successor to Glen-Riddell. He married Jean, daughter of Alexander Ferguson, of Craigdorroch, and had issue a numerous family of sons and daughters (one authority says *three* sons and *seven* daughters), of whom hereafter. Mr. Riddell's marriage was in 1781; he died in 1771; his widow died in 1792, aged 82 years. Her grandmother was Annie, daughter of Sir Robert Laurie, Baronet of Maxwelton. Was this the "Annie Laurie" who was the subject of song? The same person.

John Riddell[2] (1), second son of Walter[1] (1), of Glen-Riddell, married Helen, daughter of Sir Michael Balfour, Baronet of Denmilne, and became ancestor of the Riddells of Grange. For genealogy of his descendants, see article under that head.

Walter Riddell[2] (2), a son of Walter[1] (1), of Glen-Riddell, was born at the family residence there (parish of Glencairne), between 1705 and 1720, as proved by the parochial records. The Registrar-General of Scotland, at Edinburgh, says, however, that "the margin of the leaf has been worn off, and it is impossible to decide whether *Walter* or *William* was the name of the child." My reasons for heading this paragraph "Walter" may be found in a note attending the genealogy of the Riddells of Glasslough, Ireland, which see. Walter evidently became ancestor of that branch, having left Scotland in consequence of a quarrel with his family.

THIRD GENERATION.

Annie Riddell[3] (1), eldest daughter of Robert[2] (1), of Glen-Riddell, was married to Walter Riddell, Esq., of Newhouse, who was a son of Rev. Simon Riddell, who had married a Miss Riddell of Newhouse, the heiress (presumed) of that place, and a descendant of the Riddells of Riddell in the same parish. Rev. Simon Riddell's origin is not known, but he was probably descended from the Roxburghshire stock. Walter acquired Glen-Riddell, in right of his wife, and enjoyed it many years

---

* GLEN-RIDDELL, formerly called Gilmerston, and latterly Snade, is near the river Cairne, in the parish of Glencairne, Dumfrieshire, Scotland. It was purchased by the society for the propagation of Christian knowledge in Edinburgh. It had previously been purchased by the representative of a branch of the family of Riddell, of Riddell, in Roxburghshire, namely, Walter Riddell, Esq., who gave the place the name of Glen-Riddell; this seems to have been a custom with the Riddell family, namely, to give their name to their possessions, — a custom carried into Ireland and the United States. I do not know the date of the purchase of this place by Mr. Riddell. The ancient mansion has been dismantled, and the present house is only a ruin of the original residence; the walls are very thick, and part of the cottage is vaulted. Two families in humble circumstances now dwell there, and their cows occupy other parts of the building. The Riddells owned it in 1704.

before being followed by his son. By this marriage there were several children, of whom hereafter.

Elizabeth Riddell[4] (1), second daughter of Robert[3] (1), of Glen-Riddell, was married to Mr. John Wood (Esq.), of Largo, governor of the Isle of Man from 1761 to 1775 A. D.

Catherine Riddell[4] (1), third daughter of Robert[2] (1), of Glen-Riddell, was the wife of —— Maule, Esq.

FOURTH GENERATION.

Robert Riddell[4] (2), eldest son of Walter[3] (3), and his wife, Annie Riddell, of Glen-Riddell and Newhouse, succeeded to his mother's property; married a Miss Kennedy, but had no issue. Mr. Riddell distinguished himself as an antiquary and author. He published several small works; among them, "A Desertation on Ancient Modes of Fortifycations in Scotland"; another on "The Petrified Fortifications of Scotland." He was a member of the Philosophical Society of Manchester, and Fellow of the Antiquarian Societies of Edinburgh and London. He was a patron of Robert Burns, the poet, and is frequently mentioned by him in his poems; he was present at the celebrated convivial celebration connected with the conquest of the "Whistle," as the following lines by the great bard imply:—

> "Three joyous good fellows, with hearts clear of flaw,
> Craigdorroch, so famous for wit, worth, and law,
> And trusty Glen-Riddell, so skilled in old coins,
> And gallant Sir Robert, deep read in old wines." *

There are several other poems in which Mr. Riddell is alluded to during his lifetime, one of which was evidently sent to him with a returned newspaper, and is addressed to "Captain Riddell, of Glen-Riddell." It reads as follows:—

> "My goosequill too rude is to tell all your goodness,
> Bestowed on your servant, the poet.
> Would to God I had one like the beam of the sun,
> And then all the world, sir, should know it."

Mr. Riddell was in sympathy with those in the more lowly walks of life, and employed means to inform them by establishing a circulating library, which was owned by a society formed by his own tenants and farming neighbors. "Burns was treasurer, librarian, and censor." Mr. Riddell died April 21, 1794, and the representation of this family devolved upon the descendants of John, the second son of Walter, the first of Glen-

---

* The parties mentioned in the poem entitled "The Whistle," were Robert Riddell, the antiquary; Furguson, of Craigdorroch, — "a line that struggled for freedom under Bruce," — and Sir Robert Laurie, an admiral of the Royal Navy, all three gentlemen being connected in the ties of kinship. The lines of the poem were founded upon the challenge of a Dane, who brought the "whistle" to Scotland. The Scandinavian challenged various parties in his wine orgies, promising the whistle to the one who could outdrink him, and Sir Walter Laurie, the ancestor of the admiral, met and saw the Dane under the table, "blowing upon the whistle his requiem still." Having thus secured the trophy, Laurie and his brother-in-law, Walter Riddell, of Glen-Riddell, encountered one another in a bacchanalian contest, when the latter was victor, but his son-in-law, Robert Riddell, the "trusty Glen-Riddell" of the song, lost it to his friend Furguson, whose libations on the occasion were very wonderful, and whose representative now possesses the little ebony whistle which Walter Riddell-Carre, Esq., late of Cavers, had seen and blown upon, but not in a bacchanalian encounter.

6

Riddell, who are the nearest male heirs *if* the male line of Glen-Riddell terminated with the first Robert in 1771, as Walter Riddell-Carre says. Mr. Riddell's death seems to have taken place at a residence of the Glen-Riddell family, called "Friars' Carse," in Dunscore parish, also in Dumfrieshire, a property acquired by his grandfather, who died there in 1771.[*]

Burns was a frequent visitor at the homes of the Riddell family at Glen-Riddell and Friars' Carse, and seems to have been intimate with them from the time Robert Riddell succeeded. The following verses were composed for the anniversary of the wedding-day of Captain Riddell of Glen-Riddell, and set to the air of "A Musical Gentleman":—

> "The day returns, my bosom burns,
>   The blissful day we twa did meet;
> Though winter wild in tempest toiled,
>   Ne'er summer's sun was half sae sweet.
> Then a' the pride that loads the tide,
>   And crosses o'er the sultry line,
> Than kingly robes, than crows and globes,
>   Heaven gave me more,—it gave thee mine.
>
> While day and night can bring delight,
>   Or nature aught of pleasure give,
> While joys above my mind can move,
>   For thee, and thee alone, I live!
> When that grim foe of life below
>   Comes in between to make us part,
> The iron hand that breaks our band,
>   It breaks my bliss, it breaks my heart."

The poet Burns seems to have deeply lamented the death of his friend, and to have greatly missed his company and entertainment after his departure. He commemorates the virtues of his early friend and patron in the following lines:—

> "No more, ye warblers of the wood,—no more!
>   Nor pour your descant, grating on my soul;
> Thou young-eyed Spring, gay in thy verdant store,
>   More welcome were to me grim Winter's wildest roar.

---

[*] FRIARS' CARSE, in Nithsdale, Dumfriesshire, Scotland, was once a cell dependent upon the rich abbey of Melrose, which at the Reformation was granted by the Commendator to the Laird of Elliesland, a cadet of the Kirkpatricks of Closeburn. It passed to the Maxwells of Tinwald, and from them to the Borncleugh family, also cadets of the Lords of Maxwell. From these last owners it went into possession of the Riddells of Glen-Riddell. The old refectory, or dining-room, had walls eight feet thick, and the chimney was twelve feet wide. This ancient building having become ruinous by lapse of time, was pulled down about a hundred years ago by Robert Riddell, to give place to the present house known as Friars' Carse, now owned by Thomas Nelson, Esq. Near the house is a loch, which was the fish-pond of the friary, in the middle of which is a very curious island, artificial in construction, founded upon large piles and planks of oak, where the monks are supposed to have lodged their valuables when the English made an inroad into the Strathnith. (See plate in this work.) The estate was purchased latterly by the well-known Dr. Crichton, a very rich man and great benefactor to his country, and after the Crichton purchase, the poem entitled "The Whistle," was found there in the poet's own handwriting. The poet traced the lines "Riddell, much-lamented man," with a diamond on a window of Friars' Carse the first time he visited it after the death of his friend, the Laird of Carse; the lines read thus:—

> "To Riddell, much-lamented man,
>   This ivied cot was dear;
> Reader, dost value matchless worth?
>   This ivied cot revere."

"FRIARS CARSE."

Dumfrieshire, Scotland.

How can ye charm, ye flowers, with all your dyes?
Ye blaw upon the soil that wraps my friend;
How can I to the tuneful strain attend?
The stream flows round the untimely tomb where *Riddell* lies.

Yes, pour, ye warblers, pour the notes of woe!
And soothe the virtues weeping o'er the bier;
The man of worth who has not left his peer,
Is in his narrow house forever darkly low.
The spring again with joy shall others greet,
Me memory of my loss will only meet."

Capt. **Walter Riddell**[4] (4), second son of Walter[3] (3), of Glen-Riddell and Newhouse, and his wife Annie Riddell, who was heiress of her father, Robert Riddell, the second Laird of Glen-Riddell, became possessed by purchase of "Woodley Park,"* near Dumfries. He married Maria Woodley,† a lady of poetical gifts and accomplishments, who wrote

---

* The following extract was forwarded to me by the Rev. C. C. Culpeper, rector of Christ's Church, Nichola Town, St. Christopher Island, and should settle the question as to the maiden-name of the wife of Walter Riddell, of Woodley Park, Dumfrieshire: "1790. *Walter Riddell*, of the Island of Antigua, Gentleman, and *Maria Woodley*, of the Parish of Christ's Church, Nichola Town, Spinster, were married by licence, the 16th day of September, 1790, by me, Joseph Barnes." Witnessed as a correct extract from the register of Christ's Church, Nichola Town, by Horatio W. A. Douglas, schoolmaster. — *Author.*

† Burns having been a frequent and welcome guest at the house of Mrs. Riddell, of Woodley Park, is said, on one occasion, when under the influence of wine he had taken at her table, and the alluring charms of his fair hostess' conversation and manner, to have so far forgot himself as to attempt to kiss her, — an indignity, however, which she punished by the withdrawal of her friendship. During the continuance of this coldness, which lasted nearly two years, he weakly gave way to his wrath and wounded pride in two or three lampoons and other satirical effusions, which were not to his credit; but ultimately a kindlier feeling possessed him, under the influence of which he composed a song and sent it to Mrs. Riddell as a kind of peace-offering. To her honor, be it said, she replied to his song in a similar strain of poetic license, which she did to soothe his ruffled feelings, and help to heal the breach that kept them separated; and having the magnanimity to forgive his insult, they ultimately became thoroughly reconciled. He, at another time, took offence because she seemed to pay more attention to some officers in the company than to the poet, who had a supreme contempt for "epauletted puppies" as he delighted to call them; and while under the influence of this offence he satirized Mrs. Riddell in the following "stinging epitaph":—

"Here lies now a prey to insulting neglect,
Where once was a Butterfly gay in life's bloom;
Want only of wisdom denied her respect,
Want only of goodness denied her esteem."

He also gave vent to his feelings in the following "Monody on Mrs. Riddell, Famed for Her Caprice":—

"How cold is that bosom which folly once fir'd!
How pale is that cheek where the rouge lately glistened!
How silent that voice which the echoes oft tired,
How dull is that ear that to flattery so listened!

If sorrow and anguish await,
From friendship and dearest affection removed,
How doubly severe, Maria, thy fate!
Thou diest unwept, and thou livedst unloved.

Loves, graces, and virtues, I call not on you,
So shy, grave, and distant, ye shed not a tear;
But come, all ye offspring of Folly so true,
And flowers let us cull for Maria's cold bier.

a biographical sketch of the poet Burns, which I have seen in an edition of his poems, in which she has warmly eulogized him. I do not know whether there were children in this family.*

Sophia Riddell[4] (1), youngest daughter of Walter[3] (3), of Glen-Riddell, died unmarried in 1797.

Alexander Riddell[4] (1), presumed to be a son of Walter[3] (3), of Glen-Riddell, died at Hampton Court, in 1804; he was styled "Esquire, of Glen-Riddell."

RIDDELLS OF GRANGE, SCOTLAND.

John Riddell[1] (1), second son of Walter[1] (1), the first Laird of Glen-Riddell, became possessed of a property called "Grange," in Fifeshire. He married Helen, daughter of Sir Michael Balfour, a baronet, and had issue, of whom more hereafter. It has been supposed that the representation of Glen-Riddell and Newhouse rightfully devolved upon the male descendants of this John, and the relationship has been so stated in the published pedigrees of the family; but a claimant has been found in Ireland, who assumes, with many very well-founded evidences, to be descended from the Glen-Riddells through a nearer branch, springing from a son who became alienated from his relatives in consequence of a religious or political disagreement, and went to Ireland, where he was unknown to the younger generations of Glen-Riddell.

SECOND GENERATION.

Walter Riddell[2] (1), eldest son of John[1] (1), was styled "of Grange," in Fifeshire, and died *sine prole* in 1762.

Michael Riddell[2] (1), second son of John[1] (1), was of Grange, in Fifeshire, and was married three times; first to Miss Margaret, daughter of Henry Balfour (probably a kinswoman), by whom he had issue *one* son; by Janet, daughter of Robert Hunter, his second wife, there were *two* sons. Mr. Riddell lived to old age; the name of his third wife has not reached me.

THIRD GENERATION.

Gen. Michael Riddell[3] (2), eldest son of Michael[2] (1), was of Grange, Fifeshire; married Miss Sheridan, and had issue *two* sons, of whom here-

---

We'll search through the gardens for each silly flower,
   We'll roam through the forest for each idle weed;
But chiefly the nettle, so typical, shower,
   For none e'er approached her but rued the rash deed.

We'll sculpture the marble, we'll measure the lay,
   Here Vanity strums on her idiot lyre;
There keen Indignation shall dart on her prey,
   Which spurning Contempt shall redeem from his ire."

* There was a Miss Deborah Davies, a beautiful young English lady, connected by ties of blood with the family of Captain Riddell of Glen-Riddell, at whose house the poet Burns met her, and her beauty and accomplishments made so deep an impression upon him that he celebrated them in prose and song.

after. He was a major general in the East India Company's service, commanding the southern division of the Madras army. He died at Toronmungalalam, India, November, 1844.

John Riddell[2] (2), second son of Michael[2] (1), was in the army and died *sine prole* in 1822.

Robert Riddell[2] (1), third son of Michael[2] (1), was in the East India Company's service, and afterwards in Canada, British North America. He married in 1836, Elizabeth, daughter of Rear Admiral Henry Vansitart, and had issue *three* sons and *three* daughters, of whom hereafter. The family returned to Britain, and both Mr. and Mrs. Riddell have since deceased.

FOURTH GENERATION.

Robert-Vansitart Riddell[4] (2), eldest son of Robert[3] (1), is now (1874) serving in the Bengal Engineers, in India, and has been recognized as the representative of the families of Glen-Riddell and Grange, although he does not own any properties there, these having passed to other families.

Henry-Vansitart Riddell[4] (1), second son of Robert[3] (1), is now a soldier in the Bengal Native Infantry, in India.

Walter Riddell[4] (2), third son of Robert[3] (1), is now a soldier in the army in India, with his brothers.

Mary-Clara Riddell[4] (1), eldest daughter of Robert[3] (1).

Elizabeth-Janette Riddell[4] (1), second daughter of Robert[3] (1).

Caroline Riddell[4] (1), third daughter of Robert[3] (1).

RIDDELLS OF GRANTON, SCOTLAND.

Rev. Archibald Riddell[1] (1), the first of this denomination, was the third son of Walter, the second Baronet of Riddell, in Roxburghshire, and his wife, Jane Rigg. He was ordained as minister of Kippen about the year 1676, but preached often in field conventicles. He suffered persecution and imprisonment, and was obliged to leave Scotland and go to New Jersey, in the United States, where he spent three years as a preacher in Woodbridge. Although his name appears among those of other preachers who had drawn upon them the attention of the government by attending conventicles as early as 1674, yet the first serious proceedings against him seem to have been prompted by his connection in some way with the rising of Bothwell in 1679, the Privy Council ordering on the 24th of June that he should be sought for and offering a reward for his arrest. He was taken in September by the Laird of Graden, a relative of his wife, and sent to the Tolbooth at Jedburgh, whence he was removed to the prison at Edinburgh. On the first of October, and again in December, Mr. Riddell was called before the Council of Public Affairs, and so conducted himself as to secure the respect of his examiners. He was remitted to confinement, however, until released on the application of the Laird of Pitlochie, with the view of emigrating to New Jersey. During this period in April, 1681, he was allowed to visit his dying mother, at Riddell house, and in the following June he was charged with having broken his confinement, keeping conventicles, and baptizing children, and, in consequence, the place of his imprisonment was changed, he being sent to the Bass. He and the Rev. Thomas Patterson are described by the proprietaries as "two persons who have been in prison in Scotland for nonconformity, and are greatly esteemed among the people who are of their persuasion in matters of religion"; and as they are willing to transport themselves to East Jersey, and settle there, which will be the occasion of inviting a great number to follow them, the necessary directions were given to have two hundred acres of land allotted to each immediately on their arrival, in such places as might best accommodate them, provided they build them houses and continue their own or some other family there three years.

On board the ill-fated "Henry and Francis" we are not able to follow them. Mrs. Riddell and his children accompanied him, and she died on shipboard; the children were spared to him, to contribute to his happiness in his new home at Woodbridge, where his two hundred acres were allotted him, and where he purchased other lands. He officiated at Trinity Church at Woodbridge from 1686 to 1689, when he, having fulfilled the conditions of settlement, left the country, and started on his return to his native land, — a land having more charms for him than the "New World." He set sail with a son ten years of age, in June, 1689, but he was doomed to other sufferings and disappointments. Favorable weather attended him, but on the 2d of August, when off the coast of England, the vessel was captured by a French man-of-war, and the passengers sent to the common jail at Rochefort, whence they were subsequently marched to Toulon, chained two and two by their arms, and, at first, each ten pairs tied to a rope, but this being found an impediment to their traveling, was abandoned the second day. Mr. Riddell was chained to his little son, who was so small that he gave them no little trouble, three different bands being forged by the smith before one could be found small enough to confine his slender wrists. They were six weeks on the way to Toulon, the hardships of the journey causing the death of many, and on their arrival were conveyed to the hold of an old hulk in the harbor, but after the detention of a month, Mr. Riddell and his son and others were taken back again to Rochefort, and thence to Demain, near St. Malo, where for more than a year they were kept prisoners in the vault of an old castle. At last, after having been confined nearly two years, they were exchanged for two Romish priests and allowed to return to Scotland.* While they were imprisoned in the old castle they lay on straw, never changed save once a month, suffering every indignity and misery. But his trials were ended with his release, and he passed the rest of his

---

* The following royal letter was found by one of the Riddells some time ago in the State Paper Office, London, which was issued directly from the sovereign, William III, and directed to the Privy Council of Scotland, being to the following effect : —

"WILLIAM REX, Right Trusty and Entirely Beloved. Whereas we are informed that Mr. Archibald Riddell, Minister of the Gospel, and James Sinclair of Freshwick, are prisoners in France, and are very hardly used, whom we are resolved to have released by exchange with two Priests now Prisoners in Scotland. Therefore, WE require you to call for their friends and nearest relations of the said Mr. Archibald Riddell and James Sinclair, and signify our Royal Pleasure to them in exchange of these two Prisoners with the two Priests that shall be condescended upon, and authorise them not only to speak with the two Priests, but also to write to France anent the negotiating their friends' liberty, and that you cause these two Priests to be condescended upon and securely keeped, and make intimation to them

days in peace and security; indeed, as Woodrow states, when he returned all his losses were made up, and he and his children (his wife, who was a daughter of Henry Atkenhead, minister of North Berwick, having died on the voyage to America) were in better circumstances than if he had conformed, to which he had been instigated. He was appointed minister of Trinity College Church, a fine structure built by Mary of Guelders, in which charge he died in 1708, and his remains were deposited in Greyfriars churchyard, where the bodies of many eminent servants of God are buried, and where his brother, Sir John Riddell, the Baronet of Riddell, had been previously interred. Mr. Riddell left a great reputation behind him, and Dr. Hew Scott says : " He was a singularly pious and laborious servant of Jesus Christ." English genealogists have stated that there were *two* sons and *two* daughters in this family, but there are divers evidences pointing to a son *William* settled in New Jersey, who became the ancestor of the numerous Riddells and Riddles in Virginia and about Cincinnati, Ohio, descended from William and John, sons of the William before mentioned.

SECOND GENERATION.

Com. **Walter Riddell**[2] **(1)**, eldest son of Archibald[1] **(1)**, of Granton, married Sarah, sister of Sir John Nisbet, of Dean, but died without issue in 1738; his widow married Sir John Rutherford, of Rutherford. He was a captain in the Royal Navy, and greatly distinguished himself in the war of the Spanish succession under Queen Anne. He became commodore and was knighted. His conduct and bravery as a naval officer is noticed in a history of Europe, 1709, and he is also proved to have distinguished himself in the capture of vessels and in opposing the rebels in 1715, stimulated, no doubt, by the treatment shown his father in the reign of James II, as before shown. In the archives of the admiralty a list exists of about thirty-seven vessels, taken by him from the French while commanding the "Phœbe," frigate of war. Being attacked by a superior force on one occasion, his vessel was taken by the enemy, and he succeeded in getting off in a boat with part of the crew, unobserved. Having kept in sight of the French fleet, he observed that for some reason the "Phœbe" had fallen behind and become separated from the other ships, upon which he rowed back to his vessel, recaptured her, and made his escape. In consequence of this feat he was authorized to change his family escutcheon, and to substitute a boat with oars in place of one of the ears of rye, and to adopt the motto, "Row and Retake "; this is therefore the escutcheon of the Granton branch of Riddell. He acquired the barony of West Granton, near Edinburgh. Supposed to be the son that was chained to his father in France, before mentioned. He was succeeded by his brother in 1738.*

---

that they shall be used in the same way and manner as the French King uses the said Scots Prisoners, which they may be ordered to acquaint their friends in France with, that exchange may be more easily effected. For doing of which these Presents shall be your warrant, and so we bid you hertily farewell.

"Given at the Court of Kensington this 16th day of January, 1689, and of our Reign the first year. — By His Majesty's Command.   (Signed)   MELVILLE."

* WALTER RIDDELL was appointed captain of the "Mermaid " 21 Dec., 1703; promoted to second lieutenant of the " Chichester," of seventy guns, in 1705. The first part of his service as naval commander is barren of incident. In 1706, he commanded the "Isabella," a yacht, ordered with Sir Cloudesley Shovel, and the fleet under his command to the Mediterranean (it being, at that day, always cus-

John Riddell[2] (1), second son of Archibald[1] (1), was a physician in Edinburgh; married Jane Livingstone, an heiress, and had issue many children who died young. Dr. Riddell died in 1740, leaving a widow and *two* children, of whom hereafter. He was eminent in his profession.

Janet Riddell[2] (1), eldest daughter of Archibald[1] (1), was born in Scotland, and went to New Jersey, United States, with her father's family at the time of his banishment. She was married Jan. 26, 1686, to James, son of Sir James Dundas, who was Lord Orinston, great-grandfather of General, the Rt. Hon. Sir D. Dundas, G. C. B., of Beechwood, late commander-in-chief. Her husband was one of the party that came on the "Henry and Francis" from Scotland. These resided at Perth Amboy, his household being located on Smith Street. Mr. Dundas was selected by William Dockwra, in 1688, for one of his deputy receiver-generals, but would not accept the office; however, on being appointed by the Proprietaries, in January, 1694, receiver-general, he consented to serve, and held the office till his death in 1698. Mrs. Dundas survived her husband and administered on his estate, after which she returned to Scotland and spent her last days with her kindred.

Sarah Riddell[2] (1), second daughter of Archibald[1] (1), was born in Scotland, and presumably went to New Jersey in America, with her

---

tomary to send a vessel or two of that description with all great naval armaments, which, independent of the purposes of state and pageantry, probably first gave rise to this equipment). He returned with his gallant admiral in October, 1707. His diligence and indefatigable attention to duty, procured his promotion soon after his return to England, to the "Falmouth," of fifty guns. In the year 1708, he was ordered for New England; and, when on his voyage homeward, in 1709, with a number of ships under his convoy, signalized himself in so distinguished a manner on being attacked by a French ship-of-war of superior force, that we scarcely know whether most to applaud his intrepidity and good conduct itself, or to rejoice at the unalloyed success which attended it. He continued captain of the "Falmouth" for a considerable time after this, as in the year 1710, we find him in the same ship, accompanying Capt. George Martin, who then commanded the "Dragon," on his successful expedition against the French settlement of Port Royal, in Acadia, now called Nova Scotia. In the year 1712, he still commanded the same ship, and was then stationed off the coast of Guinea, where, in company with Capt. Mabbott, of the "Mary Galley," he had a very spirited engagement with two French ships-of-war; the enemy were, however, so fortunate as to make their escape. This is the last mention we find of Capt. Riddell. The time of his death is not known.

"Admiralty Office, May 24, 1709.— Her Majesties ship 'Falmouth,' of fifty guns, commanded by Capt. Walter Ryddell, in her passage from New England with some ships laden with masts, and others under her convoy, was on the 18th of this month, attacked by a French ship-of-war of fifty guns, about twenty-four leagues from Scilly; and Capt. Ryddell, perceiving that the enemy did intend to board him, befilled his head-sails, and laid her on board under her boltsprit directly athwart her hawse, and raked her fore and aft with his cannon. The enemy continued in this posture about an hour an a half, during which time he entered many men, but they were repulsed; however, the number of men on board being much greater than those in the 'Falmouth,' it occasioned various turns; but at length he thought fit to retire, first cut all the lanyards of the 'Falmouth' fore and mizen shrouds, believing it might prevent her following to rescue the convoy, which the enemy stood after, notwithstanding which Captain Ryddell did with such diligence follow him as enabled him to preserve them and to bring them into Plymouth. In this action the 'Falmouth' had thirteen men killed and fifty-six wounded; the captain himself received a wound in his right leg and several other hurts; and the second lieutenant and Mr. Lawrence, one of the volunteers, were shot through the body. The 'Falmouth' had on board her 20,000 pounds of New England money at the time of the engagement. Captain Ryddell's conduct on this occasion appears to have been rarely equalled and never excelled."— *Naval Biography.*

father; she was married to John Currie, minister of Haddington. No other information.

THIRD GENERATION.

John Riddell (2), eldest son of John[2] (1), of Granton, was a Writer to the Signet, Edinburgh; married Christian, daughter of Sir John Nisbet, Baronet of Dean, and had issue *two* sons, of whom hereafter. He was born in 1713, and died in 1745, and was succeeded by his son.

Esther Riddell (1), a daughter of John[2] (1), and Jane Livingstone, was married to Rev. Robert Riddell, her cousin, of Lilliesleaf, but had no issue.

FOURTH GENERATION.

John Riddell[4] (3), eldest son of John[3] (2), was born in 1740; married Betsey, daughter of John Campbell, Esq., of Clathic and Killermont, and was for some time lord provost of Glasgow. The Granton estate had become much burdened with debt by the former proprietors, and was sold during this gentleman's minority; it was purchased by the ancestors of the present Duke of Buccleuch. Mr. Riddell had issue *five* children, of whom hereafter.

Henry Riddell[4] (1), second son of John[3] (2), was styled "of Little Govan." He married his cousin Anne, daughter of John Glassford, of Dougalston, by his second wife, Anne, daughter of Sir John Nisbet, of Dean. He was a merchant in Glasgow; had issue *seven* children, and died in 1801.

FIFTH GENERATION.

John Riddell[5] (4), eldest son of John[4] (3), who was designated "younger of Granton," was a lieutenant in the Madras army, and died *sine prole* in 1828.

Archibald Riddell[5] (2), second son of John[4] (3), younger of Granton, retired early from the army; married an Austrian lady of rank, and lived at Vienna, Austria, till his death in 1877; he had issue *two* daughters; one survives.

Elizabeth Riddell[5] (1), eldest daughter of John[4] (3), younger of Granton, was married to William Horne, Esq., of Stirkoke, Caithness, and sheriff of Haddingtonshire; no issue.

Agnes Riddell[5] (1), second daughter of John[4] (3), younger of Granton, was never married; died in 1874.

Mary-Anne Riddell[5] (1), third daughter of John[4] (3), younger of Granton, was not married; died 1876.

John Riddell[5] (5), eldest son of Henry[4] (1) of Little Govan, was born Oct. 4, 1785. He was styled "of Gulane Lodge," in East Lothian, and was considered the greatest antiquary and peerage-lawyer of his day. He published works on Scotch Peerage and Consistorial Law. Lord Lindsey, now Earl Crawford, a very high authority, wrote a most interesting account of his splendid career and great attainments, from which I extract the following: "The genealogical knowledge, which gave weight and value to his opinions, was vast and profound, — the gathered stores of a lifetime spent among public and private records; almost every principal charter-chest in Scotland having at one time or other passed under his review. But this vast knowledge would have been little serviceable toward the great purposes to which he devoted it, had he not possessed that thorough familiarity with law, — feudal, consistorial, genealogical, and heraldic,

—and not of Scotland and England only, but of foreign nations,— which determined the value and regulated the application of the facts ever present before his mental eye. It was from this lofty eminence of principle and precedent that he was enabled to survey the length and breadth of Scottish genealogical antiquity; assign its limits to undue family pretensions; recall forgotten rights of representation to public recognition, and point out in many instances through which unsuspected or neglected hereditary honors might be legally claimed and vindicated. And it was from the full concurrent perception of the extent of the difficulty always attending on such processes, more especially before the House of Lords, that, acting under the impulse of that honesty which is always allied with the love of truth, as well as in accordance with his chivalric sense of honor, and his extreme disinterestedness on the point of professional remuneration, he carefully and distinctly, before engaging in such undertakings, pointed out the adverse considerations likely to attend upon them, which through deficiency of evidence, or irregular and fluctuating procedure in the tribunal where the claim must necessarily be prosecuted — anxious ever that his client should not commit himself to the pursuit without full warning of what it might entail upon him. But when once engaged in it he gave his whole soul to the object before him; and it was beautiful and inspiring to witness the play of his thoughts during the evolution of his argument; the historical breadth of his views, and their ready convergence to the required focus, however minute the particular; his subtlety of legal discrimination; his fertility in illustration; his extraordinary readiness of resource; his untiring patience and industry in working out his results, contrasting with the eager impetuosity of utterance which accompanied their birth; and lastly, the genuine professional courage springing again, as before, from his manly honesty and love of truth, with which he never evaded, but boldly faced and combated every difficulty. I speak to all this from my own experience during the prosecution of the minute and complicated Peerage claims.

"I have seldom witnessed more touching examples of that beautiful humility which is generally the sister of mental strength and moral dignity, than in Mr. Riddell. His pride was far more in the fame of his great predecessors in the same studies, and in that of the historical families of Scotland,* more especially those with whom he had become professionally related, than in his own reputation. He was as unselfish in that respect as he was disinterested in regard to the remuneration of his labours.

"Everything he wrote was stamped with the power bestowed by profound legal knowledge and a boundless command of facts, and his works will continually be resorted to as a store-house of information on matters of genealogy and Peerage law by future generations."

Such are Earl Crawford's views of his great professional acquirements and character. Mr. Riddell died issueless. The epitaph on his tomb in the Dean cemetery is as follows:—

JOHANNES RIDDELL, ESQ.
AMIGER. *Jurisconsultus, vir cojuscunque Ætatis Numbutus
Literis; Qui in Antiquitate
Et ea Præcipue Quæ Ad Originis Gentilitias Pertinet*

---

* THE GRANTON RIDDELLS are connected by marriage with the Glassfords, Gilchrists, Homes, Dares, Pringles, Stephens, Fosters, Trevalyans, Smiths, Palmers, Laws, Constables, Campbells, Seaton-Karrs, and other old and distinguished Scottish families.

*Ad Veritatem Rerum Revocandam Prodigus Laboris
Atque Etiam Felix Fuit, Eandemque Scriptis
Illustravit Auctor Omnium Consensu Gravis-
simus; Hoc In Agro, Qui Proavorum Ipsius
Olim Fuit, Sepultus Est.
Natus IV° Die Octobris MDCCLXXXV.   Decessit VIII° Die Feb-
ruarii MDCCLXII.   Vixit Annos LXXVI.*

"John Riddell, Esquire, advocate; a man imbued with the literature of every age, who in antiquities, and especially that branch of them which relates to the origin of families, by recalling it to the truth of fact, was prodigal of labor, and, moreover, felicitous. This pursuit he illustrated by his writings, being an author of the greatest weight, as all admit. In this land, once the property of his ancestors, he was buried. Born, 4th October, 1785 ; died 8th February, 1862. He lived 76 years."[*]

Rev. Henry Riddell[5] (2), second son of Henry[4] (1) of Little Govan, now a part of the city of Glasgow, was born May 23, 1789, at Glasgow ; married in 1818 Agnes Gilchrist, daughter of Archibald Gilchrist, Esq., by whom he had *one* son. His wife died at Bexhill, England, and he married secondly, in 1831, Elizabeth, daughter of John Horne, Esq., of Storkoke, Caithnesshire, and by her had issue *four* children, of whom (with the first son) hereafter. Mr. Riddell was educated at the grammar school, Glasgow, till the age of 13, and afterwards at Edinburgh, where the family removed after the death of his father in 1801. He attended the University of Edinburgh, and passed as a "Writer to His Majesty's Signet." For a short time he practised his profession at Edinburgh, but removed to London about 1822, and became solicitor there. His wife's health was delicate, and she could not live in London, so he gave up business and went to the south of England, where Mrs. Riddell died. He then returned to Scotland, determined to enter the church, and passed through the Divinity terms at St. Mary's College, St. Andrews. His first settlement was at Longformacus, a small parish in Berwickshire, in 1830. In 1843 he was appointed assistant and successor to Rev. George Cunningham, minister of Dunse, and in 1847 succeeded him in that charge, where he remained till his death, which occurred April 15, 1862. His widow still survives and lives in Edinburgh.

Rev. James Riddell[5] (1), third son of Henry[4] (1), of Little Govan, was probably born in Glasgow, Scotland, April 18, 1794 ; married Dorothy, daughter (and co-heiress) of John Foster, of Leicester Grange, and had issue several children, of whom hereafter. He was of Balliol College, Oxford, and was vicar of Hanbury, Staffordshire. He was for many years latterly at Leamington. He died in May, 1878, deeply lamented. See portrait.

Robert Riddell[5] (1), fourth son of Henry[4] (1), of Little Govan, was born May 29, 1797, presumably at Glasgow ; married in 1834 to Susan,

---

[*] In the Advocates' Library, Edinburgh, Scotland, may be found the "Riddell Note Books," about one hundred and fifty in number. In No. 43 is "Notes Relative to the Family of Carmichael," including several from the Morton Charter-chest, with pen-and-ink sketches of seals of the Rydale and Riddell family. The "Prefatory Observations" to the "Catalogue of the Riddell Papers" gives a short notice of the Papers and Note Books; a list of the published works of the late John Riddell, Esq., advocate; a letter introducing Mr. Riddell to Cardinal Gonsalvi, from the Rt. Hon. George Canning; a sketch, by Lord Lindsey, of the career and character of the great genealogical scholar, with some remarks on it by the editor of the Edinburgh *Courant;* his epitaph and mementos of Faculty of Advocate and a portrait.

daughter of James Law, Esq., of Elvington, in the county of Haddington, and by her had issue *five* children, of whom hereafter. He was educated at Edinburgh for the profession of advocate, which he became in 1820. He was appointed in 1829 to the office of sheriff substitute of the county of Haddington, which he retained till his death, April 18, 1862. He possessed considerable professional acquirements, and made a most efficient magistrate, and combined with these qualifications no ordinary degree of literary attainments, especially in that department of law and research in which his brother John was so famous. His brother once said of him, " he was tarred with the same brush."

Christiana Riddell[5] (1), eldest daughter of Henry[4] (1), of Little Govan, was born in 1784; was married to Archibald Douglas, of Glinfinnart, and was mother of that Col. John Douglas, C. B., who served in the whole Crimean war, where he led the Eleventh Hussars and miraculously escaped a desperate charge at Balaklava. She died in 1817.

Jane Riddell[5] (1), second daughter of Henry[4] (1), of Little Govan, was born Sept. 26, 1790, and resides in Edinburgh.

Catharine Riddell[5] (1), third daughter of Henry[4] (1), of Little Govan, was born in 1792 and died in 1869.

SIXTH GENERATION.

Eliza Riddell[6] (1), only surviving daughter of Archibald[5] (2), is now living with her mother in Austria.

Henry Riddell[6] (3), eldest son of Henry[5] (2), was born Aug. 4, 1819, and was educated for the profession of barrister-at-law, but was very delicate, and died at Wiseton, Northamptonshire, in 1850, aged 31 years, presumably unmarried.

John Riddell[6] (6), second son of Henry[5] (2), and eldest by second wife, was born Feb. 18, 1836; now of Dean, near Geelong, Victoria; has married, but his wife's name has not reached me. No issue.

William Riddell[6] (1), third son of Henry[5] (2), was born May 8, 1838; married in 1877, Lizzie, third daughter of the late Robert Pringle, Esq., of Carriber, Linlithgowshire. He was of Singhia, Tirhoot, East Indies, where he has been successful as a planter. He has taken a country house called Oxendean, near Dunse, in Berwickshire, Scotland, where his late father was minister. He does not believe the tradition of the New Jersey Riddells, that their ancestor was descended from the Granton family, but thinks he may have been a collateral kinsman.

James Riddell[6] (2), fourth son of Henry[5] (2), was born Dec. 28, 1840; married in 1869, Harriet-Anne, daughter of William Stevens, Esq., of Montreal, Canada, and has issue *four* children, of whom hereafter. He is of Badulipar, Assam, East Indies, where he has made money as a planter.

Elizabeth Riddell[6] (2), only daughter of Henry[5] (2), was born in 1834 (presumably at Dunse), and resides in Edinburgh with her widowed mother; unmarried.

Rev. James Riddell[6] (3), eldest son of James[5] (1), was born June 8, 1823, and was educated at Shrewsbury school, where he was one of the favorite pupils of Dr. Kennedy, and whence he was elected to a scholarship at Balliol College, in November, 1841, the colleague in the election being Dr. Matthew Arnold. He had obtained the highest honor at Shrewsbury, which was the Sydney gold medal. He was only eighteen when he went, at the head of thirty candidates from the best schools in

England, to a scholarship at Oxford. As an under-graduate he was beloved both by his seniors and contemporaries for gentleness of manner and great amiability of disposition, and the heads of the college considered him one of the best and most promising scholars that Balliol ever reared. Having obtained a first class in classics, he took his degree and was made fellow of his college, taking holy orders. Shortly after, he was appointed one of the teachers, and in this sphere he was much respected by his pupils; he was also made a public examiner, and in addition held other honorable appointments connected with the university, including a seat at the Hebdomadal Council, the governing body. He was also for one year a select preacher at St. Mary's, and in 1864 was appointed one of the Whitehall preachers, both positions being alike honorable; he was nominated to the latter by the Bishop of London. He left Oxford at the beginning of a vacation in his usual health, — never very robust, — and went to Sherburn, Dorcestershire, joined his family at a temporary residence at Tunbridge Wells, where his health, perhaps unfavorably acted upon by intense application to study for so many years, gave way, and alarming symptoms suddenly appeared, which ended in his death on the 14th of September, 1866; his remains were interred at Tunbridge Wells. His loss was greatly felt, not only among old Shrewsbury and Balliol men, but throughout the university and at Leamington, where he and his family had long resided. He enjoyed the reputation of being one of the best, — some say *the* best, — Greek scholars of his day, but it is a melancholy pleasure to his old friends to recall the fact of his singular goodness, innocence, and purity; and his former pupils will ever bear testimony to the loving industry and patience he brought to bear on his college labors for nearly twenty years. His published translations of Greek and Latin verses showed the high rank he took in such compositions, and it is not a little singular that the last production of his pen was a Latin translation of Watts' well-known hymn: —

> " There is a land of pure delight,
> Where saints immortal reign;
> Infinite day excludes the night,
> And pleasures banish pain;
> There everlasting spring abides,
> And never-withering flowers;
> Death, like a narrow sea, divides
> That heavenly land from ours."

The Rev. Canon Liddon says, "The salient features of his character, — his courage, his purity, his tenderness, his delicate and far-reaching conscientiousness, — were sufficiently obvious to all who knew him; but to show the relation of these virtues to his great intellectual life, and to mark the finer shades which would have to be distinguished, is, I fear, beyond anything that I could at present, if ever, attempt." See the portrait in this book.

John Riddell[6] (7), second son of James[5] (1), was married in 1860 to Jane Peppercorn, daughter of William Peppercorn, Esq., and is supposed to have a family of children, but I have no records.

Charlotte-Dorothy Riddell[6] (1), eldest daughter of James[5] (1), I have no particulars of; her name stands in the printed pedigree.

Anne Riddell[6] (1), second daughter of James[5] (1), was married in 1862 to the Rev. Edward-Trevelyan Smith, M. A., late scholar of St. John's College, Cambridge, and now (1862) incumbent of St. Paul's Church, Warwick.

Henrietta Riddell[6] (1), third daughter of James[5] (1), I have no particulars of; her name stands in the family pedigree.

Henry-James Riddell[6] (4), eldest son of Robert[5] (1), was born July 8, 1838, and died in 1847, aged nine years.

Robert Riddell[6] (2), second son of Robert[5] (1), was born March 23, 1840; was educated at Edinburgh, Scotland, and is now (1878) a civil engineer at Lanowlee, Bombay, India.

William-Law Riddell[6] (2), third son of Robert[5] (1), was born Oct. 16, 1843; married in 1877 Mary-Ann Frazer, and is now (1878) of Riverside, Otago, New Zealand. *One* daughter.

Jane-Anne Riddell[6] (2), eldest daughter of Robert[5] (1), was born Oct. 4, 1885; was married in 1860 to James Constable, Esq., of Cally, Perthshire, and has *four* sons and *six* daughters.

Susan-Mary Riddell[6] (1), youngest daughter of Robert[5] (1), was born Sept. 23, 1841, and resides in Edinburgh, Scotland.

SEVENTH GENERATION.

Henry-James Riddell[7] (5), eldest son of James[6] (2), was born Oct. 21, 1870. In India.

William-John Riddell[7] (3), second son of James[6] (2), was born May 19, 1872. In India.

Walter Riddell[7] (2), third son of James[6] (2), was born (probably in India) Oct. 29, 1874. A daughter was born Feb. 20, 1879.

Mary-Hepburn Riddell[7] (2), a daughter of William[6] (2), was born (probably in New Zealand) in December, 1877.

RIDDELLS OF BEESBOROUGH, SCOTLAND.

Capt. Thomas Riddell[1] (1), was the fifth son of Walter[20] (10), the fifth Baronet of Riddell (whose pedigree see). He married Elizabeth, daughter of Laughlan MacLauchlan, Esq., of an ancient Highland family, and had issue several children, of whom hereafter. He was an officer in the East India Company's naval service, and made successful voyages to India and China. A journal of one of his voyages to East India is in the British Museum, a copy of which the author of this work secured and has deposited in the archives of the New England Historical Society, in Boston, Mass. Captain Riddell made money by his adventures, and returning to Scotland, purchased a property in Berwickshire called "Kames," which he named "Beesborough," after the ship he commanded, and made it his residence. There is a fine oil-painting of Mrs. Riddell and one of her children, made when she was a young and very beautiful woman, and a photographic copy is now in the author's possession. Captain Riddell died in 1805, and was succeeded by his son.

SECOND GENERATION.

Capt. Thomas Riddell[2] (2), eldest son of Thomas[1] (1), was styled "the second of Beesborough." He was an officer in the Fourteenth Regiment of Foot, and died at Trinidad in September, 1802, "a man of ability and soldierly deportment, universally respected."

Gen. Henry-James Riddell[2] (1), second son of Thomas[1] (1) and his wife, Elizabeth MacLauchlan, was of Beesborough. He entered the navy at an early age, but left this service for the army, and obtained his first commission in 1798. His service extended through many years, and was of a very important character. He served at the siege and capture of Copenhagen, under Lord Cathcart, in 1807, and afterwards went to the Peninsula, and was prominent at the crossing of the Bidassoa, with Lord Lyndoch's Division, in 1813. He afterwards joined the army on the eastern coast of Spain, and was present at several affairs — at Villa-Franca, and before Barcelona during the blockade of that fortress, and finally embarked for Genoa with the Italian Brigade under Count Latorer, and was senior officer of the Quartermaster-general's department at the surrender of the Genoese territory, in 1814. During the Peace, General Riddell was employed in England, Scotland, and Ireland, and was never on half-pay. In 1847 he was appointed to the command of the forces in Scotland, and the governorship of Edinburgh Castle, which position he held till 1852. His commissions bear date as follows: ensign, March, 1798; lieutenant, April 19, 1798; captain, Dec. 28, 1809; major, Dec. 10, 1810; lieutenant-colonel, June 4, 1813; colonel, July 22, 1830; major-general, Nov. 23, 1841; lieutenant-general, Nov. 11, 1851; general, Sept. 26, 1857, and colonel Sixteenth Foot, June 25, 1851. He died March 8, 1861, at Oxendean, aged 79 years. He was never married. There was a very good oil-portrait of the general, painted when he was a young soldier, a copy of which is in the author's possession. He is represented in uniform with sword, and must have been a splendid-looking man.[*]

Olive Riddell[2] (1), a daughter of Thomas[1] (1), was a maiden-lady, (as also *four* other daughters, whose names have not reached me), who died March 22, 1862.

RIDDELLS OF CAMIESTON, SCOTLAND.

Thomas Riddell[1] (1) was third son of Walter[19] (9), the fourth Baronet of Riddell, and Mary, daughter of John Watt, of Rosehill. He was born in 1690 A. D.; married April 23, 1740, Margaret, daughter of Rev. William Hunter,[†] minister of Lilliesleaf and Laird of Union Hall, which

---

[*] Gen. Henry-James Riddell became involved in his financial relations, having been security for his kinsman, Sir John B. Riddell, Bart., of Riddell, and was obliged to sell "Beesborough" to make good his responsibilities, and to raise means to provide for his several maiden-sisters; some of these lived to be quite aged.

[†] The Hunters were well descended, and the minister a singularly pious and good man. This family is intimately connected with the Riddells. Union Hall was acquired by Dr. Hunter, the minister's son, who conveyed it to his son, Col. Edgar Hunter, a very popular country gentleman, who was killed by a fall from his horse in the prime of life; unmarried. At his death the succession fell to his first cousin, William Riddell, of Camieston, — well known to some still living, — whose father married Colonel Hunter's sister. The eldest daughter of the Rev. William Hunter married the Rev. Adam Milne, minister and historian of Melrose; and his only child having died young, the Linthill property passed to Mr. Riddell

is a part of the present Linthill property, Midlam Mill estate. Camieston was acquired by the fourth baronet for this son Thomas, and bestowed upon him when a young man. He died in 1750, and left issue *four* sons and *three* daughters, of whom hereafter.

SECOND GENERATION.

Walter Riddell[2] (1), eldest son of Thomas[1] (1), was born at Camieston, Roxburghshire, Scotland, in 1742, and died young.

William Riddell[2] (1), second son of Thomas[1] (1), succeeded his father at Camieston. He was born in 1746; married Jan. 13, 1776, to Elizabeth Carre, daughter and heiress of John Carre, of Cavers, in Roxburghshire, and had issue *three* sons and *three* daughters, of whom hereafter. Mr. Riddell was educated in Edinburgh, and passed as Writer to the Signet, and King's Writer for Scotland. He died Nov. 23, 1829. He acquired the estate of Union Hall, otherwise Linthill, from the Hunters, but sold it in 1822 to a Mr. Currie.

Thomas Riddell[2] (2), third son of Thomas[1] (1), was born in 1748, and died in 1756.

Robert Riddell[2] (1), fourth son of Thomas[1] (1), was born in 1750. He was in the East India Company's naval service, and perished on board the "Duchess of Athole," when that vessel was accidentally burned in Madras Roads in 1793. This occurred during the absence of the captain, and feeling his responsibility to be greater, — being in temporary command, — and being so devoted to duty (perhaps *over-devotion*) that he could not be induced to abandon the vessel, and was the only person who perished in the flames, — falling a noble sacrifice to duty.

Margaret Riddell[2] (1), eldest daughter of Thomas[1] (1), was born in 1744, and died in 1771, unmarried.

Elinor Riddell[2] (1), second daughter of Thomas[1] (1), was born in 1745, and died in 1815, unmarried.

THIRD GENERATION.

Thomas Riddell[3] (3), eldest son of William[2] (1), was born Aug. 23, 1778; married in January, 1805, to Jane, daughter of William Ferrier, of Somerford, and his wife, Lillias Wallace, heiress of the Wallaces of Crown Hill, Ayrshire, and had issue *five* sons and *four* daughters, of whom hereafter. He was entered as a Writer to the Signet, in the offices of his father, but never followed his profession. He died April 26, 1826; his widow died Jan. 11, 1833.

John Riddell[3] (1), second son of William[2] (1), was born in 1779, and was a civilian in the East India Company's service, at Madras, and died on his passage home in 1814; unmarried.

Adm'l Robert Riddell[3] (2), third son of William[2] (1), was born Feb. 27, 1782. He was a rear admiral in the Royal Navy; was a very efficient and distinguished officer, and saw much service upon the high seas. He was at Copenhagen, under Nelson, and at Algiers, under Pellew. He took the additional name, and assumed the arms of Carre (or Kerr) on succeed-

---

as the son of the younger sister. But that gentleman soon sold it, and the late Mr. Currie bought and entailed it. This estate is beautifully situated between the old Riddell House and Cavers Carre, on the river Ale. The mansion-house of Union Hall stood on the south side of the Ale, the property on the north side, where the present house of Linthill stands, having been purchased afterwards, being called Midlam Mill; the united properties were then called Linthill.

ing to the estate of Cavers Carre, on the death of his mother, who was heiress of that family, in 1828. He entered the navy in 1796, joining the "Albatross," commanded by Captain Scott, afterwards Admiral Sir George Scott. Previous to his leaving the "Albatross" the crew mutinied, but were put down by the conduct of Captain Scott and his officers, and they afterwards assisted in the capture of privateers. He afterwards served in the North Sea and Baltic stations, proceeding after those services were over to the East Indies in Sir Alexander-Collingwood Dickson's ship, the " Sceptre," seventy-four. After his return from India and further services in the Baltic and North Seas, he got the command of the "Britomart" in 1812, and in that vessel he took part in the brilliant and successful battle of Algiers. He was promoted to the rank of post-captain in 1819, and finally to that of rear-admiral. He was the recipient of a medal with bars for Copenhagen and Algiers. He died at his residence of Cavers Carre in 1860. He had long been settled at Cavers, and his life in his retirement was like his death, calm and peaceful. He was never married. Succeeded by his nephew.

Jane Riddell³ (1), eldest daughter of William² (1), was born in 1781, and died in 1849; unmarried.

Elizabeth Riddell³ (1), second daughter of William² (1), was born in 1785, and died in 1846; unmarried.

Margaret Riddell³ (1), third daughter of William² (1), was born, in 1787, and died in 1843; unmarried.

FOURTH GENERATION.

Gen. William Riddell⁴ (2), eldest son of Thomas³ (3), was born in St. George's Square, Edinburgh, Dec. 12, 1805, and succeeded his father at Camieston. He married April 9, 1837, to Margaret, daughter of Capt. John Wilkie, of the Bengal Army, and niece of Sir David Wilkie, of the Royal Army. He went out as a cadet in the Honourable East India Company's military service, in the month of April, 1823; and shortly afterwards joined as ensign the Second Battalion of the Thirtieth Native Infantry. In that regiment (subsequently numbered the sixtieth on the formation of the double battalions into single regiments), he continued to serve from junior ensign to lieutenant-colonel, and eventually succeeded to the command, which he held till his transfer, by selection, to the Thirtieth Regiment of European Infantry, in 1856, which latter corps he commanded throughout the eventful years of 1856–8, of the Indian Mutiny, till its transfer to the British service as the One Hundred and Seventh of the line. Besides holding several appointments in both civil and political employ, General Riddell was present at the siege of Bhurtpore, in 1825–6, at the forcing of the Khybur Pass, battles of Jagdulluch, Tezeen, and other actions, leading to the relief of the Jellabad garrison and the re-occupation of Cabûl, in 1842, by the Army of the Indies under Maj.-Gen. Sir George Pollock, in whose staff he served as aide-de-camp, as well as field-marshal throughout the campaign in Afghanistan, also as assistant adjutant-general to the Army of Reserve, under Sir Dudley Hill, during the Punjaub campaign of 1849, and, lastly, throughout the military campaign of 1857–8, in command of the Third Regiment of Bengal Europeans, as well as of several flying columns composed of artillery, cavalry, and infantry, sent out from Agra to co-operate with the Central India Field Force, under Sir Hugh Ross, and with the troops under the immediate command of Lord Clyde. He was present with his regiment in the severa

7

actions fought with the rebels in the vicinity of Agra, and in the Eutaws district toward Culpee, and on the Chumbal, and was in command of the fort and garrison of Agra, in which was the only remaining magazine in the upper provinces for some months, till after the fall of Delhi and the arrival of a permanent brigadier.

General Riddell received the decoration of Companion of the Most Noble, the Order of the Bath, and three medals, with one bar for Bhurtpore, Afghanistan, Cabûl, 1842, and the military campaign, and his services were twice acknowledged in the government official *Gazettes*. He retired from the army as full colonel, with rank of major-general, in December, 1861, after a continued service of upwards of thirty-eight years. He has been heard to remark on the pleasure it gave an old soldier to know when he came home to his native land that his services in the cause of his queen and country had been appreciated when abroad. Gen. Sir Hope Grant and Sir William Gomm, late field-marshal, were all in turn contemporaries and companions in arms in those trying and mutinous times. The medals received for his services were hung by the General, with a kind of military pride, upon his breast, and worn on all great occasions in connection with the volunteer meetings held at Melrose, throughout the period of his residence at the "Anchorage."

While he had reaped many honors in the far-off fields of war, of which he might truly be proud, he valued still more, perhaps, those distinctions for which he was frequently complimented by the acting government generals of the army forces, when they were inspecting the Border Battalion Volunteers, and by others, for his having been a general of the army, and yet simultaneously a full private in the ranks of the Third Roxburgh Rifle Volunteer Corps.

He took an active and prominent part in the meetings of the Border Rifle Associations, and in the social gatherings which frequently followed. He was an active and honorary member of the council of the Border Rifle Association; also, a Commissioner of Supply, and Justice of the Peace. In the most of the public events of the town of Melrose, the General, after his retirement from the army, and during his residence at the "Anchorage," took a leading part, along with the principals of the local authority. He was a director of the Exchange Company; took a deep interest in the visit of the queen at Melrose in 1867.

He was an active and esteemed member of the Border County Association; and at the Scott Centenary, in 1871, was a managing committee, and presided at the evening gathering at the Exchange. In politics he was a staunch Conservative, although his principles and opinions were never allowed to interfere with, or influence his dealings with those who held Liberal, or even Radical, views. He took a deep interest in the Episcopalian church in his neighborhood, of which he was an active supporter. About two months before his death, which occurred June 22, 1875, he had an attack of paralysis, in Edinburgh; some weeks subsequently he was so far recovered as to walk in his garden; but repeated attacks followed, and alarming tokens of his end were soon visible. He gently passed away among his friends and the clergy present, as if entering into a placid slumber. He was buried in the ancient family cemetery, in Bowden Parish. He had issue *nine* children; he left a widow, *one* son, and *four* daughters.

Walter Riddell[4] (2), second son of Thomas[3] (3) of Camieston, was born in Edinburgh, Aug. 4, 1807; married in 1830 to Elizabeth-Riddell MacLauchlan, only surviving child of Lieut.-Col. Lauchlan MacLauchlan,

"CAVERS CARRE."

Roxburghshire, Scotland.

of the Tenth Regiment; descended from the ancient Highland family of MacLauchlan of Fassifern, an estate long since sold. After a long illness, borne with great faith and patience, his admirable wife passed away in 1860, and he married secondly, in 1871, Mary, youngest daughter of William Currie, Esq., of Linthill, formerly of the East India Company's service, Madras. Mr. Riddell was educated by private tuition, and at the High School at Edinburgh. At about the age of seventeen he went to London to fill a situation in an East India house, and was for many years confidentially employed by that firm; and on retiring from business, lived some years near London, eventually returning to Scotland in 1869, where he afterward resided, — for a time near Melrose, and latterly at Cavers Carre, to which property he succeeded in 1860, on the death of his uncle, the Vice-Admiral Robert Riddell (who had assumed the additional name of Carre), and at the request of his uncle took the additional name and arms of Carre. He was a Justice of the Peace and Commissioner of Supply for the County of Roxburgh. In politics he was moderately Conservative, but he disliked the turmoil of political strife, and preferred the quiet paths of literature.

His acquaintance with the history of the border families was extensive and accurate, and he found great pleasure in imparting his knowledge through the press, lectures, correspondence, and conversation. He was an excellent lecturer, entering into his subject with much enthusiasm; and his elocution was characterized by grace and animation. He delivered several lectures on the history of the ancient families, and brought to light many valuable facts that would otherwise have been irrecoverably lost. His speeches were well prepared, and were so full of erudite and accurate information, that they were listened to with deep interest, and the reports were always read with pleasure. The mention of some old family by the local newspapers, often called forth a note from his pen, giving out of his abundant treasures valuable information.

He was a man of large heart, and the most genial sympathies; and nothing afforded him greater pleasure than to be doing good, in whatever form the opportunity presented itself. His habit of mind was serious and thoughtful, and he was strongly imbued with religious principles. He also took a deep interest in benevolent and religious societies, acting as secretary to local associations, advocating their cause on the platform, and lending his methodical and business-like capacities to their financial management. He was a great favorite with those of humble rank; he was fond of chatting with them on the road, and dropping into their cottages, would inquire kindly after their welfare.

He died at his post. He passed away at his residence at Cavers Carre * in December, 1874, his death being caused by a cold, which was followed by a severe rheumatic attack, from which the remedies applied gave him but little relief, and the poisoned blood found way to his head. He continued to grow worse, and became very incoherent in his speech, and

---

* The ancient house at Cavers Carre was built in 1532, as recorded on a stone, but has nearly disappeared. There are no less than eight stones extant that were in the old house, and when the new additions were made, were put into a court; six of these are nearly perfect, and two of them have inscribed the arms of Riddell quartered with those of Carre, — two of the ancient Carres having intermarried with the Riddells, — the oldest bearing date 1634. The early Carres were extensive land proprietors; but the acreage of Cavers Carre estate is now small, but has not passed out of the family possession.

finally was unconscious, and soon after breathed his last.   Though advanced
in years and not robust, his frame was so vigorous that a life prolonged
for many years might have been expected.   But he was prepared for the
change which came, alas! too soon; and amid his many engrossing pursuits, he was never neglectful of the great concerns of the future on which
he has entered.   He was a good man in every sense of the word.   He had
a cultured mind and a kindly heart, and was a genuine Christian.   His
mortal remains were interred at Bowden, on Dec. 7, 1874.   He left a
widow and *one* son, who succeeded to Cavers Carre.*

  Hon. John-Carre Riddell[4] (2), third son of Thomas[3] (3), was born
June 4, 1809; married in 1846, Marianna-Sibella, daughter of Justice
Stephens, of Melbourne, and had issue *three* sons and *three* daughters, of
whom hereafter.   He emigrated to Australia many years ago, and became
a squatter, in which position he continued a long time.   He subsequently
became interested, and successfully engaged in matters of polity, and was
a member of the Victorian Parliament, at Melbourne, Australia.   Is said to
have been a fine-looking man.   Deceased in 1880.

  Capt. Thomas Riddell[4] (4), fourth son of Thomas[3] (3), was born in
Edinburgh (presumably), Oct. 6, 1810; married July 24, 1848, to Ann-
Ellen, daughter of Capt. John Beckett, of the Indian Army, and had issue
one son, of whom hereafter.   He early became a soldier, and was in the
Bengal Infantry.   He was in the Punjaub campaign in 1849, with the
Army of the Reserve, and in the Afghan campaign of 1842; received a
medal for Cabûl.   Died in India, May 23, 1854.

  Robert Riddell[4] (3), fifth son of Thomas[3] (3), was born in the city of
Edinburgh (presumably), Dec. 22, 1813, and died at Bombay, India, May
29, 1839; unmarried.   He was in the East India Company's service.   A
promising young man.

  Lillias-Wallace Riddell[4] (1), eldest daughter of Thomas[3] (3), was
born in 1812; was married in 1840 to Ross Watt, and now (1873) resident in the colony of Victoria, and has issue.

  Elizabeth-Carre Riddell[4] (2), second daughter of Thomas[3] (3), was
born in 1816, and died, unmarried, in 1844.

  Georgina-Vereker Riddell[4] (1), third daughter of Thomas[3] (3), was
born in 1818; was married in 1841 to Malcolm-McNeil Rind, of the Bengal medical service, who died in 1863, leaving his widow and a numerous
family of children.†

  Jane-Ann Riddell[4] (1), fourth daughter of Thomas[3] (3), was married

---

  *The author of this work was for several years a constant correspondent
with Mr. Riddell-Carre, and much of the material incorporated into this department of his book was forwarded by that gentleman.   He was well acquainted with
the history and genealogy of all branches of the Riddell family, and seemed proud
of the ancestry from which he descended.   In reply to a letter in which the author
announced the death of his aged grandfather, Mr. Riddell-Carre said, — "I was sad
to learn of the death of your patriarchal grandfather, but you could not expect to
keep him always, and I trust he is now with the shining ones around the throne."
He was always ready to accede to my requests, and with great pains and at considerable expense, procured me portraits of eminent members of the family in England and Scotland, and views of their residences; he also introduced me to gentlemen of prominence, with whom my subsequent correspondence proved very interesting and valuable.   He always, in all his letters, manifested a deep interest in the
undertaking of the author to compile an exhaustive family history.   See his portrait
in a group in this book; also, view of Cavers Carre, his residence.
  † A cousin of the mother of this family, Susan E. Ferrier, wrote the very
popular novels "Marriage," "Inheritance," and "Destiny."

in 1843 to Elijah Imprey, Surgeon in the Bombay Medical Establishment, and died in 1859, leaving her husband and children. Dr. Imprey died in 1869.

FIFTH GENERATION.

Thomas-Carre Riddell[6] (5), eldest son of William[4] (2), was born Feb. 5, 1844, and died at sea when on the way home (to Scotland) from Calcutta, Dec. 14, 1846.

Walter-Ferrier Riddell[5] (3), second son of William[4] (2), was born Aug. 15, 1845, and died, unmarried, at Demerara, Nov. 3, 1865. He was ensign of the Second Battalion in the Sixteenth Regiment of Foot, in the East India Company's service.

Lieut. William-Carre Riddell[6] (2), third son of William[4] (2), was born March 8, 1847, and succeeded his father as "younger of Camieston." He is an officer in the One Hundred and Third Regiment Royal Bombay (India) Fusileers.

John-Wilkie Riddell[5] (3), fourth son of William[4] (2), was born March 1, 1861, and died when an infant.

Jane-Lillias Riddell[6] (2), eldest daughter of William[4] (2), was born Feb. 24, 1839; died Jan. 10, 1846.

Margaret-Sophia Riddell[6] (2), second daughter of William[4] (2), was born June 18, 1840; was married June 17, 1871, to Rev. James-Robert Crystal, D.D., minister of Cults, in Fifeshire.

Helen-Elizabeth Riddell[5] (1), third daughter of William[4] (2), was born in 1841.

Georgina-Catherine Riddell[5] (2), fourth daughter of William[4] (2), was born in 1851.

Frances-Annie Riddell[5](2), fifth daughter of William[4] (2), was born in 1863.

Capt. Thomas-Alexander Riddell[5] (6), only son of Walter[4] (2), was born in 1831; married in 1865, Elizabeth, second daughter of Alfred T. Fellows, Esq., of Beeston House, Nottingham, who was brother of Sir Charles Fellows, who received the honor of knighthood for his archæological discoveries in Lycia, and for his success in removing the "Athenian Marbles" to the British Museum. Captain Riddell was formerly in the East India Company's service, but latterly captain and Instructor of Musketry in the Ayrshire and Wigtonshire militia. He succeeded to Cavers Carre, on the death of his father, in 1874. His father wrote the author of this work, only a few weeks before his lamented death, "I hope Cavers, so long in possession of my maternal ancestors, may pass to my heirs unimpaired," little thinking that he would be called to relinquish so soon the property to which he referred. Like his father he assumed the additional surname and arms of Carre, and is the representative of the Carres of Cavers. He has issue *three* children, of whom hereafter.

Thomas-William Riddell[5] (7), eldest son of John[4] (2), was born in 1852, and is presumed to be in Australia.

John-Carre Riddell[5] (4), second son of John[4] (2), was born in 1857, and died in 1858, — probably in Australia.

Walter-John-Carre Riddell[5] (4), third son of John[4] (2), was born in 1859, and is supposed to be in Australia.

Jane-Georgina-Vereker Riddell[5] (3), eldest daughter of John[4] (2), was married in 1868 to Lieutenant Stanley, Royal Army.

Margaret-Elizabeth Riddell[5] (3), second daughter of John[4] (2), born in Australia. No other information.

Anne-Carre Riddell[5] (1), third daughter of John[4] (2), was (supposed) born in Australia. No other information.

Lieut. William-Henry Riddell[5] (4), only son of Thomas[4] (4), is an officer in the Sixteenth Regiment of Foot, British Army.

SIXTH GENERATION.

Ralph-Gervace Riddell[6] (1), a son of Thomas[5] (6), was born in 1868, and was named in honor of some early ancestors of the Roxburgh family of Riddell.

Elizabeth-Olive-Geva Riddell[6] (3), eldest daughter of Thomas[5] (6), was born Dec. 9, 1869, and was named in honor of some very early female members of the Riddell family.

Grizel-Geva Riddell[6] (1), second daughter of Thomas[5] (6), was born Oct. 6, 1871. Grizel is an old name in the family of Carre.

RIDDELLS OF NEWHOUSE, SCOTLAND.

William Riddell[1] (1), third son of Andrew[15] (2), of Haining (see Riddells of Haining in the main line of Riddells of Roxburghshire), received for his inheritance a property called "Newhouse," an old residence in the parish of Lilliesleaf, near Riddell House, and this family has since been known by that designation. William also got a charter of Muselee and Mewlie in 1618, and became ancestor of the two branches of the old Roxburghshire tree, denominated "Riddells of Newhouse" (which subsequently merged into the family of Glen-Riddell, as will afterwards appear), and "Riddells of Muselee."

SECOND GENERATION.

Rev. Simon Riddell[2] (1), who is believed to have been descended from some branch of the old border family, married Miss Riddell, the heiress of Newhouse, and became, in right of his wife, the head of this family. He was a minister of considerable distinction. In 1715 he marched to Stirling with a portion of his parishioners in defence of His Majesty and the Protestant interests, and in 1740 he was one of fifteen ministers against deposing eight seceders, of whom were Ralph and Ebenezer Erskine. Had issue *one* son, who became ancestor of Riddells of Glen-Riddell.

THIRD GENERATION.

Walter Riddell[3] (1), a son of Simon[2] (1), married the heiress of Glen-Riddell, and became head of that family.

RIDDELLS OF MINTO, SCOTLAND.

Walter Riddell[1] (1), second son of Walter[3] (1), of Newhouse, who is described as "writer in Edinburgh," acquired the barony of Minto* from

---

* MINTO is in Roxburghshire. The barony formerly belonged to the Earls of Lennox; afterwards the property of Sir Thomas Stewart, of Garlies. The Riddells

Walter Scott, of Harwood, in the year 1676, and obtained a charter under the Great Seal, dated June 23d of that year, under the terms of which the property, after his own life interest, was entailed upon his son and his second and younger daughters in succession, omitting his eldest daughter. Mr. Riddell retained Minto but a short time, and June 7, 1688, made a disposition of it in favor of his son-in-law, Thomas Rutherford, a brother of John Rutherford, of Edgerston, from whom it passed in the following year into other hands. (Disposition by Thomas Rutherford in favor of Mr. Richardson, dated July 22, 1684). But the alienation of the property by Walter Riddell was disputed by his children as heirs of entail, and legal proceedings were taken by the purchaser to enforce his rights. Ultimately, however, in the year 1687, on the purchase of the property by the Earl Ferras, all the surviving children (four daughters) joined in the conveyance of it to him.

Walter Riddell was twice married. The name of his first wife does not appear. His second wife was Isabel Riddell, but of what family I do not know. He had issue *six* children, of whom hereafter. Mr. Riddell died before January, 1685.

SECOND GENERATION.

James Riddell[2] (1), only son of Walter[1] (1), survived his father, but was dead in the year 1687, or his name would have appeared in the alienation that year.

Jean Riddell[2] (1), eldest daughter of Walter[1] (1), was married to Sir Robert Laurie, the first Baronet of Maxwelton, and had by him *three* sons and *four* daughters. Jean was the second wife of Sir Robert; and one of her daughters was "Annie Laurie," celebrated in Scottish song. She was famed for her beauty; and Mr. Douglas, of Fingland, whom she had captivated, composed in her honor the well-known verses † which are still

---

were owners between the Stewarts and Elliotts. Lord Minto informs me, that Minto House, his present residence, was rebuilt in 1814, but stands on the same site as the former one, which was the residence of the Riddells, and was supposed to be very ancient. Lord Minto kindly furnished the author a photo'-view of the south and west fronts of his magnificent and beautifully situated seat. Minto Craigs, mentioned by Sir Walter Scott, consist of a romantic assemblage of cliffs, which rise above the vale of the Tiviot, in the immediate vicinity of Minto House. A small platform on a projecting craig, commanding a beautiful prospect, is termed "Barnhills Bed." The character from whence the name was derived is said to have been a robber or outlaw. There are remains of a strong tower beneath the rocks, where the outlaw is supposed to have dwelt. On the summit of the craigs is the ruin of another tower, in a picturesque situation. Among the houses cast down by the Earl of Hartford in 1545, were the towers of Barnhills and Minto Craigs, with Minto town and place.

† "ANNIE LAURIE.

"Maxwelton braes are bonnie
    Where early fa's the dew,
And it's there that Annie Laurie
    Gie'd me her promise true —
Gie'd me her promise true,
    Which ne'er forgot will be;
And for bonnie Annie Laurie
    I'll lay me downe and dee.

"Her brow is like the snaw-drift;
    Her throat is like the swan;
Her face it is the fairest
    That e'er the sun shone on—

so popular. She was not, however, won by his poetry, but became the wife of Mr. Furguson, of Craigdorroch. See "Riddells of Glen-Riddell," in this work. The reason why Jean was excluded from the entail of Minto, was, no doubt, on account of her being already married to Sir Robert.

Susanna Riddell[2] (1), second daughter of Walter[1] (1), was the wife of Thomas Rutherford, of Tiviotdale.

Grizell Riddell[2] (1), third daughter of Walter[1] (1), died before 1687.

Elizabeth Riddell[2] (1), fourth daughter of Walter[1] (1), became the wife of James Dallas, younger of St. Martin's.

Agnes Riddell[2] (1), fifth daughter of Walter[1] (1), was under age and unmarried in January, 1687.

RIDDALLS OF ULSTER, IRELAND.

[BARONIAL BRANCH.]

Sir James Riddall[1] (1), was a son of Walter[19] (9), fourth Baronet of Riddell, and a brother of Thomas Riddell, the first of the Camieston branch of the border family. This family had intermarried with the Morrisons, who were obliged to leave Scotland and settle in Ulster, from their strict adherence to the royal cause after the battle of Worcester. He was knighted. Was this the Sir James Riddall (this family had changed the spelling to Riddall, as well as some members of the Camieston branch) who was buried in St. Mary's Church, Dublin, in 1831? The subject of this notice died issueless.

Hans Riddall[1] (1), second son of Walter[19] (9), fourth Baronet of Riddell, was Comptroller of Customs in Derry, Ireland; married, but died without issue. The name Hans was derived from the family of Hamilton, that settled in Ulster, and who were also connected by marriage with the Riddalls and Morrisons.

John Riddall[1] (1), third son of Walter[19] (9), fourth Baronet of Riddell, removed to Ulster, Ireland, with his brother, before mentioned; married, but had no children.

Gen. William Riddall[1] (1), fourth son of Walter[19] (9), fourth Baronet of Riddell, was a Knight of Hanover. He was a major-general in the army, in the Eighteenth and Sixty-second Regiments. He died in 1851, issueless.

That e'er the sun shone on—
And dark blue is her ee;
And for bonnie Annie Laurie
I'll lay me down and dee.

" Like dew on the gowan lying
Is the fa' o' fairy feet;
And like the winds in summer sighing,
Her voice is low and sweet—
Her voice is low and sweet—
And she's a' the world to me;
And for bonnie Annie Laurie
I'll lay me down and dee."

RIDDELLS OF BERMUDA, WEST INDIES.

William Riddell[1] (1) was the fourth son of Walter[19] (9), fourth Baronet of Riddell (see the main line), and his wife, Miss Watt, who was a daughter of this baronet's stepmother. William emigrated to the West Indies when young, and settled in Bermuda, as a merchant-adventurer. He married and had issue. One of his descendants wrote a medical thesis, which showed a desire to benefit humanity. This branch soon became extinct, and has now no representative. Mr. Riddell-Carre, late of Cavers, had promised me full information respecting this branch of the old family, but, alas! he died; and my very respected and reliable correspondent was lost to me. I think this branch reached only three generations.

RIDDELLS OF LILLIESLEAF, SCOTLAND.

William Riddell[1] (1), supposed to be descended from the Riddells of Riddell, in the parish of Lilliesleaf, married Margaret Hervey, resided in Lilliesleaf, and had issue *five* children, of whom hereafter. He was a carpenter by trade. I have made an effort to find where this family was broken off the old family-tree; was assisted in my work by the late Walter Riddell-Carre, of Cavers, Scotland, who had no doubt of the relationship, but could find no sufficient proof to assume the connection.

SECOND GENERATION.

John Riddell[2] (1), eldest son of William[1] (1), was born in the parish of Lilliesleaf, Roxburghshire; married Betsey Turnbull, and had issue *three* children, of whom hereafter. He was a carpenter by trade.

Thomas Riddell[2] (1), second son of William[1] (1), was born in the parish of Lilliesleaf; married Rachel Stirling, and had issue *six* children, of whom hereafter, and died in 1843. He was a thatcher by trade.

Walter Riddell[2] (1), third son of William[1] (1), was born in the parish of Lilliesleaf; married Betsey Young, and died in 1843, leaving *three* children, of whom hereafter.

Mary Riddell[2] (1), eldest daughter of William[1] (1), was born in the parish of Lilliesleaf; was married to Thomas Cochran, a merchant in Glasgow.

Margaret Riddell[2] (1), second daughter of William[1] (1), was born in the parish of Lilliesleaf, and was married to James Walker, a tailor of that place.

THIRD GENERATION.

William Riddell[3] (2), only son of John[2] (1), was born in the parish of Lilliesleaf; married Gothes Thompson, and had issue *seven* children, of whom hereafter.

Mary Riddell[3] (2), only daughter of John[2] (1), was born in the parish of Lilliesleaf, and had an infant the same day on which her father died in 1843.

William Riddell[3] (3), eldest son of Thomas[2] (1), was born in the parish of Lilliesleaf; married Agnes Deans, and had issue *five* children, of whom hereafter.

William Riddell³ (4), eldest son of Walter² (1), was born in the parish of Lilliesleaf; married April 28, 1872, to Maggie Lambert; emigrated to Philadelphia, United States, and is now residing in that city; has *two* children, of whom hereafter. He sailed from Scotland in the steamship "Iowa," Captain Overstone.

Walter Riddell³ (2), second son of Walter² (1), was born in the parish of Lilliesleaf, and came to the United States in the steamship "Australia," Captain Hederwick, in 1873; now in Philadelphia.

FOURTH GENERATION.

Jane Riddell⁴ (1), eldest daughter of William³ (2), was born in the parish of Lilliesleaf, and married James Hogg.

John Riddell⁴ (2).
Andrew Riddell⁴ (1).
George Riddell⁴ (1).
Walter Riddell⁴ (3).
Betsey Riddell⁴ (1).
Ellen Riddell⁴ (1).

} Children of William³ (2), of Lilliesleaf.

Thomas Riddell⁴ (2), eldest son of William³ (3), was born in the parish of Lilliesleaf, and is now in America; carpenter.

James Riddell⁴ (1), second son of William³ (3), was born in the parish of Lilliesleaf; is a carpenter by trade.

Walter Riddell⁴ (4), third son of William³ (3), was born in the parish of Lilliesleaf; has a family in Scotland; a baker.

Walter Riddell⁴ (5), eldest son of William³ (4), was born in Philadelphia, Penn., in 1873.

James-Bambert Riddell⁴ (2), second son of William³ (4), was born in Philadelphia, Penn., in June, 1875.

ANOTHER FAMILY.

Thomas Riddell¹ (1), a son of Isabella Riddell, was born in the parish of Lilliesleaf, Scotland, in 1815 (father's name unknown); emigrated to the United States in 1820, and settled in Lawrence, Mass., where he was employed in the mills as a dresser, until the late war. He married April 15, 1856, to Sarah S. Henderson, a woman of Scotch descent, and had issue *three* sons, of whom hereafter. Mr. Riddell was drowned (lost overboard) from a steamer between Fall River and New York, on the night of Dec. 27, 1862. His widow is in trade with her brother in Lawrence, and her sons are with their mother.

SECOND GENERATION.

James Riddell² (1), eldest son of Thomas¹ (1), was born in Lawrence, Mass., July 4, 1857; unmarried in 1874.

Walter Riddell² (1), second son of Thomas¹ (1), was born in Lawrence, Mass., Sept. 12, 1859; unmarried.

David Riddell² (1), third son of Thomas¹ (1), was born in Lawrence, Mass., Sept. 21, 1861.

RIDDELLS OF HAWICK, SCOTLAND.

Frank Riddell[1] (1), descended from the Riddells of Riddell (parents unknown), was born at Hawick, Scotland, in 1724 A. D.; married Annie Neal in 1846, and had issue, of whom hereafter. He was a gardener by occupation, and lived to old age. In an old Bible found in the home of John Fairgreaves (whose wife was a Riddell of this family), in Bridgton, Me., United States, I found the records of this branch. This old book was published in Edinburgh, Scotland, in 1734 A. D. Several members of this family hold the tradition that they are descended from the old branches of the baronial family in Roxburghshire.

SECOND GENERATION.

John Riddell[2] (1), eldest son of Frank[1] (1), was born at Hawick in 1758; married in 1780 to Peggy Parris, and had issue *twelve* children, of whom hereafter. He was gardener and sexton.

Walter Riddell[2] (1), second son of Frank[1] (1), was born at Hawick in 1760 A. D.; married Janet Hamilton, and had issue, of whom hereafter. He removed to Carlisle, England.

THIRD GENERATION.

Ann Riddell[3] (1), eldest daughter of John[2] (1), was born at Hawick, in 1784, and died when young, a single woman.

Isabella Riddell[3] (1), second daughter of John[2] (1), was born at Hawick in 1786, and died young unmarried.

Janet Riddell[3] (1), third daughter of John[2] (1), was born at Hawick in 1788, and was married to Michael Dryden.

Francis Riddell[3] (2), eldest son of John[2] (1), was born at Hawick, Nov. 22, 1792; married Euphena Scott, and died in Northumberland, Eng. He drove a mail-coach about nineteen years. Issue not known.

Isabella Riddell[3] (2), fourth daughter of John[2] (1), was born at Hawick, Aug. 4, 1795; died young.

James Riddell[3] (1), second son of John[2] (1), was born at Hawick, Sept. 1, 1797; married Janet Ray in 1820, and had issue. He was a coachman for many years.

Adam Riddell[3] (1), third son of John[2] (1), was born at Hawick, Nov. 29, 1798; married in 1821 to Martha Leatherhead, and resides in Edinburgh. Had issue; no names.

John Riddell[3] (2), fourth son of John[2] (1), was born at Hawick, April 7, 1801, and was killed in a threshing-mill, at the age of nineteen.

Jean Riddell[3] (1), fifth daughter of John[2] (1), was born at Hawick, Sept. 22, 1804; was the wife of John Watson, of Selkirk.

Katharine Riddell[3] (1), sixth daughter of John[2] (1), was born at Hawick, Sept. 22, 1806; was married to John Fairgreaves, a weaver; emigrated to Bridgton, Me., United States, and had issue (besides others) a son, who resided in Bridgton.

John Riddell[3] (3), fifth and youngest son of John[2] (1), was born at Hawick, Nov. 20, 1809; married Barbara Hall, an English lady, and had issue. He was a coachman.

Mary Riddell[3] (1), seventh and youngest daughter of John[2] (1), was born in Hawick, Feb. 9, 1810; died young.

James Riddell[3] (1), eldest son of Walter[2] (1), was born at Hawick, April 4, 1784; married and had issue *three* daughters, of whom hereafter.

Frank Riddell[3] (3), second son of Walter[2] (1), was born at Hawick, June 10, 1786, and was a clerk in a store at Leith. He died when in his prime, unmarried.

Willie Riddell[3] (1), second son at Walter[2] (1), was born at Hawick, Oct. 14, 1789, and settled at Carlisle, Eng.

Isabella Riddell[3] (3), eldest daughter of Walter[2] (1), was born at Hawick (or Carlisle, Eng.), Aug. 2, 1791.

Margaret Riddell[3] (1), second daughter of Walter[2] (1), was born at Carlisle, Eng., Sept. 6, 1793.

Walter Riddell[3] (2), a son of Walter[2] (1), was born at Hawick, and died young. He was a student for the ministry, and a very fine young man; he was greatly lamented.

FOURTH GENERATION.

Nellie Riddell[4] (1), eldest daughter of James[3] (1), was born at Hawick, and died when young, and unmarried.

Betsey Riddell[4] (1), second daughter of James[3] (1), was born at Hawick, and died young, unmarried.

Jennie Riddell[3] (1), third daughter of James[3] (1), was born at Hawick, Scotland, and became the wife of John Hislop.

RIDDELLS OF GALASHIELS, SCOTLAND.

Walter Riddell[1] (2) (parents' names unknown) married Miss Isabelle Heiton, and was a mason and builder in Galashiels. He had issue *three* children, of whom hereafter. He was a brother (presumably, as per tradition) of the ancestor of the family styled in this book "Riddells of Hawick." Mrs. Riddell belonged to the ancient family of the Heitons of Damick Lewer; see tale respecting the Heitons in Wilson's "Tales of the Border."

SECOND GENERATION.

John Riddell[2] (1), eldest son of Water[1] (1), was born in Galashiels, Scotland, 1796, and became a soldier in the Seventy-first Scottish Regiment. He fought and was wounded at Waterloo; became a pensioner in 1834, and died in his seventy-second year. He married Helen, daughter of James Leitsh, cooper, and had issue *one* son, of whom hereafter.

Thomas Riddell[2] (1), second son of Walter[1] (1), was born in Selkirk, Scotland, say 1798–9, and died young, unmarried.

Mary Riddell[2] (1), only daughter of Walter[1] (1), was born at Selkirk, Scotland, and married Thomas Hogg, a hosier and manufacturer in Selkirk; both long dead.

THIRD GENERATION.

Walter Riddell[3] (2), only son of John[2] (1), was born in Selkirk (?), Scotland, Oct. 24, 1832; married Agnes Tait (she was born in 1832), and has had issue *nine* children, of whom hereafter. Mr. Riddell writes from Galashiels, and I think he resides there,

FOURTH GENERATION.

John Riddell⁴ (2), eldest son of Walter ⁸ (2), was born 1854; dead.
Janet Riddell⁴ (1), eldest daughter of Walter⁸ (2), born July 10, 1856.
Helen Riddell⁴ (1), second daughter of Walter⁸ (2), born July 26, 1858.
Frank Riddell⁴ (1), second son of Walter⁸ (2), was born Feb. 5, 1862.
Euphemia Riddell⁴ (1), third daughter of Walter⁸ (2), born Oct. 6, 1865; dead.
Mary Riddell⁴ (1), third daughter of Walter⁸ (2), born May 5, 1864; dead.
Isabelle Riddell⁴ (1), fifth daughter of Walter⁸ (2), born April 12, 1868.
Agnes Riddell⁴ (1), sixth daughter of Walter⁸ (2), born Sept. 3, 1870.
Elizabeth Riddell⁴ (1), seventh daughter of Walter⁸ (2), born April 17, 1873.

RIDDELLS OF TIVIOTDALE, SCOTLAND.

Robert Riddell² (1) is said to have been a native of Tiviotdale.* He married a lady named Agnes Scott, a native of the same locality, and a woman of remarkable strength of mind and excellence of character. Mr. Riddell was a professional shepherd, and followed this branch of husbandry during life. A writer describes him as "a man of strong though uneducated mind." He made his home for many years in a remote district called Langshawburn; and while living in this "most friendly and hospitable district," his humble home was frequently visited by Walter Scott, Pulteney Malcolm, and James Hogg, the Ettrick shepherd. He was subsequently a resident of a place called Capplefoot, and there carried on a farm owned by Thomas Beattie; while resident here, and being remote from the school, he employed a teacher in his house to instruct his children. Mr. Riddell returned to his employment in the Forest of Ettrick under Mr. Scott, of Doleraine, to whom he had been a shepherd in his younger days; with this family and that of Mr. Borthwick, all his years were passed, save one, since he was large enough to wear the "plaid." Mr. Riddell died when in the prime of life, leaving a widow and *seven* children, six sons and one daughter, of whom hereafter.

SECOND GENERATION.

William Riddell² (1), eldest son of Robert¹ (1), was born in Tiviotdale, Roxburghshire, in the year 1789; married to Elizabeth Mill, Jan. 6, 1831, and followed farming and sheep-herding in his native district. He

---

* I am not acquainted with the history of the ancestors of this branch of the Riddells; have failed, after an extensive correspondence and liberal advertising, to trace any connection between them and the old tree planted so early in Roxburghshire. At one time there were reasons for believing that they were descended from the Glen-Riddell family of the same shire, but after a careful examination of the pedigree, no cadet was found who could have been the progenitor of this family. Tradition says these Riddells are an offshoot of the ancient stock at Riddell, and I am inclined to believe the statement; but in the absence of proof I must leave their antecedents to some one who may find access to sources of information from which I am far removed. — *Author.*

died Nov. 29, 1867, having had issue *seven* children, of whom hereafter. His wife predeceased him June 14, 1853, at the age of 53 years. The family lived at Ramcleuchburn, Scotland.

Borthwick Riddell² (1), second son of Robert¹ (1), was born in Tiviotdale, Roxburghshire; married, and followed farming as a vocation. He was a distinguished performer on the bagpipe, and for many years was known as "Riddell, the piper." He was a large, dark man, and the best player on the small pipes on the Scottish border. See a lecture in which mention is made of his playing at the wedding of the son of the Duke of Buccleuch; also see Wilson's "Songs of Scotland." He played on many important occasions, and always won the applause of the company. Mr. Riddell played at Minto House when Earl Russell married a daughter of the Earl of Minto, — the parents of Lord Amberley, — and for this service was rewarded with one of the cheapest and best farms on the estate. No children.

Henry-Scott Riddell² (1), third son of Robert¹ (1), was born at Sorbie, near Langholm, Sept. 23, 1798; married to Eliza, daughter of Mr. Clark, a merchant of Biggar, and by her had issue *three* sons, of whom hereafter. He spent his younger days as a shepherd with his father and elder brothers. His advantages for education in early life were very limited; sometimes his father employed a teacher in his house, and during a few weeks in winter sent his children to the district-school. When his father removed a distance from the schools, he was sometimes boarded for study — at Davington, Roberton and Newmill; at each of which, he says, "I only remained a short time, making, I suppose, such progress as do other boys who love the foot-ball better than the spelling-book." He early manifested a preference for literature, and read all the books he could borrow in his neighborhood; and when on the mountains with his flocks, he constantly carried a book to these lonely solitudes, and with these silent companions and his dog, surrounded by the wild scenes of nature, he passed his time most pleasantly. While thus employed he commenced the composition of poetry and, as he has said, loved to write out the thoughts that came into his mind. The following lines best show the habits of the shepherd-lad at that time :—

> " My early years were passed far on
> The hills of Ettrick wild and lone;
> Through summer sheen and winter cold,
> Tending the flocks that o'er them strolled.
> In bold, enthusiastic glee
> I sung rude strains of minstrelsy;
> Which mingling with, died o'er the dale,
> Unheeded as the plovers' wail.
> Oft where the waving rushes shed
> A shelter frail about my head,
> Weening, though not through thoughts of fame,
> To fix on these more lasting claim,
> I'd there secure in rustic scroll,
> The wayward fancies of my soul.
> Even where yon lofty rocks, arise,
> Hoar as the clouds on wintry skies,
> Wrapp'd in the plaid and dernel beneath
> The colder cone of drifted wreath,
> I noted them afar from ken,
> Till ink would freeze within the pen;
> So deep the spell that bound the heart
> Unto the bard's undying art—

"TIVIOTHEAD COTTAGE"
Near Hawick, Scotland.
RESIDENCE OF HENRY SCOTT RIDDELL, THE POET.

So rapt the charm that still beguiled
The minstrel of the mountain wild."
  .   .   .   .

He used to carry his scraps of poetry in his hat, and after a time, unlike most young authors, he got a publisher unsought for. A wind swept
his hat away and scattered his poetic productions far over hill and dale,
like a flock of wild fowl. He recovered a few of these, but others fell
into strange hands and created no little excitement in the neighborhood,
procuring for him a popularity that never died out. So strong were the
pressings of the muse, that he could not sleep, and frequently arose to
note down the thoughts that seemed to come unsought, while all others
were sound asleep. He prepared himself for college, and after the death
of his father, having accumulated considerable means from his employment as shepherd and his portion of the parental patrimony, he went to
Edinburgh and entered the university there. He proved a good scholar,
but did not apply himself to his studies with that diligence that was exercised by some, in consequence of spending much of his time in composition. After some time spent in study at St. Andrew's, he returned to
the university at Edinburgh and completed his course. After becoming
a probationer he was called to the pastoral charge of a church in the district, and for a time laid aside the pursuit of romantic literature. In consequence of there being no house provided for the preacher, he was under
the necessity of traveling nine miles to the place of his professional services, and frequently, in bad weather, preached in a very uncomfortable
condition, with the wet pouring from his sleeves upon the Bible before
him, and upon the carpet at his feet. But the Duke of Buccleuch built
a dwelling-house for him, which he occupied through the remainder of
his life. About this time Mr. Riddell fell into a melancholy state, which
terminated in insanity, and he was, of course, unable to attend to pastoral
duties for a series of years. Another minister had succeeded him, and on
his recovery he did not interfere with the new ecclesiastical arrangement;
his procedure was generously approved by the Duke of Buccleuch, who
conferred upon him the cottage at Tiviothead, a grant of land, and a small
annuity.

Mr. Riddell had formed the acquaintance of a lady of refinement and
position, Miss Eliza Clark, when a poor shepherd-lad, and the affection
bestowed by him was reciprocated; but he was too independent to ask
or receive her hand in marriage, until he had acquired an education, and
during all his college years she remained true to her first love, refusing
wealth and high standing in life, and braving the risk of embracing comparative poverty. But when he had obtained a settlement at Tiviothead,
he made his own by marriage her who had in heart been his during the
long time he was in study. She was everything that could be looked for
in the wife and mother; and during the time of his indisposition she
proved a most constant and devoted companion. Mr. Riddell spent his remaining days in comfort at his pretty cottage-home, devoting his time to
reading, lecturing, and literature. He was highly esteemed by all, and his
home was visited by the most distinguished men of his day. My space
will not admit of a more extended notice of this good man, and I must refer the reader to his complete poetical works, in which a full autobiogra-
phy, beautifully written, may be found. He died at his home at Tiviothead
Cottage, in 1870, leaving a widow and two sons to lament his death. His
widow died on the 29th of May, 1875, and now that they are dead, "the

hill-harps' notes of love " have gently died away, and she to whom the
poet "waked his harp" in the "bonnie greenwood bowers o' the birks and
willows green," has followed him to "the hames of our ain folk," and their
mortal remains are laid in the quiet

> " Church-yard that lonely is lying
> Amid the deep greenwood by Tiviot's wild strand."

Through the influence of Dr. Bydon, a monument to his memory, in
the form of a large cairn, was erected in a place overlooking the poet's
home at Tiviothead, where he lived so long, and where the most of his
poems were composed. I subjoin some lines composed by him on the
death of his mother, as a sample of his style.

" THE LAMENT.

> " In the sadness and pomp of funeral array,
>   To the grave of my father they bore her away,
> . And laid her in death's silent chambers to rest,
>   With the cold clay and church-yard turf over her breast,
>   And bade me to weep not for her who had gone
>   Away to a land where no sorrows were known;
>   To weep not for her who through regions sublime
>   Had traveled away from the troubles of time,
>   To live in the bliss of the highest abode,
>   With the angels of light and the Son of her God.

> " Yet how may it be ? Can the bosom forget
>   The form, though so cold, and the eye, though now set ?
>   Can the thoughts that away with the spirit will hie,
>   And accompany it on to the bowers of the sky,
>   There, lured and delighted, for ever remain,
>   Nor return to the earth and its sadness again ?
>   Alas ! there are shadows of darkness around,
>   With which while below we are deeply inbound ;
>   There is sorrow in all that we listen and see,
>   And pain in the heart till the spirit be free,
>   And our thoughts woe-o'erclouded, still rest on the grave
>   Where slumber the forms that we longed so to save.

> " She guarded my steps when existence was young,
>   Her lips o'er my cradle the lullaby sung,
>   Her kindness was o'er me — her arms still caressed,
>   And my head found a home on a mother's own breast ;
>   And when every eyelid in slumber was closed,
>   When the shade of creation o'er nature reposed,
>   How oft would her bosom deep tenderness prove,
>   And yearn in its hope o'er the child of her love,
>   And breathe for my welfare to Heaven a prayer,
>   When I knew not of danger, nor dreamt of her care !
>   How then shall the power of remembrance decay
>   From the form that is cold in its chamber of clay ?
>   How, how shall the heart, in its sadness of mood,
>   Forget o'er the loss of a mother to brood ?
>   And when shall the radiance be shed from the sky,
>   That finds not a tear-drop for her in mine eye ?
>   Is the house where her accents of love wont to flow,
>   Not a scene for the shadows of sadness and woe ?
>   Is the charm that was shed by her presence around
>   Not fall'n from our life, never more to be found ?
>   Do we feel not the gloom, and still live to deplore
>   The loved who is fled, and no years can restore ?

> " Oh ! there was a time when our bosoms were gay
>   As the skylark that welcomes the breezes of May ;

" When the heart heaved no sigh, and the eye shed no drop,
But was mingled with joy or enlivened by hope.
But the clouds of misfortune rose darkly the while,
And lorded their gloom o'er the light of our smile;
And the tempest burst forth all too fierce to be braved
By the feeble of form, that we fain would have saved.
It came — it hath passed, and away with it borne
The friend of our life who can never return.

" When the song of the bird, and the beauties of spring,
Delight to the land of our fathers shall bring —
When the dew-drops of morn, that no footsteps may press,
Lie lonely and long in the forest's recess —
When the mist of the mountain is melted away
By the breath of the sky and the light of the day,
And the blooms of the primrose, the flower of the thorn,
The land of the living return to adorn; —
All hearts shall be gay, and in pleasure combine,
But sorrow and sadness depart not from mine,
Since the dwelling is dark, and the chamber is cold,
Of her whom the living no more shall behold.

" When our friends, who have long been away o'er the main,
And have heard not the tale of our trial and pain,
Shall return, and shall hope in our dwelling to find
The friend who was here when they left us behind —
Oh! how, 'mid the sorrow that lies round the heart,
Shall these lips to them e'er have the power to impart
The tidings, that she whom they ask for has fled
From the home of the living, to dwell with the dead?

" Yet, yet 'mid this cold world of death and of ill.
A comfort remains in all suffering still,
For sympathy lives o'er the forms that decay,
And our hope with the dying can pass not away;
And when all the waste of our suffering proves vain,
Our spirits can gather a pleasure from pain —
A self-treasured feeling — the offspring of grief,
Which yields something more to the soul than relief.
The grass that grows green o'er the turf of the tomb
Relieves the dark thought from the depths of its gloom,
And the floweret that opens its white bosom there
Can a tale of the spirit departure declare;
And a feeling of joy like the power of a dream,
Arising to life o'er the bosom would seem,
When we think on the charms which the grave-turf has clad,
And how nature thus stoops to hold faith with the dead.

" Oh still, when the sun in the west sinks away,
And the winds from the woodlands their breathings convey —
When the song of the blackbird, aloft on the bough,
Is bidding to day's soft departure adieu,
And the whispers of nature, with voice of the stream,
Awake, and the star comes abroad with its beam,—
I will seek the lone scene, where the relics are laid
Of her whose bright memory remains undecayed;
Nor mortals shall mark there the tears that shall flow
To pleasure the heart, as they soften its woe,
Or know of the peace that can visit the breast
From the thoughts of the beauty of those that are blest."

Robert Riddell[2] **(2)**, fourth son of Robert[1] **(1)**, was born in Tiviot-dale, Roxburghshire, in 1800; married Margaret Johnston in 1819, and rented a farm in Cumberland for some years. He emigrated to America in 1832; his family consisted of *ten* children, of whom hereafter. He

8

died in Rockton, Canada, Nov. 16, 1867; his widow in 1874, aged 77 years; she was born in Canoby.

Alexander-Hay Riddell[2] (1), fifth son of Robert[1] (1), was born in Tiviotdale, Roxburghshire; married, and had issue *five* children, three sons and two daughters, of whom hereafter. He carried on farming in Cumberland, near Carlisle.

Walter Riddell[2] (1), sixth and youngest son of Robert[1] (1), was born in Tiviotdale, Roxburghshire, and died in the year 1834, unmarried.

Mary Riddell[2] (1), a daughter of Robert[1] (1), was born in Tiviotdale, Roxburghshire; married to —— Jones, and had a family of *ten*, four sons and six daughters.

THIRD GENERATION.

Margaret-Mill Riddell[3] (1), eldest daughter of William[2] (1), was born at Blackburn, Lauderdale, July 6, 1831; she was married.

Robert-Borthwick Riddell[3] (3), eldest son of William[2] (1), was born at Ramcleuchburn, in the parish of Hawick, Feb. 21, 1833, and died March 29, 1862; unmarried.

William-Mill Riddell[3] (2), second son of William[2] (1), was born at Ramcleuchburn, parish of Hawick, July 23, 1835, and is now (1878) carrying on a farm of 1,600 acres at Ramcleuchburn, Tiviothead, Hawick; is a shepherd and unmarried.

James-Scott Riddell[3] (1), third son of William[2] (1), was born at Ramcleuchburn, parish of Hawick, Sept. 27, 1837; was married at St. Boswell, Bowden, Scotland, Feb. 26, 1862, to Isabella Telper, and is now living on a farm at Grassgarth, near Carlisle, Cumberland, Eng. He has issue *seven* children, of whom hereafter.

Jessie Riddell[3] (1), second daughter of William[2] (1), was born at Ramcleuchburn, parish of Hawick, Sept. 2, 1839; was married at the same place Jan. 16, 1868, to William Easton, and has *three* children.

Agnes-Scott Riddell[3] (1), third daughter of William[2] (1), was born at Ramcleuchburn, May 24, 1842; was married Dec. 5, 1861, to Thomas Irving, of Langholm; he died there April 6, 1870, aged 34 years, leaving issue, and his widow married secondly, Jan. 9, 1873, to James Lunn, watchmaker, of Langholm, now resident at Edinburgh, Scotland.

Elizabeth Riddell[3] (1), youngest daughter of William[2] (1), was born at Ramcleuchburn, Dec. 30, 1844; died there Sept. 2, 1852.

Walter-Scott Riddell[3] (2), eldest son of Henry[2] (1), was born at Tiviothead, parish of Hawick, in 1835; married a daughter of the Rev. Dr. Arnot, of the High Church, Edinburgh, and held an office in the Hong Kong and Shanghai Bank, in China. He died in London in 1876, leaving a widow and *six* children, of whom hereafter.

· **William-Brown-Clark Riddell**[3] (3), second son of Henry[2] (1), was born at Flexhouse, near Hawick, Roxburghshire, Dec. 16, 1835. In his seventh year he was admitted a pupil in John Watson's Institution, Edinburgh, where he remained till 1850, when he entered the university. During three sessions he prosecuted his studies with extraordinary ardor and success. On the commencement of a fourth session he was seized with an illness which completely prostrated his physical, and occasionally enfeebled his mental, energies. After a period of suffering, patiently borne, he died in his father's cottage at Tiviothead, July 20, 1856, in his twenty-first year. Of an intellect singularly precocious, at the early age of seven, he composed in correct and interesting prose, and produced in his eighth year some vigorous poetry. With a highly retentive memory, he retained the results of an extended course of reading, begun almost in childhood. Conversant with general history, he was familiar with the various systems of philosophy. To an accurate knowledge of the Latin and Greek classics he added a correct acquaintance with many of the modern languages. He found consolation on his death-bed by perusing the Scriptures in the original tongues. He died in fervent hope and with Christian resignation. His was one of the most transparent intellects of his day; his qualities of mind and heart made him greatly beloved by all who knew him. The following verses were composed in his fourteenth year : —

"LAMENT OF WALLACE.

" No more by thy margin, dark Carron,
    Shall Wallace in solitude wander.
When, tranquil, the moon shines afar on
    Thy heart-stirring wildness and grandeur.
        For lost are to me
            Thy beauties forever;
        Since fallen in thee
            Lie the faithful and free,
            To waken, ah, never!

" And I, thus defeated, must suffer
    My country's reproach; yet forsaken,
A home to me Nature may offer
    Among her green forests of braken.
        But home who can find
            For heart-rending sorrow ?
        The wound who can bind
            When thus pierced is the mind
            By fate's ruthless arrow?

" 'Tis death that alone ever frees us
    Of woes too profound to be spoken,
And nought but the grave ever eases
    The pangs of a heart that is broken.
        Then, oh! that my blood
            In Carron's dark water
        Had mixed with the flood
            Of the warriors, shed
            'Mid torrents of slaughter.

" For woe to the day when, desponding,
    I read in thine aspect the story
Of those that were slain while defending
    Their homes and their mountains of glory.
        And curst be the guile
            Of treacherous knavery,
        That throws o'er our isle,
            In its tyranny vile,
            The mantle of slavery."

Robert Riddell[5] (4), youngest son of Henry[2] (1), was born at Tiviothead, near Hawick, in the year 1840 (?), and is now somewhere in Australia, engaged in agriculture. He is married, but I have no account of his family.

Nancy Riddell[5] (1), eldest daughter of Robert[2] (2), was born in Scotland (probably in Roxburghshire) in 1820, and died at Rockton, Can., March 29, 1883.

Euphemia Riddell³ (1), second daughter of Robert² (2), was born in Scotland, and died in Rockton, Can., 1845, aged 21 years.

Benjamin Riddell³ (1), eldest son of Robert² (2), was born in Scotland, and died in Canada in 1853, aged 18 years.

Thomas Riddell³ (2), second son of Robert² (2), was born in Scotland, and died in Canada in 1858.

Robert Riddell³ (5), third son of Robert² (2), was born in Scotland Feb. 24, 1821; married Charlotte Barlow, May, 12, 1846, and has had issue *fourteen* children, of whom hereafter. His wife was born in 1829. He is a farmer at Rockton, Ontario, Can.

Ann Riddell³ (1), third daughter of Robert² (2), was born in Scotland.

Walter Riddell³ (1), fourth son of Robert² (2), was born in Scotland; now living in Canada.

Walter Riddell³ (2), eldest son of Alexander² (1); married, and is now living at Sceughmire, Great Orton, Carlisle, Cumberland, Eng., as a farmer.

Thomas-Ramshay Riddell³ (1), second son of Alexander ² (1); married, and is now (1878) living at Brampton, near Carlisle, in the north of England.

Alexander-Hay Riddell³ (2), third son of Alexander² (1); married, and in 1878 was living at Beck Brow, Brampton, near Carlisle, Eng.

FOURTH GENERATION.

William Riddell⁴ (4), eldest son of James³ (1), was born at Bowden, Scotland, Feb. 27, 1863.

Robert-Bothwick Riddell⁴ (6), second son of James³ (1), was born at Ramcleuchburn, Scotland, March 29, 1865.

Elizabeth-Brown Riddell⁴ (2), eldest daughter of James³ (1), was born at Grassgarth, Cumberland, Eng., April 12, 1868.

James-Telfer Riddell⁴ (2), third son of James³ (1), was born at Grassgarth, Cumberland, Eng., July 31, 1870; died in ten weeks.

John-Telfer Riddell⁴ (1), fourth son of James³ (1), was born at Grassgarth, Cumberland, Eng., Aug. 27, 1872.

James-Scott Riddell⁴ (3), fifth son of James³ (1), was born at Grassgarth, Cumberland, Eng., Dec. 8, 1874.

Margaret-Telfer Riddell⁴ (2), second daughter of James³ (1), was born at Grassgarth, Cumberland, Eng., June 3, 1877.

Eliza-Mary Riddell⁴ (1), eldest daughter of Walter³ (2), was born at Hong Kong, China, May 22, 1867.

Helen Riddell⁴ (1), second daughter of Walter³ (2), was born in Hong Kong, China, July 28, 1868.

Henry Riddell⁴ (2), eldest son of Walter³ (2), was born in London, Eng., March 18, 1872.

Agnes-Frances Riddell⁴ (2), third daughter of Walter³ (2), was born (presumably) in London, Eng., Nov. 4, 1872.

David-Arnot Riddell⁴ (1), son of Walter³ (2), was born in London, Eng., April 3, 1875; twin.

Walter-Scott Riddell⁴ (3), son of Walter³ (2), was born in London, Eng., April 3, 1875; twin.

Robert Riddell[4] (7), eldest son of Robert[8] (5), was born in Ontario, Can., Nov. 16, 1846; married Hadann Wires in 1867, and has issue —— children; resides in Rockton.

John Riddell[4] (2), second son of Robert[8] (5), was born in Ontario, Can., May 22, 1848; resides in Rockton.

Benjamin Riddell[4] (2), third son of Robert[8] (5), was born in Ontario, Can., March 26, 1850; married Mary-Ann Wires in 1869, and has issue, —— children; resides in Rockton.

Clarisse Riddell[4] (1), eldest daughter of Robert[8] (5), was born in Ontario, Can., March 15, 1852, and was married to John Stewart in 1866 (?).

James Riddell[4] (4), fourth son of Robert[8] (5), was born in Ontario, Can., Nov. 8, 1854; married Ann Stuart in 1878, and has issue —— children. He resides in Ontario.

Harriet-A. Riddell[4] (1), second daughter of Robert[8] (5), was born in Ontario, Can., Oct. 23, 1856.

Thomas Riddell[4] (3), fifth son of Robert[8] (5), was born in Ontario, Can., April 24, 1859.

Nancy-Maria Riddell[4] (2), third daughter of Robert[8] (5), was born in Ontario, Can., Feb. 18, 1862.

Henry-S. Riddell[4] (3), sixth son of Robert[8] (5), was born in Ontario, Can., June 26, 1864; died March 9, 1865.

William-H. Riddell[4] (4), seventh son of Robert[8] (5), was born in Ontario, Can., Dec. 17, 1865.

Charles Riddell[4] (1), eighth son of Robert[8] (5), was born in Ontario, Can., Nov. 23, 1871.

Walter Riddell[4] (4), ninth son of Robert[8] (5), was born in Ontario, Can., Feb. 6, 1873.

Alexander Riddell[4] (3), tenth son of Robert[8] (5), was born in Ontario, Can., Nov. 28, 1874.

George Riddell[4] (1), eleventh son of Robert[8] (5), was born in Ontario, Can., Jan. 4, 1878.

RIDDELS OF GLENMUICK, ABERDEENSHIRE, SCOTLAND.

James Riddel[1] (1), supposed to have been born at Monymusk, Scotland, married Elizabeth Ross, and by her had issue *eight* children. The first wife died between 1791 and 1793, and he married secondly, Jane Gillanders, by whom he had *nine* children. He removed in company with two brothers, hereafter mentioned, from Monymusk to Cobbletown, Dallamurchy, in the parish of Glenmuick, Aberdeenshire, Scotland (say 1782), where he settled as blacksmith and reared his large family. He died at Glenmuick May 24, 1823, and his widow about 1835.

Peter Riddel[1] (1), a brother of the preceding, removed with his two brothers from Monymusk, Scotland, to Clackinturn, in the parish of Crathie, Aberdeenshire, and settled there as blacksmith. He married Mary Cragie, and had a family of *ten* children, of whom hereafter. It may be reasonably presumed that some of the Riddel families whose names are recorded in this book are connected with this stock, but in the absence of documentary evidence I must leave the "missing link" to be found by others.

Alexander Riddel[1] **(1)**, a brother of the preceding, was probably born at Monymusk,* in Aberdeenshire, Scotland, and removed along with his two brothers, before mentioned, to near Aberdeen, but after a short stay returned to his native parish, where he is supposed to have died. He was a blacksmith by trade. I have communicated with the parish-clerk at Monymusk, but cannot connect any Aberdeenshire family of Riddel as descended from this man, although his nephew thinks he had a large family.

SECOND GENERATION.

William Riddel[2] **(1)**, eldest son of James[1] (1), was born (presumably), at Monymusk (although the date of birth is at Glenmuick), Sept. 24, 1779, and died in infancy.

Isabella Riddel[2] **(1)**, eldest daughter of James[1] (1), was born at Glenmuick, Aberdeenshire, Nov. 25, 1780, and died in the city of Aberdeen (where she had been a dressmaker), Jan. 6, 1848.

Alexander Riddel[2] **(2)**, second son of James[1] (1), was born at Glenmuick, Aberdeenshire, in 1782 (?), and died in infancy.

Elizabeth Riddel[2] **(1)**, second daughter of James[1] (1), was born at Glenmuick, Aberdeenshire, Scotland, in 1784; was married to Alexander Morrison, shipmaster, in Aberdeen, in 1818, and died Aug. 29, 1868.

James Riddel[2] **(2)**, third son of James[1] (1), was born at Glenmuick, Aberdeenshire, Scotland, Jan. 4, 1785; married Ann, daughter of Thomas McLean, plasterer, of Aberdeen (she was born April 17, 1797, and died Aug. 18, 1852), in 1816, and by her had issue *twelve* children, of whom hereafter. Mr. Riddel was treasurer to the Harbour Trustees of Aberdeen for many years. He died Nov. 16, 1842.

Peter Riddel[2] **(2)**, fourth son of James[1] (1), was born in Glenmuick, Aberdeenshire, in 1787 (?), and settled in London, Eng., as gold- and silversmith. He died May 7, 1815. No account of a family.

John Riddel[2] **(1)**, fifth son of James[1] (1), was born in Glenmuick, Aberdeenshire, June 10, 1789, and settled in London, Eng., where he died in September, 1856. Cabinet-maker by trade. No account of a family.

Mary Riddel[2] **(1)**, third daughter of James[1] (1), was born at Glenmuick, Aberdeenshire, April 19, 1719; was married to William Morrison, of Monymusk, wood merchant, at Midmar, and died in the parish of Banshay, Invercanny, Jan. 22, 1868. Youngest child of Elizabeth Ross.

George Riddel[2] **(1)**, sixth son of James[1] (1), was born at Glenmuick, Aberdeenshire, Oct. 22, 1793; married Margaret Coults at Dorsincilley, Glenmuick, in April, 1818, and died May 11, 1855, at the city of Aberdeen, where he was a blacksmith; he had a family of children.

Alexander Riddel[2] **(3)**, seventh son of James[1] (1), was born at Glenmuick, Aberdeenshire, May 12, 1795; married June 12, 1823, at Cortachie. Elizabeth Duncan, and had *nine* children, of whom hereafter. He was a blacksmith at Aboyne, on the River Dee, and hotel keeper at Ballater, in his native county, until infirm with old age, when he went to live with his daughter, Mrs. Grant, at Mill-of-Coull. He died Dec. 27, 1874; his wife predeceased him in 1871.

Jean Riddel[2] **(1)**, fourth daughter of James[1] (1), was born at Glen-

*MONYMUSK is between the Rivers Don and Dee, in Aberdeenshire, Scotland, and not more than twelve miles (according to Murray's map) from the city of Aberdeen. Ballater-on-the-Dee is at a railway terminus near Balmoral, the Queen's summer residence. Aberdeen is the principal city in the north of Scotland, situated at the mouth of the River Dee.

muick, June 18, 1797; was married to James Ross, innkeeper, Ballater, in 1819, and died there Aug. 22, 1850.

Robert Riddel[2] (1), eighth son of James[1] (1), was born at Glenmuick, Aberdeenshire, June 30, 1801.   He is mentioned as a resident of Dundee, Scotland, but I know nothing of his history.

Margaret Riddel[2] (1), fifth daughter of James[1] (1), was born in Glenmuick, Aberdeenshire, Jan. 25, 1805; was married to —— Nelson (?), and went to New Zealand, where it is thought she died.

Ann Riddel[2] (1), sixth daughter of James[1] (1), was born in Glenmuick, Aberdeenshire, July 23, 1806.

William Riddel[2] (2), ninth son of James[1] (1), was born at Glenmuick, Aberdeenshire, April 28, 1808; married, and had a family.   He was sometime a coal merchant at Aberdeen, but in 1874 was said to live at Rochdale, Eng.   Died in 1876.

Joseph Riddel[2] (1), tenth son of James[1] (1), was born at Glenmuick, Aberdeenshire, between 1808 and 1810.   I have no other information concerning this man.

Catherine Riddel[2] (1), youngest daughter of James[1] (1) and his wife, Elizabeth Gillanders, was born at Glenmuick, Aberdeenshire, July 11, 1810; was married Sept. 25, 1836, to Francis Deans, innkeeper, near Ballater, and is the only child of James Riddel, blacksmith, known to be living (1884).

Jane Riddell[2] (2), a daughter of Peter[1] (1), was born in the parish of Crathie, Aberdeenshire.

William Riddell[2] (3), a son of Peter[1] (1), was born in the parish of Crathie, Aberdeenshire; married to Janet Gordon, and had issue.   He is a blacksmith at Dorsincilley, Aberdeenshire, Scotland.

Margaret Riddell[2] (2), second daughter of Peter[1] (1), was born in the parish of Crathie, Aberdeenshire.

Peter Riddell[2] (3), second son of Peter[1] (1), was born in the parish of Crathie, Aberdeenshire.

Catharine Riddell[2] (2), third daughter of Peter[1] (1), was born in the parish of Crathie, Aberdeenshire.

Bell Riddell[2] (1), fourth daughter of Peter[1] (1), was born in the parish of Crathie, Aberdeenshire.

Alexander Riddell[2] (4), third son of Peter[1] (1), was born in the parish of Crathie, Aberdeenshire.

James Riddell[2] (3), fourth son of Peter[1] (1), was born in the parish of Crathie, Aberdeenshire, and had issue.

Joseph Riddell[2] (2), fifth son of Peter[1] (1), was born in the parish of Crathie, Aberdeenshire.

Elizabeth Riddell[2] (2), fifth daughter of Peter[1] (1), was born in the parish of Crathie, Aberdeenshire.

THIRD GENERATION.

James Riddell[3] (4), eldest son of James[2] (2) and his wife, Ann McLean, was born at Aberdeen, Scotland, Oct. 26, 1816; married first, at Clurry, Aberdeenshire, Oct. 17, 1845, to Fanny, daughter of Alexander Fowler, merchant, Saucher, Clurry; secondly, at Banchoro, Ternan, Kincardineshire, July 28, 1864, to Jessie-Dingwall-Fordyce, daughter of Francis Adams, M. D., LL. D., and thirdly, at Guananoqui, Ontario, Can., April 15, 1869, to Margaret, daughter of Charles Fyfe, merchant, of Aberdeen.

Mr. Riddell * was liberally educated for the Scots-Law, and after some years of professional practice in Scotland, was sent to Montreal, Canada, as manager of the North American British Bank, under title of "Public Accountant and Official Assignee, Dominion of Canada." He died at Montreal, Aug. 22, 1875. No mention of children. In a communication received from Mr. Riddell in 1873, he says: "My ancestors were a plain folk, respectable in their sphere, and for the most part having the inborn desire of the Scotch for a good education, but none of us have risen out of the middle classes, so that we could never dream of parading our names in the same category with the titled aristocracy or people of ' blue blood.' We are content with the social position we occupy, and have no wish to sneak into a better, by what I may call a fortuitous chance. Let me add that I speak thus, holding as I do the aristocracy of Great Britain, as a class, in the highest respect, and recognizing in the fullest extent the beneficial influence which as a whole they exert on the movements of the body politic."

Thomas Riddell[2] (1), second son of James[2] (2), was born April 29, 1818, at Aberdeen, Scotland; married July 21, 1847, to Christian Wishart, daughter of James Blyth, manufacturer, Edinburgh. He is now (1884) actuary and cashier North Scotland Savings Bank, Aberdeen.

Peter Riddel[3] (4), third son of James[2] (2), was born Dec. 27, 1819, at Aberdeen, Scotland, and married, June 15, 1843, to Elizabeth, daughter of Daniel Anderson, shipmaster, Aberdeen, and has issue. Mr. Riddel is treasurer to the Harbour Commissioners, the same office held by his father, and is a man of good business capabilities; an excellent penman. He has manifested an interest in the genealogy and history of his family, and kindly copied from a register of his own many names and records contained in this book, and which were "collected with care, and such means as were within reach were taken to secure their verification and fulness."

Mr. Riddel entered the service of the Board, of which he has long been the chief official, in 1833, and has continued in that service ever since—a period of fifty years. The fact of Mr. Riddel's long and faithful service was fittingly referred to by the Lord Provost at the meeting of the Board in 1883, and a remit made to the Shoremaster and Convenors of Committees to present the Treasurer, who, it was stated, desired no material recognition of his services, with some suitable keepsake commemorative of the occasion. The proposal was alike fitting and modest.

Mr. Riddel was ordained to the office of deacon in the St. Clement's Free Church, Aberdeen, March 17, 1844. On the following June he was appointed session clerk. For seven years he discharged the functions of session clerk and clerk of deacons' court. On the 27th of June, 1847, he was ordained an elder of the church. During the time of his filling these offices he was for seven years also congregational treasurer. He resigned his position as session clerk in 1883, and the session, feeling themselves utterly unable to bestow a gift whose money value should indicate their appreciation of his services, decided to subscribe for a family Bible, and had inscribed in it the inscription which appears on the opposite page.

---

* It will be seen that James Riddell spells his name with the double *l*, while his brother, Peter of Aberdeen, Scotland, uses only one *l*. Peter Riddel says his ancestors used only one *l* in their surname, and he does not understand why any of his friends should deviate from the orthography of their forefathers.

" PRESENTED TO

"MR. PETER RIDDEL,

" BY THE KIRK SESSION OF

" *St. Clement's Free Church, Aberdeen,*

on the occasion of his resignation of the office of Session Clerk, as a small token of their esteem for him as a brother elder, and of their appreciation of the ability and devotion evidenced in his unusually lengthened service as Clerk."

The session, in accepting the resignation of Mr. Riddel, agreed to engross in their records the following minute, and instructed that a copy of it be transmitted to him : —

"The Session deeply regret the resignation by Mr. Riddel of the office of Clerk. With the utmost satisfaction they would have hailed the possibility of his agreeing to continue his valued services, and only in deference to his expressed wish do they, as they now most reluctantly do, accept his resignation. They cannot, however, allow him to vacate a position which he has so long and worthily held for almost forty years—his appointment having taken place on 3rd June, 1844—without putting on record their sense of the deep debt of obligation under which he has laid the Congregation for his services in the discharge of the duties of this and other offices, as also their own warm appreciation of the uniform courtesy and kindness shewn, the marked ability and deliberate judgment displayed by him in the conduct of the business of the Court. They most earnestly hope that though, from his very long tenure of the Clerkship, and also in consideration of the state of his health, he feels it incumbent on him to ask to be relieved, they will still have in Court, as often as possible, the satisfaction of his presence as its senior member, and the benefit of his wide experience and valued counsel.

" Extracted from the records by   " AND. D. DONALDSON, Clerk, *pro tem.*"

William-Ross Riddel[3] (3), fourth son of James[2] (2), was born April 29, 1821, at Aberdeen, Scotland; married March 29, 1850, to Elsy-Isabella, daughter of Alexander Paul, merchant, Bauchay, Ternan (?), and was at one time bank accountant at Aberdeen, Scotland. Mr. Riddel died Sept. 19, 1864.

Alexander Riddel[3] (5), fifth son of James[2] (2), was born Dec. 11, 1822, at Aberdeen, Scotland, and died unmarried, July 16, 1843, at Corbie, parish of Marycutter, in Aberdeenshire. He was a bank clerk at Aberdeen.

George Riddel[3] (2), sixth son of James[2] (2), was born at Aberdeen, Scotland, April 26, 1824; married Oct. 23, 1856, to Agnes, daughter of John Riddel, leather merchant, Aberdeen. Died Nov. 5, 1878. He was a commission agent in his native city.

John Riddel[3] (3), seventh son of James[2] (2), was born at Aberdeen, Scotland, Nov. 9, 1825; married at Glasgow, June 15, 1854, to Mary, daughter of Rev. Alexander Turnbull, minister Original Session Church, Glasgow. Mr. Riddel is an engine draughtsman by profession.

Isabella Riddel[3] (2), eldest daughter of James[2] (2), was born at Aberdeen, Scotland, Feb. 27, 1828; was married, Aug. 21, 1851, to Alexander Morrison, shipmaster, Aberdeen, and died in that city Feb. 25, 1870.

Anne Riddel[3] (2), second daughter of James[2] (2), was born March 10, 1830, at Aberdeen, Scotland; was married June 1, 1853, to James Middlemas, clothier, Edinburgh.

Elizabeth Riddel[3] (3), third daughter of James[2] (2), was born Aug. 30, 1832, at Aberdeen, Scotland, and is now (1884) superintendent of The Rescue Home, St. John's Hill, Edinburgh. Presumed to be a single woman.

Samuel Riddel[3] (1), seventh son of James[2] (2), was born at Aberdeen, Scotland, Sept. 7, 1834; married July 18, 1864, at Old Aberdeen, to Margaret, daughter of John Watt, leather merchant, Aberdeen, bank clerk, Glasgow.

Mary Riddel[8] (2), fourth daughter of James[2] (2), was born at Aberdeen, Scotland, Oct. 18, 1836; died Jan. 8, 1840.

George Riddell[8] (3), eldest son of George[2] (1) and his wife, Margaret Coults, was born at Dorsincilley, in Aberdeenshire, Scotland, June 15, 1819; married Aug. 3, 1849, to Jane Coults, of Glenmuick, and had issue, of whom hereafter. He was a blacksmith.

James Riddell[8] (5), second son of George[2] (1), was born at Birkhall, Aberdeenshire, Dec. 29, 1821.

James Riddell[8] (6), eldest son of Alexander[2] (3), was born in Ballater parish, Aberdeenshire, May 25, 1823.

Elizabeth Riddell[8] (4), eldest daughter of Alexander[2] (3), was born in Ballater parish, Aberdeenshire, Dec. 20, 1824.

Alexander Riddell[8] (6), second son of Alexander[2] (3), was born in Ballater parish, Aberdeen, Sept. 15, 1826.

Jane Riddell[8] (3), second daughter of Alexander[2] (3), was born in Ballater parish, Aberdeen, Oct. 27, 1828.

Margaret Riddell[8] (3), third daughter of Alexander[2] (3), was born in Ballater parish, Aberdeen, March 16, 1831.

Catherine Riddell[8] (3), fourth daughter of Alexander[2] (3), was born in the parish of Ballater, Aberdeenshire, April 25, 1833.

William Riddell[8] (4), third son of Alexander[2] (3), was born in Ballater parish, Aberdeenshire, April 21, 1837; served an apprenticeship as chemist, and sailed from the port of Glasgow on board the "Columbia," for New York, in 1871, since when, to 1874, his family in Scotland have heard nothing of him.

Charles Riddell[8] (1), fourth son of Alexander[2] (3), was born in the parish of Ballater, Aberdeenshire, Jan. 12, 1840.

Mary Riddell[8] (3), fifth daughter of Alexander[2] (3), was born in the parish of Ballater, Aberdeenshire, Nov. 7, 1840.

Ellen Riddell[8] (1), daughter of Alexander[2] (3), was born in the parish of Ballater, Aberdeenshire; was married to a Mr. Stewart, land steward for the Earl of Aberdeen, and resides at Mill-of-Coull. Her father lived with her.*

FOURTH GENERATION.

John Riddell[4] (4), eldest son of George[8] (3) and Jane Coults, his wife, was born in Glenmuick parish, Aberdeenshire, Aug. 12, 1849.

Betsey Riddell[4] (1), eldest daughter of George[8] (3), was born in Glenmuick, Aberdeenshire, Nov. 15, 1850.

Janet Riddell[4] (1), second daughter of George[8] (3), was born in Glenmuick, Aberdeenshire, Nov. 9, 1852.

William Riddell[4] (5), second son of George[8] (3), was born in Glenmuick, Aberdeenshire, Sept. 14, 1854.

---

*Mrs. Grant, Mill-of-Coull, Aberdeenshire, daughter of Alexander Riddell[2](3), informs me that her father's uncle was pressed into the Scotch army during the feudal wars, from which he deserted and went to America. He was tall. Name was not given. Probably ancestor-American of some of the United States families. Mrs. Grant's husband is land steward for the Earl of Aberdeen, on his Cromar estates.

RIDDELLS OF ABERDEEN, SCOTLAND.

James Riddell[1] (1), parents unknown, lived at Aberdeen, Scotland; married Ellen Key, and had *two* children. He was a chain-maker by trade.

SECOND GENERATION.

James Riddell[2] (2), a son of James[1] (1), was born in Aberdeen, Scotland; was pressed into the British army in 1832, and sent with the Seventy-ninth Regiment to Canada. He married Catherine O'Connell, and had issue *four* children, of whom hereafter. He died in 1846, while serving as 1st sergeant of Battery A, Second Artillery, U. S. Army.

THIRD GENERATION.

Mary Riddell[2] (1).
Ellen Riddell[2] (1).
James Riddell[2] (3). } Children of James[2] (2).
John Riddell[2] (1).

RIDDELS OF OLD MELDRUM, SCOTLAND.

[ABERDEENSHIRE BRANCH.]

Alexander Riddel[1] (1), supposed to have been descended from the same family as the " Riddells of Glenmuick, " and " Riddels of Peterhead," which see, was born at Old Meldrum, Aberdeenshire, Scotland, in 1767-8; married in 1801, at Old Mary-le-Bone Church, London, Elizabeth Turner (she was born in England, Oct. 14, 1800-1, and died June 15, 1850), and had issue *four* sons and *one* daughter, of whom hereafter. Mr. Riddel was a coach-builder at Swallow, at Argyle Street, and at Oxford Street, London ; he died at the latter place Jan. 19, 1887.

SECOND GENERATION.

Alexander Riddel[2] (2), eldest son of Alexander[1] (1), was born in April, 1802, in London, Eng. (?), and died unmarried in 1822.

William Riddel[2] (1), second son of Alexander[1] (1), was born April 11, 1805, in London, Eng. (?); was brought up to the business of coach-building ; settled in Birmingham in 1838, as a percussion-cap manufacturer ; retired in 1854, and died in 1862, unmarried.

John Riddel[2] (1), third son of Alexander[1] (1), was born in London, Eng., March 27, 1811, and succeeded to his father's business as coach-builder in London. He died April 10, 1845, at Harfleur, Normandy, unmarried.

Joseph Riddel[2] (1), fourth son of Alexander[1] (1), was born in London, Eng., July 31, 1818 ; married Jan. 19, 1859, to Martha, daughter of Edward-Hodges Baily, R. A., Fellow Royal Society, sculptor, and had issue, of whom hereafter. Mr. Riddel went in 1843 to Venezuela, South America, as secretary to Bedford-Hinton Wilson (afterwards created K. C. B.), Her Majesty's Chargé d'Affaires and Consul General to Venezuela. Resigned in 1854. During five years of this period acted as Consul General in Carácas. Now Translator and Professor of Languages in the city of London. Address, 2 Gresham Buildings, Baringhall Street, E. C. He finished this pedigree.

Elizabeth Riddel² (1), only daughter of Alexander¹ (1), was born in London, Eng., Feb. 20, 1820; was married Dec. 7, 1846, to Edward-William Wyon, sculptor, son of the late Thomas Wyon, engraver of H. M. Seals, and had *five* children. She is living. Her three sons have deceased, and the representation of this family devolves upon the son of her daughter Florence, who is the wife of Rev. Charles Goody, vicar of Whetstone church, High Barnet, Eng.

THIRD GENERATION.

Alexander Riddel² (3), only son of Joseph² (1), was born in Kent, Nov. 11, 1863, and died Oct. 23, 1864.

RIDDELS OF PETERHEAD, ABERDEENSHIRE, SCOTLAND.

John Riddel¹ (1), son of a farmer near Aberdeen, early settled near Peterhead, Scotland, and was probably a connection of the Riddells of Glenmuick, as there were branches of that family whose genealogy cannot be distinctly traced. He married Margaret, daughter of James Cochrane, weaver, Dunbar, Scotland, in 1816, and was at one time a prosperous merchant at Portsea, but by intemperance squandered his property and became a poor man. He subsequently resided in Chatham and London, Eng. Had family of *seven* children, of whom hereafter. Have no record of his death, or that of his wife. His son has heard him mention "upper and lower Metlick."

SECOND GENERATION.

John Riddel² (2), eldest son of John¹ (1), was born near Peterhead, Scotland, in 1817, and died in Auckland, New Zealand, in 1876. Was married, but his wife's name does not appear. No account of children.

Dr. Archibald-A. Riddel² (1), second son of John¹ (1), was born near Peterhead, Scotland, Dec. 10, 1819; married in 1842 to Anne Darling, of Toronto, Can., and has issue *seven* children, of whom hereafter. He came to Canada, about forty-two years ago, and worked in the city of Toronto as a practical printer for several years. He studied medicine and obtained his license in 1857. In 1859 he went to Mexico, and practised his profession in Monterey, San Miguel de Meygintal, and Fresnillo. In 1863, returned to Toronto, where his family had lived in his absence. He is coroner of Toronto and the County of York; has been city alderman. His wife has deceased.

Isabella Riddel² (1), eldest daughter of John¹ (1), was born in England in 1821, and died unmarried.

James Riddel² (1), third son of John¹ (1), was born in England, in 1823; married Margaret Birnie (his cousin), and has had a situation in the House of Commons, London, Eng., for forty years.

Catherine Riddel² (1), second daughter of John¹ (1), was born in England in 1826, and died unmarried.

Thomas Riddel² (1), fourth son of John¹ (1), was born in England about 1828, and went from London to Australia some twenty-five years ago, during gold fever there.

Alexander Riddel² (1), fifth son of John¹ (1), was born in England about 1830, and went from London to Australia.

THIRD GENERATION.

Charles-James Riddel[3] (1), eldest son of Archibald[2] (1), was born in Toronto, Can., and died young.

John Riddel[3] (3), second son of Archibald[2] (1), was born in Toronto, Can., and died young.

Sarah Riddel[3] (1), third daughter (living) of Archibald[2] (1), was born in Toronto, Can., and was married to Henry McLaren.

Mary-A. Riddel[3] (1), a daughter of Archibald[2] (1), was born in Toronto, Can., and lives at home, unmarried.

Margaret Riddel[3] (1), a daughter of Archibald[2] (1), was born in Toronto, Can., and lives at home, single.

Isabella Riddel[3] (2), a daughter of Archibald[2] (1), was born in Toronto, Can., and lives at home, single.

RIDDELS OF CUSHNIE, ABERDEENSHIRE.

Peter Riddel[2] (1), of Fletcher, Can., says his grandfather was a tailor who lived on the farm of Balnakelly, Cushnie, Aberdeenshire, Scotland, and had *seven* sons and *two* daughters, all of them six feet in height. From these sons are fifty-one grandchildren and twenty-seven great-grandchildren, some in Scotland, England, Africa, China, and Canada. The tradition of this family is that their ancestor was chief of the Clan Chatrina, and got the name Riddel in consequence of some heroic deed he had done, while acting in that capacity. Peter Riddel has written to Scotland for genealogical information, but it has not reached me. I think this family a connection of the Riddels of Glenmuick, and Riddels of Peterhead, in the same shire, from the name *Peter** in these branches and the orthography of the surname being spelled with only one *l*, a form peculiar to families in Aberdeenshire.

RIDDLES OF HERMITAGE CASTLE, SCOTLAND.

William Riddle[1] (1), parents unknown, was a native of Roxburghshire, Scotland, and his family hold the tradition that they are descended from the ancient family of Riddell of that ilk, so long settled in Lilliesleaf. William married Catherine Brydon, and had issue *nine* children, of whom hereafter. He lived some time at Hermitage Castle, a place on the Hermitage-Water, in Castleton parish, and some of his children were born there.

SECOND GENERATION.

William Riddle[2] (2), eldest son of William[1] (1), was born at Hermitage Castle, Liddesdale, Scotland, in Nov. 1801; married Jessie, daughter

---

* It seems a little singular that the Christian name *Peter* should be almost exclusively confined to the Riddels of Aberdeenshire. This name was in the family of Newcastle-on-Tyne, as early as 1500. The remote ancestors are supposed to be from the Glen-Riddell family, as the branch of Glenmuick use the same crest.

of John and Euphemia (Hillson) Watson, of Dolphiston, Ousman parish,
Roxburghshire; emigrated to Canada in 1831, and settled as a farmer in
Beverly, Ont., where he resided, — a well-known and respected citizen,—
until his death, which occurred Feb. 2, 1883.   He left issue *four* children,
of whom hereafter.

John Riddle[2] (1), second son of William[1] (1), now living in Scotland.
No account of his family.

James Riddle[2] (1), third son of William[1] (1), was born in Liddesdale, Scotland; married and had issue, of whom hereafter.   Deceased.

Thomas Riddle[2] (1), fourth son of William[1] (1), born in Liddesdale,
Scotland, and settled in Ontario, Can.   Married first, Elizabeth Truman,
and had issue *five* children, of whom hereafter.   He has married a second
wife, whose maiden-name does not appear.

Janet Riddle[2] (1), eldest daughter of William[1] (1), was born in Roxburghshire, Scotland.

Willhelmie Riddle[2] (1), second daughter of William[1] (1), was born
in Roxburghshire, Scotland.

Mary Riddle[2] (1), third daughter of William[1] (1), was born in Roxburghshire, Scotland; came to Canada with her sisters, and died in Beverly, Ont., unmarried.

Anne Riddle[2] (1), fourth daughter of William[1] (1), was born in Roxburghshire, Scotland; emigrated to Canada; was married to Hugh Smith,
and both have deceased.

Catherine Riddle[2] (1), fifth daughter of William[1] (1), was born in
Roxburghshire, Scotland; was married to Robert Craig; emigrated to
Canada; died in East Middlesex County, and left issue.

THIRD GENERATION.

William Riddle[3] (3), eldest son of William[2] (2), was born in Beverly,
Can., April 8, 1858, and lives on his father's homestead farm, unmarried
(1883).

John Riddle[3] (2), second son of William[2] (2), was born in Beverly,
Ont., April 22, 1866, and lives at home (1883).

Euphemia Riddle[3] (1), only daughter of William[2] (2), was born in
Beverly, Can., June 17, 1861.   At home, unmarried (1883).

James Riddle[3] (2), youngest son of William[2] (2), was born in Beverly, Ont., Oct. 18, 1867.   At home and single (1883).

William Riddle[3] (4), a son of James[2] (1), resides at No. 8 Wellington Street, Hawick, Scotland.

RIDDELLS OF LIDDESDALE, SCOTLAND.

James Riddell[1] (1), parents unknown, was a resident of Liddesdale,
in Roxburghshire, Scotland, where he is believed to have been a shepherd
and farmer.   He had *three* sons, of whom hereafter.   The family have
lived on the banks of the Liddell for many generations, and were, — as
stated by a descendant, — " plain Liddesdale yeomanry; frugal swains who
fed their flocks upon the Cheviot Hills."   This branch of the Riddell

family is supposed to be connected with other branches in the same county, but relationship cannot now be proven.

SECOND GENERATION.

James Riddell² (2), son of James¹ (1), was born in Liddesdale, Scotland, in 1781; married Isabella, daughter of George Hogg, an officer in the British army, and Magdalen Van Buren,* of Hackensack, N. J. The permanent home of the parents of Mrs. Riddell, when the father was not in the army, was at Berwick-on-Tweed, in England. Mr. Riddell lived at Ednam, Scotland, until 1835, when he removed to Canada with his family. His last professional work in Scotland was surveying the ground of the battle-field of "Chevy Chase." He had *three* sons, of whom hereafter. Died in Canada.

Henry Riddell² (1), a son of James¹ (1), was born in Scotland, and presumably died there. Query: Where did he settle?

William Riddell² (1), a son of James¹ (1), was born in Scotland, and is supposed to have lived and died there.

Thomas Riddell² (1), a son of James¹ (1), was born in Scotland, and presumably died there.

James-Van Buren Riddell² (3), son of James¹ (2), was born at Ednam, in Roxburghshire, Scotland, a place on the Eden, a tributary of the Tweed, and which has the honor of being the birthplace of the author of "The Seasons," James Thompson. He died when young, unmarried.

THIRD GENERATION.

George-Hogg Riddell³ (1), son of James² (2), was born at Ednam, Scotland, and died young, unmarried.

Dr. Alexander-Dow Riddell³ (1), son of James² (2), was born at Ednam, a small hamlet on the Eden, Scotland, in the year 1824; married, in 1869, Rebecca, daughter of Dr. William Wilson, sometime of Yorkshire, Eng., and is now (1883) a practising physician in Compton, P. Q., Can. Has *three* children, of whom hereafter. He removed with his parents to Canada in 1835. After acquiring a common and classical education at different places in Scotland, England, and Canada, at the age of nineteen he commenced the study of medicine with Dr. Moses Glines, of Compton, Can., a gentleman of very considerable professional eminence, particularly in the department of surgery. Having completed the usual curriculum of medical lectures and hospital attendance, he received his degree of M. D. from the University of New York City, and subsequently became a licentiate of the College of Physicians and Surgeons of Lower Canada. For the past thirty years he has resided in the township of Compton, practising medicine and farming, and has enjoyed, during the greater part of that time, a somewhat extensive rural practice in Compton and the neighboring townships.

FOURTH GENERATION.

Lizzie Riddell⁴ (1), daughter of Alexander³ (1), born in Compton, Can., and married to Rignald Bray, of Bayonne, N. J.

William-Philip Riddell⁴ (2), eldest son of Alexander³ (1), born in Compton, Can., and now (1883) at home.

George-Francis Riddell⁴ (1), second son of Alexander³ (1), was born in Compton, Can., and lives at home.

---

* Daughter of James Van Buren, a physician. The marriage took place while New York was still in the hands of the British forces.

RIDDELLS OF EAST KILBRIDE, SCOTLAND.

James Riddell[1] **(1)**, parents' names unknown, was born in 1732; married Christiana Lang in 1760 (she was born at Motherwell Farm in 1732, and died in 1818), and had issue *six* children, four daughters and two sons, of whom hereafter.   Mr. Riddell was a farmer at East Kilbride, near Glasgow.   Died in 1790.

SECOND GENERATION.

Christina Riddell[2] **(1)**, eldest daughter of James[1] **(1)**, was born at East Kilbride, June 11, 1763, and was married to a man supposed to have been a baker by trade, but his surname is not now certainly known.

Margaret Riddell[2] **(1)**, second daughter of James[1] **(1)**, was born at East Kilbride, Nov. 7, 1765 ; was married to John Ross.   Time of decease not known.

John Riddell[2] **(1)**, eldest son of James[1] **(1)**, was born at East Kilbride in 1767; married Elizabeth Branchell, of Dunbarton, Nov. 28, 1796, and had issue *four* children, three sons and a daughter, of whom hereafter.   He resided at Glasgow; died in 1832; his widow in 1842.

James Riddell[2] **(2)**, second son of James[1] **(1)**, was born at East Kilbride (say 1769) ; no other information.

Agnes Riddell[2] **(1)**, third daughter of James[1] **(1)**, was born at East Kilbride, March 18, 1773, and was married to William Patterson, blacksmith.   No record of her decease.

Jean Riddell[2] **(1)**, youngest daughter of James[1] **(1)**, was born at East Kilbride, March 29, 1776, and married —— Patterson, and became the mother of "long Will Patterson."

THIRD GENERATION.

John Riddell[3] **(2)**, eldest son of John[2] **(1)**, died in infancy.

James Riddell[3] **(3)**, second son of John[2] **(1)**, was born in Glasgow ; married Elizabeth Stewart in 1811, and had issue *eight* children, of whom hereafter.   He died Feb. 7, 1853 ; his widow April 8, 1853.

Rev. William Riddell[3] **(1)**, third son of John[2] **(1)**, was born at Glasgow, Nov. 10, 1801, and emigrated to America in early life.   Never married.   He studied a while at Lafayette College, in Pennsylvania.   Graduated at Princeton College in 1837.   After leaving college he immediately entered the Theological Seminary at Princeton, and after a three years' course graduated in 1840.   Was ordained as an evangelist by the Presbytery of Raritan, N. J., Oct. 5, 1841.   He next appears a member of the Presbytery of Mississippi in 1844, in connection with which he continued till 1859, when having removed to the Yazoo Valley, he was transferred to the Presbytery of Central Mississippi.   He labored as stated supply to several churches in the interior counties of the State till 1849, when he removed to a neighborhood of planters, near Port Gibson, where he taught the children in a private family and preached to the negroes on several adjoining plantations.   He was engaged in this work till the war of the Rebellion interrupted it, when he consented reluctantly to abandon it and return to Scotland.   (In 1859, he had removed with the family with whom he made his home to a plantation on the Yazoo River.)   In 1862, in infirm health, he left the country, sailing from New Orleans in one of the last vessels which left that port before the blockade was declared.   He died at the home of Mrs. Dick, Kim, Greenock, Scotland, Dec. 7, 1876.

While in Scotland he never (probably) exercised his ministerial office, but preached occasionally, and became a frequent contributor to the "Presbyterian," of Philadelphia, over the signature of "Rutherglen." In personal appearance he was diminutive, and was known as "little Mr. Riddell." His features were good, and his expression intelligent. He depreciated himself so much and morbidly, that he led others to do the same. He gave his confidence to few, yet his affections when bestowed were strong. His mind was vigorous, keen, and metaphysical; his tastes were delicate, and his scholarship usually exact and comprehensive. Some of his papers prepared for his Presbytery were masterly. As a preacher he was awkward in address, and his voice low and drawling. But his sermons were rich with sound and weighty thought. He was thoroughly disinterested and devoted to his work among the negroes; at the same time his idiosyncracies and peculiarities were an obstacle to his popularity. Everybody said, "Mr. Riddell is a good man." His life is said, by those who knew him best, to have been a shadowed one, but his death was no doubt a translation from darkness to light eternal.

Elizabeth Riddell³ (1), only daughter of John² (1), was born in Glasgow, in 1799; was married to John Dick (he was born in 1800), of Greenock, and has issue. Living in 1883.

FOURTH GENERATION.

Mary Riddell⁴ (1), eldest daughter of James³ (3), was born in Glasgow, Nov. 15, 1811; was married to Robert Steel; had issue, and died March 5, 1841.

Ann Riddell⁴ (1), second daughter of James³ (3), was born on June 17, 1814, and died June 21, 1823.

John Riddell⁴ (3), eldest son of James³ (3), was born Dec. 27, 1816, and died June 8, 1818.

William Riddell⁴ (2), second son of James³ (3), was born June 23, 1819, and died March 1, 1820.

Elizabeth Riddell⁴ (2), third daughter of James³ (3), born Aug. 4, 1821; was married to John Garth, and has issue.

James Riddell⁴ (4), third son of James³ (3), was born Nov. 15, 1824; married Jean Johnston, and has issue *seven* children, of whom hereafter. He resided in Glasgow, or near that city. Died.

Catherine Riddell⁴ (1), fourth daughter of James³ (3), was born Oct. 13, 1827, and died Nov. 1, 1829.

Jean Riddell⁴ (2), fifth daughter of James³ (3), was born Feb. 7, 1830, and died Feb. 22, 1837.

FIFTH GENERATION.

James Riddell⁵ (5), eldest son of James⁴ (4), was born in 1848; married Agnes Park in 1872, and has issue *five* children, of whom hereafter. He resides at Gallowflat, Rutherglen (near Glasgow). Has kindly furnished records of this family.

John-D. Riddell⁵ (4), second son of James⁴ (4), was born in 1851; married Catherine Boyle in 1874, and has issue, of whom hereafter. Resides in Glasgow.

William-D. Riddell⁵ (3), third son of James⁴ (4), was born in 1852; married Mary Orr, in 1878. No family (1883).

Robert-D. Riddell⁵ (1), fourth son of James⁴ (4), was born in 1853; married Janet Orr, in 1880, and has *one* daughter (1883).

9

Mary Riddell⁵ (2), eldest daughter of James⁴ (4), was born in 1856, and married to Thomas H. Jameson in 1876. Has issue.

Andrew Riddell⁵ (1), fifth son of James⁴ (4), was born in 1861.

Neil Riddell⁵ (1), sixth son of James⁴ (4), was born in 1864.

SIXTH GENERATION.

Elizabeth Riddell⁶ (3), eldest daughter of James⁵ (5), born in 1873.

James Riddell⁶ (6), eldest son of James⁵ (5), was born in 1874.

Robert Riddell⁶ (2), second son of James⁵ (5), was born in 1876.

Jeanie Riddell⁶ (3), second daughter of James⁵ (5), was born in 1878.

Robert Riddell⁶ (3), third son of James⁵ (5), was born in 1880.

Jeanie Riddell⁶ (4), daughter of John⁵ (4), was born in 1876.

James Riddell⁶ (7), son of John⁵ (4), was born in 1879.

RIDDELLS OF WAUCHOPE, SCOTLAND.

John Riddell¹ (1) was the son of a shepherd, who for about fifty years kept sheep at Wauchope, about twelve miles south of Hawick, and near the English border. The name of his mother does not appear. He married a Turnbull from Hawick, and had issue, of whom hereafter. He lived the most of his days at Clairlaw, one and a half miles from Lilliesleaf, where he served as shepherd thirty-seven years. He subsequently rented a farm near Melrose, called "Berryhill," adjoining "Abbotsford," the magnificent seat of Sir Walter Scott, where he continued till his death, at the age of 72. His widow survived her husband fourteen years, dying at the age of 84. Both were buried in the Bowden church-yard. Some now spell the name "Riddle."

SECOND GENERATION.

Walter Riddell² (1), a son of John¹ (1), was born at, or near, Edinburgh, Scotland; married a Miss Baxter, and had issue, of whom hereafter. He spent the most of his days as a farm-laborer, or foreman of help, near Hawick; but latterly in and about Selkirk,—for many years at Phillipshaugh, in the employ of the Murray family. He died at Selkirk, Jan. 8, 1881, and was buried by the side of his wife,—who died at Foldonside in 1857, aged 56 years,—in Bowden church-yard.

James Riddell² (1), a son of John¹ (1), was born in Scotland; married, and had issue *nine* children, of whom hereafter.* He resides at Girrick, between Kelso and Earlson, where he has been located about sixty years. He is a shepherd.

Robert Riddell² (1), a son of John¹ (1), was born in Scotland; married Elizabeth Dixon, from near St. Boswell's, and has issue *nine* children, of whom hereafter. He emigrated to Canada about 1827, and settled at Kirkwall, Beverly, where he " hewed out a fine farm in a Canadian

---

* Two of the sons of James² (1), are now (1884) in New Zealand; one a shepherd, and the other a preacher of the gospel, sent out as an evangelist by the Presbyterian church, but now a local minister.

bush," and became independent. Deceased Sept. 6, 1867. Widow living
in 1883.

John Riddell[2] (2), a son of John[1] (1), was born in Scotland; married
Margaret Grieve, daughter of a shepherd, and had *nine* children, of whom
hereafter. The parents died at Foldonside, and were buried in Bowden
church-yard.

Margaret Riddell[2] (1), a daughter of John[1] (1), was born in Scotland; was married to Walter Ballantyne, stone mason (now a prosperous merchant at St. Boswell's, Scotland), and has issue.

Turnbull Riddell[2] (1), a son of John[1] (1), was born in Scotland;
married Helen Clarkson, daughter of a gardener at Foldonside, and has
issue, of whom hereafter. He has lived on the old farm since his father's
death, — some thirty years. He was named for his mother's family.

William Riddell[2] (1), a son of John[1] (1), was a shepherd at Muselee in his young days; afterwards emigrated to Australia and made a fortune, but lost heavily by endorsing notes for others. Died when between
50 and 60 years of age. No account of a family.

Elizabeth Riddell[2] (1), youngest daughter of John[1] (1), was born in
Scotland, and died young (say 30) at Berryhill. She was buried in the
family lot in Bowden church-yard.

THIRD GENERATION.

John Riddell[3] (3), son of Walter[2] (1), was born near Edinburgh, Scotland; married a Miss Glendinnen, and has worked on a farm near Selkirk.
Now (1883) aged about 55.

James Riddell[3] (2), son of Walter[2] (1), was born near Edinburgh,
Scotland; married a Miss Murray, and had issue *five* children, of whom
hereafter. Resided in Edinburgh. Died at the age of 39 years.

Robert Riddell[3] (2), a son of Walter[2] (1), was born near Edinburgh,
Scotland, and brought up at Phillipshaugh, Selkirk. He served his apprenticeship with a blacksmith named Thomas Kedric, "a real old Scotch
worthie." He worked in Hawick, Edinburgh, Stirling, Glasgow, and subsequently emigrated to America, coming from Bromilaw to New York in
the ship "Britannia" in 1864. He worked in Galt, Can., in a foundry;
thence some time in the State of Michigan; thence returned to Canada;
thence to St. Paul, Minn.; thence to Scotland. In 1870 he came back to
Canada and settled in Chatham, where he worked in a ship-building and
engineering establishment till 1872, when the company failed, and he commenced business for himself as a manufacturer of ornamental wrought-iron
fencing. He married a Miss Tocher, who came from Banffshire, Scotland,
in 1868, and has issue *five* children, of whom hereafter. Mr. Riddell
kindly provided this family history.

Margaret Riddell[3] (2), eldest daughter of Robert[2] (1), was born in
1832 (in Scotland or Canada); was married first, in 1851, to John Clark,
who was murdered by Indians in British Columbia, in 1863, and secondly,
in 1868, to John Wight. She had *four* children by her first, and *six* by
her second husband. She lives on a farm in Beverly, Ont., Can.

Christiana Riddell[3] (1), second daughter of Robert[2] (1), was born in
Beverly, Can., in 1835; was married in 1856 to Francis Stalker, and has
had *nine* children. Lives on a farm near Godridge, Can.

Elizabeth Riddell[3] (1), third daughter of Robert[2] (1), was born in
Beverly, Can., in 1837; and became the wife of Robert McQueen in 1868.
No children. Husband, teacher of schools.

Janet Riddell[3] (1), fourth daughter of Robert[2] (1), was born in Beverly, Can., in 1839, and lives with her mother, single.

John Riddell[3] (5), eldest son of Robert[2] (1), was born in Beverly, Can., in 1841; married Nellie Manson, Nov. 30, 1882, and lives on the homestead at Kirkwall, Ont.

Robert Riddell[3] (3), second son of Robert[2] (1), was born in Beverly, Can., in 1844; married Jane Elliott, of Scottish parentage, in January, 1869, and has *three* children, of whom hereafter. Mr. Riddell is a farmer in Beverly.

Isabella Riddell[3] (1), fifth daughter of Robert[2] (1), was born in Canada, in 1846; was married in January, 1870, to James Elliot, of Scottish descent, and has had *four* children. Her husband is a manufacturer in Galt, Ont., Can.

William Riddell[3] (2), third son of Robert[2] (1), was born in Beverly, Can., in 1848; married Agnes Stewart in September, 1880, and has had issue *four* children, of whom hereafter. He lives on the parental homestead at Kirkwall, Beverly, Can.

Jane Riddell[3] (1), youngest daughter of Robert[2] (1), was born in Beverly, Can., in 1851; was married Jan. 30, 1876, to William Renwick, and has *two* daughters. Husband, a wagon-maker.

John Riddell[3] (6).   }
Robert Riddell[3] (4).   } Sons of Turnbull[2] (1) of Scotland.
William Riddell[3] (3). }

FOURTH GENERATION.

Walter-Baxter Riddell[4] (2), eldest son of Robert[3] (2), was born in Chatham, Can., March 15, 1873.

Willie-Tocher Riddell[4] (1), second son of Robert[3] (2), was born in Chatham, Can., Sept. 18, 1874. Deceased.

James-Thomson Riddell[4] (3), third son of Robert[3] (2), was born in Chatham, Can., Sept. 14, 1876.

Robert-John Riddell[4] (4), fourth son of Robert[3] (2), was born in Chatham, Can., in May 1879.

Charles-Henry Riddell[4] (1), fifth son of Robert[3] (2), was born in Chatham, Can., July 15, 1881.

RIDDELLS OF JEDBURGH, SCOTLAND.

Andrew Riddell[2] (1), a son of John[1] (1), was born in Roxburghshire, Scotland; married first, Janet Linton (no issue), and secondly, Elizabeth Archer, by whom he had issue *nine* children, of whom hereafter. He came from near Jedburgh to the township of Vaughn, near Toronto, Can., in 1835. His father was a farm laborer. There were other children who lived in Scotland. Andrew was a farmer. He died Jan. 23, 1863, aged 67. His wife died Feb. 8, 1872.

THIRD GENERATION.

Margaret Riddell[3] (1), eldest daughter of Andrew[2] (1), was born in Scotland, March 7, 1832; was married to Henry Ward, June 22, 1857, in Canada, and now (1883) resides in Wellesley, Ont.

John Riddell[2] (2), a twin son of Andrew[2] (1), was born in Scotland, Feb. 26, 1834; was brought to Canada by his parents in 1835; married Sarah Saltry, and resides on a farm in Ontario; post-office, Milverton; residence in Mornington, County of Perth. *Eight* children.

James Riddell[2] (1), a twin son of Andrew[2] (1), was born in Scotland, Feb. 26, 1834; married Ann Phillips, and is now (1888) living near Milverton, Ont., or Mornington, County Perth. Farmer. *Five* children.

Ellen Riddell[2] (1), second daughter of Andrew[2] (1), was born in Ontario, Can., Dec. 26, 1837; was married Nov. 6, 1863 to David Ferguson, and lives in Toronto, Can.

Andrew Riddell[2] (2), third son of Andrew[2] (1), was born in Canada, Feb. 29, 1840; married Louisa Phillips in August, 1864, and lives at Preston, Grey, Ont.

Thomas Riddell[2] (1), fourth son of Andrew[2] (1), was born in Canada, in March, 1848; married Jane Mason, May 23, 1872, and is living at Woodbridge, near Toronto, Ont., or Vaughan, County of York.

William Riddell[2] (1), fifth son of Andrew[2] (1), was born in Canada, July 26, 1845; unmarried. Farmer in Selkirk, Manitoba, B. C.

George Riddell[2] (1), sixth son of Andrew[2] (1), was born in Canada, in June (or July), 1847, and died Sept. 1, 1869.

Elizabeth Riddell[2] (1), third daughter of Andrew[2] (1), was born in Canada, Oct. 18, 1849, and is now living in the·city of Montreal. Post address, box 1156, care Mr. Moody.

FOURTH GENERATION.

Andrew Riddell[4] (3), son of John[3] (2), is married and living on a farm in Manitoba.

George Riddell[4] (2), son of John[3] (2).	
John-James Riddell[4] (3), son of John[3] (2).	All now (1884) at
William-Robert Riddell[4] (2), son of John[3] (2).	home, in Perth,
Albert-Edward Riddell[4] (1), son of John[3] (2).	Ont.
David Riddell[4] (1), son of John[3] (2),	
Two daughters whose names do not appear.	

Jemima-E. Riddell[4] (1), daughter of James[3] (1).	At home in
Ellen-Jane Riddell[4] (1), daughter of James[3] (1).	Perth,
Clara-Selina Riddell[4] (1), daughter of James[3] (1).	Mornington
James-Archer Riddell[4] (2), son of James[3] (1).	County, Ont.
Eliza-Ann Riddell[4] (1), daughter of James[3] (1).	(1884).

Andrew-James Riddell[4] (4).	
Elizabeth-Ann Riddell[4] (2).	Children of Andrew[3] (2). Three
George Riddell[4] (3).	others whose names do
Eliza-Jane Riddell[4] (2).	not appear.
David-Farquson Riddell[4] (2).	

Elizabeth-Ann Riddell[4] (3).	
Mary-Bertha Riddell[4] (1).	
Ellen-Isabella-J. Riddell[4] (1).	Children of Thomas[3] (1).
Mabel-Beatrice Riddell[4] (1).	
Ida-Muerial Riddell[4] (1).	
William-Archer Riddell[4] (3).	

RIDDELLS OF SELKIRK, SCOTLAND.

William Riddell[1] **(1)**, parents' names unknown, was born at Selkirk, Scotland, and had a family of sons and daughters, of whom I know only the following:—

SECOND GENERATION.

Walter Riddell[2] **(1)**, a son of William[1] (1), was born in Selkirk, Scotland; married Isabella Kedzia, who was from the State Hills, Roxburghshire, and had issue *four* sons and *two* daughters. He lived at Hawick, and died there Feb. 11, 1849; his wife predeceased him in 1839.

THIRD GENERATION.

William Riddell[2] **(2)**, eldest son of Walter[2] (1), was born at Hawick, Scotland; and in 1873 was in London, Ont., British North America.

RIDDELLS OF STIRLING, SCOTLAND.

Robert Riddell[1] **(1)**, parents unknown, was born in Glasgow, Scotland, in 1792; married Jane Buchanan and settled at Stirling. Weaver by occupation. Joined the Forty-ninth Highlanders, and went through the Peninsula war; was at the battle of Waterloo. Subsequently joined the Ninety-ninth Regiment, raised at Glasgow, and was discharged with a pension. Had issue *ten* children, of whom hereafter. He died in 1847. This family claims descent from the "Riddells of Riddell," Roxburghshire.

Anne Riddell[2] **(1)**, a daughter of Robert[1] (1), was born at Stirling, Scotland, about 1820.

Ellen Riddell[2] **(1)**, a daughter of Robert[1] (1), born in 1822.

William Riddell[2] **(1)**, eldest son of Robert[1] (1), was born at Stirling, Scotland, in 1824; learned the printer's trade; joined the Ninety-ninth Regiment, went to Australia, and while there deserted the army. Supposed to be dead.

Henry Riddell[2] **(1)**, second son of Robert[1] (1), was born in Stirling, Scotland; learned the tailor's trade; enlisted in the Ninety-ninth Regiment with his brother, and deserted the army when in Australia.

James Riddell[2] **(1)**, third son of Robert[1] (1), was born in Stirling, Scotland, and in 1857 resided in Edinburgh.

Frederick Riddell[2] **(1)**, fourth son of Robert[1] (1), was born in Stirling, Scotland; no other information.

Edward Riddell[2] **(1)**, fifth son of Robert[1] (1), was born at Stirling, Scotland; enlisted in the Forty-second Highlanders, and served in the East Indies thirteen years.

David Riddell[2] **(1)**, sixth son of Robert[1] (1), was born at Stirling, Scotland, and was at the siege of Canton, China, in the sixty-gun ship "Raynard," of the English navy.

Robert Riddell[2] **(2)**, seventh son of Robert[1] (1), was born at Stirling, Scotland; no other information.

George Riddell[2] **(1)**, eighth son of Robert[1] (1), was born at Stirling,

Scotland, in 1833; emigrated to America in 1857, and settled in Chicago, Ill. He married Mary McGary, a native of Landford, Ireland, and has (1873) issue *four* children, as follows: —

THIRD GENERATION.

Mary Riddle[3] (1).
Elizabeth Riddell[3] (1).
William Riddell[3] (2).
Ellen Riddell[3] (2).
} Children of George[2] (1).

RIDDELLS OF NEWCASTLE AND GATESHEAD.

The Riddells of Northumberland and Durham trace their lineage back to the same Norman ancestor as do the families of that surname in Scotland; indeed, they were originally one clan dwelling along the borders between England and Scotland, the boundary in early times between the two countries not being very well defined. From Primside, where Gervase Ridel, who was head of the Roxburgh family, settled, it is only three miles down the vale of Beaumont to the present English border, and during the time of the first generations of this family they probably could have lived on either side of the line without being questioned about their allegiance. It has not been clearly ascertained at what date the ancestors of this branch of the Ridel family established themselves in England, but they were in early times situated at Norham* and Twizel-on-the-Tweed, some cadets having the custody of the ancient castle at the former place. Surtees, in his "History and Antiquities of Durham," mentions three of

---

* NORHAM CASTLE was originally built by Ralph Flambard, in 1121. It was a bone of contention between the English and Scotch for centuries, and was nearly destroyed by David, King of Scots, in 1138. Cambden describes the castle as having "an outer wall of great compass, with many little towers in the angle next the river, and within, another circular wall much stronger, in the centre whereof rises a loftier tower." Part of the ruins have been undermined by the river, and little remains except the great keep-tower, seventy feet high, and the double gateway, which led to the bridge over the ancient moat. A view of this old castle, where the Riddells held custody, recalls the opening lines of Marmion: —

> " Day set on Norham's castle steep,
>   And Tweed's fair river, broad and deep,
>   And Cheviot's mountains lone ;
>   The battled towers, the donjon keep,
>   The loop-hole grates, where captives weep,
>   The flanking walls that round it sweep,
>   In yellow lustre shone.
>   The warriors on the turrets high,
>   Moving athwart the evening sky,
>   Seemed forms of giant hight :
>   Their armour, as it caught the rays,
>   Flashed back again the western blaze
>   In hues of dazzling light."

In an old history of Scotland the following relative to Norham Castle was found: " The provisions are three great vats of salt eels, forty-four kine, three hogsheads of salted salmon, forty quarters of grain, besides many cows, and four hundred sheep, lying under the castle-wall nightly; but a number of the arrows wanted feathers, and a good Fletcher (arrow-maker) was required."

the successive heads of this family, Dukentinus de Ridel, Patricius de Ridel, and Walter de Ridel, who appear to have held the lordship of the villa and manor of Whickham, in the county palitine, during the thirteenth century. The documentary records relating to the early generation are somewhat obscure and disconnected, and the printed pedigrees do not agree as to the head of the family.

FIRST GENERATION.

Sir Jordan de Ridel[1] (1), was a son of Auskittel[1] (1), of the main line of the family denominated "Riddells of Riddell," of Roxburghshire, Scotland, whose pedigree see in this work. His mother was evidently a sister of Jordanus le Flemming, and hence the name "Jordan" in the Ridel family. This man was a witness to a document in Scotland as early as 1165, and he was probably born as soon as 1140. He was a prominent man in his day, and called to various responsible offices. He was a knight and sheriff of Northumberland; acquired large estates at Tilmouth, in Durham, and held the moiety (lordship) of that manor during the reign of King Edward I. He married and had issue, but his wife's name does not appear.

SECOND GENERATION.

Walter de Ridel[2] (1), son of Jordan[1] (1), succeeded to the lordship of the villa and manor Whickham. He was Sheriff of Northumberland, — a very important office at that time, — and many times employed by his sovereign on responsible commissions in the thirteenth century. He married and had issue; wife's name not known.

THIRD GENERATION.

Sir William de Ridel[2] (1), son of Walter[2] (1), was a knight. He was appointed Sheriff of Northumberland in 1314 (seventh and eighth years of King Edward II), by patent from Bishop Kellaw, Constable of Norham Castle, and with others of his kinsman held the custody of that fortress. He was likewise employed in many public services by the king. We are also told that William was in possession of the whole manor and villa of Tillmouth,* of the manor and villa of Twizel,† of the hamlets of

---

* GURDEN RIDDELL owned Tillmouth House in 1272; whether he was a brother or uncle of Sir William we do not know.

† TWIZEL CASTLE, situated on a wooded height above the east bank of the river Till, is now a gaunt ruin eighty yards in front, with gaping windows, and round towers at the angles. It was more than forty years in building; the castle-gallery measures ninety feet by twenty-two. In the hollow below the castle is an ancient bridge, a most picturesque and lofty semi-circular arch over the Till, more than ninety feet in span and forty-two in height. A little below the bridge, and under a rock twenty feet high, is *St. Helen's Well*, a petrifying spring; and a little northwest of Twizel, is *Tillmouth*. This glen, where the ancient Ridells owned extensive lands, and defended themselves, with their retainers, in the strongholds of Norham and Twizel, is romantic and delightful, with steep banks on each side, covered with copse, particularly with hawthorn. The scenery, and fountain from which the Ridells slaked their thirst, are beautifully mentioned by Scott, in "Marmion," as follows: —

      " From Flodden ridge
      The Scots beheld the English host
      Leave Barmore-wood, their evening post,
      And heedful watched them as they crossed
         The Till by Twizel Bridge.
      High sight it is, and haughty, while
      They dive into the deep defile;

Dudhoe and Old Grindon, and two parts of the manor of Upsettlington, on the north bank of the river Tweed, about a mile south-west of Norham. These estates, held of the Bishop of Durham by an annual rent and suit at court of Norham, were inherited by his three granddaughters, of whom hereafter, and other heirs.

FOURTH GENERATION.

William de Ridel⁴ (2),* eldest son of William³ (1), acquired his father's estates and holdings, served in capacities of trust, and died during the reign of King Edward III, leaving his *three* daughters co-heirs. Wife's name unknown.

Hugh de Ridel⁴ (1), second son of William³ (1), was living in the fourth year of King Edward III (1329), and became the representative head of this family.

FIFTH GENERATION.

Isabell de Ridel⁵ (1), eldest daughter of William⁴ (2), was one of her father's co-heiresses, and became the wife of Allan Claveringe.

Constantine de Ridel⁵ (1), second daughter of William⁴ (2), was co-heir with her sisters to her father's estate. She was married to Sir John Kynges (or Kingston), a knight, and member of one of the oldest and most respectable families.

> Beneath the caverned cliff they fall,
> Beneath the castle's airy wall.
> By rock, by oak, by hawthorn tree,
>   Troop after troop are disappearing;
>   Troop after troop their banners rearing,
> Upon the eastern bank you see
> Still pouring down the rocky den
>   Where flows the sullen Till,
> And rising from the dim-wood glen,
> Standards on standards, men on men,
>   In slow succession still,
> And, sweeping o'er the Gothic arch,
> And, pressing on, in ceaseless march,
>   To gain the opposing hill.
> That morn, to many a trumpet clang,
> Twizell, thy rock's deep echo rang;
> And many a chief of birth and rank,
> Saint Helen, at thy fountain drank.
> The hawthorn-glade, which now we see
> In spring-time bloom so lavishly,
> Had then from many an axe its doom,
> To give the marching columns room."

* This Sir William Riddell was Constable of Norham Castle, being constituted such by Richard Kellow, Bishop of Durham, as well as bailiff of all his lands belonging to it; but the year is not given. In 1312, the first year of his being bishop, that prelate, as appears by a charter in the College of Arms, granted him several indulgencies with respect to Norham. He freed him from paying suit at court, and all castle-rent that should be due to him during his life. At the same time he agreed to render him the sum of ten pounds yearly, as one of his knights. When Bishop Kellow surrendered Norham Castle to Edward II, for the term of three years, in order that it might be the means of better defending the Marches, that prince entrusted the important charge of it to Sir William Riddell, as the bishop had done. In the year 1315, Sir William was appointed High Sheriff of Northumberland. To this office was also annexed the governorship of Newcastle. In the year 1321, King Edward II, who seems to have held him in high esteem, addresses him as constable of this castle, and at the same time Andrew de Harcla, and some others, as sheriffs and commanders in the northern parts, to be ready to co-operate with all

Joan de Ridel[5] (1), third daughter of William[4] (2), was co-heir with her sisters of her father; married Gerrard Widdrington, a member of the same family as the Widdringtons who have since formed alliances with the Riddells, whom see.

Thomas de Ridel[5] (1), a son of Hugh[4] (1), succeeded to his father's possessions and the representation of this family; married and had issue, wife's name unknown; made his will in the year 1358.

SIXTH GENERATION.

Thomas de Ridel[6] (2), only known son of Thomas[5] (1), was his father's heir; married and had issue a son, of whom hereafter. His wife's name does not appear.

SEVENTH GENERATION.

Thomas Ridell[7] (3), a son of Thomas[6] (2) succeeded to the paternal estates, and the representation of this family. He married the daughter and heiress of a knight named Harbottle or Harbotal, of Northumberland, and had issue, of whom hereafter. His name is spelt with the double letters and the omission of the intermediate "de."

EIGHTH GENERATION.

John Ridell[8] (1), a son of Thomas[7] (3), succeeded as his father's heir; married and had issue, of whom hereafter. He was Sheriff of Newcastle-on-Tyne, in 1478.

NINTH GENERATION.

Thomas Ridell[9] (4), eldest son of John[8] (1), was his father's successor; married Eleanor, daughter of Ralph Claxton, and sister of William Claxton, Esq., of Wyneyard (she was afterward married to Edward Swinburn, of the family of Swinburn, subsequently allied by marriage with the Riddells), and by her had issue, of whom hereafter. He was mayor of Newcastle-on-Tyne in 1510, 1521, and 1526, and "won, by his prudence and conscientious attention to public duties, the esteem of his constituency."

Peter Ridell[9] (1), second son of John[8] (1), probably died young.

---

the forces they could muster against the insurgents. The great service performed by them, and their steady attachment, it is well known, enabled Edward to completely crush the insurrection headed by the Earl of Lancaster, his own kinsman, and abetted by many powerful nobleman.

Sir William was employed on several important occasions by King Edward. In 1318, he was joined in commission with two others, to cause forty . . to be distributed to the knights who had sustained losses in Northumberland by reason of the incursion of the Scots. In 1320, his majesty, by a writ directed to Sir William, delegated to him the power of admitting to the peace any of the Scotch who should be willing to return to their allegiance; provided they gave proper security for their good conduct in future. The following year, Sir William and others were empowered to grant letters-patent for a safe conduct to John de Pilmor, who was expected to come to treat on the part of the Scotch king.

When King Edward III mounted the throne, he placed no less confidence in Sir William, whose fidelity to his father had been so conspicuous. In the very first year of his reign he commanded Sir William with others to cause the terms of truce with Scotland to be faithfully observed, and to see that the offenders were punished. He did not, however, live long to enjoy the favor of his sovereign, for he died in 1328, leaving *three* daughters, his heiresses. A part of Sir William's lands were held during life, by Hugh Ridell, a kinsman of Sir William.

William Ridell[9] (3), third son of John[8] (1), was mayor of Newcastle-on-Tyne in 1500. No account of a family.

TENTH GENERATION.

Peter Ridell[10] (2), eldest son of Thomas[9] (4), was his father's heir; he married Dorothy, daughter of John Brandling, who was mayor of the city of Newcastle in 1509, and a sister of Sir Ralph Brandling, Knt. (see "Burk's Commoners, vol. 2, page 39), and had issue, of whom hereafter. He was a merchant-adventurer in Newcastle, in 1549.

ELEVENTH GENERATION.

Thomas Ridell[11] (5), eldest son and heir of Peter[10] (2), died without children.

Peter Ridell[11] (3), second son of Peter[10] (2), was of Newcastle-on-Tyne, and succeeded his brother Thomas, before mentioned. He married Eleanor, daughter of John Swinburn, of Newcastle, and had issue several children, of whom hereafter.

William Ridell[11] (4), third son of Peter[10] (2), was of Newcastle-on-Tyne, a merchant-adventurer, and sheriff of that borough in 1575. Was mayor of Newcastle in 1582, 1590, and 1595. This worshipful citizen was married twice; his first wife, Annie, daughter and heiress of William Lawson, was the mother of *one* son, who became his father's heir. By the second wife, Barbara, daughter of Alderman Bertram Anderson (who died in 1627, and was buried on the 11th of November; *her* will bears date 30th October, 3d year of the reign of Charles 1), he had *eight* sons and *one* daughter.

Eleanor Ridell[11] (1), eldest daughter of Peter[10] (2) was the wife of Henry Lawe.

Katherine Ridell[11] (1), second daughter of Peter[10] (2), was married in 1580, to Anthony Lawe.

TWELFTH GENERATION.

William Ridell[12] (5), eldest son of Peter[11] (3), born in 1581.

Peter Ridell[12] (4), second son of Peter[11] (3), born in 1591.

Thomas Ridell[12] (6), third son of Peter[11] (3), was born in 1599.

Barbara Ridell[12] (1), a daughter of Peter[11] (3), born in 1584; was married, first, to John Southeron, and secondly, to Anthony Theabold.

Sir Thomas Ridell[12] (7), the eldest son of William[11] (4), was knighted by King James I, in the first year of his reign (1603). He was Sheriff of Newcastle-on-Tyne in 1601; mayor in 1604 and 1616, and Member of Parliament for that borough in 1620, and again with his brother Peter, before mentioned, in 1628. He was a "Knight of Gateshead in the Palatinate of Durham." He was bailiff of Gateshead in 1605, 1614, and 1620. His father had obtained, in 1569, a case from the crown of coals, "*cum les water pyttes in campis de Gatshed*"; and he himself was one of the Grand Lessees, as they were styled, of the Corporation of Newcastle, on the assignment of Thomas Sutton, founder of the Charter House, of the Lordships of Gateshead and Whickham, and the parks, wastes, and coal mines belonging to them, acquired in consideration of £12,000 paid down, but said by Dr. Craddock, archdeacon of Northumberland, to be then worth £50,000 per annum. He built him a pleasant seat out of the hospital of St. Edmund, in Gateshead, with an extensive prospect out on the fell, which

comprised thirteen hundred acres of waste or common land.   He married
Elizabeth, daughter of Sir John Conyers, Knt., of Sockburn, and had issue.
   Sir Peter Ridell[12] (5), eldest son of William[11] (4), by his second
wife, succeeded as his father's heir.   He married, first, Isabelle, daughter of
Mr. Alderman Atkinson, of Newcastle, and had by that lady, who died
in 1614, *four* sons and *four* daughters.   Sir Peter espoused, secondly,
Mary, second daughter and co-heir of Thomas Surtees, Esq. (heir male of
the Dinsdale family), and had *two* more daughters, of whom hereafter.
He was Sheriff of Newcastle-on-Tyne, in 1604; mayor in 1619 and 1635;
Member of Parliament for that borough in 1623, 1628, and 1640.   He
inherited by will the property of a younger brother, Robert, who was a
draper in Newcastle (certain lands in Lancashire), and became a very
wealthy man.   He died in 1640, and his dust lies within the hallowed
precincts of St. Nicholas' Church, Newcastle-on-Tyne.
   Henry Ridell[12] (1), second son of William[11] (4), by his second wife,
was born in 1574, and died at Elbinge, in Germany, *sine prole.*
   William Ridell[12] (6), third son of William[11] (4), by second wife, was
born in 1578; married and had issue *ten* children, of whom I have no
particulars, but presume they became the ancestors (five were sons) of
junior branches of the Northumberland family, whose connections cannot be properly made out.
   George Ridell[12] (1), fourth son of William[11] (4), by his second wife,
was born in 1580, and died when young.
   Robert Ridell[12] (1), fifth son of William[11] (4), by his second wife, was
born in 1582, and died young.
   Michael Ridell[12] (1), sixth son of William[11] (4), by his second wife, was
born in 1583, and died in 1613, probably *sine prole.*
   John Ridell[12] (2), seventh son of William[11] (4), by his second marriage.
I have no particulars concerning him.
   Robert Ridell[12] (2), eighth son of William[11] (4), by second wife, was
born in 1590, and died without issue, seized of certain lands in Lancashire,
leaving his brother, Sir Peter, his heir.   He had married in 1621, Jane Cole,
who survived as his widow in 1651.   He was a draper in the city of Newcastle, and acquired wealth.
   Alice Ridell[12] (1), only daughter of William[11] (4), was born in 1587.
No mention of her marriage.

THIRTEENTH GENERATION.

   Sir William Ridell[13] (7), eldest son of Thomas[12] (7), was his father's
heir and successor.   He was in the time of Elizabeth one of the Grand
Lessees in trust for the Corporation of Newcastle, of the Lordships of
Gateshead and Whickham.   He married first, Katherine, daughter of Sir
Henry Widdrington, of Widdrington (this family was subsequently allied
to that of Riddell, as will presently appear), and had an only surviving
child, of whom hereafter.
   Sir Thomas Ridell[13] (8), second son of Thomas[12] (7), was a Knight of
Fenham, recorder of Newcastle-on-Tyne, and representative of the borough
in Parliament in 1620 and 1628.   He was also Colonel of a regiment of
foot under Charles I, and Governor of Tynemouth Castle.   During the
troubles of his time he espoused with extraordinary zeal the royal cause,
and so distinguished himself that a reward of one thousand pounds was
offered for his apprehension.   He was a Catholic and cavalier of inflexible
spirit; and his mansion, which was situated a little to the east of the pres-

ent Trinity Chapel, in the High Street of Gateshead, suffered often and severely from the ravages of the Presbyterian forces. In the year 1640, while the Scottish army occupied Newcastle, he sent a petition to King Charles on account of the destruction of his property at the hands of the soldiers, whereby, as he alleged, he and his posterity were " like to be ruinated and undone." There was no help, however, under existing circumstances, as will appear from the following letter, which has been considered by some as apocryphal. It purports to have been written by one Captain Leslie to Sir Thomas Ridell, of Gateshead House. It runs thus : —

"SIR THOMAS. — Between me and Gad, it maks my heart blead blued to see sic wark gae thro sae trim a garden as yours. I ha been twa times we my cuslu the Generall, and sae shall I sax times mair afore the warks gae that gate. But gin awe this be dune, Sir Thamas, ye maun mak the twenty pounds thraty, and I maun hae the tagg'd-tail trooper that stands in the staw, and the wee trim-gaeing thing that stands in the newk o' the haw, chirping and chiming at the neun-tide o' day, and forty bows of bier to saw the maens withawe. And as I am a chevalier of fortin, and a limb o' the house of Rothes, as the muckle maun kist in Edinburgh Auld Kirk can weel witness for these aught hundred years and mair bygane, nought shall skaith your house, within or without, to the valedome of a twapenny checken. I am your humble sarvant, JOHN LESSLEY, Major General and Captain over sax score and twa men and some mair; Crouner of Cumberland, Northumberland, Murryland, and Riddesdale, the Merce, Tiviotdale, and Fife; Bailie of Kirkadie; Governor of Brunt Eland and the Bass; Laird of Libertone, Tilley and Whoolly; Siller-Tacker of Stirling; Constable of Leith; and Sir John Lesslie, Knight, to the bute of awe that."

After the surrender of Tynemouth Castle, which was necessitated by " the pestilence having been five weeks amongst the garrison with a great mortalitie, soe that they were glad to yeald, and to scatter themselves abroad," the knight made his way to Berwick-on-Tweed, from which place he made his escape to the Continent in a small fishing-smack. He died at Antwerp in 1652, two years after the death of his father, "a broken and banished man," his lordship of Tunstal having previously been sold to satisfy the composition levied upon him, amounting to about as much as it was worth, in the then depressed state of the land market. He married in 1629, Barbara, daughter of Sir Alexander Davidson, Knight of Blakiston, and widow of Ralph Calverly, by whom he had issue, of whom hereafter.

    Peter Ridell[12] (6), third son of Thomas[12] (7), died *sine prole.*

    Hon. George Ridell[12] (2), fourth son of Thomas[12] (7), born in 1602, was Doctor of Civil Law, Judge Advocate in the Army of the Marquis of Newcastle, and during the siege of Hull, in 1645 ; married Jane, daughand by her had a son and daughter, of whom hereafter. ter and co-heir of —— Eysdale, Chancellor of the Diocese of York, and by her had a son and daughter, of whom hereafter.

    Robert Ridell[12] (3), fifth son of Thomas[12] (7), born in 1612, married a French lady, named Magdalen. No account of a family, but he was presumably ancestor of some branch of the Riddell family that cannot now be properly made out.

    Ephraim Ridell[12] (1), sixth son of Thomas[12] (7), born in 1615.

    Annie Ridell[12] (2), eldest daughter of Thomas[12] (7), was the wife of Sir John Clavering, Knight of Callaly.

    Elizabeth Ridell[12] (1), second daughter of Thomas[12] (7), died in 1606.

    Mary Ridell[12] (1), third daughter of Thomas[12] (7), was the wife of Sir Francis Radcliffe, Baronet of Dilston.

Eleanor Ridell[13] (2), fourth daughter of Thomas[12] (7), born 1610.
Jeanie Ridell[13] (1), fifth daughter of Thomas[12] (7), was the wife of
John Forcer, Esq., of Harbor House, Durham.

FOURTEENTH GENERATION.

William Ridell[14] (8), eldest son of William[13] (7), and his wife Katherine Widdrington, was of Gateshead. He married first Isabella ——, and
by her had *one* daughter, of whom hereafter; his second wife was Margaret ——, by whom he had a son and daughter. He died in 1698.

Thomas Riddell[14] (9), eldest son of Thomas[13] (8), succeeded his father,
and was styled "of Fenham, in the county of Northumberland," which
estate he sold in the year 1695, under an act of Parliament, to John Ord,
Esq., of Newcastle. This property once belonged to the Knights of Jerusalem, called "Knight Hospitallers of St. John." The estate was granted
them by Parliament in 1324. It was annexed to the crown at the Dissolution, but afterwards came by purchase to the Riddell family; they held it
for only a few generations, however, and sold it to the Ords as above
stated. The coal mines were reserved at the time of the first sale, but
were afterwards sold to the Ords, who held the hall and lands until about
thirty years ago, when the mansion and about ninety acres of land were
sold to Colonel Bell, and he and his widow held it for fifteen years; it
was then sold to William Pears, who held it till about 1873, when it came
by purchase to William-Cochran Carr, of Newcastle-on-Tyne, the present
owner. The hall and about two hundred acres of land are all that has
been sold from the original estate by Mrs. Blackett Ord, who now owns
large tracts of valuable land in Fenham and Benwell [*vide* Gazetteer].
For the past twenty years the hall and grounds have been neglected and
allowed to go to ruin, till by the exertions of the present proprietor it has
been thoroughly renovated and put in fine condition (see plate view of
Fenham Hall in this book). The grounds are beautiful, and the trees very
large, — indeed the largest in the neighborhood, — some of them being
thirty-six inches in diameter at five feet from the ground. The rhodo-
dendrons on the terrace are of unusual size; they have come down to the
ground again, and have taken root, until from one original plant a tree
now covers about fifty feet in area. Mr. Riddell was the first of this
family whose name is found spelled with the double letters in full. He
married Mary, eldest daughter of Edward Grey, Esq., of Bichfield, Northumberland, and had (with other daughters who all died unmarried) *eight*
sons and *one* daughter, of whom hereafter. Mr. Riddell was baptized in
1632, and died in 1704.

Ralph Riddell[14] (1), second son of Thomas[13] (8), was born in 1636.
No further mention of this child.

Barbara Riddell[14] (2), eldest daughter of Thomas[13] (8), was born in
1630.

Anne Riddell[14] (3), second daughter of Thomas[13] (8), born in 1632,
was married to Francis, second son of Marmaduke Tunstal, Esq., of Wyc-
liffe, in the County of York.

Elizabeth Riddell[14] (2), third daughter of Thomas[13] (8), born in 1634;
was married to Ralph Wilson, Esq., of Field House, near Gateshead, in
the County of Durham.

Margery Riddell[14] (1), fourth daughter of Thomas[13] (8), born in 1639;
was living in 1661, a nun at Pointoise, in France.

"FENHAM HALL."

Northumberland, England

RESIDENCE OF SIR THOMAS RIDDELL.

Jane Riddell[14] (2), fifth daughter of Thomas[13] (8), born in 1641.
Eleanor Riddell[14] (3), sixth daughter of Thomas[13] (8), born in 1643.
A daughter *Angela* died 1709, aged 65 years.

Thomas Ridell[14] (10), only son of George[13] (2).   No particulars.
Margaret Ridell[14] (2), only known daughter of George[13] (2).

FIFTEENTH GENERATION.

Jane Ridell[15] (3), eldest daughter of William[14] (8), by his first wife Isabella, was married to Mark Riddell, M. D.

William Ridell[15] (9), only son of William[14] (8), by his second wife Margaret, was his father's heir and successor.   He was the last known of this family styled " of Gateshead," having died issueless in 1710.   The Gateshead property seems to have passed for a time into the family of Clavering of Callaly, Sir John Clavering, Knt., a staunch Royalist throughout the civil wars, having married Annie Ridell, William's great-aunt.   Ralph Clavering, the fourth in descent from this marriage, was an occasional resident at Gateshead House, during the Jacobite Rebellion; and in January, 1746, when the Duke of Cumberland and his army passed through the town, and a vast crowd was collected by the spectacle, several keelmen perched themselves upon the garden-wall belonging to the Ridell mansion to obtain a better view, whereupon Robert Woodness, the gardener, hounded the dogs upon them.   This gave such provocation to the mob that they broke into the garden, and proceeding from one act of destruction to another, finally destroyed the house by fire, together with the " Popish Chapel " attached to it.   And thus ended the residential connection of the Ridell family with Gateshead; for the house was never repaired, and the materials were gradually carried away, until, in 1820, the ruins were entirely removed, and on the 18th of March, 1838, the last trees of the garden were cut down by Mr. John Hopper, miller.   The only relic of the Ridell mansion now remaining is a gateway which stands at the northwest corner of the chapel.   Gateshead is only separated from the city of Newcastle by the River Tyne, and is interesting only as a manufacturing place.   Here are the great grindstone-quarries from which the celebrated " Newcastle Grindstones " are shipped to all parts of the world. The early history of Gateshead is obscure.   William the Conqueror defeated the forces of Malcolm, King of Scotland, here in 1068.

Catherine Ridell[15] (1), daughter of William[14] (8), died unmarried in 1750.

[I shall now change the designation of this family from " Riddells of Newcastle and Gateshead " to that of " Riddells of Swinburne and Felton," but shall carry forward the *generation figures* in the same rotation as before. — *Author.*]

RIDDELLS OF SWINBURNE AND FELTON.

[FIFTEENTH GENERATION FROM JORDAN DE RIDEL.]

Thomas Riddell[15] (11), eldest son of Thomas[14] (9), who sold Fenham and purchased Swinburne, was born in 1656, and died young, leaving no descendants.

William Riddell[15] (10), second son of Thomas[14] (9), was born in 1658, and died young, issueless.

Edward Riddell[16] (1), third son of Thomas[14] (9), was his father's heir and successor. Was born in 1660, and styled " of Swinburne Castle." He married Dorothy, daughter of Robert Dalton, Esq., of Thurnham, in Lancashire, and dying in 1731, was succeeded by his son, of whom hereafter.

Alexander Riddell[16] (1), fourth son of Thomas[14] (9), born in 1663.

Mark Riddell[16] (1), M. D., fifth son of Thomas[14] (9), born in 1665; was a physician, sometime of Hunton, and afterwards of Morpeth. He married Jane, daughter of William Riddell, as before mentioned, and had *one* only son living in 1731, when his father's will was proved. This will was dated 1721, and Dr. Riddell probably died about that time.

John Riddell[16] (3), sixth son of Thomas[14] (9), died in 1672.

Thomas Riddell[16] (12), seventh son of Thomas[14] (9).

William Riddell[16] (11), eighth son of Thomas[14] (9).

Elizabeth Riddell[16] (2), only daughter of Thomas[14] (9), was married to William Shaftoe, Esq., of Barrington.

SIXTEENTH GENERATION.

Thomas Riddell[16] (13), eldest son of Edward[16] (1), was styled "of Swinburne Castle, Esq." He married in 1726, Mary, daughter of William Widdrington, Esq., of Cheeseburn Grange, and sister and co-heir of Ralph Widdrington, by whom he had issue. This gentleman was involved in the rising of 1715, but saved himself by escaping from Lancashire Castle, but not being excepted from the general pardon, he was allowed to return to his estate and reside there unmolested. Swinburne Castle, the seat of this family, before mentioned, has a singular history. It was held with Gunnerton by Peter de Gunwarton, in the time of Edward I. In 1326, it belonged to John Swynburn, from whom it passed by marriage to the family of Widdrington; John de Widdrington being the first heir of that name; his descendants owned it in 1596. It was purchased by Thomas Riddell, Esq. (ante), in 1695, and has since continued in this family. The present castle is a very large stone building, situated on rising ground, and "surrounded by plantations, laid out in long straight lines, which, at a distance, have a dark and hard appearance." See plate view of Swinburne Castle in this book.

Edward Riddell[16] (2), only known son of Mark[16] (1) and Jane (Riddell), was living in 1731, when his father's will (dated 1721) was proved. He was styled "of Morpheth."

SEVENTEENTH GENERATION.

Thomas Riddell[17] (14), eldest son of Thomas[16] (13), was his father's heir and successor to Swinburne Castle. He married Elizabeth, only daughter and heiress of Edward Horsley Widdrington, Esq., of Felton Park, Northumberland, by whom he had several children, of whom hereafter. He was engaged with his father in the insurrection of 1715, and was carried up to London, where, being arraigned for treason, he pleaded guilty, but experienced the royal mercy, and was liberated. He sold the collieries of Fenham, which had been reserved at the time of the disposal of the rest of the estate, to the Ord family. He died in 1777, and was succeeded by eldest son.

Ralph Riddell[18] (2), second son of Thomas[16] (13), inherited the property of his uncle and namesake, Ralph Widdrington, called "Cheeseburn Grange," and became ancestor of the "Riddells of Cheeseburn Grange," which see.

"SWINBURN CASTLE."
Northumberland, England
RESIDENCE OF SIR...

Dorothy Riddell[18] (**1**), eldest daughter of Thomas[17] (**13**), died young.
Barbara Riddell[18] (**3**), second daughter of Thomas[17] (**13**), was the wife of a Mr. Nelson, of Lancashire, an esquire.
[One daughter, whose name does not appear, was the wife of —— Maxwell, Esq., of Scotland. Some say there was a son named Edward, who died when a child, but I cannot tell certainly about him.]

NINETEENTH GENERATION.

Thomas Riddell[19] (**15**), eldest son and heir of Thomas[18] (**14**), was of Swinburne Castle, County of Northumberland. He married, April 19, 1790, Margaret, daughter of William Salvin, Esq., of Croxdale, and by her had an only son, who predeceased him. He died himself in 1798, and was succeeded by his youngest and only surviving brother.

Edward-H.-Widdrington Riddell[19] (**3**), second son of Thomas[18] (**14**), inherited the estates of the Widdringtons through his mother, who was the heiress, and was consequently styled "of Felton and Horsley." He married, June 20, 1792, Isabella, fifth daughter of William Salvin, Esq., of Croxdale Hall, County of Durham, and sister of the wife of his brother Thomas, before mentioned; but died without issue, Jan. 26, 1793, at Stella Hall, Durham. His widow was married in 1808, to Ralph Riddell, Esq., of Cheeseburn Grange. The manor of Felton, which came to this family of Riddell from the Widdringtons, comprised Old Felton, Acton, Swarland, Framlington, Glantlees, and Over-Isger. It anciently belonged to the barony of Mitford, and was given by Henry I to William Bertram; but in the thirteenth year of the reign of Edward II it was possessed by Andromare de Valence, Earl of Pembroke, who was murdered in France, after which it passed successively to the Earls of Athol, the Perceys, the Scropes, the Lisles, and the Widdringtons. The property of Horsley came to the Riddells through the Widdringtons' intermarriage with the Horsleys, an ancient Northumberland family, long seated at Long Horsley, whence the surname.

Ralph Riddell[19] (**4**), third son of Thomas[18] (**14**), succeeded to the estates of Felton and Horsley at the decease of his brother Edward, issueless, in 1793. He married, July 23, 1801, Elizabeth, daughter of Joseph Blount, Esq., second son of Michael Blount, Esq., of Maple Durham, and had issue, of whom hereafter. Mr. Riddell was passionately fond of rearing and training race-horses, and eminently successful on the "turf"; yet he was no gambler, but of steady and retiring habits, to which deafness gave him more than a natural relish. His noted horse "Doctor Syntax," won about twenty gold cups; another called "XYZ,"— "that bonnie steed that bang'd them a' for pith and speed,"—carried off nine gold cups; and his "Don Carlos" was the winner of the same number, when he was purchased for the Russian government, and sent over to that country. Mr. Riddell gave up his racing establishment a few years before his death, which took place on the 9th of March, 1833, when he was sixty-three years of age. He was a man of unbounded kindness, and exceeding liberality to the poor. In consequence of the steady and uniform adherence of this family to the Roman Catholic faith they have not figured in the higher offices of the county.

Mary Riddell[19] (**2**), eldest daughter of Thomas[18] (**14**).
Dorothy Riddell[19] (**2**), second daughter of Thomas[18] (**14**), died unmarried.
Elizabeth Riddell[19] (**3**), third daughter of Thomas[18] (**14**), was married

10

to John Clifton, Esq., of Lytham Hall, County of Durham, and died Nov. 19, 1825.

Anne Riddell[19] (4), youngest daughter of Thomas[18] (14), was the wife of Sir Walter Blount, Bart., of Soddington, County of Worcester. The following account of the wedding will show the customs and manner of the festivities of those times:—"1792, Nov. 24,— being the anniversary of the birthday of Miss Anne Riddell, of Felton Park, the morning was ushered in by the ringing of bells; ale and other liquors were distributed to the populace, and the evening concluded with a dance at Felton Park. On the 27th, Sir Walter Blount, of Morley, in Shropshire, gave an ox to the inhabitants of Felton and its environs, which was roasted whole. Two men cooks, in proper uniforms, cut up the ox and distributed it in equal proportions to the people; the bakers of the village did the same with the bread, and the publicans with their ale. The whole was conducted with the greatest decorum, with music and firing of cannon. The favorite tune was, 'There's few good fellows when Watty's awa'.' The village exhibited a scene of laudable hospitality and harmless festivity. On the following morning Sir Walter Blount and Miss Anne Riddell were united in marriage. Immediately after the ceremony they took their departure for his seat in Shropshire, amidst the blessings of the poor, and the acclamations of the populace, who unharnessed the horses and drew the carriage from Felton Park quite through the village. He gave ten pounds to the poor of the parish, and three guineas to the people who drew the carriage, to drink; at the same time Sir Walter ordered two fat sheep to be roasted and distributed, and this was accordingly done that day." Lady Blount died in 1823, *one* only son surviving her, the eighth and present baronet, Sir Walter Blount.

TWENTIETH GENERATION.

Thomas Riddell[20] (16), eldest son of Ralph[19] (4), was born May 18, 1802; married Oct. 15, 1827, Mary, daughter of the late William Throckmorton, Esq., of Lincoln's Inn. He succeeded his father as heir of Swinburne Castle and Felton Park, on the 19th of March, 1833. He was a Commissioner of the Peace for Northumberland in 1836, and sometime Sheriff for that county. He had *four* sons by his first wife, who, having deceased, Mr. Riddell married secondly, in 1845, Laura-Anna, daughter of Thomas-Joseph de Tafford, Bart., of Tafford Park, County of Lancaster, and by her had issue. He died at his seat, Felton Park, on the 5th of April, 1870, aged 67. Throughout the winter he had been an invalid, but on Saturday before his death he was so well that he ventured upon a drive to Alnwick. In waiting for his carriage to return home he was seized with paralysis, and on being conveyed to Felton Park, under the anxious care of Mrs. Riddell and a medical attendant, he never regained consciousness, and gradually sank down to death. For many years Mr. Riddell's constitution had been giving way; and in public life he had taken little interest. Domesticated within the beautiful demesnes of Felton Park, his habits were simple and unostentatious. As a landlord, Mr. Riddell was popular; his word was his bond, and his attachments strong to the memories of generations upon his extensive estates. Sensible of the dignity of family traditions, he sustained with admirable consistency the best traits of a country gentleman. In proof of the unlimited confidence in Mr. Riddell's honor, it may be stated that occupancy upon his estates had existed for upwards of thirty-eight years without the evidence

RIGHT REV^D WILLIAM RIDDELL D.D.

of ink. Few men have passed away with deeper feelings of gratitude, affection, and regret, on the part of those who mourned his loss as a landlord, a neighbor, and a friend to the poor. His mortal remains were committed to their last resting-place in the family vault, at St. Mary's Catholic Church, Felton Park. The chief mourners were John-Giffard Riddell, Esq., Felton Park; Robert Riddell, Esq., Edward-Widdrington Riddell, Esq., York; Henry-Matthias Riddell, Esq., London; Edward Riddell, Esq., Cheeseburn Grange; John Errington, Esq., High Warden, the deceased's son-in-law; Sir Humphrey de Trafford, and Mr. Augustus de Trafford, of Trafford Hall.

[N. B. Mr. Errington of High Warden, who died in 1878, left his third wife, née Riddell of Felton Park, a widow, and also a son and daughter by her.]

Edward-Widdrington Riddell[20] (4), second son of Ralph[19] (4), was born in 1803; married July 1, 1830, Catherine, eldest daughter of Thomas Stapleton, Esq., of Carlton Hall and of the Grove, Richmond, County of York, and a sister of Miles-Thomas, eighth Lord Beaumont, father of the present baron, Henry Stapleton, by whom he had issue *three* sons and *three* daughters. Mr. Riddell was an officer in the Eighteenth Hussars, and became distinguished. He died in 1870. I think Mr. Riddell resided at Felton Park.

Right Rev. William Riddell[20] (12), third son of Ralph[19] (4), was born Feb. 5, 1807. He was endowed with superior intellectual faculties, and was early the subject of deep religious convictions. Having decided to devote himself to the work of the priesthood in the Catholic Church, of which this family have ever been supporters, he received his first lessons of knowledge and science in a celebrated house known as "Stonyhurst," from the Jesuit fathers sojourning there; and having finished his college course, he made a visit to Rome, where he entered holy orders, and was called to a most honorable and responsible office under Cardinal Wells. Then came a change in his vocation. In the autumn of 1833, he was stationed as priest at Newcastle-on-Tyne, and labored there till 1844, among the poorest classes of that great city, "always ready to receive the penitent sinner in the holy tribunal of penance, to counsel those who came to seek counsel, to encourage those who required to be reminded that, however great the guilt and ingratitude of man, the mercy of God is infinite as His infinite being, and can never be restricted by human infirmity." He was careful in teaching the flock he presided over those truths they should know, and the sacred duties required of them. He was especially devoted to the young, and spent much of his time in giving them instruction. The paramount interest of his ministry seemed to be, while in Newcastle, the founding of schools of an efficient character. He was ever ready to assist his poor brethren, and glad to part with anything in his possession in the shape of wealth, that he might be a faithful steward to the needy. In March, 1844, he was raised to the episcopal office of bishop, having been appointed by Pope Gregory XVI, coadjutor to the Right Rev. Dr. Mostyne, Vicar Apostolic of the Northern District. The new prelate, who was styled " Bishop of Lango," *in partibus infidelium*, was consecrated at Ushaw, with great pomp by the bishops in attendance. On the death of Dr. Mostyne, in 1847, Dr. Riddell became sole bishop of his district, continuing to discharge the duties of his high office with great application and acceptability. He did not confine his labors to Newcastle, but erected a church at Felling, almost exclusively by his personal

"FELTON PARK":

Northumberland, England.

"CHEESBURN GRANGE."

Northumberland, England.

1832, and was living at the time of his father's death, in 1870; but I have no particulars.

Edward Riddell[21] (5), fifth son of Thomas[20] (16), was born in January, 1836. Presumably living in 1870, as a Riddell of this name was one of the chief mourners at the death of this Edward's father; but I have no knowledge of him.

Frances-Mary Riddell[21] (1), eldest daughter of Thomas[20] (16), was born in 1838; was married Jan. 29, 1866, to John O'Shaughnessey, Esq., of Birch Grove, County Roscommon, Ireland, and had a daughter, who became a nun of St. Dominic.

Gertrude-Mary Riddell[21] (1), second daughter of Thomas[20] (16), was born in 1840; was married in 1863 to John Errington, Esq., of High Warden, County Northumberland.

Teresa-Elizabeth Riddell[21] (1), third daughter of Thomas[20] (16), was married to Thomas Metcalf, Esq., of Bath, by whom she had, besides a daughter, Maria-Teresa, a son, Thomas-Peter, who assumed, by sign manual, the surname and arms of Moore only, in compliance with the will of his paternal grandmother, who.was heiress and last lineal descendant in the direct line of the illustrious Lord High Chancellor, Sir Thomas More. [One authority states that there was another daughter of Thomas Riddell, named Laura-Elizabeth, who died in 1858, at Longborough, St. Mary's Convent.]

Rev. Edward-Widdrington Riddell[21] (6), eldest son of Edward[20] (4), was born May 10, 1831, and is in holy orders of the Roman Catholic Church. His seat is Bootham House, Yorkshire.

John-Gerard Riddell[21] (5), second son of Edward[20] (4), was born August 8, 1835; married in 1863, Catherine-Flora, youngest daughter of Edward Chaloner, Esq., of Oak Hill, near Liverpool, and is styled "of Hermiston Grange, Nottinghamshire, England." He has issue, of whom hereafter.

Arthur-George Riddell[21] (1), third son of Edward[20] (4), was born Sept. 15, 1836.

Laura-Monica Riddell[21] (1), only daughter of Edward[20] (4).

TWENTY-SECOND GENERATION.

Louisa-M.-Josephine Riddell[22] (1), only daughter of Thomas[21] (17), was born April 15, 1864.

Cuthbert-David-Giffard Riddell[22] (1), eldest son of John[21] (4), of Felton Park, was born in 1868.

Laura Riddell[22] (2), a daughter of John[21] (4), of Felton Park, was born in 1870.

Edward-Charles Riddell[22] (7), eldest son of John[21] (5), of Hermiston Grange, was born in 1867.

RIDDELLS OF CHEESEBURN GRANGE.

[EIGHTEENTH GENERATION FROM SIR JORDAN.]

Ralph Riddell[18] (2), son of Thomas[17] (13), of Felton Park (see "Riddells of Swinburne and Felton"), was born in 1774; married May 9, 1803, Isabella, daughter of William Salvin, Esq., of Croxdale Hall, County

of Durham (she was a widow of his cousin, Edward Riddell, of Felton
Park), and was the inheritor of the estates of his uncle, Ralph Widdrington, Esq., at Cheeseburn Grange. He died in 1831 (his widow in 1853),
having had issue *five* sons and *one* daughter.

NINETEENTH GENERATION.

Robert Riddell[19] (5), eldest son of Ralph[18] (2), died in 1826.
William Riddell[19] (13), second son of Ralph [18] (2), died in 1828.
Edward Riddell[19] (8), third son of Ralph[18] (2), was born in 1804, and
succeeded his father as proprietor of Cheeseburn Grange, in 1831. He
was educated at Ushaw College. Married June 16, 1866, Adelia-Maria,
third daughter of S. T. Scrope, Esq., of Danby Hall, Yorkshire. He was
a Justice of the Peace, and Doctor of Law for Northumberland; was Sheriff in 1842. Mr. Riddell died in 1871, without issue, and was succeeded
by his brother, of whom hereafter.
Frederick Riddell[19] (1), fourth son of Ralph[18] (2), was born in 1808,
and designated " of Leyburn Grove, County of York." He died in 1866,
and was succeeded by his brother.
Francis Riddell[19] (1), only surviving son of Ralph[17] (13), born in 1813;
married in 1862, Ellen, daughter of Michael Blount, Esq., of Maple Durham, Oxon, and succeeded his brother in 1871. Has a son Edward, and
probably other issue. Mr. Riddell is a magistrate for County York and
Northumberland. Residences, Cheeseburn Grange and Thornburgh House.

RIDDLES OF TROUGHEND, ENGLAND.

Edward Riddle[1] (1), supposed to have been descended from some ancient branch of the Northumberland Riddells, lived on a farm at Troughend, in that county, and raised a family of children, of whom hereafter.

SECOND GENERATION.

Robert Riddle[2] (1), eldest son of Edward[1] (1), was born on a farm at
Troughend, England, and died young, without family.
Nicholas Riddle[2] (1), second son of Edward[1] (1), was born at Trough-
end, England, and had a family of children.
John Riddle[2] (1), third son of Edward[1] (1), was born at Troughend,
England; was hind (hired man) to his brother Edward as long as he
lived. Had a family, of whom hereafter.
Edward Riddle[2] (2), fourth son of Edward[1] (1), was born at Trough-
end, England, and had a family. He was a farmer.
Ann Riddle[2] (1), only daughter of Edward[1] (1), was born at Troughend, England. No particulars.

THIRD GENERATION.

Prof. Edward Riddle[3] (3), a son of John[2] (1), was born at Troughend,
England, in 1788; married, and had issue *six* children, of whom hereafter.
Mr. Riddle first kept school at Otterburn, or Reedwater, a village not less
interesting for its romantic situation than from its historical associations;
there he became acquainted with Mr. James Thompson, a person well

known in those parts for upwards of half a century, and who was remarkable for his knowledge of many branches of science, as well as for considerable attainments in mathematics. It is not improbable that Mr. Riddle derived from him that taste for the science which clung to his mind with such tenacity to the end of his life. What renders this more likely is, that about the time, before he was twenty years of age, he made an electrical machine with his own hands, and with it showed the ordinary phenomena produced by that instrument. At that period, it is easily imagined with what wonder and alarm a ring of rustics would feel the electric impulse sent through their bodies, with a sensation unknown before.

> " And still they gazed, and still the wonder grew,
> That one small head should carry all *he* knew."

From Otterburn Mr. Riddle moved to Whitburn, in the County of Durham, and while there, in 1810, his name first appeared in the *Ladies' Diary*, then under the editorship of Dr. Hutton, whose friend he subsequently became, and who rendered him such important assistance in advancing his success in life. It then appears that at the age of twenty-two he had made great progress in mathematical studies. For many years he continued to be a distinguished contributor to the *Ladies' Diary*, in which his solutions were always remarkable for beauty and accuracy. He has said that the complete mastery of Playfair's Encylopædia, which he accomplished, produced such an effect on his mind, as to render the acquisition of any other mathematical subject easy. After continuing seven years at Whitburn, Mr. Riddle, through the recommendation of Dr. Hutton, was appointed master of the Trinity House School, Newcastle-on-Tyne, in which he remained seven years, proving by his energies and ability of the greatest service to the nautical education of the port, which had previously been in the lowest possible state. In 1821, while master of the Trinity House School, Mr. Riddle made an extensive series of observations to ascertain the longitude of that school, and to determine by actual experiments what confidence may now be placed in the results of lunar observations; these observations are given in a table in his remarks on the present state of nautical astronomy, published in 1821, and dedicated to the Master and Brethren of Trinity House, Newcastle-on-Tyne. This essay is admirably written, and proves that he was as able to become the historian of science as to extend her boundaries. In 1821, by the same powerful influence of Dr. Hutton, he was appointed Master of the Upper School, Royal Naval Asylum, Greenwich, where he remained till the period of his retirement in 1851. Soon after his removal to London he became a member of the Royal Astronomical Society, to which he contributed several valuable papers. Mr. Riddle was one of the council of that learned body, and took an active part in all its plans for the advancement of science. In the third volume of the Transactions of the Society there is an able paper by him, "On Finding the Rates of Time-keepers," in which he showed how it could be done without a transit instrument. To amateur astronomers, and to sea-faring men not having access to such an instrument, his method was valuable. In the twelfth volume of the same transactions appears another of his papers, "On Longitude of Madras, by Moon-culminating Observations," which is very elaborate, and contains valuable directions and remarks. The most valuable work which ever came from Mr. Riddle's pen is his "Treatise on Navigation and Nautical Astronomy"; — it was an immense improvement on the empirical compendium in vogue when it appeared, combining, as it did, practice and theory in luminous order. It forms a course of mathematics for the nautical men, containing as much algebra and geometry as is necessary for the demonstrations of the various problems which it comprehends. It is a text-book in the Royal Navy. Mr. Riddle was noted for the surprising quickness and accuracy with which he took celestial observations. Shortly after his retirement in 1851, his bust in marble was presented to him by his old pupils, officers in the Royal Navy, accompanied with the expression of their high esteem for his worth as a public and private man. The presentation was in the boys' department of Greenwich School, the Admiral (Sir C. Adams) and all the officers attending in full uniform. These were deserving honors for a long, useful, and honorable life. He retired on full salary. Succeeded by his son. He died in 1856, aged 68 years.

FOURTH GENERATION.

Jane Riddle[4] (1), eldest daughter of Edward[3] (3), was married in 1844, to Captain Petley, Royal Navy. Has issue.

Prof. John Riddle[4] (2), eldest son of Edward[3] (3), was born at Newcastle-on-Tyne, England, in November, 1816; married Georgiana MacKenzie, daughter of Eneas MacKenzie of Newcastle-on-Tyne, the Northumberland historian, and had issue *seven* children, of whom hereafter. At the early age of fifteen Mr. Riddle was appointed an assistant master in the Greenwich Hospital Schools, and on the retirement of his father in 1851, was chosen to succeed him as head master. In 1846, he was elected a Fellow of the Royal Astronomical Society, and from that time till his death, was a regular attendant at its meetings, and an occasional contributor to its papers. He was appointed in 1854 Examiner in Navigation to the Science and Art department of the Committee of Council on Education, and held for many years a similar appointment in the Society of Arts. By both these Institutions his services were highly valued. As a teacher Mr. John Riddle was perhaps unrivalled, and his success in instilling into the minds of mere boys not only the practice, but the theory of navigation was very remarkable. The influence he possessed with his pupils was unbounded; and the good which he has accomplished, by stamping on a vast number of the scientific officers of the Royal Navy the impress of his own vigorous mind, was so great that his untimely death, which occurred Oct. 11, 1862, was looked upon as no other than a national loss.

Mr. Riddle was not only a good mathematician and a successful teacher, but also an accomplished gentleman, with a great taste for poetry and the arts. In society he was a universal favorite; and his urbane manner and intellectual conversation will long be remembered by a large circle of sorrowing friends.

His death was the result of a fall from a platform in his class room, which produced concussion of the brain, from which, after lingering sixteen days, he expired. The following is on a monument to his memory.

To
the memory of
John Riddle, Esq., F. R. A. S.,
late Head Master of the
Nautical School,
who died 11th of Oct., 1862,
in the 46th year of his age,
from injury to the brain, caused by
an accident in his class room.

> *This tablet*
> *is erected by his colleagues,*
> *The Masters of the Royal Hospital Schools,*
> *In testimony of*
> *their high appreciation of his*
> *public services as a teacher,*
> *and the*
> *uprightness and purity of his character,*
> *as exhibited in all the relations of life.*

Mary Riddle[4] (1), second daughter of Edward[3] (3), was born March 1, 1818, and died March 19, 1823.

Margaret Riddle[4] (1), third daughter of Edward[3] (3), was born Sept. 26, 1819, and died March 15, 1839.

Eliza Riddle[4] (1), fourth daughter of Edward[3] (3), was married to Rev. George-Yates Boddy, Vicar of Colgate, near to Horsham, late Professor at the Royal Millitary Academy, Woolwich, and has issue.

William Riddle[4] (1), youngest son of Edward[3] (3), was born Nov. 2, 1824, and died Dec. 26, 1825.

FIFTH GENERATION.

Elizabeth Riddle[5] (1), eldest daughter of John[4] (2).

Edward Riddle[5] (4), eldest son of John[4] (2), married Charlotte-Jane, only daughter of Ralph-William Lucas, an old Waterloo veteran, and has issue, of whom hereafter. Mr. Riddle is an engineer of submarine telegraphy, and has been employed on almost all the great lines. He is a member of the Society of Telegraph Engineers.

Margaret-Katherine Riddle[5] (2), second daughter of John[4] (2), was married to Thomas Connorton, Esq., of Reigate, Surrey.

John-George Riddle[5] (3), second son of John[4] (2), was born in 1849, and died when an infant.

Katherine-Mary Riddle[5] (1), third daughter of John[4] (2), was married to Frank Lucas, Esq., of Blackheath.

Georgiana-Frances Riddle[5] (1), fourth daughter of John[4] (2), was born in 1853, and died an infant.

Marian-Matilda Riddle[5] (1), fifth daughter of John[4] (2).

Helen-MacKenzie Riddle[5] (1), sixth daughter of John[4] (2).

SIXTH GENERATION.

Dorothy-Margaret Riddle[6] (1), eldest daughter of Edward[5] (4), born 1874.

John Riddle[6] (4), eldest son of Edward[5] (4), born in 1877.

Willett-Lucas Riddle[6] (1), second son of Edward[5] (4), died an infant.

Infant Son of Edward[5] (4), name not known.

RIDDLES OF TWEEDMOUTH, ENGLAND.

Samuel Riddle[2] (1), was descended from an old Northumberland family long settled at Twizell-on-Tweed, and presumably an offshoot from some branch of the Riddells of Newcastle-on-Tyne, or Gateshead, and related to the Riddles of Troughend. He and his father were flour millers at Twizell mill, and both are buried in Norham church-yard. Mr.

Riddle, father of Samuel, was twice married and had several sons and daughters. The son married Elizabeth Aitchison, and left *four* sons and *two* daughters, of whom hereafter. He carried on business at Tweed-mouth as millwright and engineer; died in his 90th year, and was buried at Tweedmouth.

THIRD GENERATION.

Peter Riddle³ (1), son of Samuel² (1), and succeeded his father at Tweedmouth as millwright and engineer.

James Riddle³ (1), a son of Samuel² (1).

Samuel Riddle³ (2), a son of Samuel² (1).

Andrew Riddle³ (1), a son of Samuel² (1), was born about 1809; married Mary-Ann Steel, and has *seven* children, of whom hereafter. He is a millwright and engineer. Residence, Tweedmouth, England.

Beatrice Riddle³ (1), daughter of Samuel² (1), born at Twizell, England. Deceased.

Mary Riddle³ (1), daughter of Samuel² (1), was born at Twizell, England.

FOURTH GENERATION.

Samuel-Philip Riddle⁴ (3), eldest son of Andrew³ (1), is a mill wright and engineer at Tweedmouth.

George-Steel Riddle⁴ (1), second son of Andrew³ (1), is a millwright and engineer at Tweedmouth.

Andrew Riddle⁴ (2), third son of Andrew³ (1), was born in October, 1851, and resides at Yeavering; is the occupier of Yeavering and Kirk-newton farms, both in the parish of Kirknewton, and County of North-umberland, England.

Isabella-Bothwick Riddle⁴ (1), eldest daughter of Andrew³ (1), resides at Tweedmouth.

John Riddle⁴ (1), fourth son of Andrew³ (1), millwright and engineer at Tweedmouth.

Elizabeth-Aitchison Riddle⁴ (1), second daughter of Andrew³ (1), resides at Tweedmouth.

Mary-Ann Riddle⁴ (2), third daughter of Andrew³ (1), resides at Tweedmouth.

RIDDELLS OF PARKMOUNT, IRELAND.

[UNITED STATES BRANCH.]

James Riddell¹ (1), parents unknown, was born somewhere in the Lowlands of Scotland; became a commissioned officer in the army of William III, and being an uncompromising Presbyterian, fought from *principle* during the wars with the Catholic-Irish. He was probably at the battle of Boyne-water,* and possibly connected with the siege of Londonderry. He was rewarded for his services in the army by a grant

---

* Boyne-water, or river, in the east of Ireland, rises in the Bog of Allan, and flows through Kildare, Kings County, Meath, and Louth. The Battle of Boyne took place on the banks of Boyne-water, near Oldridge, on the 1st of July, 1690, in which William III defeated James II. An obelisk, 150 feet high, marks the scene of the battle.

of three townlands in the County of Armagh, in the North of Ireland, and subsequently went there to dwell. He is said to have married Janet Maxwell, a woman of ·Scottish descent, and by her had issue, a family of sons and daughters.

SECOND GENERATION.

James Riddell[2] (2), a son of James[1] (1), was born in the County of Armagh, Ireland, about 1670–80; married Mary Henderson, of Scotch parentage, and continued this branch family, being his father's heir. He was a man of wealth and position, and of powerful physical strength. He lived to an advanced age, and died leaving *three* children, of whom hereafter.

THIRD GENERATION.

James Riddell[3] (3), a son of James[2] (2), was born in the city of Belfast (the author thinks a few miles out of the city proper), Ireland, in 1746; married Elizabeth Cowden, and had issue *three* sons, `of whom hereafter.

FOURTH GENERATION.

Leander Riddle[4] (1), son of James[3] (3), was born in Belfast, County Antrim, Ireland, in 1766; married Mary Brooks, and had issue several children, of whom hereafter. He was in the British naval service for four years; subsequently a cotton manufacturer. Emigrated to the United States, and settled in Pennsylvania in 1827, where he died in September, 1851, aged 85 years.
James Riddle[4] (4), a son of James[3] (3), was born at (or near) Belfast, Ireland, and became ancestor of the Riddells of Belfast, which *see.* He was a half-brother of Leander.
Alexander Riddle[4] (1), a son of James[3] (3), was born near Belfast, Ireland, and never married. He is said to have been a man of herculean strength, and feats accomplished by him were remarkable.

FIFTH GENERATION.

Elizabeth Riddle[5] (1), eldest· daughter of Leander[4] (1), was born at Parkmount, near Belfast, Ireland, in 1798, and is now living at Glen-Riddle, Penn.
Samuel Riddle[5] (1), eldest son of Leander[4] (1), was born at Parkmount, near Belfast, Ireland, in 1800. He married for his first wife, Martha Mercer, and secondly, Lydia C. Doyle, of Chester, Penn., by whom he has issue *four* children, of whom hereafter. Mr. Riddle acquired a fair English education at a private academy, quitting it at an early age to enter a cotton-factory in Belfast. While at the latter place he acquired a practical knowledge of cotton-manufacturing, being thus occupied nine years. He then determined to seek a more profitable field, and in May, 1823, sailed for the United States, but was shipwrecked at Sable Island. He eventually reached Philadelphia, in the following August, his whole capital being now reduced to five Spanish dollars. He carried his sea-chest on his back to his boarding-house, and immediately obtained employment in a cotton-mill at Manayunk. He removed to Pleasant Mills, N. J., where he was employed about three years. During this time, by carefulness and thrift, he had accumulated a small amount of means, with which he commenced business on his own account. He rented a mill at Springdale, Delaware County, Penn., in 1827, and engaged in spinning cotton yarns with four hundred and eighty mule spindles, employing only ten

hands. In three years' time he removed to a larger building on Chester Creek, and commenced operations with three hundred mule spindles, and the necessary machinery used in preparation; he remained there prosperously engaged for twelve years. In 1842 he purchased property at Pennsgrove, in Delaware County, which he named "Glen-Riddle," for Glen-Riddell, the residence of a branch of the family in Scotland. This locality was well chosen; a beautiful valley on Chester Creek, about fifteen miles from Philadelphia, was the place suited to Mr. Riddle's mind, and here he has added acre to acre and mill to mill, until at present the estate consists of a tract of land of several hundred acres, worth about three hundred dollars per acre. There are five large mills and more than two hundred dwellings in the town, occupied principally by the mill-operatives, of whom there are about five hundred employed. The town, a post-office, and railway-station derive their name from their projector, Mr. Riddle. The mills operate nearly ten thousand four hundred cotton and woolen spindles, with all the machinery for the preparatory work, and two hundred and seventy power looms; these are driven by two water-wheels and a powerful Corliss engine. Here Mr. Riddle has prosecuted his business for more than thirty years, with constantly increasing prosperity, as the demand for his manufactures augments every year. Mr. Riddle's personal appearance is very marked; he is short, quite corpulent, and carries an expression of great determination in his face. In conversation he is very jocose and sarcastic; has a great fund of anecdotes, and can relate them in a peculiarly interesting way. He is fully engaged in his business operations, conducting the various branches with great system and carefulness. He has admitted other members of the family, and the business is now carried on under the firm-name of Samuel Riddle, Son & Co. In addition to the business carried on at Glen-Riddle, they have a large business as commission merchants in Philadelphia.

[The author was the guest of Samuel Riddle for a few days after the family meeting held in Philadelphia, in 1876, and will ever remember with the most pleasing emotions the hours passed in this beautiful village; every attention was bestowed by this hospitable family which could conduce to the enjoyment of my visit. On the 4th of July, Mr. Riddle's son, in company with the mother and little Maude, the youngest daughter, took me on a pleasant drive with a fine barouche drawn by a pair of noble horses; the route lay through a very rich farming district, and the prospect from some of the grand hills over which we made our way was extensive and picturesque; and the cherries that were gathered from the large trees by the roadside were delicious to the taste. Glen-Riddle was appropriately named. Beautiful hills surround the village on every side, and nestling at their base, embowered in groves of luxuriant hard-wood trees that grow along the margin of the creek, stand the mills, and neat, white dwellings, where home the families employed by Mr. Riddle. Directly in front of the mansion-house of Mr. Riddle rises a large hill, the surface in smooth pastures, except near the summit, where we reach the borders of a beautiful grove of wide-spreading trees, a cool and delightful resting-place in a summer day. The family residence is surrounded with parks and gardens, tastefully laid out and ornamented with a variety of plants and flowers; there are fountains pouring forth their sparkling waters upon the grassy banks along the garden avenues, and all overshadowed with the foliage of the wide-spreading trees that everywhere abound. The house, constructed of solid stone, is spacious and stately, situated on

"GLEN RIDDLE MILLS."

Delaware County, Pa.

a lot somewhat elevated from the parallel street, and when built was considered the most elegant country-house in that county. Nothing that a cultivated taste could suggest, or money secure, seems to have been overlooked in the arrangement and furniture of the interior of the Riddle mansion; the rooms are large and cool, the furnishing rich, and the portraits and landscapes in oil, upon the walls, are valuable and artistic. In front, over the main entrance, is a fine portico, provided with seats and large rustic chairs; here, in the evening, we gathered with the Riddle family, and in pleasant conversation touching our family history we passed genial hours; Mr. Riddle occasionally weaving in a story relating to the adventures of his ancestors in the old country. The village is surrounded by extensive farms owned by the proprietor, and the acres of ripened grain and luxuriant corn, that were standing upon the field, showed the high state of fertility to which these lands have been raised. Large droves of sleek cows go slowly to the hillside pastures in the early morning, and noble horses graze along the fields. In company with the proprietor we walked about the village and along the willow-shaded streets, having our attention called to many objects of improvement and interest at every turn.]

The following lines are taken from a poem on Glen-Riddle, composed by a lady who taught the village school: —

> " But whence camest thou, fair RIDDLE GLEN,
> Peopled by noble, active men?
> Dost thou from Scott's RYEDALE of old,
> Bear a sheaf of rye on thy armor bold?
> Or dost thou Ireland's ancestry claim,
> For him who gave thine ancient name?
> But all the same, thou canst contend
> With Scotland's or old Ireland's glen.
> But where wast thou when Doleraine
> Passed through ' ANCIENT RIDDELL's Fair Domain,'
> To seek the monk of St. Mary's Isle,
> In Melrose Abbey's most holy pile?
> Thou still wert here, as on creation's morn,
> Uncultivated, nameless, thy power unborn.
> But 't was thy fate in solitude to dwell,
> Till on thy beauties the eyes of RIDDLE fell.
> Long years ago, on our own loved shore,
> A RIDDLE stood, *one pound* his coffer bore,
> But with his own keen native wit imbued,
> America, land of the free, he viewed.
> He wandered o'er the country far and wide,
> Until he stood a gentle stream beside,
> And meditative watched its onward flow,
> His soul with new-born thoughts aglow,
> And in imagination saw an ideal Glen
> Where his free fancy painted living men;
> He invested — and his *one* pound grew
> To one pound more, then treble two.
> Oh! Perseverance. thou motto grand,
> That reared this Glen in our lovely land;
> Linked to Scotland's heraldry of old,
> Its builder from the same ancestral fold,
> Esteemed of noble heart and kind,
> Of progressive and persevering mind.
> How often with the ever-busy throng
> Beneath the willow's shade I 've moved along;
> And by the RIDDLE MANSION wend my way,
> Under whose shade the Riddle children play.

" Young *Samuel*, bent on his boyhood fun,
   As full of mischief as any other one ;
But though he 's a merry and active lad,
   And acts the rogue, we 'll not deem him bad.
And there is *Maude*, with eyes so bright,
   As sparkling as the stars of night ;
And *Lottie* too, we now must not forget,
   For she 's a winsome, cunning little pet.
Then comes wee *Willie*, who is, I ween,
   As full as any RIDDLE, of vigor keen.
And now we leave them in their childhood sport,
   For life's bright morn is at longest short.
Standing where a beautiful stream is spanned
   By a rustic bridge-way's steady band ;
Oh, this is a beautiful spot indeed,
   No better view in all GLEN-RIDDLE mead.
There I loved to go on a pleasant day,
   And watch the sparkling silvery spray ;
Or wander forth by the pale moonlight,
   And gaze on the water's surface bright,
Where it gracefully leaps in a mimic fall,
   Like old Niagara, but not quite as tall.
This same old stream that many years ago
   Pursued its quiet way, its gentle flow,
And so continued as of old, until
   A RIDDLE's mind conceived 'twould turn a mill ;
And now it lends its aid to lessen toil,
   And scatter blessings o'er GLEN-RIDDLE's soil."

Rev. James Riddle[5] (4), second son of Leander[4] (1), was born at
Parkmount, near the city of Belfast, Ireland, in 1803 ; married Hannah
Niblock, a lady of Quaker parentage, and had issue several children, of
whom hereafter. After learning to manufacture cotton goods, he emigrated to the United States, and commenced work with his brother
Samuel, at Pleasant Mills, Gloucester County, N. J. He afterwards
became manager of these mills, but subsequently entered into partnership
with his brother at Springfield, Delaware County, Penn., where their
success was so apparent that another mill was erected for them on Chester Creek, in the same county. This mill was named "Parkmount," after
the residence of the Riddells in Ireland. The brothers continued the
business at the latter place about eight years, dissolving partnership at
the end of that time. James, in company with a Mr. Lawrence, rented a
mill on Crum Creek, Avondale. Here Mr. Riddle took up his residence.
He was connected with manufacturing operations at Chester and Rose-
ville, at the same time. In 1844 he purchased the old "Gilpin estates,"
on the river Brandywine, near Wilmington, Del., where he continued his
connections with Mr. Lawrence until 1857, when he became sole proprietor. From these small beginnings the business grew to proportions of
great magnitude. The property at the time of purchase comprised one
hundred and thirty acres of land, two mansion houses, two cottages, and
several tenement houses. Now, in the cotton-mills are running three
hundred looms and eleven thousand spindles; two hundred and fifty
hands are employed, and two thousand bales of cotton used annually.
The number of tenement houses has been increased to about one hundred,
and besides the old "Kentmere Mansion," rises up the new and elegant
residence of Mr. William Field, Mr. Riddle's son-in-law. Added to perseverance and business tact, his moral and religious principles rendered
Mr. Riddle a very useful and influential citizen. Before leaving his

"RIDDLE'S BANKS."
Wilmington, Del. U. S.
RESIDENCE OF REV. JAMES RIDDLE.

native land he had been converted, and united with the Methodist church, and was a local preacher, speaking almost every Sabbath for several years. He has been heard to say he had *two calls*: one to preach the gospel, and the other to manufacture cotton goods; and he was one of the few who proved successful in both. He occupied a very leading position among the local preachers of his denomination, and was president of their National Convention in 1864. Being a natural and forcible speaker, his pulpit and platform efforts were received with great favor. Not forgetting in the tide of business the calls of duty, he provided well for the moral and religious welfare of his tenants Upon the brow of the hill, above the Brandywine River, with its graceful spire rising above the trees, is the village chapel, erected by Mr. Riddle. It is of Gothic architecture, with stained-glass windows, and being located in a pleasant and imposing situation, becomes one of the most beautiful chapels in the state. For romantic scenery "Riddle's Banks," known in song as the "Banks of Brandywine," is unsurpassed, and the shady groves of ancient oaks upon the hill back of the chapel have been the resort for many years of social and picnic parties from the neighboring cities. Mr. Riddle was devoted to his adopted country, and during the dark hours of the late Rebellion, he was always ready to attest his devotion by word and deed. In 1866 the Republican party made him their candidate for Governor of the State of Delaware; in this election he was not the successful candidate, although, owing to his great popularity, he ran ahead of his ticket in every township in the state.

His benevolence and kindly disposition were beyond question. He never received a kindness from others without fully reciprocating the same; he was always a man of peace, and was not willing to speak harshly of any one. The fact that several of his men had been in his employ for upwards of thirty years, is a sufficient evidence of the amiable disposition which his refined Christian character enabled him to manifest in all his dealings with the world. The spare time of his youth was devoted to reading and religious exercises, and the large and valuable library left by him at his decease evinced the fact that his love for books continued through life. He was fond of society, and Mrs. Riddle always had her share of visitors. His death occurred Aug. 21, 1874, from heart disease. During his sickness he received every attention from his kind and dutiful family, and his last hours were peaceful and happy. His disorder had for several years admonished him to prepare for death, and when the summons came he was found ready to depart and meet the Master he had so long loved and served. The funeral procession that followed his remains to their last resting-place was nearly two miles long, and the ceremonies in the church and at the grave were of a peculiarly impressive character, — an occasion not to be forgotten as a suitable tribute to a good man and respected citizen. In his will, Mr. Riddle left ten thousand dollars to the Church Extension Society, and five thousand dollars to the Missionary Society of the Methodist Episcopal Church. He also directed the formation of a fund for the education of young men for the ministry, with several other bequests of a similar nature, the total amount necessary to carry out the religious and charitable bequests being rising forty thousand dollars.

"*And I heard a voice from heaven, saying unto me, Write: Blessed are the dead which die in the Lord from henceforth: Yea, saith the Spirit, that they may rest from their labors, and their works do follow them.*"

[The author called at " Riddle's Banks " when returning from a western tour in the summer of 1874, and was for a few hours the guest of Mr. Riddle; and the pleasant greetings received from, and kind attentions bestowed by, this estimable family will ever be cherished among the sunny memories of life. Weary with a long journey, and weak from a serious illness of only a few weeks previous, I was made to feel at home, and while there was the recipient of every comfort that could make my stay restful, and contribute to my happiness. Mr. Riddle was then in a precarious condition of health, but was able to ride about the village with me and point out his improvements and the beauties of the place. I found him a companionable man, genial and tender-hearted. In our conversation concerning the history of his Scotch-Irish ancestors, he informed me that his family had originally spelled their names "Riddell," which *he* recognized as the correct orthography, and presumed the change of spelling was made to accommodate the pronunciation, which, he said, was invariably Riddle, in Ireland. I was holding his hand at the gate on the morning of my departure, when Mr. Riddle expressed this sentiment : "I hope to live about ten years, and then go to dwell with Jesus." His wife was found a mild, amiable lady, very quiet and modest in appearance, and was a congenial companion for her husband — a noble and godly man. I little thought Mr. Riddle's stay with his affectionate family would be so short, for in about two weeks after my return to my pastorate in Massachusetts, I received intelligence of his death. A portrait of Mr. Riddle, contributed to this work by his family, is an excellent likeness. The view of the Riddle mansion is a good representation of the house, but would have been more pleasing if it had embraced more of the grounds.]

Mary Riddle⁵ (1), second daughter of Leander⁴ (1), was born at Parkmount, near Belfast, Ireland, in 1805; was married to Alexander McDowell; emigrated to the United States many years ago, and is now (1876) residing at Glen-Riddle, Delaware County, Penn. Her son, Mr. Samuel-Riddle McDowell, is connected in the business at Glen-Riddle, with his uncle.

Jane Riddle⁵ (1), third daughter of Leander⁴ (1), was born at Parkmount, near Belfast, Ireland, in 1807; was married to Hamilton Maxwell, a man of Scottish descent, and died in 1836.

SIXTH GENERATION.

Henry Riddle⁶ (1), eldest son of Samuel⁵ (1),* was born in Philadelphia, Penn., May 30, 1850; married Oct. 23, 1873, to Annie-M. Beatty, second daughter of John C. and Jemima Beatty, of Media, Penn.

He has received an excellent literary education, besides a thorough training in the military and polytechnic schools. When but eighteen years old he had the general charge of the factory at Glen-Riddle, and was admitted into the firm March 11, 1872. Mr. Riddle has made a tour through Europe, and visited some families of his father's relatives in the city of Belfast, Ireland. No issue in 1876.

Samuel-Doyle Riddle⁶ (2), eldest son of Samuel⁵ (1), by his second wife, was born at Glen-Riddle, July 1, 1861.

Lydia-Maude Riddle⁶ (1), eldest daughter of Samuel⁵ (1), was born at Glen-Riddle, Dec. 1, 1862.

---

* There is a Samuel Riddle residing at Glen-Riddle, in some way connected with the above family, but I have not the genealogy. I was introduced to him at the Family Meeting.

Charlotte-Buffington Riddle[6] (1), second daughter of Samuel[5] (1), was born at Glen-Riddle, Nov. 2, 1864.

Leander-William Riddle[6] (2), third son of Samuel[5] (1), was born at Glen-Riddle, Penn., Oct. 25, 1868.

Hannah Riddle[6] (1), eldest daughter of James[5] (4), was born at Avondale, Penn., in 1840; died in 1844.

Hon. Leander-F. Riddle[6] (3), only son of James[5] (4), was born at Avondale, Chester County, Penn., in 1842, and has been a member of the firm of James Riddle, Son & Company since 1865; since his father's death has been at the head of the firm. His father gave him every advantage for an education, which, supplementing his great energy and determination of character, constitutes him an efficient and successful business man. He has informed himself on matters of polity, and was elected to the State Senate from Newcastle County, Del., in 1872, though scarcely thirty years old, with a large and complimentary majority, and was the only Republican member in the Senate at that session. He was secretary of Delaware State Commission at the centennial celebration at Philadelphia, in 1876, and transacted a great amount of business in that capacity. He presided at the family meeting of the Riddells, Riddles, and Ridlons, held at Philadelphia, in July, 1876, and has manifested an interest in this book. Mr. Riddle is considered one of the most promising young men in his state.

Mary Riddle[6] (2), second daughter of James[5] (4), was born (presumably) at Avondale, Chester County, Penn., in 1845, and died young.

Jeannie Riddle[6] (1), third daughter of James[5] (4), was born at Avondale (?), Penn.; was married to William Field, and resides near the home of her parents, at Riddle's Banks, near the city of Wilmington, Del. ·Mrs. Field is a lady of brilliant and amiable natural endowments, supplemented by a fine education and graceful bearing. Unassuming and modest, commanding the purest language in conversation, she exerts a charming influence over those in her company. Her husband is a member of the firm of James Riddle, Son & Company, and an enterprising business man. The residence of Mrs. Field, a stately and beautiful house of modern architecture, is situated on an elevation, almost directly in front of the parental mansion, and commands one of the widest and most picturesque prospects to be found, and from the door the shining waters of Delaware Bay may be seen in the distance. The interior of the magnificent residence is fitted up with every modern improvement, and furnished with taste and splendor.

Elizabeth Riddle[6] (2), youngest daughter of James[5] (4), was born in 1853, and died the same year.*

RIDDELLS OF BALLINAMAN, IRELAND.

James Riddell[1] (1), descended from ancestors said to have settled in Ireland in 1641; married, and had several sons and daughters. He lived

---

* Mr. James Riddle, of this family, informed the author that he had not known a branch of his family in which the Christian names, James, John, Samuel, and George, did not prevail. He also called attention to the prominent cheek-bones characteristic in his connection.

11

in the parish of Donagh, near Glasslough, in the north of Ireland, and is
presumed to have been connected with the other families of the name in
the same county. (See "Riddles of Richhill.")

SECOND GENERATION.

Robert Riddell² (1), a son of James¹ (1), was born in Ballinaman,
parish of Donagh, County Monaghan, in 1750; married twice, and had
issue by both wives, of whom hereafter. He died in 1826, aged 76 years.
He was a farmer and contractor.

James Riddell² (2), a son of James¹ (1), was born in Ballinaman,
County Monaghan, Ireland; married an English lady, and had issue, of
whom hereafter. Died in England.

THIRD GENERATION.

James Riddell² (3), eldest son of Robert² (1), was born in Ballinaman,
County Monaghan, Ireland, and died when in the prime of life, leaving
four children, who, with their mother, emigrated to Canada about thirty
years ago. Mrs. Riddell's maiden-name was Elizabeth Gilleland. She
was left a widow in 1844, sold her farm in 1849, and emigrated to Canada,
where her son James preceded her; they sailed from Belfast on the 17th
April, 1849, on board the bark "Nelsonville," and arrived in Quebec in June
following. She had expected to meet her son James at Quebec, but heard
that he had gone to Montreal. She went from place to place, seeking her
son, but died in Hamilton, Ont., on the 12th of July, without seeing him.
This son furnished means to bring her to America.

Sarah Riddell² (1), eldest daughter of Robert² (1), was born in Ballinaman, County Monaghan, Ireland; was married to a Mr. John Robinson, who went to America, and left his wife and *six* children in the care
of her father; one of her daughters married Robert Heatly, and was over
80 in 1874.

Martha Riddell² (1), second daughter of Robert² (1), was born in
Ballinaman, County Monaghan, Ireland; was married to Adam Cook,
and emigrated to America previous to 1797; these settled in Fredericksburgh, Va.

Mary Riddell² (1), third daughter of Robert² (1), was born in Ballinaman, County Monaghan, Ireland; was married to James Hamilton, settled in Manchester, Eng., and had issue; she died at the age of 56.

William Riddell² (1), second son of Robert² (1), was born in Ballinaman, Ireland; emigrated to America, and entered the army in the war
of 1812. He was a sergeant in the company of Captain Jett, Twentieth
Regiment, U. S. Infantry, and received a grant of one hundred and sixty
acres of land in the State of Illinois. He died, and the land was made
over to his sister, Mrs. Martha Cook, and the other heirs-at-law, to hold
as tenants in common. This tract of land was in Hancock County, of
which Carthage is the seat.

Dr. John Riddell² (1), third son of Robert² (1), was born in the
town of Ballinaman, County Monaghan, Ireland, and died in Rio de Janei-
ro, where he was acting as surgeon in the English army. Was at home
once, eleven months, on half-pay.

Joseph Riddell² (1), fourth son of Robert² (1), was born in the town
of Ballinaman, Ireland, in 1797; married Catherine Clark, in Ireland, and
had issue *eight* children, of whom hereafter. He sold his farm in Monaghan, Ireland, and removed to Manchester, Eng., to live with his two

daughters. His wife, to whom he was married in 1820, died in Manchester, Aug. 17, 1867. Mr. Riddell was living in 1874.

Robert Riddell[8] (2), fifth son of Robert[3] (1), was born in the town of Ballinaman, County Monaghan, Ireland, and has issue a numerous family, of whom hereafter. He lives on his father's homestead, and carries on a farm.

Thomas Riddell[8] (1), a son of James[2] (2), was born somewhere in England; no other information.

Robert Riddell[8] (3), a son of James[2] (2), was born in England, and was in the Eighty-first Regiment of Foot in 1816; since that time (when he visited his uncles) nothing is known of him.

FOURTH GENERATION.

James Riddell[4] (3), eldest son of James[8] (2), was born in the town of Ballinaman, County Monaghan, Ireland, about 1821; emigrated to Canada, in 1840-1, sailing from Warrensport, Ireland, in the ship "Dolphin"; he is now (1873) residing in Hamilton, Ont.

Jane Riddell[4] (1), eldest daughter of James[8] (2), was born in Ballinaman, Ireland, in 1819; was married to William Painter; resides in Fairport, N. Y., and has issue *three* children.

William Riddell[4] (2), second son of James[8] (2), was born in Ballinaman, Ireland, and died there at the age of 21 years.

Robert Riddle[4] (4), third son of James[8] (2), was born in Ballinaman, Ireland, in 1827; emigrated to Canada, in 1849, and is now (1873) in Rochester, N. Y., engaged in lumbering.* He married Dec. 14, 1852, to *Dolly*-Sophia Morton; no issue. Mr. Riddle (as he spells his name) was three years in the Union army during the Rebellion, and was wounded in his right fore-arm, May 8, 1864, in the battle of the Wilderness; and in the left shoulder and cheek (breaking his under jaw), April 1, 1865, at the battle of Big Five Forks. Receives a pension.

Jane Riddell[4] (2), second daughter of James[8] (2), was born in Ballinaman, Ireland, and died at the age of eleven in 1841-2.

John Riddell[4] (2), fourth son of James[8] (2), was born in Ballinaman, Ireland, in 1832-3, emigrated to Canada, in 1849, and in 1873 had built a house and was living with family in Alpena, Mich.

Jane Riddell[4] (2), eldest daughter of Joseph[8] (1), was born in Ballinaman, Ireland, Dec. 18, 1821; was married to John Aspinall, Nov. 18, 1841; emigrated to New York, and died there.

Catherine Riddell[4] (1), second daughter of Joseph[2] (1), was born in Ballinaman, Ireland, Oct. 15, 1823; died unmarried in New York.

Mary Riddell[4] (2), third daughter of Joseph[8] (1), was born in Ballinaman, Ireland, Oct. 28, 1825; was married to Richard Gleenhalgh, an engineer, at Manchester, Eng. No issue.

Elizabeth Riddell[4] (1), fourth daughter of Joseph[2] (1), was born in Ballinaman, Ireland, Sept. 18, 1828.

Sarah Riddell[4] (2), fifth daughter of Joseph[8] (1), was born in Balli-

* Robert Riddle, of Rochester, N. Y., states that his uncle Robert had children, James, Jane, Eliza, Mary, in addition to those given above; these may have deceased before I had correspondence with the family in England, in 1872, as Mr. Robert Riddle emigrated to America in 1849; or some of the preceding children may have been double-named, one authority giving one name, and another the middle name.

naman, Ireland, April 8, 1831 ; and was married to George Weller, as his
second wife, Oct. 15, 1867 ; living in 1878.

Martha Riddell[4] (2), sixth daughter of Joseph[3] (1), was born in Ballinaman, Ireland, June 28, 1833 ; died in Ireland.

Anna-Bella Riddell[4] (1), seventh daughter of Joseph[3] (1), was born in
Ballinaman, Ireland, Sept. 23, 1836 ; was married as first wife, to George
Weller, Aug. 24, 1862, and died Dec. 23, 1865, leaving *one* daughter. He
afterwards married her sister.

William Riddell[4] (3), only son of Joseph[3] (1), was born in Ballinaman, Ireland, Jan. 13, 1839 ; died there, unmarried.

John Riddell[4] (3), eldest son of Robert[3] (2), was born in Ballinaman,
Ireland, and lives on the farm with his father.

William Riddell[4] (4), second son of Robert[3] (2), was born in Ballinaman, Ireland, and lives on the home farm.

Sarah Riddell[4] (3), eldest daughter of Robert[3] (2), was born in Ballinaman, Ireland, and was at home in 1873.

Robert Riddell[4] (5), third son of Robert[3] (2), was born in Ballinaman,
Ireland, and is in business in the city of Manchester, as an iron-monger,
with his brother.

Joseph Riddell[4] (2), fourth son of Robert[3] (2), was born in Ballinaman, Ireland, and is carrying on the business of an iron-monger, at
Manchester, Eng.

Alice Riddell[4] (1), second daughter of Robert[3] (2), was born in Ballinaman, Ireland ; married and keeps a provision-shop ; do not know where.

RIDDELLS OF RAY, IRELAND.

John Riddell[1] (1), parents unknown, lived in the parish of Ray (or
Rye), in the County of Donegal, Ireland, and is supposed to be a relative
of the Riddles who emigrated from the same parish and settled in the
County of York, Penn. (see Riddles of Chambersburgh, Penn.)   He married Jane Rodgers, of the Moyle, and had issue, of whom hereafter.

SECOND GENERATION.

John Riddell[2] (2), a son of John[1] (1), was born in the parish of Ray,
County of Donegal, Ireland ; married —— Thompson, and had issue sev-
eral children, of whom hereafter. He and his family were buried in All
Saints' church-yard.

George Riddell[2] (1), a son of John[1] (1), was born in the parish of
Ray, County of Donegal, Ireland ; married and had issue, of whom hereafter. He emigrated to the United States, and acquired considerable property ; deceased many years ago, leaving will, that in case his two daughters,
then unmarried, died without issue, his estate should go to his brother *John*
and his nephew *James*, in Ireland.   One daughter married, but died issueless, and the other died single, and their property was sold, and $1,500
was deposited for his brother John, but never secured by him.   The names
of the daughters and their residence do not appear.

THIRD GENERATION.

James Riddle⁸ (1), eldest son of John² (2), was born in the parish of Ray, County of Donegal; married Maria Moffit, and emigrated to Newark, N. J. He had learned the watch-maker's trade, in Londonderry, Ireland, and carried on business some years at Strabane, in County Donegal. He had issue *two* children, of whom hereafter. He died many years ago.

John Riddle⁸ (3), youngest son of John² (2), was born in the parish of Ray, County of Donegal, Ireland; married Sarah Hamilton, sister of Dr. Hamilton; died without issue, and was buried in All Saints' churchyard. He learned the watch-maker's trade of his brother James, and had a shop at Ramelton, Ireland.

Susan Riddle⁸ (1), eldest daughter of John² (2), was born in the parish of Ray, County Donegal, Ireland, in 1796; was married to John Williams, of Moygah, and is now (1880) living.*

Catherine Riddle⁸ (2), second daughter of John² (2), was born in the parish of Ray, County of Donegal, Ireland; was married to Joseph Wilson, and resided in the city of Coleraine, Ireland; both are dead.

Mary Riddle⁸ (1), youngest daughter of John² (2), was born in the parish of Ray, County of Donegal, Ireland, and died at home, presumably unmarried.

FOURTH GENERATION.

George Biddle⁴ (2), only son of James⁸ (1), was born at Strabane, Ireland, and died in New York, unmarried.

Jane Biddle⁴ (1), only daughter of James⁸ (1), was born at Strabane, Ireland, and died in New York, unmarried.

————•❖•————

RIDDELLS OF GLASSLOUGH, IRELAND.

Walter Riddell¹ (1) was presumably descended from the family of Glen-Riddell, Dumfrieshire, Scotland, an offshoot of the baronial family of Roxburghshire, Scotland. He left his kinspeople and his native land in consequence of a quarrel concerning the Jacobite and Covenanting questions, which were agitated in Scotland, contemporary with his settlement in Ireland, in the former part of the eighteenth century. He was, it is supposed, a son,—or possibly a brother,—of Robert Riddell, the second laird of Glen-Riddell, whose genealogy and history will be found in this work, under denomination of "Riddells of Glen-Riddell," which see. He was sometime of Glasslough, in the County of Monaghan; it is not at

---

* The only male representative of this family in Ireland (so far as known) is a grandson of Mrs. Susan (Riddell) Williams, of Newton-Cunningham, who is called John-James Riddle. The surname was spelled *Riddell* by the ancestors of this family. The family Bible containing the records has been lost, and the early parish records are not extant. A gentleman, named *Marshall*, whose grandmother was a Riddell, was in Ireland some twenty-seven years ago, to learn the history of his ancestry, and visited Mrs. Susan (Riddell) Williams, informing her of her brother's death in New Jersey. There was also an American named Colon Reid who visited Ray many years ago, and said a Dr. Riddle was about to visit the parish to look up his ancestry. Was this Rev. David H. Riddle, d. d., of Martinsburgh, Va. ?

present known what influence attracted him to that place, or what was his exact condition there; it is probable, however, that he was induced to settle there by the influence of the Leslie family, who were, and are still, the principal landed proprietors of the district, and who were from Scotland. Mr. Riddell is known to have enjoyed a good social position, as became his own origin, from the marriage-connections of himself and son, and from the fact that he was possessed of considerable land-estates, part of which were situated near Blackwatertown, on the borders of the County of Armagh, where a field is still pointed out and known as "Riddell's Moor." He married a Miss Burgess, a member of a well-known county family, or of a branch thereof, now represented at Parkmaur, County of Tyrone, but formerly of Wood Park, County of Armagh. He is described as having been a very godly man, a member of the Church of Scotland, and strongly imbued with Calvinistic principles. He died 1775, having had issue *one* son, who appears to have been their only child. I append the following note, to show the grounds upon which the family base their claim to relationship with the baronial family of Scotland; the matter in the note was furnished the author by the Rev. Walter Riddall, M. A., who compiled his family pedigree for this work.*

SECOND GENERATION.

Robert Riddell² (1), son of Walter¹ (1), was born, it is supposed, about 1745–50. He grew up a very different character from his father,

* Rev. Walter Riddall says, "I am quite aware that it is stated and assumed that the Glen-Riddell family failed in the direct male line, and that it is supposed to be now represented by the descendants of John Riddell, a younger son of Walter, the first laird of Glen-Riddell. But this assumption is directly contradicted by the tradition of my branch family, and the facts of the case are such as both to confirm the tradition, and at the same time to account for the contradictory assumption; so that the common statement concerning the failure of the direct male line of the Glen-Riddell family will require to be amended, or at least modified, even if I shall not succeed in giving absolute demonstrations of the truth of the tradition of my branch family, for I shall claim to be *a* or *the* direct representative of Glen-Riddell in the male line, unless and until the tradition of my family is proved to be false, which I am sure it never can. The facts on which I rest are the following, which I beg to commend to the careful consideration of the reader. (1.) The tradition itself, which is constant and undoubted, and exists as clearly amongst the "Riddells of Richhill" (which see) as it does amongst my cousins; and I can bring many witnesses to vouch for it. Now, the tradition is a fact which requires to be accounted for. I myself often heard it as a child from a sister of my father, a godly woman, who had no knowledge on the subject but what she had received from her father and mother, a pious pair, who cared nothing about the world's rank or honor. It is every way inconceivable and impossible that such a tradition could have sprung from imagination or invention; a hundred circumstances negative such an idea. How, then, is it to be accounted for? Simply and only by accounting it to be the truth. And the tradition has not had so very far to travel down the stream of time. The first person concerned in it died in 1775, and when I first heard it there were people still living who could have discredited it if recently invented. The tradition is that 'old Walter,' my first ancestor who came to Ireland, came from Glen-Riddell, in Scotland, having separated from his family, and dropped all connections with them, owing to a dispute about politics or religion (probably both). This is my first main fact. (2.) The leading Christian names in my family precisely agree with the tradition. The first laird of Glen-Riddell was *Walter*, and the second was *Robert;* and in my family these two names have followed each other in the successive generations without any deviation from strict regularity; so that there have been at the head of each generation, successively, Walter, Robert, Walter (2), Robert (2), Walter (3), Robert (3); including my son as the last. Walter and Robert are emphatically the Glen-Riddell names. And it would seem from this that 'old

being dissolute and improvident, and was obliged to leave Glasslough after his marriage, owing to his profligate conduct, and eventually dissipated and lost all his father's property. He married, about 1768, Miss Sarah Ankittell, a daughter of Roger Ankitell, Esq., of Mount Ankitell, a grandson of the famous and gallant Matthew Ankitell, Esq., of Ankitell's Grove, County of Monaghan, who fell fighting in defence of the Protestant interest in 1688, at Drumbanagher, near Glasslough. These had issue *one* son (probably others), of whom hereafter. Soon after the birth of this son his mother died, leaving him in the care of his grandfather, his father having been obliged to quit the town. Robert married, secondly, his housekeeper, a Miss Eccles, by whom he had *three* sons, some of whose descendants have become well known in the United States. (See "Riddells of Richhill," in this work.) It is not unlikely that Robert may have had other sons besides the three mentioned. There are Riddells, or Riddles, now living in the vicinity of Glasslough, whose origin seems uncertain, but who may not improbably be considered as his descendants. Having lost all his property in gambling and dissipation, and having both talent and education, Robert turned his attention to the work of architect and builder, in which he was followed by his son, as will be hereinafter noticed. He became a converted, reformed character, under the preaching of the Methodists. The date of his death is unknown, but it probably occurred about 1800.

THIRD GENERATION.

Walter Riddell[2] (2), eldest son of Robert[2] (1), was born in or near Glasslough, County Monaghan, Ireland, 1770, and died Dec. 5, 1818. He was under the care of his grandfather, as before mentioned, until he was five years old, and received in early years seeds of religious instruction, which by God's grace he never lost. On his grandfather's death, he was kept for a time among his mother's relatives; but was afterwards restored to his father, who gave him all possible advantages of education. He was

Walter,' my ancestor, was very probably the *eldest* son of Robert, the second laird of Glen-Riddell. This is my second fact. (3.) The time at which 'old Walter' lived would agree with his having been a son of Robert, the second of Glen-Riddell. He died in 1775, five years after the birth of his grandson, who was my grandfather. (4.) The time also agrees with that portion of the tradition which refers to the family feud about politics and religion. During the former half of the last century there were fierce disputes in Scotland, with Jacobites and Covenanters. I do not know what side my ancestor may have taken; but this much is certain, that he was a very godly man, a member of the Church of Scotland, and strongly imbued with Calvinistic principles. This last I have from a statement written by my grandmother, giving a short account of her husband, after his death, but which, I fear, is lost. I have now stated the facts on which I rely, and I think it is easy to understand how, under the circumstances, my ancestor, 'old Walter,' was ignored and lost sight of by his family, and how his stiff Scotch temper would prevent his attempting to reopen communication, and thus how it came to be assumed that Glen-Riddell had died out in the direct male line, though it had survived in Ireland all the time. I do not *press* the conclusion that my ancestor was necessarily the *eldest* son of Glen-Riddell; but that he was one of the sons (or a brother, possibly), I have no doubt I only ask that the claim which I have advanced, may be fairly and fully considered and fairly stated; having no doubt but that further investigations will confirm it hereafter." Mr. Riddall will continue to investigate the history of his family and forward every new fact until the last moment before this goes to press. I should here state that Sir Walter-Buchanan Riddell, Bart., in a letter to Rev. Walter Riddall, says, "I am sure you are right to consider yourself one of the family of the Riddells of Riddell." Sir Walter's testimony should have weight, as coming from the "Chief."

early brought under Methodist influences, and began at a very early age to exhort, and finally became one of their regular preachers. He married, about 1795, Miss Anne O'Hanlon, daughter of James O'Hanlon, a merchant of Blackwatertown, County Armagh, who was a Roman Catholic, and a member of the great O'Hanlon clan, who at one time, before the plantation of Ulster, possessed about one-third of the land in the County of Armagh. His wife and daughter, however, were both pious Protestants. He had issue a numerous family, of whom hereafter.

FOURTH GENERATION.

Sarah Riddell[4] (1), eldest daughter of Walter[3] (2), was married to John Ralston, a farmer, a descendant of Richard Ralstone, one of the original patentees of the plantation of Ulster, and who held one thousand acres of land in Lemore, County Armagh. She and her husband are both dead; they had *three* sons, two of them now living.

Elizabeth Riddell[4] (1), second daughter of Walter[3] (2), married Robert Ralston (or Roulstone, as the name was originally spelt), brother of her sister's husband before mentioned, and died without issue.

Martha Riddell[4] (1), third daughter of Walter[3] (2), was married to G. Taylor, of Dangannore, and died leaving issue *one* son and *three* daughters.

Margaret Riddell[4] (1), fourth daughter of Walter[3] (2), was married to Henry Riddell, her kinsman, of Richhill, and died in Australia, without children.

Robert Riddall[4] (2), eldest son of Walter[3] (2), was born March 22, 1810; died March 24, 1873. He and his brother James adopted the spelling *Riddall*, which is continued in this family at the present time. Robert early conceived the idea of recovering the fortune and position lost by his grandfather, and was at one time about taking steps to recover by law a portion of the property lost in gambling. From this, however, he desisted; but by his energy and prudence, eventually became possessed of property in the same neighborhood, the townlands of Tyregarty and Ballytrodden, near Blackwatertown; besides other property in the County Armagh and County Tyrone. He was appointed, when quite a youth, to the important office of seneschal of the manor of Inishowen, County Donegal, and also entered into business as a corn and flour miller, at Longyvallen, near Armagh, in which he was very successful. He also held the office of Deputy Registrar of the Diocese and Province of Armagh, under his relative, George Scott, Esq., whom he eventually succeeded as Principal Registrar; and also afterwards became District Registrar of Her Majesty's Court of Probate at Armagh. He was a Justice of the Peace and a grand juror for the County Armagh. He married, in 1846, Harriet, daughter of the late Samuel Gardner, Esq., Justice of the Peace, of Armagh, who survived him and died in 1870. They had no issue. He generously took paternal charge of his brother James' family, on his early death in 1850, and they inherit the most of his estate and wealth. Mr. Riddall was a man of high character and sterling principle; and in his latter years actuated by genuine though unostentatious piety. There is a mural tablet erected to his memory in St. Mark's Church, at Armagh. The influence of his life is manifested amongst his kindred, who hold him in grateful memory.

Rev. James Riddall[4] (1), second son of Walter[3] (2), was born Sept. 21, 1816, and died Nov. 10, 1850, the perpetuator of his family line. He and his brother were educated and advanced in life by their mother's cousin, George Scott, Esq., of Armagh, Registrar of the Diocese and Province of Armagh. He (James) commenced business for himself when scarcely twenty years of age, in the city of Armagh, as an iron-monger. He married, in 1839, Miss Jemima Parkinson, daughter of Edward Parkinson, an assistant master of the Royal School, Armagh, and sister of the late Rev. William Parkinson, A. M., of Ballysillan, Belfast. They had issue *five* children, of whom hereafter. They were both pious and attached members of the Primitive Methodist Society, and of the Established Church of England and Ireland. James Riddall was a gifted favorite local preacher among the Methodists, and took the cold from which he died, while out on a preaching expedition. His wife survived him eighteen years, and died, much lamented by her family, Jan. 17, 1868. A memoir of Mr. Riddall was published by the Primitive Methodist Society, Great Georges Street, Dublin, in 1851.

FIFTH GENERATION.

Rev. Walter Riddall[5] (3), eldest son of James[4] (1), was born June 20, 1841; married, in 1867, Mary-Roe Coates, eldest daughter of Charles Coates, Esq., barrister-at-law, of Harcourt Street, Dublin, and of Jankersley, County Wicklow, by whom he has a numerous family, of whom hereafter. Educated at Armagh Royal School and Trinity College, Dublin, where he was a Royal Exhibitioner and First Honor Man, also Classical Scholar; graduated A. B. and A. M. Ordained to the ministry of the Established Church of England and Ireland, and curate of Kilmore Cathedral, County Cavan, 1866; having previously been appointed Deputy Registrar of the Diocese and Province of Ulster, under his uncle, Robert Riddall, Esq. He was subsequently appointed Vicar Choral of Armagh Cathedral, by His Grace, the present Lord Archbishop of Armagh. This appointment, however, he resigned, and went as curate in sole charge to the parish of Newtown, County Meath, of which the late well-known Rev. F. F. French was then rector. Was next appointed vicar of Glencraig, County of Down; which he resigned on account of health breaking down, and went as British Chaplain to Turin, north Italy. Returning to Ireland in December, 1870, became curate in sole charge at Killeany, County Armagh, of which the late Rev. A. Irwin, precentor of Armagh Cathedral, was then rector; and succeeded, on Rev. A. Irwin's death, as rector of Killeany (Mallaghan). Removed thence to the incumbency of St. John's, Malone, Belfast, his present appointment. He was author of one or two pamphlets, and is one of the first contributors to "Kottabos," a classical publication of T. C. D (Trinity College, Dublin); also contributes to the *Irish Church Advocate.* Mr. Riddall has manifested considerable interest in this work, and has, at great pains, collected the genealogy and history of his family as herein presented. He intends to continue his investigations concerning the ancestral connections of his family, anticipating full substantiation of the family tradition.

George-Scott Riddall[5] (1), second son of James[4] (1), was born May 1, 1843, and succeeded his uncle, Robert[4] (2), as corn and floor miller, at Longyvallen, Armagh; resides at Altavellen, Armagh. Married first, in 1869, Ellen, daughter, of Thomas Scott, Esq. She died without issue September, 1876. He married secondly, in 1878, Ida, daughter of Charles Schale, of Newcastle-on-Tyne, Eng.; who has issue *one* daughter, of whom hereafter. "Altavellen," the residence of Mr. Riddall, is a mag nificent modern house, situated on a commanding site, surrounded by ornamental shrubbery.

Rev. Edward-P. Riddall[5] (2), third son of James[4] (1), was born Nov. 4, 1846; married, in 1877, Henrietta-Seward Bayley, daughter of the late Charles-Cheetham Bayley, Esq., Justice of the Peace, of the Poplars, Plymouth Grove, Manchester, Eng.; educated at Royal School, Armagh, and Trinity College, Dublin, where he was Royal Exhibitioner, First Honor Man, and Classical Scholar; graduated A. B. and A. M. He was ordained curate of St. James', Belfast, 1870; rector of Ballymore, County Westmeath, 1872, and soon after rector of Moate, in the same County. He removed thence to Cork Cathedral, and St. Finbar's, as curate to the late well-known and lamented Very Rev. Achilles Daunt, D. D., Dean of Cork; was appointed chaplain at Argostoli, Cephalonia, Ionian Islands, where he resided for a few months without resigning his curacy of Cork Cathedral. He was appointed, in 1879, rector of Vastina, County of Westmeath, which appointment he still holds.

Anne-Eliza Riddall[5] (1), eldest daughter of James[4] (1), was born April 4, 1840; was married, in 1864, to Robert McCrum, Esq., Justice of the Peace, Milford, Armagh; died Jan. 8, 1869, having had issue a son and a daughter.

Harriet Riddall[6] (1), youngest child of James[4] (1), was born in 1850; has never married.

SIXTH GENERATION.

Robert-James Riddall[6] (3), eldest son of Walter[5] (3), was born Aug. 25, 1872.

Walter-George Riddall[6] (4), second son of Walter[5] (3), was born Feb. 8, 1874.

George-Spencer-Charles Riddall[6] (2), third son of Walter[5] (3), was born Jan. 15, 1875.

James-Edward Riddall[6] (3), fourth son of Walter[5] (3), was born Dec. 12, 1876.

Charles-Coates Riddall[6] (1), fifth son of Walter[5] (3), was born March 22, 1878.

Jane-Alice Riddall[6] (1). ⎫
Mary-Roe Riddall[6] (1). ⎬ Daughters of Walter[5] (3), all at home.
Jemima Riddall[6] (1). ⎭

RIDDELLS OF RICHHILL, IRELAND.

Robert Riddell[1] (1), a son of Walter[1] (1), and his wife Burgess, married two wives; the first was Sarah Anskittell, by whom he became ancestor of the "Riddells of Glasslough," which see, and the second was Miss Eccles (who had been his servant), by whom he became ancestor of the "Riddells of Richhill." It will be seen that both families unite in one common ancestor, namely, Walter Riddell.

SECOND GENERATION.

Robert Riddell[2] (2), eldest son of Robert[1] (1), was born Aug. 30, 1780; married in May, 1799, to Ann, daughter of Robert and Sarah Douglas, of

Annaghagh, near Grange Church, Armagh, and had issue, of whom hereafter. Mr. Riddell was a farmer in Ballylaney, near Richhill, County Armagh, Ireland; died September, 1842, and was buried at Kilmore, near Richhill.

James Riddell² (1), second son of Robert¹ (1), was born in Armagh, Ireland; married Jane Long, and had issue. He emigrated to America, and settled in Philadelphia, Penn., where he is supposed to have died. He had *two* sons, Robert and George, of whom hereafter.

Thomas Riddell² (1), third son of Robert¹ (1), was born in County Armagh, Ireland; emigrated to America before the war of 1812, and was a commissioned officer in the United States service, and lost a leg in an engagement, in consequence of which he was a pensioner during the remainder of his days. He died many years ago. No account of a family.

THIRD GENERATION.

Isabella Riddell³ (1), eldest daughter of Robert² (2) and his wife, Ann Douglas, was born in Ballylaney, County Armagh, Ireland, May 16, 1800; was married in June, 1822, to John Falloon, a farmer, and died Jan. 13, 1879.

Robert Riddell³ (3), eldest son of Robert² (2) and his wife, Ann Douglas, was born at Ballylaney, County Armagh, Ireland, April 10, 1802, and never married. He was a farmer; died Jan. 14, 1867.

James Riddell³ (2), second son of Robert² (2) and Ann Douglas, his wife, was born in Ballylaney, County Armagh, Ireland, June 24, 1804; married in August, 1829, to Alice Hayes, and died in New Zealand. He is supposed to have had a family.

John Riddell³ (2), third son of Robert² (2), was born in Ballylaney, County Armagh, Ireland, Dec. 24, 1806; married in October, 1840, to Sarah Hardy, and has issue *seven* children, of whom hereafter. He is a farmer at Richhill, County Armagh.

Walter Riddell³ (2), fourth son of Robert² (2), was born in Ballylaney, County Armagh, Ireland, Sept. 14, 1808; married Nov. 15, 1838, to Mary Rush, of Marlacoo, near Markethill, and has issue *seven* children, of whom hereafter. He is a farmer at Richhill, County Armagh,—a man of sound mind and great force of will: a characteristic type of this family.

Thomas Riddell³ (2), fifth son of Robert² (2), was born in County Armagh, Ireland, Aug. 12, 1810; married in September, 1836, to Mary-Jane O'Berry, of Portadown, and had issue *three* children, of whom hereafter. Mr. Riddell emigrated to America and died there.

Henry Riddell³ (1), sixth son of Robert² (2) and Ann Douglas, his wife, was born at Ballylaney, County Armagh, Ireland, May 16, 1812; married Margaret Riddell, his cousin, of Glasslough, County Monaghan, Ireland, and emigrated to New Zealand, where he now lives.

Sarah Riddell³ (1), second daughter of Robert² (2) and Ann Douglas, was born in Ballylaney, County Armagh, Ireland, May 28, 1814; was married Aug. 16, 1849, to David Foster, of Richhill, and died April 30, 1850.

William Riddell³ (1), seventh son of Robert² (2), was born in Ballylaney, County Armagh, Ireland, Oct. 17, 1816, and died unmarried, in August, 1848.

Samuel Riddell³ (1), eighth son of Robert² (2), was born in Ballylaney, County Armagh, Ireland, Sept. 8, 1818, and died in August, 1819.

Mary Riddell³ (1), third daughter of Robert² (2), was born in Ballylaney, County Armagh, Ireland, in March, 1820; was married in April, 1845, to Robert Chapman, and resides at Dobbin, near Portadown, Ireland.

FOURTH GENERATION.

Susannah Riddell[4] (1), eldest daughter of John[3] (2) and Sarah Hardy, his wife, was born at Richhill, County Armagh, Ireland, June 12, 1851, and was married to Charles Hardy (probably a cousin), of Richhill.

William Riddell[4] (2), eldest son of John[3] (2) and Sarah Hardy, was born at Richhill, County Armagh, Ireland, May 9, 1853, and died in New York, in September, 1876.

Annie Riddell[4] (1), second daughter of John[3] (2) and Sarah Hardy, was born at Richhill, County Armagh, Ireland, Jan. 13, 1855, and was married in Ohio.

Robert-Henry Riddell[4] (4), second son of John[3] (2) and his wife, Sarah Hardy, was born at Richhill, County Armagh, Ireland, March 16, 1857; resides at Richhill.

Sarah Riddell[4] (2), third daughter of John[3] (2) and his wife, Sarah Hardy, was born at Richhill, County of Armagh, Ireland, Oct. 4, 1858; resides at home.

Thomas-James Riddell[4] (3), third son of John[3] (2) and his wife, Sarah Hardy, was born at Richhill, County Armagh, Ireland, Jan. 28, 1860; resides at home.

Annie-Eliza Riddell[4] (2), eldest daughter of Walter[3] (2), died young.

John-Robert Riddell[4] (3), eldest son of Walter[3] (2) and his wife, Mary Rush, was born at Richhill, County Armagh, Ireland, June 15, 1850; died at home, Nov. 3, 1872.

Hugh Riddell[4] (1), second son of Walter[3] (2) and Mary Rush, was born at Richhill, County Armagh, Ireland, Sept. 18, 1853, and resides at Richhill.

William Riddell[4] (3), third son of Walter[3] (2) and Mary Rush, was born at Richhill, County Armagh, Ireland, Nov. 9, 1855, and resides at Richhill.

Annie-Eliza Riddell[4] (3), second daughter of Walter[3] (2) and Mary Rush, was born at Richhill, Nov. 6, 1857; was married to R. Magowan, of Derry-Hale.

Walter Riddell[4] (4), fourth son of Walter[3] (2) and Mary Rush, was born at Richhill, County Armagh, Ireland, Jan. 28, 1859, and resides at Richhill.

Thomas-Henry Riddell[4] (4), fifth son of Walter[3] (2) and Mary Rush, was born at Richhill, County Armagh, Ireland, Nov. 30, 1864; resides at Belfast, Ireland.

John Riddell[4] (4).
James Riddell[4] (4).
Martha Riddell[4] (1).
Letitia Riddell[4] (1).
} Children of James[3] (2).

Ann Riddell[4] (1).
Jane Riddell[4] (1).
Sarah Riddell[4] (3).
} Children of Thomas[3] (2).

RIDDELLS OF STRABANE, IRELAND.

[PENNSYLVANIA BRANCH.]

John Riddell[1] (1), whose parents are unknown, was born in Strabane,* County of Tyrone (Judge Riddell says County Donegal), in the north of Ireland, and, with his brothers, emigrated to Westmoreland County, Penn., about six months before the breaking out of the war of the Revolution. He made a "Tomahawk Improvement" on the waters of Turtle Creek, but when the war broke out entered the American army for six months as a volunteer, and at the expiration of that time he enlisted during the war. At the close of the war he returned to Turtle Creek, and continued the improvement of his land, making that his permanent home. He married Isabella Gaut, and had issue *three* children, of whom hereafter. He died in his prime, and was buried in the old "Riddle graveyard," near New Salem, and his monument, erected there by his father, has nothing but his name inscribed on it.

Robert Riddell[1] (1), a brother to the preceding, was born in Strabane, County of Tyrone, in the north of Ireland, and with his brothers, came to Westmoreland County, Penn., about six months previous to the war of the Revolution. He enlisted in the Colonial army for six months; subsequently, at the end of his first term of service, enlisted during the war, and died in camp.

William Riddell[1] (1), a half-brother of the preceding, was born in Strabane, County Tyrone, in the north of Ireland, and came to Westmoreland County, Penn., previous to the war of the Revolution. He owned a farm near New Salem, where he lived and died. He married twice; the first wife was Nancy ——, and the second wife Peggy ——; by each of these he had issue *three* children, of whom hereafter. I do not know when he died.

SECOND GENERATION.

Robert Riddle[2] (2), eldest son of John[1] (1), was born in the County of Westmoreland, Penn., in 1796, and his guardian bound him out to a distant relative, — he being about seven years old at his father's death, — and at the age of seventeen he was apprenticed to a blacksmith, and learned that trade. He was married at the age of twenty-one, to Miss Mary Williamson, and had issue *four* children, of whom hereafter. He died in 1863, aged 67 years.

John Riddle[2] (2), second son of John[1] (1), was born in the County of Westmoreland, Penn., about 1798; married to Elizabeth Williamson (probably a sister of Mary as above), and had issue *six* children, of whom hereafter. He is now (1874) living near Centreville, Butler County, Penn.

—— **Riddle**[2] (1), only daughter of John[1] (1), was born in Westmoreland County, Penn.; was married to John McMasters, who died, leaving her a widow with *one* son and *four* daughters. She married, secondly, John Gordon, and had a son and a daughter; she lived on Mill Creek, Verrango County. Her eldest son is a clergyman; the second a doctor.

---

* STRABANE is a market-town in the County of Tyrone, Ireland, on the River Mournne, one hundred and thirty miles north-north-west from Dublin, with which it is connected by railway. It communicates with Londonderry, and thus with the sea by canal and river. The chief industry is the linen trade. Four churches, — one Episcopal, two Presbyterian, and one Catholic, — besides two Methodist meeting-houses. Population in 1871 was 4615. I cannot find the name Strabane, Strawbane, nor Strawdown, on the map of County Donegal.

174   *RIDDELLS OF STRABANE, IRELAND.*

Robert Riddle² (**3**), eldest son of William¹ (**1**), was born in the County of Westmoreland, Penn., in 1769; married Ann McClellan, of Scotch-Irish descent, and settled in Clinton township, Butler County, about 1798–9. He had issue *six* children, of whom hereafter. Mr. Riddle died Jan. 25, 1853, in his 84th year; his wife died Aug. 25, 1851, in her 93d year. She was thirteen years old when she came across the ocean.

Hugh Riddle² (**1**), second son of William¹ (**1**), was born in the County of Westmoreland, Penn., March 5, 1771; married to Mary Gordon (she was born April 14, 1775), a woman of Scotch descent, and had issue *eleven* children, of whom hereafter. He settled in Clinton township, Butler County, at a place now called "Riddle's Cross-Roads," as a farmer, and died there Aug. 21, 1851. A wealthy man.

William Riddle² (**2**), a son of William¹ (**1**), was born in the County of Westmoreland, Penn., and settled on his father's homestead farm, near Salem. He married, but I have failed to procure the family records.

Nancy Riddle² (**1**), second daughter of William¹ (**1**), was born near Salem, Westmoreland County, Penn.; was married and had issue. She lived somewhere in her native State.

Betsey Riddle² (**1**), third daughter of William¹ (**1**), was born near. Salem, Westmoreland County, Penn., and was married to John McClelland-

THIRD GENERATION.

Nancy Riddle³ (**2**), eldest daughter of Robert² (**2**), was born in Westmoreland County, Penn., Sept. 11, 1807, and died Oct. 15, 1808.

Isabella Riddle³ (**1**), second daughter of Robert² (**2**), was born in Westmoreland County, Penn., June 1, 1809, and died Nov. 14, 1809.

Susan Riddle³ (**1**), third daughter of Robert² (**2**), was born in Westmoreland County, Penn., Jan. 11, 1811, and died Nov. 26, 1815.

Hon. John-W. Riddle³ (**3**), only son of Robert² (**2**), was born in Westmoreland County, Penn., in 1813; married Margaret-Jack McMahon, July 5, 1837 (her mother was of the same family of Wilson that lived in Strabane at the time Mr. Riddle's grandfather emigrated), and settled in his native County as a farmer. He commenced life poor and is now in good circumstances. He represented his County in the State Legislature in 1863–4, and is now Associate Judge of Westmoreland County. Residence at Delmont. Educated in the common schools. Is widely known and highly respected; a man of strong, practical mind and excellent ability. He had issue *three* children, of whom hereafter.*

John-W. Riddle³ (**4**), a son of John² (**2**), was born near Centerville, Butler County, Penn., and is now dead.

Robert Riddle³ (**4**), a son of John² (**2**), was born near Centerville, Butler County, Penn., and has deceased.

Samuel Riddle³ (**1**), a son of John² (**2**), was born in Butler County, Penn., and has deceased.

James Riddle³ (**1**), a son of John² (**2**), was born in Butler County, Penn.; supposed to be dead.

Isabella Riddle³ (**2**), a daughter of John² (**2**), was born in Butler County, Penn., and died in infancy.

* This family of Riddles is connected with the "Riddles of Waseon, Ohio," "Riddles of Lycoming, Pennsylvania," "Riddles of Belfont, Pennsylvania," and "Riddles of Pittsburgh, Pennsylvania," which see.

William Riddle⁸ (3), eldest son of Robert² (3), was born in Butler County, Penn., 1798–9; married Mary Cunningham for his first wife, and by her had issue *seven* children, of whom hereafter. He married, secondly, to Margaret, daughter of William Riddle² (2), who was a half-brother of Robert Riddle³ (3), and by her had issue *two* children, of whom hereafter. He lived in Clinton, Butler County, Penn. Farmer; died in 1841.

Susan Riddle⁸ (2), a daughter of Robert² (3), was born in Butler County, Penn.; was married to John McCall, and removed to the West.

Esther Riddle⁸ (1), a daughter of Robert² (3), was born in Butler County, Penn.; was married to William Culbreath, and settled in her native State.

Nancy Riddle⁸ (3), a daughter of Robert² (3), was born in Butler County, Penn.; was married to William McQueary, and removed to the West.

Betsey Riddle⁸ (1), a daughter of Robert² (3), was born in Butler County, Penn.; was married to John Duff, and lived at Ætna, Fillmore County, Minn.

Jane Riddle⁸ (1), a daughter of Robert² (3), was born in Butler County, Penn.; married John Thompson, and lived in her native State.

Jane Riddle⁸ (2), eldest daughter of Hugh² (1), was born in Butler County, Penn., Nov. 9, 1796; was married to Robert Duff, and died Aug. 27, 1874.

Matthew Riddle⁸ (1), eldest son of Hugh² (1), was born in Butler County, Penn., Sept. 20, 1798; married, and had children. He died March 21, 1860.

Elizabeth Riddle⁸ (1), second daughter of Hugh² (1), was born in Butler County, Penn.; was married to James Elliott, and resided at Sarversville, Butler County, Penn.

William Riddle⁸ (4), second son of Hugh² (1), was born in Butler County, Penn., Nov. 9, 1802; married to Margaret McClelland.

Rebeckah Riddle⁸ (1), third daughter of Hugh² (1), was born in Butler County, Penn., June 27, 1804; died Aug. 2, 1858.

Robert Riddle⁸ (5), third son of Hugh² (1), was born in Butler County, Penn., Aug. 27, 1806.

John Riddle⁸ (5), fourth son of Hugh² (1), was born in Butler County, Penn., Dec. 16, 1808, and died Aug. 9, 1851.

Mary Riddle⁸ (1), fourth daughter of Hugh² (1), was born in Butler County, Penn., Feb. 8, 1811.

Margaret Riddle⁸ (2), fifth daughter of Hugh² (1), was born in Butler County, Penn., July 16, 1813; died June 10, 1873.

Nancy Riddle⁸ (4), sixth daughter of Hugh² (1), was born in Butler County, Penn., Nov. 14, 1816, and died Jan. 18, 1875.

Isabella Riddle⁸ (3), seventh daughter of Hugh² (1), was born in Butler County, Penn., Dec. 31, 1819, and died Sept. 28, 1836.

FOURTH GENERATION.

Samuel-McMahon Riddle⁴ (2), eldest son of John³ (3), was born at Delmont, Westmoreland County, Penn., March 8, 1840, and lives on his father's homestead; unmarried in 1873.

Dr. John-Robert Riddle⁴ (6), second son of John³ (3), was born at Delmont, Westmoreland County, Penn., May 30, 1843. He was educated at Elder's Ridge Academy, and studied under the supervision of Rev. Alexander Donaldson. He read medicine under Dr. Jno. McNeil, and after attending two full courses of lectures at Jefferson Medical College, Philadelphia, he graduated in the class of 1868–9. He commenced the practice of medicine in his native County, and continued there with excellent success till 1870. He removed to Somersville, Cal., in 1871, and continued the active practice of his profession there until his death, which occurred suddenly Dec. 31, 1876. Dr. Riddle won an extensive patronage, and was doing a lucrative business. He had ordered his portrait for this book, but died before it was finished. He manifested a deep and abiding interest in this work.

Elizabeth-Mary Riddle[4] (2), only daughter of John[3] (3), was born in Westmoreland County, Penn., April 2, 1847, and was living at home with her parents in 1878, unmarried.

Robert Riddle[4] (6), eldest son of William[3] (3), was born in Butler County, Penn., Jan. 4, 1820; married Jane Esler (she was born Dec. 16, 1821), and had issue *six* children, of whom hereafter. He settled as a farmer at Riddle's Cross-Roads, Butler County, in his native State.

Hugh Riddle[4] (2), second son of William[3] (3), was born at Riddle's Cross-Roads, Butler County, Penn., and died when a child.

Nancy Riddle[4] (5), eldest daughter of William[3] (3), was born at Riddle's Cross-Roads, Butler County, Penn., in 1823; was married to John Esler, and died June 14, 1852, aged 29 years.

John-C. Riddle[4] (7), third son of William[3] (3), was born at Riddle's Cross-Roads, Butler County, Penn., May 12, 1825; married Elizabeth, daughter of John and Mary Anderson (she was born in same County, May 16, 1823), and settled near his birth-place; now (1874) living at Sharpsburg, Allegheny County. He has issue *eight* children, of whom hereafter.

William Riddle[4] (5), fourth son of William[3] (3), was born at Riddle's Cross-Roads, Butler County, Penn. (date not known), and died when a child.

James-M. Riddle[4] (2), fifth son of William[3] (3), was born at Riddle's Cross-Roads, Butler County, Penn.; married Ann ——, and died Feb. 27, 1863. His widow is living at Pittsburgh, and has *four* children living; two have deceased.

Mary-Ann Riddle[4] (2), second daughter of William[3] (3), was born at Riddle's Cross-Roads, Penn.; was married, but had no children. She died Aug. 11, 1852, in her thirtieth year.

Eliza-Jane Riddle[4] (1), third daughter of William[3] (3), was born at Riddle's Cross-Roads, Penn., and is now dead; she was presumably married, but had no children.

Rebecca-Ellen Riddle[4] (3), fourth daughter of William[3] (3) (she and Eliza were by a second wife, Margaret Riddle), was born in Butler County, enn., and was married to —— McLaughlan, and is now living. No Phildren.

FIFTH GENERATION.

William-Cunningham Riddell[5] (6), eldest son of Robert[4] (6), was born at Riddle's Cross-Roads, Butler County, Penn., Dec. 27, 1849, and is a carpenter by trade. Has kindly furnished the genealogy of this branch family. A fine penman.

James Riddle[5] (3), second son of Robert[4] (6), was born at Riddle's

Cross-Roads, Butler County, Penn., Sept. 18, 1851; married Maggie, daughter of Stephen and Jane Brewer, and lives at the Cross-Roads. No issue.

Robert-Esler Riddle[6] (7), third son of Robert[4] (6), was born at Riddle's Cross-Roads, Butler County, Penn., June 6, 1853; married Maggie, daughter of Frank and Maria Anderson, of the same County. He resides at Apollo, Armstrong County, Penn. Painter by trade.

John-Watt Riddle[5] (8), fourth son of Robert[4] (6), was born at Riddle's Cross-Roads, Butler County, Penn., April 18, 1855, and lives at home. Unmarried in 1879.

David-McClelland Riddle[6] (1), fifth son of Robert[4] (6), was born at Riddle's Cross-Roads, Butler County, Penn., Oct. 31, 1856; married Alice, daughter of James M. and Ann Riddle,—his cousin,—and lives at Markle, Westmoreland County, Penn.

Rebecca-Ann Riddle[6] (4), only daughter of Robert[4] (6), was born at Riddle's Cross-Roads, Butler County, Penn., Aug. 28, 1862, and was at home, unmarried, in 1879.

Mary-A. Riddle[5] (3), eldest daughter of John[4] (7), was born at Riddle's Cross-Roads, Butler County, Penn., Aug. 23, 1849; was married March 14, 1867, to Newton Harvey.

Margaret-A. Riddle[5] (3), second daughter of John[4] (7), was born at Riddle's Cross-Roads, Butler County, Penn., March 22, 1851; was married March 2, 1871, to Niblock Harvey, brother of Newton, husband of Mary.

Sarah-E. Riddle[5] (2), third daughter of John[4] (7), was born at Riddle's Cross-Roads, Butler County, Penn., March 21, 1853; was married April 30, 1874, to Samuel Hemphill.

Robert-A. Riddle[5] (8), eldest son of John[4] (7), was born at Riddle's Cross-Roads, Butler County, Penn., March 16, 1855. Unmarried in 1879.

Jennie Riddle[5] (1), fourth daughter of John[4] (7), was born at Riddle's Cross-Roads, Butler County, Penn., June 28, 1857. Unmarried in 1879.

Elmer-E. Riddle[5] (1), fifth daughter of John[4] (7), was born at Riddle's Cross-Roads, Butler County, Penn., Sept. 25, 1860. Unmarried in 1879.

Rebecca-M. Riddle[5] (5), fifth daughter of John[4] (7), was born at Riddle's Cross-Roads, Butler County, Penn., Jan. 22, 1862, and died Sept. 28, 1877.

John-G. Riddle[5] (9), third son of John[4](7), was born at Riddle's Cross-Roads, Butler County, Penn., March 6, 1865.

Elizabeth-A. Riddle[5] (3), sixth daughter of John[4] (7), was born at Riddle's Cross-Roads, Butler County, Penn., Aug. 1, 1867, and died March 16, 1878.

RIDDELLS OF NEWTON-STEWART, IRELAND.

[PENNSYLVANIA BRANCH.]

Christopher Riddell[1] (1), descended from Scottish ancestors, was born at Newton-Stewart,* County of Tyrone, north of Ireland, in the

---

* A town on the River Mourne, in the County Tyrone, not very far from Strabane, where other branches of the family lived.

year 1740; came to the United States in 1800, and settled in New York. He married in Ireland, and had issue several children (all born in the old country), of whom hereafter.

SECOND GENERATION.

Elizabeth Riddell[2] **(1)**, eldest daughter of Christopher[1] (1), was born at Newton-Stewart, Ireland, in 1767; came to America in 1772, and died unmarried in 1870, aged 103, probably in Philadelphia, Penn.

Jane Riddell[2] **(1)**, second daughter of Christopher[1] (1), was born at Newton-Stewart, Ireland, in 1769; came to America with her sister, in 1772, and died in 1871, at the age of 100 years, probably in Philadelphia.

Samuel Riddell[2] **(1)**, a son of Christopher[1] (1), was born at Newton-Stewart, Ireland, in the year 1770 (?), came to the United States in 1772, and held a commission in the American army during the war of 1812; he was wounded at the battle of New Orleans, and received a pension. He married, and had issue *eight* children, of whom hereafter. Died in 1852.

THIRD GENERATION.

John Riddle[3] **(1)**, a son of Samuel[2] (1), was born in 1804; married Ann B. Eardman, and settled in Philadelphia, Penn., where he deceased in 1852, leaving a widow (who died Nov. 26, 1857) and *eight* children.

Margaret Riddle[3] **(1)**, a daughter of Samuel[2] (1), was born in Philadelphia, Penn., in 1784; was married there and had a family.

Christopher Riddle[3] **(2)**, a son of Samuel[2] (1), was born in Philadelphia, Penn., and died young, unmarried.

Robert Riddle[3] **(1)**, a son of Samuel[2] (1), was born in Philadelphia, Penn.; married Miss Margaret Phipps (or Phillips), and had issue *two* children (possibly others), now living (1873). Mr. Riddle resides in Philadelphia, and is wealthy.

Eliza Riddle[3] **(1)**, a daughter of Samuel[2] (1), was born in Philadelphia, Penn., and died young, unmarried.

William Riddle[3] **(1)**, a son of Samuel[2] (1), was born in Philadelphia, Penn., in —— ; married Dec. 14, 1859, to Miss Caroline Earle, and by her had issue *five* children. He married secondly, Mrs. Mary Darnell, by whom he had *two* children, of whom (with those by first wife) hereafter. Residence in Philadelphia.

Mary Riddle[3] **(1)**, youngest daughter of Samuel[2] (1), was born in Philadelphia, and died young, unmarried.

FOURTH GENERATION.

Henry Riddle[4] **(1)**, eldest son of John[3] (1), was born in Philadelphia, Penn., Feb. 28, 1839, and died Sept. 28, 1867, presumably unmarried.

Eliza Riddle[4] **(2)**, eldest daughter of John[3] (1), was born in Philadelphia, Penn., Oct. 6, 1840, and was married to S. Desher.

Margaret Riddle[4] **(2)**, second daughter of John[3] (1), was born in Philadelphia, Penn., Nov. 1, 1842, and died Jan. 4, 1867.

Mary Riddle[4] **(2)**, third daughter of John[3] (1), was born in Philadelphia, Penn., Jan. 15, 1845, and was married to Samuel Yonker.

Julia Riddle[4] **(1)**, fourth daughter of John[3] (1), was born March 14, 1847; unmarried in 1873.

William Riddle[4] **(2)**, second son of John[3] (1), was born in Philadelphia, Penn., March 22, 1849; unmarried in 1873.

Annie Riddle[4] **(1)**, fifth daughter of John[3] (1), was born in Philadelphia, Penn., March 10, 1851; unmarried.

Caroline Riddle⁴ (1), youngest daughter of John³ (1), was born in Philadelphia, Penn., Sept. 10, 1852.

Margaret Riddle⁴ (3), a daughter of Robert³ (1), was born in Philadelphia, Penn.; was married to Mr. Fries.

Emma Riddle⁴ (1), second daughter of Robert³ (1), was born in Philadelphia, Penn., and was married to a Mr. E. Burns.

8.-Earl Riddle⁴ (1), eldest son of William³ (1), was born in Philadelphia, Penn., Feb. 22, 1852 ; married Oct. 13, 1875, to Miss M. Ella Brown, and resides in his native city. Mr. Riddle is traveling as agent for Edward K. Tryon & Co., of Philadelphia, manufacturers of arms. He has manifested a deep interest in this genealogy, and has rendered valuable assistance in securing data and subscriptions.

Mary Riddle⁴ (3), eldest daughter of William³ (1), and twin to Earl, was born in Philadelphia, Feb. 22, 1852.

Robert Riddle⁴ (2), second son of William³ (1), was born in Philadelphia, Penn., Feb. 8, 1854.

Darnel Riddle⁴ (1), third son of William³ (1), was born in Philadelphia, Penn., in 1858; unmarried.

Caroline Riddle⁴ (2), second daughter of William³ (1), was born in Philadelphia, Penn., in 1859 ; unmarried.

William Riddle⁴ (3), fourth son of William³ (1), was born in Philadelphia, Penn., and is now connected with a local telegraph company in his native city. He has provided data for this book.

ANOTHER FAMILY.

William Riddle² (4), was a native of Newton-Stewart, in County Tyrone, Ireland, and a connection of the preceding family; but the degree of kinship is not known. He was born about 1790 ; married Jane Wiley, came to New York in 1834, and settled in Philadelphia in 1835. He removed to Sudburyville, Chester County, Penn., in 1836. His wife " a woman of faithfulness." Shoemaker by trade. Had issue *eight* children, all born in Ireland, of whom hereafter.

THIRD GENERATION.

James Riddle³ (1), eldest son of William² (4), was born at Newton-Stewart, Ireland, in 1810 ; came to America in 1838, educated himself for a teacher, and became assistant principal of a high school. He died in 1843. Was twice married; second wife died of yellow fever at Galveston, Tex., in 1854. Household property destroyed by fire in 1855. Had issue *six* children, two of whom were living in 1878.

Robert Riddle³ (3), a son of William² (4), was born at Newton-Stewart, Ireland, about the year 1826 ; came to the United States in 1834, and became one of the greatest and most wealthy flour merchants in Philadelphia. He removed to Lambertville, N. J., and died there in 1878, only a few months after leaving Philadelphia. His place of business, for many years, was at the corner of Vine and Broad Streets. I have no account of a family.

Christopher Riddle² (3), a son of William² (4), was born at Newton-Stewart, Ireland, in 1828, and came to the United States with his parents when a child. He was apprenticed to learn the common painter's trade, but not being satisfied with that business, learned the art of graining in imitation of fancy woods and marble, and has been a success. He has also applied himself to the study of oratory, and sometimes receives the meed of praise for speaking in public. He has been twice married, and has a family of *five* children.

FOURTH GENERATION.

Jonathan Riddle⁴ (1), a son of James³ (1), is a merchant in Galveston, Tex., about 35 years of age.

--------◆--------

RIDDELLS OF CASTLEFINN, IRELAND.
[PENNSYLVANIA BRANCH.]

Thomas Riddell¹ (1), was a relative of the ancestors of the "Riddells of Westmoreland County, Pennsylvania," and of the "Riddells of Pittsburgh, Pennsylvania." He was engaged in business at Mar, Castlefinn, County Donegal, Ireland, but was not successful, and having failed, soon died, leaving a widow and *four* children in destitute circumstances; these, at the solicitation of relatives, came to America in 1772, and for a time made their abode in Baltimore, Md.

SECOND GENERATION.

John Riddell² (1), eldest son of Thomas¹ (1), was born at Mar, Castlefinn, County Donegal, Ireland, in 1756; came to Baltimore, Md., with his mother and brother in 1772, and lived for some years in Baltimore. He subsequently engaged in business at Philadelphia, Penn., and continued there till his death. He became financially independent. Had issue *four* children, of whom hereafter, and died about 1850. Mr. Riddell was well known in business circles as an honest man, and substantial, respectable citizen.

Eleanor Riddell² (1), a daughter of Thomas¹ (1), was born at Mar, Castlefinn, County Donegal, Ireland, in 1760; came to Baltimore, Md., in 1772; was married to a Mr. Alcern, and reared a family. Residence unknown.

Elizabeth Riddell² (1), second daughter of Thomas¹ (1), was born at Mar, Castlefinn, County Donegal, Ireland, in 1765; came to Baltimore with her mother in 1772, and is said by some to have died single, by others to have had a family.

Hon. James Riddell² (1), a son of Thomas¹ (1), was born at Mar, Castlefinn, County Donegal, Ireland, Nov. 15, 1770; came to the United States in 1772, and lived with his mother and brother at Baltimore for several years; he subsequently removed to Pittsburgh, Penn., engaged in merchandizing, and made that city his permanent residence. He was a shoemaker by trade. Was successful in business and acquired a fortune. Received the appointment of Associate Judge of the Court of Common

Pleas, and served in other positions of responsibility. He married a lady in Baltimore, also from Ireland, named Jane Adams, and had issue *nine* children, of whom hereafter. He died in 1854, aged 84 years. Mr. Riddell became acquainted with another branch of the same stock in Pittsburgh, and at their solicitation changed his surname from "Riddell" to "Riddle," a change which very much displeased his mother, but her importunities were not of sufficient force to cause him to return to his original name, he having acquired property as *James Riddle.* He was a man of sound mind and active, progressive habits, of large business capabilities, and great force of character. He was highly respected. Mr. Riddle probably had two wives, as the mother of Capt. Thomas Riddle, — his son, — was called "Elizabeth-Sin Riddle" in the records.

THIRD GENERATION.

Capt. Thomas Riddle[3] (2), eldest son of James[2] (1) and Elizabeth-Sin Riddle, was born in Shippensburgh, Penn. (Cumberland County), Oct. 17, 1795; married Charlotta, daughter of —— and Elizabeth Guthridge (she was born in Newport, Isle of Wight, Eng., July 23, 1806, where she lived until her marriage), April 16, 1826, and had issue *ten* children, of whom hereafter. At the age of seventeen he went to sea as a common sailor before the mast, and by his energy and strict attention to his business, worked himself to the position of commander. He was master of several merchant-vessels sailing between Philadelphia, Europe, and China. The last vessel he commanded in the China trade, was the "North America," making the last trip on the year of his marriage, when he quit the sea, going to Pittsburgh, Penn., where he took command of the steamboat "Neptune," plying between that city and New Orleans, it taking three months at that time to make the round trip. He located his family at Covington, Ky., and after three years' service on the "Neptune," removed to Cincinnati, O., and engaged in merchandizing for a year; thence he removed to New Albany, Ind., where he permanently located with his family in 1832, and again went on the river, taking command of a steamboat in the Louisville and New Orleans trade. He afterwards commanded the United States snag-boat "Hercules," in which he continued until the war with Mexico, when he took command of the U. S. transport, iron steamer, "Maria Burt," carrying troops from New Orleans to Vera Cruz. After the close of the war he built the steamboat "Ann Livington," and run her in the Louisville and southern coast trade for several years, when she was burned and became a total wreck. Captain Riddle died of cholera July 13, 1855, aged 57 years. He was a man of firm intellect and high social standing, and a very successful commander. He was six feet and three inches high, with an average weight of one hundred and ninety pounds, standing very erect; his complexion was dark.

John Riddle[3] (2), second son of James[2] (1), was born in Pittsburgh, Penn., Nov. 21, 1799; married, and had issue *two* sons, of whom hereafter. He resided in Philadelphia; died April 9, 1855. Was a wealthy man.

Elizabeth Riddle[3] (2), eldest daughter of James[2] (1), was born in Pittsburgh, Penn., Feb. 20, 1798; was married to Mr. M. Mason, an Englishman, dry goods merchant; secondly, to Dr. Joseph Gazzain.

James-S. Riddle[3] (2), third son of James[2] (1), was born in Pittsburgh, Penn., March 29, 1804; married ——, and had issue *four* children, of whom hereafter. He lived at or near Pittsburgh.

Mary-Ann Riddle[3] (1), second daughter of James[2] (1), was born in Pittsburgh, Penn., in 1800, and died young.

Mary-Ann Riddle[3] (2), third daughter of James[2] (1), was born in Pittsburgh, Penn., March 13, 1806; was married to Judge Charles Shaler, of Pittsburgh, and left issue.

Eleanor Riddle[3] (2), fourth daughter of James[2] (1), was born in Pittsburgh, Penn., Sept. 24, 1808; was married to Henry Forsyth, and died Jan. 20, 1858, leaving issue.

William Riddle[3] (1), fourth son of James[2] (1), was born in Pittsburgh, Penn., Oct. 8, 1810; married in 1835, to Mary Lawrence, of Louisville, Ky., and had issue *nine* children, of whom hereafter. Mr. Riddle was a merchant in the city of Louisville, and acquired wealth. Knowing that his father had changed his name from "Riddell" to "Riddle," he instructed his own children to spell their names *Riddell*. He died Dec. 13, 1855. He was a man of excellent ability, and highly esteemed by a large circle of friends.

Robert-Moore Riddle[3] (1), fifth son of James[2] (1), was born in Pittsburgh, Penn., Aug. 17, 1812; married a Miss Piers, of Pittsburgh, and had issue *five* children, of whom hereafter. He died Dec. 18, 1858, aged 46 years. Mr. Riddle was one of the most experienced editors in the city. In 1837 he became proprietor and editor of the old *Presbyterian Advocate*, but during the administration of General Harrison, he relinquished the publication of that journal to become postmaster, to which position he was appointed by the President. About the close of Mr. Tyler's term of office, he purchased of J. Heron Foster, the *Spirit of the Age*, and soon after merged it into the *Press*, now known as the *Commercial Journal*. To this paper he was constantly attached, as proprietor and active manager, until a short time before his death, when owing to failing health, his connection with that paper was discontinued. In 1853, he was elected by the Whig party as mayor of the city of Pittsburgh, which post he filled one term, with credit to himself and with benefit to the city, at the same time fulfilling his onerous duties as conductor of the aforesaid journal. As an editor he was accomplished and successful; although not ranking as a very profound reasoner, he was a most brilliant and instructive writer, and the emanations from his pen have been generally admired In person he was tall, slender, and of dignified presence; and in manner affable, courteous, and sociable,—interesting in conversation and a pleasant companion.

Charles Riddle[3] (1), youngest son of James[2] (1) was born in Pittsburgh, Penn., March 10, 1815, and died at New Orleans, La., Feb. 12, 1853, unmarried. He was a clerk.

FOURTH GENERATION.

Elizabeth-Sin Riddle[4] (3), eldest daughter of Thomas[3] (2), was born in Allegheny County, Penn., Feb. 25, 1827; died April 16, 1828.

George-William Riddle[4] (1), eldest son of Thomas[3] (2), was born in Covington, Ky., July 11, 1828, and died Aug. 2, 1830.

Samuel Riddle[4] (1), second son of Thomas[3] (2), was born in Covington, Ky., Dec. 11, 1829, and died at New Albany, Ind., May 17, 1854.

Ann-Livington Riddle[4] (1), second daughter of Thomas[3] (2), was born in Cincinnati, O., Jan. 29, 1832, and died at Hartland, Mich., April 5, 1862. She was married May 29, 1855, to Reuben C. Chambers, who with *two* children survives her.

Thomas-Franklyn Riddle[4] (3), third son of Thomas[3] (2), was born in New Albany, Ind., Oct. 23, 1834, and died in Mobile, Ala., July 12, 1863. He was married to Lizzie Beckler, in Mobile, Ala., Sept. 3, 1860. His wife and *one* child died a few months after him.

Charlotta Riddle[4] (1), third daughter of Thomas[3] (2), was born in New Albany, Ind., April 14, 1838; was married to William-Woodruff Tuley, July 24, 1856, and has but *one* child.

Jane Riddle[4] (1), fourth daughter of Thomas[3] (2), was born in New Albany, Ind., April 24, 1839, and died July 1, 1841.

Charles-Van-Dusen Riddle[4] (2), fourth son of Thomas[3] (2), was born in New Albany, Ind., July 24, 1841; married Emma A. Williams, in New Orleans, La., April 15, 1862, and died of yellow fever at Synder's Bluff, on Yazo River, twelve miles above Vicksburg, Miss., during the epidemic of 1878. His wife and *three* children are living in New Orleans; the two others died of yellow fever within a few days of their father.

William-Wray Riddle[4] (2), fifth son of Thomas[3] (2), was born in New Albany, Ind., May 19, 1843; married Miss Minnie Ferris, of Paoli, Ind., and had issue *two* children. His wife died in 1881, and he married to Miss Sue Bollman, of Pittsburgh, Penn., by whom he has *one* son, of whom hereafter.

Mary Riddle[4] (2), fifth daughter of Thomas[3] (2), was born in New Albany, Ind., May 14, 1846; was married to Henry T. Kerlin, Dec. 4, 1883, and is now living in Louisville, Ky.

John-S. Riddle[4] (3), eldest son of John[3] (2), was born at Philadelphia, Penn.; married Miss McClure, of Pittsburgh, and died leaving *one* son, of whom hereafter.

James Riddle[4] (2), second son of John[3] (2), died unmarried.

Robert-Moore Riddle[4] (2), eldest son of William[3] (1), was born in Louisville, Ky., March 30, 1837, and died June 27, 1838.

Benjamin-Lawrence Riddle[4] (1), second son of William[3] (1), was born in Louisville, Ky., May 23, 1839, and died August 2, 1840.

Leaven-Lawrence Riddle[4] (1), third son of William[3] (1), was born in Louisville, Ky., April 23, 1841; died Aug. 24, 1842.

William Riddle[4] (3), fourth son of William[3] (1), was born in Louisville, Ky., Dec. 29, 1842; died Jan. 30. 1843.

Mary-Lawrence Riddle[4] (4), eldest daughter of William[3] (1), was born in Louisville, Ky., April 17, 1845; was married to Clarence Joyes, Aug. 11, 1868, and died Oct. 25, 1876.

William Riddle[4] (4), fifth son of William[3] (1), was born in Louisville, Ky., Aug. 2, 1848; married Mollie Claxton, Oct. 8, 1874, and has issue *two* children, of whom hereafter. Farmer in Owen County, Ky.

Elias-Dorsey Riddle[4] (1), sixth son of William[3] (1), was born in Louisville, Ky., Jan. 31, 1851, and in 1873 was a clerk for Peter Wright and Sons, Philadelphia, Penn.

Charles-Lawrence Riddle[4] (3), seventh son of William[3] (1), was born in Louisville, Ky., April 22, 1853. Farmer in Owen County, Ky. Married Laura S. Ross, of Jefferson County, Ky., and has issue *three* children, of whom hereafter.

Benjamin-Howard Riddle[4] (2), eight son of William[3] (1), was born n Louisville, Ky., July 16, 1855; died Nov. 11, 1855.

Col. William Riddle⁴ (5), eldest son of Robert² (1), was on the staff of General Mead during the Rebellion, and was shot in a political altercation in a saloon in Philadelphia, about 1868.

John-Sims Riddle⁴ (4), a son of Robert² (1), was born in Pittsburgh, Penn., married Mary, daughter of John-Bradford Wallace and Mary Binney, his wife, and sister of Hon. John-William Wallace, President of the Pennsylvania Historical Society. He resided at Erie. Had issue *three* children, of whom hereafter. Buried in St. Peter's church-yard, Philadelphia, April 14, 1855, aged 54 years; his wife was born Dec. 10, 1810, and died May 13, 1852.

Robert Riddle⁴ (3), a son of Robert² (1), was born in Pittsburgh, Penn.,

Annie-D. Riddle⁴ (1), a daughter of Robert² (1), was born in Pittsburgh, Penn.; was married to Col. Thomas A. Scott, President of the Pennsylvania Railroad, and resides in Philadelphia.*

Bessie Riddle⁴ (1), youngest daughter of Robert² (1), was born in Pittsburgh, Penn. and was married to John-Harmon Fisher, of Philadelphia.

FIFTH GENERATION.

Ann-Livington Riddle⁵ (2). ⎫
Mary Riddle⁵ (5).   ⎪
Emma Riddle⁵ (1).   ⎬ Children of Charles⁴ (2).
Lotta Riddle⁵ (1).   ⎪
Thomas Riddle⁵ (4).   ⎭

Wray-T. Riddle⁵ (1), eldest son of William⁴ (2).
Irene Riddle⁵ (1), eldest daughter of William⁴ (2).
William Riddle⁵ (6), second son of William⁴ (2).

Elias-Lawrence Riddle⁵ (1), eldest son of William⁴ (4), was born in Owen County, Ky., July 2, 1878.

Nellie-H. Riddle⁵ (1), eldest daughter of William⁴ (4), was born in Owen County, Ky., Aug. 22, 1881.

Mary-L. Riddle⁵ (6), eldest daughter of Charles⁴ (3), was born in 1873, somewhere in Kentucky.

Charles Riddle⁵ (4), eldest son of Charles⁴ (3), was born in 1877, somewhere in Kentucky.

Ross Riddle⁵ (1), second son of Charles⁴ (3), was born in 1881, somewhere in Kentucky.

John-Wallace Riddle⁵ (5), eldest son of John⁴ (4), and his wife, Mary Wallace, was born Nov. 3, 1838, and died in the city of Philadelphia, Nov. 26, 1863, a promising and educated young man.

James Riddle⁵ (3), second son of John⁴ (4), was born Dec. 18, 1840, and died in Philadelphia, May, 30, 1861.

Susan-Bradford-Wallace Riddle⁵ (3), a daughter of John⁴ (4), was born, Sept. 20, 1844, and died May 3, 1852.

---

* Col. Scott was a very distinguished and wealthy man, and was sometimes called the great Pennsylvania " Railroad King." Deceased. Mrs. Scott is a lady of amiable qualities, possessing a cultivated mind and great kindness of heart. She has traveled extensively in Europe.

RIDDELLS OF BALLYBLACK, IRELAND.

[PENNSYLVANIA BRANCH.]

John Riddell[1] (1), descended from a Scottish stock, lived at Ballyblack, County of Down, province of Ulster, Ireland. He was born about 1740; married Margaret Moore, of Scottish descent, and had issue *seven* children, of whom hereafter. Mr. Riddell's ancestors came from Scotland to Ireland previous to 1620. An effort was made to trace the ancestry of this family, but as the parish registers of Ballyblack have been destroyed, connections cannot be made. They spelled the name *Riddell*. Mr. Riddell died in 1806, and his widow Feb. 1, 1816; they were buried at Ballyblack.

Matthew Riddell[1] (1), brother of the preceding, was born at Ballyblack, County of Down, province of Ulster, Ireland, in 1743; came to the County of Westmoreland, Penn.; thence in 1796 to Venango County, where he settled permanently. He married Elizabeth Gilkey, a native of Ireland (she was born in 1753, and died Nov. 26, 1817), and had issue *four* children, of whom hereafter. He died Nov. 26, 1830.

Ann Riddell[1] (1), sister of the preceding (parents' names unknown), was born at Ballyblack, County of Down, Ireland, and is supposed to have died there. Her name, with that of a sister, was found in a letter written *from* Ireland by her brother's wife.

Mary Riddell[1] (1), sister of the preceding, was born at Ballyblack, Ireland, and is supposed to have lived and died there; probably her descendants may be living there.

SECOND GENERATION.

Matthew Riddle[2] (2), a son of John[1] (1), was born at Ballyblack, County of Down, Ireland; married Sarah Findlay,* and had issue *nine* children, of whom hereafter, — all born in Ireland. After the decease of his wife he followed his kindred to the United States (1824), and settled at Howard, Centre County, Penn., where he died in 1850.

William Riddle[2] (1), son of John[1] (1), was born in Ballyblack, County of Down, Ireland; married Sarah Brittan, and had issue *seven* children, of whom hereafter. He came to America, and settled at Bellefonte, Centre County, Penn., previous to the Irish Rebellion (1796–8). He was a stone-mason by trade.

Hugh Riddle[2] (1), a son of John[1] (1), was born at Ballyblack, County of Down, Ireland, Aug. 1, 1779; married Sept. 1, 1814, to Miss Rebecca Lee, and had issue *nine* children, of whom hereafter. He came to the United States about the time of the Irish Rebellion (1796–8), and lived awhile with his brother, before mentioned, at Bellefont; while there he went to Wilmington, Del., after his baggage, and their being no public conveyances, nor bridges across the streams at that time, he started for the Susquehanna on horseback, and reached Clark's Ferry where the river was a mile wide. Having recently crossed the ocean, the distance over the Susquehanna seemed insignificant, and urging his horse forward he entered the stream; the current was strong, and horse and rider were swept down river, till, fortunately, the horse rested upon a large rock

---

* Her brother, William Findlay, lived in the County of Down, and his daughter was wife of Rev. William Mitchell, the Presbyterian minister of Ballyblack church, in 1878.

that was but a few feet below the surface. After resting awhile he pushed forward again, and by a desperate struggle succeeded in reaching the shore, where he found several persons who had been watching him in his perilous adventure, expecting to see him drowned. He was carried down the river more than a mile. An account of this undertaking was published in the newspapers at the time, and it has ever since been regarded as a feat accomplished by no other man. He removed from Bellefonte to Scrubgrass, in Venango County, where he remained nine years ; thence returned to Centre County, where he was employed for many years as superintendent of the iron-works of Roland Curtin, father of Governor Curtin. He purchased land and followed farming in Centre County until 1824, when he removed to Clearfield County, where he died March 22, 1856. He was an exemplary citizen, and for many years a devoted member of the Methodist church, highly respected for his sincere piety.

John Riddle² (2), a son of John¹ (1), was born at Ballyblack, County Down, Ireland, and died there when young.

James Riddle² (1), a son of John¹ (1), was born at Ballyblack, Ireland, and died there. Supposed to have been poisoned by a young woman.

Elizabeth Riddle² (1), a daughter of John¹ (1), was born at Ballyblack, Ireland ; was married to Samuel Ewart; had *eight* children, and died in her native country.*

Margaret Riddle² (1), a daughter of John¹ (1), was born in Ballyblack, County of Down, Ireland; was married to James Conn, and lived in Scotland, where her descendants reside.

Agnes Riddle² (1), a daughter of John¹ (1), was born in Ballyblack, County of Down, Ireland; was married to Thomas Kenney, and her descendants are living in Scotland and Ireland.

Ann Riddle² (1), eldest daughter of Matthew¹ (1), was born in Westmoreland County, Penn., March 6, 1783; was married Jan. 23, 1810, to James Pollock, a man of Scottish descent, and had issue *six* sons and *one* daughter. She died Feb. 1, 1864, aged 79 years.

John Riddle² (3), eldest son of Matthew¹ (1), was born in Westmoreland County, Penn., March 10, 1786; married July 20, 1813, to Esther Crawford (she was born April 24, 1790, and died March 10, 1877), and had issue *six* children, of whom hereafter. Farmer; died Feb. 9, 1826.

Elizabeth Riddle² (2), second daughter of Matthew¹ (1), was born in Westmoreland County, Penn., June 26, 1784, and died July 30, 1873, aged 89 years. Never married.

Robert Riddle² (1), second son of Matthew¹ (1), was born in Westmoreland County, Penn., Feb. 21, 1788; married Feb. 4, 1817, to Catherine Phipps, and had issue *ten* children, of whom hereafter. Farmer ; died Sept. 18, 1856, aged 68 years, leaving a widow who is still living.

THIRD GENERATION.

William Riddle³ (2), eldest son of Matthew² (2), was born at Bally-

---

* Her children were John, Samuel, Alexander, William, Margaret, Elizabeth, Mary, and Susanna. John Ewart is still (1880) living in Ballyblack, Ireland, without issue. Samuel died without issue. Susanna was married to Charles Robinson, and left surviving children, Charles and Eliza-Jane (my correspondent), who was married to Mr. McWilliams. Elizabeth was married to John McColloch, and is still living, with issue. Margaret was married to John Montgomery, who after her decease, went to America with his family. William (sometime dead) left issue *three* sons and *one* daughter, still alive.

black, County of Down, Ireland, March 6, 1797; married in 1829, to Isabella T. Pemberton, of Pennsylvania, and had issue *several* children, *of whom hereafter.* He died in June, 1861, aged 64 years; his widow died in 1865, aged 64 years, in the State of Pennsylvania.

John Riddle[8] (4), second son of Matthew[2] (2), was born in Ballyblack, County of Down, Ireland, about 1800; came to Pennsylvania with his father in 1824, thence went to Texas with his brother Wilson in 1842, he was taken prisoner and confined in Castle Perote, where he remained ten months, but was finally released as a subject of Great Britain, through Her Majesty's Minister, Peckenham. In 1846 he crossed into Mexico on a trading expedition and was again made a prisoner, but effected his escape two months subsequently. He suffered great deprivation during his imprisonment, which seriously impaired his health; he died in June, 1858. Never married.

James Riddle[8] (2), a son of Matthew[2] (2), was born at Ballyblack, County of Down, Ireland; came to America in 1824, and died unmarried when a young man.

Wilson Riddle[8] (1), a son of Matthew[2] (2), was born at Ballyblack, County of Down, Ireland, in 1808; married in 1841, to Miss E. M. Menesce, and had issue *two* children, of whom hereafter. He resided for several years at Howard, Centre County, Penn., and from there removed to Tennessee, and engaged in mercantile pursuits in the city of Nashville. In 1839 he removed to, and established a mercantile house in San Antonia de Bexas. As a merchant he was successful until the year 1842, when he was robbed of his entire personal property by an invading force from the Republic of Mexico, under command of General Vasquez. On the 11th day of September, 1842, he was taken prisoner by the Mexican General Wall, in the city of San Antonia, carried to Mexico, and confined (as also his brother John) in Castle Perote, where he remained ten months, and through the influence of the British Minister he was released as a subject of Great Britain. His confinement, deprivations, and sufferings, endured in prison, impaired his health, and terminated his life Sept. 12, 1847.

Margaret Riddle[8] (4), daughter of Matthew[2] (2), was born at Ballyblack, Ireland; was married to Thomas Beck, and after his death came with her family to Pennsylvania in 1844.

Anna Riddle[8] (1), second daughter of Matthew[2] (2), was born in Ballyblack, Ireland; married, and was living near Bellefonte, Penn., in 1879.

Mary Riddle[8] (3), third daughter of Matthew[2] (2), was born at Ballyblack, Ireland; came to America in 1824; was married to Thomas Moore, and lives in Centre County, Penn.

Sarah Riddle[8] (1), fourth daughter of Matthew[2] (2), was born at Ballyblack, Ireland; came to America in 1824; was married to J. H. McClure, and lived in Centre County, Penn.

Eliza Riddle[8] (1) fifth daughter of Matthew[2] (2), was born at Ballyblack, Ireland; came to America in 1824; was married to a Mr. Tipton, and deceased previous to 1879.

Betsey Riddle[8] (1), a daughter of William[2] (1), was born at Bellefonte, Centre County, Penn.; was married to John Robinson.

Margaret Riddle[8] (2), a daughter of William[2] (1), was born at Bellefonte, Centre County, Penn.; was married to —— Perry, and lives at Prairie Home, Ill.

Hugh-M. Riddle[2] (2), eldest son of William[2] (1), was born at Belle-fonte, Centre County, Penn., and died young in 1831.

William Riddle[3] (3), second son of William[2] (1), was born at Belle-fonte, Centre County, Penn., Aug. 9, 1806; married Margaret Sweeny; secondly, Agnes P. Taylor, and had issue *three* children, of whom here-after. Resided in his native town. Farmer; died Oct. 8, 1879.

Nancy Riddle[3] (1), a daughter of William[2] (1), was born at Bellefonte, Centre County, Penn.; was married to John Neil; both dead.

John-S. Riddle[3] (5), third son of William[2] (1), was born on the old Riddle farm, at the foot of the Nittany mountains, in Centre County, Penn., March 6, 1810, where he lived until three years after his marriage in 1836, to Jane Moony (she was born at Boulsburg, Centre County, Nov. 29, 1818), when he settled in Armstrong County, where he has lived ever since; the town is now called Strattonville. He is a farmer. Had issue *eight* children, of whom hereafter.

Matthew Riddle[3] (3), second son of William[2] (1), was born at Belle-fonte, Centre County, Penn., in 1813; married Eliza A. Baird, and had issue —— children, of whom hereafter. He had removed to Illinois. Farmer; killed (accidentally) in Kansas, April 11, 1878; family living near Hutchinson, Kansas.

John-M. Riddle[3] (6), eldest son of Hugh[2] (1), was born in Centre County, Penn., June 27, 1815; married May 24, 1842, to Charlotte E. Havens, and had issue *nine* children, of whom hereafter. He resides at New Washington, in his native State. Presumably a farmer; has fur-nished materials for this book; a man of sound mind and good business capacity.

William Riddle[3] (4), second son of Hugh[2] (1), was born in Centre County, Penn., March 7, 1817; emigrated to Illinois in 1841, and died there of brain fever in 1844. Carpenter by trade; no issue.

Mary-L. Riddle[3] (2), eldest daughter of Hugh[2] (1), was born in Cen-tre County, Penn., March 19, 1819; was married to John Rorabaugh, and died June 24, 1871. She was a devoted member of the Methodist church.

James Riddle[3] (3), third son of Hugh[2] (1), was born in Centre County, Penn., July 11, 1821; married March 14, 1843, to Margaret Foul-ton, and had issue *seven* children, of whom hereafter. He resides on a farm at New Washington, Clearfield County, Penn.

Margaret Riddle[3] (3), second daughter of Hugh[2] (1), was born in Centre County, Penn, in March, 1824, and died Jan. 8, 1831, of scarlet fever.

Wilson Riddle[3] (2), fourth son of Hugh[2] (1), was born in Clearfield County, Penn., in September, 1826, and died Jan. 5, 1831, of scarlet fever.

Harriet Riddle[3] (1), third daughter of Hugh[2] (1), was born in Clear-field County, Penn., in June, 1828, and died Jan. 9, 1831, of scarlet fever.

Hugh Riddle[3] (3), fifth son of Hugh[2] (1), was born in Clearfield County, Penn., Jan. 20, 1830; married in December, 1855, to Sarah J. Filbury, and had issue *two* sons, of whom hereafter Carpenter; died Feb. 14, 1865.

Elizabeth Riddle[3] (3), fourth daughter of Hugh[2] (1), was born in Clear-field County, Penn., Aug. 4, 1834, and died April 16, 1850; unmarried.

Matthew Riddle[3] (4), eldest son of John[2] (3), was born in Venango County, Penn., May 14, 1814; married Mary Moore, Sept. 5, 1839 (she was born June 5, 1820, and died Aug. 20, 1883), and had issue *six* children, of whom hereafter. Farmer by occupation; resided at Clintonville, Penn.; died Dec. 11, 1881.

John-W. Riddle[2] (7), second son of John[2] (3), was born in Venango County, Penn., Dec. 17, 1817; married Dec. 26, 1843, to Jane McCay (she was born May 6, 1819, and died Oct. 18, 1870), and had issue *five* children, of whom hereafter. He resides at Clintonville, Venango County, Penn., and carries on a farm.

William-Clark Riddle[2] (5), third son of John[2] (3), was born in Venango county, Penn.; married, and has issue —— children, of whom hereafter. He resides in his native county.

Elizabeth Riddle[2] (4), only daughter of John[2] (3), was born in Venango County, Penn.; was married to —— Moore, and lives at Big Bend, in her native County.

John-P. Riddle[2] (8), eldest son of Robert[2] (1), was born in Venango County, Penn.

James-P. Riddle[2] (4), second son of Robert[2] (1), was born in Venango County, Penn.

Elizabeth Riddle[2] (5), only daughter of Robert[2] (1), was born in Venango County, Penn.; was married to —— Calvert, and lives at Clintonville, Penn.

Matthew Riddle[2] (5), third son of Robert[2] (1), was born in Venango County, Penn.

FOURTH GENERATION.

Rev. Findlay-B. Riddle[4] (1), eldest son of William[3] (2), was born in Centre County, Penn., Dec. 3, 1829; married Mary, daughter of Samuel J. Paker, of Sunbury, and has issue *five* children, of whom hereafter. He was educated at Dickinson College, where he laid the foundation of his scholastic training, and then was a student at the Concord Biblical Institute, where he received important advantages in his theological studies. Entering the Baltimore Conference, in 1857, and becoming a member of the Central Pennsylvania Conference at its organization in 1869, he has filled some of the most important appointments; among them, at Shamokin, Berwick, Altoona, Danville and Huntingdon. He is a rapid speaker, with a logical cast of mind, uses plain, practical language, and few excel him in debate. These elements of character have given him prominence in his conference. Recognizing his scholarly acquirements, Dickinson College honored him with the degree of A. M. See portrait in this book.

James-F. Riddle[4] (5), second son of William[3] (2), was born in Centre County, Penn., July 30, 1834; married Angeline Hughes, and is a lawyer practising at Tyrone.

Nelson-P. Riddle[4] (1), third son of William[3] (2), was born in Centre County, Penn., Nov. 15, 1836; married Angeline Hughes, and has *one* child, of whom hereafter.

Francis-M. Riddle[4] (2), a daughter of William[3] (2), was born in Centre County, Penn., Sept. 5, 1841; unmarried.

Mary-E. Riddle[4] (6), eldest daughter of William[3] (2), was born in Centre County, Penn., Aug. 25, 1831; unmarried.

Matthew-M. Riddle[4] (6), fourth son of William[3] (2), was born in Centre County, Penn., May 26, 1844; married Sarah C., daughter of George

Long, and has issue *two* children, of whom hereafter. He served in the Union army in the Rebellion.

Sarah-Elizabeth Riddle[4] (3), only daughter of Wilson[3] (1), was born at San Antonia, Texas, Feb. 19, 1842; was married Sept. 18, 1866, to Robert Eagar, of Nova Scotia, and has (with other issue) *twin* daughters; resides at San Antonia.

James-Wilson Riddle[4] (6), only son of Wilson[3] (1), was born at San Antonia, Texas, April 21, 1845, and was single in 1873. At the age of sixteen he volunteered as a soldier in the Confederate army during the Rebellion, and served through the war; now (1873) a merchant at Eagle Pass, Texas.

Frank Riddle[4] (1), a son of John[3] (5), was born at Strattonville, Centre County, Penn.; married, and has *two* children, of whom hereafter; he is a farmer at Strattonville.

Sallie-E. Riddle[4] (1), eldest daughter of John[3] (5), was born at Strattonville, Penn.; was married to J. H. Martin, and lives at Limestone, Centre County.

Amanda Riddle[4] (1), second daughter of John[3] (5), was born at Strattonville, Penn.; was married to S. K. Davis, undertaker, and resides at Hubbard, O.

Lauretta Riddle[4] (1), third daughter of John[3] (5), was born at Strattonville, Penn.; was married to J. W. McIlhattan, and lives in Edenburg, Centre County, Post-office, Knox.

Asenath Riddle[4] (1), fourth daughter of John[3] (5), was born at Strattonville, Penn.; was married to Earl D. Spear, and lives in Colorado.

—— **Riddle**[4] (?), second son of John[3] (5), was born at Strattonville, Penn., and died young.

Mary-Jane Riddle[4] (4), fifth daughter of John[3] (5), was born at Strattonville, Penn., and died April 8, 1883; she was a devoted Christian.

Martha-Arminda Riddle[4] (1), eldest daughter of John[3] (6), was born in Clearfield County, Penn., Dec. 22, 1843, and died April 11, 1864.

Sarah-C. Riddle[4] (2), second daughter of John[3] (6), was born in Clearfield County, Penn., May 1, 1846; was married Feb. 14, 1866, to John E. Rorabaugh, and has issue.

Hugh Riddle[4] (5), eldest son of John[3] (6), was born in Clearfield County, Penn., July 9, 1848; died Aug. 11, 1849.

Fillmore-W. Riddle[4] (1), second son of John[3] (6), was born in Clearfield County, Penn., April 23, 1852, and in 1873 was unmarried; farmer.

Thurzah-R. Riddle[4] (1), third daughter of John[3] (6), was born in Clearfield County, Penn., Feb, 7, 1855, and was not married in 1873.

James-G. Riddle[4] (7), third son of John[3] (6), was born in Clearfield County, Penn., March 26, 1858; single in 1873.

William-Wilson Riddle[4] (6), eldest son of James[3] (3), was born in Clearfield County, Penn., Jan. 20, 1845; enlisted in the Hundred-and-fifth Regiment Pennsylvania Volunteers, in September, 1861, and served in the Union army during the Rebellion, until May 31, 1862, when he was killed at the battle of Fair Oaks, in Virginia.

Mary-E. Riddle[4] (5), second daughter of James[3] (3), was born in Clearfield County, Penn., Dec. 29, 1846, and was married Sept. 1, 1870, to Charles C. Weaver.

Hugh Riddle⁴ (6), second son of James³ (3), was born in Clearfield County, Penn., April 18, 1849; single in 1873.

Rebecca Riddle⁴ (1), third daughter of James³ (3), was born in Clearfield County, Penn., Feb. 10, 1852; was married June 18, 1871, to David G. Piper.

David-A. Riddle⁴ (2), third son of James³ (3), was born in Clearfield County, Penn., June 4, 1855; single in 1873.

. Two children died in infancy unnamed, born Jan. 1, 1844, and Dec. 20, 1857, respectively.

William Riddle⁴ (7), eldest son of Hugh³ (3), was born in Clearfield County, Penn., Dec. 4, 1857; living.

Newton Riddle⁴ (1), second son of Hugh³ (3) was born in Clearfield County, Penn., May, 1860, and died in 1865.

Julia-Ann Riddle⁴ (2), eldest daughter of Matthew³ (4), was born in Clintonville, Penn., Oct. 17, 1840; was married to John Donaldson (carpenter), and has *five* children.

Josiah-Randolph Riddle⁴ (1), eldest son of Matthew³ (4), born in Clintonville, Penn., April 1, 1844; unmarried in 1880; artist, Topeka, Kan.

Livin Riddle⁴ (1), second daughter of Matthew³ (4), was born in Clintonville, Penn., Feb. 10, 1846; was married to Joshua Huffman, and has *four* children.

John-Knox Riddle⁴ (9), second son of Matthew³ (4), was born in Clintonville, Penn., Jan. 29, 1848; single in 1880.

Rev. Clinton Riddle⁴ (1), third son of Matthew³ (4), was born in Clintonville, Penn., Sept. 29, 1851; unmarried. He resided with his parents, working on the farm and attending the common school, until the spring of 1866. In the fall and winter of 1866 and 1867, he attended a select school in Clintonville, walking, — sometimes riding, — about three miles, and returning home at noon to spend his afternoons in study and doing chores. In September, 1868, he went to Westminster College, located in New Wilmington, Lawrence County, Penn., and entering the second preparatory class, remained in that institution until he graduated in June, 1873. During the summer of 1873, he was at home in charge of the farm; in the autumn, taught for some time in the Andes Collegiate Institution, at Andes, Deleware County, N. Y. He entered the Theological Seminary at Newburgh, N. Y., Jan. 15, 1874; in 1875 was licensed to preach by the first United Presbyterian Presbytery of New York. He preached during his vacations until 1876, when he left the seminary, and after a period in Pennsylvania, went, in March, to Kansas, and spent two years as missionary in Kansas, Nebraska, and Missouri. On May 11, 1878, an unaminous call was given him at Walton, Kan., which he accepted, and received ordination the following September. Installed pastor of the United Presbyterian Church at Walton in April, 1879, and has been very successful, his congregation increasing rapidly.

Mary-Esther Riddle⁴ (7), eldest daughter of John³ (7), was born at Clintonville, Penn., Oct. 18, 1844; was married Jan. 21, 1869, to Levi Williams, and died Oct. 11, 1872, leaving issue.

Charles-Milton Riddle⁴ (1), eldest son of John³ (7), was born at Clintonville, Penn., Feb. 14, 1846; married Feb. 28, 1872, to Emma-Florence Cross, and has issue *two* children, of whom hereafter; shoemaker by occupation; lives at Clintonville.

William-McCay Riddle[4] (8), second son of John[3] (7), was born at Clintonville, Penn., May 15, 1849; married Jan. 20, 1874, to Jane-Adaline Rosenburgh, and has *two* children; farmer.

Eliza-Ann Riddle[4] (2), second daughter of John[3] (7), was born in Clintonville, Penn, July 13, 1851; unmarried in 1880.

Isabella-Jane Riddle[4] (1), third daughter of John[3] (7), was born in Clintonville, Penn., July 31, 1854; was married July 31, 1879, to Robert S. Thompson.   •

FIFTH GENERATION.

Jennie-P. Riddle[5] (1), eldest daughter of Findlay[4] (1), was born Sept. 1, 1862.

Mary-P. Riddle[5] (8), second daughter of Findlay[3] (1), was born May 27, 1865.

William-E. Riddle[5] (9), eldest son of Findlay[3] (1), was born Feb. 13, 1867.

Rachel-B. Riddle[5] (2), third daughter of Findlay[4] (1), was born July 3, 1869.

Julia-D. Riddle[5] (3), fourth daughter of Findlay[3] (1), was born Sept. 26, 1871.

Mary-Belle Riddle[5] (9), a daughter of Nelson[3] (1), was born Aug. 8. 1875.

Susan-I. Riddle[5] (3), a daughter of Matthew[4] (6), was born Feb. 4, 1872.

Mary-E. Riddle[5] (10), second daughter of Matthew[4] (6), was born June 25, 1875.

Lotta Riddle[5] (1), a daughter of Charles[4] (1).   } At Clinton-
Bertha-Alice Riddle[5] (1), a daughter of Charles[4] (1). } ville, Penn.

Eva-Jane Riddle[5] (1), a daughter of William[4] (8). } At Clintonville,
Oliver-Herbert Riddle[5] (1), a son of William[4] (8). }   Penn.

RIDDELLS OF DENMAMORA, IRELAND.

[UNITED STATES BRANCH].

John Riddell[1] (1), parents unknown, emigrated from the County of Denmamora, Ireland, in the year 1832; his wife, Mary Simpson, and some of his children came with him. He was left without parents in Ireland, when a small boy, and entrusted to the care of his grandmother named Ban. He was the youngest son; a paper-maker by trade; had a brother Robert who was a surgeon in the army, and who died at New Orleans. Two brothers came to America, and were supposed to have lived in New York under assumed names.*

---

* There were also two maiden-sisters in Philadelphia, whose names have not reached me.

SECOND GENERATION.

Rev. Walter Riddle[2] (1), sometimes spelt *Riddell*, son of John[1] (1), was born in the County of Denmamora, Ireland; came to the United States with his father in 1832. His birth was in 1822. He married in 1844, to Jane Cadmus. He was a cabinet-maker by trade, but owing to poor health he gave attention to mercantile pursuits, which were successfully carried forward to the time of his death, which occurred on Dec. 31, 1859. Mr. Riddle was for many years earnestly devoted to the cause of Christ, laboring faithfully as an elder and local preacher in the Methodist Episcopal church; he refrained from joining the ministers' conference on account of ill health. He was also an ardent supporter of the cause of temperance, and early connected himself with the Washingtonians; he has delivered many very stirring addresses on the subject of temperance. All his spare hours were devoted to the advancement of the cause of Christ, the furtherance of the temperance movement, and the general good of his fellowmen. I copy some words from a letter written by his pastor soon after his death, which prove the high estimation in which he was held by those who were intimately acquainted with him : —

"His beautifully consistent Christian character and ardent piety, combined with a faith in the promises of God that never flagged, have, ever since I have known him, been a subject of my highest admiration. Such indeed was my feeling, that whenever I was with him I felt a stronger sense of security than anywhere else; his presence was an impulse to my religious life. Oh, that I could have been with him when his last word was spoken, and have caught the last look from his sainted eyes!"

Mr. Riddle passed away in the triumphs of the faith he had so long possessed, leaving the blessed influence of life's pious example as a consolation to his family far more precious than gold that perishes. He left a widow and *two* children, of whom hereafter. Mr. Riddle is said to have had two sisters and one brother, but all are now dead.

THIRD GENERATION.

Jennie Riddle[2] (1), a daughter of Walter[2] (1), was born in the year 1849, and married to Philip W. Hammond in 1875.

Walter-W. Riddle[2] (2), eldest son of Walter[2] (1), was born in the year 1851, and is unmarried. He is connected with the Boonton Iron Works, in Boonton, N. J. He says in a letter to me, "As for myself and family (that is mother and sister) I am not ashamed to lay claim to a character and reputation untarnished." His mother says of this son, "He is the soul of honor and truthfulness."

Willie Riddle[2] (1), second son of Walter[2] (1), was born in 1855, and some time ago passed away.

RIDDELLS OF BALLAYMEATH, IRELAND.

Hugh Riddell[2] (2), a son of Hugh[1] (1) and Mary (Wilson) Riddell, was baptized in the parish of Ballaymeath, County Londonderry, Ireland, Oct. 16, 1631; married May 5, 1658, to Margery Campbell, and had issue

* This family is closely connected with others whose history is given in this book, but the same Christian names occur so often that it is impossible to make connection in genealogy without more particulars than I have been able to find.

13

seven children, five sons and two daughters, of whom hereafter. The parents are supposed to have come from Scotland, and were probably descended from the Riddells of Roxburghshire, as Walter Riddell-Carre informed me of offshoots of that family who settled in Ireland at different times.*

Robert Riddell² (1), second son of Hugh¹ (1) and Mary his wife, was baptized at Ballaymeath, Ireland, May 22, 1633; married Sept. 12, 1658, to Mary Henderson, and had issue *eight* children, of whom hereafter.

Janet Riddell² (1), daughter of Hugh¹ (1) and Mary, his wife, was baptized at Ballaymeath, Ireland, April 4, 1635; and was married Aug. 16, 1657, to James Wilson.

James Riddell² (1), son of Hugh¹ (1) and Mary Wilson, was baptized May 10, 1637; married Dec. 4, 1658, to Elizabeth Maudit, and had issue *five* children (possibly others), four sons and a daughter, of whom hereafter. Mr. Riddell died Nov. 3, 1674.

Andrew Riddell² (1), son of Hugh¹ (1) and Mary Wilson, was baptized at Ballaymeath, Ireland, Aug. 2, 1639.

John Riddell² (1), son of Hugh¹ (1) and Mary Wilson, was baptized at Ballaymeath, Ireland, Nov. 14, 1641; married June 4, 1670(?), to Janet Gordon, and had issue *nine* children, six sons and three daughters, of whom hereafter. See "Riddells of Coleraine, Massachusetts," in this book. Mr. John Riddell died Jan. 3, 1737. I think Mr. Riddell must have married a second wife, as dates of births of children seem too late to be the issue of this union. Baptisms may not have been administered till children were some years of age.

Mary Riddell² (1), daughter of Hugh¹ (1) and Mary Wilson, was baptized at Ballaymeath, Ireland, Jan. 24, 1642, and was married May 10, 1659, to Alexander Wilson.

Gavin Riddell² (1), son of Hugh¹ (1) and Mary Wilson, was baptized at Ballaymeath, Ireland, Sept. 20, 1644.

THIRD GENERATION.

Hugh Riddell³ (3), eldest son of Hugh² (2) and Margery Campbell, was baptized at Ballaymeath, Ireland, May 2, 1659; married June 3, 1681, to Janet Patten.

Mary Riddell³ (2), eldest daughter of Hugh² (2) and Margery Campbell, was baptized at Ballaymeath, Ireland, June 15, 1661, and was married May 15, 1677, to Alexander Wilson.

Robert Riddell³ (2), second son of Hugh² (2) and Margery Campbell, was baptized at Ballaymeath, June 15, 1661, and died April 4, 1671.

Ralph Riddell³ (1), third son of Hugh² (2) and Margery Campbell, was baptized at Ballaymeath, Ireland, Aug. 1, 1663, and married Sept. 20, 1678, to Elizabeth Howell.

Janet Riddell³ (2), second daughter of Hugh² (2) and Margery Campbell, was baptized at Ballaymeath, Ireland, July 14, 1665, and was married Jan. 4, 1681, to James Gordon.

John Riddell³ (2), fourth son of Hugh² (2) and Margery Campbell,

---

* Evidently this family furnished the ancestors of the Riddells and Riddles of Coleraine, Mass., and of Bedford, N. H., the history of whom see in this book. The names are identical, but dates do not agree with births and ages as recorded in the American family. There may have been mistakes in copying from original records.

was baptized at Ballaymeath, Ireland, Sept. 3, 1667, and married Dec. 15, 1681, to Mary Cowan.

Andrew Riddell (2), fifth son of Hugh[2] (2) and Margery Campbell, was baptized at Ballaymeath, Ireland, May 20, 1669.

Robert Riddell[2] (3), eldest son of Robert[2] (2) and Mary Henderson, was baptized April 3, 1663; married Aug. 22, 1682, to Margaret Campbell.

Hugh Riddell[2] (4), second son of Robert[2] (1) and Mary, his wife, was baptized at Ballaymeath, Sept. 20, 1665, and married March 2, 1684, to Betsey Patten.

John Riddell[2] (3), third son of Robert[2] (1) and Mary Henderson, was baptized at Ballaymeath, Nov. 4, 1667; married Aug. 2, 1702, Betsey Pate.

Margaret Riddell[2] (1), fourth daughter of Robert[2] (1) and Mary Henderson, was baptized at Ballaymeath, June 23, 1669.

James Riddell[2] (2), fourth son of Robert[2] (1) and Mary Henderson, was baptized at Ballaymeath, May 4, 1671.

William Riddell[2] (1), fifth son of Robert[2] (1) and Mary Henderson, was baptized at Ballaymeath, Aug. 14, 1673, and married April 4, 1694, to Mary Campbell.

Mary Riddell[2] (3), second daughter of Robert[2] (1) and Mary Henderson, was baptized at Ballaymeath, Sept. 4, 1675, and was married June 10, 1691, to William Patterson.

Alexander Riddell[2] (1), sixth son of Robert[2] (1) and Mary Henderson, was baptized at Ballaymeath, Feb. 20, 1678; married May 16, 1696, to Katherine Henderson.

Elizabeth Riddell[2] (1), third daughter of Robert[2] (1) and Mary Henderson, was baptized at Ballaymeath, April 4, 1680.

Mary Riddell[2] (4), eldest daughter of James[2] (1) and Elizabeth Maudit, was baptized at Ballaymeath, Sept. 23, 1661; married Sept. 23, 1703, to Alexander Bell.

James Riddell[2] (3), eldest son of James[2] (1) and Elizabeth Maudit, was baptized at Ballaymeath, Jan. 16, 1663.

Robert Riddell[2] (5), second son of James[2] (1) and Elizabeth Maudit, was baptized at Ballaymeath, March 2, 1665.

John Riddell[2] (4), third son of James[2] (1) and Elizabeth Maudit, was baptized at Ballaymeath, April 21, 1667.

Elizabeth Riddell[2] (2), second daughter of James[2] (1) and Elizabeth Maudit, was baptized at Ballaymeath, Sept. 3, 1669.

William Riddell[2] (2), fourth son of James[2] (1) and Elizabeth Maudit, was baptized at Ballaymeath, Dec. 16, 1672.

John Riddell[2] (5), eldest son of John[2] (1) and Janet Gordon, was baptized at Ballaymeath, Oct. 18, 1686, and died Sept. 6, 1687.

Gavin[*] **Riddell**[2] (2), second son of John[2] (1) and Janet Gordon, was baptized at Ballaymeath, May 16, 1688, and presumably emigrated to America, where he became the head of a numerous family. See "Riddells of Bedford, New Hampshire."

---

[*] This name is common in Scotland and should be spelled *Gavin;* it came to the Riddells from the Hamilton family.

Mary Riddell³ (5), eldest daughter of John² (1) and Janet Gordon, was baptized at Ballaymeath, Aug. 2, 1690.

Hugh Riddell³ (5), third son of John² (1) and Janet Gordon, was baptized at Ballaymeath, Sept. 20, 1692, and is supposed to have settled in Londonderry, N. H. See "Riddells of Coleraine, Massachusetts."

James Riddell³ (4), fourth son of John² (1) and Janet Gordon, was baptized at Ballaymeath, Dec. 3, 1695, and married Nov. 18, 1726, to Elizabeth Douglass.

Robert Riddell³ (6), fifth son of John² (1) and Janet Gordon, was baptized at Ballaymeath, March 14, 1698, and was probably one of the *four* brothers who settled in New England about the year 1718. See "Riddells of Coleraine, Massachusetts."

John Riddell³ (5), sixth son of John² (1) and Janet Gordon, was baptized at Ballaymeath, Jan. 2, 1701, and presumably came to Londonderry, N. H., with his brothers in 1718. See "Riddells of Bedford, New Hampshire."

Janet Riddell³ (3), second daughter of John² (1) and Janet Gordon, was baptized at Ballaymeath, Sept. 25, 1703, and was married April 6, 1721, to Thomas Hamilton.

Margery Riddell³ (2), third daughter of John² (1) and Janet Gordon, was baptized at Ballaymeath, Dec. 6, 1707, and married May 20, 1722, to John Clark.

Samuel Riddell³ (1), youngest son of John² (1) and Janet Gordon, was baptized at Ballaymeath, Oct. 4, 1710, and died Dec. 20, 1713.*

RIDDLES OF BALLYMONY, IRELAND.

[PENNSYLVANIA BRANCH.]

Robert Riddle¹ (1), allied to many other branches of the family of Scotch-Irish birth, lived on a farm in Ballymony, not far from the River Bann, County Antrim, Ireland; came to Pennsylvania with his son in 1835, and settled at Allegheny City, where he and wife died in 1840. He had issue several children, of whom hereafter.

SECOND GENERATION.

James Riddell² (1), a son of Robert¹ (1), was born in Ballymony, County Antrim, Ireland, and settled in Virginia many years ago. No particulars.

Charles Riddell² (1), a son of Robert¹ (1), was born in Ballymony, County Antrim, Ireland; married Elizabeth, daughter of John Dinsmore, in 1820, and had issue *seven* children, of whom hereafter. He bought a farm at Brady's Bend, about sixty miles above Pittsburgh, Penn., to which city he had emigrated in 1835, and died there in 1844. After Mr. Riddell's death the family returned to Pittsburgh, where the mother probably died.

---

* There was a James Riddell, who married Katherine Scott, July 18, 1686; she died May 23, 1733. A Mrs. Mary, wife of James Riddell, son of Hugh and Mary Riddell, died Nov. 3, 1664. All recorded with the preceding, and without doubt of the same connection.

John Riddell[2] (1), a son of Robert[1] (1), was born in the town of Ballymony, County Antrim, Ireland; married and settled at Meath Park, County Londonderry, Ireland, where his *eight* children were born. He came to America between 1850 and 1855, and died at Pittsburgh, Penn., Aug. 25, 1854, in his sixty-fifth year. His wife predeceased him June 2, 1842, in Ireland. He was a farmer.

It is presumed there were other children of Robert[1] (1).

THIRD GENERATION.

William-Dinsmore Riddell[8] (1), eldest son of Charles[2] (1), was born in Ballymony, Ireland, April 11, 1823; married Margaret, youngest daughter of Rev. Robert Hutton, of Meadville, Penn., afterwards of the M. E. Church, Lebanon, Tenn., and had issue *three* daughters and *one* son. Soon after coming to America he engaged under Dr. J. L. Reed, then in charge of the Methodist Publishing-House, at Pittsburgh, Penn., and while there, in consequence of his letters falling into the hands of others of the same name, changed his surname from "Riddell" to "Riddle," and others of the family followed suit. In 1854, in company with the Wells brothers of Wellsville, Penn., he started a whip-factory at Pittsburgh, where he died in 1864. His family removed to Tennessee a few years after, and his wife died at Lebanon in 1880.

Matilda Riddell[8] (1), eldest daughter of Charles[2] (1), was born in Ballymony, Ireland, July 15, 1825; was married to James Small of Bloomington, Ind., in 1852.

Samuel Riddell[8] (1), second son of Charles[2] (1), was born in Ballymony, Ireland, June 3, 1827; married Jennie, daughter of William Boyd,* a prominent merchant of Philadelphia, in the summer of 1854, and had issue *five* children, of whom hereafter. He early became a compositor on the *Pittsburgh Daily Gazette*, and rose by degrees to business manager, editor, and part owner of that paper. He was ten years postmaster of Allegheny City, having received his commission from President Lincoln. He was a member of the Presbyterian church, and when the war of the Rebellion broke out had a large class of young men in the Sabbath-school. When President Lincoln called for three-months' men, Mr. Riddell felt it his duty to respond, and immediately telegraphed to Washington to know if he might leave his assistant in the post-office, and go into the army, provided he could raise a company; the answer was, "Make ready and come." In less than a week he was on his way to the front, — his class among the first to follow him, — and went out with Knap's Battalion, captain of Company C. The sudden change from office duties to active field service brought on a disease that followed him ever after, hastening his death, which terminated several years of intense suffering, endured in the spirit of a true martyr, in 1877, in Charleston, S. C. During the period of his political career he was instrumental in the erection of the public building in Allegheny, and in the improvement of the park. Mr. Riddell was six feet in height, broad-shouldered, symmetrical of form; had good complexion, brown hair and eyes, and full, well-dressed beard. Two months after the death of Mr. Riddell his widow moved to Hoddonsfield,

---

* William Boyd was the youngest of a large family in Antrim, Ireland, related to the Riddells there. He was shipwrecked at the age of eighteen, when on his way to America, and washed ashore at Newfoundland. He settled in Philadelphia; possessed executive ability, firm religious principles, and soon took his place among the successful merchants of Philadelphia.

N. J., where she has built a pretty home. To her the promise, "I will establish the border of the widow," has been fully verified, and her children are ornaments in society.

Mary Riddell[5] (1), second daughter of Charles[2] (1), was born Jan. 23, 1829, and died at Pittsburgh, Penn., in June, 1872; unmarried.

Jane Riddell[5] (1), third daughter of Charles[2] (1), was born Nov. 12, 1830, and is now living in Allegheny City, Penn.

Hugh Riddell[5] (1), third son of Charles[2] (1), was born in Ballymony, Ireland, May 1, 1832, and died at the age of seven, in Pennsylvania.

Robert Riddle[5] (2), youngest son of Charles[2] (1), was born in Ballymony, Ireland, Feb. 23, 1834; came to America with his parents in 1835, and has been twice married: first, to Hannah, daughter of Francis McKinley, of Bloomington, Ind. (she and *three* children died of consumption); secondly, Elizabeth, daughter of William K. McAlister, of Nashville, Tenn., in 1872, by whom *two* children. He sold his interest in the firm of A. & D. H. Chambers & Co., glass manufacturers, Pittsburgh, Penn., in 1874, and removed to Tennessee, where, in the city of Nashville, he now carries on a sash, door, and blind factory. He is said to be six feet and two inches in height, and fine looking.

Martha Riddell[3] (1), eldest daughter of John[2] (1), was born in Ireland, Londonderry County, about 1809; was married to Hugh Cunningham, and has a son Charles, supposed to be in California. Martha and husband reside at Glengadd, Bendoorah, County Antrim, Ireland.

Thomas Riddell[3] (1), eldest son of John[2] (1), was born in Ireland, about 1810–11, and died in New York city, in 1879. He was twice married, and had *three* children, all of whom died in infancy. His last wife (whose maiden-name was Sarah Boden) survives, and lives in the United Presbyterian Home, in New York city.

Charles Riddell[3] (2), second son of John[2] (1), came to Philadelphia, and died there, aged eighteen; was a marble-cutter.

William-John Riddell[3] (2), third son of John[2] (1), was born at Meath Park, County Londonderry, Ireland; came to this country in 1848; married Agnes Fulton, in Allegheny City, Penn., April 2, 1850, and had *seven* children, of whom hereafter. He was employed as gardener in Pittsburgh, Penn., for five years, then removed to Ripley, Brown County, O., where he followed the same business; returned to Pittsburgh in 1866, where he now resides.

Holland Riddle[3] (1), fourth son of John[2] (1), was born at Meath Park, Londonderry County, Ireland, Dec. 2, 1820; came to America in 1848; married Nov. 11, 1850, in Lawrenceville, Allegheny County, Penn., Hester-Ann Reed; Rev. Nathaniel West, of the Presbyterian Church, performing the ceremony at her residence. He was first employed as clerk at Edward Healzelton's wholesale grocery in the "Diamond," Pittsburgh, Penn., where he remained one year; next, one year in the same capacity for Waterman & Clouse, on Liberty Street. He subsequently engaged in business for himself, and dealt in produce and game for five years, when the partnership of Riddle, Werts & Co. was formed and continued two years. After the dissolution of this firm he purchased stock and buildings of John D. McGill & Son, and carried on the wholesale grocery and produce business under his own name until 1871, when, having built a handsome four-story stone-front on the site of the old buildings, he admitted his son, then a young man, who had been with him many years, under the style of H. Riddle, Son & Co. He died of consumption Oct. 20, 1872, leaving a widow and several children, of whom hereafter. He was for many years a member of the Lawrenceville Presbyterian Church of Pittsburgh, Penn., and also treasurer of the society for a number of years, being such at the time of his decease. Place of residence was Lawrenceville, on the Greensburg Pike, which is now the 15th ward, and Pennsylvania Avenue, Pittsburgh, Penn.

Margaret-Jane Riddell' (1), second daughter of John² (1), was born in Ireland, and came to America when about twenty years of age. She was married to William Johnston, at Pittsburgh, Penn., Oct. 3, 1859, and has *two* daughters, one of whom is married. Mr. Johnston is connected with the O'Hara Glass Works at Pittsburgh.

Robert Riddell' (3), fifth son of John² (1), was born in County Londonderry, Ireland, and came to America in company with Margaret, and died from the effects of injuries received by a boiler-explosion in Wallace's Marble Works, Pittsburgh, Penn., Oct. 2, 1860. He was a marble-worker by occupation.

Mary-Ann Riddell' (2), third daughter of John² (1), was born in County Londonderry, Ireland, and came to America in company with Robert and Margaret. She became the wife of William J. Hammond, of Pittsburgh, Penn., in 1860, and has *four* sons. Residence, Bellevue Borough, on the P., Ft. W. & C. Railway, where they have lived since 1870. Mr. Hammond is an iron-dealer at Pittsburgh.

FOURTH GENERATION.

Mary Riddle' (3), a daughter of William³ (1), was born in Pennsylvania, and became the wife of Mr. Jacobs, now employed in the United States Patent Office.

Maggie Riddle' (2), a daughter of William³ (1), became the wife of Robert Chester, lawyer, of Jackson, Tenn., grandson of Col. Robert Chester, of Jonesboro', now of Jackson, Tenn.

Bertie Riddle' (1), a daughter of William³ (1), was born in Pennsylvania (probably at Pittsburgh), and is single.

William Riddle' (3), only son of William³ (1), born in Pennsylvania, now supposed to be in Tennessee; single.

Elizabeth-Dinsmore Riddell' (1), eldest daughter of Samuel³ (1), was born at Allegheny, Penn., in February, 1857.

Frances-Boyd Riddell' (1), second daughter of Samuel³ (1), was born at Allegheny, Penn., in April, 1861.

Charles Riddell' (3), eldest son of Samuel³ (1), was born at Allegheny, Penn., in July, 1864.

Augustus-H. Riddell' (1), second son of Samuel³ (1), was born at Allegheny, Penn., in June, 1870.

Samuel-H. Riddell' (2), youngest son of Samuel³ (1), was born at Allegheny, Penn., in January, 1872, and with his brothers and sisters lives at Haddonsfield, N. J.

Robert Riddle' (4), eldest son of Robert³ (2), was born at Pittsburgh, Penn., and died young, of consumption.

Francis Riddle' (1), second son of Robert³ (2), was born at Pittsburgh, Penn., and died young, of consumption.

Hannah Riddle[4] (1), eldest daughter of Robert[3] (2), was born at Pittsburgh, Penn., and died young, of consumption.

William-King Riddle[4] (4), a son of Robert[3] (2) and his second wife, is now living at Nashville, Tenn.

Elizabeth Riddle[4] (2), youngest daughter of Robert[3] (2), is now living at Nashville, Tenn.

Mary-Jane Riddle[4] (4), eldest daughter of William[3] (2), was born at Pittsburgh, Penn., Nov. 25, 1852; single.

Thomas-Holland Riddle[4] (2), eldest son of William[3] (2), was born at Pittsburgh, Penn., March 2, 1855; now employed in the iron-yard of W. J. Hammond, Esq.; single.

William-Lewis Riddle[4] (5), second son of William[3] (2), was born at Ripley, O., July 29, 1860; engraver on glass.

Samuel Riddle[4] (3), third son of William[3] (2), was born at Ripley, O., Sept. 8, 1862.

Charles Riddle[4] (4), fourth son of William[3] (2), was born at Ripley, O., Sept. 25, 1865; clerk A. V. R. R. freight-office, Pittsburgh, Penn.

Lilly-May Riddle[4] (1), eldest daughter of William[3] (2), was born at Pittsburgh, Penn., Dec. 6, 1867.

Blanche Riddle[4] (1), second daughter of William[3] (2), was born at Pittsburgh, Penn., Oct. 4, 1870.

Charles-Easton Riddle[4] (5), eldest son of Holland[3] (1), was born at Pittsburgh, Penn., Jan. 25, 1852; was in business with his father until the time of his death in 1872, and appointed administrator of the estate after his decease. He and his mother carried on the same business under same firm-name until 1875, when it was closed up; since that time has been clerk in various firms in one branch or other of iron-manufacturing business, being at present bookkeeper for the Iron City Tool Works (limited); unmarried.

Lilly-May Riddle[4] (2), eldest daughter of Holland[3] (1), was born at Pittsburgh, Penn., May 2, 1855, and died of scarlet fever, May 28, 1864.

William-Lewis Riddle[4] (6), second son of Holland[3] (1), was born at Pittsburgh, Penn., Oct. 4, 1857; died Feb. 22, 1858.

Bertha Riddle[4] (2), second daughter of Holland[3] (1), was born at Pittsburgh, Penn., July 8, 1859; was married Sept. 3, 1877, to Lloyd G. Brown, of Cincinnati, O., now a physician practising in Huntington, W. Va. One child.

Samuel Riddle[4] (4), third son of Holland[3] (1), was born at Pittsburgh, Penn., March 20, 1862; died June 24, 1862.

Holland-Reed Riddle[4] (2), fourth son of Holland[3] (1), was born at Pittsburgh, Penn., Nov. 23, 1863; removed to Kansas and engaged in farming for his grandmother (on his mother's side) in September, 1880. Address, Paola, Miami County, Kan.

Edgar-Adams Riddle[4] (1), fifth son of Holland[3] (1), was born at Pittsburgh, Penn., March 25, 1867; went West with his brother Holland, but returned to Pittsburgh the following year, and engaged at Union Iron Mills. Has since visited the West, but now (1884) in his native city.

Dinsmore-Lea Riddle[4] (1), youngest son of Holland[3] (1), was born at Pittsburgh, Penn., Jan. 21, 1871, and died April 6, 1872.

RIDDELLS OF GLANISH, IRELAND.

[AMERICAN BRANCH].

Andrew Riddell[1] (1), descended from Scottish ancestors (parents' names not known), early settled in Ulster, in the north of Ireland, married in the County of Monaghan,* and reared a numerous family, several of whom came to the United States and Canada. He and his ancestors spelled their names *Riddell.*

SECOND GENERATION.

John Riddle[2] (1), a son of Andrew[1] (1), was born in the County of Monaghan, town of Glanish, Ireland; married Susan Henderson, daughter of John Henderson, who was a titled land-owner in Ireland, of Scottish descent, and came to the United States in 1816, with several of his children, of whom there were *thirteen.* He died in Philadelphia, Penn., in 1827; his widow died in Allegheny City, in 1844.

Hugh Riddle[2] (1), a son of Andrew[1] (1), was born in the town of Glanish, County of Monaghan, Ireland, and came to Canada, British North America, where it is presumed he lived and died. No particulars.

Joseph Riddle[2] (1), a son of Andrew[1] (1), was born in the township of Glanish, County Monaghan, Ireland, and came to Canada, British North America, where he is supposed to have reared a family and died.

THIRD GENERATION.

William Riddle[3] (1), eldest son of John[2] (1), was born in Glanish, County Monaghan, Ireland; came to the United States with his father's family in 1816, and died at Pittsburgh, Penn., unmarried, when young.

James Riddle[3] (1), second son of John[2] (1), was born in the town of Glanish, County Monaghan, Ireland; came to the United States with his parents in 1816, and died unmarried, when quite old.

Andrew Riddle[3] (2), third son of John[2] (1), was born in Glanish, County Monaghan, Ireland; came to America with his parents in 1816, and was killed in the war of 1812, in the service of the United States.

Elizabeth Riddle[3] (1), eldest daughter of John[2] (1), was born in Glanish, County Monaghan, Ireland; came to the United States with her parents, and died when a child.

Ann Riddle[3] (1), second daughter of John[2] (1), was born in Glanish, County Monaghan, Ireland; died in infancy.

Maxwell Riddle[3] (1), fourth son of John[2] (1), was born in Glanish, County Monaghan, Ireland; married to Ann Nesbit, daughter of George and Isabella Nesbit, of Scotch descent, of Sligo, Ireland, and by her had issue *six* children. He married secondly, to Jane Riddle (I think she was his cousin), by whom he had issue *four* children. He came to the United States in 1831, and settled near Byesville, Guernsey County, O., where he died Jan. 11, 1869; his widow Nov. 20, 1873.

---

* This branch of the Riddell family is descended from Scottish, ancestors who received a grant of four townlands, named Cornasoo, Glanish, Annamacneal, and Mullacrank, County Monaghan, under Cromwell, and are all connected with other families named in this book that were from Monaghan. But few kept a register, and the degree of relationships is not made out; possibly some venerable member may, from reading this book, replace the missing link in the family chain. This branch spell the surname *Riddell* in Ireland. Some have changed to *Riddle* in the United States.

Elizabeth Riddle[3] (2), third daughter of John[2] (1), was born in Glanish, County Monaghan, Ireland; was married to James Gordon, of Philadelphia, and died of old age, at Pittsburgh, Penn., in July, 1873.

Isaac Riddle[3] (1), fifth son of John[2] (1), was born in the town of Glanish (or Glenish), County Monaghan, Ireland, and died in Pittsburgh, Penn., a young man.

John Riddle[3] (2), sixth son of John[2] (1), was born in Glanish, County Monaghan, Ireland, and settled in Pittsburgh, Penn., where he married Margaret Bell. He had issue *two* children, of whom hereafter; deceased.

Mary Riddle[3] (1), fourth daughter of John[2] (1), was born in Glanish, County Monaghan, Ireland; came to America with her parents in 1816, and was married to Henry Warner, of Pittsburgh, Penn.; died in 1876.

Hugh Riddle[3] (2), seventh son of John[2] (1), was born in Glanish, County Monaghan, Ireland; came to America in 1816, and for a few years lived with his parents in New York city; subsequently lived in Philadelphia till his father's death in 1827, when he went with his mother and the other children to Pittsburgh; there he married, Oct. 10, 1833, Miss Eliza Thomburgh, of Clinton, Penn., by whom he had *six* children, of whom hereafter. He died in 1868; his widow died in 1878.

Ann Riddle[3] (2), fifth daughter of John[2] (1), was born in Glanish, County Monaghan, Ireland; died in infancy.

FOURTH GENERATION.

James Riddle[4] (2), eldest son of Maxwell[3] (1), was born in County Monaghan, Ireland, and died there in infancy.

John Riddle[4] (3), second son of Maxwell[3] (1), was born in County Monaghan, Ireland, and died at the age of 11 years, in Allegheny County, Penn.

Hugh Riddle[4] (3), third son of Maxwell[3] (1), was born in County Monaghan, Ireland; came to America in 1832, and died in Allegheny County, Penn.

Isabella Riddle[4] (1), eldest daughter of Maxwell[3] (1), was born in County Monaghan, Ireland; came to the United States with her father in 1832; was married to Hugh Riddle, son of Robert and Jane Riddle, and grandson of Hugh Riddle, who lived in Ireland, or Scotland. (See " Riddells of Robinson Run.") Mrs. Riddle is the oldest member of the family now living; she resides at Remington, Allegheny County, Penn., and has one daughter, of whom hereafter. Mrs. Riddle has provided much valuable information for this book.

Susan Riddle[4] (1), second daughter of Maxwell[3] (1), was born in County Monaghan, Ireland; came to the United States with her father in 1832; was married to —— Maxwell, and is now with her sister, Isabella, before mentioned.

George-N. Riddle[4] (1), fourth son of Maxwell[3] (1), was born in County Monaghan, Ireland, in 1828; came to the United States in 1832; removed from Allegheny County, Penn., to Guernsey County, O., in 1855, and was married to Rachel Wilson, of said County, in 1857. He has had issue *ten* children, of whom hereafter. Mr. Riddle resides on a farm at Byesville, O.

John Riddle[4] (4), fifth son of Maxwell[3] (1), was born in Allegheny County, Penn., and died young.

Maxwell Riddle[4] (2), sixth son of Maxwell[3] (1), was born in Allegheny County, Penn., and died in youth.

Sarah Riddle[4] (1), third daughter of Maxwell[3] (1), was born in Allegheny County, Penn.; was married to Martin Hickle, of Dyson, Point Pleasant, O., and died Aug. 5, 1878, leaving children.

Anne Riddle[4] (1), fourth daughter of Maxwell[3] (1), was born in Allegheny County, Penn.; was married to John Bradshaw, of County Monaghan, Ireland, and has issue.

Susan Riddle[4] (2). ⎫ Daughters of John[3] (2).
Jane Riddle[4] (1). ⎭

Mary-Ann Riddle[4] (2), eldest daughter of Hugh[3] (2), was born in Allegheny, Penn., Aug. 1, 1834; was married to Charles Merts, of Allegheny, Oct. 1, 1855, and is now (1879) living at Ravenna, O.; she has issue.

John-Henderson Riddle[4] (5), eldest son of Hugh[3] (2), was born in Allegheny, Penn., Aug. 29, 1836; married March 26, 1862, to Nancy Mattingly, and resides in Ravenna, O.; he has issue *five* children, of whom hereafter; his wife was from Covington, Ky.

Henry-Warner Riddle[4] (1), second son of Hugh[3] (2), was born in Allegheny, Penn., Feb. 8, 1838; married Jan. 22, 1866, to Emily H. Robinson, of Ravenna, O., and is engaged extensively in manufacturing fine carriages of every description, at Ravenna, O. He has *three* children, of whom hereafter.

Susanna Riddle[4] (1), second daughter of Hugh[3] (2), was born in Allegheny, Penn., Sept. 25, 1841; was married Dec. 17, 1863, to Ewal Pitman, and lives at Ravenna, O. She has issue.

James-Thornburg Riddle[4] (3), third son of Hugh[3] (2), was born in Allegheny, Penn., March 14, 1843; married Nov. 24, 1864, to Emily Welton, and resides at Ravenna, O. He has *three* children, of whom hereafter.

Thomas-J. Riddle[4] (1), fourth son of Hugh[3] (2), was born in Allegheny, Penn., June 5, 1845; married Nov. 29, 1877, to Helen Gowey, of Ravenna, O.

FIFTH GENERATION.

Susan-N. Riddle[5] (3), eldest daughter of George[4] (1), was born in Guernsey County, O., March 22, 1859; died Aug. 13, 1859.

Thomas-A. Riddle[5] (2), twin son of George[4] (1), was born in Guernsey County, O., July 27, 1860; died Oct. 4, 1860.

Maxwell-A. Riddle[5] (3), twin to Thomas[5] (2), was born in Guernsey County, O., July 27, 1860; is living at home.

Henry-H. Riddle[5] (2), third son of George[4] (1), was born in Guernsey County, O., Sept. 7, 1861; died Sept. 30, 1861.

Lincoln-O. Riddle[5] (1), fourth son of George[4] (1), was born in Guernsey County, O., Oct. 18, 1862, and lives at home.

George Riddle[5] (2), fifth son of George[4] (1), was born in Guernsey County, O., Aug. 21, 1864; died Sept. 6, 1864.

Rachel Riddle[5] (1), second daughter of George[4] (1), was born in Guernsey County, O., Aug. 21, 1864; died Sept. 6, 1864.

Ellsworth Riddle[5] (1), sixth son of George[4] (1), was born in Guernsey County, O., Oct. 21, 1865; lives at home.

Elizabeth-J. Riddle[5] (1), third daughter of George[4] (1), was born in Guernsey County, O., Nov. 10, 1866; lives at home.

Tracy-C. Riddle[5] (1), youngest child of George[4] (1), was born in Guernsey County, O., April 12, 1868; died Oct. 13, 1878.

Charles-R. Riddle⁵ (1), eldest son of John⁴ (5), was born in Covington, Ky., Nov. 18, 1864.

Lida-B. Riddle⁵ (1), eldest daughter of John⁴ (5), was born in Covington, Ky., June 22, 1868.

Etta-J. Riddle⁵ (1), second daughter of John⁴ (5), was born in Covington, Ky., Sept. 26, 1870.

Mary-E. Riddle⁵ (3), third daughter of John⁴ (5), was born in Covington, Ky., Nov. 21, 1872.

Lizzie Riddle⁵ (1), fourth daughter of John⁴ (5), was born in Covington, Ky., April 23, 1874.

Bessie-Eleanor Riddle⁵ (1), eldest daughter of Henry⁴ (1), was born in Ravenna, O., April 3, 1867.

Maxwell-Freeman Riddle⁵ (4), eldest son of Henry⁴ (1), was born in Ravenna, O., Nov. 8, 1870.

Amy-Howard Riddle⁵ (1), second daughter of Henry⁴ (1), was born in Ravenna, O., Dec. 12, 1875.

Mary-Thornburg Riddle⁵ (4), eldest daughter of James⁴ (3), was born in Ravenna, O., March 8, 1868; died in infancy.

Charles-Welton Riddle⁵ (2), eldest son of James⁴ (3), was born in Ravenna, O., July 26, 1871.

Harry-H. Riddle⁵ (1), second son of James⁴ (3), was born in Ravenna, O., Feb. 8, 1874.

RIDDELLS OF CORNASOO, IRELAND.

[PENNSYLVANIA BRANCH.]

John Riddell[1] (1), descended from Scottish ancestors who settled in Ireland under Cromwell, resided at Cornasoo, or Mullacrank, County Monaghan, Ireland; was land-owner; had several sons and daughters; wife's name unknown. He was closely related to *Andrew*, whose name stands at the head of the preceding pedigree, but in what degree is not known.

SECOND GENERATION.

Hugh Riddell[2] (1), son of John[1] (1), was born in Glanish, County Monaghan, Ireland; married to Jane C. Rodgers, and had issue *six or seven* children, of whom hereafter.

Andrew Riddell[2] (1), a son of John[1] (1), was born in Glanish, County Monaghan, Ireland, and had issue several children, of whom hereafter ;* he lived in Glanish.

Robert Riddell[2] (1), a son of John[1] (1), was born in Glanish, County Monaghan, Ireland, and had issue *two* sons, and perhaps daughters, of whom hereafter; he lived at Glanish.

---

* ANDREW RIDDELL, uncle of Rev. John Riddell, D. D., of Robinson's Run, Penn., had a daughter who became the wife of a Mr. Bridge, whose daughter was married to John Riddell, of Annamacneal.

THIRD GENERATION.

Robert Riddell[3] (2), a son of Hugh[2] (1), was born in Glanish, County Monaghan, Ireland; married Miss Jane Graham; emigrated to the United States, and settled in Allegheny County, Penn.; had issue *nine* children, of whom hereafter. He and his wife died in the family of his son Hugh, whose wife was Isabella Riddle; see preceding pedigree.

Rev. John Riddell[3] (2), D. D., a son of Hugh[2] (1), was born in Cornasoo, County Monaghan, Ireland, in the year 1758; married for his first wife Miss Margaret Arnold, a native of Ireland, by whom he had issue *five* children. His first wife died about eleven years after their arrival in the United States. His second wife was a Mrs. Gabby, originally a Miss Mitchell, of Washington County, Penn., by whom he had issue *five* children, of whom (with the first family) hereafter. It is not certainly known in what year Mr. Riddell commenced his college-course; his diploma, however, shows that he graduated at the University of Glasgow, on the 10th of April, 1782; and from a comparison of dates it would seem that as soon as he had finished his college-course he commenced and prosecuted to a successful issue the study of theology. This he did under the supervision and instruction of the celebrated John Brown, of Haddington. He was licensed to preach on the 14th of June, 1788; and on the 18th of November of the same year he was installed pastor of the congregation in Donaghloney, County Down. In this connection he remained till the spring of 1794, when he demitted his charge and came to the United States. In August of the same year he was installed at Robinson's Run, as pastor of the united congregations of Robinson's Run and Union, in the vicinity of Pittsburgh, Penn. As these congregations rapidly increased under his ministry, he was, in a few years, released from the charge at Union and settled, agreeably to his own preference, and to the entire satisfaction of the people, for the whole of his time at Robinson's Run. The whole period of his ministry in this congregation was thirty-five years. His ministerial career extended through a period of forty-one years. When he came to the United States he connected himself with the Associate Reformed Church. He was a close student, and prepared for the pulpit with great care; he was an excellent pastor and instructive teacher. That he was not and is not more extensively known to the Christian world may be owing to the fact that none of the productions of his pen were ever published. The last public business to which he attended was the performance of the marriage ceremony. He died Sept. 4, 1829, in the seventy-second year of his age. His remains on the day after his decease were followed to the grave by a very large number of people, many of whom felt that they had sustained a loss that could not easily be made up, and amongst whom the general impression was, that a star of no mean lustre had disappeared from the firmament of the moral and ecclesiastical world.

Dr. Riddell was a man of medium size; his visage was rather long and sharp; his eyes were dark and piercing; his lips thin and slightly compressed. He became naturalized soon after coming to the United States, and ever after manifested a sober but steady interest in the welfare of his adopted country.

Thomas Riddell[3] (1), youngest son of Hugh[2] (1), was born in Glanish, County Monaghan, Ireland; married —— Sloan, and settled on land in Mullacrank, Ballabay, which came to him through the Rodgers family, of whom his mother was a member. He had *five* daughters and *four* sons, of whom hereafter.

Sarah Riddell³ (1), a daughter of Hugh² (1), was born in Monaghan, Ireland, and was married to Joseph Donaldson.

Jane Riddell³ (1), a daughter of ·Hugh² (1), was born in Monaghan, Ireland, and was married to Joseph Donaldson (?).

Eliza Riddell³ (1), a daughter of Hugh² (1), was born in Monaghan, Ireland, and was married to a Mr. Armstrong.

Joseph Riddell³ (1), a son of Andrew² (1), was born in Monaghan, Ireland; no other information.

Margaret Riddell³ (1), a daughter of Andrew² (1), was born in Monaghan, Ireland; was married to William Gipson.

Sarah Riddell³ (2), a daughter of Andrew² (1), was born in Monaghan, Ireland, and was married to a Mr. Craigh.

James Riddell³ (1), a son of Robert² (1), was born in the County Monaghan, Ireland, and died in America, issueless.

Dr. John Riddell³ (3), a son of Robert² (1), was born in the County Monaghan, Ireland, and died in America, issueless.

FOURTH GENERATION.

Hugh Riddell⁴ (2), eldest son of Robert³ (2), was born in the County Monaghan; emigrated to the United States with his father's family; married Isabella Riddell (or Riddle), daughter of Maxwell Riddle (see "Riddells of Glanish, Ireland"), and had issue, of whom hereafter. He resided in the town of Remington, Allegheny County, Penn., and cared for his parents in old age; farmer.

Margaret Riddell⁴ (2), eldest daughter of Robert³ (2), was born (presumably) in County Monaghan, Ireland, and died in Pennsylvania.

Sarah Riddell⁴ (3), second daughter of Robert³ (2), was born in Ireland (?); came to Pennsylvania with her parents in 1831; was married to John Logan, and died at Greencastle, Ia., leaving issue there.

Jane Riddle⁴ (2), third daughter of Robert³ (2), born in the County Monaghan, Ireland, was married to Maxwell Riddle, of Byesville, O., and had issue; died Nov. 30, 1873; see "Riddells of Glanish, Ireland."

Esther Riddle⁴ (1), fifth daughter of Robert³ (2).

Eliza Riddle⁴ (1), sixth daughter of Robert³ (2), was married to William McClelland, and died in Allegheny County, Penn.

Rachel Riddle⁴ (1), seventh daughter of Robert³ (2).

John Riddle⁴ (4), a son of Robert³ (2).

Robert Riddle⁴ (3), a son of Robert³ (2).

Hugh Riddell⁴ (3), eldest son of Rev. John³ (2), was born in Pittsburgh, or Robinson's Run, Allegheny County, Penn.

John Riddell⁴ (5), a son of Rev. John³ (2), was born in Washington or Allegheny County, Penn., about the year 1797; was educated at Jefferson College; studied law with Mr. Foster, of Greenburg, Westmoreland County, Penn., and was admitted to the bar. He married, about

---

* The ancestors of this family are said to have come to Ireland with Cromwell, and received grants of four townlands, namely, Cornasoo, Glanish, Annamacneal, and Mullacrank. One was William. All were farmers and linen manufacturers.

1826, Miss Elizabeth Speer, second daughter of Rev. William Speer, D. D.; settled at Meadville, Penn., but removed about 1828 to Erie in the same State. He was a successful and distinguished lawyer; was in the State Legislature; noted for eloquence and power as an advocate; espoused ardently the anti-masonic side in the bitter controversies of the period from 1830 to 1836; died of pulmonary disease, in Canonsburg, Washington County, Penn., July 4, 1837, having had issue *four* sons and *one* daughter, born between 1829 and 1836, of whom hereafter.

Nancy Riddell[4] (1), eldest daughter of Rev. John[3] (2).

Jane Riddell[4] (3), second daughter of Rev. John[3] (2), was born in Allegheny County, Penn.; was married to —— Sturgeon, and has issue.

Margaret-Ann Riddell[4] (3), third daughter of Rev. John[3] (2), was born in Pennsylvania; was married to John M. Allen, in 1837; had issue, and died Feb. 28, 1856.

Dr. George Riddell[4] (1), third son of Rev. John[3] (2), was born in Pennsylvania; married, and has a family of children;[*] is now a practising physician at Indianapolis, Ind.; considered a skilful practitioner, and has a large patronage.

Robert Riddell[4] (4), fourth son of Rev. John[3] (2), was born in Pennsylvania, and is now living at Knoxville, Jefferson County, O.; he does not reply to my letters of inquiry.

Joseph Riddell[4] (2), fifth son of Rev. John[3] (2), was born in Pennsylvania; no other information.

Eliza Riddell[4] (2), fourth daughter of Rev. John[3] (2), was born in Pennsylvania; no record of marriage.

Mary Riddell[4] (1), fifth daughter of Rev. John[3] (2), was born in Pennsylvania, and was married to —— Berry; resides in Steubenville, O.

James Riddell[4] (1), a son of Thomas[3] (1), was born in Glanish, County Monaghan, Ireland; married —— Riddell, a daughter of John, and has *seven* children, of whom hereafter. Mr. Riddell lives on a large farm in the township of Mullacrank, called a "freehold," which has come down from his remote ancestors.

William Riddell[4] (1), a son of Thomas[3] (1), was born in the County Monaghan, and is now in Victoria, Australia.

—— Riddell[4] (0), eldest daughter of Thomas[3] (1), was born in County Monaghan, Ireland; married to P. H. McPherson, and now resides in Mendota, Ill.

Elizabeth Riddell[4] (1), second daughter of Thomas[3] (1), was born in County Monaghan, Ireland; was married to a Mr. Killgour, and is now living in wealth at Greymouth, New Zealand, Australia.

Mary-Ann Riddell[4] (2), third daughter of Thomas[3] (1), was born in County Monaghan, Ireland; married —— Wooland, and is now living at Gipsland, Victoria, Australia.

Jane Riddell[4] (4), fourth daughter of Thomas[3] (1), born in County Monaghan, Ireland, was married to a Mr. White, and is now in Australia.

FIFTH GENERATION.

Annie-Nesbit Riddell[5] (1), only daughter of Hugh[4] (2) and his wife,

---

[*] Dr. J. C. RIDDELL, a son of Dr. Geo. W. Riddell, of Indianapolis, Ind., and grandson of Rev. John Riddell, D. D., formerly of Robinson's Run, Penn., has an "Opium Curative Institute" at Kansas City, Mo. I cannot prevail upon this family to provide their history or record.

Isabella, who was a daughter of Maxwell Riddle, is a school-teacher, and lives with her parents at Allegheny County, Penn.; she was born June 26, 1854.

John-W. Riddell[6] (6), eldest son of John[4] (5), was born at Erie, Penn., about 1829. He took a partial course at Jefferson College, Penn.; was appointed midshipman in the U. S. navy, about 1847, and served several years, when he resigned. Studied law at Pittsburgh, Penn., with H. S. Magran, Esq., and was there admitted to the bar, about 1854. Was several years Assistant District Attorney of Allegheny County, Penn. Resided several years in Pittsburgh, but a few years ago, 1878, went to Gilroy, Cal., where, having retired from the practice of his profession, he now (1884) resides. Wife's name not known; has one daughter.

Speer Riddell[6] (1), second son of John[4] (5), was born at Erie, Penn., about 1830; received partial classical education at private academies; was a bank-clerk with General Larimer (?), of Pittsburgh, Penn., from 1848 to 1853; in the latter year he moved to California, and has been bank-teller in San Francisco more than twenty-five years; has recently resigned his position, and is now the president of the San Bernardino Borax Mining Company. Has never married. Lives in San Francisco.

James Riddell[6] (2), third son of John[4] (5), was born at Erie, Penn., and is a druggist by profession, well acquainted with his business; he was at one time member of the large drug-importing firm of Crane & Brigham, of San Francisco. He is a man of energetic character and popular traits. Has retired in competent circumstances, and is living in the country near Gilroy, Cal., which State has been his place of residence since 1857; unmarried.

DeWitt-C. Riddell[6] (1), fourth son of John[4] (5), removed at an early age from Erie, Penn., and resided for a few years with the family of his uncle, Rev. O. A. Patterson, in New Lisbon, O.; afterwards removed to Pittsburgh, Penn., and entered the service of Alexander James, tea-merchant. In 1855, he went to California, and has been in the employ of banking and express companies till 1881, when he engaged in fruit-culture near Gilroy, on a beautiful farm he has named " Glen-Riddell," for a family seat in Scotland; see "Riddells of Glen-Riddell," in this book. Mr. Riddell has a taste for farm life and sports of the field; enjoys camping-out and hunting adventures, and has roamed over mountain and plain. He spent many years in the mining regions of California and Nevada, when connected with Wells & Fargo's Express Company. Is married, and has *two* children, of whom hereafter.

Harriet-E. Riddell[6] (1), only daughter of John[4] (5), was born in Erie, Penn.; was married to Col. Samuel C. Magill, formerly of Clinton, Ia., but now of Fargo, Dak., and has *five* living children, of whom two are married.

RIDDELLS OF ANNAMACNEAL, IRELAND.

Gordon Riddell[1] (1), descended from Scottish ancestors, said to have settled in Ireland under Cromwell, lived and died in the parish of Tully-corbit, County of Monaghan; he had issue.

Hugh Riddell[1] (1), brother of the preceding, lived in one of the townships granted his ancestors in County Monaghan; married and had issue.

SECOND GENERATION.

John Riddell[2] (1), a son of Gordon[1] (1), was born in County Monaghan, township of Annamacneal; married and had issue.

John Riddell[2] (2), a son of Hugh[1] (1), was born in County Monaghan, Ireland; married Elizabeth Bridge, a wealthy farmer's daughter, and had issue *three* sons and *eight* daughters, of whom hereafter; Mr. Riddell was a farmer.

Hugh Riddell[2] (2), a son of Hugh[1] (1), died unmarried.

THIRD GENERATION.

Hugh Riddell[3] (3), a son of John[2] (1), resides on a part of one of four townships granted his ancestors, called Annamacneal in the parish of Tullycorbit, County Monaghan, — the place where he was born, — consisting of about ten acres freeland.

Robert Riddell[3] (1), grandson of Gordon[1] (1), resides at Annamacneal, Ballybay, County Monaghan, Ireland, on twelve acres of freeland.

Gordon Riddell[3] (2), grandson of Gordon[1] (1), resides on a freeland at Ballybay* that came to him from his remote ancestors, consisting of twelve acres; I do not know the name of the father.

Rev. Hugh Riddell[3] (4), son of John[2] (2) and his wife, Elizabeth Bridge, was born in County Monaghan, Ireland, and is now a Presbyterian minister in Glasgow, Scotland.

William Riddell[3] (1), a son of John[2] (2), is now living in County Fermanaugh, Ireland; farmer; has a family.

John Riddell[3] (3), a son of John[2] (2), was born in County Monaghan, and came to Canada when a lad. He married for his first wife, Matilda Dane (or Done), who died June 8, 1879, — "an amiable Christian woman." He married secondly, Ellen B. Tate, of English extraction; she was born at Brewster, Mass., Jan. 20, 1848. Mr. Riddell moved to Michigan about 1868, and settled on a large farm at Georgetown, Ottawa County, where he now lives and has "all that heart can wish." He has issue *two* children, of whom hereafter.

Mary-Ann Riddell[3] (1), a daughter of John[2] (2); dead.

Jane Riddell[3] (1), a daughter of John[2] (2); dead.

Margaret Riddell[3] (1), a daughter of John[2] (2), was married.to —— MacKelvie, and lives at Ballybay, County Monaghan, Ireland.

Eliza Riddell[3] (1), a daughter of John[2] (2); deceased.

Esther Riddell[3] (1), a daughter of John[2] (2), is living, 1883.

Sarah Riddell[3] (1), a daughter of John[2] (2); deceased.

Matilda Riddell[3] (1), a daughter of John[2] (2); deceased.

Lettie Riddell[3] (1), a daughter of John[2] (2), living in 1883.

FOURTH GENERATION.

William Riddell[4] (2), son of John[3] (3) by first wife.

Freddie-T. Riddell[4] (1), son of John[3] (3) by second wife.

---

* Archibald Riddell lives in Glanish, Dunraymond; George Riddell in Creeragh, Ballybay; and Gordon Riddell in Edenafirkin, Ballybay, — all in County Monaghan, — and are supposed to be connected with the families before mentioned. All occupy land, and are probably small farmers.

14

RIDDLES OF YORK COUNTY, PENNSYLVANIA.

[DONEGAL BRANCH.]

John Riddell[1] **(1)**, a resident of Donegal County, in the province of Ulster, Ireland, was descended from one of several brothers who were in the army of William III, and who, for their services, were rewarded with confiscated lands in Ulster. These ancestors were Presbyterians from Scotland. (See "Riddells of Ray, Ireland.")

SECOND GENERATION.

James Riddle[2] **(1)**, a son of John[1] (1), supposed to have been born in Ireland; married in the year 16—, to Janette, daughter of Tristram Jones, of Donegal County, Ireland, and had issue *six* children, of whom hereafter.

THIRD GENERATION.

Mary Riddle[3] **(1)**, a daughter of James[2] (1), was born in Donegal, Ireland; was married to Walter McFarland, and had issue *six* children, four sons and two daughters.

John Riddle[4] **(2)**, eldest son of James[2] (1), was born in the County Donegal, Ireland; married Sarah Ewing, and died without issue.

Tristram-Jones Riddle[3] **(1)**, second son of James[2] (1), was born in Donegal, Ireland, and died unmarried.

· **Catherine Riddle**[3] **(1)**, second daughter of James[2] (1), was born in Donegal, Ireland; was married to William Young, and had issue *eight* children, five sons and three daughters.

James Riddle[3] **(2)**, third son of James[2] (1), was born in Donegal, Ireland; emigrated to America, and settled in York County, Penn., as a farmer. His wife's name has not reached me; they had issue *nine* children, of whom hereafter. There may have been daughters.

Jane Riddle[3] **(1)**, third daughter of James[2] (1), was born in Donegal, Ireland; was married and had issue *seven* children, five sons and two daughters.

FOURTH GENERATION.

John Riddle[4] **(3)**, eldest son of James[3] (2), was born in York County, Penn. (probably), Jan. 24, 1752; married April 16, 1778, to Ann McKee (aged 18 years), and by her had issue several children, of whom hereafter. He was a nail-manufacturer in early life, working on the old hand-machines at Hagerstown, Md.; afterwards principal of an academy at Chambersburgh, and then at Pittsburgh, Penn., where he died in 1818. Mr. Riddle seems to have been a prominent man in his day, and filled many positions of trust, one being that of magistrate. He was lame from white swelling, and on that account received a better education than it was usual for farmers' sons to have in those days. He had a commission from Governor Mifflin, dated 16th of February, 1792, appointing him notary public for Franklin County, Penn.; also a commission dated July 5, 1792, from the same governor, appointing him Justice of the Peace for the said County.

Robert Riddle[4] **(1)**, second son of James[3] (2), was born June 14, 1753; probably died young and unmarried, as no other mention is found concerning him.

Judge James Riddle[4] **(3)**, third son of James[3] (2), was born in Adams County, Penn., Jan. 20, 1755; married Elizabeth, daughter of Robert and

Agnes McPherson, of Gettysburgh, and had issue *seven* children, of whom hereafter. He graduated with great distinction at Princeton College, and subsequently read law at York. He was for many years tutor of languages in Princeton College; was admitted to the Chambersburgh bar in 1784. His legal abilities were very respectable, though he was not considered a great lawyer; he was well read in science, literature, and laws; was a good advocate, and very influential with the jury. He was appointed president judge in 1794, by Governor Mifflin, and continued in this position till 1804, when he resigned in consequence of the strong partisan feeling existing against him, — he being a great Federalist, — and returned to the practice of law. He was again successful and amassed a large fortune, which was impaired by payments of endorsements made for his friends. He was a soldier of the Revolution. Judge Riddle married for a second wife, Arianna, daughter of Dr. Stewart, of Blagdensburgh, and by her had *five* children. He was a gentleman of great dignity and suavity of manners; a fine specimen of old-school politeness. He died in the year 1837.

David Riddle[4] (1), fourth son of James[3] (2), was born March 29, 1757, probably in York County, Penn.; married Sarah McCune (she was probably of Harrisburg, Penn.), and settled as farmer in Amberson's valley, in eastern Pennsylvania, and died at Harrisburg. His brother George lived with him. Their old farm is now owned by Jacob B. Stewart.

William Riddle[4] (1), fifth son of James[3] (2), was born Aug. 20, 1759; married Susanna Nounce, of English parentage, and settled in Martinsburgh, Va. He was a teacher and elder of the Presbyterian Church, "with as warm and true a Scotch-Irish heart, creed, and preferences as any in his day"; these words were spoken by his son, the Rev. David H. Riddle, D. D., in an historical address. He died about the year 1812, having had issue *eleven* children, ten sons and one daughter, of whom hereafter.

Joseph Riddle[4] (1), sixth son of James[3] (2), was born in York County, Penn., April 5, 1763; married Sarah-Morrow Kearsley, second daughter of John and Nancy Kearsley, of Shepherdstown, Va., on Saturday, Sept. 12, 1789, and had issue *nine* children, of whom hereafter. Mr. Riddle was a merchant in Alexandria and Richmond, Va., many years; subsequently removed to Woodville, Miss., where he was postmaster, and where he died in 1844. His wife died in Alexandria, April 24, 1810. Mr. Riddle was quite tall and well formed, had dark gray or blue eyes, and brown hair which he wore in a cue. He was of gentlemanly and refined appearance, — very good-looking.

Joshua Riddle[4] (1), seventh son of James[3] (2), was born Aug. 15, 1766; married a Miss Harper, and was a merchant in Alexandria, Va.

Samuel Riddle[4] (1), eighth son of James[3] (2), was born Feb. 1, 1771; married a Miss Stewart, settled in Huntingdon County, Penn., and became an eminent lawyer. He studied law with his brother James, and was admitted to the bar in 1790. After his admission he removed to Huntingdon, and subsequently to Bedford, where he remained until the spring of 1794, when he went to Chambersburgh, and occupied his brother's office, succeeding to a great share of the practice held by him before he was appointed judge. He was very industrious and painstaking, and having been introduced to the people by so distinguished a lawyer as his brother, he was successful in business and acquired a fortune. He was a man of very speculative turn of mind, and wasted his large fortune by injudicious investments and improvements. When living at Bedford, he built a very large brick house, much too large for the wants of any family. He also, at a subsequent period, planted a peach-orchard, on the top of " Parnel's Knob," a high peak of the Kittanning mountain, about ten miles west of Chambersburgh, and built a still-house for the manufacture of peach-brandy at the same elevated locality. He also erected a chopping-mill and saw-mill at the same place, and thus gave it the name of " Riddle's Folly." Mr. Riddle was an ardent Federalist, and upon the establishment of a Democratic paper at Chambersburgh, in 1790, he took umbrage at some item published in its columns, and made an attempt to cowhide the editors in their sanctum, but got the worst of the battle; hence there was one Democratic victory in Franklin County that year. In person, Mr. Riddle was tall and spare, and had a very prominent arched nose. He was social and engaging in his manners, and a general favorite among those who were acquainted with him. He died in 1820, leaving a large family of children, of whom hereafter.

George Riddle[4] (1), ninth son of James[3] (2), was born in Adams County, Penn., Dec. 1, 1772; settled in the eastern part of his native State as a farmer, and lived with his brother David, before mentioned, till a great age.

FIFTH GENERATION.

Margaret Riddle[5] (1), eldest daughter of John[4] (3), was born May 20, 1779, and died May 7, 1781.

Rebecca Riddle[5] (1), second daughter of John[4] (3), was born Feb. 16, 1781; was married to Willoughby Lane, of Charleston, Va., and had issue several children.

James-McKee Riddle[5] (4), eldest son of John[4] (3), was born July 24, 1785; married Elizabeth Weaver, of Adams County, Penn., Nov. 21, 1811; studied law with his uncle, Samuel Riddle, at Huntingdon, Penn., settled at Somerset and practised his profession there for several years. He removed to the city of Pittsburgh, about 1814. He had a commission from Governor Findlay, dated Aug. 1, 1814, as colonel of a Pennsylvania militia regiment; one from the same Governor, dated March 3, 1818, as clerk of the Supreme Court of Pennsylvania; one from Governor Wolf, dated Dec. 8, 1830, as Justice of the Peace for the town (now city) of Allegheny, to which place he removed in 1829, and where he died March 20, 1832. His widow died at same place, March 27, 1857; they had issue, of whom hereafter.

Joseph Riddle[5] (2), a son of John[4] (3), died unmarried.

James Riddle[5] (5), eldest son of James[4] (3), was born in Franklin County, Penn., about the year 1784, and died young.

Eliza Riddle[5] (1), eldest daughter of James[4] (3), was born in Franklin County, Penn., (say) 1784, and died unmarried. She was one of the most pious and intellectual of young women; cultured, refined, and of delicate modesty.

John-Stewart Riddle[5] (4), second son of James[4] (3), was born in 1808; married to Miss —— Bemis, of Meadville, Penn., and had issue several children, of whom hereafter. He died in 1851. Mr. Riddle was a graduate of Union College, New York; studied law and removed to Meadville, where he was one of the most prominent men at the bar. He was a gentleman of prepossessing personal appearance; courteous and genial.

hearted, and highly respected by all who came within the circle of his acquaintance; his death was deeply lamented.

Margaret Riddle[5] (2), second daughter of James[4] (3), was born Dec. 21, 1805; was married June 30, 1836, to the Rev. B. S. Schneck, pastor of the German Reformed Church, at Chambersburgh, Penn., and for many years editor of the *Messenger*, the organ of the German Reformed Church. He died in 1874, in his 69th year.

William Riddle[5] (2), third son of James[4] (3), was born in 1805; married Miss Margaret McDowell, of Franklin County, Penn. He died at Chambersburgh in 1838, while preparing himself for the gospel ministry; a young man of remarkable natural gifts, an excellent scholar, and of charming personal address.

Horace-Ross Riddle[5] (1), fourth son of James[4] (3), was born in 1810; married Miss Sallie Hunter, of Virginia, and had issue *three* daughters. Mr. Riddle is now a merchant in Baltimore, Md.; is said to be " a very eccentric old gentleman "; has never replied to my inquiries.

Dr. Edward Riddle[5] (1), fifth son of James[4] (3), was born in 1813; studied medicine; went to California to practise his profession, and died in San Francisco in 1848, unmarried.

James-N. Riddle[5] (6), eldest son of William[4] (1), was born at Martinsburgh, Va., Jan. 25, 1796; married and had issue *six* children; he died May 10, 1863.

William-N. Riddle[5] (3), second son of William[4] (1), was born in Martinsburgh, Va., April 10, 1800; married ——, and is now (1884) living in Martinsburgh, a widower, aged 84; no children.

John Riddle[5] (5), third son of William[4] (1), was born at Martinsburgh, Va., Jan. 25, 1803; married to Susan Tabb, March 6, 1828; moved from Martinsburgh to Ely, Ralls County, Mo., in the year 1836, as a farmer. When he entered upon his new land "the wild grass was growing rank and tall upon the broad prairie, and the red deer fed unscared by the presence of man." He was an ordained elder of the church at West Ely; assisted in the building of the house of worship there, and his name rests under the corner-stone. He died April 14, 1845, leaving a widow and *eight* children, of whom hereafter.

Rev. David-H. Riddle[5] (2), D. D., LL. D., fourth son of William[4] (1), was born in Martinsburgh, Va. (now Western Virginia), April 14, 1805; married November, 1828, Elizabeth, eldest daughter of Matthew Brown, D. D., who was president of Jefferson College from 1823 to 1845, and by her (who died Dec. 3, 1858) had issue *nine* children, of whom hereafter. Mr. Riddle entered Jefferson College, Pennsylvania, in 1821; was graduated in 1823, valedictorian of a class numbering thirty-three, eighteen of whom became ministers. He studied theology at Princeton Seminary from 1825 to 1828; was licensed to preach in 1827; ordained and installed as pastor of the Presbyterian Church in Winchester, Va., Dec. 28, 1828. He removed to Pittsburgh, Penn., to become pastor of the Third Presbyterian Church there in the fall of 1833, and remained until the spring of 1857, when he became pastor of the First Reformed Dutch Church, of Jersey City, N. J., where he continued until the close of the year 1862, at which time he was elected president of Jefferson College. At the union of Washington and Jefferson Colleges, in 1865, he became professor of moral science. In 1868 he removed to Martinsburgh, to take the pastoral care of the Presbyterian church there, where he still is (1884). He was moderator of the Presbyterian General Assembly in 1852. Dr. Riddle is a man of great learning and elevated character; has been a writer of marked ability, and has delivered many able lectures. Few men have been more highly honored in their profession, or won the esteem of so wide a circle of friends.

Catherine Riddle⁵ (2), the only daughter of William⁴ (1), was married to William Stone, a planter, of McLennan County, Tex., and died in 1868, without issue.

Nancy Riddle⁵ (1), eldest daughter of Joseph⁴ (1), was born in Martinsburgh, Va., Dec. 26, 1791; was married to Dr. George Watson, of Richmond, Va., May 16, ——, and died Jan. 15, 1882.

Maria Riddle⁵ (1), second daughter of Joseph⁴ (1), was born in Shepherdstown, Va., Sept. 3, 1793; died Jan. 6, 1794, in Alexandria.

James-Dahl Riddle⁵ (7), eldest son of Joseph⁴ (1), was born in Alexandria, Va., Jan. 17, 1796, and died in Charlestown, Va., in 1825.

Eliza-Mitchell Riddle⁵ (2), third daughter of Joseph⁴ (1), was born in Alexandria, Va., Jan. 2, 1799, and died at Ionia (the country residence of Dr. George Watson), Louisa County, July 22, 1879. Never married.

John-Adams Riddle⁵ (6), second son of Joseph⁴ (1), was born in Alexandria, Va., July 3, 1800; married to Miss Susan Tabb, of Matthews County, July 8, 1823, and resided at Gloucester City, Va. He died July 29, 1823, twenty-one days after his marriage.

Julia-Maria Riddle⁵ (1), fourth daughter of Joseph⁴ (1), was born in Alexandria, Va., July 27, 1802; was married to Dr. Thomas Nelson, of Richmond, and died May 16, 1870, in Baltimore, Md.

Joseph Riddle⁵ (3), third son of Joseph⁴ (1), was born in Alexandria, Va., Jan. 24, 1804, and died Feb. 11, 1808.

Jane Riddle⁵ (2), fourth daughter of Joseph⁴ (1), was born in Alexandria, Va., Aug. 8, 1805; was married to William Ried; secondly to —— Payne, and is living at Luna Landing, Ark. She has issue.

Robert Riddle⁵ (2), fourth son of Joseph⁴ (1), was born in Alexandria, Va., Nov. 1, 1806; lived in Vicksburg, Miss.; married a lady of that place, and had one son, of whom hereafter. Died April 14, 1841.

Sarah-Arianna Riddle⁵ (1), fifth daughter of Joseph⁴ (1), was born in Alexandria, Va., July 27, 1808; was married to Dr. William A. Seldon, of Charles City County, May 16, 18 —, and had issue.

Joseph Riddle⁵ (4), fifth son of Joseph⁴ (1), was born in Alexandria, Va., April 8, 1810, and was killed in Mississippi by falling from his horse.

SIXTH GENERATION.

George-Ross Riddle⁶ (2), eldest son of James⁵ (4), was born at Somerset, Penn., Sept. 12, 1812; was married to Mary-Ann Williams, May 19, 1836, and has issue *eight* children, of whom hereafter. Mrs. Riddle's parents, Henry and Elizabeth (Jones) Williams, were natives of Wales. Mr. Riddle moved to Pittsburgh, Penn., with his father in 1814, and in 1819 to Allegheny, in which city and neighborhood he has resided ever since. He was commissioned town-clerk of Allegheny City in 1834, and held the position till 1839; was principal deputy (acting sheriff) under three sheriffs, for Allegheny County; was elected chief clerk of the civil courts of the same County from 1843 to 1846; had a commission (having been elected) from Governor Bigler, dated Feb. 4, 1854, as alderman of the city of Allegheny; also, another commission (having been elected) from Governor Hartranft, dated April 25, 1876, as Justice of the Peace for Spring Dale Township, which he resigned when he returned to Allegheny City. He was for twenty-five years the senior partner of a firm largely engaged in shipping coal, which business was discontinued in 1877. Mr. Riddle had learned the business of a conveyancer, and since his return from his residence at Spring Dale to Allegheny City, he has opened an office on Ohio Street for the transaction of that business. He is an excellent penman. Has kindly furnished much information for this book that could not have been otherwise obtained.

Mary-Ann-Lane Riddle[6] (2), eldest daughter of James[5] (4), was born at Somerset, Penn., Aug. 6, 1814; was married to Robert H. Stewart, of Lincoln Station, Spring Dale post-office. No issue.

Arianna-Rebecca Riddle[6] (1), second daughter of James[5] (4), was born at Pittsburgh, Penn., Jan. 28, 1816; was married to Dr. Robert B. Mowrey, of Allegheny City, and has issue several children, one of whom is the Rev. Philip H. Mowrey, of Chester, Penn.

John-Weaver Riddle[6] (7), second son of James[5] (4), was born at Pittsburgh, Penn., Jan. 15, 1818; married to Eliza Adams, of Milford, Eng., Sept. 24, 1841, and had issue *eleven* children, of whom hereafter. Mr. Riddle is a banker; was cashier of the Allegheny Savings Bank, but since its suspension he moved to Quincy, Ill., where he now (1879) resides.

Joseph-Ken Riddle[6] (5), third son of James[5] (4), was born at Pittsburgh, Penn., May 18, 1825; went to California, and died at New Wilmington, British Columbia; unmarried.

William Riddle[6] (4), third son of James[5] (4), was born in Pittsburgh, Penn. (presumably), and died in infancy.

Albert Riddle[6] (1), fourth son of James[5] (4), was born in Pittsburgh, Penn. (presumably), and died in infancy.

Arianna-S. Riddle[6] (2), a daughter of John[5] (5), was born (presumably) at Meadville, Penn. (where her father was in law-practice), and was married to Thomas B. Kennedy, Esq., a lawyer of prominence, and president of the Cumberland Valley and other railroad companies. They reside at Chambersburgh, Penn.

Susan-Noune Riddle[6] (1), eldest daughter of James[5] (6), was born in Martinsburgh, Va., in 1834 (?).

Elizabeth Riddle[6] (1), second daughter of James[5] (6), was born in Martinsburgh, Va., in 1836; was married to Cornelius K. Stribling, and has *four* children; now a widow in Martinsburgh.

Charles-Stuart Riddle[6] (1), son of James[5] (6), was born in Martinsburgh, Va., in 1839, and died in Jefferson College, Nov. 16, 1857.

Mary-Brown Riddle[6] (3), third daughter of James[5] (6), was born in Martinsburgh, Va.; was married; deceased.

Jane Riddle[6] (3), fourth daughter of James[5] (6), was born in Martinsburgh, Va.; was married to —— Armstrong, and is now (1884) a widow living in her native city.

—— Riddle[6] (0), youngest son of James[5] (6), was born in Martinsburgh, Va.; served with distinction in the Confederate army, and was killed in September, 1864.

Martha-Susan Riddle[6] (1), eldest daughter of John[5] (5), was born in Martinsburgh, Va., Dec. 15, 1828; was married to Samuel M. Elliott, April 8, 1854.

William-Tabb Riddle[6] (5), eldest son of John[5] (5), was born in Martinsburgh, Va., Dec. 20, 1830; married, Feb. 8, 1853, to Sarah E. Wilkinson, and has issue (1873) *seven* children, of whom hereafter. Mr. Riddle resides at Rensselaer, Ralls County, Mo.

Catherine-B. Riddle[6] (3), second daughter of John[5] (5), was born in Martinsburgh, Va., Dec. 9, 1832.

Joseph-N. Riddle[6] (6), second son of John[5] (5), was born in Martinsburgh, Va., Nov. 23, 1834.

Mary-M. Riddle[6] (4), third daughter of John[5] (5), was born near West Ely, Mo., April 3, 1837.

Elizabeth-F. Riddle[6] (2), fourth daughter of John[5] (5), was born in Ralls County, Mo., March 18, 1839.

Lovinia-Anderson Riddle[6] (1), fifth daughter of John[5] (5), was born in Ralls County, Mo., Feb. 19, 1841; she has been a teacher in the public schools; was living with her mother in 1873, unmarried. In a communication forwarded to me in 1873, Miss Riddle says: "I am the only one in our family inclined to a profession. I have taught for many years; have found much pleasure in my avocation, but like all earthly things find it an empty bubble. I am stopping at home with my mother now, and have a very good opportunity to study botany, geology, etc., besides the delightful pleasure of green fields to rest my eyes upon. I love every voice of nature, even to the chirp of the little cricket that my mother searches for with so much energy to demolish from her carpets and woolens." Her composition is elegant.

David-Hoge Riddle[6] (3), third son of John[5] (5), was born in Ralls County, Mo., Dec. 18, 1843; dead.

Mary-Brown Riddle[6] (5), eldest daughter of David[5] (2), was born in Winchester, Va. (now West Virginia); died in infancy.

William-N. Riddle[6] (6), eldest son of David[5] (2), was born at Winchester, Va., and died in the year 1836, in childhood.

Susan-N. Riddle[6] (2), second daughter of David[5] (2), was born at Winchester, Va., Nov. 1, 1834; now (1884) living in Martinsburgh, West Va.; unmarried.

Rev. Matthew-Brown Riddle[6] (1), D. D., second son of David[5] (2), was born (presumably) in Pittsburgh, Penn., Oct. 17, 1836; entered Jefferson College in 1850; was graduated in 1852, salutatorian; studied theology at Western Theological Seminary, Allegheny, Penn., 1853–6; assistant professor of Greek in Jefferson College, 1857–8; at New Brunswick Theological Seminary, 1858–60; in Europe in 1860–1. He was licensed to preach May 26, 1859; was chaplain of the three-months troops in 1861; ordained and installed pastor of the Reformed Dutch Church at Hoboken, N. J., April 15, 1862; removed to Newark, N. J., as pastor of Second Reformed Dutch Church, March 2, 1865; dismissed from the Church in 1869; in Germany until September, 1871; has been professor of New Testament Exegesis, at Hartford Theological Seminary (Conn.) since 1871, where he is now stationed. Dr. Riddle is regarded as an excellent scholar, and an author of great weight; he has accomplished a remarkable amount of literary work within the past few years. He was one of the Committee on the Revision of the Bible.

Catherine-Burton Riddle[6] (4), third daughter of David[5] (2), was born in Pittsburgh, Penn., Feb. 26, 1839; was married to G. Bogert Vroom, and is now (1884) a widow.

Alexander-Brown Riddle⁶ (1), third son of David⁵ (2), was born in Pittsburgh, Penn., and died in infancy.

Elizabeth-Herran Riddle⁶ (4), fourth daughter of David⁵ (2), was born (presumably) at Pittsburgh, Penn., Sept. 8, 1843, and was married to Rev. Meade C. Williams, of Sandusky, O.; now (1884) living at Princeton, Ill.; has *five* children.

Rev. David-H. Riddle⁶ (4), fourth son of David⁵ (2), was born (presumably) at Pittsburgh, Penn., Jan. 28, 1845; was graduated at Jefferson College in 1865; studied theology two years at Allegheny, Penn., and one at Princeton; was licensed to preach in 1869, and ordained and installed pastor of the Presbyterian Church at Falls Church,* in Fairfax County, Va., in 1871.

Henry-A. Riddle⁶ (1), fifth son of David⁵ (2), was born at Pittsburgh, Penn., June 8, 1848; married Martha Hunter, and is now a merchant at Martinsburgh, W. Va. Has *four* children, of whom hereafter.

SEVENTH GENERATION.

Elizabeth Riddle⁷ (6), eldest daughter of George⁶ (2), was born in Allegheny, Penn., March 27, 1837; was married to Rev. William Wallace, May 29, 1862, and has issue *six* children. Mr. Wallace is pastor of the United Presbyterian Church, at Newville, Cumberland County, Penn.

James-Henry Riddle⁷ (8), eldest son of George⁶ (2), was born at Allegheny, Penn., Feb. 24, 1839; married Rosanna Carson, of Franklin County, Penn., Feb. 25, 1868, and·has issue *four* children, of whom hereafter. Mr. Riddle resides at Spring Dale, Penn., and is a professional accountant and clerk.

George-Denhurst Riddle⁷ (3), second son of George⁶ (2), was born at Allegheny, Penn., March 13, 1841; married Elizabeth, daughter of Matthew and Nancy Day, Sept. 1, 1863, and has issue *six* children, of whom hereafter. Mr. Riddle was formerly in the grocery trade, in Allegheny City, but now holds the position of secretary of the Ben Franklin Insurance Company.

Arianna-Rebecca Riddle⁷ (3), second daughter of George⁶ (2), was born at Allegheny, Penn., July 2, 1843; was married to Thomas F. Marshall (civil engineer), Nov. 17, 1871, and has issue.

Edward-Dallas Riddle⁷ (2), third son of George⁶ (2), was born at Pittsburgh, Penn., Dec. 6, 1845; he is now serving as clerk, and lives at home; single.

Robert-Stewart Riddle⁷ (3), fourth son of George⁶ (2), was born at Allegheny, Penn., Feb. 6, 1848; he is living at home, single; farmer.

Joseph-Madison Riddle⁷ (7), fifth son of George⁶ (2), was born at Allegheny, Penn., Feb. 4, 1850; lives at home, a single man; farmer.

Mary-Ann Riddle⁷ (6), third daughter of George⁶ (2), was born at Allegheny, Penn., July 6, 1852; unmarried.

William-H. Riddle⁷ (7), eldest son of John⁶ (7), was born in Pittsburgh, Penn., Aug. 3, 1842; married Florence Fell, of Marietta, O., May 20, 1875; no issue. · Mr. Riddle is a prominent banker in Pittsburgh;

* The author visited Falls Church during the late war and found the ancient structure where, tradition said, George Washington was married, in a dilapidated condition, and used as a stable for cavalry-horses. The old church was some distance back from the turnpike, and in the midst of a burial-ground, after the English style.

was initiated in the Allegheny Savings Bank; thence removed to the Tradesman's National Bank; and is now teller in the People's National Bank. He is regarded as a competent and trustworthy business-man, highly respected and influential.

Albert-Findley Riddle[7] (2), second son of John[6] (6), was born in Pittsburgh, Penn., April 23, 1844; married to Martha Ogle, of Quincy, Ill., Jan. 24, 1864, and has *three* children, of whom hereafter. Mr. Riddle is superintendent of Oil Works, Butler Street, near Sharpsburgh Bridge. He is an enterprising and competent man.

Charles-Elliott Riddle[7] (2), third son of John[6] (6), was born at Pittsburgh, Penn., Nov. 19, 1845; married Elizabeth Varnum, of Parker City, Penn., Nov. 14, 1872; she died at Parker City, July 9, 1875; no issue. Mr. Riddle is an oil-merchant at Allegheny City, Penn.

James-McKee Riddle[7] (9), fourth son of John[6] (6), was born at Pittsburgh, Penn., Jan. 24, 1848; unmarried. He is in the brokerage business in Allegheny City, Penn.

Emma-Adams Riddle[7] (1), eldest daughter of John[6] (6), was born at Pittsburgh, Penn., Feb. 25, 1850; was married to Lewis-Patterson Irwin, of Allegheny, Penn., Sept. 27, 1870, and resides in the latter city.

Frank-Costen Riddle[7] (1), fifth son of John[6] (6), was born at Pittsburgh, Penn., May 24, 1852; traveling agent.

John-Weaver Riddle[7] (8), sixth son of John[6] (6), was born in Pittsburgh, Penn., Feb. 6, 1855; was formerly a lawyer at Allegheny City, but now living at Quincy, Ill., whither his father's family have removed within a few years. Unmarried in 1879.

Ida Riddle[7] (1), second daughter of John[6] (6), was born at Pittsburgh, Penn., Nov. 3, 1856; unmarried 1879.

Robert-Mowrey Riddle[7] (4), eighth son of John[6] (6), was born at Pittsburgh, Penn., Nov. 19, 1858; he is now (1879) agent for an insurance company.

Lewis-Hamnet Riddle[7] (1), ninth son of John[6] (6), was born at Pittsburgh, Penn., Nov. 10, 1860; at home.

Harry-Freemont Riddle[7] (1), tenth son of John[6] (6), was born at Pittsburgh, Penn., Nov. 15, 1861; at home.

Alice-Holmes Riddle[7] (1), eldest daughter of William[6] (5), was born at Rensselaer, Mo., Dec. 5, 1853.

Mary-V. Riddle[7] (7), second daughter of William[6] (5), was born at Rensselaer, Mo., Oct. 7, 1856.

Mason-Wilkeson Riddle[7] (1), eldest son of William[6] (5), was born at Rensselaer, Mo., Aug. 15, 1859.

Susan-Amelia Riddle[7] (4), third daughter of William[6] (5), was born at Rensselaer, Mo., June 25, 1864.

Martha-Elliott Riddle[7] (2), fourth daughter of William[6] (5), was born at Rensselaer, Mo., May 20, 1866.

Annie Riddle[7] (1), fifth daughter of William[6] (5), was born at Rensselaer, Mo., Oct. 12, 1868.

John-Travis Riddle[7] (9), second son of William[6] (5), was born at Rensselaer, Mo., July 18, 1871.

EIGHTH GENERATION.

Harry-C. Riddle[8] (2), eldest son of James[7] (8), was born at Spring Dale, Penn., Feb. 4, 1869.

Mary Riddle (8), eldest daughter of James[7] (8), was born at Spring Dale, Penn., Feb. 4, 1872.

George-Ross Riddle (4), second son of James[7] (8), was born at Spring Dale, Penn., Nov. 6, 1874.

Rebecca-M. Riddle (2), second daughter of James[7] (8), was born at Spring Dale, Penn., March 17, 1876.

Walter-D. Riddle (1), eldest son of George[7] (3), was born at Pittsburgh, Penn., July 27, 1864.

Evalyn Riddle (1), eldest son of George[7] (3), was born in Pittsburgh, Penn., Nov. 17, 1866.

Bessie Riddle (1), second daughter of George[7] (3), was born at Pittsburgh, Penn., Feb. 3, 1869.

Arianna Riddle (4), third daughter of George[7] (3), was born at Pittsburgh, Penn., June 30, 1873.

Grace Riddle (1), fourth daughter of George[7] (3), was born at Pittsburgh, Penn., Jan 12, 1871; died Oct. 8, 1877.

Clarence Riddle (1), second son of George[7] (3), was born at Pittsburgh, Penn., Jan. 13, 1876; died Dec. 29, 1877.

Joseph Riddle (8). ⎫
Albert Riddle (3). ⎬ Children of Albert[7] (2), of Pittsburgh, Penn.
Clara Riddle (1). ⎭

RIDDELLS OF BEDFORD, NEW HAMPSHIRE, NO. 1.

[GAWN BRANCH.]

Gawn Riddell[1] (1), supposed to have been born at Ballymeath, County Londonderry, Ireland, May 16, 1688; came to America in 1718. He married Mary Bell, a lady of Scottish descent (she was born in 1804), and had issue *six* children, of whom hereafter. He was a brother of Hugh, Robert, and John, who came over from Ireland at the same time. See "Riddells of Coleraine, Massachusetts," and of "Ballymeath, Ireland." His name appears on a petition to the Governor of New Hampshire, for a charter for the town of Bedford, May 10, 1750; also tythingman in Bedford the same year. In 1750, a road was laid out from William Kennedy's land to the brook near "Ghan Riddell's house." In 1751 "Gan" was constable; also took "invoice same year for 40 shillings old tenor." In 1753 "Gan" was surveyor of highways; in 1754, tythingman; in 1756, selectman and clerk of the market; in 1757, constable; in 1759, committee to build a meeting-house; 1761, surveyor of highways; 1770, collector of taxes; 1773, committee to examine town-accounts; 1775, subscribed the vote about Rev. John Houston, — in all these years he was a taxpayer in Bedford. He lived in a house east of "Riddell's Mill," —which mill was owned by him in 1754, —upon the site of the present (1874) house of S. C. Damon, and had large tract of land, which he divided among his sons.*

---

* During the autumn of 1876, the author of this book visited Bedford, N. H., and in company with John A. Riddle, Esq., a descendant in the fourth degree from

"Rev. Mr. Houston's and Gawn Riddle's farms joined each other. One Saturday they met and had some sharp and unneighborly talk together about their fences and cattle. Some townsmen were present and heard their altercation. On the next day (Sabbath) Mr. Riddle was punctually at meeting. Some of his neighbors, who had heard the contest on the day before, looked astonished, and said, 'Mr. Riddle, we thought you would not be at meeting to-day, to hear your neighbor Houston preach, after having such a quarrel with him.' Said Mr. Riddle, 'I'd have ye to know, if I did quarrel with my neighbor Houston yesterday, I did not quarrel with the gospel.'"—*History of Bedford.* He died Dec. 29, 1779, and his head-stone stands in the cemetery at Bedford Centre. The following is a *fac-simile* of his autograph: —

SECOND GENERATION.

Lieut. John Riddle[2] (1), eldest son of Gawn[1] (1), was born in Bedford, N. H., March 26, 1754; married Mary McAffee, and secondly, Sarah Hartshorn, and had by them *eleven* children, of whom hereafter. He built and resided in mill house, now (1884) occupied by Mr. Isaac C. Cutler. In 1780 he was surveyor of highways; 1781, ensign; 1784, committee to do what shall be needful to be done on "Scataquog bridge"; 1785, surveyor of highways and committee on county bridge; same year, pew No. 4 in meeting-house sold to him for $36; 1786, tythingman, juryman, committee to build a pound, and "lieutenant." He was a volunteer in the Revolution, and signed the "Association Test," which read as follows: "We the subscribers do hereby solemnly engage and promise, that we will, to the utmost of our power, at the risk of our lives and fortunes, with arms, oppose the hostile proceedings of the British Fleets and Armies against the United American Colonies." Mr. Riddle fulfilled his promise by entering the active service. He was a millwright by trade, and built nearly all the mills that were in operation in this section of the country at that time. He was a very industrious, hard-working man. He died Nov. 18, 1812.

Gawn, visited the place where the early Riddells settled; we climbed "Riddle's Hill," a beautiful elevation overlooking Bedford village, and there we could see the farms given by Gawn to his sons; beautiful lands now under a high state of cultivation, stretching away over hills and through valleys nearly as far as the eye could reach. We visited the cemetery where the Riddle fathers rest, and there saw the elegant granite tomb, erected and owned by the family. Mr. Riddle pointed out to me the lands owned by the ancestors of the family, and the homes of those families who were intermarried with the early generations; we visited the old Riddle mansion, where several generations of this family were born, and viewed many relics and antique articles of furniture that had long been in the family. The portraits in oil of Mr. and Mrs. Isaac Riddle were seen, and a curious cane brought from Russia, with which Mr. Riddle walked in his latter years. This ancient residence is situated upon an elevated and commanding position; is large and imposing, and embosomed in a beautiful grove of maples. A large green lawn surrounds the house, guarded by a circular wall of stone. The farm connected with this house is large and valuable, now owned and occupied by the three brothers, Isaac N., John A., and Silas A. Riddle; all unmarried. (See view of the Riddle mansion.)

"OLD RIDDLE MANSION-HOUSE."
Bedford, New Hampshire.
FOUNDED BY ISAAC RIDDLE

David Riddle[2] (1), second son of Gawn[1] (1), was born in Bedford, N. H., in 1756; married Mary Dunlap in 1798, and had issue *five* children, of whom hereafter. He settled near the place of his birth, in a house he erected on the hill where John D. Riddle lived in 1852, north of the mill. He was a soldier of the Revolution, and drew a pension. In 1774–5, he was pound-keeper; 1786, town voted to allow him four shillings for an endorsement on a corn note. He died Dec. 18, 1839, and was buried at Bedford Centre.

Susanna Riddle[2] (1), only daughter of Gawn[1] (1), was born in Bedford, N. H., 1759, and died in Bedford, Nov. 4, 1841, aged 82 years. She married Solomon Hutchinson; they removed to Maine, and reared a large family. One child lived in Belfast.

Hugh Riddle[2] (1), third son of Gawn[1] (1), was born in Bedford, N. H., in 1761. He married Ann M. Houston, sister of Rev. John Houston, first minister of Bedford; built and lived in a brick house about two miles south of the mill, known in 1884 as the Willard Parker house. He had issue *seven* children, and died Aug. 17, 1833. He was a soldier of the Revolution, entering the army when seventeen years old; was with General Stark at the battle of Bennington.

Capt. Isaac Riddle[2] (1), fourth son of Gawn[1] (1), was born in Bedford, N. H., June 10, 1762; married, first, Ann Aiken, in 1788; secondly, Margaret McGaw, in 1806. He built and lived in a house near the meeting-house at Bedford, one-half mile east of what was known as "Riddle's Mill," now known as the "Riddle Homestead." (See plate in this book.) He was for many years an active, public-spirited citizen of his town; and for a long time was extensively engaged in the lumber business, and one of the first proprietors of navigation by locks and canals on the Merrimack River. He superintended the building of the canals and locks belonging to the "Union Lock and Canal Company," and in company with Maj. Caleb Stark, he built and owned the first canal-boat that ever floated on the waters of the Merrimack. It was named the "Experiment"; was built at Bedford Centre, and drawn three miles on wheels by forty yokes of oxen, to "Basswood Landing," so called, at which place it was launched in the presence of the townspeople, who had gathered to witness the novelties of the day. This boat was loaded, and sailed to Boston, and the following notice relative to her arrival was taken from the *Boston Centinel* of 1812: "Arrived from Bedford, N. H., canal-boat 'Experiment,' Isaac Riddle, captain, via Merrimack River and Middlesex Canal." Upon her arrival at Boston, she was received amid cheers and the firing of cannon. From this commenced a large and extensive inland navigation on the Merrimack River, which continued until 1845, when it was interrupted by the railroads. He built factories at Souhegan, afterwards called "Riddle's Village," where, in company with his sons, William P., James, and Isaac, under the firm-name of Isaac Riddle & Sons, he carried on an extensive manufacture of cotton, wool, and nails, until the establishment was destroyed by fire in 1829. Mr. Riddle filled many offices, having been civil magistrate of his town, as well as their representative to the State Legislature. His life was a proof of his energy and active disposition. According to the "History of Manchester," when he became of age he had about fifty dollars in his pocket, mostly saved from his earnings during military service. He went to Newburyport, Mass., to purchase a stock of goods; these were transported on drays, or dray-carts, drawn by one or two horses, — if by two horses, in tandem teams, — as truck-wagons were not then in use. He occupied for a store-house the front room of his mother's dwelling, and trade increased until he was enabled to commence the manufacture of potash. But the funds were wanting to purchase a new kettle at an expense of thirty dollars. Emboldened by conscious integrity, without money or city friends, he started for Boston. On arriving at Medford, he was met by Maj. John Pinkerton, who was a man of the same stamp, the pioneer of trade in Derry, who gave him a note of introduction, and the desired utensil was secured. This line of manufacture proved lucrative; the potash was taken to Boston with ox-teams, and bartered as an article of export for imported goods. After some years had elapsed he purchased a lot of wild land at Bedford Centre, and erected a spacious mansion. By his indomitable business energy and perseverance he added acre to acre, and farm to farm, until he owned lands in several towns.

Mr. Riddle's house was literally a home for ministers, strangers, and a wide circle of acquaintances; and these were entertained with a hospitality and attention only found under the influence of the old-school gentleman. By generosity and many acts of kindness, he gained the respect of a wide-spread community. Often called upon to render pecuniary assistance, many instances are worthy of note. Judge Ebenezer Webster, of Salisbury, when on his way to Amherst to attend county court, usually passed the night at his house. On one occasion he spoke of his embarrassment on account of his son Daniel, then at college, and asked assistance, which was promptly rendered by the loan of money. Being one of the stockholders in the Concord Bank, the officers often made application to him for aid in order to meet the exigencies of the times; such calls he always effectually answered, he frequently being obliged to make a journey to Portsmouth, and obtain money in his private capacity.

In 1814, during the war with Great Britain, a public call was made by Governor Gilman, of New Hampshire, for volunteers from that class of citizens who were exempt from military duty in the ranks of the militia, to form themselves into companies for home-defence, in case of sudden invasion; this call was responded to by a veteran band of men, numbering about sixty, of fifty years of age and upwards, under the command of Capt. Isaac Riddle. He was prepared himself for military service, as previously intimated, as a volunteer soldier in the Revolution, under Colonel Nichols, and did duty at the important post of West Point, in 1780.

About 1817, an accident occurred which is still cherished in grateful remembrance. Mr. Riddle was returning from "Pembroke muster," when, seeing a ferry-boat nearing the fatal plunge of Hooksett Falls, crowded with people, without a moment's pause he sprung from his chaise, plunged into the stream, and, when all were expecting instant death, his courageous arm caught the rope attached to the boat, and thus saved thirty lives.

He had married a third wife, Mrs. Mary Vinall, of Quincy, Mass., an accomplished lady, belonging to one of the best families in the State, being a sister of the first governor, Levi Lincoln, and Captain Lincoln, one of the party who destroyed the tea in Boston harbor in 1773. Mrs. Riddle kept among her relic-treasures the axe with which her brother opened the memorable chests of tea. Mr. Riddle built a spacious mansion-house at Quincy, where, in the sunshine of earthly prosperity, he passed his last days. His death, which occurred Jan. 26, 1880, was very sudden, caused from the effects of a slight wound received at the time his factory was burned at Souhegan. He was buried with Masonic honors, and his remains interred in the family tomb at Bedford. He had a family of *eight* children, of whom hereafter.

William Riddle² (1), fifth son of Gawn¹ (1), was born in Bedford, N. H., July 5, 1765; married Janet Gilchrist in 1791, and lived on a part of the homestead with his mother. He was upwards of twenty years town-treasurer, and held the office of civil magistrate. He was frequently one of the selectmen of the town, and was seven times its representative to the General Court. At one time there were rumors afloat in his town that reflected upon the character of Rev. William Pickells, who had formerly preached in Philadelphia (a native of Wales), but then the minister in Bedford, where he had been very popular. The story soon created such bitter opposition, and the contest waxed so warm between his enemies and friends, that Lieut. John Orr offered to lay a wager of fifty dollars that the charges were true. The wager was taken by the preacher's friends, and William Riddle was chosen as agent for the parties, to proceed to Philadelphia and investigate the charges, for it was in that city where rumor located his pretended crimes. Mr. Riddle's report was to be final. He went to Philadelphia on horse-back, being on the journey two weeks, investigated the matter fully, found the charges untrue, and returning reported the result. There was great exultation on the part of the winners, and they gathered at the store of Isaac Riddle, Esq., to rejoice over the victory. Mr. Riddle was designated to go to Mr. Orr's and get the wager; he accordingly waited on that gentleman, and made known the result of his investigations. Without making a remark, Mr. Orr went to his money-drawer and paid the wager. Mr. Riddle took the money back to the winners, and it was spent at the counter in treating the company. Mr. Riddle was a man of great probity of character, firm, steadfast, and unwavering in the undertakings of life. He was a lover of peace and highly respected by all who knew him, always sustaining the unbounded confidence of his friends. He had a family of *nine* children, of whom hereafter. He died July 14, 1838, and was buried at Bedford Centre.

THIRD GENERATION.

Gawn Riddle³ (2), eldest son of John² (1), was born in Bedford, N. H., June 29, 1776; married Dollie French, had issue *three* children, and died in July, 1837, aged 61 years. He lived on a part of the homestead, and held many offices in town; he was selectman in 1822, '24, '25, '27, '28, '30, and treasurer in 1833–4; after when his name is not found on the Bedford records. He was a man of marked executive ability.

Molly Riddle³ (1), eldest daughter of John² (1), was born Dec. 11, 1778; married to —— Black, of Prospect, Me., in 1804, and resided in said town.

Nancy Riddle³ (1), second daughter of John² (1), was born Jan. 5, 1781; married William French, of Prospect, Me., in 1806, and resided in said town; died June 20, 1852.

Susanna Riddle³ (2), third daughter of John² (1), was born in 1784; married Daniel Moor in 1807, and lived in Bedford.

James Riddle³ (1), second son of John² (1), was born Jan. 9, 1786; married Anna Dole in 1815, had issue *two* children, and died in 1827, aged 41 years.

Anna Riddle³ (1), third daughter of John² (1), was born in May, 1789; married James Staples, of Prospect, Me., in 1841, and settled in said town.

John Riddle[3] (2), third son of John[2] (1), was born (probably) about 1791; died at the age of 21; no other information.

Matthew Riddle[3] (1), fourth son of John[2] (1), was born (probably) about 1793; married Sarah Dole in Ohio, in 1819; went West in 1820, and settled in Terre Haute, Ind., as cabinet-maker. He died Sept. 1, 1828, and his wife July 9, 1844; both were buried in Greenwood Cemetery, Terre Haute.

William Riddle[3] (2), fifth son of John[2] (1), was born (probably) about 1795; died in 1845; no other information.

Gilman Riddle[3] (1), sixth son of John[2] (1), was born in July, 1811; married in 1836, Mary J. Eveleth, and secondly in 1841, Emeline Henry. Had a family of *three* children, of whom hereafter. Mr. Riddle has long been identified with manufacturing operations, and has become an owner of valuable real estate. He resides in Manchester, N. H., in a spacious mansion on Chestnut Street. He is a man of quiet and unostentatious habits.

Eliza-S. Riddle[3] (1), fourth daughter of John[2] (1), was born in 1813; married and lived at Belfast, Me.

John-Dunlap Riddle[2] (3), eldest son of David[2] (1), was born in Bedford, N. H., March 20, 1802; married Sally C. Gilmore, May 12, 1831, and had issue *six* children, of whom hereafter. Mrs. Riddle died July 13, 1852, and he married, secondly, Mary-Ann Gilmore (sister of Sally C.), in 1854, but had no issue by this union. Mr. Riddle lived many years in Bedford, but removed to Manchester in 1868, and died there Aug. 5, 1876, leaving a widow and *three* children. He was a Justice of the Peace, and frequently held offices in his town; a man of considerable ability; highly respected by a wide circle of acquaintances.

Hugh Riddle[3] (2), second son of David[2] (1), was born in Bedford, N. H., April 8, 1803, and died in 1849. "When young he went to Baltimore, Md., where he was extensively engaged in constructing the public works of that city. In 1837 he built the Baltimore Custom-house, and was largely connected with the building of the first railroads terminating at that place." In 1849 he started for California by the overland route, and in the expedition lost his life, — the manner unknown. A simple head-board, carved with a rude inscription, was erected to mark his resting-place "on the plains of the Pacific."

Martha Riddle[3] (1), eldest daughter of David[2] (1), was born in Bedford, N. H., Dec. 16, 1806; married Daniel Barnard, and lived in Bedford.

Gilman Riddle[3] (2), third son of David[2] (1), was born in Bedford, N. H., and died young.

Mary Riddle[3] (1), second daughter of David[2] (1), was a twin to Gilman[3] (2); died young.

Gawn Riddle[3] (3), eldest son of Hugh[2] (1), was born in Bedford, N. H., in May, 1791; married Elizabeth, daughter of Lieut. James Moore, and settled near his father's homestead. He married, secondly, Rebecca, daughter of Robert Walker, one of the early settlers of Bedford; he had a family of *four* children, of whom hereafter, and died Aug. 20, 1867, aged 78 years; he was a farmer.

Dr. Robert Riddle[3] (1), second son of Hugh[2] (1), was born in Bedford, N. H., in 1793; was graduated at Yale College in 1818, studied medicine, and settled in his native town. "He was considered a skilful physician, and was fast rising in notice, when he died in the prime of life,

Respectfully
William P. Riddle

Dec. 17, 1828," holding the appointment of surgeon's mate in the Bedford Grenadier Company.

Anna Riddle[2] (2), eldest daughter of Hugh[2] (1), was born in Bedford, N. H., March 8, 1794; married Willard Parker, and had issue; died Oct. 7, 1876.

Polly Riddle[2] (1), second daughter of Hugh[2] (1), was born in Bedford, N. H., Feb. 12, 1796; married Oct. 10, 1820, to Rev. Daniel L. French, of Nelson, and had issue; deceased.

Sally Riddle[2] (1), third daughter of Hugh[2] (1), was born in Bedford, N. H., Nov. 7, 1799; married in 1842 to Col. Daniel Gould, and lived in Manchester. Still living, — the only one of her generation (1884).

Susanna Riddle[2] (3), fourth daughter of Hugh[2] (1), was born in Bedford; N. H., Oct. 10, 1801; married to Dea. Robert Boyd, of Londonderry, and had issue; died Jan. 21, 1849.

Jane Riddle[2] (1), fifth daughter of Hugh[2] (1), was born in Bedford, N. H., Sept. 11, 1804; married Eleazer, son of Dea. Richard Dole, in 1825, had issue, and died March 24, 1834.

Gen. William-Pickels Riddle[2] (2), eldest son of Isaac[2] (1), was born in Bedford, N. H., April 6, 1789; married Miss Sarah, daughter of Capt. John Ferguson, of Dunbarton, in 1824, and had issue *seven* children, of whom hereafter. His boyhood was passed at home, at the district school, and about his father's business, in which he early displayed aptness and activity. At Atkinson Academy, under Professor Vose, he acquired all the advanced education that it was his privilege in those days to receive, and subsequently, for a short time, he taught school in his native town. In 1811, Mr. Riddle located in Piscataquog, a village of considerable enterprise in Bedford, situated on the Merrimack River, and now a part of the city of Manchester. There he first took charge of his father's business affairs; business soon increased in importance, which led to the formation of the firm of Isaac Riddle & Sons. This firm extended its business operations throughout central New England. They owned and carried on stores, warehouses, lumber-yards, saw- and grist-mills, at Boston, Bedford Centre, and at Piscataquog; and operated cotton and nail factories, and lumber and grain mills on the Souhegan at Merrimack.

In the latter place they erected dwelling-houses, stores, and a hotel, whence it became to be known as " Riddle's Village," and was a thriving place.

During this time the construction of the " Union Locks and Canals " on the Merrimack River was inaugurated, an enterprise which rendered that river navigable for boats and barges from Amoskeag to Lowell, making connections between Concord and Boston. With this achievement Mr. Riddle became personally identified, manifesting zeal and foresight in a remarkable degree. Taking advantage of the facilities thus afforded for inland navigation, the firm of Isaac Riddle & Sons established a line of canal-boats, and in connection with their other extensive business operations, entered actively into the carrying trade. This business was continued by Mr. Riddle after the dissolution of the firm, and until the opening of the Nashua and Concord Railroad.

At the decease of his father the old firm was dissolved, and Mr. Riddle assumed and carried on the business thereafter, both at Merrimack and in Bedford, on his own account. He supplied the surrounding country with merchandise, and from his extensive wood-lots and water-powers, and

15

by way of purchase, he furnished round and manufactured lumber, largely for the cities of Nashua, Lowell, Newburyport, Boston, and supplied the navy-yard at Charlestown with spars and ship-timber; Boston and Lowell with lumber for public buildings and bridges; the railroads of New England with ties and contract stuff, and the island of Cuba with its railroad sleepers.

During this period of his business activity he also dealt extensively in hops, marketing them in Boston, New York, and Philadelphia, and in some instances shipping them abroad. Thus his mercantile enterprises and ventures continued till his retirement in 1860, having exercised a diversified, energetic, and busy life, for upwards of half a century. In 1848 he erected the Piscataquog Steam Mills, and successfully operated them for several years. About this time he received the appointment of general inspector of hops for the State of New Hampshire, the cultivation of which having become a matter of importance to the farmers of the State. In this capacity he was widely known and respected among the hop-growers and merchants of New England.

Quite early in life Mr. Riddle showed a taste for military affairs. At the age of twenty-five years he organized a company called the "Bedford Grenadiers," and was chosen its first captain. This was in 1815. He commanded this company about five years, when he was promoted to the rank of major in the "Old Ninth" Regiment, New Hampshire Militia (May 13, 1820). The next year he received further promotion to the lieutenant-colonelcy, and in June, 1824, became, through promotion, the colonel of his regiment, and commanded it for seven years. Thence he was brigadier-general, and on the 25th of June, 1833, was promoted to major-general of the division, which military office he held, with high commendations, till his resignation. Thus he had encompassed all the offices of military rank, from a fourth corporal to a major-general.

Under his command the "Old Ninth" Regiment was composed of ten full companies of infantry, two rifle companies, one artillery company, and one cavalry company, and by him was brought to a high state of discipline and efficiency; in reputation ranking first in the State.

In civil life, also, Mr. Riddle held offices of trust; was moderator at the town-meetings, representative to the State Legislature, county road-commissioner, trustee of institutions, on committees of public matters; but from constant pressure of business affairs he was often obliged to decline offices tendered him. In 1820, he was chairman of the committee appointed to build Piscataquog meeting-house, and twenty years later he was chiefly instrumental in remodeling it into an academy, of which he was trustee during its existence. In public education he always took a lively interest, fostering and promoting its advancement in every practical way; whether the common school, the academy, or the college, he warmly advocated and upheld the claims of each, and was patron of all.

As the town's committee he constructed the large bridges across the Merrimack River, — matters of public interest in these days, — and was president of the Granite Bridge Co., which erected the long lattice-bridge at Merrill's Falls, connecting the town with the city of Manchester. He also superintended the reconstruction of the large McGregor bridge, below Amoskeag Falls.

In Masonry, too, Mr. Riddle was pre-eminent and active in his time. He became a member of the Masonic order in 1823, and in the following year assisted in founding the Lafayette Lodge, being one of the chartered members. To the support and maintenance of this lodge, Mr. Riddle contributed liberally in funds and effort; giving free use of a hall for twenty-five years for its meetings. He was, in 1874, the only surviving one of its early projectors. During anti-mason times, this lodge was one of the very few in the State which kept its "altar-fires alive," and held regular communications unbroken. He was also a member of Mt. Horeb Chapter, and a member of Trinity Commandery of Knights Templars.

Amid the varied activities of a busy life, agriculture received no small share of his attention, owning several farms, which he cultivated with success, experimenting with crops and giving results to the public. He was a patron of the State and County fairs, gave much thought to improved methods of farming, and in many ways strove to aid in the advancement of the best interests of agriculture. The growing of hops was a specialty with him, and he carried it to highly successful results, establishing theories of his own, and generally improving the grade and quality of the hops raised in the State.

After the incorporation of the city of Manchester, and when military interests were dormant throughout the State, General Riddle organized the Amoskeag Veterans, — a military association composed of many of the most prominent and enterprising men of the city at that time. This was in the year 1854. Out of this association a battalion was formed, and General Riddle chosen commander. The success of this movement awakened the military spirit of the State, and soon after the whole military system was re-established and vitalized. The Veterans uniformed in Continental style, and upon parade presented a unique and attractive appearance. Its first public display worthy of mention was in Boston, on the occasion of a celebration of the Battle of Bunker Hill, at Charlestown. This assured its reputation.

In the fall of 1855, upon the invitation of President Pierce, the Amoskeag Veterans visited Washington, and became guests at the White House, freely enjoying its hospitality and receiving official honors. While there it made a notable pilgrimage to the Tomb of Washington, at Mt. Vernon. On its return homeward the battalion created much enthusiasm in the cities through which it passed; the stalwartness and martial bearing of the Veterans, the quaintness of their uniform, and their soldierly demeanor, attracted public notice. At Baltimore, Philadelphia, and New York, it received especial attention and entertainment. During the late war the Veterans evinced patriotism by volunteering their services to the Governor of New Hampshire. The corps exists to-day, highly honored and generally respected as one of the institutions among the "Granite Hills."

Mr. Riddle, though not a politician, always took manifest interest in the politics of the country. At first a staunch Whig, and subsequently an earnest Republican. He believed in advanced party principles, but had little regard for mere party policies. He ardently supported the Constitution and the Union, and ever upheld the integrity of the country. He respected the constitutional rights of all sections, and sought to sustain justice and freedom always and everywhere. Liberty of thought, speech, and action were fundamental with him. During the late Rebellion he was an earnest supporter of the government, and welcomed peace and the results of the war as a harbinger of a redeemed and glorified republic.

In religious faith Mr. Riddle was a Unitarian, though born of Scotch-Presbyterian parentage, and bred under such influences. His intellectual

J. A. J. Wilcox. Boston.

When Mr. Riddle entered the firm with his father and brothers, he located in Boston to manage the department of business there, having his office at their boat-house, at the end of the canal, which at that time ran through Canal Street (having given it that name) to Haymarket Square, and down Blackstone Street to the harbor. After the senior member of the firm gave up his share in the business, and removed to Quincy, Mass., Isaac Riddle, Jr., returned to Bedford, and his brother David took his place in the Boston office. Upon the death of Mr. Riddle's father, in 1830, the firm dissolved, and the business was divided, but he continued at Bedford. After disposing of his store, Mr. Riddle devoted himself to agriculture, — owning a valuable farm in Bedford, — and to land-surveying, being a professional of accuracy and great experience.

While living in Bedford, Mr. Riddle always manifested a lively interest in town affairs, and was prominently identified with public issues in general. He was postmaster for upwards of twenty years, and served in the Old Ninth Regiment of Militia, as adjutant, and subsequently as major.

About 1848 he built a fine large residence on Lowell Street, in Manchester, and removed to that city, — to which he had previously driven daily to attend to his business there, — and established himself as a real-estate broker. At the first sale of land by the Amoskeag Company, in 1838, he purchased a lot on Elm Street, between Concord and Lowell Streets, and erected the wooden building now standing there, which contained windows taken from the ancient church at Quincy, Mass. (which had been purchased by Isaac Riddle, Sr., and shipped to Manchester), through which John Adams and John-Quincy Adams, Presidents of the United States, used to look out, many years ago. At a subsequent sale of land Mr. Riddle bought two lots on Amherst Street, and located his office there. The block known as Riddle's Building (now owned by his son) he purchased subsequently of its builder, Ira Ballou.

He was a civil and police justice, and in these capacities did considerable business; was one of a committee to secure the incorporation of the city of Manchester, and assisted in founding the Manchester Bank, of which he was a director; was president of the Amoskeag Fire Insurance Company, and director of the Manchester Scale Company. He always manifested a deep interest in education, and was prominent in movements for the advancement of knowledge in Manchester, before the consolidation of the school-districts, and was on a committee to build the school-house at the corner of Union and Merrimack Streets.

Mr. Riddle acquired a large property in business, but was sometimes a heavy loser by the misfortunes of those he aided by his endorsements. He was widely known as an enterprising business man and public-spirited citizen, and when he died, Oct. 3, 1875, he was greatly missed. He was a typical representative of the sterling Scotch-Irish stock, and a gentleman of the old school. Of sound judgment, cautious, and conservative, his opinions were weighty, and his executions usually successful. Possessing great kindness of heart and tenderness of spirit, he was quickly moved at the appeal of the deserving, and generous in responding substantially to the calls of the needy. His remains were deposited in the family tomb at Bedford.

The excellent portrait of Mr. Riddle, engraved on steel expressly for this book, was kindly donated by his eldest son and namesake, Isaac N. Riddle, of Bedford, N. H.

Gilman Riddle³ (3), fourth son of Isaac² (1), was born in Bedford, N. H., Nov. 28, 1795, and died Oct. 8, 1799.

David Riddle³ (2), fifth son of Isaac² (1), was born in Bedford, N. H., Aug. 27, 1797. He entered Dartmouth College in 1814, but retired therefrom on account of ill-health, and made a voyage to Russia in 1815; married Mary Lincoln in 1826, and lived at Merrimack. He was engaged in business at the Boston house of the firm of Isaac Riddle & Sons. Mr. Riddle died July 23, 1835, after which his family removed to Hingham, where they were living in 1852; he had issue *four* children.

Jacob-McGaw Riddle³ (1), sixth son of Isaac² (1), and eldest child of his second wife, was born in Bedford, N. H., Dec. 30, 1807. He was educated at the Military Academy, Norwich, Vt.; was a mariner by profession, and was lost at sea, Sept. 21, 1835, on his fifth voyage, being first mate of the new brig "Washington," of Boston, bound for Cadiz. No family.

Margaret-Ann Riddle³ (1), eldest daughter of Isaac² (1), was born in Bedford, N. H., July 7, 1809; married in 1830, to Gen. Joseph C. Stevens, of Lancaster, Mass., and had issue; died at Lancaster, Mass., April 6, 1881.

Rebecca Riddle³ (1), second daughter of Isaac² (1) by his second wife, was born in Bedford, N. H., Aug. 13, 1811; died Aug. 9, 1812.

Polly Riddle³ (2), eldest daughter of William² (1), was born in Bedford, N. H., June 22, 1792; died March 19, 1819. She was the first wife of Dr. P. P. Woodbury. See Martha³ (2).

William Riddle³ (4), eldest son of William² (1), was born in Bedford, N. H., Feb. 8, 1794; married Mrs. Anna-Dole Riddle, in 1828, and had *two* children, of whom hereafter; he died Dec. 26, 1849.

Martha Riddle³ (2), second daughter of William² (1), was born in Bedford, N. H., April 18, 1796; married to Dr. P. P. Woodbury, brother of Levi Woodbury, LL. D., the distinguished associate justice of the U. S. Supreme Court. Dr. Woodbury's first wife was a sister to Martha; died Aug. 19, 1832.*

Dr. Freeman Riddle³ (1), second son of William² (1), was born in Bedford, N. H., March 13, 1798; graduated at Yale College in 1819; studied and practised medicine; settled in Upper Canada, and there died Jan. 21, 1826.

Jane Riddle³ (1), third daughter of William² (1), was born in Bedford, N. H., Sept. 3, 1800; married in 1826, to John Goff, and resided at Bedford; died Oct. 22, 1875.

Marinda Riddle³ (1), fourth daughter of William² (1), was born in Bedford, N. H., April 6, 1802; and died Oct. 24, 1840, at St. Clair, Mich.

Benjamin-Franklin Riddle³ (1), third son of William² (1), was born in Bedford, N. H., March 20, 1804; married, in 1830, Abigail D. Colley, and had issue *six* children, of whom hereafter; residence in 1852, Beloit, Wis.; died June 1, 1857.

---

* FREEMAN-PERKINS WOODBURY, son of Dr. Peter P. Woodbury, of Bedford, and Martha Riddle, engaged in mercantile pursuits in the city of New York when young, and has continued there successfully ever since. He married Harriet-Ann McGaw, and has several children, one of whom is a physician. He owns the old Goff homestead in the town of Bedford, which he has fitted up for a summer residence. He is fond of rural amusements and agriculture. A genial and generous-hearted gentleman of affluence.

Margaret-Tragallos Riddle³ (2), youngest daughter of William² (1), was born in Bedford, N. H., June 22, 1806; married Reuben Moore, in 1831, and lived at St. Clair, Mich., in 1852, having issue; no other information.

FOURTH GENERATION.

Asenath Riddle⁴ (1), eldest daughter of Gawn³ (2), was born in Bedford, N. H.; married Thomas G. Holbrook, in 1826, and had issue; died in 1845.

Albert Riddle⁴ (1)ʼ, eldest son of Gawn³ (2), was born in Bedford, N. H., 1804 (?); married Sarah Wheeler, and had *seven* children; he died Aug. 7, 1859.

Nancy Riddle⁴ (2), second daughter of Gawn³ (2), was born in Bedford, N. H.; married to William G. Campbell, and died Jan. 31, 1837, leaving issue.

Betsey-Dole Riddle⁴ (1), eldest daughter of James³ (1), was born at Bedford, N. H.; married to William Goff, and had issue; resides at Kenosha, Wis.

Sally-Dole Riddle⁴ (2), second daughter of James³ (1), was born in Bedford, N. H.; married to William-Riddle French, 1841, and had issue.

James-McAffee Riddle⁴ (3), son of Matthew³ (1), was born in Ohio, Oct. 31, 1820; married Harriet Ogden, and had issue *five* children, of whom hereafter; he resided at Matoon, Ill.; dead.

John-B. Riddle⁴ (4), second son of Matthew³ (1), was born in Terre Haute, Ind., Jan. 19, 1826; married Mary M., daughter of —— Boothe and his wife, Daphne, of Clifton, Ind., May 5, 1849, and had issue *four* daughters, of whom hereafter. Blacksmith by trade; removed to Prairie City (now Toledo), Ill., in 1853; thence to Seelyville, Ind., in 1871; thence to Cherokee, Kan., in 1877; thence to Hutchinson, Kan., in 1880, and died at the home of his daughter there, July 4, 1880. His wife predeceased him May 5, 1865.

Matthew Riddle⁴ (2), youngest son of Matthew³ (1), was born Oct. 11, 1828, at Terre Haute, Ind.; left for the far West at the age of twenty-one, and with the exception of one or two letters received by his brother John soon after his departure, nothing has been heard of him; supposed to have "died on the plains."

Gilman-Eveleth Riddle⁴ (4), eldest son of Gilman³ (1), was born in Manchester, N. H., in 1839; married; died, leaving issue.

John-Henry Riddle⁴ (5), second son of Gilman³ (1), was born in Manchester, N. H., in 1842; died in 1845.

Josephine-Henry Riddle⁴ (1), only daughter of Gilman³ (1), was born in Manchester, in 1845; married S. C. Smith, of Massachusetts, and died in 1872, without issue.

Martha-Ann Riddle⁴ (3), eldest daughter of John³ (3), was born in Bedford, N. H., Aug. 20, 1832; unmarried; resides in Manchester.

Margaret-Elizabeth Riddle⁴ (3), second daughter of John³ (3), was born in Bedford, N. H., March 2, 1834; deceased Oct. 16, 1840.

David-Brainard Riddle⁴ (3), eldest son of John³ (3), was born in Bedford, N. H., Feb. 8, 1840; deceased Oct. 8, 1840.

Mary-Louisa Riddle⁴ (2), third daughter of John³ (3), was born in Bedford, N. H., March 6, 1837; unmarried; lives in Manchester.

Sarah-Jane Riddle[4] (1), fourth daughter of John[3] (3), was born in Bedford, N. H., Jan. 7, 1842; died July 18, 1852.

Charles-Carroll Riddle[4] (1), second son of John[3] (3), was born in Bedford, N. H., March 6, 1840; married Sarah Eaton, and has *two* children, of whom hereafter. A farmer.

Hugh Riddle[4] (3), eldest son of Gawn[3] (3), was born in Bedford, N. H., Aug. 11, 1822; married Mary S. Walker, May 5, 1852, and by her had issue, of whom hereafter. His wife died Jan. 8, 1871, and he married secondly, Sept. 4, 1872, Althea E. Wetmore. Early became a civil engineer, and was employed in the location and construction of the Erie Railroad of New York. Was also identified with the location and construction of the Lake Shore and other New York railroads.

In 1853 Mr. Riddle had charge of track-repairs and construction on the Susquehanna Division of the Erie Railway, comprising a distance of one hundred and forty miles. His home at this time was at Binghamton, Broome County, N. Y. In 1854 he was appointed consulting engineer over the entire road and its branches. In 1855 he removed to Port Jervis, having been appointed superintendent of the Delaware Division, vacating, of course, the offices before mentioned. His labor while superintending this division was often unremitting and arduous. He was not absent during any emergency, day or night.

Mr. Riddle commenced on the railway as a chain carrier, at one dollar a day, and faithfully performed whatever duty was assigned him in the various grades of promotion, till he became general superintendent; and has attributed his success more to his perseverance under discouraging circumstances when a civil engineer, — even in the wilderness, during the construction of the road, — than to any talents he might possess.

Some incidents in the life of Mr. Riddle illustrate the character of the man. Soon after he established himself at Port Jervis, N. Y., he was returning to his home at a late hour of the evening, and while ascending a hill between the Erie depot and the upper village, where he lived, he heard approaching footsteps, and in a few moments a man came near and tendered him a small parcel. Mr. Riddle then discovered that it was the night-watchman of the highway-crossing near his office, and demanded of him what the package contained. The man answered, " Some money for your little boy." With a frown, and indignation of tone, Mr. Riddle replied, " Keep your money; when my child needs it I can supply him. If you ever approach me again in this way, I will discharge you the next moment." Thus foiled in his attempt to curry favors with the new superintendent, the man gave, as an excuse for his conduct, the statement that the former official in that capacity received presents. It was afterwards found out that this man wanted to build a shanty on the company's grounds. No person who may have presumed to offer a reward as an inducement for him to grant a favor ever succeeded with Hugh Riddle; and no person who had spent an hour with him in business intercourse would dare to offer him a bribe. His natural independence, supplemented by personal training during his early official experience, had prepared him to say " no " when occasion required it.

He never allowed any employé on the road to know that his services were considered indispensable. Notwithstanding his high appreciation of the abilities of some of his engineers and conductors, as adapted to peculiarly responsible positions, if they took umbrage and resigned, though Mr. Riddle was unwilling to part with them, he would never remonstrate,

George W. Riddle.

but let them take their own course; if they saw their mistake and returned for employment, however, they would be given a place.

After ten years of service as superintendent of the Delaware Division of the Erie Railway, he resigned his position, and was for some months out of business. As the office of general superintendent was vacant at this time, at the earnest solicitations of many, Mr. Riddle consented to be a candidate for that high and responsible position. This seemed a proper opportunity for the employés of the division to show their esteem for their late superintendent by procuring for him some suitable gift. A subscription was consequently started, and reached the large sum of fourteen hundred dollars. Two of Mr. Riddle's warmest friends went to New York to select the presents. A magnificent gold watch and chain, and a beautiful silver tea service, were purchased and engraved, the former with Mr. Riddle's initials, and the latter with those of his wife, the whole forming a testimonial of which any man might feel justly proud. As Mr. Riddle was known to be as independent as he was unobtrusive, the whole transaction had been kept from his knowledge lest he should strangle the arrangements by a decided command to stop them. But when the testimonials came and were offered to him, the donors were surprised to hear from him a positive refusal to accept them. Knowing it to be a law of the Erie Company that no officer shall receive a gift from the employés, and aware of his then present disconnection, they said — "Why, Mr. Riddle, you are not an officer of the company, and no rule adopted by them can be violated by your acceptance of the gifts." Mr. Riddle's answer was, "I know I am not an officer on this road now, but am I not a·candidate for the chief superintendency, and if I am elected, how can I exact proper discipline from those who have so generously contributed to purchase these presents, if I should accept them? I thank the men for their kind intentions, but I cannot receive the gifts." The presents were kept for months, the donors hoping, in vain, that Mr. Riddle would relent, so far, at least, as his wife's present was concerned, but he remained true to his first decision. The watch and chain fell into the hands of a locomotive-engineer on the road when disposed of by a raffle afterwards; and the tea service was returned to New York to be melted over.

Mr. Riddle was elected general superintendent of the road, and served in that capacity with great acceptance several years. He was afterwards offered the vice-presidency, under Jay Gould, but declined (having resigned his position of superintendent) any further service on the road.

Mr. Riddle has been a resident of Chicago for many years, and has filled the important offices of general superintendent and vice-president of the Chicago, Rock Island & Pacific Railroad.

Elizabeth Riddle⁴ (1), eldest daughter of Gawn³ (3), was born in Bedford, N. H., in 1827. Dead.

Henry-Charles Riddle⁴ (1), second son of Gawn³ (3), was born in Bedford, N. H., in 1829; married, and resides in Hawley, Penn.

Ann-Rebecca Riddle⁴ (1), second daughter of Gawn³ (3), was born in Bedford, N. H., in May, 1832; married to Lyman Eastman; resided in Manchester; was a successful school-teacher. Dead.

Margaret-Aiken Riddle⁴ (5), eldest daughter of William³ (3), was born Sept. 9, 1824; died Oct. 5, 1828.

Col. George-Washington Riddle⁴ (1), eldest son of William³ (3) and Sarah Ferguson, was born in Bedford, N. H., Nov. 9, 1826; married

Ellen M., daughter of Samuel Brown, of Manchester, N. H., Jan. 19, 1853, and has *one* daughter, of whom hereafter.

Colonel Riddle received his education at the public schools and at the academies at Hopkinton and Sanbornton, N. H. For several years he dealt extensively in lumber and hops. Possessing a taste for agricultural pursuits, he purchased a large farm in his native town, and settled there in 1860, where for eight years he carried on farming, and introduced improved stock and machinery.

While a resident in Bedford he was elected to preside in every town-meeting, with two or three exceptions; was chairman of selectmen in 1855 and '56; represented the town in the Legislature in 1863 and '64; was chosen military agent for the town during the Rebellion, and furnished one hundred and fifteen men to fill the quota called for by the government. Colonel Riddle so judiciously conducted the enlistment that the town, being in part re-imbursed by the State for advanced bounties, found itself, at the close of the war, not only free from debt, but with thousands of dollars in the treasury. This money was appropriated to build the new and beautiful town-hall at Bedford Centre.

In 1850 Colonel Riddle was appointed and commissioned quartermaster of the Ninth Regiment, New Hampshire Militia, with rank of lieutenant. At the organization of the Amoskeag Veterans, in 1854, he was one of the youngest members of that command, and his name still stands enrolled as one of the honorary members.

In 1860 he was commissioned division quartermaster on the staff of Major-General McCutchins, with rank of colonel. At the organization of the Bedford Light Infantry, in 1862, — a company composed of the best young men in town, many of whom subsequently served in the army, — Colonel Riddle was chosen captain, and commanded the company four years, during which time, by careful drill and good discipline, it was raised to a high state of military efficiency.

In 1867 he was elected treasurer of the New Hampshire State Agricultural Society, and during the seventeen years he has served in this capacity the fairs have been very successful, promoting the interest of farming throughout the State, and the introduction of various improved breeds of stock. In 1869, at the solicitation of many of the most prominent men in the State, Colonel Riddle was induced to accept the position of treasurer and general manager of the New England Agricultural Society. At this time the demands of the society required a man of large experience, executive ability, and determination, to develop its resources, and to-day, under the able management of its treasurer, the society stands second to none in New England. It has the largest number of life members (two thousand), pays liberal premiums, and its fairs are annually visited by thousands of patrons. The subject of this notice has held this important office fourteen years, and has the reputation of being one of the most successful managers of fairs in the country.

In consequence of growing business interests, and official engagements elsewhere, Colonel Riddle disposed of his farm in Bedford, in 1869, and having built an elegant mansion on Myrtle Street, Manchester, fixed his residence there. He was chosen a commissioner for Hillsboro' County in 1870; was re-elected in 1873, and during the six years he served in that capacity very important changes were effected at the County Farm, in Wilton, and at the jail, in the city of Manchester, which was under his immediate supervision; and his sympathy and kind treatment toward the unfortunate inmates of these institutions made him very popular, and insured him the highest commendations, with many a "God bless you and yours." He was offered the renomination, but declined the honor.

In 1876 Colonel Riddle was appointed State Centennial Commissioner, to represent the interests of New Hampshire at the great exhibition held that year at Philadelphia. He superintended the erection of the New Hampshire State building at Fairmount Park, and conducted the exhibit of the State during the Centennial.

After his return from Philadelphia, in 1877, in connection with other prominent men of Manchester, he promoted the organization of the Horse Railroad Company, and secured subscriptions for stock necessary to make the arrangement a success. He was appointed building agent, and in September of that year the first narrow-gauge street-railway in New England was finished, fully equipped, and put into successful operation. This continued under Colonel Riddle's management till 1880, when he resigned his position.

For many years Colonel Riddle has been identified with the material prosperity of Manchester, and connected with some of the largest and most successful financial institutions of the city. He is now director of the New Hampshire Fire Insurance Company, trustee of Amoskeag Savings Bank, trustee of the People's Bank, director of the Amoskeag National Bank, president of Manchester Driving Park Company, trustee of Elliott Hospital, and director of Franklin-street Congregational Society. In 1882 he was appointed by Gov. Chas. H. Bell, Fish and Game Commissioner of New Hampshire, and is now chairman of this important board.

Until 1883 Manchester had no suitable place for large gatherings, but in that year a meeting of the citizens was called, and a stock company organized with a large capital to establish fair grounds. Colonel Riddle was chosen one of the directors and subsequently president; was authorized to purchase the necessary land, and in the short space of four months a half-mile track was built, with commodious fair buildings, the whole ground being well laid out and transformed into a beautiful park, in which the New England Fair of 1884 was held.

While a resident of Manchester, he was moderator, assessor, and representative to the Legislature (1860). After his return from Bedford he was elected and served two years in common council of Manchester.

As chairman of a military committee during his services in the State Legislature, Colonel Riddle, by judicious management, secured an appropriation that enabled Adjt.-Gen. Natt Head to publish an excellent military history of that State.

Descending from the good Scotch-Irish stock, he is a typical representative of that noble race of men who came from the north of Ireland and settled this section of New Hampshire: transforming a howling wilderness into a blooming garden. He is a quiet, peaceful citizen; has great executive force, indomitable courage and perseverance, and achieves remarkable success in all his undertakings; liberal in his views, generous to the needy, and a firm friend. Colonel Riddle subscribed for his portrait in steel for this book.

William-Quincy Riddle[4] (5), second son of William[3] (3), was born in Bedford, N. H., June 8, 1828. He has never married. Mr. Riddle is a graduate of Harvard and Yale Colleges, and has been engaged in the practice of law in New York city for nearly fifteen years. He is regarded as an able member of the legal profession, and is employed on cases that involve very large sums of money. He is affable, genial, and conversational, and withal a refined and cultivated gentleman. Mr. Riddle attended the family meeting of the Riddles, held in Philadelphia, in the summer of 1876, and took an active part in the business of that meeting. He moved the appointment of the "Co-operative Committee," who have rendered important assistance in the furtherance of this book; he was one of the general and sub-committees, and has personally devoted valuable attention to the interests of the work. The author's acknowledgments are due this gentleman, for the timely suggestions and substantial aid given during his arduous labors in the prosecution of his work, — a work which, but for the encouragement of Mr. Riddle, might never have been published.

Daniel-Wileshire Riddle[4] (1), third son of William[3] (3), was born in Bedford, N. H., May 18, 1830; died Sept. 15, 1831, at Piscataquog Village.

Sarah-Maria Riddle[4] (2), second daughter of William[3] (3), was born in Bedford, N. H., May 24, 1832; married John F. Dinckler, and had issue; died in 1862.

Daniel-Wileshire Riddle[4] (2), fourth son of William[3] (3), was born in Bedford, N. H., July 12, 1833; married Jan. 28, 1872, Jennie Howe, of Waterloo, N. Y., and has issue. He was engaged in business in Baltimore when the war of the Rebellion broke out; volunteered into the Union service, and joined the First Philadelphia Troop, which was stationed at Winchester, Va. After his term of service had expired, he received the appointment of assistant paymaster in the navy. He was in the blockade service of the Gulf and about New Orleans; was on board Admiral Farragut's flag-ship at the naval battle off Mobile, and practically served through the war. After the close of the war, he engaged in business at New Orleans, where he continued for a time, and subsequently returned to his native town, and is now (1876) living on the homestead place.

Carroll Riddle[4] (1), youngest son of William[3] (3), was born in Bedford, N. H., Aug. 2, 1834; married Carrie Martynn, and died without issue, in December, 1871.

Charlotte-Margaret Riddle[4] (1), eldest daughter of James[3] (2), was born in Merrimack, N. H., Feb. 20, 1817; married Nathan Parker, cashier of Manchester Bank; died in Manchester, Oct. 22, 1859, leaving *one* son, Walter M. Parker.

Mary-Ann-Lincoln Riddle[4] (2), second daughter of James[3] (2), was born in Merrimack, N. H., Aug. 9, 1823; married Gilman Cheney, and had issue *one* son, William-Gilman Cheney; residence Montreal, Can.

Eliza-Frances Riddle[4] (3), third daughter of James[3] (2), was born in Merrimack, N. H., Sept. 4, 1832; married John Jackman, Oct. 11, 1860, and had issue *one* son; residence, Nashua, N. H.

Ann-Elizabeth Riddle[4] (2), eldest daughter of Isaac[3] (2), was born in Bedford, N. H., Feb. 18, 1820; she was a teacher of the public schools in her native town and of the high school in Manchester; died Jan. 26, 1850.

Isaac-Newton Riddle[4] (3), eldest son of Isaac[3] (2), was born in Bedford, N. H., Aug. 12, 1822; was in mercantile business in early life; afterwards appointed to a clerkship in the United States Custom House, in Boston, which he retained many years. He is now a Justice of the Peace and notary public at Manchester. He resides on the old Riddle homestead in Bedford; unmarried.

Jane-Aiken Riddle[4] (2), second daughter of Isaac[3] (2), was born in Bedford, July 6, 1825; was married Oct. 18, 1849, to Benjamin F. White, a merchant of Boston, Mass.; died May 10, 1862, leaving *one* daughter, Jennie-Elizabeth White.

John-Aiken Riddle[4] (5), second son of Isaac[3] (2), was born in Bedford, N. H., Sept. 8, 1826. He has been engaged in the profession of civil engineer in the location and construction of numerous railroads in New England and the Middle States; among them the Boston, Concord & Montreal; Erie; Atlantic, and Great Western. He visited California in 1858 for the purpose of inspecting the mines of that State, particularly the quartz-mines and the manner of working them. Upon his return Mr. Riddle made some researches in the State of Vermont, and extracted the first quantity of gold ever taken from the rocks of New England, having secured nearly a pound of pure metal from a single ton of ore. Mr. Riddle is Justice of the Peace, and a real-estate owner in Manchester; his office in "Riddle's Block." He has rendered much assistance in furnishing records for this work, and is a member of the Publishing Committee. He lives on the "Riddle Homestead" in Bedford with his two brothers, which town he represents in the Legislature of the State; never married.

Silas-Aiken Riddle[4] (1), youngest son of Isaac[3] (2), was born in Bedford, N. H., July 22, 1831; unmarried. He was engaged in mercantile business in Boston and St. Louis, and was in the latter city at the breaking out of the war of the Rebellion. He volunteered into the Union navy and was with Admiral Farragut in the Gulf squadron, — was on the flag-ship of the gallant Admiral at the naval battle in Mobile Bay. He now holds the office of town-clerk, in his native town, and resides with his brothers on the homestead.

Minniebel Riddle[4] (1), youngest daughter of Isaac[3] (2), died in infancy.

Mary-E. Riddle[4] (3), eldest daughter of David[3] (2), was born in Merrimack, N. H., April 16, 1827. No other information.

Gilman Riddle[4] (4), eldest son of David[3] (2), was born in Merrimack, N. H., Oct. 18, 1828; died Sept. 11, 1835.

Charles-Lincoln Riddle[4] (2), second son of David[3] (2), was born in Merrimack, N. H., Dec. 7, 1830. He probably went to Hingham after his father's death. Cashier of Webster National Bank, Boston, Mass., 1884.

Adeline Riddle[4] (1), second daughter of David[3] (2), was born in Merrimack, N. H., April 11, 1833.

Laura Riddle[4] (1), only daughter of William[3] (3), was born April 17, 1831, married to Dr. M. G. J. Tewksbury, and had issue. She died June 10, 1871.

James-W. Riddle[4] (4), only son of William[3] (3), was born March 12, 1833; died Aug. 31, 1849.

Mary-Woodbury Riddle[4] (5), eldest daughter of Benjamin[3] (1), was born at Bedford, N. H., June 9, 1832; lives in New York city.

Joseph-Colley Riddle[4] (1), eldest son of Benjamin[3] (1), was born in Bedford, N. H., March 17, 1834; married in 1864, Annie M. Segar, and has issue, of whom hereafter. He is a merchant at Marshalltown, Ia.

Lieut. William-Franklin Riddle⁴ (5), second son of Benjamin³ (1), was born in Bedford, N. H., July 22, 1835. He was in mercantile business in Detroit, Mich., at the breaking out of the war of the Rebellion; entered the Union army and served as first lieutenant in the Twenty-second Regiment, Wisconsin Volunteers. After the war he resumed business at Detroit.

Abbie-Jane Riddle⁴ (1), second daughter of Benjamin³ (1), was born at Amherst, N. H., Aug. 22, 1839; was married Oct. 23, 1869, to Frank Whipple, and resides at Port Huron, Mich. Has children.

Lieut. Freeman-Benjamin Riddle⁴ (2), third son of Benjamin³ (1), was born at Beloit, Wis., Sept. 30, 1841. He served three years in the Union army, during the war of the Rebellion, as a private in the Fifth Regiment, Wisconsin Volunteers, and was thence commissioned first lieutenant in the Thirty-seventh Regiment, Wisconsin Volunteers, in which service he fell mortally wounded while gallantly leading his troops in battle, on the 4th of June, 1864, at Petersburgh, Va.

Kittie Riddle⁴ (1), youngest daughter of Benjamin³ (1), was born at Beloit, Wis., April 8, 1852; was living at Port Huron in 1873.

FIFTH GENERATION.

Sarah-Ellen Riddle⁵ (3), eldest daughter of John⁴ (4), born in July, 1852; was married to William Richardson in 1871, at Prairie City, Ill., where they lived about three years, and where,—after several removals to Kansas and elsewhere,—they now reside, near their old homestead.

Mary-Elizabeth Riddle⁵ (6), second daughter of John⁴ (4), was born at Prairie City, Ill., July 19, 1856; was married in 1880 to Jesse Rowe, of Cherokee, Kan., and is now living at Monmouth, Kan.

Alma-Eva Riddle⁵ (1), third daughter of John⁴ (4), was born at Prairie City, Ill., June, 1858; was married in 1881 to Edmund Richardson (brother of William), in Wichita, Kan., but removed to Prairie City with her sister Sarah, and now lives there.

Harriet-Esther Riddle⁵ (2), fourth daughter of John⁴ (4), was born at Prairie City, Ill., Feb. 3, 1860; was married to V. C. Chamberlain, of Seelyville, Ind.

Freeman-Gilmore Riddle⁵ (3), eldest son of Charles⁴ (1), was born in Manchester, N. H., July 25, 1866.

Eddie Riddle⁵ (1), eldest son of Hugh⁴ (3), was born Dec. 23, 1853; died Sept. 7, 1854.

Charles-F. Riddle⁵ (3), second son of Hugh⁴ (3), was born May 13, 1855; married at Elmira, N. Y. He became identified with the Erie Railroad in early manhood.

Frederick Riddle⁵ (1), third son of Hugh⁴ (3), was born Jan. 29, 1858; died Sept. 30, 1862.

Mary Riddle⁵ (7), a daughter of Hugh⁴ (3), was born Jan. 5, 1865; died May 12, 1867.

Emma Riddle⁵ (1), only daughter of George⁴ (1), was born in Bedford, N. H., Feb. 19, 1856; was married April 24, 1884, to Walter C. Lewis, of Haverhill, Mass.

Blanch-Hayward Riddle[6] (1), daughter of Daniel[4] (2), was born April 9, 1874.

Freeman-Benjamin Riddle[6] (4), eldest son of Joseph[4] (1), was born at Marshalltown, Ia., in 1866; died in infancy.

George-Sattler Riddle[6] (3), second son of Joseph[4] (1), was born at Marshalltown, Ia., in September, 1868; died in March, 1869.

Julia-Andrews Riddle[6] (1), eldest daughter of Joseph[4] (1), was born at Marshalltown, Ia., Oct. 20, 1870.

RIDDELLS OF BEDFORD, NEW HAMPSHIRE, NO. 2.

[JOHN BRANCH.]

John Riddell[1] (1), supposed to have been a son of John Riddell and his wife, Janet Gordon, of Ballymeath, Ireland, was born Jan. 2, 1701, — an American account places his birth 1709, — and came to New England in company with his brothers in 1718, being the youngest of the four. He married Janet ——, settled in Bedford, N. H., alongside of many of his Scotch-Irish neighbors from the old country, as a farmer, and had issue, of whom hereafter. His name was signed to the original petition for a charter for the town of Bedford, May 10, 1750. He was fence-viewer June 6, 1750; fence-viewer and appraiser in 1751; he was a surveyor of highways in 1752, and a tax-payer in each of these years. His name is not found on the tax-list subsequent to 1752, but the following year, 1753, "Janet Riddell" appears as a tax-payer, and continues as such until 1764. The information found respecting this man and his family is meagre and quite disconnected; indeed, the descendants of his brothers were not aware of such a kinsman. The Rev. Samuel-Hopkins Riddell, an erudite and very accurate man, who had gathered considerable genealogical information relating to his family, was taken by surprise when, during my correspondence with him, I announced the documentary evidence of the existence of *four* original brothers, instead of the traditionary *three*, of whom he was cognizant, and for some time expressed grave doubts as to the authenticity and accuracy of my proof; at the same time he and others had before them the sketch of William P. Riddell, published in 1852, in which he mentions this John Riddell as one whose genealogical connections were left in obscurity. It has been plausibly assumed that this family was extinct in the male line; but I mention as of interest in the question, the existence of a family descended from David Riddell, who was a native of New Hampshire, and removed in early life to New York State. (See account of this family under designation of "Riddells of Rochdale, New-York.") I can find no other New Hampshire branch from which this David could have descended. John Riddell died July, 1757, and his slate-stone monument in the Bedford cemetery bears the following inscription:

> "To celebrate Jehovah's praise,
> My very body shall arise."

SECOND GENERATION.

Mary Riddell[2] (1) was a daughter of John[1] (1), of Bedford. The history of that town says of her: "John Riddle had one daughter Mary, who lived on the Isaac Atwood place, in a house by herself; she was never married, and died about 1818." Her name appears on the tax-list in 1757 (the year following her father's death), 1758, 1759, and 1782. In 1788, it was voted to excuse her from paying all past taxes. The church records of Bedford bear the names of *three* Marys of the family-name, and one of them was evidently the subject of this notice. Hon. Matthew Patten wrote in his diary, April 17, 1778, as follows: "Wrote a deed from John Clark to Mary Riddel, and a bond from Mary to him for his maintenance. 20th, went to Mary Riddel's, and took the acknowledgment of a deed from her uncle, John Clark, to her; I had writ the deed and a bond from her to him before. She gave me two dollars for my trouble." John Clark had married Mary's father's sister in Ireland, and now, — his wife having probably died, — he conveys his property to this niece, and she gives a bond for his maintenance; it is probable, then, that John Clark died in the house of Mary Riddell. David Patten, in a letter to his brother in the latter part of the last century, mentions "John Riddle, the father of Mary."

Elizabeth Riddell² (1), presumably a daughter of John¹ (1). Her name appears on the tax-list of Bedford from 1757 to 1759. I have no record of her marriage or death.

----•◦•----

RIDDELLS OF DERRYFIELD, NEW HAMPSHIRE.

John Riddell¹ (1), came from Scotland (parents unknown) in 1730, and settled in Derryfield, N. H. He was born about 1694, and had wife "Janet," as appears from her monument now standing in the southwest corner of the "Valley Cemetery," Manchester, N. H., it having been removed from an ancient burying-ground, which is now entirely obliterated by the march of improvement. In the "History of Manchester," it is said of a burying-place on an oak knoll south of Christian's Brook, and upon the farm of John McNeil, which was next to John Riddell's farm: "The oldest monument in date of death and probably in erection, was in memory of Mrs. Janet Riddel." The inscription on her monument runs thus: —

> *"Here Lyes the Body of*
> *Mrs. Janet Riddel, Wife to*
> *Mr. John Riddel. She died*
> *Septr 18, 1746, Aged 50 years."*

This ancient burying-place, whence the monument was removed, was "by the McGregor Bridge, near the present locomotive works." John's name appears on the old town records in 1751, as surveyor of highways; in 1752 as a committee to procure preaching; in 1753 as selectman and committee to supply preaching; in 1754 as fence-viewer, and in 1755–6, as a tax-payer. Some say John has a brother *Archibald*, and the *name* sounds of Scotland, but I can find no records to support the tradition; if there was such a brother he probably settled elsewhere.

SECOND GENERATION.

James Riddell² (1), a son of John¹ (1), of Derryfield, N. H., was born in 1733; married Janet, daughter of Mr. John Hall (the first town-clerk),

Sept. 27, 1759, and died at Springfield, in said State, in 1800, aged 67 years. He was a private soldier in the old French war, and also served under General Sullivan in the war of the Revolution, in a company called the "Rogers Rangers," which was sent against the notorious Indians known as the "Six Nations." He had issue *six* children, of whom hereafter. Mr. Riddell was a large, powerful man.

THIRD GENERATION.

Elizabeth Riddell³ (1), eldest daughter of James² (1), was born in Derryfield, N. H., March 28, 1761.

John Riddell³ (2), eldest son of James² (1), was born in Derryfield, N. H., Feb. 24, 1763; married a Miss Thompson, and had issue, of whom hereafter. He was a soldier in the war of the Revolution. He enlisted for three years, March, 1778, under Capt. Ebenezer Frye, Colonel Cilley's New Hampshire regiment, and General Poor's brigade; was with General Sullivan in Genessee, in 1779 and 1780, in the "Flying Camp" (so called) between the American army and the enemy. He was wounded and discharged near West Point, by Colonel Scammell, in 1781. He resided in Tunbridge, Vt., forty-three years. He married, Dec. 12, 1820, Mary Church, of Norwich, Vt. She was probably a second wife. He died Sept. 24, 1839; his widow was living at Tunbridge, in 1850, aged 74. Mr. *Riddall** (as this branch spell the name) was the father of a numerous family, of whom more hereafter, and his descendants are widely scattered.

Janet Riddell³ (1), second daughter of James² (1), was born in Derryfield, N. H., Jan. 12, 1765.

Sarah Riddell³ (1), third daughter of James² (1), was born in Derryfield, N. H., May 17, 1767; was married to Dea. James Wallace, and had issue. She was the Sarah who, when a young woman, 'tended a gristmill for Col. Daniel Moore; he directed her to take no toll from the sack of a widow, or from that of a man who brought his grain on his back. She said she was "always vexed when *two* bushels came in one sack." I do not find mention of her descendants.

Mary Riddell³ (1), fourth daughter of James² (1), was born in Derryfield, N. H., in 1769; was married, Oct. 16, 1788, to Robert Ford, and died July 26, 1848, aged 79 years. During her father's absence in the army she lived with her grandfather Hall; after his return from the war, she kept his house in Springfield until his second marriage. She walked from Andover, eleven miles through the wilderness, with only "spotted trees" for her guide.

James Riddell³ (2), youngest son of James² (1), was born in Derryfield, N. H., in 1771; married, Nov. 18, 1790, Sally (or Polly) Carr, and had issue *nine* children, of whom hereafter. He boarded at Deacon Duncan's, in Londonderry, during his father's absence in the Revolutionary army, and remained there till his settlement in Springfield. Mr. Riddell settled on a farm in Grafton, N. H., where he died Sept. 28, 1854, aged 83 years.

Martha Riddell³ (1), youngest daughter of James² (1), was born in 1773, and was probably an infant when her mother died.

FOURTH GENERATION.

Levi Riddall⁴ (1), eldest son of John³ (2), was born in Tunbridge, Vt., and died somewhere in New York, unmarried.

---

* This family use three forms of orthography, viz. : Riddall, Riddell, and Riddle, and I have followed the original authorities.

16

James Riddall⁴ (3), second son of John⁸ (2), was born in Tunbridge, Vt., and died when a young man, unmarried.

Lyman Riddall⁴ (1), third son of John⁸ (2), was born in Tunbridge, Vt., married Rhoda Alexander, and resided in Royalton until 1850, when he emigrated to Wisconsin. He died a few years ago, leaving several children, of whom hereafter. He was a farmer by occupation.

Ira Riddall⁴ (1), fourth son of John⁸ (2), was born in Tunbridge, Vt.; married Achsah Mudget, and resided for many years in his native town. After the death of his wife he removed to Canaan (?). Now dead.

Hannah Riddall⁴ (1), a daughter of John⁸ (2), was born in Tunbridge, Vt., and died there, unmarried.

Sally Riddall⁴ (1), a daughter of John⁸ (2), was born in Tunbridge, Vt.; was married to Samuel Peterson (or Patterson), and removed to the State of New York, where she died.

Jane Riddall⁴ (1), a daughter of John⁸ (2), was born in Tunbridge, Vt.; was married to James Adams, and lived and died in her native town.

Samuel Riddall⁴ (1), a son of John⁸ (2), was born in Tunbridge, Vt., Nov. 14, 1806; married the widow (Dalbar) Cilley, about 1834, and had issue *four* sons, of whom hereafter. He was a farmer in Tunbridge; died July 10, 1862.

Betsey Riddle⁴ (1), eldest daughter of James⁸ (2), was born in Grafton, N. H., Dec. 8, 1791; was married Feb. 5, 1818, to Mr. John Upton, and died March 23, 1827.

John Riddle⁴ (3), eldest son of James⁸ (2), was born in Grafton, N. H., June 11, 1794; married Oct. 20, 1814, to Polly Robinson, and had issue, of whom hereafter. He is a farmer, residing in his native town.

Rachel Riddle⁴ (1), second daughter of James⁸ (2), was born in Grafton, N. H., Oct. 6, 1796; was married Dec. 31, 1818, to Merrill Currier, and died March 23, 1852.

Enoch Riddle⁴ (1), second son of James⁸ (2), was born in Grafton, N. H., Feb. 14, 1799; married Miss Polly, daughter of Reuben and Abigail (Follet) Prescott, of Lee, N. H. (she was born March 15, 1800), March 4, 1821, and had issue *eight* children, of whom hereafter. He emigrated to the West some years ago, and died at Peotone, Ill., Oct. 11, 1865. His wife predeceased him March 20, 1856. He was a farmer.

Beriah Riddle⁴ (1), third son of James⁸ (2), was born in Grafton, N. H., March 29, 1801; drowned Aug. 14, 1814.

Robert Riddle⁴ (1), fourth son of James⁸ (2), was born in Grafton, N. H., Jan. 4, 1802; married July 3, 1827, to Sally Davis, and had issue *three* children, of whom hereafter. He was a farmer and currier; died Jan 16, 1835.

Cyrus Riddle⁴ (1), fifth son of James⁸ (2), was born in Grafton, N. H. (say 1805); married a Dutch lady named Sally-Matilda Vanhoosen, and had issue *four* children, of whom hereafter. He was a gardener; went West and died.

Hiram Riddle⁴ (1), sixth son of James⁸ (2), was born in Grafton, N. H., Nov. 2, 1809; married Jan. 13, 1831, to Betsey-Chase, daughter of Richard Whittier (she was born in Grafton, March 10, 1811), and had issue *five* children, of whom hereafter. He emigrated to Minneapolis, Minn., in 1855, where he has been engaged in farming; died at Waterford, Minn., Feb. 22, 1883, aged 74 years.

Polly Riddle[4] (1), youngest daughter of James[3] (2), was born in Grafton, N. H., Dec. 12, 1811; was married to Elkanah Whittier, of Grafton, and died at Empire City, Minn., in 1872.

FIFTH GENERATION.

Ira Riddall[5] (2), a son of Lyman[4] (1), was born in Royalton, Vt.
James Riddall[5] (4), a son of Lyman[4] (1), was born in Royalton, Vt.
John Riddall[5] (4), a son of Lyman[4] (1), was born in Royalton, Vt.

John Riddall[5] (5), eldest son of Samuel[4] (1), was born in Tunbridge, Vt., Jan. 29, 1835; married Mary-Ann Lee, April 19, 1862, and died Sept. 22, 1863.
Mahew-C. Riddall[5] (1), second son of Samuel[4] (1), was born in Tunbridge, Vt., May 5, 1837; died Sept. 25, 1857; single.
James-E. Riddall[5] (5), third son of Samuel[4] (1), was born in Tunbridge, Vt., Oct. 28, 1839; married Esther-Ann Shepherd, and resides on his father's homestead farm. He was married March 8, 1864. No mention of children.
William-H. Riddall[5] (1), fourth son of Samuel[4] (1), was born in Tunbridge, Vt., Dec. 2, 1841, and lives in Lowell, Mass.; unmarried in 1879.

James Riddle[5] (6), eldest son of John[4] (3), was born in Grafton, N. H., Nov. 16, 1815; married in Quincy, Mass., Jan. 1, 1843, to Mary-Bent Colburn, and has issue (1874) *four* children, of whom hereafter. He is a *stone-cutter* by trade. Residence unknown.
Neriah Riddle[5] (1), second son of John[4] (3), was born in Grafton, N. H., Dec. 22, 1819; a farmer. No issue.
Ira Riddle[5] (3), third son of John[4] (3), was born in Grafton, N. H., April 8, 1821; married March 6, 1844, to Candis Williams, and has issue *one* daughter, of whom hereafter. I do not know his place of residence.
Andrew-J. Riddle[5] (1), fourth son of John[4] (3), was born in Grafton, N. H., May 8, 1835; married April 28, 1859, to Janetta Martin, and has issue *two* children, of whom hereafter. Mr. Riddle is a farmer in Grafton.

Adoniram Riddle[5] (1), eldest son of Enoch[4] (1), was born in Grafton, N. H., July 17, 1822; married July 3, 1850, to Hannah J. Cook, of Centre Harbor, N. H., and has issue *three* children, of whom hereafter. He is a machinist and engineer by trade; now foreman in the Chicago, Burlington & Quincy Railroad shops, at Aurora, Ill.
Reuben-Prescott Riddle[5] (1), second son of Enoch[4] (1), was born in Grafton, N. H., Oct. 14, 1824; married, and is now (1879) living in Yuba County, Cal. He is a county surveyor; residence at Mayesville.
James-Lyman Riddle[5] (7), third son of Enoch[4] (1), was born in Grafton, N. H., April 10, 1827, and is believed to be living at Marysville, Yuba County, Cal.
Betsey-Arozina Riddle[5] (2), eldest daughter of Enoch[4] (1), was born in Grafton, N. H., Feb. 10, 1830; was married to James Webster, Oct. 5, 1848; he was killed by the cars at Lebanon, N. H., Dec. 18, 1864, aged 43 years; secondly, to Cole Vyname (?), with whom she is living near Waterman, Ill.
George-W. Riddle[5] (1), fourth son of Enoch[4] (1), was born in Grafton, N. H., May 29, 1833; married, and resides at Yarmouth, N. S. A machinist by trade.

Robert-B. Riddle[5] (1), fifth son of Enoch[4] (1), was born in Grafton, N. H., July 12, 1836; married, and is now (1879) a merchant at Kankakee, Ill.

Cyrus-S. Riddle[5] (2), sixth son of Enoch[4] (1), was born in Grafton, N. H., July 7, 1839, and died in Illinois, Oct. 11, 1857.

Charles-B. Riddle[5] (1), seventh son of Enoch[4] (1), was born in Grafton, N. H., Aug. 3, 1841; married, and is a stockdealer at Peotone, Ill. Was in the army.

Oscar-George Riddle[5] (1), only son of Robert[4] (1), was born in Grafton, N. H., Jan. 19, 1829; died March 24, 1832.

Ellen-A. Riddle[5] (1), only daughter of Robert[4] (1), was born in Grafton, N. H., Nov. 20, 1834. A teacher.

Lettice-Whittier Riddle[5] (1), eldest daughter of Hiram[4] (1), was born in Grafton, N. H., June 13, 1831; was married Dec. 8, 1852, to L. P. Elliott, and died at Farmington, Minn., Sept. 23, 1868, leaving *six* small children.

Melvina-Balch Riddle[5] (1), second daughter of Hiram[4] (1), was born in Grafton, N. H., Jan. 6, 1837; was married April 3, 1855, to George S. Dickinson. Residence unknown.

Richard-Whittier Riddle[5] (1), eldest son of Hiram[4] (1), was born in Grafton, N. H., Jan. 23, 1840; married Dec. 4, 1862, to Rachel H. Brooks, of Farmington, Minn. He is a house carpenter by trade; resides in the city of Minneapolis, Minn.; has issue *three* children, of whom hereafter.

Mary-Estelle Riddle[5] (2), third daughter of Hiram[4] (1), was born in Grafton, N. H., Aug. 3, 1844; was married Nov. 10, 1861, to William A. Smith, and lives in the West.

James-Albert Riddle[5] (8), second son of Hiram[4] (1), was born in Grafton, N. H., Dec. 25, 1848; married Oct. 22, 1872, to Hattie I. Chamberlain, and resides at Minneapolis, Minn.; house carpenter. No mention of children.

SIXTH GENERATION.

Oscar-C. Riddle[6] (2), eldest son of James[5] (6), was born in Quincy, Mass., Nov. 30, 1850; died the same year.

Sarah-Elizabeth Riddle[6] (2) eldest daughter of James[5] (6), was born in Quincy, Mass., July 22, 1852; died Nov. 28, 1855.

Henry-W. Riddle[6] (1), second son of James[5] (6), was born in Quincy, Mass., Dec. 20, 1856.

Oscar-W. Riddle[6] (3), third son of James[5] (6), was born in Quincy, Mass. (presumably), June 22, 1859.

Sarah-Jane Riddle[5] (3), only daughter of Ira[5],(3), was born Dec. 13, 1846; was married Oct. 6, 1866, to Charles H. Rogers.

Clara-Emma Riddle[6] (1), eldest daughter of Andrew[5] (1), was born Sept. 10, 1862; place unknown.

James-W. Riddle[6] (9), eldest son of Andrew[5] (1), was born Sept. 16, 1868; place unknown.

Alice Riddle[6] (1), eldest daughter of Adoniram[5] (1), was born in New Hampshire, July 26, 1858, and died Nov. 17, 1858.

Clarence-O. Riddle[6] (1), eldest son of Adoniram[5] (1), was born in Keene, N. H., Sept. 18, 1854, and is now (1879) a locomotive engineer, on the Chicago, Burlington & Quincy Railroad.

Delazon-A. Riddle[6] (1), second son of Adoniram[5] (1), was born in Aurora, Ill., March 6, 1858, and is a book-keeper in the office of the superintendent of the locomotive and car department of the Chicago, Burlington & Quincy Railroads.

Hiram-Arthur Riddle[6] (2), eldest son of Richard[5] (1), was born at Farmington, Minn., Feb. 4, 1864.

Charles-Richard Riddle[6] (2), second son of Richard[5] (1), was born at Sciota, Minn., Feb. 17, 1866.

Myrta-Betsey Riddle[6] (1), eldest daughter of Richard[5] (1), was born at Farmington, Minn., May 20, 1867.

RIDDELLS OF COLERAINE, MASSACHUSETTS, NO. 1.

[HUGH BRANCH.]

Dea. Hugh Riddell[1] (1), supposed to be a son of John Riddell and Janet Gordon, of Ballymeath, Ireland, was born Sept. 20, 1692. (See "Riddells of Ballymeath, Ireland," in this book.) The subject of this notice came to America in the year 1718, in company with his brothers, and first sat down at Londonderry, N. H. He married Mrs. Ann Aiken, a lady of Scottish descent, of Concord, Mass. He continued his residence in Londonderry until 1788, when he removed to Bedford, in the same County, where he lived for many years.* He was a pew-owner in Londonderry meeting-house in 1739, and signed an agreement for a division of land there the third day of June the same year. His name appears on a petition to the Colonial Assembly of New Hampshire about fishing at Amoskeag. In 1750 he resigned a committeeship organized to secure preaching there, and signed the resignation in presence of the town clerk. In 1752, he was a committee to build a wall around the meeting-house; in 1754, a committee to build a frame for a meeting-house; in 1756, a committee to give the Rev. John Houston a call to preach; in 1757, he had forty pounds sterling for underpinning the meeting-house; in 1759, a committee to build a bridge across the Piscataquog River; and in 1762, "Deacon Hugh Riddel" was a committee to get the pulpit built. In 1763 he removed to Coleraine, Mass., a place settled by Scotch-Irish emigrants, and named for their old home in the north of Ireland. He died at Coleraine, Feb. 25, 1775, aged,—according to the record of his birth,—eighty-three years. His widow died May 22, 1790; they were buried in an ancient cemetery in Coleraine, and in 1852 their double head-stone stood near the centre of the yard; his inscription was on one side of the stone, and that of the wife on the other. Children, of whom here-

---

* He owned the farm since known as the "MacAllister Place," esteemed one of the best in town, and situated about one and a half miles north of Bedford Centre. The site on which the house of Hugh stood was some forty rods northeast of the modern buildings (1852) on this farm, and the location only distinguishable by an indention in the ground where the cellar had been.

after, *four* in number. In 1729 his surname was found spelled "Ridell"; on May 10, 1750, it stood on a petition for a charter for Bedford, with those of his two brothers, Gawn and John, spelled "Riddell," and in 1752 it was spelt "Ridel." In Patten's journal the name is always "Riddell." Patten was a Scotchman, — or of Scottish extraction, — and understood the proper spelling of the surname. None of this branch of the Riddell family seem to have adopted the surname "Riddle" until subsequent to 1790.

Hugh Riddell was selectman in Bedford, N. H., in the years 1754 and 1755. The following is a *fac-simile* of his autograph : —

SECOND GENERATION.

Dea. Hugh Riddell[2] (2), eldest son of Hugh[1] (1) and Ann Aiken, was born in Bedford, N. H., in August, 1740. He married Jane Morris, and in the year 1763 removed to Coleraine, Mass., where he settled on a farm, and remained until within fifteen years of his death, when he went to live with his son Samuel, in Charlemont in the same State. He died June 5, 1817, aged 77 years. He was a sturdy man, and a sound orthodox deacon of the celebrated priest Taggart's church. His physical strength was remarkable, and it is said that the parson and his deacon, after refreshing the inner man, would frequently try each other's muscle in friendly wrestle, till they would pant like two bullocks; in these encounters they handled each other roughly, but always in the best spirit. Mr. Riddell had few equals in his day, where physical power was demanded. The town of Coleraine, where he lived, like that in the north of Ireland for which it was named, was noted for its large men. Dr. Adam Clark, the distinguished commentator, writes that he had seen many men in Coleraine, Ireland, whose height was seven and a half feet, and some whose stature was eight feet. Mr. Riddell's wife, by whom he had issue *nine* children, is supposed to have died at the home of her son Samuel, in Charlemont, but I have no record. See account of descendants further on.

William Riddell[2] (1), second son of Hugh[1] (1) and Ann Aiken, was born in Bedford, N. H., in the year 1742, and was lost at sea before the removal of the family from Bedford to Coleraine, Mass.; unmarried.

Robert Riddell[2] (1), third son of Hugh[1] (1) and Ann Aiken, was born in Bedford, N. H., May 11, 1744; married Jane McGee, — she was born in Deerfield, Mass., Oct. 23, 1747, — and removed from Coleraine to Ripley, Chautauqua County, N. Y., where he died Feb. 20, 1822, aged 78 years; his wife predeceased him, at Otsego, N. Y., April 5, 1805. They had issue *ten* children, of whom hereafter.

Ann Riddell[2] (1), only daughter of Hugh[1] (1), was born in Bedford, N. H., in 1747; married to Jonathan Wilson, and had issue.

THIRD GENERATION.

Letitia Riddell[3] (1), eldest daughter of Hugh[2] (2), was born in Coleraine, Mass., and died when ten months old.

Rev. William Riddel[3] (1), eldest son of Hugh[2] (2), was born in Coleraine, Mass., Feb. 4, 1768; married, Sept. 4, 1797, Lucy, daughter of Rev.

Samuel Hopkins, D. D., of Hadley, Mass. She was half-sister of the wife of Doctor Emmons, and own sister of the two wives of Dr. Samuel Spring, of Newburyport, Mass., and of Dr. Samuel Austin, of Worcester, Mass. (afterwards president of Vermont University, at Burlington), and also sister of the wife of Rev. Leonard Worcester, of Peacham, Vt. Mr. Riddel labored on the farm with his father until within one year of his majority, when, being desirous of obtaining a college-education, he proposed to his father that if he would grant him the remainder of his time, he would relinquish all claims to his share of the parental patrimony in favor of his younger brothers, and seek to acquire an education by his own exertions. This proposal was accepted by his father, and the son thereafter supported himself principally by teaching school.

When he entered Dartmouth College his mother gave him an outfit of bedding, and his father made him a present of the colt on which he rode to Hanover, and which he sold for his own benefit. This was all the aid his parents were able to give him to assist in his education. He showed remarkable application in his studies while at college, and graduated in 1793, with high honors in his class. He afterwards studied divinity with Doctor Burton, of Thetford, Vt., and with Doctor Emmons, at Franklin, Mass. His first pastorate was at Bristol, Me., commencing in 1796; second settlement in Townsend, Vt., in 1806; third pastorate in Whittingham, Vt., in 1818. He was a man of thorough scholarship, strong, logical mind, retentive memory, a sound Calvinist, an able sermonizer, serious and earnest, but not eloquent, in his style of delivery. His reading was extensive, and his mind, in riper years, was a store-house of knowledge. His nephew says, "I remember Uncle William very well in the last years of his life, when he rode the old, long, lank sorrel up and down, with immense saddle-bags under him, from which he would pull and scatter tracts as he passed taverns and naughty boys. He was avaricious, and saved large sums of money; but he was a true, honest man, a good old uncle, and at the last gave considerable money to the Tract Society. For my part he sent me a large number of the New England Catechisms to distribute, but I found them very unpopular in the West."

His wife died in 1813, from which time until his death, — a period of twenty-six years, — he remained a widower, keeping his family together until his children were educated and settled in life. He died in South Deerfield, Mass., Oct. 24, 1849, in the eighty-second year of his age. Mr. Riddel adopted an orthography unlike any other of the family, in consequence of reading the name in the poems of Robert Burns, where the name of Captain Riddell, a great favorite of the poet, was spelt with only one *l.* Mr. Riddel *supposed* this to be the most proper form; but the mistake was made by the publishers of Burns, for the Riddells of Glen-Riddell, represented by the patron of the poet, were a branch of the "Riddells of Riddell," in Roxburghshire, and they universally spelt the name with the double letters. Mr. Riddel had issue *seven* children, of whom hereafter.

Samuel Riddell[2] (1), second son of Hugh[2] (2), was born in Coleraine, Mass., June 13, 1769; married Jane Donaldson, in 1794, and had issue *nine* children, of whom hereafter. He purchased a farm, and moved from Coleraine to Charlemont, Mass., in 1796; spent thirty years on "this poor side-hill farm," and in 1835, when his family were all gone but Thomas, he left the old neighborhood, and the graves of his father, mother, and children, and went to Ann Arbor, Mich., where he spent one year, and removed to Milwaukee, Wis., where he had a son and daughter.

In 1838 he settled on a farm at Wauwatosa, six miles from the city, where he spent a happy evening of life, retaining all his faculties till his death, which occurred Aug. 8, 1851, aged 82 years. His son says, "My father was full six feet tall, and sometimes weighed two hundred pounds. His head was well poised; he was a man of great energy, of quick apprehension, and regarded as one of the first men in his town. He possessed a military taste, and was sometimes called 'General Jackson'; he was generous to a fault, and lost much as a bondsman for others. With apparent sternness was mingled the gentleness of a child. He was quick and sharp at repartee." In a communication written by the same son previously, he says, "My father was a man of the old stamp; his frame was muscular, and his mental faculties good; his memory was so tenacious that down to his death he could inform us accurately in regard to the different connections and branches of our family."

Jane Riddell³ (1), second daughter of Hugh² (2), was born in Coleraine, Mass., in 1771, and died in her seventh year.

Hugh Riddell³ (3), third son of Hugh² (2), was born in Coleraine, Mass., in 1774; died in his fourth year.

Jane Riddell³ (2), third daughter of Hugh² (2), was born in Coleraine, Mass., in 1779; died an infant.

Jane Riddell³ (3), fourth daughter of Hugh² (2), was born in Coleraine, Mass., in 1779; died in infancy.

Thomas-Morris Riddell³ (1), fourth son of Hugh² (2), was born in Coleraine, Mass., July 15, 1782; inherited the homestead, and reared a large family. His wife's name has not reached me. He was well educated, read extensively, was fond of poetry and music, a good singer, and strong controversialist. He lost his property, and in 1810 moved to Charlemont, Mass., thence to Rowe, where his family worked in the mills, and where he and his wife died.

Elisha Riddell³ (1), fifth son of Hugh² (2), was born in Coleraine, Mass., in 1785; never married. He was a soldier in the war of 1812; a bright, active man, of somewhat irregular habits. He was in the battle of Plattsburgh, after which he lost his fingers and toes by frost; twelve years subsequently he returned home and remained one year; he then went away and was never afterwards heard from.

Mary Riddell³ (1), eldest daughter of Robert² (1), was born in Coleraine, Mass., Oct. 8, 1769; time of death unknown.

Thomas Riddell³ (2), eldest son of Robert² (1), was born in Coleraine, Mass., Sept. 19, 1771; died in New York State, Nov. 8, 1832. No other information.

James Riddell³ (1), third son of Robert² (1), was born in Coleraine, Mass., Dec. 8, 1776, and died Aug. 20, 1777.

Ann Riddell³ (2), second daughter of Robert² (1), was born in Coleraine, Mass., Sept. 26, 1779; died Aug. 5, 1789.

Betsey Riddell³ (1), third daughter of Robert² (1), was born in Coleraine, Mass., June 12, 1781; married to Eleazer Hill (who died Sept. 5, 1845), and died Nov. 5, 1857, leaving issue.

William-M. Riddell³ (2), fourth son of Robert² (1), was born in Otsego County, N. Y., June 20, 1783; married Jennie Stetson, of Cherry Valley, June 7, 1804 (she was born April 17, 1783), and by her had issue *eight* children, of whom hereafter. He was a farmer in Westfield, N. Y., and died Oct. 1, 1821; his widow died June 16, 1839.

Robert Riddell[3] (2), fifth son of Robert[2] (1), was born June 5, 1786; married Olive Tucker, May 1, 1823, and had by that lady *ten* children, of whom hereafter; he died Feb. 21, 1864.

Jane Riddell[3] (4), fourth daughter of Robert[2] (1), was born June 5, 1789.

Anne Riddell[3] (3), fifth daughter of Robert[2] (1), was born Feb. 8, 1793.

FOURTH GENERATION.

Lucy Riddell[4] (1), eldest daughter of William[3] (1), was born July 17, 1798; died Oct. 31, 1798.

Rev. Samuel-Hopkins Riddel[4] (2), eldest son of William[3] (1), was born in Bristol, Me., Jan. 2, 1800; married July 12, 1827, Harriet-Angeline Ray, of North Haven, Conn., and had issue *two* children. His first wife was born May 31, 1808, and died March 15, 1856. Mr. Riddel graduated at Yale College in 1823; at Andover Theological Seminary in 1826, and was ordained at Glastonbury, Conn., June 27, 1827. He was dismissed from his first pastorate to accept the appointment of the American Educational Society, as secretary and general agent of the Connecticut branch of the society, to reside at Hartford; during the period of his residence there, the *Congregationalist*, a weekly religious newspaper, — the first in the world that bore the name, — was started by an association of gentlemen, and placed in his hands as editor. In May, 1841, he removed to Boston, to become the secretary of the American Educational Society, in which office he continued till May, 1850; having charge of the *American Quarterly Register*, published by the society until that periodical was discontinued, in 1843. After leaving the Educational Society, he became associate editor and part proprietor of the *Puritan Recorder*, a weekly religious newspaper in Boston, for five years. The *Congregationalist*, of Hartford, upon Mr. Riddel's leaving the editorship, had been merged in the *Puritan Recorder*, losing its distinctive name; and in the meantime this name was assumed by a new independent journal, started in Boston, which at length bought up the *Recorder*, and has become a first-class denominational paper. After severing his connection with the *Recorder* he was installed pastor of the Congregational Church in Tamworth, N. H., where for twelve years he labored in the ministry, until August, 1872, when he relinquished his charge. He continued his residence in Tamworth some time after closing his pastoral relations with the church there. He had married, secondly, Oct. 7, 1862, Mrs. C. D. (Douglass) Evans, of North Conway. She was born in Portland, Me., April 11, 1810; died in Conway, N. H., Jan. 28, 1866. In 1875, he went West with the intention of visiting relatives, but was prevailed upon to pass the winter with a family at Des Moines, who had formerly been in his parish in Tamworth. But when the spring came he took cold, which developed into pneumonia, of which he died June 1, 1876.

The old ministers knew Mr. Riddel well, and those who were early associated with him valued him for those qualities which made him a faithful and successful editor and secretary; for his accuracy, thoroughness, and order; for his keen interest in whatever was worth doing; for a nicety of perception, taste, and sagacity, which were peculiarly prominent characteristics of the man. He had all the marks of scholarship which impress those of educational and scholarly taste. Mr. Riddel was a clear thinker and a strong, logical writer; he had never published books, but his able articles, published in some of the leading papers and magazines, always commanded attention, as the products of a master-mind. He was a man of strong tendencies, — strong in affection and unfaltering

in his attentions and devotion to objects of his esteem. The interests
of an invalid daughter were a motive for his retirement to the quiet
country parish at Tamworth; here he tenderly watched over his child for
twelve years, during which he hardly left her for a day; he read to her,
lifted her, brought news from the outside world to her, watched her
as she sometimes passed suddenly into a world of terrible visions,
and with all this grew dull of hearing, so that he could hardly hear her
weak voice. Through all these years he lived thus without a murmur,
grateful for every little kindness, thoughtful for every one, steadfast in
his faith, unwavering in fulfilling all the duties of life. He grew prematurely old under his cares, but never lost his cheerfulness. The only
shadows of despondency passed over him when he had laid this daughter
in the grave and resigned his charge. In a letter to the author of this
work, — a work in which he took a deep interest, — he wrote, "My coal
is quenched."

As a sermonizer Mr. Riddel was not eloquent; his sermons were prepared with much study and care; were very practical, pointed, and clear,
delivered in a calm, social manner. His reading was extensive, and the
fund of information which he had acquired was almost unlimited. Social,
conversational, cautious, and with commanding gravity, he entertained
his friends. He was tall and spare, shaved clean, was quite bald, wore
glasses, and carried a calm yet pleasant expression of face. I believe all
who knew him rate him with the best of men. He was buried in Mt.
Auburn Cemetery; and the few friends who gathered at the chapel there,
drawn by love for the departed, were possessed with a feeling of thank-
fulness, that one who had endured so much was himself at rest.

William Riddell⁴ (3), second son of William³ (1), was born in Bristol,
Me., April 15, 1801: died April 24, 1801.

Jane Riddell⁴ (5), second daughter of William³ (1), was born June 20,
1802; married William Hadley, of Putnam, O., March 19, 1833. He was
born in Francestown, N. H., Aug. 7, 1793. They resided for a time at
Malta, Morgan County, and in Straitsville, Perry County, O., where she
died Aug. 30, 1862; he died March 9, 1863. They had six children.

William Riddell⁴ (4), third son of William³ (1), was born Aug. 28,
1803; died June 16, 1804.

Selma Riddell⁴ (1), third daughter of William³ (1), was born June
19, 1807; married, Nov. 8, 1832, to Caleb-Allen Cooley, of South Deerfield, Mass. He was born March 28, 1800, and died Sept. 20, 1845; she
died March 2, 1837, leaving two children.

Septima Riddell⁴ (1), fourth daughter of William³ (1), was born Oct.
29, 1810; died Nov. 4, 1810.

James-Aiken Riddell⁴ (2), eldest son of Samuel³ (1), born July 9,
1795; married Lydia Cooper in 1823; settled in Sullivan, Wis, and had
issue five children, of whom hereafter.

William Riddell⁴ (5), second son of Samuel³ (1), was born April 14,
1798; married first, in 1830, to Phebe Thayer, and secondly, June, 1843,
to Sally Artherton. His first wife died in August, 1834. He resided at
Charlemont, Mass., in 1852, and had a family of children.

Fanny-Clark Riddell⁴ (1), eldest daughter of Samuel³ (1), was born
July 17, 1800; married in July, 1825, to Isaac Allis. Her first husband
died, and she married, secondly, Oct. 25, 1841, to David Morgan; residence, Wauwatosa, Milwaukee County, Wis.

Jane Riddell⁴ (6), second daughter of Samuel³ (1), was born Sept. 29, 1802; died Aug. 29, 1805.

Antis-Ross Riddell⁴ (1), third daughter of Samuel³ (1), was born March 19, 1805; married in July, 1827, to Abaz Williams, and died at Ann Arbor, Mich., June 30, 1836.

Park Riddell⁴ (1), fourth son of Samuel³ (1), was born May 9, 1807; died in March, 1809.

Cordelia Riddell⁴ (1), fifth daughter of Samuel³ (1), was born Aug. 22, 1809; married in November, 1832, to Daniel Brown.

Samuel Riddell⁴ (3), fourth son of Samuel³ (1), was born March 2, 1812; married Jan. 1, 1836, Clarissa C. Perry. His first wife, Sarah H. Hall, died at Ann Arbor, Mich., 1835.

Thomas-Morris Riddell⁴ (3), fifth son of Samuel³ (1), was born April 22, 1816; married June 25, 1840, Adaline A. Hill, in Charlemont, Mass.; emigrated to Wauwatosa, Wis., Nov. 2, 1835, and settled as a farmer. He has been station-agent for the Milwaukee & St. Paul Railroad, postmaster, notary public, and filled many offices in his town. He was a Methodist class-leader, and his house a home for ministers. He died in Wauwatosa, Sept. 2, 1869, aged 58 years. He had *five* children, of whom hereafter.

Lovina-C. Riddell⁴ (1), eldest daughter of William³ (2), was born Dec. 31, 1806; died May 5, 1809.

Lucinda-J. Riddell⁴ (1), second daughter of William³ (2), was born Jan. 29, 1809; died Aug. 22, 1833.

Eliza-Ann Riddell⁴ (1), third daughter of William³ (2), was born Oct. 22, 1811; married to Maurice Dick, of Westfield, N. Y., and died March 20, 1852.

Joseph-McGee Riddell⁴ (1), eldest son of William³ (2), was born Nov. 9, 1813; married Isabella McWharter, 1841; had issue, of whom hereafter, and died Feb. 16, 1864.

Mary-Jane Riddell⁴ (2), second son of William³ (2), was born Feb. 17, 1816; married Jan. 7, 1836, to Oliver Minigar; resides in Ripley, N. Y.

William-Oliver Riddell⁴ (6), second son of William³ (2), was born Dec. 8, 1818; married Sept. 8, 1844, to Caroline Wilcox; she died in 1860, and he married secondly, Oct. 12, 1863, Almira J. Bassett. Mr. Riddell resides at Cherry Valley, Ill., and is a farmer; he has a family of several children, of whom hereafter.

Jannetta Riddell⁴ (1), fifth daughter of William³ (2), was born Dec. 1, 1822; married Sept. 14, 1841, to Milo McWharter, a lawyer, and lives at New Lisbon, Wis.

Hugh-Bolton Riddell⁴ (4), third son of William³ (2), was born May 7, 1826; died Aug. 10, 1831.

George Riddell⁴ (1), eldest son of Robert³ (2). ⎫
Harriet Riddell⁴ (1), eldest daughter of Robert³ (2). ⎪
Eliza Riddell⁴ (2), second daughter of Robert³ (2). ⎪ All
Jane Riddell⁴ (7), third daughter of Robert³ (2). ⎪ born
Nancy Riddell⁴ (1), fourth daughter of Robert³ (2). ⎬ in
Samuel Riddell⁴ (4), second son of Robert³ (2). ⎪ New
Charles Riddell⁴ (1), third son of Robert³ (2). ⎪ York.
Delos Riddell⁴ (1), fourth son of Robert³ (2). ⎪
Mary Riddell⁴ (3), fifth daughter of Robert³ (2). ⎪
Franklin Riddell⁴ (1), fifth son of Robert³ (2). ⎭

FIFTH GENERATION.

Harriet-Fitch Riddel[5] (2), eldest daughter of Samuel[4] (2), was born in Boston, Mass., Sept. 28, 1828; died Jan. 6, 1851; unmarried.

Lucy-Hopkins Riddell[5] (2), second daughter of Samuel[4] (2), was born in Boston, Mass., July 31, 1830; died May 18, 1873, aged 43 years. She was for many years afflicted with a nervous affection, and gradually withdrew into a single room in the parsonage, excluded the light, closed her sensitive eyes with a bandage, and lay thus year after year. She suffered intensely in body and mind; her delicate yet tenacious organization was the counterpart of a singularly gifted mind. Her solitude was broken by letters from a few friends, which were piece by piece conveyed to her by her father, who read to her a few moments each day, when she côuld bear it. Now and then some friend would call, and be led groping into the dark chamber, to hold her hand and tell a few tidings, and hear a few words from her thin lips in a fine, attenuated voice; her own communications were in pencilled notes, and oftentimes palimpsests, to the unaccustomed reader, and in short flights of song or meditation, often of great beauty. Sometimes she would take her pencil and paper to write to a friend, painfully record a few sentences, then lay her materials aside, and be able only after months to resume them again; she could then take up the same train of thought which had been held by her wonderful memory. Some of the sentences she composed seemed the product of an inspired and divinely-gifted mind, so sweet and beautiful were they. To say that she was a strangely spiritual and wonderfully gifted woman is no fitting tribute to her character and talents.

William-Park Riddell[5] (7), eldest son of James[4] (2), was born June 20, 1824; resided at Sullivan, Wis.

Jane-Maria Riddell[5] (8), eldest daughter of James[4] (2), was born April 2, 1827; married Elias W. Combs, in October, 1848. Mr. Combs died Jan. 4, 1850, leaving issue.

Mary-Eliza Riddell[5] (4), second daughter of James[4] (2), was born Nov. 20, 1831; married to Ivory Longby, in 1850, and had issue.

Sybil-Marian Riddell[5] (1), third daughter of James[4] (2), was born June 29, 1834.

Antis-Cordelia Riddell[5] (2), fourth daughter of James[4] (2), was born Nov. 24, 1836.

John-Wesley Riddell[5] (1), eldest son of William[4] (5), was born in Charlemont, Mass., August, 1834; married, and has issue, of whom hereafter. He resides at Greenfield, Mass.

Ellen-Maria Riddell[5] (1), eldest daughter of Thomas[4] (3), was born at Wauwatosa, Wis., Nov. 22, 1841; married Nov. 22, 1864, to Rev. Thomas C. Wilson, and has issue. Mr. Wilson is a Methodist presiding elder of Appleton (Wis.) District, and member of the Wisconsin Conference. He graduated at Lawrence University; residence, Waupaca, Wis.

Thomas-Morris Riddell[5] (4), eldest son of Thomas[4] (3), was born at Wauwatosa, Wis., Nov. 30, 1845; married Dec. 17, 1873, to Sophia A. Eldret, and lives at Charles City, Ia.

Charles-Hill Riddell[5] (2), second son of Thomas[4] (3), was born at Wauwatosa, Wis., Aug. 9, 1852; unmarried.

Edwin-Augustus Riddell[5] (1), third son of Thomas[4] (3), was born at Wauwatosa, Wis., April 11, 1857; unmarried.

Francis-Imogen Riddell[5] (1), fourth son of Thomas[4] (3), was born at Wauwatosa, Wis., July 22, 1859; unmarried.

Sarah-Josephine Riddell[5] (1), eldest daughter of William[4] (6), was born at Cherry Valley, Ill., Sept. 12, 1846, and married Feb. 5, 1866, to Ashley Alexander.

Eugene Riddell[5] (1), eldest son of William[4] (6), was born at Cherry Valley, Ill., Sept. 4, 1847; married Sept. 16, 1870, Nellie Maurice.

Frank Riddell[5] (2), second son of William[4] (6), was born at Cherry Valley, Ill., Feb. 22, 1849.

Mary-A. Riddell[5] (6), second daughter of William[4] (6), was born at Cherry Valley, Ill., June 3, 1854; died March 7, 1856.

William-O. Riddell[5] (8), third son of William[4] (6), was born at Cherry Valley, Ill., Oct. 12, 1867.

RIDDELLS OF COLERAINE, MASSACHUSETTS, NO. 2.

[ROBERT BRANCH.]

Robert Riddell[1] (1), presumed to be a son of John Riddell and Janet Gordon, of Ballymeath, Ireland, was born March 14, 1698, and came with his three brothers to America in 1718. He married Mary Thompson, a lady of Scottish extraction (she was born in 1706, and died May 27, 1759), and had issue, of whom hereafter. He settled in Londonderry, N. H., alongside of many Scotch-Irish families. He was surveyor of highways in Londonderry in 1748, 1749; and in 1753 was "haward." His name does not appear on the tax-list or town records of Bedford, and he probably never lived there. He removed to Coleraine (now Franklin County), Mass., and joined a Scotch-Irish settlement there; bought a large tract of land and built a spacious house, that was for many years used as a tavern for the accommodation of the traveling public. Mr. Riddell was a man of gigantic proportions, and of symmetrical form; a man of formidable strength, but of mild disposition. His eyes were blue, and his complexion fair. There are many traditions preserved in the family, among his descendants, respecting his great feats of strength, one of which was the shouldering of a cannon on muster-day, which was considered a Herculean feat. He was notorious as a bold Indian-fighter. Many of his descendants are very large men. He died at Coleraine, Sept. 14, 1787, aged (according to date on grave-stone) 79 years; if born in 1698 (as per records from Ireland), he was 89 years old at his death. His tombstone stands near the northern extremity of the old burying-ground at Coleraine, nearly concealed with rank briars, and bears the following inscription: —

> " All you advanced in years,
> You healthy and robust,
> Are tott'ring round the grave,
> And soon must turn to dust."

SECOND GENERATION.

Gavin Riddell² (1), eldest son of Robert¹ (1), was born in Londonderry, N. H., Feb. 22, 1753; married Margaret Taggart, in 1782, and had issue *eleven* children, of whom hereafter. He removed from Londonderry to Coleraine, Mass., with his parents, and kept a public-house there. He was a soldier of the Revolution, and many traditions are preserved among his descendants concerning his prowess in his frequent skirmishes with the Indians, who grievously infested those regions at that early time. He died July 29, 1812.

Robert Riddell² (2), second son of Robert¹ (1), was born in Londonderry, N. H., Jan. 27, 1758; married Jemima Long, in 1784, and removed to Sullivan County, N. Y. Mrs. Riddell was from Shelburne, Mass., born Feb. 20, 1760, and died in New York, Sept. 18, 1822. They had issue *eight* children, of whom hereafter. Mr. Riddell died Aug. 11, 1808, aged 50 years.

Susannah Riddell² (1), only daughter of Robert¹ (1), was born in Londonderry, N. H., in 1759; married —— Edwards, and had children, all of whom are deceased. She died previous to 1852.

THIRD GENERATION.

Capt. John Riddell³ (1), eldest son of Gavin² (1), was born in Coleraine, Mass., Dec. 15, 1783; married Lephe Gates,* in 1806, and had issue *ten* children, of whom hereafter. He was educated at Deerfield Academy. In 1805, he taught school at Norwich, now Preston, Chenango County, N. Y. In 1807, with his family, consisting of his wife and one son, he removed to a farm about one mile west of Preston Corners, where he built a home and permanently settled. The house stood about eighty rods northwest of the house occupied by his son Samuel T., in 1852. During the winter of 1815–16, Mr. Riddell taught school in his own district. He held the office of constable and Justice of the Peace, receiving his commission from the Governor of the State. Subsequently he was frequently elected to the office of supervisor, and ever enjoyed the entire confidence of his townsmen. He was chosen captain of the militia, at that time an office of considerable respectability, and his commission from Governor Tompkins is still (1852) preserved among the family papers. Captain Riddell was tall and rather slim; he had light blue eyes and dark hair; was noted for his large stock of general information, being an extensive reader all his days. As a leading, public-spirited man, he was highly esteemed, and was long a reliable and very useful public servant. He died May 10, 1833, deservedly lamented by all who knew him.

Susanna Riddell³ (2), eldest daughter of Gavin² (1), was born in Cole-

---

* LEPHE GATES, the mother of the above-mentioned family, was a daughter of Peter Gates, who married Mary Allen, both from Groton, Mass. (?),— then of Leyden, Mass. Lephe was born Nov. 22, 1787. "Under circumstances (says her son William) peculiarly embarrassing, after the death of her husband, she proved herself a woman of peculiar energy of character, and her efforts in behalf of the family, at that time composed chiefly of young children, are not likely soon to be forgotten by them. During the time of her greatest perplexity, after her husband's death, she seemed to receive great consolation from reading the Bible, and actually read the whole through in five months." She used to tell, with apparent satisfaction, of spinning one hundred and thirty-nine knots of yarn in a day, in early life, besides attending to the household duties; this was done in 1826. She was enjoying good health in 1852, and had the care of two of her grandsons from New Orleans, educating at the North.

raine, Mass., in 1787; married to Nathan Noyes, of Preston, N. Y., and had issue. In 1822, the family removed to Perrington, N. Y., and in April, 1833, to Novi, thence to Plymouth, Mich. Her sons were judges, lawyers, and doctors, — all distinguished. Mrs. Noyes died at Marshall, Mich., in 1850.

Robert Riddell[2.] (3), second son of Gavin[2] (1), was born in Coleraine, Mass., in 1789; married Sarah Stewart, and settled at Wilmington, Vt. For a time after the death of his father he remained at home, but subsequently kept public-houses in several places. At one time he owned and carried on the wadding-factory in Wilmington; was sheriff in his County, and filled several positions of responsibility. He was a man of large size, partaking, it is said, somewhat of the energetic character of the Taggarts, from whom he descended on his mother's side. He was a man of undisturbable good nature. He was living in 1852, but died several years ago. I have made a great effort to collect a more complete account of this branch, but the descendants of Robert cannot be prevailed upon to provide the statistics of their families; it is presumed that they shun publicity. There were *eight* children, of whom hereafter.

Thomas Riddell[3] (1), third son of Gavin[2] (1), was born in Coleraine, Mass., in 1791; had no family.

Jane Riddell[3] (1), second daughter of Gavin[2] (1), was born in Coleraine, Mass., in 1792; no family.

Harriet Riddell[3] (1), third daughter of Gavin[2] (1), was born in Coleraine, Mass., in 1793; no family.

George Riddell[3] (1), fourth son of Gavin[2] (1), was born in Coleraine, Mass., Jan. 12, 1796; married Mary Babcock (she was born Dec. 9, 1800), in 1822, and had issue *nine* children, of whom hereafter. He moved from Coleraine to Canisteo, N. Y., in 1837, and died there July 26, 1845; his widow is now (1879) living.

Mary Riddell[3] (1), fourth daughter of Gavin[2] (1), was born in Coleraine, Mass., Feb. 8, 1798; was married, first, to Benjamin Clark, by whom she had *five* children; and secondly, to John McClary, by whom she had *three* children. She lived at Onondaga, N. Y.

Lovina Riddell[3] (1), fifth daughter of Gavin[2] (1), was born in Coleraine, Mass., July 8, 1802; was married in Coleraine, Mass., Nov. 21, 1822, to Lemuel Clark, of Tully, N. Y., and had issue *twelve* children. Died March 12, 1859, and was buried in Onondaga Valley Cemetery, N. Y. Mr. Clark was born March 26, 1799, and died Sept. 21, 1869.

Gavin Riddell[3] (2), fifth son of Gavin[2] (1), was born in Coleraine' Mass., in 1804; married Arminda Babcock, and had issue *nine* children' of whom hereafter. In 1852 he was living at Coleraine, then the only one of the name (except his children) living there.

Caroline Riddell[3] (1), sixth daughter of Gavin[2] (1), was born in Coleraine, Mass., in November, 1806; was married to Mr. James Clark, of Onondaga County, N. Y., and died March 14, 1859. Buried on the same day as her sister Lovina, in the Onondaga Cemetery. No issue. Husband living in 1884, at Alden, N. Y.

Polly Riddell[3] (1), eldest daughter of Robert[2] (2), was born in Coleraine, Mass., Dec. 16, 1785; was married to Frederick Pratt, of Sullivan, N. Y., in 1808, and had issue *seven* children; she died at Fayetteville, N. Y., July 15, 1848. Mr. Pratt was a farmer.

Sally Riddell[3] (1), second daughter of Robert[2] (2), was born in Coleraine, Mass., Feb. 23, 1787; was married to Uriah Aldrich, in 1809, and had issue. She was living in Cazenovia, N. Y., in 1852. He was a blacksmith.

Jemima Riddell[3] (1), third daughter of Robert[2] (2), was born in Coleraine, Mass., May 28, 1788; was married in 1810, to Heman Williams, and had issue. She was living in Pittsfield, Mich., in 1852.

Martha Riddell[3] (1), fourth daughter of Robert[2] (2), was born in Coleraine, Mass., May 17, 1790; was married in 1811, to James Matthews; lived in Syracuse, N. Y., in 1852, and had *four* children. Mr. Matthews was a manufacturer of salt; he died before 1852.

Robert Riddell[3] (4), eldest son of Robert[2] (2), was born in Coleraine, Mass., Oct. 5, 1792; married in 1817 to ——, and had issue *five* children, of whom (with one son born of a second wife, whom he married in 1833) hereafter. He was living on a farm in Chittenango, N. Y., in 1852.

David Riddell[3] (1), second son of Robert[2] (2), was born in Coleraine, Mass., Jan. 28, 1794; married in 1817, to ——, and had issue *four* children, of whom hereafter. He was a leather manufacturer at Chittenango, N. Y., in 1852.

Susan Riddell[3] (3), youngest daughter of Robert[2] (2), was born in Coleraine,* Mass.. Sept. 15, 1795; died July 4, 1808, at Sullivan, N. Y.

Thompson Riddell[3] (1), youngest son of Robert[2] (2), was born in Coleraine, Mass., Oct. 2, 1798; married in 1823, and in 1838; the names of his wives have not reached me. He had issue *two* children, a son and daughter, of whom hereafter. Mr. Riddell was a farmer in Hamilton, Allegan County, Mich., in 1852.

FOURTH GENERATION.

Prof. John-Leonard Riddell[4] (2), eldest son of John[3] (1), was born in Leyden, Mass., Feb. 20, 1807; married, first, to Mary E. Knock, and by her had *two* children; secondly, to Ann Hennefin, and had issue several children, of whom (with the preceding) hereafter. In the autumn of 1807, he was taken by his parents to Preston, N. Y., where, according to his own diary, written in 1834, they "moved into a log-house on the middle of the farm; this house was surrounded at the time by a wilderness, but it had the advantage of being near an excellent fountain of water." He spent a portion of the years 1826–7, at the Oxford Academy; subsequently he went to the "Rensselaer School," at Troy, N. Y., where he obtained the degree of A. B.; subsequently, A. M. In 1830 he commenced giving lectures on the sciences of chemistry, botany, and geology, occupying between four and five years, embracing many cities in the United States and Canadas. In 1835 he was appointed "Adjunct Professor of Chemistry and Botany in the Cincinnati Medical College." From this college he received the degree of M. D.

In 1836, he was appointed professor of chemistry in the Medical College of Louisiana, at New Orleans; in 1852, he was connected with the medical department of the University of Louisiana, under the patronage of the State, at which date he held that chair. He was engaged by a company in 1838, to lead an exploring expedition into Texas, with the object of discovering gold and silver mines; he spent three months in the wilds of Texas with this company, penetrating nearly to the

---

* It is *presumed* that all the children of Robert[2] (2) were born in Coleraine, Mass., in want of proof to the contrary.

supposed locality of the mines; but becoming more and more annoyed by the Comanche Indians, judged it hazardous to remain very long. It was found no easy matter to discover, in so short a time, a mine, concerning which many conflicting statements had been made; yet the object of the company was in part realized, since they had obtained a knowledge of the general mineral character of the country. For his services Mr. Riddell received one share in the rights of the company, equivalent to ten thousand acres of Texas lands.

On his return to New Orleans, he learned of his appointment, by the President of the United States, as "Melter and Refiner" in the branch mint; this office he held till 1849. His contributions to science, in the meantime, had been of a varied nature. In 1885, at Cincinnati, O., he published a catalogue of plants, entitled "A Synopsis of the Flora of the Western States," including eighteen hundred different species, which may truly be styled one of the pioneers in the botany of the West. Subsequently he published a catalogue of the plants of Louisiana, comprising some twenty-three hundred species. In the West, in Louisiana, and in Texas, he was the discoverer of numerous *new* species, and has, by the consent of botanists, left his name indelibly impressed on the science, in the genus named for him, *Riddellia*.

In 1845 he published "A Monograph of the Dollar," including *fac-simile* impressions of between five and six hundred varieties of American and Mexican dollars and half-dollars, both genuine and counterfeit; with the assay of each, and if counterfeit, pointing out the method of detection. The original coins were obtained from Boston, New York, and the mints of Philadelphia and New Orleans. He was author of numerous other small publications, principally delivered as lectures, and published by his auditors and students, such as "Orrin Lindsay's Aerial Navigation," delivered before the People's Lyceum of New Orleans, in 1847; "Constitution of Matter," in 1846, published in the New Orleans *Medical and Surgical Journal;* introductory lecture on "The Natural Sciences," published in 1852, by the medical students of the University of Louisiana, also in the *Medical Journal.* In 1836, his thesis on "Miasm and Contagion" was published in Cincinnati, and republished in Boston; in which he advocated the theory that "organized and living corpuscles of various kinds" were the agents of communication in contagious diseases, and in this he was one of the earliest to adopt that theory, which has long since become settled. While an officer under the government, he published a short historic account of the mint and its operations, together with the coining process.

In 1844 he was one of five commissioners appointed by the Governor and Legislature "to devise some means to protect New Orleans from inundation." In 1852 he was giving his attention principally to microscopy, and observations connected with the animalculæ and algæ found in the swamp-waters in the vicinity of New Orleans. His widow was living in New Orleans in 1878. I do not know the date of his death. His son Sanford promised the complete genealogy and history of his father's family, but the MSS. seem to have been lost in the mails.

Lephia-Maria Riddell[4] (1), eldest daughter of John[3] (1), was born in Preston, N. Y., Jan. 1, 1809; was married in 1829, to Ruel Crumb, and had issue *four* children. She resided at Onondaga, N. Y.; died Nov. 5, 1840.

Julia-Ann Riddell[4] (1), second daughter of John[3] (1), was born in Preston, N. Y., July 19, 1812; was married in 1830 to J. S. Brown, of

East Troy, Wis., and had *six* children. Her husband was a blacksmith, formerly from Sherburne, N. Y.; born July 4, 1808.

Sanford-Allen Riddell[4] (1), second son of John[3] (1), was born in Preston, N. Y., April 9, 1816; died Aug. 25, 1828.

Samuel-Taggart Riddell[4] (1), third son of John[3] (1), was born in Preston, N. Y., July 4, 1818; married Lucy A. Beckwith in 1844, and has issue, of whom hereafter. He was named after his great-uncle, Samuel Taggart, D. D., who was a distinguished clergyman of Coleraine, Mass., the author of "Taggart's View," and for many years a member of Congress. Mr. Riddell was, during the years 1840-1-2, foreman in the melting and refining department, in the United States branch mint at New Orleans, La. He resided for a time at Preston, but moved to East Troy, Wis., in 1844; he returned to Preston, and was living on the old homestead farm in 1852. He was living in Turner, Mills County, Ia., in 1876.

Dr. George Riddell[4] (2), fourth son of John[3] (1), was born in Preston, N. Y., June 8, 1822; was married by Rev. J. T. Goodrich, Oct. 10, 1847, to Miss Harriet M., daughter of Andrew and Philena-Davis (Bowdish) Darling, of Preston, N. Y., and went back to New Orleans, where he was then employed in the mint. After attending the academies at Oxford and Norwich, N. Y., he taught school, both public and select, in various places; in the spring of 1844 he was elected town superintendent of schools for the town of Preston; he soon after commenced the study of medicine, spent three successive winters in New Orleans, attending medical lectures, and in 1848 received the degree of M. D. from the University of Louisiana. In 1840 he spent some time in the practice of his profession in Oxford, N. Y.; in 1851 he moved to Palmyra, Jefferson County, Wis., and practised there for many years; there he built a beautiful house, which was surrounded by tasteful gardens, adorned with rare flowers and shrubbery. He separated from his wife, and married a young lady while living at the latter place, his first wife retaining the house, and Mr. Riddell assisting in the support and education of his children. He removed to Rome, some nine miles from Palmyra, and practised there some three or four years, at the end of which time he went to Chippewa Falls, Wis., and seems to have entered into partnership with his nephew, Dr. Sanford S. Riddell; it is presumed that he now (1878) resides at the latter place, although he has never favored me with a reply to my communications.

Lovina Riddell[4] (2), third daughter of John[3] (1), was born in Preston, N. Y., Sept. 2, 1824; was married in January, 1848, to J. Denison Marion, of Preston, Conn., and is now living at Preston Corners, N. Y. Mr. Marion is a blacksmith by trade; is constable and collector (1852) of the town of Preston. Lovina lived with her aunt Lovina from 1832 to 1842, after which she attended the academy at Onondaga Hollow. Subsequently she attended the Norwich Academy, and a select school at Plymouth, then the academy at Oxford; in the meanwhile taught school in several places.

Margaret-Jane Riddell[4] (1), fourth daughter of John[3] (1), was born in Preston, N. Y., Nov. 8, 1826; died Sept. 20, 1845, at Preston, unmarried.

Prof. William-P. Riddell[4] (1), fifth son of John[3] (1), was born in Preston, N. Y., Oct. 1, 1828, and was only five years old when his father died. From 1838 he lived with his sister, Mrs. Brown, for nearly five years, while his mother was at New Orleans. From Oxford Academy he went to Amherst College, Massachusetts; thence in 1848, to Yale College, New Haven, Conn., where he received, in 1851, his degree of A. B.; he was there one of the five presidents of the Lionian Society. In 1852 he was at New Orleans, a student of chemistry and the natural sciences, with his brother John in the University; and in the winters of 1851–2, he gave a short course of lectures on chemistry at the Louisiana College in New Orleans. He compiled a genealogical sketch of this branch of the Riddell family in 1852, which has been the basis of the present article in this work; much, however, has been added concerning several branches of the family. Mr. Riddell was shot while near his residence in Houston, Tex., by an assassin in 1872. He married Sarah-Glenn Chalmers, of Austin Tex., and had *two* children. He is said to have been a stalwart-built man, broad-shouldered and full-chested, a regular athlete. He had dark hair and blue eyes; a receding forehead, and regular features; was social and kind-hearted.

Susan-A. Riddell[4] (4), youngest daughter of John[3] (1), was born in Preston, N. Y., March 24, 1831; was married in March, 1852, to Henry P. Marion (brother to the husband of her sister Lovina), and in that year was living on a farm in Preston, Conn. He was superintendent of schools for the town, also a Justice of the Peace and town collector. Susan, in 1838, went with her mother to New Orleans and remained there five years, returning in 1848. She attended school at Plymouth; also at Oxford Academy for two years. In 1849 she returned to New Orleans in company with her brother John and family, and remained till the following summer. She then returned and lived with her mother until her marriage.

William Riddell[4] (2), eldest son of Robert[3] (3), was born in Wilmington, Vt. (?), in 1814; died in 1816.

Thomas Riddell[4] (2), second son of Robert[3] (3), was born in Wilmington, Vt. (?), in 1816; married ——, and had issue several children, of whom hereafter. It is said he carries on the tin-ware and stove business at Bennington, Vt., and that he has been a prominent man there.

Enos Riddell[4] (1), third son of Robert[3] (3), was born in Wilmington, Vt., in 1818, and in 1852 was in Boston, Mass. Resides in Olean, N. Y. No family.

Sarah Riddell[4] (2), eldest daughter of Robert[3] (3), was born in Wilmington, Vt., in 1823; was married to Oskar L. Shafter, and had issue. Mr. Shafter was a graduate of the Harvard Law School, and esteemed one of the best lawyers in the State of Vermont; was candidate for governor in 1848. He lived in a pretty, octagonal house, situated on a lot ornamented with shade trees, some distance from the street. He was said to be " a man of plain habits and frank disposition."

Mary Riddell[4] (2), second daughter of Robert[3] (3), was born in Wilmington, Vt., in 1826; married Franklin Lamb; secondly, Addison Read, and lives in Hastings, Neb.

William Riddell[4] (3), fourth son of Robert[3] (3), was born in Wilmington, Vt., in 1829, and was of Boston in 1852; married Carrie Thayer, and has issue. Lives in Buffalo, N. Y.

Samuel-Taggart Riddell[4] (2), fifth son of Robert[3] (3), was born in Wilmington, Vt., in 1838; married Lucretia Clark; no issue. Resides in Fernandina, Florida.

Henry Riddell⁴ (1), sixth son of Robert³ (3), was born in Wilmington, Vt., March 6, 1837; married Emily C., daughter of Marlo R. Crosby, and has issue *five* children. Was of Wilmington in 1852.

Dr. George Riddell⁴ (3), eldest son of George³ (1), was born in Coleraine, Mass., Aug. 30, 1823; married Carrie Shurtleff, April 2, 1854, and by her had issue *three* children. His first wife died June 4, 1864, aged 31 years. He married, secondly, Aug. 28, 1865, Mary E. Warner, and by her has *three* children, of whom (with the other children) hereafter. He attended medical lectures at Castleton, Vt., and graduated at the University of New York, in the Medical College at New York city, March 10, 1853. He has practised medicine and surgery in Canisteo, N. Y., since his graduation, in company with his brother. He and brothers built a large hotel in Bradford, Penn., in the spring of 1878, called the "Riddell House," which was open only a little more than four months, when it was burned. Their loss above insurance was about thirty thousand dollars; they are rebuilding at a cost of about forty thousand dollars. He says: "My brothers and I are remarkable for nothing except we all work together, never disagree on any business transaction, and have always been as one family."

Mary Riddell⁴ (3), eldest daughter of George³ (1), was born in Coleraine, Mass., Aug. 11, 1825; died October, 1825.

Mary-Lovina Riddell⁴ (4), second daughter of George³ (1), was born in Coleraine, Mass., Feb. 15, 1827; was married at Canisteo, N. Y., June 19, 1851, to Jonathan Quick. She died April 26, 1852, leaving an infant ten days old.

Harriet-Arminda Riddell⁴ (2), third daughter of George³ (1), was born in Coleraine, Mass., Dec. 27, 1828; died at the age of 16, unmarried, March 10, 1845.

Dea. Lorenzo-B. Riddell⁴ (1), second son of George³ (1), was born in Coleraine, Mass., April 25, 1831; married July 4, 1855, to Caroline Frace, and has issue *four* children, of whom hereafter. He is deacon of the Presbyterian Church in Canisteo, N. Y.; carries on the business of undertaker and retail dealer in furniture. He has a good home, pleasantly situated on Academy Street. Has been intimately associated with his brothers in business.

Dr. LeRoy Riddell⁴ (1), third son of George³ (1), was born in Coleraine, Mass., Sept. 11, 1833; married Eunice L. Pratt, Dec. 17, 1863, and has issue *four* children, of whom hereafter. He is a graduate of University Medical College, New York city (1868), and is engaged in the practice of medicine and surgery, in company with his brother George, in Canisteo, N. Y., where he has an extensive patronage. He is pleasantly situated near the Canisteo Academy, on Academy Street. He was an owner in the "Riddell House," at Bradford, Penn., burned in 1878, but being rebuilt.

William Riddell⁴ (4), fourth son of George³ (1), was born in Coleraine, Mass., Feb. 21, 1836; married Helen Jones, daughter of David Jones, advocate, of New York, March 26, 1867, and has issue *three* children, of whom hereafter. He is a dealer in dry goods and groceries, in Canisteo, N. Y.; is prosperous, and owns a splendid residence near those of his brothers, on Academy Street.

Lemuel-Clark Riddell⁴ (1), fifth son of George³ (1), was born in Canisteo, N. Y., March 6, 1839, and died Aug. 23, 1868. He was in the employ of the Erie Railroad Company; was a man of great business capacity, and much esteemed by all who knew him. Unmarried.

Joseph-Marion Riddell[4] (1), youngest son of George[3] (1), was born in Canisteo, N. Y., Feb. 26, 1842; married Agnes Louder, Oct. 11, 1871, and has the care of his mother at Canisteo. He has no children; owns a farm.

William-G. Riddell[4] (5), eldest son of Gavin[3] (1), was born in Coleraine, Mass., Dec. 20, 1828; married Semira Bemis, of Whittingham, Vt., Oct. 30, 1854, and had issue. He died at Boston, March 24, 1859. His widow is still living in Charlestown.

John Riddell[4] (3), second son of Gavin[3] (1), was born in Coleraine, Mass., Oct. 7, 1830; married Martha-Ann Clark, of Boston, Oct. 5, 1857, and resided in Charlestown, Mass, where he died Oct. 3, 1859. His widow has married a Mr. Bassett. Mr. Riddell had issue *one* daughter.

Sophronia Riddell[4] (2), eldest daughter of Gavin[3] (1), was born in Coleraine, Mass., Oct. 4, 1832; died Aug. 1, 1851.

George-E. Riddell[4] (3), third son of Gavin[3] (1), was born in Coleraine, Mass., and died young, unmarried.

Hollis-T. Riddell[4] (1), fourth son of Gavin[3] (1), was born in Coleraine, Mass., March 11, 1837; died unmarried.

Elizabeth-C. Riddell[4] (1), second daughter of Gavin[3] (1), was born in Coleraine, Mass., Oct. 27, 1839; died unmarried.

Mary-E. Riddell[4] (5), third daughter of Gavin[3] (1), was born in Coleraine, Mass., June 2, 1842; died young.

Ann-E. Riddell[4] (1), fourth daughter of Gavin[3] (1), was born in Coleraine, Mass., Jan. 9, 1845; was married to Albert Robertson, of Leyden, Mass., July 3, 1864; died in Coleraine, Aug. 22, 1868.

Mary-Jane Riddell[4] (6), youngest daughter of Gavin[3] (1), was born in Coleraine, Mass., Oct. 30, 1849; died unmarried.

Charlotte-Helen Riddell[4] (1), eldest daughter of Robert[3] (4), was born in Chittenango, N. Y., May 26, 1818.

Frances-Lucretia Riddell[4] (1), second daughter of Robert[3] (4).

Henrietta-Sophia Riddell[4] (2), third daughter of Robert[3] (4), was born in Chittenango, N. Y., April 25, 1821.

Jemima Riddell[4] (2), fourth daughter of Robert[3] (4), was born in Chittenango, N. Y., April 26, 1823; died July 6, 1823.

Nancy-Marion Riddell[4] (1), fifth daughter of Robert[3] (4), was born in Chittenango, N. Y., Nov. 19, 1823.

Angeline-Fidelia Riddell[4] (1), eldest daughter of David[3] (1), was born in Chittenango, N. Y., Jan. 31, 1819.

William-Wallace Riddell[4] (6), eldest son of David[3] (1), was born in Chittenango, N. Y., Oct. 20, 1820.

Hannah-Maria Riddell[4] (1), second daughter of David[3] (1), was born in Chittenango, N. Y., Feb. 5, 1829; died Dec. 25, 1830.

Robert-David Riddell[4] (5), second son of David[3] (1), was born in Chittenango, N. Y., Nov. 2, 1834.

Sophia-R.-M. Riddell[4] (1), eldest daughter of Thompson[3] (1), was born in Hamilton, Mich., in June, 1836.

Thompson Riddell[4] (2), eldest son of Thompson[3] (1), was born in Hamilton, Mich., Jan. 31, 1845.

FIFTH GENERATION.

John-Schrager Riddell[5] (4), eldest son of John[4] (2), was born in New Orleans, La., April 2, 1837; died June 7, 1837.

Dr. Sanford-Schrager Riddell[5] (2), son of John[4] (2), was born at New Orleans, La., Aug. 22, 1838; married, December, 1866, Josephine, daughter of Roswell K. Bourne, of Cincinnatus, N. Y., and resides at Chippewa Falls, Chippewa County, Wis. His literary education was obtained in the academic department of the University of Louisiana, whence he graduated in March, 1860. He has been a resident of New Orleans, Cincinnatus, and Norwich, N. Y. He has made a special study of uterine diseases. During his youth for many years, he prepared and performed the experiments at his father's chemical lectures, and assisted at his various analyses and microscopical researches, and in perfecting the binocular microscope (first invented by his father). While still a lad he discovered, described, and named a new polygonum, "*Polygonum nova aureliensia.*" He is a member of the New Orleans Academy of Science, elected when twenty-one years of age; of the Chenango County (N. Y.), Medical Society; of the Chippewa Falls Medical Society, of which he was one of the organizers, and for some time secretary and treasurer; also, of the Chippewa County Medical Society, into which the Falls society merged. He is also a member of the American Medical Association. His contributions to professional literature consist of a few minor articles to medical journals. At the age of twenty-two he was called to the chair of chemistry and metallurgy in the New Orleans Dental College; was assistant to the Texas State Geologist, in 1860. He was three months in the Rebel army, but refused to serve after the capture of New Orleans. He was afterwards captain of a company in the Fifth Louisiana White Infantry, United States Army. Mr. Riddell is regarded as a man of scientific ability seldom excelled, and is eminent as a medical practitioner.

Edward-Henry Riddell[5] (1), third son of John[4] (2), was born in New Orleans, La., Nov. 18, 1841; married to a French lady in New Orleans.

John-William Riddell[5] (5), fourth son of John[4] (2), was born in New Orleans, La., Dec. 2, 1844; unmarried.

Lephe-Eugenia Riddell[5] (2), eldest daughter of John[4] (2), was married to York A. Woodward, a banker, of New Orleans, where they reside.

Mary-Angelica Riddell[5] (7), second daughter of John[4] (2), was born at New Orleans, La.; was married to Robert F. Hogsett, of New Orleans; deceased.

Adelaide Riddell[5] (1), third daughter of John[4] (2), was born at New Orleans, La.; married Albert P. House, and resides at New Orleans.

Robert-B. Riddell[5] (6), fifth son of John[4] (2), was born at New Orleans, La.

Peter-G. Riddell[5] (1), sixth son of John[4] (2), was born at New Orleans, La.

Jefferson-D. Riddell[5] (1), seventh son of John[4] (2), was born at New Orleans, La.

Lephe-Ann Riddell[5] (3), eldest daughter of Samuel[4] (1), was born in Preston, N. Y., Feb. 7, 1846; was married to Charles Bentley, and lives at Hastings, Mills County, Ia.

Mary-Jane Riddell[5] (8), second daughter of Samuel[4] (1), was born in Preston, N. Y., Jan. 13, 1848; was married to Elisha Lewis, and lives in Chautauqua County, N. Y.

Susan-Lovina Riddell[5] (5), third daughter of Samuel[4] (1), was born in Preston, N. Y., Jan. 4, 1850; was married.

Emma Riddell[5] (1), fourth daughter of Samuel[4] (1).

Addie-D. Riddell[5] (1), fifth daughter of Samuel[4] (1).

Harriet-Georgiana Riddell[5] (3), eldest daughter of George[4] (2), was born in Palmyra, Wis., July 2, 1851 She has acquired a good English education, and has also become a teacher of vocal and instrumental music. She is a cultured and accomplished young lady, but in a delicate condition of health. Unmarried in 1874.[*]

Frank-Darling Riddell[5] (1), eldest son of George[4] (2), was born in Palmyra, Wis, April 5, 1854; married, and has settled at Rochelle, Ill. He is a telegraph operator, and skilled in his profession.

Aurelia Riddell[5] (1), eldest daughter of Thomas[4] (2), was born in Bennington, Vt., in 1839.

Henry Riddell[5] (2), eldest son of Thomas[4] (2), was born in Bennington, Vt., in 1842.

Theodore Riddell[5] (1), second son of Thomas[4] (2), was born in Bennington, Vt., in 1845.

Robert-H. Riddell[5] (7), eldest son of Henry[4] (1), was born in Bennington, Vt., April 2, 1859; married, and has issue *one* son (1884). Mr. Riddell is a dry-goods merchant in Boston, Mass.

Sally Riddell[5] (2), eldest daughter of Henry[4] (1), died young.

Florence Riddell[5] (1), second daughter of Henry[4] (1), died young.

William-C. Riddell[5] (7), second son of Henry[4] (1), was born Dec. 13, 1868. In college at Ann Arbor, Mich.

Marlo-H. Riddell[5] (1), third son of Henry[4] (1), was born May 28, 1871-2.

Chester Riddell[5] (1), eldest son of George[4] (3), was born in Canisteo, N. Y., Feb. 14, 1855; died April 17, 1855.

Lizzie-E. Riddell[5] (1), eldest daughter of George[4] (3), was born in Canisteo, N. Y., April 11, 1856; unmarried in 1878.

Sarah-Taylor Riddell[5] (2), second daughter of George[4] (3), was born in Canisteo, N. Y., Jan. 10, 1859; died March 20, 1872.

Carrie-Lee Riddell[5] (1), third daughter of George[4] (3), was born in Canisteo, N. Y., Jan. 2, 1867.

Frank Riddell[5] (2), second son of George[4] (3), was born in Canisteo, N. Y., Aug. 13, 1870.

William-C. Riddell[5] (8), third son of George[4] (3), was born in Canisteo, N. Y., Nov. 9, 1876.

Scott Riddell[5] (1), eldest son of Lorenzo[4] (1), was born in Canisteo, N. Y., July 11, 1855.

---

[*] Mrs. Riddell, the mother of these children, married, secondly, to Simon Bunker, and is said to be "a lady in every respect," and is highly esteemed by all whose respect is worth having.

Sarah Riddell[5] (3), eldest daughter of Lorenzo[4] (1), was born in Canisteo, N. Y., May 27, 1859.

Lemuel Riddell[5] (2), second son of Lorenzo[4] (1), was born is Canisteo, N. Y., in December, 1868.

Laura-E. Riddell[5] (1), second daughter of Lorenzo[4] (1), was born in Canisteo, N. Y., July 15, 1871.

Pratt Riddell[5] (1), eldest son of LeRoy[4] (1), was born in Canisteo, N. Y., Oct. 20, 1864.

John Riddell[5] (6), second son of LeRoy[4] (1), was born in Canisteo, N. Y., Jan. 14, 1866.

Elmira Riddell[5] (1), eldest daughter of LeRoy[4] (1), was born in Canisteo, N. Y., Nov. 12, 1868.

Harriet Riddell[5] (4), second daughter of LeRoy[4] (1), was born in Canisteo, N. Y., Dec. 4, 1874.

Nettie-M. Riddell[5] (1), eldest daughter of William[4] (4), was born in Canisteo, N. Y., Oct. 5, 1868.

George Riddell[5] (4), eldest son of William[4] (4), was born in Canisteo, N. Y., Jan. 31, 1870.

Sarah-A. Riddell[5] (4), second daughter of William[4] (4), was born in Canisteo, N. Y., Aug. 9, 1876.

RIDDLES OF CHARLESTOWN, MASSACHUSETTS.

Edward Riddle[1] (1) was a well-known auctioneer many years in Boston; his parentage is not known to me. The family could have provided necessary particulars, but declined to do so. He married Charlotte, daughter of Edward and Elizabeth Cutter, Sept. 30, 1841, and fixed his residence in Charlestown, Mass. He went to England with a commission from the United States Government. Was a man of popularity; highly esteemed. Deceased.

William Riddle[1] (1), brother of the above, was many years in Boston, but went to California, and died there in the autumn of 1881, unmarried.

James Riddle[1] (1), brother of the preceding, was sometime of Boston, but removed to California, and died there in 1881, leaving a daughter.

Cordelia Riddle[1] (1), sister of the preceding, was an actress for many years. She made her *debut* at the Arch-street Theatre, Philadelphia, as Albert, in "William Tell," Jan. 23, 1834. She is now (1883) Mrs. Sanford, living at Newport, R. I., and very feeble.

Eliza Riddle[1] (1), sister of the preceding, (born in Philadelphia (?), made her first appearance as an actress, on the stage of the Walnut-street Theatre, Philadelphia, in 1823, as Charles, in "Laugh When You Can." Her first engagement in New York, though she was extremely youthful, won for her the attention and commendation of the people. She next appeared as Emily Worthington; then as Rosalie Somers Paul ("Wandering Boys") Virginia; and for her benefit, in October of that year, as Cora and Little Pickle. After an absence from New York for more than a quarter of a century, during which, as Mrs. William Smith,*— the name of her husband, — she had played with remarkable success at Philadelphia and Boston, and ranked with the first favorites of the day, particularly in comedy of every grade. She re-appeared in 1856, at Laura Keen's Theatre, and at Barton's in 1857–8, in the line of middle-aged, fashionable dowagers, country women, and Abigails of every degree, with credit to herself and satisfaction to the public. She last played in New York at the Winter Gardens, in 1859–'60. She took her farewell of the stage at the Howard Athenæum, Boston, in 1861. She died in Boston, of a lingering and painful illness, in 1861, leaving a daughter, Mrs. Sedley Brown, who has since become a favorite comedienne. Kate Field is a daughter of one of the sisters of Edward Riddle, but I do not know which one. Her father was J. M. Field.

SECOND GENERATION.

Elizabeth-Cutter Riddle[2] (1), eldest daughter of Edward[1] (1), was born in Boston (or Charlestown), Mass., Sept. 28, 1842.

Charlotta-Cordelia Riddle[2] (1), second daughter of Edward[1] (1), was born in Charlestown, Mass., Oct. 5, 1847.

Edward-Cutter Riddle[2] (2), eldest son of Edward[1] (1), was born in Charlestown, Mass., Oct. 10, 1849, and was for many years engaged in trade in Boston.

Prof. George-Peabody Riddle[2] (1), second son of Edward[1] (1), born in Charlestown, Mass., in 1851, and displayed an inclination for the theatrical profession at the age of four, having come from a family which for three generations has been represented on the American stage. When five years of age he saw played "Midsummer Night's Dream," which gave him singular emotions and greatly inspired his genius; he was when a child a promoter of amateur theatricals, and was his own manager.

His parents insisted that he should take a course at Harvard College before going upon the stage, but while at the University dreams of a theatrical career continually intruded upon his scholastic routine. At length Fechter came to Boston, and to him the aspirant for dramatic honors confided his hopes, with such result, that the great actor offered him a place in his company. How to satisfy his dearest ambition, and, at the same time, to comply with his parents' desire that he should graduate in due form was the problem that presented itself to the enthusiastic student. He thought he might become an actor, and still keep up his college studies. This plan he submitted to President Eliot, in a note, which drew forth a reply so characteristic that a quotation must be given :—

"MARCH 29, 1872.

"*Dear Sir,* — It would be quite impossible for you to be an actor, and, at the same time, keep up your college studies and take a degree. You cannot burn a candle at both ends. The stage is a very laborious and exigent profession. That you chose it at the age of four is not an argument for choosing it at twenty-four. I remember having a conviction at that age that I might be a farmer. Let me advise you strenuously to complete your education — so far, at least, as to go through college and to see a little more of real life before you commit yourself to the calling of an actor."

Excellent advice, for heeding which, Mr. Riddle now has his reward. But the dramatic instinct must needs be satisfied, and, while still an

---

* Eliza Riddle, born in Philadelphia, made her *debut* Jan. 14, 1835, as Julia in "Hunchback," at Walnut-street Theatre. Was she identical with the above Mrs. Smith ?

undergraduate, we find young Riddle giving readings in private houses. Among his auditors were Longfellow, the poet, and Professor Pierce, the mathematician, both of whom gave him the strongest encouragement to persevere in the dramatic career.   At this period he formed the acquaintance and received the encouragement of Edwin Booth.

On leaving college in 1874, Mr. Riddle sought a manager under whom to give readings.   Mr. Redpath was first applied to, but at first actually refused to listen to him.   After much persuasion, Redpath consented to hear him read, premising, by way of encouragement, "I've got to take the nine o'clock train, and you'll have to hurry."   Redpath listened and allowed himself to miss his train.   Mr. Riddle made his debut as a reader in October, 1874, at the Meionaon, and achieved a success, receiving the warm welcome of the press of the city.   At this time he began the study of Romeo, and went to New York to secure an opening there on the stage, but no manager would listen to him.   Coming back to Boston, Mr. Riddle made bold to address himself to Mr. Tompkins, of the Boston Theatre.   That gentleman, having a Saturday "off" night the following week, it was arranged then and there that Mr. Riddle should play Romeo to Mrs. Thomas Barry's Juliet.   The audience was large, and the performance a pecuniary success.   The general verdict of the critics was that Mr. Riddle's Romeo was creditable to an amateur, but his voice, still his weak point, was pronounced "too light, and lacking in body."   The following month Mr. Riddle played Titus to the Brutus of Edwin Booth. At the conclusion of the play Mr. Booth took him before the curtain to share the generous applause of the audience.   It was on this night that Mr. Booth said to Mr. Tompkins, "That young man will be famous." After this appearance, Mr. Riddle went to New York, where he gave readings at the Union Square Theatre of an afternoon.   Opinions differed in New York as to his merits as a reader.   William Winter criticised him severely; and the general verdict of New York critics, as opposed to that of Boston, was that Mr. Riddle could not read.   However, the reading was scarcely over when Mr. Palmer, of the Union Square Theatre, made him an offer to join his stock company, and at the same time came a similar offer from Mr. Field, of the Boston Museum.   Mr. Riddle accepted the Boston offer, and entered the Museum company as "walking gentleman," and then, in very reality, began to learn his trade.

He made his debut in the season of 1875–6 as Capt. Dudley Smooth, in "Money."   The part was a failure, but, although unsuccessful at the Museum, Mr. Riddle learned a good deal.   The verdict of the critics regarding his voice remained unchanged.   He was in the situation of Demosthenes when that stammering young man was told he could never become an orator.

Heartily discouraged, yet impelled by his love of the dramatic art to persevere, Mr. Riddle went to Montreal, where he found an opening in a newly-formed stock company.   He made his first appearance on the Montreal stage as Manuel, in the "Romance of a Poor Young Man."   He fairly jumped into popularity in the Canadian city, and received a handsome benefit from an enthusiastic audience.   At Montreal Mr. Riddle took all sorts of parts.   He was by turn, walking or leading man, villain, and old man.   This varied experience, playing a new part nearly every night, was of immense benefit to him.   It was there that he acquired an aptitude for the speedy acquisition of parts.   He was engaged at Montreal for a second season, but the people got wearied of their toy, the new stock company, and from Montreal Mr. Riddle went to Philadelphia, and obtained an engagement to play at the Chestnut-street Theatre. The first question addressed him, on arriving, by the manager, was, "Mr. Riddle, have you any voice?" "Let us settle that now," replied Mr. Riddle; "let me go on the stage and recite something to you." The trial was satisfactory, and he was engaged forthwith. That was a Friday, and the following Monday Mr. Riddle appeared as Clifford, in the "Hunchback." The Philadelphia press gave him a favorable verdict, and he remained at the theatre five weeks, when, being out of the bill, he came to Boston on a visit. During that visit Professor Pierce invited him to give a reading at his house in Cambridge on an afternoon. President Eliot was of the little company assembled in Professor Pierce's parlor, and took occasion to ask Mr. Riddle to accept the place of substitute to Professor Baxter, the instructor in elocution, who was then ill. Mr. Riddle declined outright, for he had, as he thought, fairly entered on his dramatic career, but President Eliot, in his quiet way, said: "I will give you two days to consider the matter," thus implying that he was not ready to take "No" for an answer. The result was that Mr. Riddle assented, and became instructor of elocution at Harvard, a position he still holds. The place has been of the greatest value to him, in that by training the voices of others he has been able to overcome his old defect of insufficient voice. Since his return to Boston, Mr. Riddle has given readings throughout New England, and has achieved great and merited success.

Mr. Riddle appeared at the Boston Theatre in 1881, playing Claude to Miss Mary Anderson's Pauline, and his performance was a great success, the audience being the largest ever seen in the theatre. He was the chief actor in the tragedy of "Œdipus" in the Greek drama at Harvard University, and proved such a success that his fame was established. Mr. Riddle's acting has been criticised as more modern than Greek, some contending that, in the Greek drama, there was little passion and forceful acting; but Mr. Riddle's conception of his part has received the approval of high classical authority, the hearty praise and commendation of learned and enthusiastic classical scholars. It is not a little curious that the classical glory which has come to the venerable university, should have come by the first actor graduated therefrom.

RIDDLES OF BOSTON, MASSACHUSETTS.

Richard Riddle[1] (1), descended from Scottish ancestors, was born in Dublin, Ireland, about 1802; married Catherine Eustes, and had issue *six* children, of whom hereafter. Mr. Riddle came to Boston, Mass., many years ago, and engaged in the blacksmith and carriage-building business. He died about 1879–80, and was succeeded in the business by his two sons, of whom hereafter. Mr. Riddle had brothers in Ireland.

SECOND GENERATION.

Sarah Riddle[2] (1), a daughter of Richard[1] (1), was married to William Conners, of Maine; resides in Boston.

John Riddle[2] (1), a son of Richard[1] (1), is in the blacksmith and carriage business, in company with his brother, in Boston, Mass., unmarried.

Mary Riddle[2] (1), a daughter of Richard[1] (1), was the wife of Thomas Dolen; deceased.

Catherine Riddle[2] (1), a daughter of Richard[1] (1), now keeping a hair store and wig manufactory in the city of Boston, where she has long been established; unmarried.

Patrick Riddle[2] (1), a son of Richard[1] (1), is in the carriage and blacksmith business in Boston.

Richard Riddle[2] (2), youngest son of Richard[1] (1), has been many years a book-keeper for dry-goods houses.

RIEDELS OF DOUGLASS, MASSACHUSETTS.

[FRENCH BRANCH.]

John-H. Riedel[1] (1) was one of the two brothers who sailed from France for America, presumably about 1760. Of his early life nothing is known. He served in an American cavalry regiment during the war of the Revolution, and passed the latter years of his life in Douglass, Mass. Whether he was a resident of that town at the time of his enlistment, or settled there after the expiration of his term of military service, is not recorded. He married an English lady named Clark, and had issue *fourteen* children,* nearly all of whom were born in Douglass. He was a Protestant in religion, and was wont to tell of the persecution his Huguenot ancestors had endured in the old country. His French Bible, sabre, camp utensils, military accoutrements, and other personal effects were in existence fifty years ago, but their present whereabouts is unknown. He died about 1800, and was buried in Douglass. The historian of the town informs me that the old family residence was known as the "Riddle House," when he was young. About 1850, and not later than 1855, a grandson, of Boston, visited Douglass for the purpose of settling the estate, and to sell the house and farm which had remained in the family, and on his return described the house as being a large, rambling affair, situated on an elevation on the "Mail Road." The estate was sold to John Floyd, — at that time connected with one of the railroads in that section, — who cleared off the timber for the road. At this time there was a dispute among some members of the family as to the propriety of spelling the surname "Riedell." The grandson, — John H. Riedel, of Boston, — after considerable search unearthed the old gentleman's sign and found his grave-stone: the name was spelled "Riedel" in both instances. Evidently this man was a direct descendant of some of the ancient houses of Ridel, in Normandy. This is the only branch in New England known to have spelled the name in the German form, except a few small families recently from Saxony and Bavaria.

---

* There are several descendants of John H. Riedel now living in New England. — some in Boston, — among them John H. Riedell, formerly editor of the *Union*, Manchester, N. H.

SECOND GENERATION.

Henry Riedel² (1), eldest son of John¹ (1), had grown to manhood when his father died, and was a carpenter by trade. He lived and died a bachelor, and was buried in Douglass or vicinity. The younger sons were apprenticed to him with one exception.

George Riedel² (1), second son of John¹ (1), went West in early life, and never returned to Massachusetts.

Armand Riedel² (1), a son of John¹ (1), was a confirmed invalid from his youth, and died when young,—presumably in Douglass.

James Riedel² (1), a son of John¹ (1), lived in Worcester, Mass., nearly all his life; was twice married, and had *one* daughter, now Mrs. Samuel Dill, Norwich, Conn.

John-St.Clair Riedel² (2), son of John¹ (1), was born in Douglass, Mass., in 1789. He resided in that town during his boyhood, and moved away after learning his trade. He married Ann Aldrich, of Smithfield, R. I., in 1811, after which he returned to his native town, and five of his *ten* children were born there. He removed to Boston in 1823, and lived in that city until his death, in 1843. He was a carpenter and builder during his residence in Douglass. His widow is still (1884) living, at the age of 88 years.

Sally Riedel² (1), a daughter of John¹ (1), was married to a man named Marsh, and lived in or near the city of Worcestor for many years, and died at Woonsocket, R. I. A daughter, Mary-Ann Marsh, was the wife of Alfred Morse, for many years a prominent manufacturer, of Farmersville, Mass.

Betsey Riedel² (1), a daughter of John¹ (1). } No records.
Fanny Riedel² (1), a daughter of John¹ (1). }

RIDDELLS OF NANTUCKET, MASSACHUSETTS.

[SCOTTISH BRANCH.]

Samuel Riddell¹ (1), supposed to have been born in Scotland,* settled in Waterford, Ireland, where he married and had issue *two* sons, of whom

---

*When Lindsey Riddell, of Nantucket, Mass., was a young man he was in the port of Glasgow, Scotland, in command of the ship "Falcon," and while there he went with the consignee to the city, where, when waiting at the hotel for the return of his friend, he observed the name "Lindsey Riddell" on a sign across the street. The store was that of a haberdasher, and being in want of some small wares Captain Riddell went over and made some purchases. The clerk asked his name for the purpose of making a bill, and when he learned it was Lindsey Riddell he gave his customer a discriminating look and asked what part of the world he was from. The reply was "Massachusetts, North America." He then inquired what information Captain Riddell could give of his family, and after hearing, stated that his father was an aged man; that many years before a favorite brother of his father went to Ireland, since when no news had reached the family in Scotland concerning him, and he had no doubt, from the account given by Captain Riddell, that this long-lost brother was his grandfather. Captain Riddell made an appointment to visit the old gentleman on another day, but returned to his ship and failed to keep it,—a neglect he always afterwards regretted. From records of marriages of Riddells with Lindseys, in Scotland, there was at one time a prospect of making genealogical connections between them and the Nantucket family, but further investigation of the family history showed the hope unfounded.

hereafter. He died in Ireland, and his widow was married to a man named Barber, — what became of him is not known, — and with her two sons came to Boston, Mass. She died in Nantucket, Sept. 10, 1793, aged 82 years, hence she was born in 1711. Her name was Susanna.

Samuel Riddell[2] (2), eldest son of Samuel[1] (1), was born in Waterford, Ireland, Dec. 22, 1748; came to Boston, Mass., with his mother and brother when a child; married, Jan. 19, 1769, to Judith, daughter of Jonathan and Mebitable Coleman (she was born Dec. 21, 1751, and died Sept. 15, 1822, aged 70 years and 9 months); the ceremony was performed by Rev. Bazaleel Shaw, at Nantucket, where Mr. Riddell had previously served his time as an apprentice to Samuel Storer, rope-maker. He settled permanently at Nantucket, and kept a hardware store and carried on the manufacture of ropes and cordage. His house was on Fair Street. Mr. Riddell was a portly, fine-looking gentleman, always dressed in what was then called "small-clothes." He was of medium height, and of fair, fresh complexion. In manners he was urbane and dignified in his general intercourse, but on occasions could be very jovial and hilarious. He was indeed a typical gentleman of the "old school." Died Oct. 20, 1823, aged 74 years, having had issue *fifteen* children, four of whom were living in 1847, and his descendants, numbering hundreds, are scattered from Maine to California.

James Riddell[2] (1), second son of Samuel[1] (1), was born in Ireland, and came with his mother to Boston, Mass., when a child or young man, before the Revolution. He married Elizabeth Rhyder, widow of Robert Rhyder, and daughter of Zachariah and Desire (Gorham) Bunker (she was born July 18, 1738), and had *one* daughter, of whom hereafter. Mr. Riddell was at one time engaged in the lumber business in Boston. He finally went to Nantucket to live, and is supposed to have died at sea. The widow Elizabeth was married to Barnabas Briggs, for her third husband.

THIRD GENERATION.

Henry Riddell[3] (1), eldest son of Samuel[2] (2), was born at Nantucket, Mass., Nov. 28, 1769; married, April 14, 1789, Sally, daughter of Joshua and Catherine Coffin (she was born Feb. 6, 1769), and secondly, Feb. 10, 1799, Hepsibah, daughter of William and Abigail Wyer, and widow of Solomon Coleman. She died Aug. 20, 1838, and he married thirdly, Peggy, widow of Alfred Coffin, who was born Oct. 8, 1784, and died Sept. 5, 1865. Mr. Riddell was a very worthy, and highly respected man; carried on rope-making; was many years a deacon of the second Congregational Church, at Nantucket, where he died Sept. 4, 1840, aged 71 years. He had issue, by two wives, *ten* children, of whom hereafter.

Capt. William Riddell[3] (1), second son of Samuel[2] (2), was born at Nantucket, Mass., April 15, 1772; married Elizabeth, daughter of Jethro and Margaret Hussey (she was born Oct. 19, 1773), by Rev. Bazaleel Shaw, June 21, 1792, and settled at Nantucket. He was a captain of merchant vessels, and made voyages to foreign countries. His house was on Maine Street, where his widow, for a number of years, kept a dry-goods store. They had *eight* children, of whom hereafter. Mr. Riddell died Aug. 4, 1817, his widow in August, 1846.

Samuel-Storer Riddell[3] (3), third son of Samuel[2] (2), was born at Nantucket, Mass., Sept. 3, 1773, and died young, unmarried.

Susan Riddell[3] (1), eldest daughter of Samuel[2] (2), was born at Nantucket, Mass., June 23, 1775; was married Nov. 8, 1797, by Josiah Coffin,

Justice of the Peace, to Timothy, son of William Wyer, and died March 31, 1842.

Capt. Lindsey Riddell² (1), fourth son of Samuel² (2), was born at Nantucket, Mass., Oct. 6, 1776; married, Feb 28, 1799, Margaret, daughter of Walter and Judith Brock, who was born May 23, 1781. He was a master of merchant ships, sailing to foreign ports. Had no children. He was a very large man, and died March 9, 1841, from injuries received from falling down stairs. His widow died March 30, 1861.

Samuel Riddell³ (4), was a twin son of Samuel² (2), born at Nantucket, Mass., Feb. 28, 1780; died March 29, 1780.

Seth Riddell³ (1) was a twin brother of Samuel³ (4), born at Nantucket, Mass., Feb. 28, 1780; died March 31, 1780.

Charles Riddell³ (1), seventh son of Samuel² (2), was born at Nantucket, Mass., April 9, 1781, and was killed by a whale at sea in the year 1799; unmarried.

Thomas Riddell³ (1), eighth son of Samuel² (2), was born at Nantucket, Mass., May 14, 1783; married Hannah, daughter of John Howland, of New Bedford; had *three* children, of whom hereafter, and died Dec. 24, 1753. He moved to New Bedford in 1810, and was a merchant and ship-owner in good circumstances. He died at Newport, R. I.

George Riddell³ (1), ninth son of Samuel² (2), was born at Nantucket, Mass., Aug. 16, 1785; and died March 20, 1789.

Nancy Riddell³ (1), second daughter of Samuel² (2), was born at Nantucket, Mass., Dec. 16, 1786, and died July, 1788.

Mary Riddell³ (1), third daughter of Samuel² (2), was born at Nantucket, Mass., June 26, 1789; was married Nov. 5, 1815, by Rev. Seth F. Swift, to James Norton, of Edgartown, and secondly, March 27, 1825 (by same clergyman), to William J. Simpson, of England.

Nancy Riddell³ (2), fourth daughter of Samuel² (2), was born at Nantucket, Mass., May 28, 1791; married by Rev. Seth F. Swift, June 22, 1815, to Reuben G., son of Seth Folger. She died July 20, 1818.

Capt. John Riddell³ (1), tenth son of Samuel² (2), was born May 28, 1791; married by Rev. Seth F. Swift, April 18, 1811, to Ann, daughter of Reuben and Anna Starbuck (she was born April 3, 1794), and settled at Nantucket. He was many years master of a packet ship. He died Nov. 2, 1873, and his widow still survives. They had *nine* children, six of whom died young.

Sophronia Riddell³ (1), fifth daughter of Samuel² (2), was born at Nantucket, Mass., Aug. 15, 1795; married Aug. 22, 1813, by Rev. Seth F. Swift, to Joseph F., son of Gideon Worth. She died Dec. 7, 1872.

Elizabeth Riddell³ (1), a daughter of that James² (1) who came from Ireland with his mother, was born Nov. 10, 1761 (probably in Boston); married Grafton, son of Peleg and Elizabeth Swain, and died May 18, 1834.

FOURTH GENERATION.

George-W. Riddell⁴ (2), eldest son of Henry³ (1), was born at Nantucket, Mass., Sept. 5, 1789; a rope-maker by trade; was lost while going to Virginia, in the schooner "Cornelia," Capt. Edmund Macy, master, Nov. 23, 1809.

Joshua-Coffin Riddell⁴ (1), second son of Henry³ (1), was born at Nantucket, Mass., Aug. 22, 1792; married, Nov. 25, 1810, by Rev. Seth Swift, Nancy, daughter of Benjamin and Judith Glover (she was born

Sept. 18, 1789), and was a rope-maker and whaleman. He died May 4, 1837, and his wife, Aug. 18, 1835.* They had *four* children, of whom hereafter.

Capt. Samuel-Storer Riddell⁴ (5), third son of Henry³ (1), was born at Nantucket, Mass., Oct. 19, 1797; married, Sept. 6, 1821, by Rev. Seth F. Swift, Judith, daughter of Zacheus Marcy, and widow of Willard Marcy (she was born June 27, 1801), and settled at Nantucket. He was captain of the whale ship "Oreno," and was killed, with the most of his men, in 1825, by the savages of the Fiji Islands. His widow married for her third husband, George H., son of Joseph Chase. These had no children.

Sarah-C. Riddell⁴ (1), eldest daughter of Henry³ (1), was born at Nantucket, Mass., Feb. 14, 1795; married, March 31, 1814, by Rev. Mr. Swift, to William J. Simpson, an Englishman. She died in New Bedford, in June, 1824.

Mary-C. Riddell⁴ (2), second daughter of Henry³ (1), and eldest by his second wife (Hepsibah Coleman), was born May 5, 1800; married in 1819, to Capt. George Pollard, Jr. Is presumed to be living, 1874.

William-Henry Riddell⁴ (2), fourth son of Henry³ (1), was born at Nantucket, Mass., Oct. 22, 1801; married, Nov. 12, 1828, by Rev. Mr. Swift, Eliza-Ann, daughter of George Pollard (she was born Feb. 5, 1805), and was a rope-maker by trade. He had *two* children, and died in Boston, Feb. 27, 1846.

Benjamin-Franklin Riddell⁴ (1), fifth son of Henry³ (1), was born at Nantucket, Mass., Nov. 28, 1802; died young.

Capt. Benjamin-Franklin Riddell⁴ (2), sixth son of Henry³ (1), was born at Nantucket, Mass., Feb. 23, 1804; married, June 20, 1831, by Rev. Mr. Swift, Lydia, daughter of Joseph and Lydia Coffin, and built a house on Center Street, Nantucket. He was a master of merchant and whale ships, and died of yellow fever, at Montego Bay, Aug. 22, 1862. His widow still survives. They had *four* children, of whom hereafter.

Capt. Timothy-W. Riddell⁴ (1), seventh son of Henry³ (1), was born at Nantucket, Mass., Jan. 5, 1806; married, April 8, 1830, by Rev. Mr. Swift, Charlotte C., daughter of Joseph, Jr., and Polly Chase. She was born July 15, 1806. He was for many years a master of whaling vessels, but was afterwards an auctioneer. He is not doing business at present (1874). His wife keeps a dry-goods store on Center Street, Nantucket; their residence is on Quincy Street. They have had *six* children, of whom hereafter.

Susan-W. Riddell⁴ (2), third daughter of Henry³ (1), was born at Nantucket, Mass., Aug. 8, 1808; was married Oct. 4, 1832, by Rev. Mr. Swift, to Cromwell Barnard, Jr.

Josiah-Hussey Riddell⁴ (1), eldest son of William³ (1), was born at Nantucket, Mass., March 13, 1793; married, Feb. 25, 1813, Eunice G., daughter of Isaac and Elizabeth Sission (she was born Oct. 19, 1793), and settled in his native town. Mr Riddell was an auctioneer and trader, and died of cholera in New York city, Sept. 5, 1832. His widow resides at Nantucket. They had *twelve* children, of whom hereafter; four died in infancy.

* His daughter says he died in June, 1836. One account states that Mrs. Nancy Riddell died of derangement, Sept. 2, 1835.

William Riddell⁴ (3), second son of William³ (1), was born at Nantucket, Mass., March 13, 1795, and died young ; unmarried.

Eliza Riddell⁴ (1), eldest daughter of William³ (1), was born at Nantucket, Mass., Feb. 20, 1798 ; was married to Frederick, son of Benjamin and Abigail Cartwright, and died at Brooklyn, N. Y., June 26, 1827.

Charles-William Riddell⁴ (2), third son of William³ (1), was born at Nantucket, Mass., April 18, 1799; married, by Rev. S. F. Swift, Sept. 25, 1821, Emeline, daughter of Moses and Hepsibah Bunker (she was born May 24, 1804), and was in early life a seaman. He moved to New York, and was for many years a police officer. He died at Williamsburgh, N. Y., Jan. 16, 1846; his widow died Dec. 25, 1865. They had *eight* children, of whom hereafter.

Capt. Alexander Riddell⁴ (1), fourth son of William³ (1), was born at Nantucket, Mass., Sept. 16, 1802; married, Jan. 1, 1826, by Rev. Daniel Filmore, Sarah, daughter of James and Polly Russell (she was born April 19, 1803), and had no children; both of them died in Benicia, Cal. He was a merchant captain. He died in April, 1855; his widow, April 24, 1865.

Peggy-Hussey Riddell⁴ (1), second daughter of William³ (1), was born at Nantucket, Mass., Aug. 2, 1803; was married to Samuel Coleman, and died in May, 1889. Mr. Coleman now (1874) lives in Boston.

Frederick-Augustus Riddell⁴ (1), fifth son of William³ (1), was born at Nantucket, Mass., Aug. 26, 1804; a cooper by trade; he was lost at sea, in the ship "Lady Adams," in the year 1823; unmarried.

Susan-Coffin Riddell⁴ (3), third daughter of William³ (1), was born at Nantucket, Mass., March 30, 1806, and died when an infant.

Lindsey-Adams Riddell⁴ (2), sixth son of William³ (1), was born at Nantucket, Mass., Jan. 30, 1807, and died an infant.

Edward-Coffin Riddell⁴ (1), seventh son of William³ (1), was born at Nantucket, Mass., Oct. 13, 1808; died single, in 1844.

George-Hussey Riddell⁴ (3), eighth son of William³ (1), was born at Nantucket, Mass., May 25, 1810; married Sept. 2, 1833, by Rev. Henry F. Edes, Eunice, daughter of Thomas and Eunice Barnard (she was born Oct. 14, 1815), and had issue *seven* children, of whom hereafter. Mr. Riddell was a clerk in a dry-goods store in Boston, from 1826 to 1832 ; was in the dry-goods business at Nantucket, from 1832 until 1836; resided in New York from that time until August, 1837, when returning to Nantucket, he re-established himself in the dry-goods trade. He closed up his business in Nantucket, and in 1849 left for California; moved his family to Benicia, in 1852; was elected Justice of the Peace in 1855, and was in that office in 1878. He was county recorder, from March, 1864, to March, 1866. He has also held other positions of responsibility, and is an efficient, public-spirited gentleman. He is now resident at Benicia, Cal.

Jethro-Hussey Riddell⁴ (1), ninth son of William³ (1), was born at Nantucket, Mass., July 21, 1812 ; died when an infant.

Thomas Riddell⁴ (2), tenth son of William³ (1), was born at Nantucket, Mass., Oct. 25, 1813 ; died when an infant.

Eliza Riddell⁴ (2), eldest daughter of Thomas³ (1), was born at Nantucket, Mass., April 23, 1808; married to Thomas R. Dix; no more information.

Charlotte Riddell⁴ (2), second daughter of Thomas³ (1), was born at

18

Nantucket, Mass., in January, 1812; married Samuel G. Stephenson, and died March 8, 1833.

Georgiana Riddell⁴ (1), third daughter of Thomas³ (1), was born in New Bedford, Mass., and married.

Harriet-Ann Riddell⁴ (1), eldest daughter of John³ (1), was born at Nantucket, Mass., Sept. 7, 1815; was married by Rev. ——— Marcus, May 7, 1839, to Albert, son of Zephaniah and Martha Wood.

Capt. Valentine-S. Riddell⁴ (1), eldest son of John³ (1), was born at Nantucket, Mass., July 7, 1817; married in March, 1841, Lydia, daughter of Elisha and Lucretia Swain (she was born May 12, 1820), and secondly, widow Amey Smith, of Ohio. He was master of a whale-ship and a trader; but now lives at Bruce Port, W. T. His first wife died Feb. 12, 1853. Mr. Riddell had *three* children by his first, and *one* by his second wife, of whom hereafter.

Nancy-F. Riddell⁴ (3), second daughter of John³ (1), was born June 5, 1822, and died unmarried, Sept. 18, 1838.

Samuel-S. Riddell⁴ (6), second son of John³ (1), was born in Nantucket, Mass., March 10, 1828; married Dec. 20, 1858, by Rev. Francis LeBaron, Elizabeth, daughter of Daniel and Eliza Whitney. Mr. Riddell is a merchant, and formerly lived in Callao, Peru; he now (1874) resides at Jamaica Plain, Mass., and has a counting-room on State Street, in Boston. They had *four* children, of whom hereafter.

Thomas Riddell⁴ (3), third son of John³ (1), was born at Nantucket, Mass., April 13, 1833, and died unmarried in Washington Territory, Aug. 31, 1868.

John Riddell⁴ (2), fourth son of John³ (1), was born at Nantucket, Mass., March 13, 1836, and lives in Washington Territory; he has no family.

FIFTH GENERATION.

Henry-G. Riddell⁵ (2), eldest son of Joshua⁴ (1), was born at Nantucket, Mass., June 3, 1812; married, July 9, 1837, Caroline Pinkham; and secondly, Lucinda ———. His first wife was born in 1810, and died Oct. 5, 1867. He now lives in Montrose County, Mo., is a mechanic, and has *one* son, of whom hereafter.

Sarah-C. Riddell⁵ (2), eldest daughter of Joshua⁴ (1), was born at Nantucket, Mass., March 6, 1817; married, July 19, 1835, by George Cobb, Justice of the Peace, William P., son of Owen Bunker.

Caroline-G. Riddell⁵ (1), second daughter of Joshua⁴ (1), was born at Nantucket, Mass., March 2, 1821; married in 1839, Horace Young, of Maine; and secondly, Capt. William H., son of William H. Swain.

George-Washington Riddell⁵ (4), second son of Joshua⁴ (1), was born at Nantucket, Mass., Sept. 24, 1824, and died unmarried, April 5, 1844, aged 19 years.

Robert-F. Riddell⁵ (2), eldest son of William⁴ (2), was born at Nantucket (supposed), and died Sept. 12, 1838, aged 2 years.

Henry-W. Riddell⁵ (3), second son of William⁴ (2), was born at Nantucket (supposed), Sept. 28, 1839; resides in New York, unmarried.

Mary-P. Riddell⁵ (3), eldest daughter of Benjamin⁴ (3), was born at Nantucket, Mass., Jan. 30, 1834; married in 1860, George P., son of Moses and Susan Smith.

Benjamin-Franklin Riddell[5] (3), eldest son of Benjamin[4] (2), was born at Nantucket, Mass., Aug. 22, 1846; now resident of Boston, where he keeps a drug-store.

Henry Riddell[5] (4), second son of Benjamin[4] (2), was born at Nantucket, Mass., May 18, 1848. No other information.

Alexander-C. Riddell[5] (2), third son of Benjamin[4] (2), was born in Nantucket, Mass., April 3, 1852, and resides in California.

Timothy-W. Riddell[5] (2), eldest son of Timothy[4] (1), was born at Nantucket, Mass., May 5, 1831, and was lost at sea, when mate of the bark "Abby," of Kingston, Mass., while coming from Malaga, in 1856.

James-Bartlett Riddell[5] (3), second son of Timothy[4] (1), was born in Nantucket, Mass., May 5, 1834, and died Feb. 18, 1836.

Charlotte-C. Riddell[5] (3), eldest daughter of Timothy[4] (1), was born at Nantucket, Mass., Jan. 29, 1838, and died single, July 27, 1851.

Mary-H. Riddell[5] (4), second daughter of Timothy[4] (1), was born at Nantucket, Mass., Sept. 11, 1839; married in November, 1864, Joseph P. Nye, of Fairhaven.

Joseph-Chase Riddell[5] (1), third son of Timothy[4] (1), was born at Nantucket, Mass., July 22, 1841, and died in September, 1847, a child.

Sarah-B. Riddell[5] (3), third daughter of Timothy[4] (1), was born at Nantucket, Mass., March 29, 1849, and died single, Jan. 27, 1873.

Isaac-Sisson Riddell[5] (1), eldest son of Josiah[4] (1), was born at Nantucket, Mass., Jan. 7, 1815; married Harriet-Louisa Berry; is a painter by trade, living in Savannah, Ga.; he has *one* son, of whom hereafter.

William-H. Riddell[5] (4), second son of Josiah[4] (1), was born at Nantucket, Mass., Oct. 19, 1819. He was mate of a vessel, and was shot at sea, Jan. 28, 1849, and buried on an uninhabited island.

Mary-P. Riddell[5] (5), eldest daughter of Charles[4] (2), was born at Nantucket, Mass., Jan. 26, 1827; married —— Parrisan. He was wounded at Antietam, and died Sept. 17, 1862.

Emeline-A. Riddell[5] (1), second daughter of Charles[4] (2), was born at Nantucket, Mass., in 1829; married John Austin. They are both dead.

Eliza-C. Riddell[5] (3), third daughter of Charles[4] (2), was born at Nantucket, Mass. (supposed), in 1830; married Allen Convey; no issue.

Josephine Riddell[5] (1), fourth daughter of Charles[4] (2), was (probably) born in New York; married Thomas Barry, and lives in Brooklyn.

Hepsibah-L. Riddell[5] (1), fifth daughter of Charles[4] (2), was (probably) born in New York; died young.

Virginia Riddell[5] (1), sixth daughter of Charles[4] (2), was (probably) born in New York, and died Dec. 14, 1845, aged 5 years.

DeWitt-C. Riddell[5] (1), a son of Charles[4] (2), died unmarried, in New York, at the age of 21, May 7, 1862.

Frederick-A. Riddell[5] (2), a son of Charles[4] (2), was born Aug. 6, 1834, and died single, in New York, May 3, 1859.

Emma-Barnard Riddell[5] (1), eldest daughter of George[4] (3), was born at Nantucket, Mass., May 27, 1834; died at Benicia, Cal., unmarried, Nov. 11, 1852.

George-William Riddell[5] (5), eldest son of George[4] (3), was (probably) born in New York, March 5, 1837; married in San Francisco to Elizabeth Hall, Jan. 16, 1872, and has issue. Mr. Riddell is a book-keeper and accountant in San Francisco, Cal.

Thomas-Barnard Riddell[5] (4), son of George[4] (3), born April 21, 1840; died May 15, 1840.

Alexander Riddell[5] (3), son of George[4] (3), born April 21, 1840; died May 17, 1840.

Mary-Coffin Riddell[5] (5), second daughter of George[4] (3), was born at Nantucket, Mass., Sept. 13, 1841; married Lieut. James L. Corley, of Barnwell, S. C., at Benicia, Cal., June 3, 1861. They now (1873) reside at Norfolk, Va.

Eliza-Starbuck Riddell[5] (3), third daughter of George[4] (3), was born at Nantucket, Mass., July 20, 1845; married, Aug. 3, 1866, to Frank Barnard (her cousin), and resides at San Francisco, Cal.

Henrietta-Herbert Riddell[5] (1), fourth daughter of George[4] (3), was born at Benicia, Cal., Dec. 8, 1855; was unmarried in 1873. She is a teacher.

Elisabeth-S. Riddell[5] (1), eldest daughter of Valentine[4] (1), was born at Nantucket, Mass., June 8, 1846. She is a teacher in the Coffin School at Nantucket.

William-S. Riddell[5] (5), eldest son of Valentine[4] (1), was born at Nantucket, Mass., March 3, 1850; married, in June, 1872, Martha A. Baskernelle, in California, and has issue.

Valentine Riddell[5] (2), second son of Valentine[4] (1), was born at Nantucket, Mass., Jan. 18, 1853, and died in California, unmarried, Jan. 18, 1871.

George-Washington Riddell[5] (6), third son of Valentine[4] (1), was born at Nantucket, Mass., about February, 1859, and was unmarried in 1874.

Charles-Whitney Riddell[5] (3), eldest son of Samuel[4] (6), was born Aug. 16, 1860.

Emma Riddell[5] (1), eldest daughter of Samuel[4] (6), was born Sept. 17, 1864.

Annie-Eliza Riddell[5] (1), second daughter of Samuel[4] (6), was born May 18, 1868.

Herbert Riddell[5] (1), second son of Samuel[4] (6), was born June 2, 1871.

SIXTH GENERATION.

John-Backman Riddell[6] (3), a son of Isaac[5] (1), was born about 1860, and lives in Savannah, Ga.

George-Lindsey Riddell[6] (7), a son of George[5] (5), was born in San Francisco, Cal.

Alice Riddell[6] (1), a daughter of William[5] (5), was born in 1873.

RIDDELLS OF MONSON, MASSACHUSETTS.

[TYRONE BRANCH.]

Thomas Ridel[1] **(1)**, or Riddell, born in County Tyrone, Ireland, in 1739, was brought to New England when a child. He married Rebecca Moulton, of Monson, Mass., and had issue *seven* children, of whom hereafter. He was a farmer. Some say he served in the Colonial Army during the war of the Revolution. I find no mention of him on the pension records at Washington, D. C. His surname, — with those of his children, — on the town records of Monson, is spelled "Ridel," hence I believe his real family name was "Riddell," and the contracted form an unauthorized assumption of some scribe. I have not found a family tradition amongst the descendants of Thomas Ridel by which the connection between him and any other American branch is assumed, or even suggested; the prevailing traits, however, so conspicuous in all branches of the old clan, are singularly prominent in this family, and they are undoubtedly of the same extraction as the numerous other Scotch-Irish branches in the United States. Mr. Ridel died in Monson, Mass., in 1809, aged 70 years.*

SECOND GENERATION.

John Riddle[2] **(1)**, eldest son of Thomas[1] **(1)**, was born in Monson, Mass., in the year 1761; married to Olive, daughter of Joshua Blodget, of Stafford, Mass., and settled in Randolph, Vt. He emigrated to Alexander, Genesee County, N. Y., in 1806 or 1807, and was, consequently, one of the pioneers on the well-known "Holland Purchase." He was a farmer by vocation, but served as Justice of the Peace for many years, and also represented his town as a supervisor for several years. Mr. Riddle died in 1849, aged 88 years; had issue *ten* children, of whom hereafter. He was reliable and straightforward; a man of honor and high respectability.

Joseph Riddle[2] **(1)**, second son of Thomas[1] **(1)**, was born at Monson, Mass. (according to Pension Records at Washington), in the year 1763; married to Mary or Polly ——, and had issue *eight* children, of whom hereafter. He resided in Monson until 1808, when he emigrated to the "Holland Purchase," in the State of New York, and settled as a farmer; here he lived the remainder of his days. In the summer of 1775 he enlisted under Capt. Isaac Cotton, in Col. David Brewster's regiment. In 1776 he enlisted under Capt. Joseph Munger, in the regiment of Col. Robert I. Woodbridge, "Massachusetts Line." July 1, 1777, he entered the service for three years under Capt. Caleb Keep, and Col. William Shepherd, of the Fourth Massachusetts Regiment, General Glover's brigade, as drum-major; and in July, 1780, was discharged by Capt. Simon Larned, who was in command of the regiment at "Robertson Farms" near West Point. He was on a short tour in the militia, and at the surrender of Burgoyne, but was not in the decisive battle preceding that event, in consequence of guarding the road to Albany. He was in the battle of Monmouth, N. J., June 28, 1778, and with General Sullivan, in Rhode Island, in August, 1778. He was probably wounded, for the Pension Records state that he was a cripple. Some say he did service in the war of 1812. I do not know the date of his death.

---

* There are traditions in other families whose Scotch-Irish ancestors settled in the Middle States, that there were relatives in New England.

Elijah Riddle² (1), third son of Thomas¹ (1) and his wife Rebecca, was born in Monson, Mass., Jan. 27, 1772; married to Clarissa Fuller (she was born Jan. 20, 1775, died Sept. 6, 1834), and early emigrated to New York State, and took up land on the "Holland Purchase," along with his brothers before mentioned. He left New York and emigrated West many years ago; died in Michigan, Oct. 10, 1842, having had issue *four* children, of whom hereafter. He was in the war of the Revolution, and fought in several engagements; also, on board a man-of-war three years.

Thomas Riddle² (2), fourth son of Thomas¹ (1), was born in Monson, Mass., Sept. 27, 1781; married to Minerva Merrick (she was born in Monson, Mass., Feb. 3, 1785), Dec. 22, 1805, and emigrated to Ohio early in the summer of 1817. He was a farmer; died at Newbury, Geauga County, O., in September, 1823, having had issue *eight* children, of whom hereafter. His widow died at Paw Paw, Ind., Jan. 11, 1866. She was a woman of remarkable intellectual powers, an excellent wife and mother.

Mary Riddle² (1), a daughter of Thomas¹ (1) (born probably in Monson, Mass., though I find no records), was married to Benjamin Blodget, of Randolph, Vt.; probably died there many years ago.

Susan Riddle² (1), a daughter of Thomas¹ (1), was born (probably in Monson, Mass.; no records) between 1772 and 1773; was married to John Squires, a farmer, and died in Alexander, N. Y., sixty years ago.

Salla Riddle² (1), fifth son of Thomas¹ (1) and Rebecca, his wife, was born in Monson, Mass., Feb. 16, 1774. I have found no other account of him, and presume he died when a child.

Sally Riddle² (1), a daughter of Thomas¹ (1), was born in Monson, Mass., Feb. 16, 1778; was married to Levi Patterson, a farmer, and died in Orangeville, N. Y.

THIRD GENERATION.

Lyman Riddle³ (1), eldest son of John² (1), was born in Monson, Mass., in 1786; married Jan. 28, 1818, to Polly, daughter of Royal Moulton, and had issue *six* children, of whom hereafter. He was a farmer; died on his father's homestead in Alexander, Genesee County, N. Y., April 9, 1872, aged 84 years.

Hannah Riddle³ (1), eldest daughter of John² (1), was born at Monson, Mass., in 1788; died in the town of Alexander, N. Y., in 1808, unmarried.

Sarah Riddle³ (1), second daughter of John² (1), was born in Monson, Mass., in 1790; died in the town of Alexander, N. Y., in 1847.

Susan Riddle³ (2), third daughter of John² (1), was born at Monson, Mass., in 1794; was married to Marshall Butterfield, and resides in Michigan.

Olive Riddle³ (1), fourth daughter of John² (1), was born at Monson, Mass., in 1796; married Leverett Seward, and resides in Alexander, N. Y.

Betsey Riddle³ (1), fifth daughter of John² (1), was born in Randolph, Vt., in 1799; was married to Harley Howe, and resides in Rochester, N. Y.

John Riddle³ (2), second son of John² (1), was born in Randolph, Vt., in 1802; died at Alexander, Genesee County, N. Y., in July, 1827.

Thomas Riddle³ (3), third son of John² (1), was born in Randolph, Vt., in 1804; married, in 1834, to Eloise A. Johnson, of LeRoy, N. Y.; resides in the town of Darien, Genesee County, N. Y., and is without issue. Mr. Riddle followed mercantile pursuits in his early days; has been postmaster, town-clerk, register of deeds, session justice, and Justice of the Peace for twenty-eight consecutive years.

Norman Riddle⁸ (1), fourth son of John² (1), was born in Alexander, N. Y., in 1806; died there in 1810.

Hannah Riddle⁸ (2), sixth daughter of John² (1), was born in Alexander, N. Y., in 1808; died there in 1812.

Salla Riddle⁸ (2), eldest son of Elijah² (1), was born March 28, 1803, in Monson, Mass., and died Feb. 17, 1863, aged 60 years. He married Olive Nelson, March 27, 1825, and had issue *seven* children, two sons and five daughters, of whom hereafter.

James-M. Riddle⁸ (1), second son of Elijah² (1), was born April 28, 1810, (probably in Monson, Mass.), but I fail to learn particulars of his family.

Harriet Riddle⁸ (1), daughter of Elijah² (1), was born March 11, 1813, probably in Monson.

Laura Riddle⁸ (1), daughter of Elijah² (1), was born July 7, 1819, (probably in New York); married to Edwin Bennet.

Orrin Riddle⁸ (1), eldest son of Joseph² (1), was born in Monson, Mass., May 18, 1790; married Bertha Chaffe, and by her had issue *four* children. He married, secondly, Harriet ——, by whom he had *four* children. He settled in Genesee County, N. Y., as a farmer, where he died. Wives both dead. For account of descendants see following pages.

Freeborn-Moulton Riddle⁸ (1), second son of Joseph² (1), was born in Monson, Mass., Sept. 18, 1793; married to Abigail Chaffe, of Alexander, N. Y., and by her (who died March 15, 1829) had *eight* children. He married, secondly, Sarah Smith, of Batavia, Genesee County, N. Y., by whom he had *three* children; thirdly, to Jemima Baston, by whom no issue. He was a farmer; died March 12, 1877; his wife predeceased him in the summer of 1874.

Rebecca Riddle⁸ (1), eldest daughter of Joseph² (1), was born in Monson, Mass., March 10, 1782; was married to Thomas Broadway, and had issue. Dead.

Polly Riddle⁸ (1), second daughter of Joseph² (1), was born in Monson, Mass., Aug. 1, 1784; was married to Daniel Moulton, and had issue. Dead.

Lina Riddle⁸ (1), third daughter of Joseph² (1), was born in Monson, Mass., June 1, 1786; was married to Maturin Allard, and had issue. Dead.

Charlotte Riddle⁸ (1), fourth daughter of Joseph² (1), was born in Monson, Mass., June 8, 1788; was married to James McKain; died in New York State.

Almon Riddle⁸ (1), eldest son of Thomas² (2), was born in Monson, Hampden County, Mass., Nov. 3, 1806; went to the "Western Reserve," Ohio, with his parents in the month of September, 1817, and settled in Newbury, Geauga County. He learned the carpenter's trade with one Joel Chapman. Purchased sixteen acres of wild land on Paw Paw Creek, Wabash County, Ind.; married Caroline-Olivia Marsh, of Springfield, Mass., Aug. 1, 1837, and moved to Noble township, Wabash County, Ind., and settled on the land he had previously purchased, in October, 1838. He had issue *three* children, of whom hereafter.

Jose-Merrick Riddle (1), second son of Thomas[2] (2), was born in Monson, Mass., July 27, 1808; married, Feb. 23, 1836, to Caroline Hayden, and by her had several children, of whom hereafter. He removed to Thetford, Genesee County, Mich., in 1849, and died there Aug. 9, 1855,—"a superior man."

Thomas-Elmer Riddle (4), third son of Thomas[2] (2), was born in Monson, Mass., Aug. 4, 1810; died there March 26, 1813.

William-Henry Riddle (1), fourth son of Thomas[2] (2), was born in Monson, Mass., April 13, 1812; went to Ohio with his parents, and became a young lawyer of great promise; he died at Plainville, Hamilton County, O., June 6, 1837, unmarried. He was the "Henry Ridgeley" in the novel written by his brother, Albert G. Riddle, of Washington, and published by Nichols & Hall, of Boston, a few years ago; it was entitled "Bart Ridgeley."

John-Adams Riddle (3), fifth son of Thomas[2] (2), was born in Monson, Hampden County, Mass., April 23, 1814; married, in October, 1837, to Lois Odell, of Manchester, Vt., and had issue. He married, secondly, Theressa Ganson; she was born in Massachusetts, and died at Chardon, O.; no issue. Mr. Riddle is now living with his youngest daughter; a carpenter.

Hon. Albert-Gallatin Riddle (1), sixth son of Thomas[2] (2), was born in Monson, Mass., May 28, 1816; married, Jan. 23, 1845, to Caroline, daughter of Judge Burton F. Avery, of Chardon, O., where he resided until 1850. After the death of his father, Mr. Riddle cared for himself, and has said, "I did it poorly." He studied law and was admitted to the bar in 1841; was elected district attorney, and served six years; was elected twice to the Ohio State Legislature; removed to Cleveland in 1850; elected to Congress in 1860; went to Cuba as United States Consul, in 1864, and to look after government interests at Nassau. On his return, he removed to Washington, and resumed the practice of law, where he still continues, having acquired an extensive patronage, and is employed on cases involving great responsibility. He is Professor of Law in the Howard University. He contributed his portrait in steel for this work, and is one of the Publishing Committee appointed at the family meeting at Philadelphia, in 1876. Mr. Riddle has issue *seven* children, of whom hereafter. He is the author of several popular novels.

Minerva Riddle (1), eldest daughter of Thomas[2] (2), born at Newbury, O., April 16, 1818; was married Jan. 24, 1839, to Varnum N. Clark, and in 1842 or '43, moved to Paw Paw, Ind. She has issue *four* children.

Roswell Riddle (1), seventh son of Thomas[2] (2), was born at Newbury, O., Dec. 4, 1820; married Romelia Smith; secondly, to Alvira Way, a widow. He served in the war of the Rebellion; has lived on the homestead. No children.

George-W. Riddle (1), eighth son of Thomas[2] (2), was born at Newbury, O., April 26, 1828; died at Paw Paw, Ind., March 23, 1843,—"as handsome and noble a youth as ever bore the name."

FOURTH GENERATION.

Pallas-Loutta Riddle (1), eldest daughter of Lyman[3] (1) and Polly (Moulton), his wife, was born at Alexander, Genesee County, N. Y., Oct. 26, 1818; was married to John Dirstine, March 17, 1842, and resides at Alexander.

Grace-Ann Riddle[4] (1), second daughter of Lyman[3] (1), was born at Alexander, N. Y., in October, 1822; was married to Royal Newland, in January, 1843, and died at Alexander, Sept. 13, 1844.

Jerome Riddle[4] (1), eldest son of Lyman[3] (1), was born at Alexander, Genesee County, N. Y., April 30, 1825; married to Adell Wright, in 1875. No children in 1878.

Elizabeth-Adell Riddle[4] (1), third daughter of Lyman[3] (1), was born at Alexander, N. Y., June 25, 1832; married to William W. Plato, Oct. 15, 1857; resides in Batavia, Genesee County, N. Y.

Thomas-Herbert Riddle[4] (5), second son of Lyman[3] (1), was born at Alexander, Genesee County, N. Y., June 3, 1839; married in February, 1862, to Elvira Blodget, and has issue, of whom hereafter. Resides at Alexander.

Albert Riddle[4] (2), eldest son of Salla[3] (1), was born in the town of Alexander, Genesee County, N. Y., Dec. 18, 1828; married Nov. 13, 1851, to Eliza J. Holt, and has had issue *five* children, of whom hereafter. Mr. Riddle has been a farmer, druggist, and engaged in the grocery business; has held every office in the township except that of constable; was twice elected county treasurer, and is now (1879) superintendent of the county poor. He resides in Howell, Livingstone County, Mich. His height is six feet three inches; his weight two hundred and sixty-five pounds. Mr. Riddle, judging from his portrait, is a fine-looking man.

Arvilla Riddle[4] (1), eldest daughter of Salla[4] (1), was born Dec. 3, 1826; was married May 25, 1845, to Riley Kinney, and died June 20, 1866.

Janett Riddle[4] (1) second daughter of Salla[3] (1), was born April 14, 1831; was married Feb. 22, 1854, to Aaron V. Holt.

Alma-S. Riddle[4] (1), third daughter of Salla[3] (1), was born Sept. 22, 1833; was married Dec. 22, 1858, to John G. Rooke.

Lucias-E. Riddle[4] (1), second son of Salla[3] (1), was born in Alexander, Genesee County, N. Y., Aug. 20, 1834; married Dec. 14, 1859, to Betsey, daughter of Henry and Lauretta Elliatte (or Elliott), of Piety Hill, Livingstone County, Mich., — he was born in Canandaigua, Ontario County, N. Y., Jan. 8, 1833, — and has issue *three* children, of whom hereafter. Mr. Riddle is a farmer in good circumstances, and has held various township offices. He resides at Oceola, Mich.

Caroline Riddle[4] (1).
Almira Riddle[4] (1).
Lyman Riddle[4] (2).
Charles Riddle[4] (1).
} Children of Orrin[3] (1).

Joseph-Montraville Riddle[4] (2), eldest son of Freeborn[3] (1), was born at Alexander, Genesee County, N. Y., June 5, 1814; married Oct. 15, 1840, to Lucy, daughter of Asa and Lucy (Bushnell) Andrus, of Pollet, Rutland County, Vt. (she was born June 5, 1815), and by her had issue *five* children, of whom hereafter. Mr. Riddle is a farmer, residing at Salamanca, N. Y.

George-Kirklin Riddle[4] (2), second son of Freeborn[3] (1), was born at Alexander, Genesee County, N. Y., Oct. 6, 1816; married in the village of Batavia, same county, April 1, 1838, to Maryette Wade (she was born in Vermont, in 1816). He settled in Batavia, Genesee County, N. Y.; worked as a mechanic; removed to Cattaraugus and engaged in

farming; thence to Pembroke, and carried on a farm; thence to Pemble-
ton as a mechanic; thence to Greenbush, Mich. (Clinton County), where
he now resides. He has issue *eleven* children, of whom hereafter.

Laura-Utley Riddle⁴ (2), eldest daughter of Freeborn³ (1), was born
at Alexander, Genesee County, N. Y.; married to Pliny Fox, a lawyer,
and lives at DeKalb, Ill.

Charlotta-Temple Riddle⁴ (2), second daughter of Freeborn³ (1),
was born at Batavia, Genesee County, N. Y.; married to Augustus Mason, of Salamanca, N. Y., and has issue.

Rosalvo-King Riddle⁴ (1), third son of Freeborn³ (1), was born at
Batavia, Genesee County, N. Y., and is now living at Independence, Van
Buren County, Ind.; is a merchant. He married Mary Wheeler, and has
issue, of whom hereafter.

Trumbull-Cary Riddle⁴ (1), fourth son of Freeborn³ (1), was born at
Batavia, Genesee County, N. Y., Aug. 12, 1823; removed to Lockport, N.
Y., at the age of 15; married Aug. 22, 1847, to Sarah-Margaret Colt; was
superintendent of canal work on Erie Canal several years; removed to
Grinnell, Poweshiek County, Ia., in 1856. In 1859 moved to Chapin,
Franklin County, Ia. He was one of the early settlers in both counties,
and suffered many hardships; his nearest market was sixty-four miles
away. He died respected, Jan. 24, 1877.

Marquis-de-Lafayette Riddle⁴ (1), fifth son of Freeborn³ (1), was
born at Batavia, Genesee County, N. Y.; married Sarah Clickner, 1848;
secondly, Emily Utley, in 1878, and resides at Royalton, Niagara County,
N. Y., as a farmer.

James-Sullivan Riddle⁴ (2), sixth son of Freeborn³ (1), was born at
Batavia, Genesee County, N. Y.; married Fluvia A. Herrighton in 1846,
and is now farming at Chapin, Franklin County, Ia.

Abigail Riddle⁴ (1), third daughter of Freeborn³ (1), was born at
Alexander, Genesee County, N. Y.; married to Morris Butterfield, a merchant of Otto, Cattaraugus County, N. Y. She died in March, 1864.

Emily-Sophia Riddle⁴ (1), second daughter of Freeborn³ (1), by his
second wife, was born at Alexander, Genesee County, N. Y.; was married
to —— Sheltersburg, and resides in Girard, Penn.

Franklin-Carlos Riddle⁴ (1), son of Freeborn³ (1), by his second
wife, was born at Alexander, N. Y.; married to Emma Jenkins, and died
in October, 1861.

Francis-Marian Riddle⁴ (1), eldest son of Almon³ (1), was born in
Wabash County, Ind., July 3, 1839; married Aug. 14, 1862, to Annette M. Stewart, and has issue *five* children, of whom hereafter. He
learned the carpenter's trade of his father. Attended school winters
until twenty years old. Was a school-teacher. Cast his first vote for
President Abraham Lincoln, in the autumn of 1860; in the following
spring, while working at his trade for money to take him to college, he
heard of the firing on Fort Sumter, and of the call of President Lincoln
for volunteers to put down the Rebellion; patriotism predominating over
every other sentiment, he responded at once to the call by enlisting in
Company H, Eighth Regiment, Indiana Volunteer Infantry, as a private;
was appointed first corporal in May, and was with his regiment at the
battle of Rich Mountain, Va., July 11, 1861, after which,—Aug. 6, 1861,
—was honorably discharged. He was offered a commission at the reorganization of the Eighth Regiment for three years, but declined doing

more infantry service. He re-enlisted, in the Third Indiana Battery, Aug. 11, 1862, to serve three years; was married on the 14th of the same month, and went immediately to Missouri to serve under General Curtis. In November, 1863, his battery was sent to Tennessee to serve with Gen. A. J. Smith against General Forrest; after two months of very severe winter campaign here, the battery was ordered to Vicksburg, to join General Sherman in a great raid on the Mobile* & Ohio Railroad, at Meridian, Miss.; returning, his battery embarked for Red River, to assist General Banks in the capture of Shreveport; was engaged in the battles at Fort De Russey, Pleasant Hill, Yellow Bayou, and several skirmishes; returned to Memphis in July, 1864, and with Gen. A. J. Smith retrieved the losses of Sturgis, at Guntown, in the battle of Lupello, July 14th, and two days later at the battle of "Old Town Creek." In September he went to Missouri, under General Smith, to assist in repelling the Price invasion. Assisted General Thomas at Nashville, Dec. 15th and 16th, in the overthrow of General Hood. In February, 1865, went to New Orleans to assist General Canby in the reduction of Mobile; was engaged in the siege of Fort Spanish, April 1st to 13th, 1865, and engaged in the storming of Fort Blakely, Alabama, late in the evening of April 9, 1865, the very last battle of the war. Although he was most of the time on detached service as provost marshal's and adjutant-general's clerk, he never missed an opportunity to stand with his comrades on the bloody field. He returned to his home, and to his wife, who had not seen him since the wedding night, — Aug. 14, 1862. He followed the occupation of a farmer for five years. In 1870 he and his family left Indiana for Washington County, Kan., where he purchased three hundred and twenty acres of land, which he cultivated till 1874, when he purchased property in the city of Blue Rapids, Marshall County, Kan., in which city he has since lived, devoting most of his time in teaching; and is now recognized as a leading educator in Marshall County, one of the most enterprising in the State. Mr. Riddle is a man of fine personal appearance.

Almaria-Melinda Riddle[4] (1), eldest daughter of Almon[3] (1), was born in Wabash County, Ind., July 3, 1841; married Sept. 3, 1871, to Charles-Frederick Hetmonsperger (German), and lives on her father's farm.

Darius-Almon Riddle[4] (1), second son of Almon[3] (1), was born in Wabash County, Ind., June 2, 1843. In June, 1862, he enlisted in Company F, Sixteenth Regiment, Indiana Volunteer Infantry; was at the battle of Richmond, Ky., Haines' Bluff, Miss., and Arkansas Post, in Arkansas. He died of typhoid pneumonia, at Point Pleasant on the Mississippi River, April 8, 1863. A brave soldier and promising young man.

Elmer Riddle[4] (1), eldest son of Jose[3] (1) and his wife, Caroline Hayden, was born at Newbury, Geauga County, O., Jan. 10, 1837; learned the carpenters' trade, and moved with his parents to Thetford, Mich., in 1845. He returned to Ohio in 1858, and married, Feb. 6, 1862, to Laura

---

* While Mr. Riddle was engaged in the siege of Mobile, during the late war, he was one day strolling about Dauphine Island, near Fort Gains, where his department was stationed, when he was suddenly brought face to face with a most beautiful monument of white marble. He read the inscription, which was as follows: "In memory of Francis M. Riddle, First Confederate Regiment, Georgia Cavalry," — his own name in full. This singular incident deeply impressed Mr. Riddle at the time, and he still looks back to it as something remarkably strange.

Robinson, by whom he has *two* daughters, of whom hereafter. He carried on a farm for ten years in Newbury, O.; is now (1879) engaged in the lumber and coal business at Chardon, O., where he resides.

Frances-Catherine Riddle[4] (2), eldest daughter of Jose[3] (1) and Caroline, was born at Newbury, Geauga County, O., May 4, 1838; was married to Philo Stafford, Oct. 4, 1857, and is resident at Zilwaukee, Saginaw County, Mich. *Five* children. Mr. Stafford is foreman in a lumbermill, and of salt-works.

Thomas-Corwin Riddle[4] (6), second son of Jose[3] (1) and his wife Caroline, was born at Newbury, Geauga County, O., Aug. 17, 1840, and went with his parents to Michigan, when five years old. He enlisted in the Union army at the first call for volunteers, June 2, 1861, and was marched three thousand miles. He was in the battles of Blue Gap, Winchester, Port Republic, and Cedar Mountain, where he was wounded. He was absent on a furlough for a short time (the only time he was at home during the war), and after returning to his regiment he was engaged in the battles of Dumfries, Fredericksburgh, Chancellorsville, Gettysburgh, Fallingwater, Lookout Mountain, Mission Ridge, Taylor Ridge, Rockyface, Dalton, Rome, Kingston Bridges, and many skirmishes. His regiment, — the Seventh Ohio Volunteer Infantry, — "had as bloody a record as any in the army." He was married to Antonetta Bartholomew soon after returning from the war, and is now living on a farm in Thetford, Mich.

Laura-Elizabeth Riddle[4] (3), second daughter of Jose[3] (1) and Caroline, his wife, was born at Thetford, Genesee County, Mich., May 13, 1848, and was a school-teacher for many years; married in December, 1878, to Jacob White, and resides at Thetford, on a farm.

Charles-Mortimer Riddle[4] (2), third son of Jose[3] (1), and his wife Caroline, was born at Thetford, Mich., Nov. 17, 1850; is an oil producer at St. Joseph, Penn.; unmarried.

Maria Riddle[4] (1), third daughter of Jose[3] (1) and Caroline, was born at Thetford, Genesee County, Mich., April 10, 1853; married to Leonard Brown, a farmer, in May, 1876. These reside at Thetford, and have *one* child.

Eleanor Riddle[4] (1), fourth daughter of Jose[3] (1) and his wife Caroline, was born at Thetford, Mich., April 11, 1855; was married to Richard Wood, in September, 1878, and resides at Keokuck, Ill. Mr. Wood is a school-teacher. *One* child.

Clarence-C. Riddle[4] (1), a son of John[3] (3), was born at Newbury, O., Sept. 26, 1840; married Helen R. Ganson, at Cleveland, O., Feb. 21, 1864, and has *two* children, of whom hereafter. His wife was born at Haverhill, N. H., Feb. 17, 1841. Mr. Riddell is a carpenter by trade. He was a gallant soldier during the war of the Rebellion, in an Ohio battery; was a sergeant, and on the second day of the battle of Stone River, distinguished himself for bravery.

Flora-E. Riddle[4] (1), eldest daughter of John[3] (3), was born at Newbury, O., April 25, 1847, and died at Russell, Dec. 2, 1853.

Harriet-J. Riddle[4] (2), second daughter of John[3] (3), was born at Newbury, O., April 4, 1849; was married to Leander S. Drew, at Okee, Wis., March 15, 1866, and has *two* children. Mr. Drew was born at Dorchester, Vt., Aug. 23, 1842. Resides at Okee, Wis.

Florence Riddle[4] (1), eldest daughter of Albert[3] (1), was born at Chardon, O., Nov. 9, 1845; was married Jan. 29, 1866, to Frank Bartlett, and resides at Washington, D. C.

Mary-Avery Riddle[4] (2), second daughter of Albert[3] (1), was born at Chardon, O., Sept. 17, 1847; unmarried in 1873. Living at home in Washington, D. C.

Caroline-Minerva Riddle[4] (2), third daughter of Albert[3] (1), was born at Cleveland, O., Jan. 22, 1850; was married to Edward Foster, and has children. She lives in Washington, D. C.

Frederick-Albert Riddle[4] (1), eldest son of Albert[3] (1), was born in Cleveland, O., Aug. 22, 1852, and died May 27, 1856.

Harriet-Williams Riddle[4] (3), fourth daughter of Albert[3] (1), was born at Cleveland, O., in October, 1854. At home in 1873.

Albert-Thomas Riddle[4] (3), second son of Albert[3] (1), was born at Cleveland, O., May 2, 1858; at home in 1873.

Alice Riddle[4] (1), fifth daughter of Albert[3] (1), was born in Cleveland, O., Dec. 8, 1860; at home in 1873.

FIFTH GENERATION.

Grace-Ann Riddle[5] (2), eldest daughter of Thomas[4] (5), was born in Alexander, N. Y., July 10, 1865.

Allan-J. Riddle[5] (1), eldest son of Thomas[4] (5), was born in Alexander, N. Y., Feb. 10, 1867.

Walter-G. Riddle[5] (1), second son of Thomas[4] (5), was born in Alexander, N. Y., Jan. 12, 1872.

Frank-D. Riddle[5] (2), eldest son of Albert[4] (2), was born Nov. 12, 1856; married, Feb. 27, 1878, to Effie Wisnean. He is in the drug business at Howell, Mich.

Wells-B. Riddle[5] (1), second son of Albert[4] (2), was born Sept. 9, 1860, and died when only three years old.

Albert-S. Riddle[5] (4), third son of Albert[4] (2), was born Jan. 9, 1864, and is now living at home.

Estelle-J. Riddle[5] (1), eldest daughter of Albert[4] (2), was born Sept. 1, 1852; was married Oct. 80, 1870, to Orrin H. Winegan, and died Feb. 11, 1872, without issue.

Elvira-J. Riddle[5] (1), second daughter of Albert[4] (2), was born Aug. 24, 1854; was married Jan. 19, 1876, to G. Dwight Wood, and has *one* daughter.

Nettie-M. Riddle[5] (1), eldest daughter of Lucius[4] (1), was born in Oceola, Mich., Dec. 12, 1865.

Jennie-M. Riddle[5] (1), second daughter of Lucius[4] (1), was born in Oceola, Mich., Dec. 21, 1868; died March 17, 1869.

Cora-M. Riddle[5] (1), third daughter of Lucius[4] (1), was born in Oceola, Mich., Feb. 2, 1871.

Lucy-E. Riddle[5] (1), eldest daughter of Joseph[4] (2), was born in Otto, Cattaraugus County, N. Y., June 25, 1841; was married to Rev. Samuel Cullen, and has *three* children.

Clark-M. Riddle[5] (1), eldest son of Joseph[4] (2), was born in Otto, Cattaraugus County, N. Y., March 16, 1848; married Elizabeth Cullen, and has *two* children, of whom hereafter.

Charles Riddle⁵ (3), second son of Joseph⁴ (2), was born in Otto, Cattaraugus County, N. Y., Dec. 19, 1848 ; married to Lodena Cybrouff (?), and has issue *one* child.

Charlotte-A. Riddle⁵ (3), second daughter of Joseph⁴ (2), was born in Clarence, Erie County, N. Y., in 1852; was married to Lorenzo Curtis, and has a family.

James-S. Riddle⁵ (3), third son of Joseph⁴ (2), was born in the town of Lockport, N. Y., Jan. 20, 1859; married March 12, 1883, Elece (or Elcie) Plow. *One* child in 1884.

Mary-E. Riddle⁵ (3), eldest daughter of George⁴ (2), was born in Otto, Cattaraugus County, N. Y., June 21, 1839; unmarried.

Susan-A. Riddle⁵ (3), second daughter of George⁴ (2), was born in Otto, Cattaraugus County, N. Y., June 4, 1841; was married to Wesley Moore, of Pembroke, N. Y., in 1862.

Zorah-A. Riddle⁵ (1), third daughter of George⁴ (2), was born in Pembroke, Genesee County, N. Y., Dec. 7, 1847; was married to William J. Havens, of Essex, Clinton County, Mich.

Alice-M. Riddle⁵ (2), fourth daughter of George⁴ (2), was born in Pembroke, Genesee County, N. Y., Aug. 6, 1848; was married to Peter Fleagle, in Clinton County, Mich.

Charles-M. Riddle⁵ (4), eldest son of George⁴ (2), was born in Genesee County, N. Y., Aug. 25, 1851; married to —— Crouls, of Canada, and has *one* son, of whom hereafter.

George-F. Riddle⁵ (3), second son of George⁴ (2), was born in Pembroke, Genesee County, N. Y., Feb. 4, 1853; died Oct. 22, 1854.

William-F. Riddle⁵ (2), third son of George⁴ (2), was born in Pendleton, Niagara County, N. Y., Jan. 18, 1855; a farmer.

Ellen-E. Riddle⁵ (1), fifth daughter of George⁴ (2), was born in Greenbush, Mich., March 1, 1857; was married to Hugh Anderson, a native of Canada, Dec. 25, 1877 (?).

George-K. Riddle⁵ (4), fourth son of George⁴ (2), was born in Greenbush, Mich., Oct. 8, 1859; died Jan. 6, 1863.

Frank-D. Riddle⁵ (1), fifth son of George⁴ (2), was born in Greenbush, Mich., May 19, 1862; a farmer.

Eliza-May Riddle⁵ (1), sixth daughter of George⁴ (2), was born in Greenbush, Mich., Nov. 11, 1864; died Oct. 6, 1867.

Robert-K. Riddle⁵ (1), seventh son of George⁴ (2), was born in Greenbush, Mich., Sept. 10, 1870.

Sarah-Jane Riddle⁵ (2), eldest daughter of Trumbull⁴ (1), was born at Lockport, N. Y., Aug. 6, 1848, and died April 11, 1851.

Ida-Elizabeth Riddle⁵ (1), second daughter of Trumbull⁴ (1), was born in Lockport, N. Y., July 22, 1849, and died April 13, 1851.

Idell-Charlotte Riddle⁵ (1), third daughter of Trumbull⁴ (1), was born at Lockport, N. Y., Aug. 5, 1850; was married July 3, 1872.

Herbert-Cary Riddle⁵ (1), eldest son of Trumbull⁴ (1), was born at Lockport, N. Y., Dec. 10, 1852; died Dec. 20, 1852.

Ida-Elizabeth Riddle⁵ (2), fourth daughter of Trumbull⁴ (1), was born in Lockport, N. Y., Dec. 10, 1853; was married Oct. 4, 1873.

Ada-Janet Riddle⁵ (1), fifth daughter of Trumbull⁴ (1), was born at Lockport, N. Y., July 22, 1855; was married Aug. 25, 1873.

Herman-Cary Riddle⁵ (1), second son of Trumbull⁴ (1), was born at

Grinnell, Ia., March 25, 1857; married Aug. 12, 1876, to Mary Drake, and has *two* children, of whom hereafter. He is a farmer at Chapin, Ill.

.**William-Avery Riddle**[5] (3), third son of Trumbull[4] (1), was born at Grinnell, Ia., Feb. 5, 1860.

Horace-Sheridan Riddle[5] (1), eldest son of Francis[4] (1), was born in Wabash County, Ind., July 1, 1867.

Della-Lorena Riddle[5] (1), eldest daughter of Francis[4] (1), was born in Wabash, Ind., Sept. 29, 1868.

Emery-Morton Riddle[5] (1), second son of Francis[4] (1), was born in Washington County, Kan., April 17, 1871; died March 9, 1880.

Anna-Caroline Riddle[5] (2), second daughter of Francis[4] (1), was born in Washington County, Kan., Oct. 7, 1872.

Omar-Ulysses Riddle[5] (1), third son of Francis[4] (1), was born in the city of Blue Rapids, Marshall County, Kan., Feb. 26, 1876; died March 26, 1880.

Lula-Marion Riddle[5] (1), youngest daughter of Francis[4] (1), was born at Wabash, Ind., April 1, 1882.

Nellie Riddle[5] (2), eldest daughter of Elmer[4] (1), was born at Newbury, O., June 14, 1863.

Emma Riddle[5] ( ), second daughter of Elmer[4] (1), was born at Newbury, O., Nov. 14, 1865.

Frederick-W. Riddle[5] (2), eldest son of Clarence[4] (1), was born in Chardon, O., June 20, 1866.

Genio Riddle[5] (1), second son of Clarence[4] (1), was born in Clyde, O., May 7, 1871.

SIXTH GENERATION.

Susan-Lilla Riddle[6] (4), eldest daughter of Herman[5] (1), was born at Chapin, Ill., June 13, 1877.

Irene Riddle[6] (1), second daughter of Herman[5] (1), was born at Chapin, Ill., July 20, 1878.

RIDDLES OF ALEXANDER, NEW YORK.

[CONNECTICUT BRANCH.]

Dr. Lyman Riddle[1] (1) moved from somewhere in the State of Connecticut to Alexander, Genesee County, N. Y., and thence to Michigan, about 1834–5. He was a surgeon in the United States army. Place of nativity unknown. Died in 1844, leaving issue. It seems quite probable that this family is connected with the "Riddells of Monson, Massachusetts," some of whom were settled in Alexander, N. Y., and had children named Lyman, but the connection is not known.

SECOND GENERATION.

Charles-Chaffee Riddle[2] (1), a son of Lyman[1] (1), was born in Alexander, N. Y., about 1813; married in 1834, moved to Michigan in 1835, and was keeping "Red Tavern" in 1844, when his father died. In 1863 he was keeping the post-office and public-house at Boston Centre, N. Y., and in 1867 was farming on the plank-road near Buffalo; sold out that year and removed to Galva, Ill., where he died in 1873, aged 60 years. Wife's maiden-name Fannie Vale.

Lyman Riddle[2] (2), a son of Lyman[1] (1), was born in Alexander, Genesee County, N. Y., and is now living at Gowrie, Webster County, Ia. No particulars. He has sisters in the State of New York, but I have not found their names and address.

THIRD GENERATION.

Henry-Seymore Riddle[3] (1), a son of Charles[2] (1), was born at Kalamazoo, Mich., and is now (1884) about forty-seven years of age; married, and has issue, a son and daughter. Mr. Riddle was not much at home when young, and knows but little of his ancestors' history. Probably living in Chicago, Ill. One sister died young; another lives in St. Paul, Minn.

FOURTH GENERATION.

George-Burnell Riddle[4] (1), a son of Henry[3] (1), was born in Buffalo, N. Y., Nov. 1, 1858; married, and has *one* daughter, born in Chicago, — where Mr. Riddle resides, — Oct. 8, 1882. He has manifested an interest in this book, and made an effort to procure a full genealogy, but his relatives did not respond. He says the Riddles are tall and of dark complexion.

RIDDELLS OF SCHENECTADY, NEW YORK.

[MONAGHAN BRANCH.]

Robert Riddell[1] (1), was born in the County of Monaghan, Ireland, about 1760; married Elizabeth Riddell, who was from the Scottish border, and had issue *five* children, of whom hereafter. He came to New York, and died at Ballston. Weaver by trade. He was a connection of the several other families from the same County, whose genealogy is given in this book.

SECOND GENERATION.

John Riddell[2] (1), eldest son of Robert[1] (1), was born in Ireland, County Monaghan, Jan. 5, 1786, and came to America in 1791. He married Sally Hall (she was born in Stockbridge, Conn., July 9, 1789, and died in Princeton, Monroe County, N. Y., May 15, 1856), and had issue *nine* children, of whom hereafter. Mr. Riddell was a carpenter by trade. Died in Van Buren, Ind., March 6, 1851.

Hugh Riddell[2] (1), second son of Robert[1] (1), was born in County Monaghan, Ireland, Dec. 6, 1787; married to Eleanor Reese, of New York, March 25, 1812, and lived at Schenectady; had issue *eight* children, of whom hereafter. He enlisted at Schenectady, N. Y., for five years, March 17, 1812, under Capt. George Nelson, in the Sixth Regiment, United States Infantry. In the fall, while at Greenbush, near Albany, he was transferred to Captain McChestney's company in the same regiment; and in the spring of 1813, marched to the western frontier, crossing Niagara River May 27, capturing Fort George. He was under Generals Winder and Chandler at

Stony Creek, where both of those officers were taken prisoners; was in the detachment of five hundred men, June 28, 1813, who marched from Fort George, under Col. Charles G. Boerstler, to Beaver Dam, to seize British stores, in which action the colonel was wounded and captured, with all his force; during this action sergeant Riddle was ordered to assist in hauling a cannon up a steep bank, and was lifting at the wheels when the drag-rope broke, letting the wheel of the cannon run across his hip and abdomen, the weight crushing his body, causing a severe hernia. He was carried a prisoner to York (now Toronto), where his injuries were dressed by a British surgeon.

After his recovery he was, with two other prisoners,—one having his arm in a sling,—put on board a batteau, with a guard of nine men under a lieutenant, to be taken to Kingston, and in the night, Riddle finding the fellow-prisoners ready to co-operate, planned a rescue, which, by throwing the arms overboard, except those retained for their own use, and by separately capturing the lieutenant, was completely successful, and the boat and prisoners triumphantly landed, July 26, 1813, at Fort George (distance sixty miles), where a large number of officers and men assembled to congratulate them upon their good fortune. Mr. Riddle was furloughed, and returned to his home at Schenectady, where he might be nursed and recover from his injuries. It is believed that Mrs. Riddle accompanied her husband in the army after their marriage, but how long, and for what purpose, is not specified. He died at Schenectady, N. Y., April 1, 1865 ; his widow was living in 1876.

Robert Riddle² (2), third son of Robert¹ (1), was born in County Monaghan, Ireland, in 1792; married Sarah Harkness, and had issue *eight* children, of whom hereafter. Resided at East Davenport, N. Y. Died July 4, 1863, aged about 71 years. He enlisted at Schenectady, N. Y., March 9, 1813, for five years, under Capt. John McChestney, in the Sixth Regiment, United States Infantry, Colonels Boyd and Brady, and was marched to Fort Oswego, N. Y., thence to Niagara frontier, and stationed at Fort Niagara for a while; thence crossing the river was at the capture of Fort George, in Canada. He received a wound at the battle of Beaver Dam, Can., in his right ankle, producing necrosis of tibia, and with his colonel and all his forces was taken prisoner and carried to Toronto, Kingston, Montreal, Quebec, and Halifax. After a captivity of nine months he was sent to Salem, Mass., and thence to the hospital at Albany, and Sackett's Harbor, N. Y.

William Riddle² (1), fourth son of Robert¹ (1), was born in the County Monaghan, Ireland; married Catherine Conley, in Delaware County, N. Y., and had issue, of whom hereafter. He lived in Delhi, Delaware County, N. Y.*

Nancy Riddle² (1), a daughter of Robert¹ (1), was born in the County Monaghan, Ireland; was married to James Riddle, of Delaware County, N. Y., and had issue, of whom hereafter. She and her husband were not relatives. He was a carpenter by trade.

THIRD GENERATION.

William Riddell³ (2), eldest son of John² (1), was born at Broadalbin,

---

* **James** Riddell's address, also his brother Robert's, is Imlay City, Lapeer County, Mich.; John's, son of William², address is Kortright Centre, Delaware County, N. Y.; Newton Riddell, son of Nancy and James, North Kortright, Delaware County, N. Y.

Fulton County, N. Y., Aug. 15, 1811; married Emma Clark, Feb. 10, 1836, in Kingsboro', N. Y., and died at White Pigeon, Mich., Aug. 26, 1847. He was a carpenter and builder. He had issue *three* sons and *one* daughter, of whom hereafter.

Nancy Riddell[2] (2), eldest daughter of John[2] (1), was born at Broadalbin, Fulton County, N. Y., Oct. 23, 1813; was married May 2, 1835, to Henry Clark, of Northampton, same County, and died at Kingsboro', Dec. 2, 1852.

Sarah-Ann Riddell[2] (1), second daughter of John[2] (1), was born in Broadalbin, N. Y., May 27, 1816, and died unmarried at Perinton (?), Monroe County, Dec. 11, 1853.

Robert Riddell[2] (3), second son of John[2] (1), was born at Mayfield, Fulton County, N. Y., Aug. 28, 1818; married Cynthia Brown (she was born in Farmington, Ontario County, N. Y., May 7, 1826) in 1843, and has had issue *ten* children, of whom hereafter. Mr. Riddell lived in his native town until nineteen years of age, when he went to Victor, Ontario County, where he learned the carpenter trade, at which he worked about eighteen years. He removed to Hanover, Jackson County, Mich., in 1866, and carried on a farm till 1880, when he removed to Juniata, Neb., and owns a farm of one hundred and sixty-eight acres, situated two and a half miles from Juniata post-office.

Betsey Riddell[2] (1), third daughter of John[2] (1), was born in Mayfield, Fulton County, N. Y., Sept. 4, 1819; was married to A. G. Northrop, Oct. 1, 1845, and is now (1883) living with her husband at Henrietta, Monroe County.

John-J. Riddell[2] (2), third son of John[2] (1), was born at Mayfield, Fulton County, N. Y., Nov. 28, 1822; married Rebecca Scrambling in 1858, of Victor, Ontario County, and died Dec. 24, 1864, in the latter town. Farmer. He had issue, of whom hereafter.

Mary-Jane Riddell[2] (1), fourth daughter of John[2] (1), was born at Mayfield, Fulton County, N. Y., Aug. 22, 1825; was married Oct. 1, 1845, to Hiram Ladd, and is now living at Victor, Ontario County.

Frances-Maria Riddell[2] (1), fifth daughter of John[2] (1), was born in Mayfield, Fulton County, N. Y., Feb. 27, 1828; was married Nov. 15, 1849, to Michael Hagerty, and died in Victor, Ontario County, Aug. 31, 1854.

Elizabeth Riddle[2] (1), eldest daughter of Hugh[2] (1), was born at Schenectady, N. Y., May 29, 1813; was married to Denis Dorsey, a painter, and resides in New York city.

William Riddle[2] (3), eldest son of Hugh[2] (1), was born at Schenectady, N. Y., March 7, 1816; farmer; unmarried.

Hugh Riddle[2] (2), second son of Hugh[2] (1), was born at Schenectady, N. Y., where he resides, unmarried; farmer.

Ellen Riddle[2] (1), second daughter of Hugh[2] (1), was born at Schenectady, N. Y., March 6, 1821, and died in New York city, in 1860 She was a milliner and dress-maker.

Nancy Riddle[2] (3), third daughter of Hugh[2] (1), was born at Schenectady, N. Y., March 28, 1823; was married to Benjamin Sheldon, merchant, and resides in Schenectady.

Rebecca Riddle[2] (1), fourth daughter of Hugh[2] (1), was born at Schenectady, N. Y., Sept. 15, 1825; was married to Henry Hathaway, contractor, and resides in her native town.

Jane Riddle² (1), fifth daughter of Hugh² (1), was born at Schenectady, N. Y., Sept. 18, 1827; was married to Thomas Riley, cartman, New York city, and has issue.

John Riddle⁵ (3), third son of Hugh² (1), was born at Schenectady, N. Y., April 8, 1848 (?); married Anna Conley, and has issue. Mason.

Nancy Riddle³ (4), eldest daughter of Robert² (2), was born at East Davenport, N. Y., Oct. 1, 1816.

Eliza Riddle³ (1), second daughter of Robert² (2), was born at East Davenport, N. Y., in 1818; was married in 1861, to Lyman Smith, of Broom County, and died Feb. 25, 1867.

Jane Riddle³ (2), third daughter of Robert² (2), was born at East Davenport, N. Y., Sept. 22, 1820; was married in 1848, to Robert Matthews, and lives at East Davenport.

James Riddle³ (1), eldest son of Robert² (2), was born at East Davenport, N. Y., May 17, 1822; married Ann Lawyer (or Sawyer) in 1848, and lives on a farm in Lapeer County, Mich.

Abigail Riddle³ (1), fourth daughter of Robert² (2), was born at East Davenport, N. Y., July 13, 1824; was married in 1838, to William Smith, and lives in Lapeer County, Mich.

Robert Riddle³ (4), second son of Robert² (2), was born at East Davenport, N. Y., March 12, 1828; married in 1856, to Jane Aldrich; farmer in Lapeer County, Mich.

Mary Riddle³ (2), fifth daughter of Robert² (2), was born at East Davenport, N. Y.; was married in 1836, to Alexander Summerville, and died in Lapeer County, Mich., March 9, 1876, aged 42 years, 10 months, and 9 days.

William-K. Riddle³ (4), youngest son of Robert² (2), was born at East Davenport, N. Y., Aug. 1, 1837; married Emma Sheldon in 1866, and had issue *five* children, of whom hereafter. He is a farmer at East Davenport.

FOURTH GENERATION.

Calvin Riddell⁴ (1), a son of William³ (2), was born in New York, or Michigan; married, and has issue. He is now living with his mother at McPherson, Kan.; farmer.

Jerome Riddell⁴ (1), second son of William³ (2), was killed in the war of the Rebellion, in 1861.

Milan Riddell⁴ (1) third son of William³ (2), is married and lives in Schuyler, Neb.

Mary Riddell⁴ (3), only daughter of William³ (2), is married and lives near Calvin, McPherson, Kan.

Mary-J. Riddell⁴ (4), eldest daughter of Robert³ (3), was born in Perinton (?), Monroe County, N. Y., June 10, 1847; went to Michigan in 1866; was married March 2, 1881, to J. W. Taylor, of Jackson, Mich., where she resides.

Alice-G. Riddell⁴ (1), second daughter of Robert³ (3), was born in Perinton (?), Monroe County, N. Y., July 6, 1849; was married to Robert Shaffer, in Hanover, Jackson County, Mich., and died there two years after marriage.

Jos-M. Riddell⁴ (1), child of Robert³ (3), was born at Perinton (?), N. Y., July 31, 1853, and lives in Jackson, Mich.; unmarried, 1883.

Ida-Dell Riddell[4] (1), third daughter of Robert[3] (3), was born in Perinton (?), N. Y., Nov. 28, 1855, and settled in Michigan in 1866; was married May 8, 1873, to James F. Nickman, of Hanover, Jackson County, Mich., and lived with him till 1881, when they parted, and she went to Chicago, Ill., where she lives, 1883.

Robert-Ray Riddell[4] (5), a son of Robert[3] (3) was born in Perinton (?), N. Y., Jan. 4, 1857, and died March 13, 1858.

Willis-B. Riddell[4] (1), a son of Robert[3] (3), was born in Perinton (?), N. Y., Jan. 21, 1859, and died Aug. 18, 1866, and was buried in Horton, Jackson County, Mich.

Paris-J. Riddell[4] (1), a child of Robert[3] (3), was born in Perinton (?), N. Y., May 12, 1862, went to Michigan with parents, and remained till 1880, when he went to Juniata, Neb., and lives with parents.

Anna-T. Riddell[4] (1), daughter of Robert[3] (3), was born in Perinton (?), N. Y., Dec. 7, 1864, and lives at home.

Carrie Riddell[4] (1), daughter of Robert[3] (3), was born in Hanover, Jackson County, Mich., July 6, 1867, and is now (1883) living at home in Juniata, Neb.

Maude-M. Riddell[4] (1), daughter of Robert[3] (3), was born in Hanover, Jackson County, Mich., Nov. 11, 1872. At home.

Rachel Riddell[4] (1), a daughter of John[3] (3), was born in Ontario County, N. Y.; was married to George Muskett, and lives in Geneva, N. Y. No issue.

Henry-Murray Riddle[4] (1), eldest son of William[3] (4), was born at East Davenport, N. Y., Sept. 7, 1867.

Mary-Augusta Riddle[4] (5), eldest daughter of William[3] (4), was born at East Davenport, N. Y., Nov. 22, 1869.

William Riddle[4] (5), second son of William[3] (4), was born at East Davenport, N. Y., Feb. 26, 1872.

Marion-Edith Riddle[4] (1), second daughter of William[3] (4), was born at East Davenport, N. Y., in February, 1874.

Bertie Riddle[4] (1), third daughter of William[3] (4), was born at Davenport, N. Y., in April, 1876.

RIDDLES OF WINCHESTER COUNTY, NEW YORK.

[SCOTCH-IRISH BRANCH.]

William Riddle[1] (1), was of Irish descent, born in New Rochelle, N. Y., in 1788. His father was an officer in the English navy, and was killed in this country during the Revolutionary war; his name has not reached me, but his wife was called "Bettie." The ancestor was said to be an "Irish nobleman." Probably this family is connected with other branches whose pedigree is found in this book, but I have no proof.

SECOND GENERATION.

Hiram Riddle[2] (1), eldest son of William[1] (1), was born in 1810, and is a produce-merchant in New York city. He has had a family of *six* children, of whom hereafter.

Charles Riddle² (1), second son of William¹ (1), was born in New York,—probably in Winchester County,—and became an active politician. Deceased.

John Riddle² (1), third son of William¹ (1), was born in New York, and died at Trenton, N. J.

Jane Riddle² (1), daughter of William¹ (1), was born in New York, and in 1873 lived in the metropolis.

James Riddle² (1), fourth son of William¹ (1), was born in New York, and is now (1880) about 70 years old. He was in the oil business at Freeport, Ill., in 1878.

THIRD GENERATION.

William Riddle³ (2), eldest son of Hiram² (1), was born in New York, and died when two years of age..

Edwin Riddle³ (1) second son of Hiram² (1), was born in New York, and in 1873 was employed in the mailing rooms of the publishing establishment of the *Christian Union* in New York city.

Elizabeth Riddle³ (1), eldest daughter of Hiram² (1), was born in New York about 1842.

Jane Riddle³ (2), second daughter of Hiram² (1), was born in New York in 1844.

James Riddle³ (2), third son of Hiram² (1), was born in 1846, and in 1873 was employed by the publishers of the *Christian Union*, Park Place, New York city.

John Riddle³ (2), fourth son of Hiram² (1), was born in New York city, and died when a child.

RIDDLES OF ROCHDALE, NEW YORK.
[NEW HAMPSHIRE BRANCH.]

David Riddle¹ (1), said to have been born and buried somewhere in New Hampshire, cannot be connected with any other family known in that State. He had *two* sons, of whom hereafter.

SECOND GENERATION.

David Riddle² (2), son of David¹ (1), was born somewhere in New Hampshire; married Martha Little, emigrated to Rochdale, N. Y. (now in New York city), and died in 1850, leaving *three* children, of whom hereafter.

James Riddle² (1), second son of David¹ (1), was born in New Hampshire, went to California, where he was living in 1848.

THIRD GENERATION.

Capt. William Riddle³ (1), eldest son of David² (2), was born in New York city, April 5, 1830, and learned the lithographer's art. He entered the Union army in the Twentieth Regiment, Massachusetts Infantry, and lost his right arm at the battle of Ball's Bluff, Oct. 21, 1861; at this date he was promoted sergeant. He was commissioned second lieutenant, Sept. 5, 1862; captain, April 12, 1863, and remained in the service till Oct. 8, 1863. Was commissioned by Abraham Lincoln, Oct. 24, 1863, as captain Veteran Reserve Corps. Mustered out June 30, 1866. Unmarried. Was living in Charlestown, Mass., in 1876.

David-James Riddle³ (3), second son of David² (2), was born in New York city, and died young.

Emily-Frances Riddle³ (1), daughter of David² (2), was born in New York city, Oct. 8, 1834; was married to Charles Halsey, who was killed in Kansas. She lives with her brother William, in Charlestown, Mass.

----•◆•----

RIDDELLS OF SARATOGA COUNTY, NEW YORK.

[SCOTCH-IRISH BRANCH].

Hugh Riddell¹ (1), parents unknown, was born in the County Armagh, north of Ireland, about the year 1740; emigrated to America when young, and settled in the southern section of the United States. He was a relative of other families in and from Armagh, but I fail to find in what degree.

David Riddell¹ (1), brother of the preceding, was born in the County Armagh, Ireland, emigrated to America with his two brothers when a young man, and settled somewhere in the Middle States. Where did he reside?

George Riddell¹ (1), brother of the preceding, was born in the County Armagh, Ireland; came with his brothers to the United States when quite small, and tarried a while in New Jersey. He removed to Massachusetts, thence to Sherburne (?), Chenango County, N. Y. He married Margaret Mulligan, and had issue *five* children, of whom hereafter. He died in 1818, aged 74 years.

SECOND GENERATION.

David Riddell² (2), a son of George¹ (1), was born in Chenango County, N. Y., in 1764; married March 18, 1790, and had issue *eleven* children, of whom hereafter. He settled near the place of his birth; learned the trade of shoe-maker with his brother-in-law, Jonathan Pettit, and removed to Albany, N. Y. He was called a "minute-man of the Revolution." Died in August, 1855, at the age of 91 years.

THIRD GENERATION.

George Riddell³ (2), eldest son of David² (2), was born in Wilton, Saratoga County, N. Y., in 1791; married April 10, 1823, to Lydia Beard, and had issue *eight* children, of whom hereafter. He lived at Porter's Corners, N. Y.

John Riddell³ (1), second son of David² (2), was born in Saratoga County, N. Y., July 19, 1793; married, Feb. 12, 1818, to Susan Rowland, and had issue *one* daughter. He died in 1871.

William Riddell³ (1), third son of David² (2), was born in Saratoga County, N. Y., Jan. 24, 1795; married in February, 1826, to Permelia Starkweather, and secondly, to Phebe Wood. He has deceased.

Israel Riddell³ (1), fourth son of David² (2), was born in Saratoga County, N. Y., Oct. 2, 1796; married, March 2, 1823, to Maria Rowland, and had issue *four* children, of whom hereafter. Mr. R. has deceased.

Margaret Riddell[2] (1), a daughter of David[2] (2), was born in Saratoga County, N. Y., Oct. 8, 1798; was married Nov. 13, 1830, to James Talmage.

David Riddell[2] (3), fifth son of David[2] (2), was born in Saratoga County, N. Y., Sept. 13, 1818; married Jan. 26, 1825, to Polly Parks, and secondly, Oct. 10, 1855, to Almira Loamis. Has issue *four* children, of whom hereafter. Mr. Riddell is a farmer and mason by occupation, and resides in Madison County, N. Y. He is a man of more than ordinary ability and force of character; has filled many positions of trust in his town and county, and is widely known and respected.

Sabrina Riddell[2] (1), second daughter of David[2] (2), was born in Saratoga County, N. Y., Aug. 1, 1802; was married Jan. 21, 1824, to David W. Fuller, and died Jan. 12, 1872.

Lucetta Riddell[2] (1), third daughter of David[2] (2), was born in Saratoga County, N. Y., April 9, 1804; was married June 1, 1825, to Joseph Banning, and died Dec. 10, 1872.

Almena Riddell[2] (1), fourth daughter of David[2] (2), was born in Saratoga County, N. Y., March 30, 1806; was married June 7, 1829, to Wheeler J. Crane; living in 1873.

Almira Riddell[2] (1), fifth daughter of David[2] (2), was born in Saratoga County, N. Y., July 1, 1808; was married April 18, 1830, to Henry Isham, and was resident, in 1873, at Ross, Kalamazoo County, Mich.

Lucy Riddell[2] (1), youngest daughter of David[2] (2), was born in Saratoga County, N. Y., April 19, 1810; was married April 18, 1831, to Morris Whitcomb; living in 1873.

FOURTH GENERATION.

Adelia Riddell[4] (1), eldest daughter of George[3] (2), was born at Porter's Corners, N. Y., Feb. 16, 1824; was married to William Rodgers, and lived, in 1873, at Rexford Flats, in Saratoga County; had *seven* children.

George Riddell[4] (3), eldest son of George[3] (2), was born at Porter's Corners, N. Y., Feb. 6, 1826, and died Feb. 9, 1867, unmarried. He was in trade in San Francisco, Cal.

Augustus Riddell[4] (1), second son of George[3] (2), was born at Porter's Corners, N. Y., July 30, 1828; married; carries on a steam bakery in Milwaukee, Wis. Has issue.

Ann Riddell[4] (1), second daughter of George[3] (2), was born at Porter's Corners, N. Y., Oct. 18, 1830; was married to Charles Blackmar; resided at Litchfield, Hillsdale County, Mich., and died Sept. 14, 1869.

John Riddell[4] (2), third son of George[3] (2), was born at Porter's Corners, N. Y., Aug. 25, 1834, and died at Milwaukee, Wis., Nov. 1, 1864, unmarried.

Caroline Riddell[4] (1), third daughter of George[3] (2), was born at Porter's Corners, N. Y., July 29, 1837; was married to Charles Latham, and lives near her birthplace.

Charles Riddell[4] (1), fourth son of George[3] (2), was born at Porter's Corners, N. Y., May 3, 1839, and in 1873 was living on a farm at Breckenridge, Mo.

Edgar Riddell[4] (1), fifth son of George[3] (2), was born at Porter's Corners, N. Y., Feb. 24, 1841, and in 1873 was practising as a dentist at Chestertown, Warren County; was married and had issue *two* children; runs a hotel at Lucerne, N. Y., called the "Riddell House."

Oscar Riddell⁴ (1), a son of William² (1), was born in New York State, Dec. 12, 1833; married Oct. 30, 1857, to Corlista E. Adams, and in 1873 had issue *five* children, of whom hereafter. He was left motherless when only a year old; was placed under the care of his aunt, Mrs. Margaret Talmage, and carried to Michigan when nine years old, where he continued to live till his father removed to that State. He followed stock-raising and farming until within a few years (1873), when he became station-master on the Lake Shore and Michigan Southern Railroad, where he now is; residence, New Carlisle, St. Joseph County, Ind.

Permelia Riddell⁴ (1), eldest daughter of William² (1), was born in New York State, Genesee County, Dec. 24, 1826, and died March 5, 1833.

Amelia Riddell⁴ (1), second daughter of William² (1), was born at Castile, N. Y., April 21, 1830; died March 3, 1833.

Rev. Mortimer Riddell⁴ (1), eldest son of David² (3), was born in Madison County, N. Y., May 8, 1827; married Maria Otis, and had issue *two* children, of whom hereafter. He commenced business as a book-seller in Watertown, N. Y., and was successful; but at the age of thirty-one entered the Theological Seminary at Hamilton, graduated in 1861, and settled as a preacher. He became a distinguished professional man; and was considered very able and eloquent as a public speaker, as well as a ripe scholar. Was settled at New Brunswick, N. J., and subsequently at Ottawa, Kan., where he called together a large and intelligent congregation, until death released him from a shepherd's care in 1870.

Rev. Rudolph-R. Riddell⁴ (1), second son of David² (3), was born in Madison County, N. Y., Feb. 11, 1847; married Annie Palmer, a lady of his native State. He entered the Union army in 1861 as a drummer-boy, then only fifteen years old, and after serving a year was promoted to first sergeant for gallant conduct. He continued to rise in the official scale until he received a commission as major, for capturing a rebel flag at Petersburgh, Va.; also received a "Medal of Honor" from Congress. He led a forlorn hope at the battle of Petersburgh, for which he was promoted to brevet-lieutenant-colonel. He was the youngest commissioned officer in the Union army, and was wounded four times; once at Fair Oaks, once at Antietam, once at Chancellorsville, and once at Gettysburg. He was engaged in *thirty-one* regular battles, and numerous skirmishes with the rebels. On returning to his home in 1865 he commenced business as wholesale and retail produce merchant, but was unsuccessful; entered a medical college at Bellevue, N. Y., but gave up that study when about to enter practice. He next entered Madison University at Hamilton, graduated in 1871, and commenced preaching for the Baptist Church at Palmer, Mass. He was subsequently settled at South Berwick, Me. He says, "My life was a curiously changeful one till the Lord took me in hand, and I became a Christian." His ordination took place Feb. 21, 1872. He stands high as a public speaker, and promises to become a very distinguished professional man. He is now (1884) settled at St. Paul, Minn., and is a D. D.

FIFTH GENERATION.

Edgar Riddell⁵ (2), eldest son of Edgar⁴ (1), was born at Chestertown, N. Y.(?), July 2, 1868.

Myran Riddell⁵ (1), second son of Edgar⁴ (1), was born at Chestertown, N. Y.(?), Aug. 29, 1869.

Alice Riddell[5] (1), eldest daughter of Oscar[4] (1), was born Sept. 12, 1860, and died Nov. 8, 1861.

Flora Riddell[5] (1), second daughter of Oscar[4] (1), was born Dec. 19, 1861.

William Riddell[5] (2), eldest son of Oscar[4] (1), was born Nov. 9, 1864.

Clara Riddell[5] (1), third daughter of Oscar[4] (1), was born Sept. 1, 1868, and died April 20, 1870.

Oscar Riddell[5] (2), second son of Oscar[4] (1), was born May 19, 1871, probably at New Carlisle, Ind.

———

Allen Riddell[5] (1) eldest son of Mortimer[4] (1), was born in Madison County, N. Y., July 2, 1859, and in 1873 was with his widowed mother in Ottawa, Kan.

Nellie Riddell[5] (1), eldest daughter of Mortimer[4] (1); no dates.

+ Coat of arms (+ p. 32)

Lineage begins p. 45-48 then pp. 63/64 thru 72+ (illustration page)

RIDDELLS OF SOMERSET COUNTY, NEW JERSEY.

[SCOTTISH BRANCH.]

See p. 70

[There are many reasons for believing that the early Riddells of New Jersey, whose genealogy will be herewith given, were descended from the ancient family in Roxburghshire, Scotland. Sir Walter Riddell succeeded as second baronet of that family in 1636; he married a very pious and accomplished woman, Janet Rigg, by whom he had *five* sons who seem to have inherited their mother's religious zeal and creed. The eldest son, Sir John, succeeded as third baronet in 1669, and being a devoted Covenanter, refused to take the test-oath in 1683; he was consequently imprisoned at Bonjedworth. The Rev. Archibald Riddell, third son of Sir Walter, was imprisoned for several years in Scotland (see "Riddelle of Granton"), and subsequently, in 1684, was banished to New Jersey, where he was settled several years contemporary with other members of the Riddell family, as will hereafter appear. William Riddell, another son of Sir Walter, became head of that branch of the family in Scotland denominated "of Glen-Riddell," in Dumfrieshire. We have now disposed of three of the five sons, and find two of which we have no particulars in the pedigree of the baronial family. It was a custom in this branch of the Scottish Riddell family to carry forward the names *John, William, and Walter,* from generation to generation; names peculiar to the Riddells for centuries, and we might reasonably look for a Walter with the William and John * in this family. Was there such a son? It is stated by one authority that Sir Walter Riddell had "several sons who suffered

———

* "SIR JOHN RIDDELL, brother of the Rev. Archibald Riddell, cousin to George Scott, was a passenger in the 'Henry and Francis.' Now Woodrow, in his list of passengers on this vessel bound for New Jersey, mentions Rev. Archibald Riddell, but does not mention George Scott or Sir John Riddell." This extract purported to be taken from a work written by Rev. Archibald Riddell, entitled "The Model of the Government of East New Jersey in America," — a work of merit, of which there are but few copies in existence.

great persecution " for their sincere devotion to the Presbyterian Church;
two of these are particularly mentioned in history, and judging from the
clannish spirit of the old Scottish families, we may believe that all members
of this noted sept would adhere to that faith so carefully taught by their
devotedly pious mother.   We shall now call the reader's attention to the
records of New Jersey, of dates contemporary with the settlement and
residence of Rev. Archibald Riddell in that colony.

In an account of disbursements by the Proprietors of East New Jersey
in 1683, it is stated that " Walter Riddell p'd Barclay £1,000. Interest for
twelve years, £1. 14. 0." This Walter Riddell was one of the proprietors
to George Willocks, in an indenture made in 1697. He was a prominent
man in the colony, and his name frequently occurs on the records with
other early proprietors. He was an educated and accomplished man, and
had a seal or coat-of-arms with which he stamped colonial documents; impressions from which, if extant, would undoubtedly prove his connection
with the Scottish border family. He and Rev. Archibald Riddell lived
within three miles of each other at one time; the former at Perth Amboy, and the latter at Woodbridge. Walter Riddell was a member of a
committee " empowered by the Society, or reputed Company of New
Jersey, to transact all the affairs of said Society," in 1697. He was deceased in 1743, as his heirs and assignees had a survey of one hundred
acres of land, "beginning at the Second Mountain," Nov. 30th of that
year.]

William Riddell (1) was a member of the " Council of Proprietors of ye
Western Division of ye Province of New Jersey," and was summoned
by Lord Cornbury, Nov. 5, 1703, to show his authority (with his colleagues)
for purchasing of lands from the Indians. This man's name appears in
many of the colonial documents, almost always in connection with some
public duty; he being, as his official responsibility shows, a person of ability
and trustworthiness.

Hugh Riddell was a resident of New Jersey, May 12, 1685, as his
goods were seized by the Custom-house officer in New York, while coming from there; Riddell beat the official most severely, and was fined
heavily. He presented a petition against the extortionate charges of the
physicians who attended the wounded man, but the court ordered that
his goods should not be restored until he paid the medical charges.

The Riddells of Perth Amboy removed to Somerset County, N. J., in
1720, and settled at Roysfield, Boundbrook, and Somerville, where they
owned extensive lands. In the Proprietors' Records the term " at Riddle's, 500 acres," appears.

It would be interesting to know the exact connections of the early generations of the Riddells of New Jersey, but no records are known that
can furnish the proof. From the fact that the names in this family and
the baronial family of Scotland correspond, with the residence of the
several Riddells in the same neighborhood, some of whom are known to
be of the border house of Riddell, of Roxburghshire, at contemporary
dates, supplemented by the possession of a seal, and the traditions of the
families, leaves but little doubt that the Riddells of Virginia and Ohio,
descended from the Boundbrook branch, are derived from an ancestry
identified with Scottish history at a very remote period.

William Riddell[2] (2), presumed to be a son of Walter Riddell, above
mentioned, was born about 1696; went to sea when a young man, and was
never heard from.

COL JOHN RIDDLE.

(son of Walter)

John Riddell [2] (1), a brother of William [2] (2), was born in New Jersey (?) about 1698; married Molly, daughter of William Anderson,* and settled as farmer on the Raritan River, near New Brunswick, in the northwestern section of the State. He was probably married twice, as may appear from the following extract from the records, which I cannot apply to any other member of the New Jersey family: "Lisence of marriage on the eleventh day of May, A. D. 1741, was granted by his Excellency, Lewis Morris, Esqr., Governor, unto John Riddell, of Princeton, in the County of Somersett, merchant, of the one party, and Rachel Stockton, of the County aforesaid, widow, of the other party." Mr. Riddell was killed by being thrown from his carriage while his horses were running away, in 1773. He had *two* children (possibly others), of whom hereafter.

THIRD GENERATION.

William Riddle [3] (3), eldest son of John [2] (1), was born in Boundbrook, N. J., Sept. 1, 1751. He left there at the age of eighteen, and settled in Fauquier County, Va., where he continued during life. He married Jemima Latham, in March, 1798. Mr. Riddle enlisted in the army of the Revolution, Oct. 1, 1775, under Capt. William Picketts, of Fauquier County, as drummer in the regiment of Col. Thomas Marshall. He reenlisted under Capt. Turner Marshall, in Colonel Churchill's regiment. He was on a tour under Captain Helm and Col. Elias Edmonds; was at the siege of York, Va., October, 1781. One tour commenced Nov. 1, 1780, and ended May, 1781; another tour commenced Sept. 1, 1781, and ended in November, 1781, after marching to Williamsburgh and Richmond. He died between March 4 and Sept. 4, 1839; his widow died in 1870, aged about 91 years. It is presumed that Mr. Riddle had a family, and it is quite probable, that some of the branches represented in this book, several of which were from Virginia, are his descendants; but in the absence of good authority I cannot make connections.

Molly Riddle [2] (1), only daughter of John [2] (1), was born in New Jersey; married to —— Casterline, of New York State, where he died. She was the mother of *one* son and *two* daughters, some of whose descendants are in northern Ohio. She was buried at Boundbrook.

Col. John Riddle [2] (2), second son of John [2] (1), was born on the banks of the Raritan River, in New Jersey, Dec. 4, 1761, and married five wives, as follows: First, in 1783, to Phebe Schmocke, of New Jersey; she was born in 1763, and died in Hamilton County, O., Sept. 9, 1792, leaving *three* children, of whom hereafter. He married, secondly, July 8, 1794, Mary James, who was born 1774, and died in Hamilton County, O., Sept. 9, 1800, leaving *two* children, of whom hereafter. He married, thirdly, in 1801, Nancy Nutt, of New Jersey, who was born Jan. 17, 1784, and died Sept. 10, 1810, leaving *four* children, of whom hereafter. He married, fourthly, Feb. 23, 1811, Jane Marshall, who was born March 14, 1789,

---

* The Andersons, descended from an ancient family in Scotland, went from the north of Ireland to Liverpool, Eng., where they acquired wealth by merchandizing; they came to New Jersey about 1750, and their descendants have frequently intermarried with the Riddells and Riddles. William and Martha Anderson had *eight* children, of whom Sarah and Willie died young, the latter on shipboard, and the mother, contrary to custom, was allowed to bring his body on shore for burial. Hannah was married to Michael Schooley; Priscilla, to Matthew Cunningham; Elizabeth, to William McDowell; Martha, to John Ross; and Peggy, to Alexander Kirkpatrick, who, with several others before mentioned, were of Scottish families.

(continues to Isaac, son, p. 305)

and died Jan. 11, 1834, leaving *nine* children, of whom hereafter. Mr. Riddle married Jane Ross, his fifth wife, Sept. 30, 1834; she was born in New Jersey, Feb. 25, 1787, and died at Spring Dale, Hamilton County, O., Jan. 4, 1859, without issue.

The subject of this notice was a very remarkable man, — a good type of the first Western pioneers. From New Jersey he emigrated to Ohio in October, 1790, twelve years before that State was admitted into the Union, and located on a tract of land about one mile from the Ohio River, on what is now a part of the city of Cincinnati, — a city boasting of nearly three hundred thousand inhabitants. At the time of Mr. Riddle's settlement it was only a small village, known as "Losantville," in the territory northwest of the Ohio River, opposite the point where the Licking River disembogues into the Ohio, and contained a population of about fifty souls. The territory around the old village was thickly timbered with heavy oak, walnut, elm, sycamore, and, indeed, all the hard-woods indigenous to the soil where forests abound in the West. At that period, and for fifteen years afterwards, the Indians were exceedingly troublesome to the white settlers; and in addition to braving the privations and hardships of frontier life, usually the lot of pioneers, the early settlers of Ohio had to encounter the cunning and craft of the merciless red-man. Volumes could be filled with legends and stories of dangers encountered by the settlers around Cincinnati, — of rapacity and cruelty of the Indians, — of bloody fights and midnight massacres, — of startling and hair-breadth escapes; but only two will be submitted, in which our subject took an active part.

In the spring of 1791, on the 21st of May, John Riddle (or Riddell), William Harris (a relative), Joseph Cutter, and Benjamin Van Cleve, were out clearing a four-acre lot, — near where the Cincinnati Hospital now stands, — preparing to sow wheat upon it. Van Cleve, as was his custom, came without his rifle. Mr. Riddle had frequently remonstrated with him relative to his imprudence, but being a large, powerful, very active and fearless man, his reply invariably was that "no red-skin's bullet could catch him." The four men had sat down at the roots of a large tree to rest and lunch about noonday, and while thus engaged noticed that the jay-birds were unusually noisy, and hearing a slight rustling in the spice-wood bushes, Riddle remarked that he believed some Indians were near. The others laughed at him, but having a small dog with them, it was urged on in the direction of the noise, and bounded fiercely into the bushes; but soon returned, manifesting every canine symptom of fear. Van Cleve at once started for the corner of the lot in a path leading toward the village, and although several shots were fired at him by the Indians, he escaped unhurt. The others took a circuitous route through the bushes, as each thought best. Cutter was captured, carried off, and never afterwards heard from. A moment after Mr. Riddle had struck the path leading to the village, he remembered that he had left behind a fine four-gallon keg. Determined, to use his own words, "not to let the rascally red-skins have that," he hastened back to secure it, and thrusting his thumb into the bung-hole, he looked and saw the Indians on the full jump toward him; but he was then young and fleet of foot, and reaching his horse, mounted and returned to his home in safety.

On the first of June following, Riddle, Van Cleve, and Harris, while working near the same place, were again attacked by Indians. Van Cleve had no rifle, and Riddle and Harris defended him and themselves as best they could; they fought from behind trees, and killed more than one of the Indians, but being outnumbered, and Riddle slightly wounded, all three took to flight. Van Cleve being very fleet of foot, was, when more than three hundred yards ahead of his companions, intercepted at a fallen tree-top by a savage in ambush, and stabbed. The Indian, seeing the white men approaching with guns, escaped to his party in the rear. They found Van Cleve lifeless, and leaving him, Riddle and Harris reached the village in safety, although closely pursued.

For many years during the early history of Cincinnati, the settlers were compelled to organize for self-defense and protection, — to work together or near each other, and, indeed, to worship God standing under arms; "for the Indians were constantly skulking around them, murdering the settlers and robbing their fields and stables."

In all these defensive operations, John Riddle took an active part, and for this he was well fitted by his experience as a soldier and sailor during the Revolutionary war. He entered the army in the month of April, 1778, at Elizabethtown, N. J., under Colonel (afterwards General) Frelinghuysen, in Capt. William Logan's company, with whom he served in the American States army nearly four years, participating in nearly all the battles fought during that period.

In the year 1782 it seems he left the army to go into the privateering service, a very powerful and useful adjunct of the army, inasmuch as our young government had no navy; and of Mr. Riddle's services and adventures as a privateersman we will let him speak for himself from an old memoir found among his papers : —

"After I left the army, in 1782, I entered the privateering service under Captain Hiller, a good seaman and a brave, patriotic man, and sailed for New Brunswick on a cruise, hovering along the coast of New York and New Jersey as far as Cape May. The first vessel we captured was a British war-sloop carrying two guns. We boarded her in the night, without loss of life, destroyed her guns and ammunition, and then ransomed her for four hundred dollars. Elated with our success, later on the same night we boarded and captured a sixteen-gun frigate, — ten eighteen-pounders and six sixteen-pounders, — in the midst of the British fleet, and after passing their guard-ships, ran her aground on a sand-bar.

"At early dawn next morning we took from this vessel fifty American prisoners-of-war, and after liberating them, made the crew prisoners. We removed from her all the stores and valuables we could find, including a large amount of ammunition, then set fire to her magazine, and blew her up. This vessel was a double-decker, fitted out for a long cruise to harass our trading-vessels. We learned from the prisoners that one hundred men were to have been added to her crew the day after her capture.

"About one month afterwards, the captain and fourteen men who had volunteered our services, took a whale-boat, sailed up the narrows into New York harbor, then occupied by the British fleet, boarded a British trading-schooner, and having ransomed her for four hundred dollars, returned to our gun-boats in Sosbury River, without injury or the loss of a single man. In turn we were frequently attacked by the enemy, and had some desperate hand-to-hand conflicts; and while on such occasions we sometimes lost men, none of our crew were ever taken prisoners.

"We had two skirmishes on shore, on Long Island. In one of these engagements a beloved comrade of mine fell back into my arms, mortally wounded; in the other, we captured a large quantity of dry goods and clothing belonging to the British, the whole of which we carried away.

"On one occasion Captain Story, who commanded a privateer from Woodbridge, N. J., fell in with us in Sosbury River, which was our rendezvous. Captains Hiller and Story ascending the heights, discovered four vessels, termed 'London traders,' at a distance, moored close to the highlands. One of the vessels, however, was an armed schooner, carrying eight guns, and was used as a guard-ship to protect the other three. Our captain determined on their capture, and we attacked them within a short distance of the British fleet. The cannonading was very severe on both sides, but after a hard-fought battle the armed schooner struck her colors, and we captured the others without difficulty. The guard-ship closed on us and poured her shot into us like hail, — a solid shot cutting our mast away just above our heads; but at last we succeeded in running the schooner first captured on a sand-bar, where we burnt her; and the other we bilged and wrecked, all in sight of the British fleet.

"A short time afterwards two good men and myself, with permission, took a small boat and in the night boarded and took a craft laden with calves, poultry, butter, eggs, etc., going to the British fleet. A prize of this kind, at the present day, would be considered of small account, but at that time it was of great value to troops who were almost starving.

"At another time we attacked a large sloop and two schooners, one of them heavily armed. They gave us a warm reception, and after a running fire of some duration, we closed with the armed schooner, and when about to board her, Captain Hiller cursed the British officer, and told him if he fired another gun he should have no quarter; whereupon he seized a match from the hand of one of his gunners and directed a shot himself, but owing to the roll of the vessels it did no execution. We then boarded her and had a most desperate hand-to-hand conflict for some minutes, Captain Hiller engaging the British captain, and I the second officer. Our commander was soon victorious, and the British captain, badly wounded, cried for quarter, which we generously gave him and all his men. These prizes we ran into a cove on the Jersey shore.

"A few days after, we sailed again, and discovered a vessel with British colors. Our captain declared he would have her, and after an exciting chase we found she was an American prize which the British had captured off the Cape of Delaware, and were sending her, filled with American prisoners, to New York, then occupied by the British troops and fleet. We soon boarded and recaptured her, threw her dead overboard, placed the crew in irons, and I was put in command to take her to a place of safety. In the evening we found that we were pursued by a sloop-of-war and two privateers, which had been sent from the British fleet to capture us, but the darkness of the night enabled us to escape them, and we ran into Shirk River, where we released the American prisoners and set fire to the ship.

"Soon after we dropped out again,— flying British colors,— for another cruise; but not finding anything along the coast, we ran into Sandy Hook, alongside the British fleet, and passed through the narrows about sunset. Here we espied a craft going across to the guard-ship, in pursuit of which our captain sent a whale-boat, well manned and armed, but perceiving a line of soldiers marching down the beach, evidently intending to waylay us at the narrows, we rowed to the shore and landed fifteen men, who were to attack in the rear, the enemy in the meantime having crossed the beach on the side we lay with our boats. We were but thirty strong, including the fifteen we had landed; the enemy about seventy. While we were looking over the beach for them from our boats, they came suddenly around a point within pistol-shot of us, and opened fire on us by a volley from a platoon; and twelve of us returned the fire with our muskets in such quick succession that the barrels burned our hands. The other three men of our boat-party managed a four-pounder loaded with langrage. It was growing very hot for us, when our captain cried, 'Men, land! land! and we will have them all'; the four-pounder was instantly discharged, we raised the yell, and with the precision of our fire from our muskets discomfitted the enemy, and they broke to run, but the fifteen men we had previously landed came up at the moment, and charging in the rear, took the British officer and nine of his men prisoners.

"Captain Hiller's privateer was a terror to the British shipping, not only because she was considered a very fast sailer, but because the captain's bravery and knowledge of the coast enabled him to thwart all their efforts to capture us. On one occasion we made a hair-breadth escape from capture. We were pursuing and fighting a large British gun-boat, between Sandy Hook and Amboy, and during the chase we ran in between a galley and a brig of the enemy that carried an eighteen-pounder at her bows. The gun-boat had struck her colors, but before we were able to board her, an eighteen-pound ball passed through our ship, which had obliged us to make the best of our way to the Jersey shore, and getting everything out of any value, under a continual fire of cannon and small arms from the British frigate which lasted until nine o'clock at night, we left 'The Fair American' to the British, our ammunition being all spent so that we could not blow her up."

After peace was declared, Mr. Riddle returned to his home at Elizabethtown, N. J., where he worked at his trade as blacksmith, until 1790, when he emigrated to Ohio. Although quietly pursuing his occupation as a farmer and blacksmith, he figured in all of the volunteer military organizations of the settlement for its defence, or for offensive operations against the Indians. He was commissioned an ensign by General St. Clair, and afterwards, Aug. 23, 1797, promoted to lieutenant, and commissioned as such by Winthrop Sargeant, acting Governor of the Territory. On the 13th of May, 1804, he was commissioned captain, by Edward Tiffin, the first Governor of the State, and on the 14th of December, 1806, he was commissioned major by the same Governor. On the 17th of March, 1811, he was elected colonel of the First Regiment of State Militia, and commissioned as such by Gov. Jonathan Meigs. In 1805 he commanded the troops during the Aaron Burr excitement, and the well-deserved honor of commanding the troops at Greenville, Dark County, O., during the making of the first and last treaty with the Indians, — a treaty which secured a lasting peace to the people of Ohio, — Gen. William Henry Harrison and General Cass being the United States Commissioners on the occasion.

Soon after the war of 1812 Colonel Riddle resigned his commission, and devoted himself to farming operations, taking little part in public affairs. That he was always passionately fond of agricultural pursuits cannot be better or more briefly shown than by the fact that he planted and raised the first crop of wheat, and the first apple and peach orchard between the Little and Big Miami Rivers. In the year 1808 he was elected a commissioner of Hamilton County, which office he filled acceptably for a term of three years. His papers show that for many years he held the office of trustee and treasurer of Mill Creek township.

He was always an active friend of popular education, and long before he died donated a valuable lot of land for a school-house site, and subscribed liberally toward the erection of the building. This lot and house are now a part of the eighteenth district graduated school of Cincinnati. He was one of the original subscribers to the organization of the first Presbyterian Church of Cincinnati, and was a member of that body till his death. Colonel Riddle was known all through the Miami valley as an honest, patriotic, and public-spirited citizen; and when he died, full of honors as well as of years, he left a fair fame behind him of which his numerous descendants may well feel proud. His career was always prosperous, and his prosperity the result of his own industry, good sense, habits, and perseverance. On the 17th of June, 1847, in the eighty-seventh year of his age, he died very suddenly of strangulated hernia. His remains were deposited in the grave in the family cemetery on his farm, and were followed to their resting-place by a large concourse of citizens and soldiers, including the old pioneers then living. The burial was conducted with military and civil honors. His remains have since been removed to the family lot in the beautiful cemetery at Spring Grove, where an elegant monument has been erected, upon which, in full relief, are emblems of his military, civil, and agricultural achievements.

The old dwelling-house in which he lived is still (1873) standing at Camp Washington, near Cincinnati, O. It was built of heavy oak timber, hewn square, and trenailed together, but has since been weatherboarded and otherwise modernized. It is two stories high, narrow, and quite long; before the front door are several very large and old cedar trees

FOURTH GENERATION.

William Riddle[4] (4), eldest son of John[3] (2), was born in New Jersey, March 19, 1785. He was a soldier in a cavalry regiment in General Hull's army; was a farmer, and died at his father's house, unmarried, March 19, 1834.

Anna Riddle[4] (1), eldest daughter of John[3] (2), was born in New Jersey, Dec. 5, 1787; died (unmarried) at her father's house, Oct. 18, 1801.

John Riddle[4] (3), second son of John[3] (2), was born in New Jersey, April 11, 1790; married, April 12, 1814, Catherine Long (she was born in Kishacoquillas Valley, Penn., Dec. 13, 1788), and died Aug. 24, 1872 (death caused by a fall), and had issue *eight* children, of whom hereafter. Mr. Riddle died on his farm at Spring Dale, Hamilton County, O., Feb. 1, 1867.

Mary Riddle[4] (1), second daughter of John[3] (2), was born in Mill Creek township, O., Sept. 10, 1797; was married, Dec. 10, 1818, to James B. Ray, Esq., afterwards governor of Indiana, and died at Brookville, Ind., July 4, 1823, leaving issue.

James Riddle[4] (1), third son of John[3] (2), was born in Mill Creek township, Hamilton County, O., May 13, 1799; married Jan. 20, 1824,

---

* Col. John Riddle's grandson, John-Jackson Riddle, and Gen. Thomas Young, who twice married members of the Riddle family, volunteered to undertake the work of compiling a biography of Col. John Riddle, and a pedigree of his descendants, and all connections of the family should feel grateful for the able manner in which each discharged his self-imposed work. General Young furnished the biographical sketch of Colonel Riddle, and John Riddle the records.

HON ADAM N RIDDLE

to Elizabeth-Haugh Jackson, daughter of John Jackson, of Redstone Creek, Penn. (she was born in Virginia, April 29, 1803, and died in Covington, Ky., May 31, 1868), and had issue *three* children, of whom hereafter. Mr. Riddle was a farmer and dealer in real estate. He died very suddenly at the residence of his son, John-Jackson Riddle, with whom he lived, Jan. 25, 1874. The paralysis of which he died was the result of a very severe sun-stroke received in the city of New York in 1851.

Jacob-Anderson Riddle[4] (1), fourth son of John[3] (2), was born in Mill Creek township, Hamilton County, O., Oct. 11, 1801; married, Aug. 7, 1823, to Charlotte Tucker (she was born in the same County and State as her husband, March 4, 1800, and died near Piqua, O., June 25, 1841), and had issue *five* children, of whom hereafter. He married, secondly, Hope Stilwell (she was born in Miami County, O., Dec. 1, 1819, and died March 16, 1855), and had issue *five* children, of whom hereafter. He married, thirdly, Patience Job (she was born in Virginia, Dec. 18, 1813), June 22, 1855, by whom no issue. Mr. Riddle died at his farm near Piqua, O., Aug. 16, 1873, of paralysis of the brain, leaving a widow.

Joseph-Ross Riddle[4] (1), fifth son of John[3] (2), was born in Mill Creek township, Hamilton County, O., March 28, 1804; married, March 18, 1829, to Eliza Smith (she was born in Adams County, Ind., 1805, and died Sept. 14, 1870), and had issue *five* children, of whom hereafter.

Hon. Adam-Nutt Riddle[4] (1), sixth son of John[3] (2), was born in Mill Creek township, Hamilton County, O., Feb. 6, 1806; married, April 28, 1835, to Elizabeth-Lecompt Cook (she was born in Baltimore, Md., Oct. 12, 1818), and had issue *six* children, of whom hereafter. Like his brothers and sisters, he worked on his father's farm in summer, and attended school in winter, until his fourteenth year. In his fifteenth year he entered the preparatory department of the Cincinnati College, and walked four miles a day, in all kinds of weather, over a bad road, and in four years graduated, receiving the highest honors of his class. He studied law with Judge D. K. Este; was admitted to the bar in 1829, and opened his law office in 1830. His urbanity, attention to business, and family influence soon secured him an extensive law practice, which he retained during his life. He was an able counsellor, but not a great advocate. Although no politician he was elected by the democracy of Hamilton County a representative to the State Legislature for the sessions of 1882 and 1833, in which capacity he served his constituents and the State faithfully; was re-elected by his party without opposition, and being thoroughly acquainted with legislative proceedings, became a leading member of the House.

At the expiration of his second term he resumed the practice of his profession. He was a delegate to the Convention in 1851, to revise the State Constitution, and a member of the Standing Committee having charge of the Executive department of the State Government. He was chosen one of the first three senators from Hamilton County, under the new constitution. At the expiration of this term he refused further official position, preferring the practice of his profession. Mr. Riddle was affable to rich and poor alike; a warm friend of the cause of education; liberal in acts of charity; long identified with the Methodist Episcopal Church as an active member, and superintendent of its Sabbath school. He died at his residence, Mount Auburn, Hamilton County, O., May 2, 1870, of congestion of the lungs and brain.

Isaac-Bates Riddle[4] (1), seventh son of John[3] (2), was born in Mill

20

(next p. 309)

Creek township, Hamilton County, O., Sept. 15, 1808; married, April 7, 1831, to Hester McL. Vanice (she was born Nov. 24, 1810, and died of hernia, at Carthage, Mo., Oct. 24, 1872), and had issue *twelve* children, of whom hereafter. Mr. Riddle lives on a farm near Lockland, O.

Nancy Riddle[4] (1), third daughter of John[3] (2), was born in Mill Creek township, Hamilton County, O., Aug. 19, 1811; married, Aug. 19, 1834, to Joseph Jackson (he was born in Virginia, Dec. 2, 1809, and died on his farm near Mount Healthy, Hamilton County, O., May 7, 1866, of paralysis), and had issue *six* children. She is now living (a widow, 1873), in a stately mansion-house near the city of Cincinnati.

Henry Riddle[4] (1), eighth son of John[3] (2), was born in Mill Creek township, Hamilton County, O., May 27, 1813, and died at his father's house, Jan. 30, 1833, of consumption.

George-W. Riddle[4] (1), ninth son of John[3] (2), was born in Mill Creek township, Hamilton County, O., April 3, 1815; married (about 1837–8) Sarah O. Pease (she was born in Massachusetts, June 2, 1816, and died in the city of Cincinnati, June 30, 1845), and had issue *three* children, of whom hereafter. He married, secondly, Dec. 26, 1850, Lydia Orr. Mr. Riddle died June 16, 1874, of dyspepsia, and was buried in the family lot in Spring Grove Cemetery, Hamilton County, O.

Thomas-Jefferson Riddle[4] (1), tenth son of John[3] (2), was born Jan. 30, 1817; married Mary E. Newell (she was born in New Brunswick, N. J., May 10, 1819; died near Spring Dale, O., Oct. 6, 1840), Jan. 24, 1837. He married, secondly, Martha A. Cooper (she was born near Cincinnati, O., Jan. 10, 1823), May 12, 1841. Mr. Riddle had *one* son by his first wife, and *three* children by the second wife, of whom hereafter.

Alfred-Columbus Riddle[4] (1), eleventh son of John[3] (2), was born Dec. 16, 1819; married Annie-Maria Olver (she was born in Ohio, Oct. 10, 1823), July 25, 1844, and settled on a farm near Mt. Healthy, Hamilton County, O. He died at his home, by a fall from his carriage, Jan. 29, 1870, leaving *three* children, of whom hereafter.

David-Wade Riddle[4] (1), twelfth son of John[3] (2), was born Oct. 10, 1821, and died at his father's house, Oct. 8, 1846, of typhoid fever; never married.

Eliza-Jane Riddle[4] (1), fourth daughter John[3] (2), was born Feb. 12, 1824; was married to Edward C. Roll, Jan. 6, 1846. Mr. Roll was born in Hamilton County, O., Oct. 25, 1815, and died July 24, 1854, leaving issue. She was married, secondly, to Elam W. Langdon, Nov. 18, 1856; he was born April 9, 1826.

Andrew-Jackson Riddle[4] (1), thirteenth son of John[3] (2), was born Dec. 26, 1825; married Martha Miller (she was born May 8, 1829; died June 23, 1861), Nov. 23, 1847. Mr. Riddle died Jan. 16, 1867, of consumption, leaving *six* children, of whom hereafter.

Samuel-Marshall Riddle[4] (1), fourteenth son of John[3] (2), was born March 25, 1830; married April 22, 1851, to Mary E. Easley, and died March 10, 1870, of consumption, leaving *four* children, of whom hereafter.

FIFTH GENERATION.

William Riddle[5] (5), eldest son of John[4] (3), was born March 15, 1815; married Nov. 9, 1854, to Lennia Burdsall; she was born near Mt. Healthy, Hamilton County, O., May 12, 1834. They reside on their farm near Glen Dale, Hamilton County, and have *three* children, of whom hereafter.

Jacob Riddle⁵ (2), second son of John⁴ (3), was born March 15, 1817, and lives on his father's farm near Spring Dale, O. Never married.

Mary Riddle⁵ (2), eldest daughter of John⁴ (3), was born near Spring Dale, Hamilton County, O., June 26, 1819; was married to Robert-Durland Hilts, March 5, 1840; he was born in New York, July 15, 1815, and died on his farm adjoining Spring Dale, Hamilton County, O., of spotted fever, Oct. 25, 1870; they had *ten* children.

John-L. Riddle⁵ (4), third son of John⁴ (3), was born near Spring Dale, Hamilton County, O., Jan. 5, 1821; married, April 6, 1843, to Elizabeth Hilts (who was born May 14, 1824), and resides on a farm one mile north of Spring Dale; he had issue *thirteen* children, of whom hereafter.

Emeline Riddle⁵ (1), second daughter of John⁴ (3), was born Feb. 9, 1823; married April 3, 1849, to Samuel-Seabury Allen; he was born in Cincinnati, O., March 2, 1820. They live on a farm near Lockwood, and have children.

Andrew-J. Riddle⁵ (2), fourth son of John⁴ (3), was born near Spring Dale, O., March 7, 1825; married Feb. 14, 1848, to Lovina Skillman. No issue. He married, secondly, Nov. 8, 1855, Louisa J. Pratt; she was born June 14, 1833, at Flemington, N. J. *Seven* children, all living.

Nancy Riddle⁵ (2), third daughter of John⁴ (3), was born Jan. 22, 1827; never married; lives on her father's home farm.

Adrian-Aten Riddle⁵ (1), fifth son of John⁴ (3), was born Sept. 26, 1830; married April 8, 1855, Henrietta-Maria Walker; she was born near Jones, Butler County, O., June 18, 1838. They live on a farm near Towanda, McLean County, Ill., and have *three* children. of whom hereafter.

John-Jackson Riddle⁵ (5), eldest son of James⁴ (1), was born at the Brighton House, Hamilton County, O., Jan. 31, 1825; married Feb. 14, 1866, to Eliza-Ann Figgans (she was born May 24, 1825), and settled in Covington, Ky. He studied law with the Hon. Bellamy Storer, and was admitted to the bar in 1850. Mr. Riddle is a thorough scholar; a genial, social-natured gentleman. He is possessed of a remarkable business capacity, and is a skilful writer. During the summer of 1873 the author formed the acquaintance of Mr. Riddle in the city of Cincinnati, and was courteously accompanied by him in searching for materials for this book. He voluntarily assumed the undertaking of furnishing the genealogy of Col. John Riddle's family, and has done the work in a careful and thorough manner. No children.

Samuel-Jackson Riddle⁵ (2), second son of James⁴ (1), was born at the Brighton House, July 10, 1827; studied law with Hon. Timothy Walker, and resides at Covington, Ky.; never married.

Melissa-Elizabeth Riddle⁵ (1), eldest daughter of James⁴ (1), was born in Green township, Hamilton County, O., March 27, 1834; was married Aug. 29, 1852, to Joseph I. Perrin; he died at Vicksburgh, Miss., Sept. 18, 1853, leaving *one* child. She married, secondly, June 11, 1856, to David D. Banta; he was born in Johnson County, Ind., May 23, 1833; graduated at Indiana State University, at Bloomington, in 1855; was admitted to the bar in 1857; was commissioned judge of the Indiana Circuit Court in 1870, and has issue *three* children.

Manning-Randolph Riddle⁵ (1), eldest son of Jacob⁴ (1), was born April 28, 1824; married April 30, 1846, to Lydia Stilwell; she died Feb. 1, 1861, leaving *four*. children.

Nancy-Jane Riddle[6] (3), eldest daughter of Jacob[4] (1), was born Feb. 22, 1827; married Jan. 3, 1850, to George Buckles; she died Aug. 13, 1855, leaving *two* daughters.

John-H. Riddle[6] (6), second son of Jacob[4] (1), was born March 26, 1830; died Sept. 4, 1832.

Mary-Tucker Riddle[6] (3), second daughter of Jacob[4] (1), was born June 30, 1834; died Aug. 23, 1839.

Asenath Riddle[6] (1), third daughter of Jacob[4] (1), was born Nov. 24, 1838; married Sept. 14, 1858, to Francis L. Bull, and has issue.

William Riddle[6] (6), third son of Jacob[4] (1), was born Sept. 1, 1842; died Aug. 19, 1863.

Joseph-M. Riddle[6] (2), fourth son of Jacob[4] (1), was born Nov. 28, 1845; died April 10, 1867.

George-W. Riddle[6] (2), fifth son of Jacob[4] (1), was born Nov. 14, 1848; married Sept. 23, 1870, to Mary J. Duncan.

Martha-A. Riddle[6] (1), fourth daughter of Jacob[4] (1), was born March 12, 1851.

Albert Riddle[6] (1), sixth son of Jacob[4] (1), was born March 17, 1854; died Oct. 11, 1867.

Martha-Jane Riddle[6] (2), eldest daughter of Joseph[4] (1), was born Dec. 21, 1829; married Aug. 18, 1847, Hon. Alpheus Cutter, and has *four* children.

George-W. Riddle[4] (3), eldest son of Joseph[4] (1), was born April 15, 1832; died Feb. 4, 1838.

Margaret-S. Riddle[6] (1), second daughter of Joseph[4] (1), was born Jan. 7, 1840; married June 15, 1858, to M. L. Jamison; he was born May 14, 1838, and died April 17, 1860. She was married, secondly, to Gen. Thomas L. Young,* of Cincinnati, O., Sept. 14, 1862; he was born near Belfast, Ireland, Dec. 14, 1832. Mrs. Young died Oct. 7, 1867, leaving issue.

John-Joseph Riddle[6] (7), second son of Joseph[4] (1), was born Feb 9, 1844; died April 24, 1844.

Joseph Riddle[6] (3), third son of Joseph[4] (1), was born May 4, 1846 lives in Colorado; unmarried.

Mary-Eliza Riddle[6] (4), eldest daughter of Adam[4] (1), was born in Cincinnati, O., Aug. 4, 1836; married to Ammi Baldwin, June 6, 1854; resides in Cincinnati. She has issue.

---

* GEN. THOMAS L. YOUNG was born near Belfast, Ireland, Dec. 14, 1832. He came to America when very young; received a common-school education, and graduated at the law school of Cincinnati College. When not quite sixteen years old he entered the United States Regular Army; this was during the last years of the Mexican war. He joined the Union army during the Southern rebellion, and was appointed captain in July, 1862; promoted to lieutenant-colonel in 1863; commissioned colonel in April, 1864; and on 13th of March, 1865, the President brevetted him brigadier-general of volunteers, for gallant conduct on the battle-field. After the war he was elected to the legislature for Hamilton County, O., and in October, 1867, he was elected recorder of said County. In 1871 he was nominated for State senator, and was the only Republican elected from Cincinnati to the State senate. When President Hayes left the governor's chair to take that of the Chief Magistrate, General Young became his successor as governor of the State of Ohio. He kindly assumed the task of compiling a biographical sketch of Col. John Riddle, and accomplished the work in a very able manner.

John-Cook Riddle[5] (8), eldest son of Adam[4] (1), was born Dec. 4, 1837; died Sept. 14, 1838.

Henry-Augustus Riddle[5] (1), second son of Adam[4] (1), was born Dec. 9, 1838; died Sept. 30, 1860.

Elizabeth-Cook Riddle[5] (1), second daughter of Adam[4] (1), was born Sept. 16, 1841; married June 7, 1864, to James McGreggor, and has issue.

Caroline Riddle[5] (1), third daughter of Adam[4] (1), was born June 7, 1843; married April 22, 1868, to Frederick H. McColloch, and has issue.

Talmage Riddle[5] (1), third son of Adam[4] (1), was born Dec. 31, 1846; died April 14, 1849.

John-V. Riddle[5] (9), eldest son of Isaac[4] (1), was born Jan. 19, 1832; died Feb. 2, 1832.

Nancy-A. Riddle[5] (4), eldest daughter of Isaac[4] (1), was born Sept. 2, 1833; died Sept. 7, 1834.

Charles-Wesley Riddle[5] (1), second son of Isaac[4] (1), was born Dec. 7, 1835; resides at Carthage, Mo.

Elizabeth Riddle[5] (2), second daughter of Isaac[4] (1), was born April 19, 1838; was married Sept. 6, 1865, to Capt. E. B. Reeder; died July 25, 1868, leaving issue.

John-M. Riddle[5] (10), third son of Isaac[4] (1), was born Nov. 20, 1840, and is living in Carthage, Mo.

Sarah-Allen Riddle[5] (1), third daughter of Isaac[4] (1), was born Dec. 28, 1842.

Caroline Riddle[5] (2), fourth daughter of Isaac[4] (1), was born March 10, 1845; died Sept. 6, 1872, in Arkansas.

George-Edward Riddle[5] (4), fourth son of Isaac[4] (1), was born Dec. 4, 1847; married, Sept. 5, 1869, to Mary-Jane Tibbetts.

Isaac-B. Riddle[5] (2), fifth son of Isaac[4] (1), was born May 12, 1850; died June 10, 1850.

Infant Riddle[5] (1), sixth son of Isaac[4] (1), was born Nov. 24, 1852; died Nov. 25, 1852.

Phebe-Townley Riddle[5] (1), fifth daughter of Isaac[4] (1), was born April 22, 1853.

Howard-Henry Riddle[5] (1), seventh son of Isaac[4] (1), was born Sept. 7, 1856.

Sarah-Elizabeth Riddle[5] (2), eldest daughter of George[4] (1), was born Jan. 7, 1842; died Feb. 1, 1868.

George-C. Riddle[5] (5), eldest son of George[4] (1), was born Nov. 30, 1844; died July 6, 1845.

Augustus Riddle[5] (1), second son of George[4] (1), was born in ——; is a merchant in the State of Texas. He served in the Washington rebel artillery company, — raised in New Orleans during the war, — with distinction.

Augustus-Newell Riddle[5] (2), eldest son of Thomas[4] (1), was born April 25, 1838; married, Dec. 12, 1866, to Eliza A. Leonard. She was born at Reading, Hamilton County, O., Nov. 1, 1838. Mr. Riddle is a carpenter by trade, and resides in Champaign City. He enlisted in the Federal army, in a regiment of cavalry, Sept. 12, 1861, and was mustered out Feb. 5, 1865. His first battle was at Shiloh; he did much scouting and skirmishing; was sick with swamp-fever, and given up for dead;

recovered and started for his regiment; was detailed by special order under General Grant to serve as clerk in the subsistence department. He served through the Atlanta campaign, and back with General Thomas, through the battles of Franklin and Nashville.   *Two* children.

Mary-Elizabeth Riddle[5] (5), eldest daughter of Thomas[4] (1), was born in Cincinnati, O., March 19, 1842; was married, Dec. 13, 1863, to John H. Johns; they reside in Columbia City, Ind.

Joseph-Cooper Riddle[5] (4), second son of Thomas[4] (1), was born of his second wife, at Reading, Hamilton County, O., Sept. 5, 1846; married and lives at Piqua, Miami County, O.

Mina-Annie Riddle[5] (1), second daughter of Thomas[4] (1), was born at Carthage, Hamilton County, O., Feb. 27, 1849; died March 12, 1849.

John-F. Riddle[5] (11), eldest son of Alfred[4] (1), was born near Mt. Healthy, Hamilton County, O., Nov. 26, 1845; married, in May, 1870, to Alice Burdsall, and has *one* child (1874).

Sarah-Agnes Riddle[5] (3), eldest daughter of Alfred[4] (1), was born June 17, 1848; was married, April 20, 1870, to Gen. Thomas L. Young (since Governor of Ohio), of Cincinnati, and has issue.   See note on preceding pages, about General Young.

Alfred-C. Riddle[5] (2), second son of Alfred[4] (1), was born Oct. 25, 1850; unmarried in 1873.

Mary-Eliza Riddle[5] (6), eldest daughter of Andrew[4] (1), was born Sept. 10, 1848; died Dec. 21, 1849.

Andrew-J. Riddle[5] (3), eldest son of Andrew[4] (1), was born Jan. 25, 1851.

Phebe-Ellen Riddle[5] (1), second daughter of Andrew[4] (1), was born April 21, 1853.

Eliza-Jane Riddle[5] (2), third daughter of Andrew[4] (1), was born Nov. 16, 1856.

Mary-Eliza Riddle[5] (7), fourth daughter of Andrew[4] (1), was born March 28, 1860.

Margaret-Jane Riddle[5] (2), eldest daughter of Samuel[4] (1), was born June 20, 1853; was married, Sept. 26, 1871, to William W. Wunder, and has issue.

Mary-Ella Riddle[5] (8), second daughter of Samuel[4] (1), was born July 10, 1854.

Samuel-Marshall Riddle[5] (3), eldest son of Samuel[4] (1), was born Oct. 21, 1858; died Jan. 28, 1860.

Miller-W. Riddle[5] (1), second son of Samuel[4] (1), was born May 13, 1862; died Sept. 17, 1862.

SIXTH GENERATION.

Lydia-Ann Riddle[6] (1), eldest daughter of William[5] (4), was born Sept. 14, 1855.

Edgar-Burdsall Riddle[6] (1), eldest son of William[5] (4), was born March 3, 1859.

Alice-Daisy Riddle[6] (1), second daughter of William[5] (4), was born Sept. 14, 1864.

Catherine-Ann Riddle[6] (3), eldest daughter of John[5] (3), was born April 18, 1844; was married March 1, 1865, to William Pratt, and has issue.

Elizabeth-Jane Riddle⁶ (3), second daughter of John⁵ (3), was born Dec. 18, 1845; was married Feb. 1, 1866, to Edward Frey, and has several children.

Cornelia Riddle⁶ (1), third daughter of John⁵ (3), was born April 9, 1847; died Aug. 20, 1848.

Frank-Adams Riddle⁶ (1), eldest son of John⁵ (3), was born June 21, 1848; died April 16, 1866.

Harriet-Hilts Riddle⁶ (1), fourth daughter of John⁵ (3), was born Sept. 29, 1849.

James Riddle⁶ (2), second son of John⁵ (3), was born November, 1850; died when four weeks old.

Clara Riddle⁶ (1), fifth daughter of John⁵ (3), was born Nov. 9, 1852.

Julia Riddle⁶ (1), sixth daughter of John⁵ (3), was born Sept. 21, 1857.

Margaret Riddle⁶ (3), seventh daughter of John⁵ (3), was born March 17, 1859.

Mary Riddle⁶ (9), eighth daughter of John⁵ (3), was born Jan. 28, 1861.

John-Long Riddle⁶ (12), third son of John⁵ (3), was born Aug. 7, 1862.

Henrietta Riddle⁶ (1), ninth daughter of John⁵ (3), was born Dec. 18, 1864.

Jacob-McPherson Riddle⁶ (3), fourth son of John⁵ (3), was born Aug. 17, 1866.

Marian-Pratt Riddle⁶ (1), eldest daughter of Andrew⁵ (2), was born Aug. 20, 1856.

Florence-Howard Riddle⁶ (1), second daughter of Andrew⁵ (2), was born Oct. 15, 1858.

Harry-Scott Riddle⁶ (1), eldest son of Andrew⁵ (2), was born Aug. 1, 1861.

Anna-Elizabeth Riddle⁶ (1), third daughter of Andrew⁵ (2), was born Aug. 1, 1861,—twin to Harry Scott.

Edward-Grant Riddle⁶ (1), second son of Andrew⁵ (2), was born Dec. 17, 1863.

Walter-Lester Riddle⁶ (1), third son of Andrew⁵ (2), was born Dec. 25, 1869.

Willie-Exton Riddle⁶ (1), twin brother of Walter⁶ (1), was born Dec. 25, 1869.

Mary-Emma Riddle⁶ (10), eldest daughter of Adrian⁵ (1), was born near Spring Dale, Hamilton County, O., Feb. 8, 1856.

Charles-Walker Riddle⁶ (2), eldest son of Adrian⁵ (1), was born near Towanda, O., June 22, 1865.

Cornelia Riddle⁶ (2), second daughter of Adrian⁵ (1), was born on her father's farm at Towanda, O., June 16, 1873.

Louisa Riddle⁶ (1), eldest daughter of Manning⁵ (1), was born Feb. 18, 1847; was married Feb. 1, 1865, to Alonzo Furrow, and has several children.

Sarah-Bell Riddle⁶ (4), second daughter of Manning⁵ (1), was born May 30, 1850.

Mary-H. Riddle⁶ (11), third daughter of Manning⁵ (1), was born Feb. 12, 1854.

Martha-J. Riddle[6] **(3)**, fourth daughter of Manning[5] (1), was born Sept. 28, 1855.

Lillie Riddle[6] **(1)**, only daughter of John[5] (11), and grand-daughter of Alfred-Columbus Riddle, was born May 22, 1871.

RIDDELLS OF MARYLAND.

Jacob Riddell[1] **(1)**, parents unknown, was descended from a Scottish ancestry, and settled in Maryland about the year 1760. He married three times (names of wives do not appear), and had issue *five* children, as follows : —

SECOND GENERATION.

Jacob Riddell[2] **(2)**, a son of Jacob[1] (1), was born in the State of Maryland; married Mary Anderson, and had issue *twelve* children, of whom hereafter. He died at the age of 40, his widow at the age of 50.

John Riddell[2] **(1)**, a son of Jacob[1] (1), was born in the State of Maryland; married Susan Johnson, and had issue; deceased many years ago.

Joseph Riddell[2] **(1)**, a son of Jacob[1] (1), was born in the State of Maryland, and died many years ago.

Elizabeth Riddell[2] **(1)**, a daughter of Jacob[1] (1), was born in Maryland, and lived in Prince George County, in 1873.

Eliza Riddell[2] **(1)**, a daughter of Jacob[1] (1), was born in Maryland, and deceased years ago.

THIRD GENERATION.

James Riddell[3] **(1)**, eldest son of Jacob[2] (2), was born in Maryland, April 9, 1820; married Ellen Sanborn, a lady of Irish descent, and has issue *six* children, of whom hereafter. Carpenter; resides in Washington, D. C.

Mary Riddell[3] **(1)**, eldest daughter of Jacob[2] (2), was born in Maryland, May 24, 1822; deceased.

Sarah Riddell[3] **(1)**, second daughter of Jacob[2] (2), was born in Maryland, May 29, 1824; deceased.

William Riddell[3] **(1)**, second son of Jacob[2] (2), was born in Maryland, June 26, 1826; resides in Washington, D. C.

Emily Riddell[3] **(1)**, third daughter of Jacob[2] (2), was born in Maryland, March 2, 1828; deceased.

Susan Riddell[3] **(1)**, fourth daughter of Jacob[2] (2), was born in Maryland, Jan. 6, 1830; lives at Blagdensburgh.

Jacob Riddell[3] **(3)**, third son of Jacob[2] (2), was born in Maryland, Oct. 3, 1832; deceased.

John Riddell[3] **(2)**, fourth son of Jacob[2] (2), was born in Maryland, Oct. 13, 1834, and lives at Washington, D. C.

Charles Riddell[3] **(1)**, fifth son of Jacob[2] (2), was born in Maryland, April 30, 1836, and resides in Virginia.

FOURTH GENERATION.

Mary Riddell[4] **(2)**, eldest daughter of James[3] (1), was born Sept. 1, 1849.

Christopher Riddell[4] (1), eldest son of James[3] (1), was born Feb. 10, 1851.

James Riddell[4] (2), second son of James[3] (1), was born March 23, 1853, and died July 15, 1853.

George Riddell[4] (1), third son of James[3] (1), was born May 10, 1854.

Luiladda Riddell[4] (1), second daughter of James[3] (1), was born Dec. 1, 1856, and died May 7, 1861.

Austin Riddell[4] (1), fourth son of James[3] (1), was born March 8, 1859, and died April 25, 1863.

RIDDELLS OF CECIL COUNTY, MARYLAND.

[SCOTCH-IRISH BRANCH.]

[The American ancestor of this branch of the Riddell family is said to have married a servant-girl in his father's family, in the north of Ireland, and being a descendant of an aristocratic stock, he was disowned by his kinspeople, and emigrated to this country. I have not found full statistics relative to the early members who were settled in Maryland; the family seem to have left that State, and those now living hold their ancestral history in tradition. It is quite probable that this is a branch of the family in Glasslough, Ireland, as the traditions in both families nearly agree.]

Levi Riddell[1] (1), whose parents' names have not reached me, was born somewhere in the north of Ireland, and emigrated to America in consequence of having married a servant-girl in his father's family. Some think this man's name was Humphrey; both names are common in the family. He settled in Cecil County, Md., and evidently reared a large family, some of whom were named as follows: —

SECOND GENERATION.

William Riddell[2] (1), a son of the preceding Levi[1] (1), was born in the State of Maryland. No other information.

Thomas Riddell[2] (1), a son of Levi[1] (1), was born in the State of Maryland; settled at Wilmington, Clinton County, O., and died in 1840, leaving *seven* children.

John Riddell[2] (1), a son of Levi[1] (1), was born in the State of Maryland (presumably); no other information.

Robert Riddell[2] (1), a son of Levi[1] (1), was (presumably) born in Cecil County, Md.; no other information.

Levi Riddell[2] (2), a son of Levi[1] (1), was born in the State of Maryland, — probably in Cecil County, — and married Lutitia Parker. He learned the shoemaker's trade with a Mr. Benjamin, in his native State. He had issue several children, of whom hereafter. Mr. Riddell died Nov. 16, 1807; his widow Jan. 5, 1853.

Jackson Riddell[2] (1), a son of Levi[1] (1), was born in the State of Maryland, and disappeared in 1833, since when nothing has been heard from him. A carpenter.

THIRD GENERATION.

Jackson Riddell³ (2), a son of Thomas² (1), married Huldah ——, and had issue *six* children, of whom hereafter. He lived at Columbus, O., and carried on an extensive business as butcher there. His widow has deceased since 1878.

Basil Riddell³ (1), a son of Thomas² (1), lived in Ohio.

William Riddell³ (2), a son of Thomas² (1), lived in Ohio.

Rachel Riddell³ (1), a daughter of Thomas² (1).

Betsey Riddell³ (1), a daughter of Thomas² (1).

Maria Riddell³ (1), a daughter of Thomas² (1).

Humphrey Riddell³ (1), eldest son of Levi² (2), was born in Cecil County, Md., Nov. 25, 1801; married Emily Tyson in 1825. His first wife died without issue, May 23, 1826. He married, secondly, Rachel Crouch, and by her had *two* children, of whom hereafter. His second wife died Oct. 6, 1833; she (as also his first wife) was a native of Maryland. After the death of his second wife he moved into Pennsylvania, and there married Mary-Ann Moore, in 1835; by her he had issue *ten* children, of whom hereafter. Mr. Riddell moved to Ohio, and continued there from 1837 to 1855, when he removed to Mercer County, Ill. He worked at shoemaking till 1852, when he took charge of the infirmary for the poor in Clinton County, O.; he continued at the latter place till 1855, when he went West and commenced farming. In the spring of 1858 he took charge of the infirmary for the poor in Mercer County, Ill., and continued there till 1868; he then moved to his farm, and lived there till his death, which occurred suddenly on the morning of Jan. 24, 1871. He was alive and apparently well only a few minutes before he was found dead in his bed. He was a member of the Methodist Church for fifty years, and lived a consistent Christian.

Silas Riddell³ (1), a son of Levi² (2), was born in Maryland, Oct. 7, 1807; married to Jane Wilson, of Mount Vernon, Penn., and by her had issue *five* children, of whom hereafter. He fell dead while on his way to his home, Jan. 6, 1872.

Jackson Riddell³ (3), a son of Levi² (2), was born in Cecil County, Md., and his history is unknown.

Levi Riddell³ (3), a son of Levi² (2), was born in Cecil County, Md., and died while young.

FOURTH GENERATION.

Corydon Riddell⁴ (1), eldest son of Jackson³ (2), is a conductor on the Pittsburgh, Cincinnati & St. Louis Railroad. Resides in Logansport, Ind.

Orlando Riddell⁴ (1), second son of Jackson³ (2), is a farmer in Columbus, O.

Wellington Riddell⁴ (1), third son of Jackson³ (2), is foreman of the fire department, Columbus, O.

Benjamin Riddell⁴ (1), fourth son of Jackson³ (2), is employed on the railroad, Logansport, Ind.

Theodore Riddell⁴ (1), fifth son of Jackson³ (2), is an ice-dealer at Columbus, O.

Isadore Riddell⁴ (1), only surviving daughter of Jackson³ (2), was living with her mother at Columbus, O., in 1878.

Elizabeth Riddell[4] (1), eldest daughter of Humphrey[8] (1), was born in Maryland, in 1828 (?); was married to Dr. W. W. Shepherd, in Clinton County, O., and lives at Sligo, in said County; has *three* children.

John-Sumerfield Riddell[4] (2), eldest son of Humphrey[8] (1), was born in Maryland, Nov. 1, 1830; married in 1855 to Mary-Catherine Peters (she was born Aug. 31, 1835), of Willington, O., and is now resident at Toledo, Mercer County, Ill. He is a shoemaker by trade, but does not follow that business. He has *seven* children, of whom hereafter. These two, — John and Elizabeth, — were the children of Humphrey's *second* wife.

Mary-Jane Riddell[4] (1), second daughter of Humphrey[8] (1), and the eldest by his third wife, was born in Chester County, Penn., March 10, 1836; was married to John H. Luner, of Chester County, June 23, 1856 (he was born Oct. 29, 1819), and resides at Millersburgh, Ill.

Harriet Riddell[4] (1), third daughter of Humphrey[8] (1), was born in Willington, Clinton County, O., Nov. 5, 1838; was married in 1856, to John Farran (he was born in Indiana, Feb. 27, 1832), and lives in Millersburgh, Mercer County, Ill.

Silas-Harrison Riddell[4] (2), second son of Humphrey[8] (1), was born in Mercer County, Ill., Aug. 30, 1840; married Dec. 10, 1861, to Sarah-Frances Vernon, daughter of James and Eliza (Duncan) Vernon, of Shelby County, Ind. Mr. Riddell was a school-teacher and farmer until 1864, when he engaged in mercantile business with his brother-in-law, T. A. Vernon. He was appointed a Justice of the Peace in 1866;· discontinued his business in 1869, and is now a clerk in a dry-goods store in Millersburgh, Mercer County, Ill. He has issue *five* children, of whom hereafter.

Levi-Parker Riddell[4] (4), third son of Humphrey[8] (1), was born in Clinton County, O , April 8, 1843; married to Elizabeth Hodge, in Mercer County, Ill., and is now living on a farm near Ketta, Keokuk County, Ia.

James-Lincoln Riddell[4] (1), fourth son of Humphrey[8] (1), was born in Clinton County, O , Nov. 6, 1844; married to Emma Lloyd (?), and is now living at David City, Neb.; a farmer.

Lutitia Riddell[4] (1), fourth daughter of Humphrey[8] (1), was born in Clinton County, O., March 27, 1847; was married to William Clegg, of Mercer County, Ill., and died at the birth of her first child.

Benjamin-Jennings Riddell[4] (2), fifth son of Humphrey[8] (1), was born in Clinton County, O., Aug. 1, 1849, and died Aug. 5, 1852.

Emily Riddell[4] (1), fifth daughter of Humphrey[8] (1), was born in Clinton County, O., Oct. 21, 1851; was married to Frank Vernon, son of Jacob and Sallie Vernon, and is now resident at Independence, Mo.

Charles-Humphrey Riddell[4] (1), sixth son of Humphrey[8] (1), was born in Mercer County, Ill., Nov. 30, 1855, and is now in California; unmarried.

Ross-Eddy Riddell[4] (1), seventh son of Humphrey[8] (1), was born in Mercer County, Ill., Aug. 2, 1858, and died April 23, 1875; presumably unmarried.

Levi-P. Riddell[4] (5), eldest son of Silas[8] (1), was born Jan. 16, 1836; married, and is now (1878) a lawyer at Xenia, O.

Robert-Wilson Riddell[4] (2), second son of Silas[8] (1), was born April 1837; married.

Humphrey Riddell[4] (2), third son of Silas[8] (1), was born Dec. 27, 38, and died Oct. 16, 1839.

Amanda Riddell⁴ (1), eldest daughter of Silas³ (1), was born July 6, 1842, and was married to Mr. Adams.

Lutitia Riddell⁴ (2), second daughter of Silas³ (1), was born Oct. 26, 1846; was married to —— Gert, and is now living at Spring Valley, O.

FIFTH GENERATION.

Sarah-Ellen Riddell⁵ (1), eldest daughter of John⁴ (2), was born Jan. 7, 1856.

Mary-Virginia Riddell⁵ (2), second daughter of John⁴ (2), was born March 20, 1858.

William-Humphrey Riddell⁵ (3), eldest son of John⁴ (2), was born Jan. 23, 1860.

Eva Riddell⁵ (1), twin daughter of John⁴ (2), was born Sept. 22, 1862.

Emma Riddell⁵ (1), twin daughter of John⁴ (2), was born Sept. 22, 1862.

Charles-Silas Riddell⁵ (2), second son of John⁴ (2), was born Feb. 16, 1865.

Merrick-Wikins Riddell⁵ (1), third son of John⁴ (2), was born Sept. 24, 1872.

Janette Riddell⁵ (1), eldest daughter of Silas⁴ (2), was born Oct. 10, 1864.

James-E. Riddell⁵ (2), eldest son of Silas⁴ (2), was born in Mercer County, Ill., Nov. 12, 1867.

Frank-Archie Riddell⁵ (1), second son of Silas⁴ (2), was born in Mercer County, Ill., Nov. 22, 1870.

Milo-Aquila Riddell⁵ (1), third son of Silas⁴ (2), was born in Mercer County, Ill., Aug. 4, 1874, and died March 18, 1875.

RIDDELLS OF LYCOMING, PENNSYLVANIA.

[SCOTCH-IRISH BRANCH.]

Robert Riddell¹ (1) was a native of the County of Derry, Ireland, and married two wives; the first was Margaret Wilson, by whom he had *nine* children; the name of his second wife, — by whom he had *three* children, — has not reached me. He was living in 1730; was a farmer and gardener, and was very aged when he died. This Mr. Riddell was an uncle to Alexander Riddle, whose name heads the article under caption of the "Riddles of Holmes County, Ohio," and father of his wife.

SECOND GENERATION.

John Riddell² (1), a son of Robert¹ (1), was born in Ireland, in 1760 (?); emigrated to the United States before the war of the Revolution, and served in the American army; he was killed at the battle of Long Island. No family.

Robert Riddell² (2) a son of Robert¹ (1), was born in Ireland, in the year 1763 (?), and emigrated to the United States with his brother John before the Revolution. He was in the war of 1812. No family.

William Riddle² (1), a son of Robert¹ (1), was born in Ireland, County of Derry or Donegal; emigrated to the United States previous to the Revolution, and settled in Lycoming County, Penn. He had a family, but after a diligent search I have failed to find the records.

· **Nancy Riddle²** (1), a daughter of Robert¹ (1), was born in Ireland, · and was married before leaving her native land; came to America before the Revolution. Had a large family.

Molly Riddle² (1), a daughter of Robert¹ (1), was born in Ireland about 1764, and lived to a great age there.

Peggy Riddle² (1), a daughter of Robert¹ (1), was born in Ireland about 1766, and reared a family there.

Charles Riddell² (1), a son of Robert¹ (1) by his first wife, was born in the County of Donegal, Ireland, in 1768; married in 1798, to Mary Beard, and having emigrated to America, settled as a farmer in Northumberland County, Penn., where he died in 1825, having had issue *ten* children, of whom hereafter.

Jane Riddle² (1), a daughter of Robert¹ (1) by his first wife, was born in Donegal County, Ireland; married to Mr. Reid in her native land, and emigrated subsequent to 1776, to Northumberland County, Penn. She had issue.

Frank Riddle² (1), a son of Robert¹ (1) by his second wife, was born in Donegal County, Ireland; emigrated to the United States subsequent to the Revolution, and settled as a farmer in Lycoming County, Penn., where he reared a family. No particulars.

Kate Riddle² (1), a daughter of Robert¹ (1), was born in the County of Donegal, Ireland; came to America after the Revolution, and lived in Lycoming County, Penn.

James Riddle² (1), a son of Robert¹ (1) by his second wife, was born in the County of Donegal, Ireland, and came to America, subsequent to the Revolution. He settled in Lycoming County, Penn.

Rachel Riddle² (1), a daughter of Robert¹ (1) by his second wife, was born in Ireland, but emigrated to Pennsylvania.

THIRD GENERATION.

Robert Riddell³ (3), a son of Charles² (1), was born in the County of Northumberland, Penn., in the year 1788; was in the war of 1812; worked at the carpenter's trade, and died in the year 1817.

Nancy Riddell³ (2), a daughter of Charles² (1), was born in the County of Northumberland, Penn., in 1790; was married to Mr. Donnelly, of Irish descent, and had issue. She now (1873) resides at Wooster, Wayne County, O., and has been blind for six years. She retains her memory, and has furnished much information for this book.

James Riddell³ (2), a son of Charles² (1), was born in the County of Northumberland, Penn., in 1793; married to Mattie Wilson, and had issue *six* children, of whom hereafter. Was a farmer. Died in the year 1843.

William Riddell³ (2), a son of Charles² (1), was born in the County of Northumberland, Penn., in April, 1796; married to Mary Berryhill, and settled on a farm in Lycoming County. He had issue *six* children. Was elected a commissioner in 1886; sheriff in 1844, and commissioner again in 1861. Mr. Riddle has been a man of strong character, and possessed a considerable share of business capabilities. He was highly respected.

Strawbridge Riddell³ (1), a son of Charles² (1), wa sborn in the County of Northumberland, Penn., in 1797; married and settled on a farm in the same County. He had issue *one* daughter, and died in 1845.

Dea. John Riddell³ (2), a son of Charles² (1), was born in the County of Northumberland, Penn., in 1799; married Laura Haynes, and moved into York township, Scioto County, O., in the year 1831; he was soon after chosen deacon of the Christian Church in that place, and has been a highly respected citizen and consistent, devoted Christian. His wife,— an eminent Christian woman,— died March 26, 1873, aged 63 years. He has *one* son.

Margery-G. Riddell³ (2), a daughter of Charles² (1), was born in the County of Northumberland, Penn., in 1800 (?); was married to Alexander Guffy, and was living at Watsontown in 1873.

Francis Riddell³ (1), a son of Charles² (1), was born in the County of Northumberland, in 1802; married to Susan Bastian in 1849, and settled on a farm in Lycoming County. He had issue *one* son; died in 1860.

Alexander Riddell³ (1), a son of Charles² (1), was born in Northumberland County, Penn., in 1804; settled in Richmond, Va. Had issue *four* children. Nothing learned from him since the Rebellion. Was a farmer.

Charles Riddell³ (2), a son of Charles² (1), was born in the County of Northumberland, Penn., in 1796; settled in said County as a farmer, and had issue *three* children, of whom hereafter; he died in 1859.

FOURTH GENERATION.

Anna-E. Riddell⁴ (1), eldest daughter of William³ (2), was born in Lycoming County, Penn., June 9, 1828; was married to William H. Rinegar, and lives at Williamsport; has issue.

John-Q. Riddell⁴ (3), eldest son of William³ (2), was born in Lycoming County, Penn., July 6, 1830; married to Nancy J. Smith, and has issue, of whom hereafter. He lives at Linden, in his native shire.

Sarah-J.-M. Riddell⁴ (1), second daughter of William³ (2), was born in Lycoming County, Penn., March 23, 1836; was married to John Blackwell, merchant, of Philadelphia, and has issue.

William-W. Riddell⁴ (3), second son of William³ (2), was born in Lycoming County, Penn., April 10, 1838; went West, and has not been heard from since.

Charles-B. Riddell⁴ (3), third son of William³ (2), was born in Lycoming County, Penn., Sept. 7, 1840; married to Maria (?) Marshall, and has issue several children, of whom hereafter. Mr. Riddell resides at Larry's Creek.

Mary-B. Riddell⁴ (1), third daughter of William³ (2), was born in Lycoming County, Penn., Jan. 24, 1843; married to J. Florence Solado, a banker, of Williamsport, and has issue.

William-Braley Riddell⁴ (4), only son of Dea. John³ (2), was born in York township, Scioto County, O., 1830 (?); married to Barbary Cupp, and has several children. A farmer.

Prof. Charles-S. Riddell⁴ (4), only son of Francis³ (1), was born in Lycoming County, Penn., March 24, 1851. After some preparation at the common school he entered Lafayette College, in the class of 1875, and after remaining about one year he located at Montoursville, and arose by promotion to the principalship of the public schools.

RIDDLES OF WASHINGTON COUNTY, PENNSYLVANIA.

[SCOTCH-IRISH BRANCH.]

David Riddle[1] (1), parents unknown, ancestor of this family, is supposed to have lived in Washington County, Penn., but where he originated, or of his history, I have learned nothing reliable. Some think he was a connexion of Judge James Riddle, of Chambersburgh, but I find no proof; others have supposed this family to be closely allied to the Riddles in the city of Cincinnati, O., but the connection is not proved. There are representatives of this family in Wellsville, O., who could undoubtedly furnish the connecting links, but they will not render assistance. Unquestionably some reader of this book will make connection with other Pennsylvania branches. Mr. Riddle had issue *four* sons; possibly daughters.

SECOND GENERATION.

John Riddle[2] (1), a son of David[1] (1), was born somewhere in Pennsylvania. No particulars.

Samuel Riddle[2] (1), a son of David[1] (1), was born in Pennsylvania, July 24, 1759; married Martha Johnson (she was born in Washington County, Jan. 11, 1766), and had issue *six* children, of whom hereafter. He removed from Pennsylvania to Trumbull County, O.

Abraham Riddle[2] (1), a son of David[1] (1), was born in Pennsylvania; married Isabella Anderson, a lady of Scottish extraction, and had issue *four* children, of whom hereafter. Presumably lived in Ohio.

William Riddle[2] (1), son of David[1] (1), was born in 1757; married Isabella, daughter of William Caldwell, and widow of Nathaniel Templeton (she was born in 1750), and had issue *four* children, of whom hereafter. He owned a "horse-mill" on the "Catfish," near the present town of Washington, Penn.; but removed to Morristown, Belmont County, O., in 1808. He died at Millford, Feb. 18, 1820, aged 63 years. Mrs. Riddle was married to Templeton as early as 1776; he was killed during "Crawford's defeat," by Indians, near Sandusky, in 1782, and she was married to Mr. Riddle in 1788. His mill was near the Caldwell farm. It is said of Mrs. Riddle: "She was one of the pioneer mothers of the West, and passed many years with her children upon an exposed frontier, compelled often to seek protection in block-houses from prowling savages." She was called "Aunt Ibbie" by her relatives; died Feb. 18, 1854, aged 104 years.

THIRD GENERATION.

David Riddle[3] (2), a son of Samuel[2] (1), was born in Trumbull County, O.; married, and had issue *two* sons, of whom hereafter.

James Riddle[3] (1), a son of Samuel[2] (1), was born in Trumbull County, O.; married, and had issue *five* children, of whom hereafter.

Dr. John Riddle[3] (2), a son of Samuel[2] (1), was born in Trumbull County, O., and was a physician. Left no children. Place of residence not known.

Samuel Riddle[3] (2), a son of Samuel[2] (1), was born in Trumbull County, O.; married, and had issue *two* sons, of whom hereafter.

Andrew-J. Riddile[3] (1), a son of Samuel[2] (1), was born in Trumbull County, O., April 20, 1799; married Matilda Taylor (she was born Dec. 10, 1798, and died Feb. 8, 1850), in 1825, and died Aug. 12, 1854. He always spelled his name "Riddile," while his relatives spelled theirs "Riddle" and "Riddell."

Catharine Riddle³ (1), a daughter of Samuel² (1), was born in Ohio. One correspondent says: "Martha was the wife of a Mr. Vannerman." He does not mention Catharine.

Ann Riddle³ (1), a daughter of Samuel² (1), was born in Ohio, and was married to a Mr. McCrady.

David Riddle³ (3), a son of Abraham² (1), was born in Ohio, and married in Virginia. Left *two* sons.

Hon. Joshua-Anderson Riddle³ (1), a son of Abraham² (1), was born in Ohio (?); married Mary A. Fawcet, and resides at Wellsville, O. He is a judge, a man of strong mind and sound judgment, maintaining an honorable standing, and commanding the highest respect from all his acquaintances. He has not furnished his family records.

Isabella Riddle³ (1), a daughter of Abraham² (1), was born in Ohio, and was married to Isaac Van, of Dutch descent.

· **Abraham Riddle³** (2), a son of Abraham² (1), was born in Ohio, went to California, and was drowned there.

David Riddle³ (4), a son of William² (1), was born in Washington County, Penn.; was a major in the army of the United States during the war of 1812, and died from wounds received in a duel at the Bay of St. Louis.

Samuel Riddle³ (3), a son of William² (1), was born in Washington County, Penn.; was in the American army during the war of 1812; died in 1820, and was buried in the military burying-ground at Baton Rouge, La. No family known.

Thomas Riddle³ (1), a son of William² (1), was born in Washington County, Penn.; commanded a company in the American army during the war of 1812; married Catherine Tice, and had *one* son.

Catherine Riddle³ (2), a daughter of William² (1), was born in Washington County, Penn.; was married to Dr. L. A. Hendrick, and has issue.

FOURTH GENERATION.

Samuel Riddle⁴ (4), a son of David³ (2). } Reside in Mahoning
John Riddle⁴ (3), was a son of David³ (2). }   County, O.

Samuel Riddle⁴ (5), a son of James³ (1). }
Ann Riddle⁴ (2), a daughter of James³ (1). } Some of this family
James Riddle⁴ (2), a son of James³ (1). } live near Lincoln, Neb.
David Riddle⁴ (5), a son of James³ (1). } Probably reside in Lin-
Stratton Riddle⁴ (1), a son of James³ (1). }   coln, Neb.

William Riddle⁴ (2), a son of Samuel³ (2). } Live in Mahoning Coun-
Samuel Riddle⁴ (6), a son of Samuel³ (2). }   ty, O.

Samuel-L. Riddle⁴ (7), eldest son of Andrew³ (1), was born in Trumbull County, O., March 12, 1827; married Mary Vannerman, 1854, and has *three* children. His post-office address is Murray, Wells County, Ind.; farmer.

George-T. Riddle⁴ (1), second son of Andrew³ (1), was born in Trumbull County, O., July 31, 1828; married Lizzie Rods, in 1855, and resides at Fort Dodge, Ia. Merchant; no issue.

Martha-S. Riddle⁴ (1), only daughter of Andrew³ (1), was born in Ohio in 1830; married to William Rankin, of Washington County, Penn., and has *two* sons; resides at Hickory, Penn.; husband a farmer.

Dr. Hiram-D. Riddle⁴ (1), third son of Andrew³ (1), was born in Trumbull County, O., April 2, 1833; married Emma Parker in 1873, and has *one* daughter; lives at Battle Ground, Ind.

William Riddle⁴ (3), only son of Thomas³ (1), died at Dayton, O., leaving *two* sons.

FIFTH GENERATION.

George Riddle⁵ (2), a son of William⁴ (3), lives in the city of Dayton, O. (1873); teamster.

RIDDELLS OF CUMBERLAND COUNTY, PENNSYLVANIA.

[ENGLISH BRANCH.]

Edward Riddell¹ (1), parents unknown, was born on the Atlantic Ocean, March 22, 1758; his father soon after died on board the same vessel, during a voyage to America, and, contrary to custom, was carried on shore for burial. The widow landed with her child at Philadelphia, where she remained for a time, then went to Cumberland County, in said state, and was again married. Growing to manhood, Edward became a miller, and carried on the milling business in Cumberland County, Penn. He entered the American army during the war of the Revolution, and was engaged in the wars with the Indians ·in western Pennsylvania, on the Ohio River. He married Agnes ——, who died in Cumberland County, without issue. He married, secondly, to Margaret McMillan, of Shippensburgh, in said State, a woman of Irish blood, descended from a noble family. After his second marriage he removed to Virginia, settling ten miles above Wheeling, where he continued till 1805, when he moved to Mercer County, Penn., and remained there till his death, which occurred in August, 1826. His ancestors were Scotch, but his immediate family had resided in England for several generations. Mr. Riddell (or Riddle, as his descendants are called), had issue *ten* children, of whom hereafter.

SECOND GENERATION.

Rebecca Riddle² (1), eldest daughter of Edward¹ (1), was born at Shippensburgh, Penn., in 1789; was married to Alexander Maccraken, of Mercer County, and had issue. Her first husband dying, she was married, secondly, to Mellen Woolly, and had other issue.

Alexander Riddle² (1), eldest son of Edward¹ (1), was born at Shippensburgh, Penn., July 24, 1793; married in Lawrence County, to Isabella Walker, a lady of Scottish descent, and had issue *two* children, of whom hereafter. Mr. Riddle was a merchant; died July 13, 1870.

James Riddle² (1), second son of Edward¹ (1), was born near Wheeling, Va., Sept. 19, 1795; married to Miss Catherine Butterbaugh, and by her had issue *nine* children, of whom hereafter. He is a merchant at Mercer, Mercer County, Penn.

Samuel Riddle[2] (1), third son of Edward[1] (1), was born near Wheeling, Va., April 13, 1797; married to Catherine Emery, and died without issue.

William Riddle[2] (1), fourth son of Edward[1] (1), was born near Wheeling, Va., July 29, 1799; married at Plain Grove, Mercer County, Penn., April 12, 1836, to Miss Elizabeth McCune, and by her had issue *ten* children, of whom hereafter. His wife deceased June 14, 1868. Mr. Riddle is a farmer at Sunville, Venango County, Penn.

Mary-Anne Riddle[2] (1), second daughter of Edward[1] (1), was born near Wheeling, Va., Aug. 5, 1801; was married at North Liberty, Mercer County, Penn., July 13, 1849, to Josiah-Scott Stevenson, and is now living at Harlensburgh, Lawrence County; no issue.

Eliza Riddle[2] (1), third daughter of Edward[1] (1), was born near Wheeling, Va., May 9, 1804; was married at Harlensburgh, Lawrence County, Penn., Aug. 30, 1827, to John Emery, an American by birth, of Hollandish ancestry; he died March 30, 1848. *Nine* children.

John-Brice Riddle[2] (1), fifth son of Edward[1] (1), was born in Mercer County, Penn., Oct. 9, 1806; married Catherine Douds, and had issue *seven* children, of whom hereafter. He lives in Mercer County, and works at the carpenters' and builders' trade.

Isabella Riddle[2] (1), fourth daughter of Edward[1] (1), was born in Mercer County, Penn., Oct. 28, 1808; was married May 7, 1829, to William Miles, of Scotch-Irish descent, and had issue *nine* children. She lives on a farm at Plain Grove, Lawrence County, Penn.

George-W. Riddle[2] (1), sixth son of Edward[1] (1), was born in Mercer County, Penn., Nov. 29, 1811; married Mary Foster, and had issue *four* children, of whom hereafter. He is a tailor at North Liberty, Mercer County.

THIRD GENERATION.

Dr. John-Walker Riddle[3] (2), a son of Alexander[2] (1), was born in Mercer County, Penn., Sept. 13, 1820; married Rebecca-Jane, second daughter of William Jennings, of Dunmanway, County Cork, Ireland, a descendant of that George Jennings who received from William of Orange the townland of Dunmanway, as a reward for services as aide-de-camp at the battle of Boyne. By this lady he had *two* sons, of whom hereafter. Mrs. Riddle died Oct. 12, 1849, at Utica, Penn., and was buried at New Vernon. He married, secondly, Rachel-Harriet Close, by whom he had issue *five* children, and from whom he was divorced Jan. 27, 1866. He married, thirdly, Susan P. Luce, Oct. 21, 1869. Dr. Riddle received a medical education at Jefferson College, Philadelphia. He served as assistant surgeon in the Sixty-first Regiment, Pennsylvania Volunteers, from Sept. 17, 1862, to Sept. 7, 1864, participating in all the battles in which the Sixth Army Corps, Army of the Potomac, was engaged. He is now in the active practice of his profession at Sandy Lake, Penn.

Margaret Riddle[3] (1), only daughter of Alexander[2] (1), was born in Mercer County, Penn.; was married to Joseph Kirk, and died issueless.

Eliza-A. Riddle[3] (2), daughter of James[2] (1), was born in Mercer County, Penn.; was married to William R. Perine, and had *four* children.

Margaret Riddle[3] (2), daughter of James[2] (1), was born in Mercer County, Penn., and was married to Perry Thompson.

James Riddle[8] (2), a son of James[2] (1), was born in Mercer County, Penn., and deceased when young.

Catharine Riddle[8] (1), daughter of James[2] (1), was born in Mercer County, Penn.; married William Roberts, and had issue *six* children.

James-W. Riddle[8] (3), son of James[2] (1), was born in Mercer County, Penn.; married Dora ——, and had issue a son and daughter. He resides at Yreka, Cal., where he carries on the carpenter business.

Alexander-W. Riddle[8] (2), a son of James[2] (1), was born in Mercer County, Penn., and resides at St. Louis, Mo.

Mary-Lucinda Riddle[8] (2), daughter of James[2] (1), was born in Mercer County, Penn.; was married to J. W. Moore, by whom *four* sons and *six* daughters.

William Riddle[8] (2), a son of James[2] (1), was born in Mercer County, Penn., and died young.

George-Taylor Riddle[8] (2), a son of James[2] (1), was born in Mercer County, Penn.; married Gertrude Lodge, and has issue *one* son. He resides on a farm in his native County.

———

Marion-C. Riddle[8] (1), eldest son of William[2] (1), was born in Mercer County, Penn., in 1840.

Joseph-B. Riddle[8] (1), second son of William[2] (1), was born in Mercer County, Penn., in 1843.

Mary-E. Riddle[8] (3), eldest daughter of William[2] (1), was born in Mercer County, Penn., in 1846.

Isabella-A. Riddle[8] (2), second daughter of William[2] (1), was born in Mercer County, Penn., in 1848.

William-A. Riddle[8] (3), third son of William[2] (1), was born in Mercer County, Penn., in 1851.

———

John-Wesley Riddle[8] (3), eldest son of John[2] (1), was born in Allegheny City, Penn., Jan. 27, 1839; married March 28, 1861, to Annie Stevenson, of Sewickley, Allegheny County (of English descent), by whom he has issue *four* children, of whom hereafter. He enlisted in the Fourth Pennsylvania Cavalry, Feb. 16, 1865, and served in the war of the Rebellion a short term; being discharged July 11, 1865, at Lynchburgh, Va. He resides at Sewickley, and is a carpenter.

George-Washington Riddle[8] (3), second son of John[2] (1), was born at Allegheny City, Penn.; married Mary A. McDonald, and had issue *three* children, of whom hereafter. He resides in Mercer County; shoemaker.

Margaret-C. Riddle[8] (3), eldest daughter of John[2] (1), was born at Allegheny City, Penn.; was married to Charles E. Waugh, a farmer, at Maquoketa, Ia.

Mary-H. Riddle[8] (4), second daughter of John[2] (1), was born at Allegheny City, Penn., March 20, 1844; was married to Henry K. Maitland, Mercer, Penn., Sept. 26, 1866. Has issue.

Amanda-W. Riddle[8] (1), third daughter of John[2] (1), was born at Allegheny City, Penn.

Zares-Coston Riddle[8] (1), third son of John[2] (1), was born at Allegheny City, Penn.

Homer-Clark Riddle[8] (1), fourth son of John[2] (1), was born at Allegheny City, Penn.

Mary-Rebecca Riddle³ (5), eldest daughter of George² (1), was born in Mercer County, Penn.

James-Madison Riddle³ (4), eldest son of George² (1), was born in Mercer County, Penn.

William-Scott Riddle³ (4), second son of George² (1), was born in Mercer County, Penn.

Alonzo-Edward Riddle³ (1), third son of George² (1), was born in Mercer County, Penn.

FOURTH GENERATION.

Alexander-Paucoust Riddle⁴ (3), eldest son of John³ (2), was born at Harlansburgh, Penn., Aug. 16, 1846.   He learned the printing-business in the office of the *Venango Spectator*, in Franklin, Penn., and is now (1876) editor of the *Press*, at Girard, Kan.   Mr. Riddle has manifested a deep interest in this family history, and contributed to its pages by providing statistics of the family of which he is a member.

Cassius-Kirk Riddle⁴ (1), second son of John³ (2), was born at Middlesex, Mercer County, Penn., April 15, 1848, and died at Utica, April 12, 1849.

Charles-Meigs Riddle⁴ (1), third son of John³ (2), was born in Mercer County, Penn., Feb. 14, 1853, and lives on a farm in Utica, Penn.

Laura-Jane Riddle⁴ (1), eldest daughter of John³ (2), was born in Mercer County, Penn., June 26, 1854; died in 1855.

Isabella-Catherine Riddle⁴ (3), second daughter of John³ (2), was born in Mercer County, Penn., March 21, 1856.

George-S.-Kemble Riddle⁴ (4), fourth son of John³ (2), was born in Mercer County, Penn., June 24, 1858.

Margaretta Riddle⁴ (4), third daughter of John³ (2), was born in Mercer County, Penn., March 14, 1861.

George-Washington Riddle⁴ (5), eldest son of James³ (3), was born in Yreka, Cal.

Indiana-Belle Riddle⁴ (1), eldest daughter of James³ (3), was born at Yreka, Cal.

Eustace-Rosecrans Riddle⁴ (1), eldest son of George³ (2), was born in Mercer County, Penn.

Mary Riddle⁴ (6).
Frances Riddle⁴ (1). } Children of John³ (3), born in Mercer Coun-
Jane Riddle⁴ (1). } ty, Penn.

George-Edward Riddle⁴ (6), a son of George³ (3).
Ida-Maude Riddle⁴ (1), a daughter of George³ (3).

RIDDLES OF PITTSBURGH, PENNSYLVANIA.
[SCOTCH-IRISH BRANCH.]

John Riddle¹ (1), came from the north of Ireland, settled at Pittsburgh, Penn., before the Revolution, and served in the American army during that war.   He married Margaret Deverse, and had issue *ten* children, of whom hereafter.   I cannot find records or traditions that would place this man in his proper connection in this book. His name may be found elsewhere and identified by some of his descendants.

SECOND GENERATION.

Nancy Riddle² (1), a daughter of John¹ (1), was born at Pittsburgh, Penn., and became the wife of John Akey.

Catherine Riddle² (1), a daughter of John¹ (1), was born at Pittsburgh, Penn., and was the wife of John Weldy.

Margaret Riddle² (1), a daughter of John¹ (1), was the wife of Philip Smith.

Elizabeth Riddle² (1), a daughter of John¹ (1), was born at Pittsburgh, Penn.

Isaac Riddle² (1), a son of John¹ (1), was born at Pittsburgh, Penn.; married, and had issue *five* children.

Samuel Riddle² (1), a son of John¹ (1), was born at Pittsburgh, Penn., and is said to have died single.

John Riddle² (2), a son of John¹ (1), was born at Pittsburgh, Penn., and died unmarried.

Joseph Riddle² (1), a son of John¹ (1), was born at Pittsburgh, Penn., and died single.

David Riddle² (1), a son of John¹ (1), was born at Pittsburgh, Penn., and died single.

James Riddle² (1), a son of John¹ (1), was born at Pittsburgh, Penn., June 15, 1792; married at Tiltonsville, O., May 5, 1816, to Elizabeth Gill, and had issue *seven* children, of whom hereafter. He served under Capt. George Steger, of the Ohio militia, from Sept. 4, 1812; also, as a substitute from Nov. 30, 1812, to Jan. 9, 1813. Assisted in building a blockhouse at Wooster, O. Discharged at Lower Sandusky. Removed to Minnesota in 1854, and died at the age of eighty-five, leaving a large estate. An extensive farmer.

THIRD GENERATION.

Mary Riddle³ (1), eldest daughter of Isaac² (1), was the wife of Cerdilis Ward, — probably of Ohio.

Sarah Riddle³ (1), second daughter of Isaac² (1), was not married.

Margaret Riddle³ (2), third daughter of Isaac² (1), was the wife of John Gill, — probably of Ohio.

David Riddle³ (2), a son of Isaac² (1), was not married.

John Riddle³ (3), a son of Isaac² (1), never married.

Sarah Riddle³ (2), eldest daughter of James² (1), was born in Ohio, — probably in Jefferson County, — and became the wife of Peter Thomas, of Steubenville, O.

Jane Riddle³ (1), second daughter of James² (1), was born in Ohio, and was married to Maj. J. Foster, and was living at Wykoff, Minn., in 1879.

William Riddle³ (1), eldest son of James² (1), was born in Ohio, and died unmarried.

John Riddle³ (4), second son of James² (1), was born in Ohio about 1816; married Barbara Thomas, of Steubenville, O., and had issue *four* children. He was a blacksmith.

Samuel Riddle³ (2), third son of James² (1), was born in Ohio; married Henrietta Eidam, and had issue *five* children, of whom hereafter. He died June 14, 1871, aged 53. Farmer in Minnesota.

James-O. Riddle³ (2), fourth son of James² (1), was born in Ohio; married Barbara Grailing, settled in Minnesota, and has *two* children.

Thomas Riddle³ (1), fifth son of James² (1), was born in Ohio; married Elizabeth Paxton, and had issue *five* children.   Mr. Riddle is a farmer at Forestville, Minn.

FOURTH GENERATION.

David Riddle⁴ (3), eldest son of John³ (4), was born in Ohio; married Martha Boyd, and had issue *five* children.   He resided in Pennsylvania, and later in Minnesota.

James-P. Riddle⁴ (3), second son of John³ (4), was born in Ohio, April 3, 1842;* married to Hannah Tedrow, and has issue *three* children. Served three years in the Union army during the Rebellion.   Farmer at Forestville, Minn.*

Eliza-A. Riddle⁴ (2), eldest daughter of John³ (4), was born in Ohio, and became the wife of John Gardner.

Elizabeth-J. Riddle⁴ (2), second daughter of John³ (4), was born in Ohio, and was married to John Atchison.

James-W. Riddle⁴ (4), eldest son of Samuel³ (2), was born in Minnesota, in 1856.   Cooper by trade.

Subina Riddle⁴ (1), eldest daughter of Samuel³ (2).   ⎫ All
Rosa-H. Riddle⁴ (1), second daughter of Samuel³ (2).   ⎪ born
Louis Riddle⁴ (1), second son of Samuel³ (2).   ⎬ in
Minnie-A. Riddle⁴ (1), third daughter of Samuel³ (2). ⎭ Minnesota.

Elizabeth-J. Riddle⁴ (3), a daughter of James³ (2). ⎫ Born in Minnesota,
Charles-N. Riddle⁴ (1), a son of James³ (2).   ⎭ unmarried.

Emma-J. Riddle⁴ (1), eldest daughter of Thomas³ (1), born in Forestville, Minn., in 1860; unmarried.

James-C. Riddle⁴ (5), eldest son of Thomas³ (1), born in 1863.

John-E. Riddle⁴ (5), second son of Thomas³ (1), born in 1871.

Frank-L. Riddle⁴ (1), third son of Thomas³ (1), born in 1873.

Laura-E. Riddle⁴ (1), second daughter of Thomas³ (1), born in 1876.

FIFTH GENERATION.   •

George Riddle⁵ (2), eldest son of James⁴ (3), born in Ohio, June 17, 1867.

Clark Riddle⁵ (1), second son of James⁴ (3), born in Pennsylvania, Oct. 10, 1873.

Emmet Riddle⁵ (1), third son of James⁴ (3), born in Minnesota, April 17, 1875.

---

* JAMES P. RIDDLE, of Forestville, Minn., writes that several sons of John Riddle, of Steubenville, O., live in Wellsburgh, Va.   He also says John Riddle, the ancestor, lived some time in Virginia.

RIDDLES OF MIFFLIN COUNTY, PENNSYLVANIA.

[SCOTCH-IRISH BRANCH.]

[It is presumed that this branch of the Riddle family is an offshoot of some other stock early settled in Pennsylvania; but no member of the family with whom I have corresponded can prove the connection. Doubtless some man will be able, when this book shall fall into his hands, to connect the several branch-families of Pennsylvania with one ancestry.]

FIRST GENERATION.

John Riddle¹ (1) is supposed to have been born somewhere in Mifflin County, Penn., but the names of his parents have not reached me. I do not find his name in the list of Revolutionary soldiers. His wife's name was Mary; they were married April 5, 1768, and had issue *thirteen* children, of whom hereafter. He was born in 1745.

SECOND GENERATION.

Elizabeth Riddle² (1), eldest daughter of John¹ (1), was born in Pennsylvania, Jan. 12, 1769.

Margaret Riddle² (1), a twin to Elizabeth² (1), was born Jan. 12, 1769.

Agnes Riddle² (1), third daughter of John¹ (1), was born in Pennsylvania, July 25, 1770; died April 13, 1776.

Susanna Riddle² (1), fourth daughter of John¹ (1), was born in Pennsylvania, March 6, 1774; married to James Mitchell.

Mary Riddle² (1), fifth daughter of John¹ (1), was born in Pennsylvania, March 6, 1776; died Dec. 5, 1778.

John Riddle² (2), eldest son of John¹ (1), was born in the State of Pennsylvania, April 13, 1778, and had issue *five* children, of whom more hereafter. His wife's name not known.

David Riddle² (1), second son of John¹ (1), was born in Mifflin County, Penn., April 20, 1780; married Mary Hamilton, of Ohio, and secondly, to Elizabeth Crocker. He removed from Pennsylvania to Ohio when young, and engaged in farming and stock-raising. In 1818 he emigrated to Illinois, and settled near St. Louis, in Washington County; from there, in October, 1822, he removed to Sangamon County, near Springfield, where he died Aug. 12, 1846, aged 66 years.

Mary Riddle² (2), sixth daughter of John¹ (1), was born in Pennsylvania, Oct. 16, 1781; married to Daniel Ruttan, and died Jan. 16, 1841, leaving issue.

Sarah Riddle² (1), seventh daughter of John¹ (1), was born in Pennsylvania, Dec. 1, 1783; married to John Smith, of Iowa.

Abner Riddle² (1), third son of John¹ (1), was born in the State of Pennsylvania, March 2, 1786, and reared a large family. His wife's name has not reached me.

Grace Riddle² (1), eighth daughter of John¹ (1), was born in Pennsylvania, Sept. 9, 1788; married to a Mr. Hurl, and died in September, 1817.

Jennie Riddle² (1), ninth daughter of John¹ (1), was born in Pennsylvania, Jan. 29, 1792; died in April, 1793.

William Riddle² (1), fourth son of John¹ (1), was born in Pennsylvania, April 4, 1772; married in 1794 to Jane Davidson; removed to Kentucky when young, and settled in Bourbon County. He removed thence to

Champaign County, O., in October, 1807, and died in the year 1818, having issue *seven* children.

THIRD GENERATION.

William Riddle³ (2).
Mary Riddle³ (3).
Abner Riddle³ (2). } Children of John Riddle² (2).
David Riddle³ (2).
Sarah Riddle³ (2).

John Riddle³ (3), eldest son of David² (1), was born in the town of Urbana, O., Jan. 8, 1809; married Sally-Han Clark, Oct. 2, 1834, and had issue *five* children, of whom hereafter. He married, secondly, Jan. 2, 1852, Martha Archer, and in 1873 was resident at Barclay, Ill., but in feeble health. Mr. Riddle was a farmer by vocation. *One* child by second wife.

James Riddle³ (1), second son of David² (1), was born at Urbana, O., April 23, 1810; married to Susan Simpson; was a farmer by vocation; died March 4, 1848, leaving issue *two* sons, of whom hereafter.

Margaret Riddle³ (2), eldest daughter of David² (1), was born at Urbana, O., Sept. 12, 1812; married to Joseph Dement.

Abner Riddle³ (3), third son of David² (1), was born at Urbana, O., Oct. 6, 1814; married Mary-Ann Pickells, and by her had *one* child. He married, secondly, Mary-Jane Clark, by whom there were *ten* children. He resides in Ottawa, Franklin County, Kan.; farmer by vocation; chairman of County Commissioners. A man of genial heart, strong mind, and excellent business capacity.

Nancy Riddle³ (1), second daughter of David² (1), was born in April, 1817; married to Abraham Bird, a farmer, and had issue. She died April 25, 1841.

Mary Riddle³ (4), third daughter of David² (1), was born in Urbana, O., May 12, 1819; married William H. Fawks, farmer.

Elizabeth Riddle³ (2), fourth daughter of David² (1), was born in July, 1822; married to Alexander Milles, a farmer.

Sarah Riddle³ (3), fifth daughter of David² (1), was born in November, 1825; married to the Rev. Alexander Semple, a presiding elder, and in 1873 lived at Decatur, Ill.

John Riddle³ (4), eldest son of William² (1), was born in Bourbon County, Ky., in 1795; married Ellen McKennison, of Vera, Ind., and had issue *four* children, of whom hereafter. Was a carpenter by trade. Died at Urbana, Champaign County, O., in 1828.

James Riddle³ (2), second son of William² (1), was born in Bourbon County, Ky., Feb. 15, 1801; married in 1822 to Mary A. McColloch (she was born Dec. 25, 1805, died Feb. 15, 1873), and by her had issue *seven* children, of whom hereafter. He was a saddler by trade. Died at Milford Centre, Union County, O., Aug. 3, 1863.

William Riddle³ (3), third son of William² (1), was born in Bourbon County, Ky., near a place called "Riddle's Station," in 1805; married Maximilia Bousman, July 13, 1826, and settled in Champaign County, O., where he continued to reside until 1839, when he removed to Sangamon County, Ill. He resided near Springfield until 1851, when he emigrated to Douglas County, Ore. When he emigrated with his family, he had a weary summer's march across the plains, moving slowly along with an ox-team. He found but few settlers in the southern part of Oregon. He went within one mile of the famous Lava Beds, and his train was completely surrounded by Modoc Indians, but finding the emigrants so well defended they did not make an attack upon them. On his way Mr. Riddle passed through the rich valley of Rogue's River, where there were no settlements. He pitched his tent in a beautiful, fertile valley called " Umpqua," on Cow Creek. No white man had made a mark in this valley when Mr. Riddle staked off his claim, and he found himself possessed of a valuable tract of land. Here he permanently settled, and reared a family. He was a blacksmith by trade ; has been a hard worker, industrious and frugal. His wife was well calculated to assist in a pioneer family ; she was tall, active, and armed with great fortitude and force of character; she died in August, 1868, leaving issue *eleven* children, of whom more hereafter.

Abner Riddle³ (4), fourth son of William² (1), was born in Bourbon County, Ky., in 1808; married April 17, 1831, to Clarissa Gooding ; she died in 1833, and he married, secondly, to Rebecca McGruder, and had issue *seven* children, of whom hereafter. He is a banker at Bellefontaine, O., and is said to be a man of fine personal appearance, and remarkable business capacity.

Nancy Riddle³ (2), eldest daughter of William² (1), was born in Bourbon County, Ky., in 1808 ; married to a Mr. Robinson, and lives at Lebanon, Boone County, Ind.

Polly Riddle³ (1), second daughter of William² (1), was born in Bourbon County, Ky., in 1810 ; died in 1814.

Jane Riddle³ (1), third daughter of William² (1), was born in Bourbon County, Ky., in 1812; married to Samuel Sherwood in 1830, and died in 1836, leaving issue.

FOURTH GENERATION.

Eliza Riddle⁴ (1), eldest daughter of John³ (3), was born in Illinois, July 1, 1835 ; deceased.

Mary-E. Riddle⁴ (5), second daughter of John³ (3), was born in Illinois, Dec. 9, 1838 ; was married to John M. Tomlinson.

Hon. Francis-Asbury Riddle⁴ (1), eldest son of John³ (3), was born in Barclay, Ill., March 19, 1843; was married to Sarah Galleher, and resides in Chicago, Ill. Mr. Riddle is a lawyer by profession ; has engaged largely in real-estate speculation ; served in the Illinois Legislature in 1878. A man of excellent legal ability, strong mind, and genial disposition.

Sarah-W. Riddle⁴ (4), third daughter of John³ (3), was born in Illinois, April 13, 1845, and lives at home.

John Riddle⁴ (5), second son of John³ (3), was born in Illinois, Feb. 29, 1849, and died young.

Nancy-E. Riddle⁴ (3), fourth daughter of John³ (3), was born in Barclay, Ill., Feb. 20, 1853, and is at home.

Rev. John Riddle⁴ (6), eldest son of James³ (1), was born in 1845; married.

David Riddle⁴ (3), second son of James³ (1), was born in 1847.

Dr. Hamilton-Rush Riddle⁴ (1), eldest son of Abner³ (3), was born in Sangamon County, Ill., Dec. 9, 1841 ; married Sept. 2, 1868, to C. F. Constant, and has *three* children, of whom hereafter. Doctor Riddle was educated in the district school, with the exception of two terms in the Illinois University, at Springfield, in the years 1862 and '65. He enlisted in Company B, One Hundred and Thirtieth Illinois Volunteer Infantry, in July, 1862, as a private; was sent to Memphis, Tenn., thence to Vicksburgh, Miss., and through the siege; from thence to the Gulf Department, under Gen. N. P. Banks; taken prisoner in the fight on Red River, and confined in prison at Tyler, Tex., fourteen months, being discharged in June, 1865. He commenced the study of medicine in the summer of 1866; attended two courses of lectures at Rush Medical College, Chicago, and graduated Doctor of Medicine, in the winter of 1873. Commenced the practice of his profession at Mechanicsburgh, Sangamon County, Ill., April 1, 1873, and now resides there. See his portrait in this work.

David-Allen Riddle[4] (4), second son of Abner[3] (3), was born in Sangamon County, Ill., Sept. 27, 1844; married to Hattie L. Rickey, Jan. 25, 1876 (she was born in Tioga, Tioga County, Penn., May 21, 1852), and has issue, of whom hereafter. Farmer in Franklin County, Kan.

Mary-Jane Riddle[4] (6), eldest daughter of Abner[3] (3), was born in Sangamon County, Ill., Dec. 3, 1846; was married to Samuel McColloch, and lives in Franklin County, Kan.

Russell-Oramel Riddle[4] (1), third son of Abner[3] (3), was born in Sangamon County, Ill., in 1848; married to Sabra Constant, and has issue, of whom hereafter. He is a farmer in his native County.

Henry-Clay Riddle[4] (1), fourth son of Abner[3] (3), was born in Sangamon County, Ill., in November, 1850, and lives at Denver, Col. A miller by occupation.

Julia-Maria Riddle[4] (1), second daughter of Abner[3] (3), was born in March, 1852.

Martha-Ellen Riddle[4] (1), third daughter of Abner[3] (3), was born in April, 1854.

Emma-Clark Riddle[4] (1), fourth daughter of Abner[3] (3), was born in April, 1856.

Ann-Eliza Riddle[4] (1), fifth daughter of Abner[3] (3), was born in June, 1858.

Willie-Lincoln Riddle[4] (1), fifth son of Abner[3] (3), was born Dec. 26, 1861.

Lizzie-Norton Riddle[4] (1), youngest daughter of Abner[3] (3), was born Nov. 4, 1864.

James Riddle[4] (3), eldest son of John[3] (4), was born June 6, 1819; married Nov. 24, 1840, to Jane Thompson, and settled at Chambersburgh, Penn. A tinner by trade. *Seven* children.

William Riddle[4] (4), second son of John[3] (4), was born at Urbana, O., Jan. 1, 1823; married July 24, 1842, to Louisa L., daughter of David and Sophia Hall, of Woodstock, O., where they continued to reside during their married life. He was a man of quiet, gentle manners and great kindness of heart. He was a tailor by trade; his education, common-school. Mr. Riddle died at the early age of 27 years, in April, 1851, having had issue *three* children, of whom hereafter.

Sarah Riddle[4] (5), eldest daughter of John[3] (4), was born at Urbana, O., Oct. 11, 1824; married to a Mr. Darling, a carpenter by trade; has issue, and lives at Mechanicsburgh, O.

John Riddle[4] (7), third son of John[3] (4), was born at Urbana, O.,

Dec. 8, 1826; married and died without issue in 1865. He was a tin-smith by trade.

William-H. Riddle⁴ (5), a son of James³ (2), was born at Milford, O., Aug. 25, 1826; a saddler by trade; died Sept. 15, 1865.

David Riddle⁴ (5), a son of James³ (2), was born at Milford, O., March 1, 1829; died Oct. 28, 1834.

Elizabeth Riddle⁴ (3), a daughter of James³ (2), was born at Milford, O., Dec. 3, 1831; died Nov. 28, 1862.

Edith Riddle⁴ (1), a daughter of James³ (2), was born in Milford, O. Aug. 3, 1836; died June 1, 1865.

Samuel Riddle⁴ (1), a son of James³ (2), was born in Milford Centre, Union County, O., June 29, 1839; died Aug. 25, 1842.

James Riddle⁴ (4), a son of James³ (2), was born in Milford, O., April 12, 1842; married Oct. 25, 1865, to Mary A. Andrews, at Pleasant Valley, O. A tinsmith by trade. Moved to Bates County, Mo., in 1868. *Four* children, of whom hereafter. Now engaged in stove, hardware, and grocery business, prosperously.

Henry Riddle⁴ (2), a son of James³ (2), was born in Milford, O., Aug. 26, 1846. A tinsmith by trade. Resided at Plain City, O., in 1879.

Jane Riddle⁴ (2), eldest daughter of William³ (3), was born in Champaign County, O., April 14, 1828; married Jan. 15, 1850, to Thomas Wilson, a Scotchman, and lives near Dawson, Sangamon County, Ill.

Artenecia Riddle⁴ (1), second daughter of William³ (3), was born in Champaign County, O., Oct. 11, 1830; married Feb. 22, 1849, to James Chapman, who died in the spring of 1851, just as they were ready to start for Oregon. Mrs. Chapman emigrated with her father, and subsequently married to William H. Merriman, of Jacksonville, Ore., where they resided in 1873, having a large family.

Isabella Riddle⁴ (1), third daughter of William³ (3), was born in Champaign County, O., Feb. 18, 1834; married to J. B. Nichols, a farmer, and has a large family. They live at Cow Creek, near Canyonville, Ore.

William Riddle⁴ (6), eldest son of William³ (3), was born in Champaign County, O., March 7, 1837, and died in Oregon, July 10, 1857; unmarried.

Hon. George-W. Riddle⁴ (1), second son of William³ (3), was born in Champaign County, O., Dec. 14, 1839; married April 20, 1865, to Anna M., daughter of Harrison and Martha-Ann Rice (she was born in Illinois, April 21, 1847, and died in Oregon, Sept. 19, 1876; an excellent woman), and had issue *three* children, of whom hereafter. He is a farmer and wool-grower. When only sixteen years old he was a volunteer Indian-fighter and scout, and was in situations "that tried the courage of the strongest men." He also acted as an interpreter in treating with the Indians. At the opening of the Rebellion he and his brother enlisted with the expectation of going South, but were employed on the frontier as scouts and escorts. Mr. Riddle was with the Superintendent of Indian Affairs, W. P. Huntington, at the first grand gathering of the blood-thirsty Modocs; the party (four men) met about two hundred, old and young, decked in hideous war-paint and ornaments; as fierce-looking as they could be. The old chief, "Sconchin,"—nearly a hundred years old,—was there and made a speech, in which he expressed disappointment in not receiving more blankets and tobacco from the "White Father." The party camped with the Indians on the night after the meeting, but Huntington complained that he could not sleep well. "Captain Jack," "Hookety Jim," and all the other chiefs that made themselves so famous in the "Lava Beds" afterwards, were present, and made arrangements for a grand pow-wow, to be held "two moons afterwards." He and brothers remained at home during the bloody Indian war of 1855–6, and built a stockade around their house; piercing the walls with loop-holes for muskets. He was reared with the rifle, and with two of his brothers was so good a shot that he could hit an Indian's eye at one hundred paces. He resides on the place where the family first sat down, in a valley among the mountains, which travelers say rivals Italy in beauty. Mr. Riddle is over six feet in height; has curly hair, and withal is a man of grand and formidable personal appearance.* He has been in the Legislature, and in every position to which he has been called by his country, or his constituency, he has fully sustained the confidence reposed in him.

Abner Riddle⁴ (5), third son of William⁸ (3), was born in Sangamon County, Ill., near Springfield, Oct. 27, 1842; married Alice-Cary, daughter of Harrison and Martha-Ann Rice, in 1865, and has issue *four* children, of whom hereafter. He is a farmer; a man of industrious habits, and a member of the Baptist Church. Early trained to frontier warfare and the use of the rifle, he has rendered much useful service as a scout and Indian-fighter. He served three years in the Union army during the late Rebellion, and was with Colonel Drew on his famous scout from Fort Klamath.

John-Bousman Riddle⁴ (8), fourth son of William⁸ (3), was born in Sangamon County, Ill., near Springfield, Nov. 9, 1844; married in 1864 to Jane Feathers, and has issue. His wife and child were drowned in the Umpqua River (Mr. Riddle was nearly drowned at the same time), and he subsequently married Mary-Frances Catchings, by whom he had (in 1873) *three* children; names unknown.

Ann-Maria Riddle⁴ (2), fourth daughter of William⁸ (3), was born in Sangamon County, Ill., near Springfield, April 13, 1847; was married to R. V. Bealle, of Jackson County, Ore., and lives on a farm there. She has issue.

Tobias-Stilley Riddle⁴ (1), fifth son of William⁸ (3), was born in Sangamon County, Ill., near Springfield, Aug. 30, 1849; married to Sarah Smyth, and had issue (in 1873) *two* children. The wife's half of the old "Donation Claim" was willed to Tobias, and after his mother's death he sold out to his brother, George W. Riddle, and removed to Fort Henry, Ore., where he is engaged in cattle-raising.

Clara-Allie Riddle⁴ (1), youngest daughter of William⁸ (3), was born in Oregon, April 8, 1853; died Oct. 10, 1855.

Clara Riddle⁴ (2), eldest daughter of Abner² (4), was born Feb. 25, 1832; married in September, 1850, to Ira W. Gorton; he died in 1871, and Mrs. Gorton married Oct. 10, 1872, to Judge William H. West.

Llewellyn Riddle⁴ (1), eldest son of Abner² (4), was born July 9, 1834, and died March 16, 1856; unmarried. He was a saddler by trade.

John-M. Riddle⁴ (9), second son of Abner² (4), was born May 29, 1836; married Jan. 1, 1868, to Maggie-Johnson, daughter of Rev. Samuel

---

* All the sons of William are full six feet in height: George W. is six feet four and a half inches.

Wallace, of Piqua, O., and has *two* children. Mr. Riddle is a banker at Bellefontaine, O.

Elizabeth Riddle⁴ (4), second daughter of Abner³ (4), was born Sept. 2, 1838, and died March 12, 1857; unmarried.

Cynthia Riddle⁴ (1), third daughter of Abner³ (4), was born Oct. 13, 1840; died Dec. 16, 1863; unmarried.

William Riddle⁴ (7), third son of Abner³ (4), was born Sept. 29, 1843, and fell at the battle of Chickamauga, Sept. 19, 1863, in charge of a company of advance skirmishers.

Guenn Riddle⁴ (1), fourth son (?) of Abner³ (4), was born Nov. 7, 1845, and died Dec. 3, 1867; unmarried.

FIFTH GENERATION.

Earl-Arthur Riddle⁵ (1), eldest son of Hamilton⁴ (1), was born at Mechanicsburgh, Ill., July 18, 1869.

Lillie-May Riddle⁵ (1), eldest daughter of Hamilton⁴ (1), was born at Mechanicsburgh, Ill., May 15, 1872.

William-Elkin Riddle⁵ (8), second son of Hamilton⁴ (1), was born at Mechanicsburgh, Ill., March 7, 1874.

Rolland-Abner Riddle⁵ (1), son of David⁴ (4), was born at Ottawa, Kan., Nov. 7, 1876.

Orlando-Thompson Riddle⁵ (1), eldest son of James⁴ (3), was born at Chambersburgh, Penn., Oct. 20, 1840; died March 7, 1842.

William-Jenison Riddle⁵ (9), second son of James⁴ (3), was born at Chambersburgh, Penn., March 7, 1843; died June 7, 1843.

Stephen-Wheeler Riddle⁵ (1), third son of James⁴ (3), was born at Chambersburgh, Penn., Sept. 29, 1844, and resides in Springfield, O. Tinsmith by trade.

Mary-Ellen Riddle⁵ (7), eldest daughter of James⁴ (3), was born at Chambersburgh, Penn., June 30, 1848.

Charles-Miller Riddle⁵ (1), fourth son of James⁴ (3), was born at Chambersburgh, Penn., Dec. 11, 1851; died same year.

John-Curtis Riddle⁵ (10), fifth son of James⁴ (3), was born at Chambersburgh, Penn., March 26, 1852; died June 13, 1859.

Versalous-Graham Riddle⁵ (1), sixth son of James⁴ (3), was born in Chambersburgh, Penn., Nov. 13, 1858.

Ellen-S. Riddle⁵ (1), eldest daughter of William⁴ (4), was born at Woodstock, O., July 9, 1843; was married March 24, 1859, to George W. Standish, youngest son of Rev. Miles and Annie Standish, of New York city.

George Riddle⁵ (2), eldest son of William⁴ (4), was born at Woodstock, O., Feb. 26, 1845; married April 21, 1869, to Ida Carlton, only child of Rev. S. P. and Linnina Carlton, of Springfield, O., and has issue *two* children, of whom hereafter. He spent the first seventeen years of his life on a farm and at school. When eighteen years old joined the Ninety-fifth Ohio Volunteer Infantry, Company G, Aug. 3, 1862; mustered into service Aug. 19, and engaged in battle of Richmond, Ky., Aug. 30, 1862; was severely wounded near the close of the battle, receiving two wounds, one through the left arm and one through the body, the ball entering the left side, passing directly through, and coming out a little to the left of the spine; was taken prisoner, remaining in the hands of the Rebels about three weeks, when he escaped, riding eighty-five miles in an ambulance-wagon, and one hundred and fifty miles by boat to Cincinnati, O. He remained at home about two years, then joined the One Hundred and Thirty-fourth Regiment, serving three months in Virginia. Received a commercial education, and fitted himself for the banking business, which he has since followed. His wounds disabling him for work, he received a pension for life. Mr. Riddle is a man of good business capacity, and served as Justice of the Peace for nine years. He is a member of the Universalist Church, and is strictly temperate in his habits.

Dennis-T. Riddle[5] (1), second son of William[4] (4), was born at Woodstock, O., July 3, 1849; married July 14, 1872, to Etta, daughter of Oliver and Sarah Ewing, of East Liberty, O., and has issue *two* children, of whom hereafter.

Willie-A. Riddle[5] (2), eldest son of James[4] (4), was born at Pleasant Valley, O., Aug. 20, 1866.

Cassius-E. Riddle[5] (1), second son of James[4] (4), was born at Pleasant Valley, O., Jan. 15, 1868.

Edith-M. Riddle[5] (2), daughter of James[4] (4), was born at Butler, Mo., Nov. 29, 1869.

Burdett-S. Riddle[5] (1), third son of James[4] (4), was born at Butler, Mo., Oct. 28, 1872.

Della-Evalyn Riddle[5] (1), eldest daughter of George[4] (1), was born in Douglas County, Ore., Feb. 6, 1866.

George-Rice Riddle[5] (3), eldest son of George[4] (1), was born in Douglas County, Ore., July 23, 1868.

Clara-Helen Riddle[5] (3), second daughter of George[4] (1), was born in Douglas County, Kan., April 4, 1871.

Ernest-Donnald Riddle[5] (1), son of Abner[4] (5), was born in Douglas County, Ore., Dec. 9, 1866.

Maude-Agnes Riddle[5] (1), eldest daughter of Abner[4] (5), was born in Douglas County, Ore., Oct. 31, 1868.

Grace-Isabella Riddle[5] (2), second daughter of Abner[4] (5), was born in Douglas County, Ore., April 15, 1871.

Blanch-Eglantine Riddle[5] (1), third daughter of Abner[4] (5), was born in Douglas County, Ore., Aug. 22, 1873.

Carrie-Lucinda Biddle[5] (4), eldest daughter of Tobias[4] (1), was born in Douglas County, Ore., in August, 1869.

Walter-Scott Riddle[5] (1), eldest son of Tobias[4] (1), was born in Douglas County, Ore., in August, 1871.

William-Wallace Riddle[5] (10), eldest son of John[4] (9), was born at Bellefontaine, O., Sept. 29, 1869.

Maggie-Gorton Riddle[5] (1), eldest daughter of John[4] (9), was born at Bellefontaine, O., Dec. 9, 1870.

RIDDLES OF HOLMES COUNTY, OHIO.

[SCOTCH-IRISH BRANCH].

Alexander Riddle[1] (1), parents' names unknown, was born in the village of Vallskill, parish of Calldoff, Barony of Eneshone, County of Donegal, Province of Ulster, Ireland; married Margaret Riddell (or Riddle), daughter of Robert and Margaret Wilson (see "Riddells of Lycoming County, Pennsylvania "), and had issue, of whom hereafter. He died about 1812.

SECOND GENERATION.

John Riddle[2] (1), a son of Alexander[1] (1), was born in Eneshone, County Donegal, Ireland, June 10, 1775; married Oct. 28, 1808, to Jane Steel, and had issue several children, of whom hereafter. He emigrated from the city of Londonderry, Ireland, on the ship "Eagle," James Killpatrick, master, July 27, 1797, and landed at Philadelphia the following October. He resided in the latter city, and superintended a department of the work on the water-works there; he subsequently removed to Pittsburgh, where he tarried a few years; thence went to Holmes County, O., and thence, in 1854, to Fulton County. He was a man of medium size, strong constitution, active temperament, kind to friends, quick to resent an insult, intelligent, and reliable. He died July 26, 1863, aged 88 years.

THIRD GENERATION.

Nathaniel Riddle[3] (1), twin son of John[2] (1), was born in Pittsburgh (?), Penn., Aug. 16, 1810; married Sarah Armstrong; secondly, Rachel Clark. He resides near Wauseon, O.; has issue *seven* children, of whom hereafter. Farmer by occupation.

Alexander Riddle[3] (2), twin son of John[2] (1), was born in Pennsylvania, Aug. 16, 1810, and died when about one year old.

Thomas Riddle[3] (1), third son of John[2] (1), was born in Pittsburgh, Penn., in 1812, and died in 1813.

James Riddle[3] (1), fourth son of John[2] (1), was born in Pittsburgh, Penn., June 29, 1813; married Nov. 21, 1833, to Matilda Siddons, and had issue *six* children, of whom hereafter. He removed from Holmes County to Fulton County, O., in 1845, and was one of the first settlers there; has filled many positions of responsibility in town and county; is a man of sound mind and business capacity.

John Riddle[3] (2), fifth son of John[2] (1), was born somewhere in Pennsylvania, Aug. 23, 1815; went to New Orleans in 1833, and was never afterwards heard from.

Charles Riddle[3] (1), youngest son of John[2] (1), was born Aug. 24, 1828, and lives at Valparaiso, Penn.

Margaret Riddle[3] (1), twin sister of Charles[3] (1), was born Aug. 24, 1828 ; was married and has a family living.

FOURTH GENERATION.

Sarah Riddle[4] (1), eldest daughter of Nathaniel[3] (1), was born in Fulton County, O., July 4, 1848.

Mary Riddle[4] (1), second daughter of Nathaniel[3] (1), was born in Fulton County, O., Jan. 7, 1850 ; deceased.

Martin Riddle[4] (1), eldest son of Nathaniel[3] (1), was born in Fulton County, O., Aug. 30, 1851.

Mary Riddle[4] (2), third daughter of Nathaniel[3] (1), was born in Fulton County, O., Feb. 28, 1854.

John Riddle[4] (3), second son of Nathaniel[3] (1), was born in Fulton County, O., Nov. 30, 1855.

Nancy Riddle[4] (1), fourth daughter of Nathaniel[3] (1), was born in Fulton County, O., Oct. 28, 1857.

James Riddle[4] (2), third son of Nathaniel[3] (1), was born in Fulton County, O., Nov. 29, 1859.

John-Q. Riddle[4] (4), eldest son of James[3] (1), was born in Holmes County, O., Oct. 21, 1833; married Feb. 9, 1863, to Mary Seeple, and had issue (1873) *two* children, of whom hereafter. He carries on an extensive business in hardware, tin-ware, and agricultural machinery; also, insurance agent at Wauseon, O. Has been very successful. Manifested a deep interest in this book; has furnished records, and a fine portrait in steel, which see. A man of active, public spirit, excellent business parts, and genial nature. Has been in the State Legislature. Traveled extensively in Europe.

Charles Riddle[4] (2), second son of James[3] (1), was born in Holmes County, O., Jan. 14, 1838; married Phebe Ely, and has issue. He is a merchant at Pioneer, O.

Thomas-H. Riddle[4] (2), third son of James[3] (1), was born in Holmes County, O., May 24, 1840, and is now (1878) a merchant in the dry- and fancy-goods business at Terre Haute, Ind. He was in the Union army during the Rebellion; was captured at Harper's Ferry, and released on parole. An active, progressive man.

James Riddle[4] (3), fourth son of James[3] (1), was born in Fulton County, O., Sept. 7, 1847; married in September, 1873, to Maude M. Joy, and was in the insurance business at Wauseon, O., in 1873.

Mary Riddle[4] (3), a daughter of James[3] (1), was born in Holmes (or Fulton) County, O., and was married to Charles Hibbard, a farmer; resides at Ledrow, O.

Louisa Riddle[4] (1), a daughter of James[3] (1), was born in Holmes (or Fulton) County, O., and was married to Willard Letcher, a merchant of Wauseon, O.

FIFTH GENERATION.

Ida Riddle[5] (1), eldest daughter of John[4] (4), was born at Wauseon, O., in March, 1864.

Arthur Riddle[5] (1), eldest son of John[4] (4), was born at Wauseon, O., in March, 1866.

Florence Riddle[5] (1), a daughter of Charles[4] (2), was born at Pioneer, O.

RIDDLES OF DAYTON, OHIO.

[SCOTCH-IRISH BRANCH.]

James Riddle[1] (1), parents and connection not known, was born (probably in Ohio) Jan. 14, 1789; married at Beaver Creek, O., Sept. 30, 1812, to Isabella —— (she was born Jan. 17, 1795, and in January, 1873, was at Dayton, O.), and had issue *ten* children, of whom hereafter. He served

J. Z. Riddle

from July 4, 1812, to April 13, 1813, under Capt. William Perry, in the "Ohio Rangers"; also from Dec. 14, 1813, to Dec. 14, 1814, on the Wabash River, in Indiana, being stationed at Vincennes. He died Aug. 14, 1854.

SECOND GENERATION.

Elizabeth Riddle[2] (1), eldest daughter of James[1] (1), was born (presumably in Ohio) Feb. 8, 1813, and was married July 6, 1834, to William Keller.

Emily-Ann Riddle[2] (1), second daughter of James[1] (1), was born June 27, 1816, and was married to William Henderson.

Isabella Riddle[2] (1), third daughter of James[1] (1), was born June 24, 1820, and was married Nov. 6, 1844, to Robert McConnell.

Abigail Riddle[2] (1), fourth daughter of James[1] (1), was born Nov. 21, 1822, and was married Feb. 25, 1840, to Jacob Criner.

James-W. Riddle[2] (2), eldest son of James[1] (1), was born Feb. 21, 1824. No other information available.

E.-B.-A. Riddle[2] (1), child of James[1] (1), was born July 11, 1827.

Jane Riddle[2] (1), fifth daughter of James[1] (1), was born Sept. 24, 1830; was married Dec. 28, 1852, to William Bennett.

Mary Riddle[2] (1), sixth daughter of James[1] (1), was born Nov. 19, 1832, and was married Nov. 18, 1852, to John Minasters.

Margaret Riddle[2] (1), supposed daughter of James[1] (1), was born Feb. 8, 1818.*

Ann-Martha Riddle[2] (1), supposed daughter of James[1] (1), was born April 6, 1835.

---·•·---

RIDDLES OF DETROIT, MICHIGAN.

[SCOTTISH BRANCH.]

Andrew Riddle[1] (1), parents' names unknown, emigrated from Scotland to the United States in 1836, with his family, and died in Michigan. Have not learned the place of his nativity.†

SECOND GENERATION.

Elizabeth Riddle[2] (1), eldest daughter of Andrew[1] (1), was born in Scotland, in 1811, and died in Michigan in 1874.

Isabella Riddle[2] (1), second daughter of Andrew[1] (1), was born in Scotland, in 1818, and resides in the State of Iowa.

Andrew Riddle[2] (2), eldest son of Andrew[1] (1), was born in Scotland, in 1815; settled in Michigan, and has issue, of whom hereafter. His wife's name does not appear.

---

* The names of Margaret and Ann-Martha are copied from the bottom of the same page of the Pension Records at Washington, on which the children of James are found; and as the dates of births correspond with spaces in the records of that family, they undoubtedly were omitted from their proper place when the others were recorded.

† I am informed that the eldest daughter of Andrew Riddle, Sr., married William McPherson, a Scotchman; a prominent merchant and banker of Howell, Mich.

William Riddle[2] (1), second son of Andrew[1] (1), was born in Scotland, in 1818; married Mary D. King in 1845, and is now a fur-dealer in Detroit, Mich.

Margaret Riddle[2] (1), third daughter of Andrew[1] (1), was born in Scotland, in 1821, and resides in Michigan.

Alexander Riddle[2] (1), third son of Andrew[1] (1), was born in Scotland, in 1824, and died in the service of the United States in 1865.

THIRD GENERATION.

William Riddle[3] (2), a son of Andrew[2] (2), was born in 1835, resides in Michigan, and has issue, of whom hereafter. His wife's name does not appear.

Nelson Riddle[3] (1), eldest son of William[2] (1), was born in Michigan in 1846; married Ella F. Dwyer in 1875, and has issue, of whom hereafter. He is a merchant in Detroit, Mich., — dealer in hats, caps, and furs.

William-E. Riddle[3] (3), second son of William[2] (1), was born in Michigan in 1858; merchant in Detroit, Mich.

Florence-S. Riddle[3] (1), eldest daughter of William[2] (1), was born in Michigan in 1854, and lives in Detroit.

Rose-I. Riddle[3] (1), second daughter of William[2] (1), was born in Michigan in 1856, and lives at home in Detroit.

FOURTH GENERATION.

Frederick-N. Riddle[4] (1), son of Nelson[3] (1), was born in Detroit, Mich., in 1876.

RIDDLES OF CALEDONIA, ILLINOIS.

[SCOTCH-IRISH BRANCH.]

[The ancestors of this family cannot be traced. The author has spent more time and money in correspondence and advertising in search of records of Capt. James Riddle's parents, than in tracing any other family of the name. It seems a little singular that Mrs. Ormstead does not know the names of her grandparents. The most plausible traditions point to Judge James Riddle of Chambersburgh, Penn., as a relative, and Captain Riddle may have been his cousin. The names James, John, and David occur in so many families of Riddle, that great confusion is occasioned in placing them. Rev. David H. Riddle, D. D., of Martinsburgh, Va., could undoubtedly give the names of the parents of Captain Riddle, but he is not disposed to impart information. An old gentleman in Covington, Ky., who knew Captain Riddle while engaged in business in Cincinnati, O., says the father's name was Hezekiah Riddle, born in Crawford County, Va.; that he settled in Columbia, Hamilton County, O., where he continued during life. Another writer says Capt. James Riddle was born at Carlisle, Penn. I must leave the ancestral history of this family,— though unwillingly, — in obscurity till some venerable relative shall read this book and supply the missing names and unknown alliances.]

Capt. James Riddle² (1), is said to have been born in Cumberland County, Penn., April 27, 1769; he married Dec. 22, 1808, Lydia Chamberlain, in Hamilton County, O., the ceremony being performed by the Rev. Joshua Wilson, M. A. He had issue by this woman. He married, secondly, about 1819, Esther, daughter of Henry and Rebecca Daniels (she was born Nov. 8, 1800); the ceremony was performed in Cincinnati, O., by Rev. Dr. Wilson, of the Presbyterian Church. Captain Riddle settled in Cincinnati as early as 1800, and was extensively engaged in business there in 1803. In 1815 or 1816, he purchased a large farm in what is now the northwest part of Covington, Ky., sold by the United States Bank to satisfy a mortgage; built him a good house on his land, on what is now Main Street, near the Ohio River; he afterwards erected a still-house at Willow Run, on his farm; this property was sold to —— Bakewell. He ran a steamboat between Cincinnati and New Orleans for many years; was an owner in the packet called the "Kentucky," — probably the first boat propelled by steam on the western rivers. He was some time commander of steamer "Scioto Valley"; was member of an importing firm at Cincinnati; president of the Miami Exporting Company; owned barges and keel-boats, and valuable real-estate in Cincinnati. He was owner of five hundred acres of land between Newport, Ky., and the ferry between Newport and Cincinnati.

Captain Riddle had an idea that the best site for a large city was near the mouth of the Ohio River, and consequently, with several other adventurers, purchased extensive lands there, — an enterprise that proved the great mistake of his life; for, although towns were laid out, roads built, buildings erected, and for a time the prospect seemed flattering, the settlement could not be sustained; the property deteriorated in value, and the whole undertaking proved disastrous to the owners. Captain Riddle carried on business in Cincinnati up to 1829, and in 1830 moved his family to a farm near Caledonia, Boone County, Ill. He had previously sent down a house for a dwelling, ready framed, and a store-house for the new town, where business was conducted by his partner and nephew, John Skiles. Mr. Riddle died in the midst of undeveloped plans and improvements, leaving a great quantity of land, mostly unimproved. He was a real specimen of the adventurer of early days; a man of great energy of character and remarkable business capacity; he was fine-looking, portly, dignified, and commanding, and moreover very attractive and influential in business circles. His death occurred in 1832. The old Riddle mansion-house is now owned by the Rev. E. B. Ormstead, who married a daughter of Mr. Riddle, and is said to be a splendid place. There is a beautiful cemetery on the homestead, where several members of the family are buried. The profile of Captain Riddle was drawn by an artist, while he (Mr. Riddle) was standing on a pavement in Cincinnati, talking with a friend, in 1831.

David Riddle² (1), a brother of Captain James, before mentioned, is not known to have had a family; indeed very little can be found concerning him. His name is found on a receipt running to his brother James, dated "Mercersburgh, April 10, 1795." This was for land in Chambersburgh, Penn. Some say David died single when quite young. His name is not found in the Bible-records with his sisters'. I have patiently investigated the matter in Chambersburgh and Mercersburgh, but can find nothing reliable about this David.

Mary Riddle² (1), eldest sister of Captain James, before mentioned, was born Dec. 17, 1767, and married James Skiles; their son, John Skiles, was in business with his uncle, James Riddle. There was a daughter who married —— King, of Mercersburgh, Penn., and one who married Doctor Patta, and settled on land inherited from her brother, in Caledonia, Boone County, Ill.

Elizabeth Riddle² (1), second sister of Captain James, before mentioned, was born Sept. 15, 1782, and married a Mr. Rutter, probably in Mercersburgh, Penn. She visited her brother James, when he was living at Covington, Ky. There were probably other children between Mary and Elizabeth; or they may have had two mothers; there was fifteen years' difference in their (the sisters') ages. Mrs. Rutter died without issue.

THIRD GENERATION.

John Riddle³ (1), eldest son of Capt. James² (1) and his wife Lydia, was born in Cincinnati, O., May 4, 1804, and was a man of splendid education and ability. He was a professional steamboat-engineer, and was much with his father on the Ohio River. He died away from home (probably at New Orleans) when young, unmarried.

Harriet Riddle³ (1), eldest daughter of James² (1) and his first wife, was born March 18, 1814, and died March 5, 1826.

Mary Riddle³ (2), eldest daughter of James²(1) by his second wife, was born in Cincinnati, O., Oct. 6, 1820; married July 10, 1839, to Rev. E. B. Ormstead, and resides on her father's old homestead at Caledonia, Ill.

James Riddle³ (2), eldest son of James² (1) by his second wife, was born at Cincinnati, O., March 16, 1822; married Elizabeth Moore, and died without issue, Oct. 16, 1851.

Dr. Henry-D. Riddle³ (1), second son of James² (1) by his second wife, was born at Covington, Ky., Feb. 16, 1824; married Minerva, daughter of Jacob Musselman, of Metropolis, Oct. 24, 1849, and had issue, of whom hereafter. He received his education at Cincinnati and Belleville, O., and studied medicine with Dr. S. S. Condon, of McLeansborough. Doctor Riddle settled down to practice at Caledonia, where he was very successful; he was a man of good ability, and extraordinary energy in the accomplishment of any chosen purpose. He was one of the original members of Caledonia Masonic lodge, and some weeks before his death, united with the Presbyterian Church, on profession of faith. He died at his residence, Oct. 15, 1871, — Sabbath evening.

Hester Riddle³ (1), second daughter of James² (1) and his second wife, was born at Covington, Ky., Sept. 5, 1826; married Henry Hughes, had issue, and died Oct. 9, 1851.

Charles-Kilgore Riddle³ (1), third son of James² (1) by his second wife, was born at Covington, Ky., Jan. 25, 1828, and died at the age of 10 years.

Margaret Riddle³ (1), third daughter of James² (1) by his second wife, was born at Caledonia, Ill., July 31, 1832, and died Sept. 12, 1834.

FOURTH GENERATION.

Mary Riddle⁴ (3), eldest daughter of Henry³ (1), was born at Caledonia, Ill., March 28, 1852; married July 4, 1872, to Benjamin Echols, and has issue.

Henry-M. Riddle⁴ (2), eldest son of Henry³ (1), was born at Caledonia, Jan. 3, 1855; a farmer, unmarried.

Sarah-S. Riddle⁴ (1), second daughter of Henry⁸ (1), was born at Caledonia, Sept. 5, 1861; unmarried.

Minnie-M. Riddle⁴ (1), third daughter of Henry⁸ (1), was born at Caledonia, Feb. 19, 1866; unmarried.

Jennie-D. Riddle⁴ (1), fourth daughter of Henry⁸ (1), was born at Caledonia, Dec. 23, 1869.

RIDDELLS OF BRUNSWICK COUNTY, VIRGINIA.
[SCOTTISH BRANCH.]

Thomas Riddell¹ (1), parents' names unknown, came from Scotland or England to Virginia at an early day, — long previous to the American Revolution, — and settled in Brunswick County, where he had grants of land. He married Polly Dean, and had issue *four* sons (and probably daughters), of whom hereafter. I believe this family connected with other families whose pedigrees are found in this book, but I cannot prove the relation.

Fountain Riddell¹ (1), a brother of the preceding, was a resident of Scotland or England. I find this very peculiar Christian name in the family in Kentucky, who trace their ancestry to an early settler of Virginia.

SECOND GENERATION.

Thomas Riddell² (2), a son of Thomas¹ (1), was born in Brunswick County, Va., about 1755; married Polly, daughter of Col. Charles Williamson, of the same County, and had issue *ten* children, of whom hereafter. He was a soldier of the Revolution, and lived many years afterwards.

Elisha Riddell² (1), a son of Thomas¹ (1), was born in Brunswick County, Va., about 1757, and was a soldier of the Revolution. He lived many years after the war, and had issue.

Reese Riddell² (1), a son of Thomas¹ (1), was born in Brunswick County, Va., about 1759, and was killed in the Revolution.

Hardy Riddell² (1), a son of Thomas¹ (1), was born in Brunswick County, Va., about 1760, and was killed in the Revolution.

THIRD GENERATION.

Thomas Riddle³ (3), eldest son of Thomas² (2), was born in Brunswick County, Va., Oct. 16, 1780; married Rebecca Riddle, his second cousin, and had issue *four* sons (possibly daughters), of whom hereafter. He settled in the State of Illinois more than seventy years ago (1808,) and is now (1879) living at Fitts Hill, Franklin County, at the great age of ninety-nine years, and can ride horse-back almost as well as a young man. His memory is growing weak, and he cannot recall all family names.

William Riddle³ (1), second son of Thomas² (2), was born in Brunswick County, Va.

Henry Riddell³ (1), third son of Thomas² (2), was born in Brunswick County, Va.

Roland Riddle³ (1), fourth son of Thomas² (2), was born in Brunswick County, Va.

John Riddle[3] (2), fifth son of Thomas[2] (2), was born in Brunswick County, Va.

Reese Riddle[3] (2), sixth son of Thomas[2] (2), was born in Brunswick County, Va.

Hardy Riddle[3] (2), seventh son of Thomas[2] (2), was born in Brunswick County, Va.

Rebecca Riddle[3] (1).
Peggy Riddle[3] (1). } Daughters of Thomas[2] (2), born in Brunswick County, Va.
Polly Riddle[3] (1).

FOURTH GENERATION.

John Riddle[4] (3), a son of Thomas[3] (3), was born in Franklin County, Ill.; deceased.

William Riddle[4] (2), second son of Thomas[3] (3), was born in Franklin County, Ill.; living in Alabama.

Nathaniel Riddle[4] (1), third son of Thomas[3] (3), was born in Franklin County, Ill.; resides at Fitts Hill.

Thomas Riddle[4] (4), fourth son of Thomas[3] (3), was born in Franklin County, Ill.; living in Cherokee County, Tex.

RIDDELLS OF LAUREL HILL, VIRGINIA.

[ENGLISH BRANCH.]

Col. George Riddell[1] (1), parents' names unknown, was descended from a family of Riddells who, with the Byrds, came over from England in their own vessels, bringing their cattle, farm-implements, plate, furniture, and servants with them. This family first landed at Philadelphia (or near), on the Schuylkill River; some of them afterwards settled in Virginia, where they purchased a large tract of land and became wealthy planters. The subject of this notice located in Shenandoah County, at Laurel Hill, which property has been in the family ever since.* They suffered almost beyond comprehension from the Indians during early days, and the women as well as the men were noted for their courage. A rifle with which one of the mothers kept at bay a number of Indians, and saved herself and children, is still in the Riddell family. Judge Byrd has never seen on record that Laurel Hill has been owned by others. Colonel Riddell resided at Red Banks at one time. A George Riddell received a grant of three hundred and forty acres of land in Henrico County, Va., March 10, 1756. Colonel Riddell married a Miss Bird, and had issue, of whom hereafter. He fought for freedom in the Revolution. Date of death unknown.

Cornelius Riddell[1] (1), brother of Colonel George[1] (1), was a resident of Shenandoah County, Va.

---

* There was a Philip Riddell attending medical lectures in Washington, D. C., a very intelligent young man, who expressed deep interest in this family history, and promised the author full data of the Laurel Hill Riddells, — he and mother, Mrs. Rebecca Riddell, were then living on the old Riddell Farm, — but failed to do so. There are numerous descendants on the female side, all well connected by marriage with the old and respected Virginian families.

SECOND GENERATION.

James Riddell[2] (1), son of George[1] (1), was born at Red Banks, Shenandoah County; married Rebecca ——, and had issue, of whom hereafter.

Mary-Ann Riddell[2] (1), daughter of George[1] (1), was born at Red Banks, Shenandoah County, Va., and lived with her uncle, Cornelius Riddell, after the death of her parents, until her marriage with Francis Sibert, of New Market, by whom she had *seven* children, four sons and three daughters. This woman was christened about the year 1772, by Peter Muhlenburg, the distinguished Lutheran divine, soldier, and statesman, and while he was performing the solemn rite, she slapped him in the face.

RIDDELLS OF PITTSYLVANIA COUNTY, VIRGINIA.

Zachariah Riddell[1] (1) lived in Albemarle County, Va., but from whence he came, whom he married, or when he deceased, is not known. His Christian name is not in any known branch of the Southern families of Riddell or Riddle. One correspondent writes by dictation of the late Ephraim Riddle, of Warrenton, Mo., that this ancestor came from Maryland to Virginia, and that he was a native of England or Ireland. If Ephraim's statement be correct, his grandfather lived in Loudoun County, Va., where he and his father were born. He had *three* children, and probably others whose names do not appear.

SECOND GENERATION.

John Riddle[2] (1), son of Zachariah[1] (1), was born in Loudoun County, Va., and had *three* sons, of whom hereafter. No record of birth or death.

THIRD GENERATION.

James-A. Riddle[3] (1), eldest son of John[2] (1), was born in Pittsylvania County, Va., in 1801 ; married Nancy A. ——, and had issue, of whom hereafter. He was called one of Virginia's best citizens. Died in 1843.

Ephraim Riddle[3] (1), second son of John[2] (1), was born in Pittsylvania County, Va., Feb. 7, 1803 ; married, Dec. 22, 1822, to Judith Graveley, and had issue *eight* children, of whom hereafter. He removed to Lincoln County, Mo., in 1838, where he lived one year, and then settled on a farm at Warrenton, in Warren County, where he lived till his death, April 15, 1874. He is represented as having been a true man in all the relations of life, a loving husband, kind and indulgent father, a sturdy and true friend and neighbor, carrying out in all he did the maxim, "Whatsoever ye would that men should do unto you, do ye even so unto them."

John Riddle[3] (2), third son of John[2] (1), was born in Pittsylvania County, Va., Feb. 14, 1804; married, and had issue *four* children. He married secondly, Martha P. Myers, and by her,—who was burned to death with one of her children in their house, Feb. 2, 1866,—had *five* children, of whom (with the other children) hereafter. Mr. Riddle escaped from his burning house in Carroll County, Va., where he resided, and died April 22, 1879, near Thorn Hill, Granger County, Tenn. He married a third wife named Mahaly Coke, by whom he had *one* son. Five sons were in the Confederate army.

Polina Riddle³ (1), only known daughter of John² (1), was the wife of Washington Johnson. No particulars.

FOURTH GENERATION.

V.-H. Riddle⁴ (1), eldest son of James³ (1), was born in Pittsylvania County, Va., April 17, 1823; married Margaret Boolling (she was born in Virginia, Dec. 2, 1834), in Georgia, Nov. 8, 1854, and had issue *ten* children, of whom hereafter. He resides at Pine Log, Bartow County, Ga., whither he removed in 1853, and where he has a farm.

Jane Riddle⁴ (1), eldest daughter of James³ (1), was born in Pittsylvania County, Va., in 1826, and became Mrs. Tayler, of Fair Mount, Ga.; has issue.

James-W. Riddle⁴ (2), second son of James³ (1), was born in Pittsylvania County, Va., Nov. 28, 1828; married and has issue *nine* children, of whom hereafter. He is a farmer living at Fair Mount, Ga.

John-H. Riddle⁴ (3), a son of James³ (1), was born in Pittsylvania County, Va., and resides (post-office address) Callands, in said County.

Frances-A. Riddle⁴ (1), eldest daughter of Ephraim³ (1), was born in Pittsylvania County, Va., Sept. 23, 1827; was married Sept. 7, 1848, to Henry Hutcherson, of Warren County, Mo.; farmer, and had *eleven* children. Husband died Feb. 19, 1881.

Elizabeth-Eleanor Riddle⁴ (1), second daughter of Ephraim³ (1), was born in Pittsylvania County, Va., Oct. 12, 1829; was married April 4, 1850, to Levi J. Garrett, farmer, of Warren County, Mo. She died Oct. 18, 1861, having had *five* children.

Jabez-Leftroich Riddle⁴ (1), eldest son of Ephraim³ (1), was born in Pittsylvania County, Va., Nov. 19, 1831; married in September, 1862, to Nancy·E. Buxton. No children. Farmer in Warren County, Mo.

Sallie-Jane Riddle⁴ (1), third daughter of Ephraim³ (1), was born in Pittsylvania County, Va., April 29, 1835; was married Nov. 4, 1852, to James Hutcherson, of Warren County, Mo., farmer, and has had *nine* children.

William-Purkins Riddle⁴ (1), second son of Ephraim³ (1), was born in Pittsylvania County, Va., Nov. 30, 1837; married in June, 1863, to Carry Moore. No issue. He is a farmer in Warren County, Mo.

James-Harrison Riddle⁴ (3), third son of Ephraim³ (1), was born in Warren County, Mo., Dec. 3, 1840; died July 19, 1878, unmarried; farmer.

Martha-Susanna Riddle⁴ (1), fourth daughter of Ephraim³ (1), was born in Warren County, Mo., Feb. 16, 1843; was married Oct. 18, 1867, to Thomas H. Hess, of Warren County, grocer. *Two* children. Died April 7, 1878.

Judith-Virginia Riddle⁴ (1), youngest daughter of Ephraim³ (1), was born in Warren County, Va., May 12, 1846; was married June 6, 1867, to Adolph Tisserand, farmer, of Warren County, and has *six* children.

John-A. Riddle⁴ (4), eldest son of John³ (2), was born (presumably) in Pittsylvania County, Va.; married —— Crouch, in Franklin County, Va., and has *four* children. He resides in Macon County (Castalian Springs), Tenn.

Thomas Riddle[4] **(1)**, second son of John[3] **(2)**, was born in Virginia; married America Hodges, of Pittsylvania County, and died in the Confederate army in 1862–3. His widow and *one* daughter reside at Black Oak (?), Weakley County, Tenn.

Martha-Ann Riddle[4] **(2)**, eldest daughter of John[3] **(2)**, was married to Christopher C. Petters, of Giles County, Va., and has several children.

Susan-P. Riddle[4] **(1)**, second daughter of John[3] **(2)**, was born in Virginia, and is the wife of John Mayhan, of Pittsylvania County; post-office address, Mamon's Store (?).

James-Steven Riddle[4] **(4)**, eldest son of John[3] **(2)** by second wife. Died at Bristol, Tenn., in 1862.

E.-P. Riddle[4] **(1)**, second son of John[3] **(2)** by second wife; lives near Thorn Hill, Granger County, Tenn. He married M. J. Prichard, daughter of Boswell and Rebecca Prichard, of Oak Ridge, N. C., Nov. 30, 1866, and has *four* children, of whom hereafter. His farm is on Clinch River (both sides), partly in Granger County, and partly in Claiborne County, Tenn. House situated on a beautiful elevation, and is surrounded by a grove of large cedar trees.

George-W. Riddle[4] **(1)**, third son of John[3] **(2)**, was burned to death with his mother, in Carroll County, Va., Feb. 2, 1866, at the burning of his father's house.

William-Asher Riddle[4] **(2)**, fourth son of John[3] **(2)** by second wife, died young.

Walter-Hew Riddle[4] **(1)**, fifth son of John[3] **(2)** by second wife, died when small.

FIFTH GENERATION.

J.-L. Riddle[5] **(?)**, eldest son of V. H.[4] **(1)**, was born in Bartow County, Ga., May 21, 1856, and is now (1880) living in Arkansas.

Henrietta Riddle[5] **(1)**, eldest daughter of V. H.[4] **(1)**, was born in Bartow County, Ga., Feb. 8, 1858, and is married.

Nancy-A. Riddle[5] **(1)**, second daughter of V. H.[4] **(1)**, was born Feb. 11, 1860, in Georgia; married.

Margaret-J. Riddle[5] **(1)**, third daughter of V. H.[4] **(1)**, was born in Georgia, Dec. 23, 1862; single.

Joseph-Wheeler Riddle[5] **(1)**, a son of V. H.[4] **(1)**, was born in Georgia, April 2, 1866, and died July 21, 1869.

Joseph Riddle[5] **(2)**, second son of V. H.[4] **(1)**, was born in Georgia, July 21, 1868; single in 1880.

Augusta-B. Riddle[5] **(1)**, fifth daughter of V. H.[4] **(1)**, was born in Georgia, July 7, 1870.

Susan-F. Riddle[5] **(2)**, sixth daughter of V. H.[4] **(1)**, was born in Georgia, Oct. 27, 1872.

Martha-L. Riddle[5] **(3)**, seventh daughter of V. H.[4] **(1)**, was born in Georgia, Dec. 27, 1874.

Paul-P. Riddle[5] **(1)**, a son of V. H.[4] **(1)**, was born in Georgia, June 16, 1877.

J.-H. Riddle[5] **(?)**, eldest son of James[4] **(2)**, was born in Georgia, March 19, 1855, and teaches school.

J.-A. Riddle[5] **(?)**, second son of James[4] **(2)**, was born in Georgia, April 1, 1857; occupation, farming.

John-Cephas Riddle[5] **(?)**, third son of James[4] **(2)**, was born in Georgia, April 19, 1859; farmer.

Charles-Glover Riddle[5] (1), eldest son of E. P.[4] (1). ⎫ All born
Arthur-Allen Riddle[5] (1), second son of E. P.[4] (1). ⎬ in Granger
Mary-Alice Riddle[5] (1), eldest daughter of E. P.[4] (1). ⎬ County,
Lilley-Lee Riddle[5] (1), second daughter of E. P.[4] (1). ⎭ Tenn.

ANOTHER FAMILY.

Lewis Riddle[1] (1), from Loudoun County, Va., of Scottish descent, whose parents are not known (probably connected with the Riddells of Orange County, Va., as the name Lewis is of frequent occurrence among them), came to Pittsylvania County, Va.,* and settled as a farmer. His wife's maiden-name was Mary Frazier (or Frazure); she had several children, of whom (some of them) hereafter. This pair died previous to 1828.

SECOND GENERATION.

Thomas Riddle[2] (1), eldest (?) son of Lewis[1] (1), was born (presumably) in Loudoun County, Va.; married Sally Blanks, of Pittsylvania County, and had issue *twelve* children. He removed to Missouri when a young man, and was subsequently sheriff of St. Charles County in that State. Stone and brick mason by trade. A man of firm mind and great force of character. He and family are supposed (by relatives in Virginia) to be dead.

James Riddle[2] (1), a son of Lewis[1] (1), was born in Pittsylvania County, Va., and married three times; firstly, Mary, daughter of John and Nancy Yeatts; secondly, Mary, daughter of John and Anna Giles, and thirdly, Susan-Christian, daughter of David and Winny McNealy, all of Pittsylvania County. He had issue *eight* children, of whom hereafter. His widow was living in 1879 as the wife of Isaac Mitchell.

William Riddle[2] (1), a son of Lewis[1] (1), was (presumably) born in Pittsylvania County, Va.; married Mildred, daughter of Joseph and Sallie Johnson, and had issue *five* children, of whom hereafter. He was a farmer; died in 1834; his widow died in 1859.

Rebecca Riddle[2] (1), only daughter of Lewis[1] (1), died young.

THIRD GENERATION.

John-Lewis Riddle[3] (1), eldest son of James[2] (1), died young.

Benjamin-Frazure Riddle[3] (1), second son of James[2] (1), was born in Pittsylvania County, Va.; married Susan F. Hardin, and died March 2, 1867 (?), leaving *two* children, of whom hereafter.

Thomas Riddle[3] (2), third son of James[2] (1), was born in Pittsylvania County, Va., and died a young man.

James-Henry Riddle[3] (3), fourth son of James[2] (1), was born in Pittsylvania County, Va., and died aged about 18.

---

* There are three Riddle brothers,—Edward, William, and Thomas,—living at Chatham, Pittsylvania County, Va., whose grandfather came from Loudoun County at the same time as his brother, Lewis Riddle, whose name stands at the head of the family whose record is above given, but they do not furnish genealogy.

Rachel Riddle[2] (1), eldest daughter of James[2] (1). ⎤ All died with
Ailsey Riddle[2] (1), second daughter of James[2] (1). ⎟ consumption,
Lydia Riddle[2] (1), third daughter of James[2] (1). ⎟ when young
Nancy Riddle[2] (1), fourth daughter of James[2] (1). ⎦ women.

Mary-Frazure Riddle[3] (1), eldest daughter of William[2] (1), was born in Pittsylvania County, Va., in 1826; was married in 1848 to John P. Wovall (?). Both dead.

Lewis-Adams Riddle[3] (2), eldest son of William[2] (1), was born in Pittsylvania County, Va., June 28, 1828; married Susan-Ann, daughter of James and Susan Glasgow, and had issue *seven* children, of whom hereafter. Mr. Riddle is a carpenter by trade, and followed that business for twenty-seven years. He now carries on two farms, consisting of six hundred and sixty-two acres, three miles apart, and employs twenty men; post-office, Whittle's Depot, Pittsylvania County, Va.

William-Blair Riddle[3] (2), second son of William[2] (1), was born in Pittsylvania County, Va., in 1830; died aged 16.

Eliza-Ann Riddle[3] (1), second daughter of William[2] (1), was born in Pittsylvania County, Va., in 1832; was married to Dudley Farthing, and had issue; deceased.

Christian-Dickson Riddle[3] (1), youngest son of William[2] (1), was born in Pittsylvania County, Va., in 1834; died aged 15.

FOURTH GENERATION.

Frazure Riddle[4] (1), only son of Benjamin[3] (1).
Agnes Riddle[4] (1), only daughter of Benjamin[3] (1).

Jane-Alstrap Riddle[4] (1), eldest daughter of Lewis[3] (2), was born in Pittsylvania County, Va., Sept. 18, 1856; was married to Joseph H. Stone, of Campbell County, Dec. 18, 1878.

Mary-Elizabeth Riddle[4] (2), second daughter of Lewis[3] (2), was born in Pittsylvania County, Va., Nov. 24, 1858; was married Aug. 11, 1875, to William P. Payne, and died Dec. 12, 1876.

James-David Riddle[4] (4), eldest son of Lewis[3] (2), was born in Pittsylvania County, Va., Oct. 6, 1860; single.

John-Lewis Riddle[4] (2), second son of Lewis[3] (2), was born in Pittsylvania County, Va., Oct. 24, 1862; single.

Sally-Bell Riddle[4] (1), third daughter of Lewis[3] (2), was born in Pittsylvania County, Va., Oct. 15, 1864; single.

William-Thomas Riddle[4] (3), third son of Lewis[3] (2), was born in Pittsylvania County, Va., Feb. 12, 1868, and died Sept. 3, 1878.

Annis-Bela Riddle[4] (1), fourth daughter of Lewis[3] (2), was born in Pittsylvania County, Va., Feb. 7, 1874, and died Feb. 10, 1876.

RIDDELLS OF GOOCHLAND COUNTY, VIRGINIA.

William Riddelle[1] (1), said to have been born in France, emigrated to Virginia about 1730. Spelled his surname *Riddelle*. Settled in Hanover County, but removed to Goochland County, where he died, aged about 80. His wife's name does not appear; he left issue *three* sons, and probably daughters. I am inclined to think this William was a relative of the other families early settled in Virginia, but as there are no records extant, connections are not proved.

SECOND GENERATION.

Robert Riddell[2] (1), a son of William[1] (1), was born in Goochland County, Va.; married Nancy Johnson, and had issue *five* children, two sons and three daughters. Stone-mason and farmer. Died about 1860, aged 88 years; his widow died in 1872, aged 94.

William Riddell[2] (2), a son of William[1] (1), was born in Goochland County, Va., and settled in Shelby County, Tenn.

John Riddell[2] (1), a son of William[1] (1), was born in Goochland County, Va., and served in the war of the Revolution under General Lafayette, and was wounded at the battle of Brandywine. He returned to his native County after the war, and followed farming. Is supposed to have had a family.

THIRD GENERATION.

Robert Riddell[3] (2), a son of Robert[2] (1), was born in Goochland County, Va., and died when 17 years old.

Dolly Riddell[3] (1), eldest daughter of Robert[2] (1), was born in Goochland County, Va., and died when young.

Sallie Riddell[3] (1), second daughter of Robert[2] (1), was born in Goochland County, Va., in 1807; was married in 1824 to R. B. Woodbury (or Woodbridge), who has deceased. She had *eight* children.

William Riddell[3] (3), second son of Robert[2] (1), was born in Goochland County, Va., in 1809; married, in 1831, Eliza, daughter of Jeremiah and Susanna (Farrar) Woodbridge, and has issue *eight* children, of whom hereafter. Resides on a farm in his native County. House-carpenter by trade.

John-M. Riddell[3] (2), third son of Robert[2] (1), was born in Goochland County, Va., in 1810; married in 1838 to Mary I. N. Clough, of the same County, and had issue *eight* children, of whom hereafter. He has been a farmer and dealer in general merchandise. His wife (who was born Dec. 12, 1819), died in 1854. He had two sons and a daughter die when young, whose names do not appear.

FOURTH GENERATION.

Matthew-M. Riddell[4] (1), eldest son of William[3] (3), was born in Goochland County, Va., April, 1835. He served in the Confederate army two and a half years during the Rebellion, belonging to the celebrated "Wise's Legion," of West Virginia, and died of disease contracted in the service. He was not married.

William-R. Riddell[4] (4), second son of William[3] (3), was born in Goochland County, Va., Feb. 11, 1837; married Eliza H., daughter of Elisha Powers and his wife, whose maiden-name was Childress, in the year 1859, and died in 1874, in his native County, leaving a widow and *five* sons. Mrs. Riddell died in 1880. He served through the war of the Rebellion in the department of the Potomac, and was a prisoner at Point Lookout eighteen months. He was a farmer.

Richard-J. Riddell[4] (1), third son of William[3] (3), was born in Goochland County, Va., Feb. 11, 1839; married Sarah E. Holland, daughter of Nathaniel and Mary-Ann (Perkins) Holland, of Louisa County, Feb. 23, 1865, and has *nine* children, of whom hereafter. He served one year in the Fifty-sixth Virginia Regiment, Confederate Infantry, under General Floyd, in the West. Occupation, farmer; residence, Louisa County, Va.

Jerry-C. Riddell[4] (1), fourth son of William[3] (3), was born in Goochland County, Va., June 18, 1841; married Mary L., daughter of Talton F. and his wife Martha (Powers) Bowles. He died Aug. 16, 1880, leaving *two* sons and *two* daughters, of whom hereafter: He served in the Confederate army during the war, under General Floyd, in artillery, in the department of the West. Was taken prisoner at the fall of Fort Donelson, in 1862.

Andrew-B. Riddell[4] (1), fifth son of William[3] (3), was born in Goochland County, Va., March 16, 1848; married Elizabeth C. Bowles, sister of the wife of his brother, in December, 1867. He served in the Confederate artillery, under General Floyd, and was captured at the fall of Fort Donelson, with his brother Jerry, in 1862. He died in June, 1876, leaving a widow and *three* daughters, of whom hereafter. Residence of family, Goochland County, Va.

Samuel-W. Riddell[4] (1), sixth son of William[3] (3), was born in Goochland County, Va., June 9, 1845; married Susie G., daughter of John M. and his wife Susan G. (Payne) Jordan, in January, 1868, and has issue *five* sons and *two* daughters, of whom hereafter. Farmer by occupation; residence, Goochland County.

Sallie-A. Riddell[4] (2), only daughter of William[3] (3), was born in Goochland County, Va., April 25, 1847, and lives at home; unmarried.

Shandy-P. Riddell[4] (1), seventh son of William[3] (3), was born in Goochland County, Va., July 5, 1849; married in 1880 to India, daughter of Richard and his wife Angelina (Singleton) Ward, of Hanover County. He died in December, 1882, leaving an infant son, who died soon after. Resided in his native County.

Dr. Thomas-Jefferson Riddell[4] (1), eldest son of John[3] (3), was born in Goochland County, Va., and is now (1880) 36 years of age. He left his native County when twelve years of age and resided in Henrico County until the war of the Rebellion, when he·was among the first to volunteer; he remained in the Confederate army until the close of the war, being in the battle of Fort Donelson and several other engagements of minor importance. After the war he commenced his collegiate course, graduated in 1869, and commenced the practice of medicine in 1870, in the city of Richmond, where he continues (1880), a competent and successful physician. A fine-looking man.

Isabella-D. Riddell[4] (1), eldest daughter of John[3] (3), was born in Goochland County, Va., and is now about 34 years of age (1880); she was married to Thomas R. Calvin, of Louisiana, in 1867.

Sarah-A. Riddell[4] (1), second daughter of John[3] (3), was born in Goochland County, Va., and is now (1880) about 32 years of age; was married in 1866 to W. A. Smith, and is living at Richmond, Va.

John-P. Riddell[4] (4), third son of John[3] (3), was born in Goochland County, Va., and is now (1880) about 31 years of age; mechanic, living in Henrico County.

Another brother (name not given), aged about 29 years, is a clerk in Henrico County.

RIDDLES OF ACCOMACK COUNTY, VIRGINIA.

Basil Riddle[1] **(1)**, a native of the north of Ireland, early came to America and settled in Virginia, in Accomack County, near the Blue Ridge. Some of his relatives settled in North Carolina, and tradition says many families in the Southern States are connected. In the absence of records I have no means of finding missing links of the family chain. Basil married and had issue, of whom hereafter. Farmer and stock-raiser.[*]

SECOND GENERATION.

Samuel Riddle[2] **(1)**, a son of Basil[1] (1), was probably born in North Carolina; married and had issue *two* [†] or more children, of whom hereafter. No record of birth, marriage, or death. Farmer.

THIRD GENERATION.

George Riddle[3] **(1)**, a son of Samuel[2] (1), was born somewhere in North Carolina; married Nancy Elkins, and had issue *six* children, of whom hereafter. He removed to Tennessee, and carried on an extensive plantation.

Randolph Riddle[3] **(1)**, supposed to be a son of Samuel[2] (1), was born in North Carolina; married Jemima ——, and had *six* children, of whom hereafter. He settled in Tennessee, and lived on a farm. Taught school. No record of birth or death.

FOURTH GENERATION.

Jeremiah Riddle[4] **(1)**, a son of George[3] (1), was born in North Carolina or Tennessee, March 3, 1818; married a daughter of Solomon and Mary (Jones) Mason (she was born Feb. 12, 1814), and had issue *eight* children, of whom hereafter. Farmer in Moore County, Tenn. Kept no records.

George Riddle[4] **(2)**, a son of George[3] (1), was born in Tennessee; married, and had a family of children, but the place of his residence is unknown.

Asa Riddle[4] **(1)**, a son of George[3] (1), was born in Tennessee; married, and had issue; residence not known.

Willis Riddle[4] **(1)**, a son of George[3] (1), was born in Tennessee; married, and is supposed to have children; his residence unknown. Some of these moved to Alabama.

Matilda Riddle[4] **(1).**
Nancy Riddle[4] **(1).** } Daughters of George[3] (1), born in Tennessee.

Stephen Riddle[4] **(1)**, eldest son of Randolph[3] (1), was born in Tennessee (Moore County?); married Sarah Weaver, of Franklin County, and had issue *twelve* children, of whom hereafter. He and wife were members of the Primitive Baptist Church, and were noted for their piety, honesty, and charity. Mr. Riddle was many years deacon of his church; farmer by occupation.

Harmon Riddle[4] **(1)**, a son of Randolph[3] (1), was born in Tennessee; married Elizabeth Easley, and by her had *ten* children. He married,

---

[*] A family of Riddells, early settled in Maryland, had a *Basel*, or *Basel*, in it. (See "Riddells of Cecil County, Maryland.")

[†] Some say Samuel's son *John* settled in Georgia, and had a family settled there. He was a soldier of the Revolution.

secondly, Annie E. Woodward, and settled near Winchester, Franklin County; he afterwards removed to Wilson County, near Lebanon, where he died in 1844; his second wife died July 5, 1861. He was a member of the Primitive Baptist Church, and a farmer by occupation.

John Riddle[4] (1), a son of Randolph[3] (1), was born in Tennessee; married Judith Easley, and had issue *seven* children, of whom hereafter. He lived on Farris Creek, in Lincoln County, many years, but removed to Alabama about 1855, where he died. He and wife were connected with the Primitive Baptist Church.

Alexander Riddle[4] (1), a son of Randolph[3] (1), settled in Alabama, and is said to be a man of talent.

Tyre Riddle[4] (1), a son of Randolph[3] (1), settled in Alabama.

Sarah Riddle[4] (1), only daughter of Randolph[3] (1).

FIFTH GENERATION.

Rebecca-Jane Riddle[5] (1), eldest daughter of Jeremiah[4] (1), was born in Tennessee, July 24, 1840; was married July 30, 1861.

Sarah Riddle[5] (2), second daughter of Jeremiah[4] (1), was born in Tennessee, June 6, 1843.

Mary-Jones Riddle[5] (1), third daughter of Jeremiah[4] (1), was born in Tennessee, Sept. 19, 1845.

Nancy Riddle[5] (2), fourth daughter of Jeremiah[4] (1), was born in Tennessee, June 18, 1849.

Susan-Frances Riddle[5] (1), fifth daughter of Jeremiah[4] (1), was born in Tennessee, Aug. 29, 1851.

Georgie-Ann Riddle[5] (1), sixth daughter of Jeremiah[4] (1), was born in Tennessee.

J.-M. Riddle[5] (2), eldest son of Jeremiah[4] (1), was called "Junior." He was born in Tennessee, Jan. 12, 1858. His address is Hunt's Station, Franklin County, Tenn.

J.-W. Riddle[5] (1), second son of Jeremiah[4] (1).

Benjamin Riddle[5] (1), eldest son of Stephen[4] (1), was born in Tennessee, married in Jackson County, Ala., and had a family of children. No particulars.

John Riddle[5] (2), second son of Stephen[4] (1), was born in Tennessee, married Rebecca Ray, of Bedford County, and had issue *seven* children. He married secondly, Caroline, daughter of William Hicks, of Bedford County, and had *six* more children, of whom, with those of first wife, hereafter. He followed farming, stock-raising, and lumber-dealing. He and wife were "strict members" of the Separate Baptist Church.

Alexander Riddle[5] (2), son of Stephen[4] (1), was born in Tennessee; married Miss Powell; secondly, Miss Dean, of Bedford County, and by his two wives he had a large family. Connected with the Separate Baptist Church. Farmer. No records of children.

Harmon Riddle[5] (2), a son of Stephen[4] (1), moved to Texas, since when no information.

Elizabeth Riddle[5] (1), eldest daughter of Stephen[4] (1), was married to Samuel Haynes, and had a family.

Randolph Riddle[5] (2), a son (fifth?) of Stephen[4] (1), was born in Tennessee; married Elizabeth Hicks, of Bedford County, and had a large family of sons and daughters. A farmer; good citizen. Family connected with Primitive Baptist Church. Place of residence not given.

Rev. Tyre Riddle⁵ (2), a son of Stephen⁴ (1), was born in Tennessee, married Eliza Lossing, by whom he had several children. He married secondly, Widow Goodlow. A minister in the communion of the Separate Baptist Church, of very acceptable ability; well beloved by a host of acquaintances. Residence unknown. He died about 1879.

Martha Riddle⁵ (1), second daughter of Stephen⁴ (1), was a very amiable and godly woman; died single.

Lucinda Riddle⁵ (1), third daughter of Stephen⁴ (1), was the wife of Chaney Smith,—a splendid man,—and had a family of *five* children. Mr. Smith is a farmer; Baptist.

Mary Riddle⁵ (2), fourth daughter of Stephen⁴ (1), was married to Carroll Marshall, a farmer, and had *three* children. A good woman.

Millie Riddle⁵ (1), fifth daughter of Stephen⁴ (1), was the wife of Thomas Mangram, and died only a few years after her marriage.

Catherine Riddle⁵ (1), sixth daughter of Stephen⁴ (1), was married to James Mangram, a school-teacher.

Lemuel Riddle⁵ (1). ⎫
John Riddle⁵ (2). ⎬ Children of Harmon⁴ (1); died single.
Jemima Riddle⁵ (2). ⎭

Lewis Riddle⁵ (1), a son of Harmon⁴ (1), married Caroline Wright, and settled in Alabama as a farmer. He had a large family; names not known. Deceased some six years ago (1884); member of Baptist Church.

Benjamin Riddle⁵ (2), a son of Harmon⁴ (1), married Sarah Carder, and settled in Jackson County, Ala. Large family; names not known. He is said to be a Baptist (Freewill) preacher; farmer.

Elizabeth Riddle⁵ (2), second daughter of Harmon⁴ (1), was married to John Chadwick, and resides in Alabama.

Sarah Riddle⁵ (3), third daughter of Harmon⁴ (1), was married to Caleb Killion, of Clark County, Ark., and had *four* children. Husband was postmaster in Deroche, Ark.; owned a farm.

Emeline Riddle⁵ (1), fourth daughter of Harmon⁴ (1), was married to a Mr. Perry, and settled in Arkansas.

Eliza Riddle⁵ (1), fifth daughter of Harmon⁴ (1), was the wife of —— Forrester, farmer, of Arkansas.

Eleanor-Jane Riddle⁵ (1), youngest daughter of Harmon⁴ (1), was married to Wesley Jarrell, and lived seven miles west of Lebanon, Tenn. *Six* children. Mr. Jarrell, who was a good farmer, Free Mason, and strict member of the Methodist Episcopal Church, died about 1866.

Martin-V. Riddle⁵ (1), youngest son of Harmon⁴ (1), was born near Winchester, Franklin County, Tenn., Oct. 23, 1835; married Theresa, daughter of Dr. William A. Tucker, of Lincoln County, Aug. 9, 1857, and had issue *ten* children, of whom hereafter. He commenced the profession of school-teaching in 1856, which he followed almost continuously till 1883, when, in consequence of hemorrhage of the lungs, he retired from the school-room. He united with the Cumberland Presbyterian Church in 1860; his wife, also. Mr. Riddle wields a facile pen, and leaves his composition as clear as print. He has kindly compiled the genealogy, — as far as available,—for this book. The various branches are widely scattered, and but few dates of births, marriages, and deaths could be had in the brief time assigned for the research.

Harmon Riddle⁵ (3), eldest son of John⁴ (1), married Margaret Hurt, and settled in Franklin County, Tenn., but in 1854 removed to Arkansas; had a large family. He was a good man in every respect. A farmer. He and wife deceased.

Stephen Riddle⁵ (2), second son of John⁴ (1), married Jane, daughter of Aulden Tucker, in Lincoln County, Tenn., but in a few years removed to Arkansas, where he had a large family born to him. Farmer; dead; widow and children still living in Arkansas.

Elizabeth Riddle⁵ (4), eldest daughter of John⁴ (1), was the spouse of George Goad, of Arkansas, and had issue. She and husband deceased. Children in Arkansas.

Frances Riddle⁵ (1), second daughter of John⁴ (1), was the wife of Wesley Turner, of Lincoln County, Tenn. He owned a farm on Cane Creek. He died many years ago, childless. Widow still living; a Baptist.

Lewis Riddle⁵ (2).   } Sons of John⁴ (1), died in Arkansas, unmar-
Alexander Riddle⁵ (3). }   ried.

William Riddle⁵ (1), a son of John⁴ (1), married Caroline Gattis, in Lincoln County, Tenn., and had issue *five* children, of whom hereafter. Good man. He and wife members of M. E. Church for many years, but in 1873 they, with three children, united with the Cumberland Presbyterian Church, at Moore Chapel, Moore County, Tenn. Mr. Riddle fell dead in 1874.

SIXTH GENERATION.

Manuel Riddle⁶ (1), eldest son of John⁵ (2), was born in Tennessee; married Sydney Pearson.

Martha-Priscilla Riddle⁶ (2), eldest daughter of John⁵ (2), was married to —— Courser.

William-Marian Riddle⁶ (2), second son of John⁵ (2), was married to Martha Byrom.

Harmon Riddle⁶ (4), third son of John⁵ (2), married Amanda Edens.

Rebecca-Caroline Riddle⁶ (3), second daughter of John⁵ (2), was married to Peter Anthony.

James Riddle⁶ (1), fourth son of John⁵ (2).

John-Henry Riddle⁶ (3), fifth son of John⁵ (2).

Minerva-Riddle⁶ (1), third daughter of John⁵ (2).

Mollie Riddle⁶ (1), fourth daughter of John⁵ (2).

Rhoda-Ellen Riddle⁶ (1), fifth daughter of John⁵ (2), was married to the Rev. E. M. Anthony, of the Lutheran Church.

Martin Riddle⁶ (2), sixth son of John⁵ (2).

Aurora Riddle⁶ (1). } Twin daughters of Martin⁶ (1), died in infancy,
Victoria Riddle⁶ (1). }   January, 1877.

Martha-Jane Riddle⁶ (3).   Children of Martin⁵ (1).
William-Benjamin Riddle⁶ (3).   William B. and James E. are
Anna-Eliza Riddle⁶ (1).   school-teachers; the other sons
James-Edmund Riddle⁶ (2).   are farming in 1884. The eight
Martin-McDonald Riddle⁶ (3).   eldest are members of Cumber-
Ophelia-Catherine Riddle⁶ (1).   land Presbyterian church, at
Mary-Emeline Riddle⁶ (3).   Moore Chapel, Moore County,
Finis-Ewing Riddle⁶ (1).   Tenn. *Twelve* children in all;
Lulu-Bell Riddle⁶ (1).   reside in Lynchburgh, Moore
Julia-Baska Riddle⁶ (1).   County, Tenn.

28

John Riddle⁶ (4).
James Riddle⁶ (3). } Sons of Harmon⁶ (3), fell in the Rebellion.

Mary-Frances Riddle⁶ (4), daughter of Harmon⁶ (3), married, and soon after died in Arkansas.

N.-M. Riddle⁶ (1).
Jane Riddle⁶ (1).
Katie Riddle⁶ (1). } Children of William⁶ (1).
John Riddle⁶ (5).
Julia Riddle⁶ (2).

RIDDLES OF VIRGINIA AND TENNESSEE.

Thomas Riddle¹ (1), said to have been born in Scotland or England. came to America about the year 1760, and settled in eastern Virginia, He enlisted in the American army, and served six years under General Marion, but was finally taken prisoner and hung. He married a Miss Roberts, and had issue *seven* children, of whom hereafter. His widow married to "Bill Ingraham," and removed to Hawkins County, but did not long survive her second marriage. This statement was by Isaac Riddle, of Richland, Pulaski County, Mo., a grandson of the above Thomas, and a man of remarkable memory. Another grandson, John Riddle of Kanosh, Utah, believes his original American progenitor was William Riddle, said to be born in what is now Western Virginia; this man served in the Revolution; married Happy Rogers, and had issue *seven* children, whose names correspond with those of Thomas Riddle, as given by my other informant. Moreover, the account of removals and settlements, etc., of the descendants given by the two writers, agree. I must leave this problem for others to solve; it has been deemed proper to give both statements for what they are worth.

SECOND GENERATION.

John Riddle² (1), a son of Thomas¹ (1), was born in Virginia previous to the Revolution; married Sarah, daughter of Moses Johnson, of Hawkins County, Tenn., and had issue *ten* children, of whom hereafter. He was a blacksmith. Removed to Bledsoe County in 1805; thence to Pulaski County, Mo., in 1830. Died in 1833; his widow in 1837.

Thomas Riddle² (2), a son of Thomas¹ (1), was born in Virginia before the Revolution; married Mary Igo, of Bledsoe County, Tenn., and had issue sons and daughters, of whom hereafter. Mr. Riddle's mother died when he was small, and he was brought up in the family of his uncle, James Roberts. He settled first in one of the upper counties of East Tennessee, and from there he and eleven others, including two of his brothers, emigrated to Sequatchee Valley, and settled on the east side of Pikeville, in Bledsoe County; they were the first settlers in this region. He married a Miss Burks for his second wife, and by her had issue *one* son, of whom hereafter. Mr. Riddle died in August, 1859, and was buried four miles west of Cleveland, Bradley County, Tenn.*

---

* Several of the grandsons of Thomas Riddle² (2) were in the Union army during the Rebellion, and one died of starvation at Andersonville.

Joseph Riddle² (1), a son of Thomas¹ (1), was born in Virginia before the Revolution, settled in Cumberland County, Ky., and had a family. A cousin believes he and family removed to Iowa.

Isaac Riddle² (1), a son of Thomas¹ (1), was said to have been born in Virginia in 1775. He married Anna Grizzel (or Griswold), daughter of William Griswold (she was born July 17, 1781), of North Carolina, and had *ten* children, of whom hereafter. Mr. Riddle settled in Hawkins County, Tenn., on the Clinch River, where he remained till 1805, when he removed to Kentucky. He was a hatter by trade, but devoted his attention principally to farming and stock-raising till his sons were old enough to guide the plough; then resumed hat-making. He was a deacon of the Baptist Church. Died in Boone County, Ky. He was a twin brother of Joseph, before mentioned.

William Riddle² (1), a son of Thomas¹ (1), was born in Virginia; married Ellen Holt, and·settled in Tennessee; had *eight* children. One says he died in Texas County, Mo. I think he has left numerous descendants in Kentucky, but they do not furnish records.

James Riddle² (1), a son of Thomas¹ (1), was born in Virginia, and settled in Cumberland County, Ky., where he raised a family, and where his numerous descendants now live.

Harriet Riddle² (1), only known daughter of Thomas¹ (1), was married in Tennessee, but I have no account of her family. One writer calls her "Happy."

THIRD GENERATION.

James Riddle³ (2), a son of John² (1), was born in Bledsoe County, Tenn.; blacksmith and carriage-maker. Killed by a man named Holman, in 1825. Unmarried.

Johnson Riddle³ (1), a son of John² (1), was born in Bledsoe County, Tenn.; married Jane Shepherd, and had issue *two* (perhaps more) children, of whom hereafter. He removed to Pulaski County, Mo., in 1830; thence to Walker County, Ala.; since when no information.

Thomas Riddle³ (3), a son of John² (1), was born in Bledsoe County, Tenn.; married Sarah Cormack in 1828, and had issue *three* children, of whom hereafter; farmer. He was accidentally killed by the discharge of his gun while hunting, in 1835; the gun was leaning against a tree, and was thrown down by his dog, and the lock sprung.

Manuel Riddle³ (1), a son of John² (1), was born in Bledsoe County, Tenn., Jan. 1, 1810; married Malinda West in 1835, and had issue *six* children, of whom hereafter. Farmer; died at Pulaski, Mo., in 1849.

Isaac Riddle³ (2), a son of John² (1), was born in Bledsoe County, Tenn., in 1812; married in 1839 to Margaret Williams, and had issue *four* children, of whom hereafter. Farmer; residence Richland, Pulaski County, Mo. Deceased.

Jesse Riddle³ (1), a son of John² (1), was born in Bledsoe County, Tenn., in 1815; married in 1834 to Narcissa Cain, and had issue *three* children, of whom hereafter. Blacksmith; died in 1863.

Elizabeth Riddle³ (1), eldest daughter of John² (1), was born in Bledsoe County, Tenn., and was married to James Weaver.

Atha Riddle³ (1), second daughter of John² (1), was born in Bledsoe County, Tenn.; was married to Thomas Lewis, who removed to Pulaski County, Mo., in 1830; he died soon after, and she was married, secondly, to Joseph Newbury. Died in 1856.

Lucinda Riddle[3] (1), third daughter of John[2] (1), was born in Bledsoe County, Tenn.; was married to Strawder Johnson, a violin-player, of Warren County, and moved to Illinois in 1827; thence to Walker County, Ala.

Abbie Riddle[3] (1), fourth daughter of John[2] (1), was born in Bledseo County, Tenn., March, 1817; was married in 1852, to Philip Henson, of Pulaski County, Mo., and in 1873 was living in Camden County.

William Riddle[3] (2), eldest son of Thomas[2] (2), was born in Tennessee, and was buried at Cleveland, Tenn. He was probably married, but no child is living.

James Riddle[3] (3), second son of Thomas[2] (2), was born in Tennessee, and is living near Arkadelphia, Clark County, Ark. He has *two* sons and *one* daughter.

Joshua Riddle[3] (1), third son of Thomas[2] (2), died near Dayton, Rhea County, and was buried at Lone Mountain Church, near Graysville, Tenn. Probably single.

Angeline Riddle[3] (1), eldest daughter of Thomas[2] (2), was married to Barclay S. Benson, and had issue. She was buried at Dayton, Rhea County, Tenn.

Margaret Riddle[3] (1), second daughter of Thomas[2] (2), was married to John H. Corbett, and settled in Arkansas. Has issue. Husband died at Little Rock.

Emereta Riddle[3] (1), third daughter of Thomas[2] (2), was married to Charles Morgan, and resides at Morgan Springs, near Dayton, Tenn. Has a large family.

Isaac Riddle[3] (3), a son of Thomas[2] (2) by his second wife. Moved to Missouri after the close of the Rebellion. No particulars.

Isaac Riddle[3] (4), eldest son of Joseph[2] (1).
James Riddle[3] (4), second son of Joseph[2] (1).

William Riddle[3] (3), eldest son of Isaac[2] (1), died when seven months old.

John Riddle[3] (2),[*] second son of Isaac[2] (1), was born in Tennessee, Dec. 23, 1803; married Elizabeth, daughter of Robert and Jane Stewart (she was born Aug. 19, 1783), Dec. 22, 1822, and by her had *eleven* children, of whom, with his other issue, hereafter; married, secondly, Abigail, daughter of John Campbell, in 1852, and had issue *two* children; married, thirdly, Eliza Bramwick, Aug. 1, 1866, and had issue *one* child. Mr. Riddle embraced religion when young, and united with the Baptist Church; was licensed to preach at the age of twenty-four; became a devoted and critical student of the Bible, and being convinced of errors in his creed, withdrew from his connections, and lectured in sympathy with the Universalists till thirty-eight years of age. He saw some printed work of the "Latter-day Saints" (Mormons), which he read carefully and critically till convinced of the scriptural soundness of the doctrines held by that

---

* JOHN RIDDLE, of Kanosh, Utah, says William, his grandfather, had a brother Moses, and a relative in Kentucky named William Ruddell, who had sons James, William, Lewis, and Valentine. If this statement is correct, the "Riddells of Orange County, Virginia," and "Riddells of Boone County, Kentucky," are of the same family as the foregoing. (See genealogy of those branches.)

people. He requested a visit from some preachers of that persuasion, and, after an extended conference with them, became confirmed in his convictions, was " baptized for the remission of sins," and has since been identified with that church. He is now eighty-one years of age, but of sound mind and retentive memory; is evidently sincere in his devotion to the Mormon communion. Resides at Kanosh, Millard County, Utah.

Elam Riddle[3] (1), second son of Isaac[2] (1), was born July 17, 1805. Probably settled in Alabama, as I find the name "Elam" in a family there.

Nancy Riddle[3] (1), eldest daughter of Isaac[2] (1), was born in Boone County, Ky., Nov. 2, 1807.

Joseph Riddle[3] (2), fourth son of Isaac[2] (1), was born in Boone County, Ky., June 9, 1810.

James Riddle[3] (5), fifth son of Isaac[2] (1), was born in Boone County, Ky., Jan. 12, 1812.

William Riddle[3] (4), sixth son of Isaac[2] (1), was born in Boone County, Ky.

Solomon Riddle[3] (1), seventh son of Isaac[2] (1), was born in 'Boone County, Ky.

Elizabeth Riddle[3] (2), second daughter of Isaac[2] (1).

Isaac Riddle[3] (5), eighth son of Isaac[2] (1).

William Riddle[3] (5), eldest son of William[2] (1). ⎫
Jinsa Riddle[3] (1), eldest daughter of William[2] (1). ⎪ Supposed to have lived
Hopa Riddle[3] (1), second daughter of William[2] (1). ⎬ in Tennessee
Alla Riddle[3] (1), third daughter of William[2] (1). ⎪ and
Susan Riddle[3] (1), fourth daughter of William[2] (1). ⎪ Kentucky.
Elizabeth Riddle[3] (3), fifth daughter of William[2] (1). ⎭

James Riddle[3] (6), eldest son of James[2] (1). ⎫ Kentuckians.
George Riddle[3] (1), second son of James[2] (1). ⎭

FOURTH GENERATION.

James Riddle[4] (7), eldest son of Johnson[3] (1).
Eliza Riddle[4] (1), a daughter of Johnson[3] (1).

John Riddle[4] (3), eldest son of Thomas[3] (3).
Jesse Riddle[4] (2), second son of Thomas[3] (3).
Caroline Riddle[4] (1), a daughter of Thomas[3] (3).

Miriam Riddle[4] (1), eldest daughter of Manuel[3] (1), was married to James Woods, of Pulaski County, Mo.

Andrew Riddle[4] (1), eldest son of Manuel[3] (1), married Lucinda Bench, of Pulaski County, Mo.

Sarah Riddle[4] (1), second daughter of Manuel[3] (1), was married to Bird Rowland, of Pulaski County, Mo.

Mary Riddle[4] (1), third daughter of Manuel[3] (1), was married to James Combs.

John Riddle[4] (4), second son of Manuel[3] (1).
James Riddle[4] (8), third son of Manuel[3] (1).

Sarah Riddle[4] (8), eldest daughter of Isaac[3] (2), was married to James E. Harrison, an historian.

Miriam Riddle[4] (2), second daughter of Isaac[3] (2), was married to John Housinger.

Lovica Riddle[4] (1), third daughter of Isaac[3] (2), was the wife of John J. Clark.

Nancy Riddle[4] (2), fourth daughter of Isaac[3] (2), was married to William D. Clark.

Parachine Riddle[4] (1), fifth daughter of Isaac[3] (2), was not married in 1878.

John Riddle[4] (5), eldest son of Jesse[3] (1), died unmarried in 1860, aged twenty years.

Isaac Riddle[4] (6), second son of Jesse[3] (1), died in the United States army in 1865.

Elias Riddle[4] (1), third son of Jesse[3] (1), married Betsey J. Hamilton.

Charles Riddle[4] (1). } Sons of James[3] (3), born in Tennessee.
Robert Riddle[4] (1). }

Milo-S. Riddle[4] (1). } Children of Joshua[3] (1), born in Tennessee.
Hiram Riddle[4] (1). } Reside at Dayton, Rhea County, Tenn.
Olivia Riddle[4] (1), }

Mary Riddle[4] (2), eldest daughter of John[3] (2), was born Sept. 22, 1823; was married to William Nichols, and died two years after marriage, leaving a son.

Elizabeth Riddle[4] (4), third daughter of John[3] (2), was married to Culver-James Hickman, Hickman County, Ky., and had *one* child. Mr. Hickman went into the army during the Mexican war and never returned home.

Maria-Jane Riddle[4] (1), fourth daughter of John[3] (2), was born in August, 1825; died in December, 1825.

Ellen Riddle[4] (1), fifth daughter of John[3] (2), was married to —— Culver, of St. Paul, Minn., and has issue. One letter places a daughter Margaret here.

Isaac Riddle[4] (7), eldest son of John[3] (2), was born March 22, 1830, in Boone County, Ky., and married Mary-Ann Levi, March 6, 1853 (she was born in Canada, July 30, 1835, and died March 4, 1871), and had issue *six* children. He married, secondly, Mary James, and by this union had *five* children. He married, thirdly, Mary-Ann Eagles, and had issue *seven* children. He is a miller, farmer, and stockman; resides at Beaver, Beaver County, Utah. A "Latter-day Saint," and has observed the Scriptural injunction to "multiply and replenish the earth."

James-Henry Riddle[4] (9), second son of John[3] (2), was a soldier in the Union army during the war of the Rebellion; married twice and had issue; lives in Kansas, near Kansas City.

Eveline Riddle[4] (1), sixth daughter of John[3] (2), was married to Joseph Grover, and lives in Montana.

Elam-D.-S. Riddle[4] (2), third son of John[3] (2), married, and has *three* sons and *one* daughter; resides at Elm Creek, Buffalo County, Neb. Landowner and stockman.

John-Thomas Riddle[4] (6), fourth son of John[3] (2), lives in Montana; unmarried.

Lucinda Riddle[4] (1), daughter of John[3] (2), in Montana.

Joseph Riddle[4] (3), youngest son of John[2] (2), dead.

Christiana Riddle[4] (1), daughter of John[2] (2), by second wife; dead.

Julia-Ann Riddle[4] (1), daughter of John[2] (2), was married to John Reed.

FIFTH GENERATION.

George Riddle[5] (2), eldest son of Isaac[4] (7), was born March 6, 1854, and died March 18, 1854.

Mary-Ann Riddle[5] (3), eldest daughter of Isaac[4] (7), was born Dec. 7, 1856, and died Oct. 12, 1857.

Isaac-J. Riddle[5] (8), second son of Isaac[4] (7), was born Dec. 17, 1858; married Nancy Russell, and resides near his father's homestead, at Grass Valley, Utah ; postmaster and stockman ; has *three* children.

Joselina-M. Riddle[5] (1), third son of Isaac[4] (7), was born July 11, 1860 ; married Lovina Jacobs, and has a family of *two* children.

Madora Riddle[5] (1), second daughter of Isaac[4] (7), was born July 9, 1862 ; died Sept. 2, 1867.

Francina Riddle[5] (1), third daughter of Isaac[4] (7), was born May 17, 1863 ; was married to W. W. Stephens in her eighteenth year, and has *two* children.

Sarah Riddle[5] (2), fourth daughter of Isaac[4] (7), was born Dec. 28, 1863 ; died Nov. 13, 1867.

Thomas-James Riddle[5] (4), fourth son of Isaac[4] (7), was born April 2, 1866, and is now at an academy in Provo City, Utah County, Utah.

Henry Riddle[5] (1), fifth son of Isaac[4] (7), was born Jan. 14, 1869.

Eva-May Riddle[5] (1), fifth daughter of Isaac[4] (7), was born March 7, 1871, and died Dec. 12, 1872.

William Riddle[5] (6), sixth son of Isaac[4] (7), was born April 7, 1874, and died May 10, 1874.

Lydia-Ann Riddle[5] (1), sixth daughter of Isaac[4] (7), was born Sept. 15, 1866, and is in the academy in Provo City, Utah County, Utah.

Sophrona Riddle[5] (1), seventh daughter of Isaac[4] (7), was born Feb. 15, 1869, and died May 4, 1877.

Lilla-Cornelia Riddle[5] (1), eighth daughter of Isaac[4] (7), was born Feb. 19, 1871.

Wallace-M. Riddle[5] (1), seventh son of Isaac[4] (7), was born Dec. 24, 1872.

Charles-Edward Riddle[5] (1), eighth son of Isaac[4] (7), was born Feb. 23, 1874.

J.-Elias Riddle[5] (1), ninth son of Isaac[4] (7), was born Feb. 25, 1874.

Isaac-Andrew Riddle[5] (9), tenth son of Isaac[4] (7),* was born April 10, 1879.

---

* It will be observed that only a few weeks intervene between the births of some of the children of Isaac Riddle[4] (7); this must be accounted for in the fact that he is a Mormon polygamist. This branch of the Riddle family is in little danger of becoming extinct.

RIDDLES OF CHATHAM COUNTY, NORTH CAROLINA.

[SCOTTISH BRANCH.]

Julius Riddle[1] (1), came early to Chatham County, N. C., from Scotland,* or the North of Ireland. He married Nancy Mentor, and had issue *seven* sons and probably daughters, but the names of the latter have not reached me. This member of the Riddle family must have been born as early as 1720 or '25; time of death unknown. He was a farmer and landowner; was presumably a connection of the ancestors of other Southern families. Died in 1756, leaving a widow and seven sons.

SECOND GENERATION.

William Riddle[2] (1), eldest son of Julius[1] (1), was born in Chatham County, N. C., March 13, 1746; married Jane —— (she was born July 27, 1761, and died July 29, 1817), Aug. 14, 1779, and had issue *eight* children, of whom hereafter. He served in the American army in the war of the Revolution, without receiving a wound. Settled in Chatham County, near Pittsborough, as a planter; died Oct. 5, 1811, aged sixty-five.

Capt. Richard Riddle[2] (1), a son of Julius[1] (1), was born about 1750, and served as captain in the American army during the Revolution, without receiving a wound. He married twice, —first, to —— Stewart; secondly, to —— Horsee, and had issue *seven* children, of whom hereafter. He settled in Chatham County, N. C., as a planter. Died about 1820. It is related of Richard Riddle, —who was just three feet across his shoulders, —that the champion fighter of Chatham County went in search of him with the intention of thrashing him, and when on his way saw a man *with a cow on his back*, and asked him where Dick Riddle lived. "I am the man," said Riddle, putting down his cow at the same time. "Well," replied the champion, "I have come thirty miles to give you a whipping, but I am satisfied by seeing you"; and bidding Mr. Riddle good-day, returned to his home.

Capt. Cato Riddle[2] (1), a son of Julius[1] (1), was born (presumably) near Haywood, Chatham County, N. C., March 10, 1755; married Martha Tomlinson (one writes Tomlin), and had issue *eight* children, of whom hereafter. He settled on Deep River, in his own native County; removed from near Pittsborough to Clark County, Ga., in 1810, thence to Washington County in 1812 or '13, where he owned a farm. He built a log-house containing two pens (rooms), in an oak and hickory grove. He served in the American army during the war of the Revolution, and was at the battles of Guilford and Cowpens; was not wounded or injured. He was short, heavy-built, and of light complexion. Died in 1823, aged sixty-eight; his widow in 1840, aged about seventy. Both were buried in the church-yard near Sandersville. They were Baptists.

John Riddle[2] (1),† a son of Julius[1] (1), was born near Haywood, Chatham County, N. C.; served in the American army during the Revo-

---

* The ancestors of this branch of Riddles were supposed to be from Scotland, as they were always telling anecdotes and fairy tales of Scotland; besides, the family had all the characteristics of the Scottish people. The seven sons of Julius Riddle[1] (1) were men of great size and extraordinary physical strength. They were of good average height and weighed from two to three hundred pounds.

† The descendants of John Riddle, son of the first Julius, cannot be found, —if any. Some think his family settled in the "Northwest." These should stand between the children of Cato and Julius.

lution, and is supposed to have settled in some Southern State, but his family history is not known. See "Gleanings and Notes" in this book. He may have been one of the John Riddles mentioned there.

Thomas Riddle² (1),* a son of Julius¹ (1), was born near Haywood, Chatham County, N. C.; entered the army of the Revolution, with his brothers, and served during the war. Tradition says a Tory stole his horse, but Riddle pursued and killed him, thus recovering his animal and reducing the enemy's strength. He removed to Moore County, in his native State, where numerous descendants now reside, but I cannot get their family records.

Julius Riddle² (2), a son of Julius¹ (1), was born near Haywood, N. C.; served in the American army during the Revolution; settled in his native County after the war, and his descendants were living near Raleigh, in 1878; some were serving in positions of responsibility.

Brantly Riddle² (1), seventh son of Julius¹ (1), was born in Chatham County, N. C., about 1760, and served in the American army in the Revolution, along with his six brothers, without injury. Some say this son's name was *Jordan*. I cannot find a descendant who has documentary proof.

THIRD GENERATION.

Elizabeth Riddle³ (1), eldest daughter of William² (1), was born in Chatham County, N. C., June 26, 1783; was married to William Ward, Oct. 8, 1801, and several of her children are now living in Alabama; three of her grandchildren, whose father was Dr. James-Riddle Ward, are living at Eutaw, Greene County, Ala., and are well allied and respectable.

John Riddle³ (2), eldest son of William² (1), was born in Chatham County, N. C., June 4, 1786, and died Aug. 22, 1797.

William Riddle³ (2), second son of William² (1), was born in Chatham County, N. C., June 27, 1789, and died Aug. 29, 1797.

Sarah Riddle³ (1), second daughter of William² (1), was born in Chatham County, N. C., Sept. 4, 1794; was married to David Smith, Oct. 19, 1809, and died May 11, 1811, as "Sarah Smith."

Joseph Riddle³ (1), third son of William² (1), was born in Chatham County, N. C., Dec. 10, 1795, and deceased May 6, 1827.

Jesse Riddle³ (1), fourth son of William² (1), was born in Chatham County, N. C., July 3, 1798, and died Nov. 25, 1819.

Hon. Thomas Riddle³ (2), fifth son of William² (1), was born in Chatham County, N. C., Jan. 15, 1803; married Elizabeth-Mary, daughter of Thompson and Huldah Chiles, April 5, 1831, and had issue *four* children, of whom hereafter. Mr. Riddle graduated at Chapel Hill University, of North Carolina, in 1825, and studied law under Judge Henderson, of the supreme court of his native State. He removed to Greene County, Ala., in 1827, and settled in the town of Springfield, where he continued to reside. In 1830 he was elected to represent his County in the State Legislature, and soon afterwards to the State Senate, where he was continued for about eight years, and during all that time was engaged in the practice of his profession.

As a politician, Colonel Riddle was mild, courteous, and respectful toward those who disagreed with him; he was firm in his opinions, but

---

* There are numerous descendants of Thomas Riddle, son of the first Julius, in Moore and adjoining Counties, in North Carolina, but they do not respond to my letters of inquiry. Daniel W. Riddle, a great-grandson of Thomas, is deputy sheriff in Moore County.

never known to use an unkind remark to or about a political opponent. Belonging to the Whig party, he was nevertheless so universally beloved by the Democrats, that at one time it was determined to have no opposition to his re-election at one term; and when a gentleman consented to oppose him, deserving the confidence and support of his party, it was impossible for him to carry its entire strength, so devoted were both parties to their former senator. He was possessed of the spirit of the true statesman, and showed great devotion to the interests of his constituency. He loved his fellow-creatures, and exerted himself to secure their happiness, and few men have been called into public service who lived more in the affections of the people. Colonel Riddle was not a brilliant, forensic debater, but nevertheless respectable; with great candor and unpretending address, he always acquitted himself to the satisfaction of all who had the pleasure of hearing him.

In his intercourse with gentlemen of his profession, both in and out of court, he was always mild, kind, and respectful. But it was in the domestic circle where his virtues shone most brilliantly; it was there that he set an example worthy of himself and the imitation of others; it was there he showed what joys a kind and affectionate husband, father, brother, friend, and master can produce by a devoted and untiring discharge of those several duties of life. Those only who knew him at home are capable of realizing to the full extent his devotion to the comfort of all who were under his care.

Colonel Riddle passed a life in the interchange of good offices with his fellow-man, without attaching himself to any religious denomination, and never made a profession of religion; but he so fully complied with so many of the precepts taught by his Divine Master for the government of his followers, and expressed such complete resignation in the hour of his dissolution, that his friends were not left without the hope that he was a believer in the Saviour of the world. He died in peace with all mankind Aug. 23, 1840, leaving a widow and *four* children; the widow and one daughter survive (1884).

At a meeting of the citizens of Eutaw, the following sentiment was adopted: — " . . . it has pleased an all-wise Providence to cut off, in the midst of his career of usefulness, one of our most valuable and beloved fellow-citizens, — a man who, in all the varied relations of life, acquitted himself with honor, and shed a lustre around the human character; whose private intercourse with his fellow-man, was ever marked with that strict integrity and honorable bearing that cannot fail to extort a tribute of respect from all who came within the circle of his influence; whose social relations were sweetened by all the virtues that give zest to domestic life; and who, in his public career, in the service of his country, has ever exhibited that probity and patriotism which imparts dignity to the councils of State, and sheds unfading lustre around his honored name."

ON THE DEATH OF THE HON. THOMAS RIDDLE.*

[THE NAME OF THE AUTHOR NOT KNOWN.]

A star has gone from virtue's crown,
Torn by the ruthless spoiler's hand;
A light from freedom's sky gone down, —
A generous spirit left the land.

---

* A stanza of this beautiful poem was accidentally lost from the copy, by the author of this book.

When die the noble and the brave,
  Who o'er their country's foes prevail,
A nation's funeral banners wave,
  And thousands chant the mournful tale.

The cenotaph and sculptured bust,
  Commemorative o'er them rise,
To consecrate their hallowed dust,
  And guard the spot where valor lies.

But when the good and virtuous die,
  They need no sculptured bust or stone;
Their virtues and their deeds supply
  A glorious monument alone.

No gilded dome or mausole'm,
  Upreared by skillful artist's hand,
Can give more glorious fame to them
  Throughout their patriot father-land.

They live, — the cherished and the dear, —
  Embalmed within a Nation's heart,
And Spring may leave the circling year,
  Ere thence their memories depart.

And this the monument of praise,
  RIDDLE! thy numerous virtues claim, —
The virtues of thy manhood's days,
  Which consecrate thy spotless name.

Thou wast not of that servile race,
  Who seek the honors of the State
And court the homage due to place,
  The vilest ends to elevate.

Thine was that steady patriot's zeal,
  That burns within the purest heart,
Which sought alone thy country's weal,
  From every selfish view apart.

Truth was thy guide, — the polar star,
  To mark the limits of thy way, —
Whose gleaming led thee from afar,
  Nor let thy feet from virtue stray.

Though fallen in thy manhood's prime,
  Freemen the meed of praise shall give,
And long as rolls the tide of time,
  Thy virtues in their hearts shall live.

In years to come the free and brave,
  Who wander near thy resting spot,
Shall pause beside thy lowly grave,
  And mourn thy sad and hapless lot.

And those who honored thee whilst here,
  Shall oft frequent thy lonely tomb,
And pay the tribute of a tear
  In mem'ry of thy early doom.

May no deceitful stone or bust,
  Its flatt'ry to thy mem'ry give; ·
Thy faults shall slumber with thy dust,
  Thy virtues in our memories live.

Riddle[3] (1), youngest son of William[2] (1), was born in Chatham
N. C., June 5, 1806; married Salina Pope, and had issue *four*

children, three sons and one daughter. He was a merchant and planter.
Died Oct. 13, 1841, aged 37 years. His widow* and daughter now (1884)
reside at Knoxville, Greene County, Ala.

Allen Riddle[3] (1), a son of Richard[2] (1), was born in Chatham County, N. C., in 1789; married April 2, 1814, Arcenia Ellington, and had issue
seven children, of whom hereafter. He served from Nov. 28, 1814, to Feb.
2, 1815, in the war of 1812, under Captain Evan in the North Carolina
militia, Fourth Regiment, Colonel Atkinson commanding. Discharged at
Norfolk, Va. Farmer in Chatham County; died Aug. 25, 1864, aged 75
years; his widow died June 14, 1874, aged 75 years.

Anderson Riddle[3] (1), a son of Richard[2] (1), was born in Chatham
County, N. C., and removed to the West.

Wiley Riddle[3] (1), a son of Richard[2] (1), was born in Chatham County, N. C., and removed to the West.

Barney Riddle[3] (1), a son of Richard[2] (1), was born in Chatham County, N. C.; married Nancy Ellington, and had issue *seven* children, of whom
hereafter. He died in his native County about six years ago (1880).

Nancy Riddle[3] (1), a daughter of Richard[2] (1), was born in Chatham
County, N. C.; married to Allen Temple, and died in her native County
twenty years ago.

Peggy Riddle[3] (1), a daughter of Richard[2] (1), was born in Chatham
County, N. C.; was married to —— Scroble, and died some twenty years
ago (1880).

Mary Riddle[3] (1), a daughter of Richard[2] (1), was born in Chatham
County, N. C.; was married to Terry Poe, and is now (1880) living in her
native County. Her husband was in the war of 1812. She has children
living in Chatham County. This family is related to the well-known poet,
Edgar-Allan Poe.

Dicy Riddle[3] (1), eldest daughter of Cato[2] (1), was born in Chatham
County, N. C., Feb. 1, 1780, and married to Aaron Brantley, of Georgia.

John Riddle[3] (3), eldest son of Cato[2] (1), was born in Chatham County, N. C., Aug. 29, 1782; married Lydia Nale, and had issue *two* children,
of whom hereafter. He was assassinated about the year 1814, somewhere
in the State of Georgia.

Anderson Riddle[3] (1), second son of Cato[2] (1), was born in Chatham
County, N. C., Feb. 28, 1788; married Lydia Burns, of North Carolina,
who died, and he married, secondly, Jane Jordan, of Georgia. Mr. Riddle was a farmer; had issue. Deceased at the home of his only son, in
his seventy-ninth year. He was tall, weighed two hundred and fifty
pounds, and considered a fine-looking man. " Riddlesville," Washington
County, Ga., founded twenty-seven years ago, has (1884) a population
of about five hundred. The land on which the village is laid out was
given by Anderson Riddle, son of Capt. Cato Riddle, with the restric-
tion that no whiskey should ever be sold there. It is six miles from a
railroad.

Sarah Riddle[3] (2), second daughter of Cato[2] (1), was born in Chatham
County, N. C., May 8, 1792; was married to Asa Sinquefield, of Georgia,
farmer.

* She was the daughter of Dr. Pope, a prominent physician of Greene County,
Ala., and her mother's maiden-name was Hobson.

Cato Riddle⁵ (2), third son of Cato² (1), was born in Chatham County, N. C., Dec. 22, 1796, and died a single man.

Mary Riddle⁵ (1), third daughter of Cato² (1), was born in Chatham County, N. C., Oct. 28, 1799; was married to Daniel MacDaniel, farmer.

Jane Riddle⁵ (1), fourth daughter of Cato² (1), was born in Chatham County, N. C., June 20, 1802; was married to Rev. William R. Stansel, and removed to Pickens County (from Georgia), Ala., in 1831, where her children now reside; among them Gen. M. L. Stansel, a prominent lawyer at Carrollton. She died Oct. 16, 1868.

Matilda Riddle⁵ (1), youngest daughter of Cato² (1), was born in Chatham County, N. C., June 11, 1805; was married to Charles Fort, of Georgia, and died Sept. 18, 1852 (?).

William Riddle⁵ (3), a son of Julius² (1), married and had issue, of whom hereafter. Lived in Chatham County, N. C.

Spencer Riddle⁵ (1), a son of Julius² (1).

Lloyd Riddle⁵ (1), a son of Julius² (2), born in Chatham County, N. C., married, and had issue, of whom hereafter. He died at Aberdeen, Miss., in 1840, aged about 60.

John Riddle⁵ (4).
German Riddle⁵ (1).
Elizabeth Riddle⁵ (2). } Children of Julius² (1).
Lucy Riddle⁵ (1).
Jane Riddle⁵ (2).
Sarah Riddle⁵ (3).

FOURTH GENERATION.

William-Thompson Riddle⁴ (4), eldest son of Thomas³ (1), was born in Greene County, Ala., July 11, 1833, and died Nov. 5, 1866. The following taken from an obituary notice written by Col. J. W. Taylor, one of the distinguished citizens of the State of Alabama, is said to be a true delineation of this young man's character: " He was a young man of rare and varied gifts of mind. His intellect was active and inquisitive, solid in its grasp, quick in its perceptions, and wonderfully discursive in its reach after knowledge. The logical and the imaginative were blended in almost equal proportions in his intellectual structure, — hence his equal aptitude and taste for the solid and æsthetic branches of learning. He was passionately fond of books, and loved literature with a clinging affection, and for its own sake. A delicate and impaired physical organization excluded him from athletic exercises and the more active pursuits of life, and he thus became a student, — almost a recluse, — from necessity as well as choice. He lived in his library, and among his books sought and found the instructive companionship coveted by intellectual natures. His tastes were scholarly and refined. His reading was extensive in nearly all departments of literature and science, and in some favored ones exhaustive and minute. The mystic problems of metaphysics had for him a special charm, and he was familiar and fully acquainted with the literature and learning of mental science. He was also peculiarly fond of that higher and nobler criticism which has for its aim the elimination of truth in all branches of knowledge. Possessing a fine library, and having ample time to indulge his literary tastes, he became one of the best read and most generally informed men that the writer ever knew. Yet his modesty, equal to his merits, led him to conceal rather than to obtrude his attainments upon the notice of others. Though learned beyond most young men, there was nothing pedantic either in his disposition or conversation. He wielded a facile and graceful pen, and it is to be regretted that he seldom employed it to minister to the amusement and instruction of others.

"The moral character of Mr. Riddle was unexceptional in its purity, and adorned with many graces. His disposition was kind and affectionate; his spirit genial and placable as childhood itself, and his domestic attachments strong and enduring. Though a great and almost constant sufferer from physical weakness and bodily ailments of various kinds, he preserved the equanimity of his spirit, bore his afflictions with philosophic fortitude, and remained to the last the idol as he was the ornament of his family circle."

Mary-Elizabeth Riddle[4] (2), eldest daughter of Thomas[8] (2), was born in Greene County, Ala., Oct. 6, 1837; was married Feb. 21, 1856, to Thomas B. McKerall, and had issue a son, William-Riddle McKerall, now a promising youth, and the only male representative of Col. Thomas Riddle. She died Dec. 15, 1872.

Irene Riddle[4] (1), second daughter of Thomas[8] (2), was born in Greene County, Ala., April 28, 1839; was married to —— McKerall, and is the only surviving child.

Thomas-Alvis Riddle[4] (3), youngest son of Thomas[8] (2), was born in Greene County, Ala., April 16, 1841, and died April 16, 1856.

Nancy Riddle[4] (2), a daughter of Allen[8] (1), was born in Chatham County, N. C.; was married to John Bishop, a carpenter.

Woodard Riddle[4] (1), a son of Allen[8] (1), was born in Chatham County, N. C., May 24, 1826; married July 17, 1866, to Civil-Ann Johnson (she was born Sept. 26, 1850), and had issue *four* children, of whom hereafter. Farmer.

Joshua Riddle[4] (1), a son of Allen[8] (1), was born in Chatham County, N. C.; married a Horton, and died in 1872–3, aged 52 years, leaving issue.

Jane Riddle[4] (3), a daughter of Allen[8] (1), was born in Chatham County, N. C.; died Feb. 18, 1872, aged 50.

Sarah-Rebecca Riddle[4] (4), a daughter of Allen[8] (1,) was born in Chatham County, N. C., Feb. 18, 1822; unmarried.

Matilda-Elizabeth Riddle[4] (2), a daughter of Allen[8] (1), was born in Chatham County, N. C., Oct. 9, 1824; single.

Arcena Riddle[4] (1), a daughter of Allen[8] (1), was born in Chatham County, N. C., Nov. 20, 1831; single.

Spencer Riddle[4] (2), a son of Allen[8] (1), was born in Chatham County, N. C., and died in 1878. He was married, and presumably left descendants.*

Richard Riddle[4] (2), a son of Barney[8] (1), was born in Chatham County, N. C.

William Riddle[4] (4), a son of Barney[8] (1), was born in Chatham County, N. C.

Alvis Riddle[4] (2), a son of Barney[8] (1), was born in Chatham County, N. C.; died in 1872.

---

* Joseph, Henderson, Adolphus, Dowal, and Adaline are grandchildren of Allen, living in Chatham County, N. C.

Margaret Riddle⁴ (1), a daughter of Barney² (1), was born in Chatham County, N. C.

Emily Riddle⁴ (1), a daughter of Barney² (1), was born in Chatham County, N. C.

Nancy Riddle⁴·⁰(3), a daughter of Barney² (1), was born in Chatham County, N. C.

Ellen Riddle⁴ (1), a daughter of Barney² (1), was born in Chatham County. N. C.

The sons of Barney Riddle are all farmers in Chatham County, N. C. Post-office address, Pittsborough, N. C.

Wealthy-Ann-Nale Riddle⁴ (1), only daughter of John³ (3), was born in Georgia about 1814; was married in 1829, to Hopkins-Rice Richardson, in Greene County, Ala., and had *nine* children, six sons and three daughters. She is now a widow living at Jamestown, Miss.; her husband died in 1878, aged 69.

Joseph-Nale Riddle⁴ (2), only son of John³ (3) was born in Georgia, about 1816, and died in Kemper County, Miss., in 1866. He was an infant when his father was killed.

Mary Riddle⁴ (3), eldest daughter of Anderson² (1), was born about 1813, and was buried on her father's homestead.

Elizabeth Riddle⁴ (3), a daughter of Anderson² (1), was born about 1815; was married to —— McEwin, and is buried at New Hope Church.

William-Cato Riddle⁴ (5), only son of Anderson² (1), was born in Chatham County, N. C., and removed to Georgia with his parents when very young. He married Seanyan-S. Brown, May 21, 1840, and had issue *ten* children, of whom hereafter. Mr. Riddle is tall, and weighs two hundred and twenty pounds. He has Scottish features, small blue eyes, and black hair. He carries on one of the most extensive cotton plantations in middle Georgia, and his crop has run as high as fifteen hundred bales in one year, the dressing of which kept fourteen gins at work. Mr. Riddle owns ten thousand acres of land in one tract. He has a fine residence, pleasantly situated, with double chimneys, and containing six rooms.

Spencer Riddle⁴ (3), a grandson of Julius² (1), is register of deeds of Wake County, and resides in Raleigh, N. C. I have forwarded letters to him, but have no reply.

William Riddle⁴ (6), a brother of the preceding, resides in Raleigh, N. C. No particulars. He had two sisters, one of whom was married to Capt. William Webster.

Dr. James Riddle⁴ (1), a son of Lloyd² (1), is now a resident of Waco, Tex. Can get no records.

John Riddle⁴ (5), a son of Lloyd² (1), resides at Waco, Tex., but I have no particulars.

FIFTH GENERATION.

Alexandretta Riddle⁵ (1), eldest daughter of Woodard⁴ (1), was born in Chatham County, N. C., Sept. 22, 1867.

Leonardas-Robert Riddle⁵ (1), eldest daughter of Woodard⁴ (1), was born in Chatham County, N. C., July 25, 1870.

Edward-Howard Riddle⁵ (1), second son of Woodard⁴ (1), was born in Chatham County, N. C., Jan. 8, 1873.

Rosanna Riddle⁵ (1), second daughter of Woodard⁴ (1), was born in Chatham County, N. C., June 6, 1876.

William-Jefferson Riddle⁵ (7), a grandson of Allen⁴ (1), was born in Chatham County, N. C., Feb. 17, 1853; married March 25, 1875, Mary-Elizabeth Bradshaw (she was born Sept. 17, 1852), and has issue; farmer.

Green Riddle⁵ (1), a grandson of Lloyd³ (1), was born in Chickasaw County, — at Egypt Station, or Gunnertown, — in 1884. No particulars.
Martha Riddle⁵ (1), a granddaughter of Lloyd³ (1), was born in Chickasaw County (as above) in 1884.

Mary-L. Riddle⁵ (4), eldest daughter of William⁴ (4), was born in Washington County, Ga., March 13, 1841; married Dec. 4, 1855, to Simon S. Thomas, and has *four* children.
Anderson-M. Riddle⁵ (2), eldest son of William⁴ (4), was born in Washington County, Ga., Aug. 3, 1842; married Sallie C. Batts, July 1, 1863. No children. Planter in his native County; served in the Confederate army.
Martha-M. Riddle⁵ (2), second daughter of William⁴ (4), was born in Washington County, Ga., Oct. 13, 1843; was married to Aaron C. Edwards, July 14, 1859, and had issue *two* daughters. She died Dec. 25, 1861. Her husband, who was a colonel in the Confederate army during the Rebellion, died about 1870.
Isabella-E. Riddle⁵ (1), third daughter of William⁴ (4), was born in Washington County, Ga., Dec. 28, 1845, and was married to Dr. Arthur F. Cheatham, Nov. 14, 1861.
Ann-E. Riddle⁵ (1), fourth daughter of William⁴ (4), was born in Washington County, Ga., Feb. 8, 1848, and was married to James F. Muriar, May 15, 1872.
John-P. Riddle⁵ (6), second son of William⁴ (4), was born in Washington County, Ga., April 16, 1850; married M. Belle Mosley, Feb. 20, 1873, and lives in Georgia.
Low-J. Riddle⁵ (1), fifth daughter of William⁴ (4), was born in Washington County, Ga., April 16, 1850, and married Nathan J. Newsome, Nov. 10, 1869.
Julia-F. Riddle⁵ (1), sixth daughter of William⁴ (4), was born in Washington County, Ga., Feb. 19, 1858, and died Oct. 19, 1882.
William-H. Riddle⁵ (8), third son of William⁴ (4), was born in Washington County, Ga., Oct. 26, 1861.
Clara-B. Riddle⁵ (1), seventh daughter of William⁴ (4), was born in Washington County, Ga., June 26, 1863, and died Oct. 13, 1865.

SIXTH GENERATION.

Ruth-Elna-J. Riddle⁶ (1), a daughter of William⁵ (7), was born in Chatham County, N. C., April 19, 1876.

The following are names of members of the Riddle family of Chatham County, N. C., but reached me without comment or even the name of the towns where they reside. Some are probably identical with those in the preceding pages: Nathaniel, Charles, Charles, Jr., Artemas, John, Richard, Robert, David C., William, William, Jr., James, Jr., Alvis A., James B., Dolph, Jefferson, David, Joseph, Henderson, Woodward, Alexander, Lounie, Edward, Cransby, Bradley.

RIDDLES OF RIDDLE'S FERRY, NORTH CAROLINA.

Stephen Riddle[1] (1) is said to have come from Ireland to this country previous to the Revolution. He settled on the Yadkin River, twelve miles west of Salem, in North Carolina, where he established a ferry, since known as "Riddle's Ferry." He was probably a native of the Northern Province, but some say came from Maryland; he was in the war of the Revolution. Wife's name not known; she had *seven* children.

SECOND GENERATION.

Benjamin Riddle[2] (1), a son of Stephen[1] (1), was born at Riddle's Ferry, N. C., in 1769; married Mary, daughter of Henry Slater, and settled on the Yadkin River, where he kept Riddle's Ferry till 1824, when he sold it to Thomas Oaks, and moved to west Tennessee. Mr. Riddle married, secondly, Nellie Harnline. He died in Hardeman County, Tenn., in 1845, aged 76 years, having had issue *ten* children, of whom hereafter.

John Riddle[2] (1), a son of Stephen[1] (1), was born at Riddle's Ferry, Rowan County, N. C., June 24, 1764; married Mary ——; settled on Yadkin River as a farmer. He is said to have been born in Maryland. Had issue *six* children. He died Oct. 15, 1826. Wealthy planter and slave-owner.

Stephen Riddle[2] (2), a son of Stephen[1] (1), was born at Riddle's Ferry, Rowan County, N. C., in 1773; married, and emigrated to the Northwest about 1816, and settled in Montgomery County, Ind.; deceased. I have failed to find the descendants of this man.

Mary-Ann Riddle[2] (1), a daughter of Stephen[1] (1), was born at Riddle's Ferry, Rowan County, N. C., and was married to Robert Markland. Lived in Davidson County, N. C. No children.

Sarah Riddle[2] (1), a daughter of Stephen[1] (1), was born in Rowan County, N. C.; was married to a Mr. Ellin.*

THIRD GENERATION.

Henry Riddle[3] (1), a son of Benjamin[2] (1), was born in Rowan County, N. C., July 31, 1796; married in the same State, Nancy Kinnick (she was born Aug. 25, 1798), and settled in Hardin County, Tenn.; thence to Marion County, Ind.; thence to Johnson County, and from there to St. Joseph County, where he owned several hundred acres of land. In 1846 he sold out and went to Iowa, but not liking the climate, returned to St. Joseph County, and purchased three hundred and twenty acres of land in Warren township, where he resided until the death of his wife (she died Jan. 18, 1854), when he removed to Kansas. He had given his two eldest sons one-half of his real estate in 1855, and sold the remainder in 1856. At the time of Mr. Riddle's settlement in Kansas, the trouble relative to its admission to the Union was rife, and he returned to St. Joseph County, Ind., where he died Feb. 14, 1857; he was buried by the side of his wife in the Price grave-yard, Warren township, Ind. By this pair were *seven* children, of whom hereafter.

John Riddle[3] (2), a son of Benjamin[2] (1), was born in Rowan County, N. C., in 1802; married Mary, a daughter of Henry Mock, and settled in Hardeman County, Tenn., about 1830, having had issue *three* children. His widow moved back to North Carolina, and died there.

---

* There were two more sisters who were married to John and Christopher Elrod. **Both** lived in Davidson County, N. C., but John moved to Indiana with his family.

Wiley-Jones Riddle (1), a son of Benjamin[2] (1), was born in Rowan (now Davie) County, N. C., June 19, 1804; married in 1833 to Ruth, daughter of Benjamin and Gillie Bowers; these two last died in 1844, in the County of Tippah, Miss. Mrs. Riddle was born May 9, 1815. Mr. Riddle is a wealthy cotton-planter, living at Cotton Plant, Tippah County, Miss.; he is an intelligent and highly respected citizen, and devoted Christian; has had issue *two* children, of whom hereafter.

Ann Riddle (1), eldest daughter of Benjamin[2] (1), was born in Rowan County, N. C.; was married to the Rev. Nathan Tuttle, of the Cumberland Presbyterian Church, and settled in Arkansas, where Tuttle died. She was married, secondly, to John Smith, and both she and her husband have died since the war.

Nancy Riddle (1), second daughter of Benjamin[2] (1), was born in Rowan County, N. C.; was married to —— Whittaker, and died soon after, in Hardeman County, Tenn.

Janette Riddle (1), third daughter of Benjamin[2] (1), was born in Rowan County, N. C.; was married to Oliver Chaffin; emigrated to Texas in 1834, and settled in Lamar County, where she still lives.

Emeline Riddle (1), fourth daughter of Benjamin[2] (1), was born in Rowan County, N. C.; was married to Daniel Sain, who died in 1873. She married, secondly, in 1877, to —— McKenney, and lives in Hardeman County, Tenn.

Adaline Riddle (1), fifth daughter of Benjamin[2] (1), was born in Rowan County, N. C.; was married to Henry Hainline (?), and died in Hardeman County, Tenn., in 1875.

Isabelle Riddle (1), sixth daughter of Benjamin[2] (1), was born in Rowan County, N. C., and died about 1850.

Sarah Riddle (1), a daughter of Benjamin[2] (1), was born in Rowan County, N. C. No other information.

William Riddle (1), a son of John[2] (1), was born in Davie County, N. C., Aug. 19, 1791; married in 1818 to Nancy, daughter of Thomas and Jennie Slater, and had issue several children, of whom hereafter. Settled on land willed by his father on the Yadkin River, half way between Wilkesborough and Salisbury. Died April 29, 1834.

Stephen Riddle (3), a son of John[2] (1), was born in Davie County, N. C., April, 1796; went West when a young man and settled in Indiana, where his family is supposed to be living. He was a farmer.

Dolly Riddle (1), a daughter of John[2] (1), was born in Davie County, N. C., Dec. 12, 1798, and was married to Jabez Grimes. One account calls her *Sarah*.

Anna Riddle (2), a daughter of John[2] (1), was born in Davie County, N. C., Aug. 3, 1800, and was married to Leonard McBride; had issue several children; all deceased but one daughter.

Mary Riddle (2), a daughter of John[2] (1), was born in Davie County, N. C., and was married to George Rector.

Penelope Riddle (1), a daughter of John[2] (1), was born in Davie County, N. C., and was married to Josiah Taylor.

FOURTH GENERATION.

Wiley Riddle (2), eldest son of Henry[3] (1), was born Jan. 9, 1818; married a Miss Price, and settled near Lakeville, St. Joseph County, Ind.,

I

and had issue several children, of whom hereafter. Mr. Riddle and wife have been dead several years; their children live at Lakeville.

Benjamin Riddle⁴ (2), second son of Henry³ (1), was born June 18, 1828, and settled in Iowa.

Mary Riddle⁴ (3), eldest daughter of Henry³ (1), was born March 6, 1825; was married to —— Johnson, and has issue; resides near St. Mary's Academy, South Bend, Ind.

William Riddle⁴ (2), third son of Henry³ (1), was born Sept. 4, 1827; married, and settled at Crum's Point, Ind. Has *three* children, of whom hereafter.

Nancy-A.-C. Riddle⁴ (2), second daughter of Henry³ (1), was born Oct. 14, 1831; was married to —— Bowland, and is living near Tekamah, Burt County, Neb.

J.-H. Riddle⁴ (3), fourth son of Henry³ (1), was born June 29, 1833; married, and had issue *eight* children, of whom hereafter. He is a farmer; has resided in Indiana and Kansas; now living at South Bend, St. Joseph County, Ind. At one time owned two hundred acres of land at Warren Centre. Was contractor on the railroad, and postmaster.

Sarah-Jane Riddle⁴ (2), third daughter of Henry³ (1), was born Feb. 25, 1836, and died at home aged 16 years.

Emeline Riddle⁴ (2), fourth daughter of Henry³ (1), was born Aug. 11, 1839; was married to —— Ammons, had issue, and died at Bangor, Mich.

Alexander Riddle⁴ (1), only son of John³ (2), was born in 1825, and went West many years ago, — some say to Texas, others, to Kansas, — since when nothing is known of him.

Ann-Janet Riddle⁴ (2), eldest daughter of John³ (2), was born April 7, 1827, and died several years ago.

Emeline Riddle⁴ (1), youngest daughter of John³ (2), was born Dec. 3, 1829; was married Nov. 20, 1845, to Richmond Sheek, and resides in Davie County, N. C.

Hon. Haywood-Yancy Riddle⁴ (1), only son of Wiley³ (1), was born in Hardeman County, Tenn., June 20, 1834; married Martha G. Shelton, of Smith County, and had issue *four* children, of whom hereafter. Mr. Riddle received his collegiate education at Union University, where, after his graduation in 1854, he was for a short time assistant professor. He was graduated at the Lebanon (Tennessee) Law School in 1857, and practised his profession for a short time at Ripley, Miss. He removed to Smith County, Tenn., in 1858, and continued there until the beginning of the war of the Rebellion; during the war he served on the staff of Gen. Marcus J. Wright. In 1865, Mr. Riddle removed to Lebanon, and was clerk and master of chancery there for ten years. He was elected to Congress in 1875, and re-elected in 1876, to a seat in the Forty-fifth Congress. His services as a statesman marked him as a man of a high order of intellect and a judicious legislator. One of his colleagues in congress said of Mr. Riddle: "No more zealous, upright, and conscientious member was ever seated in that body. His life and temper were gentle, and although firm and fearless in the advocacy of the true and the right as his studious intellect saw it, his demeanor was ever marked by a knightly courtesy and consideration for those who differed from him in opinion. His speeches, — always characterized by a scholarly grace and finish, — were replete with learning and research." Another, who was well acquainted with him, has said : "He was a man of thorough intellectual training, and in his life of unremitting labor had acquired distinction in many fields of useful knowledge. He was an exemplary and life-time member of the Baptist Church, and in that best and highest of all the walks of human life, he was distinguished for his piety and a pure and spotless life. He was courteous and affable and deservedly popular." Mr. Riddle was broken down by overwork and retired from the active business of life to his home at Lebanon, where he died on the 29th of March, 1879, greatly and deservedly lamented by all who knew him. I have before me numerous testimonials to his many eminent qualities of both head and heart, presented by his distinguished associates at the bar and in Congress, but for want of space I cannot publish them in this work. The portrait in this book was subscribed for by Mr. Riddle about one year before his death. Mrs. Riddle was a suitable companion for so good and great a man; a woman of amiable qualities and refined tastes.

Gillie-A. Riddle[4] (1), only daughter of Wiley[3] (1) and his wife, Ruth Bowers, was born in Hardeman County, Tenn., about 1838; was married to R. E. Palmer, and resides in Tippah County, Miss.

Lewis-Emerson Riddle[4] (1), eldest son of William[3] (1), was born in Davie County, N. C., June 20, 1819; married Jane, daughter of William and Jane Gullet, and had issue *eight* children, of whom hereafter. He is a farmer in Davie County, N. C.

Thomas-Calvin Riddle[4] (1), second son of William[3] (1), was born in Davie County, N. C., July 30, 1825; married Susan Vogler, daughter of Gottlieb and Martha Vogler, and settled on land, which, at his father's death, was equally divided between him and his elder brother. He says, "We are well enough to do in the world." He has issue *four* children, of whom hereafter. His first wife died in ten years after marriage, and he married secondly, Sophia-Regina Butner, daughter of John and Charlotte Butner, by whom *eight* children.

John-Wesley Riddle[4] (3), third son of William[3] (1), was born in Davie County, N. C., Sept. 11, 1832; married Eliza, daughter of Elisha and Mary Alexander, of Davie County, N. C., and moved to Indiana in 1859, where his wife died, leaving *four* children, of whom hereafter. He married secondly, a Mrs. Hawkins; moved to Texas, where he has been extensively engaged in farming.

FIFTH GENERATION.

J.-H. Riddle[5] (5), eldest son of Wiley[4] (2).
Mary-J. Riddle[5] (4), eldest daughter of Wiley[4] (2).
Nancy-A. Riddle[5] (3), second daughter of Wiley[4] (2).
William Riddle[5] (3), second son of Wiley[4] (2).
Robert Riddle[5] (1), third son of Wiley[4] (2).
Elizabeth Riddle[5] (1), third daughter of Wiley[4] (2).
James Riddle[5] (1), fourth son of Wiley[4] (2).

Alexander Riddle[5] (1), son of William[4] (2).
Harrison Riddle[5] (1), son of William[4] (2).
Francis Riddle[5] (1), son of William[4] (2).

William-R. Riddle[5] (5), eldest son of J. H.[4] (3), was born in Warren township, Ind., Aug. 19, 1855. Is in the pump business.

Thaddeus-S. Riddle[6] (1), second son of J. H.[4] (3), was born in St. Joseph County, Ind., Oct. 25, 1857, and owns a small place near the city of St. Joseph.

Ella Riddle[6] (1), eldest daughter of J. H.[4] (3), was born in St. Joseph County, Ind., May 7, 1859; was married to —— Thurston, and lives in Minnesota.

Loren-F. Riddle[6] (1), third son of J. H.[4] (3), was born in St. Joseph County, Ind., Oct. 28, 1861.

Nettie Riddle[6] (1), } Twin daughters of J. H.[4] (3), were born Oct.
Mary-E. Riddle[6] (5), } 5, 1863, and live in St. Joseph. Nettie was married to —— Jameson; Mary-E. was married to —— Garrett.

Francis Riddle[6] (2), youngest son of J. H.[4] (3), was born in St. Joseph County, Ind., Dec. 28, 1865.

Aggie-E. Riddle[6] (1), youngest daughter of J. H.[4] (3), was born in St. Joseph County, Ind., Feb. 1, 1870.

Haywood-Yancy Riddle[6] (2), eldest son of Haywood[4] (1), was born Sept. 21, 1858, at Smith County, Tenn.

Henry-Shelton Riddle[6] (2), second son of Haywood[4] (1), was born Sept. 1, 1860, in Smith County, Tenn.

Jennie-Wren Riddle[6] (1), eldest daughter of Haywood[4] (1), was born July 29, 1862, (probably) in Smith County, Tenn.

Rubie Riddle[6] (1), second daughter of Haywood[4] (1), was born Aug. 14, 1870, at Lebanon, Tenn.

Wiley-Alexander Riddle[6] (3), son of Lewis[4] (1), was born in Davie County, N. C., Nov. 28, 1850; married Ellen, daughter of James and Mary Pledger, of Forsyth County. No issue (1880).

Nancy-Elizabeth Riddle[6] (4), eldest daughter of Lewis[4] (1), was born in Davie County, N. C., Oct. 26, 1852; unmarried in 1880.

Mary-Jane Riddle[6] (6), second daughter of Lewis[4] (1), was born in Davie County, N. C., June 21, 1854.

Henry-Lewis Riddle[6] (3), second son of Lewis[4] (1), was born in Davie County, N. C., July 8, 1856.

Sarah-Malinda Riddle[6] (3), third daughter of Lewis[4] (1), was born in Davie County, N. C., July 20, 1858.

Emily-Ellen Riddle[6] (1), fourth daughter of Lewis[4] (1), was born in Davie County, N. C., June 18, 1860, and died Nov. 12, 1864.

William-Anderson Riddle[6] (6), third son of Lewis[4] (1), was born in Davie County, N. C, March 14, 1862.

John-Levin Riddle[6] (5), fourth son of Lewis[4] (1), was born in Davie County, N. C., Sept. 19, 1865.

Penelope Riddle[6] (2), eldest daughter of Thomas[4] (1), was born in Davie County, N. C., March 20, 1852; was married to George Martin, Jan. 27, 1870. Has children.

Fielding Riddle[6] (1), eldest son of Thomas[4] (1), was born in Davie County, N. C., Feb. 3, 1854; and was killed instantly by being thrown from a horse against a tree, Sept. 1, 1872.

Leander Riddle[6] (1), second son of Thomas[4] (1), was born in Davie County, N. C., Jan. 5, 1857, and died Feb. 10, 1857.

Louisa Riddle[6] (1), second daughter of Thomas[4] (1), was born in Davie County, N. C., June 9, 1858; was married to Thomas Smith, Dec. 24, 1874.

Anna Riddle[5] (**3**), third daughter of Thomas[4] (**1**), was born in Davie County, N. C., June 30, 1863, and died March 2, 1864.

Catherine Riddle[5] (**2**), fourth daughter of Thomas[4] (**1**), was born in Davie County, N. C., Oct. 22, 1865.

Ashbury Riddle[5] (**1**), third son of Thomas[4] (**1**), was born in Davie County, N. C., Nov. 8, 1867.

John Riddle[5] (**6**), fourth son of Thomas[4] (**1**), was born in Davie County, N. C., July 12, 1870.

James Riddle[5] (**3**), fifth son of Thomas[4] (**1**), was born in Davie County, N. C., Dec. 9, 1872, and died Nov. 15, 1873.

Martha Riddle[5] (**1**), fifth daughter of Thomas[4] (**1**), was born in Davie County, N. C., May 22, 1874, and died Sept. 25, 1874.

Emeline Riddle[5] (**4**), sixth daughter of Thomas[4] (**1**), was born in Davie County, N. C., Sept. 9, 1875.

Ada Riddle[5] (**1**), seventh daughter of Thomas[4] (**1**), was born in Davie County, N. C., Dec. 19, 1878.

William-Asbury Riddle[5] (**7**), eldest son of John[4] (**3**).
Elisha-Monroe Riddle[5] (**1**), second son of John[4] (**3**).
Americo Riddle[5] (**1**), eldest daughter of John[4] (**3**).
Martha Riddle[5] (**2**), second daughter of John[4] (**3**).

RIDDELLS OF ORANGE COUNTY, VIRGINIA.

[SCOTTISH BRANCH.]

James Riddell[1] (**1**), said to have been born in Scotland, came to Virginia at an early day, and settled in Orange County, where he became a wealthy planter and slave-owner. His wife's name was Mary ——, and probably came from Scotland with her husband. The names of children of this ancestor are not certainly known, and only one of his descendants could tell his name and that of his wife. His birth must have been as early as 1700 or 1705; died on his farm in Orange County in old age.

SECOND GENERATION.

William Riddell[2] (**1**), evidently a son of James[1] (**1**), was born in Orange County, Va., about 1725, and made his will in 1776. His wife's name was Joyce ——. He mentions only *seven* children in his will, which see below. It is a little singular that his son's wife should be of the same Christian name. Probably brothers of this man became the heads of other Virginian families whose records are in this book.

WILL OF WILLIAM RIDDELL.

"In the name of God, Amen: I, William Riddel, of Orange County, being of sound sense and perfect memory, thanks be to God, do make this my last will and testament, utterly revoking all other wills by me made — Imprimis. I give and bequeath my soul to Almighty God and my body to the earth to be interred at the discretion of my ex'ors hereafter named.

"*Item.* I give to my son, James Riddel, one third part of two hundred and fifty acres of land, where I now live, at my wife's decease, to him and his heirs forever.

"*Item.* I give to my son, Lewis Riddel, one third part of two hundred and fifty acres of land, said tract, at my wife's decease, to him and his heirs forever.

"*Item.* I give to my son, William Riddel, the other third part of my said land, after my wife's decease, if he is living, otherwise his part to return to my other sons, James and Lewis Riddel, to them and their heirs forever. Also, I give to my son, James Riddel, one negro cald Sampson, which he has now in possession, not to be appraised in my estate, with his paying of fifteen pounds to the estate, at the first sale of said estate. Also, I give to my son, Lewis Riddel, one negro girl cald Callamy, which he has now in possession, not to be appraised in ye sd estate, with his paying fifteen pounds at the time above mentioned.

"*Item.* I give to my daughter, Joyce Powell, one negro boy cald Joshua, with her paying fifteen pounds to the estate, at the time above mentioned, to her and her heirs forever, not to be appraised in my estate.

"*Item.* I give to my daughter, Janet Sheppard, one negro girl cald Fillis, which she has in her possession, to her and her heirs forever, not to be appraised in my estate. with her paying five pounds to the estate at the time above mentioned.

"*Item.* I give to my daughter, Winneyfrit Coursey, one negro wench cald Dafney, which she must pay sixty-five pounds to the estate at the above mentioned time, or have no more of the estate forever.

"*Item.* I give to my daughter, Sally Powell, one negro wench cald Cattenor, which she has now in possession, to her and her heirs forever, with her paying sixty-five pounds to the estate at the time above mentioned, not to be appraised in my estate.

"*Item.* I lend to my beloved wife, Joyce Riddel, three negroes, Peter, George, and Dol, during her natural life, or widowhood, and then return to the estate.

"*Item.* I give to my granddaughter, Joyce Riddel, daughter of Sally Powell, one negro boy cald Ben: to be in her possession at the age of eighteen years old, or marriage, and if he should die before, I give her seventy pounds to be raised out of my estate in lieu of the boy; also, one feather bed and furniture, worth nine pounds. and to live with her grandmother, and at her decease, under the care of Lewis Riddel, while of age or marries. My farther will is that at my decease, all the rest of my estate, be it of what kind or quality soever, be sold to the highest bidder, giving twelve months Cr., and all the money arising from the said estate, to be equally divided between my seven children, viz.: Winneyfrit, Janet, James, Joyce, William, Saley, and Lewis Riddell.

"*Item.* I constitute my beloved wife, Joyce Riddel, and my son, James Riddel, and my son, Lewis Riddel, ex'ors of this my last will and testament. As witness my hand and seal, this 22nd day of December, one thousand seven hundred and seventy-six.

" WM. RIDDELL. { Seal. }

" Signed, sealed, and delivered in presence of us.

- " James Beazley.
  " Edm. Shakelford.
- . " John Pemberton.
  " Philip Ballard."

"At a Court held for Orange County, on Thursday, 27th of Feby: 1777, this last will and testament of William Riddell deceased, being presented into Court by James Riddell and Lewis Riddell, two of the executors therein named, and proved by the oaths of James Beazley, John Pemberton, and Edmond Shakelford, three of the witnesses thereto, and ordered to be recorded — And on the motion of said ex'ors, administration is granted the said ex'ors. Whereupon, they, with James Walker, Benjamin Head, and Thomas Jones, entered into bond for the same, in the sum of two thousand pounds current money. Test— James Taylor, C. O. C."

THIRD GENERATION.

James Riddell[2] (2), a son of William[2] (1), was born in Orange County, Va., about 1750; married Mary Neal, and had issue *ten* children, of whom hereafter. He served in the American army during the Revolution. Was appointed, in conjunction with his brothers, an executor of his father's will in September, 1776. He received from the estate a third part of a lot of land containing two hundred and fifty acres, and a negro slave named Sampson. He was a farmer in Orange County, Va., and owned numerous slaves. Died about 1802, aged, — according to a letter from his grandson,—about 80. It will be seen that, if the last dates are correctly given, he was born as early as 1722. I acknowledge great inharmony of statement as given by different descendants of this man; some were old men with impaired memories, and much written was traditionary. I hope the present venerable representatives of this family will be able to disentangle the genealogical skein, and bring order out of chaos.

Lewis Riddell[3] (2), a son of William[2] (1), was born in Orange County, Va., say 1752, and is mentioned in his father's will made in 1776, as one of his executors. He receives one third section of a tract of land,— part of his father's homestead,—containing two hundred and fifty acres, and a negro girl called Callamy. This man probably left descendants, as the name Lewis prevails in several branches of the Southern family.

William Riddell[3] (2), a son of William[2] (1), was born in Orange County, Va., July 16, 1764; married Joicy Neal, a lady of Irish descent (she was born Nov. 11, 1776), Dec. 27, 1788, and had issue *thirteen* children, of whom hereafter. He settled in Boone County, Ky., about 1812, and became a wealthy farmer. He died Sept. 7, 1816, and his widow May 23, 1836. He is mentioned in his father's will in 1776 as a son, and had bequeathed to him a third part of the two hundred and fifty acres of the homestead farm, to be possessed after his mother's decease, "if he is living," otherwise his part to return to his brothers, James and Lewis. I think William must have settled in Kentucky at an earlier date than 1812. His father gave each of the other sons and daughters a negro slave, but none to William.

Winneyfrit Riddell[3] (1), a daughter of William[2] (1), was born in Orange County, Va., and became the wife of a Mr. Coursey. Her father mentions her as married, in his will in 1776, and gives her a "negro wench cald Dafney, valued at sixty-five pounds." The name of this woman in her father's will is twice spelt as above, but is elsewhere spelled "Winnefred."

Salley Riddell[3] (1), a daughter of William[2] (1), was born in Orange County, Va., was married to a Mr. Powell, and had a daughter, Joyce-Riddell Powell, at the time of her father's death. This daughter was presented by will with a "negro wench cald Cattenor, which she has now (1776) in possession," valued at sixty-five pounds, and her daughter Joyce with "a negro boy cald Ben," to be in her possession when she should be eighteen years of age; or if the boy should die before that time, she should have "seventy pounds in lieu of the boy." This granddaughter of William Riddell also received from his estate, by will, "one feather bed and furniture worth nine pounds." She was to live with her grandmother, for whom she was named, and if the grandmother deceased, to be under the care of her uncle, Lewis Riddell, until of age or married.

Joyce Riddell[3] (1), a daughter of William[2] (1), was born in Orange County, Va., and became the wife of a Mr. Powell (probably a brother of her sister's husband, before mentioned), and received by will from her father, in 1776, "one negro boy, called Joshua," valued at fifteen pounds.

Janet Riddell[3] (1), a daughter of William[2] (1), was born in Orange County, Va., and was married to —— Sheppard. Her father gave her "one negro girl, cald Fillis," valued at five pounds.

FOURTH GENERATION.

Fielding Riddell[4] (1), a son of James[3] (2), was born in Orange County, Va.; married Mildred Waits, in his native State, and resided near the place of his birth for several years. He emigrated to Ohio, and carried on farming; had issue *five* children, of whom hereafter. Mr. Riddell died in Ohio,—near Gallipolis, Gallia County,—but his widow and some of the family returned to Virginia, where some of them now reside.

James Riddell[4] (3), a son of James[3] (2), was born in Orange County, Va.; married —— Roads, and had issue *two* children, —perhaps more,— and died on a farm in his native County. I have no other information. For some reason unknown to me, the members of this family have not assisted me in my researches, and must not blame me because their genealogy is incomplete.

William Riddell[4] (3), a son of James[3] (2), was born in Orange County, Va., and died in Kentucky. Presumably had a family and left descendants.

Valentine Riddell[4] (1), a son of James[3] (2), was born in Orange County, Va.; married Elizabeth Goodall, and lived on a farm in his native County. He had issue a numerous family, some of whom now reside in Greene County, Va. He has deceased. I have not been able to get the full genealogy of this family.

Tavener Riddell[4] (1), a son of James[3] (2), was born in Orange County, Va.; married Mary Goodall, and moved to Tennessee, where his relatives suppose he died. I have not found his descendants. Did he not die in Kentucky?

John Riddell[4] (1), a son of James[3] (2), was born in Orange County, Va.; married Elizabeth Seal (?), and lived in Greene County, in his native State. He was a farmer; had a numerous family, and died many years ago. Some of his children are now living in Greene County, but I cannot prevail upon them to furnish records.

Mary Riddell[4] (1), a daughter of James[3] (2), was born in Orange County, Va.

Winnie Riddell[4] (2), a daughter of James[3] (2), was born in Orange County, Va.

Lucy Riddell[4] (1), a daughter of James[3] (2), was born in Orange County, Va.

Frances Riddell[4] (1), a daughter of James[3] (2), was born in Orange County, Va.

Charles Riddell[4] (1), eldest son of William[3] (2), was born in Orange County, Va., May 15, 1784; died June 4, 1785.

Cornelius Riddell[4] (1), second son of William[3] (2), was born in Orange County, Va., March 20, 1786; died same day.

Lewis Riddell[4] (2), third son of William[3] (2), was born in Orange County, Va., July 11, 1787; married Mildred ——, and had issue several children, of whom hereafter. He was a man of good education, for his day; was judge of the Boone County Court, and was several times elected to the Kentucky Legislature, and was a very popular man. He died Jan. 8, 1824 (another record has it 1828); his wife, Mildred, died on Friday, June 19, 1818, — both of Burlington, Ky. One account says, "He married three times, and had a family of *four* children"; but this does not agree with others, and I accept the most reliable authority.

James Riddell[4] (4), fourth son of William[3] (2), was born in Orange County, Va., Aug. 27, 1790, and after having served as a soldier in the war of 1812, married Sallie M. Craig, of Grant County, Ky. (she was born Feb. 18, 1798), Feb. 1, 1814, and died May 24, 1826. His widow died

Sept. 24, 1826. These had issue *three* sons, of whom hereafter. It is presumed that this family lived in Kentucky.

Lucy Riddell[4] (2), eldest daughter of William[3] (2), was born in Orange County, Va., Nov. 18, 1792; was married to Simeon Christy, of Boone County, Ky., and died May 11, 1822, leaving *two* children, in Missouri.

William Riddell[4] (4), fifth son of William[3] (2), was born in Orange County, Va., June 8, 1796, and died unmarried, June 19, 1818.

Neal Riddell[4] (1), sixth son of William[3] (2), was born in Orange County, Va., May 28, 1798; married, firstly, Miss Perceval; secondly, Mildred Sandy, of Hamilton County, O., Sept. 11, 1832; thirdly, a sister of his second wife, and fourthly, to a Miss Goodridge. He had issue *eight* children, of whom hereafter. He resided somewhere in Kentucky.

Valentine Riddell[4] (2), seventh son of William[3] (2), was born in Orange County, Va., May 3, 1800; married Dec. 25, 1818, to Elizabeth Garnett, by whom he had issue *three* daughters, of whom hereafter. He married secondly, March 10, 1830, to Sallie Fowler, by whom he had *two* daughters, of whom hereafter. He resided in Boone County, Ky. Was a farmer; died Jan. 11, 1834; his second wife died March 8, 1853.

Sally Riddell[4] (2), second daughter of William[3] (2), was born in Orange County, Va., April 28, 1802; was married to Wesley Mitchell, and died June 24, 1823.

John Riddell[4] (2), eighth son of William[3] (2), was born in Orange County, Va., May 17, 1804; married Florenda McKay, Oct. 23, 1825; had issue *ten* children, and died Feb. 11, 1865. His widow died Jan. 19, 1873. Mr. Riddell was a farmer in Kentucky.

Fountain Riddell[4] (1), ninth son of William[3] (2), was born in Orange County, Va., May 9, 1806. (There is a discrepancy between statements furnished by different members of this family; some state that the subject of this notice was born in Kentucky, while others state that he went to Kentucky with his father at the age of seven years.) He married when twenty-one years old to Eliza-Ann, daughter of William and Mary (Waller) Herndon, of Kenton County, Ky. Mr. Riddell lived a while in Kenton County, but at length purchased a tract of land of Thomas Stephens in the woods near Walton, on the Lexington and Covington turnpike, about eighteen miles from the city of Covington. He cleared a farm, adding tract after tract until his plantation consisted of about eight hundred acres of improved land. He kept a large stock and farmed successfully till 1870, when his wife died and he sold his personal property and divided his land among his children; since that time he has spent his days with his children at Chariton, Mo. He died at the house of Charles E. Allen, his son-in-law, July 16, 1875, aged 68 years. His wife (she was born May 2, 1810) died March 3, 1870. Both were members of the Christian Church; they had issue *eleven* children, of whom hereafter.

Elizabeth Riddell[4] (1), third daughter of William[3] (2), was born in Orange County, Va., April 1, 1808, and died in Kentucky, unmarried.

Madison Riddell[4] (1), tenth son of William[3] (2), was born in Orange County, Va., April 9, 1811; married July 4, 1832, to Francis G. Fowler, and had issue *seven* children, of whom hereafter. He died April 4, 1849.

FIFTH GENERATION.

James Riddle[5] (5), a son of Fielding[4] (1), was born in Orange County, Va.; married at Muddy Creek, to Routha-Ellen Gilmore, in Rockingham County, between 1820 and 1830, and had issue *eleven* children, of whom hereafter; was living at Minear, Tazewell County, Ill., in 1876, but deceased previous to 1877, leaving a widow. He was in Augusta County, Va., in 1873, aged 77, but soon after removed to Hopedale, Ill. He was a soldier in the company of Capt. R. Malbury, from Aug. 6 to Dec. 17, 1814, in the Virginia Militia.

Tavner Riddell[5] (2), a son of Fielding[4] (1), was born in Orange County, Va.; married Sarah Powell, and resides in Augusta County. He follows farming for a living. Has issue several children, of whom hereafter. He is now an old man with an impaired memory, and cannot provide full statistics of his family.

Charles Riddell[5] (2), a son of Fielding[4] (1), was born in Orange County, Va.; moved to Ohio with his parents when young; married Cressie Simmons, and returned to Virginia, where he settled as a farmer. I have no account of his family. He is presumed to be dead.

Thompson Riddell[5] (1), a son of Fielding[4] (1), was born in Orange County, Va.; married Mary Powell, and lived in his native shire as a farmer. He is still living, an old man, and has had a numerous family. I have made a great effort to procure full particulars, but cannot prevail upon the family to assist me.

Elizabeth Riddell[5] (2), only daughter of Fielding[4] (1), was born in Orange County, Va., and died single, aged 18 years.

Melicent Riddell[5] (1), daughter of Lewis[4] (2) and his wife Mildred, was born Aug. 7, 1810, in Boone County, Ky.; was married May 25, 1826, to John Pratt, by the Rev. C. Wilson, in Burlington, Ky. She died Sept. 24, 1841, and Mr. Pratt married, secondly, his first wife's cousin.

Joicy-Ann Riddell[5] (2), daughter of Lewis[4] (2) and his wife Mildred, was born in Boone County, Ky.; was married to a Mr. Stephens, and died June 4, 1832.

Lafayette Riddell[5] (1), a son of Lewis[4] (2) and his wife Mildred, was born in Burlington, Boone County, Ky., Nov. 22, 1824; died Sabbath morning, June 19, 1842.

Madaline Riddell[5] (1), a daughter of Lewis[4] (2), was born in Boone County, Ky.; was married to R. J. Latimer, and died leaving *two* sons. Mr. Latimer is also dead.

Lewis Riddell[5] (3), a son of Lewis[4] (2), was born in Boone County, Ky., and died young, unmarried.

Charles Riddell[5] (3), a son of Lewis[4] (2), was born in Boone County, Ky., and died young, unmarried.

Mary Riddell[5] (2), a daughter of Lewis[4] (2), was born in Boone County, Ky.; some time dead. No particulars. I do not know that these children of Lewis Riddell stand in rotation according to their ages.

Cyrus Riddell[5] (1), eldest son of James[4] (4), was born in Boone County, Ky.; married three times, and had issue *four* children, of whom hereafter. He is now the judge of Boone County Court.

Marcellus Riddell[5] (1), second son of James[4] (4), was born at Burlington, Boone County, Ky., Dec. 8, 1819; married at Petersburgh, Ky., March 18, 1845, to Martha-Catherine, daughter of William Snyder (she was born near Charlottesville, Albemarle County, Va., March 6, 1828), and had issue *two* children, of whom hereafter. Mr. Riddell died at Petersburgh, Ky., Sept. 17, 1853.

James-A. Riddell[6] (6), third son of James[4] (4), was born at Burlington, Boone County, Ky., April 10, 1822 ; married Nov. 21, 1844, to Eliza A., daughter of W. W. Eldridge, and died April 10, 1864, having had issue *eleven* children, of whom hereafter (several died in infancy), and "left an untarnished name as the principal heritage of his children."

James-M. Riddell[5] (7), a son of Neal[4] (1), was born in the State of Missouri (?) ; married Elizabeth, daughter of Jael White, of Burlington, Ky., Dec. 14, 1847, and had issue *five* children, of whom hereafter. He was a saddler by trade.

William Riddell[5] (5), a son of Neal[4] (1), was born in the State of Missouri (?) (County unknown), Dec. 27, 1825 ; married firstly, to Amanda R. Norris, at Petersburgh, Boone County, Ky., June 21, 1849 ; she died June 30, 1851, and Mr. Riddell married, secondly, Oct. 25, 1853, to Fidelia Emiley, at Petersburgh, Ky. He had issue *nine* children (one only by first wife), of whom hereafter. Mr. Riddell's mother died when he was only a few days old, and his father moved back to Kentucky when he was three weeks old. He was many years engaged in the dry-goods business in Boone and Mason Counties, Ky. In 1863 he made an engagement with the firm of Chambers, Stearns & Co., of Aurora, Ind., and moved his family to that place ; he remained in the employ of this firm eleven years, and his health having so far failed as to unfit him for business, he moved to Cincinnati, O., where he died Jan. 17, 1875, of consumption, in the fiftieth year of his age.

John Riddell[5] (3), a son of Neal[4] (1) by his second wife, was born in Boone County, Ky. ; married, and had issue *four* children, of whom hereafter. He is resident at Falmouth, Ky.

George Riddell[5] (1), a son of Neal[4] (1), was born in Boone County, Ky. ; married, and had issue *one* son. He was a very excellent man.

Catherine Riddell[5] (1), a daughter of Neal[4] (1), was born in Boone County, Ky., and was married to a Mr. Terrell, of Petersburgh, Ky.

Elizabeth Riddell[5] (3), a daughter of Neal[4] (1), was born in Boone County, Ky., and married Sanford G. Givan.

Pamelia Riddell[5] (1), a daughter of Neal[4] (1), was born in Boone County, Ky.; deceased.

Lewis Riddell[5] (4), a son of Neal[4] (1), was born in Boone County, Ky., and died young, unmarried.

Malvina-P. Riddell[5] (1), eldest daughter of Valentine[4] (2), was born Dec. 7, 1820; was married in May, 1837, to William W. Wilkie, a tailor ; residence, Union, Boone County, Ky.

Elizabeth Riddell[5] (4), second daughter of Valentine[4] (2), was born in Boone County, Ky., Oct. 13, 1823; was married to Holton Ellis, Feb. 22, 1846; he is a farmer.

Harriett-Ann Riddell[5] (1), third daughter of Valentine[4] (2), was born in Boone County, Ky., Oct. 15, 1825; was married to Lucian B. Stevens (he was born in Kenton County, Ky., Sept. 5, 1819), April 26, 1849. A farmer.

Sarah-Frances Riddell[5] (1), fourth daughter of Valentine[4] (2), was born in Boone County, Ky., Jan. 19, 1831; was married May 10, 1861, to Benjamin Clark. She is now the wife of F. Bruce Sanders, of Union, Boone County, Ky.

Augustine Riddell[5] (1), youngest daughter of Valentine[4] (2), was born in Boone County, Ky., Aug. 10, 1833; was married Feb. 22, 1853, to Jacob F. Scott, a farmer.

Lewis Riddell[5] (5), eldest son of John[4] (2), was born in Boone County, Ky., April 15, 1827, and died the same year.

Joseph Riddell[5] (1), second son of John[4] (2), was born in Boone County, Ky., Nov. 23, 1829; married Eliza Marshall, and has issue, of whom hereafter. He is a farmer by vocation.

Harriet-Ann Riddell[5] (2), eldest daughter of John[4] (2), was born in Boone County, Ky., Jan. 2, 1831; was married to Morgan Rice, April 10, 1846. Residence, Boone County.

Fountain Riddell[5] (2), third son of John[4] (2), was born in Boone County, Ky., Jan. 9, 1833; married Louisa, daughter of Nathaniel E. and Jemima (Bradford) Haws, of Virginia, March 10, 1869, and has issue, of whom hereafter. Mr. Riddell is an attorney at law, in Burlington, Ky. He was educated at the Morgan Academy; taught school about one year, then commenced the study of law; has been in the practice of his profession about twenty years; was representative to the State Legislature in the session of 1861-2, — a time that tried men's souls, — and has not been a candidate for political preferment since. He is a Democrat in politics; in religion, nondescript. Mr. Riddell has manifested considerable interest in this work, and has rendered much assistance in providing materials.

Sarah-Lucinda Riddell[5] (2), eldest daughter of John[4] (2), was born in Boone County, Ky., April 1, 1835, and died Dec. 25, 1842.

Eliza-Jane Riddell[5] (1), second daughter of John[4] (2), was born in Boone County, Ky., Sept. 12, 1837; was married Dec. 27, 1858, to Lafayette Gardner, and resides in Hamilton County, Ky.

Melicent Riddell[5] (2), third daughter of John[4] (2), was born in Boone County, Ky., Nov. 29, 1839; died April 19, 1842.

Roxanna Riddell[5] (1), fourth daughter of John[4] (2), was born in Boone County, Ky., March 22, 1841; died Aug. 17, 1842.

William-Lewis Riddell[5] (6), fourth son of John[4] (2), was born in Boone County, Ky., July 25, 1848. He has been in the grocery trade; is now (1879) an editor; unmarried.

Calvin-Garnett Riddell[5] (1), fifth son of John[4] (2), was born in Boone County, Ky., Feb. 14, 1851; a teacher.

William-Waler Riddell[5] (7), eldest son of Fountain[4] (1), was born in Boone County, Ky., Aug. 26, 1828; married July 11, 1858, to Vanelia-Victoria Rooker, of Clinton County, Mo. He resides near Rothville, Chariton County, Mo.; is a farmer and stock-dealer. *Ten* children.

Joyce-Ann Riddell[5] (3), eldest daughter of Fountain[4] (1), was born in Boone County, Ky., Aug. 4, 1832; was married to James S. Rogers, Oct. 5, 1848, and resides near Union, Boone County, Ky.

John-Lewis Riddell[5] (4), second son of Fountain[4] (1), was born in Boone County, Ky., Nov. 18, 1837; married Mary-Susan, daughter of William G. and Elizabeth Rooker, of Chariton County, Mo., March 6, 1862. Farmer and stock-raiser. Wife born Oct. 28, 1841. *Four* children. Residence, Chariton, Putnam County, Mo.

Ophelia-Winsula Riddell[5] (1), second daughter of Fountain[4] (1), was born in Boone County, Ky., Jan. 15, 1840; was married Oct. 15, 1857, to John J. Pratt, by Rev. P. Vawter, at the residence of her parents.

His first wife was her cousin. They reside at East Bend, Boone County, Ky.

James-M. Riddell[5] (8), third son of Fountain[4] (1), was born in Boone County, Ky., June 15, 1842; married Oct. 19, 1865, to Jennie, daughter of Jeremiah and Louisa Glinn, of Boone County, Ky.; moved to Rothville, Chariton County, Mo., in March, 1874, where he is now (1879) engaged in farming and stock-dealing. His wife was born July 25, 1845. They have issue *five* children, of whom hereafter.

Eliza-Madeline Riddell[5] (2), third daughter of Fountain[4] (1), was born in Boone County, Ky., April 3, 1846; was married Jan. 15, 1867, to Charles-Edward Allen; now resides near Rothville, Chariton County, Mo.

Fountain-Zachariah Riddell[5] (3), fourth son of Fountain[4] (1), was born in Boone County, Ky., March 13, 1851; married Oct. 11, 1876, to Ida-Hazeltine, daughter of James M. and Sally Akers, of Chariton County, Mo., and has *one* child, of whom hereafter. He has attended several schools, and was at one time in the Kentucky Western University. He cultivated his land in Kentucky a part of the time, and alternated between his old home in that State and Missouri, where his brothers lived, till 1873, when he sold his property in Kentucky, and located on a quartersection of land in Missouri, where he now resides.

Clara-Lotta Riddell[5] (1), fourth daughter of Fountain[4] (1), was born in Boone County, Ky., Aug. 18, 1830; deceased.

Artimesa Riddell[5] (1), fifth daughter of Fountain[4] (1), was born in Boone County, Ky., Nov. 4, 1834; deceased.

Columbus Riddell[5] (1), fifth son of Fountain[4] (1), was born in Boone County, Ky., Dec. 3, 1844; deceased.

Mary-Elizabeth Riddell[5] (3), sixth daughter of Fountain[4] (1), was born in Boone County, Ky., April 6, 1849; deceased.

Gumeorah Riddell[5] (1), eldest son of Madison[4] (1), was born in Boone County, Ky., Dec. 31, 1833; married L. W. T. Lodge, July 7, 1853, and still lives in his native shire.

William-B. Riddell[5] (8), second son of Madison[4] (1), was born in Boone County, Ky., Oct. 17, 1835; married Lucy M. Berkshire, July 1, 1862, and died May 12, 1872, leaving *two* children, of whom hereafter.

Louisa Riddell[5] (2), eldest daughter of Madison[4] (1), was born in Boone County, Ky., Oct. 29, 1837, and died Feb. 23, 1843.

Edward-F. Riddell[5] (1), third son of Madison[4] (1), was born in Boone County, Ky., Jan. 13, 1839, and died in the Confederate service during the late war, in 1862.

Martha-F. Riddell[5] (1), second daughter of Madison[4] (1), was born in Boone County, Ky., June 6, 1841; died June 14, 1845.

Robert-H. Riddell[5] (1), fourth son of Madison[4] (1), was born in Boone County, Ky., July 26, 1843.

Annie-C. Riddell[5] (1), third daughter of Madison[4] (1), was born in Boone County, Ky., Dec. 1, 1845; was married to S. B. Huley, and resides in Trimble County, Ky.

SIXTH GENERATION.

Charles Riddle[6] (4), a son of James[5] (5), was born in Orange County, Va., about 1827; married Rhoda Riddle, daughter of Talver Riddle (or Riddell), of Virginia, his cousin, and has issue *nine* children, of whom hereafter. He resides in the State of Illinois.

David Riddle⁶ (1), eldest son of James⁵ (5), was born in Virginia about 1829; married Sarah Steats, and has issue *seven* children, of whom hereafter. He is in Illinois.

James Riddle⁶ (9), third son of James⁵ (5), was born in Virginia about 1831; married Eliza Swynk, and has issue *eight* children, of whom hereafter. He lives in Illinois.

Andrew Riddle⁶ (1), fourth son of James⁵ (5), was born in Virginia about 1834; married Elizabeth Farr, and was killed in battle in the late war, in 1861. No issue known.

Gelulan Riddle⁶ (1), fifth son of James⁵ (5), was born in Virginia about 1837; married Amanda J. Prescott, and has issue, of whom hereafter. Lives in Illinois.

John Riddle⁶ (5), sixth son of James⁵ (5), was born in the State of Virginia about 1840; married Ellen Lee, and has issue, of whom hereafter. Was living in Illinois in 1876.

Martha-Jane Riddle⁶ (2), eldest daughter of James⁵ (5), was born in Virginia, and died at the age of 30.

Mary-E. Riddle⁶ (4), a daughter of James⁵ (5), was born in Virginia about 1825, and was married to Franklin Sheaks. She resides in Indiana.

Matilda Riddle⁶ (1), a daughter of James⁵ (5), was born in Virginia about 1831; was married to Joseph Woods, and lives in Virginia.

Juriah Riddle⁶ (1), a daughter of James⁵ (5), was born in Virginia about 1839; was married to Peter Bacheller, and resides in Tazewell County, Ill.

Ellen Riddle⁶ (1), a daughter of James⁵ (5), was born in Virginia about 1841; was married to Jacob Stumlaw, and resides in Illinois.

Lewis Riddle⁶ (6), a son of Tavner⁵ (2), was born in Augusta County, Va., and resides in Rockbridge County. Presumably married and has family.

Fielding Riddle⁶ (2), a son of Tavner⁵ (2), was born in Augusta County, Va., and was killed in late war.

Rhoda Riddle⁶ (1), a daughter of Tavner⁵ (2), was born in Augusta County, Va., and married to Charles Riddle, or Riddell, her cousin; resides in Illinois.

Elizabeth Riddle⁶ (5), a daughter of Tavner⁵ (2), was born in Augusta County, Va., and was married to George Calhoun, of Rockingham County, Va.

Hattie Riddle⁶ (3), a daughter of Tavner⁵ (2), was born in Augusta County, Va., and was married to —— Arrmentrout (?), of Rockingham County, Va.

Frances Riddle⁶ (2), a daughter of Tavner⁵ (2), was born in Augusta County, Va., and was married to Peter Whitesell, who lives in Indiana.

Amelia Riddle⁶ (1), a daughter of Tavner⁵ (2), was born in Augusta County, Va., and is now living at home with her father, unmarried.

James Riddell⁶ (10), eldest son of Cyrus⁵ (1), was born in Boone County, Ky.; married to a daughter of J. R. Smith.

Salley Riddell⁶ (3), a daughter of Cyrus⁵ (1), was born in Boone County, Ky.; was married to a Mr. Rigg.

Elizabeth Riddell⁶ (6), a daughter of Cyrus⁵ (1), was born in Boone County, Ky.

Catherine Riddell⁶ (2), a daughter of Cyrus⁵ (1), was born in Boone County, Ky.; was married to —— Terrell, and is now a widow at Aurora, Dearborn County, Ind.

James-Addison Riddell⁶ (11), only son of Marcellus⁵ (1), was born at Petersburgh, Ky., May 8, 1846; never married.
Marceline Riddell⁶ (1), only daughter of Marcellus⁵ (1), was born at Petersburgh, Ky., April 20, 1850; unmarried.

Cyrus-Wirt Riddell⁶ (2), eldest son of James⁵ (6) that survived infancy, was born in Boone County, Ky., Feb. 17, 1846, and died June 21, 1856. Several of this family died in infancy, and their names do not appear.
Sarah-Francis Riddell⁶ (2), eldest daughter of James⁵ (6), was born in Boone County, Ky., Oct. 10, 1847; was married June 2, 1867, to Jacob McKay, farmer, and resides in Kenton County, Ky. Post-office, Ludlow.
Charles-M. Riddell⁶ (5), second son of James⁵ (6), was born in Boone County, Ky., Sept. 4, 1849. Unmarried. Farmer at Ludlow, Kenton County, Ky.
Mary Riddell⁶ (5), second daughter of James⁵ (6), was born in Boone County, Ky., Feb. 20, 1852, and died Aug. 6, 1853.
Addison Riddell⁶ (1), third son of James⁵ (6), was born in Boone County, Ky., May 16, 1854; married Mary Phinney, Feb. 15, 1872. A farmer near Union, Boone County, Ky. Has one child, of whom hereafter.

Charles Riddell⁶ (6), eldest son of James⁵ (7), was born at Burlington, Boone County, Ky., in 1848, and is a saddler by trade. Presumably married. Lives at Williamstown, Grant County, Ky.
Horatio-B. Riddell⁶ (1), second son of James⁵ (7), was born in Boone County, Ky., Feb. 27, 1850. Has been in a saddler's store in Cincinnati, O., where I formed his acquaintance in 1870, and was kindly guided about the city by him. Now (1878) resides at Covington, Ky.
Permelia Riddell⁶ (2), eldest daughter of James⁵ (7), was born in Boone County, Ky., Nov. 13, 1852.
Hattie Riddell⁶ (4), second daughter of James⁵ (7), was born in Boone County, Ky., Jan. 9, 1855.
Neal Riddell⁶ (2), youngest son of James⁵ (7), was born in Boone County, Ky., July 29, 1863. Deceased.

Stanley Riddell⁶ (1), eldest son of William⁵ (5), was born in Boone County, Ky., Jan. 17, 1851; died Oct. 11, 1851.
Ralph Riddell⁶ (1), second son of William⁵ (5), was born in Boone County, Ky., Aug. 9, 1854; book-keeper in Cincinnati, O., for the firm of Richard Woolley & Sons.
Mary-K. Riddell⁶ (6), eldest daughter of William⁵ (5), was born in Boone County, Ky., July 8, 1856; single in 1879.
Benjamin-Franklin Riddell⁶ (1), third son of William⁵ (5), was born in Boone County, Ky., Sept. 29, 1859; is employed by a grocery firm in Cincinnati, O.
William-Anderson Riddell⁶ (9), fourth son of William⁵ (5), was born in Boone County, Ky., Sept. 11, 1861; now (1878) assistant book-keeper for the I. C. & L. grain elevator, in Cincinnati, O.

James-McClellan Riddell⁶ (12), fifth son of William⁵ (5), was born in Boone County, Ky., Feb. 1, 1864; at school.

Jane-Bush Riddell⁶ (1), twin daughter of William⁵ (5), was born in Aurora, Ind., July 15, 1868; still at school.

Laura-Bement Riddell⁶ (1), twin daughter of William⁵ (5), was born at Aurora, Ind., July, 15 1868; died Oct. 9, 1869.

Anna-Percival Riddell⁶ (1), youngest daughter of William⁵ (5), was born at Aurora, Ind., Jan. 21, 1870, and died Feb. 5, 1879. None of these children are married.

Mary Riddell⁶ (7), a daughter of John⁵ (3), was born in Falmouth, Ky.

Hattie Riddell⁶ (5), a daughter of John⁵ (5), was born in Falmouth, Ky.

Lizzie Riddell⁶ (7), a daughter of John⁵ (5), was born at Falmouth, Ky.

Lewis Riddell⁶ (7), only son of George⁵ (1), was born at Boone County, Ky.

Mary Riddell⁶ (8), a daughter of Fountain⁵ (2), was born at Burlington, Boone County, Ky., Jan. 22, 1871; died June 27, 1871.

Nathaniel-E. Riddell⁶ (1), a son of Fountain⁵ (2), was born at Burlington, Boone County, July 17, 1872.

Carry-B. Riddell⁶ (1), a daughter of Joseph⁵ (1), was born in Boone County, Ky., in August, 1866.

Mary-Waller Riddell⁶ (9), a daughter of William⁵ (7), was born in Chariton County, Mo., April 16, 1859.

Cyrus-Hutcheson Riddell⁶ (3), eldest son of William⁵ (7), was born in Chariton County, Mo., Jan. 12, 1861.

William-Fountain Riddell⁶ (10), second son of William⁵ (7), was born in Chariton County, Mo., March 13, 1863.

Clauda-Ann Riddell⁶ (1), second daughter of William⁵ (7), was born in Chariton County, Mo., March 25, 1865.

Eliza-Elizabeth Riddell⁶ (3), third daughter of William⁵ (7), was born in Chariton County, Mo., May 6, 1867.

John-Piatt Riddell⁵ (6), third son of William⁵ (7), was born in Chariton County, Mo., Dec. 17, 1871.

Charles-Allen Riddell⁶ (7), fourth son of William⁵ (7), was born in Chariton County, Mo., May 11, 1873.

James-Louis Riddell⁶ (13), fifth son of William⁵ (7), was born in Chariton County, Mo., April 28, 1875; died Jan. 24, 1877.

Vanelia Riddell⁶ (1), fourth daughter of William⁵ (7), was born in Chariton County, Mo., Feb. 28, 1878 (?).

James-Columbus Riddell⁶ (14), eldest son of John⁵ (4), was born in Chariton County, Mo., Feb. 16, 1864.

William-Rooker Riddell⁶ (11), second son of John⁵ (4), was born in Chariton County, Mo., Aug. 17, 1866.

Eliza-Dell Riddell⁶ (4), eldest daughter of John⁵ (4), was born in Chariton County, Mo., Dec. 23, 1868.

Annie-Lee Riddell⁶ (2), second daughter of John⁵ (4), was born in Chariton County, Mo., May 18, 1871.

25

Anna-Louisa Riddell⁶ (3), eldest daughter of James⁵ (8), was born in Boone County, Ky., Feb. 16, 1867.

Louis-Dudley Riddell⁶ (1), eldest son of James⁵ (8), was born in Boone County, Ky., June 3, 1869.

Mary-Ophelia Riddell⁶ (8), second daughter of James⁵ (8), was born in Boone County, Ky., March 9, 1872; died Nov. 27, 1874.

Nova-Platt Riddell⁶ (1), second son of James⁵ (8), was born in Chariton County, Mo., March 4, 1875.

Jesse-Herndon Riddell⁶ (1), third son of James⁵ (8), was born in Chariton County, Mo., Nov. 5, 1878.

Clara-Leota Riddell⁶ (3), eldest daughter of Fountain⁵ (3), was born in Chariton County, Mo., June 11, 1878.

Edward Riddell⁶ (2), eldest son of William⁵ (8), was born in Boone County, Ky., Dec. 11, 1862; died the same year.

Annie Riddell⁶ (4), eldest daughter of William⁵ (8), was born in Boone County, Ky., April 24, 1866.

SEVENTH GENERATION.

Arthur Riddell⁷ (1), eldest son of Addison⁶ (1), was born in Kenton County, Ky., Oct. 30, 1872.

RUDDELLS OF ROANOKE COUNTY, VIRGINIA.

Cornelius Ruddell¹ (1), supposed to have come from some part of England or Ireland,* was an early settler in Virginia. He married and had issue a numerous family, of whom hereafter. On an old deed from King George the surname is spelled *Ruddle*, and it may be presumed with plausibility that the "Ruddles of Ruddle's Station, Kentucky," are of the same family. It may be worth mention that the name Cornelius is a Christian name in the family designated "Riddells of Laurel Hill"; also, that the family of Byrd intermarried with both branches.

SECOND GENERATION.

Andrew Ruddell² (1), a son of Cornelius¹ (1), was born in Roanoke County, Va.; married Katie Rader, and had issue a number of children, of whom hereafter. He was a land-owner, slave-holder, and planter.

Michael Ruddell² (1), a son of Cornelius¹ (1), was born in Roanoke County, Va.; inherited valuable land from his father, but dying without a family (never married), he willed his property to his nephew.

THIRD GENERATION.

John Ruddell³ (1), eldest son of Andrew² (1), was born in Roanoke County, Va.; married Ann Hershberger, and had issue. He has deceased. Was a farmer. His widow and her family live at High Point, Ia.

---

* There are several families of Ruddell now living in Ireland, and their represen-tative uses the same crest as the Riddells of Riddell, namely, a "demi-greyhound." Walter T. R. Riddell, Esq., now of Termoyra House, Lurgan, Ireland, is a gentle-man of intelligence and means.

Betsey Ruddell³ (1), a daughter of Andrew² (1), was born in Roanoke County, Va., and was married to —— Combs.

Debbie Ruddell³ (1), a daughter of Andrew² (1), was born in Roanoke County, Va., and became the wife of John Mibblin, and had issue. Both deceased.

Mary Ruddell³ (1), a daughter of Andrew² (1), was born in Roanoke County, Va., and was married to John Rader. Her address is New Geneva, Jackson County, W. Va.

James Ruddell³ (1), a son of Andrew² (1), was born in Roanoke County, Va.; married Martha-Harris Fox (or Foss), daughter of Richard Fox, and had issue, of whom hereafter. He settled in his native County as a planter and slave-owner. Now living with his son, aged 81 years.

Andrew Ruddell³ (2), a son of Andrew² (1), was born in Roanoke County, Va., and is now living at Secor, Woodford County, Ill.; carpenter.

Cornelius Ruddell³ (2), a son of Andrew² (1), was born in Roanoke County, Va., and married, firstly, Elizabeth McGerge; secondly, Sarah Barnes, widow. He has deceased.

Igebo Ruddell³ (1), a daughter of Andrew² (1), died young.

Catherine-Ann Ruddell³ (1), a daughter of Andrew² (1); maiden.

Malinda Ruddell³ (1), a daughter of Andrew² (1), was married to George Routt, and has *three* daughters, all married. Mr. Routt is a carpenter by trade. Mrs. Routt has the family Bible containing full records.

FOURTH GENERATION.

James-Henry Ruddell⁴ (2), son of James³ (1), resides at East Bend, Ford County, Ill.

Sarah-Jane Ruddell⁴ (1), only surviving daughter of James³ (1), was married to George Gish, Roanoke, Woodford County, Ill.

John-Byrd Ruddell⁴ (2), second surviving son of James³ (1), was born in Roanoke County, Va.; married Amanda-Helen Fox, and had issue *thirteen* children, of whom hereafter. He inherited property from his uncle, Michael Ruddell, which was a part of his grandfather's estate, and lives on it, having named it "Mountain View Farm." Carpenter by trade. Now (1884) 55 years of age.

FIFTH GENERATION.

Emma Ruddell⁵ (1).
Janette Ruddell⁵ (1).
Catherine-Ann Ruddell⁵ (2).
William Ruddell⁵ (1).
Adelaide Ruddell⁵ (1).
Florence Ruddell⁵ (1).   } Children of John-Byrd⁴ (2).
George-Preston Ruddell⁵ (1).
Martha-Elizabeth Ruddell⁵ (1).
Irene Ruddell⁵ (1).
Frederick Ruddell⁵ (1).
Byrd Ruddell⁵ (1).

RIDDLES OF UNION COUNTY, KENTUCKY.*

[VIRGINIAN BRANCH.]

Jeremiah Riddle[1] **(1)**, son of a Mr. Riddle whose name is unknown, and his wife, whose maiden-name was Herindon, was born in Loudoun County, Va., 1765; married Polly, daughter of Capt. Frank Berry, of Revolutionary fame (she was born in Loudoun County, Va., in 1795, and died in her seventy-seventh year), settled on land owned by "Old Daniel Morgan, the old war-horse of Revolutionary fame," in 1802, and when the County of Union was laid off, the spot of land he had cleared was selected for the County seat; this was in 1811. Mr. Riddle was a farmer; a man of high standing, and his house was always a home for preachers. He had issue *nine* children, of whom hereafter.

SECOND GENERATION.

Hon. George-W. Riddle[2] **(1)**, eldest son of Jeremiah[1] (1), was born in Henderson County (now Union), Ky., July 18, 1807; married Eliza B., daughter of Enoch Hunt and his wife Judith, daughter of Charles Hampton (she was born in Lexington, Ky., Aug. 18, 1809; descended from Daniel Boone, the noted hunter and pioneer of Kentucky, and allied to the family of Bryant, known in pioneer history), July 2, 1826, and had issue *nine* children, of whom hereafter. Mr. Riddle was born when the country around him was a vast wilderness, and had but few educational advantages; but possessing a studious mind, he acquired a practical education and has been in the lower house of the Kentucky Legislature two or more sessions, besides filling many other positions of responsibility in his County. He is commanding in person and like all of his family noted for his courage and great force of character; his residence is on the same lot of land where he was born. He has had a shock of paralysis, and writes with difficulty. He informs me that his grandfather came to Virginia from Scotland about 1763, and his grandmother from Ireland; which statement is undoubtedly correct.

Jackson Riddle[2] **(1)**, second son of Jeremiah[1] (1), was born at Morganfield, Union County, Ky., about 1811; married Mary Finnie, of said County, and settled on a farm. He is said to have been a man who won many friends and was long called "Uncle Jack." He was killed by a mule, June 11, 1878. Issue, *four* children.

Benjamin-Franklin Riddle[2] **(1)**, third son of Jeremiah[1] (1), was born at Morganfield, Union County, Ky., July 18, 1814; married Anna F., daughter of Major Rowley, who migrated from near Wheeling, Va., at an early day, and resides on a beautiful farm near Uniontown, lying along the Ohio River, where he has been settled since early manhood. He received a medium education in his native County, and has been engaged in agricultural pursuits; has been very successful, and is now in good circumstances. He is a very handsome man; weighs about two hundred and forty pounds, and like his father and brothers is a perfect giant in

---

* This family is supposed to have been descended from those Riddell ancestors who came to Virginia in their own vessels, bringing their farm-stock, implements, furniture, plate, and servants with them. They were accompanied by families named Byrd, or Bird, now well known and highly respected in Virginia, and still allied with the Riddle family. See "Riddles of Loudoun County, Virginia," for antecedents.

physical strength, and has great courage. He is in every respect a worthy citizen, highly esteemed for his truthfulness and sterling honesty, and equally feared by all wrong-doers who may come in his way. He has suffered from paralysis. Mrs. Ann, his first wife, who died Aug. 7, 1862, was well educated at Wheeling and Fredericksburgh, Va. By his first marriage there were *six* children born, of whom hereafter. He married, secondly, Lucy A. Hundley, but has no children by this union.

Charles-H. Riddle[2] (1), fourth son of Jeremiah[1] (1), was born about 1816, in Union County, Ky.; married, and had issue *seven* children, of whom hereafter. He served in the Texas war under General Houston; settled in Hamilton County, Ill., and is now living at Moore's Prairie, Ill., a widower. Occupation, farmer.

William Riddle[2] (1), fifth son of Jeremiah[1] (1), was born at Morganfield, Union County, Ky., about 1818; married Mary Bauldwin, of Henderson, and emigrated to California in 1849. He was in the war of the Rebellion; was killed by a fall from a house on which he was at work. Do not know of any children.

Henry-B. Riddell[2] (1), sixth son of Jeremiah[1] (1), was born at Morganfield, Union County, Ky., July 22, 1826; married Julia A. Waggoner, Sept. 6, 1849, and had issue *six* children, of whom hereafter. His first wife died June 10, 1852, and he married, secondly, Elizabeth-Holland Smith, daughter of Moses and Fannie Smith (she was born Dec. 28, 1828, in Daviess County, Ky.), Dec. 5, 1854, and by her had *five* children. Mr. Riddell, — as the family spell their name, — was a farmer in Kentucky.

Sedney-C. Riddle[2] (1), eldest daughter of Jeremiah[1] (1), was born in Morganfield, Union County, Ky., in 1809; was married to William Benthall, and lived within sight of the place of her birth all her life. She lived a devoted Christian, and died at the age of 65 years, greatly lamented by a wide circle of friends.

Caroline Riddle[2] (1), second daughter of Jeremiah[1] (1), was born at Morganfield, Union County, Ky., about 1818; was married, first, to Henry Fellows; secondly, to Samuel Hunt. She had issue. Now (1879) living.

Elizabeth-A. Riddle[2] (1), youngest daughter of Jeremiah[1] (1), was born at Morganfield, Union County, Ky., say about 1828, and died in April, 1877; her residence was in Webster County, Ky. No record of marriage.

THIRD GENERATION.

John-B. Riddle[3] (1), a son of George[2] (1), was born in Union County, Ky., July 1, 1845.

William-H. Riddle[3] (2), a son of George[2] (1), was born in Union County, Ky., Feb. 14, 1848.

Charles-C.-W. Riddle[3] (2), a son of George[2] (1), was born in Morganfield, Union County, Ky., and was killed while in the Confederate army, November, 1862.

James-Samuel Riddle[3] (1), a son of George[2] (1), was born in Morganfield, Union County, Ky., and was killed while serving in the Confederate army, Aug. 21, 1864.*

George-H. Riddle[3] (3), eldest son of Jackson[2] (1), was born in Union County, Ky., Jan. 28, 1844; deceased.

---

* There were other *five* children in the family of George W. Riddle, all deceased. It is presumed some of the sons married.

Ruth-Ellen Riddle[6] (1), only daughter of Jackson[2] (1), was born in Union County, Ky., Feb. 17, 1847; was married to Isaac Reynolds, Feb. 4, 1862, and died Jan. 31, 1876.

Milton-Young Riddle[6] (1), second son of Jackson[2] (1), was born in Union County, Ky., Dec. 21, 1850; married Mary C. Taylor, Nov. 6, 1870. Post-office, Boxville, Ky.

James-William Riddle[6] (2), third son of Jackson[2] (1), was born in Union County, Ky., Dec. 17, 1854; married Carrie Combs, Nov. 2, 1876, and has *two* sons. He resides at Belle River, Jefferson County, Ill.; a farmer.

Sarah-J. Riddle[6] (1), eldest daughter of Benjamin[2] (1), was born in Union County, Ky., Feb. 25, 1839; was married to Hon. Samuel E. Flannigan, of McLeansborough, Ill., June 29, 1858, and has *six* children. Mr. Flannigan is a lawyer.*

Capt. James-M. Riddle[6] (3), eldest son of Benjamin[2] (1), was born in Union County, Ky., March 11, 1841. He was an officer in the Fifth Kentucky Confederate Cavalry, and was killed in 1865, in an engagement at Nashville, Tenn., between General Thomas, of the Federal, and General Hood, of the Confederate army. Never married.

Robert-R. Riddle[6] (1), second son of Benjamin[2] (1), was born in Union County, Ky., Dec. 24, 1845; enlisted in the Confederate army when a mere boy, and lost his life (killed) in the same engagement as his brother.

John-W. Riddle[6] (2), third son of Benjamin[2] (1), was born in Union County, Ky., Nov. 22, 1847, and is now living on his farm near Uniontown, Ky.

Augustus Riddle[6] (1), fourth son of Benjamin[2] (1), was born in Union County, Ky., July 4, 1850.

Fannie Riddle[6] (1), second daughter of Benjamin[2] (1), was born in Union County, Ky., Sept. 9, 1854.

Elizabeth-Ann Riddle[6] (2), eldest daughter of Charles[2] (1), was born in Hamilton County, Ill., in 1839; was married to Charles H. Judd, in 1858, and has children.

Abram-I. Riddle[6] (1), eldest son of Charles[2] (1), was born in Hamilton County, Ill., in 1842; married Charlotta Snerd in 1861; entered the army and died there in January, 1863, leaving a son bearing his name.

Philip-B. Riddle[6] (1), second son of Charles[2] (1), was born in Hamilton County, Ill., in 1846; married Amanda Sturman when about nineteen years of age, and has *three* children, of whom hereafter. He is a farmer in his native County.

Henry Riddle[6] (2), third son of Charles[2] (1), was born in Hamilton County, Ill., and died at the age of 3 years.

Mary Riddle[6] (1), second daughter of Charles[2] (1), was born in Hamilton County, Ill., in 1851; was married to Q. A. Wilbanks in 1871, and has issue. Residence, Belle Rive.

* HON. SAMUEL E. FLANNIGAN is the eldest son of Capt. James W. Flannigan, who is the eldest son of Samuel E. Flannigan, fifth son of David O'Flannigan, from King's County, Ireland, who was the father of ten sons, some of whom, with their father, participated in the Revolutionary War for Independence. Hon. Samuel E. Flannigan ranks among the best lawyers in Illinois, and has served on the State Board of Education and in the State Legislature.

William-I. Riddle[2] (3), fourth son of Charles[2] (1), was born in Hamilton County, Ill., in 1854; married Mary Morgan, and has issue a son and daughter. A farmer.

Charles-J. Riddle[2] (3), fifth son of Charles[2] (1), was born in Hamilton County, Ill., in 1859, and is now a barber at Belle Rive, in his native State; unmarried.

Mary-J. Riddell[2] (2), eldest daughter of Henry[2] (1), was born in Union County, Ky., July 11, 1851, and died June 28, 1864.

Kate-Wallis Riddell[2] (1), second daughter of Henry[2] (1), was born in Union County, Ky., Feb. 2, 1856; a teacher.

Henry-Fairfax Riddell[2] (3), eldest son of Henry[2] (1), was born in Union County, Ky., July 7, 1857; a farmer.

James-Gibson Riddell[2] (4), second son of Henry[2] (1), was born in Union County, Ky., Oct. 12, 1858; died Aug. 22, 1859.

Sarah-Frances Riddell[2] (2), third daughter of Henry[2] (1), was born in Union County, Ky., Feb. 7, 1860; was married March 20, 1879, to George-Edward Pepper, and lives on the Ohio River, near Raleigh, Union County; farmer.

John-Geiges Riddell[2] (3), third son of Henry[2] (1), was born in Union County, Ky., April 18, 1863; unmarried.

FOURTH GENERATION.

Robert Riddle[4] (2).
Albert Riddle[4] (1). } Children of Philip[2] (1).
Ida Riddle[4] (1).

RUDDLES OF RUDDLE'S STATION, KENTUCKY.

George Ruddle[1] (1), sometimes "Riddle" in print, settled at a place in Kentucky afterwards known as "Ruddle's Station," previous to 1780, and is supposed to have come from Virginia. He married and left issue, of whom hereafter. This family was intimate with Daniel Boone, the celebrated hunter and Indian-fighter, and associated with him in many adventures.

Abraham Ruddle[2] (1), a son of George[1] (1), was captured by the Indians and carried away; he was released, or escaped, and moved to Missouri, where he was married and reared a family. He returned to Kentucky between 1830 and 1840, and claimed a tract of land near his birth-place which he was entitled to. He became a Baptist minister and preached the remainder of his days. His descendants are supposed to be living at Point Pleasant, Mo., about eighty miles from Cairo, Ill.

Isaac Ruddle[2] (1), a son of George[1] (1), was a great hunter and Indian-fighter. He had a revolving rifle before Colonel Colt, the celebrated inventor of the revolver, was born. When hunting with a companion named Martin, on Kingston Creek, Isaac took the right hand of a hill, and Martin the left, to meet on the table-land above, where they expected to see some bison or buffalo. Martin had proceeded cautiously about a quarter of a mile when he heard the report of Ruddle's rifle, and in a few seconds another report from the same direction; he immediately ran to the top of the hill, and down to where Ruddle was, and found him scalping an Indian. He asked Martin to load his rifle while he scalped another Indian below; he had just time to get the second scalp and grasp his rifle when he was hotly pursued by two Indians; Ruddle knowing of a large oak near ran round and through its forks, where he stopped and watched his pursuers. An Indian swung round a dogwood to look for his victim, when Ruddle sent a ball through his feathered head. The other Indian came running with raised tomahawk, when Ruddle drew a heavy horse-pistol from his belt, which caused the Indian to fly to the thick woods below. It is said the lone Indian was asked by his tribe where his companions were, and replied that they had seen the devil, who killed three of them and would have shot him with his *knife* had he not run. This was the same tribe that captured Daniel Boone.

RIDDELLS OF PAKENHAM, CANADA.

[SCOTTISH BRANCH.]

James Riddell¹ (1), parents' names unknown, was probably born in Londonderry, Ireland. He married Eliza Martin, and moved with his family from Londonderry to the parish of Thurlo (or Thurlough), County Mayo, Ireland, and there made a permanent settlement. His father was born in Scotland, but the place of his nativity is not known. The family were all Presbyterians. Mr. Riddell had issue *eight* children, of whom hereafter. Funeral attended by a Rev. Mr. Hall, who was the parish minister.

SECOND GENERATION.

John Riddell² (1), eldest son of James¹ (1), was born in Londonderry, Ireland, say 1790; married Ann Ewin in the parish of Thurlo, County Mayo, in the latter part of 1803 (ceremony performed by the Rev. Mr. Hall, Presbyterian minister), and had issue *eight* children, of whom hereafter. He, with his wife and seven children, came to America in 1822, and settled in Perth, Lanark County, Can., where he is supposed to have died. He was a farmer.

David Riddell² (1), second son of James¹ (1), was (presumably) born in Londonderry, Ireland; married Cecilia Camel, and came to America in 1830; settled in or near the city of Kingston, Can., where it is believed they died many years ago; had *seven* or *eight* children, of whom hereafter.

Robert Riddell² (1), third son of James¹ (1), was born (presumably) in Londonderry, Ireland; married Bessie Booth in the parish of Thurlo, County Mayo, and had issue *two* or more children, of whom hereafter. The whole family came to America in 1832, and settled near Toronto, Can., where it is supposed they deceased and their descendants now reside.

George Riddell² (1), fourth son of James¹ (1), was born (presumably) in Londonderry, Ireland; removed to the parish of Thurlo, in the County Mayo, with his parents, where he lived and died. He was never married.

* The author believes descendants of brothers of the ancestor of this family were heads of other families mentioned in this book.

James **Riddell**[2] (2), fifth son of James[1] (1), was born (presumably)
in Londonderry, Ireland, but went with his parents to the parish of Mayo,
in County Mayo, where he remained till a young man, and then returned
to his native city in the north. No knowledge of his subsequent movements.

Mattie Riddell[2] (1), eldest daughter of James[1] (1), was probably born
in Londonderry, Ireland; she was married to Charles Otterson, in the parish of Thurlo, County Mayo, whither she went with her parents when
young, and died there. She had issue *six* children, all of whom settled
in Upper Canada.

Betty Riddell[2] (1), second daughter of James[1] (1), was probably born
in Londonderry, Ireland; went to County Mayo with her parents when
young; was married in the parish of Thurlo, to John Beekett, and had
a large family, all of whom came to Canada with them in 1832, and settled
in Pakenham.

Nancy Riddell[2] (1), youngest daughter of James[1] (1), was born (presumably) in Londonderry, Ireland, but was carried to the par sh of Thurlo,
County of Mayo, when a child. She became the wife of Jóhn Timmins,
of the latter place, had a numerous family, and came to Canada with her
children in 1832, and settled in Pakenham. Deceased.

THIRD GENERATION.

John Riddell[2] (2), eldest son of John[2] (1), was born in the parish of
Thurlo, County Mayo, Ireland, and died there young.

Eliza Riddell[2] (1), eldest daughter of John[2] (1), was born in the parish of Thurlo, County Mayo, Ireland, Dec. 19, 1804; came to Canada
with her parents in 1822, and was married to John Willson, a man of
Scottish extraction, in 1827. This was the first wedding ever celebrated
in the township by white people. In the history of the township of Fitzroy, County of Carlton, Can., the following statement is found:—" In his
magisterial capacity, Squire Laudon performed numerous marriage ceremonies, one of which, that of John Willson, who settled on the Pakenham road, and Eliza, daughter of John Riddell, of the same place, was
the first marriage-rite solemnized in the Township, as well as the first
wedding of residents of the Township." Mrs. Willson had a family of
twelve children,* and is still living. A remarkably well-informed and
strong-minded woman.

Archibald Riddell[2] (1), second son of John[2] (1), was born in the
parish of Thurlo, County Mayo, Ireland, Sept. 26, 1806; came to Canada
with his parents in 1822; married Eliza-Jane, daughter of William and
Ann (McEwin) McAdams (she was born Nov. 30, 1818), Jan. 18, 1836,
and by her had issue *nine* children, of whom hereafter. Mr. Riddell is
a resident of Pakenham, Ontario, Can.; farmer and lumberman. Possesses all the distinguishing characteristics of a genuine Scotchman:
industrious, determined, prudent, conservative, and successful.

James Riddell[2] (3), third son of John[2] (1), was born in the parish of

* DR. JAMES C. WILLSON, M. D., of Flint, Mich., a prominent physician, is her
son; and to his earnest endeavors the family is indebted for the history of this
branch of the Riddell-clan. He had promised me biographical notices of the elder
members of this family, but they do not reach me. They were pioneers in that
part of Canada where they settled, and many interesting incidents connected with
their lives could be related, and would havé enhanced the value of their family history. — *Author.*

Thurlo, County Mayo, Ireland, Aug. 15, 1808, and came to Canada with his parents in 1822. He married Mary Ritchie, a woman of Scottish descent, Feb. 5, 1836, and had issue *seven* children, of whom hereafter. Mr. Riddell lives in the town of Pakenham, Can.

George Riddell (2), fourth son of John[2] (1), was born in the parish of Thurlo, County of Mayo, Ireland, in 1810; came to Canada with his parents in 1822; married Jane Ritchie, and had issue *four* children, of whom hereafter. He died in the town of Waterford, County Norfolk, Can. His wife died some years ago.

John Riddell (3), fifth son of John[2] (1), was born in the parish of Thurlo, Mayo County, Ireland, 1812, and came to Canada with others of the family in 1822. He married Ann Fee, and had *one* son, of whom hereafter. Mr. Riddell was a farmer by occupation; deceased.

Ann Riddell (1), second daughter of John[2] (1), was born in the parish of Thurlo, County Mayo, Ireland, came to Canada with her parents in 1822; was married to Rowland Carter, and had *two* or more children. The descendants live in Dakota Territory. Mrs. Carter was born in 1814.

Robert Riddell (2), youngest son of John[2] (1), was born in the parish of Thurlo, County Mayo, Ireland, in 1816; came to Canada in 1822; married Isabella Ritchie, and has had issue *nine* children, of whom hereafter. He resides in Pakenham, County Lanark, Ontario, Can.

William Riddell (1), eldest son of David[2] (1), was born in the parish of Thurlo, County of Mayo, Ireland; came to Canada with his parents in 1830, and settled near Kingston.

George Riddell (3), second son of David, was born in the parish of Thurlo, County of Mayo, Ireland; came to Canada with his parents in 1830. No particulars.

Robert Riddell (2), third son of David[2] (1), was born in the parish of Thurlo, County Mayo, Ireland, and came to Canada with his parents in 1830. No particulars.

David Riddell (2), fourth son of David[2] (1), was born in the parish of Thurlo, County Mayo, Ireland, and came to Canada with his parents in 1830.

Eliza-Annie Riddell (2), eldest daughter of David[2] (1), was born in the parish of Thurlo, County Mayo, Ireland, and came to Canada with her parents in 1830.

Louisa Riddell (1), second daughter of David[2] (1), was born in the parish of Thurlo, County Mayo, Ireland, and came to Canada with her parents in 1830.

George Riddell (4), eldest son of Robert[2] (1), was born in the parish of Thurlo, County Mayo, Ireland, and came to Canada with his parents in 1832.

John Riddell (4), second son of Robert[2] (1), was born in the parish of Thurlo, County Mayo, Ireland, and came to Canada with his parents in 1832.

FOURTH GENERATION.

George Riddell[4] (5), eldest son of Archibald[3] (1), was born in Fitzroy, Can., Feb. 13, 1837; married Isabella Russell, May 29, 1862, and had issue *six* children, of whom hereafter. He died Nov. 27, 1880.

William Riddell[4] (2), second son of Archibald[3] (1), was born in Fitzroy, Can., Dec. 23, 1839; married Margaret McVicar, May 6, 1862, and had issue *two* children, of whom hereafter. He died Nov. 26, 1869.

John-M. Riddell[4] (5), third son of Archibald[3] (1), was born in Fitzroy, Can., Dec. 22, 1841 ; married Kate R. Dickson, Feb. 28, 1872, and has issue *five* children, of whom hereafter. He is a resident of Greenville, Mich. ; farmer.

Annie Riddell[4] (1), eldest daughter of Archibald[3] (1), was born in Fitzroy, Can., Jan. 9, 1843.

James Riddell[4] (4), fourth son of Archibald[3] (1), was born in Fitzroy, Can., April 25, 1845.

Archibald-E. Riddell[4] (2), fifth son of Archibald[3] (1), was born in Fitzroy, Can., March 9, 1847; married Jane Smith, and has issue *five* children, of whom hereafter.

Robert Riddell[4] (3), sixth son of Archibald[3] (1), was born in Fitzroy, Can., Aug. 10, 1850.

Eliza-Jane Riddell[4] (3), youngest daughter of Archibald[3] (1), was born in Fitzroy, Can., Dec. 6, 1853 ; was married to George H. Featherston, June 28, 1871, and died Aug. 19, 1880, leaving issue.

Samuel Riddell[4] (1), youngest son of Archibald[3] (1), was born in Fitzroy, Can., March 29, 1857, and died (drowned) June 23, 1863.

John Riddell[4] (6), eldest son of James[3] (3), was born in Fitzroy, Can., Feb. 11, 1838, and is now living at "Moose Man" in Manitoba.

Eliza-Jane Riddell[4] (4), eldest daughter of James[3] (3), was born in Fitzroy, Can., Nov. 23, 1840 ; was married to John Forbes, and has *six* children. Resides in Fitzroy, Ont.

James Riddell[4] (5), second son of James[3] (3), was born in Fitzroy, Can.; unmarried.

Archibald Riddell[4] (3), third son of James[3] (3), was born in Fitzroy, Can.; lives in Ottawa; unmarried.

Jane Riddell[4] (1), second daughter of James[3] (3), was born in Fitzroy, Can.; was married to Dr. Albert Armstrong, and has issue; resides in Aronprior, Ont.

William Riddell[4] (3), fourth son of James[3] (3), was born in Fitzroy, Can., and lives at "Moose Jaw," Manitoba ; single.

Matthew Riddell[4] (1) youngest son of James[3] (3), was born in Fitzroy, Can., and lives at home, unmarried.

John Riddell[4] (7), eldest son of George[3] (3), was born in Canada (?).
Eliza-Ann Riddell[4] (5), eldest daughter of George[3] (2).
Jane-Isabella Riddell[4] (2), second daughter of George[3] (2).
James Riddell[4] (6), second son of George[3] (2).

John-Fee Riddell[4] (8), a son of John[3] (3), was born Aug. 27, 1847, and is living at Winnipeg, Manitoba, British North America.

Ann Riddell[4] (2), eldest daughter of Robert[3] (2), was born in Pakenham, Can.; was married to William White, and has issue *six* children; resides at Aronprior, Ontario, Can.

George Riddell[4] (6), eldest son of Robert[3] (2), was born at Pakenham, Can.

Matthew Riddell⁴ (2), second son of Robert⁸ (2), was born in Pakenham, Can., and lives in Manitoba.

Lizzie Riddell⁴ (1), second daughter of Robert⁸ (2), was born in Pakenham, Can.

John Riddell⁴ (9), third son of Robert⁸ (2), was born in Pakenham, Can.

Robert Riddell⁴ (4), fourth son of Robert⁸ (2), was born in Pakenham, Can.

Joshua Riddell⁴ (1), fifth son of Robert⁸ (2), was born in Pakenham, Can.

Mary Riddell⁴ (1), third daughter of Robert⁸ (2), was born in Pakenham, Can.

Bella Riddell⁴ (1), fourth daughter of Robert⁸ (2), was born in Pakenham, Can.

RIDDELLS OF ST. JOHN, NEW BRUNSWICK.

Thomas Riddell¹ (1), parents unknown, was born in Scotland, but removed to London, Eng., where he continued to reside until the death of his first wife, by whom he had *twelve* children. He married a second time, emigrated to America, and settled in New Brunswick. He had *three* children by his second wife, of whom (with those previously mentioned) hereafter. He was a carpenter by trade. He died in Boston, Mass., May 28, 1882, aged 80 years and 9 months.

SECOND GENERATION.

Constance Riddell² (1), eldest daughter of Thomas¹ (1), was born in London, Eng., Oct. 7, 1826.

William Riddell² (1), eldest son of Thomas¹ (1), was born in London, Eng., Feb. 28, 1829; died in London.

Maria Riddell² (1), second daughter of Thomas¹ (1), was born in London, Eng., Oct. 26, 1830.

John Riddell² (1), second son of Thomas¹ (1), was born in London, Eng., Oct. 8, 1832; was in Boston, Mass., in 1883. Has had issue *twelve* children. Married Martha-Jane Harrington, of St. John, N. B., in 1854.

Isabella Riddell² (1), third daughter of Thomas¹ (1), was born in London, Eng., March 17, 1834; resides in London.

Thomas Riddell² (2), third son of Thomas¹ (1), was born in London, Eng., Nov. 19, 1835; lives in America.

Joseph Riddell² (1), twin brother of Thomas¹ (2), was born in London, Eng., Nov. 19, 1835; deceased.

Caroline Riddell² (1), fourth daughter of Thomas¹ (1), was born in London, Eng., Aug. 14, 1837; now in the United States.

Charles Riddell² (1), fifth son of Thomas¹ (1), was born in London, Eng., May 19, 1839, and died in London.

Josephine Riddell² (1), fifth daughter of Thomas¹ (1), was born in London, Eng., July 27, 1840, and died in London.

Frederick Riddell² (1), sixth son of Thomas¹ (1), was born in London, Eng., Nov. 1, 1842; came to America in 1850; married Mary A. Aker,

June 26, 1869, and has issue *two* children, of whom hereafter. In 1878 he was at Ellershousen Station, Hants County, N. S.

George Riddell² (1), seventh son of Thomas¹ (1), was born in London, Eng., May 31, 1845; deceased in England.

Josephine Riddell² (2), sixth daughter of Thomas¹ (1), was born in New Brunswick, Feb. 18, 1852.

Paulina Riddell² (1), seventh daughter of Thomas¹ (1), was born in St. John, N. B., Dec. 1, 1858.

Gustavus Riddell² (1), eighth son of Thomas¹ (1), was born in St. John, N. B., May 25, 1859.

THIRD GENERATION.

Roseanna Riddell³ (1), eldest daughter of John² (1), was born in St. John, N. B., May 1, 1855; was married Dec. 24, 1877.

Martha-Fearebay Riddell³ (1), second daughter of John² (1), was born in St. John, N. B., Jan. 2, 1857, and died same year.

John-Thomas Riddell³ (2), eldest son of John² (1), was born in St. John, N. B., Feb. 1, 1859.

Sophia-Josephine Riddell³ (1), third daughter of John² (1), was born in Roxbury, Mass., Jan. 14, 1861; was married June 1, 1882.

Catherine-Elizabeth Riddell³ (1), fourth daughter of John² (1), was born in Roxbury, Mass., Jan. 1, 1863.

Charles-Frederick Riddell³ (2), second son of John² (1), was born in Boston, Mass., Dec. 23, 1865.

Wilhelmina Riddell³ (1), fifth daughter of John² (1), was born in Cambridge, Mass., Jan. 2, 1867; died Jan. 15, 1868.

Floraella-Melissa Riddell³ (1), sixth daughter of John² (1), was born in Cambridge, Mass., April 18, 1869.

Alice-May Riddell³ (1), seventh daughter of John² (1), was born in Cambridge, Mass., April 18, 1871.

William-Arthur Riddell³ (2), third son of John² (1), was born in South Boston, Mass., April 15, 1875.

Harry-Sylvester Riddell³ (1), fourth son of John² (1), was born in South Boston, Mass., Aug. 11, 1878.

Gertrude-May Riddell³ (1), eighth daughter John² (1), was born in South Boston, Mass., May 15, 1880.

Willinia Riddell³ (1), eldest daughter of Frederick² (1), was born in Nova Scotia, May 22, 1870.

Thomas Riddell³ (3), eldest son of Frederick² (1), was born in Nova Scotia, June 11, 1872.

RIDDLES OF NOVA SCOTIA.

Hugh Riddle¹ (1), was a native of the County of Durham, in England, where he married, and had a family of *three* children, of whom hereafter.

SECOND GENERATION.

Robert Riddle² (1), a son of Hugh¹ (1), was born in the County of Durham, Eng.; married Phebe Johnson, and had issue *four* children, of whom hereafter.

Jane Riddle[2] (1), eldest daughter of Hugh[1] (1), was born in the County of Durham, Eng.

Susan Riddle[2] (1), second daughter of Hugh[1] (1), was born in the County of Durham, Eng.

THIRD GENERATION.

Robert Riddle[3] (2), a son of Robert[2] (1), was born in the County of Durham, Eng., in 1819; married Mary Johnson, and had issue *seven* children, of whom hereafter. He was a farmer; emigrated to New Brunswick, British North America, in 1848, and works in the coal mines.

Hugh Riddle[3] (2), a son of Robert[2] (1), was born in the County of Durham, Eng.; married Jane Ayer, and had issue; farmer.

Franklin Riddle[3] (1), a son of Robert[2] (1), was born in the County of Durham, Eng., and married Elizabeth Reed; farmer.

Margaret Riddle[3] (1), a daughter of Robert[2] (1), was born in the County of Durham, Eng.

Jane Riddle[2] (1), a daughter of Robert[2] (1), was born in the County of Durham, Eng.

FOURTH GENERATION.

Esther Riddle[4] (1), eldest daughter of Robert[3] (2), was born in England in 1838.

George Riddle[4] (1), eldest son of Robert[3] (2), was born in England in 1842.

Hugh Riddle[4] (3), second son of Robert[3] (2), was born in England in 1846.

Susan Riddle[4] (2), second daughter of Robert[3] (2), was born in New Brunswick in 1849.

Mary Riddle[4] (1), third daughter of Robert[3] (2), was born in Nova Scotia in 1854.

Isabella Riddle[4] (1), fourth daughter of Robert[3] (2), was born in Nova Scotia in 1858.

Sarah Riddle[4] (1), fifth daughter of Robert[3] (2), was born in Nova Scotia in 1860.

THE RIDLEY FAMILY OF ENGLAND AND AMERICA.

RIDLEY FAMILY OF ENGLAND.

THIS family pedigree reaches back to the time of William the Conqueror. Ridley Hall, the earliest known residence of the family, was in Cheshire, a place previously owned by the Knight Hospitallers. It is pleasantly situated in a beautiful, sequestered valley, under the shadow of the Peckferton Hills. The old hall was evidently unimposing and dilapidated at the time of the first possession of the Ridley family; but, as will appear hereafter, it was rebuilt, and became one of the most stately and elegant houses in the County. The ancient property continued in the main line of the Ridley family till it ended in an heir female, who became the wife of Robert Danyel; then the estate passed to the son and heir, Sir Robert Danyel, who quartered his arms with those of Ridley. This Sir Robert Danyel was an assistant of Sir William Standley, who became the hero of the battle at Bosworth Field, in Scotland, — probably his Esquire, or one of his body-guard, — and a veil of mystery enshrouds his history. Leland, the antiquary, in his Itinerary, says, " Ridley 'longed [belonged] to Danyel that was servant to Sir W. Standlie, and few men know what became of this Danyel." The most probable explanation is, that the owner of Ridley Hall and estate was either killed at the battle of Bosworth Field, or was put out of the way by William Standley in order to gain possession of his property. Standley went into the battle with three thousand "tall men," and turned the tide in favor of King Henry; and when King Richard died fighting, covered with wounds, Standley found his crown trampled in the mire, and placed it upon the head of King Henry. After this battle we find Sir William Standley rewarded with a great property, including Ridley Hall and Manor; this was in the year 1494. There was an abstract of a fine on the manor of Ridley in the thirty-second year of the reign of Henry VI, which intervenes between the possession of Sir Robert Danyel and that of Sir William Standley, but the parties named were probably only nominal possessors, and there is obscurity about the transfer. At any rate, Standley did not live long to enjoy his new acquisitions, for after " making it one of the fairest gentleman's houses in all Chestershire," he was, in 1494, committed to prison, and in 1495 lost his head on Tower Hill.* We find no more mention of Ridley

---

* LONDON TOWER was built by Gundulph, Bishop of Rochester, in 1078. It adjoins the River Thames at the east end of the city. The walls, sixteen feet thick, are of solid masonry. Gloomy memories associate with this ancient stronghold, in consequence of the many hapless prisoners who have been executed there, and their names on their dungeon-walls may still be seen, where they cut them centuries ago.

Hall after the death of Standley, till the year 1509, when, at the accession
of Henry VIII, he presented Ralph Egerton, who was then gentleman
usher of the king's chamber, with all the former possessions of Sir William Standley in Cheshire and Flint, which included the manor of Ridley,
a mill and certain lands in Farndon, and the Lordship of Tattanhall; and
on the 11th of February, 1514, the manor of Ridley was entailed by patent
to the heirs male of Ralph Egerton by the same king. This representative of the Egerton family had been created a knight by King Henry
VIII, for services in the army in France in 1513, and was made standard-bearer for life, with a salary of one hundred pounds a year, after the battle of Flodden Field. He was afterwards made Marshal of Chestershire,
thus having jurisdiction in office commensurate with his predecessor at
Ridley, Sir William Standley, who had also been Marshal of the County.
Egerton died in 1527, and was buried at Ridley. How came the family of
Egerton to have possession of the manor of Ridley? In the absence of specific documentary evidence, I conjecture the connections to be as follows:
As the main line of the family of Ridley had ended in Alice, the wife of
Robert Danyel, and the representation consequently devolved upon their
son and heir, who became the knight-follower of William Standley, when
this son was put out of sight in some mysterious way, his County Marshal got possession of his property, being then in great favor with the
king. Meanwhile a junior branch of the Ridley family of Chestershire,
undoubtedly the legal claimants at the death of Sir Robert Danyel, being
nearest of kin, had ended in an heir female, Margaret Ridley, who became
the wife of Richard Egerton, and had a son Thomas Egerton, her heir.
As Standley was now out of the way, the Egertons, represented in that
generation by Sir Ralph, put in their rightful claim to the manor of Ridley, and were successful in its possession, with all the costly improvements
on the estates made by William Standley. The singular circumstances
show that this ancient property, once evidently wrested from the real heirs
unjustly, came back to the legal representative after many years, so much
increased in value as to almost make good the loss of possession during the
occupancy of its unlawful holder. It will be seen by reference to the pedigrees of the Ridley family following this article, that the alliances between
the families of Ridley and Egerton had been cemented by several marriage bonds. Sir William Grosvenor, of Eton, had married Susan Ridley,
and their daughter or granddaughter became the wife of one Sir Ralph
Egerton. There had also been intermarriages between the families previous to the death of the last heiress of the junior branch of the Ridley
family.

The manor of Ridley continued in the Egerton family from 1509 to
1608, when it passed by sale to Orlando Bridgeman, Bart., Lord Keeper
of the Great Seal to King James I, thence into the possession of the family of Pepheys, in the early part of the seventeenth century, and is now
owned by William Pepheys, Earl of Cottenham. This family have never
made Ridley Hall their residence. During the civil wars the ancient house
was garrisoned by the Parliament; an unsuccessful attack was made upon
it on the 4th of June, 1645, by a party from the garrison at Beeston Castle. The Hall was burned in the year 1700.

"Ridley Chancel" was kept in repairs by the Pepheys to 1873, when
they threw it upon the wide world, their liability to keep it longer in good
condition being at that time repudiated.

The town of Ridley is in the first division of the Hundred of Edisbury,

County Palatine of Chester, six and a quarter miles from Nantwitch, and in 1850 contained one hundred and twenty-three inhabitants.

It is not known whether Ridley Hall took its name from the family, or the family their surname from the place of residence; the latter, however, is the most probable conclusion, Ridley, or Ridleigh, as the name was originally spelt, being a local name. William the Conqueror required all residents to assume surnames at his accession, in order to properly keep the records; and the family at Ridley Hall, if then resident there, probably adopted the name at that time. As one authority in a local history calls the Ridleys "a gentile family," it is possible that their ancestor came with William from Normandy, and was rewarded with the lands of Ridley for services in his army; indeed nearly all the evidence points to that as the origin of the family. I have not yet learned that the name stands on the Domesday Book.

In St. John's church-yard, in the city of Chester, is a slab, which is partly flat, and covered with flowing foliage, executed in low relief, and in part cut away in order to disclose to view a sculptured semi-effigy; the upper part, including the figure, — that of a female, — is much worn and injured by lapse of time, but the lower part of the stone is nearly entire. The tracery and border-legend within which it is contained, are still sharp and distinct, with the exception of a few letters only of the legend. The inscription in Latin on this monument is, —

> " *Hic jacet Agnes Victor Rice de-Ridlegh,*
> *Ive Obiit Dic,*
> *Sabiti Pxi aw Flu.*
> *Phi et Jacob a*
> *. . . . CCX.*"

Translated : " Here lies Agnes, wife of Richard de-Ridlegh, who died on Sabbath-day next before the feast of Philip and James, the apostles."

A junior branch of the ancient family of Ridley of Chestershire emigrated to Northumberland, and became settled upon extensive lands in the valley of the Tyne, long before the elder line became extinct at Ridley Hall. Just how their lands in Tynedale came to them has not been learned; neither what place they made their first residence in that County. They were certainly possessed of the castle and estates of Willimoteswick as early as 1280, and probably much before that date. Evidently daughters of Hudard de Willimoteswick were married to the Ridleys. Hudard or Bedard de Willimoteswick was witness to a grant of land in Whitelaw, to the Canons of Hexham, by Adam de Tynedale, in the reign of King Henry II (1154). An evidence of the connection between the families of Ridley and Willimoteswick is the fact that the singular name " Odard " or " Hudard " came into the Ridley family about this time; and the first who bore the name was undoubtedly the heir to the estate.

Willimoteswick means the *mote* or *keep* of William; the name may also represent a *villa*. Bishop Ridley, the martyr, — whose uncle was resident there, — in his farewell letter, written just before he was burned at Oxford, spells the name " Willimountwick," and his friend Doctor Turner has it " Willowmountwick." The willow tree in the dialect of Northumberland, where this old place is situated, is always called a " willey." But Willimoteswick is the ancient and most common way of spelling the name; mote is clearly Saxon, and means a *court* or *meeting-place*, both of which were anciently held in the open air in ciruse surrounded by a trench and vellum, and afterwards in castles and towers. The old distich —

" Willy willy walshale, Keep of my Castle,"

used in the north of England, in the game of " Limbo," contains the true etymon of the adjective "*willey*."

WILLIMOTESWICK CASTLE is situated on a wooded knoll, at the meeting of the South Tyne and Blackleugh Burn. The farm offices and foundation walls show that, in former times, it had been an extensive fortress. Of the early history of the place little is known. The name does not occur in the list of castles and towers of Northumberland, made out about 1460, although the family of Ridley was permanently settled there, as previously shown, long before that time, and their names are not unfrequent in private documents respecting lands in Tynedale very early.

In 1542 the "good towre" of Willimoteswick was said to be in a good state of "reparations," and so it long continued. The tower forming the entrance to a farm-yard is massive and picturesquely covered with yellow lichens; the situation is very romantic, and the prospect from the elevation on which the castle stood, embracing a wide and diversified landscape, is very pleasing. The "silver Tyne" winds among the fields and woodlands, glistening here and there like a burnished shield; beyond, the pastoral hills are covered with flocks. A rustic stone bridge crosses the burn [brook] that flows around the elevation, which is almost covered with foliage and luxuriant grasses. The tower itself is oblong,* built in substantial masonry with heavy overhanging battlements. Roger North says, "The County of Northumberland was exceedingly infested with cattle thieves (in feudal times), so that all considerable farm-houses were built of stone in the manner of a strong tower, in which the cattle were lodged every night; in the upper rooms the family lodged, and when an alarm came, they went up to the top and with hot water and stones from the battlements faught in defence of their cattle."

The cattle and estate of Willimoteswick were held by the Ridley family through a long succession of strong knights until 1652,† when, in consequence of their steady adherence to the cause of King Charles, all their lands and seats in Tynedale were confiscated and wrested from their hands; the property was then sold by the parliament to Richard Musgrave, whose daughter was the wife of William Ridley, Musgrave Ridley being the last proprietor of his name.

" Then fell the Ridley's martial line,
    Lord William's ancient towers;
Fair Ridley on the silver Tyne,
    And sweet Thorngrafton's bowers.

" All felt the plunderer's cruel hand,
When Legal rapine through the land
Stalked forth with giant stride;
    When Loyalty successless bled,
    And Truth and Honor vainly sped
        Against misfortune's tide."

---

* WILLIMOTESWICK CASTLE is a very fine example of a fortified domestic building: it forms one side of a square, the other three sides of which are offices, a large gate-way, etc.; all stone, to be fire-proof, even to the mangers of the stables.

† Willimoteswick and the Manors of Chatesworth (?), Henshaw (?), Ridley, Walltown, Hardriding, and others, chiefly in the valley of the South Tyne, are on the right side: *i. e.*, on the English side of the Roman Wall, while Parkend is on the north side. The estates of the Ridleys, on the south side of the Roman Wall, were all confiscated, in consequence of the loyalty of the family in 1652, while their lands on the north side were retained, and are still held by them.

"WILLIMOTESWICK CASTLE"
Ancient Residence of the Ridleys,
NORTHUMBERLAND, ENGLAND.

Under the Commonwealth, and in the reign of King Charles II, the estate of Willimoteswick was, with other property in that neighborhood, charged in the County rate upon a rental of seven hundred and forty pounds a year, as owned by Francis Neville, of Chewitt, in the County of York; but since the beginning of the last century, it has been owned by the Blacketts of Matfern. Willimoteswick was certainly considered the principal residence of the Ridleys of Tynedale, and here the successive chieftains, — a race of gallant and formidable knights, — long made their abode. The broad and valuable lands of the Ridleys lay along the English border, and became the scene of many a bloody hand-to-hand battle with the clans who came down upon them from across the Scottish line. Here rode forth from generation to generation the chiefs of the Ridley clan, armed to the teeth and coated in mail, followed by members of the numerous branches of the family living along the Tyne Valley at the time, to redress their wrongs and wreak vengeance upon their enemies across the border. When an attack was made upon them, every member of the clan came to the defence, called to arms by beacon-fires kindled upon the tops of towers or on the surrounding hills, and by the same signal when about to make an aggressive movement upon their foes. The Ridleys and Featherstons, of Featherston Castle, were at deadly feud, and for many years seem to have watched for every opportunity to shed each other's blood, as will appear from the following account of an engagement at Greenscheles Cleugh, where on the 24th of October, 1530, the Ridleys killed Alabamy Featherstonhaugh; an event which was made the source of the strange ballad, which Surtees pretended to have taken down from the recitation of an old woman of eighty years, the mother of a miner of Alston Moor, and which Sir Walter Scott inserted in his "Border Minstrelsy."

> " Hoot awa', lads; hoot awa',
> Ha' ye heard how the Ridleys, and Thirwalls, and a',
> Ha' set upon Albany Featherstonhaugh,
> And taken his life at Deadmans Shaw?
> There was Willimoteswick,
> And Hardriding Dick,
> And Hughy, of Hawden, and Will, of the Wall;
> I canna' tell all; I canno' tell all;
> And many a muir that the de'il may knaw.
>
> " The auld man went down, but Nichol, his son,
> Run away afore the fight was begun;
> And he run, and he run,
> And afore they were done,
> There was mony a Featherston gat sic a stun,
> As never was seen since the world begun.
>
> " I canna' tell a', I canno' tell a',
> Some gat a skelp, and some gat a claw;
> But they gae'd the Featherston's haud their jaw:
> Nichol, and Alic, and a'.
> Some gat a hurt, and some gat nane;
> Some gat a harness, and some gat sta'en,
> Ane gat a twist o' the craig;
> Ane gat a dunch o' the wame;
> Symy Haw gat lamed of a leg,
> And syne ran wallowing hame.
>
> " Hoot, hoot, the auld man is slain outright!
> Lay him now wi' his face down; — he's a sorrowful sight.

> Janet, thou donnot,
> I'll lay my best bonnet
> Thou gets a new gude-man afore it be night."

The old lady is made to say she had not heard the song sung for many years, but that, when she was a lassie, it was sung at merry-makings "till the roof rung again." The somewhat ludicrous description shows the disorderly state of society in which a murder in cold blood was not only looked upon as merely a casual circumstance, but, as stated in the succeeding verses of the old song, sometimes became the source of jest and mockery. "Willimoteswick," in the above verse, represented Sir Nicholas Ridley of that place, and proves that he was then chief of that clan, not only because his name is not given, — being well known as "Ridley of Willimoteswick," — but he is mentioned first in the list. "Hardriding Dick" was Richard Ridley, head of the family at Hardriding at that time. "Will of the Wall" was William Ridley, of Walltown, another ancient residence of the family, so named because situated on the old Roman Wall. "Hughy of Hawden" was Hugh Ridley, a resident of Hawden, a place near Willimoteswick and the other seats of the Ridleys of Northumberland. In this feudal attack an alliance was formed with the Thirwalls of the castle of that name, a compact frequently entered into in those days by families living neighbors, for the greater security of their properties. Albany Featherstonhaugh made a figure during the reign of King Edward VI, but fell at the hand of his deadly enemy, the bold and bloody "Ridley of Willimoteswick," to whose merciless power the old man was left by his son and successor, Nicholas, who ran away before the fight commenced. The following from the notes in the works of Sir Walter Scott, proves that a battle took place between the two clans: "*24 Oct. 22 do Henrici 8 vi. Inquisito capt apud Hautwhistle sup visum corpus Alexandri Featherston. Gen, apud Grensilhaugh felonici interfecti, 22 Oct, per Nicolaum Ridley de Unthauk Gen. Hugon Ridley, Nicolaum Ridley et alios ejusdem nominus.*" Nor were the Featherstons without their revenge, for, "*36 to Henrici 8 vi*" we have "*Utligatio Nicalia Featherston, ac Thome Nixson, etc., etc., pro homicitto Will Ridley de moral.*"

RIDLEY HALL, another ancient residence of the family in Northumberland, was named for their ancestral seat in Chestershire. Some authorities think Ridley Hall was possessed by the Tyndale Ridleys prior to their attainder to the Willimoteswick estates, but in the absence of proof I am unable to fix the dates of settlement with precision. This residence is near where the Allan water falls into the river Tyne. The woods are more justly celebrated for their beauty than those of any other place in Northumberland, and far surpass those of the well-known Castle Eden in the richness and variety of the scenery. They are of great extent, reaching for several miles along the shores of the Allan toward Stewart Peel. At the top of the woods, on the right bank of the Allan, a grassy terrace leads to what is known as "Billbery Hill Moss House," whence there is an extensive view up a deep glen to a promontory called "Stewart Peel"; hence a winding path descends to the "Ravens' Craig," a bold cliff of yellow sandstone which overhangs the river. A slightly-made chain bridge is swung across the stream a little lower down, whence a steep path in the hill leads through the woods to a tarn in the hill-top under a grove of dark Scotch firs, and close to a purple moorland. Thence passing the "Swiss Cottage," a place called the "Hawk's Nest" is reached by the "Craggy Pass," a narrow staircase cut in the side of the rocks which

"RIDLEY HALL"

overhang it. Different views of the woods and river are presented at every turn of these walks, which were constructed by the owner in 1878, and the foregrounds are a mixture of gray rocks, heather, and hanging-wood, with parasitic plants twining from stem to stem. The walks have recently been extended to a bold range of rocks near "Plankie Mill." Visitors are permitted to view the grounds and other attractions if they ask to do so at the house.

A most singular adventure is said to have taken place at Ridley Hall in the year 1723, when the then proprietor was absent in the city of London, and an old female servant and her son were left in charge of the place. On an evening when the old woman was sitting alone, a peddler came to the door, declaring himself half-dead with fatigue, and begging for a night's lodging. This the servant refused, when he implored that he might leave his long pack while he looked elsewhere for shelter, stating that he would return and take it away the next day. She consented to grant this favor, and directed him to put down his luggage on the shelf of the kitchen-dresser. Sometime after the man had departed the son of the old woman came in from shooting, and learning the story, and fancying he saw the pack move, in his excitement fired at it with his gun; streams of blood gushed forth, and on undoing the bundle the horror-stricken pair found the shot had killed a man who had been sewed up inside. The peddler had brought this man to the house, that in case he was not admitted himself to a lodging, the house might be opened in the night and robbed by the two, but by the accident they were foiled, and the safety of the house insured.

Some parts of Ridley Hall are very ancient, and undoubtedly formed a residence of the Ridley family before the estates were lost, but there have been many additions made at different times, until now the main building presents quite a modern appearance. The gardens and grounds around the house are quite extensive and ornamented with a rich variety of rare trees, plants, and flowers. The last known proprietor was an old lady named Davidson, and Mr. Ridley, of Parkend, was acting as her confidential agent. The colored view of Ridley Hall in this book was made from a photograph taken on the grounds, and kindly furnished by my correspondent there.

HALTWHISTLE. This ancient residence of the Ridley family of Northumberland, is a small market town of seventeen hundred and fifty inhabitants. Many of the old stone houses retain battlements and other traces of fortification. The Ridleys of Haltwhistle were long at feud with the clan of Armstrong, a family that dwelt in the strongholds of the mountain, and had several battles with them, of which accounts have been preserved. The Armstrongs were dreaded all along the border, in consequence of their bold incursions and robberies. They frequently made raids upon Haltwhistle and other property of the Ridleys on the Tyne, and carried away goods and cattle, sometimes driving large flocks before them to their impregnable rendezvous.

On one occasion the Ridleys called their clan together and pursued the Armstrong outlaws and recovered considerable of the property they were taking away. When returning to Haltwhistle, one of the Armstrongs, a chief of that clan, being more bold than the others, came out of their stronghold and pursued the clan of Ridley upon a horse, crying after them in taunting language, challenging some one to engage him in combat. This could not be long endured, and the chief of the Ridleys turned upon him, ran a spear through his body, and left him dead, with the shaft still in the wound.

This act so exasperated the Armstrongs that they vowed cruel revenge, swearing that before winter was ended they would lay the whole border waste. This destructive work was commenced by an attack on Haltwhistle, where they put fire to many houses. As a chief of the Armstrongs was running up a street with a torch in his hand, one of the Ridleys, who was in a strong stone house, made a shot and killed him; thus two chiefs of the clan of Armstrong were killed by the Ridleys that year. This deadly feud was perpetuated from father to son, and from generation to generation between the two old border families, each seeking every opportunity to work destruction of property and life.

UNTHANK HALL, near Haltwhistle, Northumberland, now the residence of the Rev. Dixon Brown, was long a residence of a scion of the Ridley family of Willimoteswick, and here the martyr Ridley was born. How long the family were seated here I have not been able to learn. The meaning of Unthank is plain enough, but no tradition remains to explain why so ungracious an appellation should have been given a beautiful place. In the year 1191 this manor belonged to Robert Rose, of Hamlake, who probably derived it from William the Lion, upon marrying his daughter Isabella. The estates have passed through many hands, but of all the family names associated with it, that of Ridley has conferred upon the place the greatest celebrity. The house is very old, and bears marks of having been built and remodeled at different periods; it is beautifully embosomed in groves, and the gardens and ornamental grounds are remarkably attractive. The broad moor of Plenmeller stretches away toward the south, while between the mansion and the River Tyne lies a tract of corn-fields and green meadows. One of the ancient chambers in the house is still known as "the bishop's room," supposed to have been occupied by that holy man during the time that Christopher Ridley, his father, resided there. In 1768, when John Tweddell, the owner of Unthank at that time, was hunting on the rocky moor of Ramshaw, and while looking for a lost hare in a cavity of rock, found a large quantity of silver coins; it was thought they were left there in 1327 by some soldiers when in pursuit of the Scottish army. I have a drawing of the house as it appeared in 1745, when the form and style were very unlike those of the present building. This view of the more ancient mansion, with several photographs of his present residence, were kindly furnished me by the proprietor, and the colored plate in this book was made from what seemed to be the most picturesque of these.

HARDRIDING. This ancient seat of the Ridleys of Northumberland was pleasantly situated, about two and a half miles from Haltwhistle, before mentioned, in the forest of Lowes, so called for the Northumbrian lakes which are included within its circuit, and on the brink of the Roman earthway, south of the Roman Wall, and not far from Hamsteads. The residence, which was sold to a Mr. Lowe, is very beautiful. It stands in an open situation, and the pleasant walks around it, especially along the banks of the Allan, among the woods and rocks, are very romantic and abundant in excellent specimens of landscape. It is said that above one of the old doors there is a date earlier than the Norman Conquest, with the initials of the builder, "N. R." There may be such a stone in the house at Hardriding, but I cannot think it was placed there as early as the Conquest, for there is no proof that the family was then settled in

"UNTHANK HALL."
Northumberland, England,
RESIDENCE OF THE RIDLEY'S.
A.D. 1855.

the County. Is it not a little singular that the date on this curious stone was not given as well as the letters, if the numbers can be made out?

WALLTOWN, so named in consequence of being situated on the Roman Wall, was long a castellated residence of a branch of the Ridley family of Tynedale, Northumberland, England. The place was romantic in its surroundings, and many interesting traditions are associated with its early history. I believe the house formerly occupied by the Ridleys has been dismantled, and at present only a farm-house marks the place. There is a fine fountain here, in which Paulinus baptized one of the Saxon kings,—perhaps Edwin,—in whose reign the wells along the wayside were provided with iron dishes for the convenience of travelers; this fountain is sometimes called "King Arthur's well," but Brand says, "At Walltown I saw the well wherein Paulinus baptized King Ecfrid." Some wrought stones lie near the well. The water is cool and limpid. Murray says, "In a farmhouse at Walltown Craigs lived Bishop Ridley's brother"; this is a mistake: it was his brother-in-law, as will appear in the pedigree of the "Ridleys of Walltown." Behind the house rise the highest of the "Walltown Craigs" known as "the nine nicks of Thirwall"; these are highly picturesque, being partly overgrown with the remains of the ancient forest which "Belted Will Howard" destroyed, because it afforded a shelter to the "Mosstroopers." Sir Walter Scott visited Walltown when young, and gathered some wild flowers near, which he presented to a young lady with the following lines : —

> "Take these flowers, which, purple waving,
> On the ruined rampart grew;
> Where, the sons of freedom braving,
> Rome's imperial standard flew.
> Warriors from the breach of danger,
> Pluck no longer laurels there;
> They but yield the passing stranger
> Wild-flower wreaths for Beauty's hair."

PARKEND, another residence of the Ridleys of Northumberland, is situated in the parish of Simonburn, and has been believed by its possessors to have been "tithe-free," and to have had other tithes in the parish, from the influence of the rectors of Simonburn. This was once the largest and wildest parish in the country, occupying an area of one hundred and three miles, from Scotland to the Roman Wall, but now divided. Here the inhabitants of Tynedale lived in the most lawless independence till 1701, when "County-keepers" were appointed, to whom a kind of protection-tribute was paid. The ancient Church of St. Simon was pulled down and restored in 1862; it contains a mutilated tomb of the Rev. Cuthbert Ridley and three of his family (1625). "Old Parkend" was inhabited for several generations by the descendants of the elder branch of the Ridleys through a younger brother of the last of the "Lords of Willimoteswick." The view from Parkend commands a fine prospect, especially of the woods and beautiful castle called Chipchase in the same parish.

TECKET was an ancient residence of the Ridleys of Northumberland. It is an "upland hamlet," where the stream called "Simonburn" tumbles in a most picturesque cascade over a chaos of fern-fringed rocks. This spot is a charming subject for the artist. The burn falls into the River Tyne near Ulmwick. There is now a stone at Tecket Farm which bears the Ridley arms. This property seems to have come into the family by a marriage of a Ridley of Willimoteswick with an heiress named *Wale;* hence we find the arms of Wale quartered with those of Ridley in some coats used by the Ridley family. The Ridleys of Tecket were once own- ers of the property of Parkend (until 1560), but it passed from them to the Earls of Suffolk; they held it until the beginning of the seventeenth century, when it again became the property of the Ridleys of Tecket.

HEATON HALL, a residence of one branch of the Ridleys of Northum- berland, was built in 1713, as a centre to the extensive collieries owned by the Ridley family, a people who represented the city of Newcastle for nearly one hundred years. This residence is delightfully situated in the parish of All Saints, Newcastle-on-Tyne, and upon the steep woody bank of Ouseburn. One of the family who resided at Heaton, from designs furnished by Mr. Newton, architect, gave the house an elegant appearance by adding the two towers (see plate-engraving in this book), and facing the front with stone. This place is to be converted into a public park for the city of Newcastle.

BLAGDON PARK, the residence of the baronial family of Ridley, present representatives of the ancient border house of Willimoteswick, was for three centuries owned by the Fenwicks, whose estates were forfeited by decree of attainder from Cromwell's parliament. The house was built before 1749, but additions were made and porticoes added from designs of Bonomi, in 1830. The name was formerly "Blakedene," from the dark dene, lined with forest trees and crossed by a handsome bridge, which runs behind the house on the north. The grounds at Blagdon are ap- proached by a gate-way, with two white bulls (the family crest) upon the piers. The arms of the family are upon one of the gables, surrounded by fine scroll-work, and also upon the front, below those before mentioned. In the grounds is preserved the ancient " *Cale Cross,*" which once stood at the foot of the side in Newcastle. In the church at Plessy Station, or Stonington Church, there is some ancient stained glass, presented by Sir Matthew W. Ridley, in 1772; this is near Blagdon Park.

Junior branches of the Ridley family located in various Counties in England and Ireland. There was an offshoot seated at BATTERSEA, in the County of York, from whom several sub-branches have descended. They anciently lived at HEXHAM,* HAWDEN, CLIFTON PARK, CREWE HALL, AT- KINTON, NEWCASTLE, GATESHEAD, and LONDON. The families have now become too numerous for me to make particular mention of all ther resi- dences.

---

* The name Ridley is not as common in Northumberland as once; from 1778 to 1790 large emigrations of Robsons and Ridleys from the North Tyne took place to the United States and Canada.

GENEALOGY AND BIOGRAPHY.

RIDLEYS OF RIDLEY HALL, CHESTERSHIRE, ENGLAND.

Bryon Ridley, of Ridley Hall, in Chestershire, England, is the first known ancestor of the Ridley family. He was "of Ridley" in the year 1157. No mention of his wife. The family surname was adopted about the time of the coming of the Conqueror; hence, previously, the family that lived at Ridley had only been known by their Christian names. . In the early generations they are frequently called "de Rideleigh," and "de Rydley." The Ridleys are one of *eleven* families out of *thirty-seven* in the north of England, that dated back to the time of the Conquest, found by Grey in 1649. They have been so independent, that some have said they "kept a boat of their own in the time of the flood, and so were under no obligation to Noah." Descended from Bryon were the following: —

SECOND GENERATION.

John Ridley (1), who married a daughter of Sir Edward Warren, of Poynton, Knt., and had issue.[*]

THIRD GENERATION.

Richard Ridley (1), who married Martha, daughter of Sir Hugh Cholmondely, by whom he had issue, of whom more hereafter. He was denominated "of Ridley."

Jane Ridley (1), only daughter of John (1), married to Sir Henry Delves, of whom is descended the Lord Sheffelde.

FOURTH GENERATION.

Mary Ridley (1), a daughter of Richard (1), married to Sir John Cotton, of whom are descended the Fitz-Herberts and Bradbournes of Chester.

John Ridley (2), eldest son and successor of Richard (1), of Ridley, married the daughter of Egerton, of Egerton, and died *sine prole* in the year 1258.

Robert Ridley (1), second son of Richard (1), of Ridley, married a daughter of Sir Henry Venables, and became the head of this family on the death of his brother John. He had issue, of whom hereafter.

---

* SIBBILLA RIDLEY, daughter of John Ridley, of Ridley, was the wife of William Phillips, "second sonne, citizen and marchantaylor [merchant tailor] of London." No date found. Cannot tell what John Ridley.

Anne Ridley[4] (1), second daughter of Richard[3] (1), of Ridley, married to —— Done, of Utkinson, or Utkinton.

FIFTH GENERATION.

James Ridley[5] (1), son and successor of Robert[4] (1), of Ridley, married a daughter of Brereton, of Brereton, Knt., and by her had issue, of whom hereafter.

SIXTH GENERATION.

Margaret Ridley[6] (1), eldest daughter of James[5] (1), of Ridley, married to John Kimpperley (Kimperley).

John Ridley[6] (3), eldest son of James[5] (1,) of Ridley, married a daughter of John Layton, of Layton, and became head of this family; he had issue, of whom hereafter.

William Ridley[6] (1), second son of James[5] (1), of Ridley, married Annie Bell, the daughter of Baron Stapleton.

Julian Ridley[6] (1), youngest daughter of James[5] (1), of Ridley, married to John Fulshust, of Crewe.

SEVENTH GENERATION.

Margaret or Barbara Ridley[7] (1), eldest daughter of John[6] (3), of Ridley, married to Sir John Holcroft or Allcroft.

Susan Ridley[7] (1), second daughter of John[6] (3), of Ridley, married to Sir William Sneade, of Staffordshire.

Anne Ridley[7] (2), third daughter of John[6] (3), of Ridley, married to Sir (one says William) Richard Savage, of Rock Savage.

Elizabeth Ridley[7] (1), fourth daughter of John[6] (3), of Ridley, married to Sir Thomas Stanley, of Howton, Cheshire.

Edmond Ridley[7] (1), only son of John[6] (3), of Ridley, married a daughter of Sir Thomas Loadstone, Knt. He was head of the Chestershire family, and had issue.

EIGHTH GENERATION.

Thomasine Ridley[8] (1), eldest daughter of Edmond[7] (1), of Ridley, married to Sir John Dutton, of Hatton.

Christian Ridley[8] (1), second daughter of Edmond[7] (1), of Ridley, married to Sir Thomas Grisley, of Staffordshire.

Jarvis or James Ridley[8] (1), a son of Edmond[7] (1), of Ridley, was head of this family, denominated "Ridley of Chestershire." He married a daughter of Sir Pearce Warburton, of Asley.

NINTH GENERATION.

Sir John Ridley[9] (4), of Ridley, in Chestershire, Knt., married Jane, daughter of Sir John Gresaker, and was head of this family; he had issue. One writer says "Sir Richard Ridley."

TENTH GENERATION.

Sir Bryan Ridley[10] (2), Knt., Lord-Chief-Justice of Ireland, and Marshal of the same; married Jane, daughter of the Viscount Roche. He was a son of Sir John[9] (4). Whether Sir Bryan had issue I cannot state; he probably settled in Ireland, and became ancestor of the Irish Ridleys. At any rate, the representation of the Chestershire family devolved upon his brother, of whom hereafter.

Sir Thomas Ridley[10] (1), eldest son of Sir John[9] (4), was of Ridley, in Chestershire, and head of this family. He was a knight, and married Anne, daughter of Lord John Samford. He had issue several children.

Judith Ridley[10] (1), eldest daughter of Sir John[9] (4), who was of Ridley, in Cheshire, married to John Lee, of Adlington.

Susan Ridley[10] (2), second daughter of Sir John[9] (4), married to William Grovesnor, or Grosvenor, of Eton, Knt.

ELEVENTH GENERATION.

Sir Henry Ridley[11] (1), eldest son and successor to Sir Thomas[10] (1), married Catherine, daughter of Sir Robert Worsley, Knt., and had issue, of whom hereafter. He was a knight.

John Ridley[11] (5), second son of Sir Thomas[10] (1), of Ridley in Cheshire, married a daughter of Sir William Tatton, of Wilsey, Knt. Nothing said of issue.

Sir Thomas Ridley[11] (2), a son of Sir Thomas[10] (1), of Ridley, in Chestershire (he was third son), married Julian, daughter (and heir) of Sir Thomas or Lambert Burdett, of Ridley in Northumberland. For the descendants of this Thomas, see "Ridleys of Ridley in Northumberland."

Isabella Ridley[11] (1), eldest daughter of Sir Thomas[10] (1), of Ridley in Cheshire, married, firstly, to Sir William Gosworthe; secondly, to Sir John Scott, Lord-Chief-Justice of Common Pleas.

Jayne Ridley[11] (1), second daughter of Sir Thomas[10] (1), of Ridley in Cheshire, married to Sir Woodgreate Harbottell, Knt.

TWELFTH GENERATION.

Sir Robert Ridley[12] (2), eldest son and successor of Sir Henry[11] (1), was of Ridley in Cheshire; married Anchitellis, daughter of Sir William Bramnowe, of Bramnowe (another pedigree reads "Bramond"), and had issue, of whom hereafter.

THIRTEENTH GENERATION.

Sir Thomas Ridley[13] (3), a son and successor of Sir Robert[12] (2), was of Ridley in Cheshire, as head of this family. He was a knight; married a daughter of Sir William Davenport, and had issue a daughter, who was his heir.

Jane Ridley[12] (2), only daughter of Sir Robert[12] (2), married to John Marbury.

FOURTEENTH GENERATION.

Margaret Ridley[14] (2), a daughter of Sir Thomas[13] (3), was the last of this branch of the Ridley family. She married Richard Egerton, and had a son Thomas Egerton, of Ridley in Cheshire. It will be seen that there was another descent in the same County, called "Lords of Ridley," which ended in an heir female married to Sir Robert Danyell, and I cannot tell how these two branches are related.

———•❦•———

RIDLEYS, LORDS OF RIDLEY, ENGLAND.

According to Ormerod's "History of Chester," this branch of the Ridley family, — or "de Rideleigh," as he calls them, — owned the manor of Ridley, in Cheshire, as per the years stated below. Mr. Lowe, a Cheshire author, says the family who lived at Ridley Hall, when it was a dependency of the Knight Hospitallers, assumed the local surname "de Ridelegh "; and according to a monument in St. John's church-yard, in Chester, the name was not spelt in the contracted orthography till it had been in use by the family for several generations.   I have no means of knowing how this branch-family is connected with that whose pedigree is recorded on the preceding pages; they are both denominated " of Ridley in Cheshire," and as both pedigrees are quite deficient in dates and details, I cannot learn which may be considered the main line of descent.   Both end in heirs female.

William Ridley[1] **(1)**, was owner of Ridley Hall previous to the reign of Edward I (1274).   His wife's name does not appear.

SECOND GENERATION.

Robert Ridley[2] **(1)**, was "Lord of Ridley, County of Chester," in the eighteenth year of the reign of Edward I (1292), and is presumably identical with "Robert, son of William de Ridley, vouchée to the warranty of John, son of William de Eggerton, in the first and second years of the reign of Edward II."   (Plea Rolls.)   He had issue, but his wife's name is not found.

THIRD GENERATION.

Hugh Ridley[3] **(1)**, a son of Robert[2] **(1)**, was "Lord of Ridelegh "; he married Cicely, a widow, in the fourteenth year of the reign of Edward III (1341), and had issue (probably) *three* children, of whom hereafter.

Robert Ridley[3] **(2)**, a son of Robert[2] **(1)**, lived during the nineteenth year of the reign of Edward II, and the fifth of Edward III (1316-32). He married (name of wife not known), and had issue.

Clement Ridley[3] **(1)**, a son of Robert[2] **(1)**, had issue, of whom hereafter.   Wife's name unknown.

Richard Ridley[3] **(1)**, a son of Robert[2] **(1)**, was styled "of Foulsehurst."   He was father of William Ridley, "of Foulsehurst," who was living in the tenth year of the reign of Edward III (1337), and was probably ancestor of Richard Ridley, who was married before 1404 to Matilda, daughter of John Rathbon, of Great Edge, sister and heir of John Rathbon, living in the ninth year of the reign of Henry V (1423).   This is probably the same Richard (subject under treatment) whose wife, Agnes, was buried in St. John's church-yard, in the city of Chester; the inscription on her monument will be found on the preceding pages.

FOURTH GENERATION.

Robert Ridley[4] **(3)**, eldest son of Hugh[3] **(1)**, was "Lord of Ridley " from the fourteenth year of the reign of Edward II (1311) to the fifth of Edward III (1332).   His wife's name is not found; but he was married and had issue, of whom hereafter.

William Ridley[4] **(1)**, second son of Hugh[3] **(1)**, married Sibyl, a widow, in the fourteenth year of the reign of Edward II (she was living twenty-three years afterwards), and died before the fourteenth year of Edward III, without issue.

Hugh Ridley[4] **(2)**, third son of Hugh[3] **(1)**, married Margaret ——, and was styled "joint Lord of Soude."   I find no mention of descendants.

William Ridley[4] **(2)**, a son of Robert[3] **(2)**, married twice; firstly, to Anice, thirteenth year of Edward III (1340); secondly (?), Katherine, daughter of Richard de Cholmundelegh, in the thirty-second year of Edward III (1861).   He had issue, of whom hereafter.

FIFTH GENERATION.

Robert Ridley[5] (4), son of Robert[4] (3), " Lord of Ridley," was twenty years old at the death of his father, in the twenty-third year of Edward III (1350).* He married Margaret, who died at the age of 36, in the thirty-ninth year of Edward III (1368), leaving issue.

Robert Ridley[5] (5), a son of William[4] (2), lived in the thirteenth year of the reign of Edward III (1340); married, firstly, Agnes, the daughter of Kenrick de Cholmondelegh, thirteenth year of Edward III (1340), and, secondly, Isabella, a widow, fourth year of Richard II (1381). There was issue by the first wife.

SIXTH GENERATION.

Kenrick Ridley[6] (1), son of Robert[5] (5), thirty-second year of Edward III (1361); married Christian ——, and is supposed to be ancestor of Richard de Ridelegh, of Tarporley, who married at Weverham in 1408 to Ellen, daughter of John Masey, of Kelsall; living in the eighth year of Henry VI (1430).

William Ridley[6] (3), a son of Robert[4] (4), was his father's heir, and became "Lord of Ridelegh." He married Alice, daughter of Richard de Prestloud, between the thirty-sixth and thirty-ninth (1365–8) years of the reign of Edward III, and had issue a daughter.

SEVENTH GENERATION.

Alice Ridley[7] (1), daughter of William[6] (3), was born in 1376; was married to Robert Danyell, and had a son, Sir Robert Danyell, who was "Lord of Ridlegh" (and heir to his mother, Alice), in the second year of the reign of Henry VI (1424). This ends the descent of this branch of the Ridley family of Cheshire.

-----•◦•-----

RIDLEYS OF WILLIMOTESWICK, NORTHUMBERLAND.

Thomas Ridley[1] (1), was the third son of Sir Thomas[10] (1), "of Ridley," in Cheshire. He married Julian, daughter of Sir Lambert Burdett, and in consequence of this alliance became possessed of landed estates in Northumberland, which were subsequently denominated "Ridley," presumably in memory of the ancient manor owned by the family in Chester. I am well satisfied that "Ridley" in Tynedale was in possession of the family of that name some time before Willimoteswick came to them. Thomas had a son.

SECOND GENERATION.

John Ridley[2] (1), a son of Thomas[1] (1), married a daughter of Sir John Grey, a Knight of Chilwick, and inherited from his mother, Julian

* In the year 1350, Robert de Rydgeleph (Ridley) held four acres of land in what is now called the township of Ridley, Edisbury Hundred, of Cheshire, — the site of the Manor house of Ridley, — from St. John of Jerusalem; and the residue of the whole manor, from John de St. Pierre, Knt., by the service of one Knight's Fee. In 1329 the Manor was called "Ridleigh," and in 1424, "Ridley."

Burdett, an estate in Northumberland which was called "Ridley"; said property held in consideration that the heirs should bear the Burdett coat-armour, quartered before those of Ridley forever; otherwise the lands were to go to the Barons of Grayslock. This John had *two* children.

Anne Ridley² (1), a daughter of Thomas¹ (1), and his wife, Julian Burdett, married to Sir John Witterington.

THIRD GENERATION.

Anthony Ridley³ (1), a son of John² (1), married Beatrice, a daughter and heiress of John Thirkell, Esq., and had issue, of whom hereafter. He was "of Ridley in Northumberland."

FOURTH GENERATION.

Nicholas Ridley⁴ (1), son of Anthony³ (1), married a daughter of Sir John Cramlington, of Cramlington, and had issue.

Odard* Ridley⁴ (1), second son of Anthony³ (1), was evidently by a second wife, who was a daughter of Odard de Willimoteswick; and became heir of that property. The pedigree is obscure in some connections. He was living in 1280.

Thomas Ridley⁴ (2), third son of Anthony³ (1), was living in 1300, and died previous to 1308. He married Majory, daughter of Whitefield, of Whitefield.

FIFTH GENERATION.

Thomas Ridley⁵ (3), eldest son of Nicholas⁴ (1), married to Audry, sister of Sir William Musgrave, and was styled "of Ridley in Northumberland" (1440). He had issue.

John Ridley⁵ (2), second son of Nicholas⁴ (1), married Margaret, daughter of Richard Horton, and had issue (1446).

Nicholas Ridley⁵ (2), third son of Nicholas⁴ (1), married to Annie, daughter of John Lawson, and had issue. He is styled in one pedigree "of Willimoteswick" (1450).

SIXTH GENERATION.

Thomas-Baron Ridley⁶ (4), son of Nicholas⁵ (2), was styled "of Hamstead Hall"; he married Alice, daughter and co-heir of Clement Skelton, Esq., of Brampton (another authority says "Alice, daughter of Arthur Skelton, of Brampton"), and died in 1820, leaving issue.

SEVENTH GENERATION.

Hugh Ridley⁷ (1), presumably a son of Thomas⁶ (4), was living as early as 1371, and was a man of great wealth and influence. His name occurs in the "*Hiis testibus*" of deeds about the manor of Haltwhistle and Colonwade in 1372, and in connection with lands in Reedsdale in the second year of the reign of Richard II (1378). The several pedigrees in the British Museum and in local histories do not agree concerning this man; one tabular pedigree calls him son of Nicholas and Alice Skelton.

---

* ODARD DE RIDLEY witnessed a charter in Northumberland in 1280. Nicholas de Ridley, son of Thomas, executed a charter in 1250; he was grandson of Nicholas de Willimoteswick, who lived in the time of King John (1166–1216), who was a son of Odard de Willimoteswick, who witnessed a charter at Hexham Abbey in the time of Henry II (1206–72). The last-named was probably a brother of John Fitz-Odard, Baron of Emildon (who was living 1161–82), and son of Odard, Viscount of Northumberland, mentioned as such in 1110 and 1130, when Governor of Banburgh; he was son of Odard de Loges, Viscount of Northumberland.

EIGHTH GENERATION.

Odard Ridley[8] (2), presumed to be son of Hugh[7] (1), was living in 1424.

NINTH GENERATION.

Nicholas Ridley[9] (3), presumed to be son of Odard[8] (2), married Anne, daughter of Eglesfield, of Eglesfield, in County Cumberland; deceased before 1467.

TENTH GENERATION.

Sir Nicholas Ridley[10] (4), son of Nicholas[9] (3), was of Willimoteswick, Northumberland, and styled "Esquire of the King's Body." He married Mary, daughter and co-heir of —— Corwin, of Workington, descended from Orne, second son of Ketd, son of Ivo de Talbois, daughter of Ethelbred, King of England. He (Nicholas) had letters of safe conduct from the King of Scotland.

Thomasine Ridley[10] (1), daughter of Nicholas[9] (3), married Thomas Carnaby, of Halton Castle, Northumberland.

Sir Hugh Ridley[10] (2), a son of Nicholas[9] (3), was styled "of Hamstead Hall and Willimoteswick, Northumberland." He was high sheriff for his County from 1508 to 1511.

ELEVENTH GENERATION.

Sir Nicholas Ridley[11] (5),* eldest son of Nicholas[10] (4), was successor to Willimoteswick. He married Mary, daughter of Simon Musgrave, of Eden Hall, and Joanna his wife, daughter of Sir William Stapleton. He was styled the "broad knight," probably in consequence of his gigantic physical proportions. He was high sheriff of Northumberland in the first, second, third, and twenty-third years of the reign of King Henry VI, and in first, second, and third of King Henry VIII. He was also commander of a division of the marauding army which invaded Scotland under Lord Dacre, in 1513,—the same year in which the battle of Flodden was fought. He was frequently engaged in border raids and family and district quarrels, which were of common occurrence in those times. He was chief of the clan when they murdered Sir Albany Featherstonhaugh, as appears on a view of the body by the coroner of Northumberland that year—1530. In 1552, Nicholas Ridley was one of the wardens appointed by Lord Wharton to have the oversight and search of the fords through the Tyne, "under the Ridley-hall, Haltwhistle, Thorngrafton, Walltown," and other places in Tynedale. In the same year he was appointed one of the Commissioners for Enclosures and Hedges from Hexhamshire to the waters of the Irthing, on both sides of the South Tyne as far as the middle marches went. His name stands at the head of the list in these commissions, followed by that of "Albany Featherstonhaugh," probably the son of that Albany to whose violent death he had contributed a few years before. He was one of the "overseers" of the river guards, in which several members of the clan were represented in subsequent years. This was the Sir Nicholas addressed by the Martyr Bishop when imprisoned at Oxford as the "bell-wether" of the Ridley family, and is faithfully admonished by his pious nephew and namesake respecting his religious faithfulness. He had issue *two* sons and *four* daughters whose names have reached us, of whom hereafter.

---

* There was a Richard de Ridley amongst the early descents of the family, but I cannot connect him with this pedigree.

John Ridley[11] (3), second son of Nicholas[10] (4), married Margaret, daughter of Richard Horton, and had issue *two* sons, of whom hereafter.

Christopher Ridley[11] (1), third son of Nicholas[10] (4), married Anne, daughter of William and Margaret Blenkinsop,* of Blenkinsop, and had issue *four* children (perhaps others), of whom hereafter. He was of Unthank Hall, Northumberland. (See engraving in this book.)

Rev. Robert Ridley[11] (1), D. D., fourth son of Nicholas[10] (4), was a relative of Bishop Tunstal. He studied at Paris a long time, and also at Cambridge University, where he commenced D. D., 1518. He became rector of St. Botolph (Bishopsgate, London), July 3, 1523, and on March 21, 1523–4, was admitted prebendary of Mora, in the Church of St. Paul. He was presented to the rectory of St. Edmunds the King, London, Feb. 20, 1526, collated to the prebend of St. Pancras, in the Church of St. Paul, Oct. 30, 1529. He was at one time rector of Simonburn, in Northumberland. Greatly assisted in the Polydon Virgil. He was collated to the sinecure rectory of Fulham, Middlesex, and the prebend of Isledon, in the Church of St. Paul, Oct. 30, 1529. He died about 1536. He was much noted for his great learning, and was a strenuous opponent of the Reformation. It was at his charge that his nephew, Nicholas Ridley, ultimately Bishop of London, was maintained at Cambridge, Paris, and Louvaine. His arms were: "Gules, a chevron between three falcons A."

TWELFTH GENERATION.

Sir Hugh Ridley[12] (3), son of Nicholas[11] (5), married Isabella, daughter of Sir John Heron, of Chipchase Castle. He was styled "of Willimoteswick," Northumberland; was a knight; had issue, of whom hereafter. Died before 1565.

William Ridley[12] (1), second son of Nicholas[11] (5), was of Battersea, County of York. See "Ridleys of Battersea."

John Ridley[12] (4), third son of Nicholas[11] (5), was of Ringwood. No other mention of him.

Thomas Ridley[12] (5), fourth son of Nicholas[11] (5), styled "Gentleman," married his cousin, Elizabeth Ridley, of Walltown. Was presented to the living of Simonburn parish, in Northumberland, and in 1532 transferred it to his cousin, John Ridley, clerk.

Jane Ridley[12] (1), eldest daughter of Nicholas[11] (5), was married to Sir John Heron, of Chipchase Castle.

Margaret Ridley[12] (1), second daughter of Nicholas[11] (5), was married to John Featherstonhaugh, of Featherston Castle.

Mabel Ridley[12] (1), third daughter of Nicholas[11] (5), was married, first to William Fenwick, of Little Harle, and secondly, to Sir John Sumley, Knt., of Axwell House.

Anne Ridley[12] (2), fourth daughter of Nicholas[11] (5), was married to William (others write John) Wallace, of Knaresdale Hall.

John Ridley[12] (5), a son of John[11] (3) (1495). No other mention, except that he had *one* son, of whom hereafter.

Rev. Lancellot Ridley[12] (1), D. D., second son of John[11] (3), was born at Willimoteswick, Northumberland. He was of Clare Hall, where he proceeded B. A., 1523–4, and commenced M. A., 1527. He was deeply skilled

---

* JOHN BLENKINSOP, kinsman of Anne, wife of Christopher Ridley, of Unthank, married a daughter of —— Ridley, of Willimoteswick. This John was granduncle of the before-mentioned Anne.

Ridley

in theology, and in the Latin, Greek, and Hebrew languages. He pro-. ceeded B. D., 1587, and on the refoundation of the Church of Canterbury, under the King's charter, April 8, 1541, was constituted one of six preachers of that cathedral. In the same year he commenced D. D., in his university. In the reign of Edward VI, he distinguished himself by the ability with which he defended the doctrines of protestantism. In 1553, he was deprived of his preachership of Canterbury for being married, but it is said he subsequently put away his wife and conformed to the change of religion which took place in the reign of Queen Mary. In 1560, he again occurs as one of the preachers of Canterbury. He also had the rectory of Stretham, in the Isle of Ely. He was collated to the rectory of Willingham, County of Cambridge, June 10, 1545, and was deprived thereof on or before May 5, 1554. He was buried at Ely, June 16, 1576. His wife, by whom he had *two* sons, was Mary, daughter of Christopher Paterson.

Hugh Ridley[12] (**4**), eldest son of Christopher[11] (**1**), of Unthank Hall, married Elizabeth ——, and had issue, of whom hereafter. He was dead in 1555, when his brother, the Bishop of London, wrote a letter to his widow and children, then living at Unthank Hall, Northumberland.*

Richard Ridley[12] (**1**), second son of Christopher[11] (**1**), settled at Newcastle-on-Tyne, and had several sons and daughters, of whom hereafter.

Elizabeth Ridley[12] (**1**), a daughter of Christopher[11] (**1**), was the wife of John Ridley, of Walltown, County of Northumberland, which John was descended from a collateral branch of the same family. She had issue. Husband died in 1562. See "Ridleys of Walltown" in this book. In his farewell letter (which see), the bishop calls Elizabeth "my gentle and loving sister," and mentions her loving him "above the rest of my brethren."

Alice Ridley[12] (**1**), a daughter of Christopher[11] (**1**), was the wife of George Shipside. Her brother, the bishop, in his letter of farewell, says of her husband, "whom I have ever found faithful, trusty, and living in all good state and conditions"; and of Alice he wrote, "I am glad to hear thou dost take Christ's cross in good part." Mr. Shipside kept near the bishop during all his imprisonment. When preparing for the stake the bishop gave this brother-in-law his gown and tippet.

Rt. Rev. Nicholas Ridley[12] (**6**), a son of Christopher[11] (**1**), was born at Unthank Hall, Northumberland, about 1500. He received his early education at Newcastle-on-Tyne, from whence he was removed to the university at Cambridge, where his great learning and distinguished abilities so recommended him that he was made master of Pembroke Hall, in that college. After being some years in this office, he left Cambridge and traveled into various parts of the continent for his advancement in knowledge. On his return to England he was made chaplain to King Henry VIII, and Bishop of Rochester, from which he was translated to the See of London, by Edward VI.

In private life he was pious, humane, and affable; in public, learned, sound, and eloquent; diligent in duty, and very popular as a preacher.

---

* **BALDWIN RIDLEY**, of Flushing, said to be a nephew of Nicholas Ridley, Bishop of London, had a daughter Appolonia, who was married to Daniel Tyssen, who was born at Flushing, in Zealand, and died there about 1647, aged 46 years. Was Baldwin a son of Hugh Ridley, who was mentioned in the farewell letter of Bishop Ridley as "of Unthank"?

Says a learned writer, "In his important offices he so diligently applied himself by preaching and teaching the true and wholesome doctrine of Christ, that no good child was more singularly loved by its parents, than he by his flock and diocese. Every holiday and Sabbath he preached in one place or other, except he was hindered by weighty matters; and to his sermons the people resorted, swarming around him like bees, and so faithfully did his life portray his doctrines that his enemies could not reprove him." His memory was so great that he himself wrote: "In my orchard* (the walls, butts, and trees, if they could speak would bear me witness) I learned without books almost all Paul's epistles; yea, and I ween all the canonical epistles, save only the Apocalypse." He had attained such reading and learning that his biographer says:

"He deserved to be compared with the best men of his age, as his works, sermons, and sundry disputations in both universities, will testify. He was wise in counsel, and very politic in all his doings. He was, in fine, so good a man in all points, so pious and spiritual, that England never saw his superior. He was comely in person, and well proportioned; took all things in good part, bearing no malice nor rancor in his heart toward any, but straightway forgave all injuries and offences done against him. He was very kind to his relatives, and yet laying down as a rule that they should look for nothing at his hand unless they lived a righteous life. He used various means to mortify himself, and was much given to prayer and meditation; for duly every morning, as soon as he was dressed, he went to his bed-chamber, and there upon his knees prayed for half an hour; which being done, he went to his study, where he continued till ten o'clock, and then came to common prayer in his house. This being over, he went to dinner, where he talked but little, and then was sober and discreet. The dinner done, he would sit for an hour talking or playing chess; he then returned to his study, and there continued, except business abroad, or visitors prevented him, until five o'clock at night, when common prayers as in the forenoon, and thence to supper, where he behaved himself as in the morning. When his labors for the day were over at eleven o'clock, he said his prayers upon his knees and retired to his bed.

"When at his manor at Fulham, he read daily lectures to his family, at the hour of common prayer, from the writings of Paul and the Psalms; so interested was he in the study of the Scriptures, that he would hire others, with money, to commit certain portions to memory. He was marvelously careful over his household that they might be patterns of virtue and honesty to others; in short, as he was godly and virtuous himself, so nothing but virtue and godliness reigned in his house.

"Ridley had been educated in the Roman Catholic religion, but was brought over to the reformed faith by reading Bertram's book on the sacrament; and he was confirmed in this belief by frequent conferences with Cranmer and Peter Martyr, so that he became a zealous promoter of the reformed doctrines and discipline during the reign of King Edward. Upon the death of Edward, he was earnest in his endeavors to seat Lady Jane Grey upon the throne; but when that design had miscarried he went to Queen Mary to do her homage, and, as he might have expected, was at once committed to the Tower of London, and afterwards to the Bocardo prison in Oxford; from whence he was removed and placed in the custody

---

* In an orchard at Cambridge he walked back and forth in his study of the Scriptures until the place was, and now is, called "Ridley's Walk."

of Mr. Irish, mayor of the city, in whose house he remained till the day of his martyrdom.

"He was several times brought before the Bishops' council, where every argument was used to make him recant, but his firm answers assured his examiners of his inflexibility. In reply to Dr. Brooks, he said, 'My lord, you know my mind fully herein; as for my doctrine, my conscience assureth me that it is sound, and according to God's word; and which doctrine, the Lord being my helper, I will maintain so long as my tongue shall move, and breath is within my body : and in confirmation thereof I am willing to seal the same with my blood.' When asked if he would not confess the pope to be head of the church, he replied, 'I marvel that ye will trouble me with any such foolish questions, — you know my mind concerning the usurped authority of that Anti-Christ.'

"When every means used to make him recant had proved unavailing, and his formal degradation, — that of putting on a priest's dress and then taking the same off with ceremony, — had commenced, he refused to assist his attendants in any way; and when told that these should be put on by force, he replied, — 'Do therein as it shall please you, I am well content with that, and more than that; the servant is not above his Master. If they dealt so cruelly with our Saviour Christ, as the Scripture maketh mention, and he suffered the same patiently, how much doth it become us, his servants!'

"On the night before he suffered, his beard * was washed, and as he sat at supper, at the house of Mr. Irish, his keeper, he invited his hostess, and the rest at the table, to his marriage; 'for,' said he, 'to-morrow I must be married,' thus showing himself as cheerful as ever. And wishing his sister at his marriage, he asked his brother, sitting at the table, whether he thought she could find in her heart to be there; he answered, 'Yes, I dare say, with all heart'; at this Ridley said he was glad to hear of her sincerity. When he saw some weeping he said, 'Quiet yourselves; though my breakfast shall be somewhat sharp and painful; yet I am sure my supper will be more pleasant and sweet.' When they arose from the table his brother-in-law offered to stay all night with him; but Ridley said, 'No, no, that you shall not; for I intend, God willing, to go to bed and sleep as quietly to-night as ever I did.' On this his brother-in-law departed, exhorting him to be of good cheer, and to take his cross quietly, for the reward was great.

"On the north side of the town, in the ditch over against Balliol College, the place of execution was appointed, and for fear that any tumult might arise to hinder the burning of God's servant, the Lord Williams was commanded by the queen's letters and the householders of the city, to be ready with an armed force to assist the execution; and when everything was in readiness, on the 15th of October, 1555, Ridley was led forth by the mayor and bailiffs. He had on a black gown furred, and faced with foins, such as he wore when bishop; a tippet of velvet, furred likewise, about his neck; a velvet cap upon his head, and slippers on his feet. When he saw the stake he held up his hands and said to Latimer, who was to be burned with him, 'God will either assuage the fury of the flames, or else strengthen us to abide it.' He then went to the stake and kneeling down prayed most fervently. Then a sermon was preached from the words, 'Though

---

* I have a picture of Ridley at the stake, purchased in London, in which he is represented with a very long, waving beard, reaching nearly to the waist.

I give my body to be burned, and have not charity, it profiteth me nothing.' Ridley asked for the liberty to reply to the discourse, but was told that he could not unless he would revoke his opinions. 'Well,' said Ridley, 'so long as breath is in my body I will never deny my Lord Christ and his known truth; God's will be done in me.' He then arose and said with a loud voice, 'I commit our cause to Almighty God, who will indifferently judge all.'

"He now disrobed himself, giving presents of his clothing to his brother-in-law, Mr. Shipside, and others who were standing near, weeping, and when he was ready for the stake he stood upon a stone, held up his hands and said, 'O Heavenly Father, I give unto Thee most hearty thanks, that Thou hast called me to be a professor of Thee, even unto death; I beseech Thee, Lord God, have mercy on this realm of England, and deliver it from all her enemies.' Then the smith took a chain of iron and brought it around his body at the waist, and as he was driving in the staple to confine him to the stake, Ridley took the chain in his hand, and looking toward the smith, said, 'Good fellow, knock it in hard, for the flesh will have its course.' They then lighted the faggots, and when Ridley saw the fire flaming up toward him, he cried with an amazing loud voice, 'Unto Thy hands, O Lord, I commend my spirit; Lord, receive my spirit.'

"From ill-making of the fire, the wood being green, and piled too high about his body, it burned fiercely underneath and was kept down by the green wood. Being in exquisite pain from the burning of his limbs, he cried out, 'For God's sake, let the fire come unto me,' and 'I cannot burn.' In all this dreadful suffering he continued to call upon God, asking for grace to sustain him. A man that stood near, with a bill-hook pulled away the green faggots, and when the flames rose around his body Ridley wrenched himself toward the side where the fire was hottest, when his head fell forward, and he was seen to move no more. His limbs were burned from his body, and so heartrending was the scene that many were in tears.

"Thus did this pious divine and steadfast believer testify with his blood, the truth of the everlasting gospel;* proving in his sufferings the sincerity of his profession and his unfaltering faith in God's promises."

The following letter of farewell, written just before his suffering, shows the gentle and affectionate spirit of the man, as well as his firm trust in God: —

" 'Farewell, my dear brother, George Shipside, whom I have ever found faithful, trusty, and living in all good state and conditions. Farewell, my [sister] Alice his wife; I am glad to hear thou dost take Christ's cross in good part. Farewell, my beloved brother, John Ridley, of Walltown; and you, my gentle and loving sister Elizabeth, whom, besides the natural league of amity your tender love, which you are said ever to bear toward me above the rest of your brethren, doth bind me to love you; your daughter Elizabeth, I bid farewell, whom I love for the gentle spirit that God hath given her, which is a precious thing in the sight of God. Farewell, my beloved sister of Unthank, with all your children, my nephews and nieces. Since the departure of my brother Hugh, my mind was to have [been a father] unto them, instead of their father. Farewell, my well beloved and worshipful cousin, Master Nicholas Ridley, of Willimoteswick, and your wife, and thank you for your kindness, shewed both to me

---

* See sermon by Bishop Ridley, in "Notes and Gleanings," in this book.

"MARTYRS MEMORIAL."
Oxford, England.
RIDLEY'S MONUMENT.

and your kinsfolks and mine; so I pray you, good cousin, as my hope and trust is in you, continue and increase in the maintenance of truth, honesty, righteousness, and all true godliness, and to the utmost of your power to withstand falsehood, untruth, unrighteousness, and all ungodliness, which are condemned by the word and laws of God. Farewell, my young cousin, Ralph Whitefield. Oh! your time was very short with me. My mind was to have done you good; but yet you caught in that little time a loss; but I trust it shall be recompensed as it shall please Almighty God. Farewell, all my whole kindred and countrymen:—farewell in Christ altogether.' "

The following poem on the martyrdom of Bishop Ridley, was composed by Miss Frances-Ridley Havergal, of Leamington, Eng., and is by her permission given a place in this book:—

" Three hundred years ago was one,
　Who held with steadfast hand
That chalice of the truth of God,
And poured its crystal stream abroad
　Upon the thirsty land.

" The moderate, the wise, the calm,
　The learned, brave, and good,
A guardian of the sacred ark,
A burning light in places dark,
For cruel, changeless Rome a mark,
　Our BISHOP RIDLEY stood.

" The vengeance of that foe naught else
　But fiery doom could still:
Too surely fell the lightning's stroke
Upon that noble English oak,
Whose acorn-memory survives
In forest ranks of earnest lives,
　And martyr souls at will.

" Rome offered life for faith laid down:
　Such ransom paid not he!
' As long as breath is in this frame,
My Lord and Saviour, Christ, His name,
And His known truth I 'll not deny ' ;
He said (and raised his head on high),
　' God's will be done in me.'

" He knelt and prayed, and kissed the stake,
　And blessed his Master's name,
That he was called his cross to take,
And counted worthy for His sake
　To suffer death and shame.

" Tho' fierce the fire and long the pain,
　The martyr's God was nigh;
Till from the awful underglow
Of torture terrible and slow,
Above the weeping round about,
Once more that powerful voice rang out,
　His Saviour's own last cry.

" Oh, faithful unto death! the crown
　Was shining on thy brow,
Before the ruddy embers paling,
And sobbing aftergusts of wailing,
Had died away, and left in silence,
That truest shrine of British islands,
　That spot so sacred now!

" In dear old England shineth yet
    The candle lit that day;
Right clear and strong the flames arise,
Undimmed, unchanged toward the skies.
By God's good grace it never dies,
    A living torch for aye.

" 'T is said that while he calmly stood
    And waited for the flame,
He gave each trifle that he had,
True relic-treasure, dear and sad,
    To each who cared to claim.
I was not there to ask a share,
But reverently forever wear
    That noble martyr's *name.*"

THIRTEENTH GENERATION.

Sir Nicholas Ridley[13] (7), eldest son of Hugh[12] (3), married Mabel, daughter of Sir Philip Dacre, of Morpeth, third son of Humphrey Dacre, a lord; was high sheriff of Northumberland in 1570; will dated 1573. Had issue *ten* children, of whom hereafter.*

John Ridley[13] (6), second son of Hugh[12] (3), married Jane, daughter of John Errington, who was a brother of Gilbert Errington, of Errington.

Cuthbert Ridley[13] (1), third son of Hugh[12] (3), went to Ireland, and is supposed to have become ancestor of the Ridleys now living in that country, whose genealogy has not been found, though many efforts have been made to procure it. There are two wealthy landed gentlemen in Ireland at present (1880), of the name.

Thomas Ridley[13] (6), fourth son of Hugh[12] (3), was married to Elizabeth, daughter and sole heir of John Ridley, of Walltown, Northumberland, before mentioned. (See "Ridleys of Walltown" in this book.)

Dorothy Ridley[13] (1), eldest daughter of Hugh[12] (3), was the wife of Henry Jackson.

There were other sisters in this family whose names do not appear; one was married to Ralph Whitefield, and another to —— Weldon.

William Ridley[13] (3), only son of John[12] (5), was styled "of Whittingham."

Henry Ridley[13] (1), eldest son of Lancellot[13] (1), married Catherine Stewart, and had issue, of whom hereafter.

Dr. Mark Ridley[13] (1), second son of Lancellot[12] (1), was born at Cambridgeshire, and was educated at Clare Hall, Cambridge University, as a member of which he proceeded A. B. in 1580, and A. M. in 1584. As a master of arts he was admitted a licentiate of the College of Physicians, Sept. 25, 1590. We gather from the annals that on April 7, 1592, he had already taken his degree of Doctor of Medicine, in his University, but he was not admitted a Fellow of the college until May 28, 1594. Immediately after this he proceeded to Russia as a physician to the English merchants trading there, and became chief physician to the czar. For the

---

* There was a Lancellot Ridley, son of Nicholas[13] (7), but the name of his wife does not appear.

NOTE — Robert Ridley, Esq., was high sheriff of Northumberland in the twenty-seventh year of the reign of Queen Elizabeth, and was no doubt a cadet of the Willimoteswick family, but his name is not found in any printed pedigree.

DR. MARK RIDLEY
DIED, 1625

Nissus ab Elisa Ruthenis quinque per annos
Anglis ni desis te Vocat illa domum
Tute mathematicis clarus. magnetica calles
Pæonias laudes doctus Vbique capis

latter office he was chosen by Lord Burghley, who recommended him as a man learned and expert in his profession. He became a great favorite at the court, and remained in Russia four years. After the death of his royal patient, he was recalled by Queen Elizabeth, and permission was granted him to return to his native country by the czar's successor, who, at the time of taking leave of Dr. Ridley, gave it to be understood, that if in future an English physician, apothecary, or other learned personage, should desire to come to Russia, he should depend upon a kind reception, due maintenance, and a free permission to return home. On Dr. Ridley's return to England he fixed his residence in London; was appointed censor in 1607, 1609, 1610, 1611, 1612, 1813, 1615, 1618; elect Sept. 20, 1609, on the death of Dr. Wilkinson; treasurer April 2, 1610, and again in 1620; consiliarius 1612, 1618, 1614, 1616, 1617, 1618, and 1621. He was dead Feb. 14, 1623–4, when Dr. Gwinne was named elect in his place. No issue. See portrait in this book.

John Ridley[18] (7), a son of Thomas[12] (5), married Anne, daughter of Edward Charlton, of Heleyside, and had issue, of whom hereafter. He was living in 1615.

FOURTEENTH GENERATION.

Sir Nicholas* **Ridley**[14] (8), eldest son of Nicholas[18] (7), married Margaret, daughter of Thomas Forster, of Ederston, died without issue in 1586, and was succeeded by his brother. He was high sheriff of Northumberland.

William Ridley[14] (4), second son of Nicholas[18] (7), married a daughter of Sir John Heron, of Chipchase Castle, and had issue, of whom hereafter. He succeeded his brother, Sir Nicholas, in the estate of Willimoteswick.

Lancellot Ridley[14] (2), third son of Nicholas[18] (7), had issue a son, of whom hereafter.

Thomas Ridley[14] (6), fourth son of Nicholas[18] (7), married his cousin Mary, daughter of John Ridley, of Walltown, and had issue, of whom hereafter. He was styled "of Hardriding, Northumberland."

Alexander Ridley[14] (1), fifth son of Nicholas[18] (7), of whom I have no particulars, except that he married Barbara, daughter of Thomas Crane.

Jane Ridley[14] (2).
Margery Ridley[14] (2).
Elizabeth Ridley[14] (2).
Mabel Ridley[14] (1).
Isabelle Ridley[14] (2).
Anne Ridley[14] (3).
} Daughters of Nicholas[18] (7).

John Ridley[14] (8), eldest son of John[18] (7), was his father's heir. He married Elizabeth, daughter of Thomas Carlton, of Carlton Hall, in the County of Cumberland, and had issue *four* sons and *four* daughters, of whom hereafter. He was of Walltown.

William Ridley[14] (5), second son of John[18] (7), was an apprentice to a dyer in Thames Street, London, 1684. He married Anne, daughter of —— Woodman, and had issue *four* children, of whom hereafter.

---

* Nicholas Ridley, the eldest son, is said in one account to be ancestor of the Ridleys of Craw Hall, a family I am not acquainted with.

Thomasine Ridley[14] (2), eldest daughter of John[13] (7), was the wife of Daniel Stoughton.

Margaret Ridley[14] (3), second daughter of John[13] (7), was the wife of Ralph Thurlway.

Elizabeth Ridley[14] (3), third daughter of John[13] (7), was the wife of William of the Morralea.

Mary Ridley[14] (1), fourth daughter of John[13] (7), was the wife of Thomas Ridley, of Hardriding, son of Nicholas Ridley.

FIFTEENTH GENERATION.

William Ridley[15] (6), son of William[14] (4), was of Willimoteswick, Northumberland, and owner of lands in Wark; married a daughter of Sir Richard Musgrave, of Norton, and had issue, of whom hereafter.

Michael Ridley[15] (1), second son of William[14] (4).

Mabel Ridley[15] (2), eldest daughter of William[14] (4).

Mary Ridley[15] (2), second daughter of William[14] (4), was the wife of Charles Ripon, of Conside Park, in 1638.

Thomas Ridley[15] (7), son of Lancellot[14] (2), was styled "Gentleman," of Bewling, in Salop; married Anne, daughter of William Day, of Wingfield, in Salop, and had issue *two* children (and probably more), of whom hereafter.

John Ridley[15] (9), eldest son of Thomas[14] (6), died without issue.

Nicholas Ridley[15] (9), second son of Thomas[14] (6), was of Hardriding, in Northumberland; married, firstly, Anne, daughter of —— Hiron, of Birtley, Northumberland; secondly, Barbara, daughter of —— Errington, of West Denton, and had issue, of whom hereafter. He stands the second proprietor of Hardriding.

Rev. Cuthbert Ridley[15] (2), D. D., third son of Thomas[14] (6), was rector of the parish of Simonburn, in Northumberland, in 1630(?), and of Tecket Tower. He was a clergyman of great learning, and able in his pulpit services. At North Tindale, Northumberland, at the east end of the south aisle of the church, are effigies of the Rev. Cuthbert Ridley, a reclining figure of a woman (one authority says "of a youth"), and a child cut in stone. The drawing now before me, forwarded by the historian of Simonburn, represents a window, before which, reclining on a pillow, is the figure of a woman, under which is an inscription in Latin, as follows:

" Sensus vionus recordor misericordiam
Dei eripientis ex hac vita in vitam eternam
Albanum Ridley filium Cuthberti Ridley,
miseri peccatoris Anno Dom. 1625."

On the left hand, in a standing position, is the figure of a child, under which are the words "*Defectus Memoriæ*," and under them, " God be merciful to Ridley, a sinner." At the right hand stands the figure of a man with long beard, in priestly costume, looking down upon the reclining figure. Under these figures in panel-work is the tomb. I think the date has not been correctly copied, as he was rector of Simonburn in 1630, as stated in the family pedigree. The church in which the tomb and effigies stood was restored in 1877.

George Ridley[15] (1), fourth son of Thomas[14] (6), was probably of Gatehouse, Northumberland, and married a daughter of Ralph Pemberton, of

Belmond Castle; either her sister or daughter married J. Reed, of Chipchase.

SIXTEENTH GENERATION.

Musgrave Ridley[16] (1), eldest son of William[15] (6), was styled "the last of the Lords of Willimoteswick," as this chief possession of the family was taken by parliament in 1652, in consequence of the steady adherence of Musgrave Ridley to the cause of Charles I, and passed into the possession of the Nevilles, by whom it was sold to the ancestor of the present Sir Edward Blackett, of Matfenn, in 1680. (See account of Willimoteswick in preceding pages.)

William Ridley[16] (7), second son of William[15] (6), of whom no more information appears.

Thomas Ridley[16] (8), third son of William[15] (6), became ancestor of the "Ridleys of Parkend," which see in this book.

Albany Ridley[16] (1), eldest son of Nicholas[15] (9), was a merchant in London, and died without issue.

John Ridley[16] (10), second son of Nicholas[15] (9), of Hardriding, in Northumberland, was born Sept. 1, 1615; married, firstly, Anne, daughter of R. Featherstonhaugh, of Stanhope; secondly, Mary, daughter of Edward Lawson, of Brumpton, and had issue *twelve* children. He was one of His Majesty's Justices of the Peace, and a major of a regiment in the army of the Rt. Hon. William, Marquis of Newcastle, for the service of King Charles I; also, major in the garrison of Carlisle, — Sir Philip Musgrave being the governor, — and afterwards major to Sir Marmaduke Langdale, afterwards Lord Langdale.

Elizabeth Ridley[16] (4), eldest daughter of Nicholas[15] (9), died when young.

Barbara Ridley[16] (1), second daughter of Nicholas[15] (9), died when young, unmarried.

Susanna Ridley[16] (1), third daughter of Nicholas[15] (9), was married to Michael Stockton, of Hedding Bridge.

Lancellot Ridley[16] (3), eldest son of Thomas[16] (7) and his wife Anne Day; married, firstly, Frances, daughter of William Acton, Esq., of Alden, ham, by whom he had issue *five* children, of whom hereafter; secondly-Elizabeth, daughter of Adam Otley, of Pitchford, in the County of Salops, by whom *six* children, of whom hereafter; thirdly, Mary, daughter of —— Iremonger, of Stafford, by whom *one* son, of whom hereafter.

Sir Thomas Ridley[16] (9), second son of Thomas[15] (7), was a knight. He was born at Ely in Cambridgeshire; bred first a scholar at Eton, then Fellow of King's College, Cambridge. He was a general scholar in all kinds of learning, especially in that which was called *melior literatura*. He was a doctor of civil laws, master in chancery, and vicar-general to Archbishop Abbott of Canterbury; also, chancellor of Winchester. He was Member of Parliament for Wycombe, in Buckinghamshire, twenty-eighth year of the reign of Queen Elizabeth. He published "A View of Civil and Ecclesiastical Law," which was of great value; also, author of a treatise on the Eucharist. He married Margaret, daughter of William Boleyne (or Bullen) and his wife Annie Duffield, a relative of Sir Thomas Boleyne, Earl of Wiltshire and Ornsond, who was the father of Queen

Anne Boleyne, mother of Queen Elizabeth, by whom he (Ridley) had issue *one* son and *two* daughters, of whom hereafter. He died Jan. 23, 1628, and was buried in St. Bennett's Church, near Paul's wharf, London. He is said to have had a son Thomas, who was father of Gloster Ridley, D. D., but he makes no mention of a son in his will, and I have no good proof that Gloster was his descendant.

COPY OF THE WILL OF SIR THOMAS RIDLEY, KNT.

"In the name of God, amen. I Thomas Ridley, Knight, Doctor of the Civill lawe, being of perfect health and sound memorie, thanckes be to Allmightie God. Considering notwithstanding the uncertainty of this life and my greate age. and therefore desirous to sett in order mine estate wherewith it hath pleased God to indowe me in this life, before I goe out of this transitorie life, doe ordaine and make this my last will and testament in manner and forme following, the eleventh daie of October, in the yeare of our lord god one thousand six hundred and twenty-eight. ffirst and principally I bequeath my sowle unto the handes of the blessed Trinitie, the ffather, the sonne, and the holighost, hoping assuredly to be saved and clensed from all my sinnes and imperfections by the innocent death and passion of my sweet saviour Jesus Christ, by whose meritts alone I trust to be delivered and acquitted from eternall death and damnation, and to be made fellowheire with him and partaker of all the ioyes in Heaven, with all his blessed angells and saintes in glory. And as touching my bodie I will the same shallbe buried in full hope of my resurrection to the ioyes eternall, with as small charges as convenientlie maybe, in such church as I shall happen to decease, Knowing that costlie funeralls are rather a shew to such as live than anie comfort to the deceased. ffirst, for my fee simple lands which is my mannor of Babridge in the parish of Owslebury, and certain other parishes thereto adioyning in the Countie of South'n, I give and bequeath the same to my dearly beloved wife Dame Margarett Ridley during her life. And after her decease according as it is alreadie devised by me, in one Indenture Tripertite bearing date the twentieth day of May one thousand six hundred and nineteen betweene myself and the parties therein named, to which Indenture for more certainetie I referr my selfe. ffor my personall estate which god of his goodnesse hath bestowed on me, I have alreadie disposed of the most of it, partly uppon my deare daughter Anne Ridley, now Dame Anne Bosevile, the wife of Sr Edward Bosevile, Knight, my deare sonne-in-lawe, for her marriage portion with him. And partly uppon my deare daughter Elizabeth Ridley for her marriage portion with such an husband as it shall please god to provide for her, if happilie shee doe marrie, or otherwise to be at her dispose as it doth and male appear by such instruments in writeing as I have heretofore made to either of them under my hand and seale before competent witnesses in full satisfaction or clayme of anie further portion of my goods. Charging my said daughter, Elizabeth (although I nothing doubt of her dutifull affection toward her mother), that shee bee advised by her deare Mother both in her marriage and in all other courses of her life besides. But as concerning my lease of Poyle farme in the parish of Hanwell, in the Countie of Midd', I give the same wholy to my loving wife Dame Margarett Ridley. All the rest of my goodes and chattells, plate, household stuffe, leases, debts, and all other my rights whatsoever and by whatsoever other name they be called, not before bequeathed to either of my loveing and dearly beloved daughters aforenamed, my funeralls first discharged, I wholy give to my loveing and best beloved wife, Dame Margarett Ridley, whom I make my full and sole executrix of this my last will and testament. ffor my servants I leave them to the discretion of my executrix aforesaid. ffor Overseers of this my last will I name the right wor'll my very worthy Kind ffriend, Sr Morrice Abbot, Knight, Governor of the East India Company, and my very loving and Kind freind and cosen, George Allington, Esq., hartilie desireing them to be assistants to my wife in anie thing she shall desire their advice concerning this my last will and testament. And to accept in remembrance of my love towards them and theirs, again towards me to each of them a peece.   THOMAS RIDLEY.

"Signed, sealed and subscribed, published and delivered for his last will and testament by the said Sr Thomas Ridley, in the presence of us.

"GILBERT DETHICKE, EDWARD PHILLIPPS, THOMAS WILLYMS, RICHARD WEBB."

The above will was proved Feb. 26, 1628–9, in the Prerogative Court of the Archbishop of Canterbury, and is now preserved at Somerset House, London.

[**Dr. Humphrey Ridley**[16] (1), M. D., was a son of Thomas Ridley, of Mansfield, County Nottingham; born in 1653, admitted a student of Merton College, Oxford, in 1661. "He left the University," says Wood, "without taking his degree, and went to Cambridge, where he was doctorated in physic. He graduated Doctor of Medicine at Leyden, in 1679, and was admitted at Cambridge, in 1688. He was admitted a candidate of the College of Physicians, 30th September, 1692. He was Gulstonian Lecturer in 1694, and performed the duties of his office to the honour of the College, to the establishment of his own reputation, and the general satisfaction of the learned auditory. He practised his profession in London. Wrote 'The Anatomy of the Brain, containing its Mechanism and Physiology; together with some new Discoveries and Corrections of antient and modern Authors upon the subject,' London, 1695; and 'A particular account of Animal Functions and Muscular Motion.' Both tracts published in 1694, were dedicated to Dr. J. Lawson, president of the College of Physicians. He died in April, 1708." *]

SEVENTEENTH GENERATION.

John Ridley[17] (11), eldest son of John[16] (10), died unmarried.
Nelville Ridley[17] (1), second son of John[16] (10), died young.
Wilford Ridley[17] (1), third son of John[16] (10), died young.
Nicholas Ridley[17] (10), fourth son of John[16] (10), was born at Hardriding, an ancient seat of the Ridley family, about 1650; married Martha, daughter of Richard March, a merchant of Newcastle, and had issue *five* sons and *four* daughters, of whom hereafter. He moved to Newcastle-on-Tyne when a young man, entered heartily into trade, and soon became an eminent merchant. He was twice mayor of the city, first in 1688, the year of the "glorious Revolution," and again in 1706, that in which the treaty of union between England and Scotland was signed. "He was," says Bourne, " esteemed a man of great honour and integrity, and an excellent magistrate." By his last will and testament, dated 7th December, 1710, he gave and bequeathed to the poor of the parish of Haltwhistle forty shillings per annum out of a little farm or tenement called Wagtail Hall. He also bequeathed an annual rent-charge of four pounds ten shillings to the poor of Newcastle, while he gave a donation of fifty pounds to the poor of Carlisle, and twenty pounds to the poor of Hexham township. He died Jan. 22, 1710–11, and lies buried in St. Nicholas' Church, at the entrance into the chancel from the body of the sacred edifice.
Godfrey Ridley[17] (1), fifth son of John[16] (10), died young.
Edward Ridley[17] (1), sixth son of John[16] (10), was born in 1652; married Dorothy, daughter of Allen Chamberlayne, and had issue *one* son and *four* daughters. He was styled " of Lincoln's Inn."
Jane Ridley[17] (3), a daughter of John[16] (10), was the wife of Christopher Barrows, Gentleman.
Mary Ridley[17] (3), a daughter of John[16] (10), was the wife of Thomas Pate, clerk vicar.
Barbara Ridley[17] (3), a daughter of John[16] (10), died young.

---

* I do not know the pedigree of this man, and place this notice here because of contemporary dates.

[Capt. **Hugh Ridley**[17] (4), parents unknown, was, on the 12th June, 1667, appointed captain of the " Star," fireship, and soon after removed to the " Tilbury," prize.   In the following year he was commissioned to the " Providence," fireship.   He had no other command till the year 1673, when he was made, by Prince Rupert, captain of the " Woolwich," sloop. On the 3d June, 1675, King Charles II, who had taken upon himself the management of all affairs relative to the navy, gave him command of the " Wivenhoe," sloop.   On the 28d February, 1681–2, he was made captain of the boats of Portsmouth, from which station he was removed into the " America," guard-ship, on the 29th July following.   After the accession of King James, he was, on the 25th May, 1685, again made captain of the " America," from which he was, on the 9th June following, removed into the " Swan."   He continued in the command of this vessel till the 15th of August, when he was appointed to the " Guardland," and sailed for the Straits on the 25th of the same month, under orders of Sir Roger Strickland.   He continued on this station till the year 1688, and arrived at Plymouth on the 30th of March.   He was, on the 9th of September, made captain of the " Antelope," one of the fleet fitted out under his old commander, Sir Roger Strickland, for the purpose of counteracting, if possible, the invasion then meditated by the Prince of Orange, afterwards King William III.   He is known to have commanded a ship of the line after the Revolution; but we have not been able to procure any farther information relative to him, except that he was still living, but unemployed, in February, 1698–9.]*

Richard Ridley[17] (2), eldest son of Lancellot[16] (3), married Jane, daughter of Robert Dockham, and had issue *two* sons, of whom hereafter.

Francis Ridley[17] (1), second son of Lancellot[16] (3), married a niece of Baron Denham.   He was of Egham, County of Surrey.

John Ridley[17] (12), eldest son of Lancellot[16] (3) by second wife.

Thomas Ridley[17] (10), second son of Lancellot[16] (3) by second wife.

Richard Ridley[17] (3), third son of Lancellot[16] (3) by second wife, was styled " of Bolding."

Mary Ridley[17] (4), eldest daughter of Lancellot[16] (3) by second wife, was married to William Putter, parson of Leneland, and vicar of Throwley, in Kent.

Jane Ridley[17] (4), second daughter of Lancellot[16] (3) by second wife, was the wife of John Cradock, Doctor of Civil Laws.

William Ridley[17] (8), only child of Lancellot[16] (3) by third wife, died *sine prole.*

Anne Ridley[17] (5), eldest daughter of Thomas[16] (9), was married to Sir Edward Bosvile, son and heir of Sir Ralph Bosvile, of Bradborne, County of Kent.   She is mentioned in her father's will as " Dame Anne Bosevile, the wife of Sir Edward Bosevile, Knt."   See will.

Elizabeth Ridley[17] (5), second daughter of Thomas[16] (9), was unmarried at her father's death, but was afterwards married to Shirley Snelling, of West Grinstead, County of Sussex.   In his will dated Oct. 11, 1628, her father charges her to " bee advised by her deare Mother, both in her marriage and in all other courses of her life besides."   See will.

* I do not know the connections of this man, and have placed the notice here because of contemporary dates.

GLOSTER RIDLEY D.D.
DIED 1774 AGED 72.

The several pedigrees of the preceding family do not correspond in placing the children.

EIGHTEENTH GENERATION.

Rev. Gloster Ridley[18] **(1),** D. D., grandson of Thomas[16] (9), was born at sea in 1702, on board the "Gloster," Indiaman, from which circumstance he received his name. He was educated at Winchester School and became Fellow of New College, Oxford, where he took his degree of B. C. L. in 1789. He manifested a great partiality for the stage in early life, and to this preference may be attributed the eloquence and graceful delivery which he afterwards displayed in the pulpit. He obtained the living of Westow, Norfolk, and the donation of Poplar, in Middlesex; and after some years spent in the peaceful obscurity of a country curacy, he was at last presented to a golden prebend in Salisbury, by Archbishop Secker, who also conferred upon him the degree of LL. D. He was an eminent scholar and divine. His publications were not numerous; he wrote a tragedy in four parts in early life, and afterwards a life of his kinsman, Bishop Nicholas Ridley. He died Nov. 3, 1774, and had his virtues recorded in an epitaph * by the learned Dr. Lowth. His widow died at Hingham, in 1837, aged 91 years; they had a family of *six* children, of whom hereafter. The following verses indicate his style of composition: —

VERSES ON PRAYER.

" Prayer is the manna, the celestial bread,
By which our hungry souls are daily fed.
Through life's wild wilderness by this sustained,
We reach the heavenly Canaan's promised land.
Bring then thy choicest lays, inspiring muse,
This glorious subject of my verse I chuse:
The various motions of the mind declare
How Heaven itself is stormed by fervent prayer,
And all the artillery of that peaceful war.

And first Contrition does the soul employ,
That pleasurable pain, that grief of joy;
Affliction's waters are of bitter kind,
And grate the palate of the mind;
But when God's grace, that Tree of Life, is cast
Therein, the streams forget their nauceous taste.
First on his knees the humble sinner falls,
And to the Lord for gracious succor calls;
He prays his God to melt his frozen soul,
To break his heart, and make, by breaking whole.
He prays his God to strike the friendly blow,
That from the rock once more the streams may flow.
The volume of his life is now displayed,
And every page impartially surveyed;
And now upon the ground behold him roll,
Expressing thus the posture of his soul;
Shame o'er his face her scarlet mantle spreads,
And his torn heart with inward anguish bleads;
His eyes of tears a grateful tribute bring,

* "*H. S. E. Glosterus Ridley, vir optimus integerrimus: Verbi Divini peritus fidelis indefensus: Ab Academiâ Oxoniensi pro meritus, et praeter ordinem, in Sacrâ Theologiâ Doctorate insignitus. Poeta natus, Oratoriæ facultati impensius studuit Quam fuerat in concionando fecundus, plurimonum animus diei insidebit; quam variâ eruditione instructus. Scripta ipsius semper testabunter. Obiit tertia die mensis Novembris, A. D. 1774.*"

From sweet Sincerity's pure crystal spring;
Deep from his heart the struggling groans arise,
And ardently he breathes the insence of his sighs.
The whole man labors in this heavenly war,
And every look and gesture is a prayer;
God's grace he still continues to implore,
Still he receives, yet still he sues for more;
Still meekly fervent is his prayer address't,
He asks for pardon for the cold request;
With tears he mourns the dryness of his eyes,
And, sighing deep, laments the want of sighs.
His grief is with an eye of pitty seen,
And sweet-tongued Mercy speaks the leeper clean.
The native pureness of his soul returns,
The Angels triumph, the Apostate mourns.

And now for praise he does his soul prepare,
Seraphic praise, that heaven of heavens is prayer!
Great God! what holy raptures does he prove!
How melt before the sacred fire of love!
'T was thus, the wondering gratitude oppres't,
He would have spoke the fulness of his breast.
"Oh righteous Lord! who sit'st enthroned on high,
Look down and view me with a gracious eye;
Accept the mighty tribute that I bring,
A mite of praise to Heaven's eternal King.
Greatly I long and ardently I burn,
To make a nobler and more large return;
But hence each thought of retribution's rain,
That thou art God, and I ignoble man:
But oh! what bright ideas shall I find
To represent thy image to my mind!
Can thought concieve the King of heaven and earth
That has in matter its plebeian birth?
And shall a word, a trancient sound, proclaim
The everlasting greatness of thy name?
Thou art, Oh Lord — O teach me what to say —
A flood, an ocean of excessive day —
A glorious sun unutterably bright,
That sheds on vast immensity its light.
Creation is contained and filled by thee,
Thou fill'st thyself, thou art immensity.
Thou wast before — Eternity 's thy name,
How great thy power! thou will'st; and strait became
A beauteous world from nothing's barren womb.
Thou frown'st, and hell and misery appear;
Thou smil'st, and heaven and happiness are there.
How boundless is thy knowledge! — thou can'st see
The perfect state of them before they be,
And the world was before it was, in thee.
To thee Time stops his never-wearied haste,
To thee is perfect still the future and the past.
But one step further does my knowledge go;
I know that thou art more than I can know;
Whene'er I tread this dark, uncertain coast,
In thy perfections mighty, vast, I 'm lost.
In vain I strive the feable hymn to raise —
Hyperbole is meanness in thy praise.

But Goodness, that fair virgin, ever blest,
Nearest and dearest to thy sacred breast,
Who with her soft enchanting voice can charm
Justice herself, and stop her lifted arm,
Demands thy praise —
An age ago, my soul, what wast thou? where?

Wast thou a lump of clay or blast of air?
Where, in the world's wide circuit did'st thou dwell?
On earth, in heaven, or in the depth of hell?
What part of vast INANE did'st thou fill?
No, then in Fate's firm fetters I was kept,
In the dark womb of non-existance slept.
In my creation thy first love began,
It gave me being, willed me into man.
In thee I think, I speak, I move, I live;
Myself from thee each moment I receive.
But here's the life of goodness, here we prove
The full protection of all-perfect love;
That he who in the world of glory shone,
The bright Paretius of the Eternal sun,
Was pleased to leave his dignity on high,
For us to live in man, for us to die.
See on the cross his bleeding body hung!
His flesh with pain, his mind with sorrow stung!
The sad, yet joyful minutes now begin,
Of Jesus' death, and of the death of sin.
In every groan he utters we revive;
He faints, we quicken; he expires, we live.
By love like this my soul is quite o'ercome;
And gratitude and wonder strike me dumb;
A theme like this requires a seraph's lays;
Give me new powers, great God, and then I'll sing thy praise."

INVITATION TO THE COUNTRY.

"Now, waiting on the Spring, soft gales
Smothe the rough waves and fill the sails.
The fields are green; the river flows,
Disburdened of its ice and snows.

"Now does the nightingale return,
In sadly pleasing notes to mourn
The unhappy boy too rashly slain!
And wakens all her grief again.

"The shepherds stretch the grass along,
Indulge the cheerful pipe and song;
Pan, patron of Arcadian swains,
Well-pleased, might listen to their strains.

"Heat brings on drought; yet, friend, scot-free
Think not to quench your thirst with me.
You are so used with Lords to dine!
—I can't afford it: earn your wine.

"Clap in your pocket prose or verse,
And freely then my hogshead pierce;
Drink till new warmpth inspire our hopes
To laugh at Grand Monarchs and Popes.

"On termes like these if you consent,
Haste here and bring the equivalent:
I am no Lord; nor think it fit
To sell my wines for less than wit.

"Come, let the press stand still to-day;
True wisdom must have some allay.
To make it stirling; tune and place
Give Folly's self a pleasing grace."

28

SELFISHNESS.

" Self spoils the sence of all mankind,
    And casts a mist before the mind;
    Whate'r 's the intrinsic of the coin,
    Yours always will be worse than mine.
    Each grovelling, despicable elf
    Damns all the world besides and deifies himself."

John Ridley[18] (12), eldest son of Nicholas[17] (10), died unmarried in 1716, and was buried in St. Nicholas' Church, Newcastle-on-Tyne.

Richard Ridley[18] (4), second son of Nicholas[17] (10), was born at Newcastle-on-Tyne; married Margaret, daughter of another eminent Newcastle merchant, Alderman Matthew White, and his wife Jane, daughter of Alderman Nicholas Fenwick, at Stannington, in 1707, and had issue, of whom hereafter.   He was alderman, mayor of Newcastle in 1713 and 1732, and Governor of the Merchants' Company.   He purchased the estate of Heaton, and built for his country-residence a large brick house named Heaton Hall (see plate in this book), on the steep and woody banks of the Ouseburn, in the neighborhood of extensive collieries owned by him. Mr. Ridley died at Heaton, Nov. 2, 1739.   The following account of his funeral will be of interest here: —

"On the 5th, in the evening, his corpse was interred in St. Nicholas' Church.   The hearse, covered with escutcheons, and drawn by six horses, was preceded by eighty-six of the deceased's tenants and agents on horseback, two and two, with mourning gloves, and three servants; the hearse was followed by a retinue of mourning and other coaches.   In this manner the corpse was conveyed from Heaton to Mr. Ridley's house on the quay, Newcastle, where the company were invited, and where the corpse was taken out of the hearse and from thence carried to the church, the pall being covered with escutcheons, and supported by eight gentlemen of note.   The master of the charity school, with a scarf, leading the charity boys of St. Nicholas, went foremost in the procession; after whom came five beadles, who were followed by twenty men in cloaks, walking two and two; betwixt these and the corpse walked three couples of servants in mourning; behind the corpse walked twenty-four chief mourners, two and two; these were succeeded by the regalia of the town in mourning, borne by the proper officers, who were followed by the mayor and aldermen, with scarfs and black gloves; next to these walked the clergy, with scarfs, who were followed by the relations of the deceased, in scarfs; to these succeeded the wardens and secretary of the Merchants' Company, with gloves, two and two, and closed with a beadle in a scarf. Then followed a multitude of gentlemen and tradesmen, in gloves; after these came the eighty-six tenants and agents on horseback, as before. During the procession through the town half-minute guns were fired, and a solemn silence was observed by the vast crowd of spectators.   When the corpse entered in at the west door of the church, a piece of solemn music was performed upon the organ.   After the funeral ceremony was over the bells rung a mourning peal, which closed the solemnities of the day."

Nicholas Ridley[18] (11), third son of Nicholas[17] (10).
Edward Ridley[18] (2), fourth son of Nicholas[17] (10).   } No
John Ridley[18] (13), was the fifth son of Nicholas[17] (10). } records.

"HEATON HALL"
Northumberland, England.
RESIDENCE OF SIR MATTHEW W. RIDLEY BART.

Mary Ridley[18] (5), eldest daughter of Nicholas[17] (10), was the wife of Garvin Ainsley, Esq., of Little Harle.

Anne Bidley[18] (6), second daughter of Nicholas[17] (10), died young and unmarried.

Anne Ridley[18] (7), third daughter of Nicholas[17] (10), was the wife of Robert Douglas, of Newcastle-on-Tyne.

Martha Ridley[18] (1), fourth daughter of Nicholas[17] (10), died young and unmarried.

Richard Ridley[18] (5), only son of Edward[17] (2), was a colonel of Guards; died unmarried, and was buried in St. Margaret's Church, Westminster.

Mary Ridley[18] (6).
Elenor Ridley[18] (1). ·
Dorothy Ridley[18] (2). } Daughters of Edward[17] (2).
Anna Ridley[18] (1).

Richard Ridley[18] (6), eldest son of Richard[17] (2).
Francis Ridley[18] (2), second son of Richard[17] (2).

NINETEENTH GENERATION.

Mary Ridley[19] (7), a daughter of Gloster[18] (1), was the wife of Capt. Edward Evans (he died in 1807), and died in 1809.

Thomas Ridley[19] (11), a son of Gloster[18] (1), died of small-pox at Madras, when young.

Rev. James Ridley[19] (1), a son of Gloster[18] (1), was educated at Winchester School and New College, Oxford, and after taking his orders succeeded his father in the living of Rumford and Essex. In 1761 he was the chaplain of a regiment, and while exposed in the discharge of his duties contracted some disorder, which, to the unspeakable sorrow of his friends and family, terminated his life in 1765, at the age of twenty; he was buried at Poplar. His father in a letter writes: "He was as hopeful a young clergyman as an affectionate father could wish his son to be. So generous a heart, such an intimate knowledge of the power and workings of nature, so serious and earnest a desire to serve God and mankind, with cheerful spirit and address in conveying his instructions, make him a loss as great to the world as to me." He was author of "The Tales of the Genii"; a humorous paper called "The Schemer," afterwards collected in a volume; "The History of James Lovegrove," and several other small works. His writings were lucid, flowing, and eloquent, as his publications show, and growing so fast in the preferment of the church, he promised to become one of the most distinguished divines that ever adorned the family of Ridley, — a family prolific in clergymen.

Matthew Ridley[19] (1), eldest son of Richard[18] (4), was born in 1712; married, firstly, Hannah, daughter of Joseph Barnes, of Newcastle, by whom (who died Nov. 17, 1741) he had *one* son. He married, secondly, Elizabeth, daughter, and at length heir, of Sir Matthew White, of Blagdon (which Matthew was brother of Margaret, wife of Richard Ridley aforesaid), Nov. 18, 1742. By the second union there were *seven* sons and *four* daughters, of whom hereafter. The first wife was buried in St. Nicholas' Church, Newcastle. Mr. Ridley's monument in St. Nicholas' Church, erected in 1782, has an inscription which epitomizes his life and virtues; it consists of a figure in statuary-marble as large as life, bearing a resemblance of the person and features of Mr. Ridley (at the period to which the medallion and inscription allude), who is represented as sitting in the curule chair, the seat of magistracy, in Roman habit, with a serious but placid countenance, as considering the general welfare of the people over whom he presided. Under the chair are placed the scales and fasces, as emblems of justice and authority; beneath this is the entablature, containing the following inscription: —

" *To the memory of*
MATTHEW RIDLEY, ESQ., *of Blagdon and Heaton,*
in the County of Northumberland,
senior Alderman of the Corporation of this Town,
and Governor of the Company of Merchant Adventurers.
He four times served in the office as Mayor,
in which station, in 1745, he rendered essential service to his country,
averting by his prudence and activity, the attack meditated against his town by the
enemies of the House of Brunswick,
and thereby materially checked the progress of their arms.
He was unanimously elected by his fellow-burgesses to represent them
in five successive parliaments,
and retired from that position only when the declining state of his health rendered him
incapable of conscientiously fulfilling the duties of it.
He lived respected and beloved, and died unfeignedly lamented,
April 6, 1778, aged 66 years." *

The base of the monument is formed by a medallion, on which the town of Newcastle is represented by a female figure, having a shield by her, bearing the arms of the town; near her is an urn, from which are issuing salmon, the peculiar attribute of the River Tyne. This female figure is attacked by a figure of Rebellion, who, treading on the crown and sceptre (insignia of royalty), bears in one hand the torch of sedition, and in the other the sword of destruction; in an attitude of supplication she inclines herself toward an armed figure, who protects her with his shield, and with a sword in his right hand resists the figure of Rebellion; on the shield are represented the arms of the family of Ridley; the helmet is ornamented with a bull, which is the crest. As a finishing, under the medallion two cornucopias are introduced, representing the general effect of plenty (attendant upon the care of good and active magistrates), connected by a civic crown, the reward among the Romans, of civil virtue. The figure of Mr. Ridley is placed against an obelisk of white marble, eight feet high, on the top of which is a very elegant urn bearing the family

---

* " April 6, 1778, died at Heaton, in the sixty-seventh year of his age, Matthew Ridley, Esq., senior alderman, and lately one of the representatives of this town (Newcastle) in Parliament. He was a gentleman of excellent natural parts, improved by a liberal education. He was of a quick and clear conception of business, and a peculiar address in the execution of it. These talents he early employed in discharging the first offices of honour and trust in the corporation, where he since continued an active, well-informed, and incorrupt magistrate. By a diligent attention to his duties in the senate he had acquired a consummate skill in the forms and business of Parliament: to this he united a more general knowledge of the constitution, applying both with a manly and disinterested spirit to the general welfare of his country. These eminent qualities of the mind were adorned with a graceful address, and polished manners. He was endeared to his friends by an hospitable, generous and affectionate temper. Such are the outlines of this distinguished character, faintly but truly sketched by a friend who knew him well."-*Newcastle Courant.*

SIR MATTHEW WHITE RIDLEY, BART.

arms emblazoned; and on the foot of it is engraved the motto, "*Constance Fideo.*" The whole is relieved by a ground of dove-colored marble. This is one of the most elaborate and beautiful monuments in England. Mr. Ridley was styled "of Newcastle," and "of Heaton" (see view of Heaton Hall), and was succeeded by his second son. He made a conspicuous figure in parliament during the American Revolution, and the records copiously represent his speeches. In an address delivered before the House of Commons, relative to the American Colonies, on Friday, Oct. 27, 1775, Mr. Ridley said: "I have gone along with the minister during the past session, upon the supposition that his information regarding America was authentic, and to be depended upon; but now I have found it otherwise. I went away last night without voting, a conduct I wish to avoid, and therefore I call upon the minister to lay sufficient information before the House that gentlemen may know the ground upon which to proceed."

Capt. Richard Ridley[19] (7), second son of Richard[18] (4), married Anne, daughter of George Roach, of Portsmouth, and died without issue. He was commander of a company of foot-guards.

Elizabeth Ridley[19] (5), eldest daughter of Richard[18] (4), was married to Robert Douglas, of Newcastle-on-Tyne.

Martha Ridley[19] (2), second daughter of Richard[18] (4), was married to Rev. Hugh Moises, A. M., lecturer of All Saints' Church, Newcastle-on-Tyne, Feb. 2, 1754.

Isabella Ridley[19] (3), third daughter of Richard[18] (4), was married to Thomas Waters, of Newcastle-on-Tyne.

Jane Ridley[19] (5), fourth daughter of Richard[18] (4), was married to Matthew Bell, of Newcastle and Woolsington.

Mary Ridley[19] (8), fifth daughter of Richard[18] (4), was married to Matthew White, Esq., of Blagdon, County of Northumberland, who, surviving her, married, secondly, Elizabeth, daughter and co-heir of John Johnson, of Newcastle, and had a daughter Elizabeth, who became the wife of Matthew Ridley, brother of his first wife.

Nicholas Ridley[19] (11), third son of Richard[18] (4), died young.

Nicholas Ridley[19] (12), fourth son of Richard[18] (4), died young.

TWENTIETH GENERATION.

Maj. Richard Ridley[20] (8), eldest son of Matthew[19] (1) by his wife Hannah Barnes, was born July 5, 1786, in the parish of St. George, Martyr Queen's Square, London. He was an officer of foot-guard, and a gallant soldier. The representation of the family devolved upon a half-brother. *

Sir Matthew-White Ridley[20] (2), second son of Matthew[19] (1), and first by his wife Elizabeth White, was born in the parish of St. John, Newcastle-on-Tyne, Oct. 28, 1745; married July 12, 1777, to Sarah, daughter of Benjamin Colburn, Esq., of Bath, by whom (who died in August, 1806) he had *five* sons and *one* daughter, of whom hereafter. Matthew White, Esq., of Blagdon, Northumberland, was high sheriff of his County in 1756; and was, on presenting an address to His Majesty, created a baronet of the kingdom, with limitations in the patent, on failure of his issue male to the heirs male of his sister Elizabeth, wife of Matthew Ridley.

---

* One pedigree names a Jane, Mary, and Martha, in this family, who died young and unmarried.

Matthew White, Bart., died March 21, 1763, and was buried in All Saints' Church, Newcastle-on-Tyne, and the subject of this notice succeeded to his title and estate, in accordance with the patent aforesaid. Mr. Ridley was one of the oldest members of the Merchants' Company, of Newcastle-on-Tyne, and was its governor for thirty-five years. In so high a degree did he possess the confidence and esteem of his townsmen, that, in eight successive parliaments, they chose him as a representative. He was a firm friend of the British Constitution; and during the long time he sat in the senate, he had the merit of maintaining perfect consistency in his political conduct. Displaying an urbanity of manners and a most endearing condescension in his general intercourse with society, he invariably performed all the relative and social duties of life in a way that threw an amiable resplendency over his whole character. As a large landed proprietor he showed himself one of the best landlords to his tenants, as all who were so connected were loud in declaiming; in years of scarcity, in particular, these experienced the liberality of his heart; and he granted indulgences to them that must have embalmed his memory among those who were the immediate objects of his generosity. Exclusive of serving his town as a Member of Parliament, he discharged, for a number of years, the duties of an active magistrate, and was three times mayor of the city of Newcastle. Early in a contemporary war, when his country was threatened with invasion, Sir Matthew-White Ridley was placed at the head of a corps of volunteers excelled by none in the kingdom, either for loyalty to their sovereign, or efficiency in military tactics. While a soldier he discharged the important functions of chief; he might be said to live in the hearts of his men, for the liberal and indulgent attention he paid to the convenience and comfort of all under his command. He died at Portland Place, London, after a two years' illness, in 1813, aged 67 years, and was succeeded by his eldest son and namesake, of whom hereafter. There is a fine monument with a statue of this man in St. Nicholas' Church, Newcastle-on-Tyne, of which the author has a photograph. (See portrait in this book.)

Nicholas Ridley[20] (13), third son of Matthew[19] (1), was born at Newcastle-on-Tyne, March 5, 1748; married, 1790, Letitia, daughter of Hugh Atkinson, a Russian merchant, and became a master in chancery; denominated "of Grey's Inn." He died at his lodgings at Bath, Jan. 1, 1804.

Edward Ridley[20] (3), fourth son of Matthew[19] (1), died young.

Lieut. John Ridley[20] (14), fifth son of Matthew[19] (1), was an officer in the Welsh Fusileers.

Rev. Henry Ridley[20] (2), D. D., sixth son of Matthew[19] (1), was born July 2, 1753; married Frances, daughter of Aubone Surtees, Esq., of Newcastle-on-Tyne (she died in June, 1830), who was sister to Elizabeth, Countess of Eldon, and had issue *two* children, of whom hereafter. He received his clerical education at University College, Oxford, where he proceeded M. A., June 12, 1776, and B. and D. D. grand compounder, June 8, 1802. In 1804 he was elected one of the prebendaries of Gloucester; and in the following year His Majesty presented him to the living of Kirby, Underdale. In 1817, the king, as Duke of Lancaster, presented him to the livings of St. Andrew's, Cumberland, and St. Mary's, Hertfordshire. He was His Majesty's Justice of the Peace for the Counties of Hertfordshire and Gloucester, and Master of the Magdalen Hospital, Newcastle-on-Tyne. He died Oct. 11, 1825, leaving *one* son.

Edward Ridley[20] (4), seventh son of Matthew[19] (1), died young.

Charles Ridley[20] (1), eighth son of Matthew[19] (1), died young.

Christiana Ridley[20] (2), eldest daughter of Matthew[19] (1); so named from being born on Christmas day.

Margaret Ridley[20] (4), second daughter of Matthew[19] (1), died at Portland Place, London, in 1813, aged 68 years. She was a maiden-lady.

Jane Ridley[20] (6), third daughter of Matthew[19] (1); married July 22, 1777, to Arthur Shakespere, Esq., of Stephney; he died in February, 1804.

Mary Ridley[20] (9), fourth daughter of Matthew[19] (1), died young.

TWENTY-FIRST GENERATION.

Sir Matthew-White Ridley[21] (3), eldest son of Matthew[20] (2), was born Aug. 8, 1778, and succeeded as second baronet at the death of his father, April 9, 1813. He married Aug. 13, 1803, to Laura, youngest daughter of George Hawkins, Esq., by whom he had issue *twelve* children, of whom hereafter. He was matriculated of Christ Church, Oxford, April 24, 1795, at the age of seventeen, and took his degree of B. A., March 6, 1798. He represented Newcastle-on-Tyne as a Member of Parliament about twenty-four years; was head of the celebrated banking-house of Sir Matthew-White Ridley, Bigge & Co., of Newcastle-on-Tyne, and extensively engaged in the coal-trade and in the manufacture of glass. His principles were those of the old Whigs, and in an address delivered by him at his last election, he declared himself a sincere and practical Reformer; but in the extreme measures which characterized the latter periods of his official career, he inclined to Conservatism. He presented a large painting, measuring seven by seventeen feet, by Tintoretto, of our Saviour washing the Apostles' feet, as an altar-piece, to St. Nicholas' Church, Newcastle, in which are the beautiful monuments of his father and grandfather, by Bacon and Flaxham. He was resident at Heaton Hall, Northumberland; his death occurred at Richmond, July 14, 1836, in the fifty-eighth year of his age. A lithograph portrait of Mr. Ridley, from a painting by Ramsey, was published by Weld Taylor, and a protracted search has been made for a copy, but without success.

Nicholas-William Ridley[21] (14), second son of Matthew[20] (2), was born April 14, 1779; married Charlotte, eldest daughter of the Rt. Hon. Thomas Steele, June 14, 1808 (she died Feb. 17, 1855), and had issue one son and *four* daughters, of whom hereafter. His mother was Sarah, sole heir of Benjamin Colborne, and he as second son, succeeded to his mother's fortunes, additional surname, and arms, and was created Baron Colborne,* of West Harling, May 15, 1839, which entitled him to a seat in parliament as a peer. He was Member of Parliament for Appleby in 1807. He lived at 19 Hill Street, Berkeley Square, London, and at Harling Hall, Thetford, Norfolk. He died May 3, 1854, when the barony became extinct.

Rev. Henry-Colburne Ridley[21] (3), D. D., third son of Matthew[20] (2), was born May 16, 1780; married, April 21, 1808, to Mary, eldest daugh-

---

* A baron has the title of "Right Honourable Lord," and is addressed as "My Lord," or "Your Lordship." His wife has also the title of "Right Honourable," and is addressed as "Madam," or "Your Ladyship." A baron in signing, sinks his Christian and family name, and subscribes his titular designation. His children enjoy the prefix "Honourable," as the "Honourable ——," mentioning Christian and surnames. A deceased baron is spoken of by his Christian name, according to his number in the list of peers of the same title, as "Nicholas, second baron." A baron's coronet is adorned with six pearls, set at equal distances on a chaplet, and is worn only on great occasions of state ceremonial.

ter of James Ferrier, Esq., of Lincoln's-Inn-Fields, London, by whom he had issue. He was of Christ Church, Oxford, B. A., 1801, M. A., April 19, 1804. He was instituted rector of Hambleden, where he served the cause of his Master for many years, as a faithful and devoted representative of the holy religion he professed. He died on Feb. 3, 1832, and a memorial sermon was subsequently preached in his church by the Rev. John-Charles Williams, M. A., which was published, but I cannot find a copy of it. His wife deceased June 13, 1837, having had *three* sons and *two* daughters, of whom hereafter.

Rev. Charles-John Ridley[21] (2), M. A., fourth son of Matthew[20] (2), was born Sept. 5, 1792, and became second Earl of Eldon. He was of University College, Oxford, B. A., June 9, 1813, M. A., Oct. 31, 1817. It is presumed he married and had a family, but I can learn no particulars relative to his history.

Rev. Richard Ridley[21] (9), M. A., fifth son of Matthew[20] (2), born Aug. 28, 1782; married, Nov. 8, 1810, Catherine-Lucy, only daughter of the Rev. Richard-Pepplewell Johnson, of Ashton-upon-Mersey, Cheshire. He was of University College, Oxford, B. A., Nov. 24, 1803, M. A., June 16, 1806, and was presented to Cramlington that year by his father; and to Leathy, in the County of York, as perpetual curate, in 1826, by the Lord Chancellor. He died at Green Hamerton, in June, 1845, aged 62 years; his widow died in 1853.

Henrietta-Elizabeth Ridley[21] (1), only daughter of Matthew[20] (2), was married, firstly, Aug. 2, 1804, to the Hon. John Scott, eldest son of John, first Earl of Eldon, who died Dec. 24, 1805, and her only son became the second Earl of Eldon. She re-married, July 7, 1811, to William Farrer, Esq., of Ingleborough, Yorkshire; he died Nov. 9, 1862, leaving issue.

Elizabeth Ridley[21] (6), only daughter of Henry[20] (2), D. D., was of Lawn Cottage, Battersea, and died unmarried in July, 1862, aged 82.

Rev. Henry-John Ridley[21] (4), a son of Henry[20] (2), was born about 1788; married, Jan. 28, 1813, to Elizabeth-M.-Antoinette, eldest daughter of John Ellis, Esq., brother of Charles, first Lord Seaford, of Mainhead House, Devonshire (she died Dec. 12, 1816), and had issue, of whom hereafter.* He was of Christ Church, Oxford, B. A., Feb. 23, 1801, M. A., Nov. 17, 1808. He was presented to a prebend at Bristol, in 1816, and to Kirby, Underwood, in 1827, by his relative, Lord Eldon. He exchanged his prebend at Bristol, for one at Norwich, in 1832. He married, secondly, in 1823, Elizabeth, daughter of Lee-Steere Steere, Esq., of Jayess, Surrey, who, surviving her husband, became the wife, Sept. 28, 1843, of Sir Robert Peel, who had been elevated to the peerage by the title of Baron Abinger, of Abinger, County of Surrey. He died April 7, 1844. (This lady has in her possession, with other relics, the chair in which Bishop Nicholas Ridley used to study.) He was instituted rector of Abinger Church, May 26, 1821; was instituted rector of Newdigate, March 3, 1814. He died Nov. 14, 1834. Pious without bigotry; generous without ostentation; kind without weakness; social without levity, — he employed the short time allotted him by his Master in the discharge of active duties, and in the exercise of benevolent affections.

---

* There was an Arthur Ridley who was styled "of Clinton Park," County Buckingham, said by one authority to have been a son of Henry[20] (2), but I query this.

Sir Matthew-White Ridley[22] (4), eldest son of Matthew[21] (3), was born Sept. 9, 1807; married, Sept. 21, 1841, to Cecilia-Anna Parkes, daughter of the well-known judge, Baron Parkes, since created Lord Wensleydale. By this union there were *three* children, of whom hereafter. Lady Ridley died in 1845. Mr. Ridley was educated at Westminster School and Christ Church College, Oxford; he took his degree of B. A., at his graduation, in 1828. He succeeded as the third baronet of the Ridley family, at the death of his father, on July 15, 1836. Such an affection existed between the father and son, that when the latter was suddenly called upon to assume the family title and honors, he was plunged into such profound sorrow that he declined, for a time, to discharge any but the most pressing public duties. Upon the death of his father he was immediately nominated for the seat which had been occupied by his father, grandfather, and great-grandfather; but when he was called upon to present an address of acceptance, he disappointed his friends by the following: —

"Gentlemen: — In consequence of the application of many kind friends to know my views as to tendering my services as your representative, I am bound not to delay addressing you, incompetent as I feel to enter upon the painful subject. In declining to offer myself to your notice, believe me, that no one can possibly entertain a higher idea of the honor of the situation than I do; and, at a happier moment, with a mind not weighed down with affliction, I assure you it would have been my pride to offer myself as a successor to one who felt that, while holding the situation of your representative, he had the most honorable of all trusts committed to his charge."

And so the family seat was lost to Blagdon, and the baronet retired for a time from political life, devoting himself to the cultivation of his paternal acres and extensive mining property, and to the oversight of the banking firm of Sir Matthew-White Ridley & Co., of which he was head. In 1839 the banking establishment ceased to have a separate existence, being incorporated into the Northumberland and Durham District Banking Company. The duties of the magistracy and of the administration of County business, which had always secured his attention, soon claimed a nearer interest, and he rapidly rose to the most eminent places which they commanded. In 1841 he was found discharging the duties of high sheriff of Northumberland. For many years previous to 1845, Sir Matthew had kept a well-appointed pack of hounds, and in 1843 was entertained at a banquet in the Assembly Rooms, Newcastle, by the members of the Northumberland Hunt, to testify their esteem and admiration of his conduct as an M. F. H. In 1845 he disposed of his hounds in London, and soon after obtained a commission in the Newcastle and Northumberland Yeomanry Cavalry, now the Northumberland Hussars. For a long time he held the rank of major in this regiment, and upon the retirement of Mr. Matthew Bell from the command, in 1867, he was promoted to the chief position in the corps. In 1852 he was created a deputy lieutenant of the County of Northumberland. In 1859 he was elected to a seat in parliament, and for seven sessions was continued. He was elected again in 1865, and continued a faithful representative till 1868, when he resolved to retire, and early in August of that year presented his farewell address to the electors, intimating that "illness of a grave character was the cause which prevented him from appealing once more for their suffrages." Being once more outside the troubled vortex of political life, when his health was re-

gained he occupied himself principally with those avocations connected
with agriculture, in which he was so well versed. Under his management
the fine pasture-lands at Blagdon were greatly improved, and the high-
bred cattle raised there were sold at the highest prices. He also made a
complete reform in the style of his laborers' cottages in the neighborhood,
providing dwellings in which his help might dwell in health and comfort.
He made like improvements at his colliery property at Blyth and Cow-
pen. For many years Sir Matthew held the office of president of the
Newcastle Farmers' Club, and until overtaken by ill health, he rarely
missed an opportunity of being present at the deliberations of that useful
body. He was also a freeman of Newcastle, being governor of the Company of Merchant Adventurers, — a position which has been almost hereditary in the family. He was also for several years chairman of the Blyth
Harbour Dock Company, and did much to improve the trade of the town,
port, and district. In parliament Sir Matthew did not distinguish himself
as a speaker,—oratory was not his forte,—but he was a hard worker, and
devoted much time to the interests of his constituents. His knowledge
of agriculture rendered his services especially invaluable in all matters relating to that interest. He was a member of the Royal Agricultural Society of England, and the Northumberland Agricultural Society received
the benefit of his experience and advice. Sir Matthew died at Blagdon
Hall, near Morpeth, on Sept. 27, 1877. He had attended a meeting of the
Visiting Justices, of which he was a member, at the Northumberland
County Lunatic Asylum, on the 5th, and after the meeting inspected some
buildings then in process of erection, and fell from a ladder to the ground.
He was immediately taken to Blagdon, in company with his physician.
Although he received some contusions to the hip and thigh, with a few
bruises, he seemed to rapidly recover from the injuries, and was able to
be in the sitting-room most of the day on which, after a relapse, he suddenly died of heart-disease.

On Saturday following his death the remains of the deceased baronet
were interred in the family-vault in Stannington church-yard, the coffin
being placed alongside that of Lady Ridley. There was a large attendance at the funeral, the deceased gentleman's urbanity of manner and
kind-heartedness having made him a great favorite with his tenantry and
others on the estates. The coffin was of polished oak, with silver mount-
ings, and a plate bearing the inscription, — "Sir Matthew-White Ridley,
Bart.; died 25th September, aged 70 years." Beautiful wreaths were
placed on the coffin. The funeral procession started from Blagdon Hall
at eleven o'clock, and on arriving at the church the burial-service, copies
of which had been printed and given to the mourners, was impressively
read by the Rev. Ambrose Jones, vicar of Stannington. At the conclusion of the service the "Dead March in Saul" was played on the organ,
after which the services at the grave were gone through in the presence
of a large concourse of people, who had traveled long distances to pay
their last respects to the memory of the departed baronet. Sir Matthew
was succeeded by his eldest son, the present Sir Matthew-White Ridley,
Bart., M. P.

Nicholas-Henry Ridley[22] (15), second son of Matthew[21] (3), probably died young.

Gen. Charles-William Ridley[22] (3), third son of Matthew[21] (3), was
born in 1812; married, April 17, 1845, to the Hon. Henrietta-Araminta-
Monck Browne, daughter of Dominick, the late Lord Oranmore (she died

March 1, 1869), and by her had, with other issue, *two* sons and *three* daughters, of whom hereafter. He entered the army as ensign and second lieutenant of the Grenadier Guards in 1828, and was promoted to major-general in 1859. On the army embarking for active service in the East, he accompanied his regiment to Turkey. He commanded the Grenadier Guards, and afterwards a brigade, at the siege of Sebastopol in 1854. In recognition of his military services while in the Eastern army, he was nominated Companion of the Bath; he was also made an officer of the "Legion of Hanover"; received both the Scandinavian and Turkish medals, and the third class order of Medjide. In 1865 he was made colonel of the Fifty-third Regiment of Foot. He died Feb. 1, 1867, aged 55 years.

Rev. Richard-Henry Ridley²² (10), fourth son of Matthew²¹ (3), was born June 12, 1815; married April 23, 1846, Georgiana-Augusta-Fredrica, daughter of Gen. Sir Thomas Bradford, G. C. B., G. C. H., and by her, who died Jan. 9, 1861, had issue a numerous family (there were *five* daughters), of whom hereafter. He was graduated at University College, Oxford, Nov. 9, 1837, and is now (1878) vicar of St. Cuthbert's, Durham, — his residence.

Sir William-John Ridley²² (9), K. C. M. G., fifth son of Matthew²¹ (3), was born in 1817, and became an officer in the Scotch Fusileers in 1835. He entered the army when about twenty years of age, and passed through the several degrees of promotion from ensign to full major-general. He saw service in the East contemporary with his brother before mentioned. He died unmarried Nov. 27, 1868, aged 51 years. He commanded the First Brigade at Malta, 1863–8; served in the Crimea, including the battles of Alma (where his horse was shot under him), Balaklava, and Inkerman. He was at the siege of Sebastopol.

Hon. George Ridley²² (3), sixth son of Matthew²¹ (3), was born in 1818; educated at Christ Church, Oxford; B. A., May 2, 1844; called to the bar at the Middle Temple, in 1845, and sat as Member of Parliament for Newcastle-on-Tyne from 1855–60. He is a copyhold inclosure and tithe commissioner. Residence, 2 Charles Street, Berkeley Square, London, W.

Sarah Ridley²² (1), eldest daughter of Matthew²¹ (3), was married April 11, 1837, to John Cookson, of Meldon Park, Northumberland, and died July 22, 1864.

Laura Ridley²² (1), second daughter of Matthew²¹ (3), was married, May 2, 1835, to Charles-Atkins, son of Sir C. Monk, Bart., who died Dec. 1, 1856, having had issue a son who became seventh baronet.

Louisa Ridley²² (1), third daughter of Matthew²¹ (3), was married, July 8, 1831, to Martin-Tucker Smith, Esq., since Member of Parliament for Wycombe, son of Mr. John Smith, Member of Parliament for Midhurst and Chichester. He died at St. Leonards-on-Sea, in 1878, aged 70.

Marianne Ridley²² (1), fourth daughter of Matthew²¹ (3), married, Jan. 5, 1839, the Rev. Andrew Corbett, rector of South Wallingham, County Lincoln, who died in 1864. Residence, 22 Kensington Gate, London, W.

Janetta-Maria Ridley²² (1), fifth daughter of Matthew²¹ (3), was married Feb. 29, 1843, to Isaac T. Cookson, Esq., of Swinburne Castle, Northumberland, and died in 1867.

Hon. William-Nicholas Ridley²² (10), only son of Nicholas²¹ (14), born July 24, 1814(?), died unmarried, March 23, 1846. He was a Member of Parliament for Richmond.

Henrietta-Susanna Ridley[22] (2), eldest daughter of Nicholas[21] (14), born June 5, 1809; was married Aug. 12, 1828, to Brampton Gurdon, son of Theophilus-Thornhaugh Gurdon, Esq., of Letton, in Norfolk, and had issue *two* children.* She died April 28, 1881.

Maria-Charlotte Ridley[22] (1), second daughter of Nicholas[21] (14), born June 3, 1810; was married July 13, 1830, to Sir George-Edmund Nugent, Bart., of Waddesdon, County Berks, late captain and lieutenant-colonel of Grenadier Guards, and had issue *two* sons and *three* daughters. She died Aug. 29, 1883. (See note.)

Emily-Frances Ridley[22] (1), third daughter of Nicholas[21] (14), born March 8, 1812; was married April 11, 1833, to John-Moyer Heathcote, Esq., of Connington Castle, Stilton, and has issue. She died Oct. 13, 1849. Mr. Heathcote, who was educated at Eton, and St. John's College, Cambridge, is a magistrate for Hants, of which he has been high sheriff, and lord of the manor and patron of Connington. Has sat in parliament.

Louisa-Harriet Ridley[22] (2), fourth daughter of Nicholas[21] (14), born Nov. 7, 1821; was married Sept. 29, 1849, to Harvie-Morton Farquhar, and was drowned while bathing, Aug. 22, 1870. She had *five* children, two sons and three daughters. (See note.) She resided at Brackley House, Northamptonshire, Eng.

Rev. William-Henry Ridley[22] (11), eldest son of Henry[21] (3), was born April 2, 1816; married Aug. 25, 1844, to Sophia-Albertine, second daughter of the Rt. Rev. Charles-Richard Sumner, D. D., lord bishop of Winchester, and has issue *one* son and *three* daughters, of whom hereafter. He was a student of Christ Church, Oxford, and obtained first class in classics; received his degree of B. A., Jan. 24, 1838, and M. A., Nov. 19, 1840. He is rector of Hambleden and Henly-on-Thames, and honorary canon of Winchester. He studied divinity with the Rev. William Havergal, of Leamington, Eng., the celebrated hymn-composer. Mr. Ridley is author of "Bible Readings for Family Prayers," "Ridley on the Holy Communion," and "Sermons in Plain Language." This gentleman's photograph is in the author's collection.

Rev. Nicholas-James Ridley[22] (16), second son of Henry[21] (3), was born Jan. 7, 1821; married Sept. 9, 1845, Frances, daughter of John Touchet, Esq., of Broomhouse, Lancashire, and has issue *seven* sons and *three* daughters, of whom hereafter. He was educated at Christ Church, Oxford, and received M. A. and second class in classics; studied divinity with the Rev. William Havergal, the well-known hymn-writer; was vicar of Woolton Hill, East Woodhay, from 1849 to 1853; in 1880 was at Hollington House, Hampshire. His degree of B. A. in 1841, and M. A. in 1845. His photograph is in the author's collection.

---

* The grandchildren of Nicholas-William Ridley (Lord Colborne), as far as known, are as follows: His daughter, Henrietta-Susanna Gurdon, had Robert-Thornhaugh, and Charlotte. Maria-Charlotte Nugent had George-Grenville, born June 19, 1837, died March 16, 1838; Edmund-Charles, born March 12, 1839, married April 30, 1863, Evelyn-Henrietta, youngest daughter of Lieut.-Gen. E. F. Gascoine, and has issue. Emily-Frances Heathcote had a son John-Moyer Heathcote, born 1834, married in 1859 Louisa-Cecilia, daughter of Norman Macleod, of Macleod, besides other issue. Louisa-Harriet Farquhar had Alfred, born in 1852, Ernest, born in 1853, Florence, Isabella, and Helen.

Rev. Oliver-Matthew Ridley[22] (1), third son of Henry[21] (3), was born May 12, 1824; married, firstly, Aug. 3, 1852, Louisa-Pole (who died Jan. 5, 1858), daughter of William Stuart, Esq., of Aldenham Abbey, Herts, by whom he had *three* sons and *two* daughters; secondly, April 17, 1860, Fanny, only surviving daughter of Col. Henry-Edward Keane, Bart., and by her has issue *three* sons and *three* daughters, of whom hereafter. He was educated at Oxford, and read divinity with the Rev. William Havergal. Was formerly rector of West Harling; now (1882) rector of Bishopstone, Hereford. His photograph is in the collection of the author of this book.

Mary Ridley[22] (10), eldest daughter of Henry[21] (3), was married to the Rev. William-Musseyre-Kirkwall Bradford, rector of West Meon, Hants, who died April 10, 1872, leaving issue *four* sons and *four* daughters.

Frances-Henrietta Ridley[22] (3), second daughter of Henry[21] (3), now living (1880), unmarried.

Lutitia-Matilda Ridley[22] (1), third daughter of Henry[21] (3), died May 30, 1831, aged 17 years.

Col. John-Ellis Ridley[22] (15), eldest son of Henry[21] (4) and his wife, Elizabeth Ellis, was born Dec. 10, 1816; married, April 25, 1848, Anna-Maria, daughter and only child of the late Rev. John-Michael Brooke, of Longfield, County of Cavan, rector of Athenage, County Cork, and has issue *two* sons and *two* daughters, of whom hereafter. Formerly of the Second Dragoon Guards, "Queen's Bays," and lieutenant-colonel Second Surrey Militia.

Augusta-Constance Ridley[22] (1), a daughter of Henry[21] (4). Unmarried.

TWENTY-THIRD GENERATION.

Sir Matthew-White Ridley[23] (5), eldest son of Matthew[22] (4), was born July 25, 1842; was educated at Harrow, and at Balliol College, Oxford. Received his degree B. A., first class in classics, in 1865, and was sometime a Fellow of All Souls' College. He married in 1873, Mary-Georgiana, daughter of Sir Dudley-Coutts Majoribanks, M. P., and has issue, of whom hereafter. At the retirement of his father in 1868, the present Sir Matthew was invited to place his services at the disposal of the electors, and was elected to represent Northumberland North. In March, 1874, he was again returned to parliament, and still continues to represent that constituency. He also held office in the Beaconsfield Administration as Under-Secretary for the Home Department, with a salary of fifteen hundred pounds a year. He is a Justice of the Peace for Northumberland, and chairman of the Quarter Sessions in that County; also, major of the Northumberland and Newcastle Yeoman Cavalry. Is patron of two livings. Seat,—Blagdon, Cramlington, Northumberland. Town residence,—10 Carlton House Terrace, S. W. Clubs,—Carlton's, White's. His photograph, with one of Lady Ridley, is in possession of the author of this book.

Hon. Edward Ridley[23] (3), second son of Matthew[22] (4), was born in 1843; educated at Harrow and at Corpus Christi College, Oxford (B. A., first class classics, 1866, and sometime Fellow of All Souls' College), called to the Bar at the Inner Temple, 1868; sat as Member of Parliament for Northumberland South 1878–80, when he was unsuccessful as a candidate. Chambers,—3 King's Bench Walk, Temple, E. C. Clubs,—

Oxford and Cambridge, Carlton. Unmarried. His photograph is in the author's collection.

Mary Ridley[23] (11), only daughter of Mâtthew[22] (4), was married June 14, 1876, to the Rev. Arthur-Octavus Medd, rector of Amble, by Warkworth, near Acklington, Northumberland, and has issue. The marriage ceremony was performed by the Rev. Henry-Richard Ridley, vicar of St. Cuthbert's, Durham, the bride's uncle. The bridesmaids were Miss Mabel Ridley and Hon. Miss Lowther, cousins of the bride. The wedding tour was in Switzerland. The author has photographs of this couple.

Edith-Harriet Ridley[23] (1), eldest daughter of Henry[22] (11), was married in 1878 to Anthony-Lax Maynard, Esq., of Newton Hall, Durham.

Mabel Ridley[23] (3), second daughter of Henry[22] (11), unmarried.

Maude Ridley[23] (1), third daughter of Henry[22] (11), unmarried.

Ethel-Louisa Ridley[23] (1), fourth daughter of Henry[22] (11), unmarried.

Bertha Ridley[23] (1), youngest daughter of Henry[22] (11), was married in 1879, to Thomas-Dundas Bruce, Esq., of Bishop's Auckland, Durham.

Henry-Monk Ridley[23] (12), eldest son of Charles[22] (3).

Charles-Colborne Ridley[23] (4), second son of Charles[22] (3).

Louisa-Katherine Ridley[23] (3), eldest daughter of Charles[22] (3), was married March 31, 1870, to Capt. Henry-Blomfield Kingscote, of the Royal Army. (B. BLOOMFIELD.)

Katherine-Louisa Ridley[23] (1), second daughter of Charles[22] (3), was married July 11, 1873, to Charles-Francis Buller, Esq., late Second Life Guards. (B. CHURSTON.)

Alice-Henrietta Ridley[23] (2), third daughter of Charles[22] (3), was married Jan. 7, 1873, to Robert Hunt, of Kelton House, Rutland. She died July 28, 1873.

Henry-Colborne-Mannoir Ridley[23] (13), eldest son of William[22] (11), was born March 19, 1854.

Mary-Sophia Ridley[23] (12), eldest daughter of William[22] (11), married Sept. 25, 1873, the Rev. Charles-Maunsell Wetherall, curate of Hambleden, Henly-on-Thames, and has issue.

Anna-Louisa-Matilda Ridley[23] (2), second daughter of William[22] (11).

Ella-Frances Ridley[23] (1), third daughter of William[22] (11).

Edward-Nicholas-Touchet Ridley[23] (4), eldest son of Nicholas[22] (16), born June 28, 1849; died Oct. 1, 1879.

Henry-Matthew Ridley[23] (14), second son of Nicholas[22] (16), was born Feb. 2, 1851; is lieutenant Seventh Hussars.

Arthur-William Ridley[23] (2), third son of Nicholas[22] (16), was born Sept. 11, 1852.

Walter-Colborne Ridley[23] (1), fourth son of Nicholas[22] (16), was born Aug. 19, 1855.

James-Francis Ridley[23] (2), fifth son of Nicholas[22] (16), was born Jan. 12, 1858.

Alfred-Bayley Ridley[23] (1), sixth son of Nicholas[22] (16), was born Dec. 14, 1859.

Reginald-Oliver Ridley[23] (1), seventh son of Nicholas[22] (16), was born May 27, 1864.

"PARKEND"
Northumberland, England.
RESIDENCE OF JOHN RIDLEY, ESQ.

Marian-Sarah Ridley[22] **(1)**, eldest daughter of Nicholas[22] **(16)**.
Helen-Elizabeth Ridley[22] **(1)**, second daughter of Nicholas[22] **(16)**.
Lucy-Frances Ridley[22] **(1)**, third daughter of Nicholas[22] **(16)**.

Stuart-Oliver Ridley[23] **(1)**, eldest son of Oliver[22] **(1)**, was born June 8, 1853.
Henry-Nicholas Ridley[23] **(15)**, second son of Oliver[22] **(1)**, was born Dec. 10, 1855.
Charles-William Ridley[23] **(4)**, third son of Oliver[22] **(1)**, was born Dec. 28, 1856.
Mary-Louisa Ridley[23] **(13)**, eldest daughter of Oliver[22] **(1)**.
Fanny-Louisa-Pole Ridley[23] **(1)**, second daughter of Oliver[22] **(1)**.
Edward-Keane Ridley[23] **(5)**, eldest son of Oliver[22] **(1)** by his second wife, was born Nov. 5, 1861.
Frank-Colborne Ridley[23] **(1)**, second son of Oliver[22] **(1)** by his second wife, was born Dec. 16, 1864.
Clarence-Oliver Ridley[23] **(1)**, third son of Oliver[22] **(1)** by his second wife, was born Aug. 9, 1869.
Letitia-Florence Ridley[23] **(2)**, second daughter of Oliver[22] **(1)**.
Alice-Catherine Ridley[23] **(3)**, third daughter of Oliver[22] **(1)**.
Helena-Lucy Ridley[23] **(2)**, fourth daughter of Oliver[22] **(1)**.

· **Holt-Warring Ridley**[23] **(1)**, eldest son of John[22] **(15)**, was born Sept. 16, 1850.
Charles-Parker Ridley[23] **(5)**, second son of John[22] **(15)**, who married Anne-Maria Brooke, was born May 12, 1855; married Aug. 14, 1879, Edyth-Hamilton, daughter of George-Beauchamp Cole, Esq., of Twickenham and Brighton. Mr. Ridley is captain in Ninety-sixth Regiment.
Louisa-Elizabeth Ridley[23] **(4)**, eldest daughter of John[22] **(15)**, was married Feb. 10, 1874, to George-Thomas-Henry Boyes, commander in the Royal Navy, and has issue.
Augusta-Constance Ridley[23] **(1)**, second daughter of John[22] **(15)**.

TWENTY-FOURTH GENERATION.

Matthew-White Ridley[24] **(6)**, eldest son of Matthew[23] **(5)**, was born in 1874, and is heir.
Cecilia-Marjorie Ridley[24] **(1)**, eldest daughter of Matthew[23] **(5)**.

RIDLEYS OF PARKEND, ENGLAND.

[The estate of Parkend came to the Ridleys through the marriage of one of the family with an heiress named *Wale*,— and in consequence of this alliance the Ridley arms were quartered with those of Wale (see article on armor in the "Compendium"), as now borne by the family. How early the property was in possession of the Ridleys does not appear, but they held the estate contemporary with Willimoteswick, Walltown, and other property in Tynedale. This property was, until 1560, in possession of the Ridleys of Tecket, from whom it passed to the Earls of Suffolk ;

they held it till the beginning of the seventeenth century, when it again became the property of the Ridleys of Tecket. Parkend was inhabited for several generations by the elder branch of the Ridleys through a younger brother of the last of the Lords of Willimoteswick, as will hereafter appear. This place, in the parish of Simonburn, has by its possessors been believed to have been tithe-free, and to have other tithes in the parish from the influence of one of the rectors, Robert Ridley, D. D., who had such power at the court of King Henry VIII, that he was deprived of his position, and the grant of the next presentation after 1532, was given to Thomas Ridley, Gentleman, who presented the parish-living to John Ridley, his cousin, who seems to have been a clerk in holy orders. Robert Ridley, D. D., who was uncle and educator of Bishop Nicholas Ridley, the martyr, was rector of Simonburn from 1510 to 1532. The family formerly, for many generations, were domiciled at "Old Parkend," but a modern residence has been erected called "New Parkend" (see engravings). In the year 1870, the estate at Parkend comprised an area of ten thousand three hundred and sixty-seven acres, and had an estimated annual rental of something more than four thousand one hundred and seventy-one pounds sterling (see tables). In the church of Simonburn is a tomb of the Rev. Cuthbert Ridley, sometime rector, with the figures in stone representing Mr. Ridley, his wife, and others of his family.]

Thomas Ridley[1] (1), third son of William[16] (6) and his wife, who was a daughter of Richard Musgrave, and a younger brother of Musgrave Ridley, the last of the Lords of Willimoteswick, was the first of Parkend. This Thomas married Anne ——, whose burial was recorded in 1691 in the registers of Simonburn parish. He had *one* son.

SECOND GENERATION.

Thomas Ridley[2] (2), who succeeded to Parkend, son of Thomas[1] (1), married to Dorothy, daughter of George Ridley, of Gate House (she had a sister who married J. Reed, of Chipchase), and his wife, who was a daughter of Ralph Pemberton, of Belmond Castle. This Thomas deceased in 1771, and was succeeded by his son, of whom hereafter.

THIRD GENERATION.

John Ridley[3] (1), a son of Thomas[2] (2), was of Parkend, and succeeded at the death of his father. He married, firstly, Susanna, daughter of Nicholas Mauhan, of Whinnatle, in 1731, and secondly, Mary, daughter of —— Ripon, of Warncyburn, in the County of Durham, and by her (as also by his first wife) had issue *five* children, of whom hereafter. Died in 1773.

Catherine Ridley[3] (1), a daughter of Thomas[2] (2). } No records.
Mary Ridley[3] (1), a daughter of Thomas[2] (2). }

FOURTH GENERATION.

Thomas Ridley[4] (3), eldest son of John[3] (1), was born at Parkend, Northumberland, and succeeded to the estate at Parkend at the death of his father in 1773. He married in 1774, Mary, the only daughter of Thomas (another says Taylor) Brown, Esq., of Corbridge, and died in 1816, leaving *five* children.

John Ridley[4] (2), second son of John[3] (1), was born at Parkend, Northumberland, and was styled "of Lincoln Hill"; he married Elizabeth Laws, and had issue *one* son, of whom hereafter.

George Ridley[4] (1), third son of John[3] (1), was born at Parkend, Northumberland, and died without issue.

Catherine Ridley[4] (2), eldest daughter of John[3] (1). }
Mary Ridley[4] (2), second daughter of John[3] (1). } No records.
Elizabeth Ridley[4] (1), third daughter of John[3] (1). }

FIFTH GENERATION.

John Ridley[5] (3), only son of Thomas[4] (3), succeeded to Parkend. He was born May 17, 1780; married Bridget, youngest daughter of Richard Atkinson, Esq., of Temple Sowerby, Westmoreland, Sept. 9, 1811, and had issue, of whom hereafter.

Mary Ridley[5] (3), eldest daughter of Thomas[4] (3). }
Susan Ridley[5] (1), second daughter of Thomas[4] (3). } No
Dorothy Ridley[5] (1), third daughter of Thomas[4] (3). } records.
Catherine Ridley[5] (3), fourth daughter of Thomas[4] (3). }

SIXTH GENERATION.

Thomas Ridley[6] (4), eldest son of John[5] (3), was born at Parkend, Northumberland, and succeeded his father in 1865. Thomas was born Feb. 12, 1817. No issue. Mr. Ridley was a magistrate. Heir presumptive his younger brother, of whom hereafter.

John-Matthew Ridley[6] (4), second son of John[5] (3), was born at Parkend, Northumberland, May 2, 1820; married June 4, 1844, Anna-Maria, youngest daughter of Henry Hilton, Esq., of Sole Street House, Kent, and has issue, of whom hereafter. He is heir presumptive to his brother Thomas. Mr. Ridley, who was educated at Jesus College, Cambridge (B. A., 1843, M. A., 1846), and was called to the Bar at Lincoln's Inn, 1846, is a magistrate for Northumberland. Residence, Walwick Hall, Hexham.

Matthew-Atkinson Ridley[6] (1), third son of John[5] (3), was born at Parkend, Northumberland, May 4, 1826.

Mary Ridley[6] (4), eldest daughter of John[5] (3), of Parkend.

Eliza Ridley[6] (1), second daughter of John[5] (3), was married Sept. 17, 1838, to Rev. Henry Carr, son of John Carr, Esq., of Dunstan Hill, County of Durham.

Jane-Mary Ridley[6] (1), third daughter of John[5] (3), of Parkend, was married March 10, 1841, to William, fourth son of Matthew Bell, Esq., of Woolsington, County of Northumberland, which Matthew was a descendant from the Ridleys of Heaton Hall, through Jane, daughter of Richard Ridley and his wife Margaret, daughter of Matthew White, of Newcastle, which Jane was the wife of Matthew Bell, who was great-grandfather of the Matthew under notice.

Susan-Catherine Ridley[6] (2), fourth daughter of John[5] (3), of Parkend, was married to Henry Venables, Esq., Slysdinan, London, County Middlesex.

SEVENTH GENERATION.

John-Hilton Ridley[7] (5), eldest son of John[6] (4), was born in June, 1848. He was educated at Eton School; B. A. of Jesus College, Cambridge.

Musgrave-Hilton Ridley[7] (1), second son of John[6] (4), was born in February, 1850.

Anna-Maria Ridley[7] (1), eldest daughter of John[6] (4).

29

RIDLEYS OF BATTERSEA, ENGLAND, NO. 1.

William Ridley[1] **(1)**, a son of Sir Nicholas Ridley (5), styled the "broad knight," of Willimoteswick, Northumberland, was of Battersea, in the County of York. William's mother was Mary, daughter of Sir Thomas Musgrave, of Musgrave, Edenhall, and granddaughter of Sir William Stapleton of the English army, 1520. William was cousin of Bishop Ridley, the martyr. He married a Miss Blackstone, and had issue, of whom hereafter. I do not know how this family became settled at Battersea; the property may have come to them by intermarriage with the Blackstones. A part of this family pedigree was found in a "visitation of Yorkshire," as recorded in the "Harleian Manuscripts," London, and a part from Rev. John Ridley, a descendant of William, and I find some links wanting in the chain.

SECOND GENERATION.

Robert Ridley[2] **(1)**, a son of William[1] (1), was styled "of Battersea in the County of York." He married Margaret, a daughter of —— Jefferson, and had issue *three* sons, of whom hereafter.

THIRD GENERATION.

Christopher Ridley[3] **(1)**, a son of Robert[2] (1), was styled "of Battersea, County of York." He married Anne, daughter and heiress of Richard Garbray, and had issue, of whom hereafter.

Nicholas Ridley[3] **(1)**, a son of Robert[2] (1), was living in 1612; married Elizabeth ——, of Marwood, and had issue, of whom hereafter. His name was found in the herald visitation, with those of his brothers, and from this I infer that he was a resident at Battersea. In the pedigree his name stands in the place of eldest son.

Robert Ridley[3] **(2)**, third son of Robert[2] (1), was born at Battersea, County of York; married Isabella Wilson, and had issue, of whom hereafter.

FOURTH GENERATION.

William Ridley[4] **(2)**, a son of Nicholas[3] (1), was born at Battersea, in 1602.

Christopher Ridley[4] **(2)**, a son of Christopher[3] (1), was born at Battersea, in 1592.

Henry Ridley[4] **(1)**, a son of Robert[3] (2), was born at Battersea, County of York, in 1610.

RIDLEYS OF BATTERSEA, ENGLAND, No. 2.

[The following statements were provided by one of the family, and I am of the opinion that full records would prove this branch and the preceding to be identical. It will be observed that the ancient Ridley Christian name, *Christopher*, occurs in both families, and as this name was first used by the father of Bishop Nicholas Ridley, who was of Unthank Hall, and according to family custom would be handed down from father to son in that branch of the ancient Willimoteswick stock, it seems plausible that the families of Battersea, as well as that denominated "of Mickley Farm" in this book, are connected with that line over which the martyr cast such a halo. It will be seen that the dates given in the "visitation," from which the preceding pedigree was taken, are contemporary with the lifetime of the first Christopher Ridley, and sufficiently early to admit of proper connections with the following records.]

Christopher Ridley[1] (1), probably descended from the family styled "of Battersea," preceding; is said to have been born at Hexham, Northumberland, about the year 1772. He settled at Battersea, in 1766-8, where he engaged in the manufacture of kid gloves; married, and had issue *five* (possibly others) children.

SECOND GENERATION.

John-Henry Ridley[2] (1), eldest son of Christopher[1] (1), was born at Battersea (?), and was a glove-maker in London. Married, and had issue *six* children, of whom hereafter.

Eliza Ridley[2] (1), eldest daughter of Christopher[1] (1), was born at Battersea, London; married a Mr. Husband, and with her companion long ago deceased.

Susannah Ridley[2] (1), second daughter of Christopher[1] (1), was born at Battersea, London; married to Samuel Smith, merchant, at Battersea; both dead.

Elizabeth Ridley[2] (1), third daughter of Christopher[1] (1), was born at Battersea; married William Phillips, Esq., who died in 1879, and is living in independent circumstances at Walpole Cottage, St. John's Hill Grove, Wandsworth, London, S. W.

Christopher Ridley[2] (2), youngest son of Christopher[1] (1), was born at Battersea, London; married, and has issue *five* children, of whom hereafter. He resides at 12 Holywell Street, Oxford, Eng.

THIRD GENERATION.

Eliza Ridley[2] (2), eldest daughter of John[2] (1), was born in 1833, and married to William B. Townsend, now of New Westminster, B. C.

James-Christopher Ridley[3] (1), eldest son of John[2] (1), was born in 1836.

Elizabeth-Susannah Ridley[2] (2), second daughter of John[2] (1), was born in 1839, and married to George Lister, now (1879) of Lindum House, Cambridge, Eng.

Emily Ridley[3] (1), third daughter of John[2] (1), was born in 1842, and married to John Worrall, of Woburn Sands, Bedfordshire, Eng.

Rev. John Ridley[2] (3), second son of John[2] (1), was born in England (probably at Battersea) in 1845; married to Caroline-Augusta Griffin, daughter of James-Kent Griffin, of Waterdown, Ontario, Can., and has been settled as a Methodist preacher at Ailsa Craig, in the same province. He returned to England in 1879, to visit his friends, and promised to secure the full particulars of the family history, but I have heard nothing from him since. He is a very fine-looking man, if one may judge from his photograph.

William Ridley[3] (1), youngest son of John[2] (1), was born in 1848, and married Mary Young, of Cambridge, Eng.

RIDLEYS OF ATKINSON, ENGLAND.

Hugh Ridley[1] **(1)**, descended from the Ridleys of Ridley in Chestershire, married the daughter and co-heir of Gymerland, and had issue, of whom hereafter. He was the first of Atkinson, County of Salop. This pedigree is taken from the visitation of Shropshire, found in the British Museum, London. Arms, Argent. an ox passant Gules. through reeds Proper; in chief a crescent charged with a crescent for differences.

SECOND GENERATION.

Randall Ridley[2] **(1)**, eldest son of Hugh[1] **(1)**, married and had issue, of whom hereafter. He was of Atkinson.

Owen Ridley[2] **(1)**, second son of Hugh[1] **(1)**, was of Atkinson; married and had issue, of whom hereafter. I think this was the same Owen Ridley who married, secondly, on Feb. 27, 1563, Ellen Franke, who was buried in St. Dionis Church, London, Oct. 25, 1587. This Owen's first wife's name is not given in the burials or records of christening in the church; nor is the name of the wife of Owen whose name stands in this pedigree given. I shall carry down the pedigree with this view; the dates agree. He died Dec. 26, 1591. Was styled "Salter."

THIRD GENERATION.

John Ridley[3] **(1)**, eldest son of Owen[2] **(1)**, died without issue.

Rignald Ridley[3] **(1)**, second son of Owen[2] **(1)**, married Alice, daughter of John Leighton, of Leighton, County Shropshire, and had issue, of whom hereafter. He was of Atkinson.

James Ridley[3] **(1)**, third son of Owen[2] **(1)**, died young.

Thomas Ridley[3] **(1)**, fourth son of Owen[2] **(1)**; baptized Feb. 9, 1547, as per records St. Dionis Church, London; buried in same church May 24, 1572; unmarried.

Martha Ridley[3] **(1)**, eldest daughter of Owen[2] **(1)**, baptized in St. Dionis Church, London, Sept. 26, 1549.

Sarah Ridley[3] **(1)**, second daughter of Owen[2] **(1)**, was baptized in St. Dionis Church, London, Jan. 4, 1550.

Ellen Ridley[3] **(1)**, third daughter of Owen[2] **(1)**, was baptized in St. Dionis Church, London, July 27, 1552.

Judith Ridley[3] **(1)**, fourth daughter of Owen[2] **(1)**, was baptized in St. Dionis Church, London, July 10, 1554.*

George Ridley[3] **(1)**, son and heir of Randall[2] **(1)**, married Rosana, daughter of Roger Blackwell, of Cronckhill, Shropshire, and had issue *seven* children, of whom hereafter. He was styled "of Broughton, in Shropshire." His sister, whose name does not appear, was married to —— Grafton, of Whitechurch.

FOURTH GENERATION.

Thomas Ridley[4] **(2)**, eldest son of George[3] **(1)**, was of Broughton, County of Shropshire; married Marcia, daughter of William Preston, of Almpton, County Stafford, and had issue.

---

* Margaret, wife of John Ridley, and John Magyar were buried in St. Dionis Church; the former, Sept. 18, 1587, and the latter, called "son-in-law to Owen Ridley," Sept. 9, 1581.

Elizabeth Ridley[4] (1), eldest daughter of George[8] (1), was married to Thomas Poyner.

Francis Ridley[4] (1), second son of George[8] (1).

John Ridley[4] (3), third son of George[8] (1).

Jane Ridley[4] (1), second daughter of George[8] (1), was married to Roger Wyken.

Alicia Ridley[4] (1), third daughter of George[8] (1), was married to Richard Seyner.

Margaret Ridley[4] (1), fourth daughter of George[8] (1), was married to Roger Howell.

Richard Ridley[4] (1), eldest son of Rignald[8] (1), was of Linley, in Shropshire (1584); married Eleanor, daughter of John Sydenham, County of Somerset. No issue mentioned.

Jane Ridley[4] (2), daughter of Rignald[8] (1), was married to Thomas Marshe, of Sedgeley, County Stafford.

FIFTH GENERATION.

Maria Ridley[5] (1), eldest daughter and co-heir of Thomas[4] (2), of Broughton; was the wife of Thomas Richardson, of Whitechurch.

Jane Ridley[5] (3), second daughter of Thomas[4] (2), was the wife of Samuel Atwood, of Overley, County Wigton.

Susanna Ridley[5] (1), third daughter of Thomas[4] (2).

Christobella Ridley[5] (1), fourth daughter of Thomas[4] (2).

RIDLEYS OF WALLTOWN, ENGLAND.

John Ridley[1] (1), parents' names unknown, of Walltown, was descended from a branch of the ancient family in Chestershire; married Elizabeth, daughter of Christopher Ridley, of Unthank Hall, and sister of Bishop Nicholas Ridley, the martyr, of London. John was called "the lord (or laird) of Walltown"; had issue, of whom hereafter, and died 1562. Buried in Haltwhistle Church, in the County of Northumberland, and the curious inscription on his monument reads as follows:—

> "JOHN REDLE
> THAT SUM
> TIM DID BE
> THEN LARD OF THE WALLTON
> GON IS HE OUT OF THES VALE OF MESRE.
> HIS BONS LIES UNDER THES STON.
> WE MUST BELEVE BE GOD'S MERSE.
> INTO THES WORLD GEVE HES SON.
> THEN FOR TO REDEM AL CHRESTENS.
> SO CHRIST HAES HES SOUL WOUN
> AL FAETHFUL PEOPLE MAY BE FAEN.
> WHEN DATH COMES THTT NON CAN.
> THE BODE KEPT THE SOUL IN PAEN.
> THROUGH CHRIST IS SET AT LIBERTE.
> AMONG BLESED COMPANE TO REMAEN.
> TO SLEP IN CHRIST NOW IS GON.

YET STEL BELEVES TO HAV AGAEN
THROUGH CHRIST A NEW RESURRECCION.
AL FRENDES MAY BE GLAD TO HAER
WHEN HES SOUL FROM PAEN DID GO
OUT OF THES WORLD AS DOETH APPEAR
IN THE YEER OF OUR LORD
A. D. 1562. XX." *

SECOND GENERATION.

Elizabeth Ridley² (1), only daughter of John¹ (1) and his wife Elizabeth, married Thomas Ridley, a great-grandson of Sir Nicholas Ridley;
hence, as the wife was a great-granddaughter of the said Sir Nicholas,
she and her husband were of the same generation, counting the descent
from the same original ancestor (see "Ridleys of Willimoteswick" and
"Ridleys of Unthank"). She had issue *one* son, and perhaps others, of
whom hereafter.

THIRD GENERATION.

John Ridley³ (2), a son of Thomas Ridley and Elizabeth Ridley² (1),
who was the daughter and sole heir of the original John Ridley, of Walltown, and Elizabeth, daughter of Christopher Ridley, of Unthank, married
to Annie, daughter and executrix of —— Charlton, of Healiside, Northumberland, and was living in the year 1615; he had issue *two* sons and
four daughters, of whom hereafter. It will be seen that the Walltown
family of Ridley became extinct in the male line with the death, in 1562,
of the first John Ridley, and that by the intermarriage of the aforesaid
Thomas, the descent counted from the male side comes down from the
Willimoteswick family.

FOURTH GENERATION.

John Ridley⁴ (3), eldest son and heir of John³ (2), of Wallsend, and
Annie Charlton, became of Walltown, Northumberland. He married
Elizabeth, daughter of Thomas Charlton, Esq., of Charlton Hall, Cumberland (of the same family as his mother), and had issue *four* sons and
four daughters, of whom hereafter.

Elizabeth Ridley⁴ (2), eldest daughter of John³ (2) and Annie Charlton, married to William of the Morrelea.

Willard Ridley⁴ (1), second son of John³ (3), of Walltown, and his
wife, Annie Charlton, married Annie, daughter of —— Woodman, and by
her had *three* sons and *one* daughter. This Willard was styled "of London and Walltown." He is presumed to be the same as referred to by
Surtees in the singular Northumberland ballad, as "Will of the Wall,"
for in a note to Sir Walter Scott he says, "'Will of the Wall' means Willard Ridley of Walltown," hence he was engaged in the encounter with
the Featherstonhaughs at the time that the clan of Ridley killed Albany,
the chief of that house.

Margaret Ridley⁴ (1), second daughter of John³ (3), of Walltown,
and his wife, Annie Charlton, married to Ralph Thurlway.

Thomasin Ridley⁴ (1), third daughter of John³ (3), of Walltown, and
his wife, Annie Charlton, married Daniel Stoughton.

---

*The above inscription was transcribed from a copy sent me by the Rev. Dixon
Brown, of Unthank Hall, Northumberland, Eng.; he lives near Haltwhistle Church-
yard, and the inscription was easily accessible. I cannot interpret all the lines,
and it is believed that some of the letters have been worn away by lapse of time.
It will be seen that the surname is spelled *Redle*, which was not unfrequent on
ancient documents and monuments.

Mary Ridley[4] (1), fourth and youngest daughter of John[3] (3) and Annie Charlton, his wife, married to Thomas Ridley, of Hardriding, Northumberland, which Thomas was a great-grandson of Nicholas Ridley, Esq., who was a son of Sir Nicholas, Knt., before mentioned (see "Ridleys of Willimoteswick").

------•------

RIDLEYS OF ALSTON MOOR.

[This branch of the Ridley family is an offshoot of the ancient Chestershire stock, so early settled in Northumberland, Eng., but where the ancestry of this family was connected with the main line does not appear.]

John Ridley[1] (1) was descended from the ancient family so early settled in Tynedale, but his parents' names are unknown. He was born in the year 1750; married in 1782 to Mary Walton; resided at Alston Moor, in the north of England; was a farmer by vocation; had issue *ten* children, and died near Alston, Dec. 3, 1882, aged 83 years; his wife predeceased him Nov. 28, 1819, aged 56 years.

SECOND GENERATION.

Elizabeth Ridley[2] (1), eldest daughter of John[1] (1) and his wife Mary, was born at Alston Moor, Sept. 20, 1783. No mention of her marriage or death.

Ann Ridley[2] (1), second daughter of John[1] (1) and Mary, his wife, was born at Alston Moor, Nov. 11, 1785, and died Nov. 4, 1808.

Mary Ridley[2] (1), third daughter of John[1] (1) and Mary, his wife, was born at Alston Moor, Sept. 20, 1788; married in 1811; resided at Quam Lodge, and died Nov. 21, ——.

William Ridley[2] (1), eldest son of John[1] (1) and his wife Mary, was born at Alston Moor, Nov. 26, 1790; lived at Alston; was a carrier by vocation; married and had issue; died in the year 1840. Family all dead.

Isabella Ridley[2] (1), fourth daughter of John[1] (1) and his wife Mary, was born at Alston Moor, Aug. 28, 1792; died May 10, 1815.

John Ridley[2] (2), second son of John[1] (1) and his wife Mary, was born at Alston Moor, Feb. 25, 1795; settled at St. Croix, West Indies.

Joseph Ridley[2] (1), third son of John[1] (1) and his wife Mary, was born at Alston Moor, Nov. 27, 1796; married, but died issueless.

Sarah Ridley[2] (1), fifth daughter of John[1] (1) and his wife Mary, was born at Alston Moor, Nov. 21, 1798; married in 1825 to David Armstrong; resided at Netheronset, parish of Kirklinton, Northumberland. No issue.

Walton Ridley[2] (1), fourth son of John[1] (1) and his wife Mary, was born at Alston Moor, April 8, 1800; married Margaret, daughter of George Hope, of Kirklinton, near Carlisle, whence he had removed from Alston when a young man. He was an architect and builder. Had issue *four* children. Died May 14, 1838.

Nancy Ridley[2] (1), youngest daughter of John[1] (1) and his wife Mary, was born at Alston Moor, Dec. 3, 1803; married to Thomas Prestman; resides at Newcastle, and has issue *five* children.

THIRD GENERATION.

Rev. John Ridley[3] (3), eldest son of Walton[2] (1) and his wife Margaret, was born at Heathersgill, parish of Kirklinton, near Carlisle, Cumberland, Sept. 11, 1828; married June 21, 1860, to Frances Antrobus (she was born April 16, 1825), and has issue *five* children, of whom hereafter. He is in Holy Orders of the Episcopal Church; vicar of Norton, in Durham, 1870. His degree in 1878 was M. A.

Rev. George Ridley[3] (1), second son of Walton[2] (1) and his wife Margaret, was born at Heathersgill, parish of Kirklinton, near Carlisle, Eng., Jan. 10, 1831; married Jan. 18, 1866, to Mary Hemingway (she was born Sept. 22, 1888), and has issue *five* children, of whom hereafter. He is in Holy Orders of the English Episcopal Church; rector of Crosby Garrett, Westmoreland.

Mary Ridley[3] (2), only daughter of Walton[2] (1) and his wife Margaret, was born in the parish of Kirklinton, Nov. 20, 1832; married Sept. 26, 1870, to John Beay, and has issue. She resides at Heathersgill, in the parish of Kirklinton, near Carlisle, Eng.

Rev. Joseph Ridley[3] (2), youngest son of Walton[2] (1), was born at Heathersgill, parish of Kirklinton, near Carlisle, Eng., April 29, 1837; married May 5, 1870, to Esther Whaley. No issue. He is a clerk in Holy Orders of the Episcopal Church of England, at Withington, near Manchester.

FOURTH GENERATION.

John-Brooke Ridley[4] (4), eldest son of John[3] (3) and his wife Frances, was born May 18, 1861.

Frances Ridley[4] (1), eldest daughter of John[3] (3) and his wife Frances, was born Oct. 21, 1862.

Edward-Hope Ridley[4] (1), second son of John[3] (3) and his wife Margaret, was born Feb. 24, 1866.

Philip-Walton Ridley[4] (1), third son of John[3] (3) and his wife Margaret, was born Sept. 30, 1868.

Florence-Grey Ridley[4] (1), second daughter of John[3] (3) and his wife Margaret, was born Oct. 4, 1870.

Christine Ridley[4] (1), eldest daughter of George[3] (1) and his wife Mary, was born Dec. 25, 1866.

Edward-Walton Ridley[4] (2), eldest son of George[3] (1) and his wife Mary, was born Feb. 9, 1867.

Nicholas-Denison Ridley[4] (1), second son of George[3] (1) and his wife Mary, was born March 16, 1871.

Frances-Havergal Ridley[4] (2), second daughter of George[3] (1) and his wfe Mary, was born Jan. 11, 1873.

George Ridley[4] (2), third son of George[3] (1) and his wife Mary, was born Feb. 23, 1875.

RIDLEYS OF GATESHEAD, ENGLAND.

Robert Ridley[1] (1), descended from the ancient family of Willimoteswick, Northumberland, was born at Gateshead in 1799; married Margaret Wight (others say Craggs), who was born at Gateshead in 1774, and had issue *six* children, of whom hereafter. He was a boat-builder, and carried on business at Newcastle-on-Tyne several years. He subsequently went to London, and carried on business at Millwall Burmandsey a number of years; he latterly returned to Newcastle, and entered the employ of T. & W. Smith, as foreman. Mr. Ridley died in 1843; his widow in 1857.

SECOND GENERATION.

Aaron Ridley[2] **(1)**, eldest son of Robert[1] **(1)**, was born at Newcastle-on-Tyne, Eng., in 1801, and died in 1869, leaving a widow and no issue. He served his time with his father as boat-builder; served on board a man-of-war as carpenter many years; married when about fifty years old, and died at Newcastle when nearly seventy.

Robert Ridley[2] **(2)**, second son of Robert[1] **(1)**, was born at Newcastle-on-Tyne, Eng., in 1803, and died in 1843, leaving a widow, *three* sons, and *two* daughters; two sons have died.

Thomas Ridley[2] **(1)**, third son of Robert[1] **(1)**, was born at Newcastle-on-Tyne, Eng., in 1805, and died in 1866, leaving a widow, *three* sons, and *two* daughters; one son has died.

John-Wright Ridley[2] **(1)**, fourth son of Robert[1] **(1)**, was born at Burmandsey, London, Eng., in 1810; married Elizabeth Parkin in 1854, and had issue several children, of whom hereafter. He was eight years old when his father returned to Newcastle; was educated at the Jubilee School, New Road, at Newcastle-on-Tyne, learned the trade of mast- and block-making of Mr. Hutton, of Northside, or Northshore, Newcastle; married as before stated, and settled at Shields about 1858. He was employed as foreman for a firm in Low Street until his poor health unfitted him for work. He died in 1877, leaving a widow and several children.

George-Stoker Ridley[2] **(1)**, fifth son of Robert[1] **(1)**, was born at Burmondsey, London, in 1815; married in 1838, in Heworth Church, Gateshead, to Mary, daughter of John Winlow, shipbuilder, of Howdon-on-Tyne. He died Oct. 18, 1838, leaving issue *six* children, of whom hereafter.

Ann Ridley[2] **(1)**, daughter of Robert[1] **(1)**, was born at Newcastle-on-Tyne, and resided in London.

Margaret Ridley[2] **(1)**, a daughter of Robert[1] **(1)**, was born at Burmondsey, London (?); no other information.

THIRD GENERATION.

John-Wright Ridley[3] **(2)**, eldest son of John[2] **(1)**, was born at Quality Row, Ballest Mills, Newcastle-on-Tyne, April 25, 1835; married in Gateshead parish, to Elizabeth, daughter of William and Elizabeth Cowell, of North Shields, in 1864, and had issue *four* children, of whom hereafter. He was educated at the Jubilee School, in the city of Newcastle; served his time as boat-builder with his father's master; went to sea; worked several years for the "River Tyne Commissioners" in various situations; has been stricken with paralysis, and is now an invalid. His wife died in Morpeth Lunatic Asylum.

Ann Ridley[3] **(2)**, eldest daughter of John[2] **(1)**, was born at Newcastle-on-Tyne, Eng., in April, 1837; was married at the Holy Saviour Church, Tynemouth, to William Kennedy, "a fitter by trade," who is foreman at the iron-works of Hawks & Cranshaw, at Gateshead. These are in comfortable circumstances.

Mary Ridley[3] **(1)**, second daughter of John[2] **(1)**, was born at Newcastle-on-Tyne, Eng., in November, 1839; was married to John Powers, and had *nine* children.

Margaret Ridley² (2), third daughter of John² (1), was born at New-castle-on-Tyne, Eng., in 1841; was married to Joseph McQueen, and had a large family.

Jane Ridley² (1), fourth daughter of John² (1), was born at New-castle-on-Tyne, Eng., in 1843; was married to William Murray, and died in 1876, leaving *one* son.

Robert Ridley² (3), second son of John² (1), was born at Newcastle-on-Tyne, in 1845; married, but has no family.

John Ridley² (3), eldest son of George² (1), was born at Newcastle-on-Tyne, June 18, 1839; died an infant.

Margaret-Ann Ridley² (3), eldest daughter of George² (1), was born at Newcastle-on-Tyne, Eng., June 18, 1840; was married in 1859 to Thomas Watson, an engineer.

Mary-Jane Ridley² (2), second daughter of George² (1), was born at Newcastle-on-Tyne, Eng., Jan. 28, 1843; was married to Robert Smith (joiner) in 1863; he died March 19, 1875.

Elizabeth Ridley² (1), third daughter of George² (1), was born at Newcastle-on-Tyne, June 16, 1845; was married in 1865 to Wiliam Etche, a carver by trade.

John Ridley² (4), second son of George² (1), was born at Newcastle-on-Tyne, Eng., Oct. 13, 1850; married Margaret Staffen in 1877, and has *one* daughter.

Ann Ridley² (3), fourth daughter of George² (1), was born at New-castle-on-Tyne, March 1, 1855; was married in 1875 to W. J. Richardson, a pattern-maker by trade, and Sabbath-school teacher by profession. Has *two* sons.

FOURTH GENERATION.

Elizabeth-W. Ridley⁴ (3), a daughter of John³ (2), was born June 26, 1866.

Elizabeth Ridley⁴ (2), a daughter of John³ (2), was born at New-castle-on-Tyne, Dec. 9, 1877.

RIDLEYS OF HEXHAM, ENGLAND.

[The Ridleys of Hexham, Northumberland, are descended from the old Willimoteswick family, — descendants from a younger son of the main line representation, consequently they have not preserved any authenti-cated pedigree. All efforts to procure full statistics of this branch have proved fruitless. Many communications have been addressed to members of several families, and no reply has been received.]

James Ridley¹ (1) was descended from some branch of the Northum-berland family (see Ridleys of Hardriding), lived in Hexham, North-umberland, and had issue, of whom hereafter. No other information.

Joseph Ridley¹ (1), was a brother of James¹ (1).

George Ridley¹ (1), was a brother of James¹ (1).

Ann Ridley¹ (1), was a sister of James¹ (1).

SECOND GENERATION.

Elizabeth Ridley² (1) was a daughter of James¹ (1).
Isabella Ridley² (1) was a daughter of James¹ (1).
Mary Ridley² (1) was the third daughter of James¹ (1).
Margaret Ridley² (1) was the fourth daughter of James¹ (1).
Ann Ridley² (2) was the fifth daughter of James¹ (1).
George Ridley² (2) was the eldest son of James¹ (1).
William Ridley² (1), second son of James¹ (1).
Joseph Ridley² (2), a son of James¹ (1), was born in Hexham, Eng., March 21, 1831; married in 1850 to Mary Tapping; emigrated to America on board the "Chimberago" in 1853, and landed in New York city. He married, secondly, in 1857, Dorothy Tapping (sister of his first wife), of London, Can. Mrs. Ridley became religiously insane in 1878, and drowned her children in a river; made an attempt to drown herself, but was rescued and placed in confinement. Mr. Ridley is a gardener and farmer; resides in Grey, Ontario, Can., and has *four* children.

THIRD GENERATION.

John Ridley³ (1), eldest son of Joseph² (2), was born in Hexham, Eng., June 11, 1851; in Canada.
James Ridley³ (2), second son of Joseph² (2), was born in Canada, Feb. 5, 1859.
William Ridley³ (2), third son of Joseph² (2), was born in Canada, Dec. 20, 1861;. twin to Jane.
Jane Ridley³ (1), only daughter of Joseph² (2), was born in Canada, Dec. 20, 1861 ; twin to William.

RIDLEYS OF MICKLEY FARM, NORTHUMBERLAND.

Cuthbert Ridley¹ (1), the first of Mickley Farm, was descended from the ancient family in Tynedale, but the parents' names are not certainly known. No record of his birth, marriage, or death, appears on the registers of the church at Ovingham,* where those of his descendants are found. These records begin with 1679, and go up to the middle of the present century, but the first mention of the Ridley family is the marriage of Jane Ridley with John Foster in 1683. The best evidence points to the Ridleys of Tecket as ancestors of this family. Cuthbert Ridley, of

---

* St. Mary's Church, Ovingham, where the Ridleys were baptized, married, buried, and worshipped God, is a well-proportioned cruciform building, with a low, square tower built of large stones, and probably Saxon. In the church-yard is the burial-place of Thomas Bewick, the celebrated engraver, and of his brother John, also an artist. Two persons were publicly excommunicated by Archbishop Sharp, in Ovingham Church, as late as 1769. The following from the Ovingham Church Registry were probably members of this branch of the Ridley family, but do not seem to apply to any mentioned in the pedigree : 1683 — John Foster and Jane Ridley married; 1713 — John Ridley and Isabella Robson married; 1745 — John Ridley and Isabella Redhead married; 1713, Feb. 18 — Mary, daughter of John Ridley, of Prudhoe, baptized; 1715, Sept. 1 — Ann, daughter of John Ridley, of Prudhoe, baptized.

Tecket, lost his lands there in 1650, in consequence of loyalty, and as his descendants are not afterwards mentioned in connection with that old family designation, they probably devoted themselves to farming. According to the family tradition Cuthbert, first of Mickley, was on friendly terms with the landed gentry in his neighborhood, and some of his children, having married well, held themselves high and looked down upon their relatives, who were farmers. Mickley is a small village about ten miles west by south of the city of Newcastle-on-Tyne.

Susan Ridley[1] **(1)**, supposed to have been a sister of Cuthbert[1] **(1)**, was the wife of —— Cromwell, of Surtees.

SECOND GENERATION.

Isabella Ridley[2] **(1)**, daughter of Cuthbert[1] **(1)**, was married to a clergyman.

Frances Ridley[2] **(1)**, daughter of Cuthbert[1] **(1)**, baptized at Ovingham Church, March 5, 1709; died in 1710. One says the name was Margaret.

Cuthbert Ridley[2] **(2)**, eldest son of Cuthbert[1] **(1)**, was born at Mickley in 1702, baptized Jan. 28, 1708, and died Feb. 15, 1793, aged 91. Married Susanna ——, who died January, 1773; he had issue *seven* children, and possibly more. He was of Mickley Farm, on Tyne, and of Hallyards.

Henry Ridley[2] **(1)**, second son of Cuthbert[1] **(1)**, baptized Feb. 2, 1707; married Ann Bell in 1728, but I find no record of a family.

THIRD GENERATION.

John Ridley[3] **(1)**, eldest son of Cuthbert[2] **(2)**, born Feb. 25, 1733; married Ann Dunn, and had issue *six* children, of whom hereafter. " Was clever in bleeding people." Was not a success. Wife "fond of reading and did not like work."[1]

Cuthbert Ridley[3] **(3)**, second son of Cuthbert[2] **(2)**, was born at Mickley Farm, Northumberland, Feb. 25, 1736; married Jane ——, and had issue *six* children, of whom hereafter. He was a farmer at Mickley; died July 17, 1779; his widow died April 17, 1801. The preceding dates are from the family records of Cuthbert Ridley, who came from Mickley in 1832, and settled in New York, a grandson, and are presumably correct. A pedigree of the family forwarded from London by Anne E. Ridley, has the date "1779" affixed to this man's name, but I do not know what it applies to.

Susan Ridley[3] **(2)**, a daughter of Cuthbert[2] **(2)**, was born at Mickley Farm, and was married to —— Ethrington, of Hallyards, and had issue.

Isabella Ridley[3] **(2)**, a daughter of Cuthbert[2] **(2)**, was born at Mickley Farm, and married to —— Weddell; and secondly, to a Mr. Johnson.

Thomas Ridley[3] **(1)**, third son of Cuthbert[2] **(2)**, was born at Mickley Farm, Northumberland, in 1738; married Ann Charlton, of Charlton Hall on the North Tyne, and had issue several children, of whom hereafter. He was a steady, hard-working farmer, very respectable and successful; thought but little of by aristocratic relations. Died in 1828.

Henry Ridley[3] **(2)**, fourth son of Cuthbert[2] **(2)**, was born at Mickley Farm; baptized at Ovingham Church, Dec. 31, 1749; married Miss Bulman, of Morpeth, and secondly, Miss Johnson, and had issue, of whom hereafter. He had a large brewery at Seaton Sluice, and two farms under Lord Delaval, whose agent he was. Spent much time visiting at Seaton and "keeping gay company." Some of his descendants are living in Newcastle.

FOURTH GENERATION.

Cuthbert Ridley[4] **(3)**, eldest son of Cuthbert[3] **(3)**, was born at Mickley Farm, Northumberland, March 10, 1770; married Elizabeth-Rowland Weatherby (she was born July 27, 1776), and had issue *ten* children, of whom hereafter. Mrs. Ridley was a sister of Captain Weatherby, a Waterloo hero, who was twice mayor of Newcastle-on-Tyne. I suppose his residence was at Mickley.

Isabella Ridley[4] **(3)**, eldest daughter of Cuthbert[3] **(3)**, was born at Mickley, Northumberland, in 1762; died in 1764.

John Ridley[4] **(3)**, second son of Cuthbert[3] **(3)**, was born at Mickley, Northumberland, in 1764; baptized in September, 1766, and is supposed to have descendants now living in England.

William Ridley[4] **(1)**, third son of Cuthbert[3] **(3)**, was born at Mickley, Northumberland, in 1774, and his descendants are said to be living in England.

Susanna Ridley[4] **(1)**, second daughter of Cuthbert[3] **(3)**, was born at Mickley, Northumberland, in 1777, and became the wife of —— Weatherby, of Craw Hall.

Cuthbert Ridley[4] **(5)**, eldest son of Thomas[3] **(1)**, was born at Mickley, Northumberland(?); baptized in 1760; married Isabella Charlton,* of Nisbit, and had issue *six* children, of whom hereafter. He died in 1848.

Thomas Ridley[4] **(2)**, a son of Thomas[3] **(1)**, baptized in 1761.

John Ridley[4] **(4)**, a son of Thomas[3] **(1)**, was baptized in 1760, and died in 1850, aged 90; no particulars.

Ann Ridley[4] **(1)**, a daughter of Thomas[3] **(1)**, was married to —— Barron.

Susan Ridley[4] **(3)**, a daughter of Thomas[3] **(1)**, was married to —— Reed, and had issue sons and daughters.

Isabella Ridley[4] **(4)**, eldest daughter of Thomas[3] **(1)**, was born at Mickley Farm(?); was married to —— Stoker, and had issue a daughter Mary,† who married —— Dryden, and descendants are now living at North Shields, Northumberland.

Mary Ridley[4] **(1)**, second daughter of Thomas[3] **(1)**, was born at Mickley Farm(?) in 1762, and became the wife of John Ridley, her cousin. She had *one* son and *three* daughters. Being a woman of ardent Wesleyan principles, she entertained the preachers of that day, who assisted in educating her children. She was left a widow in early life, and proved herself a woman of strong character. Died in 1834.

John Ridley[4] **(4)**, eldest son of John[3] **(2)**, was born in the north of

---

* THE CHARLTONS are descended from Adam de Charlton, of Charlton Tower, in Tynedale, who died in 1308. At Hesleyside, an ancient family seat, is preserved the Charlton spur, six inches long, which has existed in the family from time immemorial, and which, according to ancient border custom, was served at dinner in a covered dish when the family larder needed replenishing.

† MRS. MARY DRYDEN, from whose lips many facts found in this family history were taken, was a granddaughter of Thomas Ridley and his wife, Ann Charlton, and a woman of singularly retentive and accurate memory. She died in 1879, aged 80; her mother, Isabella Ridley, in 1850, aged 90; her grandfather, Thomas Ridley, in 1828, aged 90, and her great-grandfather, Cuthbert Ridley, in 1798, aged 91; making an unbroken chain to the first Cuthbert Ridley. The details given by this fine old lady are corroborated by others of the same family. She mentioned some cousins who went to America. Her mother often talked of her great-aunts, sisters of the first Cuthbert of Mickley Farm.

England in 1765; married Mary Ridley, daughter of Thomas[2] (1), his cousin, and had issue *four* children, of whom hereafter. He was a flour-miller by occupation; died in 1813. He was not a success.

Susan Ridley[4] (3), eldest daughter of John[3] (2), was born in the north of England, was married to a Mr. Glover, and has descendants living.

Ann Ridley[4] (1), second daughter of John[3] (2), was born in Northumberland, or Durham; was married to —— Reay, of Kenton, and had issue several children.

Ellen Ridley[4] (1), a daughter of John[3] (2), married —— Spoor, and had issue.

James Ridley[4] (2), second son of John[3] (2), married and had issue, who are said to be in America. I do not know the residence of this family.

Lieut. Charles Ridley[4] (1), eldest son of Henry[3] (2), was born in north of England, and is in the Royal army.

Frances Ridley[4] (1), eldest daughter of Henry[3] (2), was married to N. Grace, and died issueless.

Susan Ridley[4] (4), second daughter of Henry[3] (2), married —— Stratton, and resides in London.

Thomas Ridley[4] (2), second son of Henry[3] (2), resides at Newcastle-on-Tyne.

FIFTH GENERATION.

Robert Ridley[5] (2), eldest son, of Cuthbert[4] (3) and his wife, Elizabeth-Rowland Weatherby, was born at Mickley Farm, Northumberland, Aug. 12, 1801, and had deceased in 1852. No knowledge of a family.

Cuthbert Ridley[5] (6), second son of Cuthbert[4] (3), was born at Mickley Farm, Northumberland, March 9, 1803; married Mary Trotter, of Newcastle-on-Tyne; came to America in 1832, and settled in Stamford, Conn. He subsequently removed to Harlem, N. Y., and was so badly injured in 1854, by a fall through the hatchway of an india-rubber factory, that he died twenty-four hours after. *Seven* children.

John Ridley[5] (5), second son of Cuthbert[4] (3), was born at Mickley, Northumberland, Feb. 5, 1805, and had deceased in 1852. No account of a family.

William Ridley[5] (2), third son of Cuthbert[4] (3), was born at Mickley, Northumberland, Dec. 13, 1806, and when last heard from by relatives in New York, was at Berks, Berkshire, Eng.

James Ridley[5] (3), fourth son of Cuthbert[4] (3), was born at Mickley, Northumberland, Aug. 27, 1808, and when last heard from was in Melbourne, Australia.

Elizabeth-Rowland Ridley[5] (1), eldest daughter of Cuthbert[4] (3), born at Mickley, July 28, 1810.

Jane Ridley[5] (1), second daughter of Cuthbert[4] (3), was born at Mickley, July 28, 1812.

Susanna Ridley[5] (2), third daughter of Cuthbert[4] (3), was born at Mickley, July 4, 1814.

Henry Ridley[5] (3), fifth son of Cuthbert[4] (3), was born at Mickley, Sept. 19, 1816, and died Oct. 22, 1816.

Charles Ridley[5] (2), sixth son of Cuthbert[4] (3), was born at Mickley, Dec. 29, 1818, and died previous to 1854. No mention of a family.

John Ridley[5] (6), eldest son of Cuthbert[4] (5) and his wife, J. Charlton, married and had *two* sons, of whom hereafter. Resides somewhere in Northumberland.

Thomas Ridley[5] (3), second son of Cuthbert[4] (5).

Margaret Ridley[5] (1), eldest daughter of Cuthbert[4] (5), was married to a Mr. Lodge.

Mary Ridley[5] (2), second daughter of Cuthbert[4] (5).

Henry Ridley[5] (4), third son of Cuthbert[4] (5).

Isabella Ridley[5] (5), third daughter of Cuthbert[4] (5), wife of —— Weddell.

Elizabeth Ridley[5] (2), fourth daughter of Cuthbert[4] (5).

Susan Ridley[5] (4), fifth daughter of Cuthbert[4] (5).

Ann Ridley[5] (2), sixth daughter of Cuthbert[4] (5), was married to G. Swan, and had a son and daughter; died in 1869. The former, Robert Swan, is a barrister-at-law.

===

John Ridley[5] (7), eldest son of John[4] (4), was born at Hylton, near Sunderland, County of Durham, May 26, 1806. His father died when he was only five years of age, leaving him and one sister to be brought up by his mother, who being a most remarkable woman, faithfully applied herself to the instruction of her children. At the age of fifteen this lad did a man's work in the flour-mill, contriving also to read everything he could find. His mother's house was a home for the itinerant preachers of the day, who all took especial notice of the clever boy, and assisted in his development. At the age of seventeen he became a local preacher, and was noticed as full of promise. At his mother's death, when he was thirty, she was under his care. He married the daughter of Mr. Pybas, who was at the head of a large school for boys, well known in the north of England; this was at West Bolton, near Hylton, his birthplace. In 1840 he went to Australia as one of the earliest colonists. The story of his venture is worthy a place in this book. Feeling more energy than could find scope in a small country village, he made it a matter of earnest prayer that he might be sent to some place where he was needed and could work and in some way fulfil his early aspirations to become a missionary. From that day the way opened to Australia, and the first thing he heard when the ship touched land was that a public meeting had been called to consider how the wheat of the first good harvest was to be ground, as there was no mill. The meeting was unnecessary, for within a month John Ridley's mill was up and at work. A year or two later he met a still greater need by inventing a machine for reaping the corn, and gave it to the colony without reserving patent rights. In all works on the colony this machine is recognized as one of the chief agents in its advancement. Testimonials, expressive of the appreciation of the people of the colony, — including a piece of plate presented in London, — were tendered Mr. Ridley, and a county there bears his name. He lived at Close House, near Hexham, Northumberland, but for the last twenty years at 19 Belsize Park, Hampstead. He is said to resemble the portrait of Bishop Ridley, the martyr, and to be extremely like him in character. He is advanced in theological views, and now spends all his time and not a little money in the gratuitous circulation of literature advocating the liberal theology as against the eternity of punishment, a dogma from which he suffered greatly in his early years. He had issue *five* children, of whom hereafter.

Esther Ridley[6] (1), eldest daughter of John[4] (4), was born at Hylton, near Sunderland.

Ann Ridley[5] (3), second daughter of John[4] (4).

Susan Ridley[5] (5), third daughter of John[4] (4).

SIXTH GENERATION.

Elizabeth-Agnes Ridley[6] (3), eldest daughter of Cuthbert[5] (6), was born in New York city, Nov. 20, 1834. Unmarried and living in New York.

Cuthbert-Weatherby Ridley[6] (7), eldest son of Cuthbert[5] (6), was born in Brooklyn, N. Y., April 15, 1837; married Lydia Weeks in January, 1864, and has *one* child, of whom hereafter. He resides in Washington, D. C.

Charles-Henry Ridley[6] (3), second son of Cuthbert[5] (6), was born in Stamford, Conn , Sept. 25, 1839, and died Aug. 27, 1857.

James-Dent Ridley[6] (4), third son of Cuthbert[5] (6), was born at Stamford, Conn., Sept. 20, 1841; married Annie O'Hare in 1872, and has *two* children, of whom hereafter. Resides in New York city.

Rowland-Weatherby Ridley[6] (1), fourth son of Cuthbert[5] (6), was born in Stamford, Conn., Nov. 26, 1843, and is now (1883) in the druggist business, 2364 Fourth Avenue, corner 128th Street, New York city; unmarried.

Sarah-Jane Ridley[6] (1), second daughter of Cuthbert[5] (6), was born at Stamford, Conn., Feb. 5, 1846. Resides in New York city; unmarried.

Jonathan-Trotter Ridley[6] (1), fifth son of Cuthbert[5] (6), was born at Stamford, Conn., Nov. 8, 1849; married Susanna Gill in July, 1871, and has *five* children, of whom hereafter. He resides at Mount Vernon, N. Y.

John Ridley[6] (8), eldest son of John[5] (6).   } These reside in
Cuthbert Ridley[6] (8), second son of John[5] (6). } Northumberland.

Anne-Eleanor Ridley[6] (1), a daughter of John[5] (7), was born at Close House, near Hexham, Northumberland, in the year 1839, and with her sister, of whom hereafter, spends much of her time in the promotion of various philanthropic and literary undertakings, and hopes to keep up the tradition of the Ridley name and be true, in small or great ways, to the motto of the family, " *Constance Fideo.*" She lives with her father in London; manifests a deep interest in the history of her family, and has kindly furnished me with the genealogy.

Jane-Taylor Ridley[5] (2), a daughter of John[5] (7), was born at Close House, near Hexham, Northumberland, in 1845, and resides with her sister in London, in the house of their aged father. See preceding sketch.

SEVENTH GENERATION.

Nellie Ridley[7] (1), a daughter of Cuthbert[6] (7), was born in Washington, D. C.

James Ridley[7] (5), eldest son of James[6] (4).   } New York city.
Jonathan Ridley[7] (2), second son of James[6] (4). }

Cuthbert Ridley[7] (9), eldest son of Jonathan[6] (1).   ⎫
Fannie Ridley[7] (1), eldest daughter of Jonathan[6] (1).   ⎪ Reside at
Mary Ridley[7] (2), second daughter of Jonathan[6] (1).   ⎬ Mount Vernon, N. Y.
Joseph Ridley[7] (1), second son of Jonathan[6] (1).   ⎪
Agnes Ridley[7] (1), third daughter of Jonathan[6] (1).   ⎭

RIDLEYS OF BECKLEY, SUSSEX, ENGLAND.

William Ridley[1] (**1**), parents' names unknown, was born at Beckley, Sussex, Eng., Oct. 22, 1784; married Sarah Newble (she was born May 27, 1781?) Oct. 31, 1806, and had issue *four* children, of whom hereafter. Mr. Ridley was a farmer. He married, secondly, Rebecca Fiddler, and thirdly, Margaret Cornwallis, by whom *one* son. He emigrated to America in company with the son last mentioned, and has not since been heard from. His first wife was buried at Beckley, aged 35.

SECOND GENERATION.

Harriet-N. Ridley[2] (**1**), eldest daughter of William[1] (**1**), was born at Beckley, Eng., July 24, 1807, and died in Sydney, Australia; was the wife of Henry Larkins.

William Ridley[2] (**2**), eldest son of William[1] (**1**), was born at Beckley, Eng., in September, 1808; married, and sailed for America the following day.

James Ridley[2] (**1**), second son of William[1] (**1**), was born at Beckley, Eng., May 13, 1811; married Margaret Quinn, in the parish of St. Lawrence, Sydney, Australia (she was of Dublin, Ireland), in 1842, and has had issue *nine* children, of whom hereafter. Mr. Ridley emigrated to Sydney from Gravesend, in the ship "Palmyra," in 1838. He was employed in a soap-manufactory; then ten years in Kent Brewery, and then twenty-one years on the railway of New South Wales. He is now an old man, living with his children at Redfern, Sydney, Australia.[*]

Sarah-Ann Ridley[2] (**1**), second daughter of William[1] (**1**), was born at Beckley, Eng., in December, 1809; was married to John Payne, of Sussex, farmer, and died in that County about 1844.

Thomas Ridley[2] (**1**), a son of William[1] (**1**), by his third wife, married in England, and accompanied by his parents, sailed for America, but nothing has been heard from any of them since.

THIRD GENERATION.

Harriet Ridley[3] (**2**), eldest daughter of James[2] (**1**), was born in Sydney, Australia, and died in 1859, aged 18.

Margaret-Matilda Ridley[3] (**1**), second daughter of James[2] (**1**), born in Sydney, was married to William Waterman, and has issue.

James Ridley[3] (**2**), eldest son of James[2] (**1**), was born in Sydney, Australia.

Daniel Ridley[3] (**1**), second son of James[2] (**1**), was born in Sydney, Australia.

Charlotte Ridley[3] (**1**), third daughter of James[2] (**1**), was born in Sydney, Australia; twin to Daniel.

Joshua(?) Ridley[3] (**1**), third son of James[2] (**1**), was born in Sydney, New South Wales, Australia, and is employed in a government situation.

Rebecca Ridley[3] (**1**), fourth daughter of James[2] (**1**), was born in Sydney, Australia, and lives at home.

---

[*] JAMES RIDLEY, of Redfern, Sydney, says Beckley, Sussex, the ancestral home of this family, was twelve miles from any post-office at the time he left England. The family of Cornwall, or Cornwallis, with which the Ridleys intermarried, came to America before 1837; they formerly lived about twelve miles from Beckley.

30

Constance Ridley[6] (1), fifth daughter of James[2] (1), was born in Sydney, Australia.

Ambrose Ridley[2] (1), fourth son of James[2] (1), was born in Sydney, Australia, and is now (1884) at home with his aged parents.

--------·•·--------

RIDLEYS OF BURY ST. EDMUND'S, ENGLAND.

The Ridleys have been tanners at Bury St. Edmund's for a long period of time, and moved and added the tan-yards there to their business at Soham, about one hundred and fifty to one hundred and seventy years ago. Early in the sixteenth century, a Richard (or Henry) Ridley was head of the tan-yard firm at Soham, and had a son.

Lancellot Ridley[2] (1), who carried on the tannery business at Soham and St. Edmund's. From him descended directly

John Ridley[3] (1), who moved the entire business to Bury St. Edmund's. He married Mary ——, and had issue *two* sons (probably other sons and daughters), of whom hereafter. He died Sept. 3, 1779, aged 70; his wife died in 1781, and was buried in the same ground.

John Ridley[4] (2), son of John[3] (1), became head of this family, and of the tan-yard firm. He married and had issue *two* (probably others) sons, of whom hereafter.

Rev. Thomas Ridley[4] (1), son of John[3] (1), was divinity minister, from whom descended Thomas Ridley and others, of Ipswich.

FIFTH GENERATION.

John Ridley[5] (3), Esq., eldest son of John[4] (2), was born at Bury St. Edmund's, and became a magistrate for that borough. He was a prominent and learned man. He married, had issue, and died in 1853, aged 73.

William Ridley[5] (1), second son of John[4] (2), was born at Bury St. Edmund's, May 28, 1786(?); married in 1811 to Maria, eldest daughter of Thomas Dixon, of County of Essex, and had issue *eleven* children, of whom hereafter. He was a "substantial and highly respected miller," and a biographical notice of him was published in an English journal at the time of his death, June 3, 1852. His wife died May 7, 1837. Mr. Ridley was 66 years of age.

SIXTH GENERATION.

John Ridley[6] (4), a son of John[5] (3), was born at Bury St. Edmund's; married his second cousin, named Ridley, and had issue a daughter (probably other issue), who was married to a Mr. Ridley of Reading. His first wife dying, he married, secondly, Catherine E. ——, who is now living. Mr. Ridley is a magistrate of Bury, now old and infirm; his memory so impaired he could not aid me in my researches. It is though the possesses the family records.

Thomas-Dixon Ridley[6] (1), eldest son of William[5] (1), was born March 22, 1814, at Hartford End, Essex, Eng.; married June 17, 1841, Lydia, eldest daughter of William C. Wells, of Chelmsford, Essex, brewer, and had issue *five* children, of whom hereafter. He died Feb. 10, 1882. Occupation not known; supposed to have been a miller.

Rev. William Ridley[6] (2), second son of William[5] (1), was born at Hartford End, Essex, Eng., Sept. 14, 1819; married Isabella, daughter of the Rev. Joseph-Rogerson Cotter, rector of Donoughmore, and senior prebendary of Cloyne Cathedral, County Cork, Ireland, April 11, 1850, and by that lady had issue *eight* children, of whom hereafter. Mr. Ridley received his education at King's College, London, his father having intended him for the legal profession. For some time after taking his degree he continued his legal studies with great success, but he met with conscientious difficulties which caused him to abandon that profession. On one occasion he caught a thief in the act of stealing his purse, and turned him over to the authorities, but when the case came before the court he refused to be sworn, on conscientious grounds, and incurred a heavy fine for his so-called contumacy. After this he determined to devote himself to missionary work, and applied to the London Missionary Society, wishing to go to the Pacific Islands. His services were declined, but soon after, however, in 1849, he met Dr. Lang in London, and accepted an offer to become one of the professors in the Australian College. He went to Australia with Dr. Lang in the "Clifton," arriving at his destination early in 1850. He was ordained in the Presbyterian Church by Dr. Lang, in connection with the synod of New South Wales, and became professor of Greek, Latin, and Hebrew. Aided by an able staff of professors, the new college flourished, and many citizens of Sydney remember with gratitude Mr. Ridley's conscientious tuition. Whilst fulfilling the duties of his professorship he devoted much of his time to the work of the ministry. He took charge of a new church at Balmain, holding two services every Sabbath; at the same time he was active in the church-extension work in various parts of the colony. When the Australian College ceased to occupy its high position, he assumed the pastoral care of Brisbane, Portland Bay, and Manning River, successively. Then he resolved to devote himself fully to missionary work, which had been the dream of his youth. He accordingly went among the aborigines of the north-west of the colony, and of southern Queensland, particularly among the Namoi tribes. He seems to have been a natural linguist, and acquired a complete mastery of many dialects, and in later years published a grammar of the Kamilaroi tongue, with one on other languages, which received the approval of the most distinguished philologists in Europe; and an edition of this work was published by the government for the Philadelphia Exhibition of 1876. His self-denying labors were not without fruit of a moral and religious character. He so endeared himself to the aborigines, among whom he preached the gospel, that to this day (1878) the blacks of Namoi show the most enthusiastic demonstrations of joy at the mention of Mr. Ridley's name. During his missionary tours through the colony, he found many families from the Highlands of Scotland, who could not understand an English discourse, and with characteristic energy he acquired so good an acquaintance with the Gaelic as to be able to preach the gospel to them. The cares of an increasing family now caused the withdrawal of Mr. Ridley from his field of usefulness among the natives, and he returned to Sydney, where he became connected with the *Empire* newspaper. He was for many years a valued contributor to the newspapers published in Sydney, and was at one time principal editor of the *Evening News.* Notwithstanding the pressing duties of a journalist's position, he was unremitting in his attention to his ministerial profession. He was the founder of a station at

468   *RIDLEYS OF BURY ST. EDMUND'S, ENGLAND.*

Kogerah, Cook's River, and preached either there, or in one of the Sydney churches, almost every Sabbath. He was an active participator in the business of the Presbyterian Synod, and served on important committees. His great attainments were highly appreciated when placed at the service of the brotherhood of his church. For two years he assisted in editing the *Australian Witness.* He was also appointed one of the theological tutors of St. Andrew's College, and one of the examiners of candidates for the ministry. He took his degree of M. A. at Sydney University in 1864. During the last year preceding his decease he was requested by the Presbytery to enter upon a new work, one that might have daunted a man of robust health. This was nothing less than the acquirement of the Chinese language, in order to fit him to take charge of the Chinese mission in the city of Sydney. Mr. Ridley devoted one half of his time to this great undertaking, persevering with his accustomed application until he so far succeeded that he could write passages of Scripture in the language, which he distributed amongst the Chinamen. He also acquired, by private study and under the instruction of Ah Len, the Chinese missionary, an elementary knowledge of the spoken dialect. In fact, he had translated and set to music some hymns which he sang with the Chinese in their meetings for worship; but it was a source of great sorrow to him when he learned from Dr. Vrooman, a missionary of twenty years' experience in Canton, China, who visited Sydney, that his studies of the language had been prosecuted by him in mistaken lines, owing to the want of proper instruction and assistance. He spent considerable time with this missionary during his stay in the colony, in order to improve his knowledge of the Chinese language, and on the Sabbath before his death saw him off on the steamer. It was a proof of the well-balanced mind of Mr. Ridley, that, notwithstanding his enthusiasm for missionary work among the Chinese, yet on political grounds he favored moderate restrictions on emigration. In theology he was most liberal-minded. He was intensely sympathetic in his appreciation of good men of all denominations, and his broad views and spontaneous charity are manifest in the religious writings of Mr. Ridley, published in the *University Magazine.* His political views were distinctly liberal in home and foreign affairs. He had a firm grasp of the principles of popular representative government, and did not hesitate to apply them. His character, without any exaggeration, was almost perfect, and a record of his acts of self-denying kindness would fill a volume. He never made any enemy, and yet he never tampered with principles in order to conciliate opponents. He was a peace-maker in the highest sense of the word, in the church and the world. His gentleness endeared him to all with whom he associated. He was the soul of honor, and the embodiment of righteousness. Full of religious earnestness and enthusiasm, he was thoroughly practical in all his undertakings. He was never idle, and his death was undoubtedly hastened by his over-devotion to what seemed to him duty. In his service for his Master and his fellow-men, he was worn out, and in the midst of great usefulness, having only three weeks before his death preached from the text, "Put on the whole armor of God," he passed away Sept. 26, 1878. On Saturday, the 21st, he appeared in full vigor of mind and body; but on the following morning was stricken with paralysis, and never rallied from the attack. His funeral was from his late residence, "Lohort," and was attended by a large assembly of clergymen, members of the press, and other well-known and distinguished citizens. Mr. Ridley, at his own request, was buried by the side of a favorite little daughter who died many years ago. In his address at the funeral the Rev. Mr. Patterson spoke warmly of the pure, blameless, and thoroughly Christian life.of the deceased, his unassuming character, and his self-denying labors on behalf of those around him. Those who knew him were as confident as they were that they lived, that Mr. Ridley's spirit was now with his Saviour above.

The following verses were taken from the *Town and County Journal* of Oct. 5, 1878 (an Australian newspaper), from which the preceding notice was largely copied :—

"IN MEMORIAM — REV. WILLIAM RIDLEY, M. A.

" 'The world knows not its greatest men' — nor best!
And so our brother passed unto his rest,
Which darkly comes to all of mortal breath —
The solemn silence of the calm of death —
Like the good priest, who, in his Master's name,
'Did good by stealth, and blushed to find it fame,'
Has lived a life of usefulness and worth;
And through his toiling pilgrimage on earth,
Where 'en he saw a sorrow or a sin,
Saw — sorrowing for each — and tried to win
The sinner back to virtue! and for grief
And want, gave active sympathy's relief!

" His was no narrow soul, that narrow saw,
But any Heaven, justified by law,
By vengeance only! — but believed that God
Was Father always! — and affliction's rod,
His minister, to train each child of time —
Nor make of earthly sin — eternal crime!

" When far off Namois' ancient heathen tribes,
Sunk dwindling 'midst the fellow-stockmen's jibes,
Thy manly spirit saw a fitting field,
Where the true 'missionary soul' could shield
Thy sable brethren — and perchance, in time,
Sow seeds to ripen into faith sublime!
And now Kamilaroi's unlettered tongue,
Thus rescued from oblivion, has sprung
Whatever know we of that dim, dark past,
Which science craves to save from out the vast
Mysterious deep of hoary ages gone,
Whose hieroglyphs are buried flint and bone.
Nor hath thy sympathy and kindness failed,
Nor been forgotten! — to this day is hailed
Thy gentle memory, — and with fond acclaim,
The 'wild tribes' loving honor RIDLEY's name!

" Servant of Christ, — thy long day's task is done,
(His soldiers fall not till the fight is won!)
And we who sorrowing, yield back to death thy dust,
Tell, earth has lost one more good man, and just. — R. A."

John Ridley[6] (5), third son of William[5] (1), was born at Hartford End, Essex, Eng., and is now (1883) at Damerham, Wiltshire; unmarried. He has made some investigation, and could undoubtedly provide much additional genealogical information if he could find time to do so.

Maria Ridley[6] (1), daughter of William[5] (1), was born at Hartford End, Essex ; was married Sept. 17, 1839, to —— Curling, and has issue. Now (1883) a widow.

Annie Ridley[6] (1), daughter of William[5] (1), born at Hartford End, Essex; was married June 15, 1841, to Joseph Tison, and has issue. Now (1883) a widow.

Sarah-Dixon Ridley[6] (1), a daughter of William[5] (1), born at Hartford End; was married March 5, 1846, to Mr. Nash, and has issue. Now a widow (1883).

Elizabeth Ridley[6] (1), a daughter of William[5] (1), born at Hartford End, Essex; was married April 29, 1854, to John Richardson, and has issue. Now (1883) living; also her husband.

Catherine Ridley[6] (1), daughter of William[5] (1), born at Hartford End, Essex; was married Aug. 11, 1841, to Joseph L. Prentice, and has issue. Now (1883) a widow.

Susanna Ridley[6] (1), a daughter of William[5] (1), born at Hartford End, Essex; was married July 31, 1845, to Manning Prentice, and has issue. Now (1883) a widow.

Harriet Ridley[6] (1), a daughter of William[5] (1), born at Hartford End, Essex, and now of Talstead, Essex; unmarried.

Ellen Ridley[6] (1), a daughter of William[5] (1), born at Hartford End, Essex; was married Dec. 27, 1850, to —— Creak, and died Feb. 5, 1857, leaving *one* daughter.

SEVENTH GENERATION.

Mary-Ann Ridley[7] (1), a daughter of John[6] (4), the magistrate of Bury St. Edmund's, married to William Ridley, of Ipswich, Suffolk; supposed to be of the same family, and had issue, of whom hereafter. Her husband has deceased.

William-Wells Ridley[7] (3), eldest son of Thomas[6] (1), was born March 4, 1842; married and has issue.

Thomas-Herbert Ridley[7] (2), second son of Thomas[6] (1), was born Aug. 9, 1845.

Charles-Ernest Ridley[7] (1), third son of Thomas[6] (1), was born March 24, 1847, and is of "the Elms," Chelmsford, Essex.

Walter Ridley[7] (1), fourth son of Thomas[6] (1), was born July 22, 1848; married, and has issue. Lives at Hartford End, Essex.

Mary Ridley[7] (2). }
Edith Ridley[7] (1). } Daughters of Thomas[6] (1).
Gertrude Ridley[7] (1). }

William Ridley[7] (4), eldest son of William[6] (3), was born Jan. 11, 1851, and lives at Lohort, Paddington, Sydney, New South Wales, Australia. A writer in Registrar General's office. He is a "philatelist," or collector of postage-stamps. Furnished the genealogy of his family for this book.

George-Sackville Ridley[7] (1), second son of William[6] (3), was born April 6, 1858.

Francis-Arundel Ridley[7] (1), third son of William[6] (3), was born Sept. 27, 1860.

Mary-Purcell Ridley[7] (2), eldest daughter of William[6] (3).

Isabella-Grace Ridley[7] (1), second daughter of William[6] (3).

Jessie-Darroch Ridley[7] (1), third daughter of William[6] (3), died March 30, 1862. A lovely child.

Sarah-Dixon Ridley[7] (2). } Twin daughters of William[6] (3);
Ellen-Cotter Ridley[7] (1). } Ellen C. died Jan. 13, 1881.

RIDLEYS OF STAINTON, ENGLAND.

Josiah Ridley[1] **(1)**, born in Northumberland, Eng., April 24, 1812; married Jane Mownsey, and had issue *five* children, of whom hereafter. He was a farmer at Stainton,* near the city of Liverpool, to which place he moved about the year 1800.

SECOND GENERATION.

Joseph Ridley[2] **(1)**, eldest son of Josiah[1] **(1)**, was born in Stainton, Eng., in 1835, and is an inn-keeper in Liverpool. He died Nov. 2, 1878.

William Ridley[2] **(1)**, second son of Josiah[1] **(1)**, was born in Stainton, Eng., in 1838, and keeps an inn in Liverpool.

Thomas Ridley[2] **(1)**, third son of Josiah[1] **(1)**, was born in Stainton, Eng., in 1851, and died at Liverpool in 1878.

Isabella Ridley[2] **(1).** }
Annie Ridley[2] **(1).** } Daughters of Josiah[1] **(1)** ; both married.

RIDLEYS OF NEWARK, ENGLAND.

Thomas Ridley[1] **(1)** was found in the porch of Barnby Church when a small boy, and could tell nothing about his family only that he came from America. Another tradition says he was taken to England to be educated, and that his parents were lost at sea on their return to America. Was he a descendant of the family of Ridley of Virginia? He was cared for by strangers until able to support himself, when he settled in the vicinity of Newark-on-Trent; married and had issue *four* children, of whom hereafter. He was not educated, but spent his life as a laborer.

SECOND GENERATION.

Matthew Ridley[2] **(1)**, a son of Thomas[1] **(1)**, was born at Newark-on-Trent, Eng., settled at Wellingore in the same County, and had issue *three* (perhaps others) children, of whom hereafter. He was a laborer.

Thomas Ridley[2] **(2)**, a son of Thomas[1] **(1)**, was born at Newark-on-Trent, settled at Coddington, and had issue *seven* children, of whom hereafter. He was a laborer.

Ann Ridley[2] **(1)**, only daughter of Thomas[1] **(1)**, was born at Newark-on-Trent, and remained a single woman.

Frank Ridley[2] **(1)**, youngest son of Thomas[1] **(1)**, was born at Newark-on-Trent, settled at Elston, and became a soldier. He had a family of children, but I have no particulars.

---

* GEORGE RIDLEY of Stainton, near Liverpool, married Annie Atkinson in 1851, and has *seven* children. He has five brothers and three sisters (1878). The father carried on Fair Hill Farm, at Alston Moor, Northumberland, some sixty years ago. Settled at Stainton about fifty-three years ago. This family, — from which I can get no other information, — are distant relatives of the above Josiah Ridley. They all claim connection with Bishop Ridley's family.

THIRD GENERATION.

Thomas Ridley[3] (3), eldest son of Matthew[2] (1), was born at Wellingore, Eng., settled at Kirby Green, and had issue, of whom hereafter. He was a hawker.

John Ridley[3] (1), second son of Matthew[2] (1), was born at Wellingore, Eng., and had a family, but I have no records, nor could my correspondent get particulars.

Kezia Ridley[3] (1), daughter of Matthew[2] (1), was born at Wellingore, Eng. No record of her marriage.

James Ridley[3] (1), eldest son of Thomas[2] (2), was born at Coddington (presumably), lived at Potter Hanworth, and had issue *five* children, of whom hereafter. Laborer.

John Ridley[3] (2), second son of Thomas[2] (2), was born at Coddington, and lived at Hawton ; laborer.

Thomas Ridley[3] (4), third son of Thomas[2] (2), was born at Coddington, and lived at Buckingham ; laborer.

Catherine Ridley[3] (1), only daughter of Thomas[2] (2), was born at Coddington, and settled at Thorpe-on-the-Hill.

Edward Ridley[3] (1), fourth son of Thomas[2] (2), was born at Coddington, and lived at Balderton in 1848. He is called a "cottager." No record of a family.

Archibald Ridley[3] (1), youngest son of Thomas[2] (2), was born at Coddington, and is now (1878) farm bailiff at Bestwood Hall. No records of his family.

James Ridley[3] (2), a son of Frank[2] (1).   } No information.
Ann Ridley[3] (2), a daughter of Frank[2] (1). }

FOURTH GENERATION.

Matthew Ridley[4] (2), a son of Thomas[3] (3), of Kirby Green. }   No
Torn (?) Ridley[4] (1), a son of Thomas[3] (3), of Kirby Green. } records.

Thomas Ridley[4] (5), eldest son of James[3] (1), was born at Potter Hanworth, Nov. 27, 1828; married Feb. 29, 1852, and was living at Glencoyne, Villa Cooper, Nottingham, in 1878. He previously lived at Ruskington. Carpenter by trade. He says the family history is in obscurity ; also, that there are other branches in the neighborhood, but not related to him.

Ann Ridley[4] (2), daughter of James[3] (1), was born May 25, 1830, at Potter Hanworth, was married in June, 1848, and was living in her native place in 1878.

William Ridley[4] (1), second son of James[3] (1), was born June 29, 1832, and has a family. Railway signal-man in his native place.

Catherine Ridley[4] (2), eldest daughter of James[3] (1), was born in October, 1834. Living at Stanford in 1878.

Mary Ridley[4] (1), third daughter of James[3] (1), was born in June, 1836. Living at Lincoln in 1878.

RIDLEYS OF WINKFIELD, ENGLAND.

George-Jesse Ridley[1] (1) was a farmer at Berwick-on-Tweed, Scotland; descended from the Ridleys of Willimoteswick, in Northumberland, Eng.; married and had a son (perhaps other issue), of whom hereafter.

SECOND GENERATION.

Thomas Ridley[2] (1), a son of George[1] (1), was born at Berwick-on-Tweed, Scotland, and ran away from home when a boy. He visited his native place after a lapse of a quarter of a century, but took very little pains to find any relatives. He was a very eccentric character in this respect. He always told his children he was related to the family of Sir Matthew-White Ridley, Bart. He resided at Winkfield, Windsor, and was for many years a farmer and inn-keeper there. He owned lands at Winkfield. I know nothing of his education or professional life. He married Charlotte Austin, and had issue *ten* children, of whom hereafter. Died in 1871.

THIRD GENERATION.

Charlotte Ridley[3] (1), eldest daughter of Thomas[2] (1), was born at Winkfield, Northumberland, and was married to a Mr. Foster. Now dead (1883).

Ellen Ridley[3] (1), second daughter of Thomas[2] (1), was born at Winkfield, Eng., and was married to James Killenan, who is now (1883) dead.

Thomas Ridley[3] (2), eldest son of Thomas[2] (1), was born at Winkfield, Northumberland; married Amelia Nullens, and had a son (name not known), who married Jesse Blenkensop, and is now the only known male representative of this family. Mr. Ridley is dead.

William Ridley[3] (1), second son of Thomas[2] (1), was born at Winkfield, Northumberland, and lived single. Dead.

Albert Ridley[3] (1), third son of Thomas[2] (1), was born at Winkfield, Northumberland, and married in America.

Ann Ridley[3] (1), third daughter of Thomas[2] (1), was born at Winkfield, and is now living, a spinster.

George Ridley[3] (2), fourth son of Thomas[2] (1), was born at Winkfield. Living, but incompetent.

Louisa-Caroline Ridley[3] (1), fourth daughter of Thomas[2] (1), was born at Winkfield, and was married to Mr. Barnes, who died in 1873.

Emma Ridley[3] (1), fifth daughter of Thomas[2] (1), was born at Winkfield, and married Thomas Hussey.

Rose Ridley[3] (1), sixth daughter of Thomas[2] (1), was born at Winkfield; married Mr. Cooper, and died twelve years ago.

RIDLEYS OF KIMBOLTON, ENGLAND.

Doctor Ridley[1] (1), parents unknown, was surgeon to the Dukes of Manchester. Lived at Kimbolton, Huntingdonshire; married, and had issue *five* children, of whom hereafter. He was an eminent professional man, greatly respected while alive and lamented when dead. His Christian name has not reached me, nor the maiden-name of his wife. Both buried at Kimbolton.

SECOND GENERATION.

Dr. George-Nelville Ridley[2] (1), a son of Doctor Ridley[1] (1), was born at Kimbolton, Eng., and settled when a young man in Belleville, Upper Canada, where he has long been engaged in the practice of his profession, and is considered one of the most skillful professional men in Canada. He has manifested great public spirit and held important offices. Successful in his practice, he acquired a considerable property, and holds the esteem of a large and respectable circle of acquaintances. He had a family of *eight* children.

Rev. William-Charles Ridley[2] (1), son of Doctor Ridley[1] (1), was born at Kimbolton, Eng.; married Maria, daughter of R. Tidwell, Esq., of Kimbolton, and had issue *six* children, of whom hereafter. He was curate of Kimbolton, then curate of Great Stoughton, in Huntingdonshire, and afterwards incumbent of St. John's Episcopal Church, Glasgow, Scotland. He was chaplain to the Dukes of Manchester for more than twenty years. He died in Glasgow in 1855, and, with his wife, who died in 1864, was buried at Brompton Cemetery. Mr. Ridley was a man of great learning and able as a preacher. He was considered a man of eminent piety.

Sarah Ridley[2] (1), a daughter of Doctor Ridley[1] (1), was born at Kimbolton, and became the wife of Dr. R. Webster, of St. Albans, Hertfordshire, and had *three* children. She and husband are buried at St. Albans.

Louisa Ridley[2] (1), a daughter of Doctor Ridley[1] (1), was born at Kimbolton, and died there when young, single.

Sophia Ridley[2] (1), a daughter of Doctor Ridley[1] (1), was born at Kimbolton, and died unmarried, aged 61, at the home of her brother, the Rev. William C. Ridley, Place House, Great Stoughton, July 21, 1839. "A benevolent friend to the poor." She was buried with her parents at Kimbolton.

THIRD GENERATION.

William Ridley[3] (2), eldest son of George[2] (1), born (presumably) in England, and died young.

Louisa-Mary Ridley[3] (2), eldest daughter of George[2] (1), was married July 11, 1839, to Baron de Rottenburg, lieutenant-colonel, commanding at Belleville, Upper Canada.

Charles Ridley[3] (1), second son of George[2] (1), was born in Canada (?), and is supposed to be living at Belleville.

Bessie Ridley[3] (1), daughter of George[2] (1), was born in Belleville, Can.

Alfred Ridley[3] (1), a son of George[2] (1), born at Belleville, Can.; died young.

Robert-Tidwell Ridley[3] (1), eldest son of William[2] (1), was married, but had no children. He was a solicitor. Died a few years ago, and was buried at Stourbridge, Worcestershire.

Rev. Charles-George Ridley[3] (2), second son of William[2] (1), was born at Kimbolton, Feb. 22, 1822; married Jan. 22, 1861, to Mary Vine, eldest daughter of Richard Vine, Esq., of Witney(?), Oxon., and had issue *nine* children, of whom hereafter. He has been assistant master at several large grammar schools. Was appointed head-master of Spilsby Grammar School in 1856, which he held with the curacy of Spilsby, and in

1872 presented by the Baroness Willoughby de Eresby to the vicarage of Handleby(?), which he held with the chaplaincy of Spilsby Union Workhouse until 1881, when he was presented by the Lord Chancellor to the rectory of Beatoft, and by the Dean and Chapter of Lincoln to the vicarage of Isby, which two livings he now (1883) holds.

Frederick-William Ridley[2] (1), third son of William[2] (1), was born at Kimbolton, Eng.(?), and settled as a farmer in Australia. He married and has *three* children, two daughters and a son. I do not know his address.

Rev. Henry-Thomas Ridley[2] (1), fourth son of William[2] (1), was born at Kimbolton(?); married Emily-Augusta-Besant, eldest daughter of George Raggett, Esq., of Folkestone, Kent, and has *one* son, of whom hereafter. He was formerly assistant master in several schools; afterwards curate of St. James, Davenport, curate of St. Columb, Major Cornwall, St. Gabriel's, Pimlico, London, and now (1883) vicar of Bruton, Somersetshire.

Maria-Louisa Ridley[2] (1), eldest daughter of William[2] (1), is living at Sydenham, Kent, unmarried.

Adelaide-Sophia Ridley[2] (1), second daughter of William[2] (1), is now (1888) living at Sydenham, Kent, unmarried.

FOURTH GENERATION.

Maria-Louisa Ridley[4] (1), eldest daughter of Charles[8] (1), was born in December, 1861.

Nicholas-Charles Ridley[4] (1), eldest son of Charles[8] (1,) was born in 1863.

William-Alder Ridley[4] (3), second son of Charles[8] (1), born in 1864.

Ada-Tidwell Ridley[4] (1), second daughter of Charles[8] (1), born in 1866.

George-Wace Ridley[4] (2), third son of Charles[8] (1), born 1868, died 1869.

Marion-Vine Ridley[4] (1), third daughter of Charles[8] (1), born 1869.

Gerald-Walker Ridley[4] (1), fourth son of Charles[8] (1), born 1871.

Grace Ridley[4] (1), fourth daughter of Charles[8] (1), born in 1873.

Hugh Ridley[4] (1), fifth son of Charles[8] (1), born 1877, died 1877.

William-Charles-George Ridley[4] (4), only son of Henry[8] (1).

———•◦•———

RIDLEYS OF NEWARK-ON-TRENT, ENGLAND.

James-Mosley Ridley[1] (1) was born in England, Oct. 24, 1793; married Mary Moore (she was born Feb. 12, 1794, and died April 25, 1853), March 15, 1815; was a schoolmaster by profession, and died at Newark-on-Trent, Nottinghamshire, Dec. 18, 1849, having had issue *eleven* children, of whom hereafter. One says he was "keeper of Woolwich stockyard."

NOTE.—It is believed that all records of births, marriages, and deaths are to be found in the registers of Kimbolton. I have written the vicar of the church there, but have no reply.

SECOND GENERATION.

Edward Ridley[2] (1), eldest son of James[1] (1), was born at Newark-on-Trent, Nottinghamshire, Eng., June 5, 1816; married Elizabeth Smith, of Leicester, Oct. 23, 1847, and served an apprenticeship in the dry-goods business in England. He engaged in business on his own account at Leicester, and after a period of success met with reverses, and was forced into bankruptcy. He came to America when about thirty years of age, and commenced business in a small way in Albany, N. Y., and prospered. He then opened a store in Saratoga; and in 1849 went into trade on Grand Street, New York city; this new venture proved so successful that he sold his other stores and devoted all his time to its development. In 1851 he had but three employes, and carried on business in a very small store, but as his patronage increased he enlarged his capacity, adding store to store, until his place of business covered four acres of surface, and the firm employed one thousand and seven hundred hands. He was a thoroughly successful business man, and acquired a fortune estimated in the millions. Notwithstanding the growth of his business and augmentation of his wealth, he moved among his customers the same unostentatious gentleman he was when he won their confidence. It is not common to find men who have risen to fortune so free from assumption, and so considerate of those in inferior positions, as was Mr. Ridley. Rarely has any man of such extensive relations exerted so good an influence on those about him. When he suffered heavy losses he showed the same calm spirit as when all went well. He had a peculiar business experience, and was always glad to draw from its lessons to assist others; he could speak a word of encouragement when most needed, and many, when faithless, and under depressing circumstances, have found in him a sympathizing friend.

Fluent in conversation, genial in manner, amiable in temper, liberal in Christian sentiment, generous in sympathy, devout in spirit, and intelligent in the things that interested him, he proved a most entertaining companion. Ready to seize every advantage that art, science, and improved methods in business presented, he taught others by his own example. No transaction in his life shows better the integrity and conscientiousness of the man than a visit he made to England in 1879, with a view of paying debts contracted previous to his failure there more than thirty years before. These he discharged, paying principal and interest; when he could not find the parties themselves he paid their heirs, — in all about fifty thousand dollars.

Reared in the Church of England, where in his youth he was a member of the choir in one of the most ancient parishes, he ever cherished for it a profound respect; but when he became a converted man he united with the Wesleyan Communion, and was for many years a local preacher in the land of his adoption. He was truly a pillar in the church. With a purse that any proper appeal could reach, and with a munificence in giving that made both church and preacher strong, he was prominent in his influence and activities in the Parkville Methodist Church, where he was trustee, steward, class-leader, Sabbath-school superintendent, and local preacher. He may be said to have been the founder of the church, and in the support he gave, it attained its influence. As a Sabbath-school superintendent he was watchful of the members and awake to all their interests. In a single year he gave one thousand dollars for its advancement, and paid nearly three thousand dollars for the current expenses of the charge.

Six months before Mr. Ridley's death he was thrown from his carriage and sustained injuries from which he was confined to the house three months under treatment, but recovered and attended to his business as usual. On the Sabbath previous to his death he supplied the pulpit in the absence of his pastor, and addressed the school in the afternoon. In the evening he was at the service. After returning home from business Monday evening he sat with his wife on the veranda till about half-past ten o'clock; when he returned to the parlor to enjoy the music of his youngest daughter. They sang their evening hymn, "Nearer, my God, to thee," engaged in family-prayer, and retired at midnight. In a short time his wife was aroused by his heavy breathing and physical anguish, and after two brief prayers to God, apoplexy ended his life, July 31, 1883, almost before his family were aware of his danger.

His funeral was in Parkville Methodist Church, and was attended by six hundred of the employes of the dry-goods house of which he was the head. Two hundred Sabbath-school children sat in the front pews. The casket was surrounded with many elaborate offerings. After the services the employes and children filed around the church to view the remains of their departed friend, each of the children dropping a flower upon the casket as they passed. "The young of the congregation sobbed as if they had lost a father, the middle-aged wept as if he had been a brother, and the aged bowed as if feeling that a stay was gone, — sorrowing most of all that they should see his face no more." Mr. Ridley was buried in Greenwood by the side of his first wife, who died in 1863. He left issue *six* children, of whom hereafter.

In his will he left one third of his real estate, other than that employed in business, to his wife Carrie, and also gave her one hundred thousand dollars, together with his household goods and carriages. The other two thirds of his real estate go in equal shares to his children. The dry-goods business is left to his sons, — Edward, Albert, and Arthur. To his daughters twenty-five thousand dollars each is left, and to his grandson, Edward Ridley, thirty-five thousand dollars. The sum of five hundred dollars a year for seven years is left for the Parkville Methodist Church, and two hundred dollars a year for the same time for the Sabbath-school. The value of the estate is estimated at two million dollars. One clause in the will provides that if any of the legatees attempt to contest the will in a court of law, he or she shall forfeit any bequest in his or her favor.

Jane Ridley[2] (1), eldest daughter of James[1] (1), was born Nov. 12, 1818, and died Sept. 9, 1863.

William-Moor Ridley[2] (1), second son of James[1] (1), was born Oct. 22, 1821, at Newark, Nottinghamshire, Eng., and is a professor of music and organist in Liverpool. He married and has issue; names do not appear.

Eliza Ridley[2] (1), second daughter of James[1] (1), was born Jan. 19, 1824, and died Feb. 15, 1824.

Robert-Mosley Ridley[2] (1), third son of James[1] (1), was born at Newark-on-Trent, Dec. 15, 1824; deceased.

Betsey-Mosley Ridley[2] (1), third daughter of James[1] (1), was born March 16, 1826, and died July 27, 1852.

Mary-Ann Ridley[2] (1), fourth daughter of James[1] (1), was born April 16, 1829, and died May 4, 1829.

Alfred Ridley[2] (1), fourth son of James[1] (1), was born at Newark-on-

Trent, April 30, 1830, and is still (1884) living there. He was a printer, but has been paralyzed and disabled. Has the old family Bible containing the records.

Thomas-W. Ridley[2] (1), fifth son of James[1] (1), was born at Newark-on-Trent, April 28, 1833, and died June 6, 1833.

Thomas Ridley[2] (1), sixth son of James[1] (1), was born at Newark-on-Trent, Sept. 19, 1834. No information. His brother of Liverpool does not reply to any enquiries.

Robert Ridley[2] (1), youngest son of James[1] (1), was born Nov. 28, 1837. No other information.

THIRD GENERATION.

Edward-A. Ridley[3] (2), eldest son of Edward[2] (1), married, and is a member of the dry-goods firm of Edward Ridley & Sons, New York city.

Arthur-John Ridley[3] (2), second son of Edward[2] (1), married, and is a member of the dry-goods firm in New York city with his brother before mentioned.

James-M. Ridley[3] (1), third(?) son of Edward[2] (1), married, and died in 1875, leaving issue *one* son. He was buried in Greenwood Cemetery.

Emma Ridley[3] (1), a daughter of Edward[2] (1), unmarried.

Clara Ridley[3] (1), youngest daughter of Edward[2] (1), single. A daughter married Mr. Samuel Hughes, but her name does not appear.

FOURTH GENERATION.

Edward Ridley[4] (3), presumed to be a son of James[3] (1), was a legatee in his grandfather's will, and received thirty-five thousand dollars.

There are probably other grandchildren of Edward Ridley, but as the family have declined to give any genealogical information, names are not known. Every reasonable effort has been made to have Mr. Ridley's portrait and a view of his villa in this book, but without success.

RIDLEYS OF ARTHERSTONE, ENGLAND.

John Ridley[1] (1), descended from the Ridleys of Willimoteswick, Northumberland, is supposed to have been identical with John Ridley, who was called "Chief Ridley," and who, having espoused the cause of the Stuarts, had all his lands confiscated and was obliged to leave the north of England. This man was last seen at Haltwhistle in 1774, and as the John whose name heads this notice settled at Sheepy Magna, Artherstone (the post-town of Warwickshire), County of Leicester, the same year, his descendants assumed the connection. The family have handed down some old Jacobite glasses, which are supposed to have been the property of this John Ridley. He married Sarah Vincent, a sister of the Dean of Westminster, a notice of which is found in White's History of Leicestershire, and had issue *three* children, of whom hereafter. Died in 1786.

SECOND GENERATION.

Rev. John-Vincent Ridley[2] (2), eldest son of John[1] (1), died in 1785, aged 40 years. No information of his family.

James-Francis-Edward Ridley² (1), second son of John¹ (1), had the family estates of Sheepy Magna, and the record of his death stands on the church-register there. He married Jane Fairfield, and had issue *ten* children, of whom hereafter. He died in 1814, aged 55; his wife in 1820, aged 50. He is said to have been named for the "Pretender,"* whose cause his father had so ardently espoused, and for which he lost his estates.

Sarah Ridley² (1), only daughter of John¹ (1), died in 1788.

THIRD GENERATION.

James Ridley³ (2), eldest son of James² (1), died unmarried 1818.

William-Vincent Ridley³ (1), second son of James² (1), married and had a family of *eight* children of whom hereafter. He and wife (whose name does not appear) were buried at Sheepy Magna, and probably lived there.

Anne Ridley³ (1), eldest daughter of James² (1), died unmarried at Sheepy Magna in 1874.

Edward Ridley³ (1), third son of James² (1), married Eliza Eaglesfield, and had issue *four* children, of whom hereafter. He bought the shares of his brothers in the estate at Sheepy Magna, and became the virtual representative of the family. Unfortunately owing to discord the estate was thrown into chancery, and in order to clear off an incumbrance the house and lands were sold in 1878–9, and the family went to Warwick and subsequently to Liverpool, where Mr. Ridley is still (1884) living.

Louisa Ridley³ (1), second daughter of James² (1), was married to John Ashford, surgeon, Hinckley, and still lives there. She had *five* children.

Caroline Ridley³ (1), third daughter of James² (1), died unmarried at Sheepy Magna.

Dr. Charles Ridley³ (1), fourth son of James² (1), was twice married, but left no children. He died at London. A skillful surgeon.

Christiana Ridley³ (1), fourth daughter of James² (1), was married to Edward Baker, and with her husband was buried at Sheepy Magna.

Dr. Robert Ridley³ (1), fifth son of James² (1), married Sarah Walker, and died in Melbourne, Australia, issueless.

Henry Ridley³ (1), sixth son of James² (1), married and had issue, of whom hereafter. He lives at Hockley, Birmingham.

FOURTH GENERATION.

Charles Ridley⁴ (2), eldest son of William³ (1), married and lived at Artherstone; children living there.

Sophia Ridley⁴ (1), eldest daughter of William³ (1).

William-Vincent Ridley⁴ (2), second son of William³ (1).

Joseph Ridley⁴ (1), third son of William³ (1).

James Ridley⁴ (4), fourth son of William³ (1).

Jane Ridley⁴ (1), second daughter of William³ (1).

---

* JAMES-FRANCIS-EDWARD STUART, son of James II. By the forced abdication and flight of James II, in 1688, the crown of England passed to William, Prince of Orange. The "Pretender" made some vain attempts to recover the kingdom, but surrendered his claims in 1743 to his son, Charles-Edward, the "Younger Pretender," who in 1744 invaded Great Britain from France, and fought gallantly for the throne of his ancestors, but was defeated at Culloden, in 1746, and compelled to escape to the continent.

Christiana Ridley[4] (2), third daughter of William[3] (1).
John Ridley[4] (3), fifth son of William[3] (1), had issue.

Ada-Jane Ridley[4] (1), eldest daughter of Edward[3] (1), born at Sheepy Magna, Eng., and is now (1884) living with her sister at Gateshead-on-Tyne. Miss Ridley has provided family records, etc.
Eliza-Adelaid Ridley[4] (1), second daughter of Edward[3] (1).
Alfred-Edwin Ridley[4] (1), eldest son of Edward[3] (1), married Nora Patterson, a relative of Bishop Patterson who was murdered in the South Sea Islands, in 1880, and has *two* children. Mr. Ridley lives at Sparta, Ontario, Can.
Louisa-Fanny Ridley[4] (2), third daughter of Edward[3] (1), was married to Thomas Day, of Dublin, Ireland, and has issue.

Edward-Daniel Ridley[4] (2), a son of Henry[3] (1).

FIFTH GENERATION.

Joseph Ridley[5] (2), a son of Charles[4] (2).
Lizzie Ridley[5] (1), a daughter of Charles[4] (2).

Minnie Ridley[5] (1), a daughter of John[4] (3).
Christiana Ridley[5] (3), a daughter of John[4] (3).

Hilda Ridley[5] (1), a daughter of Alfred[4] (1).
Sarah-Adelaid Ridley[5] (2), a daughter of Alfred[4] (1).

RIDLEY LAND-OWNERS IN GREAT BRITAIN.

This table shows the number of acres of land accredited to the Ridleys and Ridlers in England, Scotland, and Wales, and the gross estimate of rental for 1873, as found in the "Returns of the Owners of Land," published by the Government in 1875.

NAME OF OWNER.	RESIDENCE OF OWNER.	EXTENT OF LAND.			RENTAL.	
		A.	R.	P.	£	s.
Sir Matthew W. Ridley,	Blagden, Northumberland,	9,696	2	17	31,849	5
Thomas Ridley, Esq.,	Parkend, Northumberland,	10,367	1	15	4,171	3
John M. Ridley, Esq.,	Hexham, Kent,	887	1	14	1,215	17
Samuel Ridley, Esq.,	Bridgeworth, Salop,	166	3	16	565	8
George Ridley,	Winkfield, Berks,	4	2	17	32	12
Rev. Nicholas J. Ridley,	East Woodhay, Berks,	5	2	20	12	
W. W. Ridley,	Early, Reeding, Berks,	1	2		60	
Rev. Wm. H. Ridley,	Hambleden, Bucks,	47	1	23	211	8
Elizabeth Ridley,	Market Draydon,	1	3	6	11	4
John Ridley,	Cheade, Cheshire,	38	2	3	108	
Andrew Ridley,	Newcastle-on-Tyne,	54	2	4	77	
John Ridley,	Roughsyke, Cumberland,	7	2	34	8	
John Ridley,	Greystoke, Cumberland,	2	3	9	2	
Miss Mary Ridley,	Beaumont, Cumberland,	37	1	2	39	6

NAME OF OWNER.	RESIDENCE OF OWNER.	EXTENT OF LAND.			RENTAL.	
		A.	R.	P.	£	s.
Mrs. Mary Ridley,	Berrier Head, Cumberland,	66	2	36	56	
Richard Ridley,	Field Head, Cumberland,	31	3	38	31	
Thomas Ridley,	Stainton, Cumberland,	19	1		19	
George Ridley,	Norton, Durham,	362			378	
Rev. John Ridley,	Norton, Durham,	362			378	
John Ridley,	Frosterly, Durham,	30	2	20	51	10
Mrs. Margaret Ridley,	Yarm, Durham,	3			18	
William Ridley,	Frosterly, Durham,	30	2	20	51	10
Christopher Ridley,	Chingford, Essex,	3	1	12	18	
John Ridley,	Damerham, Wilts,	57	2	26	130	16
Errington Ridley,	Hexham, Northumberland,	19	1	38	222	·
George Ridley,	Bellingham, Northum'land,	189			81	10
Henry Ridley,	Ballington (Ireland),	39			40	
John Ridley,	Hexham, Northumberland,	7	2	30	216	5
Matthew Ridley,	Keepwick, Northum'land,	191	2	7	190	
Mrs. —— Ridley,	Falstone, Northumberland,	834			240	
Sarah Ridley,	Hayden Bridge, No'm'land,	46			75	
Thomas Ridley,	Acomb Hill, Northum'land,	18	3	30	50	
Thomas D. Ridley,	Hencoats, Northum'land,	1	3		12	
Thompson Ridley,	Simonburn, Northum'land,	130			135	
William Ridley,	Ridley Stoke, No'm'land,	475			215	
Mrs. —— Ridley,	Cambdenton, Nottingham,	3	3	7	17	17
Rev. Hy T. Ridley,	Bruton, Somerset,	5	3		101	
Rev. T. Ridley,	Michialdevor, Southamp'n,	1			16	
Samuel W. Ridley,	St. Helens, Southampton,	7			15	
Rev. Thomas Ridley,	Preston, Candover, S'h'ton,	15			13	5
Rev. W. J. Ridley,	E Woodhay, Southampton,	171		20	262	5
Jane Ridley,	Pattingham, Stafford,	5	2	28	18	16
Phebe Ridley,	Tipton, Stafford,	20			29	18
Sarah Ridley,	Pattingham, Stafford,	6	1	7	36	2
Henry Ridley,	Ipswich, Suffolk,	5	1	6	119	6
John Ridley,	Bury St. Edmond's, Suf'lk,	5	2	20	288	12
Owen Ridley,	Ipswich, Suffolk,	3	1	15	511	10
Charles Ridley,	Nutly, Sussex,	4	1	8	18	
John Ridley,	Fletching, Sussex,	14	2	30	59	
Joseph Ridley,	Millbrook, Sussex,	12		14	45	10
S. Ridley,	Hemelheptead, Sussex,	18	1	2	36	16
Samuel Ridley,	Brighton, Sussex,	3	2	1	155	10
Samuel Ridley,	The Forest, Sussex,	1	3	33	14	
Rev. George Ridley,	Crosby Garett, Westm'land,	87			89	10
Mrs. —— Ridley,	Stainton, Westmoreland,	83		36	122	10
Rev. W. Ridley,	Preston Richard, W'm'land,	78	1	19	106	5
Ann Ridley,	Richmond, County York,	15		7	57	
Edward Ridley,	Whitby, County York,	73	1		35	15
RIDLER.						
John Ridler,	Brendon, Devon,	4	1	27	5	
T. W. Ridler,	Minchinham, Gloucester,	2	20	20	20	
William Ridler,	Eastcomb, Gloucester,	2	1	26	12	14
William Ridler,	Pitchcomb, Gloucester,	12		33	81	10
John Ridler,	Minehead, Somerset,	150	1	29	68	8
Joshua H. Ridler,	Felton, Somerset,	44		13	189	18
Robert Ridler,	Stogursey, Somerset,	2	3	25	30	10
William Ridler,	Malvern, Somerset,	4		35	252	

31

RIDLEYS OF SOUTHAMPTON COUNTY, VIRGINIA.

Robert Ridley[1] (1), supposed to have been a son of Christopher Ridley of Battersea, in the County of York, Eng., came to America in 1635, with his wife, Elizabeth Abridgton, to whom he was married previous to his embarkation for the New World. The record gives his age as twenty-three years, and that of his wife as twenty-eight. He came on the ship "Dorset," Captain Flowers master, and brought a certificate from a Justice of the Peace proving himself conformable to the Church of England and "no subsidy man." Mr. Ridley settled in Isle of Wight County, in the south-eastern section of Virginia, and became a wealthy land-owner and extensive planter there. He is said to have died about sixty years before the Revolution, which would make his age one hundred and three years, which is presumably incorrect, for his wife survived him and married, secondly, to Matthew Jones,* a gentleman of Welsh descent, and by him

---

* ABRIDGTON JONES, son of Matthew Jones and Elizabeth (Abridgton) Ridley, was born Sept. 22, 1720, and was married to Elizabeth Simmons, June 17, 1744, and by her had *nine* children; one died in infancy, one in early manhood, and of some others I have little knowledge. Mary, the eldest child, was married to a Mr. Jarrel, who died in a few years, leaving her in charge of *three* children, a son and two daughters, of which charge she most faithfully acquitted herself. Few women have displayed the same sound judgment and energy of character, that were visible in all the duties devolved on Mrs. Jarrel. More than sixty years of her life were spent in training her children, grandchildren, and great-grandchildren, and she descended to the tomb beloved by all who knew her. Matthew Jones, the eldest surviving son, had one son and a daughter, both of whom married and moved to the West. Agatha Jones, the second daughter, married in North Carolina, and was the mother of Dr. Simmons Baker, who was extensively known for his intelligence, usefulness, and great personal worth. Col. Abridgton Jones was the youngest of his father's children, and had just completed his twentieth year at the Declaration of Independence, yet he had already buckled on his armor and gone forth to the battle-field. He and his kinsman Ridley fought side by side throughout the Revolution, and at its close received the grateful approval of their country, the soldier's richest meed. After the toils of war Colonel Jones settled down in the old family-mansion, and being in temperament social, gathered around him a band of ardent friends. For his military services he was assigned a considerable tract of land in the State of Ohio, — joining the Ridley grant, — but in consequence of neglect, neither he nor his realized anything from it. Colonel Jones left *two* daughters and *one* son; the son has been some years dead. The eldest daughter was everything that a fond father could wish. She was united in marriage to Griffin Stith, and by a joyous sunlight of a cloudless disposition, dispensed as much happiness around her as is compatible with this fallible world. Mr. Stith was a profound lawyer and one of the most eloquent men of his day; was promoted at an early day to the circuit court bench. When on the steady march to fame he was suddenly cut down by death; and to show the inscrutable vicissitudes of time the wife of his bosom in two short years meekly bowed to the same fell destroyer. Of Colonel Jones' second daughter I will only say, she was an emblem of purity and was possessed of a charity that "suffereth long and is kind, envieth not, and thinketh no evil." In the forty-fourth year of her age she was called to enter her Father's Mansion, to receive the reward of her labors of love. Sarah Jones, the youngest daughter of the elder Abridgton, was of a cheerful disposition, disposed to look on the bright side of things, and with great felicity imparted to others her own happy mood. She married Parson Burgess, a distinguished Protestant Episcopal minister, who kept a classical school, and who, no doubt, educated more young men of lofty bearing and usefulness, including William Henry Harrison, late President of the United States, than any other man in Eastern Virginia. Mrs. Burgess had *one* daughter, who was the wife of Capt. Richard Kello, and their esteemed descendants are now resident in Virginia, their only surviving son, Dr. Samuel Kello, being present presiding justice of Southampton County Court. Mrs. Burgess had a son, Dr. Abridgton S. H.

had a son who became ancestor of a distinguished family now numerously represented in the Southern States. Mr. Ridley left issue *two* (some say *three*) sons and a daughter, of whom hereafter. It seems a little strange to me, that there is no record of a grant of land to this man in the registers at Richmond.

Capt. Nathaniel Ridley[1] **(1)**, a younger brother of Robert[1] (1), came to Virginia many years subsequent to the settlement of that gentleman, and became a wealthy land-owner and planter in the County Isle of Wight in that State, as the following grants, copied from the records in the land registry at Richmond, prove: "June 16, 1714, Capt. Nathaniel Ridley 815 acres Isle of Wight." It is presumed that Captain Ridley came to Virginia but little anterior to the date of the above-mentioned grant of land, unless he came over as an indentured servant, in which case his name would appear in connection with some grant to which it gave a constituent *heir right*, in legal virtue, of fifty acres, — the names of such, called "transports," always appearing in conjunction with grants of land. I have not found the name of Nathaniel Ridley's wife, and only know that he left *two* sons, whose names will hereafter appear.

William Ridley[1] **(1)**, a brother of Robert[1] (1) and Nathaniel[1] (1), came to Virginia and settled near his brothers in what was then Isle of Wight, but now Southampton County. The only record found of this man is of his will, dated the 1st of April and recorded the 19th of October, 1671. In his will he does not mention a single person of the Ridley name, but gives his small property, consisting mainly in chattels, to the relatives of his wife, whose maiden-name has not reached me.

SECOND GENERATION.

James Ridley[2] **(1)**, eldest son of Robert[1] (1) and his wife, Elizabeth Abridgton, was born in County Isle of Wight, now Southampton County, Va.; married, and had issue *two* sons, and perhaps other issue. He resided on a farm in Southampton County, west of Angelica Creek, and two or three miles south of the road leading from Jerusalem to Hicksford, which, in 1802, was in the possession of a Mrs. Taylor; the buildings had been good, but were then much dilapidated. There were *two* daughters in this family, of whom, with the sons, hereafter. I have no other information; no mention of the maiden-name of his wife, nor of the death of either.

William Ridley[2] **(2)**, second son of Robert[1] (1) and his wife, Elizabeth Abridgton, was born in Southampton County, Va.; married, and had issue,

---

Burgess, who, after graduating in medicine, settled in Raleigh, N. C., where he married and commanded an extensive practice. Though instinctively shunning notoriety, taking some interest in politics to while away his leisure hours, he commenced writing political essays, and such was the potency of his pen, that it acquired great notoriety, and among others attracted the particular attention of him, who by way of eminence has been called "the great Carolinian," John C. Calhoun. Dr. Burgess having lost his wife, his great desire was retirement, in search of which he returned to his native County, to reside with his sister at the paternal abode; but his light could not be hid under a bushel. He was again drawn into an extensive practice of medicine, and without the first effort on his part to procure personal popularity. When it was determined to new-model the frame-work of the State government, the public eye was turned toward him as a suitable representative in the convention, and the public voice ratified the selection, and his labors in that distinguished body were highly creditable to himself and cordially approved by his constituents. This note shows how the family of Ridley was allied with some of the most respectable families of the South.

of
the p.
his death.

in North Carolina hereafter. He is supposed to have resided on the farm now in
(See "Ridleys of Francis Ridley; I have no account of his marriage or
can be answered in his William the father of William Ridley who settled
which claimed Col. Howell grandfather of Col. Howell Ridley of that State?
Granville County, N. C., to the county, North Carolina.") If the foregoing query
issue *three* sons, of whom hereafter Ridley and Dr. James Ridley, of Oxford, native then the tradition in the other branch

James Ridley² (2), a son of Na——— second cousins, is proved true. He had
Virginia; but nothing is known of his ———
any. His name is found in the land re Nathaniel¹ (1), was probably born in
"July 10, 1740, James Ridley 820 acres." mily or descendants — if he had
Isle of Wight records, in a deed which P.ters at Richmond as follows:
brother Nathaniel in 1714, conveying land lying His name also appears in the
now in Southampton County, Va. ssed between him and his

Nathaniel Ridley² (2), a son of Nathaniel¹ (south of Notoway River,
Virginia, is mentioned in the land register as .
grants, as follows: "July 5, 1746, 340 acres in Isle of W, presumably born in
"June 18, 1755, 47 acres in Southampton County," Va. ing received two
County was taken from the Isle of Wight, and the two ght County," and
probably joined. I can find no record of family or descendants last-named
· of land

THIRD GENERATION.

Dr. James-Day Ridley³ (3), eldest son of James² (1), was born in
Southampton County, Va., about 1735. He obtained a considerable reputation as a physician, and died in the prime of life, leaving *one* son and
two daughters, of whom hereafter.

Bromfield Ridley³ (1), second son of James² (1), born in Southampton County, Va.; settled in Granville County, N. C., and became an
eminent lawyer and the ancestor of a numerous and highly respectable
posterity, now scattered through the Southern States. See "Ridleys of
North Carolina."

Mary Ridley³ (1), a daughter of James² (1), married to John Blount,*

---

* The family of Blount, or Blunt, is one of very long standing in England, and
its representatives have figured conspicuously in history during many centuries.
The family is of Norman origin, and the earliest in England came at the Conquest,
1066. A branch of this family has long been seated at Mapledurham, being intermarried with the Riddells of Felton Park, Northumberland, and the Ridleys of the
same County, and now represented by Michael-Charles Blount, Esq., Lord of the
Manor of Mapledurham. Members of the English family came early to Virginia,
became wealthy land-owners, and took high rank in public matters. John Blount,
who married Mary Ridley, was the father of *six* sons and *one* daughter; the youngest son, Richard-Augustus Blount, who married Mary-Edmunds Dawson, had a
daughter, Marianna-Ridley Blount, who was carried to Georgia when an infant,
became the wife of John W. A. Sanford, who became distinguished in the public
affairs of his State, — being commander of the Georgian troops in the Creek war as
major-general, — and had issue John-William-Augustus Sanford, who was a colonel
in the Confederate army during the Rebellion, and since the war was repeatedly
elected attorney-general of the State of Georgia; Eugene-Mandeville Sanford, now
Brigadier-General Sanford, of California, and Theodore-Gordon Sanford. now a
resident of Milledgeville, Ga. These descendants of Mary-Ridley Blount, are all
highly respectable, wealthy, and well allied by marriage with the best families of
their States.

of Southampton County, Va., and became the ancestress of a distinguished family.

Sarah Ridley[3] (1), a daughter of James[2] (1), was married to her cousin, Dr. James Ridley, and had issue *one* son, of whom, with his father, more hereafter. After the death of her first husband Mrs. Ridley was married to —— Drew, or Drewry, and died in 1807, having been many years a widow.

Dr. James Ridley[3] (4), a son of William[2] (2), was born in Southampton County, Va.; married his cousin Sarah, daughter of James Ridley[2] (1), before mentioned, and had issue *one* son, of whom hereafter. Dr. Ridley was a surgeon in the Revolutionary army.

—— **Ridley**[3] (?), a son of William[2] (2), was born in Southampton County, Va.; married, and had issue *three* children, of whom hereafter.

Col. Thomas Ridley[3] (1), youngest son of William[2] (2), was born in Southampton County, Va., say about 1740. He early obtained a commission in the Continental army, and proved himself a gallant soldier in the hour "which tried men's souls," serving with great distinction through the Revolutionary war. For meritorious conduct he was promoted to a coloneloy, and fought side by side with his kinsman, Col. Abridgton Jones, during many severe engagements. He was at the battle of Brandywine, and tradition has preserved an anecdote, which on that memorable occasion illustrated his chivalrous bearing. The day was intensely hot, and men were falling under the rays of a vertical sun as well as by the shot of the enemy. Still the battle raged, and the sound of the artillery became overwhelming. A poor soldier belonging to the Virginia regiment, catching the eye of Colonel Ridley, said in tremulous accents, "The earth is gaping and will swallow us." "Let it open," stormed Ridley, "we will sink together; to your post!" After one of the battles in which he had been engaged, he came across a wounded British officer, to whom he extended an act of kindness. The soldier drew from his pocket a gold watch, and asked Colonel Ridley to accept it as a token of his dying gratitude. That watch is now in the possession of his grandson, Francis T. Ridley. Colonel Ridley married Amy Scott, and left *two* sons, of whom hereafter. On retiring from the services of his country Colonel Ridley received, as the meed of his patriotic achievements, a bounty in land lying in the territory northwest of the Ohio River, — now in the State of Ohio, — from which his heirs realized the sum of forty thousand dollars. No record of his death.

FOURTH GENERATION.

John Ridley[4] (1), a son of James[3] (3), was born in Southampton County, Va., and died without issue.

—— **Ridley**[4] (?), a daughter of James[3] (3), was born in Southampton County, Va.; was married and had issue sons and daughters.

—— **Ridley**[4] (?), a daughter of James[3] (3), was born in Southampton County, Va.; was married and had issue sons and daughters.

Matthew Ridley[4] (1), only son of James[3] (4) and his wife, Sarah Ridley, was born in Southampton County, Va., and lived to attain his majority; died without issue.

Timothy Ridley[4] (1), a son of ——[3] (?), was born in Southampton

County, Va.; removed to Hertford County, N. C., and died without
issue.

—— **Ridley**[4] (?), a daughter of ——[3] (?), was born in Southampton
County, Va.; was married to Dr. Samuel Brown, and had issue an only
son, Dr. LaFayette Brown, to inherit the family property.

—— **Ridley**[4] (?), a daughter of ——[3] (?), was born in Southampton
County, Va.; was married to Abridgton Brown, brother of Dr. Samuel
Brown, before mentioned, and had issue.

Maj. Thomas Ridley[4] (2), eldest son of Thomas[3] (1), was born in
Southampton County, Va.; married Mary Wright, and had issue *four*
children, of whom hereafter. Married, secondly, Ann-Gilliam Wilkerson,
by whom no issue. He, like his father, became conspicuous for his military career, having commanded a cavalry company in the war of 1812.

Francis Ridley[4] (1), second son of Thomas[3] (1), was born in Southampton County, Va.; married Louisa R. Blunt, and had issue *two* sons, of
whom hereafter. Few men had more and warmer friends than the subject of this notice. For many years he represented the County of Southampton in the Virginia Legislature, and proved an able and popular member; by his foresight and prudence held his seat, while many others by
their rashness lost theirs. He died a young man.

FIFTH GENERATION.

William Ridley[5] (3), eldest son of Thomas[4] (2), was born in Southampton County, Va., and died unmarried.

Col. Thomas Ridley[5] (3), second son of Thomas[4] (2), was born in Southampton County, Va., Aug. 22, 1809; married Nov. 2, 1837, Margaret B.
Jordan, daughter of John B. Jordan, of Northampton County, N. C., the
belle and beauty of her age, and in all the bearing of life she has proven
that the homage paid her was the just tribute to her worth. They had
issue *eight* children, of whom hereafter. Colonel Ridley must have received the mantle of his grandfather of Revolutionary fame, for from his
early manhood he displayed a fondness for military life. When very young
he was made captain of a company of cavalry, keeping this position for
many years. Afterwards he was elected colonel of the militia forces of
his native County, and there he was ever the popular commander, the kind
friend, the honored gentleman. He possessed a kindness of heart, a gentleness of manner, which caused him to be ever loved and appreciated, especially in the home circle; yet in his bearing there was a dignity, a reserve of manner, that forbade anything like familiarity for even his friends.
He declined the solicitations of his friends to become a candidate for legislative duties, preferring to devote his time to the cultivation of his extensive farms. In political sentiment he was a warm Democrat, and was ever
devoted to what he regarded the best interests of his country. In the
moral relations of life his character was irreproachable. Like his ancestors, he embraced the faith and usages of the Protestant Episcopal Church.
His personal appearance was commanding; he was straight, spare, and
but little above the medium height, but from erectness of carriage and
military precision of gait, had the appearance of being tall. The cast of
his features was good; the expression of his countenance rather grave,
unless when lighted with pleasurable emotions. His advantages for acquiring an education were all that affluence could provide. By judicious
management he increased the ample fortune left him by his father, and
became the possessor of great wealth. He died March 7, 1875.

Robert Ridley[4] (2), third son of Thomas[4] (2), was born in Southampton County, Va.; married Mary-Eliza, daughter of John N. Blunt, of Greensville County, Va., and had issue *four* children, of whom hereafter. At an early period he manifested a decided taste for the legal profession. He was at one time a student at William and Mary College in Williamsburg, Va.; and subsequently at the University of Virginia. After the completion of his classical course, he entered the law-office of the distinguished John Y. Mason, as a student of law. Having passed through the usual routine of study, he appeared at the bar, and gained much distinction and a lucrative practice. He represented Southampton County in the Legislature, and served as a member of the Convention called to amend the State Constitution. As a member of the Convention and in the legislative halls he was no idle looker-on, but zealously defended the interests of the State. His urbane manners and charming conversation won him a place in the hearts of his fellow-men, and his associates were among the most respectable and cultivated of his generation. His health became somewhat impaired during his application in Conventional duties, and with short intervals of improvement continued to decline until the month of August, 1852, when his useful life was terminated. Mr. Ridley's wife was all that could be desired, proving an amiable companion and faithful helpmeet in all relations of life.

Nancy Ridley[5] (1), only daughter of Thomas[4] (2), was born in Southampton County, Va., and died single.

——— Ridley[4] (?), eldest son of Francis[4] (1), was born in Southampton County, Va., and died without issue.

Francis-Thomas Ridley[5] (2), second son of Francis[4] (1), was born in Southampton County, Va., Sept. 5, 1817; married Elizabeth-Norfleet Goodwyn, daughter of Dr. William B. Goodwyn, and had issue *six* children, of whom hereafter. Mr. Ridley inherited his father's possessions, including the old Ridley homestead, where he at present resides. He was at one time a student in Trinity College, Hartford, Conn., and afterwards at the University of Virginia. He studied law, but never practised it as a profession, preferring to devote his time to agricultural pursuits. In person he scarcely reaches the medium height, with a mould of body and limb which inclines to the stout order of men. His colloquial powers are good; his manner affable and agreeable. The eldest living member of this family.

SIXTH GENERATION.

Leonidas Ridley[6] (1), eldest son of Thomas[5] (3), was born in Southampton County, Va., Sept. 16, 1838, and died Sept. 4, 1853. He was a lad of much promise, and at the time of his death was being prepared to enter the University of Virginia.

Roberta-Mary Ridley[6] (1), eldest daughter of Thomas[5] (3), was born in Southampton County, Va., Jan. 31, 1840; she was of a very delicate constitution, and died April 6, 1872.

Eliza-Ann Ridley[6] (1), second daughter of Thomas[5] (3), was born in Southampton County, Va., Oct. 16, 1841; was married to Anseline B. Urquhart in February, 1863, and is the mother of *seven* children.

Margaret-Frances Ridley[6] (1), third daughter of Thomas[5] (3), was born in Southampton County, Va., March 18, 1843; was married to Joseph W. Urquhart in February, 1864, and is the mother of *seven* children.

Nathaniel-Thomas Ridley[6] (3), second son of Thomas[5] (3), was born in Southampton County, Va., Sept. 4, 1844; married his cousin, Mary Ridley, and has but *one* child, a daughter, of whom hereafter. Mr. Ridley is now the oldest male representative of this branch of the family, and better praise cannot be bestowed, or one that he would feel prouder to receive, than that he is in every respect "a son worthy of such a sire." He resides in his native County, and is highly respected for excellent qualities of head and heart.

Emma-Wright Ridley[6] (1), fourth daughter of Thomas[5] (3), was born in Southampton County, Va., May 9, 1846; was married to George-Pollock Burgoyne, of Northampton County, N. C., May 27, 1869; she has *three* children.

Virginia-Jordan Ridley[6] (1), fifth daughter of Thomas[5] (3), was born in Southampton County, Va., July 26, 1847, and died suddenly after arriving at the years of maturity.

John-William Ridley[6] (2), third son of Thomas[5] (3), was born in Southampton County, Va., Dec. 9, 1853; married Bettie Goodwyn, in 1875, and has issue *two* children, of whom hereafter.

Robert Ridley[6] (3), eldest son of Robert[5] (2), was born in Southampton County, Va., Sept. 27, 1844; married Lucy A. Urquhart, daughter of Charles F. Urquhart, and has issue *four* children, of whom hereafter. Mr. Ridley was educated at the Virginia Military Institute at Lexington, and after the burning of the Institute by Hunter in 1864, served with the Corps of Cadets under Breckenridge up to Jan. 1, 1865, when he was transferred to the Thirteenth Virginia Cavalry, and served till the close of the war. He resides in Southampton County, Va.

Mary-Thomas Ridley[6] (2), eldest daughter of Robert[5] (2), was born in Southampton County, Va., Aug. 29, 1846; was married to Nathaniel T. Ridley[6] (3), her cousin before mentioned, and has issue *one* daughter.

Norfleet-Blunt Ridley[6] (1), second son of Robert[5] (2), was born in Southampton County, Va., Oct. 25, 1848; married his cousin, Anna-Field Ridley, daughter of Francis T. Ridley, Dec. 18, 1873, and has issue *two* children, of whom hereafter. He was educated at Hanover Academy, Va., and at the Virginia Military School. He served the latter part of the late war as private in Company B, Corps Cadets. Mr. Ridley resides at Bellemonte, Southampton County, a locality made famous in the history of Virginia, being the place where the "Nat Turner" insurrection was quelled. Mr. Ridley has manifested a deep interest in the author's undertaking, and has rendered valuable assistance by collecting the history and genealogy of his branch-family for this work; the family will appreciate the faithful manner in which their kinsman has accomplished his task.

Sallie-Ann Ridley[6] (2), second daughter of Robert[5] (2), was born in Southampton County, Va., Oct. 23, 1850; was married Nov. 4, 1869, to John-Joseph Long, Jr., of Halifax, N. C., and was the mother of *three* children; she was left a widow, Aug. 24, 1878.

William-Goodwyn Ridley[6] (3), eldest son of Francis[5] (2), was born July 1, 1842, in Southampton County, Va. As a child he was noted for his great neatness of person, and his manner, as he grew older, was unusually refined. At the age of fourteen, having previously been carefully trained, he was sent to Brookland School, in Albemarle County, as a pupil of William Dinwiddie, M. A. At the end of the third session he had passed through the classes of his school; but Mr. Dinwiddie, having discovered in him the requisite ability of mind, was anxious to have him take the Master's Degree at the university, and persuaded him to return to Brookland another year, in order to make his success at college the more easy and certain. In October, 1860, he entered the University of Virginia, with the intention of remaining there until his education was finished. Soon after the first acts of the war he became, at the earnest solicitation of many friends, a member of Company F, a volunteer organization previously raised in Norfolk, and then stationed on Craney Island, under command of Capt. Harry Williamson. Here he had many comforts not usual to the life of a soldier, and the friends of the company *fêted* them continually. But, still, with that ardor of patriotism which characterized so many southern youths, he sighed for a more active life. He was then a beardless boy, of rather small stature, but with a good constitution. Under this rudimentary experience of "playing soldier," as it was afterwards called, his frame expanded, and he became more robust. At the reorganization in 1862, he was offered a lieutenancy in another company, but he preferred to remain with his friends in Company F. Upon the evacuation of Norfolk, this company, with others, was marched to Suffolk, and thence to Petersburgh, where it was first placed in the regiment to which it belonged, and was afterwards known as Company G, Sixth Virginia Infantry, Mahone's Brigade. The first action in which William Ridley took part was at Drury's Bluffs, his company being among those detailed to attack the gun-boats at that place. He wrote to his father, afterwards, that in his first trial he was calm and composed. Malvern Hill furnished his next experience in battle, and a friend then on a visit to the brigade described his bravery, immediately before the battle, as creditable in the highest degree to himself and his lineage. It was the twentieth anniversary of his birthday, and he wrote home that in the midst of the desperate charge the thought flashed across his mind, how unlike this to all previous celebrations of that day. After the battles about Richmond, when many were filling their places with substitutes, he was offered one. "His bleeding and injured country required *his* services, and he was unwilling to give her less."* Mahone's⎮Brigade was then stationed at Falling Creek until the middle of August, when Anderson's Division followed Longstreet's, to re-inforce Jackson and drive Pope from the Rappahannock. This brigade was not brought into action in the series of battles that culminated in the great struggle of Second Manassas, Aug. 30, 1862, until the afternoon of that day; it was then that William Ridley fell. His officers and comrades complimented his bravery on the field, but darkness intervening, no one saw him close his earthly career. On the evening of the 31st he was found dead "on the front line of the action." Thus perished this noble youth, far away from his home, his last earthly consciousness the shouts of his victorious comrades, who presently made his grave beneath the bloody sod.

Louisa-Blunt Ridley[6] (1), eldest daughter of Francis[5] (2), was born in Southampton County, Va., Dec. 28, 1844; was married to Joseph A. Drewry,* of Drewrysville, Southampton County, Dec. 2, 1869, and was left a widow the 18th of the following May.

---

* It is a little singular that there should be a "Drewry-Ridley" in England, one in Vermont, one in New York, and an intermarriage between the family of Ridley and Drewry in Virginia, without any tie of relationship known to exist between the several branches. Doubtless these several families were originally derived from one stock.

Elizabeth-Norfleet Ridley[6] (1), second daughter of Francis[5] (2), was born in Southampton County, Va., Dec. 7, 1846; was married Aug. 19, 1869, to Robert-Johnson Neely, of Bucks County, Penn., then and now of Portsmouth, Va., and has *four* children.

Anna-Field Ridley[6] (1), third daughter of Francis[5] (2), was born in Southampton County, Va., May 8, 1849; was married to her cousin, Norfleet-Blount Ridley, before mentioned, of Bellemonte, Dec. 18, 1873, and has *two* children, of whom hereafter.

Francis-Thomas Ridley[6] (3), second son of Francis[5] (2), was born in Southampton County, Va., March 28, 1851, and died Feb. 12, 1879, with heart-disease. He was a young man full of life and hope, and the pride of his family, who loved him as those only know how who have only one son. This branch has now become extinct in the male line, as he was the last male member and unmarried.

Julia-Maclin Ridley[6] (1), youngest daughter of Francis[5] (2), was born in Southampton County, Va., Aug. 23, 1853, and remains a single lady.

SEVENTH GENERATION.

Roberta-Mary Ridley[7] (1), only daughter of Nathaniel[6] (3), was born in Southampton County, Va.

Annie-B. Ridley[7] (1), eldest daughter of John[6] (2), was born in Southampton County, Va., in February, 1877.

Thomas Ridley[7] (4), eldest son of John[6] (2), was born in Southampton County, Va., in October, 1878.

Nannie-Blunt Ridley[7] (1), eldest daughter of Robert[6] (3), was born in Southampton County, Va., Sept. 11, 1868, and died Aug. 21, 1869.

Norfleet-Blunt Ridley[7] (2), eldest son of Robert[6] (3), was born in Southampton County, Va., April 2, 1870.

Thomas-Urquhart Ridley[7] (5), second son of Robert[6] (3), was born in Southampton County, Va., June 6, 1871.

Ann-Eliza Ridley[7] (2), second daughter of Robert[6] (3), was born in Southampton County, Va., Sept. 26, 1875.

Robert Ridley[7] (4), eldest son of Norfleet[6] (1), was born in Southampton County, Va., Oct. 18, 1874.

William-Goodwyn Ridley[7] (4), second son of Norfleet[6] (1), was born in Southampton County, Va., Oct. 2, 1877.

RIDLEYS OF WARWICK COUNTY, VIRGINIA.

Peter Ridley[1] (1), parents' names unknown, came from England about the year 1770, and settled in Warwick County, Va. He was born March 9, 1765; married, June 16, 1785, to Elizabeth Giles, and had issue several children, of whom hereafter. He died Feb. 7, 1809. These records were from an old Episcopal prayer-book, now preserved in the family, which was evidently brought from England. One entry reads, — "Peter Ridley, his book, 1779." This is all that is known, save that he was a wealthy planter and slave-owner.*

Gerrard Ridley[1] (1), a brother of the preceding, is supposed to have emigrated from England with Peter, and to have lived in the same County. I do not find records of children. In the prayer-book before mentioned, is the following: — "Gerrard Ridley, his book, 1772."

SECOND GENERATION.

Gerrard Ridley[2] (2), eldest son of Peter[1] (1), was born in Virginia, Sept. 11, 1787, and died Sept. 18, 1828.

Dea. John Ridley[2] (1),† a son of Peter[1] (1), was born in Virginia, Jan. 26, 1800; married, Sept. 4, 1824, to Mary-Ann Gardner (her age was sixteen), and had issue *nine* children, of whom hereafter. Mr. Ridley settled in Norfolk, Va., about 1818, and continued there till his death, Nov. 18, 1864. His education was confined to a country school in early life, but he studied and mastered several branches of science. For twenty-five years he was surveyor of the city of Norfolk. He was deacon of the Baptist church forty years; a man of strict integrity, and a devoted Christian; was of retiring disposition; owned slaves, who were alternately employed in making brick and cutting timber. Retired from active business, but held a city office at time of his death.

THIRD GENERATION.

John Ridley[3] (2), eldest son of John[2] (1), was born in Norfolk, Va., in 1828, and died in 1880.

Gerrard Ridley[3] (3), second son of John[2] (1), was born in Norfolk, Va., in 1829, and died in 1881.

Virginia Ridley[3] (1), eldest daughter of John[2] (1), was born in Norfolk, Va., in 1833, and died in 1835.

Fannie Ridley[3] (1), second daughter of John[2] (1), was born in Norfolk, Va.; was married in 1851 to John E. Shields, a hardware merchant, of Norfolk.

Virginia-Park Ridley[3] (2), third daughter of John[2] (1), was born in Norfolk, Va.; was married in 1859 to Andrew J. Nook, a lawyer, and was left a widow a few months after her marriage; now (1880) living with her mother in Norfolk.

Mattie Ridley[3] (1), fourth daughter of John[2] (1), was born in Norfolk, Va.; was married in 1868, to Rev. T. G. Jones, D. D., now pastor of the First Baptist Church of Nashville, Tenn. He has been president of Wake Forest College, N. C., and of Richmond College. A writer of great ability.

Emily Ridley[3] (1), fifth daughter of John[2] (1), was born in Norfolk, Va., and was married in 1869 to George J. Thomas, a cotton-broker. A widow, living with her mother.

---

* The Hon. Hugh-Blair Grisley, Chancellor of Virginia, in a letter, states that the records of deeds and wills of the Ridleys could be found in the Register's office of York County, but they are not there, and the records of Elizabeth City do not produce them. The records of Warwick County were destroyed during the war. This gentleman thinks one of this family was a member of the House of Burgesses before the Revolution, which is a mistake. That man was a member of the family in Southampton County, Va.

† Several sisters of John Ridley died before his marriage, and two — Mrs. Bourbon Jones and Mrs. Sands — a few weeks after his marriage. Two other sisters were married to Mr. Burnham and Mr. Ashley. I have not found the names of these sisters, nor records of their marriages and deaths.

Alice-J. Ridley[2] **(1)**, sixth daughter of John[2] (1), was born in Norfolk, Va., and was married in 1867 to Lawrence Royster, of Kent County, Va.

Sallie Ridley[2] **(1)**, seventh daughter of John[2] (1), was born in Norfolk, Va.; married in 1869, to Samuel Hodges, a wholesale boot and shoe merchant. She died in 1875.

------◆◆------

RIDLEYS OF BURKE COUNTY, NORTH CAROLINA.

William Ridley[1] **(1)**, came from England to New England before the Revolution, and settled as a school-master and tailor in or near Boston, Mass. He had married, but his wife deceased, leaving *one* son, and he then volunteered in the American army for seven years. He married Jane Pursley after the war, settled in Burke County, N. C., and had issue *four* sons, of whom hereafter.

Matthew Ridley[2] **(1)**, a son of William[1] (1), was born in Burke County, N. C. Probably settled in Jackson County, Ga. No knowledge of a family.

William Ridley[2] **(2)**, a son of William[1] (1), was born in Burke County, N. C., and settled in White County, Tenn. Probably had a family.

Francis Ridley[2] **(1)**, a son of William[1] (1), was born in Burke County, N. C., and died young.

Charles Ridley[2] **(1)**, a son of William[1] (1), was born in Burke County, N. C.; married Betsey Berry, and settled in Union County, Ga. Had issue *five* sons and *three* daughters, of whom hereafter. Farmer; died in 1865.

William Ridley[2] **(3)**,* of this family, a grandson of the first William Ridley, is now (1883) a resident of Wolf Creek, N. C., about ninety years of age. He says he was born in South Carolina. Settled in Wolf Creek about thirty years ago. Is not disposed to impart information. A man of good sense, and when in his prime was possessed of a remarkable memory; farmer. Has *one* daughter.

Alfred-Burton Ridley[3] **(1)**, eldest son of Charles[2] (1), was born in Union County, Ga.(?); married Salenia-Catherine Lance, and had issue *six* children, of whom hereafter. Farmer; died in 1851.

Hamp Ridley[3] **(1)**, a son of Charles[2] (1), lives near Trenton, Dade County, Ga. He is a man widely known, and evidently noted for his courage. I have asked for records, but do not find them.

* William Ridley, of Wolf Creek, N. C., has written the following names of members of this branch of the family, but has furnished no records by which they can be connected with the preceding: William Ridley, White County, Tenn.; Matthew Ridley, Jackson County, Ga , deceased; Joseph Ridley, Jackson County, Ga.; Henry Ridley, Murray County, Ga.; Joseph Ridley, Sr., Murray County, Ga.; William Ridley, Kansas; Alexander Ridley, Lumpkin County, Ga.; James Ridley, Pickens County, S. C.; William Ridley, west Tenn. Several letters of inquiry have been forwarded to county clerks for additional information, but without success.

James Ridley³ (1), a son of Charles² (1). ⎱
Andrew Ridley³ (1), a son of Charles² (1). ⎰ No records.
Frank Ridley³ (2), a son of Charles² (1). ⎰
Mary Ridley³ (1), a daughter of Charles² (1), was married to —— Ellerson. No particulars.
Fannie Ridley³ (1), a daughter of Charles² (1), was the wife of James Pritchard, of Tyler, Smith County, Tex.
Jane Ridley³ (1), a daughter of Charles² (1), was married to Riley Lindsey, of Murphy, N. C.

FOURTH GENERATION.

William-Pleasant Ridley⁴ (4), eldest son of Alfred³ (1), was born in Murray County, Ga.; married Mary-Henrietta Killgour, and has issue *five* children, of whom hereafter. Farmer; resides near Spring Place, Murray County, Ga.

Henry-Jacob Ridley⁴ (1), second son of Alfred³ (1), was born in Murray County, Ga.; married, but has no children.

James-Wiley Ridley⁴ (1), third son of Alfred³ (1), was born in Murray County, Ga.; married Martha-Eliza Osborn, and has *three* children, of whom hereafter. He is a farmer in his native County.

Alfred-Burton Ridley⁴ (2), fourth son of Alfred³ (1), was born in Murray County, Ga.; married Cynthia-Elizabeth Bird, and has *two* children, of whom hereafter. Farmer in his native County. Address, Spring Place.

FIFTH GENERATION.

Charles-Burton Ridley⁵ (2). ⎫
Sarah-Low Ridley⁵ (1). ⎪
Ciseral Ridley⁵ (1). ⎬ Children of William⁴ (4), all born
Madora Ridley⁵ (1). ⎪ in Murray County, Ga.
Henry Ridley⁵ (2). ⎭

George-Henry Ridley⁵ (1). ⎫ Children of Wiley⁴ (1), all born in
Alice-Cordelia Ridley⁵ (1). ⎬ Murray County, Ga.
(Infant) Ridley⁵ (?). ⎭

Murphy-Romanuel Ridley⁵ (1). ⎱ Children of Alfred⁴ (2).
Olly-Catherine Ridley⁵ (1). ⎰

RIDLEYS OF RUTHERFORD COUNTY, TENNESSEE.

Capt. George Ridley¹ (1), descended from an old and respectable family that came from England to Virginia in 1635; was born in Isle of Wight — now Southampton — County, Va., in 1727 or 1738, and died Nov. 29, 1835. He claimed to be ninety-seven years old at the time of his death; but his widow and children said he lost the count of eleven years during a severe illness, and that he was one hundred and eight years of age when he deceased. He married Elizabeth Wetherford, and by her had *eight* children. His first wife having died, he married, secondly, in 1777, Sally Vincent (she was born May 28, 1754, and died March 20, 1836), by whom he had *eight* children, of whom, with other issue, hereafter. He emigrated from Virginia when young, and settled in east Tennessee, then a part of North Carolina, on the Holston River, and followed the occupation of a "cowboy," or, to use polite parlance, a "herdsman." About the year 1790, he purchased a large tract of land in middle Tennessee, and removing, settled within one mile of where the city of Nashville now stands. Captain Ridley transported his family, household goods, and farm implements down the Holston River in large flat-boats; thence down the Tennessee River over the "mussel-shoals," and with the aid of his elder sons and eight negro-men brought his boats into the Mississippi River; thence by hard pulling and pushing with oars and poles up the Cumberland River to the present site of Nashville, where he came to anchor in the middle of the stream, and kept guard to protect himself and family from the hostile Indians then passing up and down in their canoes. Being one of the first settlers in middle Tennessee, he immediately erected a strong timber block-house, surrounded by stockades some ten feet in height, as a shelter and protection from the Indians. Here he cleared a large farm and became extensively engaged in agriculture and the raising of stock. The life of this man was attended with all the adventures and dangers incident to the pioneer of those days, and an interesting volume could be written on his experience. He was peculiarly qualified to act his part in leading the van of civilization into the wilderness, by the possession of remarkable courage, energy, fortitude, and physical endurance. Captain Ridley was a man possessed of a high sense of honor, and proverbially regarded as one in whom *truth* stood above all virtues. He was fond of prayer and the Holy Scriptures, and in sentiment a Missionary Baptist; this sentiment he practically exemplified in his relations with his fellow-men. With a force of will unyielding, whatever idea he embraced was held with a tenacity peculiarly his own; his traits of character were prominent and clearly defined; uncompromising and persistent, he would not allow any thing to stand in the way of his plans, and would drive straight on and execute where others failed. His characteristics were transmitted to his posterity, and typical representatives of the old pioneer may now be found in every branch of the Ridley family. I have not learned how the title "captain" came to the subject of this notice, but presume to say he was leader of some company during the Indian wars.

SECOND GENERATION.

Beverly Ridley² (1), eldest son of George¹ (1), was born in eastern Tennessee, July 23, 1762; married Annie Williams(?) (she was born Dec. 18, 1766, died May 30, 1825), and had issue *nine* children, four sons and five daughters, of whom hereafter. He married, secondly, Elizabeth Cooch (she was born May 5, 1798), by whom *one* child. He was a man of strong mind and undaunted courage, widely known and highly repected; died Oct. 27, 1844.

George Ridley² (2), second son of George¹ (1), was born in eastern Tennessee, Jan. 11, 1764; married and settled in northern Alabama.

John Ridley² (1), third son of George¹ (1), was born in eastern Tennessee, June 5, 1765; married a German lady in the State of Georgia, and had issue *three* children, a son and two daughters, of whom hereafter. Parents died young.

William Ridley² (1), fourth son of George¹ (1), was born in eastern Tennessee, Feb. 2, 1767. He moved from Tennessee to settle in Georgia, in the early settlement of that State, and in crossing the Tennessee River was killed by Indians, with his wife and three children. No representatives of his family now survive.

Patsey Ridley[2] (1), eldest daughter of George[1] (1), was born in eastern Tennessee, March 13, 1770; was married to James Wright, and had a family of *four* sons and *four* daughters; settled on a plantation in middle Tennessee.

Betsey Ridley[2] (1), second daughter of George[1] (1), was born in eastern Tennessee, Feb. 13, 1772; was married twice: firstly, to William Smith, of eastern Tennessee, and by him had *four* children; secondly, to —— MacMinn, a brother of Governor MacMinn, and by him had *two* sons. Her descendants are numerous and respected, — some distinguished.

Sally Ridley[2] (1), third daughter of George[1] (1), was born in eastern Tennessee, Nov. 28, 1773; was married in 1791 to Maj. John Buchanan (his second wife), and had *thirteen* children, many of whom were distinguished. She was a woman of remarkable courage and fortitude; cool and self-commanding, and being united to a husband who was a celebrated pioneer and Indian-fighter, her associations were calculated to develope those traits of character so necessary in women of the frontier settlements. Her husband had implicit confidence in his wife's judgement, and confided to her all his plans and undertakings, many of which were carefully overlooked by her, and of which she in person promptly executed during the memorable battle at his fort, on the 30th of September, 1792, when the Indians, — about nine hundred warriors from the combined Cherokees, Chickasaws, and Creeks, — made an attack at midnight, but were badly defeated by only twenty-one men in the fort. In this fierce conflict of battle, the intrepidity of Mrs. Buchanan's courage, and fearless deeds performed by her, crowned her through life as a model Indian-fighter of the West. Her son,* in a letter to the author, says of his mother: "Her many virtues vie with proud fame of Tennessee's greatness; her posterity from five generations is as numerous as the leaves on some forest tree, and, although she died in 1832, she lives in remembrance and affection among hosts of Tennessee's citizenship." She is said to have been the third white woman born in her State.

Lettie Ridley[2] (1), fourth daughter of George[1] (1), was born in eastern Tennessee, Nov. 24, 1776; was married to James Roberts, of Jackson County, and had *three* sons and *five* daughters, all of whom had large families. One of her granddaughters, Hannah Graham, is the wife of Hon. Peter Turney, one of the supreme judges of the State of Tennessee. Lettie was youngest of the first family.

Capt. Vincent Ridley[2] (1), eldest son of George[1] (1) by his second wife, was born in eastern Tennessee, June 26, 1778; married Lydia Everett, and had issue *nine* children, of whom hereafter. He was only ten

---

* Hon. HENRY-RIDLEY BUCHANAN, to whom I am indebted for much information relative to this branch of the Ridley family, was born in "Buchanan's Fort," Nov. 8, 1814, and is the youngest son of Sally Ridley. His fancy inclined him to mercantile pursuits, and in 1841 he engaged in an enterprise for trade in an expedition known as the "Santa Fé Expedition," and, with the entire company, was captured by the governor of New Mexico, and confined in a chain-gang as a slave for two years before his condition was known by his friends at home. Through the intervention of President Andrew Jackson and Judge Powhattan Ellis, who was Minister from the United States to Mexico, he was released and liberated from prison at Peubla de los Angelos in May, 1843. In 1875 he was, without opposition, elected from the Counties of Davidson and Williamson to the Senate of Tennessee.

years old when his father moved from the Holston River to west Tennessee.* Made a tour through Kentucky by way of the "Crab Orchard" when a small boy. Was with Gen. Andrew Jackson in the battle of New Orleans. Owned a large tract of land in the "New Purchase" in Kentucky. No other information.

Thomas Ridley² (1), second son of George¹ (1) by his second wife, was born on the Holston River, in Virginia (now Tennessee), Feb. 16, 1780; married Margaret Harwood (whose father was a wealthy Virginian), a lady of fine accomplishments, with a well and correctly cultivated mind, and by her had issue *seven* children, of whom hereafter. When a boy the subject of this notice moved to Nashville, Tenn. (or near that city), where he received a liberal education; he afterwards followed the profession of school-teacher, in which he acquited himself with credit; his patrons were well pleased with him; his pupils and all who knew him loved and respected him. He left "no stone unturned" to advance those placed under his care, in morals, integrity, and knowledge. After marriage he settled on his farm in Williamson County, Tenn., where he lived in affluence for many years; was confident of success and prospered in all the undertakings of life. While on his farm he was elected sheriff of his County, and held the office for nine years in immediate succession, by re-election; and during his term of service generally sympathized with the suffering and afflicted. His purse was open to all who needed or seemed to need assistance, which resulted in wasting the wealth he had hitherto accumulated. He was in every sense a Christian; he cultivated a love of justice to friend or foe; and no one could truthfully say he had wronged anyone in any manner. After having served his County as sheriff acceptably, Thomas Ridley removed to Franklin County, Tenn., where his wife died, leaving *four* children, who, — their father's attention to his business demanding his absence from home, — were carried to his father's (Capt. George Ridley), where they were tenderly cared for and educated. The latter portion of Mr. Ridley's life was spent alternately with his daughters, Mary M. Rhine, who lived in Mississippi, and Louisa A. Horton. A few years anterior to his decease he was afflicted with dyspepsia with which he suffered greatly, till he yielded to the fell disease, and (in 1854) died at the house of one of his granddaughters. He said to those present he was resigned and that all was well. His strong intellect he retained to the last. He was considered, by those who knew him well, one of the best and most honorable men the age had produced.

Moses Ridley¹ (1), third son of George¹ (1), by his second wife, was born in eastern Tennessee, June 6, 1782; married October, 1808, Kate Haward (she was born March 11, 1793; died Nov. 11, 1841), and had issue *nine* children, of whom hereafter. He resided on the Harpeth River, in Tennessee, until 1818 when he moved to Stewart's Creek, Rutherford County. Died March 16, 1864.

James Ridley² (1), fourth son of George¹ (1) by his second wife, was born in eastern Tennessee, May 24, 1784; married Feb. 9, 1806, Amy Hamilton, and had issue *nine* children, seven sons and two daughters, of whom hereafter. He lived and died in Davidson County, Tenn., near the

---

* CAPT. VINCENT RIDLEY was but ten years of age at the time his father moved from his home on the Holston River, and with a negro-man drove the horses around by land to his new home on the Cumberland River. The Indians were then hostile, and on the way young Ridley and his attendant passed by nearly forty emigrants who had recently been killed by them, but reached their destination without injury.

residence of Gen. Andrew Jackson, with whom he served in the Indian battles of the South, and acquired a lasting favoritism with the old hero for signal service and promptness in the discharge of duties in the commissary department. He was a wagon-master, and on one occasion, when an attack was about to be made by the Indians on Jackson's advanced force, intelligence was sent the commander that a number of his wagons were detained in a muddy stream and unable to move for want of help. The danger of the surroundings was iminent and prompt action was required to have the wagons moved forward. Jackson despatched an officer with a detachment of men back to the wagon-train, already buried in water and mud; it was but a short time, however, before the officer reported to the general in person that it was impossible to move the wagons. On the reception of the report Jackson straightened himself in the saddle and said, "By the Eternal! send Jimmy Ridley to me and I will have every wagon out in an hour." Ridley was soon sent forward but found the train more difficult to move than the General had anticipated. Impatience prompted Jackson to ride back to the place of detention and give his personal direction; on reaching the spot he found several officers sitting on their horses apparently unconcerned, while Ridley was at a wheel, covered with the mud and slimy water, lifting with all his power. No sooner had the General's keen eyes espied him than he dashed his horse to his side, and swinging his sword over his head, shouted at the top his voice "By the Eternal! if I had ten thousand Jimmy Ridleys, I could storm hell and capture the devil." Mr. Ridley never forgot the event and often mentioned it in after life with feelings of pride and pleasure. He and General Jackson lived and died within three miles of each other, the most profound confidence and friendship existing between them through life.

Abigail Ridley[2] (1), eldest daughter of George[1] (1) by his second wife, was born in eastern Tennessee, April 26, 1786; was married to Dr. Charles Mulherin, and had *five* sons whose descendants are farmers of wealth and note.

Winifred Ridley[2] (1), second daughter of George[1] (1) by his second wife, was born (presumably) in eastern Tennessee, Feb. 7, 1789; was married to Thomas Garrett, and had *two* sons and *two* daughters; her descendants occupy positions of respectability in Nashville and its vicinity.

Samuel-Jones Ridley[2] (1), fifth son of George[1] (1) by his second wife, was born in Tennessee (place unknown) Oct. 1, 1791; married Sally Hay, an accomplished scholar and popular teacher of Kentucky. No children.

Henry Ridley[2] (1), sixth son of George[1] (1) by his second wife, and youngest child of this family, was born in Rutherford County (presumably) Tenn., May 29, 1794; married Elizabeth Allison, and had issue *eight* children, of whom hereafter. He was a man of considerable note and of great agricultural worth; was a member of the State convention to amend the State constitution.

THIRD GENERATION.

William Ridley[2] (2), eldest son of Beverly[2] (1), was born in Davidson County, Tenn., Jan. 5, 1793; married Oct. 27, 1831, to Minerva-Tennessee Hamilton (she was born Jan. 13, 1813, and died June 28, 1853), and had issue *four* children, of whom hereafter. Mr. Ridley was a private soldier under Gen. Andrew Jackson in 1814, in fighting the Indians; undoubtedly

32

at the battle of New Orleans. He was a farmer in Williamson County, Tenn.

George-Washington Ridley (3), second son of Beverly (1), was born in Davidson County, Tenn., July 7, 1797; married and had issue several children, of whom hereafter. He was a specimen of rare genius; a native type of indomitable self-will; a man of great boldness and a stranger to all earthly fear. He enlisted under Capt. Tapley B. Andrews and Col. Thomas Williamson in the Second Tennesee Mounted Gun-men, commanded by Gen. Andrew Jackson, against the Seminole Indians. At the battle of Missisook, east Florida, April 1, 1818, he was wounded five times at one firing; once on the foot, once on the upper lip, and three times in the lower part of the abdomen, the bullets passing directly through him. He was mustered out as wounded, for a furlough, June 30, 1818, placed on board a vessel at Fort St. Mark, conveyed to New Orleans, and thence up the Cumberland River to Nashville. One of his legs was contracted an inch and a half in consequence of wounds; and he was ever afterwards subject to fits, so that he could only perform the lighter kinds of labor. In the presidential campaign between Andrew Jackson and John Q. Adams in 1824–5, he was warmly and actively in favor of the former; and after the election of Mr. Adams by the House of Representatives, his disappointment was so great that he burned his pension certificate, with a decided refusal to draw his annuity under the administration of President Adams; but, after the election of General Jackson in 1828–9, he obtained a new certificate and had his pension continued. He was a corporal in the expedition of 1818. His residence in 1866 was in Franklin, Williamson County, Tenn. During the late Rebellion he remained loyal to the Union. He died Oct. 3, 1873, leaving descendants who resemble him.

Robert Ridley (2), third son of Beverly (1), was born in Davidson County, Tenn., April 6, 1799; married Sally Houston, and had issue several children, of whom hereafter He removed to the State of Mississippi; some say he subsequently settled in Alabama, and died there.

Thomas-Jefferson Ridley (2), fourth son of Beverly (1), was born in Davidson County, Tenn., Oct. 25, 1804; married and died issueless. No other information.

Betsey Ridley (2), eldest daughter of Beverly (1), was born in Davidson County, Tenn., March 27, 1787; was married to John Weller, and had a son who married his cousin, a lady noted for her beauty.

Nancy Ridley (1), second daughter of Beverly (1), was born in Davidson County, Tenn., March 13, 1789; was married to John Ellison, a silversmith, of Nashville, Tenn., who was the father of a son and daughter; the latter was married to the distinguished Methodist divine, Rev. A. L. P. Green, who has a son of preaching talent.

Polly Ridley (1), third daughter of Beverly (1), was born in Davidson County, Tenn., Feb. 5, 1791; never married.

Rebecca Ridley (1), fourth daughter of Beverly (1), was born in Davidson County, Tenn., Aug. 4, 1795; was married to Marshall Jimmerson, who lived and died in Robertson County, Tenn., leaving, with other issue, Dr. Samuel Jimmerson, of Edgefield City, an adjunct of Nashville.

Patsey Ridley (2), fifth daughter of Beverly (1), was born in Davidson County, Tenn., March 14, 1801; was married to William Holt, of Williamson County, and became the mother of several highly respectable children.

J.-W.-B. Ridley[3] (1), only son of Beverly[2] (1) by his second wife, was born in Davidson County, Tenn., April 27, 1880.

John Ridley[3] (2), only son of John[2] (1), was born in Georgia (date unknown), and having been left an orphan when young, was brought up among his kinspeople in Tennessee. He was murdered by one Willis Mullen, of Jackson County, Tenn., who eluded the law and escaped.

Elizabeth Ridley[3] (1), eldest daughter of John[2] (1), was born in Georgia (date unknown), left an orphan, carried to Tennessee when a child, and reared among her relatives. She died when about twenty years old, unmarried.

Mary Ridley[3] (2), second daughter of John[2] (1), was born somewhere in Georgia (date unknown), and after the death of her parents was carried to Tennessee and brought up among her Ridley relatives. She became the wife of Alexander Buchanan, her cousin, and bore him *eight* children, whose descendants are now promiscuously scattered through Tennessee, as useful citizens.

George-Martin Ridley[3] (4), eldest son of Vincent[2] (1), was born in Sparta, Tenn., Oct. 2, 1800; married in 1819 to Martha-Louis, daughter of John and Elizabeth Young (she was born Aug. 18, 1800), and died Aug. 9, 1873, having had issue *ten* children, of whom hereafter. He moved with his father to Maury County, Tenn., in 1809. In 1829 he went to Claiborne parish, La., but having lost his health, he returned to his old homestead in Tennessee in 1832. In 1852 he migrated to San Marcus, Tex. He organized a Masonic Lodge at the latter place in 1853, which was one of the first west of the Rio Colorado. He cleared a farm in 1854 on the upper Gaudalope River (then in a Republic), now Kerr County, Tex. In company with his son's family, in 1859, he moved to DeWitt County, Tex.; thence to Fort Worth in 1859, and in the spring of 1865 returned to Kerr County, where he broke up house-keeping, and went to live in his daughter's family. Mr. Ridley was a mason of high standing, and assisted in the organization of many lodges in Texas; also several times elected delegate to the Grand Lodge. He was a consistent Christian, devoted to his Bible, and died in the assurance of a resurrection from the dead to immortality at the second appearing of Jesus Christ on earth.

Elizabeth Ridley[3] (2), eldest daughter of Vincent[2] (1), was born in Sparta, Tenn., and was married to —— Ward, a carpenter by trade. No particulars.

Thomas-Everett Ridley[3] (3), second son of Vincent[2] (1), was born in Sparta, Tenn., in 1803; married Asenath-Reese Hudson, and had issue *four* children, of whom hereafter. Mr. Ridley was a farmer in middle Tennessee till the excitement about California gold-mines caused him to visit that territory. He assisted in the organization of Mariposa County, and was elected to the first session of the State Legislature. On his way home to get his family he was seized with cholera, and died off Key West.

John-Topp Ridley[3] (3), third son of Vincent[2] (1), was born in Smith County, Tenn., June 22, 1806; married Lovinia Klyce, Jan. 24, 1826, and had issue *nine* children, of whom hereafter. He received a fair English education; apprenticed himself to learn the trade of wagon- and coach-builder, and acquired a handsome fortune in that business. Was a farm-overseer in Alabama a year. Carried on business at Columbia four years;

thence moved to Brownsville, Tenn., where he was engaged in business till the spring of 1838, when he moved to a new tract of land in the "New Purchase" of Kentucky, where he carried on farming and manufacturing until he and his family lost their health and were obliged to return to Tennessee. He lost heavily in injudicious investments in mail-contracts and speculation.* He is now a thrifty, money-making farmer, owning the farm upon which he lives, one and a half miles from the city of Hempstead, Tex. He has filled several civil, military, and official positions; was chief justice of Fayette County for six years; served as agent under the United States Government in removing the Creek Indians from Alabama to their reservation. He held a commission as captain in the militia. Has lived in seven states. A member of the Methodist church fifty years. Has lived with his wife fifty-three years. He is a gentleman of great worth, esteemed by all who have come within the circle of his acquaintance — a Christian in every sense.

Winifred-Hays Ridley[2] (2), second daughter of Vincent[2] (1), was born in Maury County, Tenn.; was married to Rev. James Mitchell, and is now living a widow near Johnson's Grove, west Tenn. No children.

Dr. Rufus-King Ridley[2] (1), fourth son of Vincent[2] (1), was born in Maury County, Tenn.; married —— Klyce, and had issue *four* children, of whom hereafter. He resides at Jacksonport, Jackson County, Ark., and is eminent in his profession.

Sarah-Hays Ridley[2] (1), third daughter of Vincent[2] (1), was born in Maury County, Tenn.; was married twice; firstly, to —— Klyce; secondly, to a Methodist preacher, name unknown, and resides near Bell Depot, western Tenn. Had *one* son now deceased.

Lydia Ridley[2] (1), fourth daughter of Vincent[2] (1), was born in Maury County, Tenn.; was married to Henry A. Miller, a merchant, and had *three* children.

Young-Lafayette Ridley[2] (1), youngest son of Vincent[2] (1), was born in Maury County, Tenn., and died in Kentucky, unmarried.

Sally-Vincent Ridley[2] (2), eldest daughter of Thomas[2] (1), was born in Williamson County, Tenn., July 4, 1807; was married to John-McNitt Sharp, a politician and farmer. She is long since dead.

Benjamin-L. Ridley[2] (1), eldest son of Thomas[2] (1), was born in Williamson County, Tenn., in 1809, and died young.

George-J.-M. Ridley[2] (5), second son of Thomas[2] (1), was born in 1811, and died before reaching man's estate.

Mary-M. Ridley[2] (3), second daughter of Thomas[2] (1), was born in Williamson County, Tenn., March 16, 1813; was married to George J. Rhine, and resides in Texas.

Louisa-A. Ridley[2] (1), third daughter of Thomas[2] (1), was born in Williamson County, Tenn., April 28, 1815; was married to Robertson Horton in her native State, and removed to what is now Grenada County, Miss. Her husband accumulated considerable wealth by farming, and died Jan. 9, 1878, leaving *eight* children, one of whom is a lawyer at Grenada, Miss.

Alexander Ridley[2] (1), third son of Thomas[2] (1), was born in Williamson County, Tenn., in 1817, and died young.

---

* Mr. Ridley has run stage-lines, hotels, and served as chairman of Probate Court frequently.

Benjamin-F. Ridley[3] (2), fourth son of Thomas[2] (1), was born in Williamson County, Tenn., March 16, 1819; married and had issue *one* daughter, of whom hereafter. In the death of Benjamin this family became extinct in the male line.

Dr. John-Clark Ridley[3] (4), eldest son of Moses[2] (1), was born on the Harpeth River, Tenn., Oct. 7, 1810; married, firstly, June 16, 1831, to Caroline-Elizabeth, daughter of James and Nancy Morton; secondly, March 4, 1841, to Nancy-Allison, daughter of Henry and Elizabeth Ridley, of Tennessee, and thirdly, Nov. 6, 1855, to Livonia-Candette, daughter of George-Martin and Martha-Louis Ridley. Mr. Ridley has had issue by his two last wives, *five* children, of whom hereafter. He moved with his father's family in 1818 to Stewart's Creek, Rutherford County; thence in 1848 went to Madison County, Miss. In 1850 he went to Florida, and settled the place called (in honor of his name) "Ridleyville," on the Apalachicola River, in Gadsden County. He removed to Kerr County, Tex., then unorganized; in 1858 moved to DeWitt County, and thence, in 1864, returned to Kerr County, where he has since resided, and is engaged in farming, having almost discontinued the practice of his profession.

Rev. George-Vincent Ridley[3] (6), second son of Moses[2] (1), was born in Williamson County, Tenn., July 3, 1811; married July 14, 1806, to Emma Canon, an old schoolmate (she was born April 22, 1812), and had issue *seven* children, of whom hereafter. Entered Cumberland College in 1829; was converted the same year and united with the Cumberland Presbyterian Church. Was impressed with a duty to preach the Gospel, and entered Harpeth Academy in 1831, under the care of Rev. James Otny, afterwards bishop of the Episcopal church. Was licensed to preach in 1833, and occupied a circuit one year; then entered Cumberland College the second time. Had a trouble with his eyes, which almost resulted in blindness. Taught school in 1835; ordained to the work of the ministry in 1836. He is now living at Warrensburgh, Mo. He is a staunch defender of the cause of temperance, having become a total abstainer many years ago, when intoxicants were kept by the barrel in almost every house.

—— **Ridley**[3] (1), third son of Moses[2] (1), was born in Rutherford County, Tenn., May 7, 1813. No other information.

Washington-Green Ridley[3] (1), fourth son of Moses[2] (1), was born in the County of Williamson, Tenn., Nov. 21, 1823; married Jane Carlton, Oct. 10, 1849, and died in the Confederate army during the Rebellion, April 5, 1862, leaving several children, of whom hereafter. He served in the Mexican war under General Pillow; was at the siege of Vera Cruz. He enlisted in the Confederate army in 1861, and served in the Second Tennessee Regiment until the day of his death.

Louisa-Abigail Ridley[3] (2), eldest daughter of Moses[2] (1), was born in Williamson County, Tenn., April 9, 1815; was married April 2, 1835, to Lewis Garner, and had *three* daughters. She is now living in the city of Murfreesborough, Tenn.

William-Henry Ridley[3] (3), fifth son of Moses[2] (1), was born in Rutherford County, Tenn., June 16, 1822, and died Aug. 13, 1823.

Sally-Buchanan Ridley[3] (3), second daughter of Moses[2] (1), was born in Rutherford County, Tenn., Feb. 8, 1817; married to John C. Newsom, but had no children; died Sept. 20, 1852.

Susan-Margaret Ridley[3] **(1)**, third daughter of Moses[2] (1), was born in Rutherford County, Tenn., Sept. 4, 1818; was married to Frank Newsom, and had several children; died April, 1877.

Narcissa-Frances Ridley[3] **(1)**, fourth daughter of Moses[2] (1), was born in Rutherford County, Tenn., Nov. 1, 1825; was married October, 1842, to Dr. John C. Kirkpatrick, and resided near Murfreesborough. She has had a family of children; died in February, 1863.

Samuellen-Jones Ridley[3] **(1)**, fifth daughter of Moses[2] (1), was born in Rutherford County, Tenn., Sept. 18, 1827; was married Nov. 27, 1849, to Col. Karr Patterson, of Arkansas, a lawyer by profession, and representative in the State Legislature. Has children. Now living at Smyrna, Tenn.

Mary-Josephine Ridley[3] **(4)**, sixth daughter of Moses[2] (1), was born in Rutherford County, Tenn., Nov. 16, 1829; was married April, 1858, to H. M. Jones, of Arkansas, and had *five* children.

Amanda-C. Ridley[3] **(1)**, eighth daughter of Moses[2] (1), was born in Rutherford County, Tenn., and died June 23, 1835.

Samuel-Jones Ridley[3] **(2)**, eldest son of James[2] (1), was born in Davidson County, Tenn., and died without a family.

Hance-Hamilton Ridley[3] **(1)**, second son of James[2] (1), was born in Davidson County, Tenn., Sept. 1, 1808; married Sarah B. Everett, June 9, 1830; she had *two* daughters; died Sept. 17, 1834; and he married, secondly, Sept. 19, 1839, to Amanda R. Joslin, and by her had issue *eight* children, of whom, with other issue, hereafter. Mr. Ridley died Oct. 27, 1867, aged 57 years. He lived in Tennessee.

Sarah-Vincent Ridley[3] **(3)**, eldest daughter of James[2] (1), was born in Davidson County, Tenn.; was married to Moses R. Buchanan, her cousin, and had *twelve* children.

George-Thomas Ridley[3] **(7)**, third son of James[2] (1), was born in Davidson County, Tenn., March 30, 1812; married to Mary W. Dodson, July 3, 1834, and had issue *nine* children, of whom hereafter. He died April 18, 1862.

James Ridley[3] **(2)**, fourth son of James[2] (1), was born in the County of Davidson, Tenn.; married July 4, 1836, to Hannah Williams, and had issue *seven* children, of whom hereafter. He resides near Thompson's Station, Williamson County.

John-Buchanan Ridley[3] **(5)**, fifth son of James[2] (1), was born in Davidson County, Tenn., Feb. 17, 1818; married to Mary-Agnes Fitzgerald, Jan. 9, 1845, and has issue *seven* children, of whom hereafter. He is a wealthy gentleman; resident at Thompson's Station, Williamson County, Tenn.

Moses-McNairy Ridley[3] **(2)**, sixth son of James[2] (1), was born in Davidson County, Tenn., March 18, 1816, and married twice: firstly, Aug. 5, 1841, to Ann E. Baker, and by her had issue *thirteen* children, of whom hereafter; secondly, Oct. 31, 1866, to Prudence Eason. The first wife died Jan. 19, 1862. He resides seven miles east of the city of Nashville, Davidson County, Tenn; farmer by occupation.

Anna Ridley[3] **(1)**, only daughter of James[2] (1), was born in Davidson County, Tenn., and was married to Dr. Pleasant H. Mitchell; had *seventeen* children. Residence, near Humboldt, west Tennessee.

Samuel-Jones Ridley[3] **(3)**, youngest son of James[2] (1), was born in Davidson County, Tenn., and died young.

George-Granville Ridley[3] (8), second son * of Henry[2] (1), was born in Rutherford County, Tenn., March 6, 1817; married Sally McEwen, a niece of Gov. Aaron V. Brown, and had issue, of whom hereafter (some say Mr. Ridley married Rebecca McEwen).

William-A. Ridley[3] (4), third son of Henry[2] (1), was born in Rutherford County, Tenn., March 6, 1819; married, firstly, to a daughter of Maj. Thomas Anthony, by whom no issue; secondly, to a Miss Shillcut, and had *one* child, of whom hereafter.

Samuel-Jones Ridley[3] (4), fourth son of Henry[2] (1), was born in Rutherford County, Tenn., Feb. 4, 1812; married Sally McEwen (some say Rebecca), twin sister to his brother's wife, and had issue *one* daughter, of whom hereafter. He had charge of a celebrated battery in the Confederate army, during the Southern war, and fought with desperation at the battle of Vicksburg, Miss., — his home, — where he was killed, after all his men had fallen, while defending his guns with his revolver; and after his death-blindness came on he continued to strike with his sword till he expired; his death occured May 16, 1863.

Dr. James-Allison Ridley[3] (3), fifth son of Henry[2] (1), was born in Rutherford County, Tenn., Dec. 25, 1822; married, firstly, a Miss Rusworm, and by her had *two* sons, of whom hereafter; secondly, a Miss Copeland, by whom no issue; third, a Mrs. Vanleer, daughter of Hon. James P. Clark, of Nashville, by whom no issue. He was captain in the Confederate army, and fought bravely through the war from beginning to its close; he was called "the brave old Captain Ridley" by the soldiers. He did not receive a wound during the war though frequently exposed to showers of lead. He is said to be "an uncompromising Democrat of the Andrew Jackson stripe"; and in 1873 was senator in the Tennessee Legislature. Since the war he has discontinued the practice of medicine and has turned his attention to farming; resides near the city of Nashville. Was considered a skillful physician but did not like his profession. He is tall, erect, and commanding in person; is possessed of strong intellectual powers, and an active, spirited temperament.†

Nancy-Allison Ridley[3] (2), eldest daughter of Henry[2] (1), was born in Rutherford County, Tenn., Nov. 19, 1823; was married, firstly, to her cousin, John-Clark Ridley, March 4, 1841, and secondly, to Col. Valentine S. Allen (he was born in North Carolina, Oct. 10, 1802; died Aug. 23, 1877), a lawyer by profession, who won distinction in public life. Mrs. Allen is a woman who deserves more than a passing notice; her experience during the late war brought out remarkable traits of character. Her residence was near Huntingdon, Tenn., and as her husband was prominent as a public speaker in favor of the war, he retired before the Union army, and she was left alone in charge of their large property, a place that was much frequented by the Federal soldiers, who soon carried away nearly everything available. Mrs. Allen had a very valuable young horse which she managed to keep secreted by running him from county to county; the Union soldiers swore they would have this horse, and she was equally de-

---

* JAMES-DERICK RIDLEY, eldest son of Henry[2] (1), was named in honor of a man who shot an Indian when in the act of shooting or striking Mr. Ridley, the father. This son died in infancy.

† CAPT. JAMES A. RIDLEY, had charge of a company from Rutherford County, Tenn., in the Twenty-third Regiment, under General Cleburn; was laid up with rheumatism after the battle of Shiloh, returned to his command and fought as an independent to the end of the war.

termined they should not. "As soon as the Yankees had left Huntingdon," says Mrs. Allen, "I sent for my 'Rocky Mountain' (the name of her horse), and having heard of some Confederates who were to cross the Tennessee River by night, I sent them a note requesting them to call and see me before their departure. They rode up at eleven o'clock at night, and found me with my three-year old stallion saddled and bridled; I mounted him and rode all night, reaching the river at day-break, and there, unexpectedly, I found Colonel Allen." After remaining with her husband several days she decided to return and try to save her house from being burned. Colonel Allen purchased a horse and buggy for her, hoping she would be able to collect and save her clothing which had been scattered from place to place; but the Yankees took the team and what clothing she had at home, immediately on her return. She says: "I had some meat buried in an old ash-hopper, and some salt and molasses under the kitchen floor; but one of my negroes who had watched me when these things were hid (this negro's wife being Mrs. Allen's cook, was allowed to live in a house in the yard, and all the bed-clothes belonging to the mansion were hid there), approached my door the next morning with revolver in hand. I asked him mildly what he wanted, and was answered with impudence and threats. I was determined to kill him if I could, and ran into the house for my revolver, when a lady who was stopping with me caught hold of me and said, 'for God's sake don't shoot! I see a hundred blue-coats waiting to see what you are going to do'; and in a minute my house was surrounded by Yankees; they found my revolver, and I supposed I should be killed. The negro-woman, Anna, went to her cabin and found it broken open, and the soldiers packing my bed-clothing over the fence. I went out to beg them to spare me these, when one of them drew his revolver, and cursing, threatened to shoot me. The following day they went out on the Jackson road, and my friends from Huntingdon persuaded me to leave my home and go to town, which, having packed what clothing my faithful dog could carry on his back, and what I could carry, I did. That night old Captain Kidd, who was a Federal, came to the house where I was stopping, looking for a negro waiting-man who had been our slave, and when he learned who I was, he said he had heard that I was shamefully treated. I said I had suffered everything but death. When he learned that my piano and some beds had been left at my house, he politely offered to go with me and bring them to town. When we had reached the house the front gallery was covered with fodder-oats and beef-heads; and the interior of the house was shamefully desecrated and dilapidated. When Captain Kidd saw the condition of my house he exclaimed, 'Good God, what villiany! Madam, I have heard you are a perfect lady, and I see by your deportment that you were well raised. I am sorry for you.' An old negro who had loved his master and mistress, soon came in, when Captain Kidd said, 'old man, are there horses and wagons here with which to take these things to town?' He replied, 'No, master, the Yanks have cleared the place; twenty-two fine horses and mules are gone.' 'Are there no oxen and wagon?' asked the old captain. 'I don't know, master,' said the negro; 'I saw them in the field last night.' The old negro found the oxen, and all that was in my house was taken to town." Mrs. Allen says: "My great desire was to get to my husband, and I determined to walk with a pack on my back as a beggar; but the day before I was to start on my journey, a lady friend sent me a note telling me she would let me have a horse which she desired to send to her husband over the river, and I gladly accepted her offer. I sewed up a sheet and packed what clothing I had upon the horse; then went to a neighbor's to tarry for the night, and after a supper and breakfast of opossum and sweet potatoes, with a lunch of the same food, I started on my lonely journey with no companion but my faithful, intelligent dog. I was in constant fear of being overtaken, and knowing I must cross a long, dreary bottom, I rode to the door of Mr. Bartlett's house and desired him to accompany me to the river, but he was afraid to go; consequently I rode on till I came to a long bridge, when the horse refused to go forward, and I was obliged to dismount and lead him a long distance before I could find a place suitable to get on again. The day was drawing to a close when I reached the river, and hailing the ferryman I soon found myself among acquaintances; thence pressing forward, attended by some soldiers, I reached Waverly at dark, and found Colonel Allen at the hotel; he knew my dog and came out to meet me." After boarding at Waverly several months, Mrs. Allen went to the home of her mother, near Smyrna Depot, and while at dinner on Christmas day, — her mother having made a feast, — the Union army advanced, and the shot and shell whistled around the house on every side. Colonel Allen, having no good saddle, found a boy's saddle without stirrups, and without a word of farewell escaped, leaving his wife without a dime in her pocket. She then saw her mother's property destroyed and carried away, except her money and a few things she had assisted in secreting. Her husband, who had been employed in buying supplies for the Confederate army, failed in health and retired from the service, took the oath of allegiance, and, with his wife, went back to his old home near Huntingdon. Finding their mansion very much in ruins, it was rented, and they commenced house-keeping in one of the negro cabins. Mrs. Allen says: "A neighbor let Colonel Allen have some bacon and meal, and we made out after a fashion, by no means pleasant; but I put on my best face to keep up the spirits of my husband; I reminded him that he was splendid at many games of cards, when he remarked, ' wife, I'll try it. I think I'll win some coffee to-day'; and sure enough he brought me sugar, coffee, and candles that night. I felt that I was rich, and was proud that my husband had learned to play cards. We soon moved into our house, and as there was much traveling on the Rosser ferry-road, I took in travelers and made a pretty good start by working myself almost to death; determined, however, that my husband should not know how hard it was for me to be poor." Her husband had resumed the practice of his profession, but failing in health by lapse of age, and broken down by misfortune, he did not long survive, and Mrs. Allen is now a widow, with no property save a residence at Waverly. She is now living with her sister in the city of Murfreesborough, Tenn. The author has devoted considerable space to this article to show the heroism of a noble-hearted woman and devoted wife; and to show the vicissitudes and misfortunes of war.

Mary-Jane Ridley[3] (5), second daughter of Henry[2] (1), was born in Rutherford County, Tenn., Feb. 6, 1829; was married Nov. 8, 1855, to Dr. James-Bromfield Ridley, of Jones County, Ga. (see "Ridleys of North Carolina"), and has issue; she is now a widow.

Sallie-E. Ridley[3] (4), youngest daughter of Henry[2] (1), was born in Rutherford County, Tenn., April 18, 1831; was married to her cousin, Chamelius Huggins, a banker and lawyer in the city of Murfreesborough, Tenn., and has several children. This family lives in affluence.

FOURTH GENERATION.

Thomas-B. Ridley[4] (4), eldest son of William[3] (2), was born in Williamson County, Tenn., July 9, 1832; died July 9, 1834.

Moses Ridley[4] (3), second son of William[3] (2), was born in Williamson County, Tenn., Sept. 5, 1834; died Nov. 29, 1835.

William-Thomas Ridley[4] (5), third son of William[3] (2), was born in Williamson County, Tenn., Aug. 8, 1836; married June 17, 1855, to Isabella P. Holt (she was born Dec. 26, 1839, died April 20, 1874), and has issue *seven* children, of whom hereafter. He is a farmer living near Franklin, Tenn.; was in the Twentieth Tennessee Infantry during the Southern war; was private twelve months, then captain; wounded several times, and has not fully recovered from his injuries.

John-Beverly Ridley[4] (6), fourth son of William[3] (2), was born in Williamson County, Tenn., April 17, 1838; was in the Second Tennessee (Confederate) Regiment, and was killed at the battle of Shiloh, while fighting under the " Stars and Bars," April 7, 1862. A brave and faithful soldier.

Hance-Hamilton Ridley[4] (2), fifth son of William[3] (2), was born in Williamson County, Tenn., Sept. 16, 1840, died April 2. 1843.

Michal-Ann Ridley[4] (1), eldest daughter of William[3] (2), was born in Williamson County, Tenn., Sept. 23, 1842; was married March 21, 1860, to John A. Buchanan, and lives on a farm in her native County. Has issue *seven* children.

James-Knox-Polk Ridley[4] (4), sixth son of William[3] (2), was born in Williamson County, Tenn., Dec. 8, 1844; served as a private soldier in the Twentieth Tennessee (Confederate) Infantry, known as " Bettle's Old Regiment." Now living on a farm where he was born.

George Ridley[4] (9), seventh son of William[3] (2), was born in Williamson County, Tenn., Jan. 19, 1846; died Nov. 6, 1848.

Mary-K. Ridley[4] (6), second daughter of William[3] (2), was born Sept. 11, 1849, in Williamson County, Tenn.; died Aug. 15, 1851.

Julia Ridley[4] (1), twin daughter of William[3] (2), was born in Williamson County, Tenn., Aug. 11, 1849, and died July 2, 1858.

Minerva Ridley[4] (1), twin daughter of William[3] (2), was born in Williamson County, Tenn., Aug. 11, 1849, and died Feb. 1, 1858.

William-Beverly Ridley[4] (6), eldest son of George[3] (3), was born in Williamson County, Tenn., March 15, 1821, and died Dec. 16, 1851; presumably unmarried.

Martha Ridley[4] (1), eldest daughter of George[3] (3), was born in Williamson County, Tenn., Jan. 1, 1823; was married Dec. 15, 1840, to William J. Alston, and died Aug. 25, 1848. Lived in her native County.

Elizabeth Ridley[4] (3), second daughter of George[3] (3), was born in Williamson County, Tenn., June 9, 1825; was married to Wilkin Whitefield, Nov. 15, 1847.

Thomas-Jefferson Ridley[4] (5), second son of George[3] (3), was born in Williamson County, Tenn., Nov. 15, 1827; married June 24, 1853, to Martha-Wilson Buske, and had issue *eight* children, of whom hereafter. He is a farmer in his native County.

Sarah-Columbus Ridley[4] (4), third daughter of George[3] (3), was born in Williamson County, Tenn., Sept. 11, 1829; was married to Francis-Marion Williams, Nov. 25, 1855, and died June 10, 1865, in her native County.

George-Robert Ridley[4] (10), third son of George[3] (3), was born in Williamson County, Tenn., Oct. 5, 1831, and died May 2, 1863, in his native County.

John Ridley[4] (7), youngest son of George[3] (3), was born in Williamson County, Tenn., June 11, 1834, and died Dec. 19, of the same year, in his native shire.

Elizabeth-Young Ridley[4] (4), eldest daughter of George[3] (4), was born in Maury County, Tenn., Aug. 31, 1820; was married March 15, 1843, to James M. Starkey; died Feb. 7, 1844.

Livonia-Candette Ridley[4] (1), second daughter of George[3] (4), was born in Maury County, Tenn., Nov. 11, 1824; was twice married: firstly, Oct. 20, 1841, to Francis A. Price; secondly, Nov. 6, 1855, to John-Clark Ridley.

Octavus-LeGrand Ridley[4] (1), eldest son of George[3] (4), was born in Maury County, Tenn., May 12, 1824 (probably a mistake); died July 30, 1844.

Malinda-Caroline Ridley[4] (1), third daughter of George[3] (4), was born in Maury County (?), Tenn., March 22, 1829; died Sept. 19, 1831.

Lydia-Ann-Rebecca Ridley[4] (2), fourth daughter of George[3] (4), was born in Claiborne parish, La., March 8, 1831, and died March 12, 1832.

Thomas-James Ridley[4] (6), second son of George[3] (4), was born in Maury County, Tenn., Sept. 13, 1833, and died June 24, 1835.

Volney-Barber Ridley[4] (1), third son of George[3] (4), was born in Maury County, Tenn., June 20, 1836. At the beginning of the Rebellion he volunteered and joined the "Texan Rangers" under command of Colonel Terry and remained with them till after the battle of Shiloh, Miss., April 7, 1862 (in which he distinguished himself by his bravery), when he returned home on account of poor health. After remaining at home a few months he joined "Baylors Ladies Texan Rangers," and died in this command, from exposure, near Independence, Tex., in March, 1864. One account says he died "June, 1864."

William-Rufus Ridley[4] (7), fourth son of George[3] (4), was born in Maury County, Tenn., April 9, 1838; married June 7, 1856, to Mary-Francis, daughter of Judge English, of Little Rock, Ark. Address, Frio Town, Tex. He has issue *eight* children, of whom hereafter.

Rev. George-Vincent Ridley[4] (11), fifth son of George[3] (4), was born in Maury County, Tenn., March 21, 1840; married June 7, 1865, to Sommie-Jerome Menilee (she is a niece of Col. John Thatcher, who was an officer of the United States government at Vicksburg, Miss., in its early settlement; the whole family being distinguished for wealth and high moral and intellectual cultivation. Mrs. Ridley was educated at the Ursuline Convent, Galveston, Tex.), and is now settled at Hempstead, Tex., as a preacher of the Southern Methodist Church. He was liberally educated in primary departments and licensed to preach at the age of eighteen. After having a pastoral charge for six months he again devoted his time to the pursuits of knowledge, receiving instructions in the physical sciences and in divinity from ripe scholars, being for some time under the instruction of Doctor Dickenson, D. D., M. D. After three years of hard study his application to his books was interrupted by the civil war; he

NOTE. — Mr. William T. Ridley, who kindly furnished the account of the family of George-Washington Ridley, says the dates, referring to the day of the month, may not all be correct.

did not, however, become entirely disconnected from study as were many students in the State at the time. He passed a brilliant examination before two boards, in the various branches of medical science, and received certificates of proficiency; was subsequently examined by Doctor Stone, of New Orleans, who assured him that their institution would graduate him if he would go there. He united with the Texas Annual Conference in 1863, was stationed at Texana during 1864, and at Wharton in 1865–6. In 1867–8 was stationed at Richmond, and in 1869–70, at Hempstead, Tex. In 1871–2 he located as a physician and continued till his health failed, when he purchased a drug-store which he kept till he rejoined the conference in 1878, and was stationed at Hempstead for 1879. He is a very popular man in both professions, and as a Mason his oratorical ability has been many times called into requisition. He has organized several literary societies of great worth; has been commisioned chief justice of Waller County, Tenn.; declined a nomination for the Legislature and other positions of honor. I have letters from prominent professional men in Texas who are acquainted with Rev. George V. Ridley, in which he is represented as a man of high professional and social standing, and of great personal worth.

Xarifa-Gazelle Ridley⁴ (1), youngest daughter of George⁸ (4), was born in Maury County, Tenn., July 20, 1843; died May 13, 1844.

Helen-Mar Ridley⁴ (1), eldest daughter of Thomas⁸ (4), was born in Tennessee, May 26, 1835; was married to William Cooper, and resides in Lamar County, Tex.; *five* children.

Cap. Dee-Hardman Ridley⁴ (1), eldest son of Thomas⁸ (4), was born in Tennessee, Dec. 9, 1837; married Aug. 8, 1870, to Mary F. Provins, and had issue *three* children, of whom hereafter. He entered the Confederate army in 1861, as a private in the Ninth Texas Infantry, commanded by S. B. Maxey. He was promoted to a lieutenancy, and served the latter part of the war as captain. He has held the office of district clerk for Lamar County, Tex., and served two terms as clerk of that County, where he resides.

Lydia-Everet Ridley⁴ (3), second daughter of Thomas⁸ (4), was born in Tennessee, Nov. 17, 1842; was married to William Roland, and lives in Lamar County, Tex. Four children.

Octavus-LeGrand Ridley⁴ (2), second son of Thomas⁸ (4), was born in Tennessee, Nov. 1, 1844; died in 1862 or '63·

Mary-Elizabeth Ridley⁴ (7), eldest daughter of John⁸ (3), was born in Maury County, Tenn., Oct. 28, 1829; was married to Dr. James Jones, of Mississippi, a gentleman of high culture, who, although wealthy and unembarrassed, became demented, and in a fit of insanity shot her dead in 1858; he is now confined in the Mississippi Asylum for the Insane. Mrs. Jones received a thorough collegiate education and a piece of her composition is still regarded as being one of the finest pieces of English literature by competent critics. She was also highly cultivated. Had issue.

Richard-Renshaw Ridley⁴ (1), eldest son of John⁸ (3), was born in Belmont, Ala., July 24, 1828; married Sept. 10, 1851, to Mary C. Walker, and is now (1879) living at Liberty, Tex. He graduated with highest honors at Jackson College, but returned to his trade as blacksmith. He has been a successful man in every sense; made his fortune but lost heavily by the late war.

Thomas-Jefferson Ridley[4] (7), second son of John[8] (3), was born in Belmont, Ala., June 9, 1830; married June 9, 1852, to Sarah L. Smith, and resides at Liberty, Liberty County, Tex. He was educated at Jackson College, Tennessee, but returned to his trade as coach-trimmer and builder.

Henry-Adam Ridley[4] (2), third son of John[8] (3), was born at Mount Pleasant, Maury County, Tenn., Jan. 14, 1835; married Sept. 15, 1853, to Mary Smith, and resides at Jacksonport, Ark. Educated at Jackson College, Tennessee. A skillful machinist.

Young-Lafayette Ridley[4] (2), fourth son of John[8] (3), was born in Brownsville, Tenn., March 12, 1838; married Feb. 15, 1866, to L. A. Day, and has issue *six* children, of whom hereafter. Mr. Ridley received an academic education, and was licensed to practice law at the age of twenty-one, but did not avail himself of the advantages of the legal profession in consequence of the late Rebellion; he enlisted May 6, 1861, and served through the war as lieutenant in the signal-service of the Confederate army. He is now engaged in farming, stock-raising, and general speculation, at Liberty, Liberty County, Tex.

James-Madison Ridley[4] (5), fifth son of John[8] (3), was born in Kentucky, Sept. 28, 1840; married Aug. 14, 1865, to Medora Powell, and is now (1879) in New York city. He received a good English education; left home when young, and being a musician of superior talent and execution (on any instrument), attached himself to a Spanish orchestra, went to Cuba, and played in the Ticon Theatre several years. He traveled as a high-toned gentleman the principal part of his life; has seen much of the world, and associated with the highest grade of society.

John-Vincent Ridley[4] (8), sixth son of John[8] (3), was born in Mount Pleasant, Tenn.; married March 2, 1871, to Pamila M. O'Brian, and resides at Hempstead, Tex. He received a thorough English education, and is an artist and ornamental painter.

Charles-Sumerfield Ridley[4] (1), seventh son of John[8] (3), was born at Mount Pleasant, Tenn., Jan. 12, 1852; married Nov. 30, 1876, to Helen F. Crawford, and resides at Hempstead, Waller County, Tex. He received a good education, but growing up amid the calamities of war he had not the opportunities of his elder brothers.

Martha-Jane Ridley[4] (2), second daughter of John[8] (3), was born in Columbus, Maury County, Tenn., Nov. 24, 1832, and died in infancy.

The wives of the brothers before mentioned were taken from the best families; all educated ladies of the highest type. The result of the foregoing marriages, for John-Topp Ridley and wife, is forty-nine grandchildren and four great-grandchildren.

Henry-Moses Ridley[4] (3), eldest son of John[8] (4) and his wife Nancy-Allison Ridley, was born in Rutherford County, Tenn., **Jan.** 9, 1842; enlisted in the Twelfth Tennessee Regiment at the commencement of the war, and fought through the battles of Perryville, Columbus, Shiloh, Chickamauga, Missionary Ridge, and in the engagement of Resaca. He had received seven wounds, from all of which he had recovered, till the battle of Resaca, in which the gallant young soldier, bearing the flag of his company, fell by a wound through the head, and was buried by Lieut. Stanford Avins, near the railroad, within the corporation of the village of

Resaca. He was a very brave soldier, and became justly popular with his officers. At the battle of Fort Donelson, his clothing was literally riddled with bullets. When entering battle he always went forward in the front ranks, cheering his comrades; and when a battle was over he would give every relief to the wounded of both sides. He was captured while in a hospital in Alabama, but was paroled on honor; he then made a visit to his mother in Tennessee. His mother had learned of his capture, and was almost insane with grief; but while at the table three days subsequently, he entered the house, and she was clasped in his arms. "It was the happiest moment of my life," says his mother. He was precocious in some branches of study when a boy, possessing some of the most remarkable powers of intellect. He was very kind and affectionate, and considerate of the poor; had many ardent friends; was tall, erect, and manly in his bearing, but not fond of display. It may be truly said of him, —

> "Not man or monarch half so proud
> As he whose flag becomes his shroud."

Caroline-Elizabeth Ridley⁴ (2), eldest daughter of John³ (4) and Nancy-Allison Ridley, was born in Rutherford County, Tenn., Dec. 2, 1846; died April 25, 1848.

Jerome-Bloomfield Ridley⁴ (1), second son of John³ (4), was born in Kerr County, Tex., Aug. 1, 1856; married Dec. 19, 1876, to Elizabeth C., daughter of Thomas Collins and Elizabeth North, and has issue, of whom hereafter.

Kate-Louis Ridley⁴ (1), second daughter of John³ (4), was born in DeWitt County, Tex., Sept. 20, 1860; was married May 22, 1874, to James C. Dollahite, Centre Point, Tex.

Walter-Clark Ridley⁴ (1), third son of John³ (4), was born in De-Witt County, Tex., Sept. 20, 1860; died Oct. 25, 1861.

Mary-Catherine Ridley⁴ (8), eldest daughter of George³ (6), was born in Rutherford County, Tenn., July 6, 1837; was married to Orlando H. Baker, and has *four* daughters. Mrs. Baker graduated at Cumberland (Tennessee) Female College; Mr. Baker at Asbury University, Indiana; they have taught much of their time, and have gained distinction as educators. Residence at Indianola, Ia.

Louisa-Adaline Ridley⁴ (3), second daughter of George³ (6), was born in Rutherford County, Tenn., Feb. 23, 1840; was married to James Ward, a bank cashier, and has issue. Mrs. Ward graduated at Boonville Female College, Mo., in 1863. Residence, Warrensburgh, Mo.

Almira-Jane Ridley⁴ (1), third daughter of George³ (6), was born in Rutherford County, Tenn., March 1, 1843; was married March 6, 1872 to Joseph-Albert Stewart, a salesman, and resides at St. Louis, Mo. No issue.

Eunice-Joanna Ridley⁴ (1), fourth daughter of George³ (6), was born in Rutherford County, Tenn., March 1, 1843 (twin to the preceding); was married in May, 1873, to Brennieman Barr, a live-stock dealer. No issue.

Cyrus-Canon Ridley⁴ (1), only surviving son of George³ (6), was born in Knox County, Ill., July 23, 1852; graduated in the State Normal School at Warrensburgh, Mo., in 1874; taught in Texas, but not liking the profession turned his attention to other business.

Two sons of this family have deceased; names unknown.

Knox Ridley[4] (1) eldest son of Washington[3] (1), was born in Rutherford County, Tenn., Feb. 28, 1851; married Sallie E. Crockett, November, 1874. Residence, Millersburgh.

Lewis Ridley[4] (1), second son of Washington[3] (1), was born in Rutherford County, Tenn., Feb. 20, 1856; unmarried.

Louisa Ridley[4] (4), only daughter of Washington[3] (1), was born in Rutherford County, Tenn., Dec. 9, 1860; unmarried.

Ann-Elizabeth Ridley[4] (1), eldest daughter of Hance[3] (1) and Sarah B. Everett, was born in Tennessee, Jan. 9, 1832, and became the wife of John Fitzgerald.

Eveline-J. Ridley[4] (1), second daughter of Hance[3] (1) and his wife, Sarah B. Everett, was born in Tennessee, Jan. 18, 1834, and was the wife of Charles Cuirin (?).

J.-L. Ridley[4] (?), eldest son of Hance[3] (1) and Amanda R. Joslin, was born in Tennessee, Aug. 7, 1842; married Oct. 30, 1873, to F. H. Dinwiddie. A civil engineer; lives at McKenzie, Tenn. Served four years in Confederate army.

Charles-H. Ridley[4] (2), second son of Hance[3] (1) and Amanda, was born in Tennessee, Oct. 31, 1844; married Nannie Oliver, who died April 19, 1876, and he married, secondly, Jan. 16 to Sallie Ganis. A farmer by occupation.

William Ridley[4] (8), third son of Hance[3] (1) and Amanda, was born in Tennessee, April 1, 1846, and married Sallie Cole. He lives on a farm.

Delia-C. Ridley[4] (1), eldest daughter of Hance[3] (1) and Amanda, was born in Tennessee, Oct. 7, 1848, and became the wife of Thomas J. Oliver.

George-T. Ridley[4] (12), fourth son of Hance[3] (1) and Amanda, was born in Tennessee, June 17, 1850, and married Sallie H. Dinwiddie. He is a farmer. Wife deceased.

Franklin Ridley[4] (1), fifth son of Hance[3] (1) and Amanda, was born in Tennessee, May 27, 1852; married Bettie Sund.

Henry Ridley[4] (3), sixth son of Hance[3] (1) and Amanda, was born in Tennessee, Dec. 29, 1854.

Ada Ridley[4] (1), second daughter of Hance[3] (1) and Amanda, was born in Tennesse, Sept. 11, 1857, and was married to W. H. Sharp, March 26, 1879.

It is presumed the foregoing were born in Williamson or Davidson Counties, but the author has no proof.

James-Robinson Ridley[4] (6), eldest son of George[3] (7), was born in Tennessee, April 8, 1836, and died Sept. 15, 1837.

Ann Ridley[4] (2), eldest daughter of George[3] (7), was born in Tennessee, March 2, 1838, and died Dec. 7, 1840.

Timothy Ridley[4] (1), second son of George[3] (7), was born in Tennessee, March 8, 1840, and died Dec. 15, 1840.

Sarah-Agnes Ridley[4] (5), second daughter of George[3] (7), was born in Tennessee, Oct. 28, 1841, and was married Jan. 15, 1862, to William M. Carson, a farmer. No children.

John-W.Ridley[4] (9), third son of George[3] (7), was born in Tennessee, Jan. 3, 1845, and died in the Confederate army.

George-W. Ridley[4] (13), fourth son of George[3] (7), was born in Tennessee, Sept. 10, 1848; a farmer; unmarried.

Dodson Ridley[4] (1), fifth son of George[3] (7), was born in Tennessee, April 4, 1851, and died Sept. 24, 1875.

C. Ridley[4] (?), child of George[3] (7), was born in Tennessee, Nov. 20, 1853, and died June 15, 1854.

Mary-Buchanan Ridley[4] (9), youngest daughter of George[3] (7), was born in Tennessee, July 18, 1857; died Dec. 17, 1861.

This family is supposed to have been born in Williamson or Davidson Counties, but the proof does not appear.

Adolphus Ridley[4] (1), eldest son of James[3] (2), was born in Williamson County, Tenn., April 20, 1837, and died Dec. 22, 1874.

Rev. James-A. Ridley[4] (7), second son of James[3] (2), was born in Williamson County, Tenn., June 1, 1839, and has moved to Missouri. He is a "Campbellite" preacher.

John-Buchanan Ridley[4] (10), third son of James[3] (2), was born in Williamson County, Tenn., June 7, 1841, and has moved to the State of Missouri; address unknown.

Anna Ridley[4] (2), eldest daughter of James[3] (2), was born in Williamson County, Tenn., Jan. 5, 1843; lives in Kentucky.

Rev. Robert Ridley[4] (2), fourth son of James[3] (2), was born in Williamson County, Tenn., July 4, 1845, and is now (1879) a "Campbellite" preacher somewhere in Missouri.

Sarah Ridley[4] (6), second daughter of James[3] (2), was born in Williamson County, Tenn., July 23, 1847; died in 1849.

Ann-Eliza Ridley[4] (2), third daughter of James[3] (2), was born in Williamson County, Tenn., July 29, 1849; lives in Kentucky.

Julia-Franklin Ridley[4] (2), eldest daughter of John[3] (5), was born in Williamson County, Tenn., Jan. 15, 1846; was married Aug. 30, 1863, to Thomas L. Critz.

James-Bird Ridley[4] (8),[*] eldest son of John[3] (5), was born in Williamson County, Tenn., Aug. 3, 1850, and died Aug. 6, 1852.

James-Bird Ridley[4] (9), second son of John[3] (5), was born in Williamson County, Tenn., Feb. 3, 1855, and died Dec. 29, 1856.

John-Boyd Ridley[4] (11), third son of John[3] (5), was born in Williamson County, Tenn., Sept. 7, 1857.

Fitzgerald Ridley[4] (1), fourth son of John[3] (5), was born in Williamson County, Tenn., Jan. 13, 1860.

Sallie-Morgan Ridley[4] (5), second daughter of John[3] (5), was born in Williamson County, Tenn., May 29, 1862.

Lee Ridley[4] (1), fifth son of John[3] (5), was born in Williamson County, Tenn., Aug. 30, 1864.

John-E. Baker Ridley[4] (12), eldest son of Moses[3] (2) and Ann Baker, was born near Nashville, Tenn., Oct. 6, 1842, and died in the Confederate army Jan. 13, 1862. No family.

Samuel-Jones Ridley[4] (5), second son of Moses[3] (2) and Ann Baker, was born near Nashville, Tenn., Jan. 9, 1845; married Malvina Ross, and has issue *two* small children. He lives on a farm near Nashville.

---

* These two sons were named in honor of their grandfather, James-Bird Fitzgerald.

Anna Ridley[4] (3), eldest daughter of Moses[3] (2) and Ann Baker, was born in Tennessee, near Nashville Dec. 10, 1843; was married to John-Bell Gleaves, and had *five* children. She has deceased.

James Ridley[4] (10), third son of Moses[3] (2) and Ann Baker, was born near Nashville, Tenn., June 25, 1846; married Thomas Buchanan, and has issue *three* children. He resides near the city of Nashville.

Wade-Hamilton Ridley[4] (1), fourth son of Moses[3] (2) and Ann Baker, was born near Nashville, Tenn., Aug. 19, 1848; married Ida Goodlett, and has (1879) *two* children. Resides near the city of Nashville.

William-Beasely Ridley[4] (9), fifth son of Moses[3] (2) and Ann Baker, was born near Nashville, Tenn., Jan. 28, 1858; married Lucy J. White-worth, and lives near the place of his birth; a farmer. No issue in 1878.

Moses-McNairy Ridley[4] (4), sixth son of Moses[3] (2) and his wife, Ann Baker, was born near Nashville, Tenn., June 3, 1853, and in 1878 had not married.

Mary-E. Ridley[4] (9), second daughter of Moses[3] (2) and his first wife, was born near Nashville, Tenn., Sept. 13, 1854; dead.

Watson Ridley[4] (1), seventh son of Moses[3] (2) and Ann Baker, was born in Williamson County, Tenn., Dec. 19, 1855, and is now (1879) a single man.

George-P. Ridley[4] (14), eighth son of Moses[3] (2) and Ann Baker, was born near Nashville, Tenn., Jan. 31, 1858; unmarried in 1879.

Henry Ridley[4] (4), ninth son of Moses[3] (2) and his wife Ann, was born near Nashville, Tenn., June 5, 1859. He was not married in 1879.

Vincent-Buchanan Ridley[4] (3), tenth son of Moses[3] (2) and his wife Ann, was born near Nashville, Tenn., Dec. 5, 1860; deceased.

John-E.-Baker Ridley[4] (13), eleventh son of Moses[3] (2) and his wife Ann, was born near Nashville, Tenn., Jan. 11, 1862; unmarried.

Lieut. Christopher-H. Ridley[4] (1), only son of George[3] (8), was born in Tennessee, (Williamson County), Oct. 7, 1842; entered the Confederate army at the age of twenty-three, and was in command of a company in the First Tennessee Regiment in the battle of Atlanta, and, on the 22d of July, whilst gallantly leading his company he fell pierced through the bowels by a minie ball; he survived till the 24th of July. "His last words were a most fervent prayer to the great God of Battles, for the independence of the Southern Confederacy, and that the Southern army might be enabled to drive the cruel invaders from the soil."

Sallie Ridley[4] (5), only child of William[3] (4), was born in Williamson County, Tenn.,

---

Maggie-S. Ridley[4] (1), only daughter of Samuel[3] (4), was born in Williamson County, Tenn., June 30, 1847, was married to a Mr. Gooch, and lives near Smyna Depot, Rutherford County.

Granville-S. Ridley[4] (1), eldest son of James[3] (3), was born in Williamson County, Tenn., May 12, 1847, and is now in the practice of law in the city of Murfreesborough.

Allison-J. Ridley[4] (1), second son of James[3] (3), was born in Williamson County, Tenn., Oct. 8, 1849; farmer in Texas.

Dodson Ridley[4] (1), fifth son of George[8] (7), was born in Tennessee, April 4, 1851, and died Sept. 24, 1875.

C. Ridley[4] (?), child of George[8] (7), was born in Tennessee, Nov. 20, 1853, and died June 15, 1854.

Mary-Buchanan Ridley[4] (9), youngest daughter of George[8] (7), was born in Tennessee, July 18, 1857; died Dec. 17, 1861.

This family is supposed to have been born in Williamson or Davidson Counties, but the proof does not appear.

Adolphus Ridley[4] (1), eldest son of James[8] (2), was born in Williamson County, Tenn., April 20, 1837, and died Dec. 22, 1874.

Rev. James-A. Ridley[4] (7), second son of James[8] (2), was born in Williamson County, Tenn., June 1, 1839, and has moved to Missouri. He is a "Campbellite" preacher.

John-Buchanan Ridley[4] (10), third son of James[8] (2), was born in Williamson County, Tenn., June 7, 1841, and has moved to the State of Missouri; address unknown.

Anna Ridley[4] (2), eldest daughter of James[8] (2), was born in Williamson County, Tenn., Jan. 5, 1843; lives in Kentucky.

Rev. Robert Ridley[4] (2), fourth son of James[8] (2), was born in Williamson County, Tenn., July 4, 1845, and is now (1879) a "Campbellite" preacher somewhere in Missouri.

Sarah Ridley[4] (6), second daughter of James[8] (2), was born in Williamson County, Tenn., July 23, 1847; died in 1849.

Ann-Eliza Ridley[4] (2), third daughter of James[8] (2), was born in Williamson County, Tenn., July 29, 1849; lives in Kentucky.

Julia-Franklin Ridley[4] (2), eldest daughter of John[8] (5), was born in Williamson County, Tenn., Jan. 15, 1846; was married Aug. 30, 1863, to Thomas L. Critz.

James-Bird Ridley[4] (8),[*] eldest son of John[8] (5), was born in Williamson County, Tenn., Aug. 3, 1850, and died Aug. 6, 1852.

James-Bird Ridley[4] (9), second son of John[8] (5), was born in Williamson County, Tenn., Feb. 3, 1855, and died Dec. 29, 1856.

John-Boyd Ridley[4] (11), third son of John[8] (5), was born in Williamson County, Tenn., Sept. 7, 1857.

Fitzgerald Ridley[4] (1), fourth son of John[8] (5), was born in Williamson County, Tenn., Jan. 13, 1860.

Sallie-Morgan Ridley[4] (5), second daughter of John[8] (5), was born in Williamson County, Tenn., May 29, 1862.

Lee Ridley[4] (1), fifth son of John[8] (5), was born in Williamson County, Tenn., Aug. 30, 1864.

John-E. Baker Ridley[4] (12), eldest son of Moses[8] (2) and Ann Baker, was born near Nashville, Tenn., Oct. 6, 1842, and died in the Confederate army Jan. 13, 1862. No family.

Samuel-Jones Ridley[4] (5), second son of Moses[8] (2) and Ann Baker, was born near Nashville, Tenn., Jan. 9, 1845; married Malvina Ross, and has issue *two* small children. He lives on a farm near Nashvllle.

---

[*] These two sons were named in honor of their grandfather, James-Bird Fitzgerald.

Anna Ridley⁴ (3), eldest daughter of Moses³ (2) and Ann Baker, was born in Tennessee, near Nashville Dec. 10, 1843; was married to John-Bell Gleaves, and had *five* children. She has deceased.

James Ridley⁴ (10), third son of Moses³ (2) and Ann Baker, was born near Nashville, Tenn., June 25, 1846; married Thomas Buchanan, and has issue *three* children. He resides near the city of Nashville.

Wade-Hamilton Ridley⁴ (1), fourth son of Moses³ (2) and Ann Baker, was born near Nashville, Tenn., Aug. 19, 1848; married Ida Goodlett, and has (1879) *two* children. Resides near the city of Nashville.

William-Beasely Ridley⁴ (9), fifth son of Moses³ (2) and Ann Baker, was born near Nashville, Tenn., Jan. 28, 1858; married Lucy J. Whiteworth, and lives near the place of his birth; a farmer. No issue in 1878.

Moses-McNairy Ridley⁴ (4), sixth son of Moses³ (2) and his wife, Ann Baker, was born near Nashville, Tenn., June 3, 1853, and in 1878 had not married.

Mary-E. Ridley⁴ (9), second daughter of Moses³ (2) and his first wife, was born near Nashville, Tenn., Sept. 13, 1854; dead.

Watson Ridley⁴ (1), seventh son of Moses³ (2) and Ann Baker, was born in Williamson County, Tenn., Dec. 19, 1855, and is now (1879) a single man.

George-P. Ridley⁴ (14), eighth son of Moses³ (2) and Ann Baker, was born near Nashville, Tenn., Jan. 31, 1858; unmarried in 1879.

Henry Ridley⁴ (4), ninth son of Moses³ (2) and his wife Ann, was born near Nashville, Tenn., June 5, 1859. He was not married in 1879.

Vincent-Buchanan Ridley⁴ (3), tenth son of Moses³ (2) and his wife Ann, was born near Nashville, Tenn., Dec. 5, 1860; deceased.

John-E.-Baker Ridley⁴ (13), eleventh son of Moses³ (2) and his wife Ann, was born near Nashville, Tenn., Jan. 11, 1862; unmarried.

Lieut. Christopher-H. Ridley⁴ (1), only son of George³ (8), was born in Tennessee, (Williamson County), Oct. 7, 1842; entered the Confederate army at the age of twenty-three, and was in command of a company in the First Tennessee Regiment in the battle of Atlanta, and, on the 22d of July, whilst gallantly leading his company he fell pierced through the bowels by a minie ball; he survived till the 24th of July. "His last words were a most fervent prayer to the great God of Battles, for the independence of the Southern Confederacy, and that the Southern army might be enabled to drive the cruel invaders from the soil."

Sallie Ridley⁴ (5), only child of William³ (4), was born in Williamson County, Tenn.,

---

Maggie-S. Ridley⁴ (1), only daughter of Samuel³ (4), was born in Williamson County, Tenn., June 30, 1847, was married to a Mr. Gooch, and lives near Smyna Depot, Rutherford County.

Granville-S. Ridley⁴ (1), eldest son of James³ (3), was born in Williamson County, Tenn., May 12, 1847, and is now in the practice of law in the city of Murfreesborough.

Allison-J. Ridley⁴ (1), second son of James³ (3), was born in Williamson County, Tenn., Oct. 8, 1849; farmer in Texas.

33

FIFTH GENERATION.

William-Beverly Ridley[5] (10), eldest son of William[4] (5), was born in Williamson County, Tenn., March 7, 1856, and died Sept. 5, 1856.

Mary-Maserva Ridley[5] (10), eldest daughter of William[4] (5), was born in Williamson County, Tenn., July 2, 1857, and died Feb. 12, 1858.

Thomas Ridley[5] (9), second son of William[4] (5), was born in Williamson County, Tenn., May 4, 1859; died Aug. 8, 1867.

Willie-Odia Ridley[5] (1), third son of William[4] (5), was born in Williamson County, Tenn., Sept. 3, 1865; died Oct. 30, 1865.

Nannie-Poke Ridley[5] (1), second daughter of William[4] (5), was born in Williamson County, Tenn., Dec. 11, 1866.

John-Buchanan Ridley[5] (14), fourth son of William[4] (5), was born in Williamson County, Tenn., Feb. 8, 1869; died April 2, 1870.

Bulah-Crockett Ridley[5] (1), third daughter of William[4] (5), was born in Williamson County, Tenn., Nov. 8, 1871.

William-Buchanan Ridley[5] (11), eldest son of Thomas[4] (5), was born in Williamson County, Tenn., Nov. 25, 1854.

Mary-Georgia-Ann Ridley[5] (11), eldest daughter of Thomas[4] (5), was born in Williamson County, Tenn., Feb. 18, 1856.

Johnnie (?) Florence Ridley[5] (13), second daughter of Thomas[4] (5), was born in Williamson County, Tenn., July 18, 1858.

Sarah-Eliza Ridley[5] (6), third daughter of Thomas[4] (5), was born in Williamson County, Tenn., Dec. 7, 1860.

Robert-Nathaniel Ridley[5] (3), second son of Thomas[4] (5), was born in Williamson County, Tenn., Feb. 29, 1863.

Caroline Ridley[5] (3), fourth daughter of Thomas[4] (5), was born in Williamson County, Tenn., April 6, 1865.

Lillie-Inez Ridley[5] (1), fifth daughter of Thomas[4] (5), was born in Williamson County, Tenn., Aug. 7, 1870.

Thomas-Buske Ridley[5] (9), third son of Thomas[4] (5), was born in Williamson County, Tenn., Sept. 2, 1872.

Miles-Lewis Ridley[5] (1), fourth son of Thomas[4] (5), was born in Williamson County, Tenn., April 16, 1875.

Charles-L. Ridley[5] (3), eldest son of William[4] (7), was born in Texas, Nov. 21, 1857; address, Frio Town, Tex.

Mattie-B. Ridley[5] (1), eldest daughter of William[4] (7), was born in Texas, Feb. 3, 1860.

William-Rufus Ridley[5] (12), second son of William[4] (7), was born in Texas, Oct. 15, 1862; died March 31, 1864.

Xarifa-D. Ridley[5] (1), second daughter of William[4] (7), was born in Texas, Sept. 20, 1866.

Julia Ridley[5] (3), third daughter of William[4] (7), was born in Texas in 1869.

Minnie-Louis Ridley[5] (1), fourth daughter of William[4] (7), was born in Texas, Sept. 1, 1872.

Harry-Martin Ridley[5] (1), third son of William[4] (7), was born in Texas in 1874.

Della Ridley[5] (1), fifth daughter of William[4] (7), was born in Texas in September, 1877.

Edna-E. Ridley⁶ (1), eldest daughter of Dee⁴ (1), was born in Lamar County, Tex., and is eight years old (1880).

Thomas-W. Ridley⁵ (10), a son of Dee⁴ (1), was born in Lamar County, Tex., and is now (1880) six years old.

Eugene Ridley⁵ (1), a son of Dee⁴ (1), was born in Lamar County, Tex., and died at the age of six months.

Ella-Hugh Ridley⁵ (2), eldest daughter of Young⁴ (2), was born in Liberty County, Tex., Dec. 24. 1866.

John-Day Ridley⁵ (15), eldest son of Young⁴ (2), was born in Liberty County, Tex., July 11, 1868.

Bettie-Lavinia Ridley⁵ (1), second daughter of Young⁴ (2), was born in Liberty County, Tex., July 27, 1870.

Charles-Sumerfield Ridley⁵ (4), second son of Young⁴ (2), was born in Liberty County, Tex., Feb. 4, 1872.

Mattie-Emma Ridley⁵ (2), third daughter of Young⁴ (2), was born in Liberty County, Tex., Aug. 2, 1873.

Ida-Gertrude Ridley⁵ (1), fourth daughter of Young⁴ (2), was born in Liberty County, Tex., Sept. 21, 1878.

Rufus-Jerome Ridley⁵ (3), a son of Jerome⁴ (1), was born in Kerr County, Tex., April 22, 1878.

RIDLEYS OF OXFORD, NORTH CAROLINA.
[VIRGINIAN BRANCH.]

Bromfield Ridley¹ (1), son of James Ridley, was descended from an old and distinguished family that came from England to Virginia in 1635 (see "Ridleys of Southampton County, Virginia"). He was probably educated in Virginia, but with other members of the same family early settled in North Carolina. The date of his birth is not known. He was settled as a lawyer at Oxford, Granville County, as early as 1770, and evidently several years earlier than that date. He is said to have been a man distinguished in his profession, but no published account of his life can now be found. He resided at a beautiful country-seat called "Nine Oaks," about eleven miles from Oxford, now owned and well kept by Samuel-Smith Cooper. Mr. Ridley married Frances Henderson, daughter of Judge Henderson, of Revolutionary days, and granddaughter of Judge John Williamson, whose wife was the daughter of Lord George Keiling (or Kelling) who had his property confiscated in England, and lost his seat in the House of Lords, in consequence of his Protestant religious principles, and had issue by that lady *eight* children, of whom hereafter. Mr. Ridley acquired wealth, and gave his sons a liberal education, and means sufficient for a good start in life. He died in 1796, and is thought to have been rising sixty. Tradition represents him as a gentleman of great dignity of deportment and fine appearance.

SECOND GENERATION.

Dr. James Ridley² (1), eldest son of Bromfield¹ (1), was born at Oxford, N. C., about the year 1776; married Elizabeth-Taylor Lewis, of Granville County, — a lady of remarkable beauty, and connected by ties of blood

with some of the most respectable and affluent families in the State,* — and
by her had issue *seven* children, of whom hereafter.   Doctor Ridley was
educated under the most able instructors of his day, and settled as a physician at Oxford about 1810 or 1812.†   He was a very skillful and successful practitioner, and rose to eminence in his profession.   Being introduced
into the best families in consequence of the standing of his own connections and his personal popularity, he acquired great influence as a citizen
and professional man, and soon became very wealthy.   He was a man of
integrity and great worth.   His personal appearance was fine; about five
feet nine inches in height, of perfect health and physique.   His jaw was
massive and elongated; his nose of Roman mould.   He gave his sons a college education and a good start in life.·   Doctor Ridley died Dec. 25, 1855,
aged about 81.   His widow died at LaGrange, Ga., Oct. 3, 1872, very aged.
A relative says of her, "She was a General Jackson of a woman and extraordinary in point of intellect."

   Dr. Archibald-Bromfield Ridley[2] (1), second son of Bromfield[1] (1)
and his wife, Frances Henderson, was born at Oxford, in Granville
County, N. C., about 1780; married, firstly, to Henrietta-Maria-Anderson
Lewis, and by her had *one* daughter; he was married,‡ secondly, in 1822,

---

   * JAMES TAYLOR had a daughter Elizabeth, who was married to —— Anderson,
whose daughter, Mary Anderson, became the wife of Charles Lewis and the mother
of Elizabeth-Taylor Lewis, who was married to Dr. James Ridley, of Oxford, N. C.,
and became the mother of Dr. Charles-Lewis Ridley, of Jones County, Ga.; Hon.
Bromfield-Lewis Ridley, of Murfreesborough, Tenn.; Rev. Joseph-James Ridley,
D. D., of Somerville, Tenn.; Dr. William-Snerd Ridley, of Georgia; and Dr. Robert-
Archibald Ridley, of La Grange, Ga.   This note shows how the names Taylor and
Lewis came to the Ridley family.   Mrs. Elizabeth-Taylor (Lewis) Ridley had two
brothers, Joseph-Lewis, and Thomas-Lewis who married Elizabeth Cobb, a cousin
to Gov. Henry Cobb, and by her had *two* sons, Willis and Charles, who were resident
in Granville County, N. C., when my informant, Mrs. Susan A. Ridley, widow of
Dr. Charles-Lewis Ridley, knew them.
   † The residence of Dr. James Ridley was situated about one thousand three hundred yards from the centre of the town of Oxford, and surrounded by a grove of
oaks.   The home place contained about thirty-three acres, but the present proprietors have sold off nearly one half, for which they realized $3,900.   Dr. James Rid-
ley owned a plantation in the rear of his residence, which contained three or four
hundred acres and is bounded by a stream.   The Ridley mansion, which remains
much as when occupied by the Ridley family, stands about two hundred yards from
the "old street" where the big toll-gate was, but since tolls were sold off Mr.
Kingsbury has opened a new street, running along the edge of the grove and near
the house.   I had hoped to publish a plate-view of the house and grounds above-
mentioned, but could not procure a photograph in time.   This family-seat was
called "Rural Retreat."
   ‡ MRS. SUSAN A. RIDLEY, of Jones County, Ga., a woman of culture and remarkably informed respecting the Ridleys and their collateral connections, who has provided much matter of interest now incorporated into this book, says: "Dr. Archibald-Bromfield Ridley and Mary-Ann-Ridley Blunt, — who was the only daughter
of Col. Richard A. Blunt, a good, clever Methodist man, who was never appreciated
till he had passed away, — were for a long time engaged to be married, the former
being at that time a widower with one child, now Mrs. Todd; but General Sanford
supplanted him, being younger, fine-looking, smart, of good family, and a perfect
gentleman; possessed of charming conversational powers and considerable wealth.
Mrs. Sanford was quite a belle in her day, fond of show and traveling, while her
husband was not.   Colonel Blunt and his son-in-law, General Sanford, preferred to
live on their farms alone with their servants, while their wives preferred the city of
Milledgeville for their residence; consequently they each had their choice, visiting
each other at pleasure.   Both families have visited at my house and I have visited
them, and what I write I know to be strictly true."   (See note on Sanford family
in sketch of Virginian Ridleys.)

to Harriet Blacksheare, and died in Early County, Ga., leaving an only son. His second wife was educated at Sparta, Ga., where Doctor Ridley lived and practised his profession; she was an orphan and an heiress, and in her right her husband had quite a fortune, which, said a member of the family who is well acquainted, "did not last long." Doctor Ridley was a talented man and an eminent physician; lived respected and died deservedly lamented.

Dr. Robert Ridley[2] (**1**), third son of Bromfield[1] (**1**), was born in Oxford, Granville County, N. C., about 1782; married to Sophia Cooper, of Hancock County, Ga., where he settled in the practice of his profession, and where he died. Doctor Ridley was considered a good physician; he left an only son bearing his name, of whom hereafter.

Thomas Ridley[2] (**1**), fourth son of Bromfield[1] (**1**), was born in Granville County, N. C., and was presumably a farmer; nothing is said in my correspondence about a profession. He married twice: firstly, to Betsey Blunt, who died without issue, and secondly, to a sister of his first wife, Polly Blunt, who also died childless. Mr. Ridley lived and died in his native County.

Betsey Ridley[2] (**1**), eldest daughter of Bromfield[1] (**1**), was born in Granville County, N. C., and married Mingo Burton, a lawyer of the same County; they moved to Lebanon County, Tenn., and raised a large family.

Fannie Ridley[2] (**1**), second daughter of Bromfield[1] (**1**), was born in Granville County, N. C.; married to William-Morgan Snerd, clerk of the county court of said County, and died childless in Mississippi.

Polly Ridley[2] (**1**), third daughter of Bromfield[1] (**1**), was born in Granville County, N. C.; married a Scotchman by the name of James Hamilton, a wealthy merchant in the city of New York, and had *two* children.

Sally Ridley[2] (**1**), fourth daughter of Bromfield[1] (**1**), was born in Granville County, N. C.; married to Benjamin Blunt (presumably a brother of the wife of her brother Thomas), and moved to Alabama, thence to Mississippi, where she died.

THIRD GENERATION.

Dr. Charles-Lewis Ridley[3] (**1**), eldest son of James[2] (**1**) and his wife, Elizabeth-TaylorLewis, was born at Oxford, Granville County, N. C., July 5, 1802; was educated at Chapel Hill, N. C., and graduated at the Pennsylvania Medical University in 1824. He married in Hancock County, Ga., where he was then reading medicine with his uncle, Dr. Archibald Ridley, in 1823, to Susan A. Bonner, a lady of Scottish descent, well allied with highly respectable families, and settled in Jones County, Ga., where he successfully practised his profession for nearly forty years; and when he had accumulated a fortune resigned his professional duties and devoted his attention to agricultural pursuits. He was a man of untiring industry and perseverance; of quick, ardent temperament; of sterling and stirring qualities, which gave him eminence as a physician and success as a farmer. His theory was to work with the head and with the hands; that it was the only way one could "enter the halls of learning or sit down with honor in the palace of wealth." Endowed with high qualities of head and heart, he was hasty in action but equally ready to make amends when convinced that he had done wrong. Doctor Ridley continued to prosper in his work until the Southern Rebellion, when his property shared the same fate of nearly all wealthy planters in the line of march of armies. When Sherman's army passed through Georgia, the soldiers visited Doctor

Ridley's house and took all they wished for; gave Mrs. Ridley only "three minutes to tell them where her husband was, and what he had done with his money" (they had heard that he had a bushel of silver in the house), and threatened to burn the house. Mrs. Ridley, indignant at the threat, dared them to burn; she had only two hours warning, and had given a faithful old servant such things as he could carry about his person, and sent him away. After much persuasion she had prevailed upon her husband to leave with his money, except a few hundred dollars which he overlooked; this money they found by breaking open his desk and wardrobe; took seven valuable horses, and went away swearing vengeance on Doctor Ridley if they found him, which, fortunately, they did not do. After this the unfinished houses of overseers were fitted up; and the farm restocked with the money that was saved, and they hoped to live in peace. But again they were doomed to disappointment; again the army marched that way, destroyed their stock of every kind; took from the plow eighteen "likely men and boys," and the mules with which they were plowing in wheat; (they took away twenty-nine horses and mules, and thirty-seven negroes) burned the houses and fencing; laid waste to everything; carried away the carriages, leaving nothing but the bare land. The loss of his property and the freeing of his slaves hastened Doctor Ridley's death; he could not be reconciled to his reduced circumstances, after having lived so long in comparative luxury; he gradually declined, and died March 13, 1873. Mrs. Ridley * continues to live on her farm, and has allowed thirteen families of their former slaves to build their huts on her land; not one of them self-sustaining. She is a woman of remarkable fortitude and courage; of talent, culture, and refinement, and endured their misfortunes with wonderful patience. She has provided much valuable material for this book, and has manifested a deep interest in the work since her first knowledge of my undertaking. At the age of seventy-one years she completed a braid of hair made from the combings of her own head (every hair that came out in three years was carefully preserved), which contained exactly two hundred and nineteen thousand hairs, and measured three feet in length. Doctor Ridley had issue *three* sons, of whom hereafter.

Hon. Bromfield-Lewis Ridley[3] (2), second son of James[2] (1), was born at Oxford, Granville County, N. C., Aug. 4, 1804; married Oct. 12, 1829, to Rebecca Crothwait, and had issue *nine* children, of whom hereafter. He was educated and graduated at Chapel Hill, in his native State, in a class numbering over sixty students all of whom, with one or two exceptions, have since been governors, judges, or army-officers. At the close of his collegiate course, in which he took first honors, he made choice of the

---

* There are some most remarkable traits in the character of Mrs. Susan A. Ridley. She ordered a carved black-walnut burial casket in Macon, Ga., several years ago, which had a cover shutting like a trunk and fastened with catches. This was large enough to admit a mattress, feather-bed, two pillows, and was padded within. Her burial clothes were also made with her own hands and carefully placed in the casket. For two years this was deposited in a carriage-house, but in consequence of a leak in the roof, was removed to her dining-room, where, it being as wide and high as a common table, it was used by the servants as a side-board, being covered with an oil-cloth. She says: "My reason for this is that my family all die suddenly, and anticipating such a death myself, but knowing I should not die an hour sooner, I deemed it wise to have all necessary arrangements made while alive." One of her brothers had his coffin made eleven years before his death, from boards sawed from a large walnut tree under which he played when a boy.

legal profession, and at an early period located at McMinnville, Tenn., where he continued the practice of his profession until the voice of his adopted State called him to preside as chancellor over one of the most important divisions; and he continued on the bench from his first election, in 1840, down to the second year of the Southern war; a period of more than twenty years. His commission as chancellor was from Gov. James K. Polk. He also served with distinction in the legislature of the State, and I have before me a letter to him from President Andrew Johnson, in which he refers to the acquaintance formed between them in the State Assembly. As a lawyer he was courteous, manly, and respectful to the members of the bar with whom he practised. He was a genial, social companion; warm-hearted and true in friendship. He possessed courage coupled with forebearance; independence with defference, and always held his opinion fast. He professed religion and united with the Cumberland Presbyterian Church in the autumn of 1843, in which capacity he lived a highly respected and active member; he was a ruling elder, and was frequently a lay representative from his presbytery in the general assembly of the church. Chancellor Ridley died Aug. 11, 1869. In personal appearance he was noble and commanding; born of robust stock he had a fine physique; was six feet in height, and weighed over two hundred pounds. His death was recognized and his character eulogized in the courts, and high tributes pronounced by distinguished contemporaries. In a sermon preached by his pastor at his funeral I find many beautiful expressions relative to the high esteem in which he was held in the several prominent capacities of his life. As a citizen he was said to possess a character "as high as any in the city, State, or land; none were possessed of sounder principles, purer motives, loftier patriotism, or more unselfish public-spirit. Few could claim a broader range of intelligence; none were endowed with more indomitable energy. As a statesman few men had studied more carefully and analytically the constitution and laws of the State and of the United States than he; and having no small experience in legislation, and having had the society of the greatest and best men in the land, he was not only learned but eminently practical and useful. As a Christian his practical piety, though not as active and aggressive as some, was, nevertheless, a living commentary on, and recommendation of, the Christian religion. He did not, like a comet, dash and blaze periodically, and then retire to be seen no more during long, dark intervals, but shone as steadily and truthfully as the polar star, and as modestly as that unpretending light. His religion bore the tests incidental to his diversified life; in the law, in politics, in peace, and in war, among friends or foes, with the serious or gay, in contact with Christians or men of the world, always and everywhere he maintained his integrity as a Christian." He was a noble and devoted husband; a kind, faithful, and exemplary father. Before the Rebellion Judge Ridley was considered a very wealthy man. He owned more than a hundred slaves, and after their emancipation by the President of the United States, these all took the names of their former master. The following beautiful description of Judge Ridley's home was written by his daughter and published in the *Murfreesborough Monitor* in 1867: —

"'Fairmont' is two or three miles north of a direct line from Nashville to Murfreesborough, twenty miles from the former and twelve miles from the latter, the farm lying on each side of Stones River, which cuts the Milton and Nashville turnpike at an acute angle from south to north about half a mile to the east of the homestead.

Rutherford is one of the finest counties in the State. In many portions the lands are of rare fertility, and splendid groves of oak, ash, elm, sugar-maple, and umbrageous vines give bold and vigorous testimony of richness. The face of the country is undulating, the rugged aspect of the mountain regions having gradually softened into gentle, flowing, lovely outlines. Before the desolations of the war, a traveler on any of the roads leading into Murfreesborough was impressed with the evidences of thrift, energy, and cultivated taste which he everywhere saw.

"Broad cotton and grain fields, substantial farm-houses and tasteful grounds were constantly recurring. My father's residence was in one of the most beautiful sections of the County. Stones River on the east makes a long, narrow curve through low bluffs of rock and overhanging shrubbery, and appearing again at the mill—still a little east of the houses,—runs parallel with the road for half a mile opposite the 'Fairmont' grounds; here its sloping, grassy banks, inviting seats of rock, clear, rippling, rushing current with its sheets of foaming water at the mill-dam, constitute most delightful features of the landscape. The house stood to the left and north of the road upon an approach from the east. It was situated upon one of those elevations which seems to have been fashioned by nature for architectural effects, gently sloping on all sides from base to summit, a distance of two hundred and fifty yards, and reaching in altitude about fifty feet. Flanking the road and opposite the river is a beautiful lawn containing eighty acres and embracing half the hill, excepting the yard and garden. It is thickly set with blue grass and clover, relieved on one side by a clump of small, thick-set trees, growing in tangled luxuriance over some rocks, and here and there a solitary fruit tree, dotting the smooth, open surface. The approach to the house is through a gate entering the lawn to the east and along a drive winding up the hill to the front yard gate, whence a broad gravel walk, bordered on each side by small cedars tastefully shaped, leads to the portico. The yard embraces about three acres on the brow of the hill, and is covered with green turf and adorned with those finest ornaments of all others —old, majestic, native forest trees, which stand out on the scene with bold, leafy branches and boughs, continually awakening a sensation of power and protection. There are two other gates to be seen in front, one opening into the garden on the left and another on the right into the lawn Gravel walks from the portico lead to both, with rows of small cedars similar to those in front. The house was constructed on the cottage style. It consisted of a main building one and a half stories high, with wings of one story, eight or ten feet in the rear. The portico was neatly and elegantly designed, shaded on either side by lattices and sweet-scented vines, honey-suckle, virgin-bower and roses. The roof was painted, presenting gables east and west, and in front, on each side of the portico, two dormer windows and two dormer doors in the centre. Continuing the line of the main building to the limits of the wings were two small galleries with ornamental railings, and as the whole building was elevated several feet, there were flights of stone steps leading from these as well as the front portico. On entering the house, a wide, commodious hall, extended the full length of the building—about forty-five feet,—and at the end of it a winding stair-case led to the upper hall and attic-rooms. Five doors besides the front, opened into this hall, from parlors, dining-room, chamber and back gallery, the latter extending the full length of the building in the rear.

"Such was 'Fairmont' in its palmiest days. Now, nothing remains of the house but blackened ruins. Three chimneys only stand, solitary and dismal, over the piles of rubbish. They are grim monuments over a grave—a melancholy one to us—of household treasures and dear old familiar places, hallowed by teeming recollections. The old stone steps look strangely familiar. They have worn smooth with the steps of family and friends, and often at night old Carlo sits upon them and howls piteously over the desolation."

The following account of the burning of "Fairmont" during the Rebellion was written by the same hand and copied from the same paper as the preceding:—

"You ask me to give you the particulars of 'the burning of Fairmont,' our old homestead, and it is with a very sad kind of pleasure I am seated to comply with that request. In order to understand fully our 'measure of sorrow' at that time, I must relate the situation of affairs around us, prior to the burning. Fairmont is situated immediately on the bank of Stones River, the little stream which will be ever memorable as in the battle-field upon which Bragg and Rosecrans contended with such fearful desperation for five days. During that time we witnessed from our gallery a severe skirmish between the contending parties. The flash, smoke and deafening noise of the artillery, the clicking of small arms, deploying troops in an open field, the shouts and curses of the infuriated soldiers, was a scene we will not soon forget. At last the bloody struggle ended. Bragg retreated and we were surrounded by a desperate, unscrupulous, but victorious foe. My father was compelled to leave home for safety, and took with him my young sister, thirteen years of age, fearing to leave her in the midst of such horrors. My five brothers and husband were with their respective commands, leaving ma, grandma and myself, alone, with no protector.

"This sad necessity at any time, was doubly so now, for my poor grandma was daily expected to die, and I at the same time was so ill it was not known which would survive longest. Ah! who can describe the anguish of my mother then? Husband, sons, young daughter, gone — mother and eldest daughter dying; that was a time when she could truly say, 'I've no help but God.' And through that dense darkness that enveloped her, one ray of light beamed — God heard the mother's prayer and spared to her her eldest daughter. Death — that 'reaper with the sickle keen,' entered our house though, and took for his prey our grandma, who had laid for months on a bed of suffering.

"Every road, every turnpike was strongly picketed by the Federals, and no one was permitted to pass three miles in any direction. Ma laid my grandma to rest in a coffin made by a near neighbor out of a cherry wardrobe. The outer box was made of a black board and flooring plank taken out of a house for that purpose. That precious body that we had lifted so tenderly for fear of giving her pain for months, was conveyed to her last resting place in a rough wagon, and of all her descendants, none was permitted the sad pleasure of standing by her grave, except mamma. But she rests calmly and sweetly now on the bosom of that Saviour she delighted to glorify while on earth. The thunder of artillery can't disturb her; the temporary triumph of our enemies cannot sadden her — she is safely housed.

"After grandma's death, 14th January, I continued perfectly helpless for weeks. Daily, crowds of insolent soldiers came to our house for forage, chickens, horses, meat, etc. They always got what they desired without resistance, for ma felt that excitement of any kind would endanger my life, and she would give them no cause for anger. They were always insolent and invariably taunted ma with the fact that her sons were in the rebel army. This was their apology for depredations of every kind. They instigated the negroes to steal our buried silverware, and this determined ma to make an effort to save some of the necessaries of life. In the roof of the house she concealed wheat, corn, fifty bacon hams, wool, dried fruit, etc. Almost daily we heard of threats being made to burn the house, and ma feeling almost confident of it, made an effort to save some articles of value, but our neighbors were fearing the same calamity, and we knew of no place of safety. An additional source of alarm was, almost every night, being aroused to witness some conflagration in the neighborhood — either a dwelling-house, gin, or stable. In four weeks, seventeen cotton-gins had been destroyed by fire and several dwelling-houses. Our nights, you may imagine, were full of terror, but no serious cause for alarm occurred until the 1st of February.

"A negro belonging to Mr. ——, who had a wife and child at ma's, came with a party of armed Federals and demanded his wife and child. Ma offered a stout resistance to his outrageous demands, and told him 'If he crossed that door she'd shoot him.' After some parleying, he left, saying he would return in two weeks. The negro's manner was haughty and consequential; he was armed with two pistols, strutted about the house with great freedom, talked loud and boldly, and altogether, the incident alarmed us a good deal. Nothing farther occurred though until the 11th of February. The night was cloudy, moonless, and starless. About nightfall the family assembled on the gallery to witness a burning house two miles distant, and it was with a feeling of impending evil that we all went to sleep. No one was sleeping in the dwelling-house except ma, two young ladies, and myself, and two little negroes. We had not slept long when our old watch-dog, Carlo, aroused us by jumping against the back door. It excited me very much, but ma calmed me by saying, 'Oh, it's nothing, my daughter, but Carlo trying to get in the house!' In a few moments the faithful dog came to the other door and sprang against it with an angry bark. We were fully aroused now, and ma sprang out of bed, pushed open the blinds and exclaimed 'Great God! the house is on fire! Eliza, Annie, Leila, Susan, get up, the house is burning up — be calm, my daughter, I'll save you; don't be excited — Susan, Leila, run to the kitchen and ring the bell!' In the twinkling of an eye all were up — the old plantation bell was pealing forth its first midnight alarm — servants were rushing in with shrieks and in their night clothes; some were crying 'Where's Susan? where's Leila? Save Miss Bettie; run out to the office and put out the fire,' etc., etc. Ma was calm, collected, and equal to the fearful scene.   She first gave orders to a faithful servant (Hardin), to 'wrap a blanket around Miss Bettie, give her some brandy, take her to the negro quarter, and keep her stimulated,' then secured her purse and spectacles and went to work.   As I was taken out, lying across the shoulder of the faithful Hardin, I gave one long, last, lingering look at the dear old house, so soon to be laid in ruins.   The flames were just spreading over the office — in a moment while I gazed, the roof of that room fell in with a dull, booming, crushing noise that filled my very soul with horror. The fire progressed rapidly.   Ma, Eliza, Annie, and servants were working with fearful desperation — all in their night clothes.   Only four neighbors dared to come to our relief.   The soldiers were watching from the ice-house and madly exulting in their midnight work, and all were afraid to come to our relief, or to go in any part of the yard.   The flames spread so rapidly that in two hours all that remained of our beautiful home was a heap of blackened ashes and embers.   I was taken to a negro cabin, and from that time could only see the leaping flames, the dense volumes of smoke, and hear the crackling fire and dull crushing sound of falling roof and timbers.   Everywhere it was light as noonday.   A servant standing by my bed watching the progress of the fire, exclaimed, 'Oh! Miss Bettie, look at the light upon the tombstones! you can see Miss Virginia's grave as plain as day.'   I looked and saw the pure marble shaft that marks the grave of my beloved sister, and from the depths of my heart a feeling sprung which I had never known in the eight years she had slumbered there — a feeling of perfect resignation that she had gone 'where the wicked cease from troubling,' and I exclaimed 'Thank God, my sister and grandma are at rest in the old grave-yard.'

"The morning dawned in clouds and rain: things that had been saved were in the yard thoroughly drenched; soldiers were coming in crowds demanding breakfast, and exulting in words and laughter over their work of destruction.   Then neighbors came flocking in offering us homes and comfort.   Poor ma, weary and wretched, was in a state of bold and fierce defiance.   She hurled back every insult the cowards gave, and told them in no measured terms of their cowardice in burning a house with no occupants but four defenceless women, and one of them almost dying   A carriage was sent for me the next morning by Mrs. K., to take me to her house, and after I had been lifted into it and placed upon a bed, the soldiers (?) surrounded the carriage and tried to cut the mules loose.   They were only prevented by the entreaties of my friends from doing it then, and followed the carriage to Mrs. K.'s, where, after I was taken out, they took the mules.   Poor ma! I left her behind, in the kitchen, trying to collect the remnant of her household treasures. All, all gone that she most prized — the old cradle by which she had sat so often and sang lullabies to her darlings, the little arm-chair, the little rocker, a small pillow, — sacred to her because her baby boy had died upon it, — the family Bible with its well-filled record, grandma's portrait and pa's library of books.   And what was of more vital importance just then, all her wheat, bacon, corn, and supplies that she had stored away in the roof.

"Such was the state of destitution in which we were left.   And then comes the saddest thought of all — the strong arms and brave hearts that would have sheltered us from harm, were all absent in the service of our oppressed country, and our gray-haired sire a lonely exile.   These, dear friend, are some of the facts. Your heart can better imagine our grief than I can describe it.   Indeed, that I could not do, for language fails me."

Dr. Robert-Archibald-Thomas Ridley[4] (2), third son of James[3] (1), was born at Oxford, Granville, County, N. C., March 5, 1806; married in 1831, Mary-Elizabeth Morris, and by her had issue *nine* children, of whom hereafter.   He was educated at Oxford, and graduated at the University at Chapel Hill, in 1828; was instructed in the study of medicine by his brother, Dr. Charles L. Ridley, of Georgia, and graduated in the Medical College at Charleston, S. C., in 1834.   Doctor Ridley settled permanently at La Grange Ga., in 1837.   He was a man of fine intelligence, great energy and ambition; was eminently successful in business as a planter and distinguished for his skill in the practice of his profession.   He took a great interest in politics; was a Whig, and represented the people of his County in the House of Representatives and Senate. He was in his religious faith a Methodist. He was a true friend and bitter enemy; hospitable and patriotic. His useful life terminated on Dec. 20, 1871, at his homestead, La Grange, Ga.

Rev. Joseph-James Ridley[4] (1), D. D., fourth son of James[2] (1), was born at Oxford, N. C., June 28, 1810; married to Eliza Kingsbury, — of the same family as T. B. Kingsbury, who now owns the old homestead of Dr. James Ridley, and sister of Gen. Charles P. Kingsbury, of Brooklyn, N. Y., — and died issueless, at Somerville, Tenn., March 10, 1878. He was educated partly at a military school at Oxford, and partly at the University of North Carolina, at Chapel Hill. He read medicine and commenced the practice of the medical profession at Greensborough, Ga., but did not succeed. He then abondoned medicine and studied divinity. He graduated in medicine at the University of Pennsylvania in 1837; renewed his baptismal vows, and became a candidate for Holy Orders under the late Bishop Elliott in 1841; was ordained deacon by the bishop, in North Carolina, in 1843, and advanced to the priesthood by the same bishop in 1844. From the date of his ordination he resided at Oxford, N. C., and had charge of the missions at Williamsborough and Louisburgh; and at one time held the rectorship of St. Stephen's, Oxford. In 1853 he became rector of Trinity Church, Clarksville, and held the position with great usefulness to the church, until June, 1860, when, having been elected president of the University of east Tennessee, he removed to Knoxville. Here he remained until February, 1862, when the university was closed in consequence of the war. Doctor Ridley then returned to North Carolina, but was soon invited to St. Stephen's, Milledgeville. In 1867 he returned to this diocese and accepted the rectorship of St. Thomas' Church, Somerville. He resigned the parish in 1869, and accepted the rectorship of Zion Church, Brownsville. His failing health compelled him to resign his charge in November, 1877, and he returned to Somerville to end his days. Doctor Ridley's career was one of great usefulness. His whole soul was in his work. During his seven years residence in Clarksburgh, he baptized one hundred and thirty persons, and confirmed one hundred and sixteen. On the hearts of the people his memory is stamped as that of an ever-zealous and simple-minded Christian, unwearied in well doing. This interest seems to have been specially manifested in the poor and young. No day passed during which he was not found in some poverty-stricken cottage alleviating physical wants and ministering to spirtual troubles. To youth and early manhood his house was always a pleasant home, where, aided by his excellent wife, his hospitality was always attractive, because always genial, intelligent, and refined; no one ever left his house without feeling that they were made the better and purer for having been there. His idea of serving his Master was truly evangelical; trying to copy his Master's example, Doctor Ridley did not conceive his Christian duties ended by preaching one or more sermons every week, but spent the time between public services in doing good deeds, in visiting the sick and needy. He was one of the most accomplished scholars in the ministry; a man of extensive reading and possessed of a fine literary taste and discrimination. His sermons were masterpieces of scholarly erudition, and expressive of genuine and unaffected piety. He had a strong love for nature and was a keen observer of the handiwork of his Maker; especially did he cultivate a taste for flowers. His subject-matter, gathered from every pathway in which his duties led him, was woven into his sermons in an original and graceful way. He was an untiring student of books, human nature, and God's great unwritten book whose pages were the heavens above and the green earth beneath. His nature was warm, ardent, and social. All bear witness to his real goodness, and now that he has gone, those who knew him in life are more than ever conscious of his great influence for goodness. In his latter years the approach of the disease that terminated his existence (paralysis) somewhat impaired his mind and affected his speech, but like a true disciple he continued to work on till he was worn out in the service.

Dr. William-Morgan-Snerd Ridley[2] **(1)**, fifth son of James[2] (1), was born at Oxford, Granville County, N. C., Nov. 10, 1817; married to Caroline Picket, March 11, 1838, and was a practising physician in various places in Georgia, Florida, Missouri, and Louisiana. He was a man of brilliant accomplishments as a talker and musician, and of exquisite manly beauty. He had a most reckless temper, warm to his friends and bitter toward his enemies, and was one who had great contempt of danger. His fine personal appearance, his charming conversation and agreeable deportment, rendered him a welcome guest and noted man in society. He was a surgeon in the United States army, and died of yellow fever at Galveston, Tex., after having withstood the scourge for ninety days in New Orleans and Galveston. Doctor Ridley was a graduate of New York University. His first wife died without issue, and he married twice afterwards. He left a son and a daughter living in Calcutta, India.

Mary-Frances Ridley[2] **(2)**, eldest daughter of James[2] (1), was born in Oxford, Granville County, N. C., Feb. 25, 1808; married to Thomas Speller, of Windsor, N. C.; a farmer.

Sally-Clark-Lewis Ridley[2] **(2)**, second daughter of James[2] (1) and his wife, Elizabeth-Taylor Lewis, was born at Oxford, N. C., Oct. 14, 1815; married William Lattie, merchant, of Raleigh, N. C., and died at Oxford, Sept. 5, 1836.

Maria Ridley[2] **(1)**, only daughter of Archibald[2] (1) and his first wife, Henrietta-Maria Lewis, was left motherless when a small child, and was placed under the care of her aunt, Mrs. Park, of Warren County, N. C. She married to Dr. George Kumin (?), of Virginia, for her first husband; secondly, to Oscar Britton, of Richmond, and after his death she married to a Mr. Todd, of Baltimore.

Elijah-Blackshere Ridley[2] **(1)**, only son of Archibald[2] (1), was born in Sparta, Hancock County, Ga., subsequent to 1822; married, and had issud several children.

Robert Ridley[2] **(3)**, only son of Robert[2] (1) and his wife, Sophia Cooper, died when a young man, at the age of 23.

FOURTH GENERATION.

Dr. James-Bromfield Ridley[4] **(2)**, eldest son of Charles[3] (1), was born in Jones County, Ga., Dec. 19, 1825, and was educated under the instruction of the Rev. Charles-Pollock Beman, at La Grange, Ga.; studied medicine with his father, and graduated at the New York State University in 1846-7. He married Aug. 28, 1848, to Louisa-Josephine Stamper, of Talbot County, who died, leaving *two* children, Sept. 11, 1850. He married, secondly, Nov. 8, 1855, to Mary G., daughter of Henry and Betsey-

Allison Ridley, a descendant of Capt. George Ridley, his collateral kins-woman, of Tennessee, and by her had issue *two* children, of whom here-after. Doctor Ridley was surgeon in the Eighth Georgia Regiment during the Southern war, and died April 3, 1862, of typhoid-pneumonia. He resided on his farm in Jones County, Ga., and was a successful agricul-turalist and eminent physician; a man of sound thought, deep research, and brilliant imagination. He was fine-looking, polished, and refined in manners; a friend to the poor, and a highly respected gentleman He made many friends by his social and genial deportment, and was deeply lamented at his death, which occurred at Savannah, Ga.

Dr. Hamilton-Bonner Ridley[4] (1), second son of Charles[8] (1), was born in Jones County, Ga., Oct. 21, 1825; was educated at Powelton, Ga., and Oxford, N. C., under the Rev. Mr. Geir; was a classmate of Bishop John Beckwith. He read medicine with his father, and attended lectures at the Pennsylvania State University at Philadelphia. He married Dec. 7, 1849, to his cousin, Mary-Eliza Speller, of Bertie County, N. C., whose mother was Mary Ridley. He lives on a fine farm in his native County, and being a gentleman of fortune has devoted his time to agriculture, current literature, music, and popular sports. He was a captain in the Sixth Georgia Regiment, and at the time of the war had his plantation devastated by the Union soldiers. Since the peace he has devoted him-self to the restoration of his property, and is again living at ease. He has a good farm well stocked, a large cottage-house, situated on an eminence surrounded by evergreens and choice flowers. Doctor Ridley is a fancier of fine horses, fowls, and hunting dogs, keeping a fine, large pack of fox-hounds. His home is the place of liberal hospitality, where the old and young congregate to enjoy themselves in the feast, the dance, and social pastime. He has represented his County in the State Legislature; is highly respected for his high sense of honor, his liberality, and rigid temperance. No children.

Robert-Burton Ridley[4] (4), youngest son of Charles[8] (1), was born in Hancock County, Ga., April 23, 1833; married Aug. 23, 1855, to Lu-cretia Wamble, of Talbot County, and settled on a farm at Cornucopia, Jones County, Ga., where he carried on farming successfully. He was afflicted with lameness from his eleventh year, caused by scarlet fever; consequently he was more indulged. He was not fond of books, although by nature highly endowed and talented. He was fine-looking, pleasant company, witty, and very liberal. He was ever ready to help the poor and needy; was fond of fine stock of all kinds, and enjoyed all the good things of this life, being surrounded with all human comforts. He died without issue, Sept. 19, 1863.

Maj. Jerome-Shelton Ridley[4] (1), eldest son of Bromfield[8] (2), was born in McMinnville, Warren County, Tenn., in the year 1832 (?), and was educated at Cumberland University. He graduated in the literary department in 1853; in the law department in 1855, — speaking the vale-dictory in the law department in his class. He moved to Iowa in 1856, and to Kansas in 1857; accumulated a fortune in real-estate speculation, and lost heavily in the revulsion of 1858. He was in the Confederate army during the Southern war as major and commissary of Stevenson's Divis-ion He has since devoted himself to agriculture, and was in 1878 editor of a newspaper at Elkton, Ky. Mr. Ridley is a man of high culture and finished literary attainments; is possessed of great energy of character and executive ability; determined and persevering, he allows no undertaking to drag on his hands. He has manifested a deep interest in this book and made an effort to secure a full history of his family; but his business engagements prevented complete success. He married Margaret McLean, of Todd County, and has issue *three* children, of whom hereafter.

Dr. James-Lucas Ridley[4] (3), second son of Bromfield[3] (2), was born at McMinnville, Tenn., in the year 1838. He was educated at Cumberland University; married Fannie Robertson, and is now in the practice of medicine in Huntsville, Ala. Doctor Ridley served in the Confederate army as surgeon in Dibbul's Brigade. He is regarded as a skillful practitioner, and highly respected as an accomplished gentleman and worthy citizen. *Two* children.

Capt. George-Crothwait Ridley[4] (1), third son of Bromfield[3] (2), was born in McMinnville, Tenn., in the year 1840; married Bertie Jones, who died leaving *one* child. He married, secondly, in 1871, to a widow lady named King, of Triune, Tenn., and is now living in Sumner County in that State, as a farmer and planter. He served in the Southern army during the Rebellion, as captain and inspector-general on the staff of Brig.-Gen. Ben. Hill. He was a noble soldier and rendered efficient service in his department for a long term in the field.

Capt. Bromfield-L. Ridley[4] (3), fourth son of Bromfield[3] (2), was born in Murfreesborough, Tenn., in the year 1842, and at the age of nineteen years (?) entered the service of the Confederate States as a private soldier. He was promoted for gallant conduct as a soldier, and was captain and aid-de-camp to Gen. Alexander P. Stewart, from the time he was brigadier in 1862 to the close of the war. Captain Ridley saw a great deal of service; was in many engagements and a dozen pitched battles, and was slightly wounded only once during the war. He was noticed by his general for gallantry on several fields; especially in his report after the battle of Chickamauga, in which he says: "My two aids, Lieuts. Bromfield Ridley, Jr., and R. Caruthers Stewart, though very young men, and the latter under fire for the first time, behaved with commendable gallantry." I have before me a letter from General Stewart, written after the war, in which he speaks of the subject of this notice in endearing terms, and imparts some very practical advice. I have also before me a journal kept by Captain Ridley during the war, from which many interesting extracts could be taken, but want of space in this work will not admit of its publication. He is unmarried; is now in the practice of law in the city of Murfreesborough, Tenn. His portrait represents a man of fine physique and formidable appearance; the expression, one of great determination.

Charles-Lewis Ridley[4] (2), sixth son of Bromfield[3] (2), was born at Murfreesborough, Tenn.; married in 1869, to Harriet Fitzpatrick, of western Tenn., and has issue *two* children (1878). He was aid-de-camp to Gen. Ben. Hill, in the Confederate army, during the Rebellion; now a merchant in Nashville.

Granville Ridley[4] (1), a son of Bromfield[3] (2), died in infancy.

Robert Ridley[4] (4), youngest son of Bromfield[3] (2), died in infancy.

Elizabeth Ridley[4] (1), eldest daughter of Bromfield[3] (2), was born in the year 1834; married to William Blackore (?), of Sumner County, Tenn., and died in 1863. She wrote the beautiful description of "Fairmont" her father's residence, and of the burning of the house by Northern soldiers during the war, published in this book under her father's name. She is represented as a lady of remarkable intellectual attainments and refinement of manners, possessed of a gentle, affectionate spirit.

Virginia-R. Ridley⁴ (1), second daughter of Bromfield³ (2), was a young lady of musical talent, and fine accomplishments, who died at La Grange, Ga., at the age of seventeen.

Sally Ridley⁴ (3), third daughter of Bromfield³ (2), was born in 1849; married to Thornton McLean, of Todd County, Ky., and died at Pulaski, Tenn., at the age of twenty-four. She was educated in the city of Nashville, and was a lady of remarkable mind and refinement of taste.

Thomas-Alonzo Ridley⁴ (2), eldest son of Robert³ (2), was born at La Grange, Ga., March 31, 1833; died April 24, 1851.

Rebecca Ridley⁴ (1), eldest daughter of Robert³ (2), was born at La Grange, Ga., June 8, 1837; died June 7, 1851.

Dr. Charles-Bromfield Ridley⁴ (3), second son of Robert³ (2), was born at La Grange, Ga., April 20, 1840; graduated at the State University at Athens, Ga.; served in the Confederate army during the war of the Rebellion three years; first, in the infantry, afterwards in the cavalry with General Duke, in Virginia, Tennessee, Kentucky, and Mississipi, and after the close of the war turned his attention to the study of medicine. He graduated at the Medical College in New Orleans. Married March 17, 1859, to Martha-Elizabeth Beall, and has *four* children, of whom hereafter. Doctor Ridley is a skillful and very promising physician.

Dr. Robert-Beman Ridley⁴ (5), third son of Robert³ (2), was born at La Grange, Ga., Oct. 18, 1842; was educated at the high school in his native town, and entered the Confederate army at the age of eighteen years. He was stationed at Norfolk until ordered to Richmond; was in nearly every bloody battle fought in Virginia during the war of the Rebellion. His company went out eighty strong and he was the only one left to surrender in 1864 at Appomatox Court House. He studied medicine and graduated at Jefferson Medical College in Philadelphia. Doctor Ridley married Nov. 28, 1875 to Emma-Leila, daughter of Congressman Ben. Hill, and has *one* child, of whom hereafter. He is a practising physician in Atlanta, Ga.

John-Morgan Ridley⁴ (1), fourth son of Robert³ (2), was born at La Grange, Ga., March 22, 1845, and was educated in his native town. He joined the Confederate army at the age of eighteen, and was with Gen. John B. Gordon until the close of the war, always at his post of duty regardless of impending danger. He engaged in mercantile business in New York city after the war, and continued until a short time before his death, which occurred Aug. 11, 1877, at the family residence; unmarried.

Mary-Louisa Ridley⁴ (3), second daughter of Robert³ (2), was born at La Grange, Ga., Aug. 4, 1847; died June 6, 1858.

Leila Ridley⁴ (1), third daughter of Robert³ (2), was born at La Grange, Ga., Jan. 31, 1853; died May 15, 1858.

Francis-Marion Ridley⁴ (1), fifth son of Robert³ (2), was born at La Grange, Ga., Jan. 1, 1856; was educated at the high school in his native town, and at the University at Athens, and is now in college at Nashville, Tenn.

FIFTH GENERATION.

Charles-Lewis Ridley⁵ (4), eldest son of James⁴ (2), was born in Jones County, Ga., Aug. 13, 1850, and is now (1878) living with his grandmother; a "very kind-hearted young man."

Lula-Woodson Ridley⁵ (2), eldest daughter of James⁴ (2), was born in Jones County, Ga., Aug. 28, 1853; died Oct. 9, 1854.

Roberta-Hamilton Ridley⁵ (1), a daughter of James⁴ (2) and his wife, Mary G. Ridley, was born Sept. 9, 1856; married Dec. 12, 1872, to Lu D. Ezell, of Putnam County, Ga.

James-Allison Ridley⁵ (4), a son of James⁴ (2) and his wife, Mary Ridley, was born in Jones County, Ga., Sept. 8, 1858, and died in 1860.

L.-Gray Ridley⁵ (1), eldest child of Jerome⁴ (1), was born in the year 1858; single in 1878.

Paul Ridley⁵ (1), a son of Jerome⁴ (1), was born in 1861.

Henriette Ridley⁵ (1), a daughter of Jerome⁴ (1), was born in 1868.

Melvina Ridley⁵ (1), a daughter of James⁴ (3).

Irene-G. Ridley⁵ (1), a daughter of James⁴ (3).

Birtie Ridley⁵ (1), eldest daughter of George⁴ (1).

Berthia Ridley⁵ (1).⎱ Twin daughters of George⁴ (1).
Brenda Ridley⁵ (1).⎰

Rebecca Ridley⁵ (2), a daughter of Charles⁴ (2).

Julia-Faulkner Ridley⁵ (1), eldest daughter of Charles⁴ (3), was born at La Grange, Ga., July 31, 1871.

Robert-Archibald Ridley⁵ (6), eldest son of Charles⁴ (3), was born at La Grange, Ga., Dec. 19, 1873.

Charles-Bromfield Ridley⁵ (4), second son of Charles⁴ (3).

James-Egbert Ridley⁵ (5), third son of Charles⁴ (3), was born at La Grange, Ga., March 6, 1878.

John-Francis Ridley⁵ (1), eldest son of Robert⁴ (5), was born at Atlanta, Ga., Sept. 15, 1876.

RIDLEYS OF WILKINSON COUNTY, GEORGIA.

[VIRGINIAN BRANCH.]

Robert Ridley¹ (1), descended from an ancient family in Southampton County, Va., was born about 1780, and his parents having died when he was a small boy, he emigrated to Georgia in company with other families from Virginia, and settled in Wilkinson County, where he established a permanent home. His parents' names are not certainly known. The old members of the family in Virginia were aware that some kinsmen emigrated to Georgia, but seem to have had no intercourse with them. Robert never returned to his native State. He married Nancy, daughter of William and Rebecca McKay, who went from Virginia to Georgia at the same time, and had issue *seven* children, of whom hereafter. Mr. Ridley was a farmer in moderate circumstances. He died in 1856, aged about 76 years.

SECOND GENERATION.

Jonathan Ridley[2] (1), eldest son of Robert[1] (1), was born in Wilkinson County, Ga., in 1805; married and removed to Florida, where he settled on a farm. He died in 1863, leaving a widow and several children.

Milley Ridley[2] (1), eldest daughter of Robert[1] (1), was born in Wilkinson County, Ga., in 1806; was married, but deceased many years ago.

William Ridley[2] (1), second son of Robert[1] (1), was born in Wilkinson County, Ga., in 1808; married Dec. 31, 1835, to Nancy Holley, and by her had issue *six* children, of whom hereafter. He married, secondly, Oct. 28, 1860, to Mary Narrice, and had issue *nine* children, of whom hereafter. Mr. Ridley resides on a farm in Hawkinsville, Ga.

Sarah Ridley[2] (1), second daughter of Robert[1] (1), was born in Wilkinson County, Ga. (presumably), in 1810; was married.

Dea. Everett Ridley[2] (1), third son of Robert[1] (1), was born in Wilkinson County, Ga., Feb. 8, 1813; was married Dec. 8, 1836, to Damaris Hardie, daughter of John and Damaris Hardie, of Wilkinson County, and had issue *eight* children, of whom hereafter. He united with the Missionary Baptist Church in 1837, and lived an eminent Christian until his death. He served his church in the office of deacon many years; his occupation was farming. He was a man respected alike for his noble principles and sincere piety; his life was very useful, and his death greatly lamented.

Dea. David Ridley[2] (1), fourth son of Robert[1] (1), was born in Wilkinson County, near Irwinton, Ga., July 17, 1814; married Aug. 10, 1837, to Dillie Stinsan (or Stinson), and settled in Thomas County, Ga., where he resided and successfully farmed for six years. In 1849 he removed to Baker County, and pursued the occupation of farming till 1852, when he removed to Worth County, where he now resides. He was in comfortable circumstances before the late war, but like nearly all southern people was reduced financially, and has not regained what he lost. His children were favored with the advantages of education, and have married well. His wife died Feb. 24, 1853; she was a devoted member of the Missionary Baptist Church for many years. He married, secondly, Elizabeth-Piety Cox, eldest daughter of James and Elizabeth Cox, of Worth County, Ga. Mr. Ridley resides near a well-known church called "Mount Horeb," and is now serving as deacon. He is devoted to his religious work, and is highly esteemed for his unostentatious piety. He is said to be "a fine-looking old gentleman." The residence of Mr. Ridley is beautifully situated on an elevation; in front is a fine avenue bordered with stately oaks of natural growth. The plantation lies south of the house, and consists of several hundred acres of fertile and well-cultivated land. He had issue, by both wives, *fourteen* children, of whom hereafter.

Robert Ridley[2] (2), youngest son of Robert[1] (1), was born in Wilkinson County, Ga., March 31, 1817; married Mary-Jane Manning, daughter of Wright and Nancy Manning, of said County, and then emigrated to Alabama, and is now living near Shackelville, Butler County, in that State. His first wife, who was born July 9, 1820 (to whom he was married Dec. 8, 1838), and had issue *eight* children, of whom hereafter. She died in 1856, and Mr. Ridley married, secondly, in 1860, to Flora-Elizabeth, daughter of Harmon and Sarah (Brown) Watson, of Pike County, Ala., and by her had issue *six* children, of whom hereafter. This second wife was born May 20, 1829. Mr. Ridley carried on farming till 1864, when he engaged

34

in the stone-ware business, which he still carries on. He was two years in the war.

THIRD GENERATION.

Jabez Ridley[2] (1), eldest son of William[2] (1), was born in Georgia, Oct. 10, 1836, and died in October, 1836.

Francis-J. Ridley[2] (1), second son of William[2] (1), was born in Georgia, Sept. 16, 1837, and died Feb. 8, 1838.

Samuel-Wright Ridley[3] (1), third son of William[2] (1), was born (presumably) in Pulaski County, Ga., March 10, 1839; enlisted in the Confederate army in 1861, and served under Gen. Robert E. Lee four years; he was killed at Funkstown, Md. Was a farmer previous to the war; in the army he held the office of orderly sergeant.

Benjamin Ridley[3] (1), fourth son of William[2] (1), was born in Pulaski County, Ga., Aug. 31, 1841; died Feb. 24, 1844.

William-J. Ridley[3] (2), fifth son of William[2] (1), was born in Pulaski County, Ga., June 22, 1845; enlisted in the Confederate army in 1861, was severely wounded in the second Manassas battle, and had his right leg amputated; was discharged and sent home, where he died in 1866, — a brave soldier, and noble young man.

Nancy-A. Ridley[3] (1), eldest daughter of William[2] (1), was born in Pulaski County, Ga., May 25, 1846; was married July 4, 1866, to John Taylor, and resides in Georgia.

Daniel-L. Ridley[3] (1), sixth son of William[2] (1), was born in Pulaski County, Ga., Sept. 8, 1848; enlisted in the Confederate army in 1863, and served under Gen. Joseph E. Johnston two years. Married March 22, 1873, to M. E. Singleton, and has issue *three* children, of whom hereafter. Mr. Ridley is now acting in the office of magistrate.

John-N. Ridley[3] (1), seventh son of William[2] (1), was born in Pulaski County, Ga., Nov. 26, 1853; married in 1871 to Susan Smith, and has issue *four* children, of whom hereafter. Mr. Ridley is a farmer by occupation.

Rebecca-A. Ridley[2] (1), second daughter of William[2] (1), was born in Pulaski County, Ga., July 28, 1858; single.

Mary-J. Ridley[3] (1), third daughter of William[2] (1), was born in Pulaski County, Ga., March 8, 1860; unmarried.

Willie-A. Ridley[3] (1), eighth son of William[2] (1), was born in Pulaski County, Ga., Aug. 31, 1861; unmarried.

Serena-E. Ridley[3] (1), fourth daughter of William[2] (1), was born in Pulaski County, Ga., Dec. 4, 1863; single.

Thomas-J. Ridley[2] (1), ninth son of William[2] (1), was born in Pulaski County, Ga., March 20, 1866.

Sarah-E. Ridley[3] (2), fifth daughter of William[2] (1), was born in Pulaski County, Ga., July 7, 1868.

Ravena-E. Ridley[3] (1), sixth daughter of William[2] (1), was born in Pulaski County, Ga., Dec. 17, 1871.

Martha-Ann Ridley[3] (1), eldest daughter of Everett[2] (1), was born in Wilkinson County, Ga., Dec. 2, 1837; was married July 29, 1856, to James-Franklin Hogan, a farmer of Quitman County, Ga.

John-Shelby Ridley[3] (2), eldest son of Everett[2] (1), was born in Pulaski County, Ga., Jan. 16, 1840; enlisted in the Confederate army in May, 1862, and died in August following, at Atlanta, Ga., — "a noble young man."

Nancy-Elefair Ridley³ (2), second daughter of Everett² (1), was born in Wilkinson County, Ga., May 8, 1842; was married July 29, 1862, to Christopher-Columbus Smith, a farmer; resident in her native County.

Robert-Erasmus Ridley³ (3), second son of Everett² (1), was born in Wilkinson County, Ga., Jan. 4, 1845; married Nov. 23, 1871, to Mary-Rebecca Hatfield, and has issue *four* children, of whom hereafter. Mr. Ridley is a farmer in his native County.

Sarah-Damaris Ridley³ (3), third daughter of Everett² (1), was born in Wilkinson County, Ga., July 1, 1847; was married Jan. 26, 1873, to Andrew-Jackson Porter, a farmer and carpenter, of Wilkinson County, who died Oct. 1, 1875.

Margaret-Caroline Ridley³ (1), fourth daughter of Everett² (1), was born in Wilkinson County, Ga., Dec. 4, 1849, and is a dwarf weighing only seventy pounds, and four and a half feet in height.

Joel-Galaspie Ridley³ (1), third son of Everett² (1), was born in Wilkinson County, Ga., May 14, 1852; married Dec. 20, 1877, to Dora-Jane Porter, and is a farmer. No issue.

Milton-Everett Ridley³ (1), fourth son of Everett² (1), was born in Wilkinson County, Ga., Feb. 1, 1855, and at the age of seventeen commenced to travel around the world. He has been a student for the legal profession in Tennessee, and is now (1884) principal of an academy in that State.

Mary-Jane Ridley³ (2), eldest daughter of David² (1), was born in Thomas County, Ga., July 2, 1838, and has never married. She united with the Baptist church when quite young, and has lived a " most devout observer of her Creator's laws."

Zilphia-Delaney Ridley³ (1), second daughter of David² (1), was born in Thomas County, Ga., Feb. 5, 1840, and lives with her parents a single woman. She early united with the Baptist church, and has since lived a devoted Christian.

Martha-Jane Ridley³ (2), third daughter of David² (1), was born in Thomas County, Ga., Oct. 30, 1842; was married to William Spiller in her twenty-third year, and has *four* children. She has a fair education. He is a blacksmith.

Jonathan Ridley³ (2), eldest son of David² (1), was born in Thomas County, Ga., May 4, 1844; enlisted in Company G of the "Yancy Independents,"—the first company organized in Worth County,—in the spring of 1861, and was in the command of Capt. W. A. Harris, son of Judge Iverson L. Harris, of Milledgeville, Ga.; this company, after being mustered, became a part of the Fourteenth Georgia Regiment, commanded by Col. Robert Fulson. Jonathan died with measles in northern Virginia, in the autumn of 1862.

Jesse-Ashley Ridley³ (1), second son of David² (1), was born in Thomas County, Ga., Oct. 21, 1845; died Nov. 28, 1856.

Sarah-Frances Ridley³ (4), fourth daughter of David² (1), was born in Thomas County, Ga., Nov. 4, 1847; was married to Charles G. Tipton, a Georgian, and lives on a small farm in Isabella, Worth County. Mr. Tipton is the clerk of court for Worth County; has taught school. They have *three* children.

Dr. James-Nicholas Ridley³ (1), third son of David² (1), was born either in Thomas or Baker County, Ga., Nov. 4, 1849, and was sent to school until he acquired a fair English education. In 1875 he commenced the study of medicine under Dr. T. W. Tison, of Worth County, and continued with him till 1876, when he entered Louisville Medical College, where he attended two courses of lectures, and graduated.   Dr. Ridley is in the practise of his profession at Warwick, Worth County, Ga., and his success has been wonderful, surpassing expectation.

John-Shelby Ridley[3] (3), eldest son of David[2] (1) by his second wife, was born in Worth County, Ga., Sept. 12, 1854, and died Oct. 1, 1855.

Iverson-L. Ridley[3] (1), fifth son of David[2] (1), was born in Worth County, Ga., Dec. 25, 1858; at home.

Nancy-Elizabeth Ridley[3] (3), fifth daughter of David[2] (1), was born in Worth County, Ga., March 2, 1861.

Jackson-Matthias Ridley[3] (1), sixth son of David[2] (1), was born in Worth County, Ga., March 5, 1863.

Robert-Lee Ridley[3] (4), seventh son of David[2] (1), was born in Worth County, Ga., July 11, 1865.

Theophilus-David Ridley[3] (1), eighth son of David[2] (1), was born in Worth County, Ga., Feb. 17, 1867.

Amanda-Beatrice Ridley[3] (1), sixth daughter of David[2] (1), was born in Worth County, Ga., May 6, 1870.

Robert-Wright Ridley[3] (5), eldest son of Robert[2] (2), was born in Alabama, Oct. 24, 1839, and is now at Sulphurbuff, Tex., working as a mechanic.   He was in the First Alabama Regiment, Confederate service, under General Bragg.

Nancy-Antoinette Ridley[3] (4), eldest daughter of Robert[2] (2), was born in Alabama, Nov. 10, 1841; was married Jan. 12, 1867, to James M. Redmond, and has *four* children.

Almeda-Delaney Ridley[3] (1), second daughter of Robert[2] (2), was born in Alabama, May 29, 1844, and is at Columbus; single.

Elizabeth-Elmira Ridley[3] (2), third daughter of Robert[2] (2), was born in Alabama, Dec. 16, 1846, and has deceased, 1874.

Eudotia-Rebecca Ridley[3] (1), fourth daughter of Robert[2] (2), was born in Alabama, March 6, 1850; was married Aug. 15, 1872, to John G. McLeod, and has children; lives in Troy, Pike County.

Olivia-Pemerieum Ridley[3] (1), fifth daughter of Robert[2] (2), was born in Alabama, Feb. 25, 1853.

Althena-Inglet Ridley[3] (1), sixth daughter of Robert[2] (2), was born in Butler County, Ala., Nov. 25, 1855.

Thomas-William Ridley[3] (2), second son of Robert[2] (2), was born in Butler County, Ala., Sept. 20, 1863; deceased.

Samuel-David Ridley[3] (1), third son of Robert[2] (2), was born in Butler County, Ala., May 11, 1865; deceased.

Mary-Sabrina Ridley[3] (3), seventh daughter of Robert[2] (2), was born in Alabama, Sept. 22, 1867.

John-Everett Ridley[3] (4), fourth son of Robert[2] (2), was born in Alabama, Oct. 9, 1869.

Sarah-Brown Ridley[3] (5), eighth daughter of Robert[2] (2), was born in Alabama, Feb. 14, 1872.

FOURTH GENERATION.

W.-I. Ridley[4] (1), eldest son of Daniel[3] (1), was born Jan. 1, 1874.

L.-C. Ridley[4] (1), child of Daniel[3] (1), was born March 14, 1876.

J.-C. Ridley[4] (1), child of Daniel[3] (1), was born March 1, 1878.

Lieujeney Ridley⁴ (1), eldest son of John³ (2), was born Jan. 19, 1872.

Philip-E. Ridley⁴ (1), second son of John³ (2), was born Oct. 7, 1874.

Lewis-F. Ridley⁴ (1), third son of John³ (2), was born Oct. 8, 1876.

Frederick-L. Ridley⁴ (1), fourth son of John³ (2), was born Dec. 8, 1877.

John-Franklin Ridley⁴ (5), eldest son of Robert³ (3), was born in Wilkinson County, Ga., Sept. 19, 1872.

William-Edward Ridley⁴ (3), second son of Robert³ (3), was born in Wilkinson County, Ga., May 19, 1874.

Joel-Hardie Ridley⁴ (2), third son of Robert³ (3), was born in Wilkinson County, Ga., Nov. 20, 1875.

Julia-Antoinette Ridley⁴ (2), a daughter of Robert³ (3), was born in Wilkinson County, Ga., March 12, 1878.

RIDLEYS OF WAKE COUNTY, NORTH CAROLINA.

[VIRGINIAN BRANCH.]

William Ridley¹ (1) was descended from the Ridley family of Southampton County, Virginia, and was presumably a son of William Ridley, who settled in the County Isle of Wight, Va., in the early part of the eighteenth century. Some descendants of this William say he was born in England or Wales. He went from Virginia to Gates County, N. C., when a young man, and thence removed to Wake County, where he married Elizabeth, daughter of Howell and Isabella Lewis (she was born April 10, 1761), of Granville County, where Mr. Ridley made his permanent residence. He was a farmer by occupation; died in the prime of life (previous to 1810), leaving *four* children, of whom hereafter. The family residence and plantation (consisting of five hundred acres) were sold by Mrs. Ridley to a Mr. Montague in 1810. The family was considered rich.

SECOND GENERATION.

Col. Howell-Lewis Ridley² (1), a son of William¹ (1) and his wife, Elizabeth Lewis,* born in Wake County, N. C., about 1776; married Mildred Cobb, and lived on a farm in Granville County until the death of his wife, when he went to Oxford, in the same County, and lived with his only son, of whom more hereafter. I do not know how he came by the title of colonel; he may have been in the war of 1812. He was a cultivated gentleman, wealthy, and very fond of sporting with fine horses and dogs. He died in 1823 at Oxford, N. C.

---

* It will be seen by reference to notes connected with genealogy of the Ridley family of Oxford, N. C., that they were intermarried with the families of *Lewis* and *Cobb*, evidently of the same stock as the above mother and wife of Colonel Ridley, and these double ties of blood bound the two branches of the Ridley family together. I have not learned the exact degree of relationship between Elizabeth Lewis, wife of William Ridley, and Elizabeth-Taylor Lewis, wife of Dr. James Ridley; both were of Granville County, N. C.

Dr. James-Day Ridley² (1), a son of William¹ (1), was born in Wake or Granville County, N. C., about 1781; married Elizabeth J. Ashton, of Warren County, and had issue *two* sons, of whom more hereafter. One relative says James was the eldest son. He was graduated in Philadelphia, settled as a physician at Wake Forest, N. C., and stood high in his profession. Was a handsome and popular man; his family connections and fine conversational powers gave him extensive influence. In his account-book, written by himself, is the following: "I commenced the practice of physic at Capt. Robert Crenshaw's, July 18, 1810; left there May 18, 1811." He died in 1820, leaving a fine estate of four hundred or five hundred acres, and a spacious residence. In his will he left one third to his wife, and one third to each of his two sons; but in case the sons died childless the wife was to have one half, and the other half was to go to his relatives. Mrs. Ridley was a large, dignified lady, descended from a family as good as found in the State; she deceased in 1850, leaving her property, which consisted of land and slaves, to Elbert Chuk, a nephew, and Ann-Elizabeth, wife of Dr. H. W. Montague, a niece.

Willis Ridley² (1), a son of William¹ (1), was born in Granville County, N. C.; married Mary W. Smith, of Granville County, and moved to Mount Pleasant, Maury County, Tenn., about the year 1809, where he died at the age of 52, leaving a widow and *six* children, of whom more hereafter. Mr. Ridley was a farmer.

Mary Ridley² (1), only daughter of William¹ (1), was born in Granville County, N. C., and was married to Col. Nathaniel Roberts, of Granville County.* She was the mother of *eleven* children.

THIRD GENERATION.

John-Cobb Ridley³ (1), only son of Howell² (1), was born in Granville County, N. C., in 1810; married in 1829 to Amelia Todd, and for a while resided on a farm in the County; but in 1835 moved to Oxford, where he lived for a few years. He died in Washington city in 1838, leaving a widow and *three* children, of whom hereafter. Mr. Ridley was a farmer by occupation. He was a cultivated gentleman. His widow married for her second husband a lawyer named Jeremiah Hilliard, and is now living at Scottsville, Harrison County, Tex., a very old lady.

William-James Ridley³ (2), a son of James² (1), was born in Wake County, N. C., in 1817, and died when a young man without issue; his age was 24 years. Willed all his property to his mother.

John-Alston Ridley³ (2), a son of James² (1), was born in Wake County, N. C., in 1819, and died without issue in 1850. He was married. Left property by will to his wife and Ridley family.

Mary-Ann Ridley³ (2), eldest daughter of Willis² (1), was born in Maury County, Tenn., and became the wife of a Mr. Conner, and has *three* children.

Eliza Ridley³ (1), second daughter of Willis² (1), was born in Maury County, Tenn., and died young.

---

* Mrs. Susan A. Ridley, of Georgia, remembers a visit at the house of Mary (Ridley) Roberts, where she was very kindly and attentively entertained, spending much time riding, fishing, etc. She represents Mrs. Roberts as a woman of culture and charming conversational powers, and her husband as a pleasant and dignified gentleman.

Dr. William Ridley³ (3), eldest son of Willis² (1), was born in Maury County, Tenn., and died at the age of 27.

Francis Ridley³ (1), second son of Willis² (1), was born in Maury County, Tenn.; died at the age of 29 years.

Isabella-W. Ridley³ (1), third daughter of Willis² (1), was born in Maury County, Tenn.; died at the age of 35 years.

J.-W.-S. Ridley³ (1), youngest son of Willis² (1), was born in Maury County, Tenn., about 1825; married Annie L. Pillow in 1854, and has issue *three* children, of whom hereafter. He is a wealthy man, engaged in business at Columbia, Tenn. Mr. Ridley is now (1883) extensively engaged in stock-raising and agricultural pursuits.

FOURTH GENERATION.

Virginia-L. Ridley⁴ (1), eldest daughter of John³ (1), was born in Granville County, N. C., in 1830; was married to Col. James B. Sims in 1846, and died in 1875, leaving *five* children.

Celestia-M. Ridley⁴ (1), second daughter of John³ (1), was born in Granville County, N. C., in 1833; was married to R. C. Oglesby in 1850, and died the same year.

John-David Ridley⁴ (3), only son of John³ (1), was born in Granville County, N. C., in 1836; married in 1850 to Laura C. Kent, of Blacksburgh, Va., and lived near Shreveport, La., at a place called "Ravenwood Home." He died in 1865, leaving a widow and *three* children, of whom hereafter. Mrs. Ridley was married, secondly, to a Mr. Laughlin, and resides at the home left by her first husband, who was only nineteen years of age, and his wife seventeen, when they were married.

Webb Ridley⁴ (1), eldest son of J. W. S.³ (1), was born in Maury County, Tenn., about 1859, and is being educated in his native State.

Annie-Gray Ridley⁴ (1), only daughter of J. W. S.³ (1), was born in Maury County, Tenn., in 1870; now at home.

William-P. Ridley⁴ (4), second son of J. W. S.³ (1), was born in Maury County, Tenn., in 1873; now at home.

FIFTH GENERATION.

Sallie-Amelia Ridley⁵ (1), eldest daughter of John⁴ (3), was born in Louisiana, about the year 1859. A beautiful and accomplished young lady; educated at a seminary in Virginia, and now living at "Ravenwood Home," near Shreveport, La. She represents her residence as "beautifully situated amid a variety of trees and flowers."

Laura-Kent Ridley⁵ (1), second daughter of John⁴ (3), was born near Shreveport, La., about the year 1861. Was married only a few years ago. A lady of great beauty and brilliant qualities.

John-Cobb Ridley⁵ (4), only son of John⁴ (3), was born near Shreveport, La., about the year 1863, and is now attending an agricultural, mechanical, and military school, in Blacksburgh, Va.

RIDLEYS OF TRURO, MASSACHUSETTS.

Capt. Marke Ridley¹ (1) was descended from the ancient family of Ridley in Northumberland, Eng., evidently through Albany Ridley, a

merchant in London, whose son Mark was sometime of Truro, Eng.
Captain Ridley followed the sea from boyhood, and is said to have made
voyages to New England some years previous to his settlement. His
name occurs several times in the Plymouth Colonial Records. In 1666
he was summoned to account for "bringing so much liquor into the col-
onie." At another time, — in 1668, — he was appointed administrator of
the estate of Tristram Hull, of Barnstable; and in the year 1676 his name
is connected with a law case tried in His Majesty's court at Plymouth, in
which a "cargoe of boards" was involved, said cargo having been sent
in Ridley's care to Piscataqua in 1674. He was a man of considerable
note in the old colony, as proved by the trust reposed in him by his contemporaries. From the few meagre references concerning this man in
the colonial records and contemporary history, it seems evident that he
was a roving character, who owned a small vessel and hung about the New
England coast, where he frequently became involved in legal transactions,
but always managed to elude the penalty of the law. He was brought to
trial at Newport, R. I., in 1672, on an action presented by Thomas Harte.
Marke Ridley was convicted, and Capt. John Green became his bondsman.
The records show that "Marke Ridley, defendant, was noe free inhabitant
of this collony." No estate of his was found, and the recorder was advised to secure the complainant on property of Ridley's bondsman. Tradition says he married in England, and that his son and only child,
Thomas, was born on the ocean while on the voyage to New England. I
have not found any records of births of children, nor have I found any
family who could have been descended from Marke, except through the
one son Thomas, hereafter mentioned.

SECOND GENERATION.

Thomas Ridley[2] (1), a son of Marke[1] (1), was born (presumably) on
the Atlantic ocean, in 1685, when his parents were on their way to New
England. Tradition claims that he was a seaman and master of vessels,
but I find no reliable proof. He married Mary Smalley, and had issue
ten children, of whom hereafter. Residence in Truro,* Mass. I find the
record of his death 1767.

---

* TRURO is a town on the northern extremity of the peninsula of Cape Cod, in
Massachusetts; its Indian name was "*Pamet.*" It was purchased in 1679. In 1805
the town was called "Dangerfield," and in the year 1809 it was incorporated by the
name of "Truro;" a name taken from a town in the south of England, from which
many of the early settlers emigrated. The town is fourteen miles long and three
miles wide; the soil is light and free from stones, and hardly any part will produce
English grass worth harvesting. The face of the township is composed of sand-
hills with narrow valleys between them, running at right angles with the shore;
from the top of these hills few objects can be seen except the ocean and a wide
waste of sand. The inhabitants, who derive their living mainly from the sea, are
in comfortable circumstances. The first minister in Truro was Rev. John Avery,
who was ordained in the year 1711, and died in 1754; he was succeeded by Rev.
Caleb Upham, who died in 1786. By these servants of God the early Ridleys were
baptized, married, and buried; and to their preaching they were listeners when they
attended divine service. In the "History of Truro," a locality is called "Ridler's
Bank." I think this is a mistake in spelling, and that it should be Ridley's Bank.
I have never heard of a Ridler family on Cape Cod. Upon the seacoast the early
Ridleys lived in their fisherman's cabins, and upon the waves of old ocean they
plied their rude craft. Here upon the shore their bodies repose, their requiems sung
by the roaring ocean, till that day when the trump of God shall awake the dead.
They were rude and unlettered, brave and adventuresome, but possessed of strong
bodies, noble minds, and kind hearts.

THIRD GENERATION.

Thomas Ridley[3] (2), eldest son of Thomas[2] (1), was born in Truro, Mass., Dec. 18, 1715; married Elizabeth ——, and had issue *ten* children, of whom hereafter. He was a seaman and fisherman. No record of his death or that of his wife. Tradition says he lived to a great age.*

James Ridley[3] (1), second son of Thomas[2] (1), was born in Truro, Mass., Feb. 6, 1718; married March 30, 1738, to Ruth Smalley, of Truro, and had issue several children, of whom hereafter. He resided in his native town till the year 1752, when he removed to Great Island, Harpswell, Me. (then in the colony of Massachusetts), where he settled and became the progenitor of the numerous families of the name in that State, except a small branch of the *Ridlon* family who now spell their name identical with this family, and hence great confusion was occasioned between the two. Mr. Ridley located at a place on the island since called "Ridley Point." He owned extensive lands, and carried on farming and fishing. He was a daring woodman and bold hunter; spent much of his time trapping along the eastern rivers, and could find his way through a trackless wilderness in any direction. He married, secondly, September, 1753, to Mary Bacy. He was killed by lightning at Harpswell.

John Ridley[3] (1), third son of Thomas[2] (1), was born in Truro, Mass., May 6, 1722, and probably died when young.

Mark Ridley[3] (2), fourth son of Thomas[2] (1), was born in Truro, Mass., Aug, 26, 1724; married Jan. 30, 1745, to Phebe Dyer, of Truro, and tradition says went to Harpswell with his brother James. There is a mist over this man's history, to me impenetrable. No mention of children is found in any town in Barnstable County, nor can I find his descendants anywhere in New England. Many members of the family remember of hearing the name "Old Mark" but cannot give any other information. There is a family of Ridleys in the South said to be descended from an ancestor, who, previous to the Revolution, was living somewhere in Massachusetts, but I cannot connect them with this Mark. All tradition concerning him is vague and unreliable. I must leave him to his rest.

Mary Ridley[3] (1), eldest daughter of Thomas[2] (1), was born in Truro, Mass., March 12, 1707; was married Feb. 18, 1728, to Nicholas Sparks.

Ann Ridley[3] (1), second daughter of Thomas[2] (1), was born in Truro, Mass., March 7, 1710; died Aug. 16, 1712.

Ann Ridley[3] (2), third daughter of Thomas[2] (1), was born in Truro, Mass., July 19, 1713; married to Dea. Edward Knowles.

Sarah Ridley[3] (1), fourth daughter of Thomas[2] (1), was born in Truro, Mass., April 10, 1720; was married Sept. 18, 1789, to Henry Dyer, of Truro.

Thankful Ridley[3] (1), fifth daughter of Thomas[2] (1), was born in Truro, Mass., Nov. 26, 1726; was married Sept. 15, 1737, to Taylor Smalley, of Truro.

Bette Ridley[3] (1), sixth daughter of Thomas[2] (1), was born in Truro,

* "A LONELY GRAVE. — About midway of East Harbor, near a dismal swamp, with not a habitation in sight or sound, with not a tree, or rock, or post, or sign of life, where the hills rest tier on tier, — Alps piled on Alps, — and the valleys circle deeper and deeper, is the solitary grave of Thomas Ridley, who died of small-pox, 1776. The dark slate heads-tone lay scattered in fragments about the grave. By careful matching, the name and date were made out, though part of the stone is missing." — *History of Truro.*

Mass., Jan. 16, 1728; was married, Sept. 15, 1748, to John Hatch, of Truro.

Deborah Ridley³ (1), seventh daughter of Thomas² (1), was born in Truro, Mass., May 13, 1731; was married Aug. 13, 1758, to Samuel Newcomb.

FOURTH GENERATION.

John Ridley⁴ (2), eldest son of Thomas³ (2), was born in Truro, Mass., June 19, 1738; died Dec. 6, 1738.

John Ridley⁴ (3), second son of Thomas³ (2), was born in Truro, Mass., in September, 1739; married March 20, 1760, to Hannah Grass, of Truro, and had issue *nine* children, of whom hereafter.

Isaac Ridley⁴ (1), third son of Thomas³ (2), was born in Truro, Mass., Jan. 21, 1742.

Elizabeth Ridley⁴ (1), eldest daughter of Thomas³ (2), was born in Truro, Mass., May 9, 1744; was married Oct. 31, 1768, to Daniel Combs.

Thomas Ridley⁴ (3), fourth son of Thomas³ (2), was born in Truro, Mass., June 13, 1746; died issueless.

Mary Ridley⁴ (2), second daughter of Thomas³ (2), was born in Truro, Mass., Sept. 18, 1748; was married Nov. 4, 1767, to Edward Barbour.

Jerusha Ridley⁴ (1), third daughter of Thomas³ (2), was born in Truro, Mass., March 20, 1750.

Hannah Ridely⁴ (1), fourth daughter of Thomas³ (2), was born in Truro, Mass., May 15, 1753.

Lucretia Ridley⁴ (1), fifth daughter of Thomas³ (2), was born in Truro, Mass., Sept. 7, 1755.

Deliverance Ridley⁴ (1), sixth daughter of Thomas³ (2), was born in Truro, Mass., Jan. 17, 1759.

Ann Ridley⁴ (3), eldest daughter of James³ (1), was born in Truro, Mass., Sept. 28, 1740.

Sarah Ridley⁴ (2), second daughter of James³ (1), was born in Truro, Mass., April 13, 1743.

James Ridley⁴ (2), eldest son of James³ (1), was born in Truro, Mass., June 25, 1745; married, firstly, to Isabelle Gilkey, and by her had *seven* children, of whom hereafter; secondly, to Betsey Bridges, by whom *three* children, of whom hereafter. He was a seaman. Some say it was this James who was killed by lightning.

Ambrose Ridley⁴ (1), second son of James³ (1), was born in Truro, Mass., March 16, 1747; married —— Trafton, and had issue *seven* children, of whom hereafter. He went to Harpswell, Me., with his father, when a boy, and spent his early years hunting on the eastern rivers; like his father he was a venturesome, daring man; loved the woods, and was a stranger to fear. When young he went through the wilderness from Harpswell to York, York County, Me., where he settled and lived for several years; he subsequently moved to Alfred, and lived there the remainder of his days. Mr. Ridley returned to his father's home in the East, but once after going to York, when about nineteen years of age. He was a strong-framed, muscular man, hardy, and invested with a strong constitution. He died in 1834, aged 87 years.

David Ridley⁴ (1), third son of James³ (1), was born in Truro, Mass., April 30, 1750; died when young.

Ruth Ridley⁴ (1), third daughter of James³ (1), was born in Truro,

Mass., March 28, 1752 ; was married to Crawford Staples, and settled in Prospect, Me.

David Ridley[4] (2), fourth son of James[3] (1), was born of his second wife, in Harpswell, Me., Aug. 21, 1755 ; married, and had issue *six* children, of whom hereafter.

Daniel Ridley[4] (1), fifth son of James[3] (1), was born of his second wife in Harpswell, Me., April 4, 1759 ; married, and had issue *ten* children, of whom hereafter. He enlisted for three years in the army of the Revolution, Feb. 8, 1777, under Capt. John Reed, in Colonel Alden's Massachusetts Regiment. He was in the battle of Cherry Valley, N. Y., and in Sullivan's expedition against the Six Nation Indians ; also at the surrender of General Burgoyne. At the time of his discharge at West Point (1780) Colonel Brooks was in command of the regiment. Mr. Ridley returned to his native State, and settled on a farm in Bowdoin, where he continued the remainder of his days, and lived to old age.

Capt. George Ridley[4] (1), sixth son of James[3] (1), was born in Harpswell, Me., in 1761 ; married Molly Hopkins (she was born May 7, 1776, and died in 1830), settled in Bowdoin, and had issue *nine* children, of whom hereafter. He enlisted in the army of the Revolution in February, 1777, in the company of Capt. John Reed, and served under Colonels Alden and Brooks about three years and three months. He was in General Sullivan's expedition against the Six Nation Indians ; in the battle of Long Island, and at the surrender of Burgoyne. He endured great hardships in the expedition up the Susquehannah, when five thousand men penetrated into the Indian country and attacked them in their well-constructed fortifications. Mr. Ridley said the howling of the savages was appalling and their resistance determined, but they were overpowered, and forty of their villages destroyed. He was discharged at West Point in 1780, and returned to his home in Maine, where he died Oct. 31, 1818, aged 59 years. He was a man of strong mind and generous heart.

Mark Ridley[4] (3), seventh son of James[3] (1), was born in Harpswell, Me., in 1763 ; married Abigail Webber, and settled on Great Island ; had issue *ten* children, of whom hereafter. He was a wealthy man ; owned about five hundred acres of land, nearly surrounded by water, and kept a large stock of cattle and horses. He also owned a tide grist-mill. His house was situated on an elevation which descended gradually south to the sea. He died May 9, 1818 ; his wife died Feb. 21, 1817, aged 60 years.

Rachel Ridley[4] (1) fourth daughter of James[3] (1), was born in Harpswell, Me., in 1765 ; was married, and lived in Prospect, Me.

Mary Ridley[4] (3), fifth daughter of James[3] (1), was born in Harpswell, Me., in 1767 ; was married, and settled in Prospect, Me.

Isabelle Ridley[4] (1), sixth daughter of James[3] (1), was born in Harpswell, Me., 1769 (?) ; no particulars.

FIFTH GENERATION.

Reuben Ridley[5] (1), eldest son of John[4] (3), was born in Truro, Mass., Nov. 14, 1760.

John Ridley[5] (4), second son of John[4] (3), was born in Truro, Mass., June 9, 1764.

Hannah Ridley[5] (2), eldest daughter of John[4] (3), was born in Truro, Mass., June 17, 1766.

Nathaniel Ridley[5] (1), third son of John[4] (3), was born in Truro, Mass., Nov. 29, 1768; married March 15, 1792, to Sabra Rich, of Truro, and settled first in Provincetown, in the same County. He removed to Boston in 1800; thence to New Sharon, Me., in 1813, where he died in April, 1856, aged 86 years, having had issue *eight* children, of whom hereafter.

Thomas Ridley[5] (4), fourth son of John[4] (3), was born in Truro, Mass., Nov. 25, 1771; married Nov. 16, 1796, to Rachel Cook, of Provincetown, and had issue, of whom hereafter. He lived in Boston at one time.

Elizabeth Ridley[4] (2), second daughter of John[4] (3), was born in Truro, Mass., Nov. 25, 1771; twin to Thomas.

Martha Ridley[5] (1), third daughter of John[4] (3), was born in Truro, Mass., Dec. 25, 1774.

Deborah Ridley[5] (2), fourth daughter of John[4] (3), was born in Truro, Mass., Jan. 22, 1777.

Jerusha Ridley[4] (2), fifth daughter of John[4] (3), was born in Truro, Mass., Nov. 23, 1779.

George Ridley[5] (2), eldest son of James[4] (2), was born in Harpswell, Me., in 1774; married, and settled in his native town.

James Ridley[5] (3), second son of James[4] (2), was born in Harpswell, Me., March 5, 1776; married in 1800 to Hannah Bridges, of Thomaston, and had issue *thirteen* children, of whom hereafter. He settled in Prospect when a boy, and remembered of riding to Topsham to mill horseback when twelve years old. He died Aug. 22, 1838, aged 62 years.

Daniel Ridley[5] (3), third son of James[4] (2), was born in Harpswell, Me., February, 1782; married Polly Bassick, and had issue *ten* children, of whom hereafter. He settled in Prospect and carried on a farm; died in May, 1873, aged 91.

Isabell Ridley[4] (2), eldest daughter of James[4] (2), was born in Harpswell, Me.; was married to John Campbell, and lived in her native town.

Ruth Ridley[5] (2), second daughter of James[4] (2), was born in Harpswell, Me.; was married to Crawford Staples, and lived in Prospect.

Sarah Ridley[5] (3), third daughter of James[4] (2), was born in Harpswell, Me.; was married to John Landshere, of Prospect.

Mary Ridley[5] (4), fourth daughter of James[4] (2), was born in Harpswell, Me.; was married to Robert Treat, of Prospect.

Betsey Ridley[5] (2), eldest daughter of James[4] (2) by his second wife, was born in Harpswell, Me.; was married to Thomas Park, and settled in Prospect.

John Ridley[5] (5), eldest son of James[4] (2) by his second wife, was born in Harpswell, Me.; went to sea when a young man, and was never heard from afterwards.

Ambrose Ridley[5] (2), second son of James[4] (2) by his second wife, was born in Harpswell, Me.; married Rhoda Scott, and had issue, of whom hereafter. No other information.

Ruth Ridley[4] (3), eldest daughter of Ambrose[4] (1), was born in York, Me., Dec. 3, 1773; was married to Solomon Littlefield, of Sanford, and had issue.

Joseph Ridley[5] (1), eldest son of Ambrose[4] (1), was born in York, Me., April 25, 1775, and died at sea when young.

James Ridley[5] (4), second son of Ambrose[4] (1), was born in York, Me., March 25, 1777; married in 1798 to Mary Webber, and had issue *twelve* children, of whom hereafter. He settled on a farm in Alfred, Me.; died in 1859, aged 82.

Sally Ridley[5] (1), second daughter of Ambrose[4] (1), was born in Alfred, Me., April 16, 1779; was married to John Crockett, of Shapleigh, and had issue; she lived to be very old.

Anna Ridley[5] (1), third daughter of Ambrose[4] (1), was born in Alfred, Me., April 14, 1781; was married to James Gerry, and had issue; lived in her native town.

Ambrose Ridley[5] (3), third son of Ambrose[4] (1), was born in Alfred, Me., June 10, 1786; married Betsey Thompson, and had issue *sixteen* children, of whom hereafter. He was a farmer in Sanford, Me.

Daniel Ridley[5] (4), fourth son of Ambrose[4] (1), was born in Alfred, Me., June 13, 1789; married Lucy Trafton, of Sanford, and had issue *eight* children, of whom hereafter. He was a farmer in his native town; died April, 1873, aged 84.

John Ridley[5] (6), eldest son of Daniel[4] (1)*, was born in Harpswell, Me., Jan. 17, 1782; married Susan Lincoln, and had issue *ten* children, of whom hereafter. He lived on a farm in Bowdoin, Me.

Hannah Ridley[5] (3), eldest daughter of Daniel[4] (1), was born in Harpswell, Me., Feb. 18, 1784; was married to John Adams and lived in Bowdoin, Me.

Ruben Ridley[5] (2), second son of Daniel[4] (1), was born in Bowdoin, Me., Aug. 18, 1788; married Rachel Curtis, and was lost at sea from the privateer "Dash," in 1814. No family.

Ruth Ridley[5] (4), second daughter of Daniel[4] (1), was born in Bowdoin, Me., March 17, 1791; was married to Adam Adams and resided in her native town. Had *seven* children.

Rachel Ridley[5] (2), third daughter of Daniel[4] (1), was born in Bowdoin, Me., Sept. 11, 1794; was married to Hix Small, and had *three* children, all living in Bowdoin, Me.

Mark Ridley[5] (4), third son of Daniel[4] (1), was born in Bowdoin, Me., Jan. 6, 1796; married Rhoda Combs, March 12, 1820, and had issue *ten* children, of whom hereafter. He resided in Bowdoinham on a farm.

Isaac Ridley[5] (2), fifth son of Daniel[4] (1), was born in Bowdoin, Me., Jan. 19, 1799; married Hannah Varnum, and had issue *nine* children, of whom hereafter.

Thomas Ridley[5] (5), sixth son of Daniel[4] (1), was born in Bowdoin, Me., May 20, 1802; married Julia Campbell, and had issue *three* children, of whom hereafter. He was a farmer in Bowdoinham.

Simeon Ridley[5] (1), eldest son of George[4] (2), was born in Bowdoin, Me., Aug. 1, 1785, and was lost at sea in November, 1807.

Betsey Ridley[5] (3), eldest daughter of George[4] (2), was born in Bowdoin, Me., April 1, 1788; was married in 1810 to John Snow, and died in 1870.

George Ridley[5] (3), second son of George[4] (2), was born in Bowdoin, Me., June 4, 1790; married in 1811 to Rebecca Snow; secondly, in 1825 to Martha Baker, and had issue *seven* children, of whom hereafter. He

---

* The births of Daniel Ridley's family were recorded in Bowdoin, and a part or all of them may have been born there; but my informant said they were born in Harpswell.

evidently settled in Litchfield, as will appear by the birth of his children by his first wife, who deceased in 1824. He probably moved to Bowdoin in 1826. Died Oct. 31, 18—.

Mary Ridley[5] (5), second daughter of George[4] (2), was born in Bowdoin, Me., March 5, 1792; was married in 1820 to James Potter, a farmer, and died in Wellington, Me., in 1848.

Rev. James Ridley[5] (5), third son of George[4] (2), was born in Bowdoin, Me., Nov. 11, 1794; married in 1819 to Mary Sanford, and settled in Litchfield. His first wife died in 1837, aged 44 years. He probably married twice after the death of his first wife, but the names of his wives have not reached me. He was a minister of the Calvinistic Baptist church, and was highly respected for his sincere piety and devotion to the cause of God. He lived on a farm in Monmouth, and died there in 1856, leaving issue *ten* children, of whom hereafter.

Elisha Ridley[5] (1), fourth son of George[4] (2), was born in Bowdoin, Me., April 29, 1797, and died Dec. 14, 1823.

Alexander Ridley[5] (1), fifth son of George[4] (2), was born in Bowdoin, Me., July 18, 1799, and was drowned at sea Oct. 26, 1821. No family mentioned.

Ambrose Ridley[5] (4), sixth son of George[4] (2), was born in Bowdoin, Me., Jan. 12, 1803; married in 1825 to Abigail Nash, and had issue. Settled in his native town.

Isabella Ridley[4] (3), third daughter of George[4] (2), was born in Bowdoin, Me., March 20, 1804; was married in 1830 to Waitstill Potter, and died in Bowdoinham.

William Ridley[5] (1), eldest son of Mark[4] (3), was born in Harpswell, Me., Jan. 30, 1783; married April 7, 1805, to Louisa Adams, and by her had issue *one* child. His first wife died March 25, 1806, and he married, secondly, May 19, 1807, to Mary Bowie, and by her, — who died in 1875, — had issue *eleven* children, of whom hereafter. Mr. Ridley lived on a farm in Bowdoin; he died Oct. 19, 1860, aged 77 years.

James Ridley[5] (6), second son of Mark[4] (3), was born in Harpswell, Me., in 1784, and died at his father's home in 1805, unmarried.

Mark Ridley[5] (5), third son of Mark[4] (3), was born in Harpswell, Me., in 1786; married Sarah Bowman and lived on the homestead with his parents. Was a miller. He had issue *seven* children, of whom hereafter. He died Oct. 23, 1834. One correspondent says this Mark died in 1838, and left *two* daughters and *one* son; the daughters died soon after the father, "with the same fever,"—both in one week.

David Ridley[5] (3), fourth son of Mark[4] (3), was born in Harpswell, Me., in 1788; married Ann Purington, who died in 1820; and he married, secondly, Jane Sawyer. He had issue *seven* children, of whom hereafter. He lived on a farm near his birth-place, on Great Island, Harpswell; he died March 4, 1852, aged 64 years.

Betsey Ridley[5] (4), a daughter of Mark[4] (3), was born in Harpswell, Me.; was married to Samuel Hopkins, a Quaker, and lived on a farm in Brunswick.

Mary Ridley[5] (6), a daughter of Mark[4] (3), was born in Harpswell, Me.; was married to Capt. Moses Linscott, who was lost at sea when his wife was nineteen years old. She was married, secondly, to Joshua Barstow, a harness-maker, and lived at "South-west Bend," in Durham. She died in 1840.

Sally Ridley[6] (2), a daughter of Mark[4] (3), was born in Harpswell, Me.; was married to John Toothaker, a master ship-builder, and lived at "White's Landing" in Richmond, Me. She died insane : hanged herself.

Rachel Ridley[5] (3), a daughter of Mark[4] (3), was born in Harpswell, Me.; was married to Joseph Totman, who was supposed to be lost at sea, but after an absence of fourteen years, to the great surprise of his family, returned to his home. She died in 1871.

Daniel Ridley[5] (5), youngest son of Mark[4] (3), was born in Harpswell, Me.; never married ; was an eccentric character, and wandered about the country nearly all his days. He fell dead while shutting a door in 1870.

Anna Ridley[5] (2), a daughter of Mark[4] (3), was born in Harpswell, Me.; was married to Daniel Sawyer, a seaman, and died in 1873.

SIXTH GENERATION.

Reuben Ridley[6] (3), eldest son of Nathaniel[5] (1), was born in Provincetown, Mass., July 9, 1793, and died in the West Indies, when a young man, unmarried.

Sukey Ridley[6] (1), eldest daughter of Nathaniel[5] (1), was born in Provincetown, Mass., Sept. 4, 1798, and was the wife of a Mr. Wallard ; deceased.

Sabra Ridley[6] (1), second daughter of Nathaniel[5] (1), was born in Provincetown, Mass., Feb. 1, 1801; was married to Capt. B. Payne, and resides in Boston.

Berthia Ridley[6] (1), third daughter of Nathaniel[5] (1), was born in Provincetown, Mass., in 1803; was married to a Mr. Fellows, and lived in New Orleans, La.

Abbie Ridley[6] (1), fourth daughter of Nathaniel[5] (1), was born in Boston, Mass., in 1805, and was the wife of C. S. Farnum, of said city; lives at Townsend Centre.

Nathaniel Ridley[6] (2), second son of Nathaniel[5] (1), was born in Boston, Mass., March 4, 1806; married Mercy Shaw, of New Sharon, Me., and had issue *two* children, of whom hereafter. Residence, New Sharon.

Thomas Ridley[6] (6), third son of Nathaniel[5] (1), was born in Boston, Mass., in 1813; married Susan S. Hawes, of New Sharon, and has issue *one* child, of whom hereafter. He has kept store, and traveled as agent for the Dunn Edge-Tool Company. Mr. Ridley is tall and erect; has black eyes, gray hair, and long, flowing, white beard. He is social, genial, and possessed of excellent business capacity.

Reuben Ridley[6] (4), fourth son of Nathaniel[5] (1), was born in New Sharon, Me., in 1814; married Florilla Smith, of said town (she died previous to 1865), and settled in his native town. He went to Kansas in 1865, and died in 1871.

Eliza Ridley[6] (1), youngest daughter of Nathaniel[5] (1), was born in New Sharon, say 1816, and married to Seth Higgins, and lived at Townsend Centre, Mass., in 1872.

Sally Ridley[6] (3), eldest son of James[5] (3), was born in Prospect, Me., March 9, 1801; was married to Edmund Trueworthy, of Orland, and died in 1886.

Hannah Ridley[6] (4), second daughter of James[5] (3), was born in Prospect, Me., Sept. 26, 1803; was married to Nathaniel Chase, and died in 1821.

Isabella Ridley[6] (4), third daughter of James[5] (3), was born in Prospect, Me., July 16, 1805; was married Dec. 11, 1823 to Samuel Ginn, and lives in Prospect. She is a devoted Christian, ripened for heaven.

Mary Ridley[6] (7), fourth daughter of James[5] (3), was born in Prospect, Me., July 27, 1807; was married to Amos Partridge, and is now (1879) living.

Lenity Ridley[6] (1), fifth daughter of James[5] (3), was born in Prospect, Me., July 13, 1809; was married to Wentworth Ginn, settled in Orland, and died Dec. 7, 1875.

John-B. Ridley[6] (7), eldest son of James[5] (3), was born in Prospect, Me., May 1, 1811; married, firstly, Jan. 3, 1833, Charlotte Dollard, by whom *seven* children; secondly, to Lucy Clemments, by whom *two* children, of whom hereafter. He lived on a farm at Prospect Ferry. Formerly spelled his name *Redley*. He died Nov. 9, 1868, aged 65 years.

Ruth Ridley[6] (4), sixth daughter of James[5] (3), was born in Prospect, Me., Jan. 31, 1813; died Jan. 7, 1837.

James Ridley[6] (7), second son of John[5] (3), was born in Prospect, Me., April 3, 1815; married and settled in his native town on a farm; had issue *five* children, of whom hereafter.

Betsey Ridley[6] (5), seventh daughter of James[5] (3), was born in Prospect, Me., Aug. 10, 1817; was married to Thomas Billards (?), and lived in her native town.

Henry Ridley[6] (1), third son of James[5] (3), was born in Prospect, Me., Oct. 19, 1819; married Sarah Bowden, and had issue *six* children, of whom hereafter. He is dead.

Rebecca Ridley[6] (1), eighth daughter of James[5] (3), was born in Prospect, Me., May 29, 1821; deceased when young.

Hannah Ridley[6] (5), ninth daughter of James[5] (3), was born in Prospect, Me., May 12, 1823; was married to Charles Snowman, and lived in Prospect.

Joseph Ridley[6] (2), youngest son of James[5] (3), was born in Prospect, Me., July 5, 1826; died years ago.

Dolly Ridley[6] (2), eldest daughter of Daniel[5] (3), was born in Prospect, Me., in February, 1810; was married to Joram Nichols, of Searsmont, and had issue; deceased.

Alfred Ridley[6] (1), eldest son of Daniel[5] (3), was born in Prospect, Me., in May, 1811; married Clarissa Kneeland, and had issue *eight* children, of whom hereafter. He resides in Stockton. Has manifested a deep interest in this book, and provided many data.

Daniel Ridley[6] (6), second son of Daniel[5] (3), was born in Prospect, Me., in June, 1813; went to sea and never returned; supposed to have been drowned.

Mary Ridley[6] (8), second daughter of Daniel[5] (3), was born in Prospect, Me., in May, 1817; was married to Capt. William Fletcher, and lived in Stockton; deceased.

Margaret Ridley[6] (1), third daughter of Daniel[5] (3), was born in Prospect, Me., in November, 1819; was married to Capt. Wm. Fletcher (previously married her sister), lives in Stockton.

William Ridley[6] (2), third son of Daniel[5] (3), was born in Prospect, Me., in January, 1822; married Persis B. Rice, and had issue *three* children, of whom hereafter. He settled in Searsmont, but has removed to Oregon.

Nathaniel Ridley[6] (3), fourth son of Daniel[5] (3), was born in Prospect, Me., in September, 1824; married Margaret E. Reed, and had issue *three* children, of whom hereafter. Resides on a farm in Searsport.

Enoch Ridley[6] (1), fifth son of Daniel[5] (3), was born in Prospect, Me., in February, 1827, and was drowned at sea, aged 20.

Susan Ridley[6] (2), fourth daughter of Daniel[5] (3), was born in Prospect, Me., in September, 1830; was married to William Webb, mariner; both now deceased.

Dudley Ridley[6] (1), sixth son of Daniel[5] (3), was born in Prospect, Me., in October, 1833; married Hannah Rice, and had issue *two* children, of whom hereafter; deceased.

Joseph Ridley[6] (3), only son of Ambrose[5] (2), was born June 20, 1817, and was called the "American Lambert." At the time of his birth he weighed only seven pounds; he grew very fast, and when three months old weighed seventy pounds. He lived till two and a half years old, and at the time of his death weighed two hundred and forty pounds. He was handsome, active, and well-proportioned, and possessed of great muscular strength. His mind was also remarkable, and at two years of age he could talk well and tell any piece of money. His parents carried him to Boston for exhibition, intending to visit other cities in America and Europe, but the boy grew suddenly sick and died. Some believe he was poisoned.

Annie Ridley[6] (1), eldest daughter of James[5] (4), was born in Alfred, Me., April 7, 1799; was married in 1822 to John Littlefield, son of Solomon, of Sanford, and had issue.

Ellen Ridley[6] (1), second daughter of James[5] (4), was born in Alfred, Me., April 1, 1801; was married Dec. 14, 1824, to Amos Allen, of Waterborough, and had issue.

Joseph Ridley[6] (4), eldest son of James[5] (4), was born in Alfred, Me., June 5, 1803; married Dec. 29, 1826, to Phebe Getchell (she was born Aug. 15, 1802), and had issue *eleven* children, of whom hereafter. Carpenter by trade. Residence unknown. Died Feb. 1, 1849.

James Ridley[6] (8), second son of James[5] (4), was born in Alfred, Me., Feb. 29, 1805; married Mercy, daughter of John Trafton, of Alfred, and had issue *four* children, of whom hereafter. He was a farmer and joiner. Residence in Alfred. Died May 31, 1874.

Mary Ridley[6] (9), third daughter of James[5] (4), was born in Alfred, Me., in 1807, and died when young.

Simon Ridley[6] (2), third son of James[5] (4), was born in Alfred, Me., March 29, 1809; married in 1837, to Huldah D. Webber.

Rufus Ridley[6] (1), fourth son of James[5] (4), was born in Alfred, Me., July 18, 1811; married Oct. 17, 1836, to Sarah-Ann, daughter of Samuel Bachellor, of Shapleigh; she died April 29, 1855, and he married, secondly, Dec. 25, 1863, to Esther-Ann, daughter of Ivory Ridley, of Alfred. He had issue *nine* children by his first wife, and *four* by the second wife, of whom hereafter. Mr. Ridley is a shoe-maker and farmer; has manifested a deep interest in this book, and furnished many data.

Mary Ridley[6] (10), fourth daughter of James[5] (4), was born in Alfred, Me., Oct. 28, 1813; was married to Charles Baker, a machinist, of Lyman, and had issue.

Isaiah Ridley[6] (1), fifth son of James[5] (4), was born in Alfred, Me.,

35

about 1815, and died when young. There was one child who died in infancy between Isaiah and Sarah.

Sarah Ridley[6] (**4**), fifth daughter of James[5] (**4**), was born in Alfred, Me., Oct. 29, 1820; was married to Cyrus Webber, shoe-maker, of Beverly, Mass.; secondly, to David C. Pattie, of Rockport, and is now (1877) a widow.

Joel Ridley[6] (**1**), sixth and youngest son of James[5] (**4**), was born in Alfred, Me., in 1822, and died unmarried.

Amos Ridley[6] (**1**), eldest son of Ambrose[5] (**3**), was born in Alfred (or Shapleigh), Me., Sept. 25, 1813; married Oct. 25, 1838, to Tabitha R. Jackson (she was born at Marblehead, Mass., July 13, 1812), and had issue *four* children, of whom hereafter. Carpenter by trade; residence in North Andover, Mass.

Allen Ridley[6] (**1**), second son of Ambrose[5] (**3**), was born in Alfred, Me., in 1816; married Catherine Bennett (she was born in Sanford, in 1822), and had issue *seven* children, of whom hereafter. Resides at South Sanford. Is six feet in height; weighs one hundred and forty pounds; has light complexion.

Ambrose Ridley[6] (**5**), third son of Ambrose[5] (**3**), was born in Sanford, Me.; married Abigail Evans, and had issue *two* daughters, of whom hereafter. Mr. Ridley died many years ago; his widow lives in Boston.

Isaiah Ridley[6] (**2**), a son of Ambrose[5] (**3**), was born in Sanford, Me.

Abial Ridley[5] (**1**), a son of Ambrose[5] (**3**), was born in Sanford, Me.

Theodore Ridley[6] (**1**), a son of Ambrose[5] (**3**), was born in Sanford, Me.

Jacob Ridley[6] (**1**), a son of Ambrose[5] (**3**), was born in Sanford, Me., and died young.

Jacob Ridley[6] (**2**), a son of Ambrose[5] (**3**), was born in Sanford, Me., in 1832; married Sept. 23, 1861, to Abbie R. Hamblin (she was born in 1844), and had issue *two* children, of whom hereafter. He is an operative in a mill at Lawrence, Mass.

Joseph Ridley[6] (**5**), a son of Ambrose[5] (**3**). ⎫
Sarah Ridley[6] (**5**), daughter of Ambrose[5] (**3**). ⎬ Born in Sanford, Me.
　　　　　　　　　　　　Ambrose[5] (**3**). ⎭

Ivory Ridley[6] (**1**), eldest son of Daniel[5] (**4**), was born in Alfred, Me., March 13, 1811; married May 28, 1842, to Eliza Norton, of Shapleigh, and has issue *five* children, of whom hereafter. Farmer in his native town.

Lucy Ridley[6] (**1**), eldest daughter of Daniel[5] (**4**), was born in Alfred, Me., and died young.

Hiram Ridley[6] (**2**), second son of Daniel[5] (**4**), was born in Alfred, Me., and died young.

Mary Ridley[6] (**11**), second daughter of Daniel[5] (**4**), was born in Alfred, Me., and died young (?).

Mary Ridley[6] (**12**), third daughter of Daniel[5] (**4**), was born in Alfred, Me., Aug. 25, 1815; was married to Joseph Lord, of Shapleigh, and resides in her native town.

Joseph Ridley[6] (**6**), third son of Daniel[5] (**4**), was born in Alfred, Me., and died young.

Daniel Ridley[6] (**7**), fourth son of Daniel[5] (**4**), was born in Alfred, Me., June 10, 1822; married Eliza, daughter of William Weymouth, of Berwick, and had issue *three* children, of whom hereafter. Farmer; resides in Alfred.

John Ridley⁶ (8), fifth son of Daniel⁵ (4), was born in Alfred, Me., and died young.

Joseph Ridley⁶ (7), eldest son of John⁵ (6), was born in Bowdoin, Me., March 26, 1804; married Hannah Maloon (she was born April 4, 1808), and had issue *four* children, of whom hereafter. Farmer; residence in the city of Bath, Me. Height, medium; complexion, dark.

Hannah Ridley⁶ (6), eldest daughter of John⁵ (6), was born in Bowdoin, Me., July 5, 1805; was married.

Lydia Ridley⁶ (1), second daughter of John⁵ (6), was born in Bowdoin, Me., Sept. 18, 1807; was married.

Ruth Ridley⁶ (5), third daughter of John⁵ (6), was born in Bowdoin, Me., Sept. 18, 1807; was married.

Susannah Ridley⁶ (1), fourth daughter of John⁵ (6), was born in Bowdoin, Me., July 6, 1810; died July 15, 1811.

Reuben Ridley⁶ (5), second son of John⁵ (6), was born in Bowdoin, Me., March 5, 1812.

James Ridley⁶ (9), third son of John⁵ (6), was born in Bowdoin, Me., July 1, 1814.

Obediah Ridley⁶(2), fourth son of John⁵ (6), was born in Bowdoin, Me., March 22, 1816.

Susannah Ridley⁶ (2), fifth daughter of John⁵ (6), was born in Bowdoin, Me., April 26, 1818.

Ruth Ridley⁶ (6), sixth daughter of John⁵ (6), was born in Bowdoin, Me., July 15, 1820.

Lorin Ridley⁶ (1), son of Daniel⁵ (6), was born in Bowdoinham, Me.

Daniel Ridley⁶ (8), son of Daniel⁵ (6), was born in Bowdoinham, Me.

Susan Ridley⁶ (3), daughter of Daniel⁵ (6), was born in Bowdoinham, Me.

Martha Ridley⁶ (2), eldest daughter of Mark⁵ (4), was born in Bowdoin, Me., Oct. 13, 1820; was married to William Lund, and died May 2, 1860.

Rachel Ridley⁶ (4), second daughter of Mark⁵ (4), was born in Bowdoin, Me., Jan. 6, 1822; was married to Solomon Patterson, and had issue.

Alexander Ridley⁶ (3), eldest son of Mark⁵ (4), was born in Bowdoin, Me., June 26, 1824; married Sarah A. Hinkley, of Topsham, and and had issue *ten* children, of whom hereafter. Mr. Ridley is a merchant in Brunswick.

Caleb Ridley⁶ (2), second son of Mark⁵ (4), was born in Bowdoin, Me., Sept. 6, 1826; married in November, 1850, to Ruth Morse, and had issue *seven* children, of whom hereafter. Farmer; residence, Topsham, Me.

Charlotte Ridley⁶ (1), third daughter of Mark⁵ (4), was born in Bowdoin, Me., Dec. 28, 1828; was married to Horatio MacKenney, of Brunswick, and has issue.

Hannah Ridley⁶ (7), fourth daughter of Mark⁵(4), was born in Bowdoin, Me., April 27, 1831; was married to John Owen, of Brunswick, and had issue. She resided at Jamaica Plain, near Boston, Mass., in 1873.

Daniel Ridley⁶ (9), third son of Mark⁵ (4), was born in Bowdoin, Me., Sept. 29, 1833; died in October, 1834.

Caroline Ridley⁶ (2), fifth daughter of Mark⁵ (4), was born in Bowdoin, Me., in December, 1835; was married to George Barron, of Topsham, in 1855, and has issue.

Madora Ridley⁶ (1), sixth daughter of Mark⁵ (4), was born in Bowdoin, Me., March 29, 1838; was married to George Drew, and lives at Jamaica Plain, Mass.

Julia Ridley⁶ (11), seventh daughter of Mark⁵ (4), was born in Bowdoin, Me., Dec. 10, 1841; was married to Ithina Hamilton (he was killed at the battle of Aldee during the Rebellion), and secondly, Nov. 15, 1871, to Horace Winship, of Boston, Mass.

Maria Ridley⁶ (1), eldest daughter of Isaac⁵ (2), was born in Bowdoin, Me., Feb. 22, 1827; was married June 9, 1850, to Reuben Holbrook, of Topsham, and died Aug. 13, 1878.

Charles-S. Ridley⁶ (1), eldest son of Isaac⁵ (2), was born in Bowdoin, Me., Nov. 27, 1880; died Nov. 18, 1841.

Elizabeth Ridley⁶ (3), second daughter of Isaac⁵ (2), was born in Bowdoin, Me., Jan. 27, 1887; was married May 9, 1855, to Rev. Hiram Mitchell, and lives in St. George.

Isaac-H. Ridley⁶ (3), second son of Isaac⁵ (2), was born in Bowdoin, Me., March 16, 1841; married Aug. 2, 1863, to Anna, daughter of Ayers and Matilda Haines, and has issue *three* children, of whom hereafter. Resides on a farm in his native town.

Charles-S. Ridley⁶ (2), third son of Isaac⁵ (2), was born in Bowdoin, Me., June 4, 1845; died Sept. 15, 1851.

Reuben Ridley⁶ (5), fourth son of Isaac⁵ (2), was born in Bowdoin, Me., May 7, 1849; died Sept. 8, 1851.

Abeona Ridley⁶ (1), third daughter of Isaac⁵ (2), was born in Bowdoin, Me., Oct. 16, 1852; died Nov. 16, 1861.

Ambrose Ridley⁶ (6), eldest son of Thomas⁵ (5), was born in Bowdoin, Me.

Reed Ridley⁶ (1), second son of Thomas⁵ (5), was born in Bowdoin, Me.

Eunice Ridley⁶ (1), eldest daughter of George⁵ (5), was born in Litchfield, Me., Sept. 29, 1818; was married to Capt. James Millbray, and lives in Bowdoin.

Henry Ridley⁶ (2), eldest son of George⁵ (3), was born in Litchfield, Me., Oct. 15, 1815; married July 14, 1844, to Eunice F. Purington, and has issue *seven* children, of whom hereafter. Resides in Cornville, on a farm.

Dexter-W. Ridley⁶ (1), second son of George⁵ (3), was born in Bowdoin, Me., in 1826; married and has issue. He is an engineer living in California.

Humphrey Ridley⁶ (1), third son of George⁵ (3), was born in Bowdoin, Me., in 1827-8; married Elizabeth Combs, and has issue *two* children, of whom hereafter. He resides at Richmond Village, Me. A millman.

Rebecca-R. Ridley⁶ (2), second daughter of George⁵ (3), was born in Bowdoin, Me., in 1829; was married to William A. Provins, and resides in Richmond, Me.

Emma-B. Ridley⁶ (1), third daughter of George⁵ (3), was born in

Bowdoin, Me., in 1832; was married to Vorn R. Neal, and resides in Augusta, Me.

George-R. Ridley[6] (**4**), fourth son of George[5] (**3**), was born in Bowdoin, Me., in 1834; married Annie D. Folsom, and has issue *three* children, of whom hereafter. Mr. Ridley is a millman; resides in Richmond, Me.

Mary-E. Ridley[6] (**12**), eldest daughter of James[5] (**5**), was born in Bowdoin, Me., in 1820; was married to John M. Safford, and resides in Monmouth, Me.

Abbie-E. Ridley[6] (**2**), second daughter of James[5] (**5**), was born in Bowdoin, Me., in 1822; was married to Josiah F. Purington, and resides at Gardiner, Me. She says: "After my father's death in 1856, the homestead passed into other hands, and we children were scattered, some one way and some another; we were together for the last time when I was married."

Minerva-J. Ridley[6] (**1**), third daughter of James[5] (**5**), was born in Litchfield, Me., in 1824; was married to Xenophon Goodenow, of Boston, Mass. Deceased.

Susan-W. Ridley[6] (**4**), fourth daughter of James[5] (**5**), was born in Litchfield, Me., in 1826, and was married to Xenophon Goodenow, who had previously married her sister.

Margaret Ridley[6] (**2**), fifth daughter of James[5] (**5**), was born in Litchfield, Me., in 1828, and died when young.

Horace-S. Ridley[6] (**1**), eldest son of James[5] (**5**), was born in Litchfield, Me., in 1830; married in Boston, Mass., about 1865, and has issue *three* children, of whom hereafter. Lives in San Francisco, Cal.

Sanford-S. Ridley[6] (**1**), second son of James[5] (**5**), was born in Litchfield, Me., in 1832; married Mary Leard, of Washington, Me, resided in Massachusetts, died in Monmouth, Me.

Ellen-P. Ridley[6] (**3**), sixth daughter of James[5] (**5**), was born in Litchfield, Me., in 1835; was married to Frank A. Snowman, and died at Gardiner, aged 25 years.

Melinda Ridley[6] (**1**), twin daughter of James[5] (**5**), was born in Bowdoin, Me., in 1837.

Durenda Ridley[6] (**1**), twin daughter of James[5] (**5**), was born in Bowdoin, Me., in 1837.

Alonzo Ridley[6] (**1**), eldest son of Ambrose[5] (**4**), was born about June 3, 1826, and lives somewhere in California.

Clark Ridley[6] (**1**), second son of Ambrose[5] (**4**), was born Jan. 13, 1830; married Sarah French; was a carpenter by trade. Starved to death in Andersonville during the late war.

Mark Ridley[6] (**6**), eldest son of William[5] (**1**), was born in Bowdoin, Me., July 17, 1808; married Sylvia Atherton, and had issue *six* children, of whom hereafter. He is a farmer in Canaan, Me.

Lois Ridley[6] (**1**), eldest daughter of William[5] (**1**), was born in Bowdoin, Me., Aug. 11, 1810; was married to George Sedgely (a tailor by trade), and lived in Bowdoinham.

Abigail Ridley[6] (**2**), second daughter of William[5] (**1**), was married to Joseph H. Tapley, and lived in Litchfield; she deceased in 1843.

Moses Ridley[6] (**1**), second son of William[5] (**1**), was born in Bowdoin,

Me., Sept. 17, 1814; married Huldah Robinson and had issue *five* children, of whom hereafter. Mr. Ridley is of medium height, with dark complexion. He is a farmer in Litchfield.

James Ridley[6] **(10)**, third son of William[5] **(1)**, was born in Bowdoin, Me., in 1817, and died young.

Ann Ridley[6] **(4)**, third daughter of William[5] **(1)**, was born in Bowdoin, Me., Feb. 26, 1819. No other facts.

Betsey Ridley[6] **(6)**, fourth daughter of William[5] **(1)**, was born in Bowdoin, Me., June 20, 1821; was married to Joseph H. Tapley (a merchant) before mentioned, and died in the city of Lewiston in 1874.

Deborah Ridley[6] **(3)**, fifth daughter of William[5] **(1)**, was born in Bowdoin, Me., July 8, 1825, and died in 1842.

William Ridley[6] **(3)**, fourth son of William[5] **(1)**, was born in Bowdoin, Me., March 14, 1823; married Elizabeth Gore, and had issue *six* children, of whom hereafter. He resides in Exeter, N. H.

Alexander Ridley[6] **(4)**, fifth son of William[5] **(1)**, was born in Bowdoin, Me., June 24, 1827; married Jane Atherton, and had issue *seven* children, of whom hereafter. He is a shipwright; residence in Bowdoin.

Albion Ridley[6] **(1)**, sixth son of William[5] **(1)**, was born in Bowdoin, Me., March 16, 1831; married May 16, 1854, to Harriet Gore, daughter of Elder Richard Gore, of Canaan, and has issue *five* children, of whom hereafter. Settled on a farm in his native town. Has traveled extensively through the United States and Territories. Carpenter by trade; real-estate owner in Lewiston, Me., where he has resided several years. Policeman in 1884. He is genial, conversational, and a good financier.

John Ridley[6] **(9)**, seventh son of William[5] **(1)**, was born in Bowdoin, Me., in April, 1833; married —— Flagg and has issue *four* children; ship-carpenter in Brooklyn, N. Y.

Joseph Ridley[6] **(7)**, eighth son of William[5] **(1)**, was born in Bowdoin, Me., Feb. 25, 1836; married —— Gore (?), secondly, Fannie Lane, and has issue *three* children. He is an overseer in a mill at Fall River, Mass.

James Ridley[6] **(11)**, ninth son of William[5] **(1)**, was born in Bowdoin, Me., in April, 1839, and died single.

Elizabeth Ridley[6] **(4)**, a daughter of Mark[5] **(5)**, was born in Harpswell about the year 1819, and died of a malignant fever, which swept away many of the family within a few days, in 1834, aged 15 years.

Sarah Ridley[6] **(6)**, a daughter of Mark[5] **(5)**, was born in Harpswell, Me., and died at the age of 10 years, Oct. 5, 1834, with fever.

Mark-H. Ridley[6] **(7)**, a son of Mark[5] **(5)**, was born in Harpswell, Me., and died Oct. 2, 1834, aged 19 months.

George Ridley[6] **(5)**, a son of Mark[5] **(5)**, was born in Harpswell, Me., and survived his father, but I do not know his after-history. A sister was married to William Amey and one to George Plaisted.

Robert-P. Ridley[6] **(1)**, eldest son of David[5] **(3)**, was born in Harpswell, Me., January, 1805; married Feb. 8, 1827, to Sophrona Watson, and had issue *nine* children, of whom hereafter. He purchased the mill formerly owned by James Ridley, at Harpswell, and resided in that town till 1857, when he emigrated to Iowa, where he now (1874) resides. Carpenter and millman; a man of sound mind and strong traits of character.

James Ridley[6] (12), second son of David[5] (3), was born in Harpswell, Me., in 1807; married in 1828 to Judith Watson, and died eight days after that event.

Samuel Ridley[6] (1), third son of David[5] (3), was born in Harpswell, Me., March 21, 1822; married Dec. 25, 1845, to Melvina Doyle, of Bowdoinham, and had issue *six* children, of whom hereafter. Farmer and seaman; resides in his native town.

Isaac M. Ridley[6] (4), fourth son of David[5] (3), was born in Harpswell, Me., July 21, 1832; married June 25, 1855, to Chloe A. Thompson, and had issue *three* children, of whom hereafter. Sailor; residence, Harpswell, Cumberland County, Me.

Caroline Ridley[6] (2), eldest daughter of David[5] (3), was born in Harpswell, Me., in 1812; was married to William Ray, one says Samuel Ray, and resides in Lewiston, Me.

Anne Ridley[6] (3), second daughter of David[5] (3), was born in Harpswell, Me., in 1824; was married to James Parker, and resides at Parker's Lake, Hennepin County, Minn.

Betsey Ridley[6] (7), third daughter of David[5] (3), was born in Harpswell, Me., in 1827; was married to Nelson Buzwell, and died in 1847, without children.

SEVENTH GENERATION.

Sarah Ridley[7] (7), only daughter of Nathaniel[6] (2), was born in New Sharon, Me., Jan. 1, 1833; was married and lives in East Boston, Mass.

Sewell-P. Ridley[7] (1), only son of Nathaniel (2), was born in New Sharon, Me., Feb. 9, 1838; married, and keeps a market in Boston, Mass.

Harriet Ridley[7] (2), only daughter of Thomas[6] (6), was born in New Sharon, Me.; was married to George H. Flint, and resides in Lewiston, Me.

Martha-J. Ridley[7] (3), eldest daughter of John[6] (7), was born in Prospect, Me., Oct. 4, 1834; was married.

Phebe-T. Ridley[7] (1), second daughter of John[6] (7), was born in Prospect, Me., Sept. 27, 1836.

Naomi-D. Ridley[7] (1), third daughter of John[6] (7), was born in Prospect, Me., Oct. 24, 1838; deceased.

Albert-E. Ridley[7] (2), eldest son of John[6] (7), was born in Prospect, Me., April 24, 1840; married, and resides in San Francisco, Cal, where he carries on the business of cutting stencil-plates, and has, I think, some connection with the theatre. He has issue, of whom hereafter.

Caroline-P. Ridley[7] (3), fourth daughter of John[6] (7), was born in Prospect, Me., March 10, 1842.

Amanda-S. Ridley[7] (2), fifth daughter of John[6] (7), was born in Prospect, Me., March 24, 1844.

Rev. John Ridley[7] (10), second son of John[6] (7), was born in Prospect, Me., Jan. 20, 1846; married, and has issue, of whom hereafter. He was agent for the *Portland Transcript.* Now connected with the Second Adventist denomination as a preacher. Residence in Manchester, Ia. He is of medium height, has dark complexion, and is a fluent speaker.

Jacob-T. Ridley[7] (3), third son of John[6] (7), was born in Prospect, Me., Nov. 16, 1848; deceased.

William-B. Ridley[7] (4), fourth son of John[6] (7), was born in Prospect, Me., Sept. 5, 1853.

Charles-T. Ridley[7] **(4)**, fifth son of John[6] (7), was born in Prospect, Me., Aug 30, 1856.

Herbert-F. Ridley[7] **(1)**, sixth son of John[6] (7), was born in Prospect, Me., Nov. 23, 1858.

James-A. Ridley[7] **(13)**, eldest son of James[6] (7), was born in Prospect, Me., Nov. 3, 1840; deceased.

Ruth-S. Ridley[7] **(7)**, eldest daughter of James[6] (7), was born in Prospect, Me., Jan. 10, 1844; deceased.

Orissa-D. Ridley[7] **(1)**, second daughter of James[6] (7), was born in Prospect, Me., Aug. 20, 1845; deceased.

Hugh-T. Ridley[7] **(1)**, second son of James[6] (7), was born in Prospect, Me., April 27, 1848; married, and resides in Prospect; has issue.

Samuel-G. Ridley[7] **(2)**, third son of James[6] (7), was born in Prospect, Me., Dec. 22, 1850; married —— Clements, and has issue, of whom hereafter. Residence in Monroe. An earnest Christian. Height, medium; complexion, light; farmer and woodman.

George-W. Ridley[7] **(4)**, eldest son of Henry[6] (1), was born in Prospect, Me., May 10, 1847.

Annie-M. Ridley[7] **(4)**, eldest daughter of Henry[6] (1), was born in Prospect, Me., Aug. 27, 1848.

Sarah-E. Ridley[7] **(3)**, second daughter of Henry[6] (1), was born in Prospect, Me., Sept. 14, 1850.

Benjamin-M. Ridley[7] **(1)**, second son of Henry[6] (1), was born in Prospect, Me., Oct. 15, 1852.

Rosanna-M. Ridley[7] **(1)**, third daughter of Henry[6] (1), was born in Prospect, Me., Feb. 10, 1855; deceased.

Henry-W. Ridley[7] **(3)**, third son of Henry[6] (1), was born in Prospect, Me., Dec. 22, 1856.

Hittie-B. Ridley[7] **(1)**, fourth daughter of Henry[6] (1), was born in Prospect, Me., Oct. 15, 1869.

Chesley Ridley[7] **(1)**, eldest son of Alfred[6] (1), was born in Prospect, Me., Oct. 16, 1834; married Oct. 9, 1855, and resides in his native town.

Erastus Ridley[7] **(1)**, second son of Alfred[6] (1), was born in Prospect, Me., Oct. 18, 1836, and was lost at sea in December, 1866. He was first mate of the brig "Carlann," and on the voyage from Jacksonville, Fla., about the fourth day out, they were overtaken by a gale and no one was left to tell the particulars.

Christopher-C. Ridley[7] **(1)**, third son of Alfred[6] (1), was born in Prospect, Me., July 24, 1838; married June 26, 1868, to Mary E. Kneeland, and has issue *four* children, of whom hereafter. He resides in his native town.

Annie Ridley[7] **(5)**, eldest daughter of Alfred[6] (1), was born in Prospect, Me., March 27, 1840; unmarried.

Wilber-A. Ridley[7] **(1)**, fourth son of Alfred[6] (1), was born in Prospect, Me., Sept. 3, 1843; was brought home sick with southern fever, and died five days after, Aug. 8, 1871. Probably in the Union army.

Clara-A. Ridley[7] **(1)**, second daughter of Alfred[6] (1), was born in Prospect, Me., Aug. 31, 1845; was married Oct. 30, 1870, to Henry A. Stevens, of Monroe, Me.

Mary-E. Ridley[7] (13), third daughter of Alfred[6] (1), was born in Prospect, Me., March 5, 1847 ; unmarried.

Dora-E. Ridley[7] (1), fourth daughter of Alfred[6] (1), was born in Prospect, Me., May 5, 1852; was married June 1, 1872, to A. J. Crockett, and lives in Stockton.

Frank Ridley[7] (2), eldest son of William[6] (2), was born in Searsport, Me., in December, 1849; married Mary-Evelyn Marden, and has *one* child. Residence, South Thomaston ; follows the sea.

Celia-Etta Ridley[7] (1), eldest daughter of William[6] (2), was born in Searsport, Me., in October, 1855.

Edwin-F. Ridley[7] (1), second son of William[6] (2), was born in Searsport, Me., in November, 1865.

Susan-E. Ridley[7] (4), eldest daughter of Nathaniel[6] (3), was born in Searsport, Me., in September, 1852.

Emma-A. Ridley[7] (2), second daughter of Nathaniel[6] (3), was born in Searsport, Me., in September, 1854.

Silas-Leroy Ridley[7] (1), only son of Nathaniel[6] (3), was born in Searsport, Me., in September, 1857.

Carrie-A. Ridley[7] (2), a daughter of Dudley[6] (1), was born in Searsport, Me., in April, 1855.

Adir-E. Ridley[7] (1), daughter of Dudley[6] (1), was born in Searsport, Me., in 1858.

Huldah-G. Ridley[7] (2), eldest daughter of Joseph[6] (4), was born in Alfred, Me., May 22, 1827 ; was married July 3, 1848, to George K. Frost. Residence unknown.

James Ridley[7] (14), eldest son of Joseph[6] (4), was born in Alfred, Me., May 14, 1828; married June 10, 1847, to Martha A. Morrill, and died Dec. 28, 1872.

Silas-B. Ridley[7] (2), second son of Joseph[6] (4), was born in Alfred, Me., Aug. 5, 1829; married Elizabeth Ricker.

Madison Ridley[7] (1), third son of Joseph[6] (4), was born in Alfred, Me., Sept. 13, 1830 ; married Aug. 29, 1853, to Betsey G. Trafton, and has issue *nine* children, of whom hereafter. Resides on a farm in Sanford, Me.

Mercy-B. Ridley[7] (1), second daughter of Joseph[6] (4), was born in Alfred, Me., Dec. 18, 1831; was married Dec. 8, 1848, to Humphrey S. Clark.

Mary-E. Ridley[7] (14), third daughter of Joseph[6] (4), was born in Alfred, Me., March 8, 1833 ; was married March 18, 1851, to Joseph B. Woodman; lives in Wenham, Mass.

Lydia-W. Ridley[7] (3), fourth daughter of Joseph[6] (4), was born in Alfred, Me., Aug. 29, 1834 ; was married Sept. 4, 1853, to Daniel Gould.

Lyman Ridley[7] (1), fourth son of Joseph[6] (4), was born in Alfred, Me., May 17, 1837 ; married Nov. 6, 1862 to Sarah E. Davidson. Residence unknown.

S.-Emeline Ridley[7] (?), fifth daughter of Joseph[6] (4), was born in Alfred, Me., Aug. 13, 1839. No other information.

Joseph Ridley[7] (8), fifth son of Joseph[6] (4), was born in Alfred, Me., Dec. 3, 1842; married Jan. 2, 1870, to Mary A. Lord; died April 10, 1873.

Alfred Ridley[7] (3), sixth son of Joseph[6] (4), was born in Alfred, Me., Dec. 2, 1845; married Nov. 12, 1868, to Abbie T. Littlefield.

Almira Ridley[7] (1), eldest daughter of James[6] (8), was born in Alfred, Me., in 1833; was married to Jotham Allen, of Waterborough, and has issue.

John-C. Ridley[7] (11), eldest son of James[6] (8), was born in Alfred, Me., in September, 1839; married Mary Knight, of Kennebunk, and has issue *two* children, of whom hereafter.

Olive-A. Ridley[7] (2), second daughter of James[6] (8), was born in Alfred, Me., in 1837; was married to George H. Trafton, of Alfred, and has issue.

Joseph-H Ridley[7] (9), second son of James[6] (8), was born in Alfred, Me.; married Nancy, daughter of Hiram Littlefield, of Sanford.

Francina-B. Ridley[7] (1), eldest daughter of Simon[6] (2), was born in Alfred, Me., Oct. 21, 1842; was married to William H. Walker, of Great Falls, N. H.

Cyrus-W. Ridley[7] (2), eldest son of Simon[6] (2), was born in Alfred, Me., Oct. 31, 1846, and married " a Vermont lady."

Mary-A. Ridley[7] (15), second daughter of Simon[6] (2), was born in Alfred, Me., May 26, 1850, and died in November, 1868.

Sarah-E. Ridley[7] (9), eldest daughter of Rufus[6] (1), was born in Alfred, Me., July 6, 1837, and died Oct. 20, 1838.

Charles-W. Ridley[7] (5), eldest son of Rufus[6] (1), was born in Alfred, Me., July 25, 1839, and died unmarried, March 3, 1873.

Sarah-E. Ridley[7] (10), second daughter of Rufus[6] (1), was born in Alfred, Me., Feb. 3, 1841, and died Nov. 28, 1856.

Samuel-I. Ridley[7] (4), twin son of Rufus[6] (1), was born in Alfred, Me., Sept. 24, 1843, died Jan. 17, 1844.

Lord-M Ridley[7] (1), twin son of Rufus[6] (1), was born in Alfred, Me., Sept. 24, 1843; died Jan. 17, 1844.

Abbie-E. Ridley[7] (3), third daughter of Rufus[6] (1), was born in Alfred, Me., April 11, 1848; was married to Frank Wentworth, and resides in Shapleigh.

George-H. Ridley[7] (6), fourth son of Rufus[6] (1), was born in Alfred, Me., Oct. 24, 1850; married Celia Wentworth, and has issue, of whom hereafter. Shoe-maker; resides in Shapleigh.

Huldah-F. Ridley[7] (3), fourth daughter of Rufus[6] (1), was born in Alfred, Me., Dec. 1, 1852; was married to George Bemis, and resides in Shapleigh.

Franklin Ridley[7] (3), fifth son of Rufus[6] (1), was born in Alfred, Me., March 8, 1855; died Sept. 19, 1855.

Lindsey-D. Ridley[7] (1), sixth son of Rufus[6] (1), was born in Alfred, Me., July 18, 1865.

Angie-E. Ridley[7] (1), fifth daughter of Rufus[6] (1), was born in Alfred, Me., April 26, 1867.

Rufus-P. Ridley[7] (2), seventh son of Rufus[6] (1), was born in Alfred, Me., Nov. 18, 1872, by second wife.

Alvah-D. Ridley[7] (1), eighth son of Rufus[6] (1), was born in Alfred, Me., July 25, 1874, by second wife.

John-F. Ridley[7] (12), eldest son of Amos[6] (1), was born in Andover, Mass., March 30, 1840 ; married.

Charles-W. Ridley[7] (6), second son of Amos[6] (1), was born in Andover, Mass., Aug. 14, 1842; enlisted in the First Massachusetts Regiment, Heavy Artillery, and was killed May 19, 1862, near Spottsylvania Court House, Va.

Martha-E. Ridley[7] (4), eldest daughter of Amos[6] (1), was born in Andover, Mass., Jan. 30, 1845.

Mary-Anna Ridley[7] (16), second daughter of Amos[6] (1), was born in Andover, Mass., June 28, 1847; died July 28, 1848.

Mary-E. Ridley[7] (17), eldest daughter of Allen[6] (1), was born in Sanford, Me., in 1845, and died the same year.

Lucy-E. Ridley[7] (3), second daughter of Allen[6] (1), was born in Sanford, Me., in 1850.

Isaiah-A. Ridley[7] (3), eldest son of Allen[6] (1), was born in Sanford, Me., in 1852.

Herbert-G. Ridley[7] (2), second son of Allen[6] (1), was born in Sanford, Me., in 1855.

Laura-E. Ridley[7] (2), fifth daughter of Allen[6] (1), was born in Sanford, Me., in 1856.

Mary-L. Ridley[7] (18), third daughter of Allen[6] (1), was born in Sanford, Me., in 1846, and died in 1848.

Mary-L. Ridley[7] (19), fourth daughter of Allen[6] (1), was born in Sanford, Me., in 1850.

Abbie Ridley[7] (2), daughter of Ambrose[6] (5), was born in Boston, Mass. No particulars.

Etta Ridley[7] (2), daughter of Ambrose[6] (5), was born in Boston, Mass. No particulars.

Lydia-Mabel Ridley[7] (4), eldest daughter of Jacob[6] (2), was born in Lawrence, Mass., March 27, 1863, and died Aug. 22, 1864.

Bessie-Abbey Ridley[7] (1), second daughter of Jacob[6] (2), was born in Lawrence, Mass., March 30, 1868.

James-M. Ridley[7] (15), eldest son of Ivory[6] (1), was born in Shapleigh, Me., July 16, 1844, and died Jan. 28, 1867.

Esther-Ann Ridley[7] (2), eldest daughter of Ivory[6] (1), was born in Shapleigh, Me., Aug. 20, 1846; was married to Rufus Ridley, her kinsman, of Alfred, and has issue.

Angie-M. Ridley[7] (2), second daughter of Ivory[6] (1), was born in Shapleigh, Me., Jan., 4, 1848; was married to Franklin Drew, of Milton, N. H.

Perley Ridley[7] (1), second son of Ivory[6] (1), was born in Shapleigh, Me., Dec. 27, 1849; died March 30, 1851.

Edwin-H. Ridley[7] (2), third son of Ivory[6] (1), was born in Shapleigh, Me., Nov. 2, 1853; married Jennie Bracy, of Alfred, and has issue *two* children, of whom hereafter.

Mary-A. Ridley[7] (20), eldest daughter of Daniel[6] (7), was born in Alfred, Me.; was married to James H. Hurd, of Shapleigh.

Sarah-H. Ridley[7] **(11)**, second daughter of Daniel[6] **(7)**, was born in Alfred, Me., and was married to Charles Bracy, of Alfred.

Harriet-N. Ridley[7] **(4)**, third daughter of Daniel[6] **(7)**, was born in Alfred, Me., and was married to Franklin Peabody, of Kennebunk.

John Ridley[7] **(13)**, eldest son of Joseph[6] **(7)**, was born in Bowdoin, Me., Nov. 9, 1831; married Sept. 18, 1875, to Elizabeth A. Kidder, of Dresden, and resides in the city of Bath; stone-mason; no issue.

Mary Ridley[7] **(21)**, eldest daughter of Joseph[6] **(7)**, was born in Bowdoin, Me., Dec. 25, 1836; was married to David Varner, or Varney, of Nobleborough, and resides in Bath.

Eliza-J. Ridley[7] **(3)**, second daughter of Joseph[6] **(7)**, was born in Bowdoin, Me., Jan. 6, 1839; was married to William Wormwood, and resides in Bath.

Susan Ridley[7] **(6)**, third daughter of Joseph[6] **(7)**, was born in Bowdoin, Me., Nov. 25, 1841; died May 16, 1865.

Eugene-F. Ridley[7] **(2)**, eldest son of Alexander[6] **(3)**, was born in Topsham, Me., Dec. 4, 1848.

Aaron-H. Ridley[7] **(2)**, second son of Alexander[6] **(3)**, was born in Topsham, Me., Nov. 5, 1850.

Alice Ridley[7] **(1)**, eldest daughter of Alexander[6] **(3)**, was born in Topsham, Me., December, 1852, and died in 1853.

Ernest Ridley[7] **(1)**, third son of Alexander[6] **(3)**, was born in Topsham, Me., in 1854, and died in 1855.

George-Baron Ridley[7] **(7)**, fourth son of Alexander[6] **(3)**, was born in Topsham, Me., March 18, 1856.

Annie-C. Ridley[7] **(5)**, second daughter of Alexander[6] **(3)**, was born in Topsham, Me., Jan. 1, 1858.

Eddie-A. Ridley[7] **(1)**, fifth son of Alexander[6] **(3)**, was born in Topsham, Me., Feb. 26, 1865, and died in Brunswick, March 10, 1870.

Charles-T. Ridley[7] **(7)**, sixth son of Alexander[6] **(3)**, was born in Brunswick, Me., Feb. 14, 1869.

Carrie-E. Ridley[7] **(3)**, eldest daughter of Caleb[6] **(2)**, was born in Topsham, Me., in October, 1851; was married to Edward Turner, of Bath, and has issue.

Nellie Ridley[7] **(3)**, second daughter of Caleb[6] **(2)**, was born in Topsham, Me., November, 1852.

Herbert-H. Ridley[7] **(2)**, eldest son of Caleb[6] **(2)**, was born in Topsham, Me., Jan. 8, 1858.

Fannie Ridley[7] **(1)**, third daughter of Caleb[6] **(2)**, was born in Topsham, Me., in June, 1863, — twin to Alice.

Alice Ridley[7] **(2)**, twin daughter of Caleb[6] **(2)**, was born in Topsham, Me., June, 1863, and died in July, 1865.

Alice Ridley[7] **(3)**, fifth daughter of Caleb[6] **(2)**, was born in Topsham, Me., October, 1868.

Edward-T. Ridley[7] **(1)**, second son of Caleb[6] **(2)**, was born in Topsham, Me., September, 1871.

Ida-M. Ridley[7] **(1)**, eldest daughter of Isaac[6] **(3)**, was born in Bowdoin, Me., March 15, 1865.

Cora-E. Ridley[7] (3), second daughter of Isaac[6] (3), was born in Bowdoin, Me., Dec. 17, 1867.

Lizzie-M. Ridley[7] (4), third daughter of Isaac[6] (3), was born in Bowdoin, Me., Dec. 25, 1869.

Abbie-E. Ridley[7] (4), eldest daughter of Henry[6] (2), was born Aug. 14, 1845; unmarried; lives in Athens.

James-H. Ridley[7] (16), eldest son of Henry[6] (2), was born Feb. 12, 1846, and died March 20, 1846.

George-H. Ridley[7] (8), second son of Henry[6] (2), was born April 14, 1848; married in 1874 to Elizabeth H. Merrill, and resides on a farm in Cornville.

Harriet-E. Ridley[7] (5), second daughter of Henry[6] (2), was born Dec. 3, 1850; was married in 1869 to Augustus W. Worthen, farmer, of Cornville.

Horace-D. Ridley[7] (2), third son of Henry[6] (2), was born Dec. 2, 1854; unmarried; farmer.

Rebecca-M. Ridley[7] (3), third daughter of Henry[6] (2), was born May 19, 1860, and lives at home; unmarried.

L.-M. Ridley[7] (?), fourth son of Henry[6] (2), was born Jan. 27, 1864, and died March 18, 1866.

Nellie Ridley[7] (2), eldest daughter of Humphrey[6] (1), was born in Richmond, Me., in 1858, and died in 1864.

James-P. Ridley[7] (17), eldest son of Humphrey[6] (1), was born in Richmond, Me., in 1867.

Dexter-H. Ridley[7] (2), eldest son of George[6] (4), was born in Richmond, Me., in 1856; unmarried.

Annie-S. Ridley[7] (6), eldest daughter of George[6] (4), was born in Richmond, Me., in 1862.

Rebecca-E. Ridley[7] (4), second daughter of George[6] (4), was born in Richmond, Me., in 1867.

Laura-Jane Ridley[7] (3), eldest daughter of Mark[6] (6), was born in Harpswell, Me., Nov. 1, 1832; was married to Levi Corson, a millwright, and deceased in 1855.

Samuel-A. Ridley[7] (5), eldest son of Mark[6] (6), was born in Harpswell, Me., in 1835; married Philena Brooks, and has issue *three* children, of whom hereafter. He carries on a farm in Canaan.

Hannah-A. Ridley[7] (8), second daughter of Mark[6] (6), was born in Harpswell, Me., in 1837; was married to Abner Wheeler, and resides on a farm in Canaan.

Sophia-K. Ridley[7] (2), third daughter of Mark[6] (6), was born in Harpswell, Me., Dec. 2, 1839; was married to William Drew, lumberman, and lives in Santa Cruz, Cal.

Alonzo-K. Ridley[7] (2), second son of Mark[6] (6), was born in Harpswell, Me., Oct. 21, 1841, and died in 1863.

Eliza-A. Ridley[7] (4), youngest daughter of Mark[6] (6), was born in Harpswell, Me., April 26, 1844; was married to Frank Rowe, carpenter, and resides in Bath.

Dexter-W. Ridley[7] (3), eldest son of Moses[6] (1), was born in Litchfield, Me., in January, 1835.

George Ridley[7] (9), second son of Moses[6] (1), was born in Litchfield, Me., in 1837.

Alvah Ridley[7] (1), third son of Moses[6] (1), was born in Litchfield, Me., in March, 1841.

Hattie-A. Ridley[7] (6), eldest daughter of Moses[6] (1), was born in Litchfield, Me., in 1843; was married to —— Sprague, photographer, and resides in Lewiston.

Ellen Ridley[7] (4), youngest daughter of Moses[6] (1), was born in Litchfield, Me., in 1845.

James Ridley[7] (18), eldest son of William[6] (3), was born in Bowdoin, Me., April 16, 1848.

Charles Ridley[7] (8), second son of William[6] (3), was born in Bowdoin, Me., June 5, 1850.

John Ridley[7] (14), third son of William[6] (3), was born in Bowdoin, Me., Nov. 17, 1852.

Horace Ridley[7] (3), fourth son of William[6] (3), was born in Bowdoin, Me., Nov. 15, 1855.

Edward Ridley[7] (2), fifth son of William[6] (3), was born in Bowdoin, Me., Nov. 7, 1857.

Ellen Ridley[7] (5), only daughter of William[6] (3), was born in Bowdoin, Me., April 6, 1859.

Edward Ridley[7] (3), eldest son of Alexander[6] (4), was born in Bowdoin, Me., April 30, 1852.

Cyrus Ridley[7] (1), second son of Alexander[6] (4), was born in Bowdoin, Me., June 16, 1855.

Lydia Ridley[7] (5), eldest daughter of Alexander[6] (4), was born in Bowdoin, Me., March 14, 1857.

Howard Ridley[7] (1), third son of Alexander[6] (4), was born in Bowdoin, Me., May, 1865.

Alexander Ridley[7] (5), fourth son of Alexander[6] (4), was born in Bowdoin, Me., August, 1867.

Mary-E. Ridley[7] (23), second daughter of Alexander[6] (4), was born in Bowdoin, Me., April, 1869.

William Ridley[7] (5), fifth son of Alexander[6] (4), was born in Bowdoin, Me., April, 1872.

George Ridley[7] (10), eldest son of Albion[6] (1), was born in Bowdoin, Me., April 30, 1855; a merchant in Lewiston.

Tallman-J. Ridley[7] (1), second son of Albion[6] (1), was born in Bowdoin, Me., Feb. 21, 1857; a student in Lewiston.

Winfield-Scott Ridley[7] (1), third son of Albion[6] (1), was born in Bowdoin, Me., Jan. 24, 1860; at home.

Mary-Alice Ridley[7] (24), eldest daughter of Albion[6] (1), was born in Bowdion, Me., Jan. 3, 1862; unmarried.

Bertie Ridley[7] (1), fourth son of Albion[6] (1), was born in Lewiston, Me., Dec. 24, 1869.

Arthur Ridley[7] (1), fifth son of Albion[6] (1), was born in Lewiston, Me., July 10, 1874.

Bradford Ridley[7] (1), eldest son of John[6] (9), was born Sept. 18, 1855.

Frank Ridley[7] (4), second son of John[6] (9), was born in April, 1858.

William Ridley[7] (6), third son of John[6] (9), was born in December, 1865.

—— **Ridley**[7] (?), fourth son of John[6] (9), was born in December, 1871,

Willie Ridley[7] (1), son of Joseph[6] (7), was born Oct. 4, 1860.
Joseph-Warren Ridley[7] (9), son of Joseph[6] (7), was born May, 1861.
Alice Ridley[7] (4), son of Joseph[6] (7), was born June, 1867.

James-W. Ridley[7] (19), eldest son of Robert[6] (1), was born in Harpswell, Me., in 1832; married in 1856 to Laura J. Wright, and has *one* son, of whom hereafter. He worked in the Navy Yard, at Charlestown, Mass., as ship-carpenter, until 1870, when he emigrated to Estherville, Ia., when he engaged in milling and miscellaneous trading; an excellent mechanic.

R.-Edwin Ridley[7] (3), second son of Robert[6] (1), was born in Harpswell, Me., in 1834; married in 1855 to Esther A. Allen, and the following spring (1856) emigrated to Michigan, and thence to Iowa, on the Des Moines River, seven miles from the Minnesota line. He was joined by his wife in 1857: she being the first white woman in Emmett County. He laid out a township the following year (1858) and named it Estherville for his wife. He subsequently, in company with his brothers, built a sawmill in Estherville, but soon sold his share in the mill, and purchased a farm two miles below, where he erected another mill which he still (1874) owns and operates. Has *three* children, of whom hereafter.

Algenon-H. Ridley[7] (1), third son of Robert[6] (1), was born in Harpswell, Me., in 1836; married in 1866 to Mary-Eliza Fletcher, and settled in Estherville, Ia. Carpenter by trade; served in the Union army during the Rebellion. Had his leg crushed in the horse-power of a threshing-machine in 1871, and died from the injury in 1872. No issue.

Adelia-S. Ridley[7] (1), eldest daughter of Robert[6] (1), was born in Harpswell, Me., in 1838; went to Estherville, Ia., in 1859; was married in 1860 to George Jenkins, and emigrated to Oregon in the spring of 1871.

Judith-A. Ridley[7] (1), second daughter of Robert[6] (1), was born in Harpswell, Me., in 1840, and died in the city of Bath, Me., in 1857, unmarried.

Albion-K. Ridley[7] (2), fourth son of Robert[6] (1), was born in Harpswell, Me., in 1842, and went to Estherville, Ia., with his parents in 1859. He served three years in the Union army during the Rebellion; married in 1868 to —— Graham, and carries on a farm in Estherville, Ia.; no issue.

M-Theresa Ridley[7] (1), fifth son of Robert[6] (1), was born in Harpswell, Me., in 1844; emigrated to Iowa with his parents in 1859; married in 1869 to H. W. Emery, of Chicago, Ill., and now (1874) resides in St. Louis, Mo.

Eugene-G. Ridley[7] (3), sixth son of Robert[6] (1), was born in Harpswell, Me., in 1847; emigrated to Iowa in 1859; served two years in the Union army during the Rebellion; married in 1868 to Mary C. Owen, and has issue *three* children, of whom hereafter. Carries on farming and fruit-growing in Estherville.

Lillian-E. Ridley[7] (1), third daughter of Robert[6] (1), was born in Harpswell, Me., in 1850; emigrated to Iowa with her parents in 1859; was married in 1870 to Lloyd A. Gould, and resides in Estherville, Ia.

Albert-F. Ridley[7] (3), eldest son of Samuel[6] (1), was born in Harpswell, Me., Sept. 28, 1846; married July 3, 1870, to Katie A. Hopkins, of Jamaica, West Indies, and has issue *three* children, of whom hereafter. Resides in Harpswell; seaman.

Anna-J. Ridley[7] (2), eldest daughter of Samuel[6] (1), was born in Harpswell, Me., Oct. 3, 1828; was married June 2, 1868, to D. H. Elliott, of Hartland, and resides at Cape Elizabeth.

Charles-N. Ridley[7] (9), second son of Samuel[6] (1), was born in Harpswell, Me., Oct. 22, 1850; married March 15, 1870, to Philelia A. Harrington, of Harpswell, and has issue *three* children, of whom hereafter. Sailor; resides at Cape Elizabeth.

Lucy-E. Ridley[7] (4), second daughter of Samuel[6] (1), was born in Harpswell, Me., April 28, 1858; was married Aug. 22, 1876, to E. R. Johnson, of Harpswell, a seaman.

Carrie-M. Ridley[7] (4), third daughter of Samuel[6] (1), was born in Harpswell, Me., Oct. 24, 1860.

Nellie-M. Ridley[7] (3), fourth daughter of Samuel[6] (1), was born in Harpswell, Me.; was married Dec. 10, 1867, to Charles M. Powell, of York, Me. Residence in Harpswell.

William-H. Ridley[7] (7), eldest son of Isaac[6] (4), was born in Harpswell, Me., March 23, 1856.

Emma-J. Ridley[7] (3), eldest daughter of Isaac[6] (4), was born in Harpswell, Me., June 12, 1858.

Frank-W. Ridley[7] (5), second son of Isaac[6] (4), was born in Harpswell, Me., April, 1861.

EIGHTH GENERATION.

Gracie-E. Ridley[8] (1), eldest daughter of John[7] (10), was born in Prospect, Me., November, 1871; died in Iowa in 1880.

Four other children whose names were not given.

Carrie-Emma Ridley[8] (5), eldest daughter of Christopher[7] (1), was born in Prospect, Me., Aug. 4, 1866.

Nettie-May Ridley[8] (1), second daughter of Christopher[7] (1), was born in Prospect, Me., Feb. 28, 1870.

Clara-Ella Ridley[8] (2), third daughter of Christopher[7] (1), was born in Prospect, Me., Feb. 28, 1872.

Alfred Ridley[8] (4), eldest son of Christopher[7] (1), was born in Prospect, Me., April 13, 1876.

Allie-Gertrude Ridley[8] (1), only daughter of Franklin[7] (2), was born in South Thomaston, Me.

Joseph-Albert Ridley[8] (10), eldest son of Madison[7] (1), was born in Sanford, Me., in 1854.

Alice-Ella Ridley[8] (4), eldest daughter of Madison[7] (1), was born in Sanford, Me., in 1856.

Emma-Phebe Ridley[8] (4), second daughter of Madison[7] (1), was born in Sanford, Me., in 1858.

Lucy-Rodgers Ridley[8] (5), third daughter of Madison[7] (1), was born in Sanford, Me., in 1860.

Susan-Elmore Ridley[8] (7), fourth daughter of Madison[7] (1), was born in Sanford, Me., in 1862.

Asenath-Getchell Ridley[8] (1), fifth daughter of Madison[7] (1), was born in Sanford, Me., in 1864.

Mary-Grace Ridley[8] (25), sixth daughter of Madison[7] (1), was born in Sanford, Me., in 1866.

Mattie-Ellen Ridley[8] (1), seventh daughter of Madison[7] (1), was born in Sanford, Me., in 1868.

Bessie-May Ridley[8] (1), eighth daughter of Madison[7] (1), was born in Sanford, Me., in 1870.

Gertrude Ridley[8] (1), eldest daughter of John[7] (11).

Bertie Ridley[8] (2), second daughter of John[7] (11).

Other children whose names were not given.

Annie Ridley[8] (7), eldest daughter of Edwin[7] (2), was born in Alfred, Me., Nov. 7, 1874.

William-M. Ridley[8] (8), eldest son of Edwin[7] (2), was born in Alfred, Me., May 16, 1876.

Jennie-A. Ridley[8] (1), eldest daughter of Samuel[7] (5), was born in Harpswell (or Canaan), Me., in 1865.

Alonzo-K. Ridley[8] (9), eldest son of Samuel[7] (5), was born in Harpswell (or Canaan), Me., in 1867.

Frederick-C. Ridley[8] (1), second son of Samuel[7] (5), was born in Harpswell (or Canaan), Me., in 1873.

George-I. Ridley[8] (10), a son of James[7] (19), was born in Bath, Me., in 1858, and is now in Iowa.

Anna-J. Ridley[8] (3), eldest daughter of R. Edwin[7] (3), was born in Estherville, Ia., in December, 1858; the first white child born there.

Lucy-E. Ridley[8] (6), second daughter of R. Edwin[7] (3), was born in Estherville, Ia., in October, 1860.

George-E. Ridley[8] (11), eldest son of R. Edwin[7] (3), was born in Estherville, Ia., in 1863.

R.-Etta Ridley[8] (3), eldest daughter of Eugene[7] (3), was born in Estherville, Ia., in 1870.

Harriet Ridley[8] (7), second daughter of Eugene[7] (3), was born in Estherville, Ia., in 1872.

Isa Ridley[8] (1), third daughter of Eugene[7] (3), was born in Estherville, Ia., in 1873.

Samuel-H. Ridley[8] (6), eldest son of Albert[7] (3), was born in Harpswell, Me., Dec. 3, 1871.

Archie-F. Ridley[8] (1), second son of Albert[7] (3), was born in Harpswell, Me., July 12, 1873.

Raymond-E. Ridley[8] (1), third son of Albert[7] (3), was born in Harpswell, Me., April 16, 1876.

Minnie-E. Ridley[8] (2), eldest daughter of Charles[7] (9), was born in Harpswell, Me., Nov. 28, 1871.

Charles-E. Ridley[8] (10), eldest son of Charles[7] (9), was born in Harpswell, Me., June 15, 1873.

Lizzie-S. Ridley[8] (5), second daughter of Charles[7] (9), was born in Harpswell, Me., Dec. 10, 1875.

36

. RIDLEYS OF NEW YORK -CITY.

Jesse Ridley[1] (1), parents' names unknown, was born at Gravesend, Eng., in 1823 ; married —— Gillman, at Castle Townsend, County Cork, Ireland, in 1847; emigrated to the United States in the ship "Lebanon," in 1849, landing at Philadelphia. He went thence to New York, where he worked as vessel-rigger to the time of his death in August, 1868. He was originally a seaman. He had a family of *six* children, of whom hereafter ; the widow is living in New York city.

SECOND GENERATION.

Mary-Ann Ridley[2] (1), eldest daughter of Jesse[1] (1), was born in England, or Ireland, in September, 1848, and came to New York with her parents in 1849 ; deceased since 1868.

John Ridley[2] (1), eldest son of Jesse[1] (1), was born in New York city, Aug. 27, 1850, and is now (1878) living there.

Martha Ridley[2] (1), second daughter of Jesse[1] (1), was born in New York city, Sept. 6, 1852 ; lives at home.

William Ridley[2] (1), second son of Jesse[1] (1), was born in New York city in November, 1854, and died since 1868.

Andrew Ridley[2] (1), third son of Jesse[1] (1), was born in New York city in August, 1857.

Joseph Ridley[2] (1), fourth son of Jesse[1] (1), was born in New York city Sept. 5, 1860.

RIDLEYS OF CAYUGA COUNTY, NEW YORK.

Drury Ridley[1] (1)*, parents' names unknown, was born in the County of Sussex, Eng. ; married in the parish of Worth, and had issue *nine* children, of whom hereafter.

SECOND GENERATION.

Elvydine Ridley[2] (1), eldest son of Drury[1] (1), was born in the parish of Worth, County of Sussex, Eng., and had issue *seven* children. He lives in England.

Charity Ridley[2] (1). eldest daughter of Drury[1] (1), was born in the parish of Worth, County of Sussex, Eng. No issue.

Ann Ridley[2] (1), second daughter of Drury[1] (1), was born in the parish of Worth, County of Sussex, Eng. ; has large family.

---

* The family name of Drury was derived from a place in the Duchy of Normandy ; was established in England at the Conquest (1066), and became, subsequently, divided into three distinct branches : the first settled at Rougham, the second at Welherden, and the third at Hawstead. The baronetcy expired Jan. 20, 1759. Their arms are "Arg. on a chief vert. ; a tan between two mullets perced or." The present representative of the family is the Rev. George Drury, B. A., of Clayton, Suffolk, Eng. It is a little singular that there should be a "Drury Ridley" in Virginia, another in New York, and still another in Vermont, with no apparent connection between the three families ; but the Drurys are numerous in England, and the families have evidently frequently become allied by marriage.

Mary Ridley² (2), third daughter of Drury¹ (1), was born in the parish of Worth, County of Sussex, Eng.; large family.

Elizabeth Ridley² (1), fourth daughter of Drury¹ (1), was born in the parish of Worth, County of Sussex, Eng.

Drury Ridley² (2), second son of Drury¹ (1), was born in the parish of Worth, County of Sussex, Eng., Feb. 10, 1799; married Jan. 22, 1828, to Jane Wood (she was born March 5, 1803), and had issue *seven* children, of whom hereafter. He was a farmer; emigrated to New York in 1853.

Richard Ridley² (1), third son of Drury¹ (1), was born in the parish of Worth, County Sussex, Eng., and has a large family there; farmer.

Amelia Ridley² (1), fifth daughter of Drury¹ (1), was born in the parish of Worth, County of Sussex, Eng.; large family.

Robert Ridley² (1), fourth son of Drury¹ (1), was born in the parish of Worth, County of Sussex, Eng.; married, and emigrated to America in ship " Margaret Evans," Captain Tinker, in 1850, and settled in New York State. His wife and children came over about a year subsequently. He had issue *nine* children, of whom hereafter; resides in Cayuga County, New York; farmer.

THIRD GENERATION.

Henry Ridley³ (3), a son of Elvydine² (1), was born in the parish of Worth, County of Sussex, Eng.; emigrated to New York State in 1851-2, in ship " Margaret Evans," and is now in the grocery trade at Waterloo, Seneca County, N. Y. Has *ten* children, whose names are not known. No reply to my letters of inquiry.

Peter Ridley³ (1), eldest son of Drury² (2), was born in the parish of Charlwood, County of Surrey, Eng., July 22, 1830; married May 11, 1853, to Sarah, daughter of William and Sarah Jackson (she was born in the parish of Hutton, County of Cumberland, Eng.), and has issue *eleven* children, of whom hereafter. Mr. Ridley emigrated to America with his uncle Robert in 1850, in the ship " Margaret Evans," and resides at Scipioville, Cayuga County, N. Y.

Esther Ridley³ (1), eldest daughter of Drury² (2), was born in County Surrey, Eng., March 5, 1832; married William H. Dewdney in April, 1852 (of London, Eng.), and came to America the same year. *Two* children; lives at Auburn, N. Y.; husband a machinist by occupation.

Jane Ridley³ (1), second daughter of Drury² (2), was born in County Surrey, Eng., July 10, 1834; was married to George Pattington, and resides at Scipioville, N. Y. Has *six* children; husband nurseryman.

Martin Ridley³ (1), second son of Drury² (2), was born in County Surrey, Eng., Dec. 29, 1837; unmarried. Residence, Scipioville, N. Y.; gardener by occupation.

Elizabeth Ridley³ (2), third daughter of Drury² (2), was born in County Surrey, Eng., June 12, 1840; married in 1868 to William Brooker, and has *three* children. Residence, Auburn, N. Y.; husband a blacksmith.

Emma-Ann Ridley³ (1), fourth daughter of Drury² (2), was born in County Surrey, Eng., Sept. 20, 1843, and was killed by lightning at Catskill, June 5, 1869. She was ironing at a table, and near her, children were playing (she was on a visit); she had just taken the sad-iron from the stove, where it had been left a moment before by another inmate of the house, when she dropped dead upon the floor. The bolt did little or no damage to the house and the children no harm.

John Ridley² (1), third son of Drury² (2), was born in County Surrey, Eng., Nov. 21, 1848, and died by rupturing a blood-vessel, Oct. 2, 1851.

Richard Ridley² (2), a son of Robert² (1), was born in England, and is now in the grocery business at Seneca Falls, N. Y.

James Ridley² (1), a son of Robert² (1), was born in England; came to New York in 1852; married, and has issue.

Elizabeth Ridley² (3), a daughter of Robert² (1), was married to Thomas Holland, and lives at Geneva, Ontario County, N. Y.

Ann Ridley² (2), a daughter of Robert² (1), was married to Thomas Hayes (she was born in England), and has a large family; resides at Waterloo, N. Y.

Jane Ridley² (2), daughter of Robert² (1), born in England, was married to —— Skinner, and lives at Waterloo, N. Y.; a widow with *three* children.

Amelia Ridley² (2), a daughter of Robert² (1), was born in England, and was married to Mr. French, of Geneva, Ontario County, N. Y., where they now (1879) reside.

FOURTH GENERATION.

Jane-Elizabeth Ridley⁴ (3), eldest daughter of Peter³ (1), was born in Cayuga County, N. Y., Oct. 8, 1854; died Dec. 4, 1856.

Sarah-Ann Ridley⁴ (1), second daughter of Peter³ (1), was born in Cayuga County, N. Y., Oct. 17, 1856.

George-Jackson Ridley⁴ (1), eldest son of Peter³ (1), was born in Cayuga County, N. Y., Feb. 21, 1859.

Frances-Emma Ridley⁴ (1), third daughter of Peter³ (1), was born in Cayuga County, N. Y., Jan. 2, 1861.

Harriet-Augusta Ridley⁴ (1), fourth daughter of Peter³ (1), was born in Cayuga County, N. Y., March 8, 1863; died March 4, 1869.

William-Drury Ridley⁴ (1), second son of Peter³ (1), was born in Cayuga County, N. Y., July 30, 1865.

John-Peter Ridley⁴ (2), third son of Peter³ (1), was born in Cayuga County, N. Y., Aug. 21, 1867.

Mary-Louisa Ridley⁴ (2), fifth daughter of Peter³ (1), was born in Cayuga County, N. Y., Feb. 5, 1870.

Andrew-Joseph Ridley⁴ (1), fourth son of Peter³ (1), was born in Cayuga County, N. Y., March 13, 1872.

Martin-Luther Ridley⁴ (2), fifth son of Peter³ (1), was born in Cayuga County, N. Y., June 13, 1875.

(Infant) Ridley⁴ (1), child of Peter³ (1), was born in Cayuga County, N. Y., Aug. 21, 1877, and died Oct. 3, 1877.

RIDLEYS OF DUXBURY, VERMONT.

Samuel Ridley¹ (1), parents' names unknown, was born in the city of London, Eng., March 4, 1752; served an apprenticeship of seven years as

house-carpenter; was pressed into the British service during the American Revolution; deserted and enlisted in the spring of 1777 in the company of Capt. Jacob Price, Third Maryland Regiment, Col. Mordecai
Gist, for three years, and at the end of that term of service re-enlisted in
the same command. He was a corporal. Aug. 16, 1780, he was taken a
prisoner at General Gates' defeat. He was wounded in the ankle at the
battle of Camden; was in the battle of Brandywine, Sept. 11, 1777;
Germantown, Oct. 4, 1777, and arrived at Monmouth, N. J., at the close
of the battle there June 17, 1778. He married Abiah Flemming, and
settled at Richmond, Vt.; subsequent to 1797, removed to Duxbury in
that State, where he continued the remainder of his life. He had issue
three children, of whom hereafter. Died Nov. 18, 1842, aged 90 years.

SECOND GENERATION.

Drury Ridley[2] (1), eldest son of Samuel[1] (1), was born in Vermont
about 1795, went to Canada, and died unmarried.

Samuel Ridley[2] (2), second son of Samuel[1] (1), was born in Richmond, Vt., Oct. 14, 1797; married Jan. 13, 1820, to Sally Stafford, of
Plymouth (she was born April 10, 1797), and had issue *ten* children, of
whom hereafter. He died April 10, 1866, aged 69 years; his widow in
1876 was living with her daughter, Mrs. Stewart, in Bristol, Vt.

Abigail Ridley[2] (1), a daughter of Samuel[1] (1), was born in Duxbury,
Vt., about 1799; was married to Asa Baker, and in 1876 was living with
her daughter, Mrs. Derret, in St. Albans, Vt.

THIRD GENERATION.

Ruby-S. Ridley[8] (1), eldest daughter of Samuel[2] (2), was born July
7, 1821; was married April 28, 1846, to Isaac R. Jewell, of Bolton, Vt.,
and is now (1876) in Petaluma, Cal.

Mary-A. Ridley[8] (1), second daughter of Samuel[2] (2), was born Dec.
22, 1822; was married Aug. 9, 1844, to Jesse Jewell, and died at Petaluma, Cal., Nov. 8, 1875; her husband predeceased her Oct. 4, 1874.

Drury Ridley[8] (2), eldest son of Samuel[2] (2), was born Sept. 11,
1824, and died Dec. 30, 1849, unmarried.

Sarah Ridley[8] (1), third daughter of Samuel[2] (2), was born May 28,
1826; was married April 20, 1852, to John P. Parker, and in 1876 was
resident at Waterbury, Vt.

Lucretia Ridley[8] (1), fourth daughter of Samuel[2] (2), was born Dec.
12, 1828; was married May 28, 1854, to E. R. Morse, and resides at
Montpelier, Vt.

Samuel Ridley[8] (3), second son of Samuel[2] (2), was born Feb. 9,
1830, and died Feb. 1, 1850, unmarried.

John-S. Ridley[8] (1), third son of Samuel[2] (2), was born Jan. 16,
1832; married Aug. 10, 1858, to Mary E. Houston, of Bristol, Vt., and
has *three* children, of whom hereafter; farmer.

Gideon-B. Ridley[8] (1), fourth son of Samuel[2] (2), was born Feb. 21,
1834; married Jan. 1, 1859, to Phebe Lewis, and resides on a farm in
Bristol, Vt.; no issue.

Martha-A. Ridley[8] (1), fifth daughter of Samuel[2] (2), was born
March 25, 1837; was married May 22, 1862, to Richard-Dunning Stewart,
and resides in Bristol, Vt., where her husband owns a flour-mill.

Jesse-J. Ridley[8] (1), fifth son of Samuel[2] (2), was born Oct. 9, 1838;
married Dec. 3, 1863, to Alma Caldwell, of Lincoln, Vt., and has *two*
children, of whom hereafter. He keeps a hotel at Bristol, Vt.

FOURTH GENERATION.

Anna Ridley[4] (1), eldest daughter of John[3] (1), was born May ,16, 1859.

Willie Ridley[4] (1), eldest son of John[3] (1), was born July 2, 1860.

Freddie Ridley[4] (1), second son of John[3] (1), was born Oct. 25, 1873.

Emma Ridley[4] (1), eldest daughter of Jesse[3] (1), was born July 20, 1867.

James Ridley[4] (1), eldest son of Jesse[3] (1), was born March 20, 1869.

RIDLERS OF EASTCOMB, ENGLAND.

William Ridler[1] (1), a cloth-weaver, birth-place and parents unknown, was a resident of Eastcomb, Gloucester,* Eng., married, and had issue *three* sons and probably other children.

SECOND GENERATION.

John Ridler[2] (1), son of William[1] (1), was born in 1778; married about 1818, and had *five* sons, of whom hereafter. Weaver by trade. Lived at Heavens, Strand. He died in 1864, aged 86.

William Ridler[2] (2), son of William[1] (1), was weaver by trade; lived at Heavens, Strand, and had issue *two* sons, of whom hereafter. No particulars.

Nathaniel Ridler[2] (1), son of William[1] (1), was a weaver at Heavens, Strand, and had issue *three* children, of whom hereafter.

THIRD GENERATION.

William Ridler[3] (3), eldest son of John[2] (1), was born at Heavens, Strand, in 1819; married in 1842, and lives at Eastcomb, Gloucester. He is a stone-mason by trade. He says their surname was always spelled Ridler. *Four* children.

John Ridler[3] (2), second son of John[2] (1), was born in 1821, and died unmarried in 1877; wood-cutter.

Samuel Ridler[3] (1), third son of John[2] (1), was born in 1823; married in 1858, and died in 1876; wood-cutter.

George Ridler[3] (1), fourth son of John[2] (1), was born in 1824, and resides at Eastcomb (1878), unmarried; wood-cutter.

Nathaniel Ridler[3] (2), fifth son of John[2] (1), was born in 1826; married in 1850, and lives at Eastcomb; stone-mason.

---

* The Ridler family seems to have originated in Gloucestershire. Tradition says they are an offshoot of the Ridleys of Northumberland, and that they had the same arms; but I do not find any coat-of-arms assigned to the Ridlers. William Ridler died at Cheltenham, Eng., in May, 1856, aged 59 years. He had filled the post of Manager of the Cheltenham and Gloucestershire Bank from its establishment many years ago; its business had been transferred to the County of Gloucester Bank, and Mr. Ridler had been laboriously engaged in winding up its affairs. He was found dead in his bed. He had a daughter Clara, who was married in 1860 to Augustus W. Eres, surgeon, and resident of Douglas, in the Isle of Man, son of A. Eres, Esq., M. D., of Cheltenham. (See "Gleanings and Notes" in this book.)

Nathaniel Ridler³ (3), a son of William² (2), was of Strand in 1878; weaver by occupation. No particulars.

William Ridler³ (4), a son of William² (2), was of Strand in 1878; timber-dealer by occupation.

George Ridler³ (2), son of Nathaniel² (1), settled somewhere in Upper Canada; grocer when in England.

Ann Ridler³ (1), a daughter of Nathaniel² (1), went to Upper Canada with her brother before mentioned.

Mary Ridler³ (1), a daughter of Nathaniel² (1), was somewhere in America in 1878; she was a milliner.

FOURTH GENERATION.

John Ridler⁴ (3), eldest son of William³ (3), was born at Eastcomb, Gloucester, in 1846; stone-mason.

Bartimeus Ridler⁴ (1), son of William³ (3), was born in 1848, and died at Eastcomb in 1854, unmarried.

Keziah Ridler⁴ (1), daughter of William³ (3), was born in 1850, and died at Eastcomb, unmarried.

Job Ridler⁴ (1), a son of William³ (3), was born in 1852, and in 1878 lived in Stafford, unmarried ; stone-mason.

Thomas Ridler⁴ (1), a son of Samuel³ (1), was born in 1861, lived at Eastcomb, Gloucestershire, in 1878, unmarried ; stone-mason.

RIDLERS OF BOSTON, MASSACHUSETTS.

Isaac Ridler¹ (1), parents' names unknown, was born in London, Eng., about the year 1740, and came to America at the age of nineteen years. He married Elizabeth Hemingway, and fixed his residence on Moon Street, Boston, Mass., where the Catholic church now stands. He was a professional mariner, and commanded a privateer during the war of the Revolution. A letter now in the family, dated "London, Dec. 27, 1765," forwarded to his wife in Boston, contains the following curious lines: —

> "If you have a trifle of money
>   Don't be afraid to spend it;
> But whatever you do, my honey,
>   Be sure you do not lend it."

Another letter was received from London, bearing date July 12, 1767. No record of Mr. Ridler's death; his widow was married to a Mr. Hosea, and lived to the age of 94 years. She was at one time known to be possessed of "*fifty crowns in gold*"; she spent her last days with her son, Richard Hosea, on Charter Street, Boston, opposite the cemetery; she was buried at Copp's Hill. The property and papers of Mr. Ridler went into the hands of the Hosea family. His two sisters in London forwarded many valuable presents to the widow after their brother's death.

Mary Ridler¹ (1), a sister of Isaac¹ (1), resided in London, Eng., with her parents. She forwarded a letter from London to her brother's family in Boston, dated " Aug. 9, 1763," in which her name was found. No record of marriage or death.

Ann Ridler[1] **(1)**, a sister of Isaac[1] (1), lived in London, Eng., with her parents. She forwarded a letter to the family of her brother in Boston, bearing date " May 12, 1764," in which she says, " Father and mother are well, and thank God for it; I am left to go through with the work alone. We have but nine cows at present."

SECOND GENERATION.

Jacob Ridler[2] **(1)**, a son of Isaac[1] (1), was born in Boston, Mass., and followed the sea; he was lost, with two brothers, during the war of the Revolution.

Isaac Ridler[2] **(2)**, second son of Isaac[1] (1), was born in Boston, Mass., and was lost at sea during the Revolution.

Abraham Ridler[2] **(1)**, third son of Isaac[1] (1), was born in Boston, Mass., and was lost at sea during the Revolution.

Joseph Ridler[2] **(1)**, fourth son of Isaac[1] (1), was born in Boston, Mass., Jan. 25, 1779; married Betsey Pratt, of Chelsea, Sept. 28, 1806, and had issue *ten* children, of whom hereafter. He followed the sea, and during a stay in Liverpool, Eng., in one of his early voyages, he was seized by a press-gang, but being carpenter of his ship he was liberated by the consul. He resided in Boston; originated the marine-railway; died Nov. 28, 1828.

Elizabeth Ridler[2] **(1)**, a daughter of Isaac[1] (1), was born in Boston, Mass.; was married Oct. 16, 1791, to Richard Butts, and had children. She died at the age of 93 years.

Sarah Ridler[2] **(1)**, a daughter of Isaac[1] (1), was born in Boston, Mass.; was married to Francis Holmes, had several children, and lived to a good old age.

THIRD GENERATION.

Isaac Ridler[3] **(3)**, eldest son of Joseph[2] (1), was born in Boston, Mass., Nov. 10, 1807, and died Feb. 26, 1829.

Joseph Ridler[3] **(2)**, second son of Joseph[2] (1), was born in Boston, Mass., June 9, 1809; married March 23, 1843, to Francis Oldroid, and had issue *five* children, of whom hereafter. He resides in Apalachicola, Fla.

Eliza Ridler[3] **(1)**, eldest daughter of Joseph[2] (1), was born in Boston, Mass., April 25, 1811; was married April 20, 1834, to Joseph Carlton, and had several children. She was a widow, living at Ashburnham, Mass., in 1878.

Samuel Ridler[3] **(1)**, third son of Joseph[2] (1), was born in Boston, Mass., Feb. 14, 1814, and died May 12, 1814.

James Ridler[3] **(1)**, fourth son of Joseph[2] (1), was born in Boston, Mass., and died an infant Sept. 20, 1815.

Thomas Ridler[3] **(1)**, fifth son of Joseph[2] (1), was born in Boston, Mass., July 30, 1815; married March 12, 1848, and is a farmer at Boston Highlands. No issue.

Samuel-P. Ridler[3] **(2)**, sixth son of Joseph[2] (1), was born in Boston, Mass., Feb. 1, 1818; married Aug. 15, 1841, to Charlotte Lowe, of Boston (she died Jan. 30, 1845), and secondly, Dec. 27, 1847, to Nancy Kaime, of Bramstead, N. H. He has issue *five* children, of whom hereafter. Carries on the crockery and glass-ware business in Boston.

Charles Ridler[3] **(1)**, seventh son of Joseph[2] (1), was born in Boston, Mass., Aug. 2, 1820, and died Jan. 26, 1829.

(Infant) Ridler[3] (1), a daughter of Joseph[2] (1), was born in Boston. Mass., Feb. 8, 1823, and died the same day.

George Ridler[3] (1), eighth son of Joseph[2] (1), was born in Boston, Mass., Dec. 6, 1824; married June 27, 1847, to Mary A. Robinson, of Boston, and had issue *four* children, of whom hereafter. Collector for the gas company; lives in Boston. Provided genealogy as here given.

FOURTH GENERATION.

Elizabeth Ridler[4] (2), a daughter of Joseph[3] (2), was born about the year 1842; was married to John Thygpen, and had *four* children, three of whom died previous to 1878.

Eliza Ridler[4] (2), a daughter of Joseph[3] (2), was born about the year 1847, and was married to a Mr. Lawrence, who died with small-pox two weeks after their marriage.

Annette Ridler[4] (1), a daughter of Joseph[3] (2), was married to William B. Moore. She died in 1870, aged 24 years; he died in July, 1871, aged 28 years.

Joseph Ridler[4] (4), a son of Joseph[3] (2), was drowned Feb. 24, 1871, aged 19 years.

Fannie Ridler[4] (1), a daughter of Joseph[3] (2), was born in August, 1855, and was single in 1878.

Charles Ridler[4] (2), eldest son of Samuel[3] (2), was born in Boston, Mass., in 1842; married Jennie Shepherd, of Canton, and has *one* child; school-teacher in Malden.

Samuel Ridler[4] (3), second son of Samuel[3] (2), was born in Boston, Mass., in 1844, and was single in 1873; teamster.

Parker Ridler[4] (1), third son of Samuel[3] (2), was born in Boston, Mass., in June, 1850; unmarried in 1873; clerk in silver-ware store, Boston, in 1884.

Ella Ridler[4] (1), eldest daughter of Samuel[3] (2), was born in 1852.

Irving Ridler[4] (1), youngest son of Samuel[3] (2), died in 1864, aged 8 years.

Anna Ridler[4] (1), eldest daughter of George[3] (1), was born May 15, 1848.

Alice Ridler[4] (1), second daughter of George[3] (1), was born Aug. 6, 1854.

George Ridler[4] (2), eldest son of George[3] (1), was born March 7, 1861.

Eugene Ridler[4] (1), second son of George[3] (1), was born July 26, 1863.

RHUDDLAN AND RIDLAND FAMILIES.

RHUDDLAN AND RIDLAND FAMILIES.

THE Rhuddlan, Ridland, and Redlon families, now so numerously scattered throughout Europe and America, are descended from an ancient Norman warrior named Robert d'Avranches, who, with a kinsman, Hugh d'Avranches, followed by the Normans who had settled in Chester, on the other side of the River Dee, invested Flintshire and conquered the Welsh in the twelfth century. This Robert d'Avranches fixed his residence at Rhuddlan, rebuilt and greatly strengthened the castle, and changed his original French local name to the new one of de Rhuddlan. His subsequent history is somewhat enshrouded in obscurity, but he founded a family in Wales surnamed Rhuddlan or Rydland, and his descendants are now scattered in various parts of the world under changed surnames, as will be seen by the perusal of this book.

A member of this family, supposed to have been a native of Wales,

---

*RHUDDLAN CASTLE and an ancient town of the same name, situated on the River Chwyd, in the County of Flint, Wales, derives its name from the red sandstone which abounds along the bank of the river, from which the town and castle were constructed. This castle and town have a very remote and interesting history. It is not known how early the original foundations were laid, but Rhuddlan or Rhydlan, — as the name is sometimes spelt, — was a place of considerable importance in the eighth century, and a plaintive air is still sung in North Wales, which commemorates a dreadful battle fought at "Rhuddlan Marsh," between the Britons and Saxons in the year 795, in which the Welsh were defeated and their king and leaders slain upon the bloody field. In 1283 King Edward I assembled a parliament at Rhuddlan, and divided Wales into counties; he also repealed many ancient and obnoxious laws, instituting a new code called the "Statute of Rhuddlan," which secured to the people greater advantages than they had previously enjoyed. In 1854 the town was "decayed and insignificant," but the ancient building called the "Parliament House," in which King Edward held his court, was standing, and formed part of a private residence. Rhuddlan Castle formed a square, externally, the walls being flanked by six round towers, three of which were nearly entire in 1854. The fosse around the castle walls was very wide and deep, both sides of the excavation being faced with stone; and the steep escarpment on the river side was secured by high walls and square bastions, one of which is still standing. During the civil wars the castle was garrisoned for the king; was taken in 1646, and by parliament ordered to be dismantled; from this date the ancient fortress has remained in a ruinous condition, but its bold towers and picturesque walls present a striking and beautiful appearance when approached from the river, which is navigable by small vessels as far as the village of Rhuddlan. The author has a photographic view of the castle, and a very fine cut representing the old fortress may be seen in a work entitled "Picturesque Europe."

took up his abode in the Orkney Islands alongside of his own national connections, — the Scandinavians, — who had previously settled there, but married a widow named Moar, and soon removed to Shetland, not far distant, sat down in the parish of Sandsting, Westerskeld, and became the progenitor of the families of Ridland since living there. The families of Shetland hold the tradition that their common ancestor changed his name at the time of his settlement at Orkney. The Ridlands have been a prolific family, as are the Shetlanders generally, but as nearly all the male members followed the sea, many were ship-wrecked and lost on the ocean, a circumstance that accounts for the predominace of females in that country. Nearly every family of Ridlands reside in the parish of Sandsting, neighbors to their kinspeople the Moars, who descended from the wife of Adam Ridland, the first to settle there. Like nearly all their countrymen, the families own small farms, consisting of from four to forty acres, which are mostly cultivated by the women and boys, while the men spend their time in fishing or on board the whale-ships; many of the name have gone on foreign voyages and were never afterwards heard from by their families in the north. The families now living in Shetland are in moderate circumstances and called "crofters." Some have engaged in ship-building. Many have lived to a great age, and from a comparison of photographs of typical members of the Shetland family with the aged representatives of the Redlon and Ridlon family in the United States, a marked resemblance may be observed. Sub-branches of the Shetland stock have been planted in England, Scotland, Australia, and America, but they are not numerous, with the exception of the Ridlon descent.

William Ridlon, of Boston, Mass., and Jerome Ridland who came from Shetland to that city about fifteen years ago, met in the freight-office of the Boston and Maine Railway station, and each instantly recognized the family resemblance, and by clasping hands reunited a kindred chain that had been separated across seas for six generations.

So far as I have been able to learn, the Ridland family, once resident in or near London, Eng., is now extinct in the male line. The family early settled in Charlestown, Mass., although well provided with sons, was lost sight of in two generations, and no descendant can now be found.

The descendants of Magnus Ridland, who came from Shetland in 1717, — children born by his surname, — have reached the great number of fourteen hundred on the paternal side. No branch of the Shetland family has any record, and their only history is traditionary. I have forwarded many letters of inquiry to clergymen, parish-clerks, schoolmasters, and others, and although many promises were made that copious notes would be furnished, they have not reached me up to this hour. Two or three links are missing from the family chain between the earliest known ancestor and his next descendant as now recorded on the following pages.

GENEALOGY AND BIOGRAPHY.

RIDLANDS OF SANDSTING, SHETLAND.*

Adam Ridland[1] (1), supposed to have been born in Wales and descended from an ancient Norman family, surnamed de Rhuddlan or Rhydlan, sat down first in the Orkney Islands, and is said to have changed the

<hr />

* SHETLAND consists of about one hundred islands, islets, and rocks, twenty-three of which are now inhabited. These lie between the Atlantic and the North Sea, about twenty-five leagues northeast from Orkney, and forty-four west of Norway. The largest island, called the mainland, is sixty miles long by ten broad in the widest part. Lerwick, the capital, is a fine town, with custom-house, law courts, and other public offices; it has a fine natural harbor. No wood grows in Shetland. Almost all small tenants practise spade cultivation. Nearly all the houses are of the same form, — these are called "crofters' houses," — being built of stone, with two small rooms, and covered with thatch. The cooking is done over a fire built in the centre of the common room, upon a hearth elevated above the floor, and the kettles are suspended over the fire from chains connected with the roof above. Sometimes the best room is provided with a rude chimney and fire-place. Nearly every house has its quern or hand-mill for grinding corn. Carts are not common, but the ponies numerous and very useful to the Shetlanders; these, with their fine-wooled sheep, run at large, and have registered ear-marks. The people of Shetland display many peculiarities which mark their Scandinavian origin and distinguish them from their Celtic and Saxon fellow-subjects. They are low in stature, small-featured, unrobust, symmetrically formed, light, sprightly, and almost always fair-haired. They possess much hardihood and power of physical endurance; and they are aggregately versatile and lively, fond of alternate excitement and repose. Their deportment, whether at home or among strangers, is mild, and their mode of address always modest and respectful. They are fond of music and dancing, and have many evening parties of pleasure; their songs generally Scottish, and the violin their instrument. Their dress is of woolen, homespun, their feet clad in wooden clogs, shoes of untanned leather, or boots of neat-skin. They wear a worsted head-dress, shaped like the Scottish night-cap, usually of many colors. The Shetland dialect is a soft and pleasant English, but contains many of the ancient Norse words. Many of the people eat their fish only wind-dried and slightly tainted. Oatmeal furnishes a considerable part of their food. Nearly all keep poultry, and eggs are plenty and cheap. All drink tea. Shetland is noted for its hand-knitted woolens, which are of great beauty and fineness of workmanship. No people in the known world can dress wool, and manufacture by hand, goods of equal beauty and delicacy. The women and girls spend nearly all their time in knitting. If a party is on their way to town they will be seen knitting as they walk, or ride their ponies; if they visit a neighbor they knit every step of the way; if they are guiding their ponies as they go to and from the peat-bogs, to bring their winter's fuel, they will knit on the road as they walk by their side. This note is given space in this connection, to show how our ancestors and kindred passed their lives in Shetland, — a country and people of which but little has been written until within a few years.

orthography of his name in consequence of some unlawful transaction with which he had been identified previous to his settlement in the north. He married a widow named Moar, and soon removed to Shetland, not far off, and established himself at Esterskeld, in the parish of Sandsting, where the descendants of his own body, with those of his wife named Moar, have ever since been domiciled.

THIRD GENERATION.

Thomas Ridland³ (1), a descendant of Adam¹ (1), was born in the parish of Sandsting, Shetland, and had issue *one* son (probably others), of whom hereafter.

FOURTH GENERATION.

James Ridland⁴ (1), a son of Thomas³ (1), was born in the parish of Sandsting, Shetland, and lived on a small property there; he had issue as follows :—

FIFTH GENERATION.

Lawrence Ridland⁵ (1), a son of James⁴ (1), was born in the parish of Sandsting, Shetland, and had issue a numerous family.

Thomas Ridland⁵ (2), a son of James⁴ (1), was born in the parish of Sandsting, Shetland, and married twice; first wife's name unknown; second wife, Barbary Charleson. Had issue *three* sons, — perhaps other issue.

Andrew Ridland⁵ (1), a son of James⁴ (1), was a native of Sandsting parish, Shetland; died unmarried.

Janet Ridland⁵ (1), a daughter of James⁴ (1), married William Dowall, a ship-carpenter of Scarvester, Shetland, and has issue.

Catherine Ridland⁵ (1), a daughter of James⁴ (1), was married to Lawrence Ridland, son of John Ridland (still living at the age of 90, in 1879); no children.

Ann Ridland⁵ (1), a daughter of James⁴ (1), was born in the parish of Sandsting, Shetland, and married to Lawrence Kay, a shipmaster, of Westerkeld; *four* children.

SIXTH GENERATION.

Andrew Ridland⁶ (2), a son of Thomas⁵ (2) by first wife, was born in the parish of Sandsting, Shetland, and died at sea when a young man, unmarried.

James Ridland⁶ (2), a son of Thomas⁵ (2) by first wife, was born in Sandsting, and settled in New South Wales, Australia. Post-office, Sydney.

Jerome Ridland⁶ (1), a son of Thomas⁵ (2) by second wife, was born in the parish of Sandsting, Shetland. He left home in 1870, and came to ⁿn, Mass., where he was for some time employed in the freight-office Boston & Maine Railroad Company. He was visited there by m Ridlon, and both saw a family resemblance at once. Mr. Ridland ce visited South America and San Francisco, Cal. He has returned on; married, and fixed his residence in Charlestown. He is a car- y trade; a man of good education and fine intelligence; has seen the world, having been a seaman many years. He is of medium ' trim build, and light complexion, — a genial, pleasant gentle-

John Ridland (1) was living in Sandsting in 1879, aged 90 years. Probably a son of the first Thomas Ridland. I forwarded photographs of some aged Ridlons of Maine, which are said to resemble this aged man.

Ninian Ridland (1) was a resident of Sandsting, and was old fifteen years ago. He had several children, and the sons, very powerful men, also had families.

RIDLANDS OF CHARLESTOWN, MASSACHUSETTS.

William Ridland[1] (1), was in Charlestown, Mass.; married Patience Davis, and died of fever there Dec. 2, 1694, aged sixty or upwards. He gave testimony concerning land of S. Frothingham (see Fosket) in 1682, aged 47 years; made deed of Groton land, 1694; wife, Patience, joined in a deed with B. Davis, 1685; joined in Groton deed, 1694. He had issue *six* children, as follows:

SECOND GENERATION.

William Ridland[2] (2), eldest son of William[1] (1), was born Dec. 21, 1863, probably in Charlestown.

Nathaniel Ridland[2] (1), second son of William[1] (1), was born Dec. 6, 1665, presumably in Charlestown.

Patience Ridland[2] (1), eldest daughter of William[1] (1), was born Jan. 18, 1667, presumably in Charlestown.

Joanna Ridland[2] (1), second daughter of William[1] (1), was born Aug. 15, 1670, presumably in Charlestown.

Mary Ridland[2] (1), third daughter of William[1] (1), was born Jan. 9, 1672, presumably in Charlestown.

Barnabas Ridland[2] (1), third son of William[1] (1), was born June 28, 1579, probably in Charlestown.

[**Mary Rydland** (2), daughter of William Rydland, was christened in St. Dionis' Church, London, Eng., June 19, 1625. This is the only mention of the name on the records of the church.]

NOTE.—There was a Mr. Thompson in Sandsting, who for a time was my correspondent, whose mother was a daughter of a Lawrence Ridland, but I do not know of what family.

In 1873 the representatives of Andrew Ridland held at Scarvester, Sandsting, thirty-five acres of land, worth five pounds per year. James Ridland, of Westerskeld, had forty-four acres worth three pounds per year. Jerome Ridland had at Scarvester forty-four acres, worth three pounds per year. Lawrence Ridland, Jr., had at Scarvister, Sandsting, fifty-five acres, worth five pounds a year; and Thomas Ridland, of Conziebreck, Sandwich, Orkney, held five acres, worth three pounds a year.

NOTE.—Here were three sons of William Ridland, and yet the family evidently became extinct in the male line. It is singular if all these sons died issueless. The mother and children may have left this country soon after the father's death. The name is not now known in the United States. We must leave them in obscurity.—*Author.*

HISTORY OF THE REDLON AND RIDLON FAMILIES.

RIDLON FAMILY PORTRAITS.

WHEN my genealogical researches commenced, it was hoped that some of the third generation of the Redlon and Ridlon family had left their portraits in some form; but, although several of that generation lived many years after daguerreotypes and ambrotypes were introduced, they were aged and infirm, and a considerable distance from an artist; moreover, there was a peculiar eccentricity running through the family, which caused them to have decided objections to sitting for their likenesses. John Redlon, of Waynesfield, O., who reached the great age of one hundred and six years, was quite active for many years after daguerreotypes were taken, and his descendants desired him to visit an artist, but the old patriarch did not believe in "shadows," and absolutely refused to accede to their wishes. Magnus Ridlon, of Durham, Me., youngest brother of the preceding, was once near an artist, not long before his death, but it is not known that he ever gave sittings for his picture.

After a long and persistent correspondence, and many visits to the localities where the latest survivors of this generation lived, I am very sure they left no portraits. It would have added greatly to the value and interest of this book if a good likeness of some cadet of this generation could have been engraved for its pages; but as it is, the rising generation must be contented with such descriptions of their personal appearance as I have been able to gather from those who were best acquainted with them.

Believing the younger families, and others now unborn, would have the same natural desire, as they read of their ancestors, to know how they looked, I determined to procure the portraits of all living members of the family of the fourth generation and have them copied in India ink, so they could be permanently preserved. This has been accomplished, with but one or two exceptions, at a considerable amount of money and exertion. At my request my father carried my grandfather to an artist and had his likeness taken when ninety years of age. After much entreaty, I prevailed upon two sisters of my grandfather to go with me to the rooms of Dr. Edward Peabody and sit for their pictures, and was successful in securing excellent likenesses, though both were then rising ninety years of age. Two brothers of the preceding also had their pictures made especially for my use. In the western family I found likenesses of two sons of Abraham Redlon, and two other sons and three daughters had theirs taken when very aged for me. A brother and sister, children of Jacob Redlon, had their pictures taken for my especial use, when very old. As a result of my efforts I have now between forty and fifty nice portraits, mounted, eight by ten inches each, of the Ridlons of the fourth generation, all finished in India ink, which will never fade. In one frame, which measures two feet eight inches by four feet six inches, there are twenty-one portraits of the sons and daughters of five brothers who were sons of Matthias Redlon, 1st, second son of Magnus Redlon, the original Scotch ancestor. Of the children of Matthias Ridlon, 2d, there are portraits of Sally, Mary, Rachel, and Lydia; of children of James Redlon, there are portraits of Joseph and Robert; of the children of Thomas Ridlon, there are portraits of seven, viz: Polly, Thomas,

Judith, William, Eunice, Matthias, and Samuel; of the children of Jacob Ridlon, there are portraits of Isaac and Betsey (Mrs. Mary (Ridlon) Davis was living a few years ago in Gorham, Me., but has not consented to have her likeness taken) ; of the children of Abraham Ridlon, of Ohio, there are portraits of Stephen, Samuel, Ruth, Patience, John, Rachel, and Nicholas. One of these has been taken, — that of Patience (Ridlon) Wells, — since the frame was made, and when the subject was ninety-four years old; this will be placed in a new and larger frame with the other twenty-one, if three more of the same family-connection can be found to place with it. This set of portraits cost me about $80.00. The following table shows the order in which the portraits stand :

1 POLLY RIDLON. Aged 94.	2 THOMAS RIDLON. Aged 94.	3 JUDITH RIDLON. Aged 96.	4 EUNICE RIDLON. Aged 94.	5 WILLIAM RIDLON. Aged 93.	6 MATTHIAS RIDLON. Aged 90.	7 SAMUEL RIDLON. Aged 88.
8 RUTH RIDLON. Aged 84.	9 STEPHEN RIDLON. Aged 70.	10 SAMUEL RIDLON. Aged 82.	11 JOHN RIDLON. Aged 77.	12 RACHEL RIDLON. Aged 82.	13 NICHOLAS RIDLON. Aged 75.	14 ISAAC RIDLON. Aged 82.
15 JOSEPH RIDLON. Aged 76.	16 ROBERT RIDLON. Aged 78.	17 SALLY RIDLON. Aged 75.	18 MARY RIDLON. Aged 80.	19 RACHEL RIDLON. Aged 68.	20 LYDIA RIDLON. Aged 74.	21 BETSEY RIDLON. Aged 74.

I have preserved the maiden-names of the women, and the reader is referred to the genealogy of the several families for particulars. The ages given above do not refer to the time the pictures were taken, but the respective ages of the originals as near as known at the time of death, and of those who still survive (1883).

Since the above-mentioned collection of portraits were finished I have procured twenty-eight others of Ridlons of Saco, Buxton, Limerick, and eastern Maine, which an artist is now finishing uniformly in India ink; these will be framed similarly to the others in four rows, seven in each row, and will stand arranged as follows :

1 PATIENCE RIDLON. Aged 80.	2 DANIEL RIDLON. Aged 90.	3 SALLY RIDLON. Aged 84.	4 POLLY RIDLON. Aged 79.	5 RICHARD RIDLON. Aged 85.	6 NATHANIEL RIDLON. Aged 75.	7 EDMUND RIDLON. Aged 76.
8 ALEXANDER RIDLON. Aged 75.	9 PETER RIDLON. Aged 72.	10 RUHAMA RIDLON. Aged 78.	11 MARTHA RIDLON. Aged 76.	12 REV. EBENEZER REDLON. Aged 74.	13 SALLY RIDLON. Aged —.	14 SARAH REDLON. Aged 84.
15 MARY REDLON. Aged 84.	16 JANE REDLON. Aged 75.	17 WILLIAM RIDLON. Aged 70 ?	18 JONATHAN RIDLEY. Aged 83.	19 JONATHAN RIDLON. Aged 69.	20 MARY RIDLON. Aged 74.	21 MATTHIAS RIDLEY. Aged 80.
22 HUMPHREY RIDLON. Aged 75.	23 JOHN RIDLON. Aged 79.	24 PATIENCE RIDLON. Aged 70.	25 OLIVE S. RIDLON. Aged 72.	26 SARAH A. RIDLON. Aged 67.	27 JAMES M. REDLON. Aged 74.	28 SELECTA REDLON. Aged 80.

The above were not all of the fourth generation, as will be seen by reference to the genealogies in this book, but some of them were and are advanced in life, and I have filled out the spaces in this collection with nineteen of the fifth generation. I have several hundred additional likenesses of the numerous families of Redlons, Ridlons, and Ridleys, and at some future day may have them copied in India ink for frames. I have also a fine collection of portraits and photographs of the Ridley family in England, some of them copied from paintings made more than three hundred years ago; the most ancient of these I have had copied nearly life-size in crayon for frames for my own home.

HISTORY OF THE REDLON FAMILY.

UNIVERSAL family tradition, handed down from father to son through six generations, and held in every branch of the connection, has presented our ancestor about as follows: He was born somewhere in Scotland, went to England when a young man, was pressed on board a man-of-war, taken to the New England coast, when he deserted and settled in Saco, where he married, raised his family, and died. This tradition, so far as proof is known to the contrary, is in the main supposed to be a true outline of our ancestor's early history.

Born in an inhospitable country, reared among the rude fishermen of Shetland, and invested with physical hardihood and courage, this self-reliant young man leaves the land of his nativity and goes boldly forth into the great world to seek his fortune amongst strangers. How little did he anticipate the adventitious experience that awaited him! The little stone crofter's cottage of his birth was to be left forever; parents were to be seen no more; brothers and sisters with whom he had spent the happy days of childhood were to be looked upon for the last time, and all the scenes of his early years never to be seen by him again.

Let the imagination paint the parting scene. The family hive was becoming full, and some of the eldest must give place to the increasing number; in accordance with universal custom the eldest son must remain at home as successor to his father, and Magnus was to depend upon his self-reliance in future. The hour — ever-sad hour — of parting had come, and the lad, clad in the rude costume of the northern seamen, with bundle in hand, is standing at the cottage door; around him were gathered fair-haired and blue-eyed sisters, stalwart brothers, and, conspicuous in the group, stand the parents, their foreheads furrowed by the share of time. The mother, with her head upon the shoulder of her departing son, embraces him and weeps in silence; the father, with quivering lip and voice tremulous with emotion, holds his boy by the hand and gives his last admonition and benediction; then the hands are pressed, the parting kiss given, the farewell faintly spoken, and with swelling heart the youth breaks away, climbs the stile, passes beyond the hill, and is lost to the view of the group about the door.

With tears falling like rain, the parents and children cast a last longing look after the beloved son, and in silence, their hearts too full for utterance, they go about the duties of life. What a void is left in that family-circle! What sad emotions fill the hearts of that group around the ingle and humble board! Sadly, pensively, they gaze upon the vacant seat, and for many days, their food seemed tasteless to them in consequence of the absence of their son. The father does not play the pipe, nor is the mother's song heard as she works at the wheel. But time is healing, and the demands of a laborious life soon made the recurrence of their thoughts less frequent; they cling more closely to the little ones and the wonted cheerfulness in time returns.

But turn from that home to follow the departed son. Crossing the channel to the mainland he moves south to the Scottish border, thence onward to England, where he was seized by a press-gang employed by the British naval authorities, and hurried on board a man-of-war, which, in a few hours, sailed for America. Reaching the New England coast, and being in want of fresh water, they cast anchor off " Old York," in Massachusetts colony, and went on shore to fill their casks. Among the number sent on this errand was the subject of this narrative. He had been pressed into a service which was invested with a bondage too galling to be endured, and determined to seek his liberty at all hazards ; the favored hour had now arrived, and the moment his feet touched the shore he ran for the deep and shadowy forest; if he was pursued he was not overtaken, and made good his escape.

And now consider the situation and prospects of this young adventurer. How singular the fate which had placed him upon a foreign shore !   Alone in a strange land; but worse than that, *alone* in a deep, dark, howling wilderness, and without the knowledge of the existence of any human being within hundreds of miles of him, save those from whom he had so recently escaped; exposed to wild beasts and threatened with starvation, with no weapon of defence or means of supply, his case was hard indeed. But his was not a spirit to quail in an hour like this, and he pushes boldly forward, like Abraham of old, "not knowing whither he went." The shadows of night came down upon the primeval forest, and he could see to proceed no longer; wild beasts crept from their lairs and answered each other with terrible screams from the hills around him; and weary, cold, and hungry, the young man sank upon the leaves to rest. Long and dreary was that first night in America. Fearing to sleep, he spent his time in memory of his childhood home and the dear ones there; the tears of affection that fell upon the leafy couch hallowed the place and made it a Bethel to him ever after. No sound save the howl of wild animals, the hooting of owls, the solemn note of the night-bird, and the sighing of the zephyrs in the trees above him, reached his ear. How sad his musings and dark the forebodings of that night! What numbers of questions revolved in his troubled mind ! Was he to die alone and unknown in this boundless wood, where none would ever learn his sad fate? Must his body become food for wild beasts, and his requiem be sung by the waving pines? But he sleeps at last, and dreams of home and friends, while the angels of God watch over him.

Rising from his hard bed he gathers roots and nuts to appease his hunger, and, guided by the rising sun, he staggers on, over hills, down through valleys, into tangled swamps, fording muddy streams, until, exhausted and bruised by falling over ragged stones, night spreads her mantle over him again, and he stretches himself once more upon the leaves. Another night of troubled dreams, and he is up and away: away to the highlands, and after a few hours of weary wandering he heard what made his heart leap for joy, — heard a human voice, the echoes of which, ringing through the forest, were sweeter music than he ever heard. With swelling heart and bounding step he hastens forward, till, in a little while, he hears the echoes of a woodman's axe and the lowing of cattle; the voice of the plowman urging on his team and the welcome shouts of children, proving the proximity of a settlement. And now he stands in the midst of rude log-cabins, surrounded by a crowd of curious spectators, who, viewing his naval costume and strange appearance, plied him with many questions as to his origin and adventures. When his history was briefly stated he was permitted to share the best provisions of the place. This was in the year 1717. Here, in Old York, Magnus Ridland settled and commenced life for himself; here he was united in marriage with a lady of Scottish parentage and reared a family; here, as a yeoman, he cleared his own farm and gathered his harvests.

He remained in York until 1729–30, when he sold his farm and removed to Biddeford, where he purchased land and lived until the death of his wife. He then married Massie Townsend, purchased land in Pepperellborough (now Saco), and settled on "Rendezvous Point," near the bank of Saco River. Children blessed the second union. The elder sons married and settled near their father. Grandchildren gathered round the knees of Magnus, and he told them the history of his strange life, and sung to them the wild songs learned in the island home of his childhood; here he passed a tranquil old age, surrounded by a numerous posterity; here he died and was laid down to rest, — down upon the shore of old ocean.

His trials were now over; his name stands upon the page of history as one of the original members of the first church organized in his town, and he has undoubtedly been gathered to "his fathers," where no rolling sea can separate the sainted ones. Many of his countrymen had settled around him, and every effort was made to hear from kindred left in the Orkneys, but no news ever reached the American family. The tradition of the romantic adventures of Magnus has been told at the firesides of every generation, of his descendants till scarcely one of the name can be found who has not heard it in childhood.

The aged parents of Magnus had waited and hoped for the return of their long-absent son, or of some account of his fate, but this was not to be ; old age came on apace, and bowed with a burden of years, they went down to death and were laid to rest in the "ould kirk-yard," where they had so often led their children to hear the Word of God. How many times had these parents looked toward the hill over which their son passed when last they beheld him ! With what anxiety and suspense did they look away toward the sea, hoping some approaching vessel would bring back their boy ! Alas, he never returned ! One by one the family on both sides of the Atlantic have fallen, and now the gathered ones on the celestial shore are more numerous than the family on earth. No meeting of members of the European and American families is known to have taken place till William Ridlon, of Boston, Mass., called on Jerome Ridland, who had come from Shetland to that city.

In the common tradition no mention was made of a daughter in the family of Magnus, the American ancestor; all told of the "seven sons of the little Scotchman," and had supposed they had no sister; but the records of the town of York prove there was a daughter Susanna, her mother's namesake, who died in infancy, and was buried where

"The wild waves roar on old ocean's rugged shore."

The seven sons grew to maturity, and settled in their native state, — Ebenezer, in Buxton; Matthias followed his sons to Hollis; John lived and died in Buxton; Daniel domiciled upon a part of his father's land in Saco; Abraham was a seaman, and never married; Jeremiah succeeded to the homestead farm, and Jacob, the youngest, was drowned near the place of his birth. These sons were plain folk, uneducated and uncultured; reared in the rude colonial settlement, without the privileges of schooling, they adapted themselves to the times and conditions in which they lived, and became hardy, sturdy men. They had sterling qualities, nevertheless, and possessed a high sense of honor; their courage and determination were never questioned. They cleared away the forests and led onward the tide of civilization; they established governments, and defended the claims of justice. Members of this family were upon the battle-fields of every war since their settlement in America. Magnus, the ancestor, was one of fourteen soldiers under the direction of Sir William Pepperell, to "scout along the coast eastward from Piscataqua to Casco" (now Portland). During the Revolution, all male members of the family who were of age, entered the colonial army, and some of the old men died in the service, far from home. In this struggle for independence they never shrank at duty's call, and some were specially noticed by their commanders for their brave conduct when before the enemy.

In the war of 1812, another generation represented the example of their fathers, and hastened to defend their country. Some won distinction upon the sea in the privateering service, some received wounds in engagements upon the land, and others were captured by the enemy and shut up in British prisons, from which, if they were released, they never returned to their homes and kindred.

Upon the battle-fields of Mexico another generation so bravely fought and suffered as to call forth high commendations from their superiors in rank, and some died with malarial fevers and were buried in camp.

When the memorable struggle with the South took place, our noble sons rallied at their country's call from every branch of the family, from the coast of Maine to the Pacific slope, and poured out their blood like water upon the altar of their country. Some of these were gray-haired fathers, who, when the foe pressed hardest, girded on the armor and hastened to the front. From their stores, shops, manufactories, and farms they went to the seat of war, determined to preserve the Union or die in the service. Many were shot in action, others were thrown into the filthy prison-pens of the South, and died of wounds, inhuman treatment, and starvation. Some contracted disease in the malarial swamps and returned home to linger, fail, and die, while many still live to suffer from their wounds, and relate to their children their adventures in the army. Thank God! the cause for which they fought and bled was not lost to us, nor to the poor slave. Where once stood the auction-block of the slave-master, at which families were separated ignominiously, and hearts were wrung with the keenest anguish, now waves the grand old flag, under whose starry folds our kinsmen so nobly fought and fell. Though there were no soft hands of mothers, wives, and sisters to minister to them in their last hours, and to wipe away the death-damp from their pale brows; though their graves were made, or their bones bleached, upon Southern fields, far from homes and kindred, the sweet assurance of duty well done made their death tranquil, and no tramp of marshaled hosts, or beat of drum, shall arouse them again to meet the advancing foe.

As stated in this article, the first American ancestor was a member of the church, and his numerous descendants have generally manifested a religious tendency. Hundreds have been prominent and devoted Christians; a score have filled the deacon's office, and ten or more have been ministers of the gospel.

The members of this family have excelled as farmers and mechanics; in these vocations they have manifested a commendable pride, and the exhibition of their ingenuity and skill has been conspicuous in whatever work they have accomplished. They were born with mechanical proclivities, and took naturally to the trades; they were possessed of self-reliant qualities, and never asked another to do what they could do themselves; without learning from others, they seemed ready to turn their hands successfully to the construction of their own mills, farm-buildings, and implements. They were builders of vessels at Saco; erected the first mills in towns where they settled, and constructed almost every article of husbandry and domestic use, from wood, iron, or leather. Few members have been engaged in trade or speculation, and fewer still have been good financiers. Of a quiet, retiring disposition, they did not aspire to public life or political distinction, and but few have held official stations. Many of them, however, have cultivated a taste for reading, and being generally possessed of retentive memories, they became men of wide information and profound thought. They kept close at home, and despised notoriety; read for their own comfort, kept their mouths shut, and hence few ever knew of the fund of knowledge they had acquired. Plainness of speech was a conspicuous trait of character in the family; indeed this feature prevails in all branches and has been universally recognized. Emphatic in their intercourse with others, their answers were brief and pointed, and no words were wasted. A peculiar eccentricity seems to have been stamped upon every generation and individual; this is proverbial, and noticeable where they are known; it is a hard trait to describe, and its development must be seen and known by association to be appreciated; it gives color and tone to everything they do or say. They appear cold and reserved in the presence of strangers, and visitors at their homes have sometimes felt the influence of this disposition so much that their stay was cut short, when their welcome was virtually most cordial and sincere. But when once they have opened their hearts to their friends, they remain firm and true to the end of life.

The wives and mothers taken from this family have been worthy of the highest praise. They have been the faithful assistants of their husbands, and it can be truly said of them, as of the model woman of the Bible, "she will do him good and not evil all the days of his life." They have been first and last at the sick and dying bed, proving the most careful nurses, and their discretion and sagacity were observed by all who knew them.

But I cannot undertake to delineate all the peculiar traits of character so common in the family; these seem to be stereotyped upon every generation, and until the blood of the clan shall have been neutralized by the infusion of many foreign tributaries, a Ridlon will be born, will live, will die, and will be buried in a way peculiar to *himself*.

GENEALOGY AND BIOGRAPHY.

REDLONS OF YORK, MAINE.

Magnus Redlon[1] **(1)**, whose parents' names are not certainly known, was born in Shetland, on the north coast of Scotland, in the year 1698 ; came to America in 1717, and first appears as a resident of the ancient town of York, in the County of that name, in the Province of Massachusetts, now in the State of Maine, where he married Susanna, daughter of Matthew Young,* and widow of Ichabod Austin,† of the same town, in

---

* ROLAND YOUNG, of Kittery, whose wife was Susanna, was from Scotland, and had children as follows : Joseph, Beniah, Jonathan, Matthias (on some old records spelt Mathew), Mary, Susanna, Elizabeth, Sarah, and Mercy. Matthias settled in York, and was father of Susanna, the first wife of Magnus Redlon, whose sons, Jacob and Ebenezer Redlon, also married members of the same family of Young.

† The Austens or Austins were derived from an ancient family in Surrey, Eng., and their ancestors were seated at " Shalford House," in Surrey, as early as 1600. John and George Austen, Esqrs., erected the house ever since the residence of the family, in 1608, on the site of a rectorial manor-house. These gentlemen represented Guilford in parliament, — the former in 1563, and the latter in 1603, — and to them the town was indebted for the preservation of many of its estates. The original mansion was modernized about 1760, by an uncle of the present proprietor, the exterior, however, presenting no architectural distinctions. The old dining-parlor is indicative of the age in which it was built. This room is of oak panel, having a carved oak ceiling and a chimney-piece of great beauty, on which are emblazoned the family arms, crest, and motto, with various impalements. In this ancient dining-hall several conferences took place, at which Cromwell and other leaders of the Puritan party assisted ; the house at that time belonged to Colonel Austen, whose portrait, with many others of representatives of the family, remains ; this gentleman was wounded at the battle of Worcester, and was one of those who signed the petition to the Lord Protector that he should assume the regal title. The grounds around Shalford House are extensive, and are much enhanced in beauty by the River Wey meandering through them in a most circuitous form, and the distant view of St. Catherine's Hall, with its ruinous chapel, supposed to have been erected by Henry III. The present owner of this estate is Sir Henry-Edmond Austen, a gentleman of great influence, and of commanding personal appearance.

Ichabod Austin, Jr., went to Saco with the Redlon family, and his name is found with that of Magnus Redlon, who married his mother, on a petition to Gov. William Shirley, in 1742, then of Narraganset No. 1, now Buxton, York County, Me. He settled in Nobleborough, Lincoln County, Me., as blacksmith, and Robert Redlon, the son of John Redlon and grandson of Magnus Redlon, went to Nobleborough and learned the trade with him. Ichabod Austin married and left numerous descendants now living in the eastern section of Maine. There was also an Elizabeth Austin associated with the Redlon family at Saco, presumed to have been in some way related to Ichabod.

1720 (she was born Nov. 28, 1701, — presumably in Scotland, — and died in 1780), and had issue *five* children, one daughter and four sons, whose names and births stand recorded in the ancient books of the town. This man changed his own surname, or others wrote it erroneously, several times during the first few years of his residence in the colony. In a letter from William Pepperell of Maine, to the governor of Massachusetts, dated "Kittery, May the 11th, 1717," he says, "May it please your exc'l'cy. I have sent you under the conduct of Sarg't Jon. Kingsbury, ten men imprest at York," and in the list of names that follow is that of "Magnus, Redlife." It appears from a deed in the County office at Alfred, Me., that Magnus Ridlife purchased a tract of land in York, in 1719, of Banks Bane and Prebble, "containing twenty and two acres situate between two brooks, namely ye Situate Marsh Brook upon ye north-west of ye Sawmill now in ye possession of ye said Banks Bane and Prebble, and ye Fall Mill Brook." In this deed a reservation was made "of one half acre for a landing-place for ye sawmill, and a right-of-way across said land in winter." This was the first home-farm of our ancestor in the New World. He was styled "laborer" in this deed, but when the same land was conveyed to Jedediah Prebble of York, Feb. 11, 1728, he was styled "yeoman"; the last-mentioned deed was signed by "Magnus Readlan" * and "Susanna Readlan." The subject of this notice now removed to Biddeford, purchased land, and built a house there, but after the death of his wife Susanna, he sold his property, as proved by a deed to Amos Whitney, dated Sept. 22, 1730, by which "Magnus Redlon" conveys "a certain house of thirty-eight feet long by twenty feet wide, one story, with sundry movable goods in said house, which house is standing on the east side of Saco river." He soon after married Massie, daughter of Abraham Townsend,† and purchased of his new father-in-law "a tract of land and

---

* In the list of imprest men named by William Pepperill with that of Magnus Redlife is "Henry Reedle."

† THE TOWNSHENDS — now spelt Townsend and Townson in the United States, — deduce their descent from Ladovic, a noble Norman, who settling in England during the reign of Henry I, assumed the name of the family; and by a marriage with Elizabeth, daughter and heiress of Sir Thomas de Haville, obtained the Manor of Raynham, County Norfolk, which has continued in the family, and is now their principal English residence. They have been very distinguished in Great Britain, and have for several generations enjoyed the title of viscount and marquis; and a branch, by virtue of marriage with the family of Sydney, have risen to the title of Viscount Sydney. Several representatives of this celebrated family emigrated to this country very early, since when, as authors, statesmen, and military officers, they have supported the honor of the family name. The Townsends have so frequently intermarried with the Redlons, in Maine, that some account of this branch should be placed before the readers of this genealogy.

Abraham Townsend, of Boston, in consideration of one hundred and fifty pounds current money of New England, received by conveyance from John Hobbs, of Boston, "all that tract of land which was bought of Maj. William Phillips and Bridget, his wife, by Christopher Hobbs, the grandfather of the said John Hobbs, being and lying in the town of Saco, bounded on ye Northwest with the Brook commonly called Davises Brook, and on ye Northeast by ye River of Saco, and on ye Southwest by land which was formerly Mr. John Smith's, and afterwards in ye possession of Nicholas Bulley, Gent., and by all that breadth Southwest untill three hundred acres be fully completed and ended, together with eight acres of meadow, being in ye great meadow, and called ye Wood meadow." This deed was dated April 25, 1724. "Abraham Townsend, of Biddeford, yeoman," Aug. 13, 1724, conveyed to John Center one-half of the tract of land before mentioned; deed signed by Abraham Townsend and Judith Townsend. In 1728 Abraham Townsend and his wife Judith, "late of Biddeford," convey the remaining half of the tract purchased of John Hobbs to

salt marsh in Scarborough, on " ye north side of Little river, called ye Rogers Gore." In 1742 the name of " Magnes Redlen " appears with that of his stepson, Ichabod Austin, on a petition to Gov. William Shirley, respecting the settlement of lands in Narraganset No. 1, now in Buxton, Me., and he is supposed to have been a proprietor there at that date.

Magnus Redlon purchased extensive lands in Saco, bordering on the river, and extending across Goosefair River, as proved by his will. He selected a beautiful spot on Rendezvous Point,* close to the bank of the Saco River, and within a few rods of the block-house there, for his dwelling, and Folsum, the historian of Saco, says, " The house of Magnus Redlon on Rendezvous Point was fortified with flankers and stockades." Here he lived the remainder of his days, and only a few years ago the foundation of his chimney and the depression of the cellar could be seen in his old river-field; but since, all traces of a dwelling have been obliterated by the plough.

The name of Magnus Redlon stands on the records of the first church of Saco as a charter-member. He made his will in 1766, and died in the family of his youngest surviving son, in 1772, aged 78 years. He was buried near his own house, by the side of his two wives, but no stone can now be found to distinguish their graves from others of

---

Joshua Cheaver, of Boston, cordwainer. Abraham Townsend purchased in the town of Saco, in 1728, land known as "James Gibbons' first division," and the same year other lands of Joseph, John, and Gibbons Mace, of Gossport, N. H.; this last was deeded to Abraham Townsend and Robert Edgecomb. Judith, wife of Abraham Townsend, was the daughter of Robert Edgecomb; she had brothers, Robert and Thomas, in 1733. Abraham, as above, died in 1746, and left his two sons, "Nathaniel of Lynn, blacksmith," and "Abraham of Biddeford," and several sisters, one of whom, Massie, was the second wife of Magnus Redlon. In the division of Abraham Townsend's property Judith was styled "mother-in-law," consequently was a second wife. Nathaniel Townsend, of Biddeford, son of Abraham, made his will Sept. 29, 1778, and names "wife Margaret," "Bethesda, wife of Jeremy Ridlon," and "Lucretia, wife of Thomas Deering." This will was witnessed by Rev. John Fairfield, Josiah Fairfield, M. D., and Samuel Edgecomb. Nathaniel Townsend, son of Abraham, 2d, married Judith Redlon, a daughter of Matthias Redlon, 1st, and Sarah Townsend, sister of Nathaniel, married to Jacob Redlon, who was a brother of Nathaniel's wife. Isaac Townsend, of Hollis, married Polly, a daughter of Magnus Ridlon, the blacksmith, a sister of Magnus Ridlon, blacksmith, of Parsonsfield, of the Damariscotta branch of Redlons. Abraham Townsend, brother of Nathaniel, last mentioned, emigrated to Ohio and settled near Cincinnati. There was a Jacob Townsend and Isaac Townsend, brothers of Nathaniel, and one Daniel Townsend sometime of Hollis, Me.

* The author resided in Saco about two years during his work on this book, and frequently visited the place where our ancestor spent the most of his days, and walked along the rocky shore of the river where he and his sons had moved so many years before. I there found a small off-shoot of an old apple-tree, growing in the edge of the bushes, — near where the house of Magnus Redlon stood, — that was laden with small, tart fruit, of which I ate, and I have no doubt the original tree was one planted by our ancestor, and from which he ate apples more than a hundred years ago. Rendezvous Point is a high promontory of land extending into Saco River, and partly covered with old, scrubby pines and small hardwood growth. Upon a rocky bluff, having almost perpendicular sides descending to the water, stood the block-house, built during the Indian wars, and the remains of its foundation could be distinctly seen in 1876, although overgrown with bushes, briars, and rank weeds. This point commands a wide and extended view of the river up and down, and, as the land recedes in the rear, of the inland country. In a little bay, not far above, was the old ship-yard of Coffin & Deering, where many of the early Redlons worked. While reposing in the shade of some large oaks, during my visit there in 1880, I saw fishermen plying their craft in boats, just as the Redlons had done on this river a hundred years ago.

the early generations of the Redlon family. In his will he mentions six
sons, two of whom had deceased. (See will and inventory in this book.)
The universal tradition of the family has made Magnus Redlon the father
of seven sons, but no daughter was ever mentioned or known to the grandchildren of our ancestor; there was, however, one daughter, her mother's
namesake, who died in York, and was buried there. The same tradition
represented Magnus as settled first in Saco, and Massie Townsend as the
mother of his seven sons. Documentary evidence proves these statements incorrect. Being reared among seamen, and used to the ocean from
childhood, he seemed to love the seashore ever afterwards.

He was a noted scout in the Indian wars along the New England coast.
He owned boats and spent much of his time in fishing. During the autumn and winter months he followed hunting and trapping. He also furnished many fine masts to the English, which were shipped to England.
He was supposed to be small of stature, from the fact that the name "little
Scotchman" was handed down from father to son in all branches of the
family. It was also said that the Indians called him the "white scout
with yellow hair"; hence I presume his complexion, like all his countrymen, was light. He was a stranger to fear, and his adventures would furnish materials for a volume. He must have been a man of marked traits
of character, for he has transmitted eccentric qualities to all his posterity,
since known as "Ridlon oddity."

Here on the banks of the beautiful river Saco, the Shetlander spent a
quiet and religious life after his wanderings were over; here he gathered
his grandchildren around him and told them the story of his early adventures after leaving the land of his childhood; here, when the day's
work was finished, he sat down and thought of his native land, and
the dear ones left there whom he would never see again. He acquired
extensive and valuable tracts of land, which he divided amongst his
sons. Could he have lived till the present day he could have counted
nearly *fourteen hundred descendants* on the paternal side, who have borne
the Redlon, Ridlon, or Ridley surname, and probably as many more on
the maternal side, — children of daughters whose names were changed by
marriage.

It may seem a little singular, but our ancestor was the only man known
among the early settlers of New England Christian-named Magnus, — with
the exception of some of his own descendants named in his honor, —
and we hope this grand old Norman name, derived from the ancient kings
whose subjects our remote ancestors were, may be perpetuated in our family so long as there is one who bears the surname of our common progenitor. While visiting the burial-place of Magnus Redlon in 1881, the sentiments were awakened now embodied in the following simple lines: —

> " Far from ancestral graves, and his own dear native land,
> Beneath the waving pines on old ocean's rugged strand,
> By the Saco's verdant shore,
> Near his humble cabin door,
> The exiled Northman found his earthly rest.
> The music of the waters floating on the evening breeze,
> Mingles with the song of zephyrs heard among the trees,
> And as requiems are chanted for the dead.
> The wild flowers always bloom
> Round our Father's lowly tomb,
> While the silent stars are watching o'er his bed.
> But his spirit took its flight to the world of peace and light,
> Where no ocean rolls between the kindred band,

Where no scene of earthly night will leave a shadowed blight
On the hearts of those who reach that heavenly land."

WILL OF MAGNUS REDLON.

"In the name of God, Amen, this Tenth day of December, anno Domini 1766 I
Magnus Redlon of the district of Pepperellborough in the county of York and Province of Massachusetts Bay in New England yeoman being advanced in age but of
discerning mind and memory and knowing that it is appointed unto all men once to
die do make and ordain this my last Will and Testament that is to say principally
and first of all I give and recommend my soul into the hands of God who gave it
and my Body I recommend to the earth to be burried in decent Christian burrial at
the discretion of my Executor hereafter named and as touching the Worldly Estate
wherewith it hath pleased God to Bless me in this life I give demise and dispose of
the same in the following manner and form.

"*Imprimis.* I give and Bequeath unto my beloved son Matthias Redlin his Heirs
and Assigns about fourteen acres of Land more or less it being a part of my homestead Farm in Pepperellborough aforesaid beginning at the South West end of what
he has already improved and running back North East the whole wedth of my Land
till it comes to my new Field so called.

"*Item.* I give and bequeath unto my son Ebenezer Ridlon the sum of five shillings Lawfull Money.

"*Item.* I give and bequeath unto my beloved son Daniel Redlon his Heirs or
Assigns about twenty acres of Land and Marsh being also a part of my homestead
farm beginning at the North West end of my new Field and running back from
thence the whole wedth of my land over Goosefair River, including all my Salt
Marsh on each side of said River.

"*Item.* I give and bequeath unto my beloved son Jeremiah Redlon his Heirs and
Assigns the remainder of my Homestead Farm both Land and Marsh with all the
Buildings standing thereon excepting twelve acres at the North East end of my
said Farm lying next to the middle line of the Patent.

"*Item.* I give and bequeath unto the children of my beloved son John Redlon
deceased, the sum of Five Pounds lawfull money to be equally divided betwixt them
and to be paid by my Executor within two years after my dicease.

"*Item.* I give and bequeath unto my beloved daughter-in-law Elizabeth Redlon
widow of my beloved son Jacob Redlon deceased the sum of Six Pounds, thirteen
Shillings and four pence to be paid her by my Executor within one year after my
dicease.

"*Item* I give and bequeath unto my beloved grandaughter Elizabeth Redlon
daughter of my son Jacob Redlon deceased the Sum of thirteen pounds six shillings
and eight pence lawfull money to be paid her by my Executor when she shall arrive
at the age of eighteen years.

"*Item.* I give and bequeath unto my beloved grandson Magnus Redlon son of
my son John Redlon deceased the whole sum that is due to me from the Estate of
his Father the aforesaid John Redlon deceased.

"*Item.* My will is and I order and direct that there be a road of one Rod in
wedth on the South East side of my land from the highway as far as the Land which
I have given to my son Daniel that my sons may have conveniency of passing and
repassing thro Gates or Bars as they shall have occasion.

"*Item.* My will is and I order and appoint that all my just debts and funeral
charges, also the charge of settling my Estate and the legasys herein given to the
children of my son John Redlon be paid by my Executor out of my personal Estates
and that the remainder be equally devided among all my Sons excepting my son
Ebenezer, and my will is that the other legasys herein mentioned be paid by my
Executor out of what is herein given to him.

"*Item.* My will is that if any of the Lands herein given to my Executor be
taken from him by due course of law that then he shall be oblidged to pay no more
of the legasys herein given to the widow of my son Jacob Redlon than in proportion to what of the land hereing given to him he shall finally have and enjoy.

"*Lastly.* I constitute and appoint my beloved son Jeremiah Redlon Sole Executor of this my last Will and Testament hereby revoking all other Wills or Executors
by me heretofore made or named, ratifying and confirming this and no other to be
my last Will and Testament.

"*In Witness* whereof I have hereunto set my hand and Seal the day and year beforementioned.

his
" MAGNUS - M. - REDLON (SEAL)
mark
" Signed Sealed Declared and Pronounced by the said Magnus Redlon as his last Will and Testament in presence of us —
" AMOS CHASE,
" CHASE PARKER,
" JOHN PATTERSON, JR."

INVENTORY OF MAGNUS REDLON'S ESTATE, 1773.

" A warrant issued in common form to Thomas Cutts, Esq., Amos Chase, and Chase Parker to take an Inventory of the Estate of Magnus Redlon who made return as follows, viz. : — A true inventory of all the goods, rights, credits, Lands & Chattels of Magnus Redlon late of Pepperellborough, Yeoman deceased taken by us who were appointed by the Honble. Jonathan Sayward, Esq., Judge of Probate for the county of York, so far as they have been shewn to us by the Executor according to the best of our Judgement this 16th day of September 1773, Viz. —

	£.	s.	d.
" The Homestead Land with Buildings	120	0	0
" One Bed and Bolster, Pillow, pr Blankets, 1 sheet & Bedsted 70–0, Wearing apparrell 80–0	7	10	0
" 1 Chest 6–8, 1 pr old Tongs & Shovell 4–0, 1 Iron Pot 1–6,	0	12	2
" 14lb. old Pewter 14–0, 1 Glass Bottle & Candlestick 1–0, 1 Cow 66–8	4	1	8
	£132	3	10

" THOMAS CUTTS,
" AMOS CHASE,
" CHASE PARKER."

SECOND GENERATION.

Susanna Redlon² (1), only daughter of Magnus¹ (1), was born in York, Me. (then in the Province of Massachusetts), March 4, 1721, and lived but six weeks. Her mother's namesake.

Ebenezer Redlon² (1), eldest son of Magnus¹ (1), was born in York, Me. (then in the Province of Massachusetts), Feb. 13, 1723; married Aug. 8, 1751, Sarah Young (she was presumably his own cousin and sister of the Roland Young who was captured by the Indians and carried to Canada), of York, or Pepperellborough (Saco), and settled immediately on land in Narraganset No. 1, now Buxton, Me. His descendants have universally spelled their names *Redlon*, a practice which should have been followed by all branches of the family. In the year 1762, Nathaniel Ayer, John White, Martha White, widow, Martha White, Jr., and Lydia Ayer, wife of Nathaniel, conveyed to " Ebenezer Ridley " of Narraganset No. 1, in consideration of fourteen pounds, thirteen shillings, lawful money, Lot 19, of Range D, in the First Division of the township lands. This same land was conveyed in 1768 to John Kimball of Narraganset. Mr. Redlon then purchased land at the " Hains Meadow," and established a permanent home there. His house stood on the east side of the road leading from Buxton Lower Corner to West Buxton Village, and a little above the house since owned by Capt. Lew Goodwin. According to a table found in " Goodwin's Narraganset " I find " 1798, the house of Ebenezer Redlon at Haines Meadow, is not half finished; it had six windows that comprised eighteen square feet of glass; the house covered eight hundred and ninety feet of ground, and was one story high." It was then valued at " two hundred and twenty-five dollars." The foundation of the chim-

38

ney could be seen as we passed the place in 1882, and the large and graceful elm-tree planted .by his son is still standing near; but, sad to write, some one has recently cut down the old apple-tree which stood near the door of the old Redlon house, and which was bearing fruit in 1880, being one of the oldest apple-trees in the town. A man once called at Mr. Redlon's in the night, while on the way from Saco to Moderation Falls, and asked for a drink of cider. On being informed that there was none in the house, he pointed toward this large apple-tree and said, "I saw you had a big orchard and supposed you made cider." That tree was ever after called "Redlon's Orchard" and was a grand old land-mark that should have been carefully preserved. The barn stood on the opposite side of the road from the house. The father in his will mentions Ebenezer Redlon, and bequeaths to him "the sum of five shillings, lawful money," but does not bestow upon him any part of his lands. It may be that this son, being the oldest, had received his part of the patrimony, but it is a little singular that in the will the word "beloved" does not stand with the name of Ebenezer as it does with the others. Mr. Redlon enlisted Feb. 28, 1777, in the company of Capt. Daniel Lane, in Col. Ichabod Alden's regiment "for ye service of ye Massachusetts Bay during ye war," but died from exhaustion and fatigue while in the army,—the place of his burial is not known,—May 5, 1777, aged 55 years. Tradition says that when Ebenezer went into the first battle and the shells whistled around him, "he ran like a quarter horse" some twenty rods, stopped short, ran back to the ranks, and fought like a tiger through the remainder of the battle. Some of his nephews were in the same engagement and that night said, "Uncle Ned, what in the world started you off? We thought the devil would n't scare you." The old man straightened up and replied, "Well, y-e-o-u s-e-e, them shells went to which-on-em, to which-on-em, to which-on-em, and I thought they meant me, so I got out o' the way." He stammered when excited. Mr. Redlon was quite tall, broad-shouldered, and muscular; had light hair, gray eyes, and ruddy complexion. He had issue *eight* children, and his widow survived him many years, living on the old homestead with her maiden daughters.

John Redlon² (1), second son of Magnus¹ (1), was born in York, Me., then in the Province of Massachusetts Bay, March 21, 1726; removed to Biddeford with his parents when a child; married Oct. 9, 1749, Sarah, daughter of Robert and Sarah (Roberts) Brooks, then of Biddeford, and settled in Narraganset No. 1, now Buxton, Me., May 1, 1756. He bought of the heirs of John Brown, Lot 24, in Range D, of the First Division of the Narraganset township lands; also, at the same time, "half of the common and undivided lands belonging to the right of John Brown." He settled on these lands and continued there during the rest of his days. Administration on the estate of John Redlon was granted to Abraham Redlon, of Biddeford (John's younger brother), in 1761, and he is supposed to have died that year. His father, in his will dated 1766, mentions "my son John Redlon deceased," and "the children of my son John." I find the name of "John RedLone" on a call for a Proprietors' Meeting in the township of Narraganset No. 1, in 1749, hence I suppose he was dwelling there previous to his marriage. The name of "John Radlon" stands on a petition to the Proprietors' clerk of Narraganset No. 1, in 1751. "John Redlon" signed a call for a Proprietors' Meeting in 1758. The name "John Ridling" is found in "Goodwin's Narragansett." On the muster-roll of Capt. Joseph Woodman, his name is spelled

"John Redlin," in 1756. On many old documents his name was spelled "Ridlon" and "Ridlen." These variations of spelling were undoubtedly errors of those who did the writing. In a manuscript-book, once the property of his brother Matthias, I find the following, which is a verbatim copy: "Narragansett No. 1, 1768, June ye 17th. Michael Woodsum deter to Matthias Redlon for a resate that I gave him for a haror that belongs to John Redlon's estate." His brother Matthias also charges the estate for work "fencing," in 1762. The farm was sold by his son Robert and Andrew Knowlton, in the year 1783, both being of Damariscotta, County of Lincoln, Me. This was the farm now owned by Mr. Steele, on the east side of the road leading from Buxton Centre to Moderation Village, and just south of the Benjamin Hutchinson farm. It was conveyed by the heirs of John Redlon to Joseph Leavett. Family tradition represents Mr. Redlon as tall and broad-shouldered, having brown hair and eyes, and a ruddy complexion. He had a family of *four* children, three of whom married and have left numerous descendants. He was considered "well-off," and the following inventory will show the low estimate of property at that time.

INVENTORY OF JOHN REDLON'S ESTATE.

" A true Inventory of all and Singular the real and personal Estate of John Redlon late of Narraganset No. one, Decd as was exhibited to us the Subscribers by the Administr on said Estate as follows viz : —

	£.	s.	d.
Templ. To 20 acres of Land call'd Home Lot	86	13	4
To 20 acres of Land in a second Division.	6	13	4
To an half Right of undivided Land	6	13	4
To 3d part of a Right of undivided Land.	4	0	0
	54	0	0

	£.	s.	d.
To 1 pr Breeches 16. To 1 Bed with Bedding 66-8 . . .	4	2	8
To 1 Bedsted 5-4. To 1 Platter and 6 Plates 12	0	17	4
To sundry spoons 3-4. To Sundries of Old Pewter 6 . .	0	9	4
To 1 Teapot & cups 1-4. To Sundry knives & Forks 2 . .	0	8	4
To 1 Box & Heaters 5. To Tin Ware 2. 1 Toast-iron 3-4 .	0	10	4
To 1 pr Shears 8d. 1 Gun 13-4. 1 Ring & Staple 3-4 . .	0	17	4
To 1 Frying Pan 8. 2 Old Scythes & Tacklings 2-8 1 Froe 1-6	0	4	10
To Half an Harrow 3-4. Old Iron 2-8. Wooden ware 1. .	0	7	0
To 2 Pots & 1 Kettle 12. 1 Chain 9-4. To 3d of Cross cut saw 13-4	1	14	8
To 1 Cow 60 To 1 Old mare 16. 2 Heifers 40. 1 Wheel 3 .	5	19	0
To 1 Old Saddle 6. 4 Old Chains 2-8. 1 Knife 8d. Eathern 8d.	0	9	8
To 8 Skeins Linnen Yarn 7. To 1 Old ax 2-8	0	9	0
	£18	13	6

                        TM. JORDAN,
                        ISAAC WHITNEY,
" BIDDEFORD, Dec. 17, 1761."   TIMOTHY HASSELTINE.

Matthias Redlon² (1), third son of Magnus¹ (1), was born in York, Province of Massachusetts Bay, now in York County, Me., Sept. 19, 1728, and was named for his uncle or grandfather, Matthias Young. He went to Biddeford, which then included Saco, when a child ; married Dec. 29, 1748, Rachel, daughter of Robert Edgecomb,* of Saco, descended from

---

* THE EDGECOMB FAMILY. Nicholas Edgecomb came from England and settled at Blue Point in Scarborough, Me., the same year with George Deering, and was descended from the lordly family of Mount Edgecomb, England, now represented by Earl William-Henry Edgecomb. Nicholas had several sons and daughters born in Scarborough during the twenty years of his residence there. Robert Edgecomb,

a distinguished English family, now represented by Earl Edgecomb, of Mount Edgecomb, and settled at Saco Ferry on a part of his father's homestead, where he remained until the year 1761, when he removed to Buxton, a distance of seven miles from his first home; his lands in the latter town consisted of Lots 24, 25, 26, 27, and 28, in Range D, of the First Division of Narraganset No. 1. His father, in his will of 1766, bequeaths "unto my beloved son, Matthias Redlon, about fourteen acres of land more or less, it being a part of my homestead farm in Pepperellborough (Saco), beginning at the south-west end of what he has *already improved*, and running back north-east the whole width of my land until it comes to my new field, so called." He conveyed his lands in Buxton, March 16, 1786, to Samuel Scammon, Gent., of Pepperellborough, for the considera- tion of £240, "it being the homestead farm I, the said Matthias Redlon, now dwell on," and a four-rod way given by the Proprietors. In the dis- position of this property he mentions "a house and barn thereon," and " thirty acres of land previously conveyed to my son Matthias "; this lot was " situated on the north-easterly side" of his father's land. The Old Redlon Farm is on the road leading from the present homestead of Lewis McKenney to Buxton Lower Corner, but I am not acquainted with the boundaries. Mr. Redlon probably left Buxton soon after disposing of his farm there, and followed his sons and sons-in-law to Little Falls Plantation, now Hollis,* where they settled about that time; he was settled in this plantation in 1787, as proved by charges made on his account-book there. He purchased a large tract of land bounded by Saco River, and reaching from Moderation Falls down to the homestead of the late Nathaniel Haley. He built a small house a few rods north of the present buildings of Mr. Amos Hobson, and carried on lumbering and shoe-making, keeping at the same time a small grocery and groggery store. Mr. Redlon conveyed a share of a double saw-mill situated on Moderation Falls, June 10, 1795, to one William Walkinshaw, for twenty-one pounds, lawful money. He made and shipped to Saco many shaved clapboards and "marchantable old growth shingles," as is proved by charges on his account-book. About the time Matthias Redlon sold his saw-mill at Moderation Falls he joined with his sons and sons-in-law in building their mills on Young's Meadow Brook, about a half mile up river; he worked in these mills for several years,

---

a son, married Rachel, daughter of James Gibbins and his wife Judith, daughter of John Lewis, one of the original proprietors of the Saco patent. Robert Edgecomb had several sons, among them Robert, Thomas, and James, and three or more daughters, of whom Rachel, was the wife of Matthias Redlon; Mary, the wife of David Young; and Judith, the wife of Abraham Townsend, who was brother of Massie, the second wife of Magnus Redlon, father of Matthias. These marriages prove the relationship so long existing between the Redlons, Edgecombs, Youngs, and Townsends, and show from whence came the Christian names Abraham, Gib- bins, James, Thomas, Jacob, Rachel, Judith, and others so common in the Redlon family for several generations. Matthias Redlon and David Young were first cous- ins, and their wives sisters. Descendants of Robert Edgecomb are still intermar- ried with Ridlons at Saco, and both families live on land once owned by their an- cestors.

* HOLLIS was a part of the tract of land purchased of Captain Sunday, the In- dian Sagamore, by Francis Small and Nicholas Shapleigh in 1661. Small removed to Cape Cod and died soon after, but the property was not divided till 1771. A truck-house was early erected about ten miles above Saco Lower Falls. The planta- tion name was Little Falls, which was changed at the incorporation Feb. 27, 1798, to Phillipsburgh, and subsequently to Hollis. It was at one time called the "Rope- walk."

especially the grist-mill, and when waiting for water to rise in the mill-pond, worked at a bench, making tubs, pails, and keelers, or shaved shingles, in a shed near the mill. A granddaughter now living remembers well that he used to bury her and other children in his shavings when they were playing in his shingle-camp. "Ridlon's Mills" were probably the earliest in town for grinding corn, and it was to them that Robert Martin carried his corn on a raft, after bringing it all the way from Saco Falls the same day on his shoulders. Like nearly all of the old Ridlons, Matthias was very ingenious, and could build almost anything from a "pare of shose" to a "sleaup" or "skuner," as he spelled the names of vessels upon which he worked at Saco. Shoe-making was his principal business during his residence in Saco and Buxton; but he and his sons were employed several weeks every year in the ship-yard of Coffin & Deering, at Saco Ferry. Rachel Edgecomb informed me when 95 years of age, but possessing an accurate memory, that when a girl she was hired to cook for the ship-builders, and "Old Berthias" and "Young Berthias" were often at the table. Mr. Redlon was of medium height; had broad shoulders and a very short, thick neck; his cheek-bones were high; nose large and fleshy; mouth and chin broad; upper-lip wide and full; hair and beard sandy; eyes gray and deep-set; brows thick, long, and outstanding; forehead broad, jetting, and wrinkled. He was considerably bowed over in old age. In disposition quiet and serious, but possessing a quick temper. He was firm and determined when his convictions were once settled. Several of his grandchildren remember him as resembling Matthias Ridlon, late of Sweden, Oxford County, Me., only that he was a larger man. The exact date of Mr. Redlon's death cannot be ascertained, but it was probably about the year 1810. He was then living in his house at Moderation Falls, and had a shingle-camp down the river, just back of the homestead of Robert Carl. While making shingles there he took a violent cold, was seized with colic, and started for home; he was in such distress when he reached the house of Mr. Vaughan, who then lived on the mill-brow, that he was obliged to stop. Mrs. Vaughan administered some stimulants, and he was enabled to reach his own home. His sons and daughters were immediately summoned to his bedside, and that evening the patriarch passed away. He was buried on a high knoll between the river-bank and the homestead of the late Nathaniel Haley, now in the pasture of Martin Foss, Esq., and I think upon his own land, which became the property of his daughter Judith, who married Nathaniel Townsend, after her father's decease. Mrs. Redlon went across the river and lived with her youngest son, Jacob, after her husband's death; she probably survived him many years and must have been a very aged woman. Her great-grandchildren can remember of her crossing the river in a boat to visit her sons and daughters in Hollis, and say she was called "Old Gramy Redlon," to distinguish her from the wife of her son Thomas, whom they called "Grandmarm Ridlon." Old Mrs. Redlon died at the house of her son in Buxton, and was buried by the side of her husband on Hollis side of the Saco River. She was more than 90 years of age. There were *eleven* children in this family, and the records of their births are recorded in an old account-book, by their father's hand. The descendants of Matthias Redlon and Rachel Edgecomb, his wife, have numbered more than five hundred.

Daniel Redlon[2] (1), fourth son of Magnus[1] (1), was born in York, — then in the Province of Massachusetts Bay, — York County, Me., May 4, 1730, and was carried to Biddeford by his parents the same year. He was the youngest son of the first wife of Magnus Redlon, and his name with date of birth on the records of York was spelled *Readlan*. He married Patience Sands in 1751, then of Biddeford, and settled on a part of his father's land at Saco Ferry, where he lived the remainder of his days. He owned fishing-boats, and like all of the early families at Saco spent much of his time on the water. In his father's will, dated 1766, he bequeaths "unto my beloved son, Daniel Redlon, about twenty acres of marsh and land, it being a part of my homestead farm, beginning at the north-west end of my new field, and running back from thence the whole length of my land over Goosefair River, including all my salt-marsh on both sides of said river." On Dec. 9, 1789, Daniel Redlon conveyed to Amos Chase and John Chase, then of Pepperellborough, about twenty acres of marsh, "being the same land owned by Elizabeth Odel's honoured father, late of Pepperellborough." Nov. 8, 1792, James-Odel Elwell conveyed to Daniel Redlon, of Pepperellborough, twenty acres of land, "being part of a lot lately owned by Elizabeth Odel, late of said town." Mr. Redlon died in Saco, April 29, 1804, aged 74 years, and was buried in an old cemetery at Saco Ferry. His widow lived till July 7, 1817. Mrs. Redlon was born in England, and was a little girl when the British captured Quebec. She was a very large, fleshy woman. Peter Ridlon, of Gardner, Kan., says "the Sands Ridlons were short, compact, and had light complexions, while the Townsend Ridlons were tall, spare men." He has reference to the descendants of this Daniel and his half-brother Jeremiah, who married a Townsend. Some of the old members of the family in Hollis believed this Daniel Redlon lived in Limerick during his last days, but it was his eldest son of the same name. Mr. Redlon was about medium height, broad, and somewhat corpulent in old age; he had sandy hair, gray eyes, and ruddy complexion; was serious and cool, moderate in motion, but at times, especially when he had a glass of grog, jocose and sarcastic. His name stands on his brother's account-book, and the old Ridlons in Hollis remember of his coming to visit his brother Matthias there.

Abraham Redlon[2] (1), fifth son of Magnus[1] (1), was born in Pepperellborough (now Saco), Me., Aug. 10, 1733, and was never married. I can learn but little about this son except from family tradition. He was named for his grandfather, Abraham Townsend; said to be a seaman and fisherman; hunted and trapped in winter; frequently visited his brothers and relatives in Buxton and Hollis. Was very odd and eccentric; loved to tell stories about his adventures by sea and land. He was appointed administrator of the estate of his brother, John Redlon, of Buxton, in 1761. His relatives always called him "Old Uncle Abram," to distinguish him from his nephew of the same name, who emigrated to Ohio. He died in 1798, aged 65 years.

Jeremiah Redlon[2] (1), sixth son of Magnus[1] (1), was born in Pepperellborough (now Saco), Me., Nov. 4, 1736, married March 2, 1760, Bethesda, daughter of Nathaniel and Margaret Townsend, of Biddeford, and settled on a part of his father's homestead, occupying the house on Rendezvous Point. His father in his will dated 1766, after giving his other sons a portion of his lands, bequeaths unto "my beloved son, Jeremiah Redlon, the remainder of my homestead farm, both land and marsh, with all the buildings standing thereon, excepting twelve acres on the north-east end of my farm, lying next to the middle line of the patent." His father also appoints him his executor. His name occurs in many old

documents in Saco, and in his brother's papers and accounts. He was
tall, spare, and stoop-shouldered; had dark hair, inclined to curl; gray,
deep-set eyes, regular features, and ruddy cheeks. Those who remembered him say he was moderate, of quiet, gentle disposition, honest, religious, and respected by all his townspeople. He died June 25, 1816,
aged 80 years and 7 months, and his widow Feb. 25, 1821; they had *nine*
children, but his descendants are nearly all dead.

Jacob Redlon[2] (1), youngest son of Magnus[1] (1) and his second wife,
was born in Pepperellborough (Saco), Me., May 14, 1740; married Elizabeth, daughter of Ebenezer Young, of York, Me. (she was born May 14,
1741, and was a cousin of her husband), in August, 1762, and settled in
Saco. He was drowned in Saco River, near his father's house, April 25,
1765, at the age of 25 years. After his death his widow returned to her
relatives in York, and was married Nov. 23, 1773, to Joseph Barker of
that town. I know but little of this young man, except that he was
named for Jacob Townsend, his mother's brother, and what is recorded
in his brother's papers. His father, in his will dated 1776, mentions "my
son, Jacob Redlon, deceased," and bequeaths unto "my beloved daughter-
in-law, Elizabeth Redlon, the sum of six pounds and thirteen shillings and
four pence to be paid to her within one year after my decease." The name
of Jacob Redlon was signed to a call for a Proprietors' Meeting to be
held at the house of Capt. Joseph Woodman, of Narraganset No. 1, in
1761, but he is styled "non proprietor." His relatives in Hollis and
Buxton always called him "Old Uncle Jacob," to distinguish him from
his nephew and namesake. Tradition represents him as a man of medium
height, light complexion, and ruddy face. He left *one* daughter, of whom
hereafter.

THIRD GENERATION.

David Redlon[3] (1), eldest son of Ebenezer[2] (1), was born in the Narraganset township No. 1, — now Buxton, Me., — Dec. 10, 1756; married
Mary, daughter of Capt. Daniel Lane, March 27, 1784, and settled in his
native town, near Salmon Falls Village. He was a soldier of the Revolution; enlisted in Capt. Daniel Lane's company, of Col. Ichabod Alden's
regiment, Massachusetts Volunteers, Feb. 8, 1777. He was at the battle
of Cherry Valley, where his colonel was killed, and Colonel Brooks succeeded to the regimental command. He was also in the expedition under
General Sullivan against the New York Indians, and suffered extremely
from hunger, cold, and long marches. Discharged at West Point after
serving three years. He removed to the town of Windsor about 1810–15,
where Robert Hutchinson, his son-in-law, lived, and died in that town
June 2, 1838, aged 82 years. In 1823 he applied for a pension, and the
records at Washington show that at that date the immediate members of
his family were Hannah Ridley, aged 62 years, and Hannah Palmer, aged
13 years. In the same application he mentions selling a horse in 1819 to
Mark Ridley; also uses the name of Isaac Ridley. I suppose these were
descendants of the Ridley family of Harpswell, Me., and no relation to
David.

The family traditions respecting David Redlon were numerous and conflicting. Rev. Ebenezer Redlon, formerly of Pierceville, Ind., wrote me
as follows: "Uncle David settled east of the Kennebec River, changed
his name to Ridley, and married a second wife there." Mrs. Deborah
Decker, of Hollis, sometime wife of David's son Isaac, said to me, "Old
David Ridley came back to Buxton and died near Salmon Falls." In a

letter from Sewall Hutchinson, a grandson of David Redlon, now before me, he writes: "David Ridley married Mary Lane, and never had any other wife; she survived him many years and died at the age of ninety-six." He had *three* children, all born and married in Buxton, as appears by the records of the town and church there. There were no children born afterwards. Who, then, were the "Hannah Ridley" and "Hannah Palmer" mentioned in the Pension Records as "the immediate members of his family" in 1832? There is some obscurity enshrouding the history of this man in his last days. He was of medium height, heavy built (weighing about one hundred and eighty pounds), very erect, and had light hair, gray eyes, bald crown, and long, outstanding brows. His hair turned white when he was in middle life. He was very eccentric and loved ardent spirits when young; when under the influence of drink sometimes became quarrelsome and combative. Some of the old Ridlons of Hollis remember him as he visited their father's homes when they were children, and talked over his adventures in the war of the Revolution. He was ready for any bacchanalian enjoyment, and said to be a "high-flyer."

Ebenezer Redlon³ (2), second son of Ebenezer² (1), was born in Narraganset township No. 1, now Buxton, Me., County of York, Nov. 4, 1757; married Feb. 17, 1780, Sarah, daughter of Issac Hancock,* of Buxton, and settled on a farm near the Duck Pond in the latter town. He was a shoe-maker by trade, and is said to have served his time with his uncle, Matthias Redlon, while he lived in town. He was a soldier of the Revolution in the company of Capt. Jabez Lane, and in the Sixth Massachusetts Regiment, under Col. Thomas Nixon; was at Boston, Cambridge, Connecticut, Long Island, and with the Northern Department of the Colonial Army, at Ticonderoga, and West Point under Gen. Alexander McDougall. In the book of accounts kept with his company by Captain Lane "Ebenezer Ridley" is charged with one "shurt." Mr. Redlon developed many of the eccentricities so common in the family. He was once in a store at Salmon Falls on a rainy day, where many of the farmers had gathered, — as was then a custom on such days, — among them some of the members of Parson Coffin's society, professionally very pious people. In those days the grog flowed freely and church members did not abstain, when they could frame an excuse for drinking. On this occasion one drank because he had a "bad cold"; another for a "pain in his back"; another for "rheumatism." Ebenezer understood their hypocrisy, and when all had taken a drink he walked to the counter and said, "Nothin' ails me, but I want a glass of grog *because I love it.*" At one time Parson Coffin reprimanded "Uncle Ned" because he did not attend church, and demanded a reason. The rough old fellow looked the parson in the eye, and putting on a serious expression, replied, "I have n't any sixpenny to get me a Sabba-day-hock at Marm Garland's." This woman then kept a tavern near the parson's church, and between the services, while the preacher was at dinner, some of the church-members would go there and take their drinks, which they called "Sabba-day-hocks." He was not tall, but well-formed; his shoulders were square in early life, but considerably stooping in later years; his hair was brown, eyes gray, brows long, thick, and outstanding; his features coarse, and cheeks flushed.

---

* She was aunt to Mercy Hancock, who married Isaac Ridlon, of Baldwin (widow of Joseph Ridlon), and Hannah Hancock, sister of Mercy, who married Nicholas Ridlon, of Hollis, who died in Casco, Me.

His widow died in Buxton, Me., Dec. 26, 1856, aged 100 years. She was the mother of *eleven* children, and her descendants numbered two hundred and seventy-three at the time of her death.

Jonathan Redlon³ (1), third son of Ebenezer² (1), was baptized in Buxton, Me., by Rev. Paul Coffin, April 16, 1857, and died when a young man at his father's house.

Susan Redlon³ (1), eldest daughter of Ebenezer² (1), was born in Buxton, Me., May 15, 1759, and was married May 22, 1776, to Abraham Bickford, of Falmouth.

Sarah Redlon³ (1), second daughter of Ebenezer² (1), was born in Buxton, Me., Aug. 6, 1761, and lived a single woman with her maidensister on the old homestead at the "Hains Meadow."

Jeremiah Redlon³ (2), fourth son of Ebenezer² (1), was born in Buxton, Me., June 20, 1764, and lived on the homestead farm at the "Hains Meadow" with his two maiden-sisters; never married. He sustained an injury when a child, which caused his neck to become rigid, and he could not turn his head without moving the whole body. He was an incorrigibly odd old fellow, who had a "way of his own" that he took pride in. There were days when he would not speak to any person. He seemed almost destitute of the social element, and lived as independent as any man could with his circumstances. Everybody knew "Uncle Jerry," and all the Ridlons of Hollis and the north part of Buxton called to see him and his maiden-sisters when going to and from Saco Falls. Men delighted to plague the old man, and sometimes called him from his bed while passing on cold nights, to inform him that the elevation of his house was favorable to the draining of his cellar; on these occasions he was wild with anger and would scream for an axe to kill his tormentors with. Mr. Redlon was peculiar in dress: he caught a raccoon, and made him a cap from the skin, which he wore, — with the tail hanging down behind, — so many winters that nearly all the fur came off and gave him a ludicrous appearance. The buttons on his outside garments were made of sole-leather. He died Dec. 30, 1840, aged 76 years.

Anna Redlon³ (1), fourth daughter of Ebenezer² (1), was born in Buxton, Me., Oct. 10, 1766; baptized by Rev. Paul Coffin, Feb. 29, 1766; lived with her unmarried brother and maiden-sister after the death of her parents, a single woman. She was very old at the time of her death.

Moses Redlon³ (1), the youngest (?) son of Ebenezer² (1), was born in Buxton, Me., about 1768–1772. I have several traditionary accounts concerning this man, but his name appears but once on the records. He was taxed "two shillings and sixpence" in Class No. 2, of Narraganset No. 1, in 1789; if he was not a minor at this date he must have been born as early as 1768. It is a little singular that his name cannot be found in the church-records of Rev. Paul Coffin, where those of his brothers and sisters were found. Some of the family think he entered the army of the Revolution with his brothers and never returned, but this is not consistent with his age at the time, and his name would have been on the roll. Some say he was deformed and died at the old homestead at the "Hains Meadow." When my grandfather, Thomas Ridlon, 2d, of Hollis, was nearly ninety years old, he asked me if I knew anything about "Old Moses Redlon of Buxton." When I answered in the negative, he said, "There was such a man when I was a boy." But why should he call this Moses Redlon "old," when he was about *fourteen* at the time of Thomas Ridlon's birth in 1781? His history is enshrouded in obscurity, but my con-

clusions are that he died at home, unmarried, soon after attaining to his
majority; that, as so long a time had passed since Thomas Ridlon knew
him, and having forgotten his death, he styled him "old."

Mary Redlon³ (I), youngest daughter of Ebenezer² (1), was born in
Buxton, Me., June 2, 1770, and was married March 17, 1793, to Jacob
Stevens, of Buxton.

Robert Redlon³ (1), eldest son of John² (1), was born in Narraganset No. 1 (now Buxton, York County, Me.), May 2, 1751; married
Mary Rollins, of Newcastle, or Damariscotta, in 1771, and had issue by that
lady *seven* children, of whom hereafter. He married, secondly, Betsey
Knowlton, who also predeceased him, childless. These women were both
sisters of the husbands of Mr. Redlon's sisters, as will hereafter appear.
Robert was named for his grandfather Brooks, and after his father's death
in 1761, he went to Saco and lived a few years with his grandfather, the
ancestor of the family. When quite young he made a journey to Damariscotta, or Nobleborough, Lincoln County, and learned the blacksmith's
trade there of Ichabod Austin, who was a half-brother of Robert's father.
(See note on the Austin family.) After acquiring proficiency in his chosen
occupation, he purchased land in the town of Newcastle, on the west side
of the Damariscotta River, cleared a nice farm, built a blacksmith-shop,
and established a permanent home there. His house was situated on a
hill, — the highest elevation in the neighborhood, — overlooking the river
upon which his land bordered, and about a mile above the "Scotta Bridge."
"The house, standing in 1873, was large on the ground, wide, low-
posted, and high-gabled. The interior was plain, the rooms large and low,
and were warmed by huge fire-places built in a capacious chimney, which
had a very short neck above the ridge-pole of the house. There was a
door in the front, and another in the back side of this dwelling; from the
latter, which was protected by a picturesque little porch, he reached his shop,
which was a little way in the rear, and near the present carriage-road.
His land reached from the road to the river, and his intervales were beautiful and productive. Mr. Redlon's second wife having died, and being
advanced in life, he conveyed his farm to Enoch Perkins, who provided
for him the remainder of his days; his death occurred in August, 1824,
at the age of 73. He was buried by the side of his two wives, near his
home, in a field owned in 1873 by a Mr. Elliot, who, notwithstanding the
reservations specified in his deed, has encroached upon this burial-place
with his plough until the last furrow reached one of the headstones of a
grave; he was warned against another violation of his purchase-contract,
and promised to trespass upon the reserved land no more. The graves
are only a few feet from the track of the Knox and Lincoln Railroad,
once a quiet and secluded spot, chosen by Mr. Redlon when he laid his
Mary down to rest; he little thought at that day the "iron-horse"
would course across his farm, and go screaming past his place of earthly
rest; but, alas! such are the mutations of time. In company with two of
Robert's grandchildren, — Nathan Redlon, of South China, and Hannah
Chapman, of Newcastle, — I visited the old homestead in 1873, and
stood by his grave. We crossed his broad fields and beautiful intervales;
climbed the hill by the same path from which this family-patriarch once
reached his river-fields; drank water from the old well by the road-side
near the house, still drawn by "sweep and bucket," and dug from the
ground in a corn-field where Mr. Redlon's smithy once stood, a large

forge-cinder and a piece of iron about a foot in length, both of which were preserved as memorials. There are no other buildings near, and the place now has a dreary and lonely appearance. I examined the records of the town, and found Robert's surname written *Redlon, Ridlon*, and *Ridley*. He was called a good mechanic for his day, and all his sons and many of his descendants have followed the same trade, he having marked them with a " smutty nose." Mr. Redlon was quite tall and had dark hair and eyes. His features were regular, cheeks ruddy, and his head, when in middle life, was very bald. This history will correct the tradition that Robert Redlon was a son of Magnus, the Scotchman; this no doubt obtained credence in consequence of his having lived in that family when a boy, where he was seen by many of the third generation.

Sally Redlon² (1), eldest daughter of John² (1), was born in the town of Buxton, Me., — then Narraganset No. 1, — May 20, 1753, and was married to Andrew Knowlton, of Nobleborough, Lincoln County, where she lived and died. Her husband was a brother of Robert Redlon's second wife.

Susanna Redlon³ (2), second daughter of John² (1), was born in Buxton, Me., — then Narragansett No. 1, — Jan. 20, 1756, and was married to Nathaniel Rollins, of Nobleborough, who was a brother of Robert Redlon's first wife.

Magnus Redlon² (2), second son of John² (1), was born in Buxton, Me., — then Narraganset township No. 1, — Aug. 4, 1758, and is supposed to have died when a young man, unmarried. His grandfather, for whom he was named, in his will of 1776 bequeaths unto " my beloved grandson, Magnus Redlon, son of my son, John Redlon, deceased, the whole sum that is due to me from the estate of his father." The amount is not mentioned. This child was then but eight years old. His portion of his father's lands in Buxton, were sold to Joseph Leavett, of that town, and conveyed by Robert Redlon and Andrew Knowlton, — brother and brother-in-law of Magnus, — Sept. 2, 1783. He probably died somewhere in the eastern part of the State (most likely with his brother Robert in Newcastle) just before the sale of his land in Buxton, at which time he would have been twenty-five years of age. I have found no tradition in any branch of the family concerning this Magnus.

John Redlon² (2), third son of John² (1), was born in Buxton, Me., May 14, 1760, and died in Saco in 1767.

Matthias Redlon³ (2), eldest son of Matthias² (1) and his wife, Rachel Edgecomb, was born in Saco, Me., Feb. 4, 1749 ; married by Rev. John Fairfield, of Saco, Sept. 6, 1772, to Elizabeth Field, daughter of Daniel Field, and with that lady was styled "of Buxton." He settled on a part of his father's lands in Saco, — perhaps on the line between Saco and Buxton, — about one half mile north of the road corner at the homestead of Lewis McKenney, and I think the old Redlon house was standing in 1880· Mr. Redlon was corporal in the company of Capt. Jeremiah Hill, of Biddeford, which belonged to the Thirtieth Regiment of Massachusetts Foot-Guards, commanded by Col. James Scammon, of the Revolutionary army. He was one of the soldiers drafted to go in Arnold's expedition to Quebec, Can., by way of the Kennebec and Chaudiere Rivers ; was in the expedition to Ticonderoga and Crown Point in the company of Capt. Jabez Lane; his enlistment in this department was dated May 3, 1775. He sold his lands in Saco and Buxton, say 1812-15,

and removed to Wayne, in Kennebec County, Me., where his sons had
settled. His first wife died in Saco, and he married a widow named
Dorcas Williams (I think her maiden-name was Carter), by whom he had
five children, in addition to the *six* children by the first wife. His children in Wayne changed the spelling of their names to *Ridley*, after their
removal East, but two sons who settled in Hollis, Me., and Clarendon,
Vt., held the name *Ridlon*, and their descendants so continue to this day.
He died in Turner, at the home of his daughter, in 1840, aged 89 years,*
and was buried in the family cemetery in Wayne, near the brick-house
built by his grandson, Daniel Ridley. His name upon his gravestone is
Ridley, and should have been changed long ago; the names of all his
children, with his own, on the records of Saco, are spelled *Redlon*. He
resembled his father; had broad, high shoulders, was above medium
height, had a large nose, wide mouth and chin, broad, heavy jaws, ruddy
complexion, gray eyes, long, shaggy brows, receding forehead, and wore
his hair in a long cue behind. Was very bald in old age. He is remembered as a very kind, quiet, and honorable man.

Rachel Redlon[3] (1), eldest daughter of Matthias[2] (1), was born in
Saco, Me., Oct. 10, 1751, and was married April 29, 1773, by Rev. Paul
Coffin, to Daniel Field, of Narraganset No. 1, — now Buxton. Her husband was a brother of the first wife of her brother Matthias, before mentioned. After the death of her husband she lived in the family of her
daughter Annie, who married Joseph Decker, but was subsequently carried to Greenwood, by her son-in-law, Paul Wentworth, — it is said, much
against her wishes, — who seems to have had a desire to secure her pension-
money, which was granted for her husband's five years' service in the
Revolution. She died in Greenwood at the age of 96. "She had
drawn more than a thousand dollars in money from the Government, all
of which went into the hands of the Wentworths": so says her granddaughter and namesake, Rachel Miles. Her grandson, Daniel Decker,
says, "I remember grandmother Field well; she lived with us, and at one
time was standing on the door-step, holding a smooth, slender twig in her
hand. Father was about to whip me, for some bad behavior, with a
rough, knotty apple-tree limb, when grandmother held out her hand and
said, 'Here, Joe, swap sticks with me, and lick Daniel with a smooth one.'"
Mr. Decker asks, "And who would n't remember such a grandmother as
that?" She was not tall, but quite stout in old age; her features were
coarse, and her under lip turned out prominently. She frequently fell
asleep in her chair and dropped her work.

James Redlon[3] (1), second son of Matthias[2] (1), was born in Saco,
Me., Dec. 10, 1758; married Hannah Cozens, of Kennebunk, and settled
in Little Falls Plantation, on the west side of Saco River, on a tract of
land consisting of eleven hundred and forty acres, called the "Dalton
Right," which he purchased in conjunction with his brothers and others.
Mr. Redlon's house was on the hill about one mile north of Moderation
Village, on the road from that place to Bonnie Eagle Falls, and on the farm
since owned by his son Robert, and now (1884) by Edward Whitehouse.
When he left Saco and commenced clearing his land, it was in a dense wilderness, and the screams of wild beasts could be heard around his home every
night; his first plantation was made on newly burnt ground, and the corn

---

* MATTHIAS REDLON was born in 1749, and would consequently have been 89 in
1838. If he lived till 1840 he was 91 years of age at his death.

was broken down by bears and 'coons. Neighbors were not near, roads were poor, and the family only reached Saco Falls by a bridle-path. His log-cabin was dismantled in a few years, and he erected a large, low-posted, frame-house, a little back of the more modern one in which his son lived. This was a great place for "huskings," "frolics," "quiltings," and "candy-pulls." "Uncle Jim" enjoyed company, and being jovial and generous-hearted, always had a house-full. It was here that the celebrated dance took place between Patience Redlon and Ralph Bryant. (See Ridlons of Ohio in this book.) Mr. Redlon was a soldier of the Revolution. He enlisted May 3, 1775, in the company of Capt. Jeremiah Hill, of Biddeford, in the Thirtieth Regiment of Massachusetts Foot-Guards, commanded by Col. James Scammon; he was in the expedition to Quebec with Arnold, and was one of the company who, after Captain Hill resigned his commission, joined the regiment of Col. Joseph Vose at West Point, and was at the surrender of General Burgoyne. He passed through many hardships in the army and frequently suffered for want of food when passing through the enemy's country. Mr. Redlon was qu e prominent in the early business of his town, as appears by the recordat

In 1804 he was chosen constable and collector, with the privilege that his son Joseph may act in his stead if the father would be his bondsman. He was "Lieutenant Redlon" in 1828; also appointed surveyor that year. He was tall and compactly built, and in old age grew quite corpulent; had sandy (some say red) hair, gray eyes; had ruddy complexion, and his features were of the type so general among the early members of the family. He and his brother Thomas were much together, and their families constantly visited back and forth. Mr. Redlon was a great woodsman and spent much of his time in winter cutting and hauling masts. It was often said among the early settlers at Little Falls Plantation, "Give Thamas the goard and Jeames the handspike, and their team will never get stuck." He was an owner in "Ridlon's Mills," which were on the brook near the dwelling-house of his brother Thomas. He was a good, judicious farmer, prudent in his calculations, and generally successful in the execution of his plans; was a kind, accommodating neighbor and useful citizen. He came home from a military training sick, and lived but a few hours, passing away Sept. 12, 1812, aged 61 years. He was buried in the "Old Ridlon Burying Ground," near his house, where his tombstone may be seen. Children of James and Hannah, *ten.* He always wrote his name in a strong, bold hand, and spelled it "Redlon" in every instance.

Thomas Ridlon[3] (1), third son of Matthias[2] (1), was born in Saco, Me., Dec. 28, 1755; married Jan. 24, 1779, to Martha, second daughter of Lieut. Samuel Merrill and his wife, Elizabeth Bradbury, of Buxton, and settled in Saco, on the Ferry Road, where his first two children were born. The house in which Thomas and Pattie commenced life together was near that of Dominicus Scammon, who was taken by the Indians, and sat back in what is now a pasture, on the hillside, not far in the rear of the building of the late "Uncle Nat. Ridlon," and was approached by a lane from the carriage-road; some indications of the foundation may still be seen there, and an ancient apple-tree stands near, which may have been planted by Thomas, though he was there but a short time. In 1782 he united with his brothers and relatives in the settlement of a tract of land in "Little Falls Plantation," called the "Dalton Right," which consisted of eleven hundred and forty acres.* Mr. Redlon settled on this land several years before he — with the other purchasers — had a deed made out, but I find by an old letter addressed to the Redlons of Little Falls Plantation, that they were called upon for the taxes by Jeremiah Hill, of Biddeford. When Mr. Redlon settled on his land, it was covered with a heavy growth of oak, ash, maple, elm, birch, pine, hemlock, hackmatack, and other trees indigenous to the soil of New England. He built a snug log-house, which, being well chinked with moss and mortar, and warmed by a stone fire-place, made the family a comfortable abode. The first clearings were opened on the high, sandy ground, because here, as soon as the wood was cut and burned, corn could be planted without plowing, and the ashes, constantly washed down to the roots, enriched the soil and caused everything to grow rapidly and mature early; indeed the heaviest harvests of corn and grain were grown on the newly burned and unploughed ground. During the first few years after their settlement in Little Falls Plantation, the Redlons procured much of the subsistence of their families by hunting and fishing; their groceries were purchased with pelts and shaved shingles at Saco Falls, which was the nearest trading-post, by going on foot or by horse-back. The hay for their stock, before they had cleared grass-fields, was principally drawn from the salt marshes

---

* THE DALTON RIGHT was in a section then known as "Little Falls Plantation," — since called Phillipsburgh, — now Hollis, York County, Me., on the west bank of Saco River; originally called the "Rope-walk," because a long and narrow township. I have not learned whether the plantation comprehended the whole town, but think it was only a narrow tract bordering on the river and reaching, perhaps, from the old "Smith's Bridge" to Bonnie Eagle Falls. Dalton's Right, so called, was formerly owned by Tristram Dalton, a wealthy English gentleman, and his two maiden-sisters, and is described in the deed to the Ridlons as follows: "A parcel of land containing one thousand one hundred and sixty-eight acres, being the same tract which was assigned to the Devisees of Tristram Little, deceased, by Jeremiah Hill, Joseph Bradbury, and Robert Southgate, a Committe appointed by the Supreme Judicial Court the 16th of July, 1788, and in the return of s'd Committe the 1st day of December, 1778, is thus discribed: 'beginning at Saco River one mile and a half from the upper bounds of Pattershall's Lot (so called) computed on a north-west course; thence running south-east six hundred and fifty-three rods; thence north-west two hundred and forty rods; thence north-east to Saco River; thence by s'd river to the first-mentioned bounds, and which s'd moiety or half part, I purchased of Tristram Dalton, as by his deed to me bearing date the second day of October, 1794, fully appears.'" This land was deeded by Thomas Cutts, of Saco, Aug. 10, 1797, to James Redlon, Thomas Redlon, John Bryant, Ichabod Cozens, Thomas Lewis, and Rufus Kimball, of the plantation of Little Falls, in the County of York. A tract of land, known as the "College Right," bordered on the Saco River below the "Dalton Right," and was separated from it by a "twenty-rod strip," the south-east boundary being the present line between the land of Tristram Eaton and the "Hobson Field," so called, which was the lot purchased by Daniel Field, who had married Rachel Redlon, and settled at Little Falls at the same time as his brothers-in-law. Mr. Field's original house stood on the elevation near the present line-fence between the old Martin farm and Hobson's field. After the death of Mr. Field, Joseph Decker, who had married his daughter Annie, lived in the house, and the widow lived there with them until carried to Greenwood by Paul Wentworth. The land of Daniel Field extended down the river to the present line between Amos Hobson and Daniel Decker. Zachariah Field, a son of Daniel and Rachel, once built a house on his father's land on the river bank, and near "Decker's Landing" (now in Mr. Hobson's pasture); he soon moved to Cornish, however, and some family now unknown occupied his house. Zachariah came back to Phillipsburgh, and built a house on the road-side near his father's, just back of the well-known juniper-tree, and near the creek that crosses the road there. These primitive dwellings of the early settlers have long since become obsolete, and every trace (except the indention of the old cellars and some fragments of the chimney foun-

in Scarborough on sleds in winter; at times during summer, nearly all the men and boys in the plantation were absent cutting marsh hay and stacking it for winter, while the brave, faithful wives and daughters were at home, watching the cows and growing crops, and keeping the bears away. There were no mills near, and their corn was pounded into " samp " by hand. Almost as soon as their houses were up, Thomas built a " sampmill " by cutting down a large beech tree, in the stump of which he burned out a cavity that would hold about a bushel; over this he erected a sweep and pounder, which had a long cross-bar running through it, so adjusted that a man could stand on each side and the two work the sweep in reducing the corn to the coarse meal, then called " corn-samp "; this was a laborious process, and but little was pounded at one time. Mr. Redlon's sweep and mortar was the best in the neighborhood and could be heard from morning to night, as the neighbors gathered to dress their corn and took their turns at the sweep-handles. But Mr. Redlon was gaining ground, and as soon as his farm produced sufficient hay, and food for his family, this rude instrument gave place to the wheel and water power. All the Redlons were natural mechanics, and with a few tools and plenty of lumber could construct almost anything, from a boot-jack to a saw-mill; and they determined to make the water that was daily running across their lands grind their grain. "Uncle Thomas" was always the leader in every pioneer enterprise, and he called his neighbors together one winter

---

dations) has long ago been removed. The "twenty-rod strip" of land between the Dalton and College Rights was "sold for taxes" to Elliot G. Vaughan, who conveyed it thence to John Redlon, another brother of Rachel Fields, who built a loghouse near where the present brick house stands, and commenced to clear a farm there; he sold to Thomas Ridlon, who lived above, and removed to the State of Vermont. (See Ridlons of Ohio, in this book). Thomas Ridlon conveyed the "twenty-rod strip" to his son Thomas, and David Martin, who married his daughter Eunice (she was living, in 1882, aged 95, and as active as a girl), and these young men built their houses on that land; the former, on the hill in the "Ridlon neighborhood," so called (now standing and occupied by John Sawyer), the latter, on the same site where he subsequently built the brick house now owned by Tristram Eaton. Thomas Ridlon's part of the Dalton Right commenced on the northwest side of the "twenty-rod strip," and extended up river to the land of his brother, James Redlon, the present line between the farms of Thomas C. Sawyer and Jacob Townsend. This land reached backward from Saco River southwest beyond "Young's Meadow Pond" (now known as Wales Pond), from whence issued "Ridlon's Brook," on which "Ridlon's mills" were built. Thomas built a log-cabin on the bank of the brook, near the present carding-mill. James Redlon's division of the Dalton Right extended from the northwest line of his brother's land (last mentioned) to the Cozens farm, the northwestern boundary being the present line between the farms of Col. Nicholas Ridlon and the brothers, Joseph H. Ridlon and Greenleaf Ridlon, — all descendants of the original possessor, who built his first house near where his son Robert Ridlon since lived. The Cozens portion of the Dalton Right extended from the northwestern boundary of the land of James Redlon (who had married Hannah Cozens) to the southwestern line of Thomas Lewis, who owned the farm since known as the "Uncle Joe Ridlon'place," and now owned by his eldest surviving son, Dea. Joseph Ridlon, of Gorham, Me. The lot of Thomas Lewis *seems* to have been larger than the other divisions of the Dalton Right; at any rate, it extended northwest as far as the land now owned by Abijah Usher, and possibly as far as the farm of Orrin Davis and Yates Rogers. Abraham Redlon, a younger brother of Thomas, James, and John, who first settled at "Deerwander," in the south part of Phillipsburgh, purchased the land between the Lewis farm and the present southeast line of Orrin Davis, and lived there some years before his emigration to Ohio in 1800; but I do not know the original owner of this lot. I think John Bryant and Caleb Kimball had their lots on the southwest ends of the Cozens and James Redlon lots, and they cleared farms and built houses

day, and suggested that they make preparations to erect a mill the next spring; this proposition received the favorable consideration of all, and like the servants of Nehemiah anciently, they said, "We will arise and build." A rude schedule for the frame was drawn out, and before the snow was gone, the timber was cut, hewed, mortised, and ready to raise.

Thomas yoked the oxen, and with his eldest son started across Sebago Lake to get the millstones which had been previously ordered of a stone-cutter on the other side. It was now near spring, and the ice not strong. When on their return they had reached the lake, and it was smooth sledding, the father commanded Thomas, Jr., to remove the chain from the stones with which they had been secured to the sleds; this excited the curiosity of the son, but subsequently proved the prudence of the father, for as they were coming near the southern shore the ice gave way, and the millstones sank to the bottom, while by driving hard the sprightly team was saved; had the chain which was let through the eye of the stones remained, all would have gone to the bottom together. Another pair of millstones had to be ordered, as the water was too deep to recover the first set. The grist-mill was completed and ready for grinding the corn harvested the following autumn. From this time nearly all the inhabitants of South Limington and North Buxton had their grain ground at "Ridlon's Mill"; the former bringing theirs on horse-back, and the latter taking theirs across the Saco River in boats. It must have been a pleas-

---

there, the foundations of which I saw many times in my boyhood days. The Bryant house was on the ridge southeast from "Ridlon's Brook," and now in the field of Timothy Tarbox, and once a part of the well-known "Thornton Lot," owned by Gill Thornton, of Saco. The Kimball house was situated on the high but level land far beyond "Ridlon's Brook" on the northwest, and in the well-known "old Kimball Field," since called the "Trip Field," because owned by Bill Trip, the blacksmith, of Bonnie Eagle. There was another dwelling-house in that neighborhood, called the "Temple Place." It was on the old road that once led from the house of Thomas Ridlon, the younger, in the "Ridlon neighborhood," through the woods to the County-road near the Cyrus Bean place. This house was at the foot of the hill about half a mile from Thomas Ridlon's, and only a few feet from a well-known spring of cool water, now in John Ridlon's pasture. When a boy I have spent many pleasant hours building ovens with the old bricks once in the chimney of the Temple house, and the old foundation may still be seen. William Ridlon, son of Thomas, Sr., once cleared land on the "Dalton Right," where Dr. Edward Peabody has since owned, and built a barn. I think William had a house there, but am not positive. Mr. Cozens built a barn in a small field on the back end of his lot, not far from the house of Caleb Kimball. This lot became the farm of Nicholas Ridlon, son of James, Sr. Thomas Lewis sold his lot to Joseph Ridlon, another son, who built the nice farm-buildings now known as the "Uncle Joe Ridlon Place," near the village of Bonnie Eagle. The "Dalton Right" has been divided and subdivided many times, but much of the territory is still owned by the Ridlons and their descendants; it was a valuable tract of land, and produced every kind of grain and vegetables in abundance. From early childhood I have known every acre of this land first settled by my ancestors; with my venerable grandfather I followed the mossy paths and winding wood-roads that led through the noble pine forests around the Ridlon farms; and went with my father, when, with gun in hand, at the close of the day, he hunted for partridges and pigeons. I have crept around the greenwood borders of the old, neglected clearings and bush-grown fields, where the early Ridlons followed the plough and gathered their harvests; and in maturer years I have fished and trapped along the "Ridlon Brook," until every nook and corner is familiar to me. I can still find the cool springs that bubble from the grassy margins of the woodlands, to which my ancestors went from their fields to slake their thirst, and point to places where my grandfather killed 'coons and wildcats long before my memory. Those old pioneers located well, and have left their descendants a rich patrimony.

ant sight when there were fifteen or twenty horses hitched to the trees around this mill — as was frequently the case — some being unladen and others all ready to start with their burdens, while the men, who were waiting for their grists, collected in groups to discuss the news and narrate the latest adventures of the settlement. As provisions for the family was the first necessity, a corn-mill was considered a great advantage in a new plantation; and as this first hydraulic enterprise proved a success, the settlers soon entered into a compact to build a saw-mill. Thomas and James Redlon were chosen to go down to Saco Falls and "view a good mill" from which to take a plan for the new mill. Together the neighbors went to the woods and cut timber for the mill-frame, which was hewed on the spot where it fell; this was drawn to the bank in winter and put up the following spring. The saw-mill was higher up the stream than the grist-mill, and the water was carried to the lower wheel by a long spout. It was a great day for the people of the plantation, when the saw-mill was dedicated, and started for the first time. All the settlers were duly notified, and promptly assembled at the house of "Uncle Thomas" and about the new mill; every part was carefully examined; some thought it would run and others shook their heads. A barrel of rum was brought from Saco for the occasion. The women and children were there from every home in the clearing to share in the excitement and festivities of the day, and when the hour arrived for the ceremony to commence all were seated on blocks and timber near the mill. Songs were sung, and Mr. Field made a speech in which he "named the mill." Thomas Redlon hoisted the gate and the great wheel commenced to move with a creaking sound; the saw began to rise, and the astonished people shouted "There she goes! there she goes!" while the women clapped their hands and sang, the children screamed, the dogs howled, and every wild beast escaped to the deep woods. Those were merry days for the settlers, and the festivities of such occasions served to lighten toil and drive away care. These mills were the most important adjunct of a new settlement, and the plantation was looked upon as a permanent institution from the hour they proved their capacity for grinding their grain and sawing their lumber. They could now erect good frame and finished houses, and have the corn reduced to fine meal without making their way to Saco with pack-horse or sack-on-shoulder. All went to their work with new and cheerful interest, and feelings of independence; while the stalwart men were cutting timber for their new houses, they were animated by the industrious clatter of the new mills; as the wives and daughters were at the wheel and loom, they were no longer troubled about the meal in the barrel, for while the ground produced corn, there could be no want.

There were times when the families of the Redlons were pinched for food before their mills were built, and during the first years of their settlement at Little Falls. Sometimes the mothers would sit up with their children until midnight, waiting the return of their husbands from Saco, whither they had gone to procure provisions, and would then bake bread before going to bed to satisfy their hunger. At one time Thomas Redlon's family were out of food, and he started early for Saco on foot to procure meal and groceries. When he reached Smith's (supposed to have been Daniel Smith, 1st, who lived near Smith's bridge) a woman hailed him from her door and asked him if he had any breakfast; and on learning his errand brought him a biscuit as large as his "fist," which he put in

39

his pocket and went forward. When he reached Saco Falls he could find no corn for sale, and was obliged to go down past his old home at the "Ferry" to the vessel of Colonel Cutts to fill his sack. Returning to the mill at the "Falls," he rested and ate his biscuit while his corn was being ground. About two o'clock in the afternoon he shouldered his two bushels of meal (minus the miller's toll), and with a bundle of salt fish under his arm, and a keg of molasses in his hand, he started homeward. He stopped to rest several times, and once put down his burdens and drank from a brook. It was a late hour when he reached home, and he was almost dead with weariness and hunger, but his good wife Pattie was up and soon prepared him some food. Robert Martin mentions a similar experience, and tradition proves that such was the lot of the early settlers frequently.

Thomas Redlon and his brother James were among the first in the plantation to build frame-houses, and that of Thomas was the largest in the town at that time. The timbers of which it was constructed were very large and of the best pine; the clapboards and shingles were shaved by hand; the chimney, built of stone, was so large that one could sit in the corner and look out upon the stars of heaven; the rooms were partitioned with wide pine boards, and very capacious, while hanging around the walls were the small farming tools. The fire-place over which the cooking was done was so broad and high that the crane would "swing over Pattie's head," and the wood six feet long could be burned. This dwelling stood on the same spot where the "Aunt Judith Ridlon house" now stands, and the barn was between the house and the brook. When this old mansion was taken down, the beams were sawed into boards with which to cover the present house. Mr. Redlon lived in the old house until the death of his wife, which must have been about the years 1820–24; for Thomas B. Ridlon, of Bridgton, was then living with his grandparents, and remembers when his grandfather came down to the old barn, weeping, and said, "Tommy, your grandmarm is dead"; he slept with his grandfather that summer, and says the old man groaned dreadfully as soon as he lay down upon his bed. The old house was becoming dilapidated and cold, and as the children had all married and settled in their own homes, a small house would do for "Uncle Thomas" and his two maiden-daughters, Judith and Sarah, who lived with him at that time, and the one since called the "Aunt Judith Ridlon house" was then built. Mr. Redlon continued to live in his new house until killed at his own door, in the year 1830. He had been out to his plains-lot for a load of wood, and as he went between his steers to disconnect them from the sled, they became restless, threw him down, and drew the load over him, killing him instantly. This was a solemn day for the neighbors, and as the sad news spread, the people left their work and hastened to the place. David Martin, a son-in-law, and Samuel Ridlon, a grandson, unloaded the wood, and took the body to the house. Everybody in the community, for many miles around, came to Mr. Redlon's funeral. He had been a man of great influence, and was widely known as an honest, reliable neighbor and citizen.

In personal appearance he was a most formidable man, and there were none like him. He was more than six feet in height, and so broad across his shoulders that he could lie on his back in a team-cart and touch both sides at once; his hips were so wide that, when walking, he carried his legs far apart and made a double track with his feet. His weight was about two hundred pounds, but he was never fleshy; his frame was gigantic, and clothed with muscles that were strong as iron. No man contemporary with him ever claimed to be his equal in strength, nor ever made an attempt to compete with him. His arms were so long that his hands reached his knees when walking; his neck was short and very thick; his head large and well formed; his forehead broad and high, and in old age was very smooth and fair; his hair, which was worn quite long, was jet-black, and fell in curls around his neck; his brows were exceedingly long and thick; his eyes were dark gray, deep set, and small, but remarkably sharp and expressive; his cheek-bones wide and prominent; nose short and round at the end; mouth and chin broad, and his upper-lip extremely wide and full. There was a peculiar, cool, determined expression always upon his face when undisturbed. He had great kindness of heart and generosity of disposition, and a better neighbor could not be found; but when his temper was aroused he was like a mad tiger let loose, and woe to the man or beast that stood in his way.

He was a genuine pioneer adventurer, great woodsman and hunter, and many stories have been told of his adventures in his tours through the forests. He once called his dog, and with gun on his shoulder, started for "Deerwander," some four miles away, to find large game. He soon heard his dog bark, and approaching the place he saw a large bear in the forks of an oak. Taking good aim he brought bruin to the ground. There was no means of taking his prize home but to drag it, and twisting a withe into the bear's jaws, he took it over his brawny shoulder and started toward the Saco River. When going down hill he made good headway, but when he came to an ascent the bear was so heavy he was compelled to go backwards and pull him along a few feet at a time. He reached the bank of the river just as the sun was going down, left the bear on the ice, and returned home; the next morning he took a man with him and drew the carcass home, and on weighing it the steelyards indicated over four hundred pounds.

While coming from his timber-lot one day in the latter part of winter, he discovered a bear's den under a large windfall. Taking his son Thomas and his dog, and arming himself with a long-handled axe, he started for the woods again. When he reached the den he placed the boy behind him and set the dog a-barking before the opening where the bear had gone in. He had not long to wait before her bearship put forth her head, and in an instant the axe went crashing through her skull. When she was taken out, two nice fat cubs were found in the den, which were also dispatched, and the father and son returned home loaded with game.

He once fell from a mill-frame into the falls on Saco River, and it being winter, he was carried under the ice. The people who saw him were paralyzed with fear, and no one supposed he would be seen again before the ice left the river, but to their great astonishment they saw him crawling out upon the thick ice below the falls. When he returned to his work unharmed, the master-millwright approached him and said, "Well, Thomas, I am glad it was *you* who fell in!" At this Mr. Redlon drew back his arm and would have dealt the master-workman a blow, but he made haste to apologize by saying, "Hold! hold! Thomas, I mean that no *other* man could have gone under the ice and come out alive."

He was once hanging a boom on the west bank of Saco River, and in company with several others was discussing some political question. Among the number present was one Ed. Rogers, a saucy Irishman, and as Mr. Redlon had taken the ring of a heavy chain in his hand, and was stooping down to put it around the boom-stick, Rogers called him a liar. In an instant the insulted man sprung to the bank, and with herculean strength struck at his antagonist with the chain. His son Thomas saw what was coming, and quickly pulled Rogers one side, and just saved him from being killed. The chain cut a limb from a tree overhead as large as a man's thumb.

At one time Mr. Redlon's sheep had been scattered by dogs, and it was a long time before the flock was gathered back. Hearing there was a stray wether at a barn in Limington, he went there and found it to be his own. When he could not lead the sheep, he took it across his broad shoulders and carried it nearly *nine miles*, to his home in Hollis. This was a feat of strength few men could carry out.

Thomas Redlon was a soldier of the Revolution. He served two terms in the army. His first enlistment was in John Crane's artillery, the second under Col. James Scammon, of Saco. He was at the fortification of Dorchester Heights, and at the surrender of Burgoyne. He said when he reached the army the second time he had considerable money, but finding his uncle, Daniel Field, and brother Daniel, very destitute, he divided with them.* One of his company came home from the army sick, and called at the house of Mr. Redlon to tell his family, "You will never see Thomas again, for I marched with him so far north that the north star was south of us, and *he* has been going in the same direction six weeks since I came away." Mr. Redlon returned home in a few days after, to the surprise of his friends. The heavy "Queen's-arm" gun carried by him in the army was long kept in the house of his son Thomas, and I have fired it when a boy; but my father used the barrel to burn out bow-holes in his yokes, and it was spoiled. This gun was long, clamped, and iron-trimmed, and with it Mr. Redlon killed many bears and other wild animals after his return from the army.

He was buried in the "Old Ridlon Burying-ground," on the hill beyond the homestead-buildings of his brother James, but there is now nothing but small ledge stones at his grave to mark the place of his earthly rest. Two of his *eleven* children are now living, each rising ninety-five years of age, and well preserved physically and mentally.

Mary Redlon[3] (2), second daughter of Matthias[2] (1), was born in Saco, Me., June 2, 1758, and was burned to death in the house of James Edgecomb, at "Edgecomb's Meadow," so called, April 10, 1767, together with Reliance, daughter of James Edgecomb, and Elizabeth, daughter of Samuel Fletcher. Mary was a niece of Mr. Edgecomb, and was at his home on a visit, when, while the heads of the family were absent for the night in Scarborough, the house took fire while these children were asleep, and all were burned so their bodies were not distinguishable when found in the ruins the next day. This sad occurrence was not known to Mr. Edgecomb and his wife until, as they were returning the next morning, they saw the smoke rising from the debris.

John Redlon[3] (3), fourth son of Matthias[2] (1), was born in Saco, Me., Nov. 11, 1760; married Dec. 15, 1779, Abigail Holmes, of the town of

---

* DANIEL FIELD married his sister Rachel, and was called "brother;" but who was the "Uncle Daniel Field"? Was the mother of Daniel Field, Jr., an Edgecomb and sister of Matthias Redlon's wife? He was telling this to his children and according to common custom would call his brother-in-law "brother Daniel."

Scarborough, and settled first in his native town. He subsequently followed his brothers to Little Falls Plantation, now in Hollis, York County, and cleared a farm on a twenty-rod strip between the "College Right" and "Dalton Right," so called. Mr. Redlon's house, built of logs, was near where the brick-house, known as the "Uncle David Martin house," now stands, and he owned that farm and the land on the hill in the "Ridlon Neighborhood," where Thomas Ridlon, Jr., built his house years after wards. John lived at Little Falls Plantation only about ten or twelve years when he removed to Vermont, where he purchased a large tract of land and built a house; this was about 1810. His wife died during his residence in Vermont, and becoming discouraged in cultivating a rocky soil, and hearing from his brother Abraham from Ohio, about the beauties of the western country and the fertility of the soil there, he sold out and emigrated West. Mr. Redlon's first settlement in Ohio was in Miami County, where he lived many years; but he subsequently removed with his only surviving son further north, in Auglaize County, where he continued till his death. He had married a second wife in Vermont whose name has not reached me, but he had no children by this woman, who also predeceased her husband.

The surname of this man, written by his father in his family record, was spelled "Redlon;" during his residence in Hollis and Vermont, "Ridlon," and after his settlement in the West, "Redley." He was in the war of the Revolution with his brothers, having first enlisted in John Crane's Artillery Company, and under Col. Edmund Phinney, of Gorham, Me. He was with General Knox and frequently saw Washington. Mr. Redlon spent his last days in the family of his son and namesake in Waynesfield, O., where he died in 1866, aged 106 years 3 months. He was never known to be sick, and died of old age. He retained his faculties to a remarkable degree, and when more than a hundred years old would carry a chair into his orchard and sit to shoot the birds that came for plums and cherries. He was naturally quiet and sober, but when he had taken some spirits he became communicative, and would spend hours relating his early adventures in the woods of Maine (then Massachusetts), and hardships in the army. He was not tall, but resembled his brother Thomas, before mentioned, in build. He was singularly broad across his shoulders and hips, but small at the waist. Erect and full-chested, he carried himself gracefully when walking. He had black hair, which inclined to curl; bald crown; broad, smooth forehead; heavy, outstanding brows; gray eyes, oval face, red cheeks, and a short, thick nose. Like all his relatives he had the broad mouth and chin so characteristic of the people of northern Europe, from whence his grandfather came. When a young man he was seen to spring over a line under which he could walk when erect. My grandfather has told many remarkable adventures in which this uncle was involved in the army of the Revolution. He seems to have been a courageous, unflinching soldier, and a man of peaceable, honest habits. He had kept some nice black-walnut boards in his barn for many years, from which he desired his coffin to be made when he died; this wish was complied with, but he was so broad that his body could not be placed in it, and another was made of whitewood. At the burial the remains were escorted by a detachment of military headed by two generals mounted on white horses, all attended by a band of music by which a dirge was played as the procession moved to the cemetery. His grave was also too narrow to admit the casket, and the sexton was obliged to enlarge it before he could be interred. Two years after his burial his body was exhumed for removal to another cemetery, and on opening the coffin it was found to look as fresh and natural as when he died.

A beautifully embroidered silk banner, now in the possession of his granddaughter, was made and presented to Mr. Redlon by the ladies of St. Mary on his one hundred and sixth birthday. This banner was about four feet square, corded and tasseled with blue and gold, suspended on a highly-finished rosewood staff, and bore the following inscription wrought in large letters with silk: —

JOHN REDLON,
A SOLDIER OF THE REVOLUTION.
AGED 106 YEARS.

This banner was carried in the funeral procession when Mr. Redlon was buried, and is now kept with the greatest care by his descendants. An account of his life and adventures was published in the local newspapers at the time of his death, and a condensed biographical sketch was published by the author in the New England Historical-Genealogical Register in 1876. His name on the monument at his grave is spelled "Redlon" according to his original usage, but his descendants now universally spell theirs *Redley* and *Ridley*.*

Abraham Redlon³ (2), fifth son of Matthias² (1), was born in Saco, Me., — then Pepperellborough, — Sept. 21, 1763; married Aug. 23, 1786, to Patience, daughter of Samuel Tibbetts † (sometime of Rochester, N. H.), and was then styled, — by Rev. John Fairfield, who performed the wedding ceremony, — "of Deerwander," a locality now in the south-west part of Hollis, York County, Me. From this I presume Abraham Redlon first settled in that section, somewhere near the "Warren Neighborhood," so called, and as his brother Thomas used to go frequently to "Deerwander" to hunt, I think he may have been joined by Abraham in his forest adventures. He subsequently removed to "Little Falls Plantation," where his father and brothers had previously settled, and cleared a small farm on a part of the Thomas Lewis' division of the "Dalton Right" land and now belonging to the "Uncle Joe Ridlon's place." Mr. Redlon's house is said to have been in the pasture, in front of the Yates Rod-

---

* The author visited Waynesfield, O., in 1876, and spent several days with the grandchildren of the old soldier, John Redlon. He outlived all his children, and none of the surname now live in the town; but there are several daughters of his son John living near their mother in Waynesfield; these had never seen a person of the name until the author of this book visited them. The family resembles in features and habits our New England Redlons, and expressed the deepest interest in hearing from their kindred in the East. I had the pleasure of preaching in the neighborhood.

† The family of Tibbetts is descended from Henry and his wife Eliza, who came from London, Eng., in the ship "James" in 1635, accompanied by a sister Remembrance, and his two sons, Jeremy and Samuel; the former aged four and the latter two years. In the ship's clearance Henry Tibbetts is called "Shoe-maker." He settled at Dover Neck, in New Hampshire, and had other issue. The families were remarkably prolific, and descendants are now scattered into every state of the Union. They are noted for their scholarship, mechanical capabilities, precision, order, and great will-force. They are compact of build, large of bone, muscular, and of strong constitution. Many have reached a great age. Nearly all have gray hair when young. Patience Tibbetts, who became the wife of Abraham Redlon, was aunt to Gideon Tibbetts, whose daughter Hannah was married to Samuel Ridlon, and her son is author of this book. (See note on the Bunker and Walker families in following pages.)

gers'· farm, now owned by John Lane, where there is still an old well and some other indications of a dwelling. If that was the site of Abraham Redlon's house, some of the Ridlon family were not very definite in their description of his place of residence, for they said "Uncle Abraham's house was on the *hill*, beyond Uncle Joe Ridlon's, on the old road, and close to the first school-house." This traditionary account is supported by an old document in my possession, in which is found the agreement, drawn up and signed by the settlers, to build a school-house "near the house of Abraham Ridlon." The "old road" ran back of the present oak woods, and there are still plenty of men living who went to school in the first school-house that was built there. In the year 1793 Abraham Redlon had three children to attend school there, according to the petition before mentioned, which bears his autograph written that year. Some of the family claim that Mr. Redlon once lived between his brothers, Thomas and James, on the little knoll in the field of Stephen Higgins, near the field-corner of Thomas C. Sawyer, which, if true, must have been previous to his settlement above Bonnie Eagle Village, for he was domiciled there when he sold and emigrated to Ohio in 1800.

Elder Witham, of Standish, Me., made a tour through Ohio, in the year 1788, and purchased several thousand acres of land there. He returned to New England the same year, and induced many families to go back with him to settle on his land. The letters forwarded by those who had accompanied Mr. Witham, when he came back to Maine the following autumn, gave such a glowing description of the climate, soil, timber, and water, that many families in Standish, Buxton, and Hollis (then Phillipsburgh), emigrated to Ohio the next spring. Each family was provided with a heavy covered wagon and two strong horses. Mr. Redlon employed William West to go to Haverhill, Mass., and purchase a large pair of horses; these were so broad across the back that Joseph Decker (afterwards called the "Massachusetts Prophet") stood upon one of them and rode about the yard before Thomas Redlon's house. As soon as Abraham Redlon sold his farm in Phillipsburgh he moved his family into the house of his brother Thomas, and commenced making preparation for his emigration. Old Mr. Tibbetts, Mr. Redlon's father-in-law, was a shoe-maker by trade, and was making harnesses for the horses, while his wife assisted Patience, her daughter, in making clothes for the children. Matthias Redlon, Abraham's father, and Thomas, his brother, built the body for the wagon. When all was ready the family went down to Moderation Falls, and spent their last night with their aged parents. At an early hour the next morning all the relatives and neighbors came to Old Matthias Redlon's to see Abraham's family before they left. It was a sad scene. The aged parents, brothers, sisters, and cousins, were to look upon their kindred for the last time on earth. Each moved forward and gave the parting hand; the children were handed down from the wagon and kissed for the last time; the "goodbye" was spoken amid falling tears, and the train moved away toward Salmon Falls, where it was to be joined by other families. The friends that remained behind, watched their departing kindred till out of sight, and then returned slowly and sadly homeward.

The journey was a long and tiresome one. The emigrants left New England in "flax-bloom time" (June), and did not reach their destination until "roast-ear time" (September). When they reached western Virginia their horses had become badly chafed, and their shoulders were so sore that the emigrants made a stop of several weeks to give the horses rest. They were in a Dutch settlement, and the men threshed grain and the women spun linen to pay their board and horse-keeping. One of Mr. Redlon's horses was not in a condition to travel at the time the others were ready to resume their journey, and it was exchanged for a " tight-bitted mare." Samuel Ridlen, one of the sons of Abraham, informed me that they had a very pleasant time on the way to Ohio. The men raced horses by day, and at evening tested their strength by wrestling. The women took their knitting-work with them and made the time profitable. The teams were drawn together in a circle at evening, and while the men cared for the horses, the women were busy around the camp-fires cooking food for supper. The women and children slept in the wagons, and the men took turns in watching the horses. No serious accident occurred till the train reached the Alleghany mountains, where they found a hard road. The ascent was so steep they were obliged to put two teams together and draw one wagon up the mountain a mile, and then return for another. In going down on the Ohio side, the road was so steep and rough that long poles were fastened to the sides of their carriages, and held by men on the upper side, to prevent them from capsizing. On the way down, a colt, on which Timothy Redlon, Abraham's eldest son, was riding, stumbled and threw the lad, breaking his arm. A halt was made, and the arm dressed as best it could be, but it was very painful, and the movements of the colt and the jolting of the wagons caused the arm to swell badly.

At Redstone Creek, on the bank of the Ohio River, the company tarried several days and built flat-boats upon which to transport their household goods down to Cincinnati. A young man had joined their company, who claimed to be on his way to southern Ohio, prospecting for farm-land, and as he had no horse, Abraham consented to let him ride his down the west side of the river, with the agreement that they should be delivered to him in good condition when their boats landed at their destination. Having disembarked they waited in vain for the stranger and horses to appear. Mr. Redlon went back and traced his horses till he found one of them turned out by the roadside; the other he never heard from. The recovered horse was too poor to drive, and it was exchanged for a heifer, and a note for thirty dollars, which was never collected. Abraham moved his family into some cabins owned by Abraham Townsend, who had formerly lived at Little Falls Plantation, but had joined the first company who emigrated to Ohio, and lived there that winter. He had purchased land of Mr. Witham, and was to pay for it by splitting rails; consequently he built a rude lodge in the woods by setting puncheons in a trench dug in the ground, which were chinked, and roofed over with chestnut-bark; in this cabin Mr. Redlon and family lived through the winter, and subsisted on a few bushels of meal, wild turkeys, and venison brought to them by two hunters named Van Eaton, who sometimes tarried with the family through the night. During the winter Abraham and his eldest sons were employed making fence-rails. I think one of the children was born in this bark-covered camp, and the family suffered many hardships and deprivations during the time their land was being cleared and comfortable buildings erected.

The New England families erected a church in their settlement, and Mr. Witham became their preacher; the year 1801-2 witnessed a great revival of religion in the neighborhood, and with many other families

Abraham Redlon and wife became members of the General Baptist Church, organized at that time, at a place subsequently called "Withamville," and continued consistent and devoted members of that communion as long as they lived.

Mr. Redlon died in Decatur County, Ind., in the family of his son Stephen, with whom he spent his last years, Oct. 9, 1852, aged 89 years. His wife predeceased him, but I have no date of her death. Thus this godly pair, after lives of toil and vicissitude, were laid down in graves far away from kindred ties and native land, but we trust that like his patriarchal namesake, Abraham, the Friend of God, he and his good wife Patience were "gathered to their fathers" in the "better country." No information was had of this family by their friends in New England for more than seventy years, until the work of collecting materials for this book was commenced; the author caused advertisements to be published in several western newspapers, which resulted in opening a correspondence with the family that has been continued down to the present time.

Abraham Redlon was of medium size, with broad shoulders, short neck, coarse features, brown hair, hazel eyes, and ruddy complexion. He had issue *twelve* children, of whom hereafter.

Judith Redlon[4] (1), third daughter of Matthias[2] (1), was born in Pepperellborough (now Saco), Me., Sept. 21, 1763; was married Nov. 29, 1787, to Nathaniel Townsend, of Little Falls Plantation (now Hollis, Me.), where she spent her days. She was twin-sister to Abraham, who emigrated to Ohio. The records date her birth in Biddeford, which then included Saco, but her father had moved to Narraganset No. 1, — now Buxton, Me., — in 1761-2. I do not know the date of her death; she was buried by the side of her father on the bank of Saco River, not far from her home. The Christian name *Judith* came into the Redlon family from the Townsend and Gibbins families, early proprietors in Saco, and is still retained in the western branches of the Redlon family.

Jacob Redlon[4] (2), sixth son of Matthias[2] (1), was born in Pepperellborough, — now Saco, Me., — (some say Narraganset No. 1, now in Buxton,) May 12, 1766; married Dec. 19, 1793, Mary Townsend, of Little Falls Plantation, and settled in Buxton, on what is known as the "Moses K. Wells' farm." Here Mr. Redlon cleared a farm, erected buildings, and lived for many years. It has been said by some old people that Jacob moved across the river after his father's death, and took care of his mother in her own house, but I think this a mistake, for that dear old "Grammy Redlon" was frequently taken across the Saco River in a boat, when very old, to visit her son Thomas in Hollis. Mr. Redlon died in Buxton in December, 1817, aged 50 years. He was sick only a few hours; and was buried by the side of his parents, on the west bank of Saco River, about one mile below Moderation Village; now in the pasture of Martin Foss, a place overgrown by small pines. Mr. Redlon was of medium height, broad-shouldered, and had a compact muscular form; his hair was dark, eyes gray, features coarse, complexion ruddy. Those who remember "Uncle Jacob" say he resembled his nephew, Matthias Ridlon, late of Sweeden, Me., with the exception that he was larger and had darker hair. He was a quiet, serious-minded, kind-hearted man; one who could "mind his own business" and live in peace with all the world. All speak well of "Uncle Jacob." His widow survived him many years, and died in Sebago, in the family of her son Isaac, but I have no dates.

Magnus Redlon[4] (3), youngest son of Matthias[2] (1), was born in Nar-

ing his opportunity, when all but two men were below, Ephraim threw the hatches down and bolted them; then seized the two sailors, bound them to the masts, and placed his brother at the wheel. In a moment the voice of the commander was heard below, and the following colloquy passed between the two men: "Who bolted the hatches," cried the captain. "Big Eph. Ridlon, Sir," was the reply. "Let me up, or I will put you in irons," responded the officer." "Wait till you get to port first," said Ephraim. The men below commenced with axes to cut their way through the deck, but Ephraim gave them the following warning: "The fust one of you Britishers who puts his head through this deck will git a broken skull." The birds were well and safely caged and delivered at port in Boston to the proper authorities. For this service he received a double pension during life. There are some discrepancies in the account of this adventure, as related by different members of the family, but the foregoing was from his own nephew, who had it direct from Ephraim Ridlon. He was once on guard at the head-quarters of General Knox, and saw Washington approaching, whom knowing, he allowed to come near without the usual precautions. General Washington reprimanded Ephraim for his carelessness, but on being assured that he was recognized did not punish him.

Mr. Ridlon was considered the most powerful man on the New England coast when in his prime; he could shoulder a barrel of beef, and thrashed any man who was so reckless as to provoke him to madness. Many and thrilling are the stories told around the firesides of his descendants, which were taken from his own lips, and have been handed down from generation to generation. The sword carried by him in the war of the Revolution, is now in the possession of Peter Ridlon, of Gardner, Kan.; it is a short English "hanger." The great arm-chair in which Ephraim sat in his last years, is now in the family of his grandson, Joseph-Henry Ridlon, of Easton, Mass.; it is about three feet from arm to arm, and the corner of the bottom comes directly in front; a massive, antique, and curious piece of furniture. Mr. Ridlon was a Royal Arch Freemason. He died when about 75 years of age, and was so large that the door of his house was removed from its hinges before his body could be taken out for burial. Have no record of the death of his wife. They had ten children, of whom hereafter.

Polly Ridlon (1), a daughter of Daniel (1), was born in Saco (then Pepperellborough), Me. (she was baptized Jan. 24, 1764); was married Dec. 2, 1783, to Benjamin Scammon, and lived on the "Old Orchard Road." She was called "Aunt Ben," and was widely known as a most singular woman. She wanted to be buried in the Cutts Tomb, because, as she said, "it is more healthy than a grave." She fell into the fire and was burned so badly that she soon died. Charles Granger, of Saco, drew a portrait of "Aunt Ben" Scammon many years ago, but it cannot be found.

Lewis Ridlon (1), third son of Daniel (1), was born in Saco (then Pepperellborough), Me., March 19, 1765 (he was baptized March 25, 1766); married Oct. 18, 1789, Bethesda, daughter of Jeremiah and Bethesda (Townsend) Ridlon, of Saco, and settled as a farmer on the "Ferry Road," near the Saco River. Had issue nine children; died Dec. 5, 1825. He was of medium height; complexion light.

Hannah Ridlon (2), second daughter of Daniel (1), was born in Saco between 1760 and 1765; was married Aug. 27, 1777, to Samuel Holmes, a relative of Abigail Holmes, who was the wife of John Redlon before mentioned, cousin of the subject of this notice. This couple settled in Limerick, Me., but subsequently removed to Camalis, Onandaga County, N. Y., where she probably died.

Gibbins Ridlon³ (1), a son of Daniel² (1), was born in Saco, Me. (then Pepperellborough), Aug. 10, 1770; married Lucretia, daughter of Jeremiah and Bethesda (Townsend) Ridlon, and settled at "Old Orchard" in his native town. In 1794 he and wife were members of the church in Saco. His real estate and personal property in 1797 was valued at nine hundred and fifty-two dollars. He died in Saco. *Eight* children, of whom hereafter.

Richard Ridlon³ (1), a son of Daniel² (1), was born in Saco, Me. (no dates appear); married Sally Scammon, and settled in his native town on the "Ferry Road." He carried on farming in a small way, but followed the sea the most of his time. `He was drowned on his passage home from Boston; he had a lame arm in a sling, and it was thought he must have been injured and knocked overboard by the main boom in the night. His wife, by whom he had *five* children, died in Saco, Feb. 25, 1811.

James Ridlon³ (2), youngest son of Daniel² (1), was born in Saco, Me., June 19, 1779; married March 12, 1804, to Martha Williams, and settled at "Old Orchard" in his native town. His first wife died Aug. 11, 1812, and he married, secondly, May 20, 1821, to Mary Williams, supposed to be a sister of Martha. Mr. Ridlon died March 2, 1834, aged 55 years; he had issue *five* children, of whom hereafter.

Alice Ridlon³ (1), youngest daughter of Daniel² (1), was born in Saco (baptized March 6, 1768); was married Nov. 3, 1789, to Joseph Davis, a seaman, and lived in Biddeford. Mr. Davis either died or was lost at sea, and she married, secondly, John Lowe, familiarly known as "Jack Lowe."

Jeremiah Ridlon³ (3), eldest son of Jeremiah² (1), was born in Saco, Me., Oct. 7, 1761; married Bethesda Townsend (it is a little singular that he and his father should marry women of the same name, but the records so represent), and settled in his native town. He is not known to have had a family; died or was drowned when a young man. His wife died in 1841, aged 78 years.

Bethesda Ridlon³ (1), eldest daughter of Jeremiah² (1), was born in Saco, Me., Aug. 12, 1763 (baptized Oct. 9, 1763), and was married Oct. 18, 1789, to Lewis Ridlon, her cousin; lived on the "Ferry Road," and had a large family.

Margaret Ridlon³ (1), second daughter of Jeremiah² (1), was born in Saco, Me., June 17, 1765; was baptized April 25, 1766; died Aug. 9, 1811, and was buried on her father's farm. She was a maiden lady of excellent qualities; dearly beloved.

John Ridlon³ (3), second son of Jeremiah² (1), was born in Saco, Me., in 1767, and died Oct. 16th of that year, aged 63 days.

Lucretia Ridlon³ (1), third daughter of Jeremiah² (1), was born in Saco, Me., Feb. 7, 1769 (she was baptized July 1, 1770); was married to her cousin, Gibbins Ridlon, and lived at "Old Orchard" in her native town.

Abraham Ridlon³ (3), third son of Jeremiah² (1), was born in Saco, Me., April 11, 1771, and lived with his parents as long as they survived, a single man; but at the age of seventy-one he married Katharine Cleaves, and continued to reside in Saco. His sister Bethesda and her children lived in his house at one time while she was a widow. Nathaniel Ridlon, his nephew, lived with him when young. At the time of Abraham's marriage, there was great surprise in the neighborhood, in consequence of his advanced years, and the following lines were recited by 'Squire Billings at the time he performed the ceremony, but the prayer in the closing line was not answered:—

> " When Abraham's seventieth year had fled,
> He thought with Katharine he would wed;
> May heaven bless the happy pair,
> And grant to them a noble heir."

Nathaniel Ridlon² (1), fourth son of Jeremiah² (1), was born in Saco, Me., Aug. 5, 1773; married Nov. 3, 1799, Lydia Scammon of the same town, and settled on a farm on the "Ferry Road." Mr. Ridlon was tall, and had dark hair and eyes. He was drowned in Saco River Oct. 25, 1816, having had issue *six* children, of whom hereafter.

Magnus Ridlon² (4), fifth son of Jeremiah² (1), was born in Saco, Me., July 2, 1776; married Aug. 31, 1804, Sarah Deering, of Saco, and is supposed to have died young, issueless.

Susanna Ridlon² (3), fourth daughter of Jeremiah² (1), was born in Saco, Me., Aug. 15, 1779, and probably died young.

John Ridlon² (4), youngest son of Jeremiah² (1), was born in Saco, Me., May 11, 1783, and probably died when young and unmarried. But few of this family lived to old age.

Elizabeth Redlon² (1), only child of Jacob² (1),—the youngest son of Magnus, the original ancestor of this family, and his wife Elizabeth Young, — was born in Saco, Me., about the year 1763, and after her father's death by drowning, was carried to York, the mother's native place, where she was baptized, July 28, 1765, by the name "Betty." I do not know what became of this child, but presume there are now families in York in whose blood is a strain derived from the good old Norman stock through the Redlons of Saco.

FOURTH GENERATION.

Isaac-Lane Redlon⁴ (1), eldest son of David³ (1), was born in Buxton, Me., Sept. 25, 1784; married Deborah Hanson about the year 1808, and died when a young man, issueless. His widow married, secondly, to Daniel Decker, of Hollis, and was baptized in Saco River when rising ninety years of age. She has been dead but a few years, and attended to the care of her house until about ninety-four years of age.

Susanna Redlon⁴ (4), eldest daughter of David³ (1), was born in Buxton, Me., Aug. 18, 1786; was married Feb. 22, 1807, to Edward Gordon, of Phillipsburgh (now Hollis).

Ruth Redlon⁴ (1), second daughter of David³ (1), was born in Buxton, Me., Sept. 13, 1790, and married to Robert Hutchinson, of Litchfield, Me. Died at Dublois, Me., in 1874.

Isaac-Hancock Redlon⁴ (2), eldest son of Ebenezer³ (2), was born in Buxton, Me., March 10, 1781; married Feb. 27, 1806, Mercy, daughter of Benjamin and Mercy (Moulton) Emery, and settled in his native town, near the "Duck Pond," so called. He was a successful farmer, and kind-hearted, honest man. He was quite tall and well formed; had light complexion. Died Nov. 14, 1834, aged 53 years, leaving a widow and large family of children, of whom hereafter.

Amos Redlon⁴ (1), second son of Ebenezer³ (2), was born in Buxton, Me., Dec. 10, 1788; married Oct. 28, 1802, Sally, daughter of Benjamin and Mercy (Moulton) Emery, of Buxton, sister of the wife of his brother Isaac. His first wife died Feb. 24, 1823, and Mr. Redlon married, secondly, Nov. 17, 1825, Elizabeth Berry, of Buxton. He was a farmer and shoemaker; a good and highly-esteemed man. Died March 25, 1860, aged 77 years. Had issue by both wives *fifteen* children, of whom hereafter.

Mary Redlon⁴ (3), eldest daughter of Ebenezer³ (2), was born in Buxton, Me., Oct. 15, 1785, and was married March 17, 1793, to Jacob Stevens, of Buxton.

Joanna Redlon⁴ (1), second daughter of Ebenezer³ (2), was born in Buxton, Me., Oct. 16, 1787, and was married Jan. 23, 1813, to Nathaniel Harmon, of Buxton. Some of the family say Joanna was afterwards married to Jabez Pennell, who took her sister Selecta for his second wife. She had *one* son, Charles Harmon, who is now (1882) living in Saco, and who is a good type of the early Redlons.

Mercy Redlon⁴ (1), third daughter of Ebenezer³ (2), was born in Buxton, Me., Dec. 12, 1789, and was married (according to the town records), Dec. 14, 1809, to Jabez Pennell, of Buxton.

Elizabeth Redlon⁴ (2), fourth daughter of Ebenezer³ (2), was born in Buxton, Me., Feb. 3, 1791.

Sarah Redlon⁴ (3), fifth daughter of Ebenezer³ (2), was born in Buxton, Me., April 8, 1794; never married. Died in November, 1878, at the home of John Redlon. She had a portrait in oil, painted by Mr. Treadwell.

Rebecca Redlon⁴ (1), sixth daughter of Ebenezer³ (2), was born in Buxton, Me., Aug. 3, 1796, and was married Feb. 3, 1828, to Joseph Smith, of Buxton. She was a twin-sister of Lucy.

Lucy Redlon⁴ (1), seventh daughter of Ebenezer³ (2), was born in Buxton, Me., Aug. 3, 1796, and was married April 19, 1818, to Samuel ——, of Buxton.

Rev. Ebenezer Redlon⁴ (3), third son of Ebenezer³ (2), was born in Buxton, Me., Oct. 15, 1799; married Olive Maxwell, a lady of Scottish extraction, and resided several years in Gardiner, Kennebec County. He removed to the West in 1837, and was a settled preacher many years. Deceased at Pierceville, Ind., in 1873. When a young man he embraced religion and became a gifted exhorter, but was swallowed up by the demoralizing doctrines of the notorious Jacob Cochran, and was an enthusiastic promulgator of the same ern c ous principles; but in a little time Cochran was exposed, and his fpllowers scattered abroad. Ebenezer Redlon saw the folly of the whole system and subsequently became an able defender of the doctrines of the Free Will Baptist Church. He was quite tall, broad-shouldered, and compactly built; had the type of features so common to the early Redlons. He had issue *seven* children, of whom hereafter.

Selecta Redlon⁴ (1), youngest daughter of Ebenezer³ (2), was born in Buxton, Me., Dec. 10, 1803, and was married to Jabez Pennell, who had married her sister before named. She was living at Bar Mills, on Saco River, in 1881, the only surviving member of this family.

John Redlon⁴ (5), eldest son of Robert³ (1), was born in Newcastle, Me., Nov. 7, 1772; married Nov. 14, 1791, to Mary Hall (she was born Dec. 17, 1777), and had issue *eleven* children, of whom hereafter. Mr. Redlon learned the blacksmith's trade with his father at the shop on the old homestead-farm, and after his marriage settled at Newcastle Village and carried on business there for many years; the house where he once lived, and his old shop, were standing in 1873, when the author visited the place. He was considered an excellent mechanic and was successful when he attended to his business; but he loved the cup and was unsteady in his habits. He was tall, and quite stoop-shouldered, made so from working over his anvil. He had dark hair and eyes, and was very bald at the time of his death, which took place at the home of his daughter, Mrs. William Dodge, in 1854, at the age of 82 years. He was buried on the farm of his son-in-law, Mr. Dodge, near the bank of Damariscotta River. His wife died many years previously, but I have no particulars.

Magnus Redlon (5), second son of Robert² (1), was born in Newcastle, Me., Nov. 4, 1774; married Nov. 14, 1799, Hannah, youngest daughter of Matthias and Rachel Redlon, of Hollis, then Phillipsburgh, and had issue *seven* children, of whom hereafter. He had learned the blacksmith's trade with his father at his home in Newcastle, and in making a visit to his relatives, on Saco River, became acquainted with charming Hannah, then a fair-haired and buxom lass, and decided, like the patriarchs anciently, to "take him a wife of his kindred." Mr. Redlon changed his name to *Ridlon* when he settled in the Saco Valley, to correspond with the form then used by the family in Hollis. He lived and carried on business in several places in Hollis and Buxton; at one time he had a shop near "Smith's Bridge," on Hollis side of the river; he also lived at "Shaddagee," in Buxton, and had a shop at the road-corner opposite the present house of Isaac Eaton. His first wife died in 1820, and he married, secondly, Mary, daughter of Benjamin Smith, Nov. 14, 1821. Mr. Ridlon was a competent mechanic in his day, and many are the stories told me by my grandfather illustrative of the man and his thoroughness in doing his work. At one time the mill-crank of Ridlon's mill was broken, and carried to the shop of "Uncle Mag" (as he was called to distinguish him from his wife's brother, who was known as "Uncle Magnus") to be mended. To weld a mill-crank in those days was considered a great achievement, and called forth the skill and muscle of the blacksmith. "Uncle Mag" loved his toddy and would not think of undertaking so heavy a job without some of it; so while the preliminaries were being arranged, one of the men was sent to the store with "the little brown jug." In those days they used only charcoal at the forge, and it required a large quantity to heat so heavy a piece of iron. A wooden "crane" was adjusted, to which, by chains, the crank was attached, so it could be swung quickly upon the anvil. Several of the Ridlons were present to assist, armed with heavy sledge-hammers, among them my grandfather, who had been so much with "Uncle Mag," that he was considered "second best man." The man at the bellows-pole was frequently commanded, "Blow her up, Jeams, blow her up," while "Uncle Mag" continued to pull open the coals and throw in sand. The fire was waxing hotter and hotter, and the glowing iron hissed and sparkled fearfully. The sweat dropped fast from the shaggy brow of "Uncle Mag" as he raked the fire and passed round the jug. Some thought the crank was hot enough to weld, but the blacksmith only cried the louder, "Blow her up, blow her up." The owners of the crank remonstrated, and claimed that the crank was already too hot and the iron being wasted, but all the attention they received was "Blow her up, blow her up." When all was ready and every man stationed in his place to strike, the plastic boiling iron was swung upon the anvil, and the sledge-hammers put on, "Pay on, pay on," cried "Uncle Mag," as the great drops of sweat rolled down his red face. The crank was quickly turned from side to side, while three strong men struck in concert upon the heated mass. "Hold, hold; that was a good soaking heat, and I guess she'll stick," said "Uncle Mag," as he let go the crank and took up the jug. The crank did "stick" and was soon turning slowly under "Ridlon's mill." He also understood the art of making cow-bells, then considered a great accomplishment for a common blacksmith; this was before borax was used for brazing, and the bells had to be baked in clay to melt the brass with which they were coated. Mr. Ridlon died in Buxton in 1858, aged 84 years, and was buried somewhere in that town (inconsistently), while his first wife was buried in her father's lot on Hollis side of Saco River and near the old Nat Haley homestead. Mr. Ridlon was of medium height, with broad, stooping shoulders; had dark hair, and gray eyes overshadowed with long, thick brows. He had red cheeks and fair complexion. When in good humor was full of fun, and at "huskings" and "raisings" could keep everybody in a roar of laughter by his sarcastic speeches; and notwithstanding his intemperate habits, seems to have been quite a favorite with his relatives.

Nathaniel Redlon[4] (2), third son of Robert[3] (1), was born in Newcastle, Me., April 10, 1776; married Elizabeth Pierce, of Southport, and had issue *three* children, of whom hereafter. He was also a blacksmith, and carried on business in the city of Bath. He was an expert workman and forged the ship-irons in the ship-yards of Bath and other eastern towns. An old gentleman for whom Mr. Redlon used to work told me that few men could be found at that day, who could excell him in forging heavy pieces of ship-work; this was then done by hand under sledge-hammers. Like his brothers, Nathaniel unfortunately acquired intemperate and prodigal habits, and neglected to properly provide for his family; his wife was compelled to keep boarders to support herself and children. Mr. Redlon died in Bath, Me., Oct. 6, 1851, aged 77 years, and was buried in that city. He was a man of great kindness of heart and generosity of spirit when not under the influence of drink; but when intoxicated became brutal and abused his best friends. He was tall and well formed; had dark hair and eyes, heavy brows, bald crown, regular features, red complexion, and pleasant expression; indeed he was a handsome man in his prime, but rum, that destroyer of body and soul, prematurely shattered his constitution, and his last days found him a wreck, cast upon the rocks of poverty.

Mary Redlon[4] (4), a daughter of Robert[3] (1), was born in Newcastle, Me., Oct. 26, 1778 (?), and was married to James Morton, a sea captain, of Nobleborough, and had issue. She has been dead many years — was an amiable woman.

Sally Redlon[4] (2), a daughter of Robert[3] (1), was born in Newcastle, Me., July 6, 1780 (?); was married to Capt. John Morton, of Nobleborough, and died in 1860, a very old lady.

Susan Redlon[4] (2), a daughter of Robert[3] (1), was born in Newcastle, Me., April 2, 1783 (?), and was married to Joseph Knowlton, her cousin, of Newcastle, and has been dead many years.

Robert Redlon[4] (2), a son of Robert[3] (1), born in Newcastle, Me., is supposed to have died young. No record of his name can be found. Some hold the tradition that he was lost at sea.

40

Dea. Daniel Ridlon⁴ (3), eldest son of Matthias³ (2), was born in
Saco, Me., April 4, 1773; married for his first wife a Miss Williams, who
was a daughter of his father's second wife; and secondly, Mary McKenney, of Saco, June 2, 1822. Mr. Ridlon settled on land adjoining his
father's farm in Saco, near where Lewis McKenney now lives. While
living here, and at work in his field, he heard the voice of a minister who
was preaching at Mr. McKenney's house, and was so deeply convicted for
his sins that he left his work, went to the meeting, was soundly converted,
and became a devoted Christian; he united with the primitive Freewill
Baptists and was chosen a deacon. Mr. Ridlon sold his farm in Saco, and
removed to Wayne with his brothers, subsequent to 1800, and spent the
remainder of his days there. He changed his name to *Ridley* after moving to the Kennebec Valley. He died in Wayne, and was buried near
his residence; his second wife died at the home of Lewis McKenney, in
Saco, in 1872, very aged; she was blind several years. Mr. Ridlon was
above medium height, broad-shouldered, and compactly built; his hair was
black, eyes gray, brows long and thick, features coarse, and of the old
Ridlon mould. He was of passionate temperament, and quick to resent
an insult, but generally calm and quiet in his habits. All of his relatives
have said " Uncle Daniel was a good man." He had issue *ten* children,
all by his first wife, of whom hereafter.

Samuel Ridlon⁴ (1), second son of Matthias³ (2), was born in Saco,
Me., Aug. 22, 1774, and was baptized by Rev. Paul Coffin in Buxton, July
24, 1775; the same day with his mother. The record of his birth on the
leaf of an old family Bible is "1781." I find no mention of another son
of this name, and think the first date the correct one. He married Aug.
23, 1804, to Polly, eldest daughter of Thomas and Martha (Merrill) Ridlon, his cousin, of Phillipsburgh (now Hollis). He lived some years in
Hollis, but about the year 1808 removed to Wayne, and settled near his
father and brothers; he lived in Wayne about ten years and then returned
to Hollis. Mr. Ridlon built him a house in Hollis on the exact spot
where that of Thomas C. Sawyer now stands, on the road to Bonnie
Eagle Village, from the materials taken from the house formerly owned
by his uncle, Jacob Redlon, who lived on the farm since known as the
"Wells Farm," on Buxton side of Saco River. While living in this
house he was coming from Bonnie Eagle Village in the evening, and falling down the almost perpendicular ledge that borders on the river, was
drowned. His hat was found upon the bank, but his body was not recovered till the following spring, when it was found some six miles below
where he was drowned, in the Bar Mills boom; his clothes were gone, but
he was identified by a gingham handkerchief still around his neck. There
is but little doubt that Mr. Ridlon's death was caused by rum, as a jug
containing that damning liquid was found with his hat upon the brink of
the river, where he had probably sat down to rest and drink. Mr. Ridlon
lived a while in a part of the house of his father-in-law, in Hollis, and at
a subsequent date in a house between the Stephen Higgins place and the
house he afterwards built on the knoll above. He was a carpenter and
builder, and many old houses now standing in town bear the marks of
"Uncle Sam's" tools upon their frames. He was something of a cooper
and "shingle-weaver," and had an iron stamp made with which to brand
his name on his wooden wares; this stamp bore the name "S. Ridlon,"
and I have many times burned his name with it when a boy. Mr. Ridlon
was tall, but not very broad; he had dark — nearly black — hair, gray

eyes, long, outstanding brows, and coarse features. He had issue' *nine* children, of whom hereafter. I do not know the year of his death.

Jonathan-Fields Ridlon⁴ (2), third son of Matthias⁸ (2), was born in Saco, Me., Sept. 15, 1776. He engaged in the privateering service during the war of 1812, and became fully acquainted with the New England coast. He subsequently entered the merchant service, and went to sea on a vessel owned by Col. Thomas Cutts, of Saco, and made voyages to foreign lands ; while on one of his trips the vessel was run down by a British gun-ship and captured. The American craft was relieved of all her stores and placed under the command of Aaron Eldridge, of Buxton, .who was the mate, and orders given him to " bear off and on through the night " ; this order was obeyed in one direction, for, as Mr. Eldridge subsequently said, " I bore off once too many times for them," and escaped, coming back and delivering the vessel to its owner. Mr. Ridlon was carried to England, and confined in prison there for nearly a year; he escaped, however, by digging under the walls, and made his way to Edinburgh, where he was afterwards seen and conversed with by an American seaman ; since then nothing has been known concerning him. For a time during the author's investigations it seemed probable that the Ridlands of Shetland, in the north of Scotland, were descended from Jonathan Ridlon, but subsequent information has proved that this family was established there before his birth. It is possible that he married and has left representatives in some part of Europe, who are known by names unlike that borne by their ancestors, but I can find no clue to such and must leave their history in obscurity.

Dorcas Ridlon⁴ (1), eldest daughter of Matthias⁸ (2), was born in Saco, Me., Nov. 2, 1777 ; was married by Rev. Paul Coffin, of Buxton, Feb. 11, 1811, to Samuel Leavett, of that town. I am inclined to believe there may be a mistake in foregoing dates, but they are correctly copied. She lived in Limington, and reached a good old age.

John Ridlon⁴ (6), fourth son of Matthias⁸ (2), was born in Saco, Me., Sept. 12, 1779 (so say the records, but I do not think them correct), and went to live with his grandparents in Hollis. He was a reckless, adventuresome fellow when a boy, and a source of constant anxiety to those who had the care of him. When about eight years of age he came to the house with his cap-viser torn off, and asked his aunt Hannah — wife subsequently of Magnus Ridlon, the blacksmith — who was then living at home, to sew it on. He put on his old hat, took his fishing-pole, and started for the river, near the house. When night came on he did not return, but no fears were excited until the neighborhood had been searched the next day and he could not be found. On going to the river's bank, his tracks were found, and there were indications of his having rolled a log into the water with his pole. It was thought that he ventured upon this log, lost his footing, and was drowned. The neighbors were immediately called, boats and rafts procured, and days spent in dragging the river-bottom for the lad's body; it could not be found, and his relatives returned to their homes in sorrow. About a week passed, when a Mr. Berry of Limington, who had heard that a boy was drowned, came down and informed the family that a lad of that appearance stopped at his house on the same night that John was missing. Thomas Ridlon mounted a horse and started in search of the run-away ; traced him from town to town through Maine and New Hampshire, into Vermont, where he was found at the home of his uncle John, who had moved to that state a few

years previously. He could not be prevailed upon to return, and Thomas
made haste to reach home and inform the family of his safety. He was
apprenticed to an iron-founder in Vermont, and carried on business there
for many years; subsequently settled on a farm in Clarendon, where he
spent the remainder of his days, living in a fine and beautifully situated
brick-house.

A neighbor's hogs, running loose, several times came to his moulding
sheds and rooted over his moulds. He asked the owner of the hogs to
keep them at home; but all warnings were disregarded, and the men
seized them and threw them alive into the furnace of molten iron; they did
not stand the heat as well as the three Hebrew children of the Scrip-,
tures, but were consumed in a moment. When the iron was poured into
the moulds and cooled, the castings were found so tough and flexible that
they were worthless and had to be recast. Mr. Ridlon was tall, broad-
shouldered, and muscular; had dark hair, gray eyes, long, shaggy brows,
and coarse features. His mind seemed somewhat impaired in his last years.
He visited his relatives in Hollis, Me., when advanced in life, and tarried
with them nearly all winter. I have not the date of his death; he was
buried in a field near his house. His widow was living in 1872. Children, of whom hereafter, *eight* in number.

Patience Ridlon⁴ (1), second daughter of Matthias⁸ (2), was born in
Saco, Me., June 10, 1785; was married to Benjamin Libbey at the house
of Nathaniel Townsend, Nov. 10, 1816, and always lived at South Limington, where she died in 1867, aged 82 years. Mr. Libbey died in February, 1866. One record gives the birth of Patience as " April 25, 1775,"
and I conclude the above date refers to her baptism. No children.
" Aunt Patience " was beloved by all who knew her.

Betsey Ridlon⁴ (1), third daughter of Matthias⁸ (2), was born in
Saco, Me., May 28, 1789, and was married to David Creach; secondly, to
Benjamin Young. She lived in Fayette, Me. Had children by both husbands. I have no record of her death. A woman of amiable character
and godly spirit.

David Ridlon⁴ (2), fifth son of Matthias⁸ (2), was born in Saco, Me.,
April 20, 1791; married and first settled in Wayne, where he had purchased land before his father and brothers moved to that town. His
house was on the road leading from near the brick-house built by the late
Daniel Ridley, to the farm of Charles Graves, whose wife was a Ridley; this house stood upon an elevation near a small brook. He
removed to Abbot, Piscataquis County, in 1823, thence to Bangor
in 1834, to Sangerville in 1836, to Corinth in 1838, and back to Bangor in
1843, where he died Oct. 3, 1846, aged 55 years. Mr. Ridlon was a shoe-
maker by trade. He was of medium height; had dark hair, gray eyes,
and florid complexion. *Six* children.

Mary Ridlon⁴ (5), fourth daughter of Matthias⁸ (2), was born in
Saco, Me., Aug. 3, 1794; was married to Alvin Swift, and lived in Turner,
Me. I do not know when she died. She was a stout, dark-eyed, fair-
complexioned, pretty woman.

Sally Ridlon⁴ (3), fifth daughter of Matthias⁸ (2), was born in Saco,
Me., May 28, 1798, and was married to Billings Hood and lived in Turner, Me. Her husband predeceased her, and she went to live with her son
in Gardiner. She died June 3, 1873.

Rachel Ridlon⁴ (2), sixth daughter of Matthias⁸ (2), was born in
Saco, Me., Sept. 28, 1801; was married Nov. 27, 1821, to Otis Hood,

brother of Billings Hood, and lived in Turner, Me., where she died June 3, 1864. She was a twin to Lydia

Lydia Ridlon⁴ (1), seventh daughter of Matthias² (2), was born in Saco, Me., Sept. 28, 1801; was married to Daniel True, and lived in Wayne, on a large farm, where she died Feb. 6, 1875. Deacon True is still living (1883). These two sisters (twins) were not tall, but considerably stout in old age; they had dark eyes, and coarse features. But few persons could distinguish one from the other, so close was their resemblance. The author has their portraits in India-ink, nicely framed.

Catherine Ridlon⁴ (1), eldest daughter of James² (1), was born in Saco, Me., June 4, 1779, and was married July 5, 1804, to William Hopkinson, of Limington. No record of her death.

Dea. Joseph Ridlon⁴ (1), eldest son of James² (1), was born in Saco, Me., May 26, 1782; married in March, 1802, Molly, daughter of William Hopkinson, of Buxton, Me., and lived for some time on his father's farm in Hollis. He purchased of Ebenezer Lewis a part of the farm formerly owned by his uncle, Abraham Ridlon, which joined the land of his father on the north-west, it being a part of the " Dalton Right," purchased of Col. Thomas Cutts, of Saco, and made that his permanent home. He embraced religion in early life, and became an active member of the Baptist church in Limington, maintaining a consistent Christian walk during life. He was a wheelwright by trade, and one of the most careful and thorough workmen. His motto was to attempt nothing that he could not do well. He never slighted work where it could not be seen, and whatever left his hands stood the test of time. Mr. Ridlon was a careful, judicious, and successful farmer; everything about his buildings and fields had a neat and orderly appearance, and he required of his hired · help the same thoroughness he exercised himself. He took a peculiar pride in his hay-field, and could mow so smoothly that his swaths could hardly be seen after the hay was taken off. He was careful in all his business transactions, and could not bear to be in debt to any one. Moderate in movements, and retiring in disposition, pleasant, generous, and accommodating as a neighbor, he lived in peace with all men. He was of medium height and size; had a very high forehead, regular features, gray, deep-set eyes, light complexion, and serious expression of face. He was very deeply wrinkled on his forehead and about the eyes. In walking he carried his head bent forward and his eyes turned downward, as if searching for something on the ground; and when with his ox-team, he went some distance in advance, swinging his goad-stick toward his lead-cattle. Mr. Ridlon died in his old home June 13, 1858, aged 76 years; his widow survived him, and died at the home of her son Joseph, in Gorham, Dec. 11, 1870, aged 86 years; they were buried in the "Old Ridlon Burying-ground," near his homestead. Issue *five* sons, of whom hereafter.

James Redlon⁴ (3), second son of James² (1), was born in Little Falls Plantation (now Hollis), Me., Aug. 19, 1784; married Dec. 9, 1802, Sarah, daughter of William Hopkinson, of Buxton (same County), and had issue *two* children, of whom hereafter. He settled down at Salmon Falls, on Saco River, and lived there a few years; thence removed to a part of his father's farm, and lived in a dwelling he made from an old school-house that stood near the present residence of Jacob Townsend. According to Hollis town records, he was " Lieut. James Ridlon, Field-driver," in 1818. He was esteemed as an honest and promising man.

Resembled his brother Joseph. Died at the home of his brother Robert, to which he had been removed soon after becoming ill, and was laid down to rest by the side of his father in the "Old Ridlon Burying-ground," so called, near his birth-place.

Jacob Ridlon[4] (**3**), third son of James[3] (1), was born in Little Falls Plantation (now Hollis), Me., Dec. 15, 1786; died when young and unmarried, and was buried in his father's lot, near his birth-place. The members of this branch of the family had forgotten there was such an uncle, till the author found the record of his birth on a fly-leaf of his father's old Bible. He was probably named in honor of his uncle, Jacob Ridlon, of Buxton.

Lydia Ridlon[4] (**2**), second daughter of James[3] (1), was born in Little Falls Plantation (now Hollis), Me., May 23, 1789; was married to John Wiggin, of Baldwin, Me., Dec. 1, 1814. She did not long survive, and Mr. Wiggin married her cousin, Betsey Ridlon, daughter of Jacob Ridlon, of Buxton, whose records see.

Robert Ridlon[4] (**3**), fourth son of James[3] (1), was born in Little Falls Plantation, so called (now Hollis), Me., Aug. 8, 1791; married Nov. 7, 1813, Sally, daughter of Ichabod and Dolly Cozens* (or Cousens), of Kennebunk, or Lyman, in the same County (she was born July 14, 1790), and settled on his father's homestead-farm, where he remained the rest of his days. He was surveyor of lumber in 1812–14; juror at Portland Court in 1812, 1832, and 1837. Filled several town offices. He was moderate, grave, considerate, prudent, judicious, honest, kind, and courteous; a deep thinker, careful manager, shrewd financier, ardent politician (Jackson Democrat), Universalist in sentiment, a peacemaker by practice, and a good neighbor, townsman, husband, and father. He and his good wife lived together over fifty years, and no unkind word ever passed between them. He was an excellent farmer and stock-raiser. He had great pride in keeping a pair of fat oxen, — *the fattest* in town. He kept his buildings and fences in good repair, and was very neat and precise about all his farmwork. Mr. Ridlon owned fine timber-lands, and could not bear to cut down a growing tree. His farm was one of the best in town and kept in a highly productive condition. He seldom went from home, was always busy, and never employed others to do what he could do himself. In personal appearance he resembled his brother Joseph; he was considerably stoop-shouldered, of medium height and build, had a high, bald crown, projecting forehead deeply furrowed, deep-set eyes, almost hidden by wrinkles at the temple-corners, long outstanding brows, large nose, broad mouth and chin, short neck, and when in health had a florid face. In his prime his hair was dark brown and inclined to curl at the ends. He accumulated a handsome estate, and was considered an independent farmer. His wife died Feb. 8, 1865. He died in the family of his granddaughter, Mrs. Maria (Sawyer) Whitehouse, whom he had brought up,

---

*The family of Cozens (or Cousens) is descended from John Cozens, of Casco (now Portland), Me., who was born in England in 1596, and died in York, Me., in 1689. Descendants settled in Lyman, Kennebunk, Hollis, Alfred, and Cornish, Me. Joseph Cousens lived in Cornish, but moved to Kennebunk; he was a Revolutionary soldier. Ebenezer, a cousin of the preceding, who was of Lyman, married Sarah Cousens, a kinswoman, and had issue. Either Joseph or Ebenezer was a brother of Ichabod, father of Sally, wife of Robert Ridlon, and of Hannah, wife of James Redlon, the father of Robert, and a sister of the latter became the wife of Robert Cousens, of Lyman, a collateral kinsman.

Robert Ridlon
AGED 78.

in his old home, June 29, 1869, and was buried with his relatives in the "Ridlon Burying-ground," near his own farm. His mind was impaired during his last days, but he received the tenderest care and rewarded his attendant with a handsome property. He was called "Deacon Ridlon" by his neighbors, in consequence of his serious deportment when a young man. He had issue *two* children, of whom hereafter.

Dea. Nicholas Ridlon⁴ (1), fifth son of James³ (1), was born in the town called Phillipsburgh (now Hollis), Me., Nov. 29, 1793; married March 20, 1819, Hannah, daughter of William Hancock, of Buxton, and settled on a part of the farm owned by his grandfather Cousens, adjoining that of his brother Robert; now owned by the grandsons of his brother Joseph. Mr. Ridlon built a good house and barn here, and made himself a valuable farm; but became discontented and removed to Steep Falls in Limington, in the autumn of 1840, and worked in the saw-mills there. He subsequently removed to Raymond (now Casco), and settled on the farm, where he died July 7, 1869, aged 75. His widow died Nov. 8, 1879, in Casco, but was taken to Hollis and interred by the side of her husband on the 11th of November. A few relatives gathered around her remains in the "Old Ridlon Burying-ground," only a few rods from where she and her husband commenced life together, and prayer was offered at the grave by the author of this book. She was 79 years old. Mr. Ridlon embraced religion in early life and was chosen deacon of the Freewill Baptist Church, of which he was long a consistent and devoted member. His farm in Casco was hard and rocky, but produced abundant harvests. He erected a fine stand of farm-buildings and made himself and family a comfortable home. He was a very hard-working man, and by good management and close economy acquired considerable property; but by home misunderstanding with a man who went to live with him in old age, he was drawn into litigation and encumbered his estate. Deacon Ridlon was of medium height, not broad nor heavy; his hair was soft, and as white as snow, in advanced years; his eyes were blue, and his complexion fair; his features were regular and of delicate mould; and his general appearance resembled the Cozens family more than the Ridlons. He was a quiet, peaceful man; honest, and respected by all who knew him. He had issue *six* children.

Hannah Ridlon⁴ (2), third daughter of James³ (1), was born in the town of Phillipsburgh (now Hollis), Me., Feb. 8, 1796; was married July 7, 1816, to Robert Cozens, of Lyman, who was her cousin, and settled with her husband in his native town. She had issue, and a son is said to closely resemble her brother, Magnus Ridlon, of whom hereafter. I have no record of her death.

Magnus Ridlon⁴ (6), sixth son of James³ (1), was born in Phillipsburgh (now Hollis), Me., May 12, 1798; married Feb. 5, 1819, Betsey Sanborn, of Standish, Cumberland County, and lived for several years with his brother Robert on the old homestead-farm of his father. He subsequently built the house since owned, and for many years occupied, by the widow and children of James-Hopkinson Ridlon, near Bonnie Eagle Village, and now only a few rods from the Advent Meeting-house. He afterwards removed to Norway, Oxford County, and settled on a farm there, where he made his home till the death of his wife; he then returned to Hollis, and spent the most of his remaining days with his brothers, Joseph and Robert, working on their farms in summer, and repairing and building implements for farm use in winter. Like nearly all the Ridlon family, Uncle Magnus was a natural mechanic, and, without serving an apprenticeship, could frame buildings, build wheels, carts, and sleds, and make ploughs and yokes. In personal appearance he resembled his brother Robert most; he was, however, a larger man. He was about six feet in height, broad-shouldered, round, and compactly built, and in advanced life inclined to corpulency. He stooped considerably, and had a lame ankle, caused by cutting of the tendons when young. His hair and beard were nearly black, his head bald, crown and forehead high and broad, his brows long, heavy, and outstanding, his eyes dark, small, and deep-set, his features coarse, and his face covered with very deep wrinkles, especially at the temples. He was moderate, quiet, and kind-hearted; loved children, and was constant in attendance upon divine service. Though naturally sedate and slow of speech, he sometimes became conversational and jovial. Every one loved "Uncle Magnus," for he was so kind toward all, so useful and inoffensive, that he was always a welcome guest among his relatives. Had issue *three* children, of whom hereafter. He died at his brother Robert's, but was carried to Norway and buried by the side of his wife. I have not found the date of his death.

Priscilla Ridlon[4] (1), fourth daughter of James[3] (1), was born in Phillipsburgh (now Hollis), Me., Sept. 23, 1801, and died at her brother Robert's, when young and unmarried.

Polly Ridlon[4] (2), eldest daughter of Thomas[3] (1), was born in Pepperellborough (now Saco), Me., Nov. 15, 1779; was married Aug. 23, 1804, to Samuel Ridlon, her cousin, and lived a while in a house between the present dwellings of Stephen Higgins and Thomas C. Sawyer. She lived some years in Wayne, Kennebec County, but subsequently returned to Hollis, and lived in a house that stood on the same spot where John Sawyer built his new buildings. After her husband was drowned she went to live with her son John, near her brother Thomas, and continued there until her death, which occurred April 25, 1874, in her ninety-fifth year. "Aunt Polly" was a good, quiet, gentle-spirited woman. She had a large family.

Thomas Ridlon[4] (2), eldest son of Thomas[3] (1), was born in Pepperellborough (now Saco), Me., Aug. 6, 1780; married Polly, daughter of Joshua and Sussie (Boston) Decker,* of Buxton, Aug. 22, 1804, and had

---

* The Deckers are of Dutch or German extraction, but the New England branches are descended from John Decker, a scion of an English family, who came to Exeter, Mass., as early as 1672, but subsequently settled in Kittery and York, Me., where he brought up a large family, one of whom had sons Joshua, John, and David. Joshua Decker settled in Gorham and removed to Buxton, Cumberland County, Me. He married Sussie, daughter of John Boston, or Baston, of York, and by her had *eleven* children, of whom one was Joseph Decker, the celebratetd singularly pious, and eccentric traveling preacher, known in western Maine as the "Massachusetts Prophet," who started for Jerusalem to assist in rebuilding the walls of the Holy City, but died in Spain of small-pox. Another son was Isaac Decker, a mariner by profession, who lived many years in Gardiner, Me., whose daughter, Mary D. Welcome, is the well-known contributor to the *Portland Transcript*, a woman of scholarly tastes and great information, who has devoted her talents for the enlightenment and elevation of humanity. Stephen Decker, another son of Joshua, settled on the Kennebec River, in Clinton, Me., and became an extensive land-owner and farmer there, with whom his parents lived in old age, and whose son, Isaac Decker, now resides on the homestead in Clinton. Among the other children of Joshua were Thomas, Amos, David, Joshua, and Samuel, and two daughters, — Betsey, who was married to a Mr. Russell, and Sussie, who was the

Thomas Ridlon.

AGED 94

"HILLSIDE FARM"
Hollis, Maine.
RESIDENCE OF THOMAS RIDLON.

issue *four* children, of whom hereafter. He was carried from Saco in his father's arms when but six weeks old, and passed his early days in a new clearing. He worked on his father's farm till grown to manhood, and then, having purchased land of his father, he built him a house on the hill about a half mile from the Saco River; into this house he moved with his young wife the day after their marriage, and made it his home all his days, having slept out of it but two nights for about *seventy years.* Mr. Ridlon was of nervous, impulsive temperament, and possessed a will as inflexible as iron. In all his purposes and views he was positive, determined, and persistent; never would yield to an obstacle, but with his wonderful courage and resolution encountered and surmounted everything that stood in the way of the execution of his plans. His composition seemed destitute of the element of fear. In his prejudices and preferences he was strong and unchangeable; he was raised to stormy passion with small provocation, and would as soon become calm and gentle as a summer morning. His words were few and full of meaning; when he had expressed an opinion, or gave his answer, none who knew the man ever made an attempt to change his mind. He was frank and outspoken, and his word was regarded as good as law; those who knew him reposed implicit confidence in his promises. Quick to resent an insult, he would as readily forgive when a proper confession or acknowledgment was made. He was possessed of quick perception and sound judgment; his advice was sought by many. No man knew better how to attend to his own business. He was naturally retiring and reserved in his habits, and strangers judged him cold and reticent; when he became better acquainted he was social, genial, and conversational. He embraced religion late in life, and became a devoted Christian; he maintained a consistent walk, and was literally a man of prayer. He was acknowledged by all who knew him to be a good man; it is not known that he had an enemy in the world. In his business management he was very careful, and demanded a clear statement and definite understanding of all with whom he had dealing. His papers, now in my possession, attest the extreme care with which he kept his accounts, and his promptitude in making his payments for land, cattle, and help. Whatever he undertook was done with alacrity; nothing was allowed to drag on his hands. His motto was "one thing at a time." He had been employed in running many of the town lines, and had placed so many landmarks that he was looked to as the best authority in the establishment of boundaries. His experience in working lumber made him a valuable attendant for parties who went to view trees, and he was frequently called upon to accompany timber-buyers on their exploring tours, and when his judgment was followed the purchaser never regretted it. He was a good neighbor, cheerfully adapting his circumstances to the comfort and interest of others, though at a sacrifice of time

wife of her cousin, a Mr. Boston. Joshua Decker, 2d, settled in La Grange, Me., and became the father of a most remarkable family of children, noted for their great size and gigantic physical powers. The son Samuel early settled in the British Provinces, and but little is known of his posterity. One of the other three settled at Boothbay, Me., and left descendants there. The other descendants of this branch are in Standish, Casco, and Hollis, Me., and three children of Joseph, the "Massachusetts Prophet," Daniel, Joseph, and Rachel (whose maternal grandmother, Rachel Field, was a daughter of Matthias Redlon, 1st), are now living, advanced in years. Other branches descended from John Decker, the first ancestor, are living in eastern Maine, among them, Dr. Decker of Fort Fairfield, a very erudite and able man. In the West many spell the name *Decker.*

and money. In personal appearance he resembled his father in many respects, although not as large a man. He was more than six feet in height, very broad across the shoulders and hips, and when walking carried his feet far apart. He was raw-boned and muscular; his weight was never more than one hundred and eighty pounds. His arms were unusually long, and when walking his hands reached his knees. The cords of his wrists were like ropes, and few men were his equal in strength. His neck was short and large, his jaws square and wide, his cheek-bones high, his forehead narrow and receding, his crown high and of peculiar form; his old doctor once said "Uncle Tom's head is shaped like the top of Mount Washington." He was very bald from early life; his hair in his prime was jet-black and somewhat curly; his beard was worn on the sides of his face, sometimes quite long; his brows were very long and thick, and hung out over his eyes with a peculiar curve; his eyes were gray and deep-set, and his complexion very ruddy. The expression of his face was always calm and determined. Exposure to pure air, living on plain, nutritious food, and an acquaintance with healthful exercises when young, invested him with a vigorous constitution, and fitted him to endure almost any exertion unwearied and unimpaired. Daring, full of hope and physical vitality, he drove on through heat and cold, storms or calms, frequently exposed to danger, passing almost within the jaws of death and coming out without serious harm.

He was at Saco with his father when a boy, and started to return to Hollis (then Phillipsburgh), about dark, both being mounted on one beast. The road then ran through an almost unbroken wilderness, and as they left the settlement and entered the woods, his father said, "Now, Thomas, you must hold on, or the wolves will get you." Sure enough, before they reached Salmon Falls they heard the distant howl of a wolf. "That means us," said the father. Presently another howl echoed through the deep, gloomy forest, but much nearer than the first. The horse became excited, and increased speed. Soon there was another prolonged howl, and in a moment it was answered to by others in various directions. They gave their horse the reins and let the strong beast take its own course. In a few minutes a pack of howling, hungry wolves were gathering around them, their eyeballs, in the darkness, shining like coals of fire. The lad clung to his father's coat; the horse was urged forward, and away they flew like the "wings of the wind." The number of wolves increased as they followed on, and their howls became almost deafening. Thus the race for life kept up until the father and son safely entered the clearing of his neighbors, when the lights and barking of dogs turned the wolves back in disappointment and "supperless to bed." It was a narrow escape; had the horse stumbled and the boy lost his hold, he would have been torn in pieces in a moment. Thomas never forgot that night-ride from Saco, and till old age always became much excited when relating the adventure.

He was once hunting for his cows, and failing to find them as the darkness came on, he turned his steps homeward; as he approached his field he heard a noise near his feet like the mewing of a kitten, and stooping down he found two young wild-cats coiled up at the roots of a large tree. He quickly seized them, buttoned his heavy coat around them, and ran for his house; he had not gone far, however, before he heard the angry screams of the mother-cat, and knew she had missed her babies. On he ran with all his speed, but the young cats continued to cry, and in a minute the old one sprang upon his back, cutting his coat in slits with her claws. Thomas would not relinquish his prize, but ran forward. The enraged cat continued to follow him and to spring upon his back, till his dog, taking the scent, came out to meet him, and then, to use Mr. Ridlon's words, he "shifted the responsibility," and left the cat and dog to fight the battle between themselves. He succeeded in taking his wild kittens to the house, and in a few days afterwards sent them to Portland by "'Squire Vaughan," and sold them. This adventure shows the character of the man, and in narrating the circumstances he always manifested a degree of pride in his achievement.

Mr. Ridlon worked on the Saco River driving logs when a young man, and saw many narrow escapes from death while thus employed. There were two men of herculean build in their crew, known as the "Rankin brothers," and these claimed the championship for strength; but the test came, and they lost their prestige. On a set of falls they had constructed a rude dam, connected with a sluiceway, through which they ran their logs; this had a gate at the upper end, which was raised by a lever put through a mortise in its head-post. Moving up and down as it did, through rough slides, and with a heavy pressure of water upon it from above, it demanded a powerful man to raise this gate. The Rankin brothers both did their best, but failed to move it; Robert Sawyer, a large and strong man, then took his lever and lifted till he burst the button from his shirt-collar, but could not start the heavy planking. It now came Mr. Ridlon's turn, and stepping upon the bulwarks he put his hand-spike through the mortise, adjusted the other end upon his brawny shoulder, and springing quickly, raised the gate the first time.

Mr. Ridlon was a natural mechanic, and delighted to work with tools. He constructed nearly all implements used on his farm, erected his own buildings, mended his own shoes, manufactured his own knives, and the axe-handles he made were known far and wide for more than fifty years; these last were all of one pattern of his own invention, and would sell to the backwoodsmen when no others would be used. He whittled all his axe-handles by hand, and I can see just how he looked as he sat before his bright, open fire, the long winter evenings, his bald crown shining with the reflections of light, while with his broad "scythe-knife" he dressed the rough-hewed piece of oak into symmetry and beauty of finish. He never harnessed a horse (though an expert in the saddle), never saw the cars, was never out of his native State, never called a physician but once till his last sickness, used tobacco until nearly eighty years of age, and then left it alone, invariably arose at four o'clock in the morning, lived with his congenial wife in the same house *sixty-six years*, and died in September, 1874, aged 94 years and 1 month. His wife died three years previously; they were buried in Moderation Village Cemetery, in his son's lot. The last days of this godly and venerable pair were spent in the family of the author of this book.

Judith Ridlon⁴ (2), second daughter of Thomas³ (1), was born in Phillipsburgh (now Hollis), Me., Sept. 15, 1783, and never married. She was the first white child born in her town, and lived to see it changed from a wilderness to a garden of broad and fertile farms. "Aunt Judy" lived a very useful life; was a "ministering angel" among the sick and suffering, until, by reason of age and infirmity, she became a subject of others' care and attention. Probably no person has lived contemporary with her who has watched by as many sick and dying persons. At one time a dreadfully fatal contagion swept through the town, and it was found difficult to secure nurses; during this scourge "Aunt Judy" went from house to house, and ministered to the afflicted, but she was not touched by the fever herself. She lived with a maiden-sister many years in her father's house, and at one time was possessed of considerable property; she owned land, timber, and good buildings, and had money to loan to her relatives; but, alas! the selfishness and meanness of those who had been dependent on her for a shelter for their heads and money to pay their bills, robbed her of her house and real estate; and, while she held their notes for money, they would have thrown her body upon the town for burial, had not the proper authorities forced them to provide for her funeral expenses. Such base ingratitude was too much to be endured by the real friends of this unselfish and worthy woman, and I wish to leave this enduring record as a warning against a repetition of such disgraceful conduct in the future. Miss Ridlon had no palate, and could not articulate distinctly, and this impediment of speech may have been a barrier to her matrimonial prospects in early life. She had the "old-fashioned consumption" when young, and her relatives used to shake their heads, and say, "Aunt Judy cannot stand it long, she's dreadful slim"; and still she lived on, and saw nearly all of her generation go down to their graves; the robust and sprightly passed her one by one on their "journey to the tomb," and still "Aunt Judy," with the same hollow cough and "old-fashioned consumption" (by that time) lingered upon this earthly shore, and handed the early traditions of her family down to the rising generations. She was comfortable, and retained her faculties well (except her sight), till a few days before her death. She passed quietly away, in January, 1880, aged 97 years. I have her portrait.

Martha Ridlon⁴ (1), third daughter of Thomas³ (1), was born in Phillipsburgh (now Hollis), Me., Oct. 17, 1785; was married Dec. 31, 1810, to John Mills,* of Waterborough, and lived many years in Eaton, N. H. Mr. Mills was a great axeman, and went to Georgia to cut and hew ship-timber, when his health failed, and he made his way to the hospital at New Orleans, La., where he died June 3, 1849. Mrs. Mills died March 16, 1859, aged 74 years. She was quite tall, and resembled her sister Judith in features of face; her hair was white, the last time I saw her. "Aunt Martha" was an excellent Christian woman. She left a large family, and two sons were ministers of the gospel.

Jane Ridlon⁴ (1), fourth daughter of Thomas³ (1), was born in Phillipsburgh (now Hollis), Me., Feb. 4, 1787, and died when a young woman, unmarried.

Eunice Ridlon⁴ (1), fifth daughter of Thomas³ (1), was born in Phillipsburgh (now Hollis), Me., Nov. 11, 1789; was married Feb. 2, 1812, to David Martin, of Baldwin (or Sebago), and settled on a farm adjoining her father's, where her husband erected the brick house so long known as the "Uncle David Martin house," about one half-mile from Moderation Falls, on the Bonnie Eagle road. This farm was formerly owned by that John Redlon — uncle to Mrs. Martin — who died in Ohio at the age of 106 years, and a son of his was buried near the present brick house,

* LUKE MILLS, the ancestor of the New England family of that name, came from Virginia, and settled in Saco, Me. He had a son named Elligood Mills, who married Mary Dyer and had issue Joseph, Lucy, Luke, Elligood, William, Lydia, John, and James; the latter was the well-known and eccentric old millwright. I have full records.

the second one built by Mr. Martin. Mrs. Martin is still living in the family of her daughter, Mrs. Martha Ridlon, in Hollis, and although 95 years of age she is intelligent, and actively engaged in braiding and sewing rugs. "Aunt Eunice" is a small woman with the features characteristic of her family, and in habits and disposition closely resembles her brother Matthias. She had a clear, shrill voice, and could be heard a great distance as she stood in the door and called her husband and sons from their work in the field. Like her sisters she was a nice weaver, and the author remembers the "clash" of her loom and "click" of shuttle as she threw it from side to side through her web, while making cloth for her family. She and husband were devoted Christians; they had a large family, of several of whom hereafter.

William Ridlon[4] (1), second son of Thomas[3] (1), was born in Phillipsburgh (now Hollis), Me., Feb. 26, 1792; married (the intention recorded Nov. 16, 1812) to Isabella, daughter of Robert Martin (records of Hollis say "of Standish"), and sister of the husband of his sister Eunice, before mentioned. His first wife died in the year 1843, and he married, secondly, Feb. 28, 1844, Catherine Martin, sister of Isabella. This ceremony was performed by Elder Jeremiah Bullock, of Limington. Mr. Ridlon first settled in Hollis, not far from the homestead of his brother Thomas, but was induced to sell this excellent tract of land, and moved to Bridgton or Sebago. The names of his children are recorded in Bridgton, and I think he lived some time in that town; he finally located on land in Sebago, in a neighborhood called "Folly,"—appropriately named,— where he erected farm-buildings and has lived ever since. Had he remained in Hollis he would have owned one of the best farms in town; but he has worked hard on a rocky, ungenerous little farm among the mountains, and consequently was always poor. He is still living, at the age of 93, and has attended every State election since his majority; his political sentiments are strictly Democratic. He is tall and rather slim, but has a strong, well-knit frame; his head is high, but not so broad as his brothers'; hair, originally black; brows, long and outstanding; eyes, gray; complexion, florid. He is nervous and impulsive in temperament, quick to resent an insult, or any intrusion upon what he considers his personal rights; and God pity the man who stands in his way when his temper is up. He once had a neighbor who habitually came home intoxicated and abused his wife, and "Uncle Billy" was frequently called to take the poor woman's part. When he was cutting his wood the following autumn he found a knotty, scrubby oak limb and laid it up in his wood-house; on being asked by his wife what it was for, he replied, "I am gwine to keep that to wallop O. T. with when he comes home to whip his wife." Not long after the woman was heard to scream, and "Uncle Billy" seized his club and ran for the house; he met the infuriated man at his door, and pulling him into the yard gave him such a thrashing as he never forgot, and which completely cured him from whipping his poor wife. This took place when Mr. Ridlon was an old man, and shows the spirit that was in him. He had issue *twelve* children (all by his first wife), of whom hereafter.

Dea. Matthias Ridlon[4] (3), third son of Thomas[3] (1), was born in Phillipsburgh (now Hollis), Me., March 28, 1794; married (intention recorded Jan. 30, 1818) to Rachel Pendexter, of Cornish, whose grandmother was Rachel (Redlon) Field, and settled in Eaton, N. H., where he built him a log-house, and planted a three-acre cut-down. He had no time to burn the logs and planted his corn between them on the newly burnt ground; from this plantation he sold one hundred and sixty bushels of nice corn at fifty cents per bushel toward paying for his land. After his brother Samuel married and moved from home, Matthias returned to Hollis, purchased eight acres of the Field farm, — land now owned by Hobson, where the old juniper-tree stands, — and lived in his father's house. In 1838, he sold his property in Hollis, and moved upon a tract of new land in Sweden, Oxford County, where he established a permanent home, and continued the remainder of his days. He lived in a part of Robert Morrison's house while clearing his land and building his log-cabin; but in the month of April, when his daughter Sabra was but a few weeks old, the river-drivers came to Morrison's to board, and he was compelled to move into his unfinished house, which had neither floor nor roof. He immediately hauled boards and covered a piece of the roof over his bed, and to keep out the rain, shingled it with birch bark. He built a stone chimney, chinked the walls with moss, plastered up the interstices between the logs, laid a rough board-floor, and lived in the warmest house he ever owned. He subsequently erected a good frame and clapboarded house, and suitable out-buildings for a large farm. The homestead of Mr. Ridlon was situated on a high hill, overlooking several ponds, and commanded a wide prospect of the country round about, — a rugged, mountainous, and romantic section. The soil was strong and sustained a heavy growth of hard-wood timber, especially of oak, which during later years has nearly all been manufactured into hogshead-staves, and shipped to the West Indies. The farm of Matthias was good and abundantly productive, but hard to work, and so broken that his corn-harvest was drawn to the barn on a wood-sled instead of a wheel-cart. Mr. Ridlon was not as large as his brothers, but built like them. His complexion was light, his eyes small and bright, and shaded by long, outstanding brows. His features were very coarse, — a good type of the Shetlanders from whom he was descended, — and his face florid. He was not as bald as his brothers in early life. His hair in later years was snow-white, and worn long in winter. In temperament he was like his father's family, quick, impulsive, and determined. His voice was rather harsh and sharp. He had a superabundant courage, and persisted in driving young, rampant horses when old; by these he was several times thrown from his carriage and slightly injured, but he was never afraid to try again; he frequently made journeys of a hundred miles with his "colts," as he called them, when an old, decrepit man, and greatly against the entreaties of his family. When more than eighty years of age, he purchased a horse which proved to be unsound, returned him to the original owner, and commenced legal action to recover his money. The case was tried at Portland. The old man, with his long, white hair, bowed with years, excited great interest in court, and public opinion was strong in his favor; but when he took the witness-stand, holding his memorandum in his bony hand, and with strong, clear voice, described the bargain with the circumstances; when, under a wearing cross-examination, he patiently endured, but still maintained his original testimony; and when, as his examiner intimated that he had misrepresented the statement, he stopped short, straightened himself in the witness-box, and with quivering lip and fire flashing from his eyes demanded of the lawyer as follows: "Sir, you have known me for more than forty years; do you call me a dishonest man?" and while the people in the crowded room were hushed to stillness, waiting in suspense for the answer, the attorney heartily responded, "No, Mr. Ridlon, I know you are a man of truth," every one believed he was on the right side, and could not keep back the tears of sympathy. Of course he won his case.

Deacon Ridlon embraced religion near middle life, and I think when camping in the woods, and was an earnest, devoted follower of his Master. His impulsive temper was always a source of embarrassment to him, but he kept it well in check. He was for many years a member of the Freewill Baptist Church in Sweden, but subsequently united with a Christian Church organized in his own neighborhood; this body soon lost its visibility, and it is believed he united with the Christian Church in Bridgton, some seven miles from his home. He attended his church and conference-meetings as long as age and health would admit of his going from his fireside, and during his latter years he traveled from fifty to ninety miles to attend annual and quarterly conferences. His bowed form, white hair, pleasant face, and ringing testimonies will not soon be forgotten by those who attended these gatherings.

Mr. Ridlon was very ingenious, and constructed almost any farm-implement that could be made of wood, in a neat and substantial manner. He was an excellent cooper and worked for many winters in stave-camps. In his last years he spent his winters making baskets in his own room. From boyhood till old age he loved work, and was always restless and unhappy if confined to the house. Mrs. Ridlon died in 1876, and her funeral service was conducted by the author of this book. Mr. Ridlon died in 1882 aged 88 years, and was buried by the side of his wife in a small yard, only a little way from his house. Children, of whom hereafter, *thirteen* in number.

Samuel Ridlon⁴ (2), fourth son of Thomas⁸ (1), was born in Phillipsburgh (now Hollis, Me.), Province of Massachusetts Bay, July 18, 1796; married Esther Stanley, of Cornish, March 18, 1818, and settled (presumably) in Porter, — he was called "Porter Sam" by the family in Hollis, to distinguish him from Samuel Ridlon, of that town, who married his sister, — Oxford County, and has continued in that neighborhood ever since. He first met his wife when at work for her father, William Stanley, at his mills in Cornish; she was a strapping girl, and just suited to be the helpmeet for a pioneer farmer. When her father raised his barn by the broad-side, help was scarce, and his three daughters held the foot of the posts; such girls are now hard to find. Mr. Ridlon cleared a new farm, and while at work "piling," his wife used to carry her baby to the "rick," spread a folded quilt under it upon the ground, and assist him while burning logs and brushwood; she was as strong as her husband, and never failed to carry her end of the log. Samuel sometimes came home — in his early years, when nearly all men took their glass — from "trainings" and "raisings" a little over-the-bay, and at such times was full of sport and loved to plague his wife. "Aunt Esther" — as the old folks called her — was good-natured, and endured her husband's pranks as long as she could, and then there would be a test of bone and muscle; she would lay her lord on his back upon the kitchen-floor, put her knee upon him, box his ears soundly, and say, "Now, Sammy, you keep quiet." Mr. Ridlon was a good, hard-working farmer and cooper; much of his land was covered with heavy oak growth, and in winters this timber was worked into staves for hogsheads, and became a means of placing considerable money in the manufacturer's hands. "Uncle Samuel" was short, — below the medium height, — broad-shouldered, and well formed; his neck, short, thick, and very full under the chin; his head, large, high crowned, well developed, and bald in early life; his hair and whiskers — the latter worn heavily upon the sides of his face, like those of his brother Thomas — were jet-black, and inclined to curl; his features were regular, his cheeks red, and his expression serious and thoughtful; indeed, he was a deep thinker and reasoner. Since I knew him he was moderate in his movements, and his disposition was more even and well-balanced than that of his brothers. Candid, cautious, and of sound judgment, he proved a valuable townsman and good neighbor, and few men in old age had as many real friends and well-wishers. He lived in peace with all men, and endeavored to make peace between others who were at variance. A dear lover of home, and industrious always, he did not become involved in those political broils and business embarrassments that have burdened the lives of many; he reared a large family of respectable children, who married and settled in plenty around their parental home, where he could see them all on a day. Scores of grandchildren gathered around his knee, to love and venerate him, and his descendants of the third generation have nestled their sunny heads in his patriarchal arms. In 1880 he had lived to see between eighty and ninety descendants: *fourteen* children, *fifty* grandchildren, and *twenty-four* great-grandchildren. Mr. Ridlon and his wife died within a few weeks of each other, in 1883, and were buried in a small cemetery a little north of his house, and near the South Hiram meeting-house. Funeral conducted by the author of this book.

Betsey-E. Ridlon[4] (2), sixth daughter of Thomas (1), was born in Hollis, Me. (then in Massachusetts), Oct. 4, 1799; was m   ied to David Nason, of Limington, Nov. 14, 1816, and went to live in that   She was twin to Rachel, and a remarkably pretty woman — as good as   au-tiful. She died June 24, 1841, aged 42 years, leaving a large family f children, some of whom resemble the Ridlons, and was buried in Hollis in the " Old Ridlon Burying-ground," near her father's lot.

Rachel Ridlon[4] (3), seventh daughter of Thomas[3] (1), was born in Phillipsburgh (now Hollis, Me.), Oct. 4, 1799, and died at the home of Samuel Ridlon, — who married her eldest sister, — in Baldwin, Nov. 2, 1811, but was buried with her parents.

Rebecca Ridlon[4] (2), eighth daughter of Thomas[3] (1), was born in Phillipsburgh, Mass. (now Hollis, Me.), Nov. 11, 1802, and died when a young woman, unmarried, at home.

Sarah Ridlon[4] (4), ninth daughter of Thomas[3] (1), was born in Phillipsburgh (now Hollis, Me.), Sept. 1, 1805, and lived at home with her father and maiden-sister Judith. She was in a feeble condition of health many years, and died unmarried some years after her father, but I have no date. She was laid to her earthly rest in her father's lot, in the "Old Ridlon Burying-ground," so called.

William Ridlon[4] (2), eldest son of John[3] (3), was born in Phillipsburgh (now Hollis, Me.), April 10, 1791, and was burned to death when a child by falling into the open fire from a clothes-basket, in which his mother had placed him, while she went out for some wood. This child was the first person buried in the small ground just back of the brick house subsequently built by David Martin.

Matthias Ridlon[4] (4), second son of John[3] (3), was born in Phillipsburgh (now Hollis, Me.), June 4, 1793. He was taken to Vermont with his parents, enlisted in the army during the war of 1812, and having, from exposure and over-exertion, being so young and naturally frail, contracted disease, was discharged, and died soon after his return at his father's home in Vermont. Place of burial unknown.

John Ridlon⁴ (7), third son of John³ (3), was born near Burlington, Vt., Aug. 15, 1795; married Sarah Myers, in Ohio, — after his father had emigrated to that State in 1814, — and settled first in Loveland, as a farmer. When his father became old he removed to the northern part of the State, and purchased a farm in the town of Waynesfield, Auglaize County, where he lived with his father till the time of his death in 1848. His widow, by whom he had *twelve* children, married a second husband, and was living near her first husband's old farm, in Waynesfield, in 1873, at which time I dined at her house. Mr. Ridlon — or Redley, as he spelled his name — was tall, slender, and very nervous and quick of movement; he was impulsive and high-tempered; sensitive and sure to resent an insult, but kind-hearted and pleasant when well used. His hair and beard were black, his eyes small and bright, his features rather long, and in general appearance resembled his mother's family more than the Ridlons. He was said to be a man of great physical strength, and many traditions respecting feats accomplished by him are held in his family.

Abigail Ridlon⁴ (1), eldest daughter of John³ (3), was born in Vermont, Sept. 20, 1797; went to Ohio with her parents in 1814; married Benjamin Carl, of Loveland, Clearmont County, Ohio, and had issue. She was left a widow and went to Michigan to live with her daughter, where she is said to have died at a good old age. I question the accuracy of the above date of her birth; think she was born in Maine, and at an earlier year. Her cousins now living in Hollis, Me., say, "Aunt Abby had three children when she went to Vermont, and *one* was a daughter."

Sarah Ridlon⁴ (5), second daughter of John³ (3), was born in Vermont, Jan. 17, 1798; went to Ohio with her parents in 1814, and married Roswell Graves, of Loveland, Clearmont County, in that State, and had issue. She was left a widow, her husband having died in middle life. No record of her death.

Judith Ridlon⁴ (3), third daughter of John³ (3), was born in Vermont, Sept. 10, 1800, and died in infancy.

Rachel Ridlon⁴ (4), fourth daughter of John³ (3), was born in Vermont, June 6, 1802, and died there in infancy. She was probably by John Ridlon's second wife.

Timothy-Tibbetts Ridlen⁴ (1), eldest son of Abraham³ (2), was born in Pepperellborough (now Saco, Me.), Aug. 2, 1786; was carried to Ohio by his parents in 1800; married Sarah Wright, in 1810, and settled in Clearmont County, Ohio, where he carried on farming many years. When crossing the Alleghany mountains, while on the way from Massachusetts to the Ohio River, he was thrown from a young horse he was riding and sustained a bad fracture of his arm. There was no physician to be had, and the men and women reduced the arm to as near its natural position as they could, bound splints about it, and proceeded on their way; the limb was not properly united, however, and the movements of the horse caused him such pain he was placed in a carriage, but suffered extremely all the remainder of the journey. Timothy and his brothers changed their names, after going West, to *Ridlen*. He was of medium height, well built, and very strong; his hair was brown, and his complexion ruddy. He was firm in his principles and an earnest Christian.

41

A good farmer and something of a mechanic. He died in Marian County (Indiana?), Ohio, in 1853. I have no record of his wife's death; they had issue *ten* children, of whom hereafter.

Stephen Ridlen[4] (1), second son of Abraham[2] (2), was born in Phillipsburgh (now Hollis, Me.), Province of Massachusetts, Nov. 4, 1787; went to Ohio with his parents in 1800; married Ann Bellville, and had issue *eight* children, of whom hereafter. He entered the American army in the war of 1812, under Col. Findley of the Fourth Ohio Regiment, in the company of Capt. S. B. Kyler; he was at Detroit, Mich., at the disgraceful surrender of General Hull, and with his fellow-prisoners marched to Cleveland, Ohio, where he was paroled and afterwards exchanged. He endured great hardships during his term of service; was marched from Maume to Detroit, a distance of sixty miles, bare-footed. For his services he received one hundred and sixty acres of land in Indiana, upon which he settled in 1825; he cleared a fine farm here and lived a contented, happy life. He also received a pension. He removed to Illinois in 1852, and died in the family of his son at Willow Hill, Jasper County. He was of medium height, very broad across his shoulders, and heavily, compactly built; his neck was very short and large, his jaws square, mouth and chin broad, features regular, hair white and coarse, and his facial expression calm and determined. Mr. Ridlen was esteemed a kind and honest man. The author has his portrait.

Patience Ridlen[4] (2), eldest daughter of Abraham[2] (2), was born in Phillipsburgh (now Hollis, Me.), Mass., Aug. 4, 1788, and went to Ohio with her parents in 1800. She was married in 1815, to Levi Wells, in Ohio, and is now living in the family of her daughter, Mrs. Nancy Foreman, at Rockville, Ind., in her 96th year. She has been a member of the Church of the United Brethren for many years. Date of husband's death unknown. It was supposed by the brothers and sisters of this woman that she had been many years dead, until in 1881, I found her by advertising in western newspapers; and when the news of her survival reached her friends she seemed like one raised from the dead. I have her portrait, finished in India-ink, taken in her 94th year. She had issue, and several children are still living.

Ruth Ridlen[4] (2), second daughter of Abraham[2] (2), was born in Phillipsburgh, Mass. (now Hollis, Me.), Aug. 10, 1790, and was taken to Ohio by her parents in 1800. She was married in 1816, to John Robertson, and lived at Adams, Decatur County, Ind., where she died in 1870, leaving issue. Her husband was blind for some years, and her life was one of many trials and vicissitudes; she was a good, patient, devoted servant of God, and is now at rest. A good portrait of this woman is owned by the author.

Samuel Ridlen[4] (3), third son of Abraham[2] (2), was born in the township of Phillipsburgh, Mass. (now Hollis, Me.), June 10, 1792, and was taken to Ohio in the year 1800 by his parents. He married Sarah Davis, July 18, 1813, and settled near Cincinnati, Ohio, as a blacksmith. He was in the Fourth Ohio Regiment, under Col. Findley, and served as a sergeant in the company of Capt. S. B. Kyler, from April 25, 1812, to April 24, 1813, and was at Detroit at Hull's surrender. Like his brothers, he was marched over sixty miles with bare feet. He received one hundred and sixty acres of excellent land in southern Illinois for his services in the army, and settled there when in middle life; do not know the year of his removal from Ohio, but his children were educated in that

State. He built cabins on his new land and lived there alone many weeks at a time, while clearing his farm, before moving his family. He was a good farmer and had a deep interest in breeding improved stock; indeed he took the premiums at the State fairs on his cows for many years. His farm was in Douglas County, in the well-known district called "Egypt," and the land is not only remarkable for its corn and grain producing qualities, but is also adapted to grass and all kinds of fruit. He spent his last days in the family of his only son, and was for many years nearly blind.* Two daughters lived near him, and being in good health himself, he would mount a horse, and some of his grandchildren would lead it by the bridle-rein from house to house, and thus favor the old patriarch with the privilege, almost every day in pleasant weather, of visiting his children. He was of medium height and build, and had, when in his prime, black hair and beard. His eyes were very dark and bright until he became blind. In general appearance he represented his mother's family, and said she had always told him he had a "Tibbetts nose"; this feature was large and prominent, and of a form (peculiar to the old members of the Tibbetts family in New England) that would be hard to describe without the aid of the artist's pencil. His face was naturally quite red. Mr. Ridlen's wife died in 1857. Children, *nine* in number. He died in 1878, aged 86 years.

Polly Ridlen⁴ (3), third daughter of Abraham³ (2), was born in Phillipsburgh, Mass., — now Hollis, Me., — Aug. 14, 1794; went to Ohio with her parents when six years old, and married somewhere in the West. I cannot learn anything about her family.

---

* The author of this book visited Samuel Ridlen at Webb's Prairie in 1873, and remembers with pleasure the hours spent with his kindred while there. In company with a kinsman, Alpheus G. Ridlon of Norwood, Ohio, he had stopped over night at Tamaroy, on the Illinois Central Railroad. Morning dawned bright and beautiful. We hired a team and started on our way across the rolling, blossoming prairies; the air was warm, but clear and invigorating. At noon we reached Benton, a neat little village, where we took dinner with a Mr. Nailor, who kept the hotel there. Then away through groves and wheat-fields till about 3 o'clock, P. M., when we asked a boy by the roadside how far it was to Webb's Prairie. "Why you are there now," was his quick reply. We asked if there were families named Ridlon in the neighborhood. "Just over that swell, sir; that's where they live, sir," answered the lad. But before we had passed the "swell" I discovered a venerable man sitting on the porch of a respectable cabin, and as we drew nearer I called the attention of my companion, by saying, "There, see that old man; that must be Uncle Samuel, for I see he looks like my grandfather." We stopped before the gate, and I walked along the path to the house. He heard my step as I approached, and in reply to my question, "Is this Mr. Ridlen?" said, "Yes, sir, that's my name; and pray tell me who you are." When he learned I was his kinsman from the East, he shouted with all his powers for his daughter, Mrs. Aiken, who was at that moment in her garden; she came in with haste, supposing something had happened to the old man, but to her surprise he cried out, "Good heavens! Jane, here is Mr. Ridlon from my old home in Massachusetts, and another Mr. Ridlon; do have their horse put up and get them some dinner." Taking a seat by my side he felt of my hands, arms, and shoulders, to see — as he said — if I was built like the Ridlon family. We sang a hymn — "Blest be the tie that binds our hearts in Christian love," etc., — and knelt in prayer. How that dear old man shouted praise to God! He was a Methodist of the primitive stamp, converted at a camp-meeting, and loved to relate his "experience"; he would describe all the circumstances in detail, and with considerable composure, till he reached that point where he found "peace in believing," and then he would shout as only an old-fashioned Methodist could. We had been at his daughter's of an evening, and on our return to his other daughter's (Mrs. Sarah Alexander), we called at his son's, on the way. The old man had gone to his bed in the cabin-chamber, but hearing us singing, he

Abraham Ridlen⁴ (4), fourth son of Abraham³ (2), was born in Phillipsburgh, Mass., — now Hollis, Me., — Feb. 26, 1799, and was about one year old when carried by his parents to Ohio. He married, May 9, 1822, Annis Ballard, by whom he had *five* children. His first wife died in Freestone County, Tex., Oct. 6, 1849, and he married, secondly, Phebe Vau Camp, by whom he had *three* children, of whom (with those of first wife) hereafter. He was in the war of 1812; enlisted as a musician at Springfield, O., Aug. 25, 1814, under Capt. Martin Shea, of the State militia, but afterwards served as a private soldier. He was stationed at Fort Winchester, at the mouth of the Clare, which empties into the Maume River, but was discharged at Fort Mary, Feb. 26, 1815. He was a carpenter and cabinet-maker by trade, and a Missionary Baptist preacher by profession. Mr. Ridlen was about medium height, and in old age became very stoop-shouldered and bald. Resembled his father more than either of his brothers. He visited his brothers and relatives a short time before his death, and bade them all a last farewell, telling them he should see them no more on earth. He was a man of eminent piety and very useful, and when he died at Bourbon, Douglas County, Ill., Feb. 29, 1872, he was sincerely lamented by a large number of his acquaintances.

Rachel Ridlen⁴ (4), fourth daughter of Abraham³ (2), was born in Ohio (near Cincinnati), Sept. 20, 1801; was married to Peter Teitsort, and in 1878 was living at Little York, Ind., near her brother John's farm. She is a large woman, and resembles the Tibbetts family more than the Ridlons. Her portrait, finished in India-ink, hangs in my house.

Susan Ridlen⁴ (2), youngest daughter of Abraham³ (2), was born in Ohio in 1808; married Jeremiah Mann; died in Park County, Ind., in 1870.

---

came down the ladder, saying as he descended, "Good heavens! do you suppose I can stay up here when ye sing like that?" We were sitting on the porch of Mrs. Alexander's house one hot afternoon, when on looking across the fields I saw the old patriarch approaching on horse-back, his long, white beard blowing back over his shoulders. A little granddaughter was leading the horse and chatting pleasantly with the old sire, while he sat erect, cooling himself with a large palm-leaf fan, which he carried with him everywhere. He was soon sitting at our side, telling his "experience" again; and it was indeed a rich treat every time, especially when he commenced the description of his sensations when he was converted, and interspersed his story with "Glory hallelujah!" and "Glory to God!" He was also enthusiastic in his descriptions of his fine stock of cattle, and no language at his command seemed strong enough to delineate their matchless beauty. His stories respecting his hardships in the army were painfully interesting. His beard was snowy white, with the exception of a black stripe running from his chin, which gave him a peculiar appearance. I was very ill while at the house of his daughter, and for a few hours it was thought I should never return to my home. The tender care bestowed by these relatives will never be forgotten by me. The last time I saw "Uncle-Samuel" was on the morning of our departure. He had come to the home of his daughter, Mrs. Aiken, where we were to take a public conveyance for McLeansburgh. We had all knelt in prayer, the parting hand had been given, and as we stood a moment at the gate we saw his son leading him down the orchard-path toward his own home; all at once the old man stopped, raised his broad-brimmed hat from his head, and while his white hair and beard were streaming in the breeze, he raised himself to his greatest height, and with a wave of his hand said, "Farewell, my dear kindred, farewell; we shall meet no more on earth; meet me in heaven." As he spoke these words the tears fell like rain from his blind eyes, and his trembling voice evinced how full was his heart. My last view of him was through a window of the coach, as he was passing under the garden trees leaning on the arm of his noble son, and the scene was truly patriarchal and impressive, — that of weakness leaning on strength, and old age upon vigorous manhood. I afterwards received a local newspaper which contained his obituary.

John Ridlen⁴ (8), fifth son of Abraham³ (2), was born in Ohio, March 31, 1806; married, Oct. 9, 1828, Margaret, daughter of George and Elizabeth Robinson, and lives at Little York, Washington County, Ind. His first wife having died, he married a Widow Sullivan for his second wife. Mr. Ridlen is a farmer and cooper by occupation. He is of medium height and build; has thick, bushy, white hair; long, flowing, silvery beard, and deep-set eyes. His portrait now in my possession shows him to resemble the Tibbetts family. He had issue *ten* children, all by his first wife, of whom hereafter.

Nicholas P. Ridlen⁴ (2), youngest son of Abraham³ (2), was born in Ohio, July 8, 1808; married, June 5, 1828, Hannah Bellville (she was born March 10, 1808, and died April 30, 1869), by whom he had issue *nine* children, of whom hereafter. He married, secondly, June 22, 1871, Elvira Wooten (she was born July 23, 1825), with whom he was living at Davisville, Shelby County, Ind., in 1875. His farm is near the line of the Cincinnati and Indianapolis Railroad. Farmer and cooper. He is a broad-shouldered, heavy man, with white, bushy hair, and favors in general facial appearance his mother's family. Samuel Ridlen, his brother, of Illinois, estimated his weight at three hundred pounds, but I think that was too high.

Joseph Ridlon⁴ (2), eldest son of Jacob³ (2), was born in Buxton, Me., in 1790; married Massie, daughter of William and Elizabeth (Leavett) Hancock, by whom he had *two* children, of whom hereafter. He was a millman, and lived in a house near the present mansion-house of Oliver Dow, and on the same lot now owned by Hon. Charles E. Weld, at West Buxton. He died in 1824, and requested his wife to marry his brother.

Isaac Ridlon⁴ (3), second son of Jacob³ (2), was born in Buxton, Me., July 30, 1797; married July 3, 1828, to Massie (Hancock) Ridlon, widow of his brother, before mentioned, and settled on a farm among the hills, in Baldwin, Cumberland County. He was above the medium height, and quite heavy. His head was high and bald, hair dark brown, eyes small and gray, and face ruddy. Resembled the Townsend family about the eyes and nose. He was a good-natured, honest man, and lived in peace with all the world. Died at West Baldwin, Feb. 15, 1880, aged 82 years and 6 months. His wife has deceased.

Judith Ridlon⁴ (3), eldest daughter of Jacob³ (2), was born in Buxton, Me., in 1799, and died in 1814, unmarried.

Betsey Ridlon⁴ (3), second daughter of Jacob³ (2), was born in Buxton, Me., Nov. 17, 1802; was married Sept. 4, 1831, to Daniel Wiggin, of Baldwin, whose first wife was Lydia Ridlon, her cousin. She died when aged, in Baldwin, where she had lived many years; an excellent woman. Her portrait in India-ink is in my possession.

Mary Ridlon⁴ (5), third daughter of Jacob³ (2), was born in Buxton, Me., March 10, 1807; was married May 10, 1840 (?), to William Davis, of Gorham, and lives near "White Rock." She is supposed to be living (1888), but the family will not reply to any of my communications.

Daniel Ridlon⁴ (4), eldest son of Daniel³ (2), was born in Ossipee, Mass. (now Limington, Me.), Nov. 11, 1778; baptized by Rev. John Fairfield, of Saco, March 12, 1780; married Dolly, daughter of Levi Dyer, of Limington, Nov. 21, 1799, and had issue *six* children, of whom hereafter. He lived some time in Limington or Limerick, but finally settled in Porter, Oxford County, where he owned a farm. He died in Porter, March 24, 1868, aged 90 years; his wife predeceased him Oct. 30, 1854, aged 67 years; they were buried in a small yard near his home. Mr. Ridlon was known as a very honest and pious man. He originally spelt his name *Ridley* or *Ridlea*, but changed back to Ridlon. His portrait, taken when aged, may be seen in the author's home.

Jemima Ridlon[4] (1), eldest daughter of Daniel[3] (2), was born in Limington, York County, Me., in 1782; was married to Benjamin Haines, of Buxton, Nov. 12, 1804, and this is all I can learn respecting her. The Haines family of Saco have no knowledge of such a woman.

Priscilla Ridlon[4] (2), second daughter of Daniel[3] (2), was born in Limerick (presumably), in 1784; was married to Pelatiah Brown, of that town, and lived on a farm. Her aged parents lived in her family during their last days. No record of her death.

John Ridlon[4] (9), second son of Daniel[3] (2), was born in Limerick, Me., April 4, 1786 (?); married his cousin, Mary Holmes, in 1801, and had issue *five* children, of whom hereafter. He married secondly, Tamar Wales, who survived him and was living in 1880. Mr. Ridlon owned a farm in Porter, Me., near his brother Daniel's homestead. He was of dark complexion, of medium height, compactly built, and had coarse features. Was considered a very strong man physically. Honest, quiet, and unobtrusive. He died April 4, 1849. I think there is an error either in date of birth or marriage.

Ezra Ridlon[4] (1), third son of Daniel[3] (2), was born in Limerick, Me., in 1788; married Rebecca Hutchins in 1807, and had issue *six* children, of whom hereafter. He resided on a small farm in Woodstock, Oxford County, many years, — say forty, — but had previously lived in Limerick or Porter. He was a remarkable man for one of his age. I saw him when between eighty and ninety, and he was then a hale, well-preserved, fresh-looking man. He was short, very broad across his shoulders, and compact in build; his neck thick, head large, complexion sandy, eyes gray, brows long and outstanding. He was quiet and sedate generally, and of the same eccentric, odd disposition so common with the old members of the family. Died July 23, 1881, aged 93 years. His widow died April 28, 1882.

Patience Ridlon[4] (2), fourth daughter of Daniel[3] (2), was born in Limerick, Me., June 20, 1788; was married to Simon Smith, and resided in Standish, Cumberland County. She had issue. Died July 29, 1871. Was she a twin to Ezra? Compare dates.

Sally Ridlon[4] (4), third daughter of Daniel[3] (2), was born in Limerick, Me., in April, 1791; married John Sands, of Standish, and probably lived in that town. She had issue, with one of whom (Mrs. Almon Kneeland, of Harrison),* she spent a part of her time during her last days, her husband having deceased. She died May 10, 1875, aged 84 years. I have her portrait.

Lydia Ridlon[4] (2), fifth daughter of Daniel[3] (2), was born in Limerick, Me., Aug. 25, 1793; was married to Simon Harmon, Dec. 2, 1819, and had issue. She lived in Cornish. Died Oct. 11, 1839.

---

* Mr. Kneeland kept a public house at Harrison Village, and Daniel D. Ridlon, while deputy-sheriff, used to stop there over night, when on his way to Paris to attend court; when at the table Mrs. Sands always gave him two pieces of pie, and the other guests but one. Mr. Ridlon asked her the reason for her favors, and she replied, " I know your name is Ridlon, and claim you as my relative."

Polly Ridlon⁴ (4), youngest daughter of Daniel³ (2), was born in Limerick, Me., Oct. 12, 1798; was married, June 13, 1819, to James Crowley, — he was born April 28, 1793, and died March 7, 1851, — of Cornish, Me., where she lived many years. Mr. Crowley was a blacksmith. In September, 1853, she was married to William Sargent, and removed from Cornish to Limington, in the same County. Mr. Sargent died in July, 1873, and the widow went to Ossipee, N. H., and lived with her granddaughter, Mrs. Nichols, there, until her death, which occurred July 17, 1877, at the age of 79 years. Her portrait, finished in India-ink, is in the author's collection. She had all the characteristics and features of the old Ridlon stock.

Ruth Ridlon⁴ (2), eldest daughter of Ephraim³ (1), was born in Saco, Me., Sept. 4, 1785; was married, Jan. 19, 1810, to James Dennet, and lived in her native town.

Patience Ridlon⁴ (3), second daughter of Ephraim³ (1), was born in Saco, Me., Oct. 4, 1787, and married —— Goggins. She had a daughter who married John McCollock, an Irishman, in Saco. I think Patience was not married till middle life. She was over 80 years old when she died. Her portrait is in my collection.

Henry Ridlon⁴ (1), eldest son of Ephraim³ (1), was born in Saco, Me., Feb. 15, 1790; married and had issue. He was better known as "Harry." Some of the family say he died at sea in 1821; others, that he died of hemorrhage, in Saco.

Charles Ridlon⁴ (1), second son of Ephraim³ (1), was born in Saco, Me., Jan. 15, 1792; married, Oct. 15, 1822, to Mehitable Snow, of Scarborough, and settled on a farm in Saco, on the "Ferry Road," so called. He subsequently moved to the village (now city), where he died June 20, 1843. His widow died at the home of her daughter in Portland, Feb. 17, 1859, aged 75 years. Mr. Ridlon was in the war of 1812, having enlisted in the Thirty-third Massachusetts Regiment. He was not tall, but very broad-shouldered and compact in form; his hair was dark, eyes gray, and features of the true Scottish type so prevalent in the family. He was buried in Saco. Had issue *three* children, of whom hereafter.

Mehitable Ridlon⁴ (1), third daughter of Ephraim³ (1), was born in Saco, Me., June 17, 1794, and married John Edgecomb, of Saco, Oct. 5, 1816. She lived on the "Ferry Road," so called.

Ephraim Ridlon⁴ (2), third son of Ephraim³ (1), was born in Saco, Me., April 13, 1797; married Sept. 16, 1815, Rachel Hanscomb, and had issue *three* children, of whom hereafter. He followed the sea and died in the West Indies of yellow fever. He was not tall, but very broad-shouldered and stout; hair dark, eyes gray, brows long and outstanding, features coarse. He resembled his father in disposition and habits; was eccentric, jovial, and witty. He loved the ocean from childhood, and became an excellent seaman.

Elizabeth Ridlon⁴ (3), fourth daughter of Ephraim³ (1), was born in Saco, Me., Nov. 23, 1799. She was married, but the name of her husband has not reached me. I think she lived with her father at the time of his death in 1835, but the family traditions do not agree concerning her last days.

William Ridlon⁴ (3), fourth son of Ephraim³ (1), was born in Saco, Me., March 2, 1803; married Nov. 20, 1823, Abigail Davis, and died in Saco, May 12, 1854. He lived on a small farm at the "Ferry," and left issue *four* children, of whom hereafter. His widow is still living in 1882, an active and brilliant old lady.

Lewis Ridlon⁴ (2), eldest son of Lewis³ (1), was born in Saco, Me., Jan. 21, 1791; lived with his brother Henry, on the "Ferry Road," a single man, and died of the palsy in September, 1858. He was on board the ship "Adams," of the United States Navy, during the war of 1812. This vessel was blown up on the Penobscot River, near Frankfort, Me., to prevent her being seized by the British; the crew escaped to land and made their way home.

Olive Ridlon⁴ (1), eldest daughter of Lewis³ (1), was born in Saco, Me., Jan. 7, 1792. I do not find a record of her marriage, and only know that she had a son named Enoch Ridlon, drowned at sea near Boston, at the age of 19 or 20 years.

Jeremiah Ridlon⁴ (4), second son of Lewis³ (1), was born in Saco, Me., Sept. 28, 1794, and was on board the ship "Adams," during the war of 1812.

Samuel Ridlon⁴ (3), third son of Lewis³ (1), was born in Saco, Me., Aug. 9, 1796, and died Nov. 5, 1817.

Nathaniel Ridlon⁴ (3), fourth son of Lewis³ (1), was born in Saco, Me., Aug. 30, 1798; married Jan. 26, 1827, Mercy Smith, and secondly, Jan. 23, 1832, Phebe Williams. At both weddings he was dressed in a naval uniform. He was many years a seaman, — twenty-two years, — during which he suffered severely from exposure and ill-treatment. He had sailed upon the North and Baltic seas, and passed the Straits of Gibraltar; had been in almost every European port, and passed through many dangers. At one time, coming upon the coast of Maine during very cold weather and in a driving storm, when the rigging of the vessel was clad in ice, his feet were so badly frozen he was obliged to leave the sea and remain at home all summer. The toes were all lost from one foot, and he became a cripple for the remainder of his life. "Uncle Nat" was a genuine sailor and could "spin a yarn" as well as the best seaman who rode the deck. When speaking of his sufferings with his frozen feet he delivered himself as follows: "I tell you, mister, I hed an awful time of it that summer; them ere toes was tormented sore, you better believe, and it was all I could do to hobble round on the farm. Why, sir, them toes got wus and wus, and tormented me day and night. I tried to hoe some corn, and when I reached the end of my row would sit on the grass, and with my ole jack-knife dig away at the j'ints of 'em; well, sir, I managed to unj'int 'em one by one, leetle by leetle, — gorry, how it hurt though, — till they was all off out o' my way. Them ole big fellows was hard 'nough, but when I undertook that little jack o' mine, I tell you what, sir, that was tough enough to kill. Why, that was so confounded tender, with the flesh all gone, and the bones sticking out, 't was all I could do to cripple round, But I sat down on the grass, pulled off my sock, took out my old knife, and sed I: 'Now, little jack, you've got tu cum, enyway.' Ye see, mister, the j'ints would come apart easy 'nough, but the toe held on to this ole foot by a little sinner (sinew), and by mighty, how that did hang on! Well, mister, I jist put the p'int o' the knife-blade right in a-twixt the j'int — my foot was on a block o' wood — and then, grippin' my teeth and shuttin' my eyes, I sed, 'Her'-now!' and with one mighty yank, off it flew, sinner and all; and good-Lord-a-marcy, mister, when that sinner snapped I yelled like murder. Don't you think that was a 'tarnal, all-killin' job, mister? What say?" During this description he had held his lame foot in his hands on his knee, and with contortion of body, movement of hand, and facial expression, illustrated in a forcible manner his rude amputations and sufferings. Men are few who could undergo such painful operations upon their own flesh, and with their own hands; and one must be armed with strong nerves to hear the old man tell the story unmoved. The bones of his feet were left with sharp edges and caused him great pain ever after when walking; as the motions of the foot, and weight of his body, pressed them into the flesh, keeping it always sore. "Uncle Nat" always loved the sea, and spent considerable time fishing along the coast of Maine, in after life.* He lived a while with his uncle, Abraham Ridlon, when young. He was about medium height, had round shoulders, long jutting eye-brows, gray eyes, large nose, broad mouth and chin, and short, thick neck. In his prime his hair was dark-brown. He was eccentric, odd, and willful, but quite conversational and humorous. Kind of heart and honest, "Uncle Nat" had many friends, and the many "sailors' yarns" he used to spin, after he became a "land-lubber," will never be forgotten by those who knew him. His second wife predeceased him, but I have no record. He lived with his youngest children during his last years, on his own farm, on the "Ferry Road," nearly opposite the homestead of his brother Edmund. Died in 1873, and at his request, was buried in the same suit of sailors' clothes he had been twice married in; and we may hope he made a safe voyage to the harbor of eternal rest. He had issue *twelve* children, of whom hereafter. I have his portrait.

Edmund Ridlon[4] (1), fifth son of Lewis[3] (1), was born in Saco, Me., Sept. 7, 1800; married July 15, 1820, Ruth, daughter of Jeremiah and Mercy Smith, and had issue *twelve* children, of whom hereafter. He lived on a farm on the river side of the "Ferry Road," in Saco, nearly opposite his brother Nathaniel's house, and only a little way down the hill from the cemetery. He resembled his brother last mentioned: had sandy complexion, Scottish type of features, long, shaggy eye-brows, and a surly, determined expression of face. His shoulders — unlike nearly all the Ridlons — were narrow and sloping. His constitution was vigorous till old age; he enjoyed a good dinner. Eccentric as any member of the clan; said many queer and witty things, now remembered and told by the townspeople. His wife predeceased him. Mr. Ridlon died in 1878, aged 78 years. Children now living on the homestead farm. Portrait in my home.

Henry Ridlon[4] (2), sixth son of Lewis[3] (1), was born in Saco, Me., Sept. 4, 1802; married Nancy, daughter of his uncle Gibbins Ridlon, April 11, 1826, and settled on the "Ferry Road," so called. His first wife died March 20, 1835, leaving *four* children, of whom hereafter; and Mr. Ridlon married, secondly, Feb. 6, 1845, Lucretia T. Edgecomb, of Saco; she was born Oct. 29, 1817, and is still living with her children in the city of Saco. Mr. Ridlon died Feb. 19, 1869, leaving *four* children by his second wife. He was a quiet, retiring man, honest and kind to all. Complexion light, height medium, features Scottish.

---

* For many years successively, the Ridlons of Hollis and Buxton went to Saco, and out a-fishing with Uncle Nat Ridlon, the latter always acting as "skipper." The old "tar" knew the good fishing-places, understood the management of a boat, and they always took good "fare" when under his directions.

Magnus Ridlon[4] (7), seventh son of Lewis[8] (1), was born in Saco, Me., Nov. 8, 1805; married Mary Edgecomb, of Saco, Dec. 17, 1837, and died Dec. 28, 1850, leaving *four* children, of whom hereafter. His widow died Aug. 22, 1856. He was a farmer on the "Ferry Road," but I think died at the village; was of medium height and light complexion.

Abraham Ridlon[4] (5), eighth son of Lewis[8] (1), was born in Saco, Me., Oct. 11, 1808; married Jane Ridlon, daughter of his uncle Richard, and died without issue March 5, 1834.

Richard Ridlon[4] (2), eldest son of Richard[8] (1), was born in Saco, Me., Jan. 8, 1795; married Hannah, daughter of Dea. Edward Chamberlain, of Abington, Mass., and worked for many years as a carpenter, builder, and contractor in Boston. He was very successful in business and acquired wealth. He had a fine residence on Chambers Street. Attended Unitarian church. Was large and quite a corpulent man; weighed about two hundred pounds, but was not tall. Had regular features, fair complexion, and was called fine-looking. He was somewhat reserved in appearance; nevertheless, courteous and cultured after the old-school-gentleman pattern. In latter years was troubled with paralysis and softening of the brain, and in 1879 was very much demented. Died in 1880, aged 85 years. His portrait in India-ink is in my collection.

Jane Ridlon[4] (2), eldest daughter of Richard[8] (1), was born in Saco, Me., Nov. 14, 1796; was married to her cousin, Abraham Ridlon, and died in her native town, without issue.

Lydia Ridlon[4] (3), second daughter of Richard[8] (1), was born in Saco, Me., Nov. 2, 1798. Probably died unmarried.

James Ridlon[4] (3), second son of Richard[8] (1), was born in Saco, Me., Jan. 2, 1801, married in England, and was lost at sea when a young man.

Noah Ridlon[4] (1), third son of Richard[8] (1), was born in Saco, Me., Nov. 8, 1805; married Sarah H., daughter of Capt. Thomas Hunt, of Abington, Mass., Jan. 1, 1834 (she was born Oct. 3, 1808), and had issue *one* son, of whom hereafter. Mr. Ridlon once lived in Roxbury. He was many years engaged in contracting and building. Died October, 1856, and was buried at Abington. His widow died in 1881. Mr. Ridlon is said to have been below the medium height, broad-shouldered, and quite corpulent. He was quiet and somewhat reserved in appearance.

Nancy Ridlon[4] (1), supposed to be the eldest daughter of Gibbins[8] (1), was baptized in Saco, Me., Sept. 12, 1794, " between meetings," and died of canker-rash, Jan. 31, 1798. Called "Naney."

George Ridlon[4] (1), eldest son of Gibbins[8] (1), was born in Saco, Me., May 30, 1796; baptized Sept. 18, 1796; died unmarried July 18; 1818, and was buried at "Old Orchard," so called.

Mary Ridlon[4] (6), second daughter of Gibbins[8] (1), was born in Saco, Me., Feb. 25, 1798; baptized July 15, 1798, and died unmarried, April 16, 1821. Said to have been a beautiful young woman.

Mark Ridlon[4] (1), second son of Gibbins[8] (1), was born in Saco, Me., Feb. 25, 1800, and died young, unmarried.

Capt. Gibbins* Ridlon[4] (2), third son of Gibbins[8] (1), was born in

* The name *Gibbins* was probably taken from the Gibbens family. James Gibbens was "master of the magazine" and a landed proprietor in Saco and Biddeford. He married a daughter of Thomas Lewis, one of the original owners of the

Saco, Me., Feb. 18, 1802; married Abigail Bachelder Feb. 4, 1825, and settled at "Old Orchard," so called. This family and that of James Ridlon were called "the Old Orchard Ridlons," to distinguish them from others known as "the Ferry Ridlons." His wife died Sept. 14, 1827; he died Sept. 3, 1880. This pair had several children, but I cannot find their records. His name was, by some, called and spelled "Gibbon" and "Gibeon." The family lived, died, and were buried, on the farm since owned by Ivory Fenderson. I do not know whether he was captain of the military, or of a vessel.

John Ridlon (10), fourth son of Gibbins' (1), was born in Saco, Me., Jan. 22, 1804, and died when young; some say was lost at sea.

Nancy Ridlon (2), third daughter of Gibbins' (1), was born in Saco, Me., May 7, 1806; was married to her cousin, Henry Ridlon, April 11, 1826, and died March 20, 1835.

Daniel Ridlon (5), fifth son of Gibbins' (1), was born in Saco, Me., May 26, 1809, and died Jan. 14, 1834.

Elizabeth Ridlon (4), fourth daughter of Gibbins' (1), was born in Saco, Me., Feb. 4, 1812.

Mary Ridlon (7), youngest daughter of Gibbins' (1), was born in Saco, in 1814, and died when a child.

Ruhama Ridlon (1), eldest daughter of James' (2), was born in Saco, Me., Dec. 8, 1804. She is a maiden-lady, who lived many years in her native State; now (1882) living with her sister in Monmouth, Ill. I have her portrait in my collection.

Martha Ridlon (2), second daughter of James' (2), was born in Saco, Me., April 26, 1806; was married to a Mr. Noe, and is now a widow living at Monmouth, Ill. I have her portrait.

Alexander Ridlon (1), eldest son of James' (2), was born in Saco, Me., May 3, 1808; married Anna, daughter of Luke and Lucy-Ann (Miner) Brown, and has issue *three* children, of whom hereafter. Mr. Ridlon lived on a farm at "Old Orchard," in Saco, till 1845, when, with his brother, he emigrated to Monmouth, Ill., where he lived till 1870, when he moved to Kansas, and now resides on a large farm in Middleton or Coyville, in that State. His portrait, finished in India-ink, is in my collection. One who knew him well, pronounced him one of the best men he had ever known. Deceased in March, 1883.

Peter-W. Ridlon (1), second son of James' (2), was born in Saco, Me., Aug. 29, 1810; married Abigail W. Ross, of Scottish extraction, and settled on a farm at "Old Orchard," in his native town. He emigrated to Monmouth, Ill., in 1845; but he subsequently removed to Kansas, and is now living at Gardner, in that State, in prosperous circumstances. He is a carpenter and stone-mason, — possessing the natural ingenuity of the Ridlon family, — and carries on farming and stock-raising. Is a great reader, well informed, and possessed of good abilities. He is quite a religionist, holds peculiar theological views, loves discussions, and is as firm as adamant. His memory of the early Ridlon families of Saco is remarkable, and he

---

"Lewis and Bonython Patent," and became the heir, through his wife, of his father-in-law. Rachel Edgecomb, Patience Annabel, Rebecca Wakefield, Hannah Mace, and Eliza Sharp, received portions of the estate of James Gibbens, when it was divided in 1780. There was a Gibbins Mace, Gibbins Elden, Gibbins Edgecomb, and two Gibbins Ridlons, at Saco, in early days.

has communicated much interesting information for this book.   He married a second wife, named Mary-Lyman Root.   He has had issue *four* children, of whom hereafter.   I have his portrait.

Eunice-Cutts Ridlon⁴ (2), eldest daughter of Nathaniel³ (1), was born in Saco, Me., Aug. 8, 1800; was married Sept. 30, 1822, to Abraham Forsskal (or Forsskoll), who was a native of Sweden, * and resided in her native town.   She had issue, and died June 10, 1833.   Mr. Forsskol died May 27, 1864, aged 74 years.

Betsey Ridlon⁴ (4), second daughter of Nathaniel³ (1), was born in Saco, Me., Feb. 25, 1803, and is presumed to have died young and unmarried.

Bradstreet Ridlon⁴ (1), only son of Nathaniel³ (1), was born in Saco, Me., April 6, 1806, and died unmarried.

Francis Ridlon⁴ (1), third daughter of Nathaniel³ (1), was born in Saco, Me., Oct. 29, 1808, and died Feb. 3, 1830.   I find no record of her marriage, and presume she died single.

Olive-Scammon Ridlon⁴ (2), fourth daughter of Nathaniel³ (1), was born in Saco, Me., Sept. 22, 1811; was married to Cyrenus Field, of Saco, Aug. 20, 1843, and had issue.   She is still living, and the only surviving member of her father's family; a very intelligent, active, and useful woman.   She is the youngest of the fourth generation of the Ridlon family.   I have her portrait.

Sarah-Abigail Ridlon⁴ (6), youngest daughter of Nathaniel³ (1), was born in Saco, Me., Oct. 31, 1814; was married to Barnabas Cutter, Jan. 8, 1834, and resided in Biddeford.   She died in 1881, leaving issue.   A brilliant, amiable, and cultivated lady.   Her portrait is in my collection.

FIFTH GENERATION.

Eliza-Sanborn Redlon⁵ (1), eldest daughter of Isaac⁴ (2), was born in Buxton, Me., Aug. 25, 1806, and died unmarried March 20, 1827.   An amiable and greatly beloved young woman.

William-Emery Redlon⁵ (4), eldest son of Isaac⁴ (2), was born in Buxton, Me., Jan. 7, 1808; married Grace, daughter of James Clay, of said town, and had issue *three* children, of whom hereafter.   I am not acquainted with Mr. Redlon's early life, but he carried on milling during his latter years, at a little hamlet in his native town called "Bog Mills."   He was a large, somewhat corpulent man, weighing about two hundred and twenty pounds.   Complexion sandy.   He died in the year 1872.

James-Madison Redlon⁵ (4), second son of Isaac⁴ (2), was born in Buxton, Me., Sept. 20, 1809; married March 18, 1835, Mehitable-Webster, daughter of Lemuel and Lovie (Dunnell) Sawyer, and settled on a large farm near his birth-place, at the "Duck Pond," so called.   He at one time worked on the Penobscot River about five years.   He commenced life with his wife on his grandfather's old homestead farm, but sold, and purchased his present place.   Mr. Redlon is a devoted Christian of the Primitive Free-

---

* ABRAHAM FORSSKOLL was born at Gottenburgh, Sweden, Jan. 22, 1790, and came over to America with Captain Tucker, an old shipmaster of Portland, before the war of 1812, intending to return; but the vessels of Tucker were taken for the privateering service, and young Forsskoll learned the cabinet-maker's trade in Portland.   He was a son of John-Carl Forsskoll, a physician, and left a brother and five sisters in Sweden.   One uncle was a bishop.   He settled in Saco and carried on business with Mr. Buckminster.   Was many years town-clerk; a neat penman.

will Baptist persuasion, and has frequently supplied as a lay-preacher. He is large and portly, weighing more than two hundred pounds; has sandy complexion; is moderate in movements and speech; quiet and peaceful in his habits, and an excellent farmer. Has *four* children, of whom hereafter.

Mary-Emery Redlon⁶ (8), second daughter of Isaac⁴ (2), was born in Buxton, Me., Oct. 20, 1811; was married to Joseph Sawyer, of that town, and died July 21, 1848.

Hannah Redlon⁶ (3), third daughter of Isaac⁴ (2), was born in Buxton, Me., Nov. 1, 1813; was married to Jesse Strong, of Garland, and died May 10, 1884.

Lucy-Ann Redlon⁶ (2), fourth daughter of Isaac⁴ (2), was born in Buxton, Me., Dec. 8, 1815; was married to her cousin, Marquess Emery, of that town, and died in Parsonfield, York County, where she resided, May 21, 1849, leaving a daughter.

Ammy-L. Redlon⁶ (1), third son of Isaac⁴ (2), was born in Buxton, Me., Jan. 27, 1818, and died unmarried in the eastern section of the State of Maine, July 7, 1840.

Benjamin-Emery Redlon⁶ (1), fourth son of Isaac⁴ (2), was born in Buxton, Me., June 2, 1820; married a Miss Cleverly, and lived several years in Saco, where he buried three children. He kept a shoe-store for some years at Gorham Corner, Cumberland County, but was afterwards employed as a journeyman in a shoe-factory in the city of Portland. He has settled in Kennebunk (1880), where he works at shoe-making and farming. He is said to be very stout and of light complexion. He has had issue *seven* children, of whom hereafter.

Charles Redlon⁶ (2), fifth son of Isaac⁴ (2), was born in Buxton, Me., Sept. 1, 1822; married Sarah MacLaughlan, and settled in Garland, where he now (1880) resides. He is six feet and two inches in height, and a very large, powerful man. Complexion light. Farmer. No children.

Eunice Redlon⁶ (3), fifth daughter of Isaac⁴ (2), was born in Buxton, Me., Aug. 30, 1824; married Jacob Whitten, and has issue.

Dorcas-E. Redlon⁶ (2), sixth daughter of Isaac⁴ (2), was born in Buxton, Me., Jan. 12, 1827; was married to John D. Spinney, a blacksmith, and lives at West Gorham, Cumberland County.

Isaac Redlon⁶ (3), youngest son of Isaac⁴ (2), was born in Buxton, Me., March 30, 1830; married Lydia-Ann Cleaves, — daughter of that Katherine Cleaves, of Saco, who was married to Abraham Ridlon, — and had issue *four* children, of whom hereafter. He had charge of the repair-shops of the Portland & Rochester Railroad Company, at Portland, for several years, but subsequently carried on business for himself at Buxton Centre depot. He was considered a good blacksmith. Mr. Redlon was tall and well formed, weighed about two hundred pounds, had dark-brown hair and whiskers, hazel eyes, and features of the old Redlon type; withal a fine-looking man. He was sarcastic, humorous, and greatly enjoyed a joke. He served in Company C, Twenty-seventh Regiment, Maine Volunteers, and was employed as regimental blacksmith. His wife died Jan. 10, 1878, and he lived with his sons several years. Deceased in 1884.

Benjamin Redlon⁶ (2), eldest son of Amos⁴ (1), was born in Buxton, Me., Jan. 19, 1803; married Hannah Gibson, of Waterford, and had issue *ten* children, of whom hereafter. He lived in the towns of Buxton, Standish, and Harrison, in Cumberland County, Me., and carried on farming and blacksmithing in the latter town many years. His house and shop were near the centre of the town, and on the bank of "Newcomb's Brook," so called; the barn was standing in 1880. He removed from Harrison to Springfield, in the eastern section of the State, where he continued several years; thence to Granger, N. J., and finally to Plainfield, Wis., where he was living in 1875. Mr. Redlon was a man of extraordinary natural ability; was a great reader, full of argument, retentive of memory, and tenacious in his grasp of principle. Has served as Justice of the Peace, and in other positions of responsibility. In early life he was an active member of the Freewill Baptist Church, but passed under the shadows of infidelity and is supposed to have maintained that position. He was of medium height, light-complexioned, nervous, impulsive, and passionate. A man of integrity and honesty in all his relations, and esteemed as a useful citizen. Deceased.

Sally Redlon⁴ (5), eldest daughter of Amos⁴ (1), was born in Buxton, Me., June 23, 1804; was married to Joseph McCorrison, of Standish, had issue, and died in Buckfield, Sept. 21, 1874.

Thomas-Jefferson Redlon⁵ (3), second son of Amos⁴ (1), was born in Buxton, Me., May 21, 1806; married Phebe McCorrison, of Standish, and settled in Sebago, where some of his children were born. He has also lived in the city of Portland. He is a carpenter by trade. Wife died many years ago, and he has married a second time. Resides in Kennebunk. Has been a lay-preacher many years: formerly Freewill Baptist, but now inclined to Second Adventism. Good height, well formed, portly; sandy complexion when in his prime; his hair and beard now snow-white. Mr. Redlon is possessed of many good natural parts; a great reader and easy talker; generous to a fault, charitable, and kindhearted. Has had issue *five* children, of whom hereafter.

Dr. Nathaniel Redlon⁵ (4), third son of Amos⁴ (1), was born in Buxton, Me., April 5, 1808; married Jane H. Mayberry, and had issue *eight* children, of whom hereafter. Mr. Redlon settled in Portland in 1824, and resided there till his death. He owned valuable property on Congress Street, which has greatly increased in valuation, by the growth of the city in that section. The same small dwelling and a little shop upon which his sign has hung since 1835, remain just as they were many years ago, and attract the attention of strangers, in consequence of their antiquated appearance. He was a peculiar man; extremely eccentric; a great student of books; profound in ancient lore; philosophical, critical, persistent, and single-minded. He was a practical botanist, mineralogist, and pharmacist. A shoe-maker by trade, he worked at his bench as long as his health would admit of it, and yet he was always within reach of his books, and kept a small druggist-store in a part of his shop. He accomplished many remarkable cures during his practice of medicine in Portland. He was tall, slender, and somewhat stooping; had sandy hair and beard, prominent features, bald crown, long, outstanding brows, gray eyes, and florid cheeks. Died in Portland, Oct. 21, 1881. See portrait in Redlon group in this book.

Jonathan Redlon⁵ (3), fourth son of Amos⁴ (1), was born in Buxton, Me., March 25, 1810; married Mary, daughter of Daniel Bryant, of Saco, when only nineteen years of age, and by her had *one* son. His first wife was sometimes insane, and died about the year 1840; she was married to Mr. Redlon June 24, 1829. He married, secondly, Nov. 2, 1841, Mary, daughter of Isaac Redlon (his cousin), and widow of Joseph Sawyer;

she had *twin* daughters, and died July 21, 1848. He married, thirdly, March 13, 1849, Louisa M. Cobb. He first settled in Buxton, where he worked as a joiner, shoe-maker, and farmer; moved to Saco subsequent to 1830, and lived about two miles from the "Falls." He afterwards removed to Gorham, where he lived many years, and died there Nov. 6, 1865. Mr. Redlon embraced religion in early life, and united with the Freewill Baptist Church; was a lay-preacher of acceptability, and a very useful man. He was associated with the Methodists in his latter years. He was tall, broad-shouldered, and weighed about two hundred pounds. His hair and beard were sandy, eyes gray, complexion fair, crown bald, — a pleasant, conversational, fine-looking man.

Mercy Redlon[4] (2), second daughter of Amos[4] (1), was born in Buxton, Me., March 12, 1812; was married to Nathaniel Knight, of Scarborough, and has issue.

Miranda Redlon[5] (1), third daughter of Amos[4] (1), was born in Buxton, Me., Feb. 12, 1814; was married to Joseph Elwell, of Buxton, and had issue.

Cyrus Redlon[5] (1), fifth son of Amos[4] (1), was born in Buxton, Me., March 4, 1817; married Mary A. Jordan, and had issue *two* sons, of whom hereafter. He settled at Vineland, N. J., but when last heard from was at Rockford, Minn. I have not received an answer to any communication forwarded to this man, and know but little concerning him.

Rev. Amos Redlon[5] (2), sixth son of Amos[4] (1), was born in Buxton, Me., Nov. 17, 1818, and married Eliza Sanborn. He was converted in 1834, united with the Freewill Baptist Church, and commenced preaching in 1841. Ordained in 1842, and has preached at Boston and Charlestown, Mass., Pawtucket and Scituate, R. I., Kingsley, Conn., Laconia, N. H., Berwick, Saco, Gorham, Gray, Dover, East Corinth, Dexter, Abbot, and other towns in Maine. He became editor of the *Providence Transcript* (R. I.), in 1849. Was agent for the Christian Commission, during the Rebellion. Has united with the Congregationalists within a few years, and is now settled at Hallowell, Me. Elder Redlon is a ripe scholar, able theologian, pleasant, practical preacher, and is qualified to fill any capacity where a strong, ready, well-balanced mind and executive energy are required. He is genial, social, communicative, and knows how to act the *man* as well as the *minister*. The missionary field has been successfully filled by him since his return to Maine. He is large and well-formed (weighs more than two hundred pounds), bald, light-complexioned, and withal a good type of the early Redlons. Has married a third wife. In 1878 expected to preach twenty-five years. *Seven* children.

Almira Redlon[5] (1), fourth daughter of Amos[4] (1), was born in Buxton, Me., Oct. 26, 1820, and married —— Kezar.

Mary Redlon[5] (9), fifth daughter of Amos[4] (1), was born in Buxton, Me., Feb. 26, 1823; was married to James Knight, of Scarborough, and had issue.

Apphia Redlon[5] (1), sixth daughter of Amos[4] (1), was born in Buxton, Me., Aug. 5, 1826; was married to Tristram Elwell, of that town, and had issue.

Eliza Redlon[5] (3), seventh daughter of Amos[4] (1), was born in Buxton, Me., April 26, 1828; was married to Jacob Whitney, and resides in Boston, Mass.

Nathan Redlon[5] (1), youngest son of Amos[4] (1), was born in Buxton, Me., Sept. 27, 1830; married Sarah Files, and has *one* son. Early settled in Portland, where he has been a mason and contractor for many years. Mr. Redlon is a man of marked ability, well informed, and has represented the city of Portland in the State Legislature very efficiently. His lady is also very active in benevolent and charitable work in her city, and stands at the head of organizations of this character. Mr. Redlon is of medium height, light complexion, and pleasant deportment; a useful and highly esteemed citizen and public servant.*

Olive Redlon[5] (3), eighth and youngest daughter of Amos[4] (1), was born in Buxton, Me., Sept. 25, 1832; was married to Capt. Isaac Sawyer, of Standish, and resides in that town.

John Redlon[5] (11), eldest son of Ebenezer[4] (3), was born in Buxton, Me., May 5, 1820; married Abigail Chandler, settled at "Duck Pond," in Buxton, and has issue *three* children, of whom hereafter. He is known in his neighborhood as "Honest John," and the name is appropriate to the character of the man. Wheelwright by trade. Tall, round and compact in build; has dark hair and gray eyes, and the Scottish type of features; resembles his late father.

Albion Redlon[5] (1), second son of Ebenezer[4] (3), was born in Gardiner, Me., Sept. 26, 1825; married Caroline Brown, April 14, 1850; was a private soldier in the Eighty-third Regiment Indiana Volunteers, and died at home, in 1863, from disease contracted while in the army. He was a highly respected man.

Mary-P. Redlon[5] (10), eldest daughter of Ebenezer[4] (3), was born in Buxton, Me., in 1827, and was carried to the West by her parents, when young. Was married to James D. Knight, in 1862, and resides at Irontown, Iowa.

Dr. Daniel-M. Redlon[5] (6), second son of Ebenezer[4] (3), was born in Gardiner, Me., Sept. 25, 1829, and was taken to the West by his parents, when young. Now a practising physician at Ripley, Ind. Served two years as assistant-surgeon in the Union army; subsequently as quartermaster of the Thirty-seventh Regiment Indiana Volunteers. Married Missouri Hall, Dec. 4, 1865, and has issue, of whom more hereafter. Dr. Redlon resembles his late father in many respects; head bald, features Scottish, beard long and full. Successful as a practitioner, esteemed as a citizen. See his portrait in this book.

Eliza-P. Redlon[5] (3), second daughter of Ebenezer[4] (3), was born in Gardiner, Me., in 1831; was married to Dudley Brown, in 1859, and resides at Ripley, Ind.

Ebenezer Redlon[5] (4), fourth son of Ebenezer[4] (3), was born in Gardiner, Me., in 1834; went West with his parents in 1837; served in the Thirty-seventh Regiment Indiana Volunteers, and died in 1861, in Kentucky.

Ellen Redlon[5] (1), third daughter of Ebenezer[4] (3), was born in Pierceville, Ind., in 1848; was married to John Tucker, and resides at Millhousen, Ind.

Mary Redlon[5] (11), eldest daughter of John[4] (5), was born in Newcastle, Me., Jan. 23, 1795; was married to Peleg Hall, and lived in Waldoborough in 1881. Her portrait is in my collection.

----

* NATHAN REDLON, of Gorham, Me., married Alsadia A. Cushing, of Portland, June 22, 1856. Possibly Sarah Files was a second wife.

John Redlon[5] (12), eldest son of John[4] (5), was born in Newcastle, Me., Sept. 10, 1797, and was lost at sea when young.

Jane Redlon[5] (3), second daughter of John[4] (5), was born in Newcastle, Me., July 10, 1799; was married to William Dodge, of that town, and had issue. She lived to old age. An excellent woman. I have her portrait, finished in India-ink.

Rosilla Redlon[5] (1), third daughter of John[4] (5), was born in Newcastle, Me., April 15, 1801; was married to John W. Hall, and was living in South China in 1880.

Lydia Redlon[5] (5), fourth daughter of John[4] (5), was born in Newcastle, Me., Feb. 24, 1808; was married to Andrew W. Keith, and resided in Chelsea, Mass.

Seth Redlon[5] (1), second son of John[4] (5), was born in Newcastle, Me., Nov. 4, 1805, and died young.

Robert Redlon[5] (4), third son of John[4] (5), was born in Newcastle, Me., Sept. 27, 1806; became a mariner, and is supposed to have been lost at sea, as nothing has been heard from him for many years. Is it not a little singular that he could not have been traced to his destination or death?

Joseph Redlon[5] (3), fourth son of John[4] (5), was born in Newcastle, Me., Aug. 4, 1808, and died young.

Elizabeth Redlon[5] (5), fifth daughter of John[4] (5), was born in Newcastle, Me., Oct. 6, 1810, was married to Daniel Paine, and is now (1880) living in Thomaston, Me.

Nathan Redlon[5] (2), fifth son of John[4] (5), was born in Newcastle, Me., Jan. 3, 1813; married Elizabeth Brown, and had issue, of whom hereafter. He married, secondly, Mary Martin, by whom he also has children. Mr. Redlon was "bound out" among strangers when a boy, and never knew what it was to have a home till he owned one. He says, "I had to scratch for myself, and have had a pretty hard scratch." He was formerly a merchant in Thomaston, Me., and Boston, Mass., but is now living on a beautiful farm in South China, in his native State. He has acquired a handsome pro erty, and is a prominent and highly respected citizen, having filled ppsitions of trust with the greatest acceptability to his townsmen. Mr. Redlon is of medium height, has broad shoulders, short neck, dark hair, and small, deep-set eyes. Children by two wives, *thirteen*, of whom hereafter, I have his portrait.

James Redlon[5] (5), youngest son of John[4] (5), was born in Newcastle, Me., March 8, 1815, and died when young.

John Ridlon[5] (13), eldest son Magnus[4] (5), was born in Hollis, Me., April 10, 1800; married Lucy, daughter of Daniel Smith, of Hollis, Nov. 29, 1821, and had issue *four* children, of whom hereafter. He learned the blacksmith's trade with his father, and followed that business through life. He built him a house and shop at "Smith's Bridge," so called, in Hollis, near his father-in-law's homestead, and worked there several years; he subsequently moved his house to Bonnie Eagle, and carried on a business there in company with William Tripp, their shop being at the Hollis end of the bridge there. His house was afterwards purchased by John Sawyer, and moved to the place where it now stands, at present owned by Stephen Higgins. Mr. Ridlon was a first-class mechanic. He was of medium height, had broad shoulders, and short, thick neck, gray eyes, long, outstanding brows, regular features, and ruddy complexion. He died

42

in 18—, and was buried in the "Old Ridlon Burying-ground," about one-half mile from Bonnie Eagle, but there is no stone to mark his grave.

Polly Ridlon[5] (5), eldest daughter of Magnus[4] (5), was born in Hollis (or Buxton), Me., in 1804; was married to Isaac Townsend, and had issue. "Aunt Polly" is still living in Hollis and is one of "the excellent of the earth." I have her portrait in India-ink.

Hannah Ridlon[5] (4), second daughter of Magnus[4] (5), was born in Buxton (or Hollis), Me., in 1807, and worked many years in Quincy, Mass., and Portland, Me., as a maiden-lady, and accumulated considerable money. She was married to John Eaton, of Buxton, Jan. 27, 1853, and is now living alone in her house there (1880). Mr. Eaton died in 1878.

Ann Ridlon[5] (1), third daughter of Magnus[4] (5), was born in Buxton, Me., Feb. 19, 1812; was married to Noles Rand, of Gorham (brother of the wife of Col. Nicholas Ridlon, of Hollis), and resided many years in Standish, in that County. Mr. Rand died in January, 1872, and she lives with her children and widowed sister Hannah. Draws a pension for a son killed in the Rebellion (1880).

Magnus Ridlon[5] (8), second son of Magnus[4] (5), was born in Buxton, Me., Aug. 5, 1814; married Emily, daughter of Col. Joshua Emery, of Hollis, and has had issue *seven* children, of whom hereafter. He learned the blacksmith's trade when young, and has followed that occupation through life. He located at Kezar Falls, in Parsonfield, many years ago, commenced business with John Sawyer, and has continued in the same shop ever since. He has devoted himself closely to his business, lived within his means, and acquired a good property. He has a fine stand of buildings in the village opposite his shop, and owns land and a wood-lot outside. An excellent mechanic, industrious, honest, quiet, peaceful, a good neighbor, and useful citizen; can "mind his own business" as well as any man living. He is genial, conversational, and jovial. Of medium height, round-shouldered, and muscular; has light complexion, small, gray eyes, long brows, ruddy cheeks, and pleasant expression of face. Mr. Ridlon was an officer in the military company known as "Hollis Light Infantry," and was highly esteemed by his command; is said to have been an efficient and fine-looking soldier.

Thomas Ridlon[5] (4), third son of Magnus[4] (5), was born in Buxton, Me., Feb. 4, 1820, and was adopted after his mother's death by Judith Ridlon, maiden-daughter of Thomas Ridlon, of Hollis, with whom he lived until his death when a young lad. He was buried in the "Old Ridlon Burying-ground," on the Bonnie Eagle road, in the lot of Thomas Ridlon, and next to Sarah Ridlon; a space was left, however, for the grave of "Aunt Judy," between his grave and that of Sarah, and a wide stone embedded in the ground as a warning to all sextons not to dig there. The author saw the stone removed in 1880, and the grave of the faithful guardian of "little Thomas" was then made.

James Ridlon[5] (6), youngest son of Magnus[4] (5), was born in Buxton, Me., Dec. 3, 1822 (by a second wife), and died in infancy.

Harriet Ridlon[5] (1), youngest daughter of Magnus[4] (5), was born in Buxton, Me., Feb. 4, 1825, and was married Aug. 9, 1845, to Harrison F. O. Cram. Deceased.

Robert Redlon[5] (5), eldest son of Nathaniel[4] (2), was born in Bath, Me., Aug. 4, 1798, and was lost at sea when a young man and unmarried.

Magnus Redlon[6] (9), second son of Nathaniel[4] (2), was born in Bath, Me., Oct. 10, 1799, and died in infancy.

Abigail Redlon[6] (2), eldest daughter of Nathaniel[4] (2), was born in Bath, Me., Jan. 14, 1801; became the wife of Arber Marson (now, 1875, of Boothbay, Me.) in 1825, and died in 1839.

Catherine Redlon[6] (2), second daughter of Nathaniel[4] (2), was born in Bath, Me., March 16, 1803; was married to Dennis Lines, and lived sometime in South Boston, Mass. Dead.

Sally Ridley[5] (6), eldest daughter of Daniel[4] (3), was born in Saco, Me., Nov. 30, 1793; was married to Benjamin McKenney, Feb. 27, 1812, — he was then of Scarborough, — and had issue. She died in the city of Portland many years ago. Her husband went from home during the excitement created by Jacob Cochran, and was absent many years. Mrs. McKenney's portrait is in my collection.

Matthias Ridley[5] (5), eldest son of Daniel[4] (3), was born in Saco, Me., Feb. 29, 1795; married Feb. 4, 1818, to Nancy Pratt, of Leeds, Me., and settled in Wayne, to which town he went with his parents in 1814. His house was about one-half mile north of where his brother Daniel subsequently built his brick house, and was reached by a lane from the main carriage-road. (I find he first sat down a little way east of his father's homestead, and afterwards moved his house to its present location.) He enlisted as a substitute for his father in the war of 1812, and received a pension which is now drawn by his widow, who, in a somewhat demented condition, continues on the old farm, living alone, but under the watch-care of her son. Mr. Ridlon changed his name to *Ridley*, as did all the Wayne family, and his descendants will stand thus recorded. He was tall, broad-shouldered, massive of frame, and muscular; had black hair, dark eyes, regular features, and firm but pleasant expression of face; his head was high and well developed, but not bald. He was a great reader, especially of the Scriptures, was well informed, possessed a remarkably retentive memory, and was many years a devoted Christian. He was nearly blind for some years, but recovered his sight before his death, which took place in 1875, at the age of 80 years. He was buried in the cemetery near the brick house of his brother Daniel, where so many of the family rest. His children, of whom hereafter, were *ten* in number.

Martha Ridley[5] (3), second daughter of Daniel[4] (3), was born in Saco, Me., Feb. 9, 1798, and died young.

Jonathan Ridley[5] (4), second son of Daniel[4] (3), was born in Saco, Me., Feb. 15, 1801; married Louisa Marston, of Fayette, and had issue *seven* children, of whom hereafter. He went from Saco to Wayne in 1813–14, and lived in that town during his minority, working on a farm in summer and attending or teaching school in winter. He changed the spelling of his name to *Ridley*, and all the family in that section of the State followed suit. He says, "Everybody called me Mr. Ridley, and I was weary of correcting them, so I adopted a new orthography." Mr. Ridley early manifested a taste for books, and has been a devoted reader all his life. He took front-rank as a scholar in the town-schools, and at an early age became an assistant teacher. He aspired to a thorough education, but his situation and limited means in early life made it unavailable, and he had to supplement what he acquired at the common school, by extensive reading and study at home; this he applied himself to with great persistency until his mind was well stored with practical knowledge. Mr.

Ridley settled in Jay, Franklin County, many years ago, and has been a leading, public-spirited man, filling many positions of responsibility, always to the satisfaction of his townsmen, fully sustaining the confidence reposed in him, and only declined to act in the capacity of a public servant, when advanced years and infirmities made it inconvenient for him to discharge the obligations of office with that care and faithfulness which had always characterized his administrative actions. Although he has retired from public life, and to the comparative seclusion of a farm, remote from popular society influences, he still uses the choicest language in conversation, and maintains the graceful carriage, address, suavity, and manners of a gentleman of the old school. He is communicative, argumentative, and positive, holding his principles with a peculiar tenacity of grasp; is stable-minded, impulsive, high-tempered, a keen observer of human nature discriminating in investigation, and cool in judgment. His word is taken as authority by those best acquainted with him. His home is among the mountains, surrounded by heavy woods; cool brooks and springs babble and send forth the sweetest water near his dwelling, and the specimens of landscape viewed from his door, composed of mountains, woodlands, rocky craigs, vales, green fields, and glimpses of the shining Androscoggin, are picturesque and pleasing to every lover of nature. Mr. Ridley is now in the winter of his days and past hard labor, but he is kindly cared for in the family of his dutiful son; pretty grandchildren climb upon his knee and mingle their sunny curls with the patriarch's silvery beard. He retains his faculties well, and spends nearly all his time, especially in winter, over his books and newspapers. In summer he cultivates a nice garden and takes pride in its productions. In personal appearance he resembles the old Ridlon stock, and that of the family of Field, from which he is descended maternally. He stands about the medium height, has broad shoulders, and a compact, well-knit body. His head is round, high-crowned, and intellectual, his hair (originally jet-black) almost snow-white and worn long, beard heavy, long and nearly white, falling like waves of water over his breast. His eyes are black and piercing, brows long, features regular and of the Norman type, and his facial expression calm, serious, and determined. His wife died in 1882.

Dea. Daniel Ridley[5] (7), third son of Daniel[4] (3), was born in Saco, Me., Sept. 27, 1802; married Sally Winter, and settled in the town of Wayne, whither he had gone with his parents in 1814. His father failed to meet the payments on his land purchased of Stephen Boothby, and promised him one-half of the lot if he would pay what was then due; consequently he engaged for a lumber company, entered the logging swamp, and worked hard nearly a year, but lost all his pay by the failure of his employers. He then commenced work for Mr. Boothby, and con-

---

* In a communication addressed to the author in 1872, Jonathan Ridley says: " The Ridlon family, according to my best knowledge of them, are a moral, intelligent, and hospitable people; and if they have any fame, it has been purely adventitious, for they have never sought it. Thus it was with our common progenitor: he took his life in his hands through a sturdy will and purpose to be free, to be a man. And if our kindred have not won distinctions, it was owing to their retiring disposition more than their incapability. No man can question the courage of a Ridlon when duty has called them to face danger; so we find them upon the battlefields of the Revolution, and in the army in defence of their country in every war since. But perhaps I have said enough about the male persuasion; though I venerate them, it is the women of our family who have my adoration. I have known many of them, who were too pure for sin to have any place in their hearts."

tinued till his land was paid for. He loved work from a boy, and, as soon as he became a land-owner, commenced to clear him a farm; and while the other young men of his neighborhood were away at trainings, raisings, and town-meetings, he was away in some rick, clearing new land. It is said of him that when thirsty he would *run* to a spring in the woods, drink, and *run* back to his work. Practising close economy, and turning every dollar to good account, he acquired a handsome estate, but did not live long to enjoy it; for, by overwork in building a new brick house, he impaired his constitution, and died Feb. 20, 1850. Mr. Ridley had married, for a second wife, Rebecca Graves, who brought *one* son into the family, and died Feb. 27, 1871. Daniel was of medium stature, round, and compactly made; had broad shoulders, thick neck, black hair, coarse, Scottish features, and by hard work became very much bowed over in latter years. Children, of whom hereafter, *eleven* in number.

Capt. **Benjamin Ridley**[5] (3), fourth son of Daniel[4] (3), was born in Saco, Me., June 20, 1804; married Eliza, daughter of Hamilton Jenkins,* and settled in the town of Wayne, to which he went with his parents at the age of ten. He built a house near that of his father-in-law, a few rods toward Wayne Village, and lived there several years, but subsequently removed to the town of Leeds. He lived on a farm, but worked as a stone-mason and contractor; laid the foundations for many mills, built bridges for railroads, and whatever work he superintended was done in the most thorough and workmanlike manner, as is proved by its durability. He was a prominent man; captain in the military, and representative to the legislature of his State. He availed himself of every advantage to acquire useful knowledge, and was considered a well-informed, sound-minded man. Tall, broad-shouldered, full-chested, and strong-framed, he was a man of remarkable physical powers; was a great worker, and could endure almost any tax, apparently unfatigued and unimpaired. He had dark hair and beard, gray eyes, high forehead, heavy, outstanding brows, bald crown, and regular features. His first wife having deceased when young, he married, secondly, Abiah ——, who died Jan. 7, 1807. Mr. Ridley (as he spelt his name after going East) died March 12, 1854. This family is buried in a beautiful, sequestered spot near the old Jenkins homestead. Children, *three* in number.

Pelina Ridley[5] (1), second daughter of Daniel[4] (3), was born in Saco, Me., March 7, 1807; was married to Charles Graves, of Wayne, in 1827, and died June 16, 1863, leaving issue.

Mary Ridley[5] (12), third daughter of Daniel[4] (3), was born in Saco, Me., April 4, 1809; was married to Naaman Bishop, of Wayne, and had issue. She is now (1882) living; a good woman, and a complete type of the old Ridlon family.

Betsey Ridley[5] (5), third daughter of Daniel[4] (3), was born in Saco, Me., Aug. 20, 1811; was married to Hamilton Gould, of Wilton, and had issue. Deceased.

Jannes Ridley[5] (1), fifth son of Daniel[4] (3), was born in Wayne (presumably), July 27, 1814, and became an eccentric, roving character. He would

---

* HAMILTON JENKINS, formerly from Saco, married a daughter of John Boothby, of Saco, and settled on land purchased of Stephen Boothby, his brother-in-law, who was a brother of Rev. John Boothby, late of Saco, who, as well as Stephen who died in Wayne or Leeds, lived to great age. Hamilton Jenkins was a brother of Dennis Jenkins of Wayne, and Thomas Jenkins, the centenarian, late of Saco. Sometimes *Junkins*.

leave home without giving any notice to his parents, and after an absence of years return as unexpectedly, without giving any definite account of his wanderings or adventures. He is supposed to have followed the sea for many years. At one time he claimed to have a family in New Orleans, but after a careful examination of the records of that city no mention of such a man can be found, and if he has ever lived there it was under an assumed name. Tradition says he started overland for California, with a company raised at Cincinnati, O., and died somewhere about the Rocky Mountains. But nothing has been heard from him for many years, and he may still be living. He was a small man, but very agile and muscular; something of a pugilist.

Jerome Ridley[4] (1), sixth son of Daniel[4] (3), was born in Wayne, Me., Dec. 29, 1816; married Anna Peacock, and had issue *five* children, of whom hereafter. He married, secondly, in 1845, Mary Davis, of Pittston, and by her had *ten* children. He drove the mail-coach from Portland to Augusta for many years, but latterly settled on a large farm in Richmond, Me. He was of nervous temperament, and subject to melancholy, desponding moods. He was generally cheerful, jovial, and sarcastic; conversational, rapid in speech, emphatic, determined, impulsive, and high-tempered.* A reader of general literature, and a deep thinker; a man of quick perception and ready wit, humorous and argumentative, radical in politics, firm in his religious and theological opinions, and a devoted believer of the Second Adventist doctrine. In personal appearance he closely resembled the Field family, from whom he was maternally descended. He was of good height, broad across the shoulders, full-chested, round and compact of body, and inclined to corpulency. His hair and beard were jet-black, and the latter very coarse and thick; his head was large, forehead broad, brows long and outstanding, eyes gray, features coarse, and upper-lip especially long and thick. When he smiled there was a peculiarly cunning expression about his eyes that I have never observed in any person not connected with the Field family. He was a good man. Died in 1875, leaving a large family of children, of whom hereafter.

John Ridlon[5] (14), eldest son of Samuel[4] (1), was born in Hollis, Me., Nov. 10, 1804; married Martha, eldest daughter of Thomas and Polly (Decker) Ridlon, his cousin (she was born Sept. 20, 1805, and died January, 1878), and settled in his own town, in a house near that of his father-in-law, of whom he purchased land. He has always been a farmer, but being an ingenious and capable man, has worked as a stone-mason, joiner, and cooper. He has been an extensive reader, and possesses a large fund of information. His memory is retentive, language copious, and conversation animating. Having descended from the Ridlons paternally and maternally, he inherited a double share of the traits so peculiar to the family, and stands a characteristic type of the old ancestral stock. He is tall and round-built; has very coarse Scottish features, dark hair, small gray eyes, and a high, full forehead, ornamented with a pair of eyebrows of remarkable length and shape. He is of quick movement; ner-

---

* Since my visit at the home of Jerome Ridley (he spelt his name *Ridley*, as did his brothers), I have been informed that, assisted by another old stage-driver, he once took an obnoxious fellow from his hotel, at Augusta, Me., put him into a hollow log in a pasture, closed the openings with large stones, and kept him thus imprisoned all night. He was certainly a determined, formidable man, and according to stories told by his patrons was capable of wonderful feats.

vous, impulsive temperament; radical in his political views and expressions; a devoted and consistent communicant of the Freewill Baptist Church, of which he has been a member for many years; a good and peaceful neighbor, useful citizen, and an honest man in every sense of the word. He had the misfortune to destroy the sight of one eye, many years ago, by the splinter of a nail, which flew from under his hammer and struck the pupil. He cared for his mother from the time of his father's death. His children were *four* in number — two sons and two daughters.

Ann Ridlon⁶ (2), eldest daughter of Samuel⁴ (1), was born in Hollis, Me., Sept. 4, 1806; was married to William Farr, had issue, and died many years ago somewhere in eastern Maine.

Humphrey-Merrill Ridlon⁶ (1), second son of Samuel⁴ (1), was born in Hollis, Me., Sept. 8, 1808; married and had issue *four* children, of whom hereafter. He is a farmer, in Albion, Me. Great worker; very ingenious; a free talker; small, round-shouldered, has light complexion, coarse features, small gray eyes, long brows; is quick-motioned, impulsive, passionate, radical, and determined. His powers of endurance were stronger than most of the young men of his neighborhood, when living in Hollis, and if his brothers complained of the back-ache, he used to say they were born without any "tough-leather" in them.

Jane Ridlon⁶ (4), second daughter of Samuel⁴ (1), was born in Hollis, Me., Oct. 2, 1810; was married to Arnold Bowie, of Durham, but died in Portland, leaving issue.

Patience Ridlon⁶ (5), third daughter of Samuel⁴ (1), was born in Hollis, Me., May 23, 1813; was married to Nathaniel, eldest son of David and Eunice (Ridlon) Martin, her cousin, and has issue. Now living in her native town. Rightly named "Patience."

Rev. Ira-Gould Ridlon⁶ (1), third son of Samuel⁴ (1), was born in Hollis, Me., July 15, 1815; married Mary Wagg, of Danville, May 3, 1833 (she was born in Danville, Me., Nov. 9, 1814), and had issue *five* children, of whom hereafter. He lost his father when a boy, and with his sister Patience, went to live with Magnus Ridlon, of Durham. He embraced religion in 1836, and commenced preaching in 1838; has bestowed his labors as an itinerant and evangelist, in Durham, Freeport, Lisbon, Green, Danville, Bowdoin, Brunswick, and Harpswell,— all in Maine. He has not devoted all his time to the ministry, but has carried on a farm, peddled shoes, patent medicines, and "Yankee notions." He now lives in Lisbon, on a farm. He is a good singer, interesting conversationalist, social, kind-hearted, and a pleasant exhorter in religious meeting; but is not considered a profound preacher. He is an earnest advocate of the cause of temperance, and a radical politician of the Republican stamp. Being descended from parents who were both Ridlons, he has shared largely in the elements of character so conspicuous in his family. He is tall, round, and compactly made; has dark-brown hair, gray eyes, long, outstanding brows, and regular features of face.

Roxanna-W. Ridlon⁶ (1), fourth daughter of Samuel⁴ (1), was born in Wayne, Me., Dec. 24, 1817; was married to Moses Grace, of Saco, Oct. 25, 1844, had issue, and is now living in Saco.

Mary Ridlon⁶ (13), fifth daughter of Samuel⁴ (1), was born in Hollis, Me., in 1820; was married Aug. 29, 1843, to John Buzzell, and died when a young woman, without issue. Buried in the enclosed garden of her brother John, in Hollis, where her marble headstone was set by loving hands.

Rebecca Ridlon^5 **(3)**, sixth daughter of Samuel^4 (1), was born in Hollis, Me., in 1822, and died young, unmarried.

Betsey Ridlon^5 **(6)**, eldest daughter of John^4 (6), was born in Clarendon, Vt., May 21, 1804, and was married, Oct. 29, 1822, to Alfred Colvin, a farmer of Clarendon.

Jonathan-F. Ridlon^5 **(5)**, eldest son of John^4 (6), was born in Clarendon, Vt., May 20, 1806; married Rosetta B., daughter of Benjamin and Elizabeth Colvin, in November, 1830, and had issue *five* children, of whom hereafter. Mr. Ridlon was a farmer in his native town. He was tall, broad-shouldered, and had a gigantic frame, knit with powerful muscles. His hair was black, and his beard heavy, long, and silvered with gray. He was a real mountaineer and hunter, a man of unwavering courage and fortitude, possessed of a vigor of constitution that could endure great strain. He was nervous, impulsive, quick-tempered, eccentric, and as firm as the granitic hills among which he lived. His eyes were light gray and piercing, the expression of his face determined, and his general aspect formidable and aggressive. All the peculiar traits so conspicuous in the old Ridlons seemed to be concentrated in this man.* The first sentence spoken to me when introduced to him was, "Well, sir, I can handle any Ridlon that was ever born"; at the same time he straightened himself to his greatest height, shut his mouth firmly, and looked as defiant as a Jehu. But with all his seeming coldness and sternness, he had a very kind and tender heart. He died Feb. 2, 1875, and was buried near his home. His portrait is in my collection.

Alma Ridlon^5 **(1)**, second daughter of John^4 (6), was born in Clarendon, Vt., in 1808, and died unmarried.

Thomas Ridlon^5 **(5)**, second son of John^4 (6), was born in Clarendon, Vt., March 20, 1810; married Hildee Baxter, in 1834, settled in his native town, and cultivated a farm there. He married a second wife, whose name does not appear. Children by both wives, of whom hereafter. Mr. Ridlon sold his estate in Vermont, many years ago, and emigrated to Minnesota, where he is supposed to be living at present, but nothing has been heard from this family for a long time. Mr. Ridlon is said to be tall and well formed; had black hair and beard, regular features, nervous

---

* To show the peculiar style of the man, I append the following story, told me by Jonathan Ridley, of Vermont, as an apology, when I asked him to favor us with a song. "When I was a boy my voice was the most wonderful that was ever known in the State, and people came from far and near to hear me sing. I was so bashful I could never do my best in company, but always knew there was something almost divine about my voice. Well, sir, one morning father sent me out to the pasture for the horse, and as the air was clear and balmy, and no one near to hear me, I thought I would do my best and bring my voice to the test; so, I climbed upon the gate and commenced, and my singing so filled me with astonishment that I became spell-bound and lost myself in the rapture of my own music. How long I sang I cannot tell, but when the spell was broken, behold! the birds of all kinds had gathered around me by hundreds upon the gate, and were still descending from the air in every direction; they seemed to be filled with wonder, and looked at me in complete silence; this state of things filled me with fear, and I hastened on my errand, wondering what it all meant. Well, sir, from that hour those birds have never sung, — nor have I." This was related with soberness and apparent good faith; not a smile could be detected on his face, and when he was done he looked me earnestly in the eye and asked, "And now do you blame me because I do not sing?" Of course this was a story, but it was told as but few men could have told it.

temperament, firm and settled convictions, all tempered with a very kind and generous heart.

Noel-P. Ridlon⁶ (1), third son of John⁴ (6), was born in Clarendon, Vt., Nov. 4, 1813; married Nancy B. Hallett, of Powlet, Rutland County, Nov. 8, 1849, and settled on a farm in his native town. He was killed by the cars, Oct. 12, 1866, while driving across the railroad-track with his horse-team. He had issue *three* children, of whom hereafter.

Amanda Ridlon⁶ (1), third daughter of John⁴ (6), was born in Clarendon, Vt., Feb. 1, 1815; was married to Ira Davis, Jan. 15, 1846; secondly, to M. W. Hutchinson, of Andover, Windsor County, Feb. 14, 1859.

John-Hollis Ridlon⁶ (13), fourth son of John⁴ (6), was born in Clarendon, Vt., in 1817; married Zerinda Dean, and had issue *three* children, of whom hereafter. He settled in his native town and lived there many years, but subsequently removed to Ohio, where, in 1876, he was living. He may have additional children since his settlement in the West. He once visited Hollis,* — the town for which he was named, — and spent some weeks with his Ridlon relatives there; he is spoken of by them as an eccentric character.

Loretta-P. Ridlon⁶ (1), fourth daughter of John⁴ (6), was born in Clarendon, Vt., Jan. 2, 1821; was married July 4, 1855, to Lester Jones, of Sudbury, and resides in her native town. No issue.

Rebecca Ridlon⁶ (4), youngest daughter of John⁴ (6), was born in Clarendon, Vt., July 19, 1824; was married Jan. 1, 1852, to George R. Davis, of Sudbury, and lives on a farm in her native town. She is a real Ridlon of the old type.

Orrin Ridley⁵ (1), eldest son of David⁴ (2), was born in Wayne, Me., June 8, 1814, and died in Bangor, Sept. 21, 1833.

Aphia-G. Ridley⁵ (1), eldest daughter of David⁴ (2), was born in Wayne, Me., Aug. 26, 1818; was married to Stephen H. Worth, Dec. 3, 1840, and lives on a farm in East Corinth, Me.

Rev. Isaac-G. Ridley⁵ (5), second son of David⁴ (2), was born in Wayne, Me., April 12, 1822; married Dec. 16, 1841, Harriet, daughter of Rev. Stephen Dexter, of East Corinth, and settled in that town as a carpenter. No children. His first wife, a most amiable woman, died in 1874, and he married a second wife, whose name has not reached me. Mr. Ridley embraced religion when young, and was chosen a deacon of the Baptist church in Corinth; in this sacred office, and that of a lay-minister, he served faithfully many years. In 1870 he was sent into Aroostook County, Me., as colporteur, by the Baptist Association, and in 1873 he moved to the town of Easton, in that County. He has since received ordination as an evangelist, and continues his labors as a missionary in the County, proving himself a faithful and efficient minister of the Gospel. He is tall and large, weighing, say, two hundred and twenty pounds; his head is large and bald, hair and beard nearly white, features of the family type, — withal a noble-looking man. He is social, conversational, and generous-spirited; a plain, practical preacher, who holds the confidence and esteem of the people. See portrait in this book.

David Ridley⁵ (3), third son of David⁴ (2), was born in Wayne or Abbot, March 4, 1824; married Dec. 29, 1846, Sarah Crowell, of Bangor,

----

* The town of Hollis, in York County, Me., was once called Phillipsburgh, but was probably changed in honor of the Rev. John Hollis.

and had issue *seven* children, of whom hereafter. He was a carpenter and builder, and resided at Newton Falls, Mass., where he died June 14, 1869, leaving a widow and *five* children. Mr. Ridley was tall and well formed; had light complexion, regular features, and pleasant expression of face; judging from his photograph, I should not think he resembled the Ridlon family. He was a competent mechanic, and an honest, quiet, unobtrusive young man. His widow has since married a Mr. Blaisdell, of Bangor, Me.

William-G. Ridley[5] (5), third son of David[4] (2), was born in Abbot, Me., Dec. 3, 1827, and died the same year.

Mary-G. Ridley[5] (14), second daughter of David[4] (2), was born in Abbot, Me., Dec. 3, 1828; was married to Elijah J. Clement, a wheelwright, Dec. 10, 1848, and resides at East Corinth, where she, like Dorcas of the Bible, "makes coats and garments," being a tailoress by trade.

Catharine Ridlon[5] (3), only daughter of James[4] (2), was born in Hollis, Me., May 29, 1803; was married to —— Elder, of Gorham or Standish, and lived many years in Limington. Her husband died many years ago, and she, having become insane, was placed on the town-farm, in Standish, where she still remains, and is a complete mental wreck. She was born without a palate, and could never articulate distinctly. Her bodily health, in 1880, was good.

Jacob Ridlon[5] (4), only son of James[4] (2), was born in Hollis, Me., Jan. 3, 1806, and died when young, unmarried. He was buried at his father's side, in the lot near the homestead of his uncle Robert. A young gentleman of amiable disposition and noble character, beloved by all his acquaintances. He was tall, erect, with fair complexion and stately address.

James-Hopkinson Ridlon[5] (7), eldest son of Joseph[4] (1), was born in Hollis, Me., Jan. 20, 1813; married June 8, 1843, Susan Small, of Limington, and had issue *three* sons, of whom hereafter. He acquired a good education, in the common schools and academy, and taught in winter in his native town. Served several years on the Superintending School Committee; was justice of the peace and selectman; also land-surveyor. Kept store at Bonnie Eagle Village, and engaged in the manufacture of clothing. He embraced religion while a student in Parsonsville Seminary, and on returning home united with the Freewill Baptist church at West Buxton; was many years clerk of that communion, and a member of the choir. Mr. Ridlon was a public-spirited, progressive man, manifesting a deep interest in every movement and institution calculated to enlighten and elevate his fellow-men; a useful citizen and public servant, kind and devoted husband, valued neighbor, and exemplary Christian. He was moderate, candid, serious, considerate, and generally exhibited sound judgment. He was always so absorbed in thought that he frequently passed people on the road without seeing them. Tall, broad-shouldered, and well formed; had dark-brown hair and beard, full, jutting forehead, high crown, and a deeply wrinkled face. His mouth was broad and full, chin receding, and his general features of the old Ridlon mould. He died Sept. 16, 1855, and was buried near his father's homestead, in the "Old Ridlon Burying-ground," so called, where his monument, containing his miniature, is now standing.

Dea. Joseph Ridlon[5] (4), second son of Joseph[4] (1), was born in Hollis, Me., in 1815; married March 5, 1845, Sarah, daughter of Abijah and

Susan (Nason) Usher, of Hollis, and has *two* children, of whom hereafter. He was employed as clerk in the store of Colonel Robie when young, and subsequently engaged in trade for himself in Gorham Village. He is a man of excellent business capacity, and by application and good management has built up a large trade, and is now in affluent circumstances. He has been the recipient of many honors bestowed by his townsmen; president of Gorham Bank, president of Gorham Seminary, selectman, representative, deacon of Congregational church, and has filled many other positions of trust in town and County. He is a Republican, and an outspoken advocate of the cause of temperance. Progressive and public-spirited, he is one of the foremost in all movements designed to bless his fellow-creatures, and exerts a wide and healthy influence in his community. His height is about six feet; his frame large and well-knit; his movements moderate, features regular, complexion fair, and his hair and beard now nearly white. In disposition thoughtful, serious, and straight-forward; kind of heart, courteous, graceful in his carriage, and at times conversational. He is sagacious, discriminating, far-seeing, and careful in all things. Since the death of his father he has owned the homestead farm in Hollis, now carried on by his nephew, Greenleaf Ridlon.

Dea. Jesse-Hopkinson Ridlon⁵ (1), third son of Joseph⁴ (1), was born in Hollis, Me., in 1818; married Sarah B. Hopkinson, of Limington, — his cousin, — and resided for many years in the northern part of that town. He learned the trade of carpenter and builder, and carried on farming at times. He moved to the city of Portland, and during his latter years was in the employ of Staples & Son, machinists, in their pattern-shop. He was many years a prominent member of the Calvinistic Baptist Church, and served in the office of deacon while resident in Portland. Mr. Ridlon was of medium height, round, compact build, and inclined to corpulency; his features regular, face oval, and complexion fair; hair and beard nearly white in later years. He was social, pleasant, and unassuming in manners; peaceful and honest in all his relations in life. He was in every sense a model, Christian gentleman, and was held in the highest esteem by all who knew him. He died in Portland in May, 1873, leaving a widow, by whom he had issue an only child long ago deceased.

Lieut. John-M. Ridlon⁵ (16), fourth son of Joseph⁴ (1), was born in Hollis, Me., May 16, 1822; married Sarah M. Phelps, of Oshkosh, Wis., and settled as a merchant at Lawrence, Mich. He carried on business in two stores at the same time, and was considered a successful trader, but he subsequently gave up merchandising and removed to other parts. His present place of residence (1884) is Lawrence, Mich. Mr. Ridlon was an officer in the Federal army during the war of the Rebellion, and proved a good soldier. He is quite tall, round, solid, and well porportioned; has black hair and beard, and in his features and facial expression resembled his brothers before mentioned; called a handsome man. He has issue *three* children, of whom hereafter.

Alpheus-G. Ridlon⁵ (1), fifth son of Joseph⁴ (1), was born in Hollis, Me., Jan. 8, 1822; married Sarah Stiles of Gorham, and has had issue *three* children, of whom hereafter. He has spent the most of his days on the railroad. Drove a locomotive on the Eastern Railroad between Boston and Portland, until he became a proficient engineer, then went West and found employment on the Baltimore & Ohio Railroad, which was under the management of New England men. He was thrown from a trestle-work with his locomotive, while running between Cincinnati and

Marietta, O., and sustained serious injuries; two limbs were fractured, his head badly cut, and his whole body bruised. He was so highly esteemed by the company in whose employ he was injured, that his pay was continued during his long illness, his expenses paid, and a valuable gold-watch was presented him, within the case of which is a beautifully composed inscription, which epitomizes his courage, fidelity, and disinterestedness as a man and engineer. On his recovery he was promoted to the position of conductor, and has filled that responsible station ever since, — a period of some twenty years, — to the entire satisfaction of the company, and with the highest approval of the traveling public. Mr. Ridlon has been a member of the Baptist Church from early life, and illustrates in his daily example the qualities of a true Christian. He is an excellent singer, and when in Maine was a member of the choir in the Freewill Baptist church at West Buxton. He has a fine residence at Norwood, O., about ten miles from the city of Cincinnati, and only a few rods from the railway-station. His house is situated some way back from the public street, and surrounded by beautiful grounds, ornamented with trees and shrubbery; here, with his pleasant family, he leads a quiet and happy life. His height is about five feet ten inches, shoulders broad, hair and beard nearly black, eyes hazel, features like his eldest brother, expression serious; in movement moderate, in disposition quiet, unobtrusive, and retiring. He is considered by all classes as an honest, straight-forward man.

Col. Nicholas Ridlon[5] **(3)**, only son of Robert[4] **(3)**, was born in Hollis, Me., April 18, 1815; married Mary F., daughter of John and Ruth (Blake) Rand, of Gorham, and is now (1883) living on the homestead farm where he was born. He early developed a military taste, became a commissioned officer in an independent company known as "Hollis Light Infantry," and ascended in the scale of promotions to lieutenant-colonel when a young man; he commanded a brigade, when about thirty years of age, at a general muster. Colonel Ridlon was a handsome, efficient, and respected soldier, and was held in the highest esteem by his command. His voice was clear and powerful, and could be heard at a great distance; he was equipped with splendor, was an expert rider, and when gracefully mounted upon a rampant horse he presented a grand and imposing appearance; indeed, he was as much at home in saddle, as a "Tartar of the Plains," always sitting erect, and apparently indifferent to the antic movements of his horse, the use of which, when hired, sometimes cost him ten dollars a day. He carried a sword formerly owned by Col. Joshua Emery, of Hollis, which he was always proud of; but, at the importunities of the descendants of its former owner, who desired to preserve it in their family as an heir-loom, he has sold it. Subsequent to his military career he became proprietor and landlord of a public house at North Hollis, known as the "Sweat Tavern" or "Brick Tavern," which he kept for many years, and sustained a larger patronage than any of his successors. Colonel Ridlon is about six feet in height, weighs one hundred and ninety pounds, has bald crown, sandy complexion, deeply-wrinkled face, and in features resembles the Cousens family, of which his mother and grandmother were members. He is genial, conversational, and enjoys company; has a fancy for a fine team of oxen, carries on a small farm, and

---

* The author feels under obligation to record his acknowledgments due Alpheus G. Ridlon, for his great kindness bestowed, while visiting the West, to collect data for this book, and especially for his devoted care and sacrificing attention to my needs, while sick at Webb's Prairie, Ill., — a kindness never-to-be-forgotten.

lives a peaceful, contented life. He embraced religion in 1876, and is a member of the Advent Church at Bonnie Eagle Village. No children.

Lydia Ridlon⁵ (6), only daughter of Robert⁴ (3), was born in Hollis, Me., June 24, 1818; was married Nov. 12, 1841 to John Sawyer, and has had *ten* children. She resembled her father, and was a kind-hearted, peaceful woman. She died at Rochester, N. H., Aug. 21, 1878.

Robert Ridlon⁵ (6), eldest son of Nicholas⁴ (1), was born in Hollis, Me., Sept. 20, 1820; married March 28, 1842, Susan, daughter of Peter and Sarah (Nason) Graffum, of Limington, and has lived on a farm in Standish, near Steep Falls, for many years. He is a carpenter and sash and blind maker by trade, and has worked much in the lumber-mills on Saco River during winters. He was the inventor of the first machine and concave circular-saw for cutting barrel and hogshead heading, but has realized but little money from its use. He embraced religion in 1843, and united with the Freewill Baptist Church. Mr. Ridlon is of medium height, has dark, curly hair and beard, gray eyes, and in features resembles the Hancock family. He is moderate, honest, peaceful, and respected. *Three* children.

Mary Ridlon⁵ (15), eldest daughter of Nicholas⁴ (1), was born in Hollis, Me., and died Dec. 7, 1824, aged 2 years and 6 months. Buried in "Old Ridlon Burying-ground."

Mary Ridlon⁵ (16), second daughter of Nicholas⁴ (1), was born in Hollis, Me., May 31, 1826; was married to Marshall McLucas, and has issue. Resides in Casco.

Priscilla Ridlon⁵ (3), third daughter of Nicholas⁴ (1), was born in Hollis, Me., April 20, 1829; was married to George Jones, of Casco, Cumberland County, and is now dead.

Isaac-H. Ridlon⁵ (6), second son of Nicholas⁴ (1), was born in Hollis, Me., Dec. 25, 1833; married May 16, 1857, Hannah J., daughter of James and Climelia (Lovejoy) Hobson, of Standish, and settled in Limington, near the village of Steep Falls; farmer by occupation. Has issue *five* children, of whom hereafter. Mr. Ridlon is tall, has black hair and beard, and is a free talker. Was in the army during the Rebellion, and receives a pension.

Etherlinda Ridlon⁵ (1), fourth daughter of Nicholas⁴ (1), was born in Hollis, Me., and died in Casco, Dec. 6, 1834, aged 2 years and 6 months. Buried in Hollis.

Hannah Ridlon⁵ (5), fifth daughter of Nicholas⁴ (1), was born in Hollis, Me. (presumed), May 20, 1840, and was married Feb. 14, 1858, to Cyrus Plummer, of Raymond, Cumberland County, where she now resides.

Etherlinda Ridlon⁵ (2), sixth daughter of Nicholas⁴ (1), was born in Casco, Me., Jan. 9, 1843; was married to Daniel Mann, of Casco, and lives in that town.

Susan Ridlon⁵ (4), only daughter of Magnus⁴ (6), was born in Hollis, Me.; was married to the Rev. Dudley Holt, a Methodist preacher, and, at last accounts, was living at Mechanics' Falls, Minot, Me.

Moses Ridlon⁵ (2), eldest son of Magnus⁴ (6), was born in Hollis, Me., and died when young.

James Ridlon⁵ (8), second son of Magnus⁴ (6), was born in Hollis, Me., in 1824, and was never married. He was an eccentric character from his childhood, and his humorous sayings will not soon be forgotten. He spent many winters in the backwoods of Maine and New Hampshire, "swamping roads" for the lumbermen, or acting as cook in their camps. In summer he worked on the farms of his relations, or went to the "Grand Banks" on board fishing-vessels. He almost always left his home or boarding-places unexpectedly; sometimes rising before daylight, and returning as unlooked-for after years of absence. He was several times supposed to be dead, but afterwards came back safe and sound. He enlisted in the Nineteenth Massachusetts Infantry, April 21, 1864, and was killed in battle only a few hours after he reached the army. It was only a few months before his enlistment that he was heard to say, "'Uncle Sam' must give me a very *strong invitation* (meaning a draft) before I shall enter the army." James was a noble-hearted, generous-souled man; honest, gentle, and harmless as a child. He was always watching for opportunities to do good, in cases of sickness was a ready helper, and was never a burden to any one. A welcome guest in the homes of his relatives, he kept all hearts cheerful, and being able to turn his hand to any kind of farm-work, always more than paid his way. Poor fellow! he has left a host of friends, who will never cease to remember his pleasant face and kind words. He was small, but well formed; had black hair and beard, hazel eyes, deeply-wrinkled face, and regular features of the family type.

Martha Ridlon (4), eldest daughter of Thomas (2), was born in Hollis, Me., Sept. 20, 1805; was married to John Ridlon,—her cousin,—and lived only a few rods from her father's house nearly all her days. She was a woman of great excellence, possessing every virtue that distinguishes the wife, mother, and Christian. She was the first to reach and last to leave the sick bed of her neighbors; always bestowing her sympathy upon the afflicted, and giving substantial blessings to the poor and destitute. Her mantle of charity was spread over the failings of others, and her great tenderness of heart would not admit of her speaking unkindly of any one. She was called "Aunt Martha" by old and young, relatives and acquaintances; and her loving words, gentle ministries, and pure life will not, cannot, be forgotten by any who came within the range of her heaven-born influence. She was long in feeble health, and endured her sufferings with remarkable patience and Christian fortitude. Departed to her rest on Jan. 21, 1878, aged 73 years (she had *four* children), and was buried in the village cemetery at Moderation Mills.

Joshua-Decker Ridlon (1), eldest son of Thomas (2), was born in Hollis, Me., April 4, 1807 (?), and died at the age of 18 years, unmarried. He was fond of hunting and trapping, and spent much of his time in the late autumn days in the woods; and only a few months before his death caught a large, brown eagle in his fox-trap. This bird measured nearly eight feet from tip to tip across the wings; all the aged people, with the superstition characteristic of those days, believed his death was in some way consequent upon his killing the eagle. Joshua was tall, erect, and well formed; had fair hair and complexion, and resembled the Decker family, from which he descended. He was kind of heart, noble in his bearing, and highly esteemed by a large circle of acquaintances. Buried in the "Old Ridlon Burying-ground," so called.

Judith Ridlon (4), second daughter of Thomas (2), was born in Hollis, Me., Sept. 18, 1809; was married to Joseph Decker,—her cousin, —April 25, 1833, and lived near the home of her father all her days. She was a woman of the most amiable and gentle disposition, always ready with heart and hand to bestow sympathy or substantial comforts upon the needy. She was many years in a feeble condition, but could forget her own sufferings in her efforts to alleviate those of others. She was a patient, gentle-spirited woman, and lived in peace with all the world. After a long and painful illness, endured in a calm frame of mind, and sustained by that divine arm in which she had learned in early life to trust, she passed away Aug? 17, 1862. No children.

Samuel Ridlon⁶ (4), second son of Thomas⁴ (2), was born in Hollis, Me., Feb. 28, 1815; married Hannah, fourth daughter of Gideon and Judith (Walker) Tibbetts, — she was born in Buxton, Aug. 18, 1819, and died in September, 1865, — and had issue *four* children, of whom hereafter. He being the only surviving son, remained at home with his parents, working on a farm until the decease of his wife, when he devoted himself mainly to carpenter-work and building. He was a capable man in several capacities; he moved buildings, laid stone-work, made farm-implements, surveyed lumber; he was a ready writer, and served as clerk of the church and fraternal organizations. His memory was retentive, habits studious, perceptions acute; he was always a reader and possessed a good fund of general and practical information. He was a good mathematician, but was unsystematic and without proper organization in his plans and work. He was a good farmer, so far as cultivation of the soil was concerned, but in consequence of carelessness and neglect of his farming-tools was not financially successful. In temperament passionate and impulsive, and sometimes swayed by prejudices, and an almost ungovernable temper. He was kind-hearted, generous to a fault, and remarkably unselfish in his dealings with others; in adverse circumstances naturally desponding and given to melancholy; nervous, superstitious, and imaginative, he was a strong believer in the supernatural. Strictly honest and confidential himself, he trusted everybody, and allowed them to take advantage of him in his business transactions, and frequently lost considerable sums of money, rather than press his demands. He was an active politician and advocate of the cause of temperance, and was always a promoter of education and all movements calculated to better the mental, moral, or civil condition of his fellowmen. He was pleasant, candid, concise as a public speaker, and always listened to with the most respectful attention. In personal appearance he resembled his father; full six feet in height, shoulders broad, arms very long, frame large and muscular, hair and beard black, eyes gray, brows outstanding, features regular, complexion ruddy. He died at the home of his eldest son in Saco, Nov. 14, 1880, and was buried in the family-lot in the village cemetery at Moderation Mills.

Thomas-B. Ridlon⁶ (6), eldest son of William⁴ (1), was born in Bridgton, Me., Jan. 1, 1814; married Harriet Ingalls, and settled in his native town as a farmer. He owns one of the best orchards in Cumberland County. Many of his winters have been spent driving ox-teams in the logging-swamps of Maine and New Hampshire. He is below the medium height, but broad-shouldered and compact of build; hair and beard black and inclined to curl; eyes gray and small, face florid, expression pleasant. In temperament quick, impulsive, and radical; is sarcastic, jovial, and companionable; fears nothing that walks the earth. His wife, who died many years ago, was the mother of *twelve* children. He married a second wife, but is now living with a daughter on his old homestead.

Robert-Martin Ridlon⁶ (7), second son of William⁴ (1), was born in

Bridgton, Me., May 27, 1816; married Pelina Chase, and settled upon a small, rocky farm in his native town. He emigrated to Berlin, Wis., many, years ago, and continued there until within a few years; when last heard from he was living at, or near, Juniata, Neb., on a farm. Mr. Ridlon is tall, and when young was erect and handsome of form; his hair black, eyes dark, features resemble his father's. His temperament is impulsive, his movements quick, and his expression emphatic. Genèrous and kind-hearted. He embraced religion when a young man, and maintained an exemplary and consistent Christian deportment during his residence in Maine. *Nine* children, of whom hereafter.

John-Mills Ridlon⁵ (17), third son of William⁴ (1), was born in Bridgton, Me., Dec. 10, 1819; married Martha, daughter of David and Eunice (Ridlon) Martin, — his cousin, — and settled in Sebago, where he continued several years. He subsequently removed to Hollis, York County, built a house near the homestead of his father-in-law, and has carried on a small farm ever since. He is of medium height and size, has jet-black hair and beard, small, gray eyes, florid complexion, and regular features; crown bald, brows thick and outstanding, temperament nervous, movements quick. A great talker. Many years a member of the church. A kind-hearted man and good neighbor. No children.

William Ridlon⁵ (6), fourth son of William⁴ (1), was born in Bridgton, Me., 1821, and died young, unmarried.

William Ridlon⁵ (7), fifth son of William⁴ (1), was born in Bridgton, Me., Nov. 22, 1823, and died Nov. 2, 1845, unmarried. He was a pleasant, gentle-spirited young man, beloved by all, and passed away in the triumphs of Christian faith.

Margaret Ridlon⁵ (1), eldest daughter of William⁴ (1), was born in Bridgton, Me., Feb. 4, 1826; was married to Josiah Stone, and lived several years in Lewiston, where he had a shoe-manufactory. They many years ago emigrated to California, and she is now living there (1882), a widow; her residence is at Iowa Hill, Placer County. No children.

Osborn-G. Ridlon⁵ (1), sixth son of William⁴ (1), was born in Bridgton, Me., Feb. 15, 1828; married Lucretia Day, and settled in Naples, in the "Chaplin Neighborhood," so called. He was adopted by the Chaplin family when an infant, and is now known by that surname. He is a farmer and lumberman; of medium height, shoulders broad, hair and beard jet-black, complexion dark. Has several children, of whom hereafter.

Isabella-S. Ridlon⁵ (1), second daughter of William⁴ (1), was born in Bridgton, Me., May 6, 1829; was married to Thomas Lakin, of Harrison, and has a large family. She has been a faithful wife and mother, always manifesting the deepest interest in her children.

Lydia-Ann Ridlon⁵ (7), third daughter of William⁴ (1), was born in Bridgton, Me., Feb. 24, 1832; was married to George Payne, of Sebago, but went West many years ago.

Mary Ridlon⁵ (17), fourth daughter of William⁴ (1), was born in Bridgton, Me., Aug. 4, 1834, and died young, unmarried.

Harriet Ridlon⁵ (2), fifth daughter of William⁴ (1), was born in Bridgton, Me., March 2, 1839; was married to David Jumper, and had *one* son. Lived many years in Casco.

Matilda Ridlon⁵ (1), sixth daughter of William⁴ (1), was born in Bridgton (or Sebago), Me., July 10, 1843; was married to Levi Kenniston, and lived at home with her parents, in Sebago. Mrs. Kenniston died some years ago. She had children.

Mary Ridlon[5] (18), eldest daughter of Matthias[4] (3), was born in Hollis, Me., Dec. 27, 1818, and died Aug. 28, 1825.

Martha Ridlon[5] (5), second daughter of Matthias[4] (3), was born in Eaton, N. H., July 6, 1820; was married to Zachariah Gammon, had issue, and died Jan. 26, 1843.

Sarah-Ann Ridlon[5] (7), third daughter of Matthias[4] (3), was born in Eaton, N. H., April 10, 1822, and died in Sweden, Me., Oct. 22, 1842.

Hannah Ridlon[5] (6), fourth daughter of Matthias[4] (3), was born in Eaton, N. H., May 19, 1823; was married to R. B. Morrison, of Sweden, Me., and died in December, 1848.

Thomas-E. Ridlon[5] (7), eldest son of Matthias[4] (3), was born in Hollis, Me., Feb. 27, 1825; married Philinda D., eldest daughter of John and Martha (Ridlon) Ridlon, of Hollis, in 1848, and has lived in Hollis, Sweden, Bridgton, and Alfred. He built a house and lived on a farm near his father for many years. He is a cooper by trade, very ingenious, and has followed that business and farming all his life. His first wife died in August, 1872, and he married, secondly, Ada Littlefield, of Alfred, where he now (1883) lives. He is an industrious, hard-working, honest man; steady in his habits, inoffensive and accommodating as a neighbor. About six feet in height, raw-boned, muscular, quick-motioned, and impulsive; has light hair and beard, and florid complexion. He has had issue *nine* children, all by his first wife, of whom hereafter.

William Ridlon[5] (8), second son of Matthias[4] (3), was born in Hollis, Me., Oct. 22, 1826; married Hannah E., daughter of George and Hannah (Douglas) Wentworth, of Sweden (she was born Oct. 10, 1832), Feb. 1, 1862, and has *two* children, of whom hereafter. He has always lived on the homestead with his parents, working on the farm in summer, and lumbering or coopering in winter. He is tall, broad-shouldered, and very powerfully built; indeed few men are his equal in physical strength. Hair and beard formerly jet-black, features of the old Ridlon mould, complexion ruddy. Naturally quiet and sedate; strictly honest, straight-forward, and reliable; highly esteemed in his town.

Samuel Ridlon[5] (5), third son of Matthias[4] (3), was born in Hollis, Me., Jan. 1, 1828, went to New York in 1843, and died at the residence of Lawrence Beard, in March, 1850. His father hastened to New York immediately on learning of his illness, but too late to see him alive. He was a very pure-minded, amiable young man; deeply lamented.

Edmond-P. Ridlon[5] (2), fourth son of Matthias[4] (3), was born in Hollis, Me., April 9, 1830, and died April 14, 1831.

Philena Ridlon[5] (1), fifth daughter of Matthias[4] (3), was born in Hollis, Me. (presumably), Jan. 26, 1832, and died Sept. 19, 1838.

Sabra Ridlon[5] (1), sixth daughter of Matthias[4] (3), was born in Sweden, Me., Feb. 2, 1834; was married to Robert Locklin, and has issue. Resides near her father in Sweden.

Albert Ridlon[5] (1), fifth son of Matthias[4] (3), was born in Sweden, Me., March 23, 1837, and died March 21, 1862, while away from home, where he had been at work as cooper. He was a young man of excellent principles and deportment, and was beloved by a large circle of acquaintances. He was well formed, and had fair hair and complexion.

Elizabeth Ridlon[5] (6), seventh daughter of Matthias[4] (3), was born in Sweden, Me., Jan. 1, 1840, and died April 22, 1848.

Benjamin Ridlon[5] (4), sixth son of Matthias[4] (3), was born in Sweden, Me., May 10, 1841, and died July 10, 1842.

43

Stephen Ridlon⁵ (2), seventh son of Matthias⁴ (3), was born in Sweden, Me., May 2, 1843; married and settled near his father's home, in his native town. He is tall, slender, light-complexioned, moderate in his movements, and unassuming in his manners. Farmer and cooper. He has *five* children (probably more), of whom hereafter.

Daniel-Decker Ridlon⁵ (6), eldest son of Samuel⁴ (2), was born in Cornish, Me., May 5, 1818; married Olive T. Stacy, July 12, 1840, and settled in Porter, Oxford County. His first wife died soon after their marriage, and he married, secondly, Dec. 6, 1845, Mary A. Fox. Has *ten* children, of whom hereafter. He kept a store at Cornish Village, in early life, but subsequently settled upon a large farm; has served as deputy-sheriff and selectman; deals extensively in lumber and live-stock. He is a good financier, sagacious, far-seeing, cautious, considerate, perceptive, and energetic. His mind is of a discriminating cast, his judgment generally correct. He is conversational, sarcastic, and mirthful, developing many traits closely resembling his namesake, Daniel Decker, of Hollis. He has been quite successful in business, and acquired a good property. Kind-hearted and benevolent, he ministers of his means to assist the poor and needy. He is a man of public spirit, and manifests a deep interest in matters of polity. A great reader and profound thinker, he has acquired a fund of practical information, which, supplementing his good natural ability, qualifies him to act in almost any responsible capacity, making him a very useful citizen and neighbor. He is sedate and sometimes appears cold, distant, and stern, but a warmer heart than his never beat in human breast. In personal appearance he shows the characteristics of the Ridlons and Stanleys; tall and well formed, compact and inclined to corpulency, nervous and muscular, and so strong that he has never found his equal as a wrestler. His hair and beard were originally dark, but now almost white, his eyes gray, features regular, and his upper lip long and thick.

Thomas Ridlon⁵ (8), second son of Samuel⁴ (2), was born in Cornish, Me., in 1820; married Ruth Mason, March 5, 1840, and died June 27, 1858. He was a cooper and farmer, and lived near the homestead of his father, in Hiram, Oxford County, Me. He worked very hard until his health failed; probably overwork hastened his death. He was tall, broad-shouldered, muscular, and possessed of great physical endurance; hair dark-brown, beard brown, eyes hazel, forehead broad, full, and high, features regular, expression pleasant. Mr. Ridlon was honest, kind-hearted, social; all his excellent traits, supplemented by the graces of religion, made him a useful citizen, good neighbor, husband, and father. Had issue *six* children, of whom hereafter.

William Ridlon⁵ (8), third son of Samuel⁴ (2), was born in Hiram, Me., March 20, 1822, and died in April, 1840.

Susan Ridlon⁵ (5), eldest daughter of Samuel⁴ (2), was born in Hiram, Me., Feb. 7, 1824; was married in May, 1842, to Jacob Nason (eldest son of David and Betsey (Ridlon) Nason), her cousin, and left issue. Died in 1846.

Sarah Ridlon⁵ (7), second daughter of Samuel⁴ (2), was born in Hiram, Me., Jan. 10, 1826; was married, May 7, 1848, to John Merryfield, and lived on a farm in her native town. Her husband was killed in a mill, at Kezar Falls Village, in 1874, and left issue. She was married,

"PINE GROVE COTTAGE"
RESIDENCE OF SAMUEL RIDLON,
Kezar Falls Village, Maine.

secondly, to Stephen Martin, of Parsonfield, but he died in 1884, and she is now a widow.

Olive Ridlon[5] (4), third daughter of Samuel[4] (2), was born in Hiram, Me., Dec. 1, 1827; was married in December, 1846, to Moses Fox, and resides in Porter, Me. Has had a large family.

William Ridlon[5] (9), fourth son of Samuel[4] (2), was born in Hiram, Me., in 1829, and died May 22, 1830.

Polly Ridlon[5] (6), fourth daughter of Samuel[4] (2), was born in Hiram, Me., Feb. 24, 1831; was married, in 1854, to Jeremiah Merryfield (brother of John before mentioned), and lived many years on a farm in Parsonfield. Her husband sold his farm, and now owns mills and a beautiful residence at Kezar Falls Village, where they reside. She has children and grandchildren.

Martha Ridlon[5] (6), fifth daughter of Samuel[4] (2), was born in Hiram, Me., April 21, 1833; was married, in July, 1868, to Sewell Gillpatrick, farmer, and lives at Kezar Falls Village. She has children.

Jacob Ridlon[5] (5), fifth son of Samuel[4] (2), was born in Hiram, Me., June 25, 1835; married Mehitable Cole, of Hiram, in October, 1855, and has lived on the homestead farm with his aged parents. He formerly lived on the farm previously owned by his brother Thomas. Works at the trade of stone-mason. Mr. Ridlon is tall, raw-boned, square-shouldered, and muscular, but somewhat bowed over by hard work. His hair and beard are jet-black and curly, and his complexion dark. He is good-natured, social, conversational, and an entertaining companion. Member of the Methodist Church. Honest, peaceful, and highly respected. Has had issue *eight* children, of whom hereafter.

Samuel Ridlon[5] (6), sixth son of Samuel[4] (2), was born in Hiram, Me., Aug. 31, 1837; married Sarah L. Chapman, April 5,.1859, and lived for several years on the homestead farm; he subsequently removed to Kezar Falls Village, where he erected a fine stand of buildings, and engaged in lumbering, merchandising, and general speculation. He carried on an extensive and successful business, employing many men, until 1874, when he was seized with paralysis, which deprived him of the power of speech and incapacitated him for any active employment. He had acquired a handsome property, consisting largely of real estate, and is now in good circumstances. Mr. Ridlon was a man of excellent business capacity, enterprising, progressive, far-seeing, and correct in judgment. He served as selectman and in other responsible positions. He was a reliable man in every relation of life. His business energy gave a new impetus to the village in which he lived, and when he was compelled to close his mills and shops the loss was felt by all classes. He was long an active member of the Methodist Church. His height medium, form round and portly, complexion light, eyes gray; his temperament nervous, movements quick. Conversational, jovial, and kind-hearted. He has had issue *three* children, of whom hereafter.

Narcissa-Jane Ridlon[5] (1), sixth daughter of Samuel[4] (2), was born in Hiram, Me., Dec. 10, 1840; was married in November, 1858, to William Chapman, of Porter, and has lived many years at Kezar Falls Village, where her husband carries on the shoe and harness business. She has issue.

Abbie Ridlon[5] (1), youngest daughter of Samuel[4] (2), was born in Hiram, Me., Dec. 14, 1841; was married to James Chapman, Oct. 28, 1858, and has issue. She has lived on a farm, but now resides at Kezar Falls Village.

Lewis Ridlon[5] (2), youngest son of Samuel[4] (2), was born in Hiram, Me., Nov. 25, 1844, and died Sept. 14, 1846.

Benjamin Redley[5] (5), eldest son of John[4] (7), was born in Loveland, Licking County, O., June 28, 1825; married Angeline, daughter of Harrison Knight, May 15, 1851 (she was born in Logan County, O., March 30, 1834), and resides on a farm near Marion, Ind. He is of medium height, has broad shoulders, and compact frame. He does not resemble the New England Ridlons in features of face. He has had issue *eleven* children, of whom hereafter.

Andrew Redley[5] (1), second son of John[4] (7), was born in Loveland, O., and died young, unmarried.

Alanson Redley[5] (1), third son of John[4] (7), was born in Loveland, O., and died young, unmarried.

Matthias Redley[5] (6), fourth son of John[4] (7), was born in Loveland, O., Feb. 16, 1834; married Mary Elizabeth Hendrickson, Aug. 2, 1855 (she was born Sept. 1, 1838), and lived some time at Sweetwater, Ill. In 1876 he was at Middleton, Logan County, Ill. Farmer. Has *two* children, of whom hereafter. He is tall and slender.

Esther Redley[5] (1), eldest daughter of John[4] (7), was born in Loveland, Licking County, O.; was married to Isaac Hardin, and lives in Waynesfield, Auglaize County, on the farm formerly owned by her father. She has issue.

Barbara Redley[5] (1), second daughter of John[4] (7), was born in Loveland, Licking County, O.; was married to —— Blair; and secondly, to —— Winegardner. She lives on a farm in Waynesfield, Auglaize County, O., and has issue.

Mary Redley[5] (19), third daughter of John[4] (7), was born in Loveland, Licking County, O.; was married to —— Morris, and resides in Hampshire, Auglaize County, O.

Sarah Redley[5] (8), fourth daughter of John[4] (7), was born in Loveland, Licking County, O.; was married to —— Bailey, and resides at Crystal, Montcalm County, Mich.

Abigail Redley[5] (3), fifth daughter of John[4] (7), was born in Loveland, Licking County, O.; was married to Perry Hardin, and lives on a farm in Waynesfield, Auglaize County, O.

Eliza Redley[5] (4), sixth daughter of John[4] (7), was born in Waynesfield, Auglaize County, O.; was married to —— Huffer, and lived on a farm near her birthplace in 1876.

Amanda Redley[5] (2), seventh daughter of John[4] (7), was born in Waynesfield, Auglaize County, O.; was married to Joshua Montague, and died in her native town many years ago.

Judith Redley[5] (5), eighth daughter of John[4] (7), was born in Waynesfield, Auglaize County, O.; was married to —— Winegardner, and lives in her native town.*

Stephen Ridlen[5] (3), eldest son of Timothy[4] (1), was born in Clearmont County, O., Oct. 11, 1811; married Aug. 9, 1831, and carried on a farm near St. Paul, Ind., and kept a store in the town. He was a large, corpulent man, jovial, plain-spoken, and endowed with a full share of

* I have not been able to procure full dates in this family. — *Author.*

"Ridlon oddity." Had issue *eight* children, of whom hereafter. Died in February, 1881.

Ebenezer Ridlen⁵ (5), second son of Timothy⁴ (1), was born in Clearmont County, O., July 3, 1813, and is a farmer living in Knoxville, Iowa. He has *four* children, of whom hereafter.

Miriam Ridlen⁵ (1), eldest daughter of Timothy⁴ (1), was born in Clearmont County, O., Nov. 24, 1815, and died in 1864.

Sarah Ridlen⁵ (9), second daughter of Timothy⁴ (1), was born in Clearmont County, O., Oct. 7, 1817; and was married to —— Steaves, or Stevens. Residence unknown.

William Ridlen⁵ (10), third son of Timothy⁴ (1), was born in Clearmont County, O., in 1819; married Malinda ——, and has issue *six* children, of whom hereafter. He lives on a farm in Bellefountain, Ia. Is of medium height and weight.

Joseph-Wright Ridlen⁵ (5), fourth son of Timothy⁴ (1), was born in Clearmont County, O., Feb. 17, 1822; married Matilda J. Henry, June 17, 1849; she died Nov. 17, 1859, and he married, secondly, the following spring, Julia M. Devore. He carries on a farm in Liberty township, Marion County, Ia. Medium height and build. No issue.

Samuel Ridlen⁵ (7), fifth son of Timothy⁴ (1), was born Jan. 22, 1824; married Elizabeth ——, and secondly, Elizabeth Susan —— (the former was born Dec. 15, 1828, and died Feb. 14, 1851; the latter was born Oct. 26, 1836), and has had issue *ten* children, of whom hereafter. He resides on a farm in Marion County, Ia. Six feet in height, weighs 150 pounds, is raw-boned and muscular, has prominent features, and does not resemble the old Ridlon stock in features of face.

Harriet Ridlen⁵ (3), third daughter of Timothy⁴ (1), was born in Ohio (presumably), March 22, 1826, and was married to —— Gregory.

John Ridlen⁵ (18), sixth son of Timothy⁴ (1), was born in Ohio (presumably), May 2, 1828, and died March 26, 1855.

Eley Ridlen⁵ (1), fourth daughter of Timothy⁴ (1), was born in Ohio or Indiana, Jan. 14, 1830, and was married to —— Aspaugh.

Ruth Ridlen⁵ (4), youngest daughter of Timothy⁴ (1), was born in Ohio or Indiana, June 13, 1835, and was married to —— Way.

Cynthia-A. Ridlen⁵ (1), eldest daughter of Stephen⁴ (1), was born in Clearmont County, O., Jan. 19, 1815; was married to Henry, son of John Brooks, Aug. 11, 1831, and lives at Willow Hill, Ill., near her brothers. She has issue.

Lydia Ridlen⁵ (8), second daughter of Stephen⁴ (1), was born in Clearmont County, O., in 1818; was married to —— Badaker, of German descent, and lives at Adams, Ind. A very large woman, of excellent character.

John-S. Ridlen⁵ (19), eldest son of Stephen⁴ (1), was born in Clearmont County, O., March 8, 1820; married Oct. 25, 1849, to Mary, daughter of Abel and Mary (Ashren) Bennett, of Indiana, and has had issue *seven* children, of whom hereafter. He is a farmer by occupation.

Ruth Ridlen⁵ (5), third daughter of Stephen⁴ (1), was born in Clearmont County, O., Jan. 29, 1822; was married Aug. 27, 1846, to Lemuel B. Todd, of Kentucky, and has issue.

Abraham Ridlen⁵ (6), second son of Stephen⁴ (1), was born in Clearmont County, O., Nov. 18, 1823; married Sept. 24, 1846, America Gosnell, of Kentucky, and has had issue *six* children, of whom hereafter. He resides at Willow Hill, Ill.   Farmer and stock-raiser.

James-B. Ridlen[5] (9), third son of Stephen[4] (1), was born in Decatur County, Ind., Jan. 26, 1826; married Aug. 22, 1852, Sarah A., second daughter of Ann and John Hamilton, of Decatur County, and had issue *ten* children, of whom hereafter.   He is a farmer; moderate in movement, medium height and weight; has dark hair, sandy beard, gray eyes ; is industrious and honest.   Resides at Willow Hill, Jasper County, Ill.

Stephen-T. Ridlen[5] (4), fourth son of Stephen[4] (1), was born in Decatur County, Ind., June 19, 1829; and died in Jasper County, Ill. (probably at Willow Hill), Nov. 4, 1853; was a farmer; medium height; had dark hair.

Talbut Ridlen[5] (1), fifth son of Stephen[4] (1), was born in Decatur County, Ind., May 21, 1834; married Sept. 6, 1855, Polly A., daughter of Daniel and Isabella Doty, and has issue *eight* children, of whom hereafter. Mr. Ridlen is a blacksmith and farmer; of medium size, round-shouldered, hair and beard sandy.   Industrious and honest.   Resides at Willow Hill, Jasper County, Ill.

Lucinda Ridlen[5] (1), eldest daughter of Samuel[4] (3), was born in Ohio, — probably in Clearmont County, — May 16, 1814, and died when young, unmarried.

Patience Ridlen[5] (6), second daughter of Samuel[4] (3), was born in Clearmont County (?), O., Aug. 26, 1816, and died young, unmarried.

Elizabeth Ridlen[5] (7), third daughter of Samuel[4] (3), was born in Clearmont County (?), O., Aug. 26, 1816; was married to Brooks Ross, Sept. 25, 1836, and lives at Cincinnati.

Prudence Ridlen[5] (1), fourth daughter of Samuel[4] (3), was born in Clearmont County (?), O., Nov. 20, 1818; was married to Howell Mulford, Nov. 20, 1850, and lives at St. Louis, Mo.

Nancy Ridlen[5] (3), fifth daughter of Samuel[4] (3), was born in Clearmont County (?), O., Nov. 20, 1818, and died young.

Jane-Duncan Ridlen[5] (5), sixth daughter of Samuel[4] (3), was born in Clearmont County (?), O., Dec. 31, 1820; was married Dec. 25, 1856, to Walter S. Aiken, and resides at Benton, Ill.   Has issue.

Martha-Ann Ridlen[5] (7), seventh daughter of Samuel[4] (3), was born in Ohio, Jan. 24, 1824; died unmarried.

Sarah-Ann Ridlen[5] (10), eighth daughter of Samuel[4] (3), was born in Ohio, June 10, 1826; was married Nov. 7, 1853, to Josiah Alexander, and resides at Webb's Prairie, Ill.

Samuel-Davis Ridlen[5] (8), only son of Samuel[4] (3), was born in Ohio, Sept. 28, 1832; married Margaret A. Beard, of North Carolina, and settled at Memphis, Tenn.   Carpenter by trade.   He entered the Confederate army during the war of the Rebellion, was taken prisoner by the Union army, and carried to Chicago, Ill., where he was exchanged.   He owned property in the South before the war, but lost it all.   After the war he went to Webb's Prairie, Ill., and settled on his father's farm, where he continued till his death, which occurred June 5, 1876.   He had issue *four* children, of whom hereafter.   Mr. Ridlen was of medium height, had broad shoulders, compact, well-formed body, light complexion, hair and beard ; the latter was long and heavy.   He was a genial, kind-hearted, well-read man, and was greatly beloved by his family.

Elmira Ridlen[6] (2), eldest daughter of Abraham[4] (4), was born in Illinois, June 8, 1824; was married Oct. 3, 1838, to Hugh Christia, and secondly, to —— Gauf. She died in Crawford County, Ark., in 1854, leaving children.

Lorender Ridlen[6] (1), second daughter of Abraham[4] (4), was born in Illinois, May 15, 1826; was married Oct. 3, 1868, to George W. West, of Douglas County, and is now (1881) living at Neosho, Mo.

Leander Ridlen[6] (1), eldest son of Abraham[4] (4), was born in Illinois, Sept. 12, 1828; married Julia Carter in 1847, and died in Caldwell County, Tex., Jan. 9, 1854, leaving issue *one* child, whose name is unknown.

George-W. Ridlen[6] (2), second son of Abraham[4] (4), was born in Illinois, Aug. 31, 1831; was married in 1853 to Lucien Lowe, and died in Decatur County, Ind., Dec. 23, 1855, leaving *one* child, whose name is not known.

Lafayette Ridlen[6] (1), third son of Abraham[4] (4), was born in Illinois, Oct. 30, 1834, and died unmarried Oct. 6, 1864, in Douglas County, in his native State.

Alexander-M. Ridlen[6] (2), fourth son of Abraham[4] (4), was born in Illinois, — by second wife, — Sept. 7, 1854, and is now (1881) in Neosho County, Kan.

Bettie Ridlen[6] (7), third daughter of Abraham[4] (4), was born in Illinois, Oct. 4, 1857, and died Oct. 21, 1859, in Shelby County, Ind.

Ella Ridlen[6] (1), third daughter of Abraham[4] (4), was born in Illinois, April 17, 1860, and in 1881 was living with her half-sister, Mrs. West, in Neosho, Mo., unmarried.

John-Wesley Ridlen[6] (20), eldest son of John[4] (6), was born in Little York, Ind., Oct. 17, 1829; married Maria Newbury, Oct. 24, 1850, and has issue *nine* children, of whom hereafter. Mr. Ridlen is a farmer and cooper by occupation. Resides at Little York. He says, "The Ridlens of the West are a fine-feeling people." He was orderly sergeant in the Sixty-sixth Regiment Indiana Volunteer Infantry, in the Union army during the war of the Rebellion. He does not resemble the Ridlons of New England.

George Ridlen[6] (3), second son of John[4] (6), was born in Little York, Ind., Oct. 2, 1831; married Sarah E. Hobson, Aug. 20, 1851, and had issue *two* children, who died in infancy. He married, secondly, Rosine Lester, and by her had *three* children, of whom hereafter. He was lieutenant in the Twenty-second Indiana Regiment, Volunteer Infantry, of the Union army, in the war of the Rebellion, and was killed during the engagement at Perrysville, Ky., Oct. 8, 1862, by a "minie-ball passing through his breast." He was a tall, stately young officer, and fell while bravely leading his command.

Elizabeth Ridlen[6] (8), eldest daughter of John[4] (6), was born in Little York, Ind., March 16, 1834; was married to Alfred Morris, and died June 10, 1861.

James Ridlen[6] (10), third son of John[4] (6), was born in Little York, Ind., Jan. 1, 1837, and died Nov. 14, 1852.

Samuel Ridlen[6] (9), fourth son of John[4] (6), was born in Little York, Ind., March 8, 1839; married Emeline Sullivan, and had issue (1876) *five* children, of whom hereafter. He is a cooper, living in his native town. Tall, slender, and with sharp, prominent features, he resembles the family of Tibbetts — his maternal ancestors — more than Ridlons.

Theodore Ridlen[5] **(1)**, fifth son of John[4] **(6)**, was born in Little York, Ind., July 25, 1842; married Nancy Montgomery, and had issue (1873) *two* children, of whom hereafter. He was a soldier in the Twenty-second Regiment Indiana Volunteers, of the Union army during the Rebellion. Now a resident of Seymour, Jackson County, Ind.

Pamelia-Margaret Ridlen[5] **(1)**, second daughter of John[4] **(6)**, was born in Little York, Ind., July 22, 1844; married Jesse-Lee Hobson, and lives in her native town.

Mary-Ellen Ridlen[5] **(20)**, third daughter of John[4] **(6)**, was born in Little York, Ind., Sept. 8, 1846; was married to Michael Jones, and lives in her native town.

Sarah-Louisa Ridlen[5] **(11)**, fourth daughter of John[4] **(6)**, was born in Little York, Ind., July 9, 1848; was married to Hamilton Scutchback, and resides at Caruthersville, Mo.

Nelson-F. Ridlen[5] **(1)**, sixth son of John[4] **(6)**, was born in Little York, Ind., Feb. 24, 1851; married Josephine Johnson, and has issue. Resides in his native town.

George-Robertson Ridlen[5] **(14)**, eldest son of Nicholas[4] **(2)**, was born in Indiana, July 23, 1829; married Edna Gray, July 13, 1848, and has issue, of whom hereafter. He lives at Fountaintown, Shelby County, Ind., where he carries on a farm. He is a broad-shouldered, heavy-built man, and has the mould of features so common in the Ridlon family.

Phebe Ridlen[5] **(1)**, eldest daughter of Nicholas[4] **(2)**, was born in Indiana, April 30, 1831; was married Jan. 5, 1854, to Havens Gray, and lives near Fountaintown, Ind.

Herman Ridlen[5] **(1)**, second son of Nicholas[4] **(2)**, was born in Indiana, March 7, 1833; married Maria L. Duncan, Jan. 5, 1854, and has issue *six* children (1878), of whom hereafter. He owns a steam saw-mill. Was a soldier in the Fifth Indiana Regiment, Volunteer Cavalry, during the war of the Rebellion.

Abraham-R. Ridlen[5] **(7)**, third son of Nicholas[4] **(2)**, was born in Indiana, Oct. 15, 1835; married Rebecca Williams, Dec. 8, 1864, and has issue, of whom hereafter. Mr. Ridlen is a farmer at Fountaintown, Ind.

Stephen-R. Ridlen[5] **(5)**, fourth son of Nicholas[4] **(2)**, was born in Indiana, April 5, 1837; married Laura Cobble (she died Feb. 28, 1860), Dec. 20, 1857, by whom he had *two* children. He married, secondly, Amanda Saward (?), by whom he had (1880) *three* children. Mr. Ridlen resides at Fountaintown, Ind.   Farmer.

Patience Ridlen[5] **(7)**, second daughter of Nicholas[4] **(2)**, was born in Indiana, May 13, 1839; was married Jan. 8, 1860, to Joel I. Gunn, and lives at Fountaintown, Ind.

Mary-Ann Ridlen[5] **(21)**, third daughter of Nicholas[4] **(2)**, was born in Indiana, Aug. 28, 1842; was married Sept. 26, 1858, to John Copeland. Resides at Fountaintown, Ind.

Nelson Ridlen[5] **(2)**, fifth son of Nicholas[4] **(2)**, was born in Indiana, June 18, 1846, and died Nov. 23, 1863.

Jacob-R. Ridlon[5] **(6)**, eldest son of Joseph[4] **(2)**, was born in Buxton, Me. (presumably), Oct. 25, 1822; married, and settled on a farm in Sebago, Cumberland County, where he lived many years; he subsequently removed to the town of Naples, in the same County, where he now (1883) resides. He is below the medium height, has dark complexion, and a peculiar expression about the eyes. He is a quiet, peaceful, industrious, and honest man. Had issue *six* children, of whom hereafter.

Joseph Ridlon[5] (6), second son of Joseph[4] (2), was (presumably) born in Buxton, Me., June 7, 1824, and died when young and unmarried.

Joseph Ridlon[5] (7), eldest son of Isaac[4] (3), was born in Baldwin, Cumberland County, Me., April 25, 1829; married Abbie R., daughter of Robert Hayes, of Eaton, N. H., March 25, 1853, and had issue *six* children, of whom hereafter. He became lame in early life, and manufactured clock-reels and butter-stamps; and by the practice of economy and close attention to business, he rose from small beginnings to a peddler of dry-goods and "Yankee notions," and acquired a handsome property. He was widely known as an honest, straight-forward business man. He was a man of sound judgment, cautious, far-seeing, and shrewd in his business operations. He was rather tall (some say below the medium), well formed, and sprightly; had black hair and beard, and a pleasant expression of face. He traded several years in Parsonfield, York County, but removed to his farm in Baldwin, and died in that town Oct. 17, 1872; was buried with Masonic ceremonies. His widow was living in 1881, with her children.

Isaac-H. Ridlon[5] (7), second son of Isaac[4] (3), was born in Baldwin, Me. (say in 1831); married Marona Cook, and settled on a farm in his native town. Had issue *two* children, of whom hereafter. Is said to have resembled his father's family. Died many years ago, leaving a widow, who subsequently became the wife of William Hancock (an uncle of her first husband), of Limerick, who deceased in 1879, and left her again a widow. She was living on the old Hancock farm, in Limerick, in 1881.

Martha Ridlon[5] (8), eldest daughter of Isaac[4] (3), was born in Baldwin, Me., Nov. 25, 1832; was married to Andrew J. Robinson, of Sebago, and deceased, leaving issue.

Mary Ridlon[5] (22), second daughter of Isaac[4] (3), was born in Baldwin, Me., Dec. 22, 1834. Deceased.

Betsey Ridlon[5] (8), third daughter of Isaac[4] (3), was born in Baldwin, Me., Nov. 18, 1836. Deceased.

Harriet Ridlon[5] (4), fourth daughter of Isaac[4] (3), was born in Baldwin, Me., April 29, 1839; was married to Josiah Milliken, and resides in her native town.

Daniel Ridlon[5] (8), eldest son of Daniel[4] (4), was born in Limerick, Me., Jan. 28, 1801, and married Ellen Kennell, by whom he had issue *five* children, of whom hereafter. He married, secondly, July 5, 1835, Esther Wales (she was born Jan. 11, 1811), and by her had *eight* children, of whom hereafter. He followed the sea in early life, and settled, first, in Standish, Me., but subsequently, after his second marriage, removed to Porter and settled on a farm, where he continued the remainder of his life. Mr. Ridlon was a small man of nervous temperament; he had the type of features characteristic of the early Ridlons, and was possessed of their peculiar eccentricities. Spent his last days with his daughter. Drew a pension for a son who died in the army. Died Aug. 29, 1881, aged 80.

Eunice Ridlon[5] (4), eldest daughter of Daniel[4] (4), was born in Limerick, Me. No other information.

Benjamin Ridlon[5] (6), second son of Daniel[4] (4), was born in Limerick, Me., and died young, unmarried.

682	RIDLONS OF PORTER, MAINE.

Comfort Ridlon⁵ (1), second daughter of Daniel⁴ (4), was born in Limerick, Me. Deceased; no other information.

Stephen Ridlon⁵ (6), third son of Daniel⁴ (4), was born in Limerick, Me., April 21, 1811; married Miriam, daughter of John and Miriam (Day) Wales,* Dec. 25, 1831, and has had issue *seven* children, of whom hereafter. He settled on a farm in Porter, Oxford County, where he lived several years, but subsequently removed to Hiram, in the same County, where he has continued till the present time. Mr. Ridlon is below the medium height, broad-shouldered, and compactly built; his neck is short and thick, his features of the Scottish type, and his crown high and bald. He is a characteristic Ridlon of the old stamp in every respect. He is eccentric, nervous, and high-tempered. Can tell big stories about his own feats of strength. Lives among the mountains in a remote, desolate part of his town, upon a hard, rocky farm. Has been a great woodsman; fears nothing. A professor of religion, and has meetings at his house. Is now (1880) a hale, well-preserved man, full of pluck, and bids fair to live many years.

Lydia Ridlon⁵ (9), third daughter of Daniel⁴ (4), was born in Limerick, Me.; was married to Moses Brown, in 1833, and died many years ago. Supposed to have lived in Porter.

Betsey Ridlon⁵ (8), fourth daughter of Daniel⁴ (4), was born in Limerick, Me.; was married to Joshua Robbins, Aug. 5, 1832, and is now living in Porter with her son.

Levi Ridlon⁵ (1), fourth son of Daniel⁴ (4), was born in Limerick, Me., June 4, 1818; married Hannah Lord, Aug. 7, 1838, and settled on a farm in Porter, Oxford County, Me. He is of medium height, broad-shouldered, and thick-set; his weight about one hundred and eighty pounds. He has the stamp of features common to the family. Has worked hard, and is now considerably bowed over. Honest, quiet, and talks but little. Children *five* in number, of whom hereafter. Wife deceased.

Jemima Ridlon⁵ (2), fifth daughter of Daniel⁴ (4), was born in Limerick, Me.; was married to Caleb Durgin, Feb. 12, 1835, and died many years ago.

Ephraim Ridlon⁵ (3), eldest son of John⁴ (9), was born in Limerick, Me., April 4, 1802, and died young, unmarried.

---

* The ancestor of the Wales family, of Oxford County, Me., was a singular and desperate character. He fled from Ohio to escape the vengeance of the Indians. His mother was a full-blooded squaw, and he spent his early years hunting with the tribe; but in a moment of anger had killed one of their number. He was hunted by their dogs, but eluded them by taking to the water; and after waiting in ambush, saw them approaching in a canoe. When the Indians were within range, Wales fired and sent a ball through several of them. This act so exasperated the tribe, that Wales did not dare to remain in Ohio, and made his way East. He erected a cabin on the bank of a small pond, in Hollis, York County, Me., — since known as "Wales Pond"—and lived by plunder, and burning lamp-black. He went armed with a long sheath-knife, and at one time would have killed a man, into whose store he had broken; but the gleam of his knife was a warning which saved his pursuer. His deeds were of such a criminal character, that Thomas Ridlon and his neighbors, of Hollis, whose sheep he had stolen, went to his cabin and warned him to leave the neighborhood, threatening to hang him within forty-eight hours, if he lingered. Wales left those parts, but left sons whose posterity is respectable, but whose features, complexion, and movements show the Indian blood of their dusky ancestress.

Hannah Ridlon⁵ (7) eldest daughter of John⁴ (9), was born in Limerick, Me., in 1804; was the wife of —— Stacy, of Porter, Oxford County, and died years ago.

William Ridlon⁵ (11), second son of John⁴ (9), was born in Limerick, Me., April 4, 1806; married Susan Stanley, of Porter, July 9, 1828 (she was born April 4, 1810), and settled as a farmer in the latter town. He was of medium height, heavy-built, corpulent; had black hair and beard, bald crown, and regular features. His movements were moderate; he was quiet and talked but little. Had issue *five* children, of whom hereafter. He and wife deceased.

Dorcas Ridlon⁵ (2), second daughter of John⁴ (9), was born in Limerick, Me., in 1810; was married to —— Eastman, and was living in Parkman, Me., in 1882. She has a son who is a minister of the Gospel in the Freewill Baptist Church.

Catherine Ridlon⁵ (4), third daughter of John⁴ (9), was born in Limerick, Me., in 1813; was married to John H. Howard, of Porter, Oxford County, Dec. 5, 1832, and had issue. Dead.

Ephraim Ridlon⁵ (4), third son of John⁴ (9), was born in Limerick, (or Porter), Me., in 1818; married Olive Cole, Nov. 27, 1841, and had issue. His first wife deceased, and he married, secondly, —— Hartford. He has been a roving, restless, eccentric character all his days. Was at one time a peddler; subsequently a millman. At last accounts he was living at Bar Mills Village, Buxton, Me.

Ezra Ridlon⁵ (2), only son of Ezra⁴ (1), was born in Limerick, Me., July 21, 1827; married Eliza J., daughter of Asa and Lucy (Billings) Thurlow (she was born Dec. 18, 1829), and settled in Woodstock, Me., as a farmer. He was a soldier in the Twenty-third Regiment, Maine Volunteer Infantry, during the Rebellion. Now (1882) residing at Bryant's Pond, in Woodstock, where he has engaged in lumbering. He is tall and spare; has regular features, brown hair and beard, is social, conversational, and firm in his convictions. Member of the Methodist Church. *Five* children, of whom hereafter.

Eliza Ridlon⁵ (5), a daughter of Ezra⁴ (1), was born in Limerick, Me., and was married to —— Eastman. Resides in Woodstock Oxford County.

Emma Ridlon⁵ (1), a daughter of Ezra⁴ (1), was born in Limerick, Me.; was married to —— Thurlow, and resides in Woodstock, Oxford County.

Rebecca Ridlon⁵ (5), a daughter of Ezra⁴ (1), was born in Limerick, Me.; was married to —— Benson, and lives in Woodstock, Oxford County.

Caroline Ridlon⁵ (1), a daughter of Ezra⁴ (1), was born in Limerick, Me.; was married to —— Pratt, and lives in Woodstock, Oxford County.

Abby Ridlon⁵ (2), a daughter of Ezra⁴ (1), was born in Limerick, Me.; was married to —— Farrer, and lives in West Sumner.

Dea. Charles-Francis Ridlon⁵ (3), eldest son of Charles⁴ (1), was born in Saco, Me., May 20, 1825; married Mehitable Knight, of Waterborough; secondly, Mary Keniston (or Kenison), of New Bedford, Mass., and, thirdly, to Almira Stone, of Cornish, Me. He first settled in Saco, where he remained till 1822–3, when he removed to Waterborough, and lived in that town until 1857-9, when he moved to Cornish, York County, where he now resides and owns a fine farm. He formerly drove a team. Deacon of the Freewill Baptist Church. A good and highly respected man ; somewhat eccentric and odd ; has the features and general characteristics of the old stock of Ridlons. He is a large, corpulent man. Has had issue *five* children, of whom hereafter.

Miranda-S. Ridlon[5] (2), only daughter of Charles[4] (1), was born in Saco, Me. (Ferry Neighborhood), Feb. 26, 1827; became the wife of Charles Plummer, of Portland, June 15, 1848, and is now living on Middle Street, surrounded by all the concomitants of wealth. A very useful, benevolent woman. She is large, dignified, and graceful; has the type of features common to the old Ridlon stock. No issue.

Henry-K. Ridlon[5] (3), second son of Charles[4] (1), was born in Saco, Me., June 19, 1829, and died when a child.

Thomas-H. Ridlon[5] (9), eldest son of Ephraim[4] (2), was born in Saco, Me., Jan. 17, 1815 ; married Mary-Frances Mann, and settled in Boston, or Chelsea, Mass., where he carried on the hatter's business, and acquired a handsome property. He was an extremely eccentric character, and took great pride in his peculiar costume and habits of life. He persisted in wearing clothes fashionable in the colonial days: the three-cornered hat, broad coat, long waist-coat, knee-breeches, white silk stockings, and buckled shoes. He was the subject of much attention upon the streets, and is well remembered by old Bostonians. He was generous with his money, and spent a fortune in fashionable dinners, horse-races, and the entertainment of dignitaries. He was always proud of his Scottish ancestry, and sent to the Herald College, at London, for coat-of-arms and pedigree. He was an enthusiastic antiquary and specialist, and spent considerable money in the collection of novelties and curious specimens in foreign lands. A room in his house was fitted up for a kind of museum, and filled with engravings, carvings, Yankee notions, etc. He was a cadet of the Ridlon family, who seemed to have received the mantles of four generations of odd, eccentric ancestors, and found enjoyment in what was not followed by pleasure-seekers generally. He had his grave-stones made several years before his death, the inscription being cut to his own taste, leaving only space for the date of his departure, which took place Nov. 1, 1865. He left a widow, who has married a second husband, and *two* sons, of whom hereafter. The framed coat-of-arms left in his family was supposed to be authorized for the Ridlon family, but has no connection with that family ; it is a coat belonging to a branch of the Ridleys of Northumberland, Eng.

Joseph-Henry Ridlon[5] (8), second son of Ephraim[4] (2), was born in Saco, Me., March 20, 1818 ; married Harriet Brown, June 21, 1840, and settled in Keene, N. H. He subsequently went to Boston, and engaged as a hatter with his brother before mentioned. He was possessed of considerable property. Served in the Union army, during the Rebellion. Resided many years in Chelsea, Mass., where his wife carried on the millinery and dress-making business. He has all the physical and mental characteristics of his family. Is short, corpulent, and heavy; hair and beard formerly black, now white, the latter long. He is genial, kind-hearted, and honest, but blunt, determined, and sarcastic. A very companionable man. Now living in Easton, Mass. Had issue *five* children, of whom hereafter.

JOSEPH RIDLON

Ephraim Ridlon[6] (5), youngest son of Ephraim[4] (5), was born in Saco, Me., June 8, 1820, and died when a child.

Lucinda Ridlon[6] (2), eldest daughter of William[4] (3), was born in Saco, Me., Jan. 30, 1825; was married to Amos Edgecomb, Sept. 25, 1851, and has issue. She lives on a farm near her birth-place, at Saco Ferry, so called, on land originally owned by Magnus Redlon, our common ancestor.

Ann Ridlon[6] (3), second daughter of William[4] (3), was born in Saco, Me., Sept. 22, 1827; was married to Cyrus Snow, Dec. 24, 1848, and has issue. She resides at Saco Ferry.

Marcie Ridlon[6] (1), third daughter of William[4] (3), was born in Saco, Me., April 2, 1830; was married to —— Tarbox, in 1879, and lives in a house built by her brother, near the homestead of her father, at Saco Ferry. She carried on dress-making on Factory Island, in Saco, for many years, and acquired considerable property. Marcie is a woman of enterprising spirit and sound judgment.

Leander Ridlon[6] (2), only son of William[4] (3), was born in Saco, Me., Aug. 16, 1832; married Eliza S. Haley, and has *seven* children, of whom hereafter. He built a house near the old homestead, and lived there several years, but worked in the city in a brass-foundry. He subsequently sold and moved to North Andover, Mass., where he now resides.

Betsey Ridlon[6] (9), youngest daughter of William[4] (3), was born in Saco, Me., and died there, Dec. 5, 1825.

Sabra Ridlon[6] (2), eldest daughter of Nathaniel[4] (3), was born in Saco, Me., April 15, 1827.

Luther Ridlon[6] (1), eldest son of Nathaniel[4] (3), was born in Saco, Me., Dec. 17, 1829.

Harriet Ridlon[6] (5), second daughter of Nathaniel[4] (3), was born in Saco, Me., Nov. 17, 1831.

Samuel Ridlon[6] (10), second son of Nathaniel[4] (3), was born in Saco, Me., June 11, 1836; married Sept. 29, 1860, to Lucy Kendrick, and lived in Saco. He had issue *three* children, of whom hereafter. His wife died Sept. 18, 1863. Mr. Ridlon was drowned in Saco River, subsequent to 1864. He was an Odd Fellow, and his Lodge provided for his daughter, who survived her parents. Samuel was about medium height, thick-set, and resembled his father. He formerly worked as a shoe-maker in the city.

Mary Ridlon[6] (23), third daughter of Nathaniel[4] (3), was born in Saco, Me., Dec. 21, 1837, and died unmarried.

Mark Ridlon[6] (2), third son of Nathaniel[4] (3), was born in Saco, Me., Sept. 6, 1839, and died Sept. 9, 1864.

Henry Ridlon[6] (4), fourth son of Nathaniel[4] (3), was born in Saco, Me., in 1841; married Charlotte Abbott, Oct. 5, 1862, and died in 1880, leaving a son, of whom hereafter. He served in the Twenty-seventh Regiment of Maine Infantry. He was of medium height and build, and had sandy hair and beard. He was a Second Adventist in religious faith.

Charles Ridlon[6] (3), fifth son of Nathaniel[4] (3), was born in Saco, Me., in 1845; served in the Union army during the Rebellion, in Company D, Seventh Regiment Infantry, and was killed in battle in the year 1864. A noble soldier.

Nathaniel Ridlon[5] (5), sixth son of Nathaniel[4] (3), was born in Saco, Me., in 1845; served in the Seventh Maine Infantry, in the Union army, during the Rebellion, and died in a Rebel prison.

Susan Ridlon[5] (6), fourth daughter of Nathaniel[4] (3), was born in Saco, Me. No other information.

Frank Ridlon[5] (1), seventh son of Nathaniel[4] (3), was born in Saco, Me.; married —— Edgecomb, and is now (1881) living on his father's homestead farm, on the "Ferry Road." Blacksmith; is tall, and has dark hair and complexion. Very eccentric.

Laura Ridlon[5] (1), fifth daughter of Nathaniel[4] (3), was born in Saco, Me., and was married to Alonzo Ridlon (son of Lewis, son of Edmund), Dec. 24, 1874. Resides at Saco.

Olive Ridlon[5] (5), eldest daughter of Edmund[4] (1), was born in Saco, Me., Aug. 22, 1821; was married to Jesse M. March, Aug. 11, 1839, and lives at Kennebunkport, Me.

Lewis Ridlon[5] (3), eldest son of Edmund[4] (1), was born in Saco, Me., June 22, 1823; married Susan Webster, July 24, 1848, and had issue *five* children, of whom hereafter. Mr. Ridlon is a blacksmith by trade. Resided in Biddeford. Has dark hair and beard; of medium height.

Lucinda-W. Ridlon[5] (3), second daughter of Edmund[4] (1), was born in Saco, Me., Dec. 22, 1824; was married to Joseph Wilber, Nov. 29, 1849, and has issue. Resides at Saco Ferry, near the homestead of her father. She is a *Ridlon* in every respect.

Jeremiah Ridlon[5] (5), second son of Edmund[4] (1), was born in Saco, Me., Oct. 21, 1826; married Emma Larey, Aug. 8, 1848, and has *one* daughter. Mr. Ridlon is a blacksmith, employed by the Saco Waterpower Company. Resides on the "Ferry Road" near his father's homestead. Tall and raw-boned.

Edmund Ridlon[5] (3), third son of Edmund[4] (1), was born in Saco, Me., Feb. 14, 1828; married Mary M. Hutchins, Nov. 12, 1848, and has *two* children, of whom hereafter. He is a steam-engineer. Resides at Kennebunkport.

James-W. Ridlon[5] (11), fourth son of Edmund[4] (1), was born in Saco, Me., Dec. 10, 1829; married Susan B. Hutchins, March 10, 1849, and has issue *five* children, of whom hereafter. Engineer by profession. Resides at Kennebunkport, Me.

Hannah-E. Ridlon[5] (8), third daughter of Edmund[4] (1), was born in Saco, Me., March 19, 1831, and died Sept. 20, 1832.

Hannah-E. Ridlon[5] (9), fourth daughter of Edmund[4] (1), was born in Saco, Me., May 18, 1833; was married to Josiah H. Murphy, March 27, 1851, and has issue. Resides at Kennebunkport.

Ruth-J. Ridlon[5] (6), fifth daughter of Edmund[4] (1), was born in Saco, Me., March 15, 1835; was married to John E. Seavy, July 1, 1854, and has issue. Resides at Kennebunkport.

Abraham Ridlon[5] (8), fifth son of Edmund[4] (1), was born in Saco, Me., June 21, 1837; married Jemima Page, Oct. 2, 1859, and lives at Saco, on the "Ferry Road," so called. He is of medium height and size, and has light hair and beard.

Mary-F. Ridlon[5] (24), sixth daughter of Edmund[4] (1), was born in Saco, Me., Oct. 17, 1839; was married to David Wagner, April 12, 1862, and lives at Kennebunkport.

Melinda-M. Ridlon[5] (1), seventh daughter of Edmund[4] (1), was born in Saco, March 11, 1842; was married July 30, 1860 to James Huntress, blacksmith, of Saco, and has issue.

Caroline Ridlon⁶ (2), eldest daughter of Henry⁴ (2), was born in Saco, Me., Jan. 15, 1827, and died when an infant.

Caroline Ridlon⁶ (3), second daughter of Henry⁴ (2), was born in Saco, Me., Sept. 24, 1828.

John Ridlon⁶ (21), eldest son of Henry⁴ (2), was born in Saco, Me., July 11, 1830. Resides in a house alone in Saco. An incorrigible old bachelor, and one of the most eccentric, odd characters known in the family. He moves about town moderately, and seldom speaks to any one. He is a type of the old-stamp of Ridlons; has sandy hair and beard, light eyes, and regular, but coarse features. Medium height; shoulders broad. Served in the Twenty-seventh Regiment, Maine Volunteer Infantry, during the Southern Rebellion.

Eunice Ridlon⁶ (5), third daughter of Henry⁴ (2), was born in Saco, Me., Sept. 7, 1832. Deceased.

Nancy Ridlon⁶ (4), fourth daughter of Henry⁴ (2), was born in Saco, Me., in 1834; was married to John Gordon, May 15, 1860, and probably deceased soon after, as he married her cousin two years subsequently.

Daniel-N. Ridlon⁶ (9), second son of Henry⁴ (2) by his second wife, was born in Saco, Me., Dec. 10, 1845; married in 1881, and resides in his native town.

Martha-E. Ridlon⁶ (9), fifth daughter of Henry⁴ (2), was born in Saco, Me., Nov. 3, 1850; was married to Andrew A. Strom, Feb. 8, 1876, and resides in Dayton.

Sarah-L. Ridlon⁶ (12), sixth daughter of Henry⁴ (2), was born in Saco, Me., Sept. 3, 1854; was married to Charles E. Bachelder, Nov. 26, 1874, and resides in Saco.

Marianna Ridlon⁶ (1), seventh daughter of Henry⁴ (2), was born in Saco, Me., May 27, 1858, and died in October, 1858.

Mary-E. Ridlon⁶ (25), eldest daughter of Magnus⁴ (7), was born in Saco, Me., Sept. 22, 1840; was married to John H. Gordon, Dec. 23, 1862; secondly, to Frederick Sweetser, of Saco.

Olive Ridlon⁶ (5), second daughter of Magnus⁴ (7), was born in Saco, Me., and was married to Winfield Dennet, of Saco, July 23, 1864. Mr. Dennet is a civil engineer.

Melville-Magnus Ridlon⁶ (1), only son of Magnus⁴ (7), was born in Saco, Me., married Nancy-Jane, daughter of Uran and Mary (Dearborn) Earle, of Waterborough, Dec. 24, 1868 (she was born April 8, 1851), and has had issue *six* children, of whom hereafter. He worked many years as a dyer on the York Corporation in Saco, but his health being poor has opened a market on the street. Member of the Methodist Church. Small man; hair and eyes brown. Highly respected as a citizen. He was the only one of his generation Christian-named *Magnus*, until the author of this book prevailed upon several to name children for our ancestor.

Elmira Ridlon⁶ (3), third daughter of Magnus⁴ (7), was born in Saco, Me. Unmarried in 1880.

Frank Ridlon⁶ (2), only son of Noah⁴ (1), was born Feb. 28, 1838 (probably in Abington, Mass.); married Marietta, daughter of Samuel Page, of Boston, Oct. 31, 1860, and has issue. Mr. Ridlon was at one

688REDLONS OF BUXTON, MAINE.

time agent for a company in Washington, D. C., but at last account was
connected with telephonic operations, and located in Boston. He is
a large, corpulent man. Complexion light. Business capacity good. In-
herits the peculiar traits of the family.

James-Henry Ridlon⁵ (12), eldest son of Alexander⁴ (1), was born
Jan. 20, 1854, presumably in Illinois; married Ellen, daughter of Isaac
Rodgers, and has issue, of whom hereafter. Resides in Middleton, Kan.
Farmer. Member of the Moravian Church. Resembles his father.

Albert-Aquila Ridlon⁵ (2), second sono f Alexander⁴ (1), was born
March 29, 1855, and lives at Middleton, Kan. Farmer. A member of
the Moravian Church. Unmarried in 1876.

Martha-Jane Ridlon⁵ (10), eldest daughter of Alexander⁴ (1), was
born March 22, 1857; was married to George Hibbard, and lives near
Middleton, Kan. Her uncle Peter thinks she was married to — Stout.

James-Frederick Ridlon⁵ (13), eldest son of Peter⁴ (1), was born
in Saco, Me., March, 1835; married Rachel (Sutton) Easdale, widow,
and has issue *three* children, of whom hereafter. He graduated at Bloomington University, Ill., in 1862; representative in legislature of Kansas,
in 1870. Teaches school in winter, and runs a farm in summer.

Martha-Augusta Ridlon⁵ (11), eldest daughter of Peter⁴ (1), was born
in Saco, Me., June 16, 1836. Dress-maker in Chicago. Unmarried.

Abigail-W. Ridlon⁵ (4), second daughter of Peter⁴ (1), was born in
Saco, Me., Aug. 30, 1837 [in a letter dated Dec. 28, 1882, her father
gives her birth "Septem. 12, 1837"]; both dates were from the same au-
thority]; was married to Isaac D. Webster, in New Brunswick, — where
she went to teach school, — and is now (1882) living at Mecosta, Mecosta
County, Michigan. Has issue.

Chester-Oliver Ridlon⁵ (1), second son of Peter⁴ (1), was born in
Monmouth, Ill., May 13, 1849 (he was by a second wife), married Hattie
Moor, in December, 1882, and lives near his father, in Gardner, Kan.,
where he owns a well-stocked farm of two hundred and forty acres. He
resembles his father; is mirthful, sarcastic, and humorous.

SIXTH GENERATION.

Hannah Ridlon⁶ (10), eldest daughter of William⁵ (4), was born in
Buxton, Me., May 3, 1844; supposed to be married.

Lewis-F. Ridlon⁶ (4), eldest son of William⁵ (4), was born in Buxton,
Me., Sept. 23, 1847, and died March 27, 1853.

Henry-Clay Ridlon⁶ (5), second son of William⁵ (4), was born in Buxton, Me., Jan. 24, 1856; married a daughter of Samuel Dunn, of Buxton,
and lives at "Bog Mills," so called, in that town. He learned the blacksmith's trade with his uncle, Mr. Spinney, of West Gorham, and was at
Moderation Village in 1879. A fine-looking young man; tall, well formed,
and powerful. Resembles the Redlon family in features of face and movement. Is considered an excellent mechanic.

Eliza-Sanborn Redlon⁶ (6), eldest daughter of James⁵ (4), was born
in Buxton, Me., Dec. 21, 1832; was married to Andrew Flood, and lives
on a farm in the "Spruce Swamp" neighborhood. A beautiful, gentle-
spirited woman.

Susan-Sawyer Redlon[6] (7), second daughter of James[5] (4), was born in Buxton, Me., Nov. 7, 1839; was married to John Warren, of Standish, and died July 20, 1876.

Lorenzo-Emery Redlon[6] (1), eldest son of James[5] (4), was born in Buxton, Me., April 4, 1840; married Fannie, daughter of Andrew and Elmira (Bennett) Gray, of Westbrook, in 1859, and has issue, of whom hereafter. Resides on his father's homestead farm, in Buxton. Member of the Calvinist Baptist Church. Served in the Twelfth Regiment Maine Infantry, in the Department of the Gulf from 1861 to 1866, in Union army, war of the Rebellion. Saw much hard service. Below the medium height; thick-set, and weighs over two hundred pounds. Complexion light. A man of sound mind; highly respected.

Ammy-L. Redlon[6] (2), second son of James[5] (4), was born in Buxton, Me., Aug. 28, 1842. Deceased young.

William-Ammy Redlon[6] (12), eldest son of Benjamin[5] (1), was born in Boston, Mass., May 29, 1843; married Abbie A. Frost, Jan. 26, 1873, by whom *one* son. His wife died in October, 1874, and he married Helen M. Patrick. Resides at Kennebunk, Me.

Eugene-F. Redlon[6] (1), second son of Benjamin[5] (1), was born in Boston, Mass., Aug. 22, 1844; married Susan Harmon, and has *five* children, of whom hereafter. He resides at Kennebunk, Me.

Nehemiah-Rich Redlon[6] (1), third son of Benjamin[5] (1), was born in Buxton, Me., April 16, 1846; married Olive Woodman, Nov. 26, 1869, and has issue, of whom hereafter. Mr. Ridlon is a harness-maker by trade, and has long worked for Jason Beaty, at Saco. Lives at Kennebunk.

Lucy Redlon[6] (3), eldest daughter of Benjamin[5] (1), was born May 8, 1850, and died April 8, 1852.

Charles-Sumner Redlon[6] (4), fourth son of Benjamin[5] (1), was born Dec. 26, 1853, and died Aug. 21, 1857.

Frederick-S. Redlon[6] (1), eldest son of Isaac[5] (4), was born in Buxton, Me., Jan. 22, 1855; married Mary Delaney, of Saco, in February, 1881 (ceremony by the author), and resides in that city. Tall, slender, dark hair and eyes. Fond of horses. Had a leg badly fractured in 1880. Has issue.

Melville-H. Redlon[6] (2), second son of Isaac[5] (4), was born in Buxton, Me., Feb. 19, 1857.

William Redlon[6] (13), third son of Isaac[5] (4), was born in Buxton, Me., Nov. 3, 1862.

George-Albert Redlon[6] (5), fourth son of Isaac[5] (4), was born in Buxton, Me., July 19, 1864.

Capt. Silas Redlon[6] (1), eldest son of Benjamin[5] (2), was born in Buxton, Me., April 4, 1822; married Mary-Ann Symnet, and had issue, of whom hereafter. He was an officer in the Florida war. He was a man of great physical strength and proportions. Brave, adventuresome, uncompromising, but possessed of generosity and kindness of heart. He died at Key West, in 1865.

Sarah Redlon[6] (13), eldest daughter of Benjamin[5] (2), was born in Buxton, Me., Feb. 2, 1824; was married to Oliver M. Gilpatric, of Granger, N. J., — where she now (1876) resides, — and has issue.

44

Benjamin-Carsley Redlon' (7), second son of Benjamin⁵ (2), was born in Harrison, Me., Oct. 9, 1827; married Eliza C. Smith, of Granger, N. J., and is now (1876) living in Kansas, engaged in farming and stock-raising. He has had issue several children, of whom hereafter.

Elizabeth Redlon' (9), second daughter of Benjamin⁵ (2), was born in Harrison, Me., Jan. 5, 1830; was married, in 1846, to Lewis Youngs, and (presumably) lives in Wisconsin.

Mary Redlon' (26), third daughter of Benjamin⁵ (2), was born in Springfield, Me., April 18, 1832; was married, in 1852, to Dr. Y. B. Griffith, of Oramel, N. J.

Nathaniel-K. Redlon' (6), third son of Benjamin⁵ (2), was born in Springfield, Me., March 5, 1834; married Elizabeth B. Griffith, of Granger, N. J., and has issue, of whom hereafter. He served in the Eighth Wisconsin Battery during the Rebellion. Has been Justice of the Peace. Carries on mercantile business. A man of sound judgment and ability.

Abigail-C. Redlon' (5), fourth daughter of Benjamin⁵ (2), was born in Springfield, Me., Aug. 2, 1838, and was married, in 1855, to William Hall, of Plainfield, Wis.

Cerena Redlon' (1), youngest daughter of Benjamin⁵ (2), was born in Springfield, Me., Aug. 3, 1840; was married Sept. 4, 1855, to Thomas Hall, of Plainfield, Wis.

Amos-M. Redlon' (3), fourth son of Benjamin⁵ (2), was born in Granger, N. J., Dec. 18, 1844. He served three years in the Seventh Regiment Wisconsin Infantry, during the Rebellion, and was in every engagement in which the Army of the Potomac participated, from the second battle of Bull Run until the battle of Getteysburgh, and it was during the long march from Fredericksburgh and back, that he contracted disease and went to the hospital. He subsequently returned to his father's home and died there Sept. 4, 1864, unmarried. A brave soldier.

Thomas-Leonard Redlon' (10), fifth son of Benjamin⁵ (1), was born in Granger, N. J., Oct. 5, 1846; married Delia Richardson, and has issue. He served in the First Regiment of Wisconsin Cavalry, and afterwards in the Eighth Battery, with his brother before mentioned, until the end of the war. After his return from the army he studied law, and at the age of twenty-three was admitted to the Bar of Crawford County, Wis. He is a man of clear, strong mind, and a successful practitioner.

Maj. Benjamin-M. Redlon' (8), eldest son of Thomas⁵ (3), was born in Sebago, Me., Oct. 15, 1833; married Mary, daughter of John and Susan (Libbey) Houston, of Portland, and has had issue *five* children, of whom hereafter. He enlisted in the First Maine Infantry; was mustered into the army May 3, 1861; mustered into the Tenth Regiment Infantry, Oct. 4, 1862; and was subsequently in the Twenty-ninth Regiment Infantry. His commissions and promotions were as follows: Second lieutenant Company C, First Regiment, April 28, 1861; first lieutenant Company C, Tenth Regiment, Oct. 5, 1861; first lieutenant, Dec. 11, 1863; captain Company B, Twenty-ninth Regiment, Dec. 24, 1863, and brevet-major — "for faithful and meritorious service during the war " — March 13, 1865. He was in the following engagements: Winchester, May 25, 1862; Cedar Mountain, Aug. 9, 1862; Rappahannock, Aug. 20, 1862; Sulphur Springs, Aug. 24, 1862; South Mountain, Sept. 4, 1862; Antietam, Sept. 17, 1862; Mansfield Cross-roads, Pleasant Hill, Mansura Plain, and Cane River Crossing, — the last four in Louisiana. He was in the service from May 3, 1861, to

June 26, 1865, and among all the Maine officers during the war, none had so complete a record. One who was much with him in the army says, "Neither heat, nor cold, rain or dust, good dinners or starvation, could affect him; he kept pegging away from the beginning to the end, the same 'old Ben' from year to year. He was strict and exacting as an officer, but beloved and respected by his men." He had a beautiful sword presented him by his command, — members of Company C, Tenth Maine Regiment of Infantry, — inscribed as follows: —

> *" Presented to*
> LIEUT. B. M. REDLON,
> *By the Members of Company C, Tenth Maine Volunteers,*
> *As a Token of Respect,*
> *March, 1863."*

Major Redlon is a carpenter and builder by trade, and since the war has resided in Portland, where he has been a contractor. His wife and eldest daughter were in the South during the war, and while at his headquarters were taken prisoners by Ashby's Cavalry, at Winchester, Va., during Banks' retreat, and carried to Richmond; they were, however, sent into the Union lines under a flag of truce. Major Redlon's trunk and dress-uniform were also carried away, but he afterwards recovered them. He is of medium height, corpulent, and has dark hair and beard; is fine-looking, social, jovial, and companionable. He has always possessed a military spirit, and still becomes very animated when speaking of the war.

Christiana Redlon[6] (1), eldest daughter of Thomas[5] (3), was married to George Hillard, a painter.

Sarah Jane Redlon[6] (14), second daughter of Thomas[5] (3), was married to William Vaughan, of Portland, Me.

Clementine Redlon[6] (1), third daughter of Thomas[5] (3), was married to Benjamin Vaughan, of Portland, Me.

Francena Redlon[6] (1), fourth daughter of Thomas[5] (3), died unmarried.

Emily-Jane Redlon[6] (2), eldest daughter of Nathaniel[5] (4), was born in Portland, Me., Jan. 18, 1836, and died June 11, 1846.

Lucretia Redlon[6] (2), second daughter of Nathaniel[5] (4), was born in Portland, Me., June 14, 1839, and died Sept. 19, 1839.

Albert Redlon[6] (3), eldest son of Nathaniel[5] (4), was born in Portland, Me., Jan. 6, 1842; married Helen S. Allen, and died Feb. 16, 1870, leaving one child.

Augusta Redlon[6] (1), third daughter of Nathaniel[5] (4), was born in Portland, Me., May 5, 1843; a maiden-lady.

Luther Redlon[6] (1), second son of Nathaniel[5] (4), was born in Portland, Me., Nov. 25, 1844; married Mary M. Law, of Jersey City, N. J., Nov. 13, 1873, and is now manufacturing brooms in Portland.

Roscoe Redlon[6] (1), third son of Nathaniel[5] (4), was born in Portland, Me., July 21, 1846, and died Sept. 9, 1846.

Edward Redlon[6] (1), fourth son of Nathaniel[5] (4), was born in Portland, Me., March 25, 1847, and died Sept. 25, 1847.

Abbie-Jane Redlon[6] (3), youngest daughter of Nathaniel[5] (4), was born in Portland, Me., Dec. 14, 1849, and was married to Albert G. Randall, of North Bridgewater, Mass.

Alvan-Bryant Redlon[6] (1), only son of Jonathan[5] (3), was born in Buxton, Me., Jan. 25, 1830; married June 11, 1861, and is a resident of

Pekin, Ill. No children. He has had a most singular, adventitious, and wandering life; full of vicissitudes and discouragements. His mother died when he was a small boy, and he was left to drift about from place to place. In 1845 he went to Portland to learn the art of printing; thence, after a few months, to Dedham, Mass., and worked in a woolen mill; thence to Boston, and worked in a printing office. He continued to go·from city to city, losing his situation and seeking employment, constantly attended by misfortune, until he had traversed New England. He was employed on the *Providence Transcript* when his uncle Amos was editor; also for Brown, Thurston & Co., in Portland. During his indisposition he spent his winters with relatives. In 1859 he commenced work on the *Register* at Pekin, Ill., and by hard work and strict economy has managed to get a little home. In a communication to the author, written in 1875, he says: "My mother was subject to fits of insanity when I was a child, and at one time attempted to throw me into the fire, but was prevented by some one in the house. I have wished a thousand times she had accomplished her purpose, which, in her insensibility, she would have done; for my life, so far, has been one of trouble and disappointment, and I have accomplished nothing worthy of our name."

Annette-A. Redlon⁶ (1), a twin daughter of Jonathan⁵ (3) and Mary Redlon, was born in Buxton, Me., April 6, 1847; was married Dec. 11, 1868, to Johnson Varney, and resides at East Windham, Cumberland County, Me.

Mary-F. Redlon⁶ (27), a twin daughter of Jonathan⁵ (3) and Mary Redlon, was born in Buxton, Me., April 6, 1847, and died March 16, 1865, unmarried.

Frederick Redlon⁶ (2), eldest son of Cyrus⁵ (1). ⎫ I have failed to
Cyrus Redlon⁶ (2), second son of Cyrus⁵ (1). ⎬ find any other in-
Deborah Redlon⁶ (1), daughter of Cyrus⁵ (1). ⎭ formation.

Albert-G. Redlon⁶ (4), eldest son of Amos⁵ (2), was born in Massachusetts, June 26, 1842, and died in Hallowell, Me., Sept. 8, 1843.

Lydia-Maria Redlon⁶ (10), eldest daughter of Amos⁵ (2), was born in Maine (Berwick?), March 4, 1844; died Nov. 24, 1864.

Martin-Luther Redlon⁶ (1), second son of Amos⁵ (2), was born in Maine, Oct. 22, 1845; died Aug. 28, 1846.

Frederick-D. Redlon⁶ (3), third son of Amos⁵ (2), was born in Maine, Nov. 5, 1847; died Oct. 28, 1849.

Etta-F. Redlon⁶ (1), second daughter of Amos⁵ (2), was born in Maine (?), Sept. 4, 1857; was married and lives in Boston, but I do not know her husband's name.

Ida-Luella Redlon⁶ (1), third daughter of Amos⁵ (2), was born Dec. 28, 1858; died Nov. 9, 1861.

Mary-E. Redlon⁶ (28), fourth daughter of Amos⁵ (2), was born May 17, 1863.

Franklin Redlon⁶ (2), only son of Nathan⁵ (1); is married and lives in Portland, Me. Mason by trade.

Lephe-Anna Redlon⁶ (1), eldest daughter of John⁵ (11), was born in Buxton, Me., Oct. 23, 1851. Married.

Horatio Redlon⁶ (1), a son of John⁵ (11), was born in Buxton, Me., Nov. 19, 1853. Married.

Sarah-Elizabeth Redlon⁶ (15), youngest daughter of John⁵ (11), was born in Buxton, Me., Dec. 17, 1855; died Nov. 29, 1870.

Stanley-E. Redlon⁶ (1), eldest son of Daniel⁵ (6), was born at Pierceville, Ind., July 9, 1866.

Atlee Redlon⁶ (1), second son of Daniel⁵ (6), was born at Pierceville, Ind., Sept. 21, 1869.

Clare-W. Redlon⁶ (1), third son of Daniel⁵ (6), was born at Pierceville, Ind., Sept. 20, 1872.

Leon-H. Redlon⁶ (1), fourth son of Daniel⁵ (6), was born at Pierceville, Ind., Nov. 8, 1873.

Burton Redlon⁶ (1), fifth son of Daniel⁵ (6), was born in Pierceville, Ind., April 3, 1876.

Blanche Redlon⁶ (1), only daughter of Daniel⁵ (6), was born in Pierceville, Ind., April 3, 1876. (Twin to Burton).

James Redlon⁶ (14), eldest son of Nathan⁵ (2), was born May 12, 1838, and died June 1, 1838.

George-M. Redlon⁶ (6), second son of Nathan⁵ (2), was born March 28, 1839, and died Oct. 19, 1862.

Frances-A. Redlon⁶ (2), eldest daughter of Nathan⁵ (2), was born Sept. 28, 1840, and died April 10, 1870.

Julia-A. Redlon⁶ (1), second daughter of Nathan⁵ (2), was born Aug. 20, 1842, and died Sept. 12, 1843.

James-F. Redlon⁶ (14), third son of Nathan⁵ (2), was born May 1, 1845, and died June 10, 1866.

Charles Redlon⁶ (5), fourth son of Nathan⁵ (2), was born June 30, 1852, and died Dec. 26, 1853.

Mary-E. Redlon⁶ (29), third daughter of Nathan⁵ (2), was born July 18, 1853. She was for several years a writer in the publishing-house of Allen & Co., Augusta, Me.; she is an accomplished, sweet-spirited lady, who should frequently read Proverbs 25 : 25.

William-B. Redlon⁶ (14), fifth son of Nathan⁵ (2), was born in China, Me., Jan. 21, 1857.

Eva-M. Redlon⁶ (1), fourth daughter of Nathan⁵ (2), was born in China, Me., April 18, 1859, and died April 29, 1859.

Helen-L. Redlon⁶ (1), fifth daughter of Nathan⁵ (2), was born in China, Me., Feb. 28, 1861.

George-B. Redlon⁵ (7), sixth son of Nathan⁵ (2), was born in China, Me., Oct. 31, 1868.

Jennie-D. Redlon⁶ (1), sixth daughter of Nathan⁵ (2), was born in China, Me., Jan. 27, 1867.

Albert-E. Redlon⁶ (5), seventh son of Nathan⁵ (2), was born in China, Me., Nov. 7, 1868.

Ambrose-A. Redlon⁶ (1), eighth son of Nathan⁵ (2), was born in China, Me., Oct. 3, 1872.

Artemas Ridlon⁶ (1), only son of John⁵ (13), was born in Hollis, Me., about 1822; married Ann Tripp, of New Bedford, Mass., and settled at Taunton, in that State. He was a blacksmith and machinist, an excellent workman, and accumulated considerable property. He became a prominent Odd Fellow. Finally grew insane, and was placed under treatment in the asylum at Somerville, where, at the end of three years, he died, leaving *one* daughter. He was a very interesting and promising young man.

Mary Ridlon⁶ (30), eldest daughter of John⁵ (13), was born in Hollis, Me., and was married, firstly, to Thomas Dyer; she was married, secondly, to C. L. Drown, of Newburyport, Mass. She is a dress-maker.

Ardelia Ridlon⁶ (1), second daughter of John⁵ (13), was born in Hollis, Me.; was married to Brackett Pillsbury, of Portland, and has issue. Now (1880) a widow.

Emery-S. Ridlon⁶ (1), eldest son of Magnus⁵ (8), was born April 21, 1841, presumably in Parsonfield, Me.; married Ida M. Bickford, April 30, 1864, and has issue *one* son. He was educated at North Parsonfield Seminary, and Albany University, New York, where he graduated, May 7, 1867, with degree of LL. B. He studied law with Hon. Caleb R. Ayer, of Cornish, Me., and opened an office at Kezar Falls Village, near his birth-place, where he practised his profession till 1872, when he sold out to Francis W. Ridlon, Esq., and removed to Portland, where he has gained prominence in his practice and has an extensive business. He is one of those who, fortunately, has found the position in life for which he was especially adapted, and promises to be one of the most influential lawyers in the city of Portland. Affable and social, pleasant in conversation, prompt in his attention to the interest of his clients, and foremost in all issues pertaining to the public good, he has won a large circle of warm friends and patrons. As a progressive and clear-headed lawyer he attracts the public attention, and has been honored with official positions in the city government. Esquire Ridlon is below the medium height, thick-set, corpulent; has dark hair and beard, and in general movements and personal appearance resembles his mother's family. He wears spectacles. He was a member of the committee chosen at the Family Meeting in Philadelphia, in 1876, to aid in the publication of this book.

Elizabeth-B. Ridlon⁶ (10), eldest daughter of Magnus⁵ (8), was born in Parsonfield, Me., Jan. 18, 1844. Deceased young.

John-F. Ridlon⁶ (?), second son of Magnus⁵ (8), was born in Parsonfield, Me., Sept. 7, 1846; learned the blacksmith's trade with his father, and worked some years in Massachusetts. He has latterly returned to his native village and resumed business with his father. Is an owner of real estate at Kezar Falls. Has been deputy sheriff in York County. He is tall, broad-shouldered, and corpulent; a remarkably fine-looking young man, an influential citizen, and excellent mechanic.

Stilman-J. Ridlon⁶ (1), third son of Magnus⁵ (8), was born in Parsonfield, Me., Dec. 7, 1849; married Nellie A., daughter of Horace M. and Sarah M. Quimby, of Newport, Me., and has issue, of whom hereafter. He learned the blacksmith's trade with his father, and, before marriage, lived at home. He was deputy-sheriff several years before his brother, before mentioned, served. He is now living on a farm with his father-in-law at Newport. He is short, heavy, and corpulent; resembles the Emery family.

Emily-F. Ridlon⁶ (3), second daughter of Magnus⁵ (8), was born in Parsonfield, Me., Oct. 6, 1853, and never married. Lives at home with her parents. A lady of amiable disposition.

Marcie-E. Ridlon[6] (2), third daughter of Magnus[5] (8), was born in Parsonfield, Me., July 25, 1857. She has acquired a thorough education, being a graduate of Farmington Normal School, and is now a teacher in the public schools in Portland, Me.

Nellie Ridlon[6] (?), youngest daughter of Magnus[5] (8), was born in Parsonfield, Me., Nov. 28, 1867. Nellie has a very precocious mind, and is an interesting young lady, beloved by all.

Clark Ridley[6] (1), eldest son of Matthias[5] (5), was born in Wayne, Me., June 25, 1819, and never married. He spent many years in the gold-mines of California, having gone out amongst the early explorers of that country. He acquired a passion for camp-life, and became a good cook. He is an eccentric character, and keeps away from society as much as possible. In 1879 he was living in New Bedford, Mass., where he is said to own considerable property. Lives alone. Medium height, broad shoulders, short, thick neck, dark hair and beard, gray eyes, and is a typical specimen of the old Redlon ancestral stock in looks and movements.

Matthias Ridley[6] (7), second son of Matthias[5] (5), was born in Wayne, Me., March 7, 1822; married Lydia D. Rolf, Aug. 27, 1849 (another authority states his wife to be Mary-Ann Tibbetts, daughter of Isaac Tibbetts, of Rumford, Me.), and resides at Dedham, Mass., where he carries on a mill. He was a watchman for several years in Lowell, and it is said his wife owned considerable property in that city; she was helpless for several years. He sometime lived in Charlestown, and worked in the navy yard there. Kept a store in Boston. Possibly married twice: the "skein is tangled." He was a man of great physical powers when in his prime. Resembles the old Redlons. Reserved and retiring in disposition. He has had issue *four* children, of whom hereafter.

Nancy Ridley[6] (4), eldest daughter of Matthias[5] (5), was born in Wayne, Me., Dec. 30, 1824; was married, Sept. 4, 1844, by Rev. A. A. Miner, to Philip Sargent, of New Hampshire, and resided in Lowell, Mass. Died Dec. 12, 1854.

Hannah Ridley[6] (11), second daughter of Matthias[5] (5), was born in Wayne, Me., July 17, 1826; was married Nov. 24, 1847, to Daniel Kimball, of New Hampshire, and died in Lowell, Mass., Nov. 14, 1856.

Mary Ridley[6] (31), third daughter of Matthias[5] (5), was born in Wayne, Me., May 26, 1828; was married Oct. 6, 1855, at Boston, to David Patterson, and resides in Lowell, Mass.

Isaac Ridley[6] (8), third son of Matthias[5] (5), was born in Wayne, Me., June 21, 1831; married Mary M., daughter of Dea. Snow Keene and his wife, Sophronia Maxum, Oct. 1, 1856, settled in Leeds, and had issue *one* son, of whom hereafter. His wife died in 1858, and he went to California the same year. He worked on a farm in Sacramento Valley; thence went to Oregon, and mined on the Powder River; then worked in a lumber-yard, at Fort Walla Walla, Washington Territory; thence mined on the Columbia River; thence up that river seven hundred miles, prospecting in a log-canoe; dragged canoe two miles to Courtney River, in British Columbia; thence down that river to Courtney mines; thence alone on a pony six hundred miles, to Fort Colville, where he carried on a farm two years. He engaged in speculations, on the Columbia; went back from Portland, Oregon, to San Francisco and Sacramento; thence home to Maine, and settled down upon a part of his father's old homestead farm. He married, secondly, July 20, 1874, to Annetta, daughter of Didimus and Harriet (Gould) Edgecomb, of Lisbon, Me. (she was born April 5, 1832), and lives a quiet, contented, and peaceful life. His early years were full of adventure, and an interesting volume could be written on his travels and engagements with the Indians. Mr. Ridley is tall and slender, and has the features of face and movements of his ancestors. He is honest, frugal, and very kind of heart. A neat, systematic, prudent, and successful farmer.

Sophronia Ridley[6] (1), fourth daughter of Matthias[5] (5), was born in Wayne, Me., July 1, 1833; was married July 12, 1854, to Jeremiah Tuck, of Lowell, Mass. Kept hotel at Mattawaumkeag, Me. Resided a while at Frederickton, N. B.; now (1880) in San Francisco, Cal. Her husband is a photographer.

Delaney Ridley[6] (1), fifth daughter of Matthias[5] (5), was born in Wayne, Me., Nov. 15, 1834; was married to Charles Hull, and resides at Sacramento, Cal., on a stock-farm. She is a woman of literary tastes and refined, well-stored mind.

Abiah Ridley[6] (1), sixth daughter of Matthias[5] (5), was born in Wayne, Me., April 11, 1838; was married Feb. 6, 1862, to Reuben Weld, of Livermore, a carpenter, and is now (1879) living at Strickland's Ferry, Kennebec County, Me. Has a daughter.

Abington Ridley[6](1), youngest son of Matthias[5] (5), was born in Wayne, Me., July 5, 1842; married Harriet-Elizabeth, daughter of Didimus and Harriet (Gould) Edgecomb, of Lisbon, Me., and lived some time on the homestead farm. He served in the Eighth Regiment, Maine Volunteer Infantry, during the Rebellion, for four years. He went West in 1871, and lived a while at Santa Cruz; thence to Barnard's Inlet, British Columbia. He has *five* children, of whom hereafter. He resembles his brothers in features and habits, — reserved, reticent, eccentric.

Lieut. Billings-Hood Ridley[6] (1), eldest son of Jonathan[5] (4), was born in Wayne, Me., May 9, 1826; married Mary S. Dickey, of Manchester, N. H., and has *six* children, of whom hereafter. In 1852 he went on board the steamship "Ohio," bound for California, and when crossing the gulf-stream they encountered a terrible tempest, and the vessel was so badly disabled that for hours they despaired of being saved; but through the remarkable efficiency of the commander, and the untiring exertions of the crew, they outrode the storm. After spending four years in the gold State, he started on his return home; had a pleasant voyage on the Pacific, and at Aspinwall embarked on the ill-fated "Central America." When they were in nearly the same waters where they were wrecked on the outward-bound voyage, they were overtaken by a severe gale, and the vessel became unmanageable. The six hundred passengers took turns at bailing, for two days and a night, when the vessel went down with nearly all on board. A vessel picked up forty-nine, at midnight, and three days later, three others were taken from a piece of the wreck, upon which they had floated in the gulf-stream about six hundred miles. Mr. Ridley was twice injured by falling buckets, which cut his head, and has never fully recovered from his injuries. He was an officer in the Twenty-eighth Regiment of Maine Volunteer Infantry, during the Rebellion, and proved himself a good soldier. He now lives on a farm with his aged father, in the town of Jay, surrounded by his pleasant family and all the temporal comforts of life. He has an inventive cast of mind, and has spent considerable time and study on a new motor, which was not a success. He has been a great reader, is well informed, conversational, and an interesting and social gentleman. Of medium height; dark complexion; hair and beard formerly black, the latter curly and worn long and heavy. He has been a great worker, and his hardships and exposure have caused him to grow prematurely old and gray.

Eliza-H. Ridley[6] (7), eldest daughter of Jonathan[5] (4), was born in Wayne, Me., Aug. 23, 1828; was married to Artson K. Pratt, Jan. 25, 1849, and is now living in the West.

Nancy-E. Ridley[6] (5), second daughter of Jonathan[5] (4), was born in Wayne, Me., Feb. 17, 1830; was married to Annah(?) B. Beal, Aug. 30, 1843, and lives in Canton, near her father's home.

Jonathan Ridley[6] (6), second son of Jonathan[5] (4), was born Aug. 18, 1832; married Frances Pollard, of Berlin, Mass., in 1873, and lives on a farm in Jackson, Me. He served in the Union army, during the Rebellion, being mustered, Feb. 19, 1862. He is tall, and has dark hair, beard, and eyes; his features are of the old Ridlon type. A steady, honest, industrious, and quiet man. No issue.

Sarah-M. Ridley[6] (16), third daughter of Jonathan[5] (4), was born Dec. 11, 1834; was married to Daniel M. Howard, April 5, 1854; secondly, to —— Palmer. She lives at Caribou, Aroostook County, Me.

Benjamin Ridley[6] (9), third son of Jonathan[5] (4), was born in November, 1837, and died at home, unmarried, May 31, 1858.

Martha-Louisa Ridley[6] (12), youngest daughter of Jonathan[5] (4), was born Dec. 13, 1842; was married to Elijah F. Purington, Feb. 6, 1857, and lives on a hillside farm, in Wilton, Me.[*] Martha is a woman of many virtues, and possessed of a well-stored and discriminating mind. She is fond of books and flowers, and admires the beauties of nature; is endowed with a gentle and tender spirit, and develops many traits characteristic of the old Ridlon mothers. She takes pride in her family, and has contributed toward the portrait of her beloved and patriarchal father, for this book. No children.

Paulina Ridley[6] (2), eldest daughter of Daniel[5] (7), was born in Wayne, Me., Dec. 13, 1828, and was married to Joseph Lovett.

Silas-C. Ridley[6] (1), eldest son of Daniel[5] (7), was born in Wayne, Me., April 3, 1830, and died Nov. 10, 1870. He was married, and left a widow, who has married —— Wentworth, of Bangor, Me.

Joseph-W. Ridley[6] (9), second son of Daniel[5] (7), was born in Wayne,

[*] Several visits at the home of Mr. and Mrs. Purington, during the compilation of this book, will long be remembered by the author, as among the most restful and happy of his experiences in the country. The cordial and unpretentious greeting received, with the generous and simple hospitality bestowed, were calculated to enhance the enjoyment of one who, with weary brain, was seeking for a quiet retreat, for rest and recuperation. The home, situated upon a high elevation, commanding a wide and beautiful prospect, diversified with almost every specimen of landscape, — mountains, forests, farms, broad, green valleys, winding streams, and neat villages, — is cool and spacious; and being so far removed from the highway, — the approach is by a gate-way and circuitous lane, — there is no sound to disturb the serenity of the place; the tinkling of the sheep-bells, bleating of lambs, and sweet song of birds in pasture, roof-tree, and orchard, produce a peaceful spirit, and contribute to the pleasure of one who loves rural scenery and association. The fresh berries, snow-white bread, gilt-edged butter, cool milk, and all the wholesome products of the orchard and garden, loaded a table that would make a king smack his lips. A few days' tarry at this home invigorated health, made the muscles stronger, and toned the brain to clearer work.

Me., July 9, 1832; married Mary A., daughter of E. W. Robbins, and lives on a farm in Hudson, Penobscot County, Me. Has issue, of whom hereafter. ' He served in Company B, Seventh Regiment Maine Volunteer Infantry, during the Rebellion, being mustered into the army Oct. 20, 1862.

Betsey Ridley[6] (11), second daughter of Daniel[5] (7), was born in Wayne, Me., Feb. 28, 1833, and was married to Theodore B. Knox, a farmer, of Livermore.

Joshua-G. Ridley[6] (3), third son of Daniel[5] (7), was born in Wayne, Me., May 30, 1834, and has been in California many years. He is said to be a wealthy man. No record of his marriage. Is well-formed and fine-looking; has black hair and beard.

Jerome-R. Ridley[6] (2), fourth son of Daniel[5] (7), was born in Wayne, Me., March 22, 1835; married Clara Knowlton, and has issue, of whom hereafter. Carpenter by trade. Formerly worked in the city of Lewiston; latterly resided in Wayne Village. He is dark-complexioned, of medium height, and a real Ridlon.

Charles-G. Ridley[6] (6), fifth son of Daniel[5] (7), was born in Wayne, Me., Oct. 3, 1837; married Vienna-Melissa Goodwin, and in 1873, was a farmer at River Falls, Wis. Has issue, of whom hereafter. He is five feet ten inches in height, and weighs one hundred and sixty pounds.

Sarah Ridley[6] (17), third daughter of Daniel[5] (7), was born in Wayne, Me., Oct. 4, 1838. Never married, but lived at home with her mother, till the latter died; now in Lewiston mills. A lady of excellent character, and a true type of our old Ridlon mothers, in features of face and movements.

Jason-M. Ridley[6] (1), sixth son of Daniel[5] (7), was born in Wayne, Me., March 15, 1841; married Abbie L. Stinchfield, and lives at Wayne Village. Works in shovel-handle factory.

Dean-K. Ridley[6] (1), seventh son of Daniel[5] (7), was born in Wayne, Me., Jan. 12, 1843, and is now (1879) working as a blacksmith at Wayne Village. Unmarried.

Lee-S. Ridley[6] (1), eighth son of Daniel[5] (7), was born in Wayne, Me., Dec. 24, 1844. He lived on the home-farm, and engaged in breeding fine horses, till the death of his mother, when he went to Lewiston and kept a livery stable. He and his brothers have raised some of the most valuable horses ever owned in the State of Maine, and have sold at fancy prices; but they lost heavily by too extensive outlays and bad management. He has every characteristic of the Ridlon family.

Horatio-N. Ridley[6] (2), a half-brother to the preceding, was born March 11, 1828; married and has issue. Resides at North Dartmouth, Mass. I have no particulars of this family.

Hamilton-Jenkins Ridley[6] (1), eldest son of Benjamin[5] (3), was born in Wayne, Me., Jan. 11, 1824; married Sarah R., daughter of Dea. Daniel and Lydia (Ridlon) True, of Wayne, and has had issue *seven* children, of whom hereafter. Mr. Ridley lives on the old Hamilton Jenkins farm, in his native town. He is an able, influential, public-spirited citizen. A great reader; well-informed. Has served as enrolling officer, selectman, juryman, and in many other positions of trust. Free Mason of high degree. Has quick perception, sound judgment, and executive ability. An active and radical politician, and fluent speaker. He is naturally logical and argumentative. Memory very retentive and accurate. Tall, well-formed, and of nervous temperament. Dark-brown hair, eyes, and whiskers. Resembles his grandmother's family — the Boothbys — more than the Ridlons.

Hallet Ridley[6] (1), second son of Benjamin[5] (3), was born in Wayne, Me., May 15, 1827; married Frances, daughter of Otis and Rachel (Ridlon) Hood, of Turner, March 21, 1848, and had issue *six* children, of whom hereafter. Mr. Ridley kept a boarding-house in the city of Bangor, several years. Subsequently kept boarders in the city of Lewiston. He was in poor health for many years, could do no heavy work, and during the winter of 1876, had a shock of paralysis, which destroyed his power of speech, and from which he died the 24th of July following. He was buried in Wayne, by the side of his children, who predeceased him, in a beautifully sequestered spot, bordered by woodlands, and near the home of his surviving brother. He was a quiet, serious, thoughtful man; good-natured, generous, and conversational, when in the company of those he esteemed. He was light-complexioned, tall, heavy-built, and corpulent, sometimes weighing two hundred pounds.

Eliza Ridley[6] (8), only daughter of Benjamin[5] (3), was born in Wayne, Me., June 17, 1831; was married to Osgood Graves, her cousin, and had issue *five* children. She died June 27, 1854.

Paulina Ridley[6] (3), eldest daughter of Jerome[5] (1), was born in Richmond, Me., Jan. 30, 1837; was married, in 1856, to Sumner Cunningham, of Gardiner, and has issue.

Luther-Martin Ridley[6] (3), a twin son of Jerome[5] (1), was born in Richmond, Me., Sept. 15, 1840. He was mustered into the First Maine Cavalry, Oct. 20, 1861, and served in the Union army till the close of the Rebellion. A good soldier.

Martin-Luther Ridley[6] (2), a twin son of Jerome[5] (1), was born in Richmond, Me., Sept. 15, 1840. He was mustered into Company A, Twenty-fourth Regiment, Maine Volunteer Infantry, Oct. 11, 1862.

Hezekiah Ridley[6] (1), third son of Jerome[5] (1), was born in Richmond, Me., March 12, 1842; married Arvilla Paris, of Dresden, in 1865, and lives in his native town.

Jerome Ridley[6] (3), fourth son of Jerome[5] (1), was born in Richmond, Me., July 1, 1843. He was mustered into the Union army, Oct. 20, 1861, as a member of the First Regiment of Maine Cavalry, and died of wounds received in a skirmish, at "Ream's Station," Virginia, Aug. 23, 1864. He was a brave soldier.

Benjamin Ridley[6] (10), fifth son of Jerome[5] (1), was born in Richmond, Me., June 10, 1846; was mustered into the Union army, in Company A, Twenty-fourth Regiment Maine Volunteer Infantry, and died at Chicago, Ill., Aug. 19, 1863, from disease contracted near Bonnet Carre, La. He served from Oct. 11, 1862.

Augusta-Eliza Ridley[6] (2), second daughter of Jerome[5] (1), was born in Richmond, Me., Sept. 19, 1847; unmarried in 1876. She is an amiable, Christian lady; an ornament to the family.

Mary-L. Ridley[6] (32), third daughter of Jerome[5] (1), was born in Richmond, Me., Sept. 2, 1849. Unmarried in 1876.

Dr. Davis-A. Ridley[6] (1), sixth son of Jerome[5] (1), was born in Richmond, Me., March 25, 1851; married, and has issue, of whom hereafter. He was educated for the medical profession, and has practised at Wayne Village and Palermo. He was considered skillful for one so young.

Newton-J. Ridley[6] (1), seventh son of Jerome[5] (1), was born in Richmond, Me., Jan. 23, 1853.

Banks-W. Ridley[6] (1), eighth son of Jerome[5] (1), was born in Richmond, Me., May 29, 1855.

Daniel-W. Ridley[6] (10), ninth son of Jerome[5] (1), was born in Richmond, Me., May 10, 1858.

Walter-E. Ridley[6] (1), tenth son of Jerome[5] (1), was born in Richmond, Me., Feb. 19, 1860.

Frank-B. Ridley[6] (3), eleventh son of Jerome[5] (1), was born in Richmond, Me., April 23, 1862.

Alberta-J. Ridley[6] (1), fourth daughter of Jerome[5] (1), was born in Richmond, Me., April 28, 1867.

Phylinda-Decker Ridley[6] (1), eldest daughter of John[5] (14), was born in Hollis, Me., Jan. 29, 1828 ; was married to Thomas, son of Matthias and Rachel (Pendexter) Ridlon, of Sweden, Me., in April, 1854, and had a large family, of whom hereafter. She died at North Bridgton, Me., Aug. 20, 1873.

Albion-L. Ridlon[6] (2), eldest son of John[5] (14), was born in Hollis, Me., Aug. 30, 1831 ; married Harriet, daughter of Ferdinand Libby, of Limington, in 1858, and had issue *four* children, of whom hereafter. He settled at Moderation Village in his native town, and worked many years in a box-factory. He was a natural mechanic, and could do a neat piece of cabinet work. He was mustered into the First Regiment District Columbia Cavalry, Feb. 9, 1864, went to the seat of war, and while on a march, and when foraging, was captured by the Rebels ; was carried to Richmond, confined in Libbey Prison, and after suffering every abuse and indignity died of starvation His widow married Nathan Lane for a second husband, and died in 1875. He was tall and slender ; had black hair, beard, and eyes ; was featured like his mother ; was steady, industrious, kindhearted, and a professed Christian.

Asenath-F. Ridlon[6] (1), second daughter of John[5] (14), was born in Hollis, Me., Dec. 11, 1829, and has always lived at home with her parents ; a maiden-lady of many virtues.

Stephen Ridlon[6] (7), second son of John[5] (14), was born in Hollis, Me., Sept. 28, 1840 ; died Feb. 25, 1843.

James-Allen Ridlon[6] (16), eldest son of Humphrey[5] (1), was born in Albion (?), Me., Nov. 28, 1831 ; married Elizabeth-Rachel, daughter of Ezra and Sarah (Doe) Wiggin, of China (she was born in China, Me., May 5, 1837, and died Jan. 2, 1871), by whom he had *six* children. He married, secondly, April 4, 1871, Orvilla, daughter of Ira and Sally (Balcom) Shorey, of Palermo, Me. (she was born in China, Nov. 27, 1847), by whom he had issue *two* (possibly others) children, of whom, with those of first wife, hereafter. Mr. Ridlon is a shoe-maker and farmer. He is well informed. Does not resemble the Ridlon family.

Pelena-F. Ridlon[6] (4), eldest daughter of Humphrey[5] (1), was born in Albion (?), Me., Jan. 26, 1833 ; was married to Miles S. Leonard, and has issue.

Albina Ridlon[6] (1), second daughter of Humphrey[5] (1), was born in Albion (?), Me., June 30, 1835 ; was married to George M. Wiggin, and has issue.

John-Wesley Ridlon[6] (22), second son of Humphrey[6] (1), was born in Albion (?), Me., Jan. 15, 1888 ; married and has issue *three* children, of whom hereafter. He has lived on the homestead farm with his parents, in Albion.

Mary-A. Ridlon[6] (33), eldest daughter of Ira[5] (1), was born Dec. 25, 1833, and died Dec. 22, 1837.
Oraville-A. Ridlon[6] (1), second daughter of Ira[5] (1), was born Sept. 25, 1839, and died Nov. 2, 1860.
Lizzie-W. Ridlon[6] (11), third daughter of Ira[5] (1), was born June 8, 1842, and died Aug. 19, 1860.
Alfred-B. Ridlon[6] (2), only son of Ira[5] (1), was born in Durham, Me., Sept. 21, 1846 ; married firstly, Lucy C. Irish; secondly, Jan. 9, 1873, Mary A. Goodwin, of Reading, Mass., by whom he has issue *four* sons, of whom hereafter. Mr. Ridlon served in the war of the Rebellion about four years, being in many engagements and hard marches; receives a pen-pension for injuries sustained in the service. Carpenter by trade. Resides in Franklin, N. H. He is of medium height, slender build, and has dark complexion.
Maria-S. Ridlon[6] (1), youngest daughter of Ira[5] (1), was born Dec. 28, 1851; was married to Charles-Hiram Libbey, March 28, 1870.

Olive-O. Ridlon[6] (6), eldest daughter of Jonathan[6] (5), was born in Clarendon, Vt., April 1, 1831; was married to Noah Fisk, of Danby, a carpenter, Nov. 10, 1852, and lives near her birth-place.
George-M. Ridlon[6] (8), eldest son of Jonathan[6] (5), was born in Clarendon, Vt., May 28, 1834; married Delaney Shearman, of Wells, Rut-land County, July 13, 1859, and has issue *two* children, of whom hereafter. Mr. Ridlon carries on a large dairy-farm near the place of his birth. He was the first member of this branch of the family with whom correspond-ence was opened respecting this genealogy; the family was not aware that they had any kindred of their name, until they saw my advertisement in a Vermont newspaper. George is of medium height, broad-shouldered, and muscular; has brown hair and beard. He seems to be a kind-hearted, genial, well-informed man.
Freelove-T. Ridlon[6] (1), second daughter of Jonathan[6] (5), was born in Clarendon, Vt., Dec. 18, 1843; was married in 1866, to George T. Pha-lon, of Cuttingsville, Rutland County, merchant, and is supposed to be living there.
Elizabeth Ridlon[6] (12), third daughter of Jonathan[6] (5), was born in Clarendon, Vt., Jan. 4, 1847.
Edgar-J. Ridlon[6] (1), youngest son of Jonathan[6] (5), was born in Clarendon, Vt., May 9, 1852.

John-H. Ridlon[6] (23), eldest son of Thomas[5] (5), was born in Claren-don, Vt., Dec. 20, 1835; married Adelaide, daughter of Lovings and Betsey Seamans, of Tinmouth, March 10, 1862, and has issue *two* children, of whom hereafter. Mason by trade. Resembles his Ridlon ancestors.
Lorada-C. Ridlon[6] (1), eldest daughter of Thomas[5] (5), was born in Clarendon, Vt., Dec. 31, 1837; was married Dec. 25, 1856, to Julius C. Gilmore, a farmer, in Rutland.
Paulina-W. Ridlon[6] (5), second daughter of Thomas[5] (5), was born in Clarendon, Vt., Feb. 16, 1837; was married Dec. 25, 1864, to George

W. Potter, a farmer, of Castleton, and died in Illinois, whither she had emigrated in April, 1868.

Delilah-B. Ridlon⁶ (1), third daughter of Thomas⁵ (5), was born in Clarendon, Vt., April 5, 1841; was married Oct. 26, 1861, to James D. Everest, a farmer in Clarendon.

Eddie Ridlon⁶ (1), second son of Thomas⁵ (5).

Mary Ridlon⁶ (34), fourth daughter of Thomas⁵ (5).

Eudora Ridlon⁶ (1), fifth daughter of Thomas⁵ (5).

Vesta Ridlon⁶ (1), sixth daughter of Thomas⁵ (5).

Alvin Ridlon⁶ (2), third son of Thomas⁵ (5).

Dr. John-F. Ridlon⁶ (24), eldest son of Noel⁵ (1), was born in the southwestern part of the town of Clarendon, Vt., Nov. 24, 1852, and was named for his two grandfathers, "John-Joshua," but he disliked his middle name, and changed it to *Frederick.* He commenced to attend the district school in his eighth year, walking two miles each way; the term lasted thirteen weeks, and the great distance made his attendance very irregular. He continued at school during the summer and winter terms until his twelfth year, when he was kept at home for work on the farm. In his fourteenth year his father was killed, and he became virtually the head of the household; to the extent, at least, that nothing was done without his consent, and what he advised was carried forward. At this time his highest ambition, founded on the best type of manhood he knew of, was to become a clerk in a country store, and afterwards to have a store of his own. With this end in view the homestead was rented, in 1867, and the family took lodgings at Poultney, Vt., that he might attend Lansley's Commercial College; he graduated from this institution in May following (1868), having been taught commercial arithmetic, commercial law, and bookkeeping. He also imbibed a desire for a higher education, but without any definite end in view, and on the following September found himself at Uncle Jake Spaulding's Barre Academy, at Barre, Vt., which at that time had the reputation of being the best school of the kind in the State. After a year in this academy he gave up study, and commenced canvassing for a book entitled "Our Great, New West." This proved disagreeable business, and he gave it up, and engaged as clerk in a store at Granville, N. Y., for one hundred and twenty-five dollars a year and board. About this time his mother, who had been his guardian, was married, and their property (the farm in Vermont had been sold in 1868) was divided, and he assumed absolute control of his share, amounting to about eleven thousand dollars. At the end of his engagement in the store, he went to Momence, Ill., to visit his mother, and while there (summer of 1870), he joined a civil-engineer corps, on the Chicago, Danville, and Vincennes Railroad, and carried "level-rod" for some weeks. In October, 1870, he came East, and began fitting for college, at Goddard Seminary (then called Green Mountain Central Institute), at Barre, Vt., under L. L. Barrington. Here he worked hard, and by reading Latin and Greek, during the summer vacation, did his three years' course in two, graduating in June, 1872, and delivering the first Latin oration ever delivered in that institution. From the latter place he went to Tufts College, entering the class of '76. He did only enough studying during his freshman year to keep his place in his class. He joined the Θ Δ Χ society, which was made up of the "good fellows" of the college, and took a leading part in all the amusements to be found. On Saturday he always dined

John F. Ridlon M.D.

at Parker's (Boston), and went to see the Zaostaske Sisters, or Ada Richmond, at the Howard Athenæum, or Lydia Thompson's troup, at the Globe. He knew many of the city "sports," and had friendly bouts with "the gloves" with Sol Aaron, and most of the "fraternity" of Howard Street. He spent a good deal of money, and just before the end of the year, was called before the faculty and mildly disciplined. Appreciating their consideration, he reformed, and during his sophomore year worked hard. Two weeks before the end of the year, however, he was again called before the faculty, and accused of breach of rules, of which (he says) he was not guilty. An example was wanted, and having no proof but his own statement, and having a bad reputation the year before, he was expelled from the college. Stung by this injustice, he went to Chicago, Ill., and entered the University of Chicago; by working hard during all the summer vacation, he made up some junior studies, and was allowed to enter the senior class of '75. He now gave up his connection with the Θ Δ Χ society, and became a Δ Κ Ε. He made up the remainder of his junior studies, and was so successful in his senior work that he was chosen class-poet on class day, and had the salutatory oration awarded him at commencement day; thus having the satisfaction of receiving the degree of A. B. from a college of a higher standing than that from which he had been expelled, and that a year sooner. As he now looks back, his expulsion from Tuft's College seems to him the most fortunate thing that ever occurred to him. He now became a member of Momence Lodge 481, of Free and Accepted Masons. His graduating oration was upon the infallibility of the Pope, and because he treated the subject in what seemed to him a purely logical and scientific way, he was roundly denounced as a Catholic, in a speech made by an ex-president of the college, at the alumni-dinner. "Hereafter," he said, "we shall see to it that no Roman Catholic graduates from our (Baptist) institution." The following September found him in New York city, studying medicine at the College of Physicians and Surgeons, with Prof. E. C. Seguin as preceptor. He took the three years' course and graduated in March, 1878. In June following the University of Chicago conferred upon him the degree of A. M. He entered the competitive examination for interne at St. Luke's Hospital, and gained the position, going on duty July 1, 1878, and serving as assistant-surgeon, assistant-physician, house-surgeon, and house-physician till April 1, 1880. In the midst of this service he was married. The New York *Evening Express* printed the following: "Special dispatch — Newport, June 4 (1879). At the hour of eleven this forenoon Trinity Church was well filled with the *élite* of this place, to witness the performance of a marriage ceremony in the upper ranks of fashion. The high-contracting parties were Dr. J. F. Ridlon, of New York city, and Miss Emily C. Robinson, daughter of Madame M. J. Robinson, of Newport and New York. The ceremony was performed by Rev. George J. Magill, rector of Trinity. The ushers were Messrs. R. O. Harris and F. E. Cabot, of Boston, and George F. Crane and Dr. Walter Mendelson, of New York. There were four bridesmaids: Miss A. M. Harris, of Boston, Miss Ernestine Houget, of New York, and Miss Josie Gorton and Miss Annie Gorton, of Newport. The bride was elegantly attired in heavy corded white silk dress, *en train*, with tulle veil, and a profusion of orange-blossoms. She carried a magnificent boquet of white roses. After the wedding a reception was held at Madame Robinson's cottage. Numerous elegant and costly gifts were received by the bride. The happy couple leave this af-

ternoon on a month's wedding tour, after which they will settle in their
new home, in New York." From the *Home Journal* (New York) we
quote the following extract: "The bridesmaids wore white French organ-
die, beautifully trimmed with white satin. Their tulle veils were arranged
to form turbans on the head, being fastened at the back with a bunch of
roses, and caught at the neck in the same manner. The boquets of jacque-
minot and tea-roses were the gift of the groom. The groom and ushers
wore frock-coats and light trousers, with *boutonnieres* to match the bridesmaids' boquets. Immediately after the ceremony, the favored guests repaired to Madame Robinson's cottage, in Catherine Street, where a colla-
tion was spread. The table and room were beautifully decorated with
flowers. The ceremony of cutting the wedding-cake was novel and pretty. The bride sat on an ottoman, while the four bridesmaids held the
cake over her head, the officiating clergyman, of course, wielding the
sacrificial knife. Telegrams and letters of congratulation, and presents
were showered upon the happy couple."

On leaving the hospital, April 1, 1880, Dr. Ridlon began practice in
that part of the city known as Washington Heights. In April, 1881, he
was appointed on the attending staff of St. Luke's Hospital as assistant
orthopordic surgeon; and in June following as assistant-surgeon to the
New York Orthopordic Dispensary and Hospital. In May, 1882, he gave
up his general practice, and moved into the centre of the city, in order to
devote himself entirely to surgery, especially as applied to the treatment
of deformities by mechanical means. In October, 1882, he was appointed
first clinical assistant to the chair of orthopordic surgery of the medical department of the University of the city of New York, and since,
during the sessions, has lectured twice a week on the subject of orthopordic surgery. In June, 1883, he was appointed attending surgeon to
the dispensary of the University Medical College. Of medical societies
he is a member of the County Medical Society and the Parthological
Society.

From his first school attendance to his graduation, Dr. Ridlon proved
himself a very proficient student, and his rapid advancement in his profession, since he commenced practice, shows conclusively that his skill and
judgment are something quite remarkable for one of his years and experience. He was converted while attending school in Vermont, and
became connected with the Methodist Church there, but has continued
to modify his religious views, and says he is now as near an Agnostic as
anything. He has issue *three* children, of whom hereafter. The accompanying steel engraved portrait was kindly furnished by Dr. Ridlon for
this book, at a cost of seventy-five dollars, and is a very fine work of art.

Emmet-N. Ridlon⁶ (1), second son of Noel⁵ (1), was born in Clarendon, Vt., Aug. 29 —— ; died Dec. 15, 1859.

Charles Ridlon⁶ (7), third son of Noel⁵ (1), was born in Clarendon,
Vt., July 31, 1861; died May 9, 1863.

Ada Ridlon⁶ (1), eldest daughter of John⁵ (15), was born in Clarendon, Vt.; was married to N. B. Potter, in 1861.

John Ridlon⁶ (25), eldest son of John⁵ (15), was born in Clarendon, Vt., and deceased when young.

Jerome Ridlon⁶ (4), second son of John⁵ (15), was born in Clarendon, Vt., and deceased when young.

Oren-M. Ridley[6] (2), eldest son of David[5] (3), was born in Bangor, Me., Feb. 19, 1847; died Jan. 8, 1854.

Mary-J. Ridley[6] (35), eldest daughter of David[5] (3), was born in Bangor, Me., Oct. 24, 1849; was married to Henry W. Russell, of Corinth, Oct. 26, 1862, and died Feb. 8, 1878.

Annie-C. Ridley[6] (1), second daughter of David[5] (3), was born in Bangor, Me., Nov. 5, 1851; was married in Corinth, March 18, 1870, to L. D. Cole, and died Dec. 19, 1872.

Louisa-A. Ridley[6] (1), third daughter of David[5] (3), was born in Bangor, Me., Jan. 29, 1853; was married in Corinth, March 18, 1871, to Edwin A. Cole, and died Sept. 21, 1873.

Lizzie-E. Ridley[6] (13), fourth daughter of David[5] (3), was born in Bangor, Me., Oct. 11, 1857, and died Dec. 4, 1873.

Ada-F. Ridley[6] (2), fifth daughter of David[5] (3), was born in Corinth, Me., May 29, 1860, and died in Bangor, Nov. 28, 1878.

Bertha-G. Ridley[6] (1), sixth daughter of David[5] (3), was born in Corinth, Me., May 9, 1863, and died July 22, 1864.

James-Greenleaf Ridlon[6] (17), eldest son of James[5] (7), was born in Hollis, Me., April 28, 1847; married Mary F., daughter of Elisha and Lovina (Haley) Davis, and lives on the homestead farm of his grandfather, now owned by his uncle Joseph. He is tall, broad-shouldered, raw-boned, muscular; has dark-brown hair, and in features of face and movements resembles the old Ridlon ancestors. He is a quiet, industrious, honest man, respected citizen and Christian. No issue.

Joseph-Henry Ridlon[6] (10), second son of James[5] (7), was born in Hollis, Me., Aug. 28, 1848, and lives at home with his mother, on the old Nicholas Ridlon farm, about half a mile south of Bonnie Eagle Village, now owned by Mrs. Ridlon and her sons. Joseph resembles his father in every respect. He is tall, very broad, and square-shouldered, somewhat stooping, moderate in movements, and naturally of a serious, reflective mind. He is a hard-working, steady, highly-esteemed young man, and devoted Christian.

Willie-Hopkinson Ridlon[6] (15), youngest son of James[5] (7), was born in Hollis, Me., in February, 1852, and died unmarried, in 1874. He was in delicate health from a child, and could do no heavy work. He spent his time mostly in clerking in grocery-stores, until his strength so far failed him that he was compelled to retire to his mother's home, where he endured with great patience a long and painful illness. He was quite tall, but slender; walked with bowed head, like his father; was always conscientious and honest, and left an untarnished reputation.

Frank Ridlon[6] (4), only son of Joseph[5] (4), was born in Gorham, Me., and is now in business with his father, at Gorham Village. He was formerly a clerk in the city of Portland. Was educated for commercial pursuits, and is an efficient business manager, book-keeper, and financier.

Mary-Susan Ridlon[6] (36), only daughter of Joseph[5] (4), was born in Gorham, Me.; was married Sept. 22, 1880, to Nathan-Clifford Cummings, grandson of Judge Nathan Clifford, formerly of the United States Supreme Court.

Emma-Frances Ridlon[6] (1), only child of Jesse[5] (1), was born in Limington, Me., Feb. 8, 1847, and died Oct. 27, 1850.

45

Jennie-Frances Ridlon[6] (2), eldest daughter of John[5] (16), was born in Paw Paw, Mich., Nov. 80, 1855 ; was married to Sylvester M. Hess, and resides at Lawrence, Mich.

Addie-Blanch Ridlon[6] (1), second daughter of John[5] (16), was born in Paw Paw, Mich., Sept. 28, 1861 ; was married to J. H. Yund, and lives at Grand Island, Neb.

Charles-Alpheus Ridlon[6] (8), a son of John[5] (16), was born in Paw Paw, Mich., Aug. 20, 1864.

Emma-F. Ridlon[6] (2), eldest daughter of Alpheus[5] (1), was born in Salem, Mass., March 17, 1852 ; died May 28, 1860.

Nellie Ridlon[6] (2), second daughter of Alpheus[5] (1), was born in Harmer, O., Feb. 28, 1860 ; was married to Jerome H. Smith, March 1, 1882, and lives at Avondale, O. Has issue.

Mary-N. Ridlon[6] (37), youngest daughter of Alpheus[5] (1), was born in Harmer, O., March 8, 1861. Single in 1883.

Franklin-Demick Ridlon[6] (5), eldest son of Robert[5] (6), was born in Standish, Me. (?), Feb. 8, 1843 ; married Sarah A., daughter of Moses and Phebe Wood, of Limington, and has issue *seven* children, of whom hereafter. He resides at Steep Falls Village, Standish, and is engaged in the lumber-mills there. He enlisted at the age of twenty-one in the Maine Volunteer Infantry, and was mustered into the Thirtieth Regiment (Company I), Jan. 6, 1864, for service in crushing the Southern Rebellion.

Andrew-Bryant Ridlon[6] (2), second son of Robert[5] (6), was born (presumably) in Standish, Me., Dec. 16, 1845 ; married Eva F., daughter of Luke Rich, of Standish, Jan. 1, 1866, and has issue *three* children, of whom hereafter. He was mustered into the Thirtieth Regiment Maine Infantry, — in the same company with his brother, — Jan. 6, 1864, and served in the Union army in the Rebellion. Resides at Steep Falls Village.

Robert-Herbert Ridlon[6] (8), third son of Robert[5] (6), was born in Standish, Me. (?), Aug. 25, 1852 ; married Sarah, daughter of Freedom and Catherine (Pendexter) Berry, of Cornish, and has issue *three* children, of whom hereafter.

Clarence Ridlon[6] (1), eldest son of Isaac[5] (6), was born in Limington, Me., March 1, 1858.

Minnie-H. Ridlon[6] (1), eldest daughter of Isaac[5] (6), was born in Limington, Me., Aug. 5, 1860.

Jane-E. Ridlon[6] (6), second daughter of Isaac[5] (6), was born in Limington, Me., Nov. 25, 1866.

Mary-M. Ridlon[6] (38), third daughter of Isaac[5] (6), was born in Limington, Me., Jan. 31, 1869.

Nellie Ridlon[6] (2), fourth daughter of Isaac[5] (6), was born in Limington, Me., Dec. 15, 1872.

Rev. Nathaniel-Townsend Ridlon[6] (7), eldest son of Samuel[5] (4), was born in Hollis, Me., Nov. 16, 1837 ; married Rhoda A., daughter of Ezra Fluent, of Waterborough, June 19, 1855, and settled as a carpenter at Moderation Village, near his birth-place, on Saco River. He worked at his trade till his twenty-fourth year, when, having been converted in an extensive reformation, which prevailed in town two years previously, he commenced to preach the Gospel; his first attempt was at Lovell, Me., in the autumn of 1861. He became a member of the "York and Cumberland Christian Conference," and was ordained in the Christian chapel, — which he had built, — in Hollis, during a session of conference held there. He supplied several pulpits, and worked with his tools during the week, until his settlement as pastor of the church at Northampton, N. H., where he was continued about seven years; he removed from that place to Saco, to accept the pastoral charge of the Christian Church in that town, where he has continued rising ten years as a successful shepherd of the flock. He retains his taste for mechanical pursuits, and spends considerable time in building stairs and cabinet-work. He acquired skill as an architect in early years, and still draws plans for houses. Within a few years he has studied dentistry, and being settled in a rural district some miles from town, he has a considerable patronage in this profession. He is a good singer, and sometimes teaches music in winter. He has chosen to live a quiet and unobtrusive life, and is not widely known as a preacher.

Having no children, and enjoying uniformly excellent health, he has always been comparatively free from pressing cares and confinement at home; hence the current of his life flows smoothly onward. As a public speaker he always delivers himself fluently without notes, and is a very ready and acceptable preacher. His theological views are well settled and held firmly. In personal appearance and temperament he has all the prominent characteristics of the old Ridlon stock, supplemented with an overshoot woven from the maternal family loom. Strong of will impulsive; is passionate, sometimes mirthful and jocose. He has been president of his conference, and is a progressive, rising preacher. Hair black and wavy, eyes gray, complexion florid.

Rev. Gideon-Tibbetts Ridlon[6] (1), second son of Samuel[5] (4), was born in Hollis, York County, Me., July 1, 1841; married Lydia-Ellen, twin daughter of John and Lydia (Ridlon) Sawyer, Sept. 30, 1860, and has had issue *four* children, of whom hereafter. He worked on the homestead farm, attending school in winter, until his fifteenth year, when he went to the city to learn the iron machinist's trade; this business he followed, being employed in several cities in Maine, and in traveling to introduce cotton-spinning machinery into new mills in the South and West, until his twenty-fourth year, when, having been converted the winter previous, he commenced preaching as an evangelist, traveling from place to place about two years, and was ordained and settled as pastor over a Christian church he had gathered in Harrison, Me., where he continued nearly four years, during which time he baptized about one hundred and forty members.

His next settlement was at Salisbury Point, Mass., where he bestowed his labors one year; he then commenced evangelistic work at Amesbury, Mass., gathered a church, and was continued there about three years, till the financial revulsion of 1878 so reduced the resources of the new society that he was obliged to resign his charge. At this time the two Christian churches at Harrison, Me., where Mr. Ridlon had been settled previously, were without preaching, and at their call he returned and became their pastor, continuing about three years; during this time he preached one summer at Lovell, Me. He subsequently preached at Lewiston, Fairfield, Dixmont, and Newburg, and was encouraged by seeing many begin a Christian life.

During these years Mr. Ridlon had devoted much time to this work, and in writing for the press, and by overwork so taxed his brain that he suffered a partial paralysis of the right side, which so impaired his memory and the right hand that he was compelled to turn away from study and the use of his pen, and seek rest for his weary mind and body. After consulting the best medical advisers with but little encouragement and no permanent improvement, he resumed work at his trade for one year, and was so far recovered that he settled as pastor of the Christian church at Manchester, N. H., a city with a population of forty thousand, where he has continued about three years. He has baptized over five hundred souls during the past fourteen years, and gathered four new churches. Served as secretary of the New England Christian Convention. Was a member of a conference in western Maine about eight years, but declared his independence and left to escape a spirit of intolerance and coercion, and has since been one of God's freemen, looking to no man or body of men for his authority, but to Him who commissioned him to preach the gospel to all the world.

Mr. Ridlon served during the war of the Rebellion in the Seventeenth Regiment of Maine Volunteer Infantry, and endured many hardships from long marches and exposure. During his early years, possessing an ardent love for the woods, and a spirit of adventure, he spent many weeks each year with dog and gun, roaming along the rivers and lake shores of northern Maine and New Hampshire, and in camp among the mountains, hunting and trapping. He has always been a student of nature, and is charmed by the beauties of shady woodland and flowery field; he sees the wisdom and goodness of the Creator as clearly revealed in His handiwork as displayed in the great, unwritten book, as in the inspired volume, and draws much of the subject matter, woven into his sermons, from these sources.

From early years a persistent reader, he has cherished a love for books, and has now a rare collection, many of them purchased in Europe. He has also many interesting, beautiful, and rare pictures and engravings. Having an interest in antiquarian pursuits, he has spent considerable time in researches for ancient documents, and has much valuable material of . an historical, biographical, and genealogical character stored away, which may some day be found in print. He has been a correspondent for several English and Scottish historical and genealogical publications, and has contributed frequently to the historical magazines of this country. Being a member of several historical and literary societies, he has formed the acquaintance of, and corresponded with, many distinguished historians and men of books, and his files of letters contain the autographs of men that are of eminence in America and Europe.

Mr. Ridlon has written and published works entitled "The Early Settlers of Harrison, Maine," and "Contributions to the Genealogy of the Burbank Family," and has assisted in compiling several other genealogies and town histories. He has devoted much attention to the science of heraldry, and has become sufficiently acquainted with the system to draw coats-of-arms from the heraldic descriptions in abbreviation. During the fourteen years in which he has applied himself to this book, he has gratified his love for traveling and sight-seeing, by several tours through the Western and Southern States; going there in search of genealogical information, and for the purpose of seeing his kindred, for whom he entertains a profound esteem. He proposes making a tour through England,

Scotland, and Shetland, to visit his kindred and view the lands and home of his ancestors.

Mr. Ridlon's life has been a singularly changeable and adventuresome one from his early years. Being possessed of a daring, impulsive temperament, he has moved in many dangerous ways, and accidents have frequently befallen him that came near terminating his life. When only a lad he fell from the great beams of the barn and was taken up unconscious, but without broken limbs. A few years subsequently he accidentally cut an artery in his head, and before a physician could reach him, nearly died from loss of blood. He once fell from a bridge on Saco River, eighteen feet into the falls, and sustained injuries from which he was slow to recover, but managed to swim to the shore, where he lay till men carried him to his home. At the age of fourteen he was thrown from a horse, and had his right arm badly fractured and dislocated; and in the winter of 1881 he was carried down through an iron bridge, in a train of cars on the Boston & Maine Railroad, and seriously injured, barely escaping with his life. In all these experiences a wonderful protective power has seemed to attend him, and he has good grounds to believe that God has preserved him for a wise end.

The subject of this notice is tall and erect, has dark brown, curly hair, hazel eyes, clean-cut features, nervous temperament, and great adhesiveness of will. He delivers his public speeches extemporaneously and fluently, in a clear, distinct voice.

The following verses were composed soon after Mr. Ridlon commenced to preach, and are expressive of his feelings at the time.

" WAYMARKS IN EXPERIENCE.

" Among New England's noble hills,
   Where flow the cool, refreshing rills,
   My Christian mother gave me birth,
   And reared me at the fireside hearth.

" While dwelling in that peaceful home,
   Before my feet had learned to roam,
   My parents read the Scriptures there,
   And daily joined in humble prayer.

" From early dawn to close of day,
   I through the woodlands loved to stray,
   Breathing the fragrant mountain air,
   Guarded with kind, parental care;

" But soon the leadings of my mind
   Caused me to leave these scenes behind,
   And tread, the remnant of my days,
   Life's rugged steeps and thorny ways.

" The counsels of those early years
   Oft caused mine eyes to flow with tears;
   The memory of the good-night kiss
   Still moves my heart to tenderness.

" In later years the tempter's hand
   Would bind me with its iron band;
   Yet thoughts of home and mother's prayer,
   Oft kept me from his fatal snare.

" When on Virginia's tented field,
   God proved my guide and guardian shield,
   He strengthened me to live, and bear
   The hardships I must there endure.

" While in the dark and dreary night,
Around the camp-fire's glimmering light,
Where sleeping comrades near me lay,
I bowed my head and tried to pray.

" When there upon the cold, damp ground,
No peaceful angels gathered round,
But chains of guilt my soul confined,
And weighed upon my troubled mind.

" As on the lonely picket's line
I walked, these thoughts employed my mind,
Of home and friends, who gathered there
At nine o'clock, to kneel in prayer.

" Yet through these scenes of toil and strife,
The Lord preserved my worthless life,
And through his care and guardian grace,
Restored me to my friends' embrace.

" When safe at home the vows I made,
And calls of God I disobeyed;
I walked destruction's awful road,
And shunned the just commands of God.

" But soon my darling, dark-eyed child
Was taken to the spirit world;
My home was made a lonely place,
And still I spurned my Saviour's grace.

" While wicked thoughts my mind employed,
A messenger in haste appeared;
He said my mother soon must die,
And wished to see and counsel me.

" Her loving heart soon ceased to beat;
The work of life was made complete;
And while her friends around her mourned,
The angel took her spirit home.

" I then my life and works reviewed,
And solemn promises renewed;
I changed my course, and sins confessed;
God heard, and oh! how I was blessed!

" My soul was filled with holy love,
And all my thoughts were raised above;
I loved the straight and narrow way,
And praised my Saviour night and day.

" My home was like a paradise,
My heart the Spirit's dwelling-place;
I told the news to all around,
What glorious comfort I had found.

" I had to leave my friends and home,
Through valleys, and o'er hills to roam;
A 'woe' upon my soul was laid,
If I refused, and disobeyed.

" My home I loved, my friends were dear;
More precious still did souls appear;
Through storms and calms I since have been
To warn my dying fellowmen.

" The gospel trump I love to sound,
When anxious sinners gather round.
God gives me raiment, food, and friends,
And I must preach till life shall end.

> " And when I lay my armor down,
> I hope to gain a warrior's crown,
> And with the blissful, happy throng
> To sing the victor's conquering song."

Susan-Ellen Ridlon (8), only daughter of Samuel[5] (4), was born May 4, 1847, and died when about four years of age. She was a dark-eyed, sunny-haired, and lovely child.

Edwin-Franklin Ridlon (1), youngest son of Samuel[5] (4), was born in Hollis, Me., Nov. 25, 1854; married Sarah, daughter of William and Mary (Libbey) Spencer, of Gorham, and lived several years on the homestead farm. He is a carpenter and builder by trade. Tall, raw-boned, light-complexioned, quick of motion, passionate, conversational. No children. Now (1883) living in Boston.

Albert-P. Ridlon (6), eldest son of Robert[5] (7), was born in Bridgton, Me., Aug. 18, 1887; married.

Mary-J. Ridlon (38), eldest daughter of Robert[5] (7), was born in Bridgton, Me., Aug. 14, 1889; married.

Margaret Ridlon (2), second daughter of Robert[5] (7), was born in Letter B township, Me., Dec. 25, 1841; died young.

Nathan-O. Ridlon (3), second son of Robert[5] (7), was born in Bridgton, Me., Dec. 24, 1843; married, but name of wife does not appear.

Calvin-H. Ridlon (1), third son of Robert[5] (7), was born in Bridgton, Me., March 27, 1846; married, but wife's name has not reached me.

Emily-S. Ridlon (3), third daughter of Robert[5] (7), was born in Bridgton, Me., Oct. 22, 1828; was married, but name of husband is unknown.

Daniel-C. Ridlon (11), fourth son of Robert[5] (7), was born in Bridgton, Me., Feb. 2, 1851; married, but I have no particulars.

Fernando-A. Ridlon (1), fifth son of Robert[5] (7), was born in Bridgton(?), Me., or Berlin, Wis.,* March 12, 1856; supposed to be married.

Isabella Ridlon (2), fourth daughter of Robert[5] (7), was born in Berlin, Wis., Nov. 12, 1857; is married, but husband's name unknown.

Nettie Ridlon (1), fifth daughter of Robert[5] (7), was born in Berlin, Wis., Jan. 1, 1859; no particulars.

Granville Ridlon (2), eldest son of Thomas[5] (6), was born in Bridgton, Me., July 7, 1835, and died July 28, 1835.

Almon-H. Ridlon (1), second son of Thomas[5] (6), was born in Bridgton, Me., Sept. 10, 1837; married Mary Mariner, of Sebago, and had issue *two* children, of whom hereafter. He followed the sea, and was many years in the United States Navy. When the war of the Rebellion commenced he came home from sea and enlisted in the army, becoming a member of the Thirtieth Maine Infantry, in 1864. He was once buried alive, but recovered consciousness and called the attention of some officers passing over the battle-field, who had him removed to a hospital. After his recovery from his wounds he returned to his regiment, was taken prisoner, and starved to death in a Southern prison.

Francina-B. Ridlon (1), eldest daughter of Thomas[5] (6), was born in Bridgton, Me., Sept. 31, 1838; was married to Andrew J. Martin, son of David and Eunice (Ridlon) Martin, of Hollis, and had *three* daugh-

---

* It is supposed Robert Ridlon emigrated West, between 1851 and 1856.

ters. She was divorced from her first husband, and was married, secondly, to —— Floyd. She died in Massachusetts in 1876, and was buried in Bridgton. Francina was a woman of great beauty, and possessed of many excellent qualities.

Lucy-M. Ridlon (4), second daughter of Thomas (6), was born in Bridgton, Me., March 25, 1841; was married to Nathaniel York, of Naples, and has *one* daughter. Lives on a farm in Naples, on the bank of Long Pond.

Louisa-A. Ridlon (2), third daughter of Thomas (6), was born in Bridgton, Me., Nov. 2, 1848; is married, and lives at home with her father.

Ruxley-J. Ridlon (1), fourth daughter of Thomas (6), was born in Bridgton, Me., Dec. 6, 1848; died Jan. 4, 1852.

Martha-Jane Ridlon (13), twin daughter of Thomas (6), was born in Bridgton, Me., July 7, 1851; was married to —— Libbey, blacksmith, and lives in Bridgton. Has issue.

Edward-Eugene Ridlon (2), twin son of Thomas (6), was born in Bridgton, Me., July 7, 1851.

Elizabeth-Ann Ridlon (5), sixth daughter of Thomas (6), was born in Bridgton, Me., Oct. 3, 1853; was married to Alphonzo York (brother of Nathaniel before mentioned), and lives on a farm in Naples, Cumberland County.

Isabella Ridlon (3), seventh daughter of Thomas (6), was born in Bridgton, Me., March 9, 1856; was married to Charles Hill, of Sebago, and lived for some time at home. She was in Massachusetts when last heard from.

Thomas-Bertram Ridlon (11), youngest son of Thomas (6), was born in Bridgton, Me., date unknown.

Almira-Ellen Ridlon (4), eldest daughter of Osborn (1), was born in Naples, Me., Jan. 13, 1863. Unmarried.

Nancy-Estelle Ridlon (6), second daughter of Osborn (1), was born in Naples, Me., June 7, 1866. Unmarried.

James-Bertwill Ridlon (18), eldest son of Osborn (1), was born in Naples, Me., Sept. 29, 1868; died Sept. 24, 1870.

Hittie-Eugenia Ridlon (1), third daughter of Osborn (1), was born in Naples, Me., Feb. 22, 1870.

Henry-Everett Ridlon (6), second son of Osborn (1), was born in Naples, Me., March 9, 1872.

Fannie-Emma Ridlon (1), fourth daughter of Osborn (1), was born in Naples, Me., June 20, 1874.

Marcie-A. Ridlon (3), fifth daughter of Osborn (1), was born in Naples, Me., March 25, 1877; twin.

Bertie-L. Ridlon (2), sixth daughter of Osborn (1), was born in Naples, Me., March 25, 1877; twin.

Clara-L. Ridlon (1), seventh daughter of Osborn (1), was born in Naples, Me., July 4, 1878.

Luie-Bell Ridlon (1), eighth daughter of Osborn (1), was born in Naples, Me., May 17, 1881.

Martha-Ann Ridlon (14), eldest daughter of Thomas (7), was born in Sweden, Me., May 7, 1849; was married to Ansel Holden, of Sweden, and is now living somewhere in the Western States. She has issue.

Mary-Eliza Ridlon (39), second daughter of Thomas (7), was born in Sweden, Me., Dec. 11, 1850; was married to Samuel Quint, of Brownfield, Dec. 24, 1874, and has issue. She was brought up by her maternal grandfather, John Ridlon, of Hollis, and now lives in Alfred, Me.

Clarence-Waldo Ridlon⁶ (2), eldest son of Thomas⁵ (7), was born in Hollis, Me., in August, 1853, and died Oct. 2, 1855.

Sarah-Frances Ridlon⁶ (18), third daughter of Thomas⁵ (7), was born in Sweden, Me., in 1854; was married to George Kimball, of Sweden, in 1879, and resides in that town.

Samuel-Herbert Ridlon⁶ (11), second son of Thomas⁵ (7), was born in Sweden, Me., in 1856, and works in that town. A steady, industrious young man; resembles his grandfather. Married, and is now living in North Berwick, Me.

Marilla-Marks Ridlon⁶ (1), fourth daughter of Thomas⁵ (7), was born in Sweden, Me., in 1858, and died an infant.

Maria-Josephine Ridlon⁶ (2), twin daughter of Thomas⁵ (7), was born in Sweden, Me., June 10, 1861; was married to Jethro Bodwell, of Sanford, and settled in the West; was brought home sick, and died Sept. 9, 1879.

Marilla-Aristene Ridlon⁶ (2), twin daughter of Thomas⁵ (7), was born in Sweden, Me., June 10, 1861, and lives at home.

Judith-Llewella Ridlon⁶ (6), sixth daughter of Thomas⁵ (7), was born in Sweden, Me., and died in 1873.

Jesse-Levi Ridlon⁶ (2), a son of William⁵ (8), was born in Sweden, Me., Feb. 20, 1866 (one record says Oct. 10, 1866).

Martha-Ellen Ridlon⁶ (15), daughter of William⁵ (8), was born in Sweden, Me., Sept. 1, 1871.

Mary Ridlon⁶ (40), eldest daughter of Stephen⁵ (2), was born in Sweden, Me., May 17, 1865.

Samuel Ridlon⁶ (12), eldest son of Stephen⁵ (2), was born in Sweden, Me., April 6, 1867.

Walter Ridlon⁶ (2), second son of Stephen⁵ (2), was born in Sweden, Me., March 10, 1869.

Susan Ridlon⁶ (9), second daughter of Stephen⁵ (2), was born in Sweden, Me., May 12, 1871.

Eddie Ridlon⁶ (2), third son of Stephen⁵ (2), was born in Sweden, Me., 1873.

Genette Ridlon⁶ (1), third daughter of Stephen⁵ (2), was born in Sweden, Me., 1876.

Jennie Ridlon⁶ (2), fourth daughter of Stephen⁵ (2), was born in Sweden, Me., Feb. 2, 1879.

George Ridlon⁶ (9), fourth son of Stephen⁵ (2), was born in Sweden, Me., Nov. 18, 1881.

Nellie Ridlon⁶ (3), fifth daughter of Stephen⁵ (2), was born in Sweden, Me., Feb. 9, 1883.

Walter-H. Ridlon⁶ (3), eldest son of Daniel⁵ (8), was born in Porter (?), Me., July 26, 1848; married Carrie E. Wakefield, May 25, 1867, and has issue *four* children, of whom hereafter. He built a fine stand at Kezar Falls Village, in Porter, and lived there several years; but having engaged in the shook business in several towns in New Hampshire, he has sold his house, and lived in other places. Mr. Ridlon is of medium height, has dark complexion, is energetic and nervous, resembles his father in general movement and personal appearance.

Olive Ridlon[6] (7), eldest daughter of Daniel[5] (8), was born in Porter, Me., June 15, 1850; was married to Samuel Gilpatrick, of Hiram, and lives at Kezar Falls Village, in the latter town. She is a dressmaker; a picture of her father. Has had *two* children, both deceased.

Mary-A. Ridlon[6] (41), second daughter of Daniel[5] (8), was born in Porter, Me., Feb. 24, 1852; was married to W. A. Treadwell, Sept. 15, 1873, and has issue. She lives in Charlestown, Mass., where her husband is in business.

John-G.-F. Ridlon[6] (26), second son of Daniel[5] (8), was born in Porter, Me., May 3, 1856; married Alphia-May Chapman, daughter of Hanson Chapman, of Porter, and has issue, of whom hereafter. Resides at Kezar Falls Village, in his native town. Has black hair and eyes. Cooper by trade. A skillful player on the violin.

Emma-F. Ridlon[6] (3), third daughter of Daniel[5] (8), was born in Porter, Me., Aug. 2, 1860; was married to Robert Durgin, of Hiram, and has issue. Lived at Kezar Falls. Died in 1884.

Edwin-R. Ridlon[6] (2), third son of Daniel[5] (8), was born in Porter, Me., Oct. 11, 1862; married, and is now (1883) at home. Has light complexion.

Esther-Susan Ridlon[6] (1), fourth daughter of Daniel[5] (8), was born in Porter, Me., Dec. 9, 1864; was married to Hebert L. Ridlon, of Porter, and has issue.

Helen Ridlon[6] (2), fifth daughter of Daniel[5] (8), was born in Porter, Me., Nov. 22, 1866, and died Oct. 2, 1867.

Ada Ridlon[6] (3), sixth daughter of Daniel[5] (8), was born in Porter, Me., June 24, 1868. Unmarried in 1883.

Frank Ridlon[6] (5), fourth son of Daniel[5] (8), was born in Porter, Me., Nov. 1, 1870. Unmarried in 1883.

Hannah-A. Ridlon[6] (12), eldest daughter of Thomas[5] (8), was born in Hiram, Me., May 18, 1841. Died when young.

William-R. Ridlon[6] (16), eldest son of Thomas[5] (8), was born in Hiram, Me., Jan. 1, 1843; married Mary M. Gilpatrick, of Hiram, Nov. 7, 1865, and has issue *six* children, of whom hereafter. He served in the Twenty-seventh Maine Regiment Volunteer Infantry, during the Rebellion. Lives at Kezar Falls Village. Cooper by trade. Below the medium height, broad-shouldered, thick-set, muscular, and compact; has dark hair, nervous temperament, is conversational, and somewhat sarcastic; a steady, industrious man.

George-S. Ridlon[6] (10), second son of Thomas[5] (8), was born in Hiram, Me., March 26, 1845; married Adelaide Weeks, in May, 1867, and settled at Kezar Falls Village. Served in the Twenty-third Regiment Maine Infantry during the Rebellion. His first wife died in 1875, and he married, secondly, Mary Bartlett, of Conway, N. H. He is short and thick-set, has light complexion, features like his father. Cooper by trade. A steady, hard-working young man. No issue.

Esther-Jane Ridlon[6] (2), second daughter of Thomas[5] (8), was born in Hiram, Me., Jan. 24, 1847; was married to William Scribner, in December, 1866, and has issue.

Charles-Freeman Ridlon[6] (9), youngest son of Thomas[5] (8), was born in Hiram, Me., April 11, 1854; married Sarah Hurd, Oct. 10, 1875,

and had issue *one* child. He was left a child at his father's death, and
went to live with his grandfather Ridlon, where he remained till maturity.
He is a cooper by trade. A devoted Christian, and is highly esteemed.
Now (1884) living at Kezar Falls, but in a feeble condition. Tall, broad-
shouldered, and slender; has dark hair.

Ruth-Ella Ridlon⁶ (7), youngest daughter of Thomas⁵ (8), was born
in Hiram, Me., Jan. 11, 1856, and died young.

Lewis-A. Ridlon⁶ (5), eldest son of Jacob⁵ (5), was born in Hiram,
Me., Feb. 4, 1857; married Mary, daughter of Robert and Sabra (Ridlon)
Locklin, of Sweden, Me., May 20, 1877, and had issue *one* child, deceased
in infancy. Lewis is short, thick, and compactly built; has dark eyes and
complexion, and curly hair. Cooper and farmer. Has been in the West,
but has since settled in Sweden, Me.

Susan-Ellen Ridlon⁶ (10), eldest daughter of Jacob⁵ (5), was born in
Hiram, Me., March 4, 1854, and died April 21, 1854.

Thomas-J. Ridlon⁶ (12), second son of Jacob⁵ (5), was born in Hiram,
Me., June 11, 1863. He is a humorous, eccentric fellow.

Charles-C. Ridlon⁶ (10), third son of Jacob⁵ (5), was born in Hiram,
Me., July 21, 1865, and died Aug. 2, 1866.

Charles-F. Ridlon⁶ (11), fourth son of Jacob⁵ (5), was born in Hiram,
Me., Jan. 20, 1871. Now (1883) at home.

Carrie-E. Ridlon⁶ (1), second daughter of Jacob⁵ (5), was born in
Hiram, Me., April 4, 1867. Living at home.

Edward-C. Ridlon⁶ (3), youngest son of Jacob⁵ (5), was born in Hiram,
Me., June 17, 1874.

Herbert-L. Ridlon⁶ (1), son of Samuel⁵ (6), was born in Hiram, Me.,
Oct. 8, 1860; married Ella, daughter of Jeremiah Davis, of Porter, in
1882, and has issue *two* children (1884). Of medium size and complexion.
Cooper and farmer. He lives at Kezar Falls Village, Oxford County, Me.

Lillian Ridlon⁶ (4), eldest daughter of Samuel⁵ (6), was born in Hiram,
Me., Jan. 25, 1863, and died Sept. 18, 1865.

Lilla-E. Ridlon⁶ (1), second daughter of Samuel⁵ (6), was born in
Porter, Me., Aug. 15, 1869. A meek and lowly Christian.

John-Wesley Ridley⁶ (27), eldest son of Benjamin⁵ (5), was born in
Ohio (presumably), Oct. 30, 1853, and died Oct. 21, 1854.

Mary-Jane Ridley⁶ (42), eldest daughter of Benjamin⁵ (5), was born
in Ohio (presumably), March 10, 1855; died Oct. 6, 1860.

William-Harrison Ridley⁶ (17), second son of Benjamin⁵ (5), was
born April 11, 1857. Lives at Van Buren, Ind.

Phebe-Ann Ridley⁶ (1), second daughter of Benjamin⁵ (5), was born
Feb. 24, 1859; was married to John Cemer, of Grant County, Ind., March
15, 1881.

Judith-Almeda-Minerva Ridley⁶ (6), third daughter of Benjamin⁵(5),
was born in Indiana, July 2, 1863.

Charles-Homer Ridley⁶ (12), third son of Benjamin⁵ (5), was born in
Indiana, June 20, 1869, and died Jan. 6, 1870.

Benjamin-Lavaner-Cory Ridley⁶ (11), fourth son of Benjamin⁵ (5),
was born in Indiana, Jan. 28, 1871.

Jesse-Andrew Ridley⁶ (3), fifth son of Benjamin⁵ (5), was born in
Indiana, Feb. 21, 1874.

Daniel-Marshall Ridley[6] **(12)**, youngest son of Benjamin[5] **(5)**, was born in Indiana, Jan. 17, 1880.

Mary-Ann Ridley[6] **(43)**, eldest daughter of Matthias[5] **(6)**, was born at Sweetwater, Ill. (presumably), June 16, 1857.

Sarah-Alice Ridley[6] **(19)**, second daughter of Matthias[5] **(6)**, was born at Sweetwater, Ill. (presumably), Aug. 16, 1860.

Cumberland Ridlen[6] **(1)**, eldest son of Stephen[5] **(3)**, was born at St. Paul, Ind., Feb. 2, 1833; married Lucinda Perry, and has *two* children, of whom hereafter. Lives at St. Paul.

Charles-W.-W. Ridlen[6] **(13)**, second son of Stephen[5] **(3)**, was born at St. Paul, Ind., Nov. 17, 1835; married Dorcas Russell, and has issue, of whom hereafter. Lives in St. Paul.

Ebenezer-V. Ridlen[6] **(6)**, third son of Stephen[5] **(3)**, was born in St. Paul, Ind., June 22, 1840; married Albina McKee, and has issue, of whom hereafter. He lives in Indiana.

Samuel Ridlen[6] **(13)**, fourth son of Stephen[5] **(3)**, was born in St. Paul, Ind. (say 1842), and was killed in battle during the war of the Rebellion. He was married.

Ann-Wright Ridlen[6] **(4)**, eldest daughter of Stephen[5] **(3)**, was born in Decatur County, Ind., Nov. 19, 1833; was married to John Wright, and lives at St. Paul, or near there.

Emeline-Amanda Ridlen[6] **(1)**, second daughter of Stephen[5] **(3)**, was born in Decatur County, Ind., Dec. 9, 1887; was married to John Sheffler, and has issue.

Orphia-Wilder Ridlen[6] **(1)**, third daughter of Stephen[5] **(3)**, was born in Decatur County, Ind., May 29, 1846; was married to Ellis Sliffer, and resides in her native State.

Sarah-Wilder Ridlen[6] **(20)**, fourth daughter of Stephen[5] **(3)**, was born in Decatur County, Ind., Sept. 17, 1849; was married to John Wisley, and lives at St. Paul.

Matilda-J. Ridlen[6] **(2)**, eldest daughter of William[5] **(10)**, was born at Bellefountain, Ia., Sept. 26, 1847.

William-B. Ridlen[6] **(18)**, eldest son of William[5] **(10)**, was born at Bellefountain, Ia., July 29, 1849.

Eliza-E. Ridlen[6] **(8)**, second daughter of William[5] **(10)**, was born at Bellefountain, Ia., May 20, 1853.

Rachel-R. Ridlen[6] **(5)**, third daughter of William[5] **(10)**, was born at Bellefountain, Ia., Sept. 6, 1855.

Sabra Ridlen[6] **(3)**, fourth daughter of William[5] **(10)**, was born at Bellefountain, Ia., June 12, 1859.

Mary Ridlen[6] **(44)**, fifth daughter of William[5] **(10)**, was born at Bellefountain, Ia., Jan. 11, 1864.

Elizabeth-Susan Ridlen[6] **(13)**, eldest daughter of Samuel[5] **(7)**, was born in Clay, Marion County, Ia., Oct. 26, 1836.

Stephen Ridlen[6] **(7)**, eldest son of Samuel[5] **(7)**, was born in Marion County, Ia., Feb. 17, 1849.

George-T. Ridlen[6] **(11)**, second son of Samuel[5] **(7)**, was born in Marion County, Ia., Dec. 25, 1850; died Feb. 14, 1865.

Frances-Marion Ridlen⁶ (3), second daughter of Samuel⁵ (7), was born in Marion County, Ia., March 31, 1855; died Aug. 5, 1869.

Samuel-B. Ridlen⁶ (14), third son of Samuel⁵ (7), was born in Marion County, Ia., Dec. 21, 1856.

Sarah-E. Ridlen⁶ (21), third daughter of Samuel⁵ (7), was born in Marion County, Ia., Jan. 27, 1858.

Mary-Jane Ridlen⁶ (45), fourth daughter of Samuel⁵ (7), was born in Marion County, Ia., Sept. 5, 1860.

Ann-Eliza Ridlen⁶ (5), fifth daughter of Samuel⁵ (7), was born in Marion County, Ia., May 1, 1862; died Jan. 9, 1870.

Ada Ridlen⁶ (4), sixth daughter of Samuel⁵ (7), was born in Marion County, Ia., May 31, 1867.

Arizona Ridlen⁶ (1), seventh son of Samuel⁵ (7), was born in Marion County, Ia., Feb. 3, 1870.

Rebecca-J. Ridlen⁶ (6), eldest daughter of Ebenezer⁵ (5), was born at Knoxville, Ia., Aug. 6, 1837.

Calvin-C. Ridlen⁶ (2), eldest son of Ebenezer⁵ (5), was born in Knoxville, Ia., Nov. 18, 1839.

Timothy Ridlen⁶ (2), second son of Ebenezer⁵ (5), was born in Knoxville, Ia., June 19, 1841.

Sarah-E. Ridlen⁶ (22), second daughter of Ebenezer⁵ (5), was born in Knoxville, Ia., May 9, 1846.

Martha-E. Ridlen⁶ (16), eldest daughter of John⁵ (19), was born in Hancock County, Ind., Sept. 24, 1850; was married Oct. 11, 1868, to John E. Parr, eldest son of Isaac B. and Mary (Stretcher) Parr, of Jasper County, Ill. She died Jan. 28, 1870, leaving issue. She was a devoted Christian, and beloved by all who knew her.

Margaret-A. Ridlen⁶ (3), second daughter of John⁵ (19), was born in Hancock County, Ind., June 6, 1852; was married July 25, 1872, to James Bartley, eldest son of James and Rachel (Conrad) Bartley, of Jasper County, Ill., and has issue.

Eliza-J. Ridlen⁶ (9), third daughter of John⁵ (19), was born in Hancock County, Ind., June 1, 1854; was married July 25, 1872, to James R., son of James and Rachel (Kimbrel) Manning, of Jasper County, Ill., and has issue.

Lydia-C. Ridlen⁶ (11), fourth daughter of John⁵ (19), was born July 18, 1859; unmarried.

Sarah-F. Ridlen⁶ (23), fifth daughter of John⁵ (19), was born Feb. 26, 1862; unmarried.

William-P. Ridlen⁶ (19), eldest son of John⁵ (19), was born Feb. 15, 1864; unmarried.

Mary-C. Ridlen⁶ (46), sixth daughter of John⁵ (19), was born Feb. 9, 1868; unmarried.

Nancy Ridlen⁶ (7), eldest daughter of Abraham⁵ (6), was born in Hancock County, Ind., July 17, 1847; was married Oct. 8, 1866, to William Ping, son of William and Elizabeth (Reed) Ping, of Jasper County, Ill., and has several children.

Lydia Ridlen⁶ (12), second daughter of Abraham⁵ (6), was born in Hancock County, Ind., Dec. 7, 1849.

James-William Ridlen[6] (18), eldest son of Abraham[5] (6), was born April 11, 1853.

Amanda-J. Ridlen[6] (3), third daughter of Abraham[5] (6), was born Jan. 14, 1859.

Eliza-A. Ridlen[6] (10), fourth daughter of Abraham[5] (6), was born Aug. 17, 1861.

John-F. Ridlen[6] (28), second son of Abraham[5] (6), was born Feb. 14, 1868.

Andrew Ridlen[6] (3), eldest son of James[5] (9), was born May 12, 1854; died June 29, 1854.

Ann Ridlen[6] (6), eldest daughter of James[5] (9), was born April 28, 1855; was married Oct. 21, 1874, to Geo. W. Hicks, son of John F. and Mary C. Hicks, of Jasper County, Ill., and had issue.

Mary Ridlen[6] (47), second daughter of James[5] (9), was born in Jasper County, Ill., Oct. 31, 1856; was married March 12, 1874, to Richard J. Ferguson, son of Sanford and Iorlinda J. (Ireland) Ferguson, and has issue.

Elizabeth Ridlen[6] (14), third daughter of James[5] (9), was born Aug. 10, 1858; unmarried.

Martha-J. Ridlen[6] (17), fourth daughter of James[5] (9), was born June 11, 1860; unmarried.

Emma Ridlen[6] (4), fifth daughter of James[5] (9), was born June 15, 1862; unmarried.

John Ridlen[6] (29), second son of James[5] (9), was born May 16, 1864; unmarried.

Louisa Ridlen[6] (3), sixth daughter of James[5] (9), was born Oct. 26, 1865; unmarried.

James Ridlen[6] (19), third son of James[5] (9), was born Jan. 7, 1873.

John-F. Ridlen[6] (30), eldest son of Talbut[5] (1), was born Oct. 7, 1856; died Feb. 1, 1857.

Eliza-J. Ridlen[6] (11), eldest daughter of Talbut[5] (1), was born Nov. 22, 1857; died March 18, 1859.

George-A. Ridlen[6] (12), second son of Talbut[5] (1), was born Feb. 13, 1860.

Nancy-J. Ridlen[6] (8), second daughter of Talbut[5] (1), was born Jan. 19, 1862.

Marion Ridlen[6] (1), third daughter of Talbut[5] (1), was born Jan. 25, 1867.

Arminta-V. Ridlen[6] (1), fourth daughter of Talbut[5] (1), was born Aug. 22, 1869.

Daniel-S. Ridlen[6] (13), third son of Talbut[5] (1), was born Dec. 2, 1871; died Sept. 13, 1872.

Norris Ridlen[6] (1), fourth son of Talbut[5] (1), was born May 28, 1874.

Ida Ridlen[6] (2), eldest daughter of Samuel[5] (8), was born in Memphis, Tenn., June 9, 1859.

Samuel Ridlen[6] (15), eldest son of Samuel[5] (8), was born in Memphis, Tenn., Nov. 2, 1862.

Arena Ridlen[6] (1), second daughter of Samuel[5] (8), was born at Webb's Prairie, Ill., April 17, 1867.

Thomas-Ridlon Ridlen[6] (13), youngest son of Samuel[5] (8), was born at Webb's Prairie, Ill., March 8, 1869, and is the namesake of Thomas Ridlon, late of Hollis, Me., who was a cousin of this child's grandfather.

George Ridlen[6] (13), eldest son of John[5] (20), was born in Little York, Ind., July 25, 1851; married.

Alice-Elizabeth Ridlen[6] (2), eldest daughter of John[5] (20), was born at Little York, Ind., July 11, 1853; was married.

John-Stanford Ridlen[6] (31), second son of John[5] (20), was born at Little York, Ind., Feb. 1, 1856, and died Oct. 6, 1857.

Almira Ridlen[6] (5), second daughter of John[5] (20), was born at Little York, Ind., Aug. 21, 1859; was married.

James-Albert Ridlen[6] (20), third son of John[5] (20), was born at Little York, Ind., Jan. 25, 1861.

Dora-Bell Ridlen[6] (1), third daughter of John[5] (20), was born at Little York, Ind., Aug. 8, 1866.

Ida-Ellen Ridlen[6] (3), fourth daughter of John[5] (20), was born at Little York, Ind., June 14, 1869.

Warren Ridlen[6] (1), twin son of John[5] (20), was born at Little York, Ind., Oct. 29, 1870.

Willis Ridlen[6] (1), twin son of John[5] (20), was born at Little York, Ind., Oct. 29, 1870.

Margaret Ridlen[6] (4), a daughter of George[5] (3), was born at Little York, Ind.

Almon Ridlen[6] (2), eldest son of George[5] (3), was born at Little York, Ind.

George Ridlen[6] (14), second son of George[5] (3), was born at Little York, Ind.

Mary-Etta Ridlen[6] (48), a daughter of Samuel[5] (9).
Minnie-Margaret Ridlen[6] (2), a daughter of Samuel[5] (9).
George Ridlen[6] (15), eldest son of Samuel[5] (9).
Julia-Adaline Ridlen[6] (2), a daughter of Samuel[5] (9).
Stella Ridlen[6] (1), a daughter of Samuel[5] (9).

All born in Indiana.

John-Richard Ridlen[6] (32), a son of Theodore[5] (1).
Charles Ridlen[6] (14), a son of Theodore[5] (1).

Born in Indiana.

Perry Ridlen[6] (1), a son of Nelson[5] (1), was born in Indiana.

Nicholas Ridlen[6] (4), eldest son of George[5] (4), was born in Indiana, Sept. 3, 1849; married, May 16, 1871, to Mary-Jane Baker, and in 1878, had *two* children, of whom hereafter. Photographer at Fountaintown, Ind.

Catherine Ridlen[6] (5), eldest daughter of George[5] (4), was born in Indiana, Feb. 20, 1851, and was married, Aug. 4, 1870, to Sylvester Baker, a relative of Jane.

Hannah Ridlen[6] (13), second daughter of George[5] (4), was born in Indiana, May 1, 1852, and was married, Jan. 21, 1869, to Lafayette Baker, brother of Sylvester.

Isaac-Newton Ridlen[6] (8), second son of George[5] (4), was born in Indiana, July 24, 1858. Unmarried in 1878.

George-Washington Ridlen⁶ (16), third son of George⁶ (4), was born in Indiana, Oct. 21, 1855; died Feb. 14, 1856.

Abraham Ridlen⁶ (9), fourth son of George⁶ (4), was born in Indiana, Dec. 25, 1856.

Mary-Jane Ridlen⁶ (49), third daughter of George⁶ (4), was born in Indiana, March 26, 1858, and died same year.

Peter Ridlen⁶ (2), fifth son of George⁶ (4), was born in Indiana, April 2, 1859.

Nancy-Maria Ridlen⁶ (9), fourth daughter of George⁶ (4), was born in Indiana, July 31, 1860.

Nancy-Ellen Ridlen⁶ (10), eldest daughter of Hermon⁵ (1), was born in Indiana, Oct. 15, 1854, and died Oct. 19, 1855.

Missouri-Evaline Ridlen⁶ (1), second daughter of Hermon⁵ (1), was born in Indiana, May 28, 1856; died Aug. 7, 1861.

Mary-Isabella Ridlen⁶ (50), third daughter of Hermon⁵ (1), was born in Indiana, Feb. 5, 1859.

John-Henry Ridlen⁶ (33), eldest son of Hermon⁵ (1), was born in Indiana, March 28, 1862.

Sarah-Alice Ridlen⁶ (24), fourth daughter of Hermon⁵ (1), was born in Indiana, July 8, 1865.

Charles-Wesley Ridlen⁶ (15), second son of Hermon⁵ (1), was born in Indiana, April 28, 1867.

George-Franklin Ridlen⁶ (17), eldest son of Abraham⁵ (7), was born in Indiana in 1870.

Charles-Elzy Ridlen⁶ (16), second son of Abraham⁵ (7), was born in Indiana in 1873.

Eliza-Annis Ridlen⁶ (12), eldest daughter of Stephen⁵ (5).
Albert-Orias Ridlen⁶ (7), eldest son of Stephen⁵ (5). Dead.
Perry Ridlen⁶ (1), second son of Stephen⁵ (5).
Ida-May Ridlen⁶ (4), second daughter of Stephen⁵ (5).
Rhoda-Alice Ridlen⁶ (1), third daughter of Stephen⁵ (5).
Ephraim-Pryer Ridlen⁶ (6), third son of Stephen⁵ (5). Dead.
Jemima-Laura Ridlen⁶ (3), fourth daughter of Stephen⁵ (5).

Charles Ridlon⁶ (17), eldest son of Jacob⁵ (6), was born in Sebago, Me., April 18, 1850; died Jan. 6, 1874.

Joseph-M. Ridlon⁶ (11), second son of Jacob⁵ (6), was born in Sebago, Me., Aug. 23, 1852; unmarried in 1888.

Isaac-M.Ridlon⁶ (9), third son of Jacob⁵ (6), was born in Sebago, Me., July 14, 1854; unmarried in 1883.

Mary-E. Ridlon⁶ (51), eldest daughter of Jacob⁵ (6), was born in Sebago, Me., Sept. 7, 1857; married Roscoe A. Leavett, of Sebago.

Betsey-J. Ridlon⁶ (12), second daughter of Jacob⁵ (6), was born in Sebago, Me., Aug. 2, 1859; died June 5, 1881.

Annie-C. Ridlon⁶ (1), third daughter of Jacob⁵ (6), was born in Sebago, Me., Nov. 7, 1861; died in infancy.

Joseph-Millard Ridlon⁶ (12), eldest son of Joseph⁵ (7), was born in Parsonfield, Me., July 7, 1855; married June 28, 1876, to Georgie A. Benford, of Baldwin. No issue in 1878. He has kept a grocery and dry-goods store in Parsonfield, where his father previously traded. He is small, has light complexion, and in features of face resembles the Hancock family, from which he is descended through his paternal grandmother. He is an active, enterprising business man.

Willie-Francis Ridlon[6] (20), second son of Joseph[5] (7), was born in Parsonfield, Me., Jan. 1, 1857; died Oct. 4, 1865.

Woodbridge-Gordon Ridlon[6] (1), third son of Joseph[5] (7), was born in Parsonfield, Me., Jan. 9, 1860. He is a young man of scholarly tastes, and desires a classical education, but a trouble in his eyes has deprived him of the advantages of study. He has carried on business in the store with his brother.

John-Franklin Ridlon[6] (34), fourth* son of Joseph[5] (7), was born in Parsonfield, Me., June 4, 1868. Now (1878) in a store, clerking for his brothers, before mentioned.

Willie-Francis Ridlon[6] (21), fifth son of Joseph[5] (7), was born in Parsonfield, Me., April 3, 1869; died Oct. 5, 1869.

Frederick-Murch Ridlon[6] (4), eldest son of Isaac[5] (7), was born in Baldwin, Me., June 8, 1856; married June 8, 1878, to Hattie-Jane, daughter of Charles and Abigail (Edgecomb) Tufts, of Limerick, where he now (1879) resides, and carries on the well-known "William Hancock farm." No children.

Franklin-M. Ridlon[6] (4), second son of Isaac[5] (7), was born in Baldwin, Me., April 12, 1861, and is now (1879) living with his mother in Limerick, unmarried.

Mary-Jane Ridlon[6] (51), eldest daughter of Daniel[5] (8), was born in Standish, Cumberland County, Me., in 1816; was married to Col. Joseph Shaw of that town, and is now (1878) living there.

Charlotte Ridlon[6] (1), second daughter of Daniel[5] (8), was born in Standish, Me., Aug. 20, 1821; was married in 1844 to Andrew-Hobson Wiggin, of Baldwin; he died July 4, 1857, and she married, secondly, in 1861, Ethiel Flanders, of Buxton. Mr. Flanders has deceased, and she is again a widow. No children.

Olive Ridlon[6] (8), third daughter of Daniel[5] (8), was born in Standish, Me., and was married to Charles MacDonald, of Leominster, Mass.

Recilphia Ridlon[6] (1), fourth daughter of Daniel[5] (8), was born in Standish, Me., and died unmarried in 1868, aged 42. One of the most amiable of women.

Almond-Shirlock Ridlon[6] (3), eldest son of Daniel[5] (8), was born in Standish, Me., in 1829; married Carrie Gardner, and has *three* children, of whom hereafter. Mr. Ridlon is a large man, weighing over two hundred pounds. He has light complexion, and is called handsome. He is superintendent of a nail-factory in Somerset, Mass. This son, and his four sisters before named, were by Daniel Ridlon's first wife, Ellen Kennell.

Comfort-A. Ridlon[6] (2), eldest daughter of Daniel[5] (8) by his second wife, was born in Brownfield, Me., Nov. 12, 1835; died in Porter, Me., Sept. 27, 1871, and was buried near her father's homestead in that town.

Susan Ridlon[6] (11), second daughter of Daniel[5] (8) by his second wife, was born in Porter, Me., Jan. 16, 1838; was married April 12, 1862, to William B. Davis, and lives on a farm near Kezar Falls, Parsonfield, Me.

*An infant born Feb. 21, 1862, died the next day.

46

Benjamin-H. Ridlon⁶ (12), a son of Daniel⁵ (8), was born in Porter, Me., Dec. 31, 1840. He enlisted in the Ninth Maine Regiment Infantry, and served in the Union army till 1865, when he was mortally wounded in the head while skirmishing at Bermuda Hundred. He was sent to Fortress Monroe, and I suppose died there. His father drew a pension on his behalf.

John-W. Ridlon⁶ (35), a son of Daniel⁵ (8), was born in Porter, Me., Feb. 1, 1843, and died (drowned?) May 2, 1857.

George-W. Ridlon⁶ (18), third son of Daniel⁵ (8) by his second wife, was born in Porter, Me., Feb. 25, 1846, and died Aug. 22, 1859.

Dorothy Ridlon⁶ (1), third daughter of Daniel⁵ (8) by his second wife, was born in Porter, Me., July 26, 1849; was married Dec. 12, 1865, to Samuel Durgin, of Porter, Me. Deceased.

Mary Ridlon⁶ (53), fourth daughter of Daniel⁵ (8) by his second wife, was born in Porter, Me., July 25, 1849; was married to Edward Clemmons (or Clements), and has issue.

Martha-Ellen Ridlon⁶ (18), youngest daughter of Daniel⁵ (8), was born in Porter, Me., Aug. 15, 1850; was married July 18, 1866, to Winfield S. MacDonald. Deceased.

Nancy Ridlon⁶ (11), eldest daughter of Stephen⁵ (6), was born in Porter, Me., July 28, 1833; was married July 25, 1852, to Benjamin Goodwin, of Biddeford, and died Sept. 25, 1859.

Moses Ridlon⁶ (3), eldest son of Stephen⁵ (6), was born in Porter, Me., Dec. 15, 1834, and died July 5, 1838.

Elizabeth Ridlon⁶ (15), second daughter of Stephen⁵ (6), was born in Porter, Me., Feb. 27, 1836; was married Oct. 25, 1852, to Henry Benson, of Hollis, York County, and died Aug. 6, 1858.

Joshua-Robbins Ridlon⁶ (3), second son of Stephen⁵ (6), was born in Hiram, Me., July 31, 1838; married to Eunice Gould, Dec. 2, 1861, and has issue *four* (perhaps more) children, of whom hereafter. Mr. Ridlon is of medium height, broad-shouldered, and possessed of great physical strength. Somewhat eccentric in his habits and speech. Farmer. Resides among the mountains of Hiram, near his father.

Benjamin-Hawkins Ridlon⁶ (13), third son of Stephen⁵ (6), was born in Hiram, Me., July 23, 1840; married March 16, 1851, to Elizabeth Durgin, and died Nov. 19, 1870, leaving *two* children, of whom hereafter. He enlisted in the Thirteenth Regiment Maine Volunteer Infantry, and served from Dec. 12, 1862, to August, 1865, proving himself a noble and true-hearted soldier. He returned from the army and settled on a farm near his father's homestead in Hiram. Deceased.

Mary-Ann Ridlon⁶ (54), third daughter of Stephen⁵ (6), was born in Hiram, Me., April 7, 1842; was married Dec. 25, 1860, to Josiah Fly. Residence unknown.

James-Harmon Ridlon⁶ (21), fourth son of Stephen⁵ (6), was born in Hiram, Me., April 1, 1844; married June 18, 1864, to Joanna Goodwin, and settled on the homestead farm with his aged parents. Experienced religion in 1874, and became a gifted exhorter. Has served as deputy-sheriff, and in other positions of trust. A man of good natural ability, and great kindness of heart. Married, secondly, Irene Cotton, of Hiram, June 21, 1884. Has *three* children, of whom hereafter.

Henry Ridlon⁶ (7), eldest son of Levi⁵ (1), was born in Porter, Me.,

April 19, 1889; married Dec. 25, 1857, to Julia A. Stanley, and had issue *three* children, of whom hereafter. He lived in his native town. A young man of excellent character. Died March 24, 1864.

Francis Ridlon[6] (1), second son of Levi[5] (1), was born in Porter, Me., Oct. 8, 1840; died Dec. 12, 1842.

David Ridlon[6] (4), third son of Levi[5] (1), was born in Porter, Me., Nov. 26, 1842, and died May 24, 1857.

Hon. Francis-W. Ridlon[6] (2), fourth son of Levi[5] (1), was born in Porter, Me., Nov. 18, 1846; married Feb. 25, 1871, Nellie E., daughter of Rev. John Mitchell, a Methodist clergyman, and has issue *two* children, of whom hereafter. He was educated at Limington Academy, Parsonfield Academy, and the Nichols Latin School at Lewiston; studied law with Emery S. Ridlon, Esq., and with Mattox & Fox of Portland; served as deputy-sheriff in 1871 and 1872 for Oxford and York Counties; was admitted to the bar in 1873; served three years as town-clerk; member of school committee in Porter; taught school, and has, latterly, for several years been actively engaged in the practice of law at Kezar Falls, a village in Oxford County, Me., having succeeded Emery S. Ridlon, Esq., when he removed to Portland. He was elected to the State senate and served in 1878-9. Manifests a live public spirit, and is identified with matters of polity. Foremost in all movements calculated to advance the moral and educational advantages of his fellow-men. Successful as a lawyer, respected as a citizen and neighbor. Deals in real-estate quite extensively. Is tall, slender, and erect; has dark hair and eyes; temperament nervous. He has kindly donated the steel portrait in this book.

Eunice-M. Ridlon[6] (5), eldest daughter of Levi[5] (1), was born in Porter, Me., April 26, 1848; was married Feb. 14, 1874, to Dana Cotton, and has issue.

Abbie-E. Ridlon[6] (4), second daughter of Levi[5] (1), was born in Porter, Me., Feb. 26, 1852; was married Sept. 5, 1875, to Wyman Cotton.

Charles-D. Ridlon[6] (18), fifth son of Levi[5] (1), was born in Porter, Me., Jan. 20, 1854; married Sept. 5, 1875, to a Miss Cotton, and lives on the homestead farm. Short and thick-set.

John-C. Ridlon[6] (36), eldest son of Ezra[5] (2), was born in Woodstock, Me., March 21, 1850; married Clara Chase, in March, 1871, and has *two* children, of whom hereafter. He was living in Paris, Oxford County, Me., when last heard from, and was engaged in selling fruit-trees. Tall, erect, active; complexion sandy, features of Scottish mould. Business ability good.

George-W. Ridlon[6] (19), second son of Ezra[5] (2), was born in Woodstock, Me., Jan. 23, 1856. Unmarried in 1882.

Lucy-A. Ridlon[6] (5), eldest daughter of Ezra[5] (2), was born in Woodstock, Me., June 7, 1858; died in April, 1862.

Nellie-F. Ridlon[6] (4), second daughter of Ezra[5] (2), was born in Woodstock, Me., Oct. 30, 1862. Unmarried.

Charles-A. Ridlon[6] (19), third son of Ezra[5] (2), was born in Woodstock, Me., May 22, 1869. Unmarried in 1882.

George-Washington Ridlon[6] (20), eldest son of William[5] (11), was born in Porter, Me., Oct. 14, 1832; married Mary A. Poor, Nov. 8, 1864; she died, and he married, secondly, Mary A. Sullivan, of Irish extraction. He has *five* children, of whom hereafter. Mr. Ridlon was employed by his brother William, in Boston, several years. He subsequently settled on a farm in Porter. He is a very large, corpulent man; has dark hair and gray eyes. A successful farmer. Quite eccentric in his habits.

Mary-Jane Ridlon' (55), only daughter of William⁶ (11), was born in Porter, Me., Aug. 27, 1835; was married to Daniel Durgin, and has issue. Lives in Porter.

John-R. Ridlon' (37), second son of William⁶(11), was born in Porter, Me., March 8, 1838, and died unmarried, Aug. 25, 1860. He had black hair and beard, the latter very heavy; was well formed, erect, commanding, and handsome in person.

William Ridlon' (22), third son of William⁶ (11), was born in Porter Me., Jan. 18, 1842; married Dec. 26, 1863, to Ruth R., daughter of William Taylor, and has *two* beautiful daughters, of whom hereafter. He went to Boston, Mass., in 1858, and worked in a brick-yard. In 1862 he drove a piano-team in Boston. Taught winter school in Maine in 1865-6 and 1867-8. Was town-clerk of Porter from 1866 to 1869, when he returned to Boston and commenced business as an expressman, where he has since continued successfully. From a small beginning, by close attention to the requirements of his customers, he has augmented his business, constantly winning new patrons and adding to his facilities, until he has a large number of men and many fine teams employed. He has become fully acquainted with the piano trade, and conducts his business on a plan so systematic that his customers esteem him very highly, and repose perfect confidence in his honesty and ability. He gives his personal attention to his office-business, and fills his orders with promptness and precision. Few men stand higher in business relations in the city. His office is on La Grange Street, near Washington. He stands nearly six feet and six inches in height, weighs about two hundred and sixty pounds; has very broad chest and shoulders, thick neck, and fine, well-poised head. His hair and beard are black, eyes dark-hazel, features regular, expression of face pleasant. He has a noble, generous heart, and is a genial, social gentleman. He is always cool-headed and self-possessed; he is firm in his grasp of opinion, considerate, and of sound judgment. Physically, intellectually, and socially, he is as fine a specimen of manhood as can be found in New England. He has fitted up a beautiful home in Somerville, where, when the business of the day is over, with his amiable, pleasant family around him, he finds a quiet rest; and there his guests will find a hospitality of the most generous and interesting character. Mr. Ridlon has acquired a competency and is able to surround himself with all the material concomitants of life. The fine steel engraving of Mr. Ridlon in this book was kindly donated by him at a cost of seventy-five dollars, and is an excellent likeness and nice specimen of art. William has kindly assisted the author in the publication of this book, and to him the family are largely indebted for its early issue.

Joseph-S. Ridlon' (13), third son of William⁶ (11), was born in Porter, Me., June 15, 1845; married Frances L. Tripp, and resides in Boston, Mass., where he has been employed for many years by his brother William in the express business. He is tall and heavy, weighing about two hundred and twenty pounds; has light hair and eyes; good-natured and jovial. *One* son, of whom hereafter.

Mary Ridlon' (56), eldest daughter of Ephraim⁶ (4).

Wm. Ridlon.

Levi Ridlon⁶ (2), eldest son of Ephraim⁵ (4).
Charles Ridlon⁶ (20), second son of Ephraim⁵ (4).
Weller Ridlon⁶ (1), third son of Ephraim⁵ (4).
Ida Ridlon⁶ (5), a daughter of Ephraim⁵ (4).

George-H. Ridlon⁶ (21), eldest son of Charles⁵ (2), was born in Saco, Me., June 9, 1851, and died in Waterborough, May 11, 1853.
Mary-E. Ridlon⁶ (57), eldest daughter of Charles⁵ (2), was born in Waterborough, Me., Oct. 25, 1854; was married Oct. 10, 1873, to Albion Stone, and lives in Cornish.
Stephen-K. Ridlon⁶ (9), second son of Charles⁵ (2), was born in Waterborough, Me., Feb. 10, 1856, and is married.
Charles-H. Ridlon⁶ (21), third son of Charles⁵ (2), was born in Cornish, Me., May 11, 1859.
Lorenzo-D. Ridlon⁶ (2), fourth son of Charles⁵ (2), was born in Cornish, Me., Aug. 11, 1862.

Sarah-E. Ridlon⁶ (25), eldest daughter of Joseph⁵ (8), was born in Chelsea, Mass., June 8, 1841; died Nov. 13, 1843.
Hattie-Amelia Ridlon⁶ (6), second daughter of Joseph⁵ (8), was born in Chelsea, Mass., Oct. 13, 1843, and has been twice married: first, to James T. Kendall, Sept. 4, 1864; secondly, to —— Burr. Had issue.
Joseph-T. Ridlon⁶ (14), eldest son of Joseph⁵ (8), was born in Chelsea, Mass., May 25, 1844, and died Aug. 25, 1844.
Leonce-F. Ridlon⁶ (1), third daughter of Joseph⁵ (8), was born in Chelsea, Mass., July 4, 1845, and died Sept. 26, 1845.
Ida-E. Ridlon⁶ (6), fourth daughter of Joseph⁵ (8), was born in Chelsea, Mass., Oct. 2, 1849, and died Dec. 9, 1849.

Sebastian-S. Ridlon⁶ (1), eldest son of Thomas⁵ (9), was born in Boston (?), Mass., in 1837, and died in 1849.
Granville-H. Ridlon⁶ (1), second son of Thomas⁵ (9), was born in Boston (?), Mass., Oct. 3, 1847; married Sarah J. Merrill, and has issue, of whom hereafter. Mr. Ridlon has kept a crockery and glassware store in Boston for many years, and is a man of very energetic character. He is small, of dark complexion, and somewhat eccentric. Does not resemble the Ridlon family in build or features of face.
Charles-T. Ridlon⁶ (22), third son of Thomas⁵ (9), was born in Chelsea (?), Mass., May 15, 1849; married Adelaide-Grafton Legg, and has issue, of whom hereafter. Charles is with his brother before mentioned, in a Boston crockery-ware store. He is short and thick, and in no way resembles the Ridlon family in his personal appearance, but is said to have many traits like his father. Resides in Chelsea.

Leander Ridlon⁶ (3), eldest son of Leander⁵ (2), was born in Biddeford, Me., Dec. 30, 1855.
William Ridlon⁶ (23), second son of Leander⁵ (2), was born in Saco, Me., March 26, 1858; married, and is now (1884) living at Skowhegan, Me.
Mary Ridlon⁶ (58), eldest daughter of Leander⁵ (2), was born in Saco, Me., April 4, 1862. Deceased.
Mary Ridlon⁶ (59), second daughter of Leander⁵ (2), was born in Saco,

Me., July 28, 1863; was married to —— Haliday, and resides at North Andover, Mass.

Elizabeth Ridlon[6] (16), third daughter of Leander[5] (2), was born in Saco, Me.

Evalena Ridlon[6] (1), fourth daughter of Leander[5] (2), was born in Saco, Me.

Marcie Ridlon[6] (4), fifth daughter of Leander[5] (2), was born in Saco, Me.

James-F. Ridlon[6] (21), eldest son of Lewis[5] (3), was born in Saco, Me., March 24, 1849; died Sept. 10, 1852.

Charles-F. Ridlon[6] (23), second son of Lewis[5] (3), was born in Saco, Me., April 18, 1851; married June 4, 1875, to Ida M. King, and settled in the city of Saco. He is a blacksmith by trade. Has issue, of whom hereafter.

Eliza-J. Ridlon[6] (13), eldest daughter of Lewis[5] (3), was born in Saco, Me., May 27, 1853; was married April 20, 1881, to John Q. Smith, and resides in the city of Biddeford.

Alonzo Ridlon[6] (2), third son of Lewis[5] (3), was born in Saco, Me., May 17, 1855; married Dec. 24, 1874, to Laura Ridlon, daughter of Nathaniel, of the "Ferry Road," and resides in the city of Saco. Blacksmith.

Lillian-Rose Ridlon[6] (2), second daughter of Lewis[5] (3), was born in Saco, Me., Oct. 3, 1857; was married July 2, 1879, to Frank Macomber, and has issue.

Fannie-S. Ridlon[6] (1), third daughter of Lewis[5] (3), was born in Saco, Me., May 11, 1862; that "funny Fan" was not married in 1881.

Ella-F. Ridlon[6] (2), only daughter of Jeremiah[5] (5), was born in Saco, Me., April 14, 1862; lives at Saco.

Addie-E. Ridlon[6] (1), a daughter of Edmund[5] (3), was born in Kennebunk, Me., June 8, 1851; married to Christopher Perkins, and resides at Kennebunkport.

Simon-H. Ridlon[6] (1), a son of Edmund[5] (3), was born in Kennebunk, Me., Oct. 8, 1857; lives at Kennebunkport.

Abbie-R. Ridlon[6] (5), eldest daughter of James[5] (11), was born (probably) in Kennebunk, Me., June 10, 1850; married Feb. 8, 1867, to William C. Stinson; lives in Kennebunkport.

Asa-F. Ridlon[6] (1), eldest son of James[5] (11), was born in (probably) Kennebunk, Me., Sept. 9, 1852; married June 28, 1872, to Annie F. Tibbets, and lives in Lynn, Mass. Has issue, of whom hereafter.

Lenella-F. Ridlon[6] (1), second daughter of James[5] (11), was (probably) born in Kennebunk, Me., Jan. 28, 1856; married, March 6, 1873, to James E. Tarbox, and lives in Lynn, Mass.

Gardner-P. Ridlon[6] (1), second son of James[5] (11), was born in Kennebunk, Me., Jan. 26, 1860; lives at Kennebunkport.

Lucy-J. Ridlon[6] (6), third daughter of James[5] (11), was born in Kennebunk, Me., March 17, 1862; lives at home.

Cora-L. Ridlon[6] (2), fourth daughter of James[5] (11), was born in Kennebunk, Me., June 25, 1865; lives at home.

Josephine-M. Ridlon⁶ (1), only daughter of Abraham⁵ (8), was born Sept. 8, 1861; died March 4, 1863.

Lizzie Ridlon⁶ (17), twin daughter of Samuel⁵ (10), was born in Saco, Me., and died in infancy.

Ellen Ridlon⁶ (5), twin daughter of Samuel⁵ (10), was born in Saco, Me., and lived in the family of a Mr. Nutter, under the care of the Odd Fellows.

George Ridlon⁶ (22), only son of Henry⁵ (8), was born in Saco, Me., Aug. 28, 1864.

Alice-M. Ridlon⁶ (3), eldest daughter of Melville⁵ (1), was born in Saco, Me., Nov. 12, 1872.

Carrie-E. Ridlon⁶ (2), second daughter of Melville⁵ (1), was born in Saco, Me., May 17, 1869. Deceased.

Charles-A. Ridlon⁶ (24), eldest son of Melville⁵ (1), was born in Saco, Me., Dec. 10, 1875. Deceased.

Everett Ridlon⁶ (1). } Son and daughter of Melville⁵ (1), were born
Eveline Ridlon⁶ (2). } in Saco, Me., May 9, 1880. Deceased.

Everett-L. Ridlon⁶ (2), youngest son of Melville⁵ (1), was born in Saco, Me., Oct. 1, 1882.

Belle Ridlon⁶ (2), only daughter of Frank⁵ (2), was born in Washington, D. C., Aug. 9, 1861.

William-Clark Ridlon⁶ (24), a son of James⁵ (12), was born in Middleton, Kan., June 22, 1879.

Albert-Clark Ridlon⁶ (8), a son of James⁵ (12), was born in Middleton, Kan., Oct. 16, 1881.

Gussie Ridlon⁶ (1). }
Ida-May Ridlon⁶ (7). } Children of James⁵ (13), born in Kansas.
George Ridlon⁶ (23). }

SEVENTH GENERATION.

Harrison-Gray Redlon⁷ (1), son of Lorenzo⁶ (1), was born in Buxton, Me., Oct. 13, 1872.

Mabel-Florence Redlon⁷ (1), daughter of Lorenzo⁶ (1), was born in Buxton, Me., Nov. 15, 1876.

John Redlon⁷ (38), eldest son of Silas⁶ (1), was born Dec. 9, 1846, and died the same month.

Benjamin-W. Redlon⁷ (14), second son of Silas⁶ (1), was born Dec. 30, 1848' and died young.

Charles Redlon⁷ (25), third son of Silas⁶ (1), was born in 1854. Blacksmith.

Five children of Silas⁶ (1) died in infancy.

Eli Redlon⁷ (1), eldest son of Benjamin⁶ (7), was born in March, 1847, and died young.

Lloyd Redlon⁷ (1), second son of Benjamin⁶ (7), was born in Granger, N. J.

Hannah Redlon[7] (**14**), eldest daughter of Benjamin[6] (**7**), was born in Wisconsin, in May, 1852.

Nancy Redlon[7] (**12**), second daughter of Benjamin[6] (**7**), was born in April, 1855, and died in September, 1869.

Charles Redlon[7] (**26**), third son of Benjamin[6] (**7**), was born in Wisconsin in 1853. Farmer.

Alice-A. Redlon[7] (**4**), a daughter of Benjamin[6] (**7**), was born in March, 1857.

Eliza-P. Redlon[7] (**14**), a daughter of Benjamin[6] (**7**), was born in June, 1859.

Flora Redlon[7] (**1**), a daughter of Benjamin[6] (**7**), was born in July, 1861.

Marianna Redlon[7] (**2**), a daughter of Benjamin[6] (**7**), was born in December, 1868.

Jessie Redlon[7] (**3**), a daughter of Nathaniel[6] (**6**), was born in Plainfield, Wis., Nov. 8, 1856.

Janette Redlon[7] (**2**), a daughter of Nathaniel[6] (**6**), was born in 1858; died in 1862.

Eva Redlon[7] (**2**), a daughter of Nathaniel[6] (**6**), was born in Plainfield, in May, 1866.

Amos Redlon[7] (**4**), a son of Nathaniel[6] (**6**), was born in January, 1871.

Marilla Redlon[7] (**3**), a daughter of Thomas[6] (**10**), was born in February, 1867.

Minnie Redlon[7] (**3**), a daughter of Thomas[6] (**10**), was born in 1869.

Bertha Redlon[7] (**2**), a daughter of Thomas[6] (**10**), was born in ——.

Lorana Redlon[7] (**1**), a daughter of Thomas[6] (**10**), was born in ——.

Charles-Lewis Redlon[7] (**27**), eldest son of Benjamin[6] (**8**), was born in Portland, Me., July 18, 1855; died July 30, 1861.

Georgia-Anna Redlon[7] (**1**), eldest daughter of Benjamin[6] (**8**), was born in Portland, Me., May 24, 1858; was taken prisoner with her mother at Winchester, Va., during the Southern Rebellion, and sent by the Rebels into the Union lines under a flag of truce, after three days.

Charles-Henry Redlon[7] (**28**), second son of Benjamin[6] (**8**), was born in Portland, Me., May 12, 1864.

Willie-Lincoln Redlon[7] (**25**), third son of Benjamin[6] (**8**), was born in Portland, Me., April 8, 1868.

Alice-May Redlon[7] (**5**), second daughter of Benjamin[6] (**8**), was born in Portland, Me., Sept. 24, 1875; died June 9, 1881.

Elizabeth Redlon[7] (**17**), only child of Albert[6] (**3**), was born in Portland; lives with her mother, Mrs. Samuel Dunn, in Hallowell, Me.

William-Howard Redlon[7] (**26**), son of William[6] (**12**), was born in April, 1874.

Fannie Redlon[7] (**2**), eldest daughter of Eugene[6] (**1**), was born in October, 1864.

Bennie Redlon[7] (**15**), eldest son of Eugene[6] (**1**), was born in May, 1869.

Abbie Redlon[7] (6), second daughter of Eugene[6] (1), was born April 30, 1875.

Hattie Redlon[7] (7), third daughter of Eugene[6] (1), was born in October, 1877.

Herbert Redlon[7] (2), second son of Eugene[6] (1), was born in February, 1880.

Winnefred-Adams Redlon[7] (1), only child of Nehemiah[6] (1), was born May 30, 1874.

Ada Ridlon[7] (6), only child of Artemas[6] (1), was born in Taunton, Mass., and died young.

Bertrand-D. Ridlon[7] (1), only son of Emery[6] (1), was born in Parsonfield, Me., June 11, 1868.

Horace-Denber Ridlon[7] (1), eldest son of Stillman[6] (1), was born Feb. 24, 1876.

Harry-Emery Ridlon[7] (2), second son of Stillman[6] (1), was born Aug. 27, 1877.

Emma-C. Ridley[7] (5), eldest daughter of Matthias[6] (7), was born June 8, 1850; was married to Albert Dean, a farmer, and resides in Dedham, Mass.

Olive-M. Ridley[7] (9), second daughter of Matthias[6] (7), was born Nov. 25, 1854; was married to Daniel Ballou, a blacksmith, and lives in Norwood, Mass.

Minnie-H. Ridley[7] (4), third daughter of Matthias[6](7), was born June 10, 1858. Unmarried in 1876.

George-P. Ridley[7] (24), only son of Isaac[6] (8), was born Sept. 8, 1857, and is now in Maine (1879). He is tall and slender; has black hair. Fond of books; has a remarkable memory; very quiet.

Hannah-P. Ridley[7] (15), eldest daughter of Billings[6] (1), was born in Jay, Me., April 26, 1860, and attended school at Manchester, N. H., and Rockbottom, Mass.; was married to Herbert P. Underwood, a railroad man, and has *two* children. Residence, Fitchburg, Mass.

Benjamin Ridley[7] (16), eldest son of Billings[6] (1), was born in Jay, Me., Dec. 26, 1861.

Mary-Eliza Ridley[7] (60), second daughter of Billings[6] (1), was born in Jay, Me., Aug. 21, 1865; has taught school. Was married in 1884.

John-D. Ridley[7] (39), second son of Billings[6] (1), was born in Jay, Me., Aug. 21, 1867.

Emma-S. Ridley[7] (6), third daughter of Billings[6] (1), was born in Jay, Me., Nov. 7, 1869.

Jonathan-D. Ridley[7] (7), third son of Billings[6] (1), was born in Jay, Me., Sept. 12, 1871.

Lydia-J. Ridley[7] (13), eldest daughter of Hamilton[6] (1), was born in Wayne, Me., Feb. 15, 1846; married to T. F. Storer, of Vienna, and resides in Leeds, Me.

Benjamin-H. Ridley[7] (17), eldest son of Hamilton[6] (1), was born in

Wayne, Me., April 20, 1847; married Charlotte B. Haskel, and has issue *three* children, of whom hereafter. Resides in Wayne; blacksmith.

Eliza-M.-J. Ridley[7] (15), second daughter of Hamilton[6] (1), was born in Wayne, Me., Dec. 30, 1848; married Feb. 9, 1869, to Greenleaf Hodgsdon, of Byron, and had issue. Died July 28, 1882.

Daniel-Frank Ridley[7] (14), second son of Hamilton[6] (1), was born in Wayne, Me., Dec. 16, 1852; married Sarah H. Roberts, Nov. 28, 1882, and has *one* daughter.

Alvah-M. Ridley[7] (1), third son of Hamilton[6] (1), was born in Wayne, Me., Feb. 28, 1860.

Jessie-E. Ridley[7] (2), third daughter of Hamilton[6] (1), was born in Wayne, Me., Feb. 28, 1862; died Sept. 30, 1879.

Hannah-S.-E. Ridley[7] (16), fourth daughter of Hamilton[6] (1), was born in Wayne, Me., Oct. 20, 1867.

Leonard-S. Ridley[7] (2), eldest son of Hallet[6] (1), was born in Wayne, Me., Feb. 21, 1849; died in Turner, July 9, 1870.

Rachel-A. Ridley[7] (6), eldest daughter of Hallet[6] (1), was born in Wayne, Me., Feb. 7, 1851; died in Bangor, April 4, 1869.

Melvina-B. Ridley[7] (1), second daughter of Hallet[6] (1), was born in Wayne, Me., May 25, 1852; died in Bangor, Dec. 29, 1866.

Eliza-E. Ridley[7] (16), third daughter of Hallet[6] (1), was born in Wayne, Me., Jan. 16, 1855; was married, in 1880, to —— Sawyer, of Lewiston, Me.

Mary-F. Ridley[7] (61), fourth daughter of Hallet[6] (1), was born in Wayne, Me., March 6, 1857; was married, in 1880, to —— Bradford, of Lewiston, Me.

William-H. Ridley[7] (27), second son of Hallet[6](1), was born in Wayne, Me., May 5, 1859.

Orman Ridley[7] (1), eldest son of Joseph[6] (9), was born in Hudson, Me., Oct. 11, 1858.

Corlista Ridley[7] (1), eldest daughter of Joseph[6] (9), was born in Hudson, Me., Jan. 7, 1860.

Myrtle Ridley[7] (1), second daughter of Joseph[6] (9), was born in Hudson, Me., May 4, 1864.

Naaman-B. Ridley[7] (1), eldest son of Jerome[6] (2), was born in Wayne, Me., June 3, 1871.

Scott-K. Ridley[7] (1), second son of Jerome[6] (2), was born in Wayne, Me., March 16, 1873.

Minnie-Belle Ridley[7] (5), eldest daughter of Charles[6] (6), was born at River Falls, Wis., Nov. 24, 1865.

George Ridley[7] (25), eldest son of Charles[6] (6), was born at River Falls, Wis., Sept. 8, 1869.

Lee Ridley[7] (2), second son of Charles[6] (6), was born at River Falls, Wis., Jan. 16, 1872.

Abbie-Jane Ridlon[7] (7), eldest daughter of Albion[6] (2), was born in Hollis, Me., Dec. 15, 1854; married April 23, 1874, to George Richardson, of Limington.

Oliver-Howard Ridlon[7] (1), eldest son of Albion[6] (2), was born in

Hollis, Me., Jan. 22, 1857; lives with his grandfather, in Hollis. Unmarried in 1882.

Alice-M.Ridlon[7] (6), second daughter of Albion[6] (2), was born in Hollis, Me., May 23, 1860; was married in 1878 to Charles Graffum, of Buxton, Me., and lives in that town.

Cora-Bell Ridlon[7] (3), third daughter of Albion[6] (2), was born in Hollis, Me., July 23, 1862; died Aug. 1, 1867.

Walter-A. Ridlon[7] (4), eldest son of James[6] (16), was born in Albion, Me., Aug. 31, 1857; married Feb. 22, 1878, to Ella-Elizabeth, daughter of Solomon and Harriet (Whiting) Townsend, of Turner, Me., and has issue. He is a shoemaker. Lives in Turner.

Sarah-E. Ridlon[7] (26), eldest daughter of James[6] (16), was born in Albion, Me., Dec. 8, 1860. She died when a young woman; was remarkably beautiful.

James-F. Ridlon[7] (22), second son of James[6] (16), was born in Albion, Me., Sept. 12, 1864. Deceased.

James-F. Ridlon[7] (23), third son of James[6] (16), was born in Albion, Me., Dec. 29, 1867.

Clarence-E. Ridlon[7] (2), fourth son of James[6] (16), was born in Albion, Me., Dec. 20, 1870, and died Aug. 20, 1871; a twin.

Claribell-E. Ridlon[7] (1), second daughter of James[6] (16), was born in Albion, Me., Dec. 20, 1870, and died Sept. 23, 1871.

Inez-G. Ridlon[7] (1), third daughter of James[6] (16), was born Feb. 24, 1872.

Wesley-T. Ridlon[7] (1), fifth son of James[6] (16), was born Dec. 4, 1878.

Oraville-F. Ridlon[7] (2), eldest daughter of John[6] (22), was born in Albion, Me., May 4, 1868.

James-Wesley Ridlon[7] (24), eldest son of John[6] (22), was born in Albion, Me., March 16, 1872.

Rosa-Belle Ridlon[7] (1), second daughter of John[6] (22), was born in Albion, Me. Date not known.

Clara Ridlon[7] (2), third daughter of John[6] (22), was born in Albion, Me., Oct. 20, 1878.

Frederick-Walter Ridlon[7] (5), eldest son of Alfred[6] (2), was born Aug. 6, 1873.

George-Wales Ridlon[7] (26), second son of Alfred[6] (2), was born June 21, 1875.

Charles-Augustus Ridlon[7] (29), third son of Alfred[6] (2), was born Nov. 20, 1877.

Irvin-Ira Ridlon[7] (1), fourth son of Alfred[6] (2), was born Sept. 12, 1879.

Merritt-H.-S. Ridlon[7] (1), eldest son of George[6] (8), was born in Rutland, Vt., Jan. 25, 1864.

Ermenie-L. Ridlon[7] (1), a daughter of George[6] (8), was born in Clarendon, Vt., Aug. 25, 1866.

Lila-Bell Ridlon[7] (2), eldest daughter of John[6] (23), was born in Clarendon, Vt., May 10, 1863; died March 18, 1864.

Alice-J. Ridlon[7] (7), second daughter of John[6] (23), was born in Clarendon, Vt., Jan. 30, 1865.

Hester Ridlon[7] (2), eldest daughter of John[6] (24), was born in New York city, April 4, 1880.

Constance Ridlon[7] (1), second daughter of John[6] (24), was born in New York city, Oct. 17, 1881, and died Sept. 25, 1882.

Robert Ridlon[7] (9), a son of John[6] (24), was born in New York city, Feb. 6, 1888.

Frank-Berleigh Ridlon[7] (6), eldest son of Franklin[6] (3), was born in Standish, Me., Nov. 11, 1863.

William-Moses Ridlon[7] (28), second son of Franklin[6] (3), was born in Standish, Me., July 19, 1865.

David-Harry Ridlon[7] (5), third son of Franklin[6] (3), was born in Standish, Me., March 16, 1867.

Octavia Ridlon[7] (1), eldest daughter of Franklin[6] (3), was born in Standish, Me., Sept. 7, 1869.

Sarah-Ada Ridlon[7] (27), second daughter of Franklin[6] (3), was born in Standish, Me., Oct. 28, 1871.

Robert Ridlon[7] (10), fourth son of Franklin[6] (3), was born in Standish, Me., Nov. 1, 1873.

Nellie Ridlon[7] (6), third daughter of Franklin[6] (3), was born March 26, 1876.

Phebe-Jane Ridlon[7] (2), fourth daughter of Franklin[6] (3), was born in 1878.

Gardner-Rich Ridlon[7] (1), eldest son of Andrew[6] (2), was born in Standish, Me., March 18, 1868.

Annie-Susan Ridlon[7] (2), eldest daughter of Andrew[6] (2), was born in Standish, Me., Dec. 19, 1870.

Laura-Richardson Ridlon[7] (3), second daughter of Andrew[6] (2), was born in Standish, Me., Jan. 28, 1873.

Elizabeth Ridlon[7] (18), eldest daughter of Robert[6] (8).

Herbert-Eugene Ridlon[7] (3), eldest son of Robert[6] (8).

Susan-Catherine Ridlon[7] (12), second daughter of Robert[6] (8).

Annie-Decker Ridlon[7] (3), eldest daughter of Gideon[6] (1), was born in Hollis, Me., April 28, 1861. She closely resembles her paternal grandmother, Hannah Tibbetts; has light, wavy hair, brown eyes, and a clear complexion; has a remarkably fine treble voice, and sings select pieces to public assemblies with great power and beauty. She was married to Charles-S. Whitney, of Harrison, and has issue a son and a daughter.

Gennette Ridlon[7] (2), second daughter of Gideon[6] (1), was born in Hollis, Me., Jan. 16, 1863; died Sept. 28, 1864. She was a dark-eyed, curly-haired, lovely little creature.

Harvey Ridlon[7] (1), eldest son of Gideon[6] (1), was born in Hollis, Me., Aug. 8, 1865; died in September, 1867. He had fair, sunny hair, black eyes, and the type of features so common in the family.

Gideon-T. Ridlon[7] (2), second son of Gideon[6] (1), was born in Hollis, Me., Nov. 26, 1867; has the Ridlon type of features, gray eyes, and brown, curly hair; is even-tempered, moderate, and affectionate; a good scholar, and very ingenious.

Greenleaf-Herbert Ridlon[7] (1), eldest son of Almon[6] (1), was born in Bridgton, Me., Nov. 17, 1856.

Charles-M.-W. Ridlon[7] (30), second son of Almon[6] (1), was born in Bridgton, Me., June 9, 1858.

Georgie Ridlon[7] (2), eldest daughter of Walter[6] (3), was born in Porter, Me., Nov. 16, 1868.

Benjamin Ridlon[7] (18), eldest son of Walter[6] (3), was born in Porter, Me., Sept. 27, 1870.

Daniel-D. Ridlon[7] (15), second son of Walter[6] (3), was born in Porter, Me., Feb. 2, 1873.

Walter-Sumner Ridlon[7] (5), third son of Walter[6] (3), was born in Porter, Me., May 15, 1878.

Magnus-Gervace Ridlon[7] (10), fourth son of Walter[6] (3), was born in Porter, Me., Nov. 29, 1879.

Addison Ridlon[7] (1), a son of John[6] (26), was born in Porter, Me., June 2, 1879.

Nova Ridlon[7] (1), eldest daughter of John[6] (26), was born in Porter, Me., Oct. 21, 1881.

Norman Ridlon[7] (1), second son of John[6] (26), was born in Porter, Me., Dec. 2, 1883.

Ida-May Ridlon[7] (8), eldest daughter of William[6] (16), was born at Chest Springs, Cambria County, Penn., Jan. 28, 1868.

Alwilda Ridlon[7] (1), second daughter of William[6] (16), was born at Porter, Me., Jan. 2, 1871.

Guy-Leroy Ridlon[7] (1), eldest son of William[6] (16), was born in Porter, Me., Aug. 28, 1872.

Grace-Gertrude Ridlon[7] (1), third daughter of William[6] (16), was born in Porter, Me., Nov. 23, 1874.

Lova-Alberta Ridlon[7] (1), fourth daughter of William[6] (16), was born in Porter, Me., July 4, 1878.

Arthur-Wendell Ridlon[7] (1), second son of William[6] (16), was born in Porter, Me., May 5, 1882.

Bertha-May Ridlon[7] (2), a daughter of Lewis[6] (5), was born in Hiram, Me., May 5, 1880, and died Nov. 28, 1880.

Gertrude Ridlon[7] (2), a daughter of Herbert[6] (1), was born in Porter, Me., June 15, 1882.

Myron-Abbott Ridlon[7] (1), a son of Herbert[6] (1), was born in Porter, Me., Aug. 14, 1883.

Mary-Belle Ridlen[7] (62), eldest daughter of Cumberland[6] (1), was born in Indiana.

Ida Ridlen[7] (9), second daughter of Cumberland[6] (1), was born in Indiana.

Samuel Ridlen[7] (16), a son of Charles[6] (13).
Stephen Ridlen[7] (10), a son of Charles[6] (13).
Ally Ridlen[7] (1), a daughter of Charles[6] (13).
Mary Ridlen[7] (63), a daughter of Charles[6] (13).
} Born in Indiana.

Mary Ridlen[7] **(64)**, a daughter of Ebenezer[6] (6), was born in Indiana.

Jefferson Ridlon[7] **(1)**, eldest son of Joshua[6] (4), was born in Hiram, Me., Oct. 2, 1862; died in 1881.

Sarah-French Ridlon[7] **(28)**, eldest daughter of Joshua[6] (4), was born in Hiram, Me., March 11, 1866.

Charles-Gould Ridlon[7] **(31)**, second son of Joshua[6] (4), was born in Hiram, Me., Sept. 10, 1870.

Octavius Ridlon[7] **(1)**, third son of Joshua[6] (4), was born in Hiram, Me., June 10, 1872.

Elizabeth Ridlon[7] **(19)**, second daughter of Joshua[6] (4), was born in Hiram, Me., Nov. 10, 1874.

John-Spring Ridlon[7] **(40)**, eldest son of Benjamin[6] (13), was born in Hiram, Me., March 16, 1868; died May 10, 1870.

Caleb-Durgin Ridlon[7] **(1)**, second son of Benjamin[6] (13), was born in Hiram, Me., Sept. 12, 1869; died July 2, 1870.

Ruth-Goodwin Ridlon[7] **(8)**, eldest daughter of James[6] (21), was born in Hiram, Me., Dec. 8, 1864.

Fanny-J. Ridlon[7] **(3)**, second daughter of James[6] (21), was born in Hiram, Me., April 7, 1866.

Marcia Ridlon[7] **(5)**, third daughter of James[6] (21), was born in Hiram, Me., Nov. 8, 1867.

David Ridlon[7] **(5)**, eldest son of Henry[6] (7), was born in Porter, Me., Sept. 23, 1858.

Herbert-L. Ridlon[7] **(4)**, second son of Henry[6] (7), was born in Porter, Me., Dec. 15, 1860; married Susan, daughter of Daniel D. Ridlon, of Hiram, and has issue, of whom hereafter.

Elmer-E. Ridlon[7] **(1)**, third son of Henry[6] (7), was born in Porter, Me., Feb. 18, 1863.

Wirt-V. Ridlon[7] **(1)**, son of Francis[6] (2), was born in Parsonfield, Me., Feb. 14, 1875.

Lizzie-F. Ridlon[7] **(20)**, daughter of Francis[6] (2), was born in Parsonfield, Me., Aug. 22, 1875.

Dora-M. Ridlon[7] **(2)**, eldest daughter of John[6] (36), was born in May, 1873, probably in Paris, Me.

Della-C. Ridlon[7] **(1)**, second daughter of John[6] (36), was born in November, 1878, probably in Paris, Me.

Oscar-Gould Ridlon[7] **(2)**, eldest son of George[6] (20), was born in Porter, Me., Oct. 4, 1855; married Hannah Cummings, and lives in Boston. Express-teamster. *One* child.

Emma-Tibbetts Ridlon[7] **(7)**, eldest daughter of George[6] (20), was born in Porter, Me., Jan. 18, 1859; died in 1860.

John-Sullivan Ridlon[7] **(41)**, second son of George[6] (20), was born in Porter, Me., June 22, 1866.

Nellie-C. Ridlon[7] **(7)**, second daughter of George[6] (20), was born in Porter, Me., June 10, 1870.

Charles-Chester Ridlon[7] **(32)**, third son of George[6] (20), was born in Boston, Mass., May 22, 1875.

Eva-S. Ridlon[7] (2), eldest daughter of William[6] (22), was born in Porter, Me., Nov. 23, 1868.

Bertha-May Ridlon[7] (3), second daughter of William[6] (22), was born in Boston, Mass., May 24, 1874.

Chalmers-E. Ridlon[7] (1), son of Joseph[6] (13), was born in Boston, Mass. (presumably), and is now (1884) about seventeen years of age.

George Ridlon[7] (27), eldest son of Granville[6] (1), was born in Chelsea, Mass.

Walter-Mann Ridlon[7] (6), eldest son of Charles[6] (22), was born in Chelsea, Mass., Dec. 23, 1872.

Irving-Francis Ridlon[7] (2), second son of Charles[6] (22), was born in Chelsea, Mass., March 5, 1876.

James-A. Ridlon[7] (25), eldest son of Asa[6] (1), was born in Lynn, Mass., Jan. 10, 1873; died Sept. 9, 1873.

Bertram-E. Ridlon[7] (1), second son of Asa[6] (1), was born in Lynn, Mass., July 29, 1874.

EIGHTH GENERATION.

Scott Ridley[8] (2), eldest son of Benjamin[7] (17), was born in Wayne, Me., March 8, 1874.

James-A. Ridley[8] (26), second son of Benjamin[7] (17), was born Aug. 28, 1876.

Gracie-E. Ridley[8] (2), a daughter of Benjamin[7] (17), was born March 25, 1878.

Mary-Jessie Ridley[8] (65), eldest daughter of Daniel[7] (14), was born March 26, 1884.

Angie-Olive Ridlon[8] (2), a daughter of Herbert[7] (4) and Susan Ridlon, was born in Sandwich, N. H., May 13, 1882. This child is the only known descendant of Daniel Redlon, 1st, of the eighth generation from Magnus Redlon, our ancestor, born by the Ridlon surname; this degree is second from the father's side.

Willie Ridlon[8] (29), eldest son of Oscar[7] (1), was born in Boston, Mass., Feb. 4, 1882.

Gervase-Everett Ridlon[8] (1), twin son of Oscar[7] (1), was born in Boston, Mass., May 27, 1884.

Galfred-Oscar Ridlon[8] (1), twin son of Oscar[7] (1), was born in Boston, Mass., May 27, 1884.

NOTE. — On the foregoing pages are the names of nearly twelve hundred descendants of our common ancestor, Magnus Redlon, on the paternal side, all born within one hundred and sixty years; and there are probably many others, born during the compilation of this book, whose names have not reached the author, — truly a prolific family.

APPENDIX.

APPENDIX.

APPENDIX.

LAND-OWNERS IN GREAT BRITAIN AND IRELAND.

The following table shows the number of acres of land accredited to the Riddells and Riddles in England, Scotland, Ireland, and Wales, and the gross estimated rental, as found in the "Return of the Owners of Land," published by the government in 1875: —

NAME OF OWNER.	RESIDENCE OF OWNER.	EXTENT OF LAND.			RENTAL.	
RIDDELL.		A.	R.	P.	£	s.
Sir Thomas M. Riddell,	Strontian, County Argyle,	54,418			3,672	18
Sir Walter B. Riddell,	Hepple, Rothbury,	4,482	1	18	1,576	9
Francis Riddell, Esq.,	Cheeseburn Grange,	2,570			2,890	
John G. Riddell, Esq.,	Felton Park,	12,911	3	32	11,119	18
Rev. John C. Riddell,	Harrietsham, Kent,	61	2	37		
Rev. James Riddell,	Leamington, Prior's,	72			118	
E. M. H. Riddell,	Carlton, Nott's,	42	3	4	196	10
William Riddell,	Lympsham, Somerset,	86	1	35	231	18
Rev. James Riddell,	Warwick,	47	3	4	76	19
Francis Riddell,	Leyburn Grove,	595	2	5	791	13
Capt. George W. Riddell,	Melton, Berwick,	119			417	10
William Riddell,	Wellgreen, Glassford,	112			120	
John Riddell,	Bankfield, Chappelton,	67			67	
John Riddell,	Todshill, St. Stratheren,	5			32	
Jane Riddell,	Edinburgh, Scotland,	8			55	10
Gen. William Riddell,	Anchorage, Melrose,	297			441	
RIDDLE.						
Charles Riddle,	Amphill, Bedford,	3	1	17	5	5
John Riddle,	Millpool, Cornwall,	4	1	30	14	10
E. Riddle,	Cardyerham,	31	1	3	36	11
Elizabeth Riddle,	Stoke Bishop, Gloucester,	3	3	31	150	
F. T. Riddle,	Fishponds, Gloucester,	1	1	3	30	2
Herbert Riddle,	Bristol, Gloucester,	61	26		117	14
T. H. Riddle,	Stapleton, Gloucester,	38		6	201	5
John Riddle,	Wolverhampton, Hertd.,	7	2	38	57	6
Thomas Riddle,	Ashford, Kent,	5	3	20	17	5
Mrs. Riddle,	Southampton,	5	2	36	75	
Andrew Riddle,	Tweedmouth,	12	2	37	321	18
Jane Riddle,	Berwick,	2	3	35	32	13
Joseph Riddle,	Haining Ridge,	12			9	
Robert Riddle,	Chesterhope,	9	24		31	
Edwin Riddle,	Wallsall, Salop,	22	3	4	46	
Mrs. William Riddle,	Cleredon, Somerset,	11	3	10	31	16
William Riddle,	Lympsham, Somerset,	238	11		582	7
Edward Riddle,	Newcastle-on-Tyne,	119	2	19	99	
Sellwood Riddle,	Wolverhampton,	95	1	34	74	10

RIDDLES, RIDDELLS, RIDDALLS, AND RUDDELLS IN IRELAND.

NAME.	RESIDENCE OF OWNER.	EXTENT OF LAND.			RENTAL.	
		A.	R.	P.	£	s.
James T. Riddle,	Grange, Kilkenny,	312	3	30	235	5
William Riddell,	Beachmont, Antrim,	1	1	10	680	10
David Riddell,	Richhill, Armagh,	14	0	10	17	5
Mrs. Riddell,	Armagh, ——,	300	1	10	379	15
Archibald Riddel,	Glenish, Monaghan Co.	10	0	35	6	15
George Riddel,	Creevah, Monaghan Co.	26	3	5	19	15
Gordon Riddel,	Annamacnell, Monaghan Co.	11	2	0	9	5
Gordon Riddel,	Edenafirkin, Monaghan Co.	12	2	30	28	5
Hugh Riddel,	Comasoo, Monaghan Co.	5	3	5	4	15
James Riddel,	Mullycrock, Monaghan Co.	23	0	25	19	15
Robert Riddel,	Annamacnell, Monaghan Co.	12	2	5	13	5
James Riddall,	Corteenahilla, Rathdowny,	432	1	30	290	0
George Riddall,	Knockaneagh, Armagh,	22	2	35	23	10
George S. Riddall,	Armagh, ——,	17	2	5	291	5
Robert Riddall,	Armagh, Tyrone Co.	190	0	25	174	5
David Ruddell,	Smithfield, Antrim,	1	2	35	227	15
David Ruddell,	Peacefield, Armagh,	98	0	30	221	10
Nelson Ruddell,	Aghacommon, Lurgan,	15	3	0	92	15
Samuel Ruddell,	Turmoyra, Lurgan,	28	2	15	36	10
Thomas Ruddell,	Knockramer, Lurgan,	5	3	30	93	10
David Ruddell,	Lurgan, County Down,	10	0	35	12	5
Frederick Ruddell,	Portadown, County Down,	130	2	10	148	5

RIDDLES OF TROUGHEND, ENGLAND.

[ADDENDA TO PAGE 150.]

ROBERT RIDDLE, of Bellingham, Northumberland, Eng., says, "Our forefathers as far as we know were tenant-farmers, and although not possessed of great wealth, have always been looked upon as men of sterling integrity and honor. It is presumed they originally came from Scotland, as the earliest traditions we know, find them farming a farm called the 'Bog,' near Otterburn in Northumberland, about thirty miles from the Scottish border, and the whole family, with few exceptions, may be found located within a radius of thirty miles from the same place at this day." Mr. Riddle, above mentioned, says, the earliest known ancestor was

Robert Riddle[1] (1), who married and had issue a son.

SECOND GENERATION.

Edward Riddle[2] (1), who married Jane Headley, from the Hillock, Reedwater, and by her had *four* sons and *one* daughter.

THIRD GENERATION.

Robert Riddle[3] (2), eldest son of Edward[2] (1), died young.

Nicholas Riddle[3] (1), second son of Edward[2] (1), was born in 1746; married Christiana Adamson in 1783, by whom he had issue *two* children. He married, secondly, Mrs. Ann Headley, of Monkridge, by whom he had *two* children, of whom hereafter. Mr. Riddle died in 1818.

John Riddle[3] (1), third son Edward[2] (1), was father of Edward, the master of the Greenwich Naval School. See body of book.

Ann Riddle[8] (1), only daughter of Edward[2] (1), was married to Michael Hall.

Edward Riddle[8] (2), fourth son of Edward[2] (1), was born in 1754; married Ann Davidson in 1793, by whom he had issue *eight* children, of whom hereafter. He died in 1832.

FOURTH GENERATION.

Jane Riddle[4] (1), eldest child of Nicholas[8] (1), born in 1784, was married to Thomas Snaith.

Edward Riddle[4] (3), eldest son of Nicholas[8] (1), born in 1786; married, first, Ursula Davidson, in 1808, by whom he had issue *seven* children, of whom hereafter. He married, secondly, Ann Milburn, and had issue *two* children. He died in 1874.

Ursula Riddle[4] (1), second daughter of Nicholas[8] (1), born in 1809, was married to James Heron, of "Soppit."

Nicholas Riddle[4] (2), second son of Nicholas[8] (1), was born in 1811; married Mary Patterson, of Overacres, and had a large family.

[For descendants of John[8] (1), see page 150.]

Edward Riddle[4] (4), eldest son of Edward[8] (2), was born in 1794; married Ann Buckons, of Rawfoot, and had issue *eight* children, of whom hereafter. He died in 1880.

Thomas Riddle[4] (1), second son of Edward[8] (2), born in 1796; married Elizabeth Pearson, of the Hole Farm, in 1826, and had issue *three* children, of whom hereafter. He died in 1874.

Elizabeth Riddle[4] (1), eldest daughter of Edward[8] (2), born in 1798; was married in 1823 to Lancelot Fenwick, of "Brieredge." No children.

Nicholas Riddle[4] (3), third son of Edward[8] (2), born in 1800, died in 1822, unmarried.

Jane Riddle[4] (2), second daughter of Edward[8] (2), born in 1802; was married in 1828, to John Thompson, of Barmoor, and died in 1868.

Robert Riddle[4] (3), fourth son of Edward[8] (2), born in 1805; married Ann English, of Woodburn, in 1831, by whom he had issue *ten* children, of whom hereafter. Mr. Riddle still survives, an old and feeble man.

John Riddle[4] (2), fifth son of Edward[8] (2), born in 1807; died young.

William Riddle[4] (1), sixth son of Edward[8] (2), born in 1810; married Ann Davidson, of Buteland, and died issueless in 1855.

FIFTH GENERATION.

Christiana Riddle[5] (1), eldest daughter of Edward[4] (3).
Nicholas Riddle[5] (4), eldest son of Edward[4] (3).
John Riddle[5] (3), second son of Edward[4] (3).
Edward Riddle[5] (5), third son of Edward[4] (3).
Jane Riddle[5] (3), second daughter of Edward[4] (3).
William Riddle[5] (2), fourth son of Edward[4] (3).
Alexander Riddle[5] (1), fifth son of Edward[4] (3).
Sarah Riddle[5] (1), third daughter of Edward[4] (3), was married to William Thompson, of "the Brigg."
Robert Riddle[5] (4), sixth son of Edward[4] (3), unmarried.

Margaret Riddle[5] (1), eldest daughter of Edward[4] (4), was married to Thomas Martinson, of Woodburn.

Edward Riddle[5] (6), eldest son of Edward[4] (4), married Elizabeth Wallace, of Woodburn, by whom he had a family of daughters, all of whom, with one exception, died young.

Nicholas Riddle[5] (5), second son of Edward[4] (4), married Elizabeth Wood, of Woodburn, Lounhead, by whom he had *four* sons and *five* daughters, of whom none are married.

Ann Riddle[5] (2), second daughter of Edward[4] (4), unmarried.

Thomas Riddle[5] (2), third son of Edward[4] (4), unmarried.

William Riddle[5] (3), fourth son of Edward[4] (4), unmarried.

Elizabeth Riddle[5] (2), third daughter of Edward[4] (4), was married to George Headley, of Whickhope.

John Riddle[5] (4), fifth son of Edward[4] (4), died in childhood.

John Riddle[5] (5), son of Thomas[4] (1), married Mary Coulson, of Yarridge, near Hexham, by whom *five* sons.

Edward Riddle[5] (7), son of Thomas[4] (1), married Mary Baty, of Hexham, by whom he had *two* sons and *three* daughters. Mr. Riddle is an extensive draper in Hexham.

William Riddle[5] (4), son of Thomas[4] (1), married Jane Bell, of Hexham, but has no issue. He has a large business as chemist and druggist in Hexham, Northumberland.

Edward Riddle[5] (8), eldest son of Robert[4] (3), was born in 1832; married Ann Headley, of Monkridge, in 1873, and died in 1874, without children.

Mary Riddle[5] (1), eldest daughter of Robert[4] (3), born in 1834, was married to Robert Headley, of Garretshields.

Joseph Riddle[5] (1), second son of Robert[4] (3), married in 1866 to Ann Langhorne, of Haydonbridge, and has issue *four* children, of whom hereafter.

John Riddle[5] (6), third son of Robert[4] (3), born in 1838, married in 1870 to Elizabeth Patterson, of Potts Durtrees, and has issue *four* children, of whom hereafter.

Ann Riddle[5] (3), second daughter of Robert[4] (3), born in 1840, died in infancy.

Robert Riddle[5] (5), fourth son of Robert[4] (3), born in 1843; married in 1870 to Isabella Robson, of Garretshields, and has issue *seven* children, of whom hereafter. Mr. Riddle is a clerk and resides at Bellingham. He kindly provided the genealogy of this family, but too late for its proper place in the book.

Thomas-Lancelot Riddle[5] (3), fifth son of Robert[4] (3), born in 1845, died in infancy.

Ann Riddle[5] (4), third daughter of Robert[4] (3), born in 1848, unmarried.

William Riddle[5] (5), sixth son of Robert[4] (3), born in 1852, unmarried.

SIXTH GENERATION.

Ann Riddle[6] (5), only surviving daughter of Edward[5] (6), was married to Thomas Snowdon, and has a family.

William-G.-L. Riddle[6] (6), eldest son of Joseph[5] (1), born in 1868.

Robert Riddle[6] (6), second son of Joseph[5] (1), born in 1871.

Ann-Temple Riddle⁶ (6), eldest daughter of Joseph⁵ (1), born in 1873.
Thomas-Edward Riddle⁶ (4), third son of Joseph⁵ (1), born in 1875.

Robert-Christopher Riddle⁶ (7), eldest son of John⁵ (6), born in 1871.
William Riddle⁶ (7), second son of John⁵ (6), born in 1873.
John Riddle⁶ (7), third son of John⁵ (6), born in 1875.
Edward Riddle⁶ (9), fourth son of John⁵ (6), born in 1881.

Margaret Riddle⁶ (2), eldest daughter of Robert⁵ (5), born in 1870.
Annie Riddle⁶ (1), second daughter of Robert⁵ (5), born in 1872.
Robert-Edward Riddle⁶ (8), eldest son of Robert⁵ (5), born in 1874.
John Riddle⁶ (8), second son of Robert⁵ (5), born in 1876.
Isabella Riddle⁶ (2), third daughter of Robert⁵ (5), born in 1879.
William Riddle⁶ (8), third son of Robert⁵ (5), born in 1881.
Joseph-Lancelot Riddle⁶ (2), fourth son of Robert⁵ (5), born in 1883.

RIDDLES OF NEWCASTLE, DELAWARE.*

James Riddle¹ (1), was of Scottish descent, but probably born in the north of Ireland, as James Riddle of "Riddle Banks," near Wilmington, Delaware, informed me that he was of the same ancestry as his own family. The name of Mr. Riddle's wife is not known by his surviving grandchildren. He was probably a resident of Newcastle on the Delaware River. He was a large man, with light complexion and blue eyes. Occupation unknown. Children, *six* in number.

James Riddle² (2), eldest son of James¹ (1), was born at Newcastle, Del. (presumably), but never married. I have no particulars.
John Riddle² (1), second son of James¹ (1), was born at Newcastle, Del., and made that town his place of residence. He married Margaret Kirkbride, and had *seven* children, of whom hereafter. Occupation unknown.
Gunning-B. Riddle² (1), third son of James¹ (1), was born at Newcastle, Del., and died single.
Mary Riddle² (1), a daughter of James¹ (1), was born in Newcastle, Del. Never married.
Sally Riddle² (1), second daughter of James¹ (1), was born in Newcastle, Del. Never married.
Elizabeth Riddle² (1), third daughter of James¹ (1), was born in Newcastle, Del. Never married.

James Riddle² (3), eldest son of John² (1), was born at Newcastle, Del., and was married to a Miss White, but left no children. He died about 1863. Was in the Navy at one time, but held a position in the custom-house at Philadelphia latterly.

* In consequence of the loss of the original MS., containing the genealogy of this family, it was overlooked and could not stand in its proper place in the body of the book. The author regrets this very much, but the omission was discovered too late.

Hon. George-Read Riddle[2] **(1)**, second son of John[2] (1), was born in Newcastle, Del., in 1817; married a Miss Opie, of Virginia, and settled in his native town. He was descended from George Reed, one of the signers of the Declaration of Independence, on his mother's side. He graduated at Delaware College, and at an early age turned his attention to civil-engineering. For some time he engaged in surveying and laying out railroads in Maryland and Virginia, prior to 1842. About this period he evinced a disposition to enter the political arena, and commenced the publication of a Democratic newspaper in the city of Baltimore; but the enterprise did not prove successful, and was abandoned after the first issue. Subsequently he was engaged as chief-engineer on the Philadelphia, Wilmington & Baltimore Railroad, and took up his residence in Wilmington, with his parents, who were then under his care.

In 1844 he studied law, and at the same time, till 1847, was employed as a contributor to the *Delaware Gazette*. In 1846 he was elected a member of the city council by the Democrats, and exercised great influence in that capacity. About this time his taste and judgment as an engineer, led the originators of the Wilmington and Brandywine cemetery to seek his services in laying out their grounds, and to him the people are indebted for those designs which adorn that beautiful place. In 1848 he was admitted to the bar, and was appointed Deputy Attorney-General for the State. In 1850 he was nominated by his party as a candidate for congress, and was elected. Again in 1852 he was elected to the same position by a complimentary majority. He received his third nomination in 1854, but was not the successful candidate. While a member of the House of Representatives, Mr. Riddle, by his good judgment and great influence, secured an appropriation for the erection of the new post-office and custom-house buildings in Wilmington. On the resignation of a United States senator in 1864, Mr. Riddle was elected by the legislature to succeed him, and took his seat in the senate in February, a few days after his election. Having an active and obliging mind, he was courteous and attentive to every one; added to this, his great fund of useful knowledge acquired in his early training, was known to many of his contemporaries in congress before he took his seat in that body, and, consequently, Mr. Riddle was placed upon many important committees during his term of service. His willingness to assume the most wearing duties of such positions, and the disposition of many of his colleagues to shun the labors of committees, threw an immense amount upon him. This devotion to what seemed to be duty, impaired the health of Mr. Riddle, and when he returned home at the close of a session he was very much weakened and careworn. He resorted to various watering-places, and had the ablest medical advice, but without permanent improvement, and he returned to his work at Washington totally unfitted to assume the harassing labor that devolved upon him; but being buoyant in spirit, and anxious to do all in his power for his state and constituents, he could not be prevailed upon to leave his post.

The subject of this notice, died in Washington, D. C., in 1867, and his remains were deposited in the Wilmington and Brandywine cemetery. A committee from both houses of congress attended the body from Washington to Wilmington, and a committee appointed at a meeting of the bar, met the remains at the station; these, with a large number of friends and acquaintances, followed the body to the family mansion. The flags on the public buildings and shipping were at half-mast, and large numbers visited the house to take a last look of one they loved. His funeral was under the direction of Hon. Messrs. Davis and Nye, of the senate, and Glossbrenner and Benton, of the House of Representatives. The assembly was very large, and the mayor and city council attended in a body; also, numerous members of the bar. During the passage of the funeral cortege to the cemetery, the city bells were tolled, and the flags were at half-mast. The services at the grave were performed in an impressive manner by Revs. Messrs. Hinckley, of the Swedenborgian, and Spottswood of the Presbyterian Churches. Mr. Riddle left a widow, but no children, to mourn his departure.

Mr. Riddle's social qualities were esteemed by all who knew him, and made him a very popular man. No man was ever more devoted to his state, and few die at his age leaving behind them, in their community, so many who sincerely feel their loss.

Richard Riddle³ (1), third son of John² (1), was born in Newcastle, Del., and was captain of a ship. Died at New Orleans, unmarried.

William Riddle³ (1), fourth son of John² (1), was born in Newcastle, Del., and never married.

Eliza Riddle³ (1), eldest daughter of John² (1), was born in Newcastle, Del., and was married in 1842 to William H. Jewett, of Skaneateles, N. Y., a lawyer by profession, by whom she had *one* son, Freeborn G. Jewett, who has been in the Secretary of State's office at Albany, N. Y. Mr. Jewett died in 1859, and in 1866, Eliza was married to Judge William Marvin, of Key West, Fla., with whom she is now living at Skaneateles, N. Y., in wealth. Mrs. Marvin has manifested a deep interest in this book from the first knowledge of the undertaking, and generously subscribed for a portrait of her brother, Hon. George R. Riddle. She has traveled extensively in Europe.

Sally Riddle³ (1), second daughter of John² .(1), was born at Newcastle, Del., and never married.

Emily Riddle³ (1), third daughter of John² (1), was born in Newcastle, Del., and became the wife of a Mr. Truss, a grain and coal merchant of that town, by whom *two* children. Mrs. Truss is still living in Newcastle, a beautiful, thriving town, and the County seat, on the Delaware River, where the author of this book spent a summer several years ago.

RIDDLES OF BOSTON, MASSACHUSETTS.

[ADDENDA TO PAGE 267.]

John Riddel¹ (1) married Mary Kelch, of Ballybriggan County, Dublin, Ireland, about the year 1793, and had issue *six* children, of whom hereafter.

SECOND GENERATION.

Ambrose Riddel² (1), son of John¹ (1), died in Ireland, aged 25.

Patrick Riddel² (1), son of John¹ (1), enlisted in the dragoons of the English army, and went to India; returned home in 1848, married, and emigrated to Canada.

Michael Riddel² (1), son of John¹ (1), married and emigrated to Boston, Mass., about the year 1850; died there in 1866, and was buried in

Hollyhood (?) cemetery. He left *four* children, who are somewhere in Massachusetts.

Richard Riddle⁸ (1), son of John¹ (1), married Catherine, daughter of Edward Eustace, of Ballybriggan County, Dublin, Ireland, and had issue, *twelve* children, of whom hereafter. He emigrated to Boston, Mass., in 1848, with his wife and five children, the other seven having died in Ireland. He died in Boston, April 24, 1882, aged 81 years, and was buried by his wife, — who died in Boston, Aug. 6, 1878, aged 72, — in Calvary cemetery.

John Riddel² (1), son of John¹ (1), was a baker by trade; married, had a family, and was living in Dublin, Ireland, when last heard from. If living, is about 72 years of age.

Margaret Riddel² (1), daughter of John¹ (1), emigrated to America in 1849, and is supposed to be dead; unmarried.

THIRD GENERATION.

Sarah Riddel⁸ (1), married William Cromer, and had *seven* children.
John Riddel⁸ (2).
Kate Riddel⁸ (1). } See pages 267–68.
Mary Riddel⁸ (1), married Thomas Dolan, and had *one* son.
Patrick-E. Riddel⁸ (2).
Richard Riddel⁸ (2). } See pages 267–68.

RIDLEYS OF SHINCLIFFE, ENGLAND.

William Ridley¹ (1), supposed to have been a son of Walter Ridley, was a resident of a small village called Shincliffe, about one mile east of Durham,* Eng., where his children were born and settled. He used to follow his son with the game-bag, during the shooting season, when old.

SECOND GENERATION.

William Ridley² (2), a son of William¹ (1), was born at Shincliffe; married Elizabeth Robinson, of Durham, and had issue *four* children, of whom hereafter. He was a gardener and gamekeeper. Emigrated to Wisconsin, many years ago, and when last heard from was living with a grandson, in Illinois.

Alice Ridley² (1), a daughter of William¹ (1).
Rose Ridley² (1), a daughter of William¹ (1).

THIRD GENERATION.

Walter Ridley⁸ (2), a son of William² (2), was born at Shincliffe, Durham, Eng., about the year 1826, and emigrated to the United States in 1844. He married Mary-Ann Frost, from Devonshire, Eng., in Wisconsin, — where he then resided, — and by her had issue *five* children, of whom hereafter. He is now living at Lamar, Barton County, Mo.

---

* There were other families of Ridley living in the same neighborhood, in some way connected with this family, closely resembling them, who frequently visited Durham and Shincliffe.

William Ridley² (3), a son of William² (2), was born in Shincliffe, Eng.; emigrated to the United States, and when last heard from was in Texas or Missouri.

John-G. Ridley² (1), a son of William² (2), was born in the County of Durham, Eng., and emigrated to the United States, many years ago; present residence not known, but supposed to be St. Joseph, Mo.

Alice Ridley² (1), only daughter of William² (2), was born in County Durham, Eng., and died in Wisconsin, U. S., soon after the emigration to that State.

FOURTH GENERATION.

Alice Ridley⁴ (2), eldest daughter of Walter³ (2), was born April 12 1857; was married to Byron Fast, of Barton County, Mo.

Emma Ridley⁴ (1), second daughter of Walter³ (2), was born April 12, 1859, and was married to Charles H. Chace.

Walter Ridley⁴ (3), only son of Walter³ (2), was born April 26, 1861, and married Eddy-Ann Millard, daughter of John Millard, of Barton County, Mo

Mary Ridley⁴ (1), third daughter of Walter³ (2), was born Nov. 5, 1863.

Jane Ridley⁴ (1), fourth daughter of Walter³ (2), was born Dec. 5, 1865.

RIDLEYS OF SUSSEX, ENGLAND.

John Ridley¹ (1), descended from the ancient family in Tynedale, Northumberland, was a native of the parish of East Grinstid, County of Sussex, Eng., but lived many years in a seaport town, called Hastings, where he was the superintendent of a large poor-house. Wife's name not known; she predeceased her husband at the age of ninety-five. Mr. Ridley died at the home of his son in Frant, Sussex, about the year 1810, aged ninety-eight. He was a large man, weighing two hundred and fifty pounds, with light complexion and dark hair. There were *four* children.

SECOND GENERATION.

William Ridley² (1), a son of John¹ (1), was born at East Grinstid, Sussex, Aug. 26, 1790; married Hannah Eridge, — she was born at Eastbourne, Sussex, Oct. 5, 1795, — and had issue several children, of whom hereafter. He had dark hair, but fair complexion; weighed one hundred and seventy-five pounds. Emigrated from London to Canada in 1837; thence moved to the States in 1840. Carpenter by trade. Died at Rochester, N. Y., aged one hundred and eight years. *Eight* children, of whom hereafter.

James Ridley² (1), a son of John¹ (1), was born at East Grinstid, Sussex, and lived in a seaport town in County Sussex, named Eastbourne. He was many years employed by the English government.

John Ridley² (2), a son of John¹ (1), was born in the County of Sussex, married, and resided at Frant, in his native shire, till 1837, when he emigrated to Quebec, Canada, in company with the family of his brother William. He settled in Canada and died there some twenty years ago, say 1864, leaving his widow Mary, since deceased, and *six* children, of whom hereafter.

Elizabeth Ridley[2] (1), a daughter of John[1] (1), of whom no other information.

THIRD GENERATION.

William Ridley[3] (2), a son of William[2] (1), was born in Frant, Sussex, Dec. 16, 1816; married a Scotch lady from Berwick-on-Tweed, by whom he had issue (she died at Rochester, N. Y., in 1847), and secondly, to Lucy-Ann Graves (she was born in Oneida, N. Y.), by whom issue. Resides at Binghamton, N. Y. Carpenter by trade.

Esther Ridley[3] (1), eldest daughter of William[2] (1), born Dec. 12, 1817; was married to Thomas Martin (from Briton, Sussex, Eng.) in Canada, in 1838, and had children. She died in Rochester, N. Y., in 1874.

Elizabeth Ridley[3] (2), second daughter of William[2] (1), was born at Frant, Sussex, June 4, 1819; was married to Calvin Buckley, and died at Mount Morris, N. Y., in 1860. Husband also deceased.

Lucy Ridley[3] (1), third daughter of William[2](1), was born at Frant, Sussex, Jan. 11, 1820; was married to Joseph T. Cox, an Englishman, in Rochester, N. Y., in 1842, and has *five* children.

Abigail Ridley[3] (1), fourth daughter of William[2] (1), was born in County Sussex, June 20, 1822; was married at Mount Morris, N. Y., to John Buckley, in 1850, and has removed to the West.

Barzilla Ridley[3] (1), second son of William[2] (1), was born in County Sussex, June 5, 1827; married Elizabeth Sperry, of Oswego, N. Y., and has a daughter. He resides at Elmira, N. Y. Carpenter by trade.

Benjamin Ridley[3] (1), third son of William[2] (1), was born in County Sussex, Dec. 22, 1834; married an Irish woman, and had *one* son. Mr. Ridley died in Rochester, N. Y., in September, 1880.

Mary Ridley[3] (1), youngest daughter of William[2] (1), was born Dec. 12, 1836, in Sussex County, Eng.; was married to an American farmer, and lives in the West. No children.

J

Mary Ridley[3]
Mira Ridley[4] (1).   } to Canada in 1837.
Sarah Ridley[3] (1).

FOURTH GENERATION.

Henry Ridley[4] (1), eldest son of William[3] (2), was born in Rochester N. Y., in 1841, and was killed in Oil City in 1868.

Violet-Lewis Ridley[4] (1), eldest daughter of William[3] (2), was born in Rochester, N. Y., in 1843, and was married to an engineer of the New York Central Railroad.

Hannah Ridley[4] (1), second daughter of William[3] (2), was born in Rochester, N. Y., in 1844, and was married to a boiler-maker.

Anna Ridley[4] (1), third daughter of William[3] (2), was born in Rochester, N. Y., and is married.

William Ridley[4] (3), a son of William[3] (2) by his second wife, died at the age of seven, in Binghamton, N. Y.

Lafayette Ridley[4] (1), a son of William[3](2) by his second wife, died at Binghamton, N. Y., aged 5 years.

Dora Ridley[4] (1), a daughter of William[3] (2) by his second wife, was born in Binghamton, N. Y., and (now 25 years of age) was married to Alonzo Strong, of Ithaca, N. Y., and has issue.

Elizabeth Ridley[4] (3), a daughter of Barzilla[3] (1).

Benjamin Ridley[4] (2), a son of Benjamin[3] (1).

------ •◦• ------ .

SERMON BY BISHOP RIDLEY.[*]

[FROM RIDLEY'S "PITEOUS LAMENTATION OF THE MISERABLE ESTATE OF THE CHURCH IN ENGLAND."]

" Of God's gracious aid in extreme perils toward them that put their trust in Him, all Scripture is full, both old and new. What dangers were the patriarchs often brought into, as Abraham, Isaac, and Jacob, but of all others, Joseph; and how mercifully were they delivered again! In what perils was Moses when he was fain to fly for the safeguard of his life! And when was he sent again to deliver the Israelites from the servile bondage? And when did the Lord mightily deliver his people from Pharaoh's sword? Not before they were brought into such straits that they were compassed on every side (the main sea on the one side, and the main host on the other), that they could look for no other (yea, what did they else look for, then?) but either to have been drowned in the sea, or else to have fallen on the edge of Pharaoh his sword. Those Judges, which wrought most wonderful things in delivery of the people, were ever given when the people were brought to most misery before; as Othniel, Aioth [Ehud], Sangar, Gedeon, Jepthah, and Samson. And so was Saul endued with strength and boldness from above, against the Ammonites, Philistines, and Amalechites, for the defence of the people of God. David, likewise, felt God's help, most sensibly ever in his extreme persecutions.

" What shall I speak of the Prophets of God, whom God suffered so oft to be brought into extreme perils, and so mightily delivered them again; as Helias, Heremy, Daniel, Micheas, and Jonas, and many others, whom it were too long to rehearse and set out at large? And did the Lord use his servants otherwise in the new law after Christ's incarnation? Read the Acts of the Apostles and you shall see, no. Were not the Apostles cast into prison, and brought out by the mighty hand of God? Did not the angel deliver Peter out of the strong prison, and bring him out by the iron gates of the city and set him free? And when, I pray you? Even the same night before Herod appointed to have brought him in judgment for to have slain him, as he had a little before killed James, the brother of John. Paul and Silas, when after they had been sore scourged, and were put into the inner prison, and there were held fast in stocks; I pray you, what appearance was there that the magistrates should be glad to come the next day themselves to them, to desire them to be content, and to depart in peace? Who provided for Paul, that he should be safely conducted out of all dangers, and brought to Felix, the Emperor's deputy, — when, as both the high priests, the Pharesees, and rulers of the Jews had conspired

------

[*] The spelling and composition of this sermon are just as in original, and show the quaint style of the time, — say 1550 A. D.

to require judgment of death against him, he being fast in prison, and also more than forty men had sworn each one to other that they would never eat nor drink until they had slain Paul! A thing wonderful, that no reason could have invented, or man could have looked for: God provided Paul his own sister's son, a young man, that disappointed that conspiracy and all their former conjuration. The manner how the thing came to pass, thou mayest read in the twenty-third of the Acts; I will not be tedious unto thee here with the rehearsal thereof.

"Now, to descend from the Apostles to the Martyrs that followed next in Christ's church, and in them likewise to declare how gracious our good God ever hath been to work wonderfully with them which in His cause have been in extreme perils, it were a matter enough to write a long book. I will here name but one man and woman, that is, Athanasias, the great clerk and godly man, stoutly standing in Christ's cause against the Arians; and that holy woman, Blandina, so constantly in all extreme pains, in the simple confession of Christ. If thou wilt have examples of more, look and thou shalt have both these and a hundred more in Ecclesiastica Historia of Eusebius, and in *Tripartita Historia.* But for all these examples, both of holy Scriptures and of other histories, I fear me the weak man of God, encumbered with the frailty and infirmity of the flesh, will have now and then such thoughts and qualms (as they call them) to run over his heart, and think thus: All these things which are rehearsed out of the Scriptures I believe to be true, and of the rest truly I do think well, and can believe them also to be true; but all these we must needs grant were special miricles of God, which now in our hands are ceased, we see; and to require them of God's hands, were it not to tempt God?

"Well-beloved brother, I grant such were great wonderful works of God, and we have not seen many of such miricles in our time; either for that our sight is not clear (for truly God worketh with us his part in all times), or else because we have not the like faith of them for whose cause God wrought such things, or because after that he had set forth the truth of his doctrine by such miricles then sufficiently, the time of so many miricles to be done was expired withal. Which of these is the most special cause of all other, or whether there be any other, God knoweth; I leave that to God. But know thou this, my well-beloved in God, that God's hand is as strong as ever it was; he may do what His gracious pleasure is, and He is as good and gracious as ever he was. Man changeth as the garment cloth; but God, our heavenly Father, is even the same now that he was, and shall be for evermore.

"The world without doubt (this I do believe, and therefore say) draweth toward an end, and in all ages God hath had his own manner, after his secret unsearchable wisdom, to use his elect: sometimes to deliver them, and to keep them safe; and sometimes to suffer them to drink of Christ's cup, that is, to feel the smart, and to feel of the whip. And though the flesh smarteth at the one, and feeleth ease in the other, is glad of the one, and sore vexed in the other; yet the Lord is all one toward them in both, and loveth them no less when he suffereth them to be beaten, yea, and to be put to bodily death, than when he worketh wonders for their marvelous delivery. Nay, rather he doth more for them, when in anguish of the torments he standeth by them, and strengtheneth them in their faith, to suffer in the confession of the truth and his faith the bitter pains of death, than when he openeth the prison doors and letteth them go loose: for here he doth but respite them to another time, and leaveth them in danger to fall in like peril again; and there he maketh them perfect, to be without danger, pain, or peril, after that for evermore. But this his love toward them, howsoever the world doth judge of it, is all one, both when he delivereth and when he suffereth them to be put to death. He loveth as well Peter and Paul, when (after they had, according to his blessed will, pleasure, and providence, finished their courses, and done their services appointed them by him in preaching his Gospel), the one was beheaded, and the other was hanged or crucified of the cruel tyrant Nero (as the Ecclesiastical History saith), as when he sent the angel to bring Peter out of prison, and for Paul's delivery, He made all the doors of the prison to fly wide open, and the foundation of the same, like an earthquake, to tremble and shake.

"Thinkest thou, O man of God, that Christ, our Savior, had less affection to the first martyr, Stephen, because he suffered his enemies, even at the first conflict, to stone him to death? No, surely; nor James, John's brother, which was one of the three that Paul calleth primates or principals amongst the Apostles of Christ. He loved him never a whit the worse than he did the other, although he suffered Herod the tyrant's sword to cut off his head. Nay, doth not Daniel say, speaking of the cruelty of Anti-Christ in his time: 'And the learned [he meaneth truly learned in God's law] shall teach many, and shall fall upon the sword, and in the flame [that is, shall be burnt in the flaming fire], and in captivity [that is, shall be in prison], and be spoiled and robbed of their goods for a long season.' And after a little, in the same place of Daniel, it followeth: 'And of the learned there be which shall fall or be overthrown, that they may be known, tried, chosen, and be made white,'—he meaneth, be banished and scourged anew, picked and chosen, and made fresh and lusty. If that, then, was foreseen for to be done to the godly learned, and for so gracious causes, let every one to whom any such thing by the will of God doth chance, be merry in God and rejoice, for it is to God's glory and to his own everlasting wealth. Wherefore well is he that ever he was born, for whom thus graciously God hath provided, having grace of God, and strength of the Holy Ghost, to stand steadfastly in the height of the storm. Happy is he that ever he was born, whom God, his heavenly Father, hath vouchsafed to appoint to glorify him, and to edify his church by the effusion of his blood.

"To die in Christ's cause is an high honor, to which no man certainly shall or can aspire, but to whom God vouchsafeth that dignity; for no man is allowed to presume for to take unto himself any office of honour but he which is thereunto called of God. Therefore John saith well, speaking of them which have obtained the victory by the blood of the Lamb, and by the word of his testimony, that they loved not their own lives even unto death."

GLEANINGS AND NOTES.

RIDDELLS AND RIDDLES.

JOHN RIDDLE born in Morristown, N. J., in 1760. While residing in Dutchess County, N. Y., he was drafted for six months, in May, 1778, under Captain Dodge, in the regiment of Colonel Wisonpett, and marched in that command from Fishkill to Newburgh, N. Y.; thence to Albany, where he remained in garrison some time; thence fifteen miles up the Mohawk River; thence to Johnston, where he was under the command of General Sullivan, in the battle of that place with Canadians and Indians. He then returned to be stationed at Saratoga during the remainder of his service, and was employed in erecting a block-house. In 1779 he re-entered for three months, rendezvousing at Fishkill, under Colonel Stark, and remained in garrison until the end of his term of service; he then re-enlisted for and during the war under Captain Savage, and was conducted to New Windsor, where he received a bounty of sixteen dollars in silver money. He was now marched to West Point, where he was in garrison until the end of the war, in 1788, attached to the artillery under Colonel Lamb; the garrison was commanded by General Putnam. He went back to Morristown, N. J., after the war, where he lived only a few years, and removed to the State of Pennsylvania; thence to Frederick County, Va., where he resided two years; thence to Lexington, Ky., for one year, when he returned to Morristown, N. J., where he lived eight years; thence to Shelby and Henry Counties, Ky., and was living in the latter subsequent to 1816.

JOHN RIDDLE, born in Hanover County, Va., in 1762, enlisted in Goochland County, in the fall of 1779, to guard the prisoners at Albemarle barracks, in Albemarle County, Va. Served under Capt. Elisha Leake, Capt. Josiah Leake, and Capt. Humphrey Parrish, about four months; also one month in guarding prisoners from Goochland County to Winchester, under Capt. Elisha Leake; also three months under Capt. Stokely Fowles, when Arnold burnt Manchester warehouses, and for a time at Richmond, stationed at Morbin Hills, below the town. He also volunteered for six months under Capt. Jonathan Price, in command of Col. Holt Richardson, and marched south, joining General Gates at the time of his defeat, Aug. 16, 1780, and was then wounded in the foot; retreated to Hillsborough, N. C., where, after remaining some time, he was discharged by Col. Nathaniel Morris. He served in another tour under Capt. Stokely Fowles, when Lord Cornwallis invaded Virginia, and was present at his surrender; also guarded prisoners who were conveyed to Win-

chester. He resided, after the war of the Revolution, in Goochland County,
Va. In 1858 his son, John Riddle, was living in Jefferson County, O.,
probably at Steubenville.

JOHN RIDDLE, born Oct. 11, 1760, in Virginia, enlisted in February,
1779, for one month, under Capt. Josiah Leake, rendering service as guard
at Albemarle barracks. In January, 1780, he served one month under
Ted Curd, at the same barracks, under Colonels Lewis and Taylor. At
the time of Arnold's invasion, he was drafted for three months, and served
under Gideon Hollister, in the regiment of Col. Charles Flemming, going
to Richmond, thence down the river, crossing to Smithfield and Isle of
Wight Counties; thence to Petersburgh, where he was discharged. Soon
after his return home he went into Captain Curd's company (who was succeeded by Robert Bradshaw) for six weeks; marched down into the lower
country, crossing the James River near Williamsburgh, and was discharged
at Cabin Point. He lived many years at Lickinghole Creek, Goochland
County, Va., but early in 1838 moved to Monroe County, Ga., where he
owned land, and where many relatives resided.

JOHN RIDDLE was born near Flat River, N. C. (probably in Orange
County), and in September, 1833, was residing in the north-west corner of
Rockingham County, N. C., a few perches north-east from Stoke County,
and stated his age to be 83. He enlisted in 1776, in Grayson County, Va.,
under Capt. John Cox, near Chisels Lead Mines, on New River; marched
to Long Islands, of the Holston River, against the Cherokee Indians, serving over four months. He again entered the army in Henry County, Va.,
in September, 1781, under Captain Hill; marched to York, and engaged in
the siege of that place until the surrender of Lord Cornwallis, after which
he served as guard when the British prisoners were taken to Winchester.

WILLIAM RIDDELL died at Selkirk, Scotland, in 1780, aged 116 years.
This man was, in early life, a considerable smuggler, and remarkable for
his love of brandy, which he drank in large quantities. He was always
so fond of good ale, that he frequently declared that he could not remember that he ever drank water. He was not a regular drunkard, but had
frequent paroxysms of drinking, which lasted several successive days.
After his ninetieth year he at one time drank for a fortnight together,
with only a few intervals of sleep in his chair. He married his third wife
when ninety-five years old. For the last two years he subsisted on bread
infused with spirit and ale. He retained his faculties till death.

JAMES W. RIDDLE, ensign United States Infantry, April 5, 1814; second lieutenant, Nov. 14, 1814; appointed from District of Columbia;
resigned March 4, 1815. Aged 77 in March, 1871. His company took
twenty "44-pounders" from a French vessel commanded by Commodore
Barney, and by orders of Commodore Rogers, mounted the guns in Fort
McHenry, near Baltimore, which rendered efficient aid in repulsing and
bombarding the attack of the British fleet in 1814. He married, Nov.
22, 1824, Eliza Goain, in Brooklyn, N. Y. Resided in 1871 at corner
of Carondolet and Calliope Streets, New Orleans. Had a family. Drew
a pension.

ALEXANDER RIDDLE, a native of Aberdeenshire, Scotland, settled at
Hollinwood, near Oldham, Eng., and had *two* or more children. A
daughter was married to a Mr. Burgess, and in 1871-3 was living at Fall
River, Mass. Her brother was killed and left a son, *John Riddle*, brought

48

up in the family of his grandfather, before mentioned, who came to America, but his place of residence was unknown in 1878. This family is probably connected with the Riddels of Mill of Cull or Moneymusk, Aberdeenshire (whose records see in this book), as there were relatives said to have settled in England.

JEREMIAH RIDDLE enlisted from Randolph County, Va., serving in the militia from Sept. 13, 1814, to Feb. 13, 1815, at Norfolk, under Capt. Jonathan Wormsby. He married, in Randolph County, May 11, 1811, to Margaret Hardman, and died at Cedar Creek, Lawson County, Va., Oct. 17, 1818. His widow was living at Grass Run, Gilmore County, W. Va., in May, 1871, aged 81. This man had issue *three* sons and a daughter (possibly others), who were living in Virginia in 1878, named as follows: —

JOHN B. RIDDLE, Glenville, Gilmore County, W. Va.

GEORGE M. RIDDLE, Newburgh, Ritchie County, W. Va.

REBECCA (RIDDLE) SHORT, Troy, Gilmore County, W. Va.

COL. JAMES RIDDLE, a noted loyalist of Surrey County, N. C., had a son, Capt. William Riddle, who became a reckless Tory leader. He was captured, court-martialed, and hung at Wilkesborough, Wilkes County, N. C., in 1781. The oak on which this man, and Bill Nichols who married his sister, were hung, is now standing on a hill adjoining the village. Mrs. Riddle, who accompanied her husband on his wild marauds, was present, and witnessed his execution. There is a locality called "Riddle's Knob" in Watauga County, which may have derived its name from this family. I have not found any descendants.

JOHN RIDDLE moved from Pennsylvania to Washington County, Md., when twenty-five years of age, and died in 1845, aged nearly ninety-four. His sister Catherine settled in Maryland at the same time. Parents and birthplace unknown. Supposed to be of German descent. No children. Left an adopted daughter named Elizabeth Riddle, now (1878) living at Funkstown; she has forwarded two old documents, found amongst the papers of Mr. Riddle, written in German, supposed to be a baptismal and a marriage certificate.

SAMUEL RIDDLE and his brother DAVID settled in a township in Bedford County, Penn., in 1808, and called it *Riddlesburg*. They owned coal-mines, and carried on quite an extensive business, shipping coal to Havre de Grace. Their coal-banks were near the Susquehanna River, and this gave them advantage over many dealers. The Riddle brothers left about 1820, and went to Kentucky or Tennessee. The township is now owned by a New York firm, known as the "Kemble Coal and Iron Company."

BRADLEY G. RIDDLE, born in South Carolina in 1800, removed to Georgia when young, and lived there 16 years. Enlisted in Edgefield District, S. C., Feb. 4, 1815. Married Mary-Ann Sharp, in Monroe County, Ga., at the age of twenty-six. Moved to Alabama, and resides at Clopton, Dale County. Seventy-nine years of age in 1879; wife seventy-one. Had a brother and two sisters. Mary Riddle died at the age of sixteen. The others lived in South Carolina. Mr. Riddle is a blacksmith.

WILLIAM RIDDELL, of Hundalee, Jedburgh, in Roxburghshire, Scotland, is a prominent man in all Border agricultural interests, and a breeder of fine stock. He has been president of agricultural societies, and is considered an excellent judge of blooded sheep. He owns twenty-eight acres of land. I have forwarded several communications to this gentleman, but have no reply to them. He is known to be connected with other Border-families of Riddell, however.

JACOB RIDDELL, of White Hall Inn, Old Market Street, London, died in 1820, aged 62 years. His death was occasioned by a severe fall, which fractured his left limb in two or three places, and it was deemed advisable to resort to amputation; a mortification soon ensued, however, which deprived him of life. He bore his sufferings with great Christian resignation. His loss was sincerely lamented by his relatives and a large circle of friends, by whom he was beloved.

DAVID RIDDLE (Pennsylvania), second-lieutenant Fifteenth Infantry, 9th April, 1812; first-lieutenant, March, 1813; brevet-captain for distinguished service in battle of Niagara Falls, July 25, 1814; distinguished in Gaines' victory at Fort Erie; brevet-major for gallant conduct in sortie from Fort Erie, Sept. 17, 1814 (Jan. 15), in which he was wounded; retained December, 1815, in Infantry; captain, December, 1816; died July 9, 1820.

WILLIAM RIDDEL was born in Westchester County, N. Y., in the year 1788. He was the son of a Riddel who held a commission in the English army or navy, and came to this country during the Revolutionary war, and was killed; he was born in the north of Ireland. William S. Riddel, before mentioned, left New York about 1820, and went South; his son, *Hiram H. Riddle*, in 1873, was residing in New York city, aged 63 years.

HUGH RIDDELL, May 12, 1685, presented a petition in New York, against the extortionate charges of the physicians who attended Mr. Vaughton, the custom-house officer wounded by him at the seizure of his goods. Mr. Riddell's goods were taken when coming from New Jersey to New York, and he beat the officer nearly to death. The court ordered that his goods should be restored, provided he pay the medical charges.

REV. ARTHUR-JOHN RIDDLE, Stratford, Bucks, Jesus College, Oxford, Eng., B. A. 1872, M. A. 1877, deacon 1872, priest by Bishop of Oxford. Former chaplain of Oxford diocese, Sch. Cowley, 1872-8; curate of Wycomb 1876-7; Crowmarsh-Gifford, near Wallingford, 1877-8. After retiring from the latter place he took a curacy at Stoney Strafford, Bucks. In the "Clergy List" of 1883 he was chaplain at Cronstadt, in Russia.

SAMUEL RIDDLE, sergeant Light Dragoons, May 20, 1813; exchanged to Fifteenth Infantry in September, 1813; brevet second-lieutenant for gallant conduct in sortie from Fort Erie, Sept. 17, 1814, and second-lieutenant, September, 1814; retained December, 1815, in Eighth Infantry; first-lieutenant, August, 1817; captain, April, 1819; company disbanded in June, 1821; was sutler at Fort Barrancas in 1821; died in 1823.

WILLIAM RIDDLE, of Selkirk, Scotland, had a son, *Walter Riddle*, who married Isabella Kellzie, who was from the State Hills, Roxburghshire, and had *four* sons and *two* daughters. Walter died at Hawick, Scotland, Feb. 11, 1849, aged between sixty and seventy years; his wife predeceased him at the same place about 1839. The eldest son, *William Riddle*, was at London, Ont., Can., in 1873, with Watterman, Englehart & Co.

MRS. CHARLOTTE RIDDELL, youngest child of James Cowan, of Carrickfergus, County Antrim, Ireland, is wife of J. H. Riddell, Esq., a civil-engineer, and is known as the author of many popular novels, including "Too Much Alone," "City and Suburbs," "George Geith," "A Life's Assize," "Mortomley's Estate" (1874), "Above Suspicion" (1875), and "Her Mother's Darling" (1877).

WILLIAM RIDDELL lived in the parish of Dromara, townland of Grassquare, County Down, Ireland; married a Barr, and had *seven* or more children; died before 1873, and left a widow and six children in Ireland. A son, *James Riddle*, was at Malden Bridge, N. Y., in 1873; had many relatives in America, but could not find them; he emigrated in 1863. Presbyterian.

A RIDDELL bore the chief part in the arrest of the Earl of Argyle, who was a Campbell. On this account the whole race of Riddells was, during more than a century, held in abhorrence by the great tribe of Campbell, and within living memory, when a Riddell visited a fair in Argyleshire, he found it necessary to assume another name. The arrest was in 1685.

JOSIAH RIDDLE came from London, Eng., to Canada in 1846, with his wife and several children. He had married previously and had issue. His eldest son by first wife, *William-Josiah Riddle*, was living at St. Andrews, Can., in 1873; the widow and other children were in Montreal. William J. was born in London, Jan. 31, 1830.

JOHN RIDDELL and his wife Mary were born in Birmingham, Eng., and settled at Wallsworth. *Henry Riddell*, son of the preceding, married in England, and had *five* children, when, in 1853, they came to America. He died at Trenton, N. J., April 6, 1863, leaving a widow, E. M. Riddell, at Providence, in 1873. He had brothers.

SAMUEL RIDDLE was sergeant in Capt. William Mitchell's Independent Blues, Pennsylvania Militia, in 1818. In March, on the second night of his arrival at Fort Mifflin, on the Delaware, while on guard, it being icy, slipped and fell twenty feet from ramparts, and was taken up insensible; conveyed to his own dwelling next day.

JESSE RIDDLE was a resident of Edgefield District, S. C., and had *two* daughters. Annie-Cox Riddle, born Dec. 29, 1810, was married to James-Alexander Bradford, of Georgia, and died Jan. 17, 1843, leaving issue. Pamelia Riddle, second daughter, was the wife of Nelson Baird, of Mobile in Alabama, but has deceased.

JOHN RIDDELL (or Riddle) resided at Princeton, and kept a store of goods there; married a woman of good estate, real and personal, and had sundry negroes and other personal property. Built a house there. Had good reputation and respect of community, and was recommended for appointment as sheriff. No date.

JAMES-WILSON RIDDLE enlisted under Captain Pugh, in Company F, Fourth Regiment Ohio Volunteers, Colonel Brough, May 5, 1847, during the war with Mexico. While at Matamoras was ordered to discharge boxes of arms from a steam-ship, by which he was injured and discharged Oct. 6, 1847. Occupation, laborer.

WILLIAM, HUGH, and GEORGE RIDDLE went from near Petersburgh, Va., about 1804, and settled in Kentucky; Hugh and George on the Kentucky River, near Frankfort or Lexington, and William between Bedford, Trimble County, and the mouth of the river. The adopted grandson, W. A. Riddle, lives at St. Joseph, Mo.

REV. ARTHUR-ESMOND RIDDLE, Lockhampton, Cheltenham, Worcester College, Oxford, Eng.; third class theological B. A. 1875; deacon 1875; ordained priest in 1876 by Bishop of Hereford. Formerly curate of Madley, Tiverton, diocese of Hereford, 1875–7. All S., Chapton Park, Middlesex, 1878–9.

TAVNER RIDDLE, Burk's Mill, Augusta County, Va., and his son, LEWIS G. RIDDLE, Livingstone, Nelson County, Va., in 1878. The father, seventy-five or eighty years of age. Some of their connections are in this book. Neither of the above will reply to my letters of inquiry.

JAMES RIDDLE was born in the city of Londonderry, Ireland; emigrated to Philadelphia, where he resided till death. His son lived in Delaware, where he died about 1889–40, leaving a son, A. J. Riddle, — 46 years old in 1874, — who owns the "Thewalla House," at Eufaula, Ala.

LAWSON RIDDLE in 1871 was living at Clark's Mills, Howard County, Md., aged 84. Served under Capt. Henry Woodward, from Aug. 13 to Sept. 1, 1813, and under Capt. T. T. Simmons, from Oct. 1 to Dec. 1814. He married Aug. 15, 1820, at Union Factory, to Mary ——.

ROSE-CHRISTIANA RIDDELL, second daughter of J. R. Riddell, Esq., of Banghurst House, Hants, was married at St. Saviour's, Bath, in October, 1858, to Herbert-Croft Ryder, Esq., of the Third Regiment, Bombay, youngest son of the Rev. T. R. Ryder, vicar of Ecclesfield.

BENJAMIN RIDDLE, of Beloit, Wis., died in June, 1857, aged 53 years. He was one of the early settlers, having moved there in 1839; as a citizen, he was highly respected and esteemed. Left a wife and several children, and a large circle of relatives, to mourn.

JAMES RIDDLE, commander of the "Hornet," took the brig "Penguin," March 23, 1815, off the island Tristan da Cunha. The engagement lasted only twenty-two minutes. There were one hundred and thirty-two men in the "Hornet"; one killed, ten wounded.

JOHN RIDDLE served under Capt. William Kendricks in South Carolina Militia, from Oct. 1, 1814, to March 7, 1815, in the regiment of Colonel Means, stationed at Charleston, S. C., and neighboring islands. Married after Feb. 17, 1815. Died July 1, 1871.

ANNIE-MARIA RIDDELL, second daughter of Gabriel Riddell, Esq., of Brixton, was married, April 11, 1866, to the Rev. Richard-Lee Allnuth, M. A., incumbent of St. Stephen's, Tunbridge, second son of Henry Allnuth, Esq., of Loose, near Maidstone.

JOHN RIDDELL, of the colony of Virginia, was granted permission to pass from any port in the province to Europe, with his baggage, June 24, 1776, he having first produced a passport from the Committee of Safety of Virginia, licensing such departure.

JOHN RIDDLE served under Capt. William Fleming in Virginia Militia, from Sept. 2 to Sept. 21, 1814. He married June 29, 1820, at Fincastle,

Va., to Ann Washburn. In August, 1871, lived at Woodland, Md., aged 75 years. Died Feb. 28, 1872.

CHARLES RIDDELL (or Riddle), of Martinsburgh, Va., died at Canonsburgh, Nov. 16, 1857. He was nephew of Dr. Riddle, of Pittsburgh, Penn., a member of the senior class of Jefferson College; respected and beloved by all who knew him.

JOHN A. RIDDLE died in Matthews County, Va., in July 29, 1823. Sometime a resident of Richmond, and probably of Washington, D. C. His autograph is in a book owned by Robert Brock, as "John A. Riddle, Washington, D. C."

HENRY RIDDLE, of Onandago, Ontario, Can. (1874), was the son and grandson of Riddles who came to America from County Down, Ireland, with his aunt, many years ago; subsequently went from Canada to Philadelphia (?).

JAMES RIDDELL was born in the townland of Durmain, County Monaghan, Ireland,—two miles from the *town* of Monaghan,—and had sons, *Alexander, John, Joseph,* and *James,* who, in 1873, were at Smithfield, Can.

WILLIAM RIDDELL, of Roxburghshire, Scotland, had a son, *Thomas,* who was in St. John, N. B., in 1873. A brother of William, before mentioned, came to America, married, and left *two* children, a son and daughter.

ALMENA RIDDELL was married to Rev. Wheeler Ingalls, East Pembroke, N. Y.; their son, Charles-Crane, married Regina-Augusta Cook; resident at Chicago, Ill.; merchant. Almena lives at Franklin, Ill.

COL. THOMAS RIDDELL, member-elect of the State Senate of Alabama, died at Springfield, in that State, in August, 1840. (See records of descendants of Capt. Cato Riddle, of North Carolina, in this book.)

WILLIAM RIDDELL, of Wellgreen, Glassford, Lanark, Scotland, owned one thousand and twelve acres of land, worth one hundred and twenty pounds a year in 1878. Know nothing of his family connections.

ANDREW-NISBIT-EDWARDS RIDDELL, ESQ., H. E. Q. C. S., only son of Capt. A. N. Riddell, Second Regiment, B. N., I., was married to Frances, youngest daughter of S. Wilson, Esq., of Kensington Place, Bath, Eng.

CAPT. MICHAEL RIDDELL, of Madras Cavalry, married Caroline-Alicia, third daughter of C. F. Sheridan, Esq., and niece of the Rt. Hon. R. B. Sheridan, at Cheltenham, Eng., in 1810.

COL. JOHN RIDDELL had a son, A. N. Riddell, who married, Oct. 12, 1819, Mary-Anne, daughter of Lieutenant-Colonel Edwards, of the Seventy-third Regiment, at Bombay, India.

JOSEPH RIDDLE was vice-consul at La Guayra, Venezuela, from October, 1844, to October, 1854, when he resigned. He was acting consul from June 5, 1848, to Aug. 23, 1853.

THOMAS RIDDLE (Ohio), ensign Twenty-seventh Infantry, May 20, 1813; transferred to Nineteenth Infantry; third-lieutenant in September; company disbanded in June, 1814.

JOHN RIDDLE died in Northampton County, Penn., Nov. 10, 1767, and WILLIAM RIDDLE March 2, 1857. These possibly belong to families whose genealogies are found in this book.

WILLIAM RIDDELL, for more than thirty years Registrar to Her Majesty's Board of Inland Revenue, died at his residence, Mayfield Place, Dalton, Eng., in 1861, aged 70 years.

REV. J. E. RIDDLE, incumbent of St. Philip's and St. John's, Leckhampton, Gloucestershire, died at his residence, Tudor-lodge, Cheltenham, in October, 1859, aged 55 years.

WILLIAM RIDDELL, aged 19 years (1862), of Stockbridge, Mass., mustered into the Second Regiment Infantry, May 25, 1861; mustered out, May 28, 1864.

RILEY RIDDLE was living with Walker Gan, Bestonville, Stokes County, N. C., in 1878. A relative to "old John Riddle," of Rockingham County, a mile distant.

FREDERICK-JUSTUS RIEDEL, a German *littérateur*, was born near Erfurt, in 1742. Among his works are "Satires" (three volumes, 1786). He died in 1787.

JAMES RIDDELL, stocking-weaver, lived in Halifax, Nova Scotia, in 1873; he was a son of Thomas Riddell, of Barony Parish, Lanarkshire, Scotland.

MRS. ELIZABETH RIDDLE, wife of William Riddle, of Martinsburgh, Va., daughter of Richard Ragan, Esq., of Hagerstown, Md., died Dec. 28, 1857.

GEORGE-JAMES RIDDELL, Esq., of Beauchamp House, married Laura, youngest daughter of Rev. Thomas Wood, of Tiverton, Devon, in 1808.

ROBERT-ANDREW RIDDELL, Esq., married in 1808, Miss Mills, daughter of the late William Mills, Esq., merchant and alderman of Bristol, Eng.

MRS. ELIZABETH RIDDELL, widow of William Horne, Esq., sheriff of East Lothian, died at Belhaven House, Dunbar, Scotland, Feb. 26, 1857.

EDWARD RIDDLE, attorney, was tried for killing Captain Lidburn in a duel in the Nuns' Garden, Newcastle, Eng., in 1723, but was acquitted.

CALVIN T., EMERSON, and WILEY RIDDLE were living at Farmington, Davie County, N. C., in 1879, but neither will reply to my inquiries.

JOHN RIDDELL, a relative of others mentioned, owned land at Strathaven and Chapelton, in the County of Lanark, Scotland, in 1873.

JOHN RIDDELL, son of John and Lucy Riddell, died in Boston, Mass., Dec. 28, 1770, and was buried in King's Chapel burying-ground.

REV. JAMES-GIBSON RIDDELL, M. A., formerly minister of Portland and Portman chapels, died at Edgeware Road, Dec. 7, 1814.

LIEUTENANT-COLONEL RIDDALL, K. H., was married to Anne, daughter of George Daysh, Esq., at Worthing, June 16, 1831.

ROBERT RIDDLE, a native of Durham, Eng., had a wife, Mary, and was living at Stockton, Luzerne County, Penn., in 1873.

MRS. RIDDELL, of Brynston (or Bryanstan), St. Portman's Square, London, was married in 1793, to Captain Douglas.

MRS. KEZIA RIDDLE, formerly of Arlington Street, Westminster, died at Great Portland Street, July 11, 1856, aged 90.

AUGUSTUS RIEDEL, a celebrated German painter, was born at Baireuth in 1780. He worked several years in Rome.

ROBERT RIDDELL, Esq., of Kenny's Hall, Dumfriesshire, Scotland, died at Musselburg in 1805, aged 83 years.

JOHN RIDDELL, of Bath, Eng., left a widow (daughter of Samuel Short, Esq.), who died at Exmouth in 1804.

JANE RIDDLE, wife of Andrew (before mentioned), died at Jamaica Plain, Mass., Sept. 18, 1830, aged 56.

WILLIAM, WILLIAM-P., and JABEZ-L. RIDDLE were living at Warrenton, Warren County, Mo., in 1878.

WILLIAM RIDDELL came to Virginia, July 6, 1685, in a vessel commanded by Capt. Leonard Betts.

J. B. F. RIDDLE, son of JOHN RIDDLE, and GEORGE L. RIDDLE Zeno P. O., York County, S. C., in 1878.

HENRY RIDDLE, son of Walter and Margaret (Brown), was baptized at Albany, N. Y., Oct. 4, 1757.

ANDREW, JOHN, and SAMUEL RIDDELL lived in Jersey City, N. J., in 1878; all at 308 Grand Street.

JEREMIAH RIDDLE, of Capt. Daniel Morgan's company, was taken prisoner at Quebec, Dec. 3, 1775.

G. J. RIDDELL, Esq., of Bingwell-house, died at Budleigh, Salterton, Aug. 5, 1833, aged 23 years.   •

JOHN B. RIDDELL (sometimes Ruddell) was living at Gish's Mill, Roanoke County, Va., in 1878.

JAMES RIDDLE and PELAGIE RIDEL were in Newark, N. J., in 1878. No reply to my inquiries.

SAMUEL and J. W. RIDDLE were at Cassville, and J. D. RIDDLE, at Corsicana, Mo., in 1878.

BENJAMIN RIDELL was in an expedition to Crown Point, under Major Nichols, June 30, 1755.

CHARLES RIDDLES, and JOHN, GEORGE, and THOMAS RIDDLE were at Cleveland, O., in 1878.

JEAN RIDDELL, daughter of John and Mary, was baptized at Albany, N. Y., June 28, 1756.

WATKINS P. RIDDLE, of New Canton (or Gilliamsville), Buckingham County, Va., in 1878.

JOHN RIDDELL kept a perfumery, brush, and carpet warehouse, in Dublin, Ireland, in 1868.

AMBROSE RIDDELL, Esq., had a daughter married in 1808, to Sir Philip Manoux, Bart.

GRACE RIDDELL, of Hull, was married in 1822, to Rev. George Brown, of St. Albans.

WILLIAM RIDDLE's name was on the County record at Tours River, N. J., in 1878.

HENRY, WILLIAM C., and JAMES RIDDLE were living at Buffalo, N. Y., in 1879.

WILLIAM RIDDELL was acting consul at Cyprus, from July 19 till Dec. 7, 1871.

GEORGE W. RIDDLE was living at Clarkville, Howard County, Md., in 1878.

HARRISON RIDDLE lived at Mechum's River, Albemarle County, Va., in 1878.

WILLIAM RUDDELL, in business at 147 Francis Street, Dublin, Ireland, in 1868.

ANDREW RIDDLE died at Jamaica Plain, Mass., Dec. 14, 1830, aged 58 years.

FRANCIS RIDDELL, SR., died at St. Phillips, Bristol, in 1808, aged 75 years.

ANDREW RIDDEL,
ROYAL W. RIDDELL,
ALFRED G. RIDDLE, } Commissioned officers in the war of the Rebel-
JOHN W. RIDDLE, lion, from Pennsylvania.
WILLIAM RIDDLE,

JOHN RIDDLE died at Jamaica Plain, Mass., July 24, 1836, aged 29 years.

THOMAS RIDDELL, of Hull, Eng., merchant, died in 1810, aged 46 years.

JAMES RIDDELL, printer and bookseller, died at Bodmin, Eng., in 1839.

A. R. RIDDELL was in the army under Lord Exmouth, in 1816.

THOMAS RIDDLE, at Huffstutters store, Blount County, Tenn., in 1878.

J. RIDDLE, of Wellsville, Montgomery County, Mo., in 1878.

JAMES RIDDELL married Jane Hall, in Pennsylvania, June 21, 1763.

ROBERT RIDDELL, District Register, Armagh, Ireland, 1868.

E. T. RIDDLE, Thorn Hill, Grainger County, Tenn., 1878.

MRS. JANE RIDDELL, 93 Grafton Street, Dublin, Ireland, 1868.

JAMES-SELWOOD RIDDELL, ESQ., died at Bristol in 1813.

GEORGE RIDDELL, married Anne Freight, in Pennsylvania, Dec. 3, 1770.

REV. J. E. RIDDELL, author of "Ecclesiastical Chronology."

EDWARD RIDDELL, of Hull, died in 1881, aged 79 years.

THOMAS RIDDELL was at Hamilton, Ont., in 1878.

JAMES W. RIDDLE was at Warsaw, Benton County, Mo., in 1879.

REV. T. RIDDELL was at Sudbury, N. Y., in 1840.

JAMES RIDDLE, of Butler, Bates County, Mo., in 1878.

SERGT. JOSEPH RIDDLE was at Marshfield, Mass., in 1664.

ROBERT RIDDELL, M. D., Lauder, Berwickshire; L. R. C. S. 1858.

ROLLIN RIDDLE, of Morgantown, N. C., in 1878.

CHRISTIAN RIDDLE, of Delaware, O., in 1878.

ISAAC RIDDELL owned pew No. 5 in the old church at Quincy, Mass.

RIDDELL GRADUATES OF OXFORD COLLEGE, ENGLAND.

SIR WALTER B. RIDDELL, BART. Christ's Church, B. A. June 16, 1831; M. A. March 6, 1834.

JOHN C. B. RIDDELL. Christ's Church, B. A. Oct. 26, 1837; All Souls', M. A. March 6, 1841.

JOSEPH-ESMOND RIDDLE. Eden Hall, B. A. Dec. 4, 1828; M. A. June 23, 1831.

THOMAS RIDDELL. Eden Hall, B. A. Dec. 17, 1825; M. A. June 19, 1828.

JOHN-BRIMBLE RIDDLE. Wadh., B.A. Dec. 7, 1837; M.A. June 6, 1844.

SIR JAMES RIDDELL, BART. Christ's Church, B. A. May 19, 1807.

JAMES RIDDELL. Ball, B. A. May 2, 1845; M. A. Dec. 17, 1847.

JAMES RIDDELL. Ball, B. A. June 5, 1816; M. A. May 6, 1819.

GEORGE-JAMES RIDDELL. New Inn Hall, B. A. May 24, 1832.

RIDDELL AND RIDDLE AUTHORS.

JOSEPH-ESMOND RIDDLE ("see preceding Notes") was the author of many valuable works of a theological and educational character, among them—I. Family Reader: Explanatory of St. Matthew. London. 8vo. II. Churchman's Companion: Commentary on Prayer. 18mo. III. Illustrations of Aristotle from Shakespeare. 1832. 8vo. IV. Commentary on First Epistle of St. Peter. 1834. 8vo. V. Letters from a Godfather. 1837. 8vo. VI. Luther and his Times. 1838. 12mo. VII. Eighteen Sermons. 1838. 8vo. VIII. Manual of Christian Antiquities. 1839, '41, '43. 8vo. IX. Ecclesiastical Chronology. 1840. 8vo. X. British Commentary on the Gospels. 1843. 8vo. XI. First Sundays in Church. 8vo.; several editions. XII. Churchman's Guide to the Use of the Liturgy. 1848. 8vo. XIII. Natural History of Infidelity: eight lectures. 1852. 8vo. XIV. Popular History of the Papacy in the Reformation. 1854. 2 vols. 8vo. XV. Household Prayers for Four Weeks. 1857. 8vo.; several editions. XVI. Manual of Scripture History. London, 1857. 8vo. XVII. Words of Truth and Love: six sermons. 1860. 8vo. XVIII. Dictionary, Latin-English. London, 1836. 8vo.; several editions. XIX. Dictionary, English-Latin. 1838. XX. Dictionary, English-Latin and Latin-English. 1838. 8vo.; this work is considered the best of its kind in the language. XXI. A Copious and Critical Latin-English Lexicon. 1849. 4to. XXII. A Copious and Critical English-Latin Lexicon. 1849. 8vo.; many editions. XXIII. The Gospels in Greek for Schools. 1845. 8vo. XXIV. Progressive Latin-English Vocabulary. 1847. 12mo. XXV. Questions in Latin Style. 1849. 12mo. He was a contributor to the *Encyclopædia Metropolitana*. His works are everywhere highly commended. At the time of his death he had promised (D. V.) an English-Latin Thesaurus, designed for Latin writers.

JOHN RIDDELL, an eminent Scotch antiquary. I. The Sadfoot Contro-
versy; relating to the Family History of the Stewarts of Allanton.
Edinburgh, 1818. 8vo. [See *Blackwood's Magazine*, No. 18.] II. Remarks upon Scottish Peerage Law. Edinburgh, 1832. 8vo. III. Legal
and Historical Tracts. 1835. 8vo. IV. Law and Practise in Scottish
Peerages. 1842. 2 vols. 8vo. V. Chartularies, Stewartiana. 1843. 8vo.

JOHN L. RIDDELL. I. Synopsis of the Flora of the Western States.
1835. 8vo. II. Memoir Advocating the Organic Nature of Miasm and
Contagion. 1836. 8vo. III. A Monograph of the Silver Dollar. 1845.
8vo. IV. Memoir on the Constitution of Matter. 1847. 8vo. V. Report
upon the Epidemic of 1853–4. Many articles in the *American Journal of
Science* and other medical and scientific publications.

EDWARD RIDDLE (see "Riddles of Troughend") was a large contributor
to the *Ladies' Diary* and the Transactions of the Royal Astronomical
Society, and author of the following valuable work: Treatise on Navigation and Nautical Astronomy. 1842. 8vo.; has passed through many
editions, with various changes by Mr. Riddle and others.

MRS. J. H. RIDDELL. I. The Race for Wealth. London, 1866. 3 vols.
8vo. II. Phemie Keller. London, 1866. 8vo. III. The Rich Husband.
1866. 8vo. IV. Far above Rubies. 1867. 3 vols. 8vo. In 1867 Mrs.
Riddell became co-proprietor and editor of *St. James Magazine*, London.

ROBERT RIDDELL. I. Hand-railing Simplified. Philadelphia, 1856; 3d
edition, 1860. 4to. II. Scientific Stair Builder. 1856. Folio. III. The
Modern Carpenter and Builder. 1867. 4to. IV. The Carpenter, Joiner,
and Elements of Hand-railing, with 34 plates. 1868. 4to. $7.

JOHN RIDDELL, architect, of Philadelphia. Architectural Designs for
Model Country Residences, with 23 Colored Drawings of Front Elevations and 44 Plates of General Plans, with Descriptions, Specifications,
and Estimates. 1867. $15.

H. SCOTT RIDDELL. I. Songs of the Ark. 12mo. II. Poems, Songs,
etc. 1847. 12mo. III. Book of Psalms in Lowland Scotch. London,
1857. 8vo. For Prince Louis-Lucian Bonaparte.

WILLIAM-PITT RIDDELL. Genealogical Sketch of the Riddell Family.
New Orleans, 1852. 8vo. He also published several chemical analyses of
mineral waters, soils, etc.

HENRY RIDDELL. I. Railway Parliamentary Practise. London, 1842.
8vo. II. Index to Public Statutes, from 9 Henry III, to 10 and 11 Victoria. 1848. 8vo.

REV. MATTHEW B. RIDDLE, D. D. Author of numerous theological
works; one of the American Revision Committee to revise New Testament, etc.

JOHN RIDDLE (see "Riddles of Troughend") edited Guy's Elements of
Astronomy, of which the seventh edition was issued in 1855. 12mo.

REV. SAMUEL H. RIDDEL. Author of many papers in historical and
religious journals; at one time editor of the *Puritan Recorder*.

REV. WILLIAM RIDDEL. Author of papers published in the Presbyterian newspapers, under name *Rutherglen*.

MARIA RIDDELL. Voyages to the Madeira and Leeward Caribbean Islands. Edinburgh, 1792. 12mo.

COL. ROBERT RIDDELL. The Riddellian System; or, New Medical Improvements. 1808. 8vo.

ROBERT RIDDELL, of Glen-Riddell. Antiquarian papers in *Archæologia.* 1789–90–92–94.

REV. ARCHIBALD RIDDELL. Model of the Government of New Jersey in America. (Rare.)

C. I. RIDDELL. Remarks on the Organization of the British Royal Artillery.

JOHN RIDDELL. Continued Fevers. Glasgow, 1788.

WALTER RIDDELL-CARRE. Memoirs of Scottish Border.

RIDLEYS AND RIDLERS.

MATTHEW RIDLEY, of Baltimore, married Catherine, second daughter of Gov. William Livingstone, of New Jersey, whose family was one of the most cultivated and distinguished in the days of the Revolution; seated at a fine place called "Liberty Hall," near Elizabethtown. I do not know the connections of Mr. Ridley; but he was engaged in business at Nantez, in 1778. He was styled "of Baltimore," at the time of his marriage with the celebrated "Kitty Livingstone," and his alliance with that well-known family seems good ground for believing he was a gentleman of wealth and education. The name "Matthew" prevails in the English family of Ridley, and as many of the Northumberland stock came to America about this time, he may have been one of them. He lived but a few years.

SAMUEL RIDLEY, a person of penurious habits, died at Boston, Lincolnshire, in January, 1858, aged 73 years. He lived alone in a little, old cottage, and performed all his household work without assistance, keeping everything very clean. Until within a few days of his death he worked on his land as hard as any of his laborers, whom he watched from an old hovel, where he was wont to lie down to rest when too weak to work. His death was, no doubt, accelerated by the want of sustenance, and his poor horses bore testimony to their partaking of a singularly hard fare. He was possessed of property to the amount of two thousand pounds.

REV. THOMAS-YATES RIDLEY died at Heysham, near Lancaster, in 1838, aged 42 years. Rector of that parish. He was of Peterhouse, Cambridge, B. A. 1820, M. A. 1823; and was instituted to his living in 1824, on his own petition. Thinking it to be the duty of a clergyman to look to the temporal comforts as well as the spiritual wants of his people, he studied medicine at Edinburgh. He was at once the eloquent and faithful minister, the kind and bountiful, and the attentive and skilful physician of the poor people in his parish, who lived in a village six miles distant from other medical aid.

RT. REV. WILLIAM RIDLEY, D. D., Lord Bishop of Caledonia, British Columbia. Stationed at Metta Katta, Victoria. He was formerly chaplain of the English Church in the Krenz Strasse, Dresden, 1867–72; vicar of Shelley, near Huddersfield; vicar of Moldgreen, 1873–4; vicar of St. Paul, Huddersfield, 1874–9. This is a recently formed Bishopric, New Westminster and Caledonia, being sub-divisions of Columbia. Bishop Ridley is not a graduate, but was trained for missionary work in India (where he was for a short time) at the Missionary College, Islington, London.*

JAMES RIDLEY, M. D., Frankfort, Kings County, Ireland; L. K. Q. C. P. Ireland, 1866; L. R. C. S. I., 1866 (R. C. S. Ireland); Med. Off. Frankfort Disp. Dist., and R. I. Constable; late Hon. Surg. Liverpool Disp.; Res. Surg. Parish Infirm. and Fever Hospt., and Asst. Med. Off. East Disp. Liverpool, and Med. Off. Phillippstown Disp., Ireland; Contrib. " Anomalous Anatomy," *Med. Press Circ.*, 1865 ; "Dislocation of Atlas forward, with fracture of Atlas, Occipital, Parietal, and Temporal Bones."

"MRS. MARY RIDLEY, widow of Benjamin Ridley, a painter, died at Little Mary-le-Bone Street, London, Eng., in the year 1800. The cause of her death was almost for want of food and the necessary comforts of life, in the midst of plenty, because of a stingy disposition. She had two good houses, money in the bank, and ready money in her house, which she left to her two sisters, one of whom, on hearing of her good fortune (?), died only a few hours afterwards."

JOHN-THOMAS RIDLEY, now manager of a bank at Hartlepool, Eng., is descended from a respectable family of the Tynedale Ridleys, but I have not succeeded in procuring records. Mr. Ridley is a very fine-looking man, and is described as "most erudite." He kindly furnished a photographic copy of Sir Matthew-White Ridley's portrait, from which the steel engraving was made, now in this book.

WILLIAM RIDLEY, of Westwood, married Dorothie, daughter of William Ridley, of Tecket (or Ticket) Farm, Eng., and by her had a son, *William Ridley*, who married, firstly, Anne, daughter of Matthew Bell, of Newbanks, and had a daughter, *Mary Ridley*; secondly, Anne, daughter of Mark Errington, of England, and was living at Westwood in 1615 (See Ridleys of Parkend, England.)

" A mastiff dog belonging to MATTHEW-WHITE RIDLEY, Esq., of Heaton, near Newcastle-on-Tyne, being frequently teased by a mongrel (1818), that followed barking when his master was being driven to the city, at last took the little fellow up by the back, and with the greatest composure dropped it over the quay into the river without any attempt to injure it further."

CAPTAIN RIDLEY, "Annapolis, Md., May 25, 1776." At this date the " Maryland Committee of Safety" wrote to Captain Ridley, " This Board have been requested by the convention to countermand your orders for sailing. You are therefore not to move from your station till you have further directions; or, if you have moved, you are to return to the River Patapsco."

---

* I have held correspondence with Bishop Ridley of the above family, but too late to secure full date. He says he and his brothers have no ambition to emerge from the obscurity they inherited and are content with.

RICHARD RIDLEY held lands in Ribbleton, in the parish of Preston, and died there Feb. 27, 1602–3. An inquisition was taken at Preston, Aug. 17, 1607, when it was found that he left a son, JOHN RIDLEY, then aged 22 years, who was his heir. A Latin abstract of this inquisition has been printed in Volume XCIX, page 163, of the publications of the Chatham Society.

RICHARD RIDLEY, of Abbotsastley, Shropshire; FRANCIS RIDLEY, of Windsor, Berkshire; WILLIAM RADLEY, of the Hall of the Hill, Lancashire; CHARLES RADLEY, of Lowth, Lincolnshire; and NATHANIEL RIDLER, of Bisley, Gloucestershire, Esquires, are mentioned in 1673 as Gentlemen of England.

MARTHA RIDLEY, widow, was married Feb. 27, 1719, to Harbord Harriot, single man, son of James, citizen and cloth-worker, of London. She was buried in St. Bride's Church, London, April 17, 1723, and her daughter, *Sarah Harriot* (who was born Jan. 13, 1720), buried July 29, 1721.

ELIZABETH RIDLEY, daughter of Jannet Bayley, who was buried in Westminster Abbey, and granddaughter of the Rev. Thomas Yates, D. D. She was born June 10, and baptized at St. James', Westminster, July 9, 1748; was unmarried in 1776, but living Oct. 28, 1782, as above named.

MRS. FRANCES RIDLEY, widow of W. T. Ridley, and daughter of the late Capt. Alexander Innes, R. N., granddaughter of the Rev. N. Ellison, M. A., vicar of Newcastle-on-Tyne, was married June 4, 1864, at Wallsend, to the Rev. E. H. Augustine Geake, B. A., rector of Willington.

REV. JOHN RIDLEY, Brownhill, Bristol, Leeds; London College of Divinity second class, 1875; deacon, 1875, by Bishop of Winchester for Bishop of Ripon; curate of Brownhill, diocese of Ripon, 1875. In 1883, was vicar of Yorkshire parish. Brothers mentioned.

JOHN RIDLEY, Esq., of Hawthorne, County of Durham, Eng., had a son, John-Frederick Ridley, Esq., his successor, who died *sine prole* in February, 1829, and a daughter Catherine, who married, Oct. 31, 1816, Robert Atkins, Esq., of Firville, County of Cork, Ireland.

GEORGE RIDLEY, of Newcastle-on-Tyne, brother of John-Thomas, is an engineer. Mr. William Coulson, an old and well-informed Northumberland man, says this gentleman is a representative of the elder line of the ancient Willimoteswick family, but I have no particulars.

WILLIAM-WELLS RIDLEY, ESQ., of Leamington, son of T. D. Ridley, Esq., of the Elms, Chelmsford, Essex, was married at St. Luke's, Cheltenham, in 1864, to Emily-Mary, youngest daughter of the late Maj. Christopher Newport, of the Royal army, Bombay, India.

REV. CHRISTOPHER RIDLEY, Aylesbury; University of London, B. A., 1876; deacon, 1877; priest in 1878 by Bishop of Oxford; curate of Aylesbury, diocese of Oxford, 1877. He was master of a grammar-school in 1883. He is a brother of the bishop.

JOSEPH-SIMPSON RIDLEY, M. D., 10 Lune Street, Preston, Lancashire; M. D. St. And. 1859; M. R. C. S., Eng., and L. M. 1858; L. S. A. 1867 (St. Barthol.); Med. Off. 8th Dist., and Workh., Preston Union; Med. Ref. Briton Med. Gen. Life Association.

APPOLONIA RIDLEY, daughter of Baldwin Ridley, of Flushing, Zealand, was married to Daniel Tysson, who was born in Flushing, and died there in 1647, aged about 46 years. Baldwin Ridley was said to be "nephew of Bishop Ridley."

RICHARD RIDLEY was found to have a copy of the proclamation of General Howe in his pocket (or possession), by the New York Committee of Safety, Nov. 6, 1776. He with others were arming to resist troops at Hellesburgh.

MRS. RIDLEY, widow of the late W. Ridley, Gentleman, of Walton-upon-Thames, Eng., and daughter of the late Rev. Roger Simpkinson, rector of Dew Church, Magna, County of Hereford, died in 1812, aged 89 years.

MARIA-CHARLOTTE RIDLEY, second daughter of N. W. Ridley-Colburn, Esq., M. P., was married at St. George's, Hanover Square, 1830, to George-Edmund Nugent, Esq., Grenadier Guards, son of Gen. Sir G. Nugent, Bart.

JAMES RIDLEY, M. D., 47 West Street, Gateshead-on-Tyne, Eng.; L. R. C. S., Edinburgh, and L. M. 1868 (Newcastle-on-Tyne); Med. Off. House, Gateshead, U. Dist.; late Med. Off. Gateshead Small-pox Hospital.

RICHARD, ROBERT, and ELIZABETH RIDLEY were among passengers on board the "Dorsett," John Flowers, master, in 1685, from London, Eng., bound for St. Christopher Island. See "Ridleys of Virginia."

REV. THOMAS RIDLEY, Sunnyside, Leyland Road, Southport; Magdalen College, Oxford, B. A. 1833, M. A. 1838; deacon, 1833; priest, 1834. Formerly priest-curate of St. Mary, Sowerby, Yorkshire, 1848-67.

CLARA-JANE RIDLEY, daughter of the late Samuel Ridley, Esq., was married Nov. 28, 1862, at St. James, Piccadilly, to the Rev. William-Pakenham Walsh, M. A., chaplain of Sanford, Dublin, Ireland.

AGNES RIDLEY, youngest daughter of the late Samuel Ridley, of Hastings, was married at her father's residence, Feb. 24, 1858, to the Rev. George Burnet, incumbent of St. James', Birkenhead.

REV. LANCELOT RIDLEY, St. Thomas, Salsbury; Lincoln College, Oxford, B. A. 1876; deacon, 1878; priest, 1879, by Bishop of Sarum; curate of St. Thomas', city and diocese of Sarum, 1878.

"MASTER RIDLEY" was one of thirty gentlemen on board a vessel commanded by Captain Hore, of London, bound for Newfoundland, in 1536. The voyage ended in "great misery."

EVELYN-CLARA RIDLEY, second surviving daughter of Henry-Stephen Ridley, of Vincent Square, Westminster, died at Kingston-on-Thames in 1859, after a short illness, aged 18 years.

JOHN RIDLEY, Esq., of Bedford Place, Russell Square, London, died at Newcastle-on-Tyne, in 1854, aged 45 years. Mr. Ridley was formerly a councilman of the city of Newcastle.

LOUISA-MARY RIDLEY, daughter of George-Nelville Ridley, Esq., was married July 11, 1839, to Baron de Rothenbury, commanding at Bellville Upper Canada, as lieutenant-colonel.

JOHN RIDLEY, M. D., Tullamore,* Kings County, Ireland. Glasg., 1838; L. K. Q. C. P. Ireland; F. R. C. S. I. 1844, L. 1837; L. M. Rot. Hosp. 1836; Surg. Kings Co. Infirm. Gaol; Med. Off. Disp. Dist.

REV. H. J. RIDLEY left a widow, who was married in September, 1843, to the Rt. Hon. Lord Abinger, at Oakley, Surrey. She was Elizabeth, daughter of Lee Steere, Esq., Jayess.

JULIA G. RIDLEY, daughter of the late Samuel Ridley, Esq., of Hastings, was married to John W. Hulke, of London, who was a son of William Hulke, Esq., of Deal, Kent.

CHARLES RIDLEY, ESQ., of Charlotte Street, Bedford Square, London, married at Nottingham, July, 1858, Sarah, daughter of the late John Wild, Esq., The Park, Nottingham.

MISS RIDLEY, a sister of the Rev. W. C. Ridley, died at the residence of the latter, Place House, Great Stoughton, July 21, 1839, aged 61 years. "A benevolent friend to the poor."

MARTHA RIDLEY, widow, Feb. 27, 1720, married to Harbord Herriott, "single man," youngest son of James Herriott, citizen and cloth-worker, of London, by his wife Mary.

ELIZABETH RIDLEY, daughter of the late William Ridley, Esq., of Falstead, was married April 29, 1854, to John Richardson, Esq., at Falstead, County Essex.

RICHARD RIDLEY, Esq., of Hapstone, the ancient family residence in Claverly, after an illness of two days, and on the eve of marriage, died May 15, 1829.

ELIZABETH RIDLEY had a brother, Yates Bayley, Esq., who died in 1782, aged 36 years, leaving her five pounds sterling. (See preceding for family connections).

JOHN RIDLEY, late of Lincoln's Hill (an ensign in the army), died at Haddington barracks, in 1814. He was of the Northumberland Militia. Eldest son.

JOSEPH RIDLEY, ESQ., of the Plantations near Whitby, was married in 1810 to Lutitia, youngest daughter of the late Doctor Wells, of Willingham.

EDWARD RIDLEY, artist, took premiums for the best drawings from the Antique, the silver medal and the "Lectures of the Professors Orpie and Fuseli."

WILLIAM RIDLEY, sometime an eminent engraver, died at Addleston, Aug. 15, 1838, aged 74 years. He had been a resident of the village 25 years.

WILLIAM-WHITE RIDLEY, merchant of Plymouth, died at his residence Portland Square, aged 69 years. He was a gentleman of high standing.

NICHOLAS RIDLEY, bachelor, of London, Eng., married Elizabeth Turner, widow (by license), of St. Dunstan's, Stepney, May 18, 1696.

---

* JOHN RIDLEY, of Tullamore, owns 724 acres of land, valued at £365 per annum. GEORGE, of Tullamore, has 523 acres, valued at £243.

JAMES-HUTTON-WILKIE RIDLEY, M. D., Millfield House, Hexham Road, Gateshead; M. R. C. S., England, 1852 (Newcastle-on-Tyne).

NICHOLAS RIDLEY, ESQ., a Master in Chancery, and one of the benchers of Grey's Inn, died at his lodgings in Bath, in the year 1805.

WILLIAM RIDLEY, Esq., predeceased his wife, who died at Addleston, near Chertely (or Chertsey), Sept. 11, 1841, aged 67 years.

MARGARET RIDLEY, eldest daughter of Mr. Ridley, of Sidmouth Street, George's Road, London, died April 21, 1811, aged 26 years.

ELIZA RIDLEY, only daughter of R. Ridley, Esq., of Essequibo, was married in 1834 to the Rev. H. McKenzie, of Torrydon, N. B.

CATHERINE-LUCY RIDLEY, widow of the late Rev. R. Ridley, died at Green Hammerton Hall, Yorkshire, in 1853, aged 70.

MARGARET RIDLEY, wife of John Ridley, was buried in the church of St. Dionis, Blackchurch, London, Sept. 18, 1587.

REV. WILLIAM-CHARLES RIDLEY, M. A., incumbent of St. John's Episcopal Chapel, Glasgow, Scotland, died in 1855.

REV. HENRY-JOHN RIDLEY was married, in 1813, to Eliza, daughter of John Ellis, Esq., of Mamhead House, Devon.

FANNY-MERCY RIDLEY, wife of Arthur S. Ridley, Esq., of Newgate Street, Ipswich, died in 1854, aged 24 years.

ANTHONY RIDLEY, of St. Botolph, London, married Margaret Harris, of Whitechapel, by license, June 6, 1727.

MRS. JOYCE RIDLEY, widow of the late Thomas Ridley, wine-merchant, of Ipswich, died in 1818, aged 52 years.

MISS PATIENCE RIDLEY was the wife of George Bennett, of Saleman's Cross, London. She was of Croydon.

COL. C. W. B. RIDLEY was promoted in March, 1859, to be gentleman usher to H. R. M. the Prince Consort.

ANNA RIDLEY was married May 31, 1650, to Richard Jarvis, of the parish of St. Thomas', London, Eng.

ELIZABETH RIDLEY was married June 13, 1579, to William Raunce, of London, Eng., in St. Thomas' parish.

MARGARET RIDLEY, eldest daughter of Mr. Ridley, of Sidmouth Street, Grey's-Inn Road, died April 21, 1811.

SAMUEL RIDLEY, SR., died in 1816 at Rindleford, in the parish of Worthfield, County of Salop.

SARAH RIDLEY was married to Giles Coleman, of St. Thomas' parish, London, Eng., Nov. 26, 1642.

JOHN RIDLEY, ESQ., for many years a magistrate of Bury St. Edmund's, died in 1853, aged 73 years.

WILLIAM-BEVERLY RIDLEY, provision-merchant, Akinside Hill and Farnley Grove, Corlridge.

REV. W. D. RIDLEY was married in 1819 to Maria, daughter of Robert Tidwell, Esq., of Oporto.

49

ROBERT RIDLEY, son of Mr. Cuthbert Ridley, spirit-merchant, Sunderland, died June 13, 1831.

GEORGE RIDLEY, son of Thomas, died in the parish of St. Mary, London, Eng., May 20, 1618.

ELIZABETH RIDLEY, wife of Anthony Ridley, Esq., of Hyde Park, Eng., died in 1860.

REV. J. W. RIDLEY received preferment to H. M. S. Nankin, 50 Chatham, in the year 1855.

MATTHEW RIDLEY, ESQ., of Heaton, presented a Curate to Rev. John Brand, in 1774.

ANTHONY RIDLEY, M. D. (address uncommunicated) ; L. R. C. S. Edinburgh, 1852.

GEORGE-ROBERT RIDLEY, M. D., Brunswick Street, Melbourne, Victoria, Australia.

MUSGRAVE RIDLEY, timber-merchant, Carliol Square and 28 Archibald Terrace.

REV. H. T. RIDLEY, M. A., promoted to a Prebend in Bristol Cathedral, in 1816.

REV. HENRY-RIDLEY MOODY, M. A., Chatham R., Kent. Preferment, 1822.

CHARLES RIDLEY, M. D., 6 Charlotte Street, Bedford Square, London, W.C.

REV. J. H. RIDLEY, Prebendary of Bristol ; lost his wife in 1817.

Ridleys of Birmingham, England.

WILLIAM RIDLEY, 39 King Edward's Road.

HENRY RIDLEY, 222 TcKneild Port Road.

ROBERT-WOOD RIDLEY, 22 Heath Street.

ALFRED RIDLEY, 90 Lower Hurst Street.

JOHN RIDLEY, 88 Great Francis Street.

HOWARD RIDLEY, 40 Augusta Street.

WILLIAM RIDLEY, 129 Varna Road.·

HENRY RIDLEY, 16½ Hockley Hill.

ALFRED RIDLEY, Clissold Street.

JOHN RIDLEY, 32 Fazely Street.

JOHN RIDLEY, 317 Farm Street.

Ridleys of Liverpool, England.

WILLIAM RIDLEY, F. C. O., professor of music and organist of West Derby Parish Church, 19 Ivy Leigh, Tue Brook.

CLAUDE RIDLEY, professor of music and organist of St. John's Church, Tue Brook, 19 Ivy Leigh.

JOHN RIDLEY, of the firm of Ridley & Co., 30 Derby Road, Bootle, and 9 Scotland Road.

GOWLAND C. RIDLEY, joiner and builder, Claremont Cottage, Stourton Road, Oxton.

WILLIAM RIDLEY, beer-seller, 19 Lower Ivy Street, Birkenhead.

JAMES RIDLEY, shipwright, 404 Mill Street, Toxteth Park.

SAMUEL C. RIDLEY, contractor, Wellington Road, New Brighton.

WILLIAM RIDLEY, Wheat Sheaf, 184 Scotland Road.

WILLIAM RIDLEY, plasterer, Woodchuck Road, Oxton.

WILLIAM RIDLEY, whitesmith, 11 Bute Street.

ROBERT RIDLEY, plasterer, 233 Burlington Street.

WILLIAM RIDLEY, paper-hanger, 6 George's Terrace, Plumpton Street.

GEORGE RIDLEY, joiner, Stourton Road, Oxton.

ELIZABETH RIDLEY, 15 Royston Street.

JOSEPH RIDLEY, victualler, 7 Great Homer Street.

Ridleys of Newcastle-on-Tyne, England, 1877-78.

THOMAS RIDLEY, store-manager, 137 Clifford Street.

THOMAS RIDLEY, barrister-at-law, 30 Grey Street.

MRS. ELIZABETH RIDLEY, lodgings, 8 Albert Street.

JAMES-TAYLOR RIDLEY, engineer, 18 Alexander Place.

THOMAS RIDLEY, Penn Street and Stockbridge.

DAVID-NICHOLAS RIDLEY, agent, 91 Henry Street.

MISS ANN RIDLEY, 17 Regent Terrace.

MISS JANE RIDLEY, 1 Belle Grove Terrace.

ANDREW RIDLEY, beer-retailer, 22 Churchill Street.

MRS. SARAH RIDLEY, 13 Victoria Square.

THOMAS RIDLEY, bottle-maker, 113 Northumberland Street.

JAMES-CARTMELL RIDLEY, 3 Summerhill Grove.

SAMUEL-JOHN RIDLEY, 13 Victoria Square.

JOHN-HILTON RIDLEY, Wellburn, Ovingham, N. C.

HENRY RIDLEY, chemist, 153 Newgate Street.

WILLIAM RIDLEY, confectioner, 37 Tyne Side.

WILLIAM RIDLEY, corn-factor, 101 Addison Road.

MRS. ISABELLA RIDLEY, 1 High Swinburn Place.

JONATHAN RIDLEY, tinplate-worker, 31 Buckingham Street.

THOMAS RIDLEY, photographer, 35 Park Road.

WILLIAM RIDLEY, waterproof-paper maker, 31 Maple Street.

MRS. H. C. RIDLEY, academy, 73 Park Road.

THOMAS RIDLEY, Blackhill County, Durham.

THOMAS-HARRISON RIDLEY, Grace Church Buildings, London.

GEORGE RIDLEY, gas manager.

MRS. JANE RIDLEY, 13 Victoria Square.

RIDLEY GRADUATES OF OXFORD COLLEGE, ENGLAND.[*]

HENRY RIDLEY. University B. A. Feb. 11, 1774; M. A. June 12, 1776; B. and D. D. June 3, 1802.

HENRY-COLBORN RIDLEY. Christ's Church, B. A. June 25, 1801; M. A. April 19, 1804.

WILLIAM-HENRY RIDLEY. Christ's Church, B. A. Jan. 24, 1838; M. A. Nov. 19, 1840.

HENRY-JOHN RIDLEY. Christ's Church, B. A. Feb. 23, 1801; M. A. Nov. 17, 1813.

CHARLES-JOHN RIDLEY. University B. A. June 9, 1813; M. A. Oct. 31, 1817.

GLOSTER RIDLEY. New College, B. C. L. April 19, 1729; D. D. Feb. 2, 1767.

RICHARD RIDLEY. University, B. A. Nov. 24, 1803; M. A. June 16, 1806.

THOMAS RIDLEY. Magdalen Hall, B. A. May 30, 1833; M. A. June 6, 1838.

GILES RIDLEY. Eden Hall, B. A. May 23, 1704; M. A. May 20, 1708.

MATTHEW-WHITE RIDLEY. Christ's Church, B. A. March 6, 1798.

MATTHEW-WHITE RIDLEY. Christ's Church, B. A. May 28, 1828.

OLIVER-MATTHEW RIDLEY. Christ's Church, B. A. Oct. 22, 1846.

NICHOLAS-JAMES RIDLEY. Christ's Church, B. A. June, 1800.

HENRY-RICHARD RIDLEY. University, B. A. Nov. 9, 1837.

GEORGE RIDLEY. Christ's Church, B. A. May 2, 1844.

JAMES RIDLEY. New College, B. A. Feb. 16, 1760.

MATTHEW RIDLEY, Esq. Cr. M. A. July 1, 1730.

RIDLEY AUTHORS.

NICHOLAS RIDLEY, D. D. A collection of his works, with Biographical Notice, by Rev. Henry Christmas, was published at Cambridge in 1841. 8vo. Contents: Declaration of the Lord's Supper; Piteous Lamentations of the Miserable State of the Church; Treatise on the Worship of Images; Conference with Latimer, and with Secretary Bourne; Disputation of Oxford; Examination before the Queen's Commissioners; and many minor pieces. "For his piety, learning, and solid judgment, the ablest man of all that advanced the Reformation." — *Bishop Burnet.* "He was a person small in stature, but great in learning, and profoundly read in divinity." — *Wood.*

---

[*] Many other representatives of the Ridley family in England were graduated from other colleges, as will be seen by reference to personal sketches in the Genealogical and Biographical department in this book.

GLOSTER RIDLEY, D. D. Published many sermons and the following volumes: I. Eight Sermons on the Holy Ghost. London, 1740–2. 8vo.; new edition, Oxford, 1802. 8vo. II. De Syriacarum Novi Fœderis Virsionum Indole atque Usa Dissertatio, etc. London, 1761. 4to. III. Life of Dr. Nicholas Ridley, Bishop of London, 1763. 4to. Also, his Voice of the Church. 1840. 2 vols.; 8vo. IV. Review of Mr. Phillips's History of the Life of Reginald Pole. 1765–6. 8vo. V. Three Letters to the Author of the Confessional. 1768. 8vo. VI. Melampus; or, The Religious Groves: a Poem. 1781. 4to.

REV. WILLIAM H. RIDLEY, rector of Hambleden, Buckinghamshire. I. Master and his Servants: an Allegory. London, 1848. 12mo. II. The Holy Communion. 1854. 18mo. III. Ascension Day. 1857. 12mo. IV. What can we do for our Fellow-subjects in India? 1857. 12mo. V. On Confirmation. 1858. 12mo. VI. Letters to a Layman. 1858. 12mo. VII. Daily Service. 1858. 12mo. 8. Sermons in Plain Language adapted to the Poor. 1863. 8vo. IX. Every-day Companion. 1865–6. 8vo. X. Bible Readings. 1869. 2 vols. 8vo.

SIR THOMAS RIDLEY. Master of Eton School (see genealogy). Author of A View of the Civile and Ecclesiastical Law. Oxford, 1607. 4to; second edition, with Notes, by John Gregory. 1634. 4to; several other editions. "His work, while it established the reputation of the author, contributed to revive the declining credit of that jurisdiction." James I. greatly admired Ridley's "View."

HUMPHREY RIDLEY, M. D. I. Dissert. Inaug. Leyden, 1679. 4to. II. Anatomy of the Brain. London, 1695. 8vo.; Latin, Leyden, 1725. 8vo. III. Observationes Medico-Practicæ Phys. de Asthmate et Hydrophobia. London, 1703. 8vo.; Leyden, 1738. 8vo.

REV. WILLIAM A. RIDLEY, M. A. University of Sydney. I. The Aborigines of Australia: a Lecture at Sydney, Sept. 14, 1864–5. II. Kamilaroi, Dippie, and Turrubue: Languages Spoken by Australian Aborigines. 1868. 4to.

REV. JAMES RIDLEY, son of Gloster, who died in 1765, was author of The History of James Lovegrove, Esq.: a Novel. Tales of the Genii; 2 vols., many editions; and The Schemer.

MARK RIDLEY, M. D. I. Magnetical Bodies and Motions. London, 1613. Folio. II. Animadversions on a Late Work, entitled Magnetical Advertisement, etc. 1617. 4to.

LANCELOT RIDLEY, of Canterbury, published in 1540: Commentaries on Ephesians, Philippians, Colossians, and St. Jude. See Lownder's Bible Manual, 1562.

ANNE E. RIDLEY. Under the Waves; or, The Hermit Crab "In Society." London, 1865. 16mo.

J. H. RIDLEY. Losses at Sea, their Causes and Means of Prevention. London, 1855. 8vo.

JOHN RIDLEY. A Sermon of Walking Humbly with God. London, 1649. 4to.

INDEX OF SURNAMES.